Freedom in the World
2010

D0904332

The findings of *Freedom in the World 2010* include events from January 1, 2009, through December 31, 2009.

Freedom in the World 2010

The Annual Survey of Political Rights & Civil Liberties

Arch Puddington
General Editor

Aili Piano
Managing Editor

Eliza Young and Tyler Roylance
Assistant Editors

Freedom House • New York, NY and Washington, DC
Rowman & Littlefield Publishers, Inc. • Lanham, Boulder,
New York, Toronto, Oxford

ROWMAN & LITTLEFIELD PUBLISHERS, INC.

Published in the United States of America
by Rowman & Littlefield Publishers, Inc.
A wholly owned subsidiary of The Rowman & Littlefield Publishing Group, Inc.
4501 Forbes Boulevard, Suite 200, Lanham, Maryland 20706
www.rowmanlittlefield.com

Estover Road, Plymouth PL6 7PY, United Kingdom

British Library Cataloguing in Publication Information Available

Library of Congress Cataloging-in-Publication Data

Freedom in the world / —1978–
New York : Freedom House, 1978–
v. : map; 25 cm.—(Freedom House Book)
Annual.
ISSN 0732-6610=Freedom in the World.
1. Civil rights—Periodicals. I. R. Adrian Karatnycky, et al. I. Series.
JC571 .F66 323.4'05—dc 19 82-642048
AACR 2   MARC-S
Library of Congress [84101]

ISBN: 978-1-4422-0494-2 (cloth : alk. paper)
ISBN: 978-1-4422-0495-9 (pbk. : alk. paper)
ISBN: 978-1-4422-0496-6 (electronic)
ISSN: 0732-6610

Printed in the United States of America

Contents

Acknowledgments 1

Freedom in the World 2010:
Erosion of Freedom Intensifies *Arch Puddington* 3

Introduction 15

Country Reports 16

Related and Disputed Territory Reports 740

Survey Methodology 796

Tables and Ratings
 Table of Independent Countries 815
 Table of Disputed Territories 817
 Table of Related Territories 817
 Combined Average Ratings: Independent Countries 818
 Combined Average Ratings: Related and Disputed Territories 819
 Table of Electoral Democracies 820

The Survey Team 822

Selected Sources 831

Freedom House Board of Trustees 838

About Freedom House 839

Acknowledgments

Freedom in the World 2010 could not have been completed without the contributions of numerous Freedom House staff and consultants. The section titled "The Survey Team" contains a detailed list of the writers and advisers without whose efforts this project would not have been possible.

Critical administrative, research, and editorial support was provided by Ellena Fotinatos, Eva Hoier Greene, Jennifer Lam, Charlie Liebling, Katherine Prizeman, Sheena Reiter, Josh Siegel, and Kelly Tek. Overall guidance for the project was provided by Jennifer Windsor, executive director of Freedom House, and Thomas Melia, deputy executive director of Freedom House. A number of Freedom House staff provided valuable additional input on the country reports and/or ratings process.

Freedom House would like to acknowledge the generous financial support for *Freedom in the World* by The Lynde and Harry Bradley Foundation, Smith Richardson Foundation, Lilly Endowment, F.M. Kirby Foundation, 21st Century ILGWU Heritage Fund, Walter J. Schloss, and Freedom House Board of Trustees.

Findings of *Freedom in the World 2010*
Erosion of Freedom Intensifies

Arch Puddington

In a year of intensified repression against human rights defenders and democratic activists by many of the world's most powerful authoritarian regimes, Freedom House found a continued erosion of freedom worldwide, with setbacks in Latin America, Africa, the former Soviet Union, and the Middle East. For the fourth consecutive year, declines have trumped gains. This represents the longest continuous period of deterioration in the nearly 40-year history of *Freedom in the World*, House's annual assessment of the state of political rights and civil liberties in every country in the world.

In 2009, declines for freedom were registered in 40 countries, representing 20 percent of the world's polities. In 22 of those countries, the problems were significant enough to merit downgrades in the numerical ratings for political rights or civil liberties. Six countries moved downward in their overall status designation, either from Free to Partly Free or from Partly Free to Not Free. The year also featured a drop in the number of electoral democracies from 119 to 116, the lowest figure since 1995.

A series of disturbing events at year's end reinforced the magnitude of the challenge to fundamental freedoms, including the violent repression of protesters on the streets of Iran, lengthy prison sentences meted out to peaceful dissidents in China, attacks on leading human rights activists in Russia, and continued terrorist and insurgent violence in Pakistan, Afghanistan, Iraq, Somalia, and Yemen.

There were a few bright spots. Of the 194 countries assessed, 16 experienced gains in freedom. Broad improvements were recorded in the Balkans, as Montenegro moved into the Free category and Kosovo moved up to Partly Free, while ratings increases were seen for Croatia, Moldova, and Serbia. Countries including Iraq, Lebanon, Malawi, and Togo also made noteworthy gains. There were advances for freedom in South Asia for the second consecutive year, and political institutions in major Asian democracies showed impressive strength in the face of global economic upheaval.

By absolute historical standards, the overall state of freedom in the world has improved over the last two decades. Many more countries were in the Free category and were designated as electoral democracies in 2009 than in 1989, and the majority of countries that made major progress 20 years ago have retained those improvements.

Indeed, as the world marks the 20th anniversary of the fall of the Berlin Wall, the democratic institutions of the post-communist countries of Central Europe, the Baltic region, and the Balkans have shown encouraging resilience despite mounting stresses. The majority of new democracies in Latin America have not seen major ratings declines, and a number of young democracies in the Asia-Pacific region have maintained or improved their ratings.

But over the last four years, the dominant pattern has been one of growing restrictions on the fundamental freedoms of expression and association in authoritarian settings, and a failure to continue democratic progress in previously improving countries due to unchecked corruption and weaknesses in the rule of law.

The continued downward spiral throughout Central Asia in 2009, with Kyrgyzstan moving from Partly Free to Not Free, gave it the dubious distinction of becoming the world's least free subregion. The Kazakh government notably failed to enact the fundamental political reforms it had promised during its campaign to secure the chairmanship of the Organization for Security and Cooperation in Europe (OSCE) for 2010.

Sub-Saharan Africa suffered the largest setbacks, with 15 countries registering declines and 4 securing gains. Nigeria and Kenya, both large and influential states that had demonstrated some democratic improvements in the past, saw continued backsliding. They were joined by a number of other African countries that had earned records of democratic achievement, including Botswana, Lesotho, Madagascar, and Mozambique.

Several parts of the Arab Middle East also saw deterioration, causing three countries in the region—Bahrain, Jordan, and Yemen—to drop into the Not Free category.

Other notable trends in 2009 include:

Authoritarian crackdowns on frontline human rights defenders. In Russia, human rights lawyer Stanislav Markelov, journalist Anastasia Baburova, and human rights advocate Natalya Estemirova were among the victims of unsolved political murders. In China, Liu Xiaobo, an organizer of the Charter 08 democracy movement, received an 11-year prison sentence, though he was only one among dozens of civic activists sentenced to long prison terms during the year. In Vietnam, a group of dissidents were given five-year prison sentences for advocating multiparty politics. And in Iran, hundreds of regime critics were detained, tortured, or killed in the aftermath of the June presidential election.

Attacks on journalists and new threats to new media. The massacre of 29 journalists in a single incident in the Philippines stood out in a year of killings in such disparate locations as Russia, Pakistan, Mexico, and Somalia. Meanwhile, authoritarian governments expanded their efforts to stifle free expression by systematically blocking the use of new media for any activity they saw as a threat to their power. China remained at the cutting edge of this campaign, developing and deploying new forms of internet control and cracking down on bloggers and internet journalists who crossed political redlines. Bloggers in other authoritarian countries—including Iran and Azerbaijan—also faced increased threats, censorship, and prosecution for their activities.

Coups d'etat. Coups have been a rare phenomenon in the last two decades. During 2009, however, a number of countries experienced what amounted to coups. In Guinea, a classic military takeover that began at the end of 2008 took hold during the year, while in Honduras, Niger, and

Madagascar, extraconstitutional mechanisms were used to remove or extend the rule of sitting leaders.

Challenges from nonstate actors, including religious extremists and drug lords. Violent Islamic extremism continued to plague a number of countries from Africa to South Asia, including Somalia, Yemen, Afghanistan, and Pakistan. At the same time, regimes continued to use such problems to justify their crackdowns on civic activists or ethnic minorities, as China did with its concerted repression of the Uighur population. Organized drug trafficking contributed to insecurity and corruption in Afghanistan as well as in parts of Central America and Africa.

Freedom in the World—2010 Survey

The population of the world as estimated in mid-2009 was 6,790 million persons, who reside in 194 sovereign states. The level of political rights and civil liberties as shown comparatively by the Freedom House Survey is:

Free: 3,088.7 million (46.00 percent of the world's population) live in 89 of the states.

Partly Free: 1,367.4 million (20 percent of the world's population) live in 58 of the states.

Not Free: 2,333.9 million (34.00 percent of the world's population) live in 47 of the states.

A Record of the Survey
(population in millions)

Year under Review	FREE	PARTLY FREE	NOT FREE	WORLD POPULATION
Mid-1992	1,352.2 (24.83%)	2,403.3 (44.11%)	1,690.4 (31.06%)	5,446.0
Mid-1993	1,046.2 (19.00%)	2,224.4 (40.41%)	2,234.6 (40.59%)	5,505.2
Mid-1994	1,119.7 (19.97%)	2,243.4 (40.01%)	2,243.9 (40.02%)	5,607.0
Mid-1995	1,114.5 (19.55%)	2,365.8 (41.49%)	2,221.2 (38.96%)	5,701.5
Mid-1996	1,250.3 (21.67%)	2,260.1 (39.16%)	2,260.6 (39.17%)	5,771.0
Mid-1997	1,266.0 (21.71%)	2,281.9 (39.12%)	2,284.6 (39.17%)	5,832.5
Mid-1998	2,354.0 (39.84%)	1,570.6 (26.59%)	1,984.1 (33.58%)	5,908.7
Mid-1999	2,324.9 (38.90%)	1,529.0 (25.58%)	2,122.4 (35.51%)	5,976.3
Mid-2000	2,465.2 (40.69%)	1,435.8 (23.70%)	2,157.5 (35.61%)	6,058.5
Mid-2001	2,500.7 (40.79%)	1,462.9 (23.86%)	2,167.1 (35.35%)	6,130.7
Mid-2002	2,717.6 (43.85%)	1,293.1 (20.87%)	2,186.3 (35.28%)	6,197.0
Mid-2003	2,780.1 (44.03%)	1,324.0 (20.97%)	2,209.9 (35.00%)	6,314.0
Mid-2004	2,819.1 (44.08%)	1,189.0 (18.59%)	2,387.3 (37.33%)	6,395.4
Mid-2005	2,968.8 (45.97%)	1,157.7 (17.93%)	2,331.2 (36.10%)	6,457.7
Mid-2006	3,005.0 (46.00%)	1,083.2 (17.00%)	2,448.6 (37.00%)	6,536.8
Mid-2007	3,028.2 (45.85%)	1,185.3 (17.94%)	2,391.4 (36.21%)	6,604.9
Mid-2008	3,055.9 (45.73%)	1,351.0 (20.21%)	2,276.3 (34.06%)	6,683.2
Mid-2009	3,088.7 (45.49%)	1,367.4 (20.14%)	2,333.9 (34.37%)	6,790.0

* The large shift in the population figure between 1997 and 1998 is due to India's change in status from Partly Free to Free.

FIVE-YEAR TRENDS FOR POLITICAL RIGHTS AND CIVIL LIBERTIES

An analysis of *Freedom in the World* subcategories under the broader political rights and civil liberties rubrics from 2005 through 2009 shows that the past year was not an anomaly. Throughout this period, there have been growing pressures on freedom of expression, including press freedom, as well as on civic activists engaged in promoting political reform and respect for human rights, including the rights of workers to organize.

Overall, however, the most significant declines were in the rule of law arena.

Judicial systems on the whole remain weak, unable to act independently or apply the law equally to all members of society. Arbitrary detention and human rights violations by both state and nonstate actors continue to hamper progress toward the institutionalization of democratic gains in many societies.

On a positive note, most regions have shown an outright improvement in the conduct of elections over the last five years. Globally, the elections scores in *Freedom in the World* would have improved by a significant degree were it not for a broad decline in one subregion: the former Soviet Union. Asian countries registered a substantial improvement on indicators tied to the conduct of elections and the ability of the political opposition to compete on a level playing field.

Thus, despite the vote rigging, fraud, and other manipulations that occurred in a number of countries in 2009, the global picture over the last five years suggests that governments are more likely to permit relatively honest elections than to allow an uncensored press, a robust civil society, and an independent judiciary.

The Global Trend

Year Under Review	Free	Partly Free	Not Free
1979	51	54	56
1989	61	44	62
1999	85	60	47
2009	89	58	47

Tracking Electoral Democracy

Year Under Review	Number of Electoral Democracies
1999	120
2004	119
2009	116

THE STATE OF FREEDOM IN 2009: A SNAPSHOT

The number of countries assessed by *Freedom in the World* to be Free in 2009 stood at 89, representing 46 percent of the world's 194 countries and 3,088,704,000 people—46 percent of the global population. The number of Free countries remained unchanged from the previous year's survey.

The number of countries qualifying as Partly Free stood at 58, or 30 percent of all countries, and they comprised 1,367,440,000 people, or 20 percent of the world's total. The number of Partly Free countries declined by four from the previous year. (Among the Partly Free countries for 2009 was Kosovo, which in previous editions of *Freedom in the World* had been listed as a disputed territory.)

Forty-seven countries were deemed Not Free, representing 24 percent of the total. The number of people living under Not Free conditions stood at 2,333,869,000, or 34 percent of the world population, though it is important to note that more than half of these people live in just one country: China. The number of Not Free countries increased by five from 2008.

Two countries, both in the Balkans, registered positive changes in status during the year. Montenegro moved from Partly Free to Free, and Kosovo rose from Not Free to Partly Free. Six countries experienced declines in status: Lesotho moved from Free to Partly Free, while Bahrain, Gabon, Jordan, Kyrgyzstan, and Yemen fell from Partly Free to Not Free.

The number of electoral democracies dropped by 3 and stands at 116. Setbacks in four countries—Honduras, Madagascar, Mozambique, and Niger—led to their removal from the electoral democracy list. One country, the Maldives, joined the ranks of the world's electoral democracies.

ANALYSIS OF REGIONAL TRENDS
LATIN AMERICA: REGIONAL AND INTERNAL CHALLENGES

Declines for freedom in Honduras and Nicaragua were signal developments in a year of general deterioration in Central America.

The elite classes' fear of a power grab by Honduran president Manuel Zelaya provoked a coup that resulted in his forced exile. This clear democratic rupture was complicated by an institutional clash: Zelaya's ouster, though disapproved of in opinion polls, was supported by the country's legislature and Supreme Court, and it came after Zelaya himself had acted in ways that many felt violated the checks and balances of the Honduran constitution. But while Zelaya's actions provided his opponents with much fodder, his forced exile and the restrictions imposed on civil liberties by his successors resulted in declines for the country's political rights and civil liberties ratings.

In Nicaragua, civil liberties declined due to President Daniel Ortega's continued use of violent intimidation and politicized courts to overcome obstacles to his plans for reelection. Guatemala's political rights rating fell as a result of the government's inability to implement policies and legislation in the face of rampant organized crime and related violence. Indeed, the violence perpetrated by nonstate actors, including drug traffickers, have over the years led to declines in civil liberties in a number of countries in Central America, as well as in Mexico and Colombia.

Political rights in Venezuela have deteriorated due to the ongoing concentration of power by President Hugo Chavez and the further marginalization of the political opposition. These developments in turn have influenced politics in the rest of the region. Chavez's populist message resonates in some places, and left-of-center candidates have scored electoral victories in a number of countries, most notably in the Andean and Central American subregions. Unfortunately, fears of growing Venezuelan influence also helped motivate the coup in Honduras. Nevertheless, many in Latin America have both rejected the populist-authoritarian model of Venezuela and strengthened their countries' democratic institutions. This has been the case in Chile, Brazil, and Uruguay.

There remained one Not Free country in the Western Hemisphere in 2009: Cuba. The Cuban government took no significant measures during the year to open up the political system or allow citizens to exercise their freedoms of expression and association. At year's end, Cuban authorities arrested an American who was in the country to distribute telecommunications equipment to political dissidents. Cuba remains one of the handful of countries worldwide that treats the distribution of laptops and mobile telephones to civil society groups as a crime.

MIDDLE EAST AND NORTH AFRICA: SOME GAINS, BUT REVERSALS PREVAIL

News from the region was dominated by the upheaval in Iran, where election rigging, deadly state violence against civilians, and repression of the political opposition were met by a protest movement that impressed the world with its size, courage, commitment to democratic values, and staying power. Overall, the Middle East and North Africa region suffered a number of significant setbacks, and these were often centered in countries that had produced some evidence of reformist intentions in the recent past. Declines in 2009 brought the portion of the region's residents who live in Not Free societies to 88 percent.

Three countries—Jordan, Bahrain, and Yemen—dropped from the Partly Free to the Not Free category. Jordan suffered a decline in political rights due to the king's decision to dissolve the parliament and postpone elections. In Bahrain, political rights suffered as a result of the harassment of opposition political figures and discrimination by the minority Sunni elite against the Shiite majority. Yemen's political rights rating declined due to rapidly deteriorating security conditions and the increased marginalization of the parliament and other political institutions. Although Morocco's status did not decline in 2009, the increased concentration of power in the hands of forces aligned with King Mohammed VI, along with stepped-up harassment of opposition critics, increased concerns about the erosion of political rights in that country.

Improvements were noted in two countries that have experienced conflict in recent years: Iraq and Lebanon. Iraq's political rights rating improved in light of provincial elections, which were generally regarded as fair and competitive, and due to the government's enhanced autonomy as the phased withdrawal of U.S. troops got under way. Lebanon benefited from a decline in political violence, which resulted in an improvement in its civil liberties rating.

Nevertheless, violence remains a dominant theme in the politics of the region and a significant impediment to the exercise of fundamental freedoms in many countries, including Iraq. The beginning of the year was marred by fierce fighting between the Israeli military and the Hamas movement in the Gaza Strip. While Israel remains the only country in the region to hold a *Freedom in the World* designation of Free, freedoms of assembly and association came under pressure there during the year. Hundreds of people were arrested during demonstrations against the Gaza conflict, and the parliamentary elections committee passed a measure banning two political parties from national elections, though the ban was quickly overturned by the Supreme Court.

SUB-SAHARAN AFRICA: YEAR OF MAJOR SETBACKS

While the advances made in sub-Saharan Africa in recent decades have not eroded overall, the region suffered the largest setbacks of 2009, with 15 countries registering declines and only 4 countries marking gains.

Botswana and Lesotho both experienced reversals, with Lesotho moving from Free to Partly Free status. A decline in Botswana's political rights rating was attributed to growing secrecy in the government. In Lesotho, political rights deteriorated as a result of the government's failure to negotiate in good faith with the opposition over flaws in the election system that emerged during balloting in 2008.

Three countries experienced coups: Guinea, Madagascar, and Niger. In the case of Guinea, the military takeover was followed by a terrifying rampage in which soldiers massacred and raped peaceful protesters.

Among the region's most repressive or least free states, declines were recorded in Eritrea, Gabon, and the Democratic Republic of Congo.

Perhaps the most disturbing trend in the region is the decline over several years of some of sub-Saharan Africa's largest and most influential countries, which had previously made important democratic progress. Kenya continued to see declines in freedom stemming from charges of vote rigging during the 2007 elections, the violence that came in the election's wake, and a failure to hold those responsible to account.

Another regional powerhouse, Nigeria, continued on its downward path of recent years, which have featured flawed elections, pervasive corruption, and troubling levels of sectarian and religious violence. These problems have eroded some of the gains the country made following the transition from military rule in 1999.

Ethiopia's trajectory has also been negative for a number of years, as Prime Minister Meles Zenawi has persecuted the political opposition, tilted the political playing field, and suppressed civil society.

Improvements were noted in four countries: Malawi, Burundi, Togo, and Zimbabwe. While harsh conditions in Zimbabwe eased somewhat after opposition leader Morgan Tsvangirai was brought into a unity government as prime minister and a parliament led by his party was sworn in, the country remained among the continent's most repressive. The authoritarian president, Robert Mugabe, remained in office, and his allies in the security forces continued to harass, arrest, and torture opposition figures.

CENTRAL AND EASTERN EUROPE/FORMER SOVIET UNION: BALKAN PROGRESS, CENTRAL ASIAN DECAY

The year 2009 marked the 20th anniversary of the fall of the Berlin Wall. It was also a year when many of the countries that had won their freedom from Soviet domination found themselves under increased pressure from the global economic downturn. Latvia, Hungary, and Bulgaria were among those most severely affected by the crisis, but the entire region suffered to some degree, with skyrocketing rates of unemployment, increased poverty, financial instability, and waning confidence in free-market capitalism. Despite these pressures, the institutions of freedom remained remarkably resilient throughout Central Europe, the Baltics, and the Balkans.

Five countries in the western Balkans experienced gains for freedom during the year. The most notable improvements occurred in Kosovo, which advanced from Not Free to Partly Free status after holding elections that were deemed to be in compliance with international standards and strengthening the protection of minority rights. The other countries registering gains were Croatia, Serbia, Macedonia, and Montenegro, with the last moving from Partly Free to Free.

Meanwhile, the countries of the non-Baltic former Soviet Union continued their decade-long backslide during 2009. Conditions in this subregion have deteriorated to the point that almost every country ranks at the very bottom on multiple indicators measured by *Freedom in the World*. The area's average political rights score— which covers the spheres of electoral process, political pluralism, and functioning of government—has dropped sharply over the past four years and is now comparable to that of the Middle East and North Africa. The non-Baltic former Soviet Union lags far behind sub-Saharan Africa on the average scores for political rights and civil liberties, as well as on the majority of individual indicators, including freedom of expression, freedom of association, and the rule of law.

The dominant regional power, Russia, suffered further deterioration despite assurances from President Dmitry Medvedev that reform is in the offing. While Medvedev announced policies to fight corruption, loosen controls on civil society organizations, strengthen the rule of law, and enhance freedom of expression, the country met with a range of setbacks for political rights and civil liberties. Credible reports suggest that local and regional elections were suffused with irregularities. New restrictions were placed on religious minorities. A new commission was established to influence the presentation of history in schools and elsewhere, a move consistent with the Kremlin's wider efforts to manage and manipulate information in the public sphere. Human rights defenders and journalists remained vulnerable to persecution and murder, and there was a distinct lack of progress in punishing those responsible for previous politically motivated killings.

Central Asia remained one of the repressive areas in the world. Uzbekistan and Turkmenistan have long ranked at or near the bottom of the *Freedom in the World* scale. The decline of Kyrgyzstan from Partly Free to Not Free was of particular concern, as the country seemed to have been embarked on a reformist course at various times in the post-Soviet period. Kazakhstan, Central Asia's wealthiest state, also registered a decline. It has made no progress toward implementation of reforms it had promised in advance of its assumption of the chairmanship of the OSCE. During 2009, the Kazakh authorities took a further step backward, when they arrested and sentenced Yevgenii Zhovtis, a prominent human rights advocate.

The regimes in other authoritarian states on Russia's periphery, including Belarus, Armenia, and Azerbaijan, have shown no signs of abandoning their repressive policies. Ukraine, which has also suffered heavily from the economic downturn and is burdened by enormous corruption problems, remains the only Free state in the non-Baltic former Soviet Union.

ASIA-PACIFIC: MODEST IMPROVEMENTS

As the world's most populous region, Asia is home to some of the globe's largest democracies as well as its biggest authoritarian regime, presenting a unique dynamic for democratic development. While most regions experienced various degrees of decline for freedom in 2009, the Asia-Pacific region as a whole experienced modest gains. Three of its most strategically significant countries—India, Indonesia, and Japan—held competitive and fair general elections, with the historic victory of Japan's opposition Democratic Party reconfirming that Japanese citizens can change their government when they choose to do so.

Other gains for political rights were seen in Bangladesh, where an elected civilian government replaced a military-backed administration, and the Maldives, where the first democratic parliamentary elections passed peacefully. Polls in Mongolia and both Indian and Pakistani Kashmir similarly contributed to improvements in the realization of political rights.

Not all election-related developments were positive, however. In Afghanistan, which saw a decline in its political rights rating, a deeply flawed presidential poll exacerbated an already unstable security situation and exposed the prevalence of corruption within the government. And in the Philippines, the massacre of civilians in connection with a local official's attempt to register his candidacy, and the government's subsequent declaration of martial law in the area, were indicative of heightened political violence in the run-up to 2010 elections.

Among civil liberties, particular pressure was placed on the rule of law and respect for freedom of expression, with reversals noted in both authoritarian and democratic societies. In Cambodia, the government recriminalized defamation and then used the new legislation to intimidate independent journalists. In Vietnam, a prominent independent think tank was shut down and prodemocracy civic activists were imprisoned. In Indonesia, top law enforcement officials were implicated in efforts to undermine anticorruption bodies. In Taiwan, increased government efforts to enforce anticorruption laws were marred by flaws in the protection of criminal defendants' rights, and new legislation restricted the political expression of academics. And in China, Communist Party leaders sought to tighten control over judges, while embarking on a sweeping crackdown against leading human rights lawyers and nonprofits offering legal services.

Indeed, as China's leaders showed greater confidence on the world stage, their actions at home demonstrated continued insecurity and intolerance with respect to citizens' demands for legal rights and accountable governance. The authorities' paranoid handling of a series of politically sensitive anniversaries—such as the 60-year mark of the Communist Party's time in power—included lockdowns on major cities, new restrictions on the internet, the creation of special extralegal task forces, and harsh punishments meted out to democracy activists, petitioners, Tibetans, Falun Gong adherents, and human rights defenders. Separately, long-standing government policies of altering the demography and repressing religious freedom in the Xinjiang region came to a head in 2009, when an eruption of ethnic violence was followed by forced "disappearances" of Uighur Muslims, a series of executions, and tightened internet censorship. Often at great personal risk, many of China's bloggers, journalists, legal professionals, workers, and religious believers nevertheless pushed the limits of permissible activity in increasingly sophisticated ways. They managed to expose cases of official corruption, circulate underground political publications, and play a role in forcing the government's partial retraction of a policy to install monitoring and censorship software on personal computers. Growing labor unrest and better organized strikes reflected workers' ability to bypass the party-controlled union, sometimes resulting in concessions by employers.

South Asia saw several improvements in 2009. Bangladesh's new civilian-led government enacted important legislation to improve transparency, and while the issue of detainee deaths remained a serious concern, lower levels of politically motivated violence and detentions, as well as fewer restrictions on the media, led to better scores for the country in a number of categories. Scores for the Maldives also improved, thanks to the holding of generally free legislative elections and a series of reforms in the areas of accountability, anticorruption, free assembly and association, and prison conditions.

While Pakistan remained mired in official corruption and extremist violence, positive signs were noted in initial reforms of the administration of the tribal areas and especially in the peaceful resolution of the judicial crisis, which included the reinstatement of the chief justice of the Supreme Court and the restoration of a large measure of judicial independence.

In Sri Lanka, improvements in political freedom following the end of the long-running civil war were balanced by the government's unwillingness to meaningfully address ethnic grievances, the internment in squalid conditions of several hundred thousand displaced civilians for much of the year, and increased hostility toward journalists and nongovernmental organizations.

W. EUROPE AND N. AMERICA:
SOME CHANGE IN U.S., ASSIMILATION CRISIS ENDURES IN EUROPE

The countries of Western Europe and North America continued to register the highest scores on the *Freedom in the World* scale despite their ongoing struggle to assimilate large numbers of immigrants from developing countries, the continued tension between security and civil liberties, and problems stemming from libel tourism and other threats to freedom of expression.

In the United States, the presidency of Barack Obama was greeted with enthusiasm by civil libertarians, as his campaign platform had suggested a major rollback of controversial antiterrorism policies instituted by his predecessor, George W. Bush. In some areas, Obama did pursue a markedly different course than did Bush. For example, at year's end, Obama issued an order that will result in the release to the public of millions of documents that had been classified during World War II, the Cold War, and other conflict periods. The new administration also issued a policy that forbade the use of torture by U.S. personnel; announced plans to close down the military detention facility at Guantanamo Bay, Cuba; and decided that some of the terrorism suspects held at Guantanamo would be tried in U.S. civilian courts, while others would be brought before military tribunals. More broadly, however, Obama decided against reversing course on many Bush-era security policies. Furthermore, the goal of shutting down the Guantanamo facility was complicated by the revelation that a number of previously freed detainees had joined jihadist groups in Afghanistan, Yemen, and elsewhere; by a nearly successful attempt to destroy an American airliner at year's end; and by political resistance to the relocation of terrorism detainees to facilities in the United States.

In Europe, cultural tensions driven by an influx of immigrants from Muslim countries continued to pose challenges to the region's tradition of tolerance and civil liberties. A number of countries have experienced political disputes over the building of mosques and minarets, the wearing of headscarves and burqas, the treatment of women in Muslim families, and similar issues. Apprehensions over immigration have led to the growth of right-wing political parties whose platforms are centered on demands for immigration restrictions. Switzerland, home to the region's most politically successful anti-immigrant party, suffered a decline in its *Freedom in the World* score after its citizens voted in a referendum to ban the construction of minarets. Malta also suffered a decline due to its record of often refusing to come to the aid of foundering boats carrying immigrants from North Africa, as well as the poor condition of its immigrant detention centers. Turkey experienced a modest score decline due to a court decision that outlawed a political party representing the interests of Kurds, an action that seriously undermined the government's efforts to end the Kurdish insurgency.

Challenges to freedom of expression remained a problem, especially in the United Kingdom, where journalists and scholars have been brought to court on libel charges by individuals from foreign countries—most often countries under authoritarian rule. The problem has prompted press freedom advocates to cite such "libel tourism" as a serious menace to intellectual inquiry and the robust exchange of ideas. The controversy deepened in 2009, when libel charges were advanced against scientists who had written critiques of the conclusions of fellow scholars. Meanwhile, several states in the United States have passed laws that would effectively nullify monetary awards for libel or defamation issued by foreign courts in most instances. In a positive development, a court decision in Canada significantly narrowed the conditions under which cases of libel or defamation can be brought before the judicial system.

CONCLUSION
MEETING THE AUTHORITARIAN CHALLENGE

Despite the record of global setbacks during the past year, the overall state of freedom in the world remains quite positive by any historical measurement. With some exceptions, the societies that embraced democracy during the Cold War's waning years and immediately after the dissolution of the Soviet Union have retained their array of free institutions. The apparent durability of democracy in a number of Asia's most important countries represents a bright spot, as do the gains for freedom in the Balkans, a region that was mired in civil war and ethnic hatred during the 1990s. The fact that more societies did not seek authoritarian alternatives in the face of a severe worldwide economic crisis last year could be held up as a testament to the strength of the democratic idea.

Still, the notion that things could have been worse is poor consolation for a year in which freedom showed some measure of decline in roughly 40 countries. And the results for 2009 were no isolated occurrence: they marked the fourth consecutive year of overall decline, the longest such stretch of negative data in the history of *Freedom in the World*. This is a phenomenon that should be galvanizing civic leaders and governments throughout the democratic world, no less than it should be concerning to those men and women elsewhere who aspire to live in free societies. Yet, it comes at a time when American public opinion, at least, is experiencing a resurgence of isolationism in key respects.

According to a survey published by the Pew Research Center for the People and the Press on December 3, 2009, for the first time since World War II, a plurality of Americans (49 percent) believe the United States should, "mind its own business and let other countries get along the best they can." The steepest specific change in general public attitudes surveyed is the decline in interest in "spreading democracy around the world," from 44 percent just after the 2001 terrorist attacks to a mere 10 percent today. As was the case when Freedom House was founded in 1941, the reluctance of American public opinion to support active engagement in a messy world, despite clear infringements on democratic liberties overseas, makes it extremely difficult for American foreign policy to defend democracy from its enemies.

Another source of concern is the growing paranoia of even the largest and most headstrong among the world's authoritarian powers. No country can compete in this respect with China, which—despite its waxing economic and military prowess—behaves as if it were under siege by its own citizens. The prison sentence recently issued to democracy advocate Liu Xiaobo is reminiscent of the antidissident campaigns of the Soviet Union under Leonid Brezhnev. Similarly disturbing is Beijing's persecution of lawyers who have represented defendants in politically sensitive cases, including ethnic and religious minorities and independent journalists. While China asserts that its relations with the rest of the world are based on a fundamental principle of noninterference, it recently tried to intimidate foreign cultural officials into silencing regime critics at conferences and exhibition venues in Germany, Australia, South Korea, and Bangladesh. It has likewise badgered foreign countries to return Uighurs seeking asylum abroad, and succeeded in persuading Pakistan and Cambodia to do so despite a credible risk of torture and execution.

While these acts of repression are disturbing, so is the absence of protest from the democratic world. When the Soviet Union arrested a dissident or suppressed religious expression, it drew widespread condemnation by figures ranging from heads of state to trade union leaders, as well as by human rights organizations and prominent humanitarians. China's current actions, by contrast, elicit little more than boilerplate criticism, and just as often they provoke no response whatsoever. Nor is China the only authoritarian power that has managed to avoid global attention for its breaches of democratic standards. Kazakhstan holds the chairmanship of the OSCE for the year 2010 despite a record of fraudulent elections and repression of independent critics in the media and civil society—behavior that only grew worse as 2010 approached. Venezuela's Hugo Chavez has beguiled many and escaped censure by the Organization of American States despite his increasingly contemptuous attitude toward pluralism and his own country's constitution. Egypt, Saudi Arabia, and other influential authoritarian states in the Middle East similarly avoid criticism for their assaults on citizens who seek to improve the climate for rights and freedoms in their countries.

The Cold War has ended, but the tendency of authoritarians of various stripes to band together and pursue common strategic, diplomatic, and occasionally economic interests remains a reality of international behavior. Authoritarians prefer alliances with other authoritarians and continue to regard the United States and the world's other democracies as adversaries. They are deeply unsettled by citizen-driven movements for change, such as the one witnessed in the U.S. electoral campaign of 2008, or those that—in very different contexts—currently threaten the forces of repression in Iran and Zimbabwe. Authoritarian rulers fear their own citizens, hence their frequently expressed apprehensions about an American-inspired "velvet revolution." In response, they devote more and more strategic thought and material resources to the challenge of keeping their people under control and the democratic world at bay.

While a "freedom recession" and an authoritarian resurgence have clearly emerged as global trends, they are subject to reversal. Democracy remains the preferred form of government; indeed, no other system or model has gained widespread support. The United States and other democracies should take the initiative to meet the authoritarian challenge, and democratic leaders should make the case to their wary publics about the importance of doing so now, while the balance remains relatively favorable, rather than waiting for a further erosion in the global state of freedom.

This report was prepared with the assistance of Eliza Young.

Introduction

The *Freedom in the World 2010* survey contains reports on 194 countries and 14 related and disputed territories. Each country report begins with a section containing the following information: **population, capital, political rights** (numerical rating), **civil liberties** (numerical rating), **status** (Free, Partly Free, or Not Free), and a **10-year ratings timeline**. Each territory report begins with a section containing the same information, except for capital. The figures are drawn primarily from the *2009 World Population Data Sheet* of the Population Reference Bureau.

The **political rights** and **civil liberties** categories contain numerical ratings between 1 and 7 for each country or territory, with 1 representing the most free and 7 the least free. The **status** designation of Free, Partly Free, or Not Free, which is determined by the combination of the political rights and civil liberties ratings, indicates the general state of freedom in a country or territory. The ratings of countries or territories that have improved or declined since the previous survey are indicated by notations next to the ratings. Positive or negative trends that do not warrant a ratings change since the previous year may be indicated by upward or downward trend arrows, which are located next to the name of the country or territory. A brief explanation of ratings changes or trend arrows is provided for each country or territory as required. For a full description of the methods used to determine the survey's ratings, please see the chapter on the survey's methodology.

The **10-year ratings timeline** lists the political rights and civil liberties ratings and status for each of the last 10 years. Each year that is included in the timeline refers to the year under review, *not* the edition of the survey. Thus, the ratings and status from the *Freedom in the World 2010* edition are listed under "2009" (the year that was under review for the 2010 survey edition).

Following the section described above, each country and territory report is divided into two parts: an **overview** and an analysis of **political rights and civil liberties**. The overview provides a brief historical background and a description of major recent events. The political rights and civil liberties section summarizes each country or territory's degree of respect for the rights and liberties that Freedom House uses to evaluate freedom in the world.

Afghanistan

Political Rights: 6*
Civil Liberties: 6
Status: Not Free

Population: 28,396,000
Capital: Kabul

Ratings Change: Afghanistan's political rights rating declined from 5 to 6 due to a deeply flawed presidential election that included massive fraud, a compromised electoral management body, and low voter turnout due to intimidation.

Ten-Year Ratings Timeline For Year Under Review (Political Rights, Civil Liberties, Status)

2000	2001	2002	2003	2004	2005	2006	2007	2008	2009
7,7NF	7,7NF	6,6NF	6,6NF	5,6NF	5,5PF	5,5PF	5,5PF	5,6NF	6,6NF

Overview: President Hamid Karzai secured a new term in 2009 after his main challenger, Abdullah Abdullah, withdrew in protest from a runoff election scheduled for November. The runoff had been called after the discovery of massive fraud reduced Karzai's lead in the first round, which was held in August following a controversial four-month delay. The deeply flawed voting took place as insurgent and other violence continued to mount, spreading to the capital and previously calmer areas in the north, and further hampering local and international efforts to rebuild Afghanistan's shattered infrastructure and institutions.

After decades of intermittent attempts to assert control and ward off Russian influence in the country, Britain recognized Afghanistan as a fully independent monarchy in 1921. Muhammad Zahir Shah ruled from 1933, until he was deposed in a 1973 coup, and a republic was declared. Afghanistan entered a period of continuous civil conflict in 1978, when a Marxist faction staged a coup and set out to transform the country's highly traditional society. The Soviet Union invaded to support its allies in 1979, but was defeated by U.S.-backed guerrillas and forced to withdraw in 1989.

The mujahideen guerrilla factions finally overthrew the Marxist government in 1992 and then battled one another for control of Kabul, killing more than 25,000 civilians in the capital by 1995. The Islamist Taliban movement entered the fray, seizing Kabul in 1996 and quickly establishing control over most of the country, the rest of which remained in the hands of other factions. In response to the terrorist attacks of September 11, 2001, the United States launched a military campaign to topple the Taliban regime and eliminate Saudi militant Osama bin Laden's terrorist network, al-Qaeda.

As a result of the December 2001 Bonn Agreement, an interim administration took office to replace the ousted Taliban. In June 2002, the United Nations oversaw an emergency *loya jirga* (gathering of representatives) that appointed a Transitional Administration (TA) to rule Afghanistan for a further two years. Interim leader Hamid Karzai won the votes of more than 80 percent of the delegates to become president and head of the TA.

A new constitution was ratified January 2004. It described Afghanistan as an

Islamic republic and called for a presidential system and a bicameral National Assembly. Later that year, Karzai won the landmark presidential election—Afghanistan's first in more than three decades—with 55 percent of the vote, and in December, he formed a cabinet that was a mix of technocrats and regional power brokers. Relatively peaceful elections for the new National Assembly and 34 provincial councils were held in September 2005. However, a large number of warlords and others involved in organized crime and human rights abuses were elected.

The new parliament convened in December 2005, and over the next several years, it made little progress on addressing political and economic reforms or passing key legislation. While some analysts had expressed concern that the legislative branch would be weak and largely subservient to the executive, it was often at odds with the president, making it difficult for him to advance the government's agenda. A new political alliance, the United National Front of Afghanistan (UNFA), formed in February 2007, with the goal of switching to a parliamentary system and empowering a strong prime minister.

The UN-mandated International Security Assistance Force (ISAF), which had been managed by NATO since August 2003, completed the expansion of its security and reconstruction mission from Kabul to the rest of the country in 2006. In addition to the roughly 50,000 ISAF troops, a separate force of about 10,000 U.S. troops pursued a parallel counterterrorism mission. Despite the multinational troop presence and the development of the Afghan army, Afghanistan largely remained under the sway of local military commanders, tribal leaders, warlords, drug traffickers, and petty bandits. Meanwhile, resurgent Taliban stepped up their attacks on the government and international forces, and steadily extended their influence over vast swaths of territory, particularly in the southern provinces of Kandahar and Helmand, but also in previously quiet areas of the north and west.

Recognizing the failures of the military campaign and the growing frustration of their own citizens, the United States and its NATO allies struggled in 2009 to implement better counterinsurgency practices and accelerate the training of Afghan soldiers and police. They also boosted their troop commitments, in part to maintain security during the year's presidential election, while the Afghan government continued with attempts to contain the Taliban insurgency by nonmilitary means, partly through "reconciliation" efforts aimed at bringing former antigovernment actors into the official fold. Nevertheless, thousands of civilians, security personnel, government officials, and foreign-aid workers were killed or injured during 2009 in an increasing number of insurgent attacks, air strikes by coalition forces, and clashes among factional militias and criminal gangs. Kidnapping also remained as a major concern.

The presidential election, held in August after a four-month delay, was characterized by low turnout, massive fraud, and international paralysis. After Karzai initially emerged as the outright winner with more than 50 percent of the vote, the confirmation of large-scale fraud significantly reduced his total, necessitating a November runoff against his main opponent, former foreign minister Abdullah Abdullah. However, Abdullah withdrew before the vote could be held, arguing that the flaws in the electoral system had not been adequately addressed, and Karzai was declared the winner.

Lingering doubts about the Karzai administration's legitimacy and integrity, combined with the continued deterioration in security, posed a major challenge to the central and provincial governments as they struggled to control areas under their jurisdiction, deliver basic services, and engage in vital reconstruction efforts. These problems also had a negative effect on the ability of civil society and humanitarian organizations to operate freely.

Political Rights and Civil Liberties: Afghanistan is not an electoral democracy. While elections have been held, significant problems remain with regard to the political framework, effective governance, and transparency. The directly elected president serves five-year terms and has the power to appoint ministers, subject to parliamentary approval. In the directly elected lower house of the National Assembly, the 249-seat Wolesi Jirga (House of the People), members stand for five-year terms. In the 102-seat Meshrano Jirga (House of Elders), the upper house, two-thirds of members are indirectly elected by the provinces, while one-third are appointed by the president. At least 68 of the Wolesi Jirga seats are reserved for women, while 10 are reserved for the nomadic Kuchi community. Provisions for women's representation have also been made for the Meshrano Jirga and provincial councils.

The 2004 presidential election was judged to be relatively free and fair despite allegations of intimidation by militias and insurgent groups, partisanship within the electoral administration, and other irregularities. Legislative elections originally scheduled for 2004 were postponed until September 2005 to allow more time for the government to map out district boundaries, conduct a census, enact election laws, and improve the security situation. These polls were also marred by what the electoral commission termed "serious localized fraud," intimidation, some violence, and other problems, although the overall results were broadly accepted by Afghans and the international community.

The 2009 presidential election, however, dashed any remaining confidence in the democratic strength of the Afghan political system. The constitution called for the election to be held by April, with incumbent president Hamid Karzai's term due to expire in May, but delays in passing the electoral law and slow international coordination resulted in the election being delayed until August. Fraud and manipulation during the voter registration process, low voter turnout, a compromised electoral management body, and insecurity in most of the country produced a preliminary victory for Karzai. The outcome was challenged by his main opponent, former foreign minister Abdullah Abdullah, and the two remained locked in a dispute over the election results for over two months. Though the extent of the fraud was not fully investigated or reported, election officials concluded that enough fraud had occurred to merit a runoff between Karzai and Abdullah in November. However, before the runoff could take place, Abdullah withdrew from the race, arguing that the electoral and judicial systems remained too corrupt to ensure a fair vote. Karzai was consequently declared the winner.

Restrictions on political activity continue. Levels of political freedom are higher in urban centers, but violence, insecurity, and repression prevail nationwide. Critics have warned that the 2003 Political Parties Law's vague language could be exploited to deny registration to parties on flimsy grounds. In addition, analysts viewed the adoption of the single-nontransferable-vote system for the 2005 legislative elections as a disadvantage for new political parties. Parties lack a formal role within the legislature, which further weakens their ability to contribute to stable political, policy-making, and legislative processes. There have been a number of violent attacks against members of the Afghan government, including assassination attempts on President Karzai.

The international community, concerned that government corruption is crippling the counterinsurgency campaign, has called on the new Karzai administration to make the issue its top priority, but it remains to be seen whether antigraft efforts will bear fruit. Corruption, nepotism, and cronyism are rampant, and woefully inadequate salaries exacerbate corrupt behavior by public sector workers. In addition, government transparency and accountability are often undermined by disjointed international involvement. Afghanistan was ranked 179 out of 180 countries surveyed in Transparency International's 2009 Corruption Perceptions Index.

Afghan media continue to grow and diversify but faced rising threats in 2009, mostly in the form of physical attacks and intimidation. Though a 2007 media law was intended to clarify press freedoms and limit government interference, a growing number of journalists have been arrested, threatened, or harassed by politicians, security services, and others in positions of power as a result of their coverage. The most high-profile case of state intimidation of the press has been that of Parwez Kambakhsh, a journalist with the daily newspaper *Janan-e-Naw,* who was sentenced to death for blasphemy in January 2008, though his sentence was commuted to 20 years in prison in October of that year, and he was ultimately pardoned in 2009. Media diversity and freedom are markedly higher in Kabul than elsewhere in the country, but some local warlords display limited tolerance for independent media in their areas. Dozens of private radio stations and several private television channels currently operate. Some independent outlets and publications have been criticized by conservative clerics for airing programs that "oppose Islam and national values," or fined by the authorities for similar reasons. The use of the internet and mobile telephones continues to grow rapidly and has broadened the flow of news and other information, particularly for urban residents.

Religious freedom has improved since the fall of the ultraconservative Taliban in late 2001, but it is still hampered by violence and harassment aimed at religious minorities and reformist Muslims. The constitution establishes Islam as the official religion. Blasphemy and apostasy by Muslims are considered capital crimes. While faiths other than Islam are permitted, non-Muslim proselytizing is strongly discouraged. A 2007 court ruling found the minority Baha'i faith to be a form of blasphemy, jeopardizing the legal status of that community. Hindus, Sikhs, and Shiite Muslims—particularly those from the Hazara ethnic group—have also faced official obstacles and discrimination by the Sunni Muslim majority. Militant groups have occasionally targeted mosques and clerics as part of the larger civil conflict.

Academic freedom is not officially restricted. In an effort to counter the teaching of extremist ideologies in Taliban-dominated religious schools, the government announced plans in 2007 to open state-run madrassahs. Militant attacks on schools worsened in 2006 and 2007, but the trend reversed somewhat in 2008, and incidents were sporadic in 2009. Meanwhile, the quality of school instruction and resources remains poor, and higher education is subject to bribery and prohibitively expensive for most Afghans.

The constitution has formally restored rights to assembly and association, subject to some restrictions, but they are upheld erratically from region to region. Police and other security personnel have occasionally used excessive force when confronted with demonstrations or protests.

The work of hundreds of international and Afghan nongovernmental organizations (NGOs) is not formally constrained by the authorities, but their ability to operate freely and effectively is impeded by the worsening security situation and increasingly restrictive bureaucratic rules. Following the death of seven UN staff members in a brazen attack on a guesthouse in November 2009, half of the UN staff in the country were evacuated. Both foreign and Afghan NGO staff have been targeted in kidnappings and violent attacks by criminals and insurgents, and security incidents against NGOs are on the rise. Civil society activists, particularly those who focus on human rights or accountability issues, continue to face some threats and harassment. Despite broad constitutional protections for workers, labor rights are not well defined, and there are currently no enforcement or dispute-resolution mechanisms. Child labor is reportedly common.

The judicial system operates haphazardly, and justice in many places is administered on the basis of a mixture of legal codes by inadequately trained judges. Corruption in the judiciary is extensive, and judges and lawyers are often subject to threats from local leaders or armed groups. Traditional justice remains the main recourse for the population, particularly in rural areas. The Supreme Court, composed of religious scholars who have little knowledge of civil jurisprudence, is particularly in need of reform. Prison conditions are extremely poor, with many detainees held illegally, and a massive June 2008 prison break by the Taliban in Kandahar freed hundreds of inmates. The national intelligence agency, as well as some warlords and political leaders, maintain their own prisons and do not allow access to detainees.

In a prevailing climate of impunity, government ministers, as well as warlords in some provinces, sanction widespread abuses by the police, military, and intelligence forces under their command, including arbitrary arrest and detention, torture, extortion, and extrajudicial killings. The Afghan Independent Human Rights Commission (AIHRC), which was formed in 2002 and focuses on raising awareness of human rights issues as well as monitoring and investigating abuses, receives hundreds of complaints of rights violations each year. In addition to the abuses by security forces, reported violations have involved land theft, displacement, kidnapping, child trafficking, domestic violence, and forced marriage.

A facet of the new counterinsurgency doctrine adopted by international forces involves reforming detention policies at facilities like the U.S.-controlled Bagram air base. Human Rights Watch has documented numerous cases of abuse of Afghan detainees by U.S. forces over the past several years, and eight detainees are confirmed to have died in U.S. custody. Few of the service personnel involved have been charged or punished. Human Rights First has reported that Afghan detainees who are handed over by the U.S. government continue to suffer abuses at the hands of Afghan officials.

The Afghan National Army continued to grow in 2009, with strong support from international donors. Existing soldiers are reportedly well trained and have participated ably in a variety of counterterrorism and counterinsurgency operations. In contrast, the National Police remains plagued by inadequate training, illiteracy, corruption, involvement in drug trafficking, and high levels of desertion, but donors continue to press for the force's expansion at the cost of quality and standards. The intelligence service, the National Directorate of Security, lacks transparency and stands accused of serious human rights violations.

An estimated 2,000 illegal armed groups, with as many as 125,000 members, continue to operate. A voluntary disarmament, demobilization, and reintegration (DDR) program targeting irregular militia forces between 2003 and 2005, and the follow-up Disbandment of Illegal Armed Groups (DIAG) initiative, succeeded in demobilizing over 60,000 militiamen and collected a considerable amount of weaponry. However, the disarmament process never moved to the enforcement stage as planned, and international programs supported by the United States, Britain, and Canada to rearm informal militias as a counterinsurgency force are actively undermining efforts to curtail and regulate the use of illegal arms. Afghan law demands that illegal armed groups be excluded from elections, but Afghan institutions lack the will and capacity to enforce this ban meaningfully. Such groups continue to reinforce their power bases through legitimate and illegitimate means, and pose a troubling threat to stability and good governance.

More than 230,000 civilians remain displaced within the country, according to a recent report released by the Office of the United Nations High Commissioner for Refugees. Humanitarian agencies and Afghan authorities are ill-equipped to deal with the displaced. Factors like the poor security situation and widespread land-grabbing have prevented refugees from returning to their homes, and many congregate instead around major urban centers. In the absence of a properly functioning legal system, the state remains unable to protect property rights.

Women's formal rights to education and employment have been restored, and in some areas, women are once again participating in public life. Women accounted for about 10 percent of the candidates in the 2005 parliamentary elections, and roughly 41 percent of registered voters were women. There were two women among the 41 candidates for the 2009 presidential election, but on the whole, female participation was limited by threats, harassment, and social restrictions on traveling alone and appearing in public. Another major setback to women's rights came with the passage in 2009 of new legislation that derogated many constitutional rights for women belonging to the Shiite Muslim minority, leaving questions of inheritance, marriage, and personal freedoms to be determined by conservative Shiite religious authorities. Social discrimination and violence remain pervasive, with domestic violence occurring in an estimated 95 percent of households, according to one survey. Women's choices regarding marriage and divorce remain circumscribed by custom and discriminatory laws, and the forced marriage of young girls to older men or widows to their husbands' male relations is a problem. Nearly 60 percent of Afghan girls are married before the legal age of 16, according to UNICEF.

Albania

Political Rights: 3
Civil Liberties: 3
Status: Partly Free

Population: 3,196,000
Capital: Tirana

Ten-Year Ratings Timeline For Year Under Review (Political Rights, Civil Liberties, Status)

2000	2001	2002	2003	2004	2005	2006	2007	2008	2009
4,5PF	3,4PF	3,3PF	3,3PF	3,3PF	3,3PF	3,3PF	3,3PF	3,3PF	3,3PF

Overview: Prime Minister Sali Berisha retained his post after his Democratic Party won parliamentary elections in June. However, the opposition Socialist Party mounted protests to demand a recount and boycotted the new parliament through the end of the year. Albania achieved a major goal in April, when it formally joined NATO; it filed an application to join the European Union later that month.

Ruling from World War II until his death in 1985, communist dictator Enver Hoxha turned Albania into the most isolated country in Europe. The regime began to adopt more liberal policies in the late 1980s, and multiparty elections in 1992 brought the Democratic Party (PD), led by Sali Berisha, to power. Continuing poverty and corruption, along with unrest after the 1997 collapse of several vast investment scams, resulted in the election of a new government led by the Socialist Party (PS).

Berisha and the PD returned to power in the 2005 parliamentary elections. While the poll was not free from fraud, it was praised for bringing Albania's first postcommunist rotation of power without significant violence. In 2007, the parliament elected PD candidate Bamir Topi as the country's new president.

Berisha's government was plagued by allegations of corruption and abuse of office in 2008, including a case stemming from a weapons depot explosion that killed 26 people and destroyed hundreds of homes in March. Nevertheless, the PD secured a narrow victory in the June 2009 parliamentary elections, which were held under a new electoral code passed in late 2008. The ruling party took 68 seats in the 140-seat parliament and eventually formed a coalition government with four much smaller parties: the Socialist Movement for Integration, a PS splinter group that won four seats; the Republican Party, with one seat; the Union for Human Rights, an ethnic Greek party, with one seat; and the Union for Justice and Integration, a party representing the Cham minority, with one seat. This left the PS, with 65 seats, in opposition. It boycotted the new parliament, which convened in September, and mounted a series of street protests to demand a fraud investigation and a partial ballot recount. Berisha countered that the courts had approved the results. The opposition boycott continued at year's end.

Albania was formally welcomed into NATO in April 2009, and later that month, it filed its application to join the European Union (EU), with which it already had a Stabilization and Association Agreement. However, EU accession remained uncertain and would not come before 2015.

Political Rights and Civil Liberties: Albania is an electoral democracy. International observers of the 2009 parliamentary elections hailed improvements in a number of areas, but also cited problems including media bias, abuse of state resources, political pressure on public employees, and flaws in the tabulation process. Under a new electoral code passed in late 2008, the unicameral, 140-member Kuvendi Popullor (People's Assembly) was elected through proportional representation in 12 regional districts of varying size. All members serve four-year terms. The prime minister is designated by the majority party or coalition, and the president—who does not hold executive powers but heads the military and plays an important role in selecting senior judges—is chosen by the parliament for a five-year term.

Despite their sharp, personality-driven rivalry, the two major political parties, the PD and the PS, ran on nearly identical platforms and pledges of EU integration. They also cooperated in 2008 to pass the new electoral rules, which, as expected, strongly disadvantaged smaller parties. Minor parties held some 40 seats after the 2005 elections, but this fell to just 7 seats—split among four parties—in 2009.

Corruption is pervasive, and the EU has called for rigorous implementation of anticorruption measures. However, Prime Minister Sali Berisha has refused to dismiss key allies facing indictments by Prosecutor General Ina Rama, who has resisted government pressure with support from U.S. and EU officials. Fatmir Mediu, leader of the Republican Party, resigned as defense minister after the 2008 depot explosion, and his parliamentary immunity was lifted that year. He was indicted along with 28 other defendants in the depot case in early 2009, but the Supreme Court ruled in September that his reelection to the parliament in June effectively restored his immunity, and he was named environment minister in Berisha's new government. Similarly, Foreign Minister Lulzim Basha was indicted for corruption related to road-building projects, but he remained in government as interior minister after the elections. Former deputy transport minister Nikolin Jaka had been sentenced for related crimes in 2008, but was acquitted on appeal in 2009. In a survey released in 2009, 52 percent of respondents said they had to pay a bribe within the last year. Albania was ranked 95 out of 180 countries surveyed in Transparency International's 2009 Corruption Perceptions Index.

While the constitution guarantees freedom of expression, the intermingling of powerful business, political, and media interests inhibits the development of independent outlets. During the 2009 campaign period, most outlets were seen as biased toward either the PS or PD. Reporters have little job security and remain subject to lawsuits, intimidation, and in some cases, physical attacks by those facing media scrutiny. Berisha routinely denigrates the media, and his government has placed financial pressure on critical outlets. In January, the authorities evicted a critical newspaper, *Tema*, from its offices in a state-owned building despite a court order to halt the action. In February, an editorial in a paper that was close to Berisha called for the murder of Mero Baze, *Tema*'s publisher. Baze was allegedly beaten severely in November by oil magnate and Berisha associate Rezart Taci and his bodyguards, after the journalist accused Taci of tax evasion on his television show. Taci and two of his guards were subsequently arrested for the attack, and the case was pending at year's end. The government does not limit internet access.

The constitution provides for freedom of religion, and it is usually upheld in practice. In October 2009, an imam in Durres was arrested for allegedly inciting terrorism. The government generally does not limit academic freedom, although both students and teachers were reportedly pressured to support the PD ahead of the 2009 elections.

Freedoms of association and assembly are generally respected. Independent NGOs are active even if underfunded, and their influence on the government is slowly growing. The constitution guarantees workers the rights to organize and bargain collectively, and most have the right to strike. However, effective collective bargaining remains limited, and contracts are often difficult to enforce. Child labor is a problem, particularly in the garment industry.

The constitution provides for an independent judiciary, but the courts are subject to political pressure. The judiciary and law enforcement agencies are inefficient and prone to corruption, and judicial proceedings can be unjustifiably delayed. Enforcement of court decisions is weak, especially when they go against government interests. In February 2009, the Constitutional Court suspended a controversial new lustration law, pending a ruling on its constitutionality. The law, passed in December 2008, would allow a special commission to purge judges and prosecutors based on their role in the communist regime. Opponents said it could result in the dismissal of many top judges and cripple ongoing corruption cases.

Police reportedly engage in abuse of suspects during arrest and interrogation, and such ill-treatment is lightly if ever punished despite vigorous criticism from the country's human rights ombudsman. New prison facilities have been constructed, but inmates continue to suffer from overcrowding and lack of adequate medical treatment.

High-level crimes associated with the Balkan wars of the 1990s have gone unpunished. In 2009, former security service commander Arben Sefgjini and three former colleagues were on trial for the 1995 torture and murder of a man who may have witnessed conversations between then president Berisha and Yugoslav leader Slobodan Milosevic about oil smuggling. Berisha fired Sefgjini as head of the tax service in January.

Weak state institutions have augmented the power of crime syndicates, and Albania is reportedly a key transshipment point for drug smugglers. Traditional tribal law and revenge killings are practiced in parts of the north. In two high-profile crimes in 2009, Supreme Court judge Ardian Nuni was shot and seriously wounded in February, and PS lawmaker Fatmir Xhindi was assassinated by two gunmen in May. The cases remained unsolved at year's end, and Nuni reportedly sought asylum in the United States.

Roma face significant social and economic marginalization, but other minorities are generally well integrated. In 2009, an ethnic Greek mayor who has advocated regional autonomy was sentenced to six months in jail and a fine for removing road signs on the grounds that they did not include Greek translations.

Berisha announced plans in July to legalize gay marriage, drawing objections from religious leaders. Homosexuality was decriminalized in 1995, but discrimination in society and by law enforcement officials remains strong.

Women are underrepresented in most governmental institutions. A new 30 percent quota for party candidate lists helped to raise women's presence in the parliament to 23 seats in 2009, from 10 in 2005, though the quota rules contained a number of loopholes. Domestic violence, which is believed to be widespread, is rarely punished by the authorities. Albania is a source country for trafficking in women and children, with the latter typically exploited as beggars in European countries. The EU reported in 2009 that the government has made an effort to combat the practice, but that human and financial resources remain insufficient.

Algeria

Political Rights: 6
Civil Liberties: 5
Status: Not Free

Population: 35,370,000
Capital: Algiers

Ten-Year Ratings Timeline For Year Under Review (Political Rights, Civil Liberties, Status)

2000	2001	2002	2003	2004	2005	2006	2007	2008	2009
6,5NF	6,5NF	6,5NF	6,5NF	6,5NF	6,5NF	6,5NF	6,5NF	6,5NF	6,5NF

Overview: Press freedom was severely curtailed prior to the April 2009 presidential elections, which President Abdelaziz Bouteflika won with over 90 percent of the vote amid protests of fraud by his opponents. The government consolidated its internet monitoring power during the year, and international observers reported that the authorities began blocking websites. Meanwhile, as the terrorist group al-Qaeda in the Islamic Maghreb continued to attack military, state, and foreign targets in the country, the government joined forces with neighboring countries to combat the regional threat of terrorism.

Unlike many other French colonies, Algeria was considered an integral part of France, leading to an especially bloody war of independence that lasted from 1954 to 1962. After the military overthrew the country's first president in 1965, it dominated Algerian politics for the next four decades, backing the National Liberation Front (FLN) to the exclusion of all other parties for most of that time. President Chadli Benjedid permitted the establishment of legal opposition parties in 1988, and Islamist groups quickly gained popularity in the face of the government's failures; the Islamic Salvation Front (FIS) became the main opposition faction. With the FIS poised to win parliamentary elections in 1991, the army canceled the elections, forced Benjedid from office, and summarily imprisoned FIS leaders under a declared state of emergency.

Over the next decade, various Islamist groups engaged in a bloody civil conflict against the military and one another. All sides targeted civilians and perpetrated large-scale human rights abuses, causing well over 150,000 deaths and the disappearance of at least 6,000 people. Journalists and intellectuals were also targeted. In 1999, the military-backed candidate—former foreign minister Abdelaziz Bouteflika—easily won the presidential election after his opponents withdrew to protest alleged fraud. Bouteflika's first attempt at resolving the civil war was the promulgation of a civil harmony law, which granted partial amnesty to combatants who renounced violence. A few thousand militants surrendered, but the more uncompromising groups—including one which later renamed itself al-Qaeda in the Islamic Maghreb (AQIM)—continued to kill government personnel and civilians. The next several years saw occasional outbursts of violence, and the government continued to commit human rights abuses.

The FLN gained power in the 2002 elections to the lower house of Parliament and the 2003 elections to the upper house, while the number of seats won by the army-backed

National Democratic Rally (RND) fell considerably in both. Bouteflika, who to distance himself from the military, won reelection in 2004 with 85 percent of the vote.

In 2005, Algerians overwhelmingly approved a referendum on the Charter for Peace and National Reconciliation. The document offered a general amnesty to most militants and government agents for crimes committed during the civil war, and it called for victims to receive compensation. Victims' groups criticized the charter for not addressing the issue of the disappeared, and international human rights groups denounced it for not allowing perpetrators to be brought to justice.

Elections for Parliament's lower house in May 2007 drew a turnout of just 35 percent, the lowest in Algerian history. Many opposition groups, both Islamist and leftist, asked supporters not to participate, arguing that the results would be rigged. The FLN lost 63 seats in the voting, though it remained the largest party, followed by the RND, the Rally for Culture and Democracy (RCD), and the Movement for Peaceful Society. Indirect elections for the upper house in December 2009 saw the FLN again secure the largest number of seats, followed by the RND.

On April 9, 2009, Bouteflika won his third term, with around 90 percent of the vote, amid accusations of fraud from the other five candidates. Although officials announced a 74 percent voter turnout, an informal poll conducted by the Associated Press at 17 randomly chosen voting stations indicated that turnout was about half that number.

Algeria continued to be racked by terrorist attacks against government and foreign targets throughout 2009. AQIM claimed responsibility for a series of attacks throughout the year, including a March suicide bombing that killed two guards; a June ambush that left 18 national gendarmeries officers dead; a July ambush on a military supply convoy that killed 23 soldiers; and an October attack that left seven Algerian security guards at a Canadian water project dead. Immediately before the April presidential election, terror groups linked to al-Qaeda carried out three ambushes, killing five security guards, and six voting stations were set on fire. Algerian nationals with ties to AQIM have been increasingly implicated in terrorist plots abroad. In November, Italian police broke up a terrorist cell based in Milan, arresting 17 men living in Italy and neighboring countries. Similar arrests occurred in France and the United Kingdom, although on a smaller scale.

In response to terrorist attacks, the government appeared to be increasing its antiterrorism efforts throughout the year. In March, it announced that 150 militants had been killed and another 50 had surrendered in exchange for amnesty, including Ali Ben Touati, a senior commanding officer of AQIM. In May, eight militants were killed in a government raid of AQIM strongholds just east of Algiers. Meanwhile, in August, Algeria hosted a meeting between high-level military commanders from Mali, Niger, and Mauritania in an effort to generate regional cooperation in an antiterrorism initiative. Several thousand additional Algerian troops were sent to the already-large contingent of troops protecting the country's southern border.

Political Rights and Civil Liberties: Algeria is not an electoral democracy. However, Algerian parliamentary elections are more democratic than those in many other Arab states. The military still plays an important role in politics despite fluctuations in its prominence in recent years. The June 2008 appointment of Ahmed Ouyahia as prime minister in a cabinet shuffle appeared to signal an increase in military influence, as he had first held the post as part of the military-dominated regime of the 1990s.

The People's National Assembly (APN), the lower house of the bicameral Parliament, has 389 members directly elected for five-year terms. The upper house, the National Council (CN), has 144 members serving six-year term; 96 members are chosen through indirect elections by local assemblies, and the president appoints the remaining 48. The president is directly elected for five-year terms, and constitutional amendments passed in November 2008 allowed President Abdelaziz Bouteflika to run for a third term in April 2009. The amendments, which were approved 500 to 21 in a joint session of Parliament and without recourse to a referendum, also increased the president's powers relative to the premiership and other entities, drawing criticism from segments of the press and opposition parties.

The Ministry of the Interior must approve political parties before they can operate legally. While there are dozens of active political parties, movements that are deemed too radically Islamist are outlawed, and many of the Islamist groups that were banned in the 1990s remain illegal.

High levels of corruption still plague Algeria's business and public sectors. Customs police face particular scrutiny, both in the press and by government monitors; by the end of May 2009, 202 customs officers had been arrested on bribery charges. Algeria was ranked 111 out of 180 countries surveyed in Transparency International's 2009 Corruption Perceptions Index.

Journalists face an array of government tools designed to control the press, but current restrictions bear little resemblance to those during the peak of the civil war in the mid-1990s, when journalists were regularly murdered for their work. Private newspapers have been published in Algeria for nearly two decades, and journalists have been aggressive in their coverage of government affairs. While Arabic- and French-language satellite channels are popular, the government keeps tight control over local television and radio broadcasts. In late 2009, the information minister announced a proposed centralized system for monitoring incoming and outgoing internet information. The purported purpose of the system was to inhibit cyber terrorists and online piracy, as well as limit access to pornography.

International press freedom groups continued to document numerous cases of harassment of critical journalists in 2009. During the April presidential elections, the government banned multiple publications that criticized the president. Foreign journalists often faced obstacles in covering the election, including being arrested or otherwise physically prevented from reporting on the polls. Defamation remains a criminal offense. According to the U.S.-based Committee to Protect Journalists, the managing editor of the news website al-Waha, Nedjar Hadj Daoud, began serving a six-month prison sentence in March 2009 after being convicted in 2005 of defamation over an article he wrote that was critical of a local government official; however, he was released days later for medical reasons. Rabah Lamouchi, the local correspondent of the national Arabic-language daily *Ennahar*, was charged with defamation and lacking press credentials; he was convicted in July and sentenced to six months in prison. The privately owned daily newspaper, *El Watan*, also faced continued pressure from government officials and private entities. In December 2008, the editor of *El Watan* and one reporter were convicted of libeling a faith healer in articles published in 2004 and were sentenced to three months imprisonment and a fine of 50,000 dinars (US$678); both remained free at the end of 2009 pending their appeals. The editor was summoned before the court again in December 2008, facing libel charges for three different articles. Two charges were brought by the CEO of Air Algerie, one related to an article that covered fare hikes by the airline. Police brought a third charge connected to a 2001 article that claimed the police had killed over 100 protesters in Bouira. In the first quarter of 2009, the editor was summoned before police at least 14 times for questioning related to defamation charges, sparking criticism from international observers who considered the police questioning to be harassment.

Algeria's population is overwhelmingly Sunni Muslim, and the small non-Muslim communities are able to practice their faiths without systematic harassment. However, non-Muslims may only gather to worship at state-approved locations, proselytizing by non-Muslims is illegal, and the government in February 2008 began enforcing an ordinance that tightened restrictions on minority faiths. Given Algeria's civil conflict, security services monitor mosques for radical Islamist activity. Academic freedom is largely respected.

The police sometimes disperse peaceful gatherings, and the government generally discourages demonstrations featuring clear or implicit criticism of the authorities. As terrorist attacks continued in 2009, the government remained wary of large public gatherings and restricted freedom of assembly. An attempt by minority parties in April to stage demonstrations in favor of boycotting the 2009 presidential elections was stopped by the authorities, who blocked marchers from taking to the streets of an Algiers suburb. In July, police dispersed a conference organized by the Collective of the Families of the Disappeared in Algeria. Permits are required to establish nongovernmental organizations, and those with Islamist leanings are regarded with suspicion by the government. Workers can establish independent trade unions. The main labor federation, the General Union of Algerian Workers, has been criticized for being too close to the government and failing to advance workers' interests aggressively.

The judiciary is not independent and is susceptible to government pressure. International human rights activists have accused the security forces of practicing torture. The human rights situation remains poor, though there have been significant gains since the peak of the civil war. As of October 2009, most of the eight Algerian citizens who had been repatriated after having been in U.S. custody in Guantanamo Bay were released pending domestic trials on terrorism-related charges. Prison conditions generally do not meet international standards. Overcrowding remains the primary issue; other conditions, including nutrition and hygiene, are also substandard. In September, the justice minister announced that 14 prison workers had been prosecuted and jailed for mistreating their charges, and stated that abuse of inmates by prison officials would not be tolerated in general.

Algeria's ethnic composition is a mixture of Arabs and Berbers. Those who identify themselves as Arabs have traditionally formed the country's elite. In the last few years, following outbreaks of antigovernment violence in the Berber community, officials have made more of an effort to recognize Berber cultural demands. Tamazight, the Berber language, is now a national language.

While most citizens are free to move throughout the country and abroad with little government interference, the authorities closely monitor and limit the movement of suspected terrorists. The long-standing state of emergency permits the government to restrict where certain people live and work. Men of military draft age are not allowed to leave the country without government consent.

Women continue to face discrimination at both the legal and societal levels. Under the family code, which is based on Islamic law, women do not enjoy equal rights in marriage, divorce, and inheritance. They are poorly represented in parliament, holding only 5.2 percent of the upper house and 7.2 percent of the popularly elected lower house. In 2009, presidential candidate Louisa Hanoun came in a distant second place, with about 4 percent of the vote. Under legislative changes made to the nationality law in 2005, Algeria is one of the few countries in the region to allow women to transfer their nationality to their children, regardless of their father's nationality. A law adopted in January 2009 criminalizes all forms of trafficking in persons, but had not gone into effect by year's end.

Andorra

Political Rights: 1
Civil Liberties: 1
Status: Free

Population: 86,000
Capital: Andorra la Vela

Ten-Year Ratings Timeline For Year Under Review (Political Rights, Civil Liberties, Status)

2000	2001	2002	2003	2004	2005	2006	2007	2008	2009
1,1F	1,1F	1,1F	1,1F	1,1F	1,1F	1,1F	1,1F	1,1F	1,1F

Overview:
In March 2009, French president Nicolas Sarkozy threatened to resign as co-prince of Andorra if the principality did not improve its banking laws and increase transparency. The Andorran government proposed legislation in September that would ease bank-secrecy rules. The Social Democratic Party took power in the April parliamentary elections, defeating the incumbent Liberal Party of Andorra.

As a co-principality, Andorra was ruled for centuries by the French head of state and the bishop of Seu d'Urgel, Spain. The 1993 constitution retained the titular co-princes but transformed the government into a parliamentary democracy. Andorra joined the United Nations that year and the Council of Europe in 1994, but it is not a member of the European Union (EU).

In April 2009, the country held national elections, bringing the Social Democratic Party to power with 14 out of the 28 seats in the Consell General, or parliament. The Reformist Coalition, including the incumbent Liberal Party of Andorra which had ruled for 15 years, won 11 seats, and the remaining 3 seats were taken by Andorra for Change. Jaume Bartumeu of the Social Democratic Party replaced Albert Pintat as the Cap de Govern (Head of Government) in June.

In the first half of the year, the Pintat government continued to implement banking reforms as required by the Organization for Economic Cooperation and Development (OECD), which led to Andorra's removal from the OECD "gray list" in April

2009. The country has participated in the EU Savings Tax Directive since 2005, which provided a way to tax revenue from savings accounts held by EU citizens in a member state other than their country of residence or in certain non-EU countries.

In March 2009, French president Nicolas Sarkozy threatened to renounce his title as co-prince if Andorra did not increase the transparency of its banking system. The government proposed a law in September that lifts bank secrecy on information requested by other countries; the law was expected to be implemented in 2010.

Political Rights and Civil Liberties: Andorra is an electoral democracy. Popular elections to the 28-member Consell General, which selects the executive council president, or head of government, are held every four years. Half of the members are chosen in two-seat constituencies known as parishes, and the other half are chosen through a national system of proportional representation.

The people have the right to establish and join different political parties. However, more than 60 percent of the population consists of noncitizens, who have no right to vote.

Transparency International did not review or rank Andorra in its 2009 Corruption Perceptions Index. However, the country implemented several financial reforms during the year in an attempt to open its economy, which resulted in Andorra's removal from the OECD "gray list" in April.

Freedom of speech is respected across the country. There are two independent daily newspapers (*Diari d'Andorra* and *El Periodic d'Andorra*), and residents have access to broadcasts from neighboring France and Spain as well as unrestricted internet access.

Although the constitution recognizes the state's special relationship with the Roman Catholic Church, the government no longer subsidizes the Church. Religious minorities like Mormons and Jehovah's Witnesses are free to seek converts. Despite years of negotiations between the Muslim community and the government, a proper mosque for the country's roughly 2,000 Muslims has still not been built. While requests to convert public buildings or former churches for this purpose have been denied, the government does provide the Muslim community with public facilities for various religious functions. Academic freedom is respected.

Freedoms of assembly and association are generally respected, and domestic and international human rights organizations operate freely. Although the government recognizes that both workers and employers have the right to defend their interests, there are no laws guaranteeing the right to strike, penalizing antiunion discrimination, or regulating collective bargaining. There have been few advances in labor rights since the creation of a registry for associations in 2001, which enabled trade unions to gain the legal recognition that they previously lacked. However, the government passed a law in January 2009 that guarantees unions the right to operate.

The judicial system, which is based on Spanish and French civil codes, does not include the power of judicial review of legislative acts. Police can detain suspects for up to 48 hours without charging them. Prison conditions meet international standards.

Under Andorra's restrictive naturalization criteria, one must marry a resident

Andorran or live in the country for more than 20 years to qualify for citizenship. Prospective citizens are also required to learn Catalan, the national language. Although they do not have the right to vote, noncitizen residents receive most of the social and economic benefits of citizenship.

Immigrant workers, primarily from North Africa, complain that they lack the rights of citizens. Nearly 7,000 such immigrants have legal status, but many hold only "temporary work authorizations." Temporary workers are in a precarious position, as they must leave the country when their job contract expires.

Citizens have the right to own property. Legislation passed in November 2008 fully opened up 200 key economic sectors to foreign investment. Also under the new law, noncitizens can now hold up to 49 percent capital in other established sectors. All foreign investment restrictions are expected to be lifted within five years.

Women enjoy the same legal rights as men, and recently gained significant representation in government, taking 10 out of 28 seats in the April 2009 parliamentary elections. There are no specific laws addressing violence against women, which remains a problem. In 2009, there was a 40 percent increase in reports of physical abuse over the previous year. There are no government departments for women's issues or government-run shelters for battered women. Abortion is illegal, except to save the life of the mother.

Angola

Political Rights: 6　　　　　　　　　　　　　**Population:** 17,074,000
Civil Liberties: 5　　　　　　　　　　　　　**Capital:** Luanda
Status: Not Free

Ten-Year Ratings Timeline For Year Under Review (Political Rights, Civil Liberties, Status)

2000	2001	2002	2003	2004	2005	2006	2007	2008	2009
6,6NF	6,6NF	6,5NF	6,5NF	6,5NF	6,5NF	6,5NF	6,5NF	6,5NF	6,5NF

Overview:　　A presidential election that had been scheduled for 2009 after repeated delays was postponed yet again during the year, as a commission dominated by the ruling party failed to meet its deadline to present a new draft constitution. Also in 2009, Angola and the Democratic Republic of Congo engaged in tit-for-tat refugee expulsions, sending thousands of Angolans back over the border without adequate humanitarian preparations.

Angola was racked by civil war for nearly three decades following independence from Portugal in 1975. Peace accords in 1991 and 1994 failed to end fighting between the rebel National Union for the Total Independence of Angola (UNITA) and the government, controlled by the Popular Movement for the Liberation of Angola (MPLA), but the death of UNITA leader Jonas Savimbi in 2002 helped to spur a successful ceasefire deal later that year. UNITA subsequently transformed itself into Angola's largest opposition party.

The conflict claimed an estimated one million lives, displaced more than four million people, and forced over half a million to flee to neighboring countries. Many resettled people have remained without land, basic resources, or even identification documents. The resettlement process was slowed by the presence of an estimated 500,000 land mines and a war-ruined infrastructure, which made large tracts of the country inaccessible to humanitarian aid. The United Nations concluded its voluntary refugee repatriation program in 2007, and between August and October 2009, Angola and the neighboring Democratic Republic of Congo (DRC) engaged in a series of tit-for-tat expulsions. The resulting return of some 32,000 Angolans and 19,000 Congolese to their home countries raised concerns about a humanitarian crisis.

Legislative elections, delayed repeatedly since 1997, were finally held in September 2008. As expected, the ruling MPLA won a sweeping victory, taking 191 of 220 seats. UNITA placed second among 14 parties, with 16 seats. While both domestic and international observers found that the results reflected the people's will, the voting was less than free and fair. The run-up to the elections was marred by political violence, pro-MPLA bias in the state media, and other problems, and many polling places in the capital failed to open on election day. UNITA accepted the outcome after an initial challenge of the Luanda results was rejected by the electoral commission.

The presidential election, scheduled for 2009 after a number of delays, was postponed once again that year. The MPLA made a new constitution a precondition for the presidential vote, and in July 2009, the country's Constitutional Commission announced that it would not meet the September deadline for presenting its draft. The commission was made up of members of the MPLA-dominated parliament.

Angola, Africa's second-largest oil producer, has enjoyed an economic boom in recent years, though it slowed in 2009 following a drop in oil prices. Corruption and mismanagement have prevented the country's wealth from reaching most residents. Eighty-five percent of the population engages in subsistence agriculture, and the United Nations estimates that 54 percent of the population lives on less than $1.25 a day.

Political Rights and Civil Liberties:

Angola is not an electoral democracy. Long-delayed legislative elections held in September 2008, while largely reflective of the people's will, were not free and fair. The 220-seat National Assembly, whose members serve four-year terms, has little power, and 90 percent of legislation originates in the executive branch. The president, who is supposed to serve five-year terms, directly appoints the prime minister, cabinet, and provincial governors. Presidential elections, repeatedly delayed since 1997, were postponed again in 2009.

The 2008 legislative elections were contested by 14 parties, but the electoral framework was highly advantageous to the ruling MPLA; aside from UNITA, the main opposition party, just three smaller parties won seats. The National Electoral Commission (CNE), which was dominated by MPLA loyalists, denied opposition parties access to the voter registry and obstructed the accreditation of domestic monitors who were not aligned with the government. In addition, the government released state funding for opposition parties later than mandated, and the MPLA exploited additional state resources to support its own campaign. Voting in Luanda—

home to between one-quarter and one-third of registered voters—was marred by serious irregularities, including late delivery of ballot papers, 320 polling stations that failed to open, and a breakdown in the use of voter rolls to check identities. While political violence rose in the run-up to the elections, it has decreased significantly since 2002, and the government provided security for opposition rallies around the country.

Corruption and patronage are endemic in the government, and bribery often underpins business activity. Business regulations are reportedly outdated and poorly implemented, and state budget-making and spending processes have been criticized for extreme opacity and other weaknesses. In November 2009, President Jose Eduardo dos Santos called for a crackdown on corruption, alleging that MPLA members had squandered large portions of the country's oil revenues; the president himself is alleged to be one the country's richest men. Angola was ranked 162 out of 180 countries surveyed in Transparency International's 2009 Corruption Perceptions Index.

Media restrictions were eased somewhat after 2002, but despite constitutional guarantees of freedom of expression, journalists are driven to self-censorship by the threat of dismissal, detention, and legal sanction by authorities. Defamation of the president or his representatives and libel are criminal offenses, punishable by imprisonment or fines. The 2006 Press Law ended the state monopoly on television broadcasting, called for the creation of a public service broadcaster, and allowed journalists to use truth as a defense in libel and defamation trials. However, the law includes onerous registration requirements as well as restrictive provisions concerning journalistic "duties" and access to information. Moreover, almost none of the legislation required for the law's implementation had been passed by the end of 2009.

The state owns the only daily newspaper and national radio station, as well as the main television stations. In December 2008, however, the country's first private television station, TV Zimbo, was launched. The state outlets favored the ruling party ahead of the 2008 elections, and private media are often denied access to official information and events. There are several independent weeklies and radio stations in Luanda that criticize the government, but they have reported funding problems, and the state dominates media elsewhere. In 2009, authorities continued to prevent the outspoken Roman Catholic radio station Radio Ecclesia from broadcasting outside the capital. Internet access is limited to a small elite, as most citizens lack computers or even electricity.

In 2008, journalist Fernando Lelo was sentenced to 12 years in prison after being tried along with several soldiers before a military court in the restive region of Cabinda; the defendants were accused of rebel activity, but Human Rights Watch (HRW) and other groups said Lelo was mainly targeted for critical opinions he had expressed while working for Voice of America. Separately, in April 2009, two newspaper editors were charged with inciting criminal activity after publishing photographs of the corpses of the recently slain president of Guinea-Bissau and his military chief. One of the editors, William Tonet of the biweekly *Folha 8*, was barred from foreign travel in May.

Religious freedom is widely respected, despite colonial-era statutes that ban non-Christian religious groups. The educational system barely functions, suffering from underpaid and often corrupt teachers and severely damaged infrastructure.

The constitution guarantees freedom of assembly and association. Increasingly, authorities are allowing opposition groups to hold demonstrations in Luanda, though crackdowns are common in the interior. The right to strike and form unions is provided by the constitution, but the MPLA dominates the labor movement and only a few independent unions exist. Hundreds of nongovernmental organizations (NGOs) operate in Angola, many of them demanding political reform, government accountability, and human rights protections. Churches in particular have grown more outspoken. However, the government has occasionally threatened organizations with closure. In 2008, the government ordered the local representatives of the UN High Commissioner for Human Rights to cease activities and leave the country. Ahead of that year's elections, the government accused the local Association for Justice, Peace, and Democracy (AJPD) of having illegal statutes and threatened to close the organization. The Constitutional Court heard the case in September 2009, and a decision was pending at year's end.

The judiciary is subject to extensive executive influence, though courts occasionally rule against the government. Supreme Court judges are appointed to life terms by the president without legislative input or approval. The courts in general are hampered by a lack of training and infrastructure, a large backlog of cases, and corruption. While the government has sought to train more municipal magistrates, municipal courts are rarely operational. As a result, traditional or informal courts are utilized.

Lengthy pretrial detention is common, and prisoners are subject to torture, severe overcrowding, sexual abuse, extortion, and a lack of basic services. Despite increased resources and human rights training, security forces continue to commit abuses with impunity. An estimated four million weapons in civilian hands threaten to contribute to lawlessness, and the diamond-mining industry is afflicted by murders and other abuses by government and private security personnel.

In 2006, the government signed a peace agreement with secessionists in the oil-rich northern exclave of Cabinda, hoping to end a conflict that had continued intermittently since 1975. While between 80 and 90 percent of the rebel fighters have reportedly joined the army or demobilized, some violence has continued. According to a June 2009 report by HRW, the Angolan military had arrested at least 38 people in Cabinda between September 2007 and March 2009 and accused them of state security crimes. Most of these detainees were allegedly denied basic due process rights and subjected to torture and other cruel or inhumane treatment. In May 2009, a civilian judge acquitted four such detainees for lack of evidence, though prosecutors have appealed.

China has invested heavily in Angola in recent years, funding major infrastructure projects, but there are signs that the large Chinese presence has bred resentment and opportunistic criminality. The British Broadcasting Corporation (BBC) reported in November 2009 that Chinese workers in Luanda were being targeted in a wave of violent robberies.

Eight provinces representing about 50 percent of the country contain areas that were heavily mined, restricting freedom of movement. At least 80,000 people have lost limbs to mines over the years.

Angolans' property rights are tenuous in practice. Since 2001, security forces have evicted thousands of people from informal settlements in and around Luanda without adequate notice, compensation, or resettlement provisions. The government claims the residents are trespassing on state land that is needed for development purposes. In July 2009, authorities displaced some 3,000 families from the Bagdad and Iraque neighborhoods of Luanda.

Women enjoy legal protections and occupy cabinet positions and National Assembly seats, but de facto discrimination and violence against women remain common, particularly in rural areas. Women are often killed or injured by land mines as they search for food and firewood. Child labor is a major problem, and there have been reports of trafficking in women and children for prostitution or forced labor. A recent study by Angola's National Children's Institute and UNICEF found "a significant and growing" trend of abuse and abandonment of children who are accused of witchcraft after the death of a family member, usually from AIDS.

AntiguaandBarbuda

Political Rights: 3*
Civil Liberties: 2
Status: Free

Population: 88,000
Capital: St. John's

Ratings Change: Antigua and Barbuda's political rights rating declined from 2 to 3 due to the collapse of a massive fraudulent investment scheme, which revealed how deeply the government had been influenced and corrupted by foreign business interests.

Ten-Year Ratings Timeline For Year Under Review (Political Rights, Civil Liberties, Status)

2000	2001	2002	2003	2004	2005	2006	2007	2008	2009
4,2PF	4,2PF	4,2PF	4,2PF	2,2F	2,2F	2,2F	2,2F	2,2F	3,2F

Overview: In 2009, the sudden implosion of the Stanford Financial Group due to an alleged $8 billion investment fraud exposed strong ties between billionaire financier R. Allen Stanford and the government of Antigua and Barbuda. Several defrauded investors filed lawsuits claiming that the government had benefited from the schemes and aided in the cover-up, heightening political tensions in the country.

Antigua and Barbuda, a member of the Commonwealth, gained independence from Britain in 1981. In the 2004 elections, the opposition United Progressive Party (UPP), led by Baldwin Spencer, defeated Prime Minister Lester Bird and the ruling Antigua Labour Party (ALP). The transfer of power ended the rule of the Bird political dynasty, which had governed the country continuously since 1976.

The March 2009 parliamentary elections returned Baldwin Spencer and the UPP to power with 9 seats in the 17-seat lower house; the ALP took 7 seats, while the Barbuda People's Movement (BPM) retained the single seat representing Barbuda. The elections were deemed fair and competitive by the Organization of American States, which sent an observer mission. However, the voting was preceded by instances of violence, including the firebombing and vandalizing of three ALP offices.

In 2009, the collapse of the $8 billion Stanford Financial Group, run by U.S. financier R. Allen Stanford, revealed deep ties between Stanford and the government of Antigua and Barbuda. The resulting scandal rocked the country's politics. A consortium of defrauded investors sued the government, claiming that top officials had been aware of the scheme and benefited from it. They specifically accused the leadership of accepting preferential loans from Stanford's companies in exchange for not investigating his operations. The company's high-profile collapse accelerated a 6.5 percent economic contraction in 2009 that crippled the country's finances.

Political Rights and Civil Liberties: Antigua and Barbuda is an electoral democracy. The 1981 constitution establishes a parliamentary system, with a governor-general representing the British monarch as ceremonial head of state. The bicameral Parliament is composed of the 17-seat House of Representatives (16 seats for Antigua, 1 for Barbuda), to which members are elected for five-year terms, and an appointed Senate. Of the senators, 11 are appointed by the governor-general on the advice of the prime minister, 4 on the advice of the parliamentary opposition leader, 1 on the advice of the Barbuda Council (an 11-member local government body that runs Barbuda's internal affairs), and 1 at the governor-general's discretion. Antigua and Barbuda's prime minister is typically the leader of the majority party or coalition that emerges from the legislative elections. The Antigua and Barbuda Electoral Commission (ABEC) was established in 2008 to reform the country's electoral system, including introducing voter-identification cards. Political parties can organize freely.

The government has overseen the enactment of anticorruption and transparency legislation in recent years, but implementation has been slow. In 2009, elected officials faced charges of corruption and vote buying during the campaign season, and the repercussions from the collapse of the Stanford Financial Group included the surrender of the former chief financial regulator to U.S. authorities on charges of fraud. Antigua and Barbuda was not ranked by Transparency International in its 2009 Corruption Perceptions Index.

Antigua and Barbuda generally respects freedom of the press, but in practice, media outlets are concentrated among a small number of firms affiliated with either the current government or its predecessor. The Bird family continues to control television, cable, and radio outlets. The government owns one of three radio stations and the public television station. Some instances of intimidation related to the fallout of the Stanford Financial Group scandal were reported, including alleged government pressure on journalists to shape how they covered the case.

The government generally respects religious and academic freedoms.

Nongovernmental organizations are active, but lack adequate funding and are often strongly influenced by government. Labor unions can organize freely. The Industrial Court mediates labor disputes, but public sector unions tend to be under the sway of the ruling party. Demonstrators are occasionally subject to police harassment.

The country's legal system is based on English common law. During the Bird years, the ALP government manipulated the nominally independent judicial system, which was powerless to address corruption in the executive branch. The UPP's efforts to prevent corruption were deeply discredited by the fallout in 2009 from the Stanford Financial Group fraud.

The police generally respect human rights; basic police statistics, however, are confidential. The country's prison is in primitive condition, and the abuse of inmates has been reported, though visits by independent human rights groups are permitted. The government has responded to higher levels of crime with increased patrols, the reintroduction of roadblocks, and stiffer fines for firearms violations. The authorities attribute the high crime rate to a new trend of gun possession among youth and an influx of criminal deportees, with links to the drug trade, from the United States and Europe.

The 2005 Equal Opportunity Act bars discrimination on the basis of race, gender, class, political affinity, or place of origin. Social discrimination and violence against women remain problems, however. In October 2009, the Directorate of Gender Affairs launched a public awareness campaign against gender-related violence following a number of highly publicized rape cases.

Argentina

Political Rights: 2
Civil Liberties: 2
Status: Free

Population: 40,276,000
Capital: Buenos Aires

Ten-Year Ratings Timeline For Year Under Review (Political Rights, Civil Liberties, Status)

2000	2001	2002	2003	2004	2005	2006	2007	2008	2009
1,2F	3,3PF	3,3PF	2,2F	2,2F	2,2F	2,2F	2,2F	2,2F	2,2F

Overview: President Cristina Fernandez de Kirchner and her Front for Victory (FV) Peronist party were left without a majority in either house of Congress following the June 2009 midterm elections. The president became increasingly isolated politically, her powers diminished by her unpopularity and an economic recession following six years of uninterrupted growth. Meanwhile, a new media bill adopted in October contained provisions that could potentially limit freedom of expression.

Argentina gained independence from Spain in 1816. Democratic rule was often interrupted by war and military coups over the following century. The end of Juan Peron's populist and authoritarian regime in 1955 led to a series of right-wing military dictatorships that lasted until 1983. The beginning of civilian rule brought an end to Argentina's dirty war, waged against real or suspected dissidents by the far-right military regime.

Carlos Menem, a populist of the Peronist party who ran on a platform of nationalism and state intervention in the economy, was elected president in 1989 amid hyperinflation and food riots. As president, however, he implemented an economic liberalization program and unconditionally allied the country with the United States. His convertibility plan, which pegged the peso to the U.S. dollar through a currency board, ended the country's chronic bouts of hyperinflation.

Buenos Aires mayor Fernando de la Rua, of the center-left Alianza coalition, was elected president in October 1999. Record unemployment and reduced government wages, effects of the highly overvalued and inflexible currency, spurred protests and unprecedented economic insecurity. In December 2001, government efforts to stop a run on Argentina's banking system sparked violent protests that forced de la Rua to resign. He was replaced by an interim president, who was himself forced to quit less than a week later. On December 31, Menem's former vice president, Eduardo Duhalde, was selected by Congress as Argentina's new president. A steep devaluation of the peso and a debilitating default on its foreign debt left Argentina teetering on the brink of political and economic collapse throughout 2002. Unemployment soared to levels unheard of since the founding of the republic, and violent crime spiraled out of control.

Nestor Kirchner was elected president in 2003 on a Peronist ticket. While working to stabilize the economy, Kirchner moved to purge the country's military and police leadership of authoritarian elements. Seeking to make human rights a trademark of his administration, Kirchner also took steps to remove justices from the highly politicized Supreme Court—considered the country's most corrupt institution—and signed a decree that permitted the extradition of former military officials accused of human rights abuses. Kirchner also presided over a long-hoped-for economic recovery bolstered by high international soya prices and increased demand for Argentina's principal exports. By March 2005, Argentina was able to declare an end to the three-year battle to restructure its defaulted debt. Growing economic stability helped the Peronists increase their legislative majority in the October 2005 parliamentary elections.

In 2006, Kirchner implemented a series of measures to centralize power in the executive branch. Congress granted the president the authority to reallocate government spending, as long as the overall appropriation remained the same. Kirchner also changed the tax system to limit the influence of historically powerful provincial governors, and he created new state-owned enterprises while nationalizing privatized ones. He was able to pass this concentrated power to his wife, Senator Cristina Fernandez de Kirchner, after she won the October 2007 presidential election by a comfortable margin. In practice, she began to govern in tandem with her husband. The new president experienced numerous challenges during her first year in office, most notably a standoff with Argentina's agricultural sector, stemming from her administration's failed attempt to increase export taxes on certain farm products. Kirchner's once-strong political alliance and majority in Congress were fractured after the farmers' standoff, reducing the power her husband had amassed as president.

Nestor Kirchner left his wife a legacy of corruption scandals. Several corruption cases involved government officials, including Kirchner's economy, and defense ministers. In August 2007, $800,000 in cash was seized from a Venezuelan businessman, Franklin Duran, at the Buenos Aires airport; the funds were an illicit campaign contribution from Venezuela's state oil company, Petroleos de Venezuela, to then-Senator Kirchner. The 2008 trial in Miami revealed an extensive cover-up effort by Venezuelan officials, and Duran was sentenced in March to four years in prison.

Mid-term elections held in June 2009—described as a plebiscite on the Kirchner regime—brought significant losses to the Kirchners. The Union-PRO coalition fared especially well, capturing 47 seats in the Senate, up from 33. In the lower house, progovernment party representation fell from 141 to 112 of the 257 seats. The government lost 4 seats in the Senate, bringing the total of Kirchner's Front for Victory

(FV) Peronist party down to 36—1 less than needed for a majority. Nestor Kirchner resigned his post as leader of the Peronist Party. The government's defeat was influenced by growing unemployment and poverty as the country experienced a recession following six years of uninterrupted growth, and by the Kirchners' resulting diminished powers of patronage. Low approval ratings were also driven by the couple's personal fortune, which had increased six-fold since the 2003 election, leading to claims that they exploited political connections.

Political Rights and Civil Liberties:

Argentina is an electoral democracy. As amended in 1994, the constitution provides for a president elected for four years, with the option of reelection for one additional term. Presidential candidates must win 45 percent of the vote to avoid a runoff. The National Congress consists of the 257-member Chamber of Deputies, directly elected for four years, with half of the seats up for election every two years; and the 72-member Senate, directly elected for six-year terms, with one-third of the seats up for election every two years. The midterm legislative elections in June 2009 were considered free and fair.

The right to organize political parties is generally respected. Major parties include the Justicialist Party (PJ, commonly known as the Peronist Party); the FV; the centrist Radical Civic Union (UCR), factions of which support the Peronists; the center-left Support for a Republic of Equals (ARI); and the center-right Union-PRO. The Peronists have been a dominant force in politics since 1946.

Former president Nestor Kirchner's government initially made anticorruption efforts a central theme, establishing the public's right to information and other transparency guarantees. However, subsequent corruption scandals tainted his administration and undermined this decree, revealing a degree of entrenched corruption. Secretary of Transportation Ricardo Jaime was forced to resign in June 2009 over 25 reported charges of corruption. In December, Argentine courts upheld the indictments of former presidents Carlos Menem and Fernando de la Rua on separate corruption charges. Argentina was ranked 106 out of 180 countries surveyed in Transparency International's 2009 Corruption Perceptions Index.

Freedom of expression is guaranteed by law. A June 2008 ruling by the Supreme Court unanimously asserted the press's right to criticize government officials, and a February 2009 court ruling ordered the government to place state advertising in critical publications. However, faced with an increasingly uncertain economic environment, President Cristina Fernandez de Kirchner began cracking down on the press. In May 2009, the president offered to cancel the tax debts of five private media companies in exchange for official advertising space portraying the Kirchners in a positive light. In September, 200 tax agents raided the offices of Argentina's largest daily, *Clarin*, after it ran a story alleging the improper allocation of a large subsidy by a government farm trade agency. The raid, which came in the midst of a debate on a media reform bill backed by President Kirchner, was decried by *Clarin* as government intimidation. The bill, passed by Congress in October, overhauls antiquated broadcasting regulations, but it contains provisions that limit freedom of expression, such as the creation of a politically appointed regulatory body. Critics contend that the reform bill was an attempt to control Argentina's largest media conglomerate, Grupo Clarin, which is largely critical of the government. By setting limits on the number of media outlets any one company can own, the bill forces Grupo Clarin to sell off some of its holdings within a year.

The constitution guarantees freedom of religion. Nevertheless, Argentina's Jewish community, the largest in Latin America, is a frequent target of discrimination and vandalism. Neo-Nazi and other anti-Semitic groups remain active, and the memory of the 1994 bombing of a Jewish cultural center still looms. No one has been convicted of the bombing, although the Argentine judiciary has formally accused Iran and Hezbollah of responsibility. Academic freedom is a cherished Argentine tradition and is largely observed in practice.

The rights to freedom of assembly and association are generally respected. Civic organizations are robust and play a major role in society, although some fall victim to Argentina's pervasive corruption. Labor is dominated by Peronist unions. Union influence, however, has diminished dramatically in recent years because of internal divisions.

While Nestor Kirchner appointed magistrates of professional quality, the tenure of scores of incompetent and corrupt judges remains a serious problem. Moreover, in February 2006, Congress voted to change the composition of the body responsible for selecting judges, making it less professional and more political. Police misconduct, including torture and brutality of suspects in police custody, is endemic. The Buenos Aires provincial police have been involved in drug trafficking, extortion, and other crimes. Arbitrary arrests and abuse by police are rarely punished in the courts owing to intimidation of witnesses and judges, particularly in Buenos Aires province. Prison conditions remain substandard throughout the country.

In 2005, the Supreme Court ruled that laws passed in the 1980s to protect the military from prosecution—justified at the time as a way to help avoid a military coup—were unconstitutional, thus making Argentina a world leader in efforts to fight military impunity. The decision laid the foundation for the prosecution of other military crimes. Nestor Kirchner's pursuit of former officials involved in the dirty war included the 2006 sentencing of a police sergeant connected with the military junta, and the reversal of presidential pardons granted by Menem to three military leaders. Other prosecutions included former president Isabel Peron in 2007 for her alleged role in the disappearance of students during her time in power and a former navy captain, Ricardo Cavallo, in 2008 for 431 cases of kidnapping, abuse, and disappearance. Cavallo was later extradited to Argentina from Spain and was scheduled to stand trial in January 2010. A former navy pilot arrested in September 2009 for his alleged role in "death flights," in which prisoners were thrown into the sea, faces extradition from Spain to Argentina.

Argentina's indigenous peoples, who represent between 3 and 5 percent of the total population, are largely neglected by the government. Approximately 70 percent of the country's rural indigenous communities lack title to their lands. While the Nestor Kirchner administration returned lands to several communities, most such disputes remain unresolved. In 2002, Buenos Aires became the first South American city to pass a domestic partnership law, and the city has established a reputation for its tolerance of homosexuality.

Women actively participate in politics in Argentina, as reflected by the 2007 election of President Kirchner and decrees mandating that one-third of Congress members be women. However, domestic abuse remains a serious problem. More than 3,000 children are homeless in Buenos Aires, more than double the number prior to Argentina's 2001 economic collapse.

Armenia

Political Rights: 6
Civil Liberties: 4
Status: Partly Free

Population: 3,097,000
Capital: Yerevan

Note: The numerical ratings and status listed above do not reflect conditions in Nagorno-Karabakh, which is examined in a separate report.

Ten-Year Ratings Timeline For Year Under Review (Political Rights, Civil Liberties, Status)

2000	2001	2002	2003	2004	2005	2006	2007	2008	2009
4,4PF	4,4PF	4,4PF	4,4PF	5,4PF	5,4PF	5,4PF	5,4PF	6,4PF	6,4PF

Overview: The ruling Republican Party won municipal elections in the capital in May 2009, securing a majority of council seats and confirmation of the appointed incumbent as mayor. International observers alleged widespread fraud, and opposition parties refused to recognize the results. Meanwhile, police abuses committed during the violence that followed the 2008 presidential election remained largely unpunished, and a number of opposition supporters who were arrested during the 2008 crackdown were still behind bars at year's end.

After a short period of independence amid the turmoil at the end of World War I, Armenia was divided between Turkey and the Soviet Union by 1922. Most of the Armenians in the Turkish portion were killed or driven abroad during the war and its aftermath, but those in the east survived Soviet rule. The Soviet republic of Armenia declared its independence in 1991, propelled by a nationalist movement that had gained strength during the tenure of Soviet leader Mikhail Gorbachev in the 1980s. The movement had initially focused on demands to transfer the substantially ethnic Armenian region of Nagorno-Karabakh from Azerbaijan to Armenia; Nagorno-Karabakh was recognized internationally as part of Azerbaijan, but by the late 1990s, it was held by ethnic Armenian forces who claimed independence. Prime Minister Robert Kocharian, the former president of Nagorno-Karabakh, was elected president of Armenia in 1998.

The country was thrust into a political crisis on October 27, 1999, when five gunmen stormed into the National Assembly and assassinated Prime Minister Vazgen Sarkisian, assembly speaker Karen Demirchian, and several other senior officials. The leader of the gunmen, Nairi Hunanian, maintained that he and the other assailants had acted alone in an attempt to incite a popular revolt against the government. Allegations that Kocharian or members of his inner circle had orchestrated the shootings prompted opposition calls for the president to resign. Citing a lack of evidence, however, prosecutors did not press charges against Kocharian, who gradually consolidated his power during the following year.

In 2003, Kocharian was reelected in a presidential vote that was widely regarded as flawed, with the Organization for Security and Cooperation in Europe (OSCE) alleging widespread ballot-box stuffing. During the runoff, authorities placed more than 200 opposition supporters in administrative detention for over 15 days; they were sentenced on charges of hooliganism and participation in unsanctioned demonstrations. The Constitutional Court upheld the election results, but it proposed holding a "referendum of confidence" on Kocharian within the next year; Kocharian rejected the proposal. Opposition parties boycotted subsequent sessions of the National Assembly, and police violently dispersed protests mounted in the spring of 2004 over the government's failure to redress the problems of the 2003 vote.

The Republican Party of Armenia (HHK)—the party of Prime Minister Serzh Sarkisian, a close Kocharian ally—won 65 of 131 seats in the May 2007 National Assembly elections. Two other propresidential parties took a total of 41 seats, giving the government a clear majority. Opposition parties suffered from disadvantages regarding media coverage and the abuse of state resources ahead of the vote.

The 2008 presidential election was held on February 19. Five days after the balloting, the Central Election Commission announced that Sarkisian had won 52.8 percent, and the main opposition candidate, former president Levon Ter-Petrosian, had taken 21.5 percent. The results, which the opposition disputed, allowed Sarkisian to avoid a runoff vote. Peaceful opposition demonstrations that began on February 21 turned violent a week later, when the police engaged the protesters. According to the OSCE, 10 people were killed, and more than 200 were injured during the clashes. Outgoing president Kocharian declared a 20-day state of emergency, and more than 100 people were arrested in the wake of the upheaval. The OSCE's final observation report stated that the electoral deficiencies had "resulted primarily from a lack of sufficient will to implement legal provisions effectively and impartially."

By the end of 2009, little had been done to punish police officers for abuse during the 2008 postelection violence. Though there were reportedly hundreds of internal inquiries, only a handful of officers were charged with using excessive force. In late 2009, investigators for the Parliamentary Assembly of the Council of Europe (PACE) criticized the results of an Armenian parliamentary inquiry, which found that the crackdown on the postelection protests had been "by and large legitimate and adequate." A general amnesty bill passed in June freed 30 protesters, but more than a dozen reportedly remained in prison at year's end.

Municipal elections for Yerevan were held in May 2009. The HHK secured 35 of 65 seats in the city council, meaning the appointed HHK incumbent was reinstated as mayor. Opposition parties refused to recognize the results, accusing the ruling party of fraud. Observers with the International Foundation for Electoral Systems (IFES) reported witnessing "egregious violations," and the Council of Europe similarly cited "serious deficiencies."

Political Rights and Civil Liberties: Armenia is not an electoral democracy. The unicameral National Assembly is elected for four-year terms, with 90 seats chosen by proportional representation and 41 through races in single-member districts. The president is elected by popular vote for up to two five-year terms. However, elections since the 1990s have been marred by serious irregularities. The May 2007 parliamentary vote was described by the OSCE as an improvement, albeit flawed, over previous polls, but the 2008 presidential election was seriously marred by problems with the vote count, a biased and restricted media environment, and the abuse of administrative resources in favor of ruling party candidate Serzh Sarkisian. The Yerevan municipal elections held in May 2009 were the first in which the capital's mayor was indirectly elected rather than appointed by the president. They also suffered from serious violations, though international observers claimed that the fraud did not jeopardize the overall legitimacy of the results.

Bribery and nepotism are reportedly common among government officials, who are rarely prosecuted or removed for abuse of office. Corruption is also believed to be a serious problem in law enforcement. Armenia was ranked 120 out of 180 countries surveyed in Transparency International's 2009 Corruption Perceptions Index.

There are limits on press freedom in Armenia. The authorities use informal pressure to maintain control over broadcast outlets, the chief source of news for most Armenians. State-run Armenian Public Television is the only station with nationwide coverage, and the owners of most private channels have close government ties. The independent television company A1+ continued to be denied a license in 2009 despite a 2008 ruling in its favor by the European Court of Human Rights. Libel is considered a criminal offense, and violence against journalists is a problem. The Helsinki Committee of Armenia reported that attacks on journalists increased in both frequency and cruelty in 2009. Among other assaults during the year, Argishti Kivirian, the founding editor of the news website Armenia Today, was severely beaten in late April, and a week later two assailants attacked Nver Mnatsakanian, a television journalist and commentator. Amnesty International reported that independent media outlets that covered the political activities of the opposition were often harassed. The authorities generally do not interfere with internet access.

Freedom of religion is generally respected, though the dominant Armenian Apostolic Church enjoys certain exclusive privileges, and members of minority faiths sometimes face societal discrimination. At the end of 2009, there were 76 Jehovah's Witnesses serving prison terms for refusing to participate in either military service or the military-administered alternative service for conscientious objectors.

The government generally does not restrict academic freedom. Public schools are required to display portraits of the president and the head of the Armenian Apostolic Church, and to teach the church's history.

In the aftermath of the 2008 postelection violence, the government imposed restrictions on freedom of assembly. The majority of opposition requests to hold demonstrations in 2009 were rejected, and the authorities allegedly restricted road access to the capital ahead of planned opposition rallies. Police also reportedly continued to use force to disperse some opposition gatherings. In December, four police officers were convicted of abusing protesters in the 2008 clashes, but they avoided jail time under a general amnesty enacted in June.

Registration requirements for nongovernmental organizations (NGOs) are cumbersome and time-consuming. Some 3,000 NGOs are registered with the Ministry of Justice, although many are not active in a meaningful way. While the constitution provides for the right to form and join trade unions, labor organizations are weak and relatively inactive in practice.

The judicial branch is subject to political pressure from the executive branch and suffers from considerable corruption. Police make arbitrary arrests without warrants, beat detainees during arrest and interrogation, and use torture to extract confessions. conditions in Armenia are poor, and threats to prisoner health are significant.

Although members of the country's tiny ethnic minority population rarely report cases of overt discrimination, they have complained about difficulties in receiving education in their native languages. Members of the Yezidi community have sometimes reported discrimination by police and local authorities.

Citizens have the right to own private property and establish businesses, but an inefficient and often corrupt court system and unfair business competition hinder such activities. Key industries remain in the hands of so-called oligarchs and influential cliques who received preferential treatment in the early stages of privatization.

According to the current election code, women must account for 15 percent of a party's candidate list for the parliament's proportional representation seats and occupy every tenth position on the list. Women currently hold 12 of the 131 National Assembly seats. Domestic violence and trafficking in women and girls for the purpose of prostitution are believed to be serious problems. Though homosexuality was decriminalized in 2003, homosexual individuals still face violence and persecution.

Australia

Political Rights: 1
Civil Liberties: 1
Status: Free

Population: 21,852,000
Capital: Canberra

Ten-Year Ratings Timeline For Year Under Review (Political Rights, Civil Liberties, Status)

2000	2001	2002	2003	2004	2005	2006	2007	2008	2009
1,1F	1,1F	1,1F	1,1F	1,1F	1,1F	1,1F	1,1F	1,1F	1,1F

Overview: The Labor Party government in 2009 continued to grapple with the complex problems of immigration, racially motivated violence, and poor conditions in Aboriginal settlements. Also during the year, a quadriplegic man won a court battle to stop being fed and be allowed to die, advancing the cause of voluntary euthanasia or assisted suicide.

The British colonies in Australia, first settled in 1788, were organized as a federative commonwealth in 1901, and gradually gained full independence from Britain. Since World War II, political power has alternated between the center-left Labor Party and a conservative coalition of the Liberal Party and the smaller, rural-based National Party. In the 2007 elections, Labor captured 83 seats in the 150-seat lower house and gained 18 Senate seats for a new total of 32 in the 76-seat upper chamber, allowing party leader Kevin Rudd to replace John Howard of the Liberal Party as prime minister.

The Rudd government reversed a number of its predecessor's policies, ending Australia's combat role in Iraq, issuing a formal apology for past laws and policies that had "inflicted profound grief, suffering, and loss" on the country's Aborigines, and announcing the creation of a reparations fund for health and education programs benefitting all Aborigines. The new government also closed detention centers in Nauru and Papua New Guinea that had been created by the Howard government in response to an influx of asylum seekers from South Asia. It pledged to assure adjudication of asylum claims within a year, barred detention for women and children, and implemented a system of three-year temporary visas.

However, by the end of 2008, the government had to open a new detention center on Christmas Island to receive the increasing number of asylum seekers. By October 2009, the facility had nearly reached its capacity of 1,200, and the government said it would expand the center to accommodate 2,000 in order to meet increasing demand. Prime Minister Rudd also appealed to Indonesian authorities to stop boats carrying asylum seekers toward Australian waters, and even visited Jakarta in October to meet with his counterpart on this matter. When the Indonesian navy intercepted a vessel carrying 250 Sri Lankans in October, Rudd insisted that they were the responsibility of the United Nations, refusing to allow them to enter Australia despite their threat of a hunger strike.

On Aboriginal issues, the federal government and local council members attempted in 2009 to negotiate a rescue plan for a settlement of some 3,000 people in Alice Springs, Northern Territory, that was plagued by chronic overcrowding, poor sanitation, and crime. However, the talks broke down as the government threatened to seize control of the settlement and local leaders argued that this would constitute a federal land grab. The federal government had intervened in the Northern Territory in 2007 in response to evidence of rampant pedophilia, juvenile prostitution, domestic abuse, and other problems in Aboriginal communities there.

Also in 2009, racial violence involving immigrant groups continued to simmer. In May, more than 2,000 South Asian students and their supporters marched in Melbourne to protest alleged racial attacks. In June, more than 200 South Asians held a street protest in Sydney after an Indian man said he was attacked by a Lebanese group. Violence broke out and police intervened when a Lebanese man alleged assault by the South Asian protesters. In August, another four South Asians alleged attacks in Melbourne. The government said it would consider increasing penalties for hate crimes. The number of Indian students in Australia is projected to fall in 2010, costing the country some US$70 million.

In light of new allegations of attempted terrorist attacks, the government announced plans to allow the police to search property without a warrant, and to expand the definition of terrorism to include both physical and psychological harm. However, detention without charges would be restricted to a maximum of eight days. In August, four Australian citizens of Somali and Lebanese descent were arrested in Melbourne for allegedly planning a suicide attack on an army base. Antiterrorism laws were also used in September to sentence former airport worker Bela Khazaal to 12 years in prison for producing an instructional book that encouraged terrorist acts.

In August, a quadriplegic man in Perth won a court battle to refuse feeding and be allowed to die, weakening a legal ban on voluntary euthanasia or assisted suicide. The man, Christian Rossiter, died the following month.

In another effort to own up to past wrongdoings committed by the state, Rudd apologized in November to tens of thousands of men and women who were abused or neglected in state care as children between 1930 and 1970. Many of the affected individuals were brought to Australia as children from Britain, without the knowledge or consent of their parents, under a British government-sponsored migrant scheme.

Political Rights and Civil Liberties: Australia is an electoral democracy. The British monarch is represented as head of state by a governor-general, who is appointed on the recommendation of the prime minister. Quentin Bryce, a former governor of Queensland, became the first female governor-general in 2008. The prime minister is the leader of the majority party or coalition in Parliament.

Voting is compulsory, and citizens participate in free and fair multiparty elections to choose representatives for the bicameral Parliament. The Senate, the upper house, has 76 seats, with 12 senators from each of the six states and 2 from each of the two mainland territories. Half of the state members, who serve six-year terms, are up for election every three years; all territory members are elected every three years. The House of Representatives, the lower house, has 150 seats. All members are elected by popular preferential voting to serve three-year terms, and no state can have fewer than five representatives.

The Liberal and Labor parties are the two major parties. Others include the National Party, the Green Party, the Family First Party, and the Best Party of Allah, formed in 2005 by Muslim Australians.

Australia is regarded as one of the least corrupt societies in the world, ranking 8 out of 180 countries surveyed in Transparency International's 2009 Corruption Perceptions Index. Defence Minister Joel Fitzgibbon resigned in June 2009, when it was revealed that he had failed to declare gifts and that there was possible conflict of interest related to contacts between the government and his brother's company.

There are no constitutional protections for freedom of speech and the press, but citizens and the media freely criticize the government without reprisal. Some laws restrict publication and dissemination of material that promotes or incites terrorist acts. The Australian Broadcasting Corporation operates national and local public television and radio stations. A second public station delivers multilingual radio and television broadcasts. There are three major commercial television networks and many commercial radio stations. Internet access and mobile telephone use are widespread and competitively priced.

Freedom of religion is respected, as is academic freedom, although mosques and Islamic schools are barred from disseminating anti-Australian messages.

The rights of assembly and association are not codified in law, but the government respects these rights in practice. Workers can organize and bargain collectively. The Fair Work Act of 2009 replaced the Workplace Relations Act (WRA) of the Howard administration. Labor groups disliked the WRA, alleging that it undermined collective bargaining.

The judiciary is independent, and prison conditions are generally good by international standards. Antiterrorism legislation enacted in 2005, with a 10-year sunset clause, includes police powers to detain suspects without charge, "shoot to kill" provisions, the criminalization of violence against the public and Australian troops overseas, and authorization for the limited use of soldiers to meet terrorist threats on domestic soil.

Aborigines, comprising about 12 percent of the population, are underrepresented at all levels of political leadership and lag far behind other groups in key social and economic development indicators. A national report published in July 2009 indicated that the gap between Aborigines and other Australians continues to widen.

For Aborigines, life expectancy is 20 years shorter, the rate of unemployment is 3 times higher, homicide is 7 times higher, child abuse is 6 times higher, and imprisonment is 13 times higher. There are also claims of routine mistreatment by police and prison officials.

Although women enjoy equal rights and freedoms and have attained greater parity in pay and promotion in public and private sector jobs, violence against women remains a serious problem, particularly within the Aboriginal population. In 2009, the first shelter for domestic abuse victims opened in the Northern Territory to help Aboriginal women. Homosexuals can serve in the military, and federal law grants legal residence to foreign same-sex partners of Australian citizens. However, federal laws do not bar discrimination based on sexual orientation. A 2004 amendment to the Federal Marriage Act defines marriage as a union between a man and a woman "to the exclusion of all others," and a local law in the Australian Capital Territory that granted formal recognition to same-sex partnerships was struck down in 2006.

Austria

Political Rights: 1
Civil Liberties: 1
Status: Free

Population: 8,374,000
Capital: Vienna

Ten-Year Ratings Timeline For Year Under Review (Political Rights, Civil Liberties, Status)

2000	2001	2002	2003	2004	2005	2006	2007	2008	2009
1,1F	1,1F	1,1F	1,1F	1,1F	1,1F	1,1F	1,1F	1,1F	1,1F

Overview: The far-right Freedom Party made significant gains in the February 2009 provincial elections, largely at the expense of the Social Democratic Party of Austria (SPO). Austria's police were criticized for failing to act on warnings of expected violence following the fatal shooting of a Sikh leader in an Austrian mosque in May. Meanwhile, parliament adopted legislation in December permitting civil partnerships for same-sex couples.

Modern Austria emerged after World War I, when the Austro-Hungarian Empire broke apart. It was annexed to Nazi Germany in 1938 until defeat in World War II. Austria remained neutral during the Cold War, focusing instead on economic growth.

From 1986 until 2000, the two biggest political parties—the center-left Social Democratic Party of Austria (SPO) and the center-right People's Party of Austria (OVP)—governed together in a grand coalition. The 1999 elections produced the first government since 1970 not to include the SPO. Instead, the OVP formed a coalition with the Freedom Party, a far-right nationalist party with vestigial Nazi sympathies, which won 27 percent of the popular vote. Its support had risen steadily as voters became disaffected with the large parties' power-sharing arrangement and its barriers to major political change. In 2000, the European Union (EU) briefly suspended ties with Austria in response to the Freedom Party's inclusion, though perceived EU interference bolstered party support.

Due to the sanctions, the controversial Joerg Haider stepped down as leader of the Freedom Party. Austrian politics returned to near normality thereafter, as the party was moderated by the day-to-day realities of governing. After an internal leadership struggle, the party withdrew from the coalition in September 2002. November 2002 parliamentary elections saw the Freedom Party's share of the vote fall to 10 percent. It rejoined the coalition with the OVP, but as a clear junior partner. Subsequent poor election performances, including European Parliament elections, furthered rifts within the party. Most of its members of parliament, as well as Haider, left the party in spring 2005 to form the Alliance for the Future of Austria (BZO). The Freedom Party remained in parliament as a rump, though with many activists. The BZO became OVP's junior coalition partner.

In October 2006, parliamentary elections confirmed an OVP decline, with the SPO winning by a small margin and the two parties forming another grand coalition. The SPO's Alfred Gusenbauer became chancellor, but top ministries including foreign affairs and finance went to the OVP, continuing the parties' struggle for dominance within the government. The SPO's investigation into the previous OVP government's purchase of 18 Eurofighter jets antagonized its coalition partner; the two also struggled over health, tax, and pension reforms, as well as policy toward the EU. In the summer of 2008, the OVP announced its exit from the coalition.

New elections were held in September, with Werner Faymann leading the SPO. Support for the SPO fell to 29 percent, and the OVP's declined to 26 percent. The BZO and Freedom Party surged to 18 and 11 percent, respectively, buoyed by anti-foreigner sentiment, skepticism toward the EU, and frustration with the squabbling grand coalition. Both major parties refused coalitions with the far right. Shortly after the vote, Haider was killed in a car accident. In late 2008, the SPO and OVP revived their grand coalition, under Faymann as chancellor with an OVP vice-chancellor.

The February 2009 provincial elections suggested a continued movement towards the right, with the SPO suffering dramatic losses. The OVP retained power in Upper Austria and Vorarlberg, while the Freedom Party nearly doubled its presence in both regions, winning 25 percent of the vote in Vorarlberg as it absorbed support from the much-diminished BZO. However, the OVP again ruled out a coalition with the Freedom Party.

In May, a Sikh religious leader visiting from India was fatally shot by rival Sikhs during a religious service in an Austrian mosque; another 16 people were injured during the attacks, and several suspects were arrested. The shootings triggered riots in northern India among supporters of the slain cleric. Meanwhile, Austrian police were accused of failing to act on warnings that a rival Sikh temple had threatened violence if the cleric proceeded with his visit as planned.

Members of the Hapsburg family, which ruled the Austro-Hungarian Empire until 1918, applied to the country's Constitutional Court in September for an end to a 90-year ban prohibiting them from running for Austria's largely ceremonial presidency. In December, the Constitutional Court ruled that the Hapsburgs could proceed with an appeal only after a family member had applied as a candidate and been formally rejected.

Political Rights and Civil Liberties: Austria is an electoral democracy. The lower house of the Federal Assembly, the Nationalrat (National Council), has 183 members chosen through proportional representation at the district, state, and federal levels. Members serve five-year terms, extended from four in 2008. The chancellor, appointed by the president, needs the support of the legislature to govern. The 62 members of the upper house, the Bundesrat (Federal Council), are chosen by state legislatures. In 2008, the voting age was lowered to 16.

Though Austria has competitive political parties and free and fair elections, the traditional practice of grand coalitions has fostered disillusionment with the political process. Frustration with the cozy relationship between the OVP and the SPO contributed to the rise of the Freedom Party, though its time in government brought it temporarily closer to the mainstream right. Minority participation in government remains frustrated despite the high number of foreigners in Austria.

Austria is now less corrupt than it was during the 1980s, following tightened campaign donation laws. However, the 2006 collapse of Bawag, a union-owned bank with strong ties to the SPO, led to a flurry of media stories about bad loans, concealed losses, and lavish lifestyles among executives. Austria was ranked 16 out of 180 countries surveyed in Transparency International's 2009 Corruption Perceptions Index.

The media are free, though not highly pluralistic. The end of monopoly by the state broadcaster, ORF, has not brought significant competition, and print media ownership is concentrated in a few hands. Harassment and libel lawsuits by politicians—notably from the Freedom Party—against critical journalists have hampered the work of reporters. Austria has lost more press-freedom cases before the European Court of Human Rights than any country but Turkey. There are no restrictions on internet access.

Nazi and anti-Semitic speech and writing are banned, and in 2005, David Irving, a British historian, was arrested on charges of Holocaust denial. He was sentenced to three years in prison in February 2006, but he was released on probation later that year. During 2008, the Freedom Party campaigned in favor of relaxing some bans on Nazi symbols.

Religious freedom in Austria is respected and constitutionally guaranteed. Thirteen officially recognized religions can draw on state funds for religious education. Obtaining this status requires a membership equaling at least 0.05 percent of Austria's population and a period of 10 years as a "confessional community" with fewer privileges. The Jehovah's Witnesses, currently a confessional community, have complained that these rules violate their freedom of religion. The Church of Scientology has third-tier status as an "association." Academic freedom is respected.

Freedoms of assembly and association are protected in the constitution. Civic and nongovernmental organizations operate without restrictions. Trade unions, which traditionally have been close to the SPO, are free to organize and strike and are considered an essential partner in national policy making.

The judiciary is independent, and the Constitutional Court examines the compatibility of legislation with the constitution. Austria is a member of the Council of Europe, and its citizens have recourse to the European Court of Human Rights in Strasbourg, France. The quality of prisons generally meet high European standards, though isolated incidents of police brutality and harsh or crowded prison conditions are reported.

Residents generally are afforded equal protection under the law. However, immigration has fueled some resentment toward minorities and foreigners; Austria has one of the world's highest numbers of asylum seekers per capita. The UN High Commissioner for Refugees (UNHCR) has criticized the country's asylum law, which is among the strictest in the developed world. Some asylum seekers can be deported while appeals are pending, and new arrivals are asked for full statements within 72 hours. The UNHCR has also criticized shortages of qualified legal advisers and interpreters for detainees.

A 1979 law guarantees women's freedom from discrimination in various areas, including the workplace. A 1993 law sought to increase women's employment in government agencies, where they were underrepresented. The June 2009 Second Protection Against Violence Act increases penalties for domestic violence and takes further measures against chronic offenders.

In December 2009, parliament adopted legislation permitting civil partnerships for same-sex couples. The law, which enters into effect in January 2010, provides them with equal rights to pensions and alimony and allows them to take each other's names, but does not provide them with the same adoption rights as married couples.

Azerbaijan

Political Rights: 6
Civil Liberties: 5
Status: Not Free

Population: 8,781,000
Capital: Baku

Note: The numerical ratings and status listed above do not reflect conditions in Nagorno-Karabakh, which is examined in a separate report.

Ten-Year Ratings Timeline For Year Under Review (Political Rights, Civil Liberties, Status)

2000	2001	2002	2003	2004	2005	2006	2007	2008	2009
6,5PF	6,5PF	6,5PF	6,5NF	6,5NF	6,5NF	6,5NF	6,5NF	6,5NF	6,5NF

Overview: President Ilham Aliyev consolidated his authoritarian rule with a March 2009 referendum that eliminated presidential term limits. Also during the year, the government increased regulatory restrictions on civil society groups and implemented a ban on foreign radio broadcasts.

After a short period of independence from 1918 to 1920, Azerbaijan was occupied by Soviet forces and formally entered the Soviet Union in 1922 as part of the Transcaucasian Soviet Federated Socialist Republic. It became a separate Soviet republic in 1936. Following a referendum in 1991, Azerbaijan declared independence from the disintegrating Soviet Union.

In 1992, Abulfaz Elchibey, leader of the nationalist opposition Azerbaijan Popular Front, was elected president in a generally free and fair vote. A military coup one year later ousted him from power and installed the former first secretary of the Azerbaijan Communist Party, Heydar Aliyev, in his place. In the October 1993 presidential election, Aliyev was credited with receiving nearly 99 percent of the vote. Five leading opposition parties and some 600 independent candidates were barred from Azerbaijan's first post-Soviet parliamentary elections in 1995, allowing Aliyev's Yeni Azerbaijan Party (YAP) to win the most seats. In 1998, Aliyev was reelected with more than 70 percent of the vote in balloting that was marred by irregularities.

The ruling YAP captured the majority of seats in the 2000 parliamentary elections. International monitors from the Organization for Security and Cooperation in Europe (OSCE) and the Council of Europe cited widespread electoral fraud, including the stuffing of ballot boxes.

A 2002 referendum approved a series of constitutional amendments, some of which critics said would strengthen the ruling party's grip on power. One amendment stipulated that the prime minister would become president if the head of state resigned or was incapacitated, which ultimately allowed the ailing Aliyev to appoint his son, Ilham, to the premiership and facilitate a transfer of power within the Aliyev family. Opposition groups and the OSCE charged that the referendum was marred by fraud, intimidation of election monitors and officials, and an inflated voter-turnout figure of nearly 90 percent.

Heydar Aliyev collapsed during a live television broadcast in April 2003 and left Azerbaijan that summer to receive medical treatment abroad. In June, Prime Minister Ilham Aliyev was officially nominated as a presidential candidate for the October election, and the elder Aliyev withdrew his candidacy just two weeks before the vote.

Final election results showed Ilham Aliyev defeating seven challengers with nearly 77 percent of the vote. His closest rival, opposition Musavat Party leader Isa Gambar, received only 14 percent, while six other candidates received less than 4 percent each. According to OSCE observers, the vote was again tainted by widespread fraud. During violent clashes between security forces and demonstrators in Baku that month, at least one person was reportedly killed and several hundred were injured, and the authorities unleashed a crackdown against the opposition in which more than 600 people were detained. Among those arrested were election officials who refused to certify fraudulent results. Heydar Aliyev died in December 2003.

Less than half of all registered voters cast ballots in the 2005 parliamentary elections, the lowest turnout in a decade. The opposition captured just 10 of 125 seats in the Milli Majlis (National Assembly), with a substantial majority going to the ruling YAP and its allies. The results were contested by the opposition, which organized a number of rallies in the capital.

Aliyev easily won a second term in the October 2008 presidential election, taking 89 percent of the vote amid 75 percent turnout, according to official results. Most of the political opposition chose to boycott the poll, citing barriers to meaningful media access and the overwhelming influence of administrative resources deployed by the YAP. In March 2009, a constitutional amendment that removed term limits for the president reportedly passed a referendum with more than 90 percent of the vote, allowing Aliyev to run again in 2013.

International mediators have failed to make progress on negotiations for a final settlement of the dispute over Nagorno-Karabakh, a region of Azerbaijan that has been ruled by ethnic Armenian separatists since the early 1990s. No country or international organization recognizes Nagorno-Karabakh's self-proclaimed independence.

Political Rights and Civil Liberties: Azerbaijan is not an electoral democracy. The country's constitution provides for a strong presidency, and the parliament, the 125-member Milli Majlis, exercises little or no independence from the executive branch. The president and members of parliament serve five-year terms, and a referendum held in March 2009 eliminated presidential term limits. Although the PACE indicated that the vote was "transparent, well organized, and held in a peaceful atmosphere," it criticized the lack of public debate on the issue in the media.

Elections since the early 1990s have been considered neither free nor fair by international observers. The most recent parliamentary elections, in 2005, were afflicted by extensive irregularities. The OSCE cited the "interference of local authorities, disproportionate use of force to thwart rallies, arbitrary detentions, restrictive interpretations of campaign provisions and an unbalanced composition of election commissions."

The 2008 presidential election, though largely peaceful, was no exception to this pattern. The OSCE's monitoring report noted a number of problems, including "a lack of robust competition, a lack of vibrant political discourse, and a restrictive media environment." President Ilham Aliyev said he would not campaign personally, but he reportedly stepped up his official activities and opened a number of infrastructure projects during the campaign period, garnering extensive coverage from the biased media. The OSCE also noted that public officials and YAP operatives worked cooperatively to mobilize support and increase turnout.

Corruption is pervasive in government and society. Officials reportedly made improvements in the business sector and raised awareness about the need to combat corruption in 2009, but 46 percent of respondents to a Transparency International (TI) survey said they or a member of their household had paid a bribe in the past year, and 62 percent assessed the government's anticorruption efforts as "ineffective." Azerbaijan was ranked 143 out of 180 countries surveyed in TI's 2009 Corruption Perceptions Index.

While Azerbaijan's constitution guarantees freedom of speech and the press, the authorities severely limit press freedom in practice. Broadcast media are the main source of information for the vast majority of the population, and privately owned television stations with national reach generally reflect progovernment views. While there is some pluralism in the print media, newspapers have relatively small circulations, are not distributed regularly in rural areas, and are frequently too expensive for many people to purchase. Independent and opposition newspapers struggle financially in the face of limited advertising revenues and heavy fines or imprisonment of their staff. State-owned companies rarely if ever advertise in opposition newspapers.

As of January 1, 2009, foreign radio broadcasts—including the British Broadcasting Corporation (BBC), Radio Free Europe/Radio Liberty (RFE/RL), and Voice of America—were banned from Azerbaijan's airwaves. RFE/RL began broadcasting via satellite in April to bypass the ban. A number of media editors, including the editor of a progovernment newspaper, were jailed on charges of defamation during the year. The government also restricted freedom of speech on the internet. In November, two bloggers were sentenced to two and two and a half years in prison for a July incident in which they were apparently attacked by two men and then arrested for "hooliganism," while their attackers were set free. The bloggers had recently participated in online criticism of the government, including a satirical video in which a donkey holds a news conference.

The government restricts the activities of "nontraditional" minority religious groups through burdensome registration requirements and interference in the importation and distribution of printed religious materials. A new law adopted in May 2009 required religious groups to reregister with the authorities and religious figures to be recertified. It also forbids foreign citizens from leading prayers.

The authorities generally do not restrict academic freedom. However, some faculty and students have experienced political pressure, including reported threats to lower the grades of students who participate in opposition political activity. Some professors and teachers have said they were dismissed because of their membership in opposition parties or for political activity during campaign periods. Private and open discussion was limited in 2009. Authorities in the Naxcivan autonomous republic in 2009 banned the leaking of information to the media, leading to house arrests and threats aimed at those who have provided information to opposition newspapers. In March, the government banned a book depicting a gay relationship between an Armenian and an Azeri, claiming it was "against Azerbaijan's values."

The government restricts freedom of assembly, especially for opposition parties. Legal amendments enacted in 2009 require NGOs to register their grants with the authorities and foreign NGOs to reach agreements with the government before opening offices in the country. Although the law permits the formation of trade unions and the right to strike, the majority of trade unions remain closely affiliated with the government, and most major industries are state owned.

The judiciary is corrupt, inefficient, and subservient to the executive branch. Arbitrary arrest and detention are common, particularly for members of the political opposition. Detainees are often held for long periods before trial, and their access to lawyers is restricted. Police abuse of suspects during arrest and interrogation reportedly remains common, with torture sometimes used to extract confessions. Prison conditions are severe, with many inmates suffering from overcrowding and inadequate medical care. In August 2009, a jailed editor died in a Baku prison after allegedly receiving inadequate medical care.

Some members of ethnic minority groups, including the small ethnic Armenian population, have complained of discrimination in areas including education, employment, and housing. Hundreds of thousands of ethnic Azeris, who were displaced by the war in Nagorno-Karabakh in the early 1990s, remain subject to restrictions on their place of residence and often live in dreadful conditions.

Significant parts of the economy are controlled by a corrupt elite, which severely limits equality of opportunity. Supporters of the political opposition face job discrimination, demotion, and dismissal.

Traditional societal norms and poor economic conditions restrict women's professional roles, and they remain underrepresented in government. Women hold 14 seats in the 125-seat parliament. Domestic violence is a problem, and there are no laws regarding spousal abuse. The country is believed to be a source and a transit point for the trafficking of women for prostitution. A 2005 law criminalized human trafficking, but the U.S. State Department's 2009 Trafficking in Persons Report kept Azerbaijan on the Tier 2 Watch List, citing only modest improvements.

Bahamas

Political Rights: 1
Civil Liberties: 1
Status: Free

Population: 341,000
Capital: Nassau

Ten-Year Ratings Timeline For Year Under Review (Political Rights, Civil Liberties, Status)

2000	2001	2002	2003	2004	2005	2006	2007	2008	2009
1,1F	1,1F	1,1F	1,1F	1,1F	1,1F	1,1F	1,1F	1,1F	1,1F

Overview: In 2009, the Bahamas faced increasing challenges to its traditional record of good governance due to economic instability, rising crime, and increased tensions over migration issues.

The Bahamas, a former British colony, became an independent state within the Commonwealth in 1973. Lynden Pindling served as the country's first prime minister and head of the Progressive Liberal Party (PLP) for a quarter-century. After years of allegations of corruption and involvement by high officials in narcotics trafficking, Pindling and the PLP were defeated by the Free National Movement (FNM) party in the 1992 elections.

The FNM ruled the Bahamas for 10 years under Prime Minister Hubert Ingraham, until the 2002 elections brought the PLP, led by Perry Christie, back to power. In May 2007, the FNM triumphed at the polls, winning 23 parliamentary seats to the PLP's 18, thereby restoring Ingraham to the premiership and demoting Christie to leader of the opposition. Christie retained this position by winning an overwhelming majority of votes in the PLP leadership conference in October 2009.

As the Caribbean's only upper-income country, the Bahamas has established a model service economy based on an impressive tourism sector—which accounts for a large share of national income—and offshore financial services. However, in 2009, the worsening global economy cut into the Bahamian tourism industry and posed new challenges to the Ingraham government. Marijuana cultivation and trafficking by foreign nationals residing in the country has led the United States to keep the Bahamas on the list of major drug-producing or drug-transit countries. The country is also a major transit point for migrants coming from elsewhere in the Caribbean, especially Cuba and Haiti, in the hope of reaching the United States.

In January 2009, an ambulance driver and a member of Parliament were arrested on charges of attempting to extort money from American actor John Travolta following his son's death in the Bahamas. A mistrial was later declared when another lawmaker prematurely announced an acquittal.

Political Rights and Civil Liberties: The Bahamas is an electoral democracy. The lower house of the bicameral Parliament, the 41-member House of Assembly, is directly elected for five-year terms. The 16 members of the upper house, the Senate, are appointed for five-year terms by the governor-general, who represents the British monarch as head of state. Nine of the senators are appointed on the recommendation of the prime minister, four on the recommendation of the opposition leader, and three on the recommendation of the prime minister after consulting with the opposition leader. The head of the majority party or coalition in Parliament typically serves as prime minister.

Political parties can organize freely. The two leading parties are the FNM, headed by Prime Minister Hubert Ingraham, and the PLP, led by former prime minister Perry Christie.

The Bahamas was not ranked by Transparency International in its 2009 Corruption Perceptions Index, but police corruption remained a major concern and top officials frequently face allegations of administrative graft.

The Bahamas has a well-developed tradition of respecting freedom of the press. Daily and weekly newspapers, all privately owned, express a variety of views, as do the government-run radio station and four privately owned radio broadcasters. Strict and antiquated libel laws dating to British legal codes are seldom invoked. Access to the internet is unrestricted.

The people's rights to religious and academic freedoms are respected.

The Bahamas upholds freedom of assembly. Constitutional guarantees of the right to form nongovernmental organizations (NGOs) are generally respected, and human rights organizations have broad access to institutions and individuals. Labor, business, and professional organizations are generally free from government interference. Unions have the right to strike, and collective bargaining is prevalent. In 2009, the government sought to liberalize its telecom industry by offering controlling shares of the Bahamas Telecommunications Industry, thus opening up a state monopoly to private investors.

The judicial system is headed by the Supreme Court and a court of appeals, with the additional right of appeal under certain circumstances to the Privy Council in London. Some progress has been reported in reducing both the duration of court cases and the backlog of criminal appeals. Nevertheless, some murder suspects have been held for up to four years before being brought to trial. In 2006, the Privy Council ruled that mandatory death sentences for individuals convicted of murder in the Bahamas are unconstitutional. However, a higher than normal homicide tally in 2009, exceeding 70 murders by October, reopened the death penalty debate. In practice, the death penalty was last carried out in January 2000.

NGOs have documented the occasional abuse of prisoners and arbitrary arrest. Prison overcrowding remains a major problem. Juveniles are often housed with adults, increasing the risk of sexual abuse. The establishment of a "correctional training institute" in 2005 was intended to improve segregation of violent and nonviolent offenders, and has since achieved positive results. However, the institute continues to face problems of limited capacity.

Discrimination against people of Haitian descent persists, and between 30,000 and 40,000 Haitians reside illegally in the Bahamas. Strict citizenship requirements and a stringent work-permit system leave Haitians with few rights. In May 2009, a boat carrying Haitian refugees capsized near the Bahamas, and some dozen people drowned.

The government is strongly opposed to homosexuality. However, the Bahamas spends more than US$1 million annually on antiretroviral drugs for HIV-infected patients. Gender equality has not been achieved, and only 12.2 percent of the seats in the Bahamian parliament are held by women. There is, however, better representation for women in the Senate than in the House of Assembly. Domestic violence remains a problem. In the fall of 2009, the government sought to amend the Sexual Offenses Act to outlaw marital rape, a move that generated significant controversy and was deferred until the 2010 legislative session.

Bahrain

Political Rights: 6*
Civil Liberties: 5
Status: Not Free

Population: 1,217,000
Capital: Manama

Status Change: Bahrain's political rights rating declined from 5 to 6 and its status from Partly Free to Not Free due to arrests of prominent members of the Haq political society, an increase in systematic harassment of opposition figures, and worsening sectarian discrimination.

Ten-Year Ratings Timeline For Year Under Review (Political Rights, Civil Liberties, Status)

2000	2001	2002	2003	2004	2005	2006	2007	2008	2009
7,6NF	6,5NF	5,5PF	5,5PF	5,5PF	5,5PF	5,5PF	5,5PF	5,5PF	6,5NF

Overview: Tensions between the country's Shiite majority and the ruling Sunni minority intensified in 2009. In January, authorities arrested three leaders of the mostly Shiite opposition political society Haq, sparking a series of violent protests. Also that month, the information minister ordered internet service providers to block access to websites with political content that was critical of the government. In June, the government briefly closed the daily newspaper *Akhbar al-Khaleej* for an article that was critical of Iran's leadership.

The al-Khalifa family, which belongs to Bahrain's Sunni Muslim minority, has ruled the Shiite-majority country for more than two centuries. Bahrain gained independence in 1971 after more than a hundred years as a British protectorate. The first constitution provided for a national assembly with both elected and appointed members, but the monarch dissolved the assembly in 1975 for attempting to end al-Khalifa rule.

In 1994, the arrest of prominent individuals who had petitioned for the reestablishment of democratic institutions sparked protests. The disturbances left more than 40 people dead, thousands arrested, and hundreds either imprisoned or exiled.

After Sheikh Hamad bin Isa al-Khalifa ascended to the throne in 1999, he released political prisoners, permitted the return of exiles, and eliminated emergency laws and courts. He also introduced the National Charter, which aimed to create a constitutional monarchy with an elected parliament, an independent judicial branch, and rights guaranteeing women's political participation.

Voters approved the National Charter in 2001, and the country was proclaimed a constitutional kingdom the following year. However, the process of political reform had disappointed many Bahrainis by the time local and parliamentary elections were held in May and October 2002, respectively. Leading Shiite groups and leftists boycotted the elections to protest campaigning restrictions and electoral gerrymandering aimed at diminishing the power of the Shiite majority. The government banned international organizations from monitoring the elections, and Sunni groups won most of the seats in the new National Assembly.

Shiite groups that boycotted the 2002 voting took part in the next elections in 2006. Al-Wefaq, a Shiite political society, won 42 percent of the vote and 17 in the Council of Representatives, the lower house of the bicameral National Assembly. The overall results represented a victory for Islamist groups, which took 30 of the lower chamber's 40 seats. The remaining 10 were awarded to liberal candidates. King Hamad appointed a liberal Consultative Council, the upper house, to offset the Islamist electoral gains. In wake of the elections, claims emerged that a senior official was determined to keep the Shiite majority underrepresented. Critics also alleged that the authorities had stepped up the naturalization of foreign workers and non-Bahraini Arabs in advance of the elections to boost the number of Sunni voters.

Security forces cracked down on the government's most outspoken critics in 2007, and the campaign continued through 2008, with dozens of Shiite activists claiming that they were tortured in custody. Violence escalated following the January 2009 arrest of Hassan Mushaima, Abduljalil al-Singace, and Mohammed Habib al-Muqdad, three leaders of the opposition political association Haq. Authorities compounded tensions that month when they arrested the popular human rights activist Abdulhadi al-Khawaja for a speech that was critical of the government. Al-Khawaja was charged with "instigating hatred and disrespect" against the government and faced a possible 10-year prison sentence, but subsequently received a royal pardon in April. While the pardon provided al-Khawaja his freedom, royal pardons are temporary. The charges and the possibility of future imprisonment remain in place. Protests and clashes between mostly young Shiites and security forces broke out regularly between January and April, with police using live ammunition to disperse demonstrators.

In a bid to calm the unrest, the government released Mushaima, al-Singace, and al-Muqdad in April, and the king pardoned 22 Shiite activists who had been imprisoned for 10 months on charges of "promoting regime change through terrorism." In October, 19 Shiites were acquitted of murdering a police officer in 2008.

Political Rights and Civil Liberties:

Bahrain is not an electoral democracy. The 2002 constitution gives the king power over the executive, legislative, and judicial authorities. He appoints cabinet ministers and members of the 40-seat Consultative Council, the upper house of the National Assembly. The lower house, or Council of Representatives, consists of 40 elected members serving four-year terms. The National Assembly may propose legislation, but the cabinet must draft the laws.

Formal political parties are illegal, but the government allows political societies or groupings to operate. A 2005 law makes it illegal to form political associations based on class, profession, or religion, and requires all political associations to register with the Ministry of Justice.

Although Bahrain has some anticorruption laws, enforcement is weak, and high-ranking officials suspected of corruption are rarely punished. Bahrain was ranked 46 out of 180 countries surveyed in Transparency International's 2009 Corruption Perceptions Index.

Freedom of expression is restricted, and the authorities routinely harass activists who criticize them publicly. The government owns all broadcast media outlets, and the private owners of the three main newspapers have close ties to the government. Self-censorship is encouraged by the vaguely worded 2002 Press Law, which allows the state to imprison journalists for criticizing the king or Islam, or for threatening "national security." In January 2009, the information minister ordered internet service providers to continue blocking websites with critical political content. In June the government temporarily shut down the newspaper *Akhbar al-Khaleej* for an article denouncing Iran's leadership. The government and its supporters have also used the press to criticize and smear human rights and opposition activists. Despite these restrictions, print outlets feature some debate regarding reform, the parliament's effectiveness, and sectarianism.

Islam is the state religion. However, non-Muslim minorities are generally free to practice their faiths. All religious groups must obtain a permit from the Ministry of Justice and Islamic Affairs to operate legally, although the government has not punished groups that operate without a permit.

Academic freedom is not formally restricted, but teachers and professors tend to avoid politically sensitive issues, and scholars who criticize the government are subject to dismissal. While there are some limits to public speech, Bahrainis engage in robust private discussion in their homes, cafes, and political salons.

Severe restrictions on freedom of assembly were enacted in 2006. Citizens must obtain a license to hold demonstrations, which are now banned from sunrise to sunset in any public arena. Police regularly use violence to break up political protests, most of which occur in Shiite villages. The 1989 Societies Law prohibits any nongovernmental organization from operating without a permit. The Bahrain Center for Human Rights was closed by the government in 2004, although its members continue to operate. In September 2009, Mohammad al-Maskati, president of the Bahrain Youth Society for Human Rights, was charged for operating the organization without a registration; he faced up to six months' imprisonment.

Bahrainis have the right to establish independent labor unions, but workers must give two weeks' notice before a strike, and strikes are banned in vital sectors such as security, civil defense, transportation, health care, communications, and basic infrastructure. A 2006 amendment to the labor law stipulates that private sector employees cannot be dismissed for union activities, but harassment of workers continues. Foreign workers are not protected by the labor law and lack the right to organize and seek help from Bahraini unions. In August 2009, the labor minister announced that the Labor Market Regulatory Authority would take over responsibility for sponsoring foreign workers, removing the power of sponsorship from employers. While the move was expected to protect foreign workers from some abuses, it did not apply to household servants, who are particularly vulnerable to exploitation.

The king appoints all judges, and courts have been subject to government pressure. Members of the royal family hold all security-related offices. Bahrain's antiterrorism law prescribes the death penalty for members of terrorist groups and prison terms for those who use religion to spread extremism. This legislation has been criticized on the grounds that its definition of terrorist crimes is too broad and that it has led to the use of torture and arbitrary detention.

Shiites are underrepresented in government and face various forms of discrimination. Fears of Shiite power and suspicions about their loyalties have limited employment opportunities for young Shiite men and fueled attempts by the government to erode the Shiite majority, mostly by granting citizenship to foreign-born Sunnis. Bahrainis have the right to travel freely inside and outside the country.

Although women have the right to vote and participate in elections, they are underrepresented politically. One-quarter of Consultative Council members are women, and the first woman in the Council of Representatives won her seat in 2006 after running unopposed. In May 2008, Bahrain named Hoda Nono as its first female (and Jewish) ambassador to the United States. While they are often partners in family decision making, women are generally not afforded equal protections under the law. The government drafted a personal status law in 2008 but withdrew it in February 2009 under pressure from the country's Shiite clergy; the Sunni portion was resubmitted and passed in parliament. Personal status and family law issues for Shiite Bahrainis are still subject to Sharia court rulings based on the interpretation of predominantly male religious scholars and are not included in the recently enacted law.

Bangladesh

Political Rights: 3*
Civil Liberties: 4
Status: Partly Free

Population: 162,221,000
Capital: Dhaka

Ratings Change: Bangladesh's political rights rating improved from 4 to 3 due to the installation of a new elected civilian government and related gains in government functioning and accountability

Ten-Year Ratings Timeline For Year Under Review (Political Rights, Civil Liberties, Status)

2000	2001	2002	2003	2004	2005	2006	2007	2008	2009
3,4PF	3,4PF	4,4PF	4,4PF	4,4PF	4,4PF	4,4PF	5,4PF	4,4PF	3,4PF

Overview: A new civilian government took office in January 2009 after the Awami League party won a sweeping victory in December 2008 elections, ending a period of indirect military rule. It moved to implement an ambitious reform agenda, which called for trials for those suspected of committing war crimes during the 1971 war of independence, restoration of the 1972 constitution, and a crackdown on Islamist political and militant groups. The government demonstrated its staying power in February, when it effectively quelled a mutiny by paramilitary Bangladesh Rifles troops in which dozens of officers were killed. Despite significant openings in the political environment, human rights abuses—particularly extrajudicial executions—remained a concern during the year.

Bangladesh gained independence from Britain in 1947 as part of the newly formed state of Pakistan, and successfully split from Pakistan in December 1971, after a nine-month war. The 1975 assassination of independence leader and prime minister Sheikh Mujibur Rahman by soldiers precipitated 15 years of military rule and continues to polarize Bangladeshi politics. The last military ruler resigned in 1990 after weeks of prodemocracy demonstrations. Elections in 1991 brought the Bangladesh Nationalist Party (BNP) to power under Prime Minister Khaleda Zia.

A long political deadlock began in 1994, when Sheikh Hasina Wajed's center-left Awami League (AL) party began boycotting Parliament to protest alleged corruption in Zia's government. The AL and the BNP differed little on domestic policy; their disputes often reflected the personal animosity between Hasina, the daughter of Rahman, and Zia, the widow of a military ruler, who was allegedly complicit in his assassination. The AL boycotted the February 1996 elections, then forced Zia's resignation in March, and triumphed in elections held in June. The BNP also marked its time in opposition by boycotting Parliament and organizing periodic nationwide strikes.

In 2001, the AL was voted out of office in elections marred by political violence and intimidation, and a new BNP-led coalition that included two Islamist parties took power. The AL initially refused to accept the election results and turned to parliamentary boycotts, countrywide hartals (general strikes), and other forms of protest to pressure the government on various issues. Political violence and general lawlessness mounted in 2004 and 2005, partly due to bombings and other attacks by Islamist extremist groups. Two of the largest—the Jamiat-ul-Mujahideen Bangladesh (JMB) and the Jagrata Muslim Janata Bangladesh (JMJB)—were banned in 2005, and a government crackdown in 2006 yielded the arrest of the two groups' leaders, along with some 800 members; six militant leaders were eventually executed. The threat of Islamist violence subsided after the crackdown, but it did not disappear altogether.

Partisan disagreement over the planned 2007 general elections led to heightened political tension and violence throughout 2006. The AL and its allies demanded reform of Bangladesh's caretaker government (CG) system, in which a theoretically nonpartisan government takes power temporarily to oversee parliamentary elections. The AL also questioned the conduct and impartiality of the Election Commission (EC) and its preparation of a new voter list. Faced with the possibility of an election that lacked credibility, in January 2007 the army pressured President Iajuddin Ahmed to declare a state of emergency and cancel the elections. A new, military-backed CG, headed by technocrat Fakhruddin Ahmed, announced plans to tackle endemic corruption and prepare for new elections. Under emergency regulations, freedoms of assembly and association were suspended, controls were placed on the media, and all political activity was banned.

While the "soft coup" was carried out partly within the constitutional framework, stopping short of martial law and leaving a civilian CG in nominal control, creeping military influence was extended over key institutions. A new Anti-Corruption Commission (ACC), headed by a former army chief, was formed in January 2007. An unprecedented number of high-level politicians and their business allies—including Hasina, Zia, and their immediate family members—were arrested and held pending investigations of their finances; some were subsequently convicted by a special court. The new government also made efforts to remove executive influence from the increasingly politicized judiciary.

After antimilitary student demonstrations in August 2007 left several people dead and hundreds injured, the authorities responded with university closures, arrests, and a temporary shutdown of the internet and mobile-telephone network.

Economic woes—including inflation, a decline in investment, and increasing food shortages—also progressively weakened public support for the administration.

The CG spent much of 2008 attempting to balance its anticorruption drive and electoral reforms with the need to win the cooperation of the dominant political parties and ensure the success of the planned elections. Early in the year, Hasina (along with several family members) was formally charged with extortion, and other high-level politicians continued to face arrest as well. By May, the main parties jointly decided to boycott preelection talks with the EC unless their leaders were released. A series of CG capitulations regarding the release of Hasina, Zia, and Zia's sons marked the de facto collapse of the anticorruption campaign. The new EC also failed to address the issue of suspected war criminals' continued involvement in politics. Of particular concern was the Jamaat-e-Islami (Islamic Party), whose leaders and student wing played a well-documented role in atrocities against civilians during the 1971 war of independence.

The emergency regulations, which had been eased in August and early December, were fully lifted on December 17, and the elections followed on December 29. Although the long-standing party leaders remained in place, there was a considerable infusion of new blood into the parties' candidate lists. Turnout was extremely high, at 87 percent, and included a large proportion of first-time, women, and minority voters. An electoral alliance led by the AL won a landslide of 263 seats (230 for the AL), while the BNP-led coalition took 32 seats (29 for the BNP and just 2 for the Jamaat-e-Islami). After initial protests, Zia accepted the results, and with Hasina taking office as prime minister, Bangladesh returned to civilian rule after a two-year hiatus.

AL-backed candidates also won a majority of leadership positions in the January 2009 upazila parishad (subdistrict) elections, the first local government polls to be held for 19 years. In contrast to the national elections, the January balloting was marred by more extensive violence and intimidation, as well as electoral irregularities and suspected rigging. Separately, veteran AL politician Zillur Rahman was chosen by Parliament as the new president in February. In July, Hasina reshuffled and expanded her cabinet to improve ministerial performance. She also reasserted control over the AL by engineering the removal of four key party officials who had challenged her dominance.

The new government moved quickly to implement its campaign promises and ratify most of the ordinances passed by the CG. Several war crimes suspects were arrested, and in July, the government submitted draft legislation regarding the establishment of a tribunal to oversee prosecutions. Another key part of the AL's agenda was to restore the 1972 constitution, nullifying all amendments enacted since then. Among other effects, this would reinstate a ban on religious parties, posing a clear threat to parties like the Jamaat-e-Islami. The government took a harder line on Islamist militants during the year, and by July security forces had arrested more than 40 JMB activists.

The BNP-led opposition continued to boycott Parliament and assail most of the AL government's initiatives, including the constitutional restoration, proposed revisions to education policy, and a shift toward amicable dispute resolution with neighboring India. However, the BNP did not resort to the use of hartals during the year.

The government faced an early test in February, when troops from the Bangladesh Rifles (BDR), a paramilitary force tasked with border security, mutinied in Dhaka and killed some 70 officers and civilians, including the BDR commander and several officers' families. The mutiny quickly ended after Hasina, with the army's support, threatened to use force. An official investigation, released in May, ruled out the involvement of politicians, Islamist militants, or foreign governments, but failed to clearly identify the cause of the revolt by the BDR, which was known to harbor resentments over poor pay and other conditions of service. At the urging of the army, the government said it would prosecute suspected mutineers, and at least 3,500 BDR members had been arrested by August. Several dozen of the detainees died under suspicious circumstances, leading the government to promise an inquiry. The Supreme Court ruled in September that alleged mutineers would not be prosecuted under the Army Act (which called for the death penalty), but would instead be tried under either the BDR Act for minor offenses or a special tribunal under the penal code for criminal offenses. The trial of a first group of BDR members accused of taking part in the mutiny started in late November.

Political Rights and Civil Liberties: Bangladesh is an electoral democracy. It regained that status through the December 2008 parliamentary elections, which were deemed free and fair by European Union observers and other monitoring groups. Terms for both the unicameral National Parliament and the largely ceremonial presidency are five years. Parliament is composed of 345 members, of which 300 are directly elected, and 45 are women nominated by political parties—based on their share of the elected seats—and then voted on by their fellow lawmakers. The president is elected by Parliament. The 1996 polls were the first held under a constitutional amendment requiring a CG to oversee the election process.

A primary justification for the postponement of the 2007 elections was the need for an overhaul of electoral procedures. A series of reforms announced in July 2008 mandated that parties disband their student, labor, and overseas units; obliged parties to reserve a third of all positions for women; reduced the number of seats a parliamentary candidate could simultaneously contest from five to three; tripled campaign spending limits to 1.5 million taka (US$22,000) per candidate; and gave voters in each constituency the option of rejecting all candidates. The new regulations were designed to curtail the widespread bribery, rigging, and violence that had characterized recent elections. A new voter registry completed the same month was considerably smaller than its predecessor, which contained around 12 million invalid names. Hopes that voters in the December 2008 elections would reject tainted politicians did not materialize; at least two candidates who were facing corruption charges won landslide victories from jail. The level of political violence remained relatively high in 2009; local rights group Odhikar registered 251 deaths and more than 15,000 injured as a result of inter- or intraparty clashes during the year, with a spike surrounding the January 2009 local government polls.

Endemic corruption and criminality, weak rule of law, limited bureaucratic transparency, and political polarization have long undermined government accountability. Moreover, boycotts by both major parties while in opposition have regularly crippled the parliamentary system and led to a process by which the legislature effectively rubber-stamps decisions by the executive and dominant party. This phenomenon reemerged in 2009, as the BNP boycotted Parliament through the end of the year. The two parties have also maintained links to criminal networks.

Bangladesh was ranked 139 out of 180 countries surveyed by Transparency International (TI) in its 2009 Corruption Perceptions Index. The local branch of TI noted in 2008 that although the CG's campaign had effectively reduced large-scale corruption, graft and bribery on a smaller scale remained rampant. In 2009, the ACC continued to investigate and prosecute high-level cases, opening a new case in March against Arafat "Koko" Rahman, Zia's son, for alleged money laundering. However, watchdog groups such as Odhikar expressed concern that political interference remained an impediment to the effective work and independence of the commission. In June, the state prosecution service decided to withdraw more than 60 cases, most of which had been brought against leading AL politicians under the CG, after deeming them politically motivated. The dropped cases included 12 against Prime Minister Sheikh Hasina.

Bangladesh's media environment opened up considerably in 2009. In late 2008, the CG had lifted the Emergency Powers Rules (EPR), which limited coverage of sensitive topics, allowed censorship of print and broadcast outlets, criminalized "provocative" criticism of the government, and imposed penalties—including up to five years in prison and hefty fines—for violations. Media were allowed to cover freely the December 2008 elections, and despite occasional cases of censorship, the print media were generally given more leeway when covering sensitive topics than broadcasters, particularly the private television channels that provide 24-hour news coverage. Atiqullah Khan Masud, editor of the national daily *Janakantha*, was released in January 2009 after being held for 22 months under the EPR. Separately, a journalist and writer who was first arrested in 2003, Salah Uddin Shoaib Choudhury, still faced sedition, treason, and blasphemy charges; his trial began in June 2008 and was ongoing during 2009, but he was allowed to travel abroad while the proceedings continued. A new Right to Information Act took effect in July 2009. According to the press freedom group Article 19, the measure would apply to all information held by public bodies, simplify the fees required to access information, override existing secrecy legislation, and grant greater independence to the Information Commission charged with overseeing and promoting the law.

Journalists continue to be threatened and attacked with impunity by organized crime groups, party activists, and Islamist groups, although the level of harassment has declined and no journalists have been killed for the past four years, according to the Committee to Protect Journalists. In February, journalist Farid Alam fled the country after receiving death threats from the JMB in connection with his new book on militant Islam. Several cases of arbitrary arrest, prolonged detention, and custodial torture of journalists were documented during 2009, including that of *New Age* reporter F. M. Masum, who was tortured by a member of a government paramilitary unit in October. Journalists have also reported receiving threatening telephone calls from intelligence agencies seeking to prevent negative coverage, and many practice self-censorship when reporting on sensitive topics.

Islam is the official religion, but about 10 percent of the population is Hindu, and there are smaller numbers of Buddhists and Christians. Although religious minorities have the right to worship freely, they face societal discrimination and remain underrepresented in politics and state employment. A trend of increased intolerance and attacks on minorities was reversed in 2009, as the new government made explicit commitments to defend minority rights and deployed police to protect vulnerable groups like the 100,000-strong Ahmadiyya sect. Ahmadis are considered heretical by some mainstream Muslims, and they have faced physical attacks, boycotts, and demands by extremist groups that they be declared non-Muslims by the state. Other positive steps taken by the avowedly secular AL government included the appointment of several individuals from minority groups to leadership positions, the initiation of curriculum reform in the religious schools (madrassahs), and the provision of additional security at religious celebrations.

While authorities largely respect academic freedom, research on sensitive political and religious topics is discouraged, according to the U.S. State Department's human rights report. Political polarization at many universities inhibits education and occasionally leads to clashes between students and security forces. Fighting between AL and BNP student groups at Jahangirnagar University led to temporary closures at a number of universities in January 2009, while in February, more than 200 people were injured in clashes between police and students at technical colleges across the country.

Restrictions on rights of assembly and association under the EPR were fully lifted by the end of 2008. Occasional demonstrations continued to take place, and protesters have sometimes been killed or injured during clashes with police. Numerous world-class nongovernmental organizations (NGOs) operate in Bangladesh and meet basic needs in fields such as education, health care, and microcredit. However, those perceived to be overly critical of the government, particularly on human rights issues, are subject to intense official scrutiny and occasional harassment or denial of permission for proposed projects. Amnesty International has noted that at least eight human rights defenders have been assassinated since 2000, and that many have been injured or threatened by criminal gangs or party factions. Others have faced arbitrary arrest and torture by the authorities.

Labor rights were simplified and codified in the Bangladesh Labour Act (BLA) of 2006, although the new law carried over many of the restrictions contained in previous legislation. For example, labor union formation is hampered by a 30 percent employee-approval requirement, restrictions on organizing by unregistered unions, and rules against union formation by certain categories of civil servants. Conditions for workers improved in 2009 following the lifting of the EPR. In April, the AFL-CIO reported that modest improvements had been made in workers' rights, particularly in the shrimp-processing and ready-made garment industries, as well as in the Export Processing Zones (EPZs), which fall outside the purview of the BLA. Labor activists occasionally face harassment, and worker grievances sometimes fuel unrest at factories. In June, violence erupted at several garment factories outside of Dhaka, resulting in considerable property damage, several worker fatalities, and hundreds of injuries.

Prior to 2007, the judiciary had become increasingly politicized, with frequent instances of executive-branch meddling in lower-court decisions. The military-backed CG, unlike previous governments, worked to carry out a 1999 Supreme Court directive ordering the separation of the judiciary from the executive. In 2007, the power to appoint judges and magistrates was transferred from the executive branch to the Supreme Court. However, the Supreme Court's appellate division resumed the practice of overturning politically-motivated judicial decisions of the high court, according to the U.S. State Department's human rights report, a practice that often favored the ruling AL party. In July 2009, approximately 100 judges attended a demonstration organized by the Bangladesh Judicial Service Association to protest administrative interference in the judiciary. According to the Asian Human Rights Commission, the AL government initially attempted to force two of the judges who organized the protest into retirement, in violation of the 2007 reforms, but then backed down in August.

The court system is prone to corruption and severely backlogged; pretrial detention is lengthy, and many defendants lack counsel. The indigent have little access to justice through the courts. In August 2009, the government launched an initiative to form small courts in 500 rural administrative councils that could settle disputes outside of traditional court settings, reducing pressure on the legal system. Prison conditions are extremely poor, and severe overcrowding is common, to the extent that prisoners have to sleep in shifts. According to the New Delhi–based Asian Centre for Human Rights, hundreds of juveniles are illegally held in prisons in contravention of the 1974 Children's Act. Suspects are routinely subjected to warrantless arrest and detention, demands for bribes, and physical abuse (including torture) at the hands of law enforcement officials. Torture is routinely used to extract confessions and intimidate political detainees.

Many abuses are perpetrated by the Rapid Action Battalion (RAB), a paramilitary unit composed of some 4,500 military and police personnel that was formed in 2004 to combat widespread lawlessness. Although initially popular, the RAB and other units engaged in anticrime campaigns have been criticized for excesses like extrajudicial executions. According to local rights watchdog Odhikar, there were 154 extrajudicial killings by law enforcement agencies in 2009, a similar number to the previous year. During 2009, several dozen suspected BDR mutineers died in custody under suspicious circumstances, with some bodies bearing marks of torture and other abuse. The Directorate General–Forces Intelligence (DGFI), a military intelligence unit, has also been responsible for a number of cases of abuse during interrogations. Although the new government initially promised a "zero-tolerance" approach to issues of torture and extrajudicial executions, key ministers appeared to back away from this promise as the year wore on.

Law enforcement abuses are facilitated by legislation such as the 1974 Special Powers Act, which permits arbitrary detention without charge, as well as Section 54 of the Criminal Procedure Code, which allows detention without a warrant. Rights groups also expressed concern about a June 2008 counterterrorism ordinance that included an overly broad definition of terrorism and generally did not meet international standards. In February 2009, the new government adopted this ordinance as a bill without modifying its troubling provisions. On a positive note, legislation introduced in July 2009 was designed to bring the existing International War Crimes Tribunal Act of 1973 into line with international standards concerning the right to a fair trial.

The CG approved an ordinance to set up a national human rights commission in December 2007, and the new government passed the National Human Rights Commission Bill in July 2009. However, rights groups expressed concern over the independence of the commission, which would be appointed by a seven-member selection committee composed of government officials, all but one of whom would belong to the ruling party. In addition, the commission would have no powers to initiate legal action against those suspected of abuse.

Islamist militant groups continue to operate and maintain contact with regional allies, but Islamist violence has been negligible since the 2006 crackdown. However, such groups continue to operate, and in late October, several high-ranking JMB members were arrested by government forces. Casualties from clashes involving Maoist militants have declined somewhat in the past several years; according to the South Asia Terrorism Portal, 86 people, the vast majority of them militants, were killed in 2009.

Land rights for the Hindu minority remain tenuous despite the annulment of the Vested Property Act in 2001. Tribal minorities have little control over land decisions affecting them, and Bengali-speaking settlers continue to encroach illegally on tribal lands in the Chittagong Hill Tracts (CHT) with the reported connivance of government officials and the army. A 1997 accord ended a 24-year insurgency by indigenous groups in the CHT that had resulted in the deaths of 8,500 people. However, as documented by the Asian Centre for Human Rights, the accord has not been fully implemented, tribal inhabitants continue to be displaced to make way for army camps, and returning refugees have been unable to reclaim their land. Security forces are also occasionally implicated in the suppression of protests, the arrest of political activists, and extrajudicial killings. Moreover, indigenous people remain subject to physical attacks and property destruction by Bengali settlers, according to the World Organization Against Torture and other groups. In July 2009, the new government said it would immediately withdraw more than 2,000 troops from the CHT and dismantle several dozen military camps. It also announced plans to set up a commission that would allocate land to indigenous tribes.

Roughly 260,000 ethnic Rohingyas fleeing forced labor, discrimination, and other abuses in Burma, entered Bangladesh in the early 1990s; some 28,000 registered refugees and at least 200,000 other Rohingyas who are not formally documented as refugees remain in the country and are subject to some harassment. Bangladesh also hosts camp-like settlements of some 300,000 non-Bengali Muslims, often called Biharis, who had emigrated from India in 1947 and were rendered stateless at independence in 1971, as many had sided with and initially sought repatriation to Pakistan. In May 2008, a landmark court ruling granted citizenship rights to this group, enabling their access to social services and the right to vote.

Rape, dowry-related assaults, acid throwing, and other forms of violence against women occur regularly. A law requiring rape victims to file police reports and obtain medical certificates within 24 hours of the crime in order to press charges prevents most rape cases from reaching the courts. Police also accept bribes to quash rape cases and rarely enforce existing laws protecting women. The Acid Survivors Foundation (ASF), a local NGO, recorded 115 acid attacks during 2009; they affected 145 victims, most of them women. While investigation of acid-related crimes remains inadequate, attacks have steadily declined since the passage of the Acid Crime Prevention Act in 2002.

Under the legal codes pertaining to Muslims, women have fewer divorce and inheritance rights than men. In rural areas, religious leaders sometimes impose flogging and other punishments on women accused of violating strict moral codes. Women also face some discrimination in health care, education, and employment. They remain underrepresented in government, although a 2004 constitutional amendment reserves 45 parliamentary seats for women, and a large number of women participated in the December 2008 elections. Trafficking in both women and children remains extensive, but the government has taken steps to raise awareness and prosecute traffickers more vigorously; several dozen were convicted during 2009, with many receiving life sentences. Child labor is widespread.

Barbados

Political Rights: 1
Civil Liberties: 1
Status: Free

Population: 281,000
Capital: Bridgetown

Ten-Year Ratings Timeline For Year Under Review (Political Rights, Civil Liberties, Status)

2000	2001	2002	2003	2004	2005	2006	2007	2008	2009
1,1F	1,1F	1,1F	1,1F	1,1F	1,1F	1,1F	1,1F	1,1F	1,1F

Overview: In 2009, the new Barbadian government, led by Prime Minister David Thompson of the Democratic Labour Party, grappled with the impact of the economic recession.

Barbados gained its independence from Britain in 1966 but remained a member of the Commonwealth. The Barbados Labour Party (BLP) under Prime Minister Owen Arthur governed from 1994 to 2008, when the opposition Democratic Labour Party (DLP) won a clear majority of 20 seats in the lower house of Parliament. The BLP was left with the remaining 10 seats. Despite this stunning upset, the new government, led by David Thompson of the DLP, did not break markedly from the policies pursued by the Arthur government.

In 2009, Barbados was an active member of the Caribbean Community and enjoyed warm relations with most of its neighbors. However, heavy migration flows from Guyana to Barbados continued to cause tension between the countries, and Barbados remained outside the Venezuelan-backed regional energy pact known as PetroCaribe due to concerns about accumulating additional debt. The pact offered Caribbean countries a guarantee of Venezuelan oil shipments on favorable financial terms. The International Monetary Fund forecast that Barbados would face a major economic recession by the end of 2009, forcing the government to cut expenditures, stabilize prices, and shore up the country's foreign reserves.

Barbados has been more successful than other Caribbean countries in combating violent crime, which remained at low levels. The country experienced only 19 murders in 2009, the lowest recorded number in a decade. Joint patrols of the Royal Barbados Police Force and the Barbados Defence Force have managed to contain the problem, which was often linked to narcotics trafficking. The attorney general called for focusing more attention on curtailing the drug trade, which remained a significant problem in 2009.

Political Rights and Civil Liberties: Barbados is an electoral democracy. Members of the 30-member House of Assembly, the lower house of the bicameral Parliament, are directly elected for five-year terms. The governor-general, who represents the British monarch as head of state, appoints the 21 members of the Senate: 12 on the advice of the prime minister, 2 on the advice of the leader of the opposition, and the remaining 7 at his own discretion. The prime minister is the leader of the political party with a majority in the House.

Political parties are free to organize. Historically, power has alternated between two centrist parties—the DLP and the BLP. In addition to the parties holding parliamentary seats, other political organizations include the small, left-wing Worker's Party of Barbados and the People's Empowerment Party (PEP), an opposition force favoring trade union rights and greater state intervention in the economy.

Barbados was ranked 20 out of 180 countries surveyed in Transparency International's 2009 Corruption Perceptions Index.

Freedom of expression is respected. Public opinion expressed through the news media, which are free of censorship and government control, has a powerful influence on policy. Newspapers, including the two major dailies, are privately owned. Four private and two government radio stations operate. The single television station, operated by the government-owned Caribbean Broadcasting Corporation, presents a wide range of political viewpoints. There is unrestricted access to the internet.

The constitution guarantees freedom of religion, which is widely respected for mainstream religious groups, although members of Barbados's small Rastafarian community have protested prison regulations that require inmates to have their long dreadlocks cut off while in detention. Academic freedom is fully respected.

Barbados's legal framework provides important guarantees for freedom of assembly, which are upheld in practice. The right to form civic organizations and labor unions is respected. Two major labor unions, as well as various smaller ones, are active.

The judicial system is independent, and the Supreme Court includes a high court and a court of appeals. Lower-court officials are appointed on the advice of the Judicial and Legal Service Commission. Barbados has ratified the Caribbean Court of Justice (CCJ) as its highest appellate court. There are occasional reports and complaints of the use of excessive force by the Royal Barbados Police Force to extract confessions, along with reports that police do not always seek warrants before searching homes.

The prison system has taken steps to relieve overcrowding. A new prison facility with the capacity to house 1,250 inmates was completed in 2007, after a fire destroyed the island's largest penitentiary in 2005. Barbados is considering judicial reform that would reduce overcrowding by keeping courts open longer to hear more cases per year, but no reforms have been implemented, and overcrowding remains a problem. Although the authorities have made significant efforts to discharge prison personnel alleged to have beaten inmates, their prosecution has not made substantial progress.

The country's crime rate, fueled by an increase in drug abuse and narcotics trafficking, has given rise to human rights concerns. In May 2009, the government examined reforming the constitution to abolish mandatory death sentences for murder convicts. The death penalty remains a mandatory punishment for certain capital crimes, although in practice it has not been implemented since 1984.

Women comprise roughly half of the country's workforce, however, violence against women and children continue to be serious social concerns.

Belarus

Political Rights: 7
Civil Liberties: 6
Status: Not Free

Population: 9,662,000
Capital: Minsk

Ten-Year Ratings Timeline For Year Under Review (Political Rights, Civil Liberties, Status)

2000	2001	2002	2003	2004	2005	2006	2007	2008	2009
6,6NF	6,6NF	6,6NF	6,6NF	7,6NF	7,6NF	7,6NF	7,6NF	7,6NF	7,6NF

Overview:
Despite incentives from the European Union to introduce reforms, President Alyaksandr Lukashenka maintained a tight grip over Belarus's political and economic systems in 2009. He continued to use police violence and other forms of harassment against the political opposition, and blocked independent media from covering demonstrations through systematic intimidation. After releasing all of its political prisoners in 2008, the regime incarcerated more activists in 2009. The country made no substantial progress in reforming its electoral code, and overall hopes for an improvement in the political situation went unrealized.

Belarus declared independence in 1991, ending centuries of rule by Poland, Russia, and the Soviet Union. In 1994, voters made Alyaksandr Lukashenka, a member of parliament with close links to the security services, Belarus's first post-Soviet president. He pursued reunification with Russia and subordinated the government, legislature, and courts to his political whims while denying citizens basic rights and liberties. A widely criticized 1996 referendum approved constitutional amendments that extended Lukashenka's term through 2001, broadened presidential powers, and created a new bicameral parliament (the National Assembly).

In October 2000, Belarus held deeply flawed elections to the lower house. State media coverage of the campaign was limited and biased, and roughly half of all opposition candidates were denied registration. Following a boycott by seven opposition parties, only three opposition candidates were elected.

Lukashenka won a second term through disputed elections held in September 2001, amid accusations by former security-service officials that the president was directing a death squad aimed at silencing his opponents. Four politicians and journalists who had been critical of the regime disappeared during 1999 and 2000. By 2002, Lukashenka had launched a campaign of political retribution against those who had opposed him during the presidential campaign.

Legislative elections and a parallel referendum on the presidency were held in October 2004. According to official results, not a single opposition candidate entered the National Assembly, while voters ostensibly endorsed the government's proposal to allow Lukashenka to run for a third term in 2006. As with previous votes, the Organization for Security and Cooperation in Europe (OSCE) declared that the parliamentary elections fell "significantly short" of Belarus's commitments. Following Ukraine's Orange Revolution, in which protesters helped overturn the results of a fraudulent election, Lukashenka bolstered the law enforcement agencies and purged their ranks of potential dissenters. Amendments to the Law on Interior Troops introduced in February 2005 allowed for the discretionary use of firearms against protesters on orders from the president.

The March 19, 2006, presidential election, in which Lukashenka won a third term, did not meet democratic standards, according to the OSCE. The government took harsh repressive measures against the opposition, detaining and beating many activists, including Alyaksandr Kazulin, one of three opposition candidates. Though there were no reliable exit polls, the opposition asserted that Lukashenka could not have won the 83 percent of the vote that he claimed. Lukashenka subsequently asserted that his vote total had been much higher, but that the numbers were manipulated downward to make it look more realistic.

The election provoked the largest public protest of Lukashenka's tenure, bringing 10,000 to 15,000 activists onto Minsk's October Square on election day. Between 500 and 1,000 individuals were arrested on March 25, including Kazulin, who was sentenced to five and a half years in prison for protesting the flawed election and the subsequent crackdown. Opposition activity dwindled after the protests, as the government typically jailed opposition leaders and intimidated their rank-and-file supporters with fees and warnings.

In an effort to bolster his international standing, Lukashenka released all the political prisoners identified by the European Union (EU) and United States by August 19, 2008. However, hopes for further progress dimmed when no opposition candidates won seats in the September 2008 parliamentary elections.

The EU nevertheless indicated a strong interest in improved ties in 2009, releasing Lukashenka from a 13-year travel ban and allowing him to visit Italy and Lithuania. Italian prime minister Silvio Berlusconi returned the visit in November, making him the first Western leader to call in over a decade. Belarus also joined the EU's Eastern Partnership program. While taking advantage of these overtures, Lukashenka simultaneously launched a new political crackdown, describing opposition activists as "enemies of the Belarusian nation." In February, the regime arrested more political prisoners, according to local human rights workers. These included Mikalai Autukhovich, Yury Lyavonau, and Uladzimir Asipenka. Autukhovich and Lyavonau had previously been held as political prisoners. The authorities charged Autukhovich with preparing a terrorist act in June and pressed similar charges against Asipenka in November, but released Lyavonau on August 8. Among other cases, the courts sentenced "Young Front" activist Dubski to one year in prison on July 7, and in October, United Civil Party member Andrey Bandarenka, a former parliamentary candidate, received a seven-year sentence. As in previous years, the police regularly used violence to break up demonstrations and blocked the media from documenting such events. Toward the end of the year, the security services kidnapped at least three opposition activists and, after threatening them, dumped them in the forest far from home.

Political Rights and Civil Liberties: Belarus is not an electoral democracy. Serious and widespread irregularities have marred all recent elections. The 110 members of the Chamber of Representatives, the lower house of the bicameral National Assembly, are popularly elected for four years on the basis of single-mandate constituencies. The upper house, the Council of the

Republic, consists of 64 members serving four-year terms; 56 are elected by regional councils, and 8 are appointed by the president. The constitution vests most power in the president, giving him control over the government, courts, and even the legislative process by stating that presidential decrees have a higher legal force than ordinary legislation. The National Assembly serves largely as a rubber-stamp body. The president is elected for five-year terms, and there are no term limits.

With power concentrated in the presidency, parties play a negligible role in the political process. Opposition parties have no representation in the National Assembly, while propresidential parties serve only superficial functions. Members of opposition parties claim that they are drafted into the military because of their political views. A 2009 law makes it illegal for soldiers to belong to political parties, forcing these opposition members to give up their affiliations. Amendments to the electoral law adopted in 2009 give the parties more opportunities to campaign but still do not provide for a transparent vote count.

Corruption is fed by the state's dominance of the economy and the overall lack of transparency and accountability in government. Belarus was ranked 139 out of 180 countries surveyed in Transparency International's 2009 Corruption Perceptions Index.

President Alyaksandr Lukashenka systematically curtails press freedom. Libel is both a civil and a criminal offense, and an August 2008 media law gives the state a monopoly over information about political, social, and economic affairs. The authorities routinely harass and censor independent media outlets, including through physical force and revocation of journalists' credentials. Belarusian national television is completely under the control of the state and does not provide coverage of alternative and opposition views. The state-run press distribution monopoly limits the availability of private newspapers. Under the 2008 media law, the federal government revoked the registration of several independent newspapers toward the end of 2009. The new media law also allowed local authorities to close down independent publications for minor violations. According to the law, the cabinet will exercise control over internet media, which are now legally subject to the same restrictions as traditional media. While the government had not yet applied the internet restrictions in 2009, its ownership of the country's sole internet service provider gives it the power to do so.

Despite constitutional guarantees that "all religions and faiths shall be equal before the law," government decrees and registration requirements have increasingly restricted religious activity. Amendments to the Law on Religions in 2002 provided for government censorship of religious publications and prevented foreign citizens from leading religious groups. The amendments also placed strict limitations on religious groups that have been active in Belarus for fewer than 20 years. The government in 2003 signed a concordat with the Belarusian Orthodox Church, which enjoys a privileged position. The authorities have discriminated against Protestant clergy and ignored anti-Semitic attacks, according to the U.S. State Department.

Academic freedom is subject to intense state ideological pressures, and institutions that use a liberal curriculum, promote national consciousness, or are suspected of disloyalty face harassment and liquidation. Official regulations stipulate immediate dismissal and revocation of degrees for students and professors who join opposition protests. Wiretapping by state security agencies limits the right to privacy.

The Lukashenka government restricts freedom of assembly for critical independent groups. Protests and rallies require authorization from local authorities, who can arbitrarily withhold or revoke permission. When public demonstrations do occur, police frequently break them up and arrest participants, a pattern that was repeated in 2009.

Freedom of association is severely restricted. More than a hundred of the most active nongovernmental organizations (NGOs) were forced to close between 2003 and 2005. In December 2005, Lukashenka signed amendments to the penal code that criminalized participation in an unregistered or liquidated political party or organization, allowing further punitive measures against groups that refused to shut down. As a result, most human rights activists operating in the country face potential jail terms ranging from six months to two years. Regulations introduced in 2005 ban foreign assistance to NGOs, parties, and individuals deemed to have promoted "meddling in the internal affairs" of Belarus from abroad. The government signaled a slight thaw in December 2008, however, when it registered the Movement for Freedom, an NGO led by former presidential candidate Alyaksandr Milinkevich. Independent trade unions face harassment, and their leaders are frequently dismissed from employment and prosecuted for peaceful protests. Over 90 percent of workers have fixed-term contracts, meaning the government can dismiss them for any reason when the contract expires.

Although the country's constitution calls for judicial independence, courts are subject to significant executive influence. The right to a fair trial is often not respected in cases with political overtones. Human rights groups continue to document instances of beatings, torture, and inadequate protection during detention in cases involving leaders of the democratic opposition, and their trials are frequently held in secret.

An internal passport system, in which a passport is required for domestic travel and to secure permanent housing, limits freedom of movement and choice of residence. As of January 2008, citizens no longer need a travel permit before going abroad, but the government has created a database that will include nearly 100,000 people who cannot leave the country. The country's command economy severely limits economic freedom.

Ethnic Poles and Roma often face discrimination. Women are not specifically targeted for discrimination, but there are significant discrepancies in income between men and women, and women are poorly represented in leading government positions. As a result of extreme poverty, many women have become victims of the international sex trade.

Belgium

Political Rights: 1
Civil Liberties: 1
Status: Free

Population: 10,792,000
Capital: Brussels

Ten-Year Ratings Timeline For Year Under Review (Political Rights, Civil Liberties, Status)

2000	2001	2002	2003	2004	2005	2006	2007	2008	2009
1,2F	1,2F	1,1F	1,1F	1,1F	1,1F	1,1F	1,1F	1,1F	1,1F

Overview: Herman Van Rompuy, a Flemish Christian Democrat who had ended 18 months of political crisis in Belgium after becoming prime minister in December 2008, resigned in November 2009 to assume his new post as the first permanent president of the European Council. He was replaced as prime minister by his predecessor and fellow Christian Democrat, Yves Leterme.

Modern Belgium dates to 1830, when the territory broke away from the Netherlands and formed an independent constitutional monarchy. The territory that constitutes present-day Belgium had previously been in the possession of the Spanish and Austrian Habsburgs and Napoleonic France, as well as briefly the Netherlands. History accounts for its rich cultural and linguistic diversity, and to some extent, tension. In the 20th century, Belgium became one of the founding members of the European Union (EU) and still hosts the organization's central administration in Brussels.

Ethnic and linguistic conflicts prompted a series of constitutional amendments in 1970, 1971, and 1993 that devolved considerable power from the central government to the three regions in the federation: French-speaking Wallonia in the south, Dutch-speaking Flanders in the north, and Brussels, the capital, where French and Flemish share the same official status. The small German minority in Wallonia, which consists of around 70,000 people, has also been accorded cultural autonomy.

Prior to the 2007 parliamentary elections, cultural and economic differences between the country's regions had contributed to political rifts between Flemish and Francophone parties across the ideological spectrum, with the wealthier Flemish north seeking increased self-rule and reduced taxpayer support for the less prosperous Wallonia. Flanders premier Yves Leterme's centrist Christian Democratic and Flemish (CDV) party—in an electoral bloc with the New Flemish Alliance (N-VA)— led the June elections with 30 of 150 seats in the lower house. The remaining seats were divided among 10 other factions. Leterme was invited by King Albert II to form a new government, but because the Flemish and Walloon parties were unable to agree on coalition terms after an extraordinary 196 days of negotiations, outgoing prime minister Guy Verhofstadt stayed on as a caretaker. In December 2007, Verhofstadt agreed to the request of King Albert II to form an interim government with the authority to act on pressing economic and other concerns.

In February 2008, a majority of political parties agreed on an outline for limited constitutional reform, which cleared the way for Leterme to become prime minister the following month. However, he was unable to consolidate support after taking office. The king rejected his offer to resign in July, after he failed to win approval for a regional autonomy plan, and lawmakers began to leave the ruling coalition during the fall. Leterme's government was ultimately brought down at the end of the year after being accused of interfering in a court case concerning the failed bank, Fortis. The prime minister offered his resignation again in December, this time refusing to return to his post. On December 30, the king swore in Herman Van Rompuy, also of the CDV, to replace him.

Van Rompuy's time in office proved to be brief, but noteworthy. His 11-month term is regarded as a time during which the instabilities and divisions of the recent past were laid to rest. In part due to his burgeoning reputation as a consensus-builder, Van Rompuy emerged in the fall of 2009 as a leading candidate to fill the new position of the first permanent president of the European Council, the supreme intergovernmental decision-making body in the EU, comprising the heads of state and government of the member states. The post was created by the Lisbon Treaty to end the six-month rotation of the Council's presidency between the heads of state of the country holding the presidency of the EU. Van Rompuy was unanimously appointed by the 27 EU member states on November 19. On November 24, it was announced that Leterme would succeed Van Rompuy as prime minister.

Political Rights and Civil Liberties: Belgium is an electoral democracy. Parliament consists of two houses: the Chamber of Deputies and the Senate. The 150 members of the Chamber of Deputies are elected directly by proportional representation. In the Senate, there are 71 seats, with 40 filled by direct popular vote and 31 by indirect vote. In both houses, members serve four-year terms. The prime minister, who is the leader of the majority party or coalition, is appointed by the monarch and approved by Parliament. The party system is highly fragmented, with each standard ideological niche occupied by separate Flemish and Walloon parties.

In November 2004, Belgian courts banned the xenophobic Vlaams Blok party for violating the country's antiracism laws. The party changed its name to Vlaams Belang (Flemish Interest) and removed some of the most overtly racist elements from its platform. However, the party maintains its opposition to immigration and commitment to an independent Flanders. The party was the third-largest vote-earner in the 2007 Chamber of Deputies elections, taking 12 percent of the vote and 17 seats. It won 16 percent of the Dutch-speaking vote in the 2009 European Parliament election.

Belgium has minimal issues regarding corruption and was ranked 21 out of 180 countries surveyed in Transparency International's 2009 Corruption Perceptions Index.

Freedoms of speech and the press are guaranteed by the constitution and generally respected by the government. Belgians have access to numerous private media outlets. However, concentration of newspaper ownership has progressed in recent decades, leaving most of the country's papers in the hands of a few corporations. A law on the protection of journalists' sources was enacted in 2005, in the wake of a 2004 incident in which police raided the home and office of a Brussels reporter. In early 2009, Belgian prosecutors dismissed a complaint of bribery brought by the EU Anti-Fraud Office against Hans-Martin Tillack, a German journalist for *Stern* magazine working in Brussels; Tillack had been investigating EU-related fraud and corruption. The government does not limit access to the internet.

Freedom of religion is protected. About half of the country's population identifies itself as Roman Catholic. However, members of a number of minority religions have complained of discrimination by the government, which has been criticized for its characterization of some non-Catholic groups as "sects." The government does not restrict academic freedom.

Freedom of association is guaranteed by law, except for groups that practice discrimination "overtly and repeatedly." Freedom of assembly is also respected. About 63 percent of the workforce is unionized. Employers found guilty of firing workers because of union activities are required to reinstate the workers or pay an indemnity.

The judiciary is independent, and the rule of law generally prevails in civil and criminal matters. Although conditions in prisons and detention centers meet most international standards, many continue to suffer from overcrowding.

Specific antiracism laws prohibit and penalize the incitement of discrimination, of hatred, and violence based on race, ethnicity, or nationality. However, there have been complaints about the treatment of rejected asylum seekers and illegal immigrants awaiting deportation, who have often been held in unsanitary conditions in Brussels national airport, sometimes for several months. The European Court of Human Rights in 2008 ordered Belgium to pay two Palestinian asylum seekers 15,000 euros each (roughly US$22,000) in damages after they were detained in the airport in 2002. Belgium decided in 2009 to regularize 25,000 illegal immigrants. The wearing of the *hijab* is prohibited in several municipalities in Flanders.

The law provides for the free movement of citizens at home and abroad, and the government does not interfere with these rights.

The government actively promotes equality for women. In 2003, it created the Institute for the Equality of Men and Women, formerly the Ministry of Labor's Division of Equal Opportunity, which is empowered to initiate sex-discrimination lawsuits. Women won more than 35 percent of the seats in the of Deputies, and 38 percent of the seats in the Senate, during the 2007 elections. Belgium is a destination and transit point for trafficked persons. However, according to the 2009 U.S. State Department's Trafficking in Persons Report, the country complies fully with the minimum standards for eliminating trafficking, including financing nongovernmental organizations that assist victims.

Belize

Political Rights: 1
Civil Liberties: 2
Status: Free

Population: 329,000
Capital: Belmopan

Ten-Year Ratings Timeline For Year Under Review (Political Rights, Civil Liberties, Status)

2000	2001	2002	2003	2004	2005	2006	2007	2008	2009
1,1F	1,2F	1,2F	1,2F	1,2F	1,2F	1,2F	1,2F	1,2F	1,2F

Overview:
The political establishment was shaken by several high-profile cases of corruption and financial mismanagement

during 2009, including the arrest of Belize City's mayor and charges—later dismissed—against a former prime minister. Also in 2009, violent crime continued, and Prime Minister Dean Barrow failed to make progress on proposed constitutional amendments that would have, among other things, allowed for wiretapping, preventative detentions, and government seizure of lands containing mineral resources.

Belize achieved independence from Britain in 1981 but remained a member of the Commonwealth. The government has since changed hands a number of times, alternating between the center-right United Democratic Party (UDP) and the center-left People's United Party (PUP).

Said Wilbert Musa of the PUP was elected as prime minister in 1998, and he became the country's first prime minister to secure a consecutive term after the PUP won again in 2003. However, the opposition UDP swept the 2006 local elections amid public dissatisfaction with corruption scandals, increased taxation, and rising crime rates. In 2007, public protests broke out, focusing on issues including education and financial mismanagement. The Musa government's plan to take over the debt of Universal Health Services (UHS), a private company, was particularly controversial. Belize received a US$10 million grant from the Venezuelan government that year for the construction and repair of housing, but the funds were diverted to Belize Bank to assist in the repayment of a government-guaranteed loan to UHS.

The UDP, led by Dean Barrow, ousted Musa and the PUP in February 2008 parliamentary elections, taking 25 out of 31 seats in the lower house of the National Assembly and leaving the PUP with just six seats. Voter turnout was lower than in the last elections, but the balloting was determined to be free and fair.

In April 2008, the Barrow government proposed amendments to the constitution that would allow for wiretapping and preventative detention. The package also provided the government with the right to seize property if mineral resources are discovered on it. Opponents argued that this power could easily be abused and did not respect the land rights of Mayan minority groups. The legislation was passed by the National Assembly in August, but the Court of Appeal ruled in March 2009 that the government had to hold a referendum on the amendments before they could become law. The measure remained stalled at year's end.

Barrow was also criticized in 2009 for a controversial government takeover of Belize Telemedia, the country's largest telecommunications company, in August. In reaction to a conflict with the company, lawmakers had quickly amended the Belize Telecommunications Act to allow for the takeover, which was subsequently denounced as illegal and unconstitutional by business groups.

Belize has strengthened ties with Venezuela in recent years, joining its PetroCaribe program, which supplies the majority of the country's oil imports on favorable terms, in 2006. Belize has also worked with Venezuela and Taiwan to develop its own nascent oil production. Meanwhile, a long-standing border dispute with Guatemala has continued. The two countries agreed in December 2008 to hold referendums on whether to submit the issue to the International Court of Justice, but there were no concrete plans for the votes at the end of 2009.

Political Rights and Civil Liberties: Belize is an electoral democracy. The head of state is the British monarch, represented by a governor-general. The

31-seat House of Representatives, the lower house of the bicameral National Assembly, is elected for five-year terms. The 12 members of the Senate are appointed to five-year terms, with 6 appointed by the governor-general on the advice of the prime minister, 3 on the advice of the opposition leader, and 3 on the advice of major civil society groups. There are no restrictions on the right to organize political parties, and the interests of Mestizo, Creole, Mayan, and Garifuna ethnic groups are represented in the National Assembly. The country's major parties are the center-right UDP and the center-left PUP.

Government corruption is a serious problem, but in a sign of growing intolerance for graft, a number of scandals shook the political scene during 2009. In March, Minister of Human Development and Social Transformation Juan Coy was suspended from his post for six months for an alleged abuse of power in which he intervened to secure the release of seized contraband goods. In September, Belize City mayor Zenaida Moya was arrested on charges linked to the alleged misappropriation of some US$140,000 in public funds. Former prime minister Said Wilbert Musa was cleared in June of corruption charges related to his government's diversion of funds to aid the private company UHS. Musa rejected the charges, filed in late 2008, as politically motivated. Belize was not included in Transparency International's 2009 Corruption Perceptions Index.

Belize has a generally open media environment, with little fear of government reprisal for criticism. The authorities may imprison (for up to three years) or fine (up to US$2,500) journalists or others who criticize the financial disclosures of government officials, but this law has not been applied in recent years. The Belize Broadcasting Authority has the right to prior restraint of all broadcasts for national security or emergency reasons, though this too is rarely invoked. Belize has one daily newspaper and 10 weeklies, including 2 that are supported directly by political parties. There are 10 radio stations and two television networks, along with a variety of cable outlets. The internet penetration rate is one of the highest in Central America.

There is full freedom of religion in Belize, and academic freedom is respected.

Freedoms of assembly and association are generally upheld, and demonstrations are usually peaceful. In late January and early February 2009, protests by sugarcane workers turned violent, as police attempted to break up a roadblock, resulting in one death and injuries to at least 10 people. A large number of nongovernmental organizations are active, and labor unions remain politically influential despite their shrinking ranks. Official boards of inquiry adjudicate labor disputes, and businesses are penalized for labor-code violations. However, the government has done little to combat antiunion discrimination, and workers who are fired for organizing rarely receive compensation. In a positive development, the Supreme Court in July 2009 ruled in favor of six workers who were fired from a Maya King banana farm in 2001 for attempting to join a union.

The judiciary is independent and nondiscriminatory, and the rule of law is generally respected. Court cases are often prolonged for years amid a heavy backlog, while defendants remain free on bail or in lengthy pretrial detention. Reports of police misconduct are investigated by the department's internal affairs office or by an ombudsman's office. Extrajudicial killing and use of excessive force are among the country's primary human rights concerns.

According to the International Center for Prison Studies, Belize has the 12th-highest prisoner-to-public ratio, with about 476 inmates per 100,000 inhabitants. Prisons do not meet minimum standards, although the Hattieville Prison is now run by a nonprofit foundation that has improved conditions somewhat. There have been investigations into the brutalization of inmates by prison authorities, and at least three senior prison officers have been dismissed over brutality and bribery allegations. The prison occupancy level is at 96.5 percent; about a quarter of detainees are awaiting trial.

Violent crime, money laundering, and drug trafficking continued unabated in 2009 due to insufficient countermeasures and government corruption. There were 97 reported homicides in 2009, down 6 percent from the 103 reported in 2008.

The government actively discourages ethnic discrimination. Although the Mayans claim to be the original inhabitants of Belize, the government has designated only 77,000 acres as Mayan preserves, and there has been little action on the 500,000 acres of disputed land. Most of the indigenous population lives in the south, the poorest part of the country. The Belize Human Rights Commission is independent and effective, although it is allocated limited resources.

Most of the estimated 40,000 Spanish-speaking immigrants in the country lack legal status, and undocumented workers continue to be exploited. A number of cases involving the trafficking of workers from South Asia and China for forced labor have also been uncovered in recent years.

Belize is a source, transit, and destination country for women and children trafficked for prostitution and forced labor, and the majority of women working in the country's brothels are from Guatemala, Honduras, and El Salvador. The U.S. State Department's 2009 Trafficking in Persons Report placed Belize on its Tier 2 Watch List, citing the government's failure to make progress in trying and convicting offenders.

Violence against women and children remains a serious concern, as does the prevalence of child labor in agriculture. According to UNAIDS, as of September 2009, the adult HIV-prevalence rate had remained relatively unchanged at about 2.6 percent, compared to 2.4 percent in 2007. There were reports of discrimination against persons living with HIV/AIDS in recent years, despite the government's efforts to educate the public about the illness.

Benin

Political Rights: 2
Civil Liberties: 2
Status: Free

Population: 8,935,000
Capital: Porto-Novo

Ten-Year Ratings Timeline For Year Under Review (Political Rights, Civil Liberties, Status)

2000	2001	2002	2003	2004	2005	2006	2007	2008	2009
2,2F	3,2F	3,2F	2,2F	2,2F	2,2F	2,2F	2,2F	2,2F	2,2F

Overview: President Boni Yayi's popularity continued to wane in 2009, as his fragile political alliances in the National Assembly prevented him from following through on campaign promises involving decentralization, privatization, and improved government efficiency.

Six decades of French rule in Benin ended in 1960. Mathieu Kerekou took power 12 years later, ending a series of coups and imposing a one-party system along with other communist policies. However, by 1990, economic hardship and rising internal unrest forced Kerekou to hold a national conference that eventually ushered in democracy. The transition culminated in his defeat by Nicephore Soglo in the 1991 presidential election, and the country's human rights record subsequently improved. Kerekou returned to power in 1996 through a democratic election, and he secured another term in 2001, after his two main opponents boycotted a runoff due to administrative problems and alleged fraud.

In 2003, legislative elections gave the ruling coalition a majority in the National Assembly for the first time since democratization, and the voting was generally considered free and fair. Pro-Kerekou candidates also performed well in local elections, which were held for the first time that year in a move toward decentralization.

The 2006 presidential election featured unprecedented competition, since both Kerekou and Soglo were ineligible due to their ages, and Kerekou had refused to name a successor. Boni Yayi, an independent candidate and former president of the regional development bank, emerged as the victor and promised to tackle corruption, decentralize government, and privatize state companies.

A coalition of parties supporting Yayi, led by the Cowrie Forces for an Emerging Benin (FCBE), won a majority of seats in the 2007 legislative elections. All but three seats changed hands in generally free and fair voting, demonstrating the public's desire for new leadership.

While the country's poverty and limited infrastructure often lead to technical problems during elections, particularly serious irregularities caused the 2008 local elections to be postponed by two months and led to the eventual annulment and rerun of contests in 24 districts. In the run-up to the elections, the Supreme Court reprimanded the Autonomous National Electoral Commission (CENA) three separate times for instances of politicization.

By 2009, the optimism that followed Yayi's 2006 election had waned, as the growing instability of his legislative coalition and of political parties in general hampered his efforts to enact promised reforms and improve government efficiency. A referendum on the president's proposed constitutional revisions, originally slated for early 2009, was postponed indefinitely due to resistance from opposition politicians in the National Assembly. The president's proposed constitutional reforms did not extend the presidential term limit or otherwise increase presidential power as the opposition had anticipated, and instead focused primarily on bureaucratic changes to improve the functioning of government and the operations of the civil service. Nevertheless, the opposition hindered any progress on these measures in what appeared to be a power play in advance of the 2011 presidential elections.

The government decentralization program moved forward in May, when officials announced that the country's 12 current regional departments would be increased to 29. However, there were protests in a number of small towns that were not selected as department capitals, casting doubt on implementation of the plan. Meanwhile, although the administration successfully sold its stake in the largest local bank in 2008, it encountered delays in its attempts to privatize the state-owned telecommunications and power companies in 2009.

Political Rights and Civil Liberties: Benin is an electoral democracy. Despite delays and disorganization, the 25-member CENA effectively oversaw the 2007 legislative polls, which were considered free and fair. However, the commission's performance noticeably deteriorated during the 2008 local elections.

The president is elected by popular vote for up to two five-year terms and serves as both the chief of state and head of government. Delegates to the 83-member, unicameral National Assembly serve four-year terms.

Historically, Benin has been divided between northern and southern ethnic groups, which are the main support bases of many of the current political parties. However, since the 2006 presidential election, traditional party structures have given way to a plethora of smaller parties—currently more than 50—and fragile political alliances.

President Boni Yayi has made the fight against endemic corruption a top priority, garnering praise from international officials. In 2006, he signed into law an official code of conduct for government officials that led to the arrest of an influential petroleum tycoon on fraud charges and the audit of 60 state-run companies as well as overseas Beninese embassies. In 2009, major corruption was also uncovered in both the microfinance and water sectors. Benin was ranked 106 out of 180 countries surveyed in Transparency International's 2009 Corruption Perceptions Index.

Constitutional guarantees of freedom of expression are largely respected in practice. An independent and pluralistic press publishes articles that are highly critical of government and party leaders. However, in July 2009, three journalists were subjected to physical attacks—rare events in a country where journalists usually operate unhindered. The government does not restrict internet access, though the country's connection was temporarily disrupted during the year when an undersea cable running from South Africa was damaged.

The government actively seeks to ensure religious and academic freedom. While more than half of Benin's citizens practice voodoo, most of them also associate with another religion like Christianity or Islam. Through a number of recent high-profile cases, the Constitutional Court has reaffirmed religious rights and the separation of church and state. Primary education is mandatory under the constitution, and the state is working to facilitate access to education by eliminating tuition fees.

Freedom of assembly is respected, and requirements for permits and registration are often ignored. Large opposition demonstrations on a range of issues were allowed to proceed peacefully during 2009. Numerous nongovernmental organizations and human rights groups operate freely.

The right to organize and join labor unions is constitutionally guaranteed. Unions played a central role in the country's democratization and remain powerful today. The medical unions, seeking increased pay, were on strike for the first half of 2009. Although it received support from the opposition, the strike led to a deterioration in care and the cancellation of a major polio vaccination campaign.

The judiciary's independence is generally respected by the executive branch, but the courts are considered to be highly inefficient and susceptible to corruption. More than 90 percent of cases involving overdue payments are never resolved in the courts, and there are currently more pretrial detainees than convicts behind bars. Harsh prison conditions aggravate the situation; cells in Cotonou and Abomey prisons, for example, hold six times the intended number of inmates. While the government announced in 2008 that it intended to abolish the death penalty, it had yet to do so by the end of 2009.

A sharp increase in armed robberies and violent crime was reported in Cotonou in late 2008. The government linked this to an increase in small-arms trafficking and smuggling in the poorest areas of the city. In March 2009, police discovered 50 kilograms of cannabis during a drug raid and arrested 45 suspects.

Relations among Benin's ethnic groups are generally good, although regional divisions occasionally flare up, particularly between the north, where Yayi is from, and the south. Minority ethnic groups are well represented in government agencies, the civil service, and the armed forces. Societal prejudices against women in the workplace and open homosexuality are evident, though not ubiquitous. In 2008, Benin signed the International Convention on the Rights of Persons with Disabilities.

Although the constitution provides for gender equality, women enjoy fewer educational and employment opportunities than men, particularly in rural areas. A family code promulgated in 2004 improved women's inheritance, property, and marriage rights, and prohibited forced marriage and polygamy. However, legal rights pertaining to family matters are frequently unknown or ignored. In April 2009, to address the country's high maternal mortality rate, the government began helping women pay for caesarean births.

Human trafficking is widespread in Benin; most victims are girls trafficked inside the country from rural to urban areas. A law formally outlawing human trafficking was passed in 2006. While a number of traffickers were arrested in 2007 and 2008, there were no reported arrests in 2009, and the prison sentences handed down to date—ranging from 3 months to 1 year—are far short of the 20-year maximum provided by the law.

Bhutan

Political Rights: 4
Civil Liberties: 5
Status: Partly Free

Population: 683,000
Capital: Thimphu

Ten-Year Ratings Timeline For Year Under Review (Political Rights, Civil Liberties, Status)

2000	2001	2002	2003	2004	2005	2006	2007	2008	2009
7,6NF	7,6NF	6,5NF	6,5NF	6,5NF	6,5NF	6,5NF	6,5NF	4,5PF	4,5PF

Overview: Bhutan's new elected legislature passed several new laws in 2009, and declared an end to strict enforcement of cultural traditions such as the national dress code. While several thousand Nepali-speaking Bhutanese refugees who were displaced in the 1990s have been resettled in other countries in recent years, 95,000 remain in camps in Nepal.

Britain began guiding Bhutan's affairs in 1865, and in 1907, the British helped install the Wangchuck dynasty. A 1949 treaty allowed newly independent India to assume Britain's role in conducting Bhutan's foreign and defense policies. In 1971, Jigme Singye Wangchuck succeeded his father as king.

Reversing its long-standing tolerance of cultural diversity, the government in the 1980s began imposing restrictions on Nepali speakers, also known as Southern Bhutanese, ostensibly to protect the culture of the ruling Ngalong Drukpa ethnic group. In 1988, the government began stripping thousands of Nepali speakers of their citizenship. The newly formed Bhutanese People's Party (BPP) responded in 1990 with sometimes violent demonstrations, prompting a government crackdown. Tens of thousands of Southern Bhutanese fled or were expelled to Nepal in the early 1990s, with credible accounts suggesting that soldiers raped and beat many villagers and detained thousands as "antinationals."

As part of a major transition toward democracy led by the king, political parties were legalized in June 2007, and elections for an upper house of Parliament were held in two rounds, in December 2007 and January 2008. Elections for a lower house, the National Assembly, took place in March 2008. With voter turnout at about 80 percent, the Bhutan Peace and Prosperity Party (DPT) won 45 of the 47 seats. A new constitution promulgated in July provided for some fundamental rights, but upheld the primacy of the monarchy, and analysts noted that it did not adequately protect the rights of Nepali speakers.

Jigme Khesar Namgyel Wangchuck formally succeeded his father as king in November 2008, although he had been in power since the outgoing king's abdication in 2006. The monarchy remains highly popular with the public, and many Bhutanese have expressed reservations about the shift toward democracy.

The new elected political institutions were relatively active in 2009, passing bills related to local governance, tobacco sales, and the police. In July, the National Assembly declared that Driglam Namzha (traditional etiquette) would no longer be strictly enforced, instead stipulating that cultural traditions such as the national dress code would be sustained through education alone.

Political Rights and Civil Liberties:

Bhutan is not an electoral democracy, though the 2008 elections represented a significant step toward that status. A European Union (EU) monitoring team reported that the National Assembly elections "generally met international standards," although it noted problems with freedom of expression and association during the campaign. The new constitution provides for a bicameral Parliament, with a 25-seat upper house, the nonpartisan National Council, and a 47-seat lower house, the National Assembly, both serving five-year terms. The king appoints 5 members of the National Council, and the remaining 20 are elected; the lower house is entirely elected, and the head of the majority party is nominated by the king to serve as prime minister. The cabinet is nominated by the king and approved by the National Assembly. The king remains the head of state and appoints members of the Supreme Court, the attorney general, and the heads of national commissions. He can return legislation to the government with objections or amendments, but once it has been reconsidered and resubmitted, the king must sign it into law.

Political parties, previously illegal, were allowed to begin registering in 2007. Only two parties—the DPT and PDP, both of which have ties to the royal family—participated in the 2008 National Assembly elections. The parties do not differ significantly in policy goals. The constitution forbids parties based on sex, religion, language, or region, and a 2007 election law bars individuals without bachelor's degrees from participating in government. In November 2007, the election commission denied registration to the Bhutan People's United Party, commenting that it did not "have the capacity to fulfill ... national aspirations, visions and goals." Nine ethnic Nepali candidates were elected to office in 2008, although the EU monitors noted that a rule requiring candidates to obtain a security clearance certificate may have been an obstacle for some Nepalis.

The government operates with limited transparency and accountability, but steps have been taken in recent years to improve both. The Anti-Corruption Commission (ACC), created in 2006, is tasked with investigating and preventing graft, and the Anti-Corruption Act, passed that year, also established protections for whistle-blowers. However, police and local officials routinely ask for bribes. From 2006 through November 2009, the ACC fielded 2,073 complaints, with the majority related to corruption in local government. Of the 249 complaints that qualified for investigation, only 78 were actually investigated; the rest are pending review. In late 2008, the cabinet appointed a chief executive for Bhutan Post over the objections of the ACC, which uncovered corruption in the appointment process. Bhutan was ranked 49 of 180 countries surveyed in Transparency International's 2009 Corruption Perceptions Index.

The authorities restrict freedom of expression, and a 1992 law prohibits criticism of the king and the political system. A 2006 media law overhaul led to the establishment of two independent radio stations, but it did not provide specific protections for journalists or guarantee freedom of information. Two independent weeklies, *Bhutan Times* and *Daily Observer*, were launched that year. Both papers, along with the state-owned *Kuensel*, generally publish progovernment articles but occasionally cover criticism of the government. A new paper, the *Bhutan Daily*, opened in October 2008. Cable television services, which air uncensored foreign programming, thrive in some areas but are hampered by a high sales tax and regulatory obstacles. A June 2009 decision by the National Assembly to discontinue live television broadcasts of its debates drew objections from Bhutanese press freedom advocates; National Council debates continue to be broadcast live. Shanti Ram Acharya, a journalist working for the *Bhutan Reporter*, a monthly published by refugees in Nepal, was sentenced to seven and half years in prison in January 2009. He had been arrested for alleged "subversive activities" while visiting Bhutan in 2007. The government claims that he was photographing an army outpost.

The constitution protects freedom of religion, and a 2007 election law bars any ordained religious figure or "religious personality" from voting or running for office. While Bhutanese of all faiths can worship relatively freely, the Drukpa Kagyupa school of Mahayana Buddhism is the official religion and reportedly receives various subsidies. A 9,287-member Monastic Body is the sole arbiter of religious matters, and monks also wield political influence. The religious services of the small Christian minority are reportedly often held out of sight to avoid harassment by the authorities, and permits for the construction of Hindu temples are apparently difficult to obtain. Restrictions on academic freedom have been reported, although nongovernmental organizations (NGOs) claim that the teaching of Nepali and Sanskrit is banned.

Freedoms of assembly and association are restricted. The constitution guarantees freedom of assembly, but the government must approve the purpose of any protests. In recent years, security forces have arrested Southern Bhutanese refugees based in Nepal who entered Bhutan to demonstrate for the right to return home.

NGOs that work on human rights, the refugee issue, or other sensitive matters are not legally allowed to operate. The 2007 Civil Society Organization Act requires all new NGOs to register with the government. The constitution guarantees freedom of association, but only for groups "not harmful to the peace and unity of the country." Several NGOs are currently operating, with the majority focusing on women's rights or environmental issues. The government prohibits independent trade unions and strikes, though some 85 percent of the workforce is engaged in subsistence agriculture. A 2007 labor and employment law prohibits forced labor, child labor, discrimination, and sexual harassment.

The 2007 Judicial Service Act created an independent Judicial Service Council to control judicial appointments and promotions. Courts are also now required to make decisions within a year, and citizens are guaranteed legal counsel in court cases. Arbitrary arrest, detention, and torture remain areas of concern, and dozens of political prisoners continue to serve lengthy sentences.

Prior to the mass expulsions of Nepali speakers in the early 1990s, the government had stripped thousands of their citizenship under a 1985 law that required both parents to be Bhutanese citizens. Individuals also had to prove that they or both of their parents resided in Bhutan in 1958. While the Office of the UN High Commissioner for Refugees (UNHCR) asserts that the overwhelming majority of refugees have proof of Bhutanese nationality, the government maintains that many left voluntarily or had been illegal immigrants. The refugees live in extremely poor conditions in Nepal. Even if permitted to reenter Bhutan, ethnic Nepalis would face a difficult citizenship process and would not be compensated for lost property. The government has also sought to settle Bhutanese from the north in lands formerly occupied by the refugees. A resettlement process aimed at transferring the refugees to third countries including the United States began in 2008, but it was reported in June 2009 that approximately 95,000 ethnic Nepalis remained in refugee camps.

According to a 2007 Human Rights Watch report, ethnic Nepalis living in Bhutan must obtain certificates verifying that they do not present a threat to the state in order to enter schools, receive health care, take government jobs, or travel within the country or abroad. Schools in the south restrict even Nepali speakers with certificates. Bhutan's first private college, the Royal Thimphu College, opened in July 2009.

The Bhutanese Communist Party, modeled on Nepal's Maoist party and dominated by Nepali refugees, has launched an armed struggle to overthrow the monarchy, and a number of bomb attacks were reported in 2008. The Bhutanese group has received training and supplies from Indian separatist groups such as the United Liberation Front of Assam (ULFA), which reportedly operates from guerrilla bases in southern Bhutan. There were no reports of major attacks or deaths in 2009.

Restrictions on dress and cultural practices were imposed in the late 1980s in an attempt to safeguard Bhutan's heritage. However, the National Assembly in 2009 declared that cultural traditions should no longer be enforced, but instead sustained only through education.

Women participate freely in social and economic life but continue to be underrepresented in government and politics, despite some recent gains. The application of religious or ethnically based customary laws regarding inheritance, marriage, and divorce sometimes results in discrimination against women. There are no reports that trafficking of women or children is a problem in Bhutan.

Bolivia

Political Rights: 3
Civil Liberties: 3
Status: Partly Free

Population: 9,863,000
Capital: La Paz (administrative), Sucre (judicial)

Ten-Year RatingsTimeline ForYear Under Review (Political Rights, Civil Liberties, Status)

2000	2001	2002	2003	2004	2005	2006	2007	2008	2009
1,3F	1,3F	2,3F	3,3PF	3,3PF	3,3PF	3,3PF	3,3PF	3,3PF	3,3PF

Overview: Referendum voters approved a new constitution in January. In December, President Evo Morales was reelected by a wide margin, while members of the ruling party garnered more than two-thirds of the seats in both houses of the legislature. Although the level of political violence declined compared with 2008, the breakup of an alleged plot to assassinate Morales helped to keep political polarization sharp throughout the year.

After achieving independence from Spain in 1825, the Republic of Bolivia endured recurrent instability and military rule. However, the armed forces, responsible for more than 180 coups in 157 years, refrained from political intervention after 1982, allowing a regular succession of civilian presidents over the next two decades.

No candidate in the 2002 presidential election won a majority of the popular vote, and under Bolivia's constitution, members of the National Congress were tasked with deciding the outcome. They selected Gonzalo Sanchez de Lozada, a wealthy businessman and former president (1993–97) associated with economic privatization and forced coca-eradication programs, who had received a small plurality of votes. The runner-up, confrontational indigenous leader Evo Morales, had gained prominence by capitalizing on the unpopularity of U.S.-sponsored antidrug efforts among Bolivia's majority indigenous population, many of whom spoke Spanish as a second language and used the coca leaf for traditional cultural and medical purposes.

In 2003, indigenous groups, workers, students, and coca growers mounted mass protests against government plans for a $5 billion pipeline to export Bolivian natural gas via longtime rival Chile to the United States and Mexico. The movement was also fueled by resentment over the failure of nearly two decades of democratic reform and economic restructuring to improve the lot of the indigenous majority in a country where over 60 percent of the population lived in poverty. The president ordered harsh repression of the protests, but after the crackdown led to at least 120 deaths, Sanchez de Lozada resigned in October and fled to the United States.

The nonpartisan vice president, Carlos Mesa, assumed the presidency. Despite successfully increasing state control over natural resources, he failed to quell mounting protests over gas revenues, regional autonomy, and other issues, and he ultimately resigned in June 2005. The chief justice of the Supreme Court temporarily assumed the presidency to oversee new elections, which were held in December. Morales won the presidential poll with 53.7 percent of the ballots. He pledged to implement anticorruption reforms and act on the long-standing call for a Constituent Assembly that would draft a new constitution. Morales's Movement toward Socialism (MAS) also emerged as the largest party in Congress and won three of nine races for departmental prefect (provincial governor); the latter posts were being filled through direct elections for the first time.

In May 2006, the Morales government announced additional state controls over oil and gas resources. It also introduced a land-reform plan that was opposed by the owners of large estates in the eastern lowlands. Voters handed the MAS a majority in the Constituent Assembly in July, and in a concurrent vote on the question of regional autonomy, four departments supported greater autonomy, while five rejected the idea.

Although the assembly reached compromise in February 2007 on a paralyzing disagreement over the size of the majority needed to adopt changes to individual constitutional articles, disputes continued over regional autonomy, indigenous rights, state structure, and the issue of whether La Paz or Sucre should be the capital. The resulting polarization increased regional and ethnic friction, and violent confrontations throughout the year left several people dead and scores wounded.

Wrangling over the capital proved an insurmountable obstacle for the assembly, and after pro-Sucre protesters repeatedly blocked the body's attempts to meet, a rump composed largely of MAS delegates met on November 24 outside the city and approved a draft constitution without the support (or presence) of the opposition. Protesters in Sucre responded with two days of riots that left three people dead and several hundred injured. On December 9, a similar MAS-dominated group of delegates met in Oruro to approve the final draft, which called for autonomy at the departmental, regional, municipal, and indigenous levels. It also authorized the selection of high-court judges by popular vote rather than by Congress.

Controversy over the tactics used to pass the draft charter continued for most of 2008. Two government attempts to call a national vote on the draft were blocked by the National Electoral Court (CNE). In May and June, opposition supporters easily won referendums confirming statutes detailing local control in four departments, but the CNE ruled all four votes illegal. In May, the opposition-led Senate approved a recall referendum on the president and all departmental prefects. However, Morales accepted the challenge, and on August 10, over 67 percent of voters affirmed his mandate, while two prefects, from La Paz and Cochabamba, were forced from office.

After the recall referendum, conflict increased significantly, with roadblocks, marches, and strikes throughout the country. The violence peaked on September 11, when a confrontation between peasant supporters of Morales and followers of prefect Leopoldo Fernandez in Pando resulted in the shooting deaths of at least 11 of the government supporters. The central government declared a state of emergency in the department and arrested a number of suspects, including the prefect.

Following the Pando incident, the government and opposition resumed dialogue on the constitution. On October 20, with government supporters surrounding the

Congress, the two sides announced a compromise draft that retained most articles but made notable changes, including an easing of potentially restrictive media language, a higher bar for future constitutional amendments, expansion of the electoral commission, and the limitation of consecutive presidential terms to two. After a brief but intense campaign, on January 25, 2009, over 61 percent of voters approved the new constitution, with a turnout of over 90 percent.

Polarization remained acute throughout 2009, but the overall level of violence decreased. In the year's most serious incident, police in April killed three men and detained two others at a Santa Cruz hotel who had stockpiled weapons and were allegedly conspiring to assassinate Morales and other leaders. All elements of the episode, including the nature of the plot, the circumstances of the deaths, the government's adherence to due-process rights, and the extent of lowland elites' involvement in the alleged conspiracy, remained in dispute for the rest of the year. Following incriminating testimony by supposed plot participants, several prominent Santa Cruz business and political leaders were among those placed under investigation or charged, fueling opposition complaints that the case was devolving into a witch hunt.

A transitional electoral law was passed in April, and the CNE was charged with producing a new, biometrically based electoral roll; the ensuing process vastly exceeded expectations in both efficiency and comprehensiveness. Despite scattered instances of violence, the run-up to the December balloting was largely calm. The main opposition party, the Progressive Plan for Bolivia (PPB), selected former Cochabamba city mayor and department prefect Manfred Reyes Villa as its presidential candidate. He ran on an anti-MAS platform, signified by his choice of Fernandez, the jailed former prefect of Pando, as his running mate. Reyes Villa was also hampered by a history of corruption allegations and the fallout from the alleged assassination plot, while Morales's popularity was bolstered by continuing economic growth. Morales was reelected with 64 percent of the vote amid a record 95 percent turnout. The MAS also captured 26 of 36 Senate seats and 90 of 130 seats in the Chamber of Deputies. Five departments overwhelmingly approved autonomy statutes, joining the four that had already done so.

Opposition electoral complaints centered on the abuse of state resources and a flurry of criminal charges brought against opposition politicians, including Reyes Villa, who was barred from leaving the country during the campaign as multiple corruption-related investigations proceeded. Monitors from the European Union characterized the elections as generally free and fair, but they also confirmed the misuse of state resources and noted that the judiciary's paralysis left those facing criminal charges with inadequate legal recourse. After the elections, Reyes Villa fled to the United States.

Bolivia's relations with the United States remained poor in 2009 after a sharp deterioration in 2008. That year, the two countries had expelled each other's ambassadors and markedly reduced cooperation on aid, trade, and counternarcotics due to disagreements over issues including coca eradication and alleged U.S. meddling. The two sides held talks on a new bilateral accord during 2009, but no agreement was finalized by year's end.

Political Rights and Civil Liberties: Bolivia is an electoral democracy. Elections and referendums since 2005 have been deemed free and fair by international observers. Bolivians residing abroad were granted voting rights for the first time in the December 2009 elections. Under the new constitution, presidential and congressional terms are both five years, with up to two consecutive terms permitted. The Plurinational Legislative Assembly consists of a 130-member Chamber of Deputies and a 36-member Senate, in which all senators and 53 deputies are elected by proportional representation and 70 deputies are elected in individual districts. Seven Chamber of Deputies seats reserved for indigenous representatives. The new constitution includes a presidential runoff provision to replace the previous system, in which. Congress had decided elections when no candidate won an outright majority.

Bolivians have the right to organize political parties. The current dominant electoral vehicle is President Evo Morales's MAS, an alliance of social movements whose disputes Morales must mediate. The opposition had been led by the center-right Social Democratic Power (PODEMOS) party, but in 2008, it split over the negotiations on the draft constitution, and most prominent opposition members ran under the PPB banner in 2009.

Graft and nepotism remain common, and the administration has yet to build successful institutional anticorruption mechanisms. A major scandal broke in February 2009, when the murder of a businessman carrying $450,000 led to the arrest on corruption charges of Santos Ramirez, the head of the national oil and gas company and one of Morales's closest allies. Bolivia was ranked 120 out of 180 countries surveyed in Transparency International's 2009 Corruption Perceptions Index.

Although the constitution guarantees freedom of expression, the media are subject to some limitations in practice. Most outlets are privately owned, and radio is the leading source of information. Many newspapers and television stations tend to feature opposition rather than progovernment opinion pieces; the opposite holds true in state media. A general climate of hostility toward journalists has increased along with political tensions. A local watchdog group registered 64 incidents of physical aggression between January and October 2009. As in previous years, Morales sparred bitterly with the press, and in March he brought a *desacato* (disrespect) lawsuit against the La Paz newspaper *La Prensa*. The government does not restrict access to the internet.

Freedom of religion is guaranteed by the constitution. Tensions between the Roman Catholic Church and the government have risen considerably in recent years. The new constitution ended the Church's official status and created a secular state. The government does not restrict academic freedom, and the law grants public universities an autonomous status, which students defend vigorously.

Bolivian law provides for the rights of peaceful assembly and freedom of association, although social protests sometimes turn violent. While politicians on all sides continued to use protests to obtain political leverage in 2009, the demonstrations' size and ferocity declined. Nongovernmental organizations, including independent human rights groups, operate freely. The right to form labor unions is guaranteed by the constitution, and unions are an active force in society.

The judiciary remains corrupt, inefficient, and inaccessible to many Bolivians, especially non-Spanish speakers. Although the government has pushed reforms designed to make the courts more responsive to the needs of poor and rural citizens, a lack of resources and political difficulties have limited progress. The system for selecting Supreme Court and Constitutional Tribunal (TC) justices broke down starting in 2007, leading to a crisis that included a wave of resignations and legal charges against several justices for dereliction of duty. In May 2009, the last TC justice resigned, and by year's end, a backlog of over 5,000 cases had accumulated at the tribunal. Following the suspension of Chief Justice Eddy Fernandez in May 2009, the Supreme Court was also largely paralyzed.

Prison conditions are harsh, and over 70 percent of detainees are in pretrial detention. Although the criminal procedure code recognizes indigenous conflict-resolution traditions, judicial reform to date have not effectively codified and incorporated indigenous customary law. This lack of clarity has led perpetrators of vigilante crimes, including lynching, to portray, with no basis, their acts as a form of indigenous justice. The local office of the UN High Commissioner for Human Rights noted at least 15 lynching deaths in 2009. Communal justice also served as the justification for the eviction of former vice president Victor Hugo Cardenas from his home in March; the government condemned the act.

Detentions related to the September 2008 Pando massacre appeared to violate legal norms on warrant approval, habeas corpus, and other elements of due process. The government argued that given the volatile climate, speedy detentions were necessary, but continuing arrests, a change of jurisdiction from Pando to La Paz, and the slow pace of investigations caused concern among the opposition and some human rights observers. More than 25 people were charged with serious crimes in the case in October 2009, but trials had not begun at year's end.

Both the human rights ombudsman and independent human rights organizations are able to report on brutality by the security forces, although impunity remains the norm. Attempts to seek justice for human rights abuses under past dictatorships gained momentum in 2009, despite investigators' meager resources and an ongoing lack of cooperation from the military. In some cases, such as the Pando killings, security forces were accused of passivity in the face of violence.

Coca cultivation, much of which is authorized, has increased in recent years, as have drug seizures and arrests. Morales's policy of distinguishing between authorized and unauthorized production zones, and his government's greater cooperation with coca growers, have resulted in a significant decline in rights violations. However, cocaine production appears to be on the rise, as does the transit of Peruvian narcotics through Bolivia to Brazil and Argentina. Crime rates in La Paz and other major cities are increasing, though crime in Bolivia remains at a lower level than in many other South American countries.

The new constitution recognizes 36 indigenous nationalities, declares Bolivia a "plurinational" state, and formalizes local political and judicial control within indigenous territories. However, some groups were dissatisfied with receiving just seven reserved legislative seats. In general, racism is rife in the country, especially by mestizos and whites against indigenous groups from the highlands. Several people were charged in 2009 for a May 2008 incident in which a small group of indigenous government supporters were subjected to violence and humiliation by a crowd of antigovernment activists in Sucre. Some rural employers keep indigenous workers in debt peonage, particularly in the Chaco region.

While the law protects and the government generally respects freedom of movement, protesters often block highways and city streets, causing serious economic losses. There have been clashes between landowners in the lowlands and migrants from the highlands, and sporadic land invasions by landless peasants continue to occur. A 2006 law allowed for the redistribution of land deemed idle or with unclear ownership, and the government has since reallocated millions of hectares. Meanwhile, foreign investors have been discouraged by the government's aggressive renegotiation of contract terms in the energy, mining, and telecommunications industries.

Women's political representation has increased notably in recent years, and ballot-alternation requirements resulted in women winning 44 percent of the seats in the new Senate, though only 28 percent of the seats in the Chamber of Deputies. Violence against women is pervasive, and the justice system is ineffective at safeguarding women's broader legal rights. Child prostitution and child labor are problems, particularly in urban areas and in the Chaco and Chapare regions.

Bosnia and Herzegovina

Political Rights: 4
Civil Liberties: 3
Status: Partly Free

Population: 3,843,000
Capital: Sarajevo

Ten-Year Ratings Timeline For Year Under Review (Political Rights, Civil Liberties, Status)

2000	2001	2002	2003	2004	2005	2006	2007	2008	2009
5,4PF	5,4PF	4,4PF	4,4PF	4,3PF	4,3PF	3,3PF	4,3PF	4,3PF	4,3PF

Overview: Nationalist rhetoric began to rise in 2009, as Bosnia and Herzegovina prepared for the 2010 parliamentary and presidential elections. Political tensions were also fueled by obstructionism on the part of the Republika Srpska government and ongoing disagreement among leaders of the three main ethnic groups over the country's territorial and administrative structure. Attempts to institute meaningful constitutional reform yielded little success, apart from a confirmation of the final status of the Brcko district in March.

Formerly a constituent republic within socialist Yugoslavia, Bosnia and Herzegovina (BiH) is among the most ethnically diverse countries in the region. The bulk of the population consists of three ethnic groups: Bosniaks, who are mainly Muslim; Serbs, who are Orthodox Christian; and Croats, who identify with the Roman Catholic Church. As Yugoslavia began to disintegrate in the early 1990s, BiH was recognized as an independent state in April 1992. A 43-month-long civil war ensued, resulting in the deaths of tens of thousands of people and the forced resettlement of approximately half of BiH's population.

In November 1995, the Dayton Peace Accords brought an end to the war by creating a loosely knit state composed of the Bosniak-Croat "Federation of Bosnia and Herzegovina" (the Federation) and the largely Serb "Republika Srpska." The final status of the Brcko district was decided in 1999 by a special arbitration council, which defined it as a self-governing administrative unit that is formally part of both the Federation and Republika Srpska. The political structure established by the

Dayton treaty allowed for peace and power sharing, but it also resulted in a weak state that was unable to effectively implement major reforms.

The Dayton Accords gave the international community a decisive role in running postwar BiH, with significant authority granted to international civilian agencies such as the Office of the High Representative (OHR). Despite years of considerable efforts by the international community to aid the country's integration, most aspects of political, social, and economic life remained divided along ethnic lines. The October 2006 elections shifted power to arguably more moderate parties, but they took strong nationalist stances to appeal to their respective ethnic constituencies. The Alliance of Independent Social Democrats (SNSD) emerged as the winner in Republika Srpska, and the Party for BiH (SzBiH) won the most votes in the Federation. The Croat Democratic Union (HDZ) remained the most popular party among Bosnian Croats.

After lengthy postelection negotiations, a new coalition government—led by Nikola Spiric of the SNSD—was formed in February 2007. However, the coalition proved to be highly unstable, particularly due to a thorny working relationship between SNSD leader Milorad Dodik, who was determined to maintain Republika Srpska's autonomy, and SzBiH leader Haris Silajdzic, who sought to create a unitary BiH. Meanwhile, most Croat officials advocated further decentralization and the creation of a third constituent entity for Croat-majority areas.

Although Republika Srpska leaders raised the threat of secession after Kosovo declared independence from Serbia in early 2008, the BiH government made some progress on the centralization of police functions later in the year. In June, the European Union (EU) and BiH signed a Stabilization and Association Agreement, a key step toward EU membership.

Nationalist rhetoric among politicians and the ethnically divided media began to increase in 2009 as the country prepared for presidential and parliamentary elections scheduled for 2010. Dodik and the Bosnian Serb authorities continued to stress Republika Srpska's autonomy and assert its right to seek independence from BiH. The entity's parliament in June passed a resolution that would have prevented any future transfer of power to the central government, but the measure was annulled by the OHR. Meanwhile, internal divisions plagued the government of the Federation. In May, Federation prime minister Nedzad Brankovic of the mainly Bosniak Party of Democratic Action (SDA) submitted his resignation after Sulejman Tihic was reelected as the SDA leader. Tihic had accused Brankovic of presiding over an ineffective government.

In March 2009, Austrian diplomat Valentin Inzko was appointed as the new High Representative, replacing Miroslav Lajcak, who had resigned in January to become the foreign minister of Slovakia. Tensions between the OHR and the Bosnian Serb leadership continued, with the latter challenging several of Inzko's decisions and denying the OHR's authority to impose laws or fire officials. In December, Inzko accused Bosnian Serb leaders of violating the Dayton Peace Accords by undermining his authority.

While the country's rival factions were unable to agree during the year on reforms that would put the country's constitution in line with European requirements, the BiH parliament in March passed an amendment on the less controversial issue of Brcko's status, confirming the 1999 arbitration ruling. This marked the first time the constitution had been amended since the Dayton Accords.

Political Rights and Civil Liberties: The Republic of Bosnia and Herzegovina (BiH) is an electoral democracy. In general, voters can freely elect their representatives, although the OHR has the authority to remove elected officials if they are deemed to be obstructing the peace process. The government is led by a prime minister, and the role of head of state is performed by a three-member presidency composed of one Bosniak, one Serb, and one Croat. The Parliamentary Assembly is a bicameral body. The 15-seat upper house, the House of Peoples, consists of five members from each of the three main ethnic groups, elected by the Federation and Republika Srpska legislatures for four-year terms. The lower house, the House of Representatives, has 42 popularly elected members serving four-year terms, with 28 seats assigned to the Federation and 14 to Republika Srpska. The most important parties include the SNSD, the SDA, the SzBiH, the Serb Democratic Party (SDS), and the HDZ.

Corruption remains a serious problem. Political parties, the police, the healthcare system, the customs service, and the governments of the two entities are thought to be the most corrupt institutions in the country. In recent years, under international pressure, the BiH government has passed some legislation designed to combat corruption. However, enforcement of these laws has been weak, due in part to the lack of strong and independent anticorruption agencies. In February 2009, the State Investigation and Protection Agency (SIPA) issued a report charging Republika Srpska prime minister Milorad Dodik and 10 other government officials with fraud, corruption, and misuse of state finances in several public contracts. In response, Dodik challenged SIPA's authority and the constitutionality of its mandate, while refusing to cooperate with the investigation. BiH was ranked 99 out of 180 countries surveyed in Transparency International's 2009 Corruption Perceptions Index.

The constitution and the human rights annex to the Dayton Peace Accords provide for freedom of the press, although this right is not always respected in practice. A large number of independent broadcast and print media outlets operate, but they are plagued by a relatively low level of professionalism and a tendency to appeal to narrow ethnic audiences. State-owned companies sometimes withhold advertising from media outlets whose coverage is critical of the government. Instances of attacks against journalists continued in 2009. In March, an angry crowd attacked a television crew filming outside an Orthodox church in the southeastern town of Trebinje. The editor in chief of the news program *60 Minutes* received death threats during the year for his coverage of alleged ties between government officials and organized crime. According to the Helsinki Committee for BiH, most attacks against journalists are ordered by politicians or religious leaders. Internet access in the country is unrestricted.

Citizens enjoy full freedom of religion, but only in areas where their particular group represents a majority. The 2004 Law on Religious Freedom grants religious communities a legal status akin to that of nongovernmental organizations (NGOs). Acts of vandalism against holy sites of all three major faiths—Islam, Orthodox Christianity, and Roman Catholicism—continue to occur. Religious symbols are often exploited for political purposes. In February 2009, a local magistrate in the Republika Srpska capital of Banja Luka ruled that the city authorities must pay $42 million to the local Muslim community for the destruction of mosques during the 1992–95 war; however, a Banja Luka district court overturned the decision in November.

While the authorities do not restrict academic freedom at institutions of higher education, academic appointments are subject to ethnic favoritism and politicization. Primary- and secondary-school curriculums are heavily politicized. Depending on their ethnicity, children use textbooks printed in Croatia, Serbia, or Sarajevo. In parts of the region of Herzegovina, students are divided by ethnicity, with separate classrooms, entrances, textbooks, and time shifts. The educational sector is among the most corrupt in BiH, with studies showing that bribery and inappropriate expenditures are pervasive.

The constitution provides for freedoms of assembly and association, and the various levels of government generally respect these rights in practice. Although there are no legal restrictions on the right of workers to form and join labor unions, discrimination against union members persists.

Despite evidence of growing independence, the judiciary remains influenced by nationalist political parties and faces pressure from the executive branch. In 2008 and 2009, the government of Republika Srpska instructed its ministries not to cooperate with state-level law enforcement agencies investigating allegations of corruption involving the entity's building contracts. The country has made some efforts to reduce its case backlog, but the total number of pending court cases continues to be high. The Court of Bosnia and Herzegovina—established in 2002 to handle organized crime, war crimes, corruption, and terrorism cases—employs about two dozen foreign judges and prosecutors whose mandate was to expire at the end of 2009. Despite heavy protests by the Republika Srpska government, the OHR in December renewed the mandate of the international judges and prosecutors handling war crimes for three years, while retaining those handling corruption, organized crime, and terrorism cases as advisers to the local staff.

Ethnic nationalism presents a major obstacle to the country's integration. Individuals face discrimination in employment, housing, and social services in regions that are not dominated by their own ethnic group. Under the constitution, only Bosniaks, Croats, and Serbs are able to run for the presidency or serve in the upper house of parliament. In 2006, two would-be presidential candidates—one Jewish and the other Romany—brought a discrimination case to the European Court of Human Rights, which in December 2009, ruled that the constitution was indeed discriminatory and must be reformed.

The vast majority of property restitution cases stemming from the war have been resolved. However, many people returned to their prewar homes only to sell their property and move back to areas where their ethnicity forms a majority. When returnees decide to stay in areas where their group constitutes a minority, they are often subject to discrimination and threats. The Brcko district is an exceptional case, having achieved a relatively high level of ethnic integration.

Women are legally entitled to full equality with men. However, they are underrepresented in politics and government and face discrimination in the workplace. The issue of sexual harassment is poorly understood, and improper behavior frequently goes unpunished. Political parties are required to include 3 women among the top 10 names on their candidate lists. Women currently hold nine seats in the BiH House of Representatives and two in the House of Peoples. Domestic violence is a problem, and the police are still largely unresponsive to violent domestic disputes, particularly in rural areas. Women are trafficked domestically for the purpose of prostitution, and BiH is to a lesser extent a transit country for trafficking to other parts of Europe.

Botswana

Political Rights: 3*
Civil Liberties: 2
Status: Free

Population: 1,991,000
Capital: Gaborone

Ratings Change: Botswana's political rights rating declined from 2 to 3 due to decreased transparency and accountability in the executive branch under President Seretse Khama Ian Khama's administration.

Ten-Year Ratings Timeline For Year Under Review (Political Rights, Civil Liberties, Status)

2000	2001	2002	2003	2004	2005	2006	2007	2008	2009
2,2F	2,2F	2,2F	2,2F	2,2F	2,2F	2,2F	2,2F	2,2F	3,2F

Overview:

The ruling Botswana Democratic Party swept parliamentary elections in October 2009, and Parliament confirmed President Seretse Khama Ian Khama for a full term in office. Khama, previously the vice president, had risen to the presidency in 2008 after the incumbent retired, and government transparency has been reduced under his administration. In May 2009, he was accused of ordering the extrajudicial killing of a suspected criminal, amid a spate of similar killings by security forces that began in 2008.

Elected governments, all led by the Botswana Democratic Party (BDP), have ruled the country since it gained independence from Britain in 1966. Vice President Mogae, a former central bank chief, rose to the presidency when longtime president Ketumile Masire retired in 1998, and he was confirmed as the country's leader after the BDP easily won legislative elections in 1999. The BDP took 44 of the 57 contested seats in the 2004 elections, securing a second presidential term for Mogae. International observers declared the polling free and fair but recommended giving the opposition equal access to state-run media and setting the date for elections well in advance.

In April 2008, Mogae—like Masire before him—retired before the end of his term, leaving Vice President Khama Ian Khama to assume the presidency. Khama, the son of independence leader and first president Seretse Khama, had been appointed vice president by Mogae in 1998 and was elected chairman of the BDP in 2003. He quickly shuffled the cabinet and appointed former foreign minister Mompati Merafhe as vice president. Critics have accused the BDP of subverting democratic institutions through this "automatic succession" process.

Significant rifts within the ruling party emerged before legislative elections in October 2009. Most notably, Khama suspended his rival, BDP secretary general Gomolemo Motswaledi, preventing him from standing as a candidate for Parliament. In September, the High Court rejected Motswaledi's related lawsuit against Khama, citing the head of state's constitutional immunity from civil suits.

In the elections, the BDP won 45 of 57 seats with 53.3 percent of the vote. The Botswana National Front (BNF) won 6 seats and almost 22 percent of the vote, while the Botswana Congress Party (BCP) won 4 seats and 19 percent. Two other parties each captured one seat. Parliament confirmed Khama for a full presidential term later that month, and preliminary observer reports declared the elections free and fair.

A spate of extrajudicial killings by police and other security forces that began in 2008 continued in 2009. According to government statistics and media reports, there were between 10 and 12 such killings from April 2008 to the end of 2009. In May, the killing of alleged criminal John Kalafatis sparked a major controversy after press reports claimed that security forces were involved and that President Khama had ordered Kalafatis's death. The government vociferously denied the charge.

More than 17.5 percent of Botswana's population is infected with HIV, and the UN Children's Fund estimates that AIDS has created more than 120,000 orphans in the country. Nevertheless, the government announced in February 2009 that revenue shortfalls would force cuts to its HIV/AIDS programs, which have included free antiretroviral drugs and routine HIV testing in all public health facilities.

Political Rights and Civil Liberties: Botswana is an electoral democracy. The 63-seat National Assembly, elected for five years, chooses the president to serve a concurrent five-year term. Of the Assembly's 63 members, 57 are directly elected, 4 are nominated by the president and approved by the Assembly, and 2—the president and the attorney general—are ex-officio members. Despite being elected indirectly, the president holds significant power; while he can prolong or dismiss the legislature, the legislature is not empowered to impeach the president. Democracy advocates have alleged that power has become increasingly centralized around current president Seretse Khama Ian Khama, with many top jobs going to military officers and family members.

The 15-member House of Chiefs, which serves primarily as an advisory body, represents the country's eight major Setswana-speaking tribes and some smaller ones. Groups other than the eight major tribes tend to be left out of the political process; under the Territories Act, land in ethnic territory is distributed under the jurisdiction of majority groups. Due in part to their lack of representation in the House of Chiefs, minority groups are subject to patriarchal Tswana customary law despite having their own traditional rules for inheritance, marriage, and succession.

The BDP's control of the National Assembly and the presidency has never faced a serious challenge, and opposition parties, namely the BCP and the BNF, have accused the government of effectively institutionalizing the BDP's dominant status. Nevertheless, the Independent Election Commission, created in 1996, has helped consolidate Botswana's reputation for fairness in voting.

An anticorruption body set up in 1994 has special powers of investigation, arrest, and search and seizure, and the resulting conviction rate has been more than 80 percent. Nevertheless, there are almost no restrictions on the private business activities of public servants. Botswana was ranked 37 out of 180 countries surveyed in Transparency International's 2009 Corruption Perceptions Index, and has had the best rank among African countries for several years running.

A free and vigorous press thrives in cities and towns, with several independent newspapers and magazines published in the capital. The private Gaborone Broadcasting Corporation television system and two private radio stations have limited reach, though Botswana easily receives broadcasts from neighboring South Africa. State-owned outlets dominate the local broadcast media, which reach far more residents than the print media, and provide inadequate access to the opposition and government critics. In addition, the government sometimes censors or otherwise restricts news sources or stories that it finds undesirable. In December 2008, the government passed a new Media Practitioners Act, which set up a media regulatory body and mandated the registration of all media workers, without holding promised consultations with the bill's detractors. The government does not restrict internet access, though such access is rare outside cities.

Botswana does not have a freedom of information law, and critics accuse the government of excessive secrecy. President Khama had yet to hold a press conference as of the end of 2009. In May, he threatened to sue the *Sunday Standard* for reporting that linked him to the murder of alleged criminal John Kalafatis by security forces; the *Sunday Standard* announced that it would countersue.

Freedom of religion is guaranteed, but all religious organizations must register with the government. There are over 1,000 church groups in Botswana.

Academic freedom is generally respected. However, in 2005, the authorities deported Australian-born academic Kenneth Good after he criticized the institution of "automatic succession" and said the government was run by a small elite and manipulated state media. While free and private discussion is largely protected, the government in 2008 mandated the registration of all prepaid mobile-telephone SIM cards, at risk of disconnection; only 15 percent of such cards had been registered by the December 2009 deadline. The November 2009 arrest and overnight detention of a South African woman for insulting the president also raised concerns about freedom of expression.

The government generally respects the constitutional rights of assembly and association. Nongovernmental organizations (NGOs), including human rights groups, operate openly without harassment. However, the government has barred San rights organizations from entering the Central Kgalagadi Game Reserve (CKGR), the subject of a long-running land dispute, and demonstrations at the reserve have been forcibly dispersed. While independent labor unions are permitted, workers' rights to strike and bargain collectively are restricted.

The courts are generally considered to be fair and free of direct political interference, although the legal system is affected by staffing shortages and a large backlog of cases. Trials are usually public, and those accused of the most serious violent crimes are provided with attorneys. Civil cases, however, are sometimes tried in customary courts, where defendants have no legal counsel.

Occasional police abuse to obtain evidence or confessions has been reported, and Botswana has been criticized by rights groups for continuing to use corporal and capital punishment. The 2007 Intelligence and Security Services Act created a Directorate of Intelligence and Security (DIS) in the office of the president. Critics said it vested too much power in the agency's director—allowing him to authorize arrests without warrants, for instance—and lacked parliamentary oversight mechanisms. DIS officers were implicated in a number of extrajudicial killings in 2008 and 2009. Prisons are overcrowded and suffer from poor health conditions, though the government has responded by building new facilities and providing HIV testing to inmates.

Discrimination against ethnic minorities is a problem. Since 1985, authorities have relocated about 5,000 San to settlements outside the CKGR. Almost all of those remaining, 530 people, left in 2002 when the government cut off water, food, health, and social services. A three-judge panel of the High Court in Lobaste ruled in favor of the San in 2006, ordering the government to allow them to return. Several hundred San have since gone back to the CKGR, although disagreement remains as to how many will be allowed to live in the reserve. The government insists that the San have been adequately compensated and are provided with decent education and health facilities in the new settlements, and it rejects claims that it simply wanted unrestricted access to diamond reserves in the region. In September 2009, a report by the Bench Marks Foundation alleged that mining operations in the CKGR had been excluded from environmental impact assessments and were making it difficult for San to access local water sources. The San tend to be marginalized in education and employment opportunities.

Illegal immigrants from Zimbabwe face increasing xenophobia and are accused, sometimes legitimately, of criminal activity. These immigrants are subject to exploitation in the labor market. Botswana is building an electric fence along its border with Zimbabwe, ostensibly to control foot-and-mouth disease among livestock, but the barrier is popularly supported as a means of halting illegal immigration; thousands of Zimbabweans have been deported in recent years.

Botswana features a vibrant market economy and was ranked highest among African countries in the Heritage Foundation's 2009 Index of Economic Freedom.

Women enjoy the same rights as men under the constitution, but customary laws limit their property rights. Women married under traditional laws are deemed legal minors. However, the 2004 Abolition of Marital Powers Act established equal control of marriage estates and equal custody of children, removed restrictive domicile rules, and set the minimum marriage age at 18. A 2007 report by Physicians for Human Rights stated that women's disempowerment perpetuated the HIV/AIDS pandemic in Botswana. Domestic violence is rampant, and trafficking in women and children for the purposes of prostitution and labor is a problem. The law prohibits homosexuality.

Brazil

Political Rights: 2
Civil Liberties: 2
Status: Free

Population: 191,481,000
Capital: Brasilia

Ten-Year Ratings Timeline For Year Under Review (Political Rights, Civil Liberties, Status)

2000	2001	2002	2003	2004	2005	2006	2007	2008	2009
3,3PF	3,3PF	2,3F	2,3F	2,3F	2,2F	2,2F	2,2F	2,2F	2,2F

Overview: President Luiz Inacio "Lula" da Silva unveiled plans for social spending and increased state control over the oil sector in 2009 as he sought to bolster popular support for his chosen successor ahead of the 2010 presidential election. Criminal violence remained an immense problem in Brazil's major cities during the year, and official corruption continued to stoke political debate.

After gaining independence from Portugal in 1822, Brazil retained a monarchical system until a republic was established in 1889. Democratic governance was interrupted by long periods of authoritarian rule, and the last military regime gave way to an elected civilian government in 1985. However, Brazil's democracy has been marred by frequent corruption scandals. One scandal eventually led Congress to impeach President Fernando Collor de Mello in 1992.

Brazilian Social Democracy Party (PSDB) leader Fernando Henrique Cardoso—a market-oriented, centrist finance minister—was elected president in 1994, and he subsequently oversaw a highly successful currency-stabilization program that included fiscal reform, privatization of state enterprises, and a new currency pegged to the U.S. dollar. He also ushered in a new era of dialogue with international human rights and good-governance groups. In 1998, Cardoso handily won a second term in a rematch against his 1994 opponent, former labor leader and political prisoner Luiz Inacio "Lula" da Silva of the left-leaning Workers' Party (PT).

Da Silva finally won the presidency in 2002, promising to maintain orthodox economic policies while initiating meaningful social-welfare programs. These included "Bolsa Familia," a cash-transfer program that benefited approximately one-fourth of the population, and "ProUni," a fund providing low-income students with scholarships to private colleges.

Da Silva was reelected by a comfortable margin in the October 2006 presidential runoff, drawing on his popularity among working-class voters. Despite the fact that the legislature was widely seen as the most corrupt in the country's history, the PT did not suffer losses in the concurrent congressional elections.

In August 2007, the government released a report outlining the fate of political dissidents who were "disappeared" by the military between 1961 and 1988. Unlike in other Latin American countries with recent histories of military rule, former officials in Brazil remained protected by a 1979 amnesty law, and none had faced charges for human rights violations. In response to increasing pressure from victims' families, however, da Silva in October 2009 announced plans to create a truth commission to investigate crimes committed during the military regime. The exact mandate and powers of the proposed panel remained unclear at year's end.

In municipal elections held in October 2008, the ruling coalition won nearly two-thirds of the mayoral races, a 36 percent increase from the 2004 local polls. However, despite da Silva's explicit backing, the PT's candidate for mayor of Sao Paulo, Marta Suplicy, lost to incumbent Gilberto Kassab of the conservative Democratic Party. As mayors are traditionally important vote gatherers for presidential elections, Kassab's victory represented an important loss for the PT.

A series of major government corruption scandals that began in 2004 continued into 2009. The earlier affairs had involved vote buying and kickbacks for public-works contracts, but the Senate faced new scrutiny in 2009 over some 660 "secret acts" it had passed since 1995 to award jobs, salary increases, and other benefits to staff members and senators' relatives. The leader of the Senate, former president Jose Sarney, was accused of personally benefiting from such measures. Despite calls for his resignation, Sarney held on to his seat with da Silva's support. However, the president's decision to back Sarney, whose Brazilian Democratic Movement Party (PMDB) was a crucial component of his ruling coalition, alienated many in the PT. In November 2009, the governor of the Federal District—the quasi-state that includes the capital Brasilia—was accused of accepting bribes.

In August 2009, da Silva announced plans to channel Brazil's burgeoning oil revenues into poverty-reduction programs and augment the role of the state oil company at the expense of foreign investors. The proposed legislation was seen in part as an effort to rally public support behind the administration and specifically da Silva's chief of staff, Dilma Rousseff, who was expected to run as his successor in the 2010 presidential election.

Political Rights and Civil Liberties:

Brazil is an electoral democracy. The 2006 national elections and 2008 municipal elections were free and fair. The constitution provides for a president, to be elected for up to two four-year terms, and a bicameral National Congress. The Senate's 81 members serve eight-year terms, with a portion coming up for election every four years, and the 513-member Chamber of Deputies is elected for four-year terms.

The four largest political parties, accounting for more than half of the seats in the Chamber of Deputies and the Senate, are the centrist , the leftist PT, the conservative Democratic Party, and the center-left PSDB. Fourteen other parties are also represented in Congress. The electoral system encourages the proliferation of parties, a number of which are based in a single state, and lawmakers have sometimes switched parties for financial and other inducements. However, the Supreme Court in 2007 upheld a decision by the electoral tribunal to outlaw party switching after elections.

Corruption is an endemic problem in Brazil, which was ranked 75 out of 180 countries surveyed in Transparency International's 2009 Corruption Perceptions Index. Despite a constitutional right of access to public information, the country does not have specific laws to regulate and guarantee transparency.

The constitution guarantees freedom of expression. The press is privately owned, but foreigners can acquire only a 30 percent stake in a media company and are restricted in their ability to influence editorial decisions and management selection. There are dozens of daily newspapers and a variety of television and radio stations across the country. The print media have played a central role in exposing official corruption, including the 2009 scandal surrounding Senator Jose Sarney. At the same time, journalists—especially those who focus on organized crime, corruption, or military-era human rights violations—are frequently the targets of violence. In a positive step, Brazil's highest court in May 2009 struck down a 1967 press law that criminalized libel and slander. The law had been used to harass critical journalists and encourage self-censorship. However, civil suits against journalists remain common. The government does not impose restrictions on access to the internet.

The constitution guarantees freedom of religion, and the government generally respects this right in practice. The government does not restrict academic freedom.

The freedoms of association and assembly are generally respected, as is the right to strike. Industrial labor unions are well organized. Although they are politically connected, Brazilian unions tend to be freer from political party control than their counterparts in most other Latin American countries. Labor issues are adjudicated in a system of special labor courts. Intimidation of rural union leaders continued to be a problem in 2009.

The country's largely independent judiciary is overburdened, plagued by corruption, and virtually powerless in the face of organized crime. Public complaints about the judiciary's inefficiency are frequent, and it has thwarted widely supported reforms. For example, judges regularly employ legal formalisms to overturn government modernization efforts, including those aimed at privatizing state-owned industries and reforming the public welfare system.

Brazil has one of the highest homicide rates in the world. Most violent crime in the country is related to the illegal drug trade. Highly organized and well-armed drug gangs frequently fight against the military police as well as private militias composed of off-duty police officers, prison guards, and firefighters. These militias have intimidated human rights activists and instituted their own form of extortion, charging citizens a mandatory tax for ousting drug traffickers from their areas. While a crackdown in the summer of 2008 led to the arrest of several important militia leaders, the groups continued to control and terrorize countless *favelas*, or shantytowns, in 2009. In an indication of the severity of Rio de Janeiro's criminal violence, a police helicopter was shot down in October 2009 while flying over a shoot-out between rival gangs in one of the city's slums. In an effort to bolster Rio's security ahead of the 2016 Summer Olympic Games, President Luiz Inacio "Lula" da Silva committed federal police and $60 million in federal aid to the city.

Brazil's police are among the world's most violent and corrupt. While reports of killings by police in Rio and Sao Paulo fell by 10 percent between 2007 to 2008, killings still exceeded 1,000 annually in 2008. Torture is used systematically to extract confessions from suspects, and extrajudicial killings are portrayed as shootouts with dangerous criminals. Police officers are rarely prosecuted for abuses, and those charged are almost never convicted; typically the cases are dismissed for "lack of evidence."

The prison system is anarchic, overcrowded, and largely unfit for human habitation. According to official estimates, Brazil's prisons hold some 400,000 inmates, 40 percent over the system's intended capacity. Overcrowding sometimes results in men and women being held in the same facilities, and human rights groups claim that the torture and other abuses common to most of the country's detention centers have the effect of turning petty thieves into hardened criminals.

Racial discrimination, long officially denied as a problem in Brazil, began to receive both recognition and remediation from da Silva during his first term. Afro-Brazilians earn less than 50 percent of the average earnings of other citizens, and they suffer from the highest homicide, poverty, and illiteracy rates. When he assumed office, da Silva took the unprecedented step of naming four Afro-Brazilians to his cabinet (three of whom remained in 2009), and appointed the country's first Afro-Brazilian Supreme Court justice. There are currently 17 Afro-Brazilians in Congress.

The owners of large estates control nearly 60 percent of the country's arable land, while the poorest 30 percent of the population hold less than 2 percent. There were an estimated two million landless rural families in 2009. Land invasions are organized by the grassroots Landless Workers' Movement (MST), which claims that the seized land is unused or illegally held. The da Silva administration has promised to implement land reform, but progress has been slow; the government has instead focused on increased access to credit as a way to reduce rural poverty.

Although Brazil abolished slavery in 1888 and has benefited in recent years from a relatively successful antislavery taskforce, between 6,000 and 8,000 rural laborers still work under slavery-like conditions. Landowners who enslave workers face two to eight years in prison, in addition to fines. However, the fines are minimal, and no one has ever been imprisoned for using slave labor.

Brazil's indigenous population numbers around 460,000. The government promised in 2003 to demarcate large swaths of ancestral lands as the first step in creating indigenous reserves. In a landmark ruling in March 2009, the Supreme Court ended a 30-year battle by upholding the 2005 creation of one of the largest protected indigenous areas in the world. The ruling paves the way for the eviction of rice farmers who have resisted leaving the four-million-acre territory. Violence and discrimination against indigenous people continues; half of the indigenous population lives in poverty, and most indigenous communities lack adequate sanitation and education services.

A 2001 decree granted same-sex partners the same rights as married couples with respect to pensions, social security benefits, and taxation. While discrimination based on sexual orientation is prohibited by law, violence against homosexuals remains a problem.

In 2003, a new legal code made women equal to men under the law for the first time in the country's history. However, violence against women and children is a common problem, and protective laws are rarely enforced. Forced prostitution of children is widespread. While the number of child workers has fallen over the past 15 years, 4.85 million children between the ages of 5 and 17 still work in Brazil. The government has sought to address the problem by cooperating with various NGOs, increasing inspections, and offering cash incentives to keep children in school.

While illegal, human trafficking continues from and within Brazil for the purpose of forced labor and commercial sexual exploitation. According to the U.S. State Department's 2009 Trafficking in Persons Report, Brazil still does not comply with the minimum standards for eliminating human trafficking, and prosecutions for forced labor remain deficient. However, the report notes the government's efforts to improve its record, most notably through mobile inspection operations in the Amazon and other remote areas.

Brunei

Political Rights: 6
Civil Liberties: 5
Status: Not Free

Population: 383,000
Capital: Bandar Seri Begawan

Ten-Year Ratings Timeline For Year Under Review (Political Rights, Civil Liberties, Status)

2000	2001	2002	2003	2004	2005	2006	2007	2008	2009
7,5NF	7,5NF	6,5NF	6,5NF	6,5NF	6,5NF	6,5NF	6,5NF	6,5NF	6,5NF

Overview: Marking 25 years of independence, the sultanate experienced little political change in 2009, with the Legislative Council continuing to demonstrate an increased but still minor oversight role. However, in two positive steps for women during the year, married female civil servants secured new rights, and Brunei's first female attorney general was appointed.

The oil-rich sultanate of Brunei became a British protectorate in 1888. The 1959 constitution vested full executive powers in the sultan, while providing for five advisory councils, including a Legislative Council. In 1962, Sultan Omar Ali annulled legislative election results after the leftist Brunei People's Party (BPP), which sought to end the monarchy, won all 10 elected seats in the 21-member council. British troops crushed an insurrection mounted by the BPP, and Omar declared a state of emergency, which has remained in force ever since. Continuing his father's absolute rule, Hassanal Bolkiah Mu'izzaddin Waddaulah became Brunei's 29th sultan in 1967. The British granted Brunei full independence in 1984.

In 2004, Hassanal reconvened the Legislative Council, which had been suspended since 1984. The body passed a constitutional amendment to expand its size to 45 seats, with 15 elected positions. However, Hassanal in September 2005 convened a new, 29-member Legislative Council, including 5 indirectly elected members representing village councils. Plans for the 45-person legislature with 15 directly elected slots have remained on the table, but elections have yet to be scheduled. While the sultan's family and appointees continue to hold all state power, with the Internal Security Act (ISA) reserving virtually untrammeled authority for the sultan himself, the existing Legislative Council has assumed budget review as a regular function, meeting annually to scrutinize government expenditures.

The revival of the Legislative Council, the plans for elected members, and parallel efforts to promote the private sector, while curbing corruption and radical Islam, are all considered preparations for the eventual depletion of the country's oil and gas reserves, which currently account for 90 percent of state revenues and are expected to run out in two to three decades. Energy wealth has long allowed the government to stave off demands for political reform by employing most of the population, providing citizens with extensive benefits, and sparing them an income tax. However, a French energy company discovered some new oil and gas supplies in late 2008, and the country's 25th anniversary of independence in 2009 was marked by the absence of further political reform.

Political Rights and Civil Liberties: Brunei is not an electoral democracy. The sultan wields broad powers under a long-standing state of emergency, and no direct legislative elections have been held since 1962. Citizens convey concerns to their leaders through government-vetted councils of elected village chiefs. The government promotes a combination of Islamic values, local Malay culture, and allegiance to the monarchy through a national ideology called Malay Muslim Monarchy, and portrays abandonment of these values as treason and *haram* (sin).

The reform efforts of Sultan Hassanal Bolkiah Mu'izzaddin Waddaulah have been largely superficial and are designed to attract foreign investment. The unicameral Legislative Council has no political standing independent of the sultan. However, the council's mounting oversight activity and queries aimed at the government reflect a growing demand for accountability and responsible spending.

Despite long-standing plans to establish a 45-member legislature with 15 popularly elected members, political activity remains extremely limited. In 2007, the Registrar of Societies disbanded the People's Awareness Party (PAKAR) and forced the president of the Brunei National Solidarity Party (PPKB) to resign. The PPKB was then deregistered without explanation in 2008, leaving the National Development

Party (NDP) as Brunei's sole remaining political party. Headed by a former political prisoner, exile, and insurgent leader, the NDP was permitted to register in 2005 after pledging to work as a partner with the government and swearing loyalty to the sultan.

The government claims to have a zero-tolerance policy on corruption, and its Anti-Corruption Bureau has made efforts to cooperate with regional partners and the Ministry of Education in recent years. In June 2008, an arrest warrant was issued for the sultan's brother and former finance minister, Prince Jefri Bolkiah, who had skipped a court appearance concerning his failure to compensate the sultanate for billions of dollars in misappropriated oil revenues. The compensation had been ordered in 2006 by a Brunei court, and the prince has reportedly exhausted his opportunities to appeal. Having resided abroad for many years, the prince was pictured alongside the sultan in Brunei in September 2009, suggesting the possibility of a more united front and near-term resolution. Brunei was ranked 39 out of 180 countries surveyed in Transparency International's 2009 Corruption Perceptions Index.

Journalists in Brunei face considerable restrictions. Legislation enacted in 2001 allows officials to close newspapers without cause and to fine and jail journalists for articles deemed "false and malicious." The national sedition law was amended in 2005 to strengthen prohibitions on criticizing the sultan and the national ideology. The largest daily, the *Borneo Bulletin*, practices self-censorship, though it does publish letters to the editor that criticize government policies. A second English-language daily, the *Brunei Times*, was launched by prominent businessmen in 2006 to attract foreign investors. A smaller, Malay-language newspaper and several Chinese-language newspapers are also published. Brunei's only television station is state run, but residents can receive Malaysian broadcasts and satellite channels. The country's internet practice code stipulates that content must not be subversive or encourage illegitimate reform efforts. Access to the internet is reportedly unrestricted.

The constitution allows for the practice of religions other than the official Shafeite school of Sunni Islam, but proselytizing and the importation of religious literature by non-Muslims is prohibited. Christianity is the most common target of censorship, and the Baha'i faith is banned. Nevertheless, the country's various religious groups coexist peacefully. All residents must carry identity cards stating their religion, and marriage between Muslims and non-Muslims is not allowed. Muslims require permission from the Ministry of Religious Affairs to convert to other faiths, though official and societal pressure make conversion nearly impossible. Radical Islam is discouraged, in part due to the government's interest in attracting investment.

The study of Islam, Malay Muslim Monarchy ideology, and the Jawi (Arabic script used for writing the Malay language) is mandatory in all public schools. The teaching of all other religions is prohibited. With a particular focus on youth, the government reportedly held a number of events in 2009 at University of Brunei Darussalam reinforcing the Malay Muslim Monarchy ideology.

Emergency laws continue to restrict freedom of assembly. Most nongovernmental organizations are professional or business groups, and under the 2005 Societies Order, all must register and name their members. No more than 10 people can associate for a purpose without registering, and all meeting minutes must be submitted to the Registrar of Societies. Registration can be refused for any reason. In late 2008, the government disbanded 55 associations for not complying with regulations. Brunei's three, largely inactive, trade unions, which must also register, are all in the oil sector and represent only about 15,000 workers. Strikes are illegal, and collective bargaining is not recognized.

The constitution does not provide for an independent judiciary. Although the courts generally appear to act independently, they have yet to be tested in political cases. Magistrates' courts try most cases, while more serious matters are handled by the High Court. Final recourse for civil cases is managed by the Privy Council in the United Kingdom. Sharia (Islamic law) takes precedence in areas including divorce, inheritance, and some sex crimes, though it does not apply to non-Muslims. A backlog of capital cases results in lengthy pretrial detention for those accused of serious crimes. According to the U.S. State Department's human rights report, caning is mandatory for 42 criminal offenses, including immigration violations, and is commonly carried out.

Religious enforcement officers raid homes to punish the mingling of unrelated Muslim men and women. According to the U.S. State Department's 2009 International Religious Freedom Report, Bruneian religious authorities reported 54 official "khalwat" cases between July 2008 and June 2009. However, some of these charges were dropped due to lack of evidence. The authorities also detain suspected antigovernment activists under the ISA, which permits detention without trial for renewable two-year periods. Prison conditions generally meet international standards.

Brunei's many "stateless" people, mostly longtime ethnic Chinese residents, are denied the full rights and benefits of citizens, while migrant workers, who comprise 30 to 40 percent of the workforce, are largely unprotected by the labor laws. Authorities are very strict on illegal entry, and workers who overstay visas are regularly imprisoned and, in some cases, caned or whipped.

Islamic law generally places women at a disadvantage in areas such as divorce, but an increasing number of women have entered the workforce in recent years. In April 2009, the government abolished a policy whereby female civil servants' employment contracts were terminated upon marriage, which had meant that they could only be reemployed on a month-to-month basis. In August, Brunei appointed its first female attorney general, Hayati Salleh, who had formerly been the country's first female High Court judge. Women in government-run institutions and non-Muslim female students are required or pressured to wear traditional Muslim head coverings.

Bulgaria

Political Rights: 2
Civil Liberties: 2
Status: Free

Population: 7,590,000
Capital: Sofia

Ten-Year Ratings Timeline For Year Under Review (Political Rights, Civil Liberties, Status)

2000	2001	2002	2003	2004	2005	2006	2007	2008	2009
2,3F	1,3F	1,2F	1,2F	1,2F	1,2F	1,2F	1,2F	2,2F	2,2F

Overview: A new right-wing government led by Prime Minister Boyko Borisov took office in July following parliamentary elections. Borisov pledged to combat organized crime and corruption in order to restore European Union (EU) aid funds that had been frozen in 2008. The EU released some of the aid during 2009, but decided to extend its monitoring mechanism into 2010 amid continued problems with the judiciary and the handling of high-profile cases.

Bulgaria gained autonomy within the Ottoman Empire in 1878 and full independence in 1908. Its monarchy was replaced by communist rule after Soviet forces occupied the country during World War II. Communist leader Todor Zhivkov governed Bulgaria from 1954 to 1989, when the broader political changes sweeping the region inspired a massive prodemocracy rally in Sofia.

Over the next 12 years, power alternated between the Bulgarian Socialist Party (BSP), successor to the Communist Party, and the center-right Union of Democratic Forces (UDF). The latter achieved significant economic restructuring and won an invitation for European Union (EU) membership talks, which began in 2000. In 2001, the National Movement for Simeon II (NDSV), led by the former king, won national elections and a governing coalition with the Movement for Rights and Freedoms (DPS), a party representing the country's ethnic Turkish minority. However, both parties became junior partners in a BSP-led coalition government after the 2005 elections.

Bulgaria formally joined the EU in January 2007, and its first elections for the European Parliament in May featured the emergence of a new center-right opposition party, Citizens for the European Development of Bulgaria (GERB), led by Sofia mayor Boyko Borisov. The party gained popularity as the BSP and its allies were blamed for unchecked corruption, particularly after the EU decided to suspend hundreds of millions of dollars in aid funds over the issue in July 2008.

GERB led the European Parliament elections in June 2009, taking 5 of Bulgaria's 17 seats, and went on to capture 116 of 240 seats in the national parliament elections in July. Borisov took office as prime minister with the support of the ultranationalist Ataka party (21 seats), the center-right Blue Coalition (15 seats), and the new Order, Law, and Justice party (10 seats). The BSP-led Coalition for Bulgaria was left in opposition with 40 seats, as was the DPS, with 38.

The new GERB government pledged to tackle corruption and organized crime, including misdeeds by the previous government, and took several steps to that end during its first months in office. Meanwhile, the EU released several tranches of frozen aid for transportation and agriculture over the course of the year, but withheld some of the suspended funds and decided to extend its monitoring of Bulgaria's performance into 2010.

Political Rights and Civil Liberties: Bulgaria is an electoral democracy. The unicameral National Assembly, composed of 240 members, is elected every four years. Georgi Parvanov of the BSP is currently serving his second five-year term as president, having won reelection in 2006. The president is the head of state, but his powers are very limited. The legislature chooses the prime minister, who serves as head of government.

The 2009 parliamentary elections were held under new rules enacted less than three months before the voting. The changes created 31 single-member constituencies that varied widely by population, leaving the other 209 seats under the existing system of regional proportional representation. Vote buying remained a problem, although monitors from the Organization for Security and Cooperation in Europe (OSCE) found that open discussion of the practice during the campaign helped to alleviate its effects. The authorities had increased penalties for vote buying before the elections and made a number of arrests after the balloting; a deputy emergency situations minister was among those charged. Voter turnout was 60 percent, up from 56 percent in 2005 and 39 percent in the June 2009 European Parliament elections.

Bulgaria's multiparty system includes a variety of left- and right-leaning factions, and the ethnic Turkish minority is represented by the DPS. Roma are not as well represented, with just one Romany candidate winning a National Assembly seat in 2009. Roma are also seen as vulnerable to vote-buying and intimidation efforts.

Corruption is a serious concern in Bulgaria. The European Commission's July 2009 progress report cited a lack of political will for the paucity of law enforcement action, though it noted some progress with respect to misappropriation of EU funds. Among other corruption cases during the year, a deputy interior minister resigned amid bribery allegations in June, a former DPS lawmaker was sentenced to three and a half years in prison in July for profiting from public contracts, and a former agriculture minister was charged in September for allegedly illegal land swaps. Investigations were launched against at least two other cabinet ministers after they left office following the elections. Margarita Popova, who had led an antifraud unit that won praise from the EU, was named justice minister in the new GERB government, and a respected World Bank economist was named finance minister. The new government also launched an overhaul of the graft-prone customs service, firing more than 500 officials and forcing 3,000 others to reapply for their jobs. Bulgaria was ranked 71 out of 180 countries surveyed in Transparency International's 2009 Corruption Perceptions Index, tying with Greece and Romania for the worst performance in the EU.

Bulgarian media have improved considerably since 1989, due in part to increasing foreign ownership, but political and economic pressures sometimes lead to self-censorship. Although the state-owned media have at times been critical of the government, ineffective legislation leaves them vulnerable to political influence. The OSCE found that state television favored the incumbents in the 2009 elections, while the major private stations and print outlets provided more balanced coverage. Unlike in previous years, no major cases of violence or intimidation aimed at journalists were reported in 2009. The government does not place restrictions on internet access, but broad information retention rules allow it to access user information when investigating even minor crimes.

Members of minority faiths report occasional instances of harassment and discrimination despite constitutional guarantees of religious freedom. The authorities in some areas have blocked the construction of new mosques, and the European Court of Human Rights ruled in January 2009 that the government had violated religious freedom beginning in 2002 by intervening on behalf of one side in a Bulgarian Orthodox Church schism. The government does not restrict academic freedom.

The authorities generally respect constitutional freedoms of assembly and association. Workers have the right to join trade unions, but public employees cannot strike or bargain collectively, and private employers often discriminate against union members. An antigovernment protest in January 2009 turned violent, leading to over 170 arrests. Other protests during the year remained peaceful, including labor-related demonstrations by policemen in March and workers from many sectors in June.

Bulgaria's judiciary has benefited from a series of structural reforms associated with EU accession. However, the July 2009 European Commission report found that some judges and prosecutors were allegedly subject to outside influence, and criticized procedural rules that effectively allowed criminal defendants to stall their trials indefinitely. It noted that while some organized crime figures had been convicted, the cases were resolved through plea bargaining rather than successful trials.

Organized crime remains a serious problem, and scores of suspected contract killings over the past decade have gone unsolved. Small-scale bombings with suspected links to organized crime continued to occur in 2009, as did attacks on prominent businessmen and local officials. High-profile lawyer Petar Loupov was murdered in March, while construction magnate Kiro Kirov, who was abducted that month, was released by his kidnappers in April after his son paid a ransom. A similar abduction, allegedly by the same group, was reported in October. In September, a bomb blast killed the wife and child of the interim mayor in Razlog. Incidents of mistreatment by police have been reported, and prison conditions remain inadequate in many places.

Ethnic minorities, particularly Roma, continue to face discrimination in employment, health care, education, and housing. Sexual minorities also face discrimination.

Women remain underrepresented in political life, accounting for 21 percent of the National Assembly seats after the latest elections. However, the new chamber elected the first female Speaker, and Sofia elected its first female mayor to replace newly elected prime minister Boyko Borisov. Domestic violence is an ongoing concern. The country is a source of human-trafficking victims, of whom Roma make up a disproportionate share. Several Bulgarians were arrested during 2009 for allegedly selling infants across the border in Greece.

Burkina Faso

Political Rights: 5
Civil Liberties: 3
Status: Partly Free

Population: 15,757,000
Capital: Ouagadougou

Ten-Year Ratings Timeline For Year Under Review (Political Rights, Civil Liberties, Status)

2000	2001	2002	2003	2004	2005	2006	2007	2008	2009
4,4PF	4,4PF	4,4PF	4,4PF	5,4PF	5,3PF	5,3PF	5,3PF	5,3PF	5,3PF

Overview: Thibault Nana, an opposition party leader who had been sentenced to three years in prison for his role in 2008 protests, was released in January 2009. Electoral reforms enacted in the spring created a gender quota for party lists and extended suffrage to Burkinabe living abroad. In September, severe rainfall and flooding left over 100,000 people homeless and damaged the country's infrastructure.

Burkina Faso experienced a series of military coups after gaining independence from France in 1960. In 1987, Thomas Sankara, a populist president who had risen to power through a coup in 1983, was ousted by army captain Blaise Compaore; Sankara and several of his supporters were killed. In 1991, a democratic constitution was approved in a referendum, and Compaore easily won that year's presidential election due to an opposition boycott. Compaore secured another seven-year term in the 1998 election.

The government undertook a series of political reforms after 1998, including the introduction of an independent electoral commission, a single-ballot voting system, public campaign financing, and a third vice presidential position in the legislature for the opposition leader. However, in December 1998, Norbert Zongo, a journalist investigating the death of an employee of Compaore's brother, was assassinated. An independent investigative body concluded in 1999 that the murder was linked to his reporting and identified six members of the presidential guard as suspects. Only one suspect was charged, and an appeals court dismissed the charges in August 2006, citing lack of evidence.

The 2002 National Assembly elections were the first conducted without a significant opposition boycott. Compaore's Congress for Democracy and Progress (CDP) party won only 57 of 111 seats, compared with 101 in 1997. Compaore secured a third term as president in 2005, though it was shortened to five years by a 2000 constitutional amendment. A 2001 amendment had imposed a two-term limit for presidents, but the CDP argued that it was not retroactive. The country's first municipal elections were held in 2006, with the CDP capturing nearly two-thirds of the local council seats. The CDP gained 16 seats in the 2007 National Assembly elections, for a total of 73, while the largest opposition party, the Alliance for Democracy and Federation–African Democratic Rally (ADF-RDA) lost 3 seats, for a total of 14.

In January 2009, Compaore pardoned Thibault Nana, leader of the opposition Democratic and Popular Rally (RDP) party, who had been sentenced to three years in prison in 2008 for allegedly orchestrating violent protests against high food prices that year. To cope with the price increases, the World Food Programme launched a $5.9 million voucher program in February 2009, providing vouchers to 200,000 residents of Ouagadougou and Bobo-Dioulasso.

Also in 2009, Burkina Faso embarked on further electoral reforms. The National Assembly voted in April to establish a quota of 30 percent for women on all party candidate lists in municipal and legislative elections. In May, the Assembly extended the right to vote in presidential elections and referendums to millions of Burkinabe living abroad.

On September 1, 2009, severe rainfall and flooding left more than 100,000 people homeless. Thousands of the displaced were taken in by local families, but thousands more slept in schools, churches, and government buildings. The flooding put further strains on health facilities and sanitary infrastructure, which were already underequipped. Earlier in the year, a measles outbreak led to more than 45,000 infections and 300 deaths. The 2009 UN Human Development Report ranked Burkina Faso at 177 of 182 countries based on key development indicators.

Political Rights and Civil Liberties: Burkina Faso is not an electoral democracy. International monitors have judged the most recent presidential, municipal, and legislative elections to be generally free but not entirely fair, due to the ruling CDP's privileged access to state resources and the media. President Blaise Compaore is currently serving his third term in office, and he is expected to seek another five-year term in 2010. The 111-seat National Assembly is unicameral, and members serve five-year terms. The legislature is independent, but subject to executive influence.

The constitution guarantees the right to form political parties, and 13 parties are currently represented in the legislature. Opposition members have argued that 2004 revisions to the electoral code, which tripled the number of electoral districts, gave an undue advantage to larger parties, particularly the CDP. Some civil society groups have also criticized the 2009 electoral reforms, which established a gender quota and extended suffrage to citizens living abroad. The CDP has notably higher numbers of female members, and there are concerns that the overseas polling will be managed exclusively by embassies, with fewer monitoring opportunities for the opposition and civil society. Opposition parties remain weak; in the 2007 legislative elections, only two parties, the CDP and ADF-RDA, reached the 5 percent vote threshold needed to qualify for campaign financing. Another April 2009 electoral reform reduced that threshold to 3 percent of the vote so as to include a greater number of parties.

Corruption remains widespread, despite a number of public and private anticorruption initiatives. The courts have been unwilling or unable to prosecute adequately many senior officials charged with corruption. Burkina Faso was ranked 79 out of 180 countries surveyed in Transparency International's 2009 Corruption Perceptions Index. It also ranked 147 out of 183 in the World Bank's 2010 Doing Business Report on business regulations and enforcement, though this represented the best performance among all Francophone African states except Madagascar.

Although freedom of expression is constitutionally guaranteed and generally respected, many media outlets practice self-censorship. Journalists occasionally face criminal libel prosecutions, death threats, and other forms of harassment and intimidation. There are over 50 private radio stations, a private television station, and several independent newspapers, and the government does not restrict internet access.

Burkina Faso is a secular state, and freedom of religion is respected. Academic freedom is also unrestricted.

The constitution provides for the right to assemble, though demonstrations are sometimes suppressed or banned, as evidenced by the authorities' crackdown on protests in 2008. Many nongovernmental organizations, including human rights groups that have reported abuses by security forces, operate openly and freely. The constitution guarantees the right to strike, and unions are able to engage freely in strikes and collective bargaining, although only a minority of the workforce is unionized. In April 2009, a 23-day strike by employees of the French oil company Total closed all of its gas stations in Ouagadougou.

The judicial system is formally independent, but it is subject to executive influence and corruption. The courts are further weakened by a lack of resources and citizens' poor knowledge of their rights. Although the right to own property is legally guaranteed, the inadequate judicial system and the frequent recourse to traditional courts in rural areas limit this right in practice.

Human rights advocates in Burkina Faso have repeatedly criticized the military and police for committing abuses with impunity. Police often use excessive force and disregard pretrial detention limits.

Discrimination against various ethnic minorities occurs but is not widespread. However, the disabled, homosexuals, and those infected with HIV routinely experience discrimination.

The constitution provides for freedom of movement within the country, although security checks on travelers are common. Equality of opportunity is hampered in part by the advantages conferred on CDP members, who receive preferential treatment in securing public contracts.

Gender discrimination, though illegal, remains common in employment, education, property, and family rights, particularly in rural areas. In the north, early marriage contributes to lower female school enrollment and a heightened incidence of fistula. Female genital mutilation still occurs despite being banned in 1996.

Unpaid child labor is illegal but common. Burkina Faso is a source, transit, and destination country for trafficking in women and children, who are subject to forced labor and sexual exploitation. According to the U.S. State Department's 2009 Trafficking in Persons Report, Burkina Faso does not comply with the minimum standards for eliminating human trafficking. However, the report notes the government's efforts to reform, including May 2008 legislation that criminalizes all forms of human trafficking and assigns more stringent penalties to those convicted.

Burma (Myanmar)

Political Rights: 7
Civil Liberties: 7
Status: Not Free

Population: 50,020,000
Capital: Rangoon
[Note: Nay Pyi Taw serves as the administrative capital]

Ten-Year Ratings Timeline For Year Under Review (Political Rights, Civil Liberties, Status)

2000	2001	2002	2003	2004	2005	2006	2007	2008	2009
7,7NF	7,7NF	7,7NF	7,7NF	7,7NF	7,7NF	7,7NF	7,7NF	7,7NF	7,7NF

Overview:

The military regime forged ahead in 2009 with its "road map to democracy," a plan intended to legitimize its grip on power. The process called for national elections that were expected to be held in 2010, and the junta continued to arrest and imprison political dissidents in 2009, ensuring their marginalization ahead of the voting. It also extended the house arrest of opposition leader Daw Aung San Suu Kyi in August, ostensibly punishing her for a bizarre incident in which an American man swam across a lake and stayed uninvited in her home for two days. Tensions between the military and armed ethnic groups increased in the fall, as the groups refused to incorporate themselves into the military's Border Guard Force, impeding the government's goal of national unity by 2010.

Burma gained independence from Britain in 1948. The military has ruled the country since 1962, when General Ne Win led a coup that toppled an elected civilian government. The ruling Revolutionary Council consolidated all legislative, executive, and judicial power and pursued radical socialist and isolationist policies. Burma, once one of the wealthiest countries in Southeast Asia, eventually became one of the most impoverished in the region.

The present junta, led by General Than Shwe, dramatically asserted its power in 1988, when the army opened fire on peaceful, student-led, prodemocracy protesters, killing an estimated 3,000 people. In the aftermath, a younger generation of army commanders created the State Law and Order Restoration Council (SLORC) to rule the country. The SLORC refused to cede power after it was defeated in a landslide election by the National League for Democracy (NLD) in 1990. The NLD won 392 of the 485 parliamentary seats in Burma's first free elections in three decades. The junta responded by nullifying the results and jailing dozens of members of the NLD, including party leader Daw Aung San Suu Kyi. She went on to spend 14 of the next 20 years in detention. Aung San Suu Kyi was awarded the Nobel Peace Prize in 1991 for her nonviolent struggle for democracy and human rights.

The SLORC refashioned itself into the State Peace and Development Council (SPDC) in 1997. In late 2000, the government began holding talks with Aung San Suu Kyi, leading to an easing of restrictions on the NLD by mid-2002. However, the party's revitalization apparently rattled hard-liners within the regime during the first half of 2003. On May 30, 2003, scores of NLD leaders and supporters were killed when SPDC thugs ambushed an NLD motorcade. Arrests and detentions of political activists, journalists, and students followed the attack, which came to be known as the Depayin massacre.

In a surprise move in 2005, General Than Shwe announced a decision to relocate the country's capital 600 kilometers (370 miles) inland to Nay Pyi Taw, citing congestion and lack of space in Rangoon. Many Burmese believe the decision was made on the advice of astrologers who serve the notoriously superstitious generals.

The largest demonstrations in nearly 20 years broke out in cities across the country in August and September 2007, triggered by a 500 percent fuel-price increase. The 88 Generation Students, a group composed of dissidents active in the 1988 protests, were at the forefront of many of the demonstrations. The protest movement expanded to include thousands of Buddhist monks and nuns, who were encouraged by the general populace. Soldiers, riot police, and members of the paramilitary Union Solidarity and Development Association (USDA) and the Swan Arr Shin militia group responded brutally, killing at least 31 people. The crackdown targeted important religious sites and included the public beating, shooting, and arrest of monks, further delegitimizing the regime in the eyes of many Burmese.

Cyclone Nargis struck the Irrawaddy Delta on May 2, 2008. It was the worst natural disaster in Burma's modern history, causing over 150,000 deaths and severely affecting another 2.4 million people. The SPDC attempted to control all foreign and domestic relief efforts, which effectively blocked much of the desperately needed aid. In the absence of a government response, local Burmese civil society actors stepped in, and monasteries became distribution points and shelters for survivors. Domestic and international relief efforts expanded in June after the Association of Southeast Asian Nations (ASEAN) mediated dialogues with the regime, but the delay worsened conditions for storm victims. Many Burmese volunteers were detained for trying to deliver aid to cyclone victims, including the popular comedian Zarganar, who was sentenced to 59 years in prison in November 2008.

Despite the severity of the cyclone, the SPDC pushed through a constitutional referendum on May 10, 2008. The process of drafting the constitution, which had proceeded intermittently for 15 years, was tightly controlled by the junta and excluded key stakeholders. The regime delayed balloting in areas affected by the cyclone, but after just five days of voting, the government claimed that 99 percent of eligible voters had turned out and that 92.4 percent had voted in favor of the constitution. Burmese political opposition and international human rights groups called the referendum a sham. The new charter paved the way for national elections expected in 2010, part of a seven-step "road map" toward a "disciplined" democracy that the junta had laid out in 2003.

In an apparent bid to remove potential obstacles to the elections, the authorities continued to arrest and imprison dissidents throughout 2009. More than 300 activists, ranging from political and labor figures to artists and internet bloggers, received harsh sentences after closed trials, with some prison terms exceeding 100 years. In August, Aung San Suu Kyi was sentenced to 18 additional months of house arrest after a bizarre incident in which an American man swam across Inya lake and stayed for two days in her home, claiming he was protecting her from assassination. Other leading opposition figures remained in detention; Khun Tun Oo, leader of the Shan Nationalities League for Democracy, was serving a 93-year term.

Also in 2009, the regime pursued a parallel effort to consolidate its control over the country by incorporating armed ethnic minority groups—with which it had established ceasefire agreements—into a government-led Border Guard Force. In August, the military showed its willingness to risk the ire of China by clashing with the Kokang ethnic group in the north and driving a flood of refugees over the border. Nevertheless, ethnic factions such as the United Wa State Army (UWSA) and the National Democratic Alliance Army (NDAA) in Shan State refused to go along with the regime's plan, and a deadline set for October was allowed to pass. The minority groups stepped up their drug-trafficking activities during the year, aiming to raise funds and buy weapons in preparation for hostilities with the government.

Although the United States sought "constructive engagement" with the Burmese regime in 2009, economic sanctions remained in place. The global recession added to the country's difficulties, which include a lack of contract enforcement and effective property rights, as well as arbitrary and ill-informed macroeconomic policy making.

Political Rights and Civil Liberties:

Burma is not an electoral democracy. The SPDC rules by decree; controls all executive, legislative, and judicial powers; suppresses nearly all basic rights; and commits human rights abuses with impunity. Military officers occupy almost all cabinet positions, and active or retired officers hold the top posts in all ministries as well as key positions in the private sector. The SPDC does not tolerate dissent and has a long history of imprisoning anyone who is critical of the government.

The 2008 constitution retains the existing division of the country into seven ethnic states and seven other regions, though these will now include six new autonomous subunits for ethnic minorities. Each of the 14 states and regions will have a legislature with limited authority. At the national level, the charter establishes a bicameral legislature called the Pyidaungsu Hluttaw, which elects the president. A quarter of the seats in all legislatures are reserved for the military and filled through appointment by the commander-in-chief, an officer who has broad powers and is selected by the military-dominated National Defense and Security Council. The military members of the national legislature have the right to nominate one of the three presidential candidates, with the other two nominated by the elected members of each chamber. The constitution includes a bill of rights, but many of the rights are limited by existing laws and may be suspended in a state of emergency. Constitutional amendments require a three-quarters majority in the national legislature and in some cases a national referendum. Criticism of the constitution is banned by a 1996 order that carries a penalty of 20 years in prison. Under the new charter, the military retains the right to administer its own affairs, and members of the outgoing military regime receive blanket immunity for all official acts.

Political party activity remains sharply restricted in Burma. Since it rejected the results of the 1990 elections and prevented the unicameral legislature from convening, the junta has all but paralyzed the victorious NLD. The authorities regularly jail NLD leaders, pressure members to resign, close party offices, and harass members' families. The activities of over 20 other political parties, most of them formed along ethnic lines, are similarly suppressed.

Individuals are relentlessly imprisoned for expressing their political views. About 43 prisons hold political prisoners, and there are over 50 hard-labor camps in the country. A September 2009 Human Rights Watch report estimates that there are over 2,100 political prisoners in Burma—more than double the number in early 2007.

The SPDC has announced that it will hold elections in 2010, but has not set a date or promulgated laws and regulations governing the electoral process and the registration of political parties. Citing the inability to freely organize, the NLD has said it will not participate, but it has yet to call for a voter boycott. Some ethnic parties have indicated that they will take part and have requested international support to ensure an inclusive and fair process. It remains unclear what approach the military will take in establishing a loyalist political party.

In a system that lacks transparency and accountability, corruption and economic mismanagement are rampant at both the national and local levels. The country was ranked 178 out of 180 countries surveyed in Transparency International's 2009 Corruption Perceptions Index. The SPDC's arbitrary economic policies, such as an official fixed exchange rate that overvalues the kyat by 150 percent, facilitate corruption through erroneous bookkeeping.

The junta drastically restricts press freedom and owns or controls all newspapers and broadcast media. While the market for private publications is growing, the military censors private periodicals before publication and impedes the importation of foreign news sources. Media crackdowns continued in 2009, with at least 17 journalists in detention at the year's end. The authorities practice surveillance at internet cafes and regularly jail bloggers.

The 2008 constitution provides for freedom of religion. It distinguishes Buddhism as the majority religion but also recognizes Christianity, Islam, Hinduism, and animism. At times, the government interferes with religious assemblies and discriminates against minority religious groups. Buddhist temples and monasteries have been kept under close surveillance since the 2007 protests and crackdown.

Academic freedom is severely limited. Teachers are subject to restrictions on freedom of expression and are held accountable for the political activities of their students. Since the 1988 student prodemocracy demonstrations, the junta has sporadically closed universities and relocated many campuses to relatively isolated areas to disperse the student population.

Freedoms of association and assembly are restricted. Unauthorized outdoor gatherings of more than five people are banned. Authorities regularly use force to break up or prevent demonstrations and meetings, most notably during the 2007 protests.

The junta repeatedly violates worker rights and represses union activity. Some public sector employees and ordinary citizens are compelled to join the USDA. Independent trade unions, collective bargaining, and strikes are illegal, and several labor activists are serving long prison terms. The regime continues to use forced labor despite formally banning the practice in 2000. Nongovernmental organizations providing social services in remote areas regularly face threats to their activities. International humanitarian organizations have expanded their work in the country but continue to face severe restrictions and monitoring.

The judiciary is not independent. Judges are appointed or approved by the junta and adjudicate cases according to its decrees. Administrative detention laws allow people to be held without charge, trial, or access to legal counsel for up to five years if the SPDC concludes that they have threatened the state's security or sovereignty. The frequently used Decree 5/96 authorizes prison terms of up to 20 years for aiding activities "which adversely affect the national interest." Political prisoners are frequently held incommunicado in pretrial detention, facilitating torture. Impunity for crimes and human rights violations committed by state security forces is deeply entrenched.

Some of the worst human rights abuses take place in areas populated by ethnic minorities, who comprise roughly 35 percent of Burma's population. In these border regions the military kills, beats, rapes, and arbitrarily detains civilians. The Chin, Karen, and Rohingya minorities are frequent victims. Tens of thousands of ethnic minorities in Shan, Karenni, Karen, and Mon states live in squalid relocation centers set up by the military. Over the years, several million Burmese have fled as refugees to neighboring countries. Some ethnic rebel armies maintain low-grade insurgencies, and have reportedly displaced villagers and used forced labor. Both the Burmese armed forces and rebel armies recruit child soldiers.

Burmese women have traditionally enjoyed high social and economic status, but domestic violence and trafficking are growing concerns, and women remain underrepresented in the government and civil service. The Women's League of Burma has accused the military of systematically using rape and forced marriage as a weapon against ethnic minorities.

☛ Burundi

Political Rights: 4
Civil Liberties: 5
Status: Partly Free

Population: 8,303,000
Capital: Bujumbura

Trend Arrow: Burundi received an upward trend arrow due to the integration of the last remaining rebel group into the political process and the establishment of an independent electoral commission.

Ten-Year Ratings Timeline For Year Under Review (Political Rights, Civil Liberties, Status)

2000	2001	2002	2003	2004	2005	2006	2007	2008	2009
6,6NF	6,6NF	6,5NF	5,5PF	5,5PF	3,5PF	4,5PF	4,5PF	4,5PF	4,5PF

Overview:

In 2009, the last rebel guerrilla movement, the National Liberation Forces, laid down its arms and was recognized as a legal political party. Also during the year, an electoral code was adopted, and an independent election commission was appointed to prepare for presidential, parliamentary, and local elections due in 2010.

The minority Tutsi ethnic group governed Burundi for most of the period since independence from Belgium in 1962. The military, judiciary, education system, business sector, and news media have also traditionally been dominated by the Tutsi. Violence between them and the majority Hutu has broken out repeatedly since independence. A 1992 constitution introduced multiparty politics, but the 1993 assassination of the newly elected Hutu president, Melchior Ndadaye of the Front for Democracy in Burundi (FRODEBU) party, resulted in sustained and widespread ethnic violence.

Ndadaye's successor was killed in 1994, along with Rwandan president Juvenal Habyarimana, when their plane was apparently shot down as it approached Kigali airport in Rwanda. This event triggered the Rwandan genocide and intensified the fighting in Burundi.

A 1994 power-sharing arrangement between FRODEBU and the mainly Tutsi-led Unity for National Progress (UPRONA) party installed Hutu politician Sylvestre Ntibantunganya as Burundi's new president, but he was ousted in a 1996 military coup led by former president Pierre Buyoya, a Tutsi whom Ndadaye had defeated in the 1993 election. Peace and political stability remained elusive, as insurgents sporadically staged attacks and government forces pursued a campaign of intimidation.

In 2000, 19 groups from across the political spectrum agreed in principle on a future political solution to the conflict, and in 2001, a transitional government was installed, with Buyoya temporarily remaining chief of state and FRODEBU's Domitien Ndayizeye serving as vice president. The failure of key elements of two Hutu rebel groups, the Forces for the Defense of Democracy (FDD) and the National Liberation Forces (FNL), to participate in the transition resulted in both continued negotiations and additional violence.

By the end of 2002, most of the factions had agreed to stop the fighting and participate in transitional arrangements leading to national elections, initially scheduled for late 2004. In April 2003, Buyoya stepped down and was replaced as president by Ndayizeye. In October of that year, the FDD reached an agreement with the government. Progress continued in 2004, with an August agreement on the shape of new democratic institutions—designed to balance the interests of the Hutu and Tutsi populations—and on the holding of elections.

In 2005, Burundi held the first local and national elections since 1993. The largely Hutu National Council for the Defense of Democracy (CNDD), the political wing of the FDD, emerged as the country's largest party, and Parliament chose Pierre Nkurunziza as president. Domestic and international observers generally regarded the voting as legitimate and reflective of the people's will.

A key faction of the sole remaining rebel group, the FNL, agreed to lay down its arms and participate in the political process in 2006. The country was shaken, however, when several senior figures, including opposition leaders, were temporarily arrested in connection with an alleged coup plot. In addition, the CNDD leadership showed increasing signs of intolerance toward opposition and independent viewpoints.

A tentative ceasefire agreement was reached with the last significant FNL faction in June 2007, but violence involving the group flared again in the spring of 2008. In addition, the Constitutional Court ruled in favor of a government claim that a number of lawmakers should be replaced by government supporters. Nonetheless, FNL leader Agathon Rwasa returned to Bujumbura in late May to participate in negotiations on the demobilization of his guerrillas and the transformation of the FNL into a political party. These discussions were complicated by complaints regarding repressive actions taken by the CNDD, such as the arrest of a well-known journalist and opposition political leader, and counterclaims that the FNL was continuing to recruit military cadres.

The talks finally bore fruit in 2009, when the rebel group laid down its arms and was recognized as a legal political party. In April, an independent election commission was sworn in to prepare for presidential, parliamentary, and local elections due in 2010, and a new electoral code was adopted in September. Political uncertainty and tension remained, however. Opposition parties harshly criticized an alleged attempt by the government to manipulate the electoral process, and a leading anticorruption campaigner was murdered in April under mysterious circumstances.

Political Rights and Civil Liberties: Burundi is an electoral democracy. In 2005, citizens were able to change their government democratically. Restrictions on political parties were lifted, and parties and civic organizations now function with relative freedom. Burundi currently has representative institutions at the local, municipal, and national levels, in both the legislative and executive branches of government. In 2009, a new independent election commission was appointed, although its suffered from tense relations with the government, which at one point withheld funding. In elections set for 2010, the president will be directly elected by popular vote for a five-year term; Parliament had elected the president in 2005. The president appoints two vice presidents, one Tutsi and one Hutu, and they must be approved separately by a two-thirds majority in the lower and upper houses. Governments must include all parties that have won at least 5 percent of the votes cast in parliamentary elections.

While the lower house of Parliament—the 100-seat National Assembly—is directly elected for a five-year term, locally elected officials choose members of the Senate, also for five-year terms. Each of Burundi's 17 provinces chooses two senators—one Tutsi and one Hutu. Carefully crafted constitutional arrangements require the National Assembly to be 60 percent Hutu and 40 percent Tutsi, with three additional deputies from the Twa ethnic minority, who are also allocated three senators. In both houses, a minimum of 30 percent of the legislators must be women. In 2008, the ruling CNDD party successfully pressured the Constitutional Court to permit the removal of 22 dissident lawmakers and their replacement with loyal party members.

There are more than two dozen active political parties in the country, ranging from those that champion radical Tutsi positions to those that hold extremist Hutu views. Most are small in terms of membership. Many Tutsi have now joined formerly Hutu-dominated parties. According to Human Rights Watch, both the ruling and other parties have sometimes employed violence and intimidation against opponents and internal dissent.

Corruption is a significant problem. Some government revenues and expenditures have not been regularly listed on the budget. In April 2009, Ernest Manirumva—the deputy head of Burundi's main anticorruption organization, the Anticorruption and Economic Malpractice Observatory (OLUCOME)—was killed by unknown assailants at his home in the capital. OLUCOME alleged that high-ranking government officials were complicit, and called for an international investigation. Burundi was ranked 168 out of 180 countries surveyed in Transparency International's 2009 Corruption Perceptions Index.

Freedom of speech is legally guaranteed and exists in practice, although journalists have been subject to self-censorship and occasional government censorship. The media have presented a wider range of political perspectives in recent years, and there is an opposition press, though it functions sporadically. Print runs of most newspapers are small, and readership is limited by low literacy levels. Radio is the main source of information for most Burundians. The government runs the sole television station and the only radio station with national reach, as well as the only newspaper that publishes regularly. The British Broadcasting Corporation (BBC), Radio France Internationale, and the Voice of America are available on FM radio in the capital. Several private radio stations exist, but they generally have a short broadcast range. Access to the internet remains largely confined to urban areas.

Freedom of religion is generally observed. For many years, the ongoing civil strife and the Tutsi social and institutional dominance impeded academic freedom by limiting educational opportunities for the Hutu, but this situation has improved in recent years. In June 2009, university students demonstrated to protest increases in administrative fees.

The constitution provides for freedoms of assembly and association, although past governments occasionally restricted these rights in practice. There is modest but important civil society activity with a focus on human rights. Constitutional protections for organized labor are in place, and the right to strike is guaranteed by the labor code. The Confederation of Burundi Trade Unions has been independent since its establishment in 1995. Most union members are civil servants and have bargained collectively with the government. Most of Burundi's doctors, who earn an average of $100 per month, went on strike in May 2009 to focus attention on their calls for salary increases.

The judicial system is seriously burdened by corruption and a lack of resources and training, and crimes often go unreported. There are far more pending cases than can easily be handled by the current judiciary, and many of them are politically sensitive. According to a June 2009 Human Rights Watch statement, the government has stalled on the creation of a truth and reconciliation commission to address past human rights violations, and has failed to adequately investigate or prosecute such crimes. Amnesty International has reported that prison conditions continue to be "subhuman" and at times life-threatening.

With the improvement in the political environment, many of Burundi's internally displaced and refugee populations have returned home in recent years. According to the Office of the UN High Commissioner for Refugees, more than 300,000 Burundians returned from Tanzania between 2002 and 2008. Since 2004, UNICEF has assisted the demobilization of 3,013 child soldiers, and the last had reportedly returned home by May 2009.

A new penal code adopted in 2009 criminalizes same-sex relationships. Women have limited opportunities for advancement in the economic and political spheres, especially in rural areas. According to UNICEF, only 12 percent of eligible females were enrolled in secondary school in 2008. A 2007 study by Amnesty International and a Burundian partner organization found that minors are the victims in 60 percent of reported rapes in the country. Albinos face a particular threat from discrimination and violence; eight murderers of Albinos were convicted and sentenced to prison in 2009.

◆ Cambodia

Political Rights: 6
Civil Liberties: 5
Status: Not Free

Population: 14,805,000
Capital: Phnom Penh

Trend Arrow: Cambodia received a downward trend arrow due to the deportation of 20 Uighur asylum seekers to China in December 2009.

Ten-Year Ratings Timeline For Year Under Review (Political Rights, Civil Liberties, Status)

2000	2001	2002	2003	2004	2005	2006	2007	2008	2009
6,6NF	6,5NF	6,5NF	6,5NF	6,5NF	6,5NF	6,5NF	6,5NF	6,5NF	6,5NF

Overview: Land grabs and official corruption continued in 2009, and the government's harassment of its critics appeared to worsen. Two opposition members of parliament were stripped of immunity; one was tried in absentia for defaming the prime minister, and the other was threatened with arrest for allegedly claiming that Vietnam is encroaching on Cambodia. The parliament also approved a new penal code which opponents argue will allow for government abuse. Separately, the international tribunal trying former high-ranking officials of the Khmer Rouge regime heard its first testimony in March, and

Cambodian authorities in December deported 20 Uighur asylum seekers to China despite human rights concerns.

Cambodia won independence from France in 1953. King Norodom Sihanouk ruled until he was ousted in 1970 by U.S.-backed military commander Lon Nol, and the Chinese-supported Khmer Rouge (KR) seized power in 1975. Between 250,000 and two million of Cambodia's seven million people died from disease, overwork, starvation, or execution under the KR before Vietnamese forces toppled the regime and installed a new communist government in 1979. Fighting continued in the 1980s between the Hanoi-backed government and the allied armies of Sihanouk, the KR, and other political contenders. The 1991 Paris Peace Accords halted open warfare, but the KR waged a low-grade insurgency until its disintegration in the late 1990s.

Prime Minister Hun Sen, who first entered government as part of the Vietnamese-backed regime in 1979, came to dominate national politics through his Cambodian People's Party (CPP), which controlled the National Assembly, military, courts and police. They quashed any challenge to their authority with lawsuits, prosecutions, or extralegal actions. Opposition figures, journalists, and democracy advocates were given criminal sentences or faced violent attacks by unknown assailants in public spaces. Hun Sen's divide-and-rule tactics succeeded in fracturing and weakening the opposition even further, as he formed coalitions with one opposition party to outmaneuver another.

A special tribunal, officially known as the Extraordinary Chambers in the Courts of Cambodia, was established in 2007 to try former KR officials for genocide and other crimes against humanity. The tribunal's launch was delayed for years by bureaucratic and funding obstacles. It was given three years to complete its work. Cases are decided by majority vote among five justices (three are Cambodian), and victims must file complaints as a group; the maximum penalty is life imprisonment. Five former high-level KR leaders were charged at the end of 2008—the first time anyone had been charged for the atrocities committed by the KR. The accused were former head of state Khieu Samphan, former foreign minister Ieng Sary, former social affairs minister Ieng Thirith, former second-in-command of the KR Nuon Chea, and former chief of the Tuol Sleng prison Kang Kek Ieu (also known as Duch). KR mastermind Pol Pot and his successor, Ta Mok, died before they could be brought to trial.

In the 2008 elections, the CPP took 90 of 123 parliamentary seats, and Hun Sen was reelected as prime minister. The opposition Sam Rainsy Party (SRP) took 26 seats, up from 24; the Funcinpec party took 2 seats, down from 26; and two new parties, the Human Rights Party and the Norodom Ranariddh Party, took 3 and 2 seats, respectively. Opposition parties rejected the results, citing political intimidation and violence. They also alleged that the National Election Committee worked with pro-CPP local authorities to delete potential opposition supporters from the voter rolls, changed polling stations shortly before voting began to confuse opposition supporters, and issued fraudulent forms that allowed people not on the rolls to vote. With the opposition divided and unproven in the eyes of the voters, and the country enjoying relative political stability and sustained moderate economic growth, the CPP commanded a measure of credibility despite public frustration with widespread corruption and other problems. Local and international election observers said there were fewer incidents of violence and flagrant use of fraud tactics than in previous elections, though they still fell short of international standards.

In March 2009, testimony began at the special tribunal for former KR officials. Only Kang Kek Ieu publicly apologized for his part in the atrocities committed; the other four defendants denied any knowledge of the crimes. Meanwhile, the tribunal was running low on funds, jeopardizing its operations, and critics said corruption and abuse, including nepotism in hiring, remained serious problems.

Throughout 2009, critics of the government continued to face legal harassment. In June, Hang Chakra, publisher and editor in chief of the *Khmer Machas Srok* newspaper, was tried and sentenced in absentia to one year in prison and a $2,250 fine for "misinformation" and "dishonoring public officials." Hang had published articles in May alleging corruption in the office of the deputy prime minister. His defense attorney had only one day to prepare for the trial. Separately, opposition lawmaker Mu Sochua, a former minister for women's and veterans' affairs, was stripped of parliamentary immunity and convicted of defamation in absentia in August. In November, opposition leader Sam Rainsy was also stripped of parliamentary immunity and threatened with arrest for allegedly claiming that Vietnam is encroaching on Cambodia— a matter of considerable political sensitivity given the history between the two countries. To give legal basis to these actions, the parliament approved a new penal code in October to replace the 1992 code adopted under the United Nations Transitional Authority. Critics argue that the language in the new penal code is too vague and gives excessive authority to judges to interpret laws in a system where the judiciary is not independent.

In an indication of China's growing influence in the country, Cambodian authorities forcibly deported 20 Uighur asylum seekers, including two infants, to China in December, despite warnings from UN officials and human rights groups that they could face torture or other mistreatment for alleged involvement in fomenting unrest.

Political Rights and Civil Liberties: Cambodia is not an electoral democracy. The current constitution was promulgated in 1993 by the king, who serves as head of state. The monarchy remains highly revered as a symbol of national unity. Prince Sihamoni, who has lived abroad for much of his life, succeeded his father, King Norodom Sihanouk, in 2004, after the latter abdicated for health reasons.

The prime minister and cabinet must be approved by a two-thirds vote in the 123-seat National Assembly. Assembly members are elected by popular vote to serve five-year terms. The upper house of the bicameral parliament, the Senate, has 61 members, of whom 2 are appointed by the king, 2 are elected by the National Assembly, and 57 are chosen by functional constituencies. Senators serve five-year terms. Voting is tied to a citizen's permanent resident status in a village, township, or urban district, and this status cannot be changed easily. The CPP's strong influence in rural areas, with its presence of party members and control of government officials, gives it an advantage over the opposition SRP, which finds support mainly in urban centers.

Corruption and abuse of power are serious problems that hinder economic development and social stability. Many in the ruling elite abuse their positions for private gain. While economic growth in recent years has been sustained by increased investment in mining, forestry, agriculture, textile manufacturing, tourism, and real estate, these enterprises frequently involve land grabs by powerful politicians, bureaucrats, and military officers. Cambodia was ranked 158 out of 180 countries surveyed in Transparency International's 2009 Corruption Perceptions Index.

The government does not fully respect freedom of speech. Media controls are largely focused on local broadcast outlets, which are the primary source of information for most Cambodians. There are many newspapers and private television and radio stations, including several owned and operated by the CPP and opposition parties. There are no restrictions on privately owned satellite dishes receiving foreign broadcasts. Print journalists are somewhat freer to criticize government policies and senior officials, but the print media reach only about 10 percent of the population. Moreover, critical journalists are subject to lawsuits and criminal prosecution. A new penal code passed in October 2009 confirmed defamation as a criminal offense and contained language allowing for liberal interpretation of defamation. Although imprisonment was eliminated as a penalty for defamation in 2006, it can be imposed for spreading false information or insulting public officials. Journalists also remain vulnerable to intimidation and violence, which are rarely punished. A journalists' association claims that at least 10 media workers have been killed by government agents over the past two years, and that there have been no arrests or charges in their cases. The internet is fairly free of government control, but access is largely limited to urban centers. Mobile telephone use, though spreading, is still low because of cost and infrastructure constraints. The majority of Cambodians are Theravada Buddhists and can generally practice their faith freely, but discrimination against ethnic Cham Muslims is widespread. Terrorist attacks by Islamist militants in the broader region in recent years have raised new suspicions about Muslims. The government generally respects academic freedom, although criticism of the state is not tolerated.

Freedoms of association and assembly are respected by the government to a certain degree because of pressure and scrutiny by international donors. Civil society groups work on a broad spectrum of issues and offer social services, frequently with funding from overseas. Those that work on social or health issues generally face less harassment from the state. Public gatherings, protests, and marches occur and are rarely violent. However, the government occasionally uses police and other forces to intimidate participants. Democracy advocates fear that the new penal code, which limits protests to fewer than 20 participants, will allow the government to further restrict freedoms of assembly and speech. The government also appears keen to limit the influence of civil society groups. In 2008, the government proposed a new local associations and nongovernmental organizations law that would require international funds to be channeled through government bodies. The proposed law also imposes complex regulatory requirements on groups and bans activities deemed too political. Toward the end of 2009, Prime Minister Hun Sen pledged to push for its passage by the parliament.

Cambodia has a small number of independent unions. Workers have the right to strike, and many have done so to protest low wages and poor or dangerous working conditions. Lack of resources and experience limits union success in collective bargaining, and union leaders report harassment and physical threats. Labor conditions and workers' ability to hold public protests and bargain collectively reportedly worsened in 2009. Wages have not kept up with rising costs of living, and the global economic slowdown exacerbated the hardships of low-income workers.

The judiciary is marred by inefficiency, corruption, and a lack of independence.

There is a severe shortage of lawyers, and the system's poorly trained judges are subject to political pressure from the CPP. Abuse by law enforcement officers, including illegal detention and the torture of suspects, is common. Delays in the judicial process and corruption allow many suspects to escape prosecution. Jails are seriously overcrowded, and inmates often lack sufficient food, water, and health care. Police, soldiers, and government officials are widely believed to tolerate, or be involved in, the trafficking of guns, drugs, and people, as well as other crimes.

The constitution guarantees the right to freedom of travel and movement. The government generally respects this right, but there have been reports of authorities restricting travel for opposition politicians, particularly during election campaigns. Land and property rights are regularly abused for the sake of private development projects. Over the past several years, tens of thousands of people have been forcibly removed—from both rural and urban areas, and with little or no compensation or relocation assistance—to make room for commercial plantations, mine operations, factories, and high-end office and residential developments. High-ranking officials and their family members are frequently involved in these ventures, alongside international investors.

Women suffer widespread economic and social discrimination, lagging behind men in secondary and higher education, and many die from difficulties related to pregnancy and childbirth. Rape and domestic violence are common and are often tied to alcohol and drug abuse by men. Women and girls are trafficked inside and outside of Cambodia for prostitution, and the sex trade has fueled the spread of HIV/AIDS. A 2008 law against human trafficking imposes tougher penalties, but enforcement is said to be weak.

Cameroon

Political Rights: 6
Civil Liberties: 6
Status: Not Free

Population: 18,879,000
Capital: Yaounde

Ten-Year Ratings Timeline For Year Under Review (Political Rights, Civil Liberties, Status)

2000	2001	2002	2003	2004	2005	2006	2007	2008	2009
7,6NF	6,6NF	6,6NF	6,6NF	6,6NF	6,6NF	6,6NF	6,6NF	6,6NF	6,6NF

Overview: The government continued to resist electoral reforms in 2009, and the opposition Social Democratic Front party launched a legal challenge to the nomination of election commissioners who it argued were ruling party loyalists. Restrictions on the press also continued during the year, but the publication of a critical report by the government-created National Commission on Human Rights and Freedoms marked a step toward open public discussion.

Colonized by Germany in the late 19th century, Cameroon was later administered by Britain and France, first through League of Nations mandates and then as a UN trust territory after World War II. Independence for French Cameroon in 1960 was followed a year later by independence for Anglophone Cameroon, part of which opted for union with Nigeria. The rest joined Francophone Cameroon in a federation, which became a unitary state in 1972.

The country's first president, Ahmadou Ahidjo, oversaw a repressive, one-party system until his resignation in 1982. He was succeeded by Paul Biya, whose Cameroon People's Democratic Movement (CPDM) did not face multiparty legislative elections until 1992. It failed to win an absolute majority, despite a boycott by the main opposition party, the Anglophone-led Social Democratic Front (SDF). Also in 1992, Biya was reelected in a vote that was condemned by international observers.

Municipal elections in 1996 led the CPDM to lose control of all major councils in the country. A constitutional revision that year extended the presidential term from five to seven years, and Biya won subsequent presidential elections in 1997 and 2004 amid numerous irregularities. The CPDM's victories in 1997 and 2002 legislative and 2002 municipal elections were similarly tainted. Electoral gerrymandering provided the CPDM with significant inroads into the SDF support base in the 2007 legislative and municipal polls, and SDF parliamentary representation decreased to 16 seats, from 22 in 2002 and 43 in 1997.

In 2008, Biya secured a constitutional amendment to remove the two-term presidential limit set in 1996, allowing him to stand for reelection in 2011. However, action by taxi drivers in Douala that year spurred broader antigovernment riots in several cities, as citizens used the opportunity to protest the president's move as well as the rising cost of living. The protests were the largest in many years, and local human rights groups estimated that 100 people were killed and 1,500 arrested as riot police clashed with the protesters.

In a June 2009 cabinet reshuffle, Prime Minister Ephraim Inoni was replaced by Philemon Yang, another Anglophone and CPDM politician. The defense minister, Remy Ze Meka, was also replaced. The ousted officials had both been linked to a corruption scandal involving the purchase of a presidential aircraft in 2004.

The trial of SDF leader John Fru Ndi and 21 other party members, who were accused of murdering another SDF member in 2006, was postponed indefinitely in July 2009. Many party members had been held in pretrial detention since 2006, and had died in custody. Critics had denounced the trial as politically motivated.

Political Rights and Civil Liberties:

Cameroon is not an electoral democracy. Although the 1996 constitutional revisions created an upper chamber for the legislature, a decentralized system of regional government, and a Constitutional Court, none of these provisions have been implemented. A 2008 constitutional amendment removed the 1996 limit of two seven-year terms for the president, allowing President Paul Biya to run again in 2011. The president is not required to consult the National Assembly, and the Supreme Court may review the constitutionality of a law only at the president's request. Since 1992, the executive has initiated every bill passed by the legislature. The unicameral National Assembly has 180 seats, 153 of which are held by the ruling CPDM. Members are elected by direct popular vote to serve five-year terms.

The National Elections Observatory (NEO) has little influence, and the Ministry of Territorial Administration and Decentralization effectively controls elections. An elections commission, Elections Cameroon (ELECAM), was created in 2006, but the commissioners were not named until December 2008. No civil society or opposition members were included, and 11 out of the 12 appointees were reputedly CPDM loyalists. The SDF launched legal action in January 2009 to contest the body's impartiality.

There are more than 180 recognized political parties, but Biya's CPDM and the Anglophone SDF are dominant. Continued marginalization of the Anglophone community is fueling a campaign for independence led by the Southern Cameroons National Council (SCNC). In October 2009, the Commission on Human and People's Rights ruled on a six-year case brought by the SCNC against the government, dismissing the SCNC's secessionist claims while simultaneously condemning discrimination against Anglophones.

Despite some high-profile convictions of former regime officials, corruption remains endemic. Biya's many years in power and the large number of cabinet ministries have encouraged cronyism, with members of the president's Beti ethnic group dominating key positions. Cameroon signed on to the Extractive Industries Transparency Initiative (EITI) in 2007, but revenues from the oil, gas, and mining sectors are not openly reported. A constitutional provision requiring all top civil servants to declare their assets before and after leaving office has been ignored. In June 2009, a French nongovernmental organization (NGO), the Catholic Committee against Hunger and for Development (CCFD), published a report the embezzlement of public funds by Biya and his relatives. Biya's lavish lifestyle came under more scrutiny in September 2009, when it emerged that he was spending $40,000 a day on 43 hotel rooms during a vacation in France. Cameroon was ranked 146 out of 180 countries in Transparency International's 2009 Corruption Perceptions Index and 171 out of 183 countries in the World Bank's 2010 Doing Business index.

The constitution guarantees free speech, but genuine freedom of expression remains elusive. Although the 1996 constitution ended prepublication censorship, the charter's Article 17 gives officials the power to ban newspapers based on a claimed threat to public order. Libel and defamation remain criminal offenses, and judicial harassment and arrests of journalists have engendered self-censorship. Editor Medjo of *La Detente Libre*was sentenced in January 2009 to three years in prison for publishing a story about the president's alleged attempts to manipulate the Supreme Court. Jean-Bosco Talla, editor of the private weekly *Germinal*, received death threats after republishing the CCFD's report on corruption in June; he was then detained in December and given a suspended one-year jail sentence on a charge of insulting the president, after *Germinal* published excerpts from a banned book. Separately, a military court in June sentenced journalists to five years in prison after their paper, *La Nouvelle*, published articles that were critical of the former defense minister. The journalists were not present at their own trial. The government has not attempted to restrict or monitor internet communications.

Freedom of religion is generally respected. There are no legal restrictions on academic freedom, but state security informants operate on university campuses, and many professors exercise self-censorship.

The requisite administrative authorization for public meetings is often used to restrict freedoms of assembly and association. Meetings of the banned SCNC are routinely disrupted. In April 2009, 50 members of the group were arrested for allegedly holding an illegal public meeting. Trade union formation is permitted, but subject to numerous restrictions.

The judiciary is subordinate to the Ministry of Justice, and the courts are weakened by political influence and corruption. Military tribunals exercise jurisdiction over civilians in cases involving civil unrest or organized armed violence, and various intelligence agencies operate with impunity. Torture, ill-treatment of detainees, and lengthy pretrial detention are routine. In August 2009, the government-created National Commission on Human Rights and Freedoms published a report that was highly critical of the government and detailed appalling prison conditions. The absence of habeas corpus provisions in Francophone civil law further undermines due process. In the north, traditional rulers (*lamibee*) operate private militias, courts, and prisons, which are used against political opponents.

Slavery reportedly persists in parts of the north, and indigenous groups and ethnic minorities, particularly the Baka (Pygmies), face discrimination. Many laws contain gender-biased provisions and penalties. There is widespread violence and discrimination against women, who often are denied inheritance and property rights. Female genital mutilation is practiced in the Southwest and Far North Regions, and homosexuality is illegal. Cameroon is a child labor market and a transit center for child trafficking. Abortion is prohibited except in cases of rape or to preserve the life of the mother.

Canada

Political Rights: 1
Civil Liberties: 1
Status: Free

Population: 33,700,000
Capital: Ottawa

Ten-Year Ratings Timeline For Year Under Review (Political Rights, Civil Liberties, Status)

2000	2001	2002	2003	2004	2005	2006	2007	2008	2009
1,1F	1,1F	1,1F	1,1F	1,1F	1,1F	1,1F	1,1F	1,1F	1,1F

Overview:　　　　Prime Minister Stephen Harper suspended Parliament in December 2009, thereby postponing criticism stemming from allegations of abuse of Afghan detainees. It was the second consecutive year in which Harper had ended the legislative session prematurely. In what some observers regarded as a major achievement for freedom of expression, the Supreme Court issued two decisions in December that restricted the grounds on which libel judgments could be brought against journalists and others.

Colonized by French and British settlers in the 17th and 18th centuries, Canada was secured by the British Crown under the terms of the Treaty of Paris in 1763. After granting home rule in 1867, Britain retained a theoretical right to override the Canadian Parliament until 1982, when Canadians established complete control over their own constitution.

After a dozen years of center-left Liberal Party rule, the Conservative Party emerged from the 2006 parliamentary elections with a plurality and established a fragile minority government. Following setbacks in several of the 2007 provincial elections, the Conservatives expanded their position in the 2008 national elections. While capturing 143 seats in Parliament, the Conservatives failed to attain a majority. The Liberals, the principal opposition party, secured only 77 seats, but subsequently formed an alliance with the social democratic New Democratic Party (NDP) and the Quebec-based Bloc Quebecois, in an attempt to displace the Conservatives with a coalition government. Prime Minister Stephen Harper, the leader of the Conservative Party, suspended Parliament in December 2008 to prevent a confidence vote, which his government was likely to lose.

Since the 2001 terrorist attacks on the United States, Canada has struggled to find a balance between ensuring the country's security and safeguarding civil liberties. A number of laws adopted soon after the 2001 attacks have been modified or struck down by the courts. In May 2008, the Supreme Court determined that the United States violated the rights of Omar Khadr, a Canadian who had been held at the Guantanamo Bay prison facility since the age of 15. The court rebuked the Canadian government for having allowed its intelligence agents to interview Khadr and share information with U.S. officials. The government has also been criticized for its policy of handing over prisoners detained in conflict in Afghanistan to Afghan authorities. Diplomats have asserted that many of those given over to Afghan officials were tortured. A parliamentary committee launched an investigation of the detainee issue in fall 2009, and opposition critics claimed that Prime Minister Harper dismissed Parliament on December 30 in part to avoid the controversy that would have surrounded the committee's findings.

Two Supreme Court decisions, both issued in December 2009, significantly changed the terms under which libel cases could be brought against journalists. The rulings establish a "responsible journalism" defense for reporters whose stories are deemed in the public interest. The decisions also extend protection against libel suits to internet journalists.

An intense debate has raged over Canada's participation in a NATO-led mission to fight the Taliban in Afghanistan. In November 2009, the government announced its intention to withdraw its forces from the military zone in 2011.

Political Rights and Civil Liberties: Canada is an electoral democracy. The country is governed by a prime minister, a cabinet, and Parliament, which consists of an elected 308-member House of Commons and an appointed 105-member Senate. Senators may serve until age 75, and elections for the lower house have been held at least every five years. However, a law enacted in 2007 stipulated that lower-house elections would be held every four years, with early elections called only if the government lost a parliamentary no-confidence vote. The British monarch remains head of state, represented by a ceremonial governor-general who is appointed on the advice of the prime minister. As a result of government canvassing, Canada has nearly 100 percent voter registration. Prisoners have the right to vote in federal elections, as do citizens who have lived abroad for fewer than five years. However, voter turnout in the 2008 election, at 60 percent, was one of the lowest in Canadian history.

Political parties operate freely. The main parties are the Conservative Party, the Liberal Party, the Bloc Quebecois, and the NDP.

Civil liberties have been protected since 1982 by the federal Charter of Rights and Freedoms, but they are limited by the constitutional "notwithstanding" clause, which permits provincial governments to exempt themselves with respect to individual provisions in their jurisdictions. Quebec has used the clause to retain its provincial language law, which restricts the use of languages other than French on signs. The provincial governments exercise significant autonomy.

In 2004, the Supreme Court upheld legislation that places a limit on the amount lobbying groups can spend on advertisements that support or oppose political candidates, a measure designed to prevent corruption. While Canada has a reputation for vigorous prosecution of corruption involving public officials, the country has endured several high-profile scandals in recent years. Nonetheless, Canada is regarded as a society with a low level of official corruption. Canada was ranked 8 out of 180 countries surveyed in Transparency International's 2009 Corruption Perceptions Index.

The media are generally free, although they exercise self-censorship in areas such as violence on television, and there is concern that this tendency may also apply to coverage of the country's minority groups, especially Muslims. Limitations on freedom of expression range from unevenly enforced "hate laws" and restrictions on pornography to rules on reporting. Some civil libertarians have expressed concern over an amendment to the criminal code that gives judges wide latitude in determining what constitutes hate speech on the internet. However, in 2009, the country's human rights tribunal found unconstitutional an anti-hate speech law that targeted telephone and internet messages. The decision is expected to restrict the Canadian Human Rights Commission's efforts to bring cases against alleged hate speech on the internet. Advocates of freedom of expression have grown increasingly concerned over legal cases filed by the human rights commission against journalists who write critically about Muslims and Islam, as well as other minority groups. There is a high degree of media concentration. On a positive note, in December 2009, the Supreme Court issued two decisions strengthening protections for journalists by restricting the ground on which libel judgments can be brought against journalists and others.

Religious expression is free and diverse. Academic freedom is respected.

Freedom of assembly is respected, and many political and quasi-political organizations function freely. Trade unions and business associations enjoy high levels of membership and are free and well organized.

The judiciary is independent. Canada's criminal law is based on legislation enacted by Parliament; its tort and contract law is based on English common law, with the exception of Quebec, where it is based on the French civil code. While Canada's crime rate is low by regional standards, it has experienced a growing problem from the growth of criminal gangs, often involved in the illegal drug trade. Recently, civil liberties' groups have criticized the police over the use of Tasers on criminal suspects. In 2009, Amnesty International reported that 26 people have died in Canada since 2003 after being subjected to Tasers.

Canada maintains relatively liberal immigration policies. However, concern has mounted over the possible entry into Canada of immigrants involved in terrorist missions. The 2002 Immigration and Refugee Protection Act seeks to continue the tradition of liberal immigration by providing additional protection for refugees while making it more difficult for potential terrorists, people involved in organized crime, and war criminals to enter the country. Some officials have also raised questions about Canada's rules allowing immigrants to maintain dual citizenship. About 10 percent of foreign-born Canadians hold passports from another country, leading critics to charge that some immigrants use Canadian citizenship primarily as a safety net while maintaining principal loyalty to their country of origin. Others have objected more broadly to Canada's policies of multiculturalism in education, law, and social life.

The authorities have taken important steps to protect the rights of native groups, although some contend that indigenous people remain subject to discrimination. Indigenous groups continue to lag badly on practically every social indicator, including those for education, health, and unemployment. There are frequent controversies over control of land in various provinces. At the same time, government proposals to facilitate the assimilation of native groups have met with stiff opposition from the groups' chiefs.

The country boasts a generous welfare system that supplements the largely open, competitive economy.

Women's rights are protected in law and practice. Women hold 22 percent of seats in Parliament, have made major gains in the economy, and are well represented in such professions as medicine and law. However, women's rights advocates report high rates of violence against women in indigenous communities. Canada in 2005 became one of the few countries in the world to legalize same-sex marriage.

CapeVerde

Political Rights: 1
Civil Liberties: 1
Status: Free

Population: 509,000
Capital: Praia

Ten-Year Ratings Timeline For Year Under Review (Political Rights, Civil Liberties, Status)

2000	2001	2002	2003	2004	2005	2006	2007	2008	2009
1,2F	1,2F	1,2F	1,1F	1,1F	1,1F	1,1F	1,1F	1,1F	1,1F

Overview:

Cape Verde continued to serve as a model for political rights and civil liberties in Africa in 2009. In a sign of the country's generally good governance, the World Food Programme agreed to transfer its school feeding responsibilities to Cape Verdean authorities, and swift government action late in the year helped to contain the country's first outbreak of dengue fever.

After achieving independence from Portugal in 1975, Cape Verde was governed for 16 years as a Marxist, one-party state under the African Party for the Independence of Guinea and Cape Verde, later renamed the African Party for the Independence of Cape Verde (PAICV). In 1991, the country became the first former Portuguese colony in Africa to abandon Marxist political and economic systems, and the Movement for Democracy (MPD) won a landslide victory in the first democratic elections that year. In 1995, the MPD was returned to power with 59 percent of the vote.

President Antonio Mascarenhas Monteiro's mandate ended in 2001, after he had served two terms. That February's presidential election was spectacularly close, with PAICV candidate Pedro Verona Rodrigues Pires defeating Carlos Alberto

Wahnon de Carvalho Veiga of the MPD by just 13 votes in the second round. Despite the thin margin, the results were widely accepted. The PAICV had also captured a majority in legislative elections the previous month.

The January 2006 legislative elections had a similar outcome, with the PAICV taking 41 of the 72 seats, the MPD placing second with 29, and the Democratic and Independent Cape Verdean Union(UCID), a smaller opposition party, securing the remaining 2 seats. Pires won a new five-year mandate in the February presidential election, garnering 51.2 percent of the vote. His closest rival, Veiga, claimed that the results were fraudulent, but they were endorsed by international election monitors.

In June 2007, the parliament unanimously passed new electoral code provisions aimed at strengthening the National Electoral Commission's transparency and independence. Voter registration for municipal elections held in May 2008 marked the debut of a biometric registry. The opposition MPD won a marginal victory, capturing 11 out of 22 municipalities, including the capital.

Large numbers of migrants from other African countries continue to stop in Cape Verde while trying to reach Europe. In 2007, the government announced that it would seek to negotiate exemptions from clauses guaranteeing free movement between members of the Economic Community of West African States (ECOWAS). Cape Verde and the European Union (EU) signed an agreement the following year under which Cape Verdeans would have easier access to certain EU member states, in particular for seasonal work, while Cape Verde would undertake specific commitments to contain illegal migration to Europe.

In addition to its role in the flow of migrants, Cape Verde is increasingly serving as a transit point for drug trafficking between Latin America and Europe. According to data cited by the Associated Press in 2008, Cape Verdean passport-holders accounted for 25 percent of all West African drug traffickers arrested in Europe. The United Nations, ECOWAS, the EU, and the United States have recognized this increase and have committed funds to aid in Cape Verde's policing activities.

Cape Verde lacks natural resources and has little arable land; unemployment rates remain at roughly 20 percent, and there is growing income inequality. Nevertheless, the economy has benefited from high levels of remittances from citizens working overseas, a boom in service-oriented industries, and increasing tourism. Cape Verde joined the World Trade Organization in 2008, capping nine years of negotiations. And in an indication of the country's good governance, the UN World Food Programme announced in 2009 that it would hand over its school feeding program to Cape Verdean officials in 2010.

In November 2009, Cape Verde declared a national emergency to contain its first dengue fever outbreak, which affected more than 14,000 people, including Prime Minister Jose Maria Pereira Neves. Swift government action and foreign assistance were credited with mitigating the outbreak.

Political Rights and Civil Liberties:

Cape Verde is an electoral democracy. The president and members of the 72-seat National Assembly are elected by universal suffrage for five-year terms. The prime minister, who nominates the other members of the cabinet, is nominated by the National Assembly and appointed by the president. International observers considered the 2006 presidential and legislative elections to be free and fair.

The left-leaning PAICV has dominated Cape Verdean politics for most of the period since independence. The main opposition party is the centrist MPD. The only other party holding seats in the National Assembly is the UCID.

Cape Verde received the second-highest ranking in the 2009 Ibrahim Index of African Governance, and placed in the top five in all of the index's categories. The U.S. government gave the country a vote of confidence in 2005 by agreeing to provide $110 million in aid from the Millennium Challenge Account, based on a positive evaluation of its governance and anticorruption initiatives. However, the U.S. State Department reported in 2009 that police corruption was increasing. Cape Verde was ranked 46 out of 180 countries in Transparency International's 2009 Corruption Perceptions Index, making it the third-best performer in Africa.

While government authorization is needed to publish newspapers and other periodicals, freedom of the press is legally guaranteed and generally respected in practice. The independent press is small but vigorous, and there are several private and community-run radio stations. State-run media include a radio broadcaster and a television station. Licenses were issued to four private television stations in 2007, but only two were operating as of 2009. The government does not impede or monitor internet access.

According to the 2009 U.S. Department of State's International Religious Freedom Report, there were no societal or governmental incidents of religious intolerance, and the constitution requires the separation of church and state. However, the vast majority of Cape Verdeans belong to the Roman Catholic Church, which enjoys a somewhat privileged status. Academic freedom is respected.

Freedoms of assembly and association are legally guaranteed and observed in practice. Nongovernmental organizations operate freely. The constitution also protects the right to unionize, and workers may form and join unions without restriction. Roughly 25 percent of the workforce is unionized, but collective bargaining is reportedly rare.

Cape Verde's judiciary is independent. However, the capacity and efficiency of the courts are limited, and the U.S. State Department has reported that pretrial detentions of a year or more are common. In May 2007, National Assembly president Aristides Lima acknowledged that the judicial police force lacked funding and was unable to cover the entire country. Prison conditions are poor and characterized by overcrowding. While police beatings of detainees have been reported, increased reform and media coverage have seemingly mitigated such abuses. Juveniles are often incarcerated with adult populations.

Ethnic divisions are not a salient problem in Cape Verde, although tensions occasionally flare between the authorities and West African immigrants.

Three new female members of parliament were elected in 2006, bringing the total to 11. The government amended the penal code in 2004 to include sex crimes and verbal and mental abuse against women and children as punishable acts, but the government has not effectively enforced the law, according to the U.S. State Department. The government is a signatory to the African Protocol on the Rights of Women, which came into force in 2005. The protocol seeks to set international legal standards for women's rights, such as the criminalization of female genital mutilation and the prohibition of abuse of women in advertising and pornography. However, despite legal prohibitions, domestic violence and discrimination against women remain commonplace.

Central African Republic

Political Rights: 5
Civil Liberties: 5
Status: Partly Free

Population: 4,511,000
Capital: Tirana

Ten-Year Ratings Timeline For Year Under Review (Political Rights, Civil Liberties, Status)

2000	2001	2002	2003	2004	2005	2006	2007	2008	2009
3,4PF	5,5PF	5,5PF	7,5NF	6,5NF	5,4PF	5,4PF	5,5PF	5,5PF	5,5PF

Overview: Despite the installation of a consensus government in January 2009, rebel groups continued to clash with government forces during the year, creating thousands of new internally displaced persons and refugees. In October, former president Ange-Felix Patasse returned to the country after six years in exile with the intention of running in the 2010 presidential election.

The Central African Republic (CAR) gained independence from France in 1960 after a period of brutal colonial exploitation. Colonel Jean-Bedel Bokassa seized power from President David Dacko in a 1966 coup, but French forces helped to restore Dacko in 1979. He was then deposed again by General Andre Kolingba in 1981.

Mounting political pressure led Kolingba to introduce a multiparty system in 1991, and Ange-Felix Patasse, leader of the Movement for the Liberation of the Central African People (MLPC), was elected president in 1993. With French assistance, he survived three attempted coups between 1996 and 1997. French forces were replaced by African peacekeepers in 1997, and the United Nations took over peacekeeping duties the following year.

Patasse won a second six-year term in 1999. International observers judged the election to be relatively free, although irregularities were reported. UN peacekeepers withdrew in 2000, and while Patasse overcame a coup attempt by Kolingba in 2001, he was ousted by General Francois Bozize in 2003, allegedly with backing from Chadian president Idriss Deby.

Bozize initiated a transition back to civilian rule, and voters approved a new constitution in December 2004. The general then ran for president as an independent with the backing of the National Convergence Kwa Na Kwa (KNK) coalition, winning 65 percent of the vote in a May 2005 runoff against MLPC candidate Martin Ziguele. The KNK won 42 of 105 seats in the National Assembly, securing a majority with the help of several smaller parties and independents. The MLPC, the second-largest grouping, won just 11 seats.

In early 2005, the rebel Army for the Restoration of the Republic and Democracy (APRD), supported by forces loyal to Patasse, launched an insurgency in the northwest. In the northeast, another conflict erupted between the government and the Union of Democratic Forces for Unity (UFDR), consisting of former Bozize supporters and members of the largely Muslim Gula ethnic group. Destructive rebel assaults on Birao and other towns continued through 2006, and in early 2007, the Central African People's Democratic Front (FDPC) launched yet another insurgency in the northwest.

In September 2007, the UN Security Council authorized a new UN mission in the Central African Republic and Chad (MINURCAT) and a related European Union (EU) peacekeeping force, but these were limited to the northeastern CAR and tasked primarily with addressing the spillover effects of the conflict in Sudan's Darfur region.

After a number of abortive peace agreements, the National Assembly in September 2008 passed an amnesty law providing government and rebel forces with immunity for abuses committed after March 15, 2003. Talks resumed in December when President Bozize, rebel groups, and opposition leaders agreed on the establishment of an interim government to lead the country until the next presidential and legislative elections in 2010. The December peace talks, known as the Inclusive Political Dialogue, outlined a Disarmament, Demobilization, and Reintegration (DDR) program in preparation for the 2010 elections.

The "consensus government" was installed in January 2009, but some rebel groups remained dissatisfied with government performance. In February, the FDPC and the Movement of Central African Liberators for Justice (MLCJ) declared that they would resume violence, and raids against the government by the FDPC continued through May. Both groups signed onto the DDR program in July. By December 2009, the UN reported that the all rebel groups were participating in the peace process except the Convention of Patriots for Justice and Peace (CPJP). CPJP has led attacks against the government in the northeast, displacing some 6,400 people internally and driving an additional 9,000 into Chad. CPJP leader Charles Massi, who served as defense minister under Patasse, was arrested by Chadian authorities in May. Massi was released in July, but re-arrested in December.

Beginning in June, clashes between the Ugandan military and the Lord's Resistance Army, a Ugandan rebel group, intensified in southeastern CAR, near Obo and M'Boki. The International Committee of the Red Cross estimated in October 2009 that the cross-border fighting had internally displaced over 4,500 CAR residents and forced 1,400 refugees into the country from the Democratic Republic of Congo (DRC).

UNICEF estimated in early 2008 that there are some 197,000 internally displaced persons in the CAR, and that roughly a quarter of the country's four million citizens have been affected by armed conflict. Despite the country's abundant natural resources, some 80 percent of the population relies on subsistence agriculture. Decades of conflict and poor governance have led to economic and social collapse. The CAR earned the fourth-worst ranking on the UN Development Programme's 2009 Human Development Index.

Political Rights and Civil Liberties: The CAR is not an electoral democracy. Although presidential and parliamentary elections were held in 2005, they were marked by some irregularities and criticized by opposition candidates as unfair. The president, who is limited to two five-year terms, appoints the cabinet and dominates the legislative and judicial branches. Members of the unicameral, 105-seat National Assembly are elected by popular vote for five-year terms. Though the KNK coalition is the country's leading political force, other parties operate freely, including the MLPC and former coup leader Andre Kolingba's Central African Democratic Assembly.

After much negotiation, the government passed a revised electoral code in November 2009 and formed an electoral commission for the 2010 presidential and legislative races. First-round voting will take place on April 18, 2010. In October 2009, former president Ange-Felix Patasse returned from a six-year exile in Togo and announced his candidacy for president. He will run as an independent, as the MLPC had already selected former prime minister Martin Ziguele as its candidate. Patasse is also tainted by past associations with Jean-Pierre Bemba, a former DRC rebel leader, who was currently facing trial before the International Criminal Court for alleged war crimes and crimes against humanity.

Corruption remains pervasive, despite some steps toward reform in recent years. Diamonds account for about half of the country's export earnings, but a large percentage of the stones are thought to circumvent official channels. The Central African Republic ranks 158 out of 180 countries surveyed in Transparency International's 2009 Corruption Perceptions Index.

The government generally respects the right to free speech, but many journalists practice self-censorship. It remains a crime to broadcast information that is "false" or that could incite ethnic or religious tension. According to the U.S. State Department, laws providing journalists with access to information do not specifically guarantee access to government information. Insecurity prevents journalists from traveling freely outside the capital. The state dominates the broadcast media, but some private radio stations exist, including a Roman Catholic station and a UN-supported station. Several private newspapers offer competing views, though they have limited influence due to low literacy levels and high poverty rates. There are no government restrictions on the internet, but the vast majority of the population is unable to access this resource.

The constitution guarantees religious freedom. However, the government prohibits activities that it considers subversive or fundamentalist, and the constitution bans the formation of religion-based parties. Academic freedom is generally respected.

Freedoms of assembly and association are constitutionally protected and generally upheld in practice. However, permission is required to hold public meetings and demonstrations; authorities sometimes deny such requests on the grounds that they could stoke ethnic or religious tensions. Insecurity in the north continues to hinder the operations of aid groups, forcing a number to withdraw from volatile areas. In June 2009, a Red Cross employee was killed by armed men in Birao, and two French aid workers were abducted there in November. All associations must register with the Interior Ministry. The rights to unionize and strike are constitutionally protected and generally respected, though only a small percentage of workers are unionized, primarily those in the public sector.

Corruption, political interference, and lack of training undermine the judiciary. Judges are appointed by the president, and proceedings are prone to executive influence. Limitations on police searches and detention are often ignored. While the penal code prohibits torture, police brutality remains a serious problem. Prison conditions are poor. The military and members of the presidential guard have committed human rights abuses, including extrajudicial killings, with impunity.

Members of northern ethnic groups, especially President Francois Bozize's Baya group, hold all key positions in the government and the military, and discrimination against indigenous ethnic groups, such as the Aka, persists. Insecurity restricts the movement of citizens and greatly undermines the protection of private property.

Constitutional guarantees for women's rights are not enforced, especially in rural areas. Violence against women is common, with instances of rape widespread in conflict areas. Abortion is prohibited in all circumstances. The U.S. State Department's 2009 Trafficking in Persons Report placed the CAR on its Tier 2 Watch List due to the government's failure to pass a 2006 draft law against trafficking. In January 2009, new labor code articles outlawed forced and bonded labor.

Chad

Political Rights: 7
Civil Liberties: 6
Status: Not Free

Population: 10,329,000
Capital: N'Djamena

Ten-Year Ratings Timeline For Year Under Review (Political Rights, Civil Liberties, Status)

2000	2001	2002	2003	2004	2005	2006	2007	2008	2009
6,5NF	6,5NF	6,5NF	6,5NF	6,5NF	6,5NF	6,6NF	7,6NF	7,6NF	7,6NF

Overview:
In May 2009, less than a week after the governments of Chad and Sudan signed an accord on normalizing their relations, a new alliance of Chadian rebel groups launched an offensive from bases in Sudan's Darfur region. Chadian and Sudanese officials met again in October to reaffirm their commitment to peace. A UN peacekeeping mission replaced a European Union force in eastern Chad in March, but as of September the UN force still had less than half of the recommended personnel.

Since gaining independence from France in 1960, Chad has been beset by civil conflict and rebellions. Hissene Habre seized control in 1982 and led a one-party dictatorship characterized by widespread atrocities against individuals and ethnic groups that were perceived as threats to the regime. In 1989, Idriss Deby, a military commander, launched a rebellion against Habre from Sudan. With support from Libya and no opposition from French troops stationed in Chad, Deby overthrew Habre in 1990.

Deby won a presidential election held under a new constitution in 1996 despite the ongoing threat of rebel violence. In 1997 legislative elections, Deby's Patriotic Salvation Movement (MPS) party won 65 of the 125 seats. International observers charged that both elections were marred by irregularities.

Deby was reelected president in 2001, and the six opposition candidates were briefly detained for alleging that the election results were fraudulent. The MPS secured 110 seats in the recently enlarged, 155-seat National Assembly during the 2002 legislative elections, which were boycotted by several opposition parties. Voters approved the elimination of presidential term limits in a 2005 constitutional referendum, although the balloting featured irregularities and the government cracked down on the media during the campaign.

Security forces, assisted by French intelligence and air support, repelled an April 2006 attack on the capital by the United Front for Change (FUC) rebel group. The May presidential election was then held on schedule despite an opposition boycott, and Deby secured a third term. The military, again with French support, launched a new assault on rebel forces in September, and in November the government declared a six-month state of emergency for the capital and most of the east, including a ban on media coverage of sensitive issues.

Several hundred Chadians were killed in March 2007 attacks that the government attributed to Sudanese and Chadian Arab militias. The government and four rebel groups reached an agreement to end fighting in early October 2007, but renewed clashes soon erupted between the government and several rebel alliances.

In early February 2008, a formation of some 2,000 rebel fighters attacked the capital. Although the two sides soon agreed on a ceasefire and the rebels withdrew, Deby declared a state of emergency, suspending due process rights and tightening already harsh media restrictions. Human rights groups accused the regime of extrajudicial detention and killing of suspected rebels, their supporters, and members of the Goran ethnic group, some of whom were involved in the rebel assault. Three prominent opposition politicians—Lol Mahamat Choua, Ngarjely Yorongar, and Ibni Oumar Mahamat Saleh—were arrested during the attack. Choua was later released and then placed under house arrest, while Yorongar was freed and ultimately received asylum in France, and Saleh was revealed to have died in custody. The state of emergency was lifted on March 15, but fighting continued in the east during the year.

Deby and Sudanese president Omar al-Bashir continued to trade accusations in 2008 that one was supporting rebels on the other's territory. Al-Bashir cut diplomatic ties with Chad in May following a rebel attack on Khartoum that al-Bashir accused Deby of supporting, but the Sudanese leader agreed to restore ties at a meeting in July.

On May 3, 2009, the Chadian and Sudanese governments signed an accord aimed at normalizing relations between the two countries. However, less than a week later, the Union of Resistance Forces (UFR)—an alliance of eight rebel groups that had formed in January—launched an attack from its base in Sudan's Darfur region. Violence along the border increased over the subsequent months, and in July Chadian planes bombed targets in Darfur. Also in July, the government signed a peace agreement with a coalition of smaller rebel groups, the National Movement, which had been active in eastern Chad. In October Chadian and Sudanese authorities met again and reaffirmed their commitment to "definitive peace."

After years of regular fighting in the region, Chad is now home to some 180,000 internally displaced persons as well as more than 320,000 refugees from Darfur and the Central African Republic. The UN Mission in the Central African Republic and Chad (MINURCAT), formed in 2007 to help care for and protect these civilians, added a military component in March 2009 to take over the responsibilities of a parallel European Union peacekeeping force (EUFOR). However, as of September, the new UN force had less than half of the 5,200 personnel recommended for the mission.

Chad remains mired in poverty despite its substantial oil revenues. In September 2008, the World Bank withdrew from a project launched in 2001, in which the bank financed development of the oil sector and Chad agreed to invest the revenue in poverty-alleviation projects. The Chadian government had repeatedly sought greater control over revenues, and the bank had suspended loans for half of 2006 due to breaches of the agreement.

Political Rights and Civil Liberties: Chad is not an electoral democracy. The country has never experienced a free and fair transfer of power through elections. The president is elected for five-year terms, and a 2005 constitutional amendment abolished term limits. The 2006 presidential election was held shortly after a rebel assault on the capital despite calls for a postponement. Many opposition members boycotted the balloting, which was reportedly marred by irregularities, and voter turnout may have been as low as 10 percent in some areas. The executive branch dominates the judicial and legislative branches, and the president appoints the prime minister. The unicameral National Assembly consists of 155 members elected for four-year terms. The last legislative elections, in 2002, also featured widespread irregularities. The legislative elections originally due in 2006 have been repeatedly postponed; they are currently scheduled for 2010.

There are over 70 political parties, although a number were created by the government to divide the opposition. Only the ruling MPS has significant influence. Despite rivalries within President Idriss Deby's northeastern Zaghawa ethnic group, members of that and other northern ethnic groups continue to control Chad's political and economic systems, causing resentment among the country's more than 200 other ethnic groups.

Corruption is rampant within Deby's inner circle. Weaknesses in revenue management and oversight facilitate the diversion of oil revenues from national development projects to private interests as well as growing military expenditures. Chad was ranked 175 out of 180 countries surveyed in Transparency International's 2009 Corruption Perceptions Index.

Freedom of expression is severely restricted, and self-censorship is common. Broadcast media are controlled by the state. The High Council of Communication (HCC) exerts control over the content of most radio broadcasts, and while there are roughly a dozen private stations, they face high licensing fees and the threat of closure for critical coverage. Following the 2008 rebel attack on the capital, the government imposed a new press law that increased the maximum penalty for false news and defamation to three years in prison, and the maximum penalty for insulting the president to five years. It also requires permission from both the prosecutor's office and the HCC to establish a newspaper. Meanwhile, the HCC banned reporting on the activities of rebels or any other information that could harm national unity. A small number of private newspapers have circulated in the capital, and internet access is not restricted, but the reach of both print and online media is limited by poverty, illiteracy, and inadequate infrastructure. In October 2009, Cameroonian-born editor Innocent Ebode was expelled for writing a column that criticized a minister's suggestion that President Deby be awarded the Nobel Peace Prize. After the government ordered the suspension of his newspaper, *La Voix*, Ebode returned to Ndjamena to challenge the ruling. Ebode was abducted from his home in December and was reportedly being held at the Cameroonian border.

Although Chad is a secular state, religion is a divisive force. Muslims, who make up slightly more than half of the population, hold a disproportionately large number of senior government posts, and some policies favor Islam in practice, such as government sponsorship of the pilgrimage to Mecca. At the same time, the authorities have banned Muslim groups that are seen as promoting violence, and security forces clashed with supporters of a radical Islamist preacher in 2008. The government does not restrict academic freedom.

Despite the constitutional guarantee of free assembly, the authorities ban demonstrations by groups thought to be critical of the government. Insecurity in the east and south has severely hindered the activities of humanitarian organizations in recent years. The constitution guarantees the rights to strike and unionize, but a 2007 law imposed new limits on public sector workers' right to strike.

The rule of law and the judicial system remain weak, with courts heavily influenced by the political leadership. Former president Hissene Habre was sentenced to death in absentia—along with 11 suspected rebel leaders—by a Chadian court in August 2008; an additional 31 suspected rebels received life sentences. Habre, who lives in exile in Senegal, was scheduled to face a trial there for crimes against humanity allegedly committed during his presidency. However, in its first ruling in December 2009, the African Court on Human and People's Rights dismissed the case for lack of jurisdiction.

Civilian leaders do not maintain effective control of the security forces, which routinely ignore constitutional protections regarding search, seizure, and detention. Human rights groups credibly accuse the security forces and rebel groups of killing and torturing with impunity. Overcrowding, disease, and malnutrition make prison conditions harsh, and many inmates are held for years without charge.

Clashes are common between Christian farmers of the various southern ethnic groups and Muslim Arab groups living largely in the north. Turmoil linked to ethnic and religious differences is exacerbated by clan rivalries and external interference along the insecure borders. Communal tensions in eastern Chad have worsened due to the proliferation of small arms and ongoing disputes over the use of land and water resources.

The government restricts the movement of citizens within the country, a practice that has increased in tandem with the civil conflicts. In February 2008, Deby called for the destruction of "illegal" structures in N'Djamena, and Amnesty International estimates that 3,700 homes in the city were demolished by January 2009. Most affected residents received no warning, compensation, or alternative housing.

The army and its paramilitary forces, as well as rebel forces, have recruited child soldiers. The government has been slow to follow through on its agreement to demobilize them. UNICEF and the Red Cross demanded that the government release 80 child soldiers who were captured during a May 2009 battle.

Chadian women face widespread discrimination and violence. Female genital mutilation is illegal but routinely practiced by several ethnic groups. Chad is a source, transit, and destination country for child trafficking, and the government has not made significant efforts to eliminate the problem. The U.S. State Department demoted Chad to Tier 3, the worst-possible rating, in its 2009 Trafficking in Persons Report.

Chile

Political Rights: 1
Civil Liberties: 1
Status: Free

Population: 16,970,000
Capital: Santiago

Ten-Year Ratings Timeline For Year Under Review (Political Rights, Civil Liberties, Status)

2000	2001	2002	2003	2004	2005	2006	2007	2008	2009
2,2F	2,2F	2,1F	1,1F	1,1F	1,1F	1,1F	1,1F	1,1F	1,1F

Overview:
Sebastian Pinera of the center-right Coalition for Change led the first round of the presidential election in December, and a runoff was scheduled for January 2010. His candidacy was supported by several high-level defectors from the ruling center-left Concertacion bloc, whose nominee—former president Eduardo Frei—would be Pinera's runoff opponent. Pinera's early success came despite the popularity of outgoing president Michelle Bachelet and her administration's robust social-welfare programs.

The Republic of Chile was founded after independence from Spain in 1818. Democratic rule predominated in the 20th century until 1973, when General Augusto Pinochet led a military coup against President Salvador Allende. An estimated 3,000 people were killed or "disappeared" under Pinochet's regime. The 1980 constitution provided for a plebiscite in which voters could bar another presidential term for the general. When the poll was held in 1988, some 55 percent of voters rejected eight more years of military rule, and competitive presidential and legislative elections were scheduled for the following year.

Christian Democrat Patricio Aylwin of the center-left bloc Concertacion (Coalition of Parties for Democracy) won the presidential vote, ushering in a period of regular democratic power transfers. He was succeeded by Concertacion candidates Eduardo Frei, elected in 1993, and Ricardo Lagos, elected in 1999.

In the first step in what would become a years-long effort to hold Pinochet responsible for human rights atrocities, the former leader was detained in London in 1998 under an extradition order from Spain. After being released for health reasons in 2000, he returned to Chile, where he was eventually indicted in 2004 for tax evasion and two outstanding human rights cases. A series of pretrial legal battles over his health status and immunity from prosecution ended with a September 2006 Supreme Court decision that cleared the way for his trial. However, Pinochet died in December of that year.

Michelle Bachelet, Lagos's health and defense minister, was elected president in January 2006. Because of Concertacion's strong performance in the 2005 legislative elections and a reform that eliminated the institution of unelected senators, she became the first president to govern with majorities in both houses of Congress. However, this advantage was relatively short-lived. In December 2007, the Christian Democratic Party suffered a serious split, causing six of its lawmakers to break away and end Concertacion's majority.

Early in her term, Bachelet faced huge student demonstrations demanding education improvements, and oversaw a botched reform of Santiago's public transit system. Concertacion's strength was also undermined in 2009 by infighting among its four member parties, three of which suffered defections. However, Bachelet presided over popular spending projects, including the construction of new hospitals, homes, and nursery schools. In 2009, the government was able to continue social spending despite the global economic downturn, as it had saved copper revenues aggressively during the previous commodities boom. Additional welfare programs in 2009 included monthly cash transfers to senior citizens without a pension in the poorest 50 percent of the population.

Despite Bachelet's personal popularity, Concertacion candidate Eduardo Frei, the former president, garnered only 30 percent in the first round of the presidential election in December. Businessman and former senator Sebastian Pinera of the center-right Coalition for Change led the voting with 44 percent, and he was set to face Frei in a January 2010 runoff. Frei's candidacy was weakened in part by Marco Enriquez-Ominami, a renegade Concertacion lawmaker, who ran as an independent and won 20 percent of the first-round vote. In the concurrent legislative election, the Coalition for Change edged out Concertacion in the 120-seat lower house, 58 seats to 57, with the remainder going to small parties and independents. The Concertacion also picked up one seat in the Senate.

Political Rights and Civil Liberties:

Chile is an electoral democracy. Elections are considered free and fair. The constitution, which took effect in 1981 and has been amended several times, currently calls for a president elected for a single four-year term, and a bicameral National Congress. The Senate's 38 members serve eight-year terms, with half coming up for election every four years, and the 120-member Chamber of Deputies is elected for four years.

In 2005, the Senate passed reforms that repealed some of the last vestiges of military rule, ending authoritarian curbs on the legislative branch and restoring the president's right to remove top military commanders. The reform package included the abolition of the Senate's nine unelected seats and reduced the presidential term from six years to four. In September 2009, a bill was introduced to repeal another relic of the former regime, the Copper Reserve Law, which obliged the state-owned copper producer Codelco to transfer 10 percent of its earnings to the military.

The major political groupings in Chile include the center-left Concertacion, composed of the Christian Democratic Party, the Socialist Party, the Party for Democracy, and the Social Democratic Radical Party; the center-right Alliance coalition, consisting of the Independent Democratic Union and the National Renewal party; and the Communist Party. The Coalition for Change, encompassing the Alliance coalition, independents, and some Concertacion defectors, was formed in May 2009.

Congress passed significant transparency and campaign finance laws in 2003 that contributed to Chile's reputation as Latin America's best-governed country. In 2007, Congress passed a law designed to further improve transparency, in part by protecting public employees who expose corruption. Transparency International's 2009 Corruption Perceptions Index gave Chile a ranking of 25 out of 180 countries surveyed, making it the best performer in Latin America.

Guarantees of free speech are generally respected, and the media operate without constraint. Some laws barring defamation of state institutions remain on the books. The print media are dominated by two right-leaning companies, but the television market is considered highly diverse. A freedom of information law enacted in 2008 was praised by civil society groups. There are no government restrictions on the internet.

The constitution provides for freedom of religion, and the government generally upholds this right in practice. The government does not restrict academic freedom.

The right to assemble peacefully is largely respected, and the constitution guarantees the right of association and collective bargaining, which the government has also upheld. Despite laws protecting worker and union rights, antiunion practices by private employers are reportedly common.

The constitution provides for an independent judiciary, and the courts are generally free from political interference. The right to legal counsel is constitutionally guaranteed, but indigent defendants have not always received effective representation. Chilean courts have convicted several former military officers of committing heinous crimes during military rule. In September 2009, arrest warrants were issued for 129 former security officials tied to disappearances and killings from that period.

The government has developed effective mechanisms to investigate and punish police abuse and corruption. Chile's prisons are overcrowded, and inmates suffer from physical abuse as well as substandard medical and food services.

Indigenous groups comprise approximately 5 percent of Chile's population. While they still experience societal discrimination, indigenous poverty levels are declining, aided by government scholarships and land transfers. However, violence and land seizures increased in 2009 due to frustration among indigenous groups over the pace of the government's land return program.

Violence against women and children remains a problem, though gender discrimination is on the decline. In 2004, Congress passed a law that legalized divorce; Chile had been one of only a handful of countries in the world to prohibit divorce. President Michelle Bachelet made great strides to reduce gender discrimination. She initially fulfilled a campaign promise by appointing women to half of the positions in her cabinet, and in 2006, she helped enact a new public sector labor code that removed job candidates' gender from applications and mandated job training during regular working hours. A breastfeeding law passed in 2007 expanded the rights of women to nurse their infants during working hours, and pension reforms in 2008 provided a range of benefits for female homemakers, particularly those with low incomes. While a quota law to promote political participation by women is still pending, Congress passed a law in May 2009 that aimed to eliminate the pay gap between men and women performing the same work.

China

Political Rights: 7
Civil Liberties: 6
Status: Not Free

Population: 1,331,398,000
Capital: Beijing

Note: The numerical ratings and status listed above do not reflect conditions in Hong Kong or Tibet, which are examined in separate reports.

Ten-Year Ratings Timeline For Year Under Review (Political Rights, Civil Liberties, Status)

2000	2001	2002	2003	2004	2005	2006	2007	2008	2009
7,6NF	7,6NF	7,6NF	7,6NF	7,6NF	7,6NF	7,6NF	7,6NF	7,6NF	7,6NF

Overview: The Chinese government continued in 2009 to demonstrate high levels of insecurity and intolerance regarding citizens' political activism and demands for human rights protection. Aiming to suppress protests during politically sensitive anniversaries during the year, including the 60-year mark of the Communist Party's rise to power, the authorities resorted to lockdowns on major cities and new restrictions on the internet. The government also engaged in a renewed campaign against democracy activists, human rights lawyers, and religious or ethnic minorities, which included sentencing dozens to long prison terms following unfair trials. Repressive measures were intensified in the northwestern region of Xinjiang, especially after ethnic violence erupted there in July. Nevertheless, many citizens defied government hostility and asserted their rights to free expression and association.

The Chinese Communist Party (CCP) took power in mainland China in 1949. Party leader Mao Zedong subsequently oversaw devastating mass-mobilization campaigns, such as the Great Leap Forward (1958–61) and the Cultural Revolution (1966–76), which resulted in tens of millions of deaths. Following Mao's death in 1976, Deng Xiaoping emerged as paramount leader. Over the next two decades, he maintained the CCP's absolute rule in the political sphere while initiating limited market-based reforms to stimulate the economy.

The CCP signaled its resolve to avoid democratization with the deadly 1989 assault on prodemocracy protesters in Beijing's Tiananmen Square and surrounding areas. Following the crackdown, Jiang Zemin replaced Zhao Ziyang as general secretary of the party. Jiang was named state president in 1993 and became China's top leader following Deng's death in 1997. He continued Deng's policy of rapid economic growth, recognizing that regime legitimacy now rested largely on the CCP's ability to boost living standards. In the political sphere, Jiang maintained a hard line.

Hu Jintao succeeded Jiang as CCP general secretary in 2002, state president in 2003, and head of the military in 2004. Many observers expected Hu and Premier Wen Jiabao to implement modest political reforms to address pressing socioeconomic problems, including a rising income gap, unemployment, the lack of a social safety net, environmental degradation, and corruption. However, while it proved moderately more responsive to certain constituencies—especially the urban middle class—the government continued to exercise tight control over key institutions and intensified repression of perceived threats to the CCP's authority.

In March 2008, the National People's Congress bestowed additional five-year terms on Hu and Wen, while Shanghai party boss Xi Jinping was appointed vice president, setting the stage for him to potentially succeed Hu in 2012. In August, China hosted the Olympic Games in Beijing. Despite its pledges to ensure an open media environment and improved human rights protections surrounding the games, the government engaged in large-scale evictions, greater restrictions on freedom of movement, internet censorship for foreign journalists, and crackdowns on dissidents and minorities.

The atmosphere of heightened repression continued in 2009, as the global economic crisis, rising public protests, and the arrival of several politically sensitive anniversaries strengthened hard-liners within the CCP. The major dates included the 50th anniversary of the Dalai Lama's flight from Tibet in March, the 20th anniversary of the Tiananmen Square crackdown in June, the 10th anniversary of the CCP's ongoing suppression of the Falun Gong spiritual movement in July, and the 60th anniversary of the CCP's rise to power in October. Following the model used for the Olympics, the authorities imposed anniversary-related security measures including lockdowns on major cities, increased restrictions on internet access, and systematic arrests of rights activists, petitioners, and religious and ethnic minorities. Conditions in the Xinjiang Uighur Autonomous Region deteriorated during the year, both before and after ethnic violence erupted in July.

Popular unrest was not limited to Xinjiang. Growing anger over corruption, abuse of power, and impunity fueled tens of thousands of protests, particularly in rural areas. In response, CCP leaders committed more resources to tackling corruption, spurring the investigation of hundreds of mid- and high-ranking officials and a well-publicized crackdown on organized crime, although the effort stopped short of much-needed legal and institutional reforms. The CCP also tightened political control over the judiciary, expanded the use of surveillance equipment, and established a network of extralegal taskforces to coordinate the suppression of grassroots discontent.

Despite government repression, a growing nonprofit sector continued to provide crucial social services and increase citizens' rights awareness. In addition, bloggers, journalists, legal professionals, workers, and religious believers pushed the limits of permissible activity, sometimes effectively asserting the rights to free expression and association. Citizens managed to expose official corruption, obtain compensation for unpaid wages, and force the partial retraction of a plan to install monitoring and censorship software on personal computers. According to reports by activists and references on official websites, banned political publications continued to circulate—especially online—including the newly released memoir of ousted CCP leader Zhao Ziyang, the prodemocracy manifesto Charter 08, and the *Nine Commentaries*, a collection of editorials highly critical of CCP rule.

Also during the year, reconstruction continued in the wake of a May 2008 earthquake in Sichuan province that led to an estimated 70,000 deaths. The effort was marred, however, by the alleged misuse of relief funds and ongoing government attempts to cover up the disproportionate toll among children due to shoddily constructed school buildings. Under public pressure, the government published the death toll among children in May, setting the figure at 5,335, though many observers argued that the true count was probably much higher.

China weathered the global economic downturn better than many other countries, thanks in part to a $580 billion stimulus package. However, critics raised concerns that the government spending could boost large, underperforming state-owned enterprises at the expense of small and medium-sized companies that typically account for much of the country's tax revenue and economic dynamism. Some observers also warned that the increased investment in infrastructure could stir unrest related to land disputes.

At the international level, the CCP made concerted efforts to extend its propaganda and censorship beyond China's borders. The government invested billions of dollars in new international versions of party mouthpieces such as Xinhua News Agency, while pressuring foreign officials to silence critics at cultural events in Germany, Australia, South Korea, Bangladesh, and Taiwan. Chinese officials also successfully pressured Pakistan and Cambodia to repatriate Uighur asylum seekers, who faced possible torture and execution in China. Relations between China and Taiwan continued to thaw, as new bilateral agreements facilitated transportation links, judicial assistance, and economic investment.

Political Rights and Civil Liberties:

China is not an electoral democracy. The CCP has a monopoly on political power and its nine-member Politburo Standing Committee makes most important political decisions and sets government policy. Party members hold almost all top posts in government, the military, and the internal security services, as well as in many economic entities and social organizations.

The 3,000-member National People's Congress (NPC), which is elected for five-year terms by subnational congresses, formally elects the state president for up to two five-year terms, and confirms the premier after he is nominated by the president. However, the NPC is a largely symbolic body, meeting for just two weeks a year and serving primarily to approve proposed legislation, though members sometimes question bills before passing them. The country's only competitive elections are for village committees and urban residency councils, which hold limited authority and are generally subordinate to the local CCP committees. The nomination of candidates remains tightly controlled, and many of these elections have been marred by fraud, violence, corruption, and attacks on independent candidates. Plans to expand polls to higher levels of governance, such as townships, have stalled.

Opposition groups like the China Democracy Party are suppressed, and members are imprisoned. Prominent democracy advocate Liu Xiaobo was sentenced in December 2009 to 11 years in prison for his involvement in drafting and circulating Charter 08. At least 100 other signers of the prodemocracy manifesto were reportedly summoned for questioning following its publication. Several other democracy activists received long prison sentences during the year, including Xie Changfa, sentenced to 13 years for organizing a Hunan province branch of the China Democracy Party, and Guo Quan, an online writer and professor who launched the China New People's Party, sentenced to 10 years. In October, the U.S. Congressional-Executive Commission on China published a partial list of over 1,200 political prisoners, while the San Francisco-based Dui Hua Foundation estimated that 1,150 new arrests for "endangering state security" were made in 2009. Tens of thousands of others are thought to be held in extrajudicial forms of detention for their political or religious views.

In February 2009, the government of the Macau Special Administrative Region, a Portuguese-ruled colony until 1999, passed legislation that stipulates long prison terms for crimes such as "secession," "subversion," and "association with foreign political organizations that harm state security." Human rights groups raised concerns that, as in the rest of China, such provisions could be used to restrict freedom of expression and imprison critics of the Macau or Beijing authorities. Macau immigration officers reportedly cited the law in barring entry to several prodemocracy lawmakers and activists from Hong Kong shortly after its passage.

Corruption remains endemic despite increased government antigraft efforts, generating growing public resentment. The problem is most acute in sectors with extensive state involvement, such as construction, land procurement, and banking. While multiple bodies track and prosecute corruption, there is no independent anticorruption agency. Tens of thousands of cases were investigated at all levels in 2009, with suspects including several assistant ministers and heads of state-run conglomerates. A crackdown on organized crime in Chongqing that began in June swept up thousands of suspects, exposing criminal infiltration of key industries as well as crime bosses' collusion with senior officers in local party committees, the police, and the judiciary. Prosecution in such cases is often selective, as informal personal networks and internal CCP power struggles influence the choice of targets. Also in 2009, censors heavily restricted reporting on a Namibian bribery probe involving a state-owned company formerly headed by President Hu Jintao's son.

CCP officials increasingly seek input from academics and civic groups on pending legislation and occasionally hold public hearings, though without relinquishing control over the decision-making process. New open-government regulations took effect in 2008, but implementation has been incomplete. While some agencies have been more forthcoming in publishing accounting details or official regulations, courts have hesitated to enforce citizens' information requests, and a precise accounting of economic stimulus funds had not been released by the end of 2009 despite promises of transparency. Local officials continued to hide vital information on topics including mining disasters, tainted food products, and polluting companies. China was ranked 79 out of 180 countries surveyed in Transparency International's 2009 Corruption Perceptions Index.

Despite relative freedom in private discussion and journalists' efforts to push the limits of permissible speech, China's media environment remains extremely restrictive. The authorities employ sophisticated means to control news reporting, particularly on sensitive topics. This includes setting the agenda by allowing key state-run media outlets to cover events—including negative news—in a timely but selective manner, and requiring that other outlets restrict their coverage to such approved accounts. Party directives in 2009 curbed reporting related to sensitive anniversaries, public health, environmental accidents, deaths in police custody, foreign policy, and other topics. Journalists who fail to comply with official guidance are harassed, fired, or jailed. According to international watchdog groups, at least 30 journalists, mostly freelancers, and 68 cyberdissidents remained imprisoned at year's end for disseminating proscribed information, though the actual number is likely much higher. In one prominent case, online activist Huang Qi was sentenced in November to three years in prison for publishing criticism of the authorities' response to the 2008 Sichuan earthquake. Tan Zuoren, an activist who had coordinated citizen efforts to document the death toll from school collapses during the quake, was put on trial in August, and several witnesses were beaten on their way to testify. At year's end, Tan remained in detention but had not been sentenced.

In addition to restrictions on media coverage imposed by the central government, lower-level officials also take measures to repress reports that expose shortcomings in their performance. Several journalists were assaulted during 2009 while trying to cover pollution or corruption. Others faced criminal defamation charges or were jailed on bribery charges in an apparent effort to stifle investigative reporting. Activist Wu Baoquan was sentenced in September to 18 months in prison after posting online allegations that officials in Inner Mongolia had profited from forced evictions. In December, Fu Hua of *China Business News* was sentenced to three years in prison for allegedly accepting bribes in relation to a story exposing safety problems in the construction of an airport in northeastern China. In November, the editor in chief Hu Shuli and other key staff resigned from the business magazine *Caijing* amid clashes with owners over financial matters and pressure to tone down its aggressive reporting on corruption.

Regulations have allowed greater freedom of movement for foreign journalists since 2007, but local officials continue to block, harass, and sometimes assault foreign reporters while intimidating their Chinese sources and assistants. In February 2009, the government issued a code of conduct for Chinese assistants of foreign correspondents that threatens punishment for those who engage in "independent reporting." Some international radio and television broadcasts, including the U.S. government–funded Radio Free Asia, remain jammed. The signal of the Falun Gong–affiliated satellite station New Tang Dynasty TV remained cut off in 2009, after the French company Eutelsat, apparently under pressure from Beijing, stopped its broadcasts in June 2008.

In 2009, China was home to the largest number of internet users globally, reaching 360 million by September 2009, according to official figures. However, the government maintains an elaborate apparatus for censoring and monitoring internet use and personal communications, including via mobile telephones. The authorities block websites they deem politically threatening and detain those who post the content. In 2009, they repeatedly blocked social-networking and microblogging sites, removed political content and shut down blogs in the name of antipornography campaigns, required users to register their real identities when posting comments on news websites, and stepped up obstruction of technologies used to circumvent censorship. In May, the government announced regulations requiring the installation of censorship and surveillance software called Green Dam Youth Escort on all computers sold in China; following protests from the international business community, human rights groups, and Chinese internet users, the authorities withdrew the directive in June, but said installation would proceed for computers in schools and internet cafes. For all the government's controls, the technology's flexibility, circumvention tools, and the large volume of online communications have allowed many users to nonetheless access censored content, expose official corruption, mobilize protests, and circulate banned political texts.

The number of religious believers, including Christians, has expanded in recent years. Nevertheless, religious freedom remains sharply curtailed, and religious minorities remained a key target of repression during 2009. All religious groups are required to register with the government, which regulates their activities and guides their theology. Some faiths, such as Falun Gong as well as certain Buddhist and Christian groups, are formally outlawed, and their members face harassment, imprisonment, and torture. Other unregistered groups, such as unofficial Protestant and Roman Catholic congregations, operate in a legal gray zone, and state tolerance of them varies from place to place. In September, police and thugs destroyed the Linfen-Fushan megachurch in Shanxi; church leaders were subsequently sentenced to as much as seven years in prison. Unregistered Buddhist temples were similarly targeted for demolition during the year, particularly in Jiangxi province. Security forces led by the 6-10 Office, an extralegal agency created in 1999, continued to target Falun Gong adherents nationwide for surveillance, imprisonment, torture, and forced conversion, sometimes leading to deaths in custody. In January 2009, Chongqing resident Jiang Xiqing died while held at a "reeducation through labor" camp for practicing Falun Gong; lawyers seeking to investigate his death were detained and beaten.

Academic freedom remains restricted with respect to politically sensitive issues. The CCP controls the appointment of university officials, and many scholars practice self-censorship to preserve their positions and personal safety. Pressure to self-censor increased during 2009, particularly surrounding the June and October anniversaries. Political indoctrination is a required component of the curriculum at all levels of education.

Freedoms of assembly and association are severely restricted. Both central and local authorities issued regulations in 2009 aimed at preventing petitioners from traveling to Beijing to report injustices to senior officials. Local officials continued to face penalties if they failed to limit the flow of petitioners to the capital; as a result, petitioners were routinely intercepted, harassed, detained in illegal detention centers termed "black jails," or sent to labor camps. Thousands of detained petitioners were reportedly subjected to beatings, psychological abuse, and sexual violence. Despite such repression, workers, farmers, and others held tens of thousands of protests during the year, reflecting growing public anger over wrongdoing by officials, especially land confiscation, corruption, and fatal police beatings. Security agencies and hired thugs often use excessive force to put down demonstrations; in several instances during 2009, this drove protesters to violently attack symbols of authority, such as police cars and government buildings. In June, riot police used batons to disperse an estimated 10,000 residents of Shishou in Hubei province, who had mustered after police refused to investigate the mysterious death of a 24-year-old hotel chef. At least eight people were subsequently sentenced to jail terms, including relatives of the deceased. In some cases, officials tolerate demonstrations as an outlet for pent-up frustration, or agree to protesters' demands.

Nongovernmental organizations (NGOs) are required to register and follow strict regulations, including vague prohibitions on advocating non-CCP rule, "damaging national unity," or "upsetting ethnic harmony." Many groups seeking more independence organize informally or register as businesses, though they are vulnerable to closure at any time. A government crackdown on several public interest groups in 2009 generated a chilling effect among civil society activists, with many putting projects on hold. In July, Beijing authorities shut down the Open Constitution Initiative, a legal aid NGO known for defending victims of the 2008 tainted-milk scandal and commissioning a report on government policies in Tibet, and raided the offices of the Yi Ren Ping Center, an organization assisting hepatitis B patients.

The only legal labor union is the government-controlled All-China Federation of Trade Unions. Collective bargaining is legal but does not occur in practice, and independent labor leaders are harassed and jailed. Nevertheless, workers have increasingly asserted themselves informally via strikes, collective petitioning, and selection of negotiating representatives. Such tactics repeatedly yielded concessions from employers or drew government intervention on behalf of workers in 2009. Three labor laws that took effect in 2008 were designed to protect workers, counter discrimination, and facilitate complaints against employers, while also empowering CCP-controlled unions. Initial promising signs on implementation—including a sharp rise in the number of labor-dispute cases filed by workers—were overshadowed by the economic downturn, the lack of independent arbitration bodies, and a growing backlog of complaints. Dangerous workplace conditions continued to claim lives. The official number of workplace accidents during the first three months of 2009 declined compared with the same period in 2008, but the death toll for the first quarter remained high at 18,501. Forced labor, including child labor through government-sanctioned "work-study" programs and in "reeducation through labor" camps, remains a serious problem.

The CCP controls the judiciary and directs verdicts and sentences, particularly in politically sensitive cases. Judicial autonomy is greater in commercial litigation and civil suits involving private individuals. A party veteran with no formal legal training was appointed as chief justice in 2008, and he subsequently issued a doctrine emphasizing the "Supremacy of the Cause of the Party" over the law. In 2009, the government accelerated a crackdown on civil rights lawyers, law firms, and NGOs offering legal services. In March, authorities shut down the Beijing-based law firm Yitong, known for representing victims of corruption or rights abuses. In May, over 20 lawyers were effectively disbarred when their license registrations were rejected, and several were physically assaulted during the year. In November, Wang Yonghang, a lawyer from Dalian in northeastern China, was sentenced to seven years in prison for defending Falun Gong practitioners, the harshest term given to an attorney in recent memory. Prominent lawyer Gao Zhisheng remained "disappeared" and at severe risk of torture following his abduction by security forces in February.

Despite recent criminal procedure reforms, trials—which often amount to mere sentencing announcements—are frequently closed to the public. Torture remains widespread, with coerced confessions routinely admitted as evidence. Endemic corruption exacerbates the lack of due process. Since late 2008, about a dozen senior judges have been detained on bribery charges, including the vice president of the Supreme People's Court. Many suspects are deprived of court hearings altogether, detained instead by bureaucratic fiat in "reeducation through labor" camps. Based on interviews with recently released detainees, a February 2009 study by the Chinese Human Rights Defenders group reported that in addition to petty thieves and drug addicts, Falun Gong practitioners, Christians, and petitioners constituted a significant percentage of those incarcerated in the camps. The use of various forms of extralegal detention has increased in recent years, including secret jails and psychiatric arrest of petitioners and dissidents. Together, detention facilities are estimated to hold a total of three to five million detainees. Conditions in such facilities are generally harsh, with detainees reporting inadequate food, regular beatings, and deprivation of medical care; the government generally does not permit visits by independent monitoring groups, including the International Committee of the Red Cross. Some 65 crimes—including nonviolent offenses—carry the death penalty. The number of executions remains a state secret but was thought to be close to 5,000 in 2009. Recent reforms enabling the Supreme People's Court to review capital cases have apparently led to a modest reduction in executions. In 2009, state-run media reported that executed prisoners "provide the major source of [organ] transplants in China"; some experts have also raised concerns over the possible use of those imprisoned for their religious beliefs or ethnic identity as sources for organs.

Security forces work closely with the CCP leadership at all levels, and special departments under the Ministry of Public Security are dedicated to maintaining the party's monopoly on political power. Hired thugs and urban management officers also engage in intimidation and abuse of petitioners, protesters, and whistle-blowers. During 2009, the CCP significantly expanded its network of extralegal "stability maintenance" offices, including at the neighborhood level and in some enterprises. As part of their mandate, these agencies are tasked with suppressing the peaceful exercise of basic civil liberties.

In April 2009, the government published its first National Human Rights Action Plan, outlining measures that, if implemented, would lead to improvements in human rights protection. However, observers questioned its likely impact given that it imposed no specific obligations or envisioned any change in trajectory from the regime's current priorities or ongoing systemic abuses.

In the Xinjiang Uighur Autonomous Region, political indoctrination programs, curbs on Muslim religious practice, and policies marginalizing the use of Uighur language in education intensified throughout 2009. The government continued decade-old policies to alter the region's demography, offering incentives to ethnic Han to move to the area and instituting a program to transfer Uighur laborers, sometimes by force, to work in other parts of China. In February, the government began a project to demolish most buildings in the historic core of the city of Kashgar and resettle some 200,000 Uighur residents. On July 5, police forcibly suppressed a peaceful demonstration in Urumqi by Uighurs voicing frustration over the limited investigation into the deaths of Uighur factory workers in a brawl with Han employees in southern China. The police action—which, according to Amnesty International, included using tear gas and shooting with live ammunition into crowds of peaceful protesters—sparked an outbreak of violence between Uighurs and Han residents. State-run media reported that 197 people were killed, but the details of events that day could not be fully verified due to tight government control of information and the intimidation of witnesses. The July 5 clashes were followed by a harsh crackdown that included large-scale "disappearances" of Uighurs, imprisonment and execution of Uighurs and some Han residents following questionable legal proceedings, and an almost complete shutdown of internet access in the region that remained in effect for several months. Among those detained were the managers of websites reporting on Uighur issues. A state propaganda campaign vilifying Uighurs and the U.S.-based Uighur activist Rebiya Kadeer fueled further ethnic tensions and increased discrimination against Uighurs throughout the country.

Minorities, the disabled, and people with HIV/AIDS or hepatitis B face severe societal discrimination. In a positive development, a court ruled in October 2009 that mandatory hepatitis B testing violated the 2008 Employment Promotion Law. A household registration, or hukou, system remains in place, mostly affecting China's 150 million internal migrants. Some local governments have experimented with reforms to allow greater mobility, but citizens continue to face restrictions on changing employers or residence, and many migrants are unable to fully access social services as a result. Other restrictions on freedom of movement remained substantial during 2009, as the authorities imposed lockdowns on Beijing and neighboring provinces surrounding the October anniversary. Dissidents were restricted from traveling abroad or placed under house arrest, particularly around the June anniversary and during U.S. President Barack Obama's visit in November. Law enforcement agencies continued to seek out and repatriate North Korean refugees, who face imprisonment or execution upon return. In August, a court in Inner Mongolia sentenced two Chinese citizens to 7 and 10 years in prison for helping 61 North Korean refugees cross into neighboring Mongolia.

Despite a growing body of property rights legislation, protection remains weak in practice, and all land is formally owned by the state. Tens of thousands of forced evictions and illegal land confiscations occurred in 2009, generally to provide land for private development, state-led infrastructure projects, or upcoming international events such as the World Expo in Shanghai. Residents who resist eviction, seek legal redress, or organize protests face violence at the hands of local police or hired thugs. In May 2009, over 1,000 villagers in Hunan reportedly clashed with police after a local man was beaten to death by security guards for a company that had begun building on confiscated land. Reforms to rural land use announced at the end of 2008 were put on hold in 2009, ostensibly due to the economic downturn.

China's policy of allowing only one child per couple remains in place, though many rural families are allowed a second child if the first is female. Although compulsory abortion and sterilization by local officials are less common than in the past, they still occur fairly frequently. According to official websites, authorities in some areas of Yunnan and Fujian mandated the use of abortion in 2009, while in other provinces officials imposed fines on families that resisted the one-child policy. These controls and a cultural preference for boys have led to sex-selective abortion and a general shortage of females, exacerbating the problem of human trafficking.

Domestic violence and sexual harassment affect one-third of Chinese families, according to statistics published in November 2008 by the CCP-controlled All-China Women's Federation. The government has taken steps in recent years to improve the legal framework related to violence against women, but implementation remains weak. The case of female hotel worker Deng Yujiao, who killed a local official as he tried to rape her in May 2009, drew public sympathy and stimulated discussion of the need to protect women's rights.

Colombia

Political Rights: 3
Civil Liberties: 4
Status: Partly Free

Population: 45,065,000
Capital: Bogota

Ten-Year Ratings Timeline For Year Under Review (Political Rights, Civil Liberties, Status)

2000	2001	2002	2003	2004	2005	2006	2007	2008	2009
4,4PF	4,4PF	4,4PF	4,4PF	4,4PF	3,3PF	3,3PF	3,3PF	3,4PF	3,4PF

Overview:
Political uncertainty increased in 2009, as President Alvaro Uribe's supporters took steps to allow him to seek a third term in 2010. A scandal involving government surveillance of civil society members, opposition politicians, and judges sharpened existing tensions between the president and the Supreme Court. Meanwhile, the significant security gains of recent years appeared to level off, as violence rose in some cities and rural zones. Relations with neighboring Venezuela continued to worsen amid recriminations over a U.S.-Colombian military accord and Caracas's alleged toleration of Colombian rebel activity on Venezuelan territory.

Following independence from Spain in 1819, Gran Colombia broke into what became Venezuela, Ecuador, and modern Colombia. The 1903 secession of Panama, engineered by the United States, left Colombia with its present boundaries. A civil war between Liberals and Conservatives, known as La Violencia, erupted in 1948 and resulted in some 200,000 deaths before subsiding after 1953. From 1958 to 1974, the two parties alternated in the presidency under the terms of a 1957 coalition pact (the National Front) aimed at ending civil strife. Colombia has since been marked by corrupt politics as well as by left-wing guerrilla insurgencies, right-wing paramilitary violence, the emergence of vicious drug cartels, and human rights abuses committed by all sides.

Conservative candidate Andres Pastrana won the 1998 presidential election, and as part of the peace process, he arranged for the leftist Revolutionary Armed Forces of Colombia (FARC) rebel group to occupy a so-called demilitarized zone in the south. However, in 2001 it became clear that the FARC was using its territory to coordinate military and criminal operations, and the government began a new offensive.

In the 2002 presidential election, Colombians chose Alvaro Uribe, a former provincial governor, who ran as an independent and pledged to crush the rebels by military means. Soon after his inauguration, he decreed a state of emergency and created special combat zones in 27 municipalities in which the military was allowed to restrict civilian movement and conduct searches without a warrant. Right-wing paramilitary death squads, grouped together as the United Self-Defense Forces of Colombia (AUC), also battled the guerrillas in both rural and urban areas, sometimes with the tolerance or covert complicity of government forces. However, the country continued to be racked by massacres, drug trafficking, and kidnappings. Uribe was praised for his diligent leadership and communications skills, but critics faulted him for his authoritarian bent and apparent lack of concern for human rights. The Constitutional Court in 2003 stripped him of the emergency powers he had assumed in 2002, and he triggered protests by proposing an amnesty that would grant paramilitaries reduced prison sentences or allow them to pay reparations in lieu of jail time.

Although by 2005 the leftist guerrillas had largely ceded control of major cities to the paramilitaries, the FARC and the smaller National Liberation Army (ELN) appeared determined to hold out in remote areas, using the narcotics trade and extortion for financial support. Moreover, social and human rights conditions in newly recaptured rural areas sometimes deteriorated further as paramilitaries replaced the guerrillas. In subsequent years, the government attempted to better integrate its military presence with social development in former conflict zones, with limited impact.

Debate continued over the paramilitaries' demobilization. Human rights groups claimed that the Justice and Peace Law, adopted in June 2005, failed to ensure the permanent dismantling of paramilitary organizations and did not allow adequate time for their many crimes to be investigated. The government denied that the law encouraged impunity—combatants could be required to spend between five and eight years in prison—and noted that it did not apply to drug-related offenses. In May 2006, the Constitutional Court struck down certain elements of the law and mandated full confessions, the seizure of illicitly acquired assets, and the provision of reparations to victims.

In the run-up to the March 2006 legislative elections, the FARC and paramilitaries sometimes attacked local politicians and intimidated civilians. However, violence declined prior to the May presidential election, in which Uribe's prospects were bolstered by a growing economy and the perception of improved security. He was reelected with 62 percent of the vote, fully 40 points ahead of his closest rival.

By late 2006, more than 30,000 paramilitaries had formally demobilized. However, human rights groups reported subsequent problems with civilian reintegration, violence against former combatants, a lack of resources for investigations, nonparticipation in the justice and peace process, and delays in reparation payments and physical protection for victims. In some cases, the FARC moved into territory vacated by demobilized paramilitaries, while other areas were held by new factions that were at least partly composed of recalcitrant or recidivist members of the disbanded paramilitary groups. These organizations often mimicked the AUC, reportedly engaging in extortion, assassinations, and in some cases collaboration with security forces or guerrillas, although they lacked the AUC's unified command structure. While drug trafficking was their primary focus, they also frequently directed aggression against social and human rights activists, particularly those advocating on behalf of victims of AUC crimes.

Top AUC leaders continued in 2007 and 2008 to testify about their crimes. In certain instances, they refused to admit culpability, but others yielded valuable information on paramilitary operations and thousands of unsolved murders. In April 2008, 14 paramilitary chiefs were extradited to the United States, where they faced long prison sentences for drug trafficking. The Colombian government argued that this would break their ongoing control over drug distribution networks, but rights groups feared that the transfers would truncate the confessions process, a concern validated in 2009 as testimony from some of the most important leaders ceased. In August 2009, the Colombian Supreme Court prohibited further extraditions of former paramilitary leaders still involved in the justice and peace process.

Observers also raised concerns that the extraditions effectively removed potential witnesses in the ongoing "parapolitics" scandal, which linked scores of politicians to paramilitaries. By the end of 2009, over 80 congressmen—including the president's cousin, Mario Uribe—had been arrested, convicted, or were under investigation. The case stoked tensions between the president and the Supreme Court, which is tasked with investigating sitting lawmakers. Several dozen congressmen resigned to remove their cases from the court's purview, but in 2009, the Court ruled that it would retain jurisdiction over investigations of resigned congressmen.

Meanwhile, in February 2009, evidence emerged of a massive telephone, e-mail, and personal surveillance operation initiated in 2003 by Colombia's intelligence agency, the Administrative Security Department (DAS). Among its targets were journalists, nongovernmental organization (NGO) workers, politicians, and Supreme Court justices. Dozens of DAS employees were dismissed, and 10 were charged. Nonetheless, signs of continued wiretapping were revealed in August. In September, Uribe announced that the DAS would be disbanded, with most of its functions absorbed by the police.

The DAS scandal added to the strains in the relationship between the president and the Supreme Court. Among other contributing factors, the administration lodged accusations of corruption within the Court, the Court rejected all attorney general candidates proposed by Uribe, and a series of Court-led investigations focused on supposed exchanges of favors surrounding the passage of a 2004 constitutional amendment that had allowed Uribe's reelection in 2006.

FARC activity appeared to increase somewhat in 2009, although signs of rebel weakness—including desertions, information leaks, and reports of paranoia-induced internal brutality—continued to emerge. The government had made major gains against the FARC in 2008, killing a top commander, Raul Reyes, in a March raid on a rebel camp across the Ecuadorean border and rescuing a group of high-profile FARC hostages in July. Also that year, another FARC leader, Ivan Rios, was killed by one of his own guards, and the group's founder, Manuel Marulanda, died of natural causes. Six additional hostages were released in February 2009.

According to police figures, the country's overall homicide rate declined slightly in 2009, but murders increased in the country's three largest cities, Bogota, Medellin, and Cali. The sharp rise in Medellin reflected competition to fill a criminal power vacuum created by the extradition of paramilitary boss and drug kingpin Diego Murillo Bejarano.

Colombia's relations with its neighbors have been turbulent in recent years. Both Ecuador and Venezuela cut off diplomatic ties after Colombia's 2008 cross-border raid in Ecuador; many, though not all, ties with Ecuador were subsequently reestablished. In October 2009, the United States and Colombia signed a defense pact granting U.S. military personnel and aircraft increased access to seven Colombian bases. The agreement's broad language led Venezuelan president Hugo Chavez to denounce it in bellicose terms, prompting fears of a border conflict.

Political Rights and Civil Liberties: Colombia is an electoral democracy. The 2006 legislative elections, while an improvement over the 2002 contest, were marred by vote buying, district switching, opaque financing, paramilitary intimidation, and violence. The 2006 presidential election was comparatively peaceful, and the 2007 regional and local elections repeated some of the flaws of the congressional polls but marked an improvement over the last such elections in 2003.

The Congress is comprised of the Senate and the Chamber of Representatives, with all seats up for election every four years. Of the Senate's 102 members, 2 are chosen by indigenous communities and 100 by the nation at large, using a party-list system. The Chamber of Deputies consists of 166 members elected by party-list proportional representation in multimember districts.

President Alvaro Uribe's 2006 reelection came after a drawn-out constitutional amendment campaign to allow a second four-year presidential term. Starting in 2008, Uribe supporters collected enough petition signatures to launch a constitutional amendment referendum for a third term, but the effort was marred by serious doubts about its financing, the wording of the question to voters, and the procedures used to move the measure through Congress. The opposition boycotted the August and September 2009 votes in which progovernment legislators barely secured passage of the referendum law. Meanwhile, Uribe maintained a calculated ambiguity about his electoral intentions, adding to institutional uncertainty.

The traditional Liberal-Conservative partisan duopoly in Congress has in recent years been supplanted by a rough division between anti-Uribe forces on the left and pro-Uribe forces on the right. The shift was partly the result of 2003 reforms designed to open the system and contain the problem of party fragmentation. Further political reform efforts in 2008 and 2009 proved contentious, especially the opposition's argument that seats vacated by lawmakers implicated in the parapolitics scandal should be left empty rather than filled by the next candidate on their party list. A bill passed in June 2009 included the "empty seat" provision for crimes tying politicians to armed groups but did not apply it to the parapolitics-linked legislators in the 2006–10 congressional term. The measure also provided a period during which current legislators could change parties without penalty, leading to a flurry of party-switching between July and September. Late in the year, several new parties formed as vehicles for members of the groups most implicated in the parapolitics scandal to maintain influence, in many cases by using relatives as proxy candidates.

Corruption occurs at multiple levels of public administration. In 2009, public attention focused on an agricultural subsidies program that benefited large landowners and suspected front men at the expense of poor rural farmers. Controversy also raged around the allegation that Uribe's two sons improperly profited from a zoning change affecting recently purchased property. Colombia was ranked 75 out of 180 countries surveyed in Transparency International's 2009 Corruption Perceptions Index.

The constitution guarantees freedom of expression, and opposition viewpoints are commonly expressed. However, crime and conflict make it difficult for journalists to conduct their work. Dozens of journalists have been murdered since the mid-1990s, many for reporting on drug trafficking and corruption. Most of the cases remain unsolved; in 2009, material perpetrators—though not intellectual authors—were convicted in three murders. At least one reporter was killed in 2009 in connection with his work, and self-censorship remained common. The Uribe administration has repeatedly accused journalists of antigovernment bias or links to guerrillas. Journalist Hollman Morris, a target of particular executive opprobrium in 2009, was also among 16 reporters confirmed as subjects of DAS surveillance. Slander and defamation remain criminalized. The government does not limit or block access to the internet or censor websites.

The constitution provides for freedom of religion, and the government generally respects this right in practice. The authorities also uphold academic freedom, and university debates are often vigorous, although armed groups maintain a presence on many campuses to generate political support and intimidate opponents.

Constitutional rights regarding freedoms of assembly and association are restricted in practice by violence. Although the government provides extensive protection to several thousand threatened human rights workers, trust in the program varies widely, and numerous activists have been murdered by all armed groups. Uribe's rhetorical hostility toward NGOs and the sometimes baseless legal cases brought against human rights defenders are on occasion interpreted as a green light to physically attack them, and threats against activists have increased in recent years. From 2006 to 2009, at least 20 victims' rights and land activists were killed; advocates for the displaced face special risk as former paramilitaries seek to smother criticism of their ill-gotten assets.

Colombia is considered the world's most dangerous country for organized labor. More than 2,600 union activists and leaders have been killed over the last two decades, with an impunity rate of over 95 percent. Labor leaders are frequently targeted by paramilitary groups, guerrillas, and narcotics traffickers. Although killings declined from 49 in 2008 to 39 in 2009, the issue continued to hold up ratification of a bilateral free-trade agreement by the U.S. Congress. In response, the government has worked with the International Labour Organization and formed a special unit of prosecutors that, starting in 2007, substantially increased prosecutions for assassinations of union members. More than 180 convictions have been secured since 2007, compared to 50 between 2000 and 2006. Nonetheless, most convictions have involved material rather than intellectual authors, and the impunity rate remains above 90 percent.

The justice system remains compromised by corruption and extortion. The Constitutional Court and Supreme Court have, on multiple occasions, demonstrated independence from the executive. Lower courts are more susceptible to political and criminal influence.

Many soldiers operating in Colombia's complex security environment work under limited civilian oversight. The government has in recent years increased human rights training and investigated a greater number of military personnel for grave human rights abuses. Collaboration between security forces and illegal armed groups declined considerably following AUC demobilization, but rights groups report toleration of the new paramilitary formations in some regions. Primary responsibility for combating them rests with the police, who are underresourced compared with the military and lack a presence in many rural areas where combatants are active.

In 2008, the army chief and several dozen other officers were fired over a scandal involving the systematic killing of civilians to fraudulently inflate guerrilla death tolls. More than 2,000 people may have been killed in this way, although the pace declined substantially in 2009. By year's end, the attorney general's office was investigating over 2,000 security force members and had arrested several hundred.

All of the illegal armed groups systematically abuse human rights. FARC guerrillas regularly extort payments from businesspeople and intimidate suspected government informants. The increasing use of landmines has added to casualties among both civilians and the military. Impunity is rampant for all criminals, and victims of human rights abuses often express frustration with the government's level of commitment to obtaining economic reparations and prosecuting perpetrators. In June 2009, a victims' rights bill that would have increased reparations was shelved after congressmen were unable to agree on its terms. The government insisted that the version preferred by victims was too expensive and improperly placed state violations on an equal footing with those of nonstate groups. Meanwhile, victims and rights groups expressed concern that demobilized paramilitaries had returned just a fraction of the millions of acres of land they had seized while ostensibly fighting the guerrillas.

Colombia's more than 1.7 million indigenous inhabitants live on more than 34 million hectares granted to them by the government, often in resource-rich, strategic regions that are contested by the various armed groups. Indigenous people are frequently targeted by all sides. Despite a January 2009 Constitutional Court ruling that extended guarantees of protection, murders of indigenous people increased significantly during the year, including several massacres of members of the Awa group by the FARC and other, unknown actors.

Afro-Colombians, who account for as much as 25 percent of the population, make up the largest sector of Colombia's nearly 4 million displaced people, and 80 percent of Afro-Colombians fall below the poverty line. In March 2009 the Inter-American Human Rights Commission reported ongoing, grievous violations of Afro-Colombians' legal rights. The displaced population as a whole suffers from social stigma, arbitrary arrest, and exploitation, as well as generalized poverty.

Homosexuals face active discrimination, but in 2007, the Constitutional Court ruled that homosexual couples must be made eligible for various benefits, which were expanded in April 2008 and January 2009.

Child labor is a serious problem in Colombia, as are child recruitment into illegal armed groups and related sexual abuse. Sexual harassment, violence against women, and the trafficking of women for sexual exploitation remain major concerns. Almost 60 percent of the displaced population is female. The country's active abortion-rights movement has challenged restrictive laws, and in 2006 a Constitutional Court ruling allowed abortion in cases of rape or incest, or to protect the mother's life.

Comoros

Political Rights: 3
Civil Liberties: 4
Status: Partly Free

Population: 676,000
Capital: Moroni

Ten-Year Ratings Timeline For Year Under Review (Political Rights, Civil Liberties, Status)

2000	2001	2002	2003	2004	2005	2006	2007	2008	2009
6,4PF	6,4PF	5,4PF	5,4PF	4,4PF	4,4PF	3,4PF	4,4PF	3,4PF	3,4PF

Overview: Referendum voters in May approved a constitutional overhaul that strengthened the powers of the central government, in part by extending the president's term and reducing the authority of each island's leader. In parliamentary elections held in December, President Ahmed Abdallah Sambi's supporters won 19 of the 24 directly elected seats in the 33-seat legislature.

The Union of the Comoros comprises three islands: Grande Comore, Anjouan, and Moheli. Residents of Mayotte, the fourth island of the archipelago, voted to remain under French rule in a 1974 referendum.

Two mercenary invasions and at least 18 other coups and attempted coups have shaken the Comoros since it gained independence from France in 1975. The 1996 presidential election was considered free and fair by international monitors, but Anjouan and Moheli fell under the control of separatists the following year. Colonel Azali Assoumani staged a coup in 1999 in a bid to restore order. A reconciliation agreement was signed in 2000, and a 2001 referendum approved a new constitution that gave greater autonomy to the three islands. The 2002 elections for the island presidencies were deemed largely free and fair, but Azali won the federal presidency after his two opponents claimed fraud and withdrew.

In the 2004 federal legislative elections, Azali supporters captured only 6 of the 33 seats. A moderate Islamist preacher and businessman, Ahmed Abdallah Sambi, won the federal presidency in May 2006, taking 58 percent of the vote in an election that was also deemed legitimate by most observers.

Colonel Mohamed Bacar, president of Anjouan, refused to leave office at the end of his term in April 2007. He organized unauthorized elections in June to extend his rule, and claimed to have won with 90 percent of the vote. However, in March 2008 an African Union military force removed him from power, and three months later, a supporter of President Sambi was elected in his place.

In May 2009, referendum voters approved constitutional reforms that increased the powers of the federal government at the expense of the individual island governments, whose presidents would be downgraded to governors and left with reduced authority. Among other changes, the reforms altered the composition of the federal parliament to included 24 directly elected seats and 9 seats elected by the three island assemblies, compared with 18 directly elected and 15 indirectly elected seats under the old system. Legislative elections were held under the new rules in December, and the president's supporters—grouped under the Baobab coalition—won 19 of the 24 directly elected seats, providing Sambi with sufficient support to enact a one-year extension of his term as called for in the constitutional reforms.

Large numbers of Comorans illegally emigrate to Mayotte, either to settle there or to seek entry into metropolitan France, and the economy depends heavily on remittances and foreign aid. In 2009, the global economic downturn contributed to delays or suspensions of public sector salary payments and a continued decline in public services.

Political Rights and Civil Liberties:

The Comoros is an electoral democracy. Since 1996, Comorans have voted freely in several parliamentary and presidential elections. Under the 2001 constitution, the federal presidency rotates among the islands every four years, but a constitutional referendum in May 2009 extended the presidential term to five years. The reform also downgraded individual island presidents to the status of governors, limited the size of cabinets, empowered the president to dissolve the federal parliament, and allowed the president to rule by decree with the parliament's approval.

The unicameral Assembly of the Union consists of 33 members, with 9 selected by the islands' local assemblies and 24 by direct popular vote; before the 2009 referendum, there were 15 indirectly elected and 18 directly elected seats. All members serve five-year terms. Political parties are mainly defined by their positions regarding the division of power between the federal and local governments.

Corruption remains a major problem. In 2007, former Moheli president Said Mohamed Fazul received an 18-month suspended prison term and a fine for fraud. There have also been complaints of corruption among the security forces. The Comoros was ranked 143 out of 180 countries surveyed in Transparency International's 2009 Corruption Perceptions Index.

The constitution and laws provide for freedom of speech and of the press, but the government partially restricts press freedom. The authorities have arrested journalists, seized newspapers, and silenced broadcast outlets for reports that are found to be objectionable, although these practices are less common under the current administration. Several private newspapers that are at times critical of the government are sporadically published in the capital. Two state-run radio stations broadcast, as do about 20 regional radio stations and five local private television stations. Internet access is extremely limited for economic reasons.

Islam is the state religion. Tensions have sometimes arisen between Sunni and Shiite Muslims, and non-Muslims are reportedly subject to restrictions, detentions, and harassment. Conversion from Islam and non-Muslim proselytizing are illegal. Academic freedom is generally respected.

The government typically upholds freedoms of assembly and association. However, security forces have responded to demonstrations with excessive force in the past. A few human rights and other nongovernmental organizations operate in the country. Workers have the right to bargain collectively and to strike, but collective bargaining is rare. In 2009, teachers went on strike to protest nonpayment of salaries.

The judicial system is based on both Sharia (Islamic law) and the French legal code and is subject to influence by the executive branch and other elites. Minor disputes are often settled informally by village elders. Harsh prison conditions include severe overcrowding and inadequate sanitation, medical care, and nutrition.

Women possess constitutional protections, but in practice they enjoy little political or economic power and have far fewer opportunities for education and salaried employment than men, especially in rural areas.

➼ Congo, Democratic Republic of (Kinshasa)

Political Rights: 6
Civil Liberties: 6
Status: Not Free

Population: 68,693,000
Capital: Kinshasa

Trend Arrow: The Democratic Republic of Congo received a downward trend arrow due to the government's continued harassment of human rights groups and an increasingly dangerous working environment for journalists.

Ten-Year Ratings Timeline For Year Under Review (Political Rights, Civil Liberties, Status)

2000	2001	2002	2003	2004	2005	2006	2007	2008	2009
7,6NF	6,6,NF	6,6,NF	6,6,NF	6,6,NF	6,6,NF	5,6NF	5,6NF	6,6,NF	6,6,NF

Overview:

The government undertook several military operations against militia groups in the east in 2009, but civilians suffered widespread displacement and abuses as a result of the intensified fighting, including at the hands of the Congolese army. National Assembly speaker Vital Kamerhe, a vocal critic of the government's military actions, was forced to resign amid growing indications that President Joseph Kabila was seeking to centralize power. Opposition politicians, human rights activists, and the press continued to be targeted for attacks and harassment, and the third journalist in as many years was killed in the eastern city of Bukavu.

The king of Belgium claimed a vast area of Central Africa as his private colony in the late 19th century, and the territory was exploited with a brutality that was extreme even for the imperialist era. After it gained independence from Belgium in 1960, the country became an arena for Cold War rivalries, and Colonel Joseph Mobutu seized power with CIA backing in 1965. Mobutu changed the country's name from the Democratic Republic of Congo (DRC) to Zaire in 1971, renamed himself Mobutu Sese Seko, and assumed dictatorial powers.

Mobutu largely overcame pressure to open up the political process following the end of the Cold War, but after the 1994 genocide in neighboring Rwanda, the Rwandan and Ugandan governments turned their cross-border pursuit of Rwandan Hutu militia members into an advance on Kinshasa. Rwandan troops, accompanied by representatives of the Alliance of Democratic Forces for the Liberation of Congo-Zaire (AFDL), a coalition led by former Zairian rebel leader Laurent-Desire Kabila, entered eastern Zaire in October 1996 and reached Kinshasa in May 1997; Mobutu fled to Morocco, where he died. Kabila declared himself president and changed the country's name back to the Democratic Republic of Congo.

Relations between Kabila and his Rwandan and Ugandan backers deteriorated after he ordered all foreign troops to leave the DRC in 1998. Rwanda intervened in support of a newly formed rebel group, the Congolese Rally for Democracy (RCD), but the DRC government was defended by Angolan, Namibian, and Zimbabwean troops. Uganda later backed a rival rebel group, the Movement for the Liberation of the Congo (MLC), establishing control over the northern third of the DRC, while the RCD held much of the eastern Kivu region. The country's vast mineral wealth spurred the involvement of multinational companies, criminal networks, and other foreign governments.

Military stalemate led to the signing of the Lusaka Peace Agreement in 1999. The accord called for a ceasefire, the deployment of UN peacekeepers, the withdrawal of foreign troops, and a transitional government. Kabila drew international criticism for blocking the deployment of UN troops and suppressing internal political activity. He was assassinated in 2001 and succeeded by his son Joseph, who revived the peace process. The Sun City Peace Agreement, signed in South Africa in 2002, led to the creation of a transitional government in 2003 and a formal end to the war.

A new constitution was passed by the bicameral transitional legislature and approved by referendum in 2005. Presidential and legislative elections, the first multiparty polls since independence, were held in 2006. Despite daunting logistical challenges, the elections were largely peaceful and drew a voter turnout of over 70 percent. Kabila's People's Party for Reconstruction and Democracy (PPRD) gained the most seats in the National Assembly, the legislature's lower house, but fell short of an outright majority. In a field of 33 presidential candidates, Kabila won about 45 percent of the vote. He then won the runoff against MLC leader and transitional vice president Jean-Pierre Bemba.

Following the elections, two broad alliances emerged in the 500-seat National Assembly: the Alliance of the Presidential Majority (AMP), comprising 332 seats, and the opposition Union for the Nation (UpN), comprising 116 seats. Eleven provincial assemblies voted in the January 2007 Senate elections, granting the AMP 58 seats and the UpN 21. Gubernatorial polls that year handed 10 governorships to AMP-affiliated candidates and 1 to the UpN. In March 2007, fighting broke out in Kinshasa between the authorities and Bemba loyalists. Bemba went into exile in Europe, adding to doubts as to whether Kabila would allow genuine political pluralism.

In September 2008, Prime Minister Antoine Gizenga resigned amid growing tensions with the president, though he cited health concerns. Kabila appointed Adolphe Muzito, a member of Gizenga's Unified Party for Lumumba (PALU), to replace him.

Despite the 2002 peace agreement, competition to control earnings from the country's massive deposits of cobalt, diamonds, coltan, gold, and copper continued to fuel fighting in the eastern DRC, internally displacing at least 1.2 million people, according to the United Nations. In January 2008, a peace agreement was signed between the government and 22 armed groups operating in the east. Notably, the agreement did not include the Rwandan government or the Democratic Liberation Forces of Rwanda (FDLR), an ethnic Hutu–dominated militia group led by perpetrators of the 1994 Rwandan genocide who had fled to the DRC. Heavy fighting broke out in August 2008 between government troops and the ethnic Tutsi rebel leader Laurent Nkunda's National Congress for the Defense of the People (CNDP), which allegedly received Rwandan government backing, leading to further civilian displacement and human rights abuses.

Relations between the Congolese and Rwandan governments began to improve significantly in late 2008, and the two governments signed an agreement to begin a joint military operation against the FDLR. The operation, which lasted from January to February 2009, coincided with the surprise arrest in Rwanda of the CNDP's Nkunda. Rwandan authorities agreed to extradite him to the DRC, but this had not yet occurred at year's end. The DRC also embarked on a joint military operation with Uganda from December 2008 to March 2009 to pursue the Lord's Resistance Army (LRA), a Ugandan rebel group.

Kabila made the decision to proceed with the joint operations without informing the National Assembly, and this drew criticism from figures including the chamber's speaker, PPRD member Vital Kamerhe. The AMP boycotted the opening of the National Assembly in March, after Kamerhe rejected calls for his resignation, but he relented later that month, announcing that he would establish a new political party. Evariste Boshab of the PPRD was elected as the new speaker, though the opposition alleged vote fraud by the AMP.

Meanwhile, with Nkunda under arrest in Rwanda, the Congolese government and the CNDP signed a peace accord in March, and an amnesty bill for acts of war in the affected provinces was passed into law, despite objections that the CNDP was the primary beneficiary. The CNDP subsequently transformed itself into a political party under the leadership of Desire Kamandji.

In March, Congolese and UN forces began a military operation against the FDLR. As with previous campaigns, it led to severe suffering for civilians, including reprisal killings by the FDLR. In July, the United Nations estimated that a total of 400,000 people had been displaced in North Kivu and South Kivu provinces. The operation ended in December, but the Congolese army and the United Nations signed a new joint military operational order to begin in 2010.

Aside from the east, most parts of the country were relatively stable in 2009. However, large-scale violence broke out in October over fishing rights in the western province of Equateur, causing the displacement of approximately 70,000 people. All of the DRC has been devastated by the combined effects of war, economic crisis, and the breakdown of political and social institutions. At least four million people have died since fighting began in 1994, and humanitarian groups estimate that 1,000 people continue to die each day. Critical health and social services are nonexistent in many areas, and much of the country's infrastructure has disintegrated. Congo was ranked 176 out of 182 countries on the UN Development Programme's 2009 Human Development Index.

The DRC was granted access to the International Monetary Fund/World Bank Heavily Indebted Poor Countries (HIPC) initiative in 2003. Despite significant efforts to restore economic vitality, the economy has yet to improve. Kabila has tried to break with the tradition of printing money to meet budget shortfalls, but there have been reports that the central bank has counterfeited its own currency. In 2008, the state signed a loan deal worth close to $9 billion with China's Exim Bank. In return, China obtained a significant stake in a joint venture with Gecamines, the state mining company, as well as rights to two large mining concessions. The opaque terms of this agreement, as well as the debt it entails, have impeded negotiations between the government and the International Monetary Fund over a new Poverty Reduction and Growth Facility.

Political Rights and Civil Liberties: The DRC is not an electoral democracy. Though the 2006 elections were a significant improvement over previous voting, serious problems remained. The opposition Union for Social Democracy and Progress (UDPS) party did not participate as a result of its call for a boycott of the constitutional referendum, international observers noted voter registration irregularities, and the campaign period included clashes between opposition militants and government forces as well as an attempt on opposition leader Jean-Pierre Bemba's life. The 2007 Senate elections were marred by allegations of vote buying. Local elections initially scheduled for 2008 have been delayed until at least 2010. Voter registration began in June 2009, but no election date was set.

Under the new constitution, the president is elected to a five-year term, which is renewable once. The president nominates a prime minister from the leading party or coalition in the 500-seat National Assembly, the lower house of the bicameral legislature, whose members are popularly elected to serve five-year terms. The provincial assemblies elect the upper house, the 108-seat Senate, as well as the provincial governors, for five-year terms.

Of the approximately 247 registered political parties, only a dozen have broad representation. President Joseph Kabila's coalition, the AMP, currently holds 332 seats in the National Assembly and 58 in the Senate. The 2007 exile of Bemba, whose MLC is the largest opposition party, represented a severe blow to political pluralism.

Opposition politicians have increasingly faced violence and harassment. In 2008, MLC politician Daniel Botethi was killed in Kinshasa. A military tribunal sentenced three soldiers to death in connection with his murder, and one of those convicted initially claimed that the Kinshasa governor had ordered the killing. In March 2009, Norbert Luyeye Binzunga, the leader of a small opposition party, the Union of Republicans, was arrested after organizing a peaceful demonstration against the presence of foreign troops in the DRC. Another opposition leader, Gabriel Mokia of the Congolese Democratic Party, was imprisoned in April after criticizing the government during a televised debate. The mounting pressure on opposition figures has raised concerns that Kabila is leading the DRC back toward a highly centralized presidential system that allows no more than the formalities of representative governance.

Corruption is rampant in the DRC, particularly in the mining sector. The country ranked 182 out of 183 countries in the World Bank's 2010 Doing Business survey, and 162 out of 180 countries surveyed in Transparency International's 2009 Corruption Perceptions Index. In 2006, the government approved new investment and mining codes and established a commercial court to protect foreign investment. The National Assembly's Lutundula Commission implicated a number of senior officials in corruption that year, some of whom were fired. In 2007, Kabila bowed to international pressure and announced a review of 61 mining contracts with foreign companies, but rejected calls for independent oversight. The first stage of the mining review was completed in 2008, and the government noted that 26 contracts required renegotiation and 21 faced termination. In 2009, the government began completing negotiations of new contracts and revisions of contract terms. Separately, the government in 2008 announced the results of a World Bank–backed, three-year review of logging contracts, stating that it would cancel more than two-thirds of the contracts and continue a moratorium on logging deals for another three years.

Although guaranteed by the constitution, freedoms of speech and expression are limited. Independent journalists are frequently threatened, arrested, and attacked, and have occasionally been killed. Radio is the dominant medium in the country, which suffers from low literacy rates and limited access to television. The United Nations and a Swiss-based organization, Fondation Hirondelle, launched Radio Okapi in 2002 to provide independent news. The government banned 40 television and radio stations for improper licenses in 2007, and more were banned in 2008. In July 2009, the government banned transmission of the French public radio station Radio France Internationale (RFI). Radio Start news presenter Bruno Koko Chirambiza was killed in August in Bukavu, South Kivu, province, making him the third journalist to be murdered in the city in as many years. In addition, three female radio journalists in Bukavu received death threats in September. The government does not restrict access to the internet, but it is limited by poor infrastructure.

The constitution guarantees religious freedom, which is generally respected in practice, although religious groups must register with the government to be recognized. In early 2008, the national police carried out operations against Bundu Dia Kongo (BDK), a politico-religious movement based in Bas-Congo province. More than 150 BDK members were arrested, and at least 100 people were killed. The United Nations called for an investigation into these incidents, which the government rejected. Nine of the arrested BDK members were sentenced to death, and four others died while in detention. The government also designated the movement illegal. Academic freedom is restricted by fears of government harassment, which often lead university professors to engage in self-censorship.

The rights to freedom of assembly and association are limited under the pretext of maintaining public order, and groups holding public events must inform local authorities in advance. Nongovernmental organizations (NGOs) are able to operate, but they face pressure from the government and nonstate actors if they offend powerful interests. In March 2009, three human rights defenders—Floribert Chebeya Bahizire, Dolly Inefo Mbunga, and Donat Tshikaya—were arrested and held incommunicado for 48 hours after calling for a protest against the AMP's attempts to force Vital Kamerhe to resign. Also during the year, the president of the human rights group ASADHO-Katanga, Golden Misabiko, was sentenced to one year in jail after the organization published a report alleging official kickbacks from illegal mining. Labor unions, though legal, exist only in urban areas and are largely inactive. Some unions are affiliated with political parties, and labor leaders and activists have faced harassment. In 2008, there were strikes by transport workers, health workers, teachers, and magistrates, who were concerned about low salaries and delayed remuneration. In January 2009, trade union leader Pepe Nginamau Malaba was arrested and charged with falsifying documents after he wrote a memorandum alleging the embezzlement of public money by the minister of national economy and trade.

Despite guarantees of independence, the judiciary remains subject to corruption and manipulation, and the court system lacks both trained personnel and resources. In July 2009, the president dismissed 165 prosecutors and magistrates, including the first president of the Supreme Court, for abuse of office. Kabila's role in the replacement process has been a source of concern. Prison conditions are often abysmal, and long periods of pretrial detention are common. In a landmark ruling in March 2009, a military court convicted a Mai Mai militia leader, Gedeon Kyungu

Mutanga, and 20 other Mai Mai fighters for crimes against humanity in addition to finding the government responsible for not disarming the Mai Mai. However, most government and government-allied forces still enjoy apparent impunity for even the most heinous crimes.

The International Criminal Court (ICC) continues to pursue cases in the DRC, including those against rebel leaders Mathieu Ngudjolo Chui, Thomas Lubanga, and Germain Katanga, as well as exiled opposition leader Jean-Pierre Bemba, who was transferred to the ICC in 2008. The trials of Bemba and Lubanga began in early 2009; the latter is particularly notable as the first international prosecution treating the use of child soldiers as a war crime. The ICC also issued a warrant in 2008 for the arrest of Jean-Bosco Ntaganda, who replaced Laurent Nkunda as CNDP military chief of staff in January 2009. The Congolese authorities have yet to arrest Ntaganda.

Civilian authorities do not maintain effective control of the security forces. Soldiers and police regularly commit serious human rights abuses, including rape. Human Rights Watch identified 250 cases of rape between January and May 2009, 143 of which were reportedly committed by army soldiers. Low pay and inadequate provisions commonly lead soldiers to seize goods from civilians, and demobilized combatants have not been successfully integrated into the civilian economy. The incorporation of former rebel groups into the military has resulted in competing chains of command and factional conflicts, with many fighters answering to former commanders and political leaders rather than their formal superiors. In 2009, an estimated 12,000 CNDP and other rebel fighters were rapidly integrated into the military.

Societal discrimination based on ethnicity is practiced widely among the country's 200 ethnic groups, particularly against indigenous Pygmy tribes and the Congolese Banyamulenge Tutsis. The ongoing fighting in the eastern Kivu region is driven in part by ethnic rivalries.

Although the law provides for freedom of movement, security forces seeking bribes or travel permits restrict it in practice, and foreigners must regularly submit to immigration controls when traveling internally. In conflict zones, various armed groups and soldiers have seized private property and destroyed homes.

Despite constitutional guarantees, women face discrimination in nearly every aspect of their lives, especially in rural areas, where there is little government presence. Violence against women, including rape and sexual slavery, has soared since fighting began in 1994. Congolese women are also subjugated as agricultural laborers, and armed groups regularly loot their harvests. Abortion is prohibited. Save the Children has ranked the DRC among the world's five worst conflict zones in which to be a woman or child. The number of children abducted to serve as soldiers continues to increase.

🔳 Congo, Republic of (Brazzaville)

Political Rights: 6
Civil Liberties: 5
Status: Not Free

Population: 3,683,000
Capital: Brazzaville

Trend Arrow: Congo received a downward trend arrow due to President Denis Sassou-Nguesso's increasing concentration of power and the authorities' handling of the July 2009 presidential election and its aftermath, including the disqualification of several opposition candidates and the intimidation of journalists.

Ten-Year Ratings Timeline For Year Under Review (Political Rights, Civil Liberties, Status)

2000	2001	2002	2003	2004	2005	2006	2007	2008	2009
6,4PF	5,4PF	6,4PF	5,4PF	5,4PF	5,5PF	6,5NF	6,5NF	6,5NF	6,5NF

Overview:

President Denis Sassou-Nguesso secured a new term in the July 2009 presidential election, which was marred by the lack of an independent electoral commission, the disqualification of several opposition candidates, and the intimidation of journalists. Sassou-Nguesso subsequently eliminated the position of prime minister, further concentrating executive power in his own hands. A postelection demonstration by the opposition was forcefully halted by the police, and opposition leaders were barred from leaving the country.

Congo's history since independence from France in 1960 has been marked by conflict and military coups. Colonel Denis Sassou-Nguesso seized power from another military officer in 1979, but domestic and international pressure finally forced him to hold multiparty presidential elections in 1992. He lost, placing third in the first round. In the runoff, former prime minister Pascal Lissouba defeated the late veteran oppositionist Bernard Kollas.

Disputed parliamentary elections in 1993 triggered violent clashes between rival militia groups. The fighting ended in 1997, when Sassou-Nguesso ousted Lissouba with the help of Angolan troops and French political support. Referendum voters adopted a new constitution in 2002, and Sassou-Nguesso easily won the presidential election that year after his main challenger, former National Assembly president Andre Milongo, claimed fraud and withdrew. In the 2002 legislative elections, Sassou-Nguesso's Congolese Labor Party (PCT) and its allies obtained 90 percent of the seats. The polls failed to foster genuine reconciliation, although a 2003 peace agreement was signed by virtually all of the country's rebel factions.

The 2007 legislative elections were boycotted by the main opposition parties after the government ignored calls to create an independent electoral commission. The PCT and its allies won 125 out of 137 seats in the National Assembly. The participation of Frederic Bintsangou's National Resistance Council (CNR), a former rebel group based in the southern Pool region, was hailed as a major step toward peace.

Sassou-Nguesso made minor cabinet changes in late 2007, notably including of Kolelas's Congolese Movement for Democracy and Integral Development (MCDDI) for the first time. A new political coalition, the Rally of the Presidential Majority

(RMP), was formed by the PCT and some 60 other parties in early 2008, with the goal of broadening the government's support ahead of the 2009 presidential election.

The RMP won 564 out of 864 council seats in June 2008 local elections, which featured low voter turnout. Councilors from seven departments subsequently elected members of the national Senate, marking the first time the departments of Pool and Pointe-Noire chose senators. The RMP secured 34 out of the 42 seats at stake.

In the July 2009 presidential election, Sassou-Nguesso won another term with 79 percent of the vote. His closest challenger was independent candidate Joseph Kignoumbi Kia Mboungou, who took 7 percent. Six of the original opposition candidates had withdrawn to protest poor electoral conditions. The government had again rejected calls to establish an independent electoral commission, and the existing National Commission on Elections (CONEL) had disqualified four of the initial opposition candidates, most notably Ange Edouard Poungui of the Pan-African Union for Social Democracy (UPADS), the largest opposition party in the National Assembly.

While the government reported voter turnout of 66 percent, the opposition claimed that the figure was closer to 10 percent. The African Union and the Economic Community of Central African States sent some poll observers, but the European Union did not. In advance of the elections, the government had updated the existing voter registry rather than carrying out a new census, despite evidence of inaccuracies.

Sassou-Nguesso made major cabinet changes after the election, including the elimination of the position of prime minister. The move meant that the president would be both head of state and head of government, further concentrating executive power.

Congo is one of sub-Saharan Africa's major oil producers, which has led to strong economic ties with France and other European states. However, corruption and decades of instability have contributed to poor humanitarian conditions. Congo ranked 136 out of 182 countries on the 2009 UN Human Development Index.

Political Rights and Civil Liberties:

The Republic of Congo is not an electoral democracy. Recent elections have been marred by irregularities, opposition boycotts and disqualifications, and the absence of an independent electoral commission. The constitution of 2002 limits the president to two seven-year terms, although current president Denis Sassou-Nguesso has been in office since he seized power in 1997; he previously ruled from 1979 to 1992. The Senate, the upper house of Parliament, consists of 72 members, with councilors from each department electing six senators for six-year terms; half of the total ordinarily come up for election every three years, although 42 seats were at stake in 2008. Members of the 137-seat National Assembly, the lower house, are directly elected for five-year terms. Most of the over 200 registered political parties are personality driven and ethnically based. The ruling RMP coalition faces a weak and fragmented opposition.

Corruption in Congo's extractive industries remains pervasive. The country's Corruption Observatory (ACO), tasked with increasing government accountability, became operational in 2008, but the International Monetary Fund and the World Bank have found that the government maintains inadequate internal controls and accounting systems. Sassou-Nguesso and his family have been beset by allegations of graft. In 2008, the watchdog organization Global Witness reported extravagant personal spending by one of the president's sons and evidence of kickbacks involving the state oil company. Congo was ranked 162 out of 180 countries surveyed in Transparency International's 2009 Corruption Perceptions Index.

The government's respect for press freedom is limited. Harassment and violence against journalists were reported during the 2009 presidential campaign period, and police attacked French and British journalists and confiscated their equipment during an opposition protest following the election. Speech that incites ethnic hatred, violence, or civil war is illegal. The government monopolizes the broadcast media, which reach a much larger audience than print publications. However, about 10 private weekly newspapers in Brazzaville often publish articles and editorials that are critical of the government. There are no government restrictions on internet access.

Religious and academic freedoms are guaranteed and respected. Freedoms of assembly and association are generally upheld, although public demonstrations are rare. The opposition's postelection protest in 2009 was halted by police, who allegedly fired live rounds at demonstrators. Several leaders of opposition parties, including Edouard Poungui of the UPADS, were subsequently barred from leaving the country. Nongovernmental organizations operate more or less without interference as long as they do not challenge the ruling elite. Workers' rights to join trade unions and to strike are protected, and collective bargaining is practiced freely. Most workers in the formal business sector, including the oil industry, are union members, and unions have made efforts to organize informal sectors, such as agriculture and retail trade.

Congo's weak judiciary is subject to corruption and political influence. Members of the poorly coordinated security forces act with impunity, and there have been reports of suspects dying during apprehension or in custody. Prison conditions are life threatening. Women and men, as well as juveniles and adults, are incarcerated together, and rape is common.

Ethnic discrimination persists. Members of Sassou-Nguesso's northern ethnic group and related clans dominate key government posts. Pygmy groups suffer discrimination, and many are effectively held in lifetime servitude through customary ties to ethnic Bantu "patrons." Members of virtually all ethnicities favor their own groups in hiring practices, and urban neighborhoods tend to be segregated.

Harassment by military personnel and militia groups inhibits travel, though such practices have declined. The judicial system offers few protections for business and property rights. Congo ranked 179 out of 183 countries surveyed in the World Bank's 2010 Doing Business index.

Despite constitutional safeguards, legal and societal discrimination against women persists. Their access to education and employment is limited, and civil codes and traditional practices regarding marriage formalize women's inferior status; for example, adultery is illegal for women but not for men. In traditional marriages, widows often do not inherit any portion of their spouses' estates, and divorce is difficult for women. Violence against women is reportedly widespread. Abortion is prohibited.

Costa Rica

Political Rights: 1
Civil Liberties: 1
Status: Free

Population: 4,509,000
Capital: San José

Ten-Year Ratings Timeline For Year Under Review (Political Rights, Civil Liberties, Status)

2000	2001	2002	2003	2004	2005	2006	2007	2008	2009
1,2F	1,2F	1,2F	1,2F	1,1F	1,1F	1,1F	1,1F	1,1F	1,1F

Overview: Former president and 2010 presidential candidate Rafael Angel Calderon was convicted of corruption in October 2009 and sentenced to five years in prison related to kickbacks obtained during his first presidency. Public perception of crime and insecurity rose unabated in 2009, as did the incidence of the warehousing and transportation of cocaine destined for the United States. President Oscar Arias introduced emergency measures to mitigate the effects of the global economic crisis on Costa Rica's most vulnerable populations.

Costa Rica achieved independence from Spain in 1821 and gained full sovereignty in 1838. The country enjoyed relative political stability until 1948, when Jose "Pepe" Figueres launched a 40-day civil war to restore power to the rightful winner of that year's presidential election and successfully pushed to disband Costa Rica's military. In 1949, the country adopted a new constitution that ultimately strengthened democratic rule. Figueres later served as president for two separate terms under the banner of the National Liberation Party (PLN). Since 1949, power has alternated between the PLN and the Social Christian Unity Party (PUSC).

The PUSC's Abel Pacheco won the 2002 presidential election, succeeding Miguel Angel Rodriguez, also of the PUSC. However, in 2006, former president Oscar Arias recaptured the presidency for the PLN, narrowly defeating Citizens' Action Party (PAC) candidate Otton Solis. Meanwhile, the PUSC lost its former prominence after Rodriguez was sentenced on corruption charges. The 2006 balloting also resulted in a divided Legislative Assembly; the PLN won 25 seats, the PAC 17, the Libertarian Movement Party (PML) 6, and the PUSC 5; other small parties won the remaining 4 seats.

Candidates for the February 2010 general elections began campaigning in 2009, including former vice president Laura Chinchilla of the PLN—who is backed by President Arias—PAC candidate Otton Solis, and the PML's Otto Guevara. The PUSC's popularity was further damaged in October, when candidate and former president Rafael Angel Calderon was sentenced to five years in jail on corruption charges. With Calderon unexpectedly withdrawing from the race, Guevara was poised to capture many of the PUSC votes. Meanwhile, in anticipation of the 2010 elections, Costa Rica in August approved new reforms to its electoral law, including the prohibition of anonymous and foreign campaign donations, revised regulations surrounding government financing of political parties, and new quotas designed to promote women's leadership roles within political parties.

Concerns about public security, crime, and narcotics trafficking continued to grow in 2009. A January 2009 poll conducted by the company Unimer revealed that 27 percent of Costa Ricans surveyed cited security as a major concern. This fear has manifested itself in a move towards public armament in a country with no standing army; the number of gun licenses issued increased by 73 percent in 2008. The spread of violent crime is closely tied to drug trafficking, as Costa Rica is increasingly being used as a storage and transportation route. Organized criminal networks are also suspected of having infiltrated police and political institutions. In September, 10 Costa Rican police officers were arrested for aiding Colombian drug traffickers, including the former head of the antidrug program in the country's central Pacific region. About 1,500 police corruption cases remained open at year's end, but fewer than 200 officers have been discharged on corruption allegations in the past six years.

While quality of life in Costa Rica is relatively high for the region, economic growth is hampered by the national debt, inflation, and a rising cost of living. The global economic crisis has further threatened economic stability in the country, causing President Arias in January to announce a 23-point plan to mitigate the effects of the global downturn on the country's most vulnerable populations. The plan includes a 15 percent increase in welfare payments for the poorest sectors of society and mortgage debt forgiveness for approximately 2,100 families facing foreclosure. The Dominican Republic–Central America Free Trade Agreement (DR-CAFTA) with the United States—narrowly approved by voters in a 2007 referendum—went into effect on January 1, 2009, though its impact is yet to be seen.

Political Rights and Civil Liberties: Costa Rica is an electoral democracy. Legislative and presidential elections held in 2006 were generally considered free and fair. The president and members of the 57-seat, unicameral Legislative Assembly are elected for single four-year terms and can seek a nonconsecutive second term. The main political parties are the PLN, the PAC, the PML, and the PUSC. A special chamber of the Supreme Court chooses an independent national election commission.

Every president since 1990 has been accused of corruption after leaving office. Former president Rafael Angel Calderon was convicted in 2008 of taking an $800,000 kickback from a Finnish firm. In October 2009, he was convicted once again for graft, this time related to a loan from the Finnish government, and was sentenced to five years in jail. Costa Rica was ranked 43 out of 180 countries surveyed in Transparency International's 2009 Corruption Perceptions Index.

The Costa Rican media are generally free from state interference. There are six privately owned dailies, and both public and commercial broadcast outlets are available, including at least four private television stations and more than 100 private radio stations. Abuse of government advertising and direct pressure from senior officials to influence media content has been reported. The government had not modernized its defamation laws or removed excessive penalties as of the end of 2009. Internet access is unrestricted.

Freedom of religion is recognized, and there is complete academic freedom. President Oscar Arias backed a bill in September 2009 proposing that Costa Rica be declared a "secular state," rather than a Roman Catholic state; the move created controversy in 2009 and was publicly rejected by the Catholic Church.

The constitution provides for freedom of assembly and association, and numerous nongovernmental organizations (NGOs) are active. Although labor unions organize and mount frequent protests with minimal governmental interference, employers often ignore minimum-wage and social security laws, and the resulting fines are insignificant.

The judicial branch is independent, with members elected by the legislature. There are often substantial delays in the judicial process, including long pretrial detention. There have been some police brutality complaints, which are collected by an ombudsman's office. Prisons are notoriously overcrowded and offer inadequate medical services, though the government has made efforts to reduce overcrowding. In July 2009, the Inter-American Court of Human Rights ruled that Costa Rica had not fully complied with a 2004 ruling regarding the criminal appeals process; Costa Rica took actions in 2009 towards full compliance and submitted a report to the IACHR in October.

As the drug trade expands in Costa Rica, the country has experienced a significant increase in homicides in recent years, with a homicide rate of approximately 11 murders per every 100,000 people. There were 525 homicides reported in 2009, up from 435 in 2008. Costa Rica has become a popular location for the warehousing and transport of cocaine destined for the United States. The number of large shipments (between 500 and 1,000 kilograms) of cocaine passing through the country has increased by an estimated 400 percent between 2008 and 2009, with the majority of narcotics entering the country through maritime routes. Costa Rican authorities seized 20.6 tons of cocaine in 2009. Costa Rica received $5.3 million in counternarcotics funding from the United States as part of the Merida Initiative that was introduced in June 2009 to combat drug trafficking and money laundering.

At least 500,000 Nicaraguan immigrants live in the country illegally, and a 2006 law permits security forces to raid any home, business, or vehicle where they suspect the presence of undocumented immigrants, who can be detained indefinitely. There have been reports of abuse and extortion of migrants by the border guard. Costa Rica reformed its migration law in 2009, implementing fines for employers who hire illegal immigrants and creating stricter controls over marriages between Costa Ricans and foreigners in an effort to prevent "marriages of convenience."

Indigenous rights are not a government priority, and NGOs estimate that about 73 percent of the country's 70,000 indigenous people have little access to health and education services, electricity, or potable water. According to UNICEF, only 21 percent of indigenous youth have more than a primary-school education. Costa Ricans of African descent have also faced racial and economic discrimination.

Women still face discrimination in the economic realm, and only about a third of the economically active population is female. Most female employment is in the informal sector, where women on average earn 50 percent less than men. There are 22 women in the Legislative Assembly. Domestic workers have long been subject to exploitation; they lack legal protection, have the lowest minimum wage of all wage categories, and are excluded from social security programs.

Violence against women and children is a major problem. The number of female homicides in Costa Rica more than doubled in the past two years, with 16 reported in 2007 and 39 reported in 2009. An increasing number of sex tourists visit Costa Rica, and approximately 3,500 children were victims of sexual exploitation in 2007. Costa Rica has failed to enforce antitrafficking legislation and remains a transit and destination country for trafficked persons. However, reforms to the migration law in 2009 increased jail sentences for human traffickers.

Cote d'Ivoire

Political Rights: 6
Civil Liberties: 5
Status: Not Free

Population: 21,395,000
Capital: Yamoussoukro (official); Abidjan (de facto)

Ten-Year Ratings Timeline For Year Under Review (Political Rights, Civil Liberties, Status)

2000	2001	2002	2003	2004	2005	2006	2007	2008	2009
6,5PF	5,4PF	6,6NF	6,5NF	6,6NF	6,6NF	7,6NF	7,5NF	6,5NF	6,5NF

Overview:

Long-delayed national elections, required under a 2007 peace accord signed by President Laurent Gbagbo and rebel leader Guillaume Soro, were again postponed in 2009. Progress had stalled on voter registration, militia disarmament, the integration of rebel fighters into the military, and the restoration of government institutions in the rebel-held north, and both sides appeared to lack the political will to change the status quo.

Cote d'Ivoire gained independence from France in 1960, and President Felix Houphouet-Boigny ruled until his death in 1993. Henri Konan Bedie, then the Speaker of the National Assembly, assumed power and won a fraudulent election in 1995. Opposition candidate Alassane Ouattara was disqualified on the grounds of his alleged Burkinabe origins.

General Robert Guei seized power in 1999 and declared himself the winner of an October 2000 presidential election after initial results showed that he was losing to Laurent Gbagbo. He was soon toppled by a popular uprising, and Gbagbo, who was eventually declared the winner, refused to call new polls. The postelection violence cost hundreds of civilian lives and deepened the divisions between north and south as well as between Muslims and Christians. In the December 2000 legislative elections, Gbagbo's Ivorian Popular Front (FPI) won 96 seats, while Bedie's Democratic Party of Cote d'Ivoire–African Democratic Rally (PDCI-RDA) took 94 and smaller parties and independents won the remainder.

Civil war erupted in September 2002, when some 700 soldiers mounted a coup attempt, and government forces killed Guei in unclear circumstances on the first day of fighting. Clashes intensified between loyalist troops and the rebels, who quickly took control of the north and called for Gbagbo to step down. This call was echoed by similar forces in the west. By December 2002, the rebel factions had united to form the New Forces (FN), led by Guillaume Soro.

Gbagbo's government and the FN signed a ceasefire brokered by France in 2003, but it soon broke down. In 2004, following the deaths of nine French peacekeepers in a government bombing campaign against the FN, France destroyed the Ivorian air force and—with the backing of the African Union (AU)—persuaded the UN Security Council to impose a strict arms embargo on the country. In April 2005, South African president Thabo Mbeki brokered a new peace accord that set general elections for the end of that year. However, because the requisite disarmament and poll preparations were not completed in time, the AU postponed the elections, extended Gbagbo's term, and appointed an interim prime minister, economist Charles Konan Banny.

Similar disarmament and voter-identification delays prevented elections from taking place in 2006. With the expiration of Gbagbo's extended mandate in October 2006, the UN Security Council passed a resolution transferring all political and military power to the prime minister until the next elections. Gbagbo refused to accept the move and called for the withdrawal of all foreign troops.

In March 2007, Gbagbo and Soro met in Burkina Faso and signed an entirely new bilateral peace deal, the Ouagadougou Political Accord (APO), according to which Soro was appointed interim prime minister until elections could be held. Opposition political parties were left out, but the pact was seen as having a greater chance of success than its predecessors. Gbagbo soon visited the north for the first time since 2002, and the "confidence zone" separating the two parts of the country was officially dismantled. Despite the more peaceful climate, the elections envisioned in the APO were repeatedly postponed due to a combination of stalled preparations and lack of political will. Preelection hurdles included the distribution of identity cards, creation of a voter registry, integration of rebel forces into the army, disarmament of other armed groups, and restoration of administrative institutions in the north.

In 2008, notable progress was made in identifying voters; 600,000 new birth certificates were reportedly distributed by the middle of the year. Yet the process for formally registering voters was badly organized and cumbersome, involving five separate bodies with overlapping responsibilities. While the electoral commission announced in June 2009 that over 6 million voters had been successfully enrolled (short of the anticipated 8.6 million), the official registry had yet to be approved by all political parties at year's end.

The disarmament of both rebel and progovernment militias and the integration of rebel troops into the military have proven to be more problematic than the voter registration process. The United Nations reported that 7,704 former rebels had joined the reintegration program as of September 2009—a notable increase over the 2008 figure of 2,600. However, the program had found new civilian roles for only 675 of them, and the government estimated that over 18,000 formal rebel troops and over 20,000 progovernment and rebel-aligned militiamen had not yet disarmed. The government has also proven unwilling to provide the US$1,000 in assistance promised to each former combatant under the APO, or the estimated US$87 million it would cost to create a joint police force. Most parties have now accepted that the planned integration of 5,000 rebel soldiers into the military will not take place until after an election.

Rebel military leaders in the north handed over nominal administrative authority to government officials in May 2009. However, it remained unclear at year's end how much power was actually relinquished. The rebels retained their military structures and appeared to continue collecting taxes, while the new government administrators lacked even basic office supplies.

Political Rights and Civil Liberties: Cote d'Ivoire is not an electoral democracy. The constitution provides for the popular election of a president and a 225-seat unicameral National Assembly for five-year terms. However, the last legislative and presidential elections were held in 2000, and new voting has been repeatedly postponed; elections were most recently scheduled for November 2009, but they were pushed back indefinitely during the year. The president traditionally appoints the prime minister; in 2007, President Laurent Gbagbo replaced UN-backed prime minister Charles Konan Banny with rebel leader Guillaume Soro in keeping with the 2007 APO. The president's party, the FPI, dominates the legislature. Other major parties include the PDCI-RDA and the Rally of Republicans (RDR), led by Alassane Ouattara.

Corruption is a serious problem. Earnings from informal taxes and the sale of cocoa, cotton, and weapons have given many of those in power—including members of the military and rebel forces—an incentive to obstruct peace and political normalization. In the only successful high-profile corruption case of 2009, Gbagbo's secretary was convicted of extorting roughly US$150,000 from the president of a telecommunications company. She was sentenced to five years in prison, stripped of her civil rights, and ordered to pay some US$600 in damages directly to Gbagbo for dishonoring the presidency. Cote d'Ivoire ranked 154 out of 180 countries surveyed in Transparency International's 2009 Corruption Perceptions Index.

Despite constitutional protections, press freedom is generally not respected in practice, though violence against journalists appears to have declined since the signing of the APO in 2007. The government maintains a virtual monopoly on national television and radio broadcasting and owns the largest daily newspaper. Reporters who criticize powerful political figures often face defamation charges. Journalists convicted of insulting the president in an article detailing government corruption were fined about $US40,000 in March 2009, and others found guilty of libeling the prime minister were fined some US$10,000 in October. The government does not restrict internet access, but penetration is limited by poverty and infrastructural obstacles.

Legal guarantees of religious freedom are generally respected in practice. In the past, the government has shown a preference for Christians, particularly as the north-south divide corresponds roughly with the distribution of the Muslim and Christian populations. The marginal success of the voter-identification and registration process in the north in 2008 eased Muslim complaints about discrimination to some degree.

The government, which owns most educational facilities, inhibits academic freedom by requiring authorization for all political meetings held on campuses. However, the greatest restriction on academic freedom is the impunity enjoyed by the progovernment udent Federation of Cote d'Ivoire (FESCI), which engages in systematic violent intimidation.

The constitution protects the right to free assembly, but it is often denied in practice. In recent years, opposition demonstrations have been violently dispersed by progovernment forces like FESCI and the Young Patriots, leaving many dead. There have been a number of peaceful antigovernment demonstrations since the signing of the APO, but militia protests over the slow demobilization process often turn violent, as they did in two instances in September 2009. The activities of human rights groups are often hindered by progovernment forces, especially those that take a critical stance against the Gbagbo administration or those that attempt to operate in the north. While the situation has marginally improved ahead of the ever-anticipated elections, many human rights activists still face death threats and harassment from groups like the Young Patriots.

The right to organize and join labor unions is constitutionally guaranteed, and workers have the right to bargain collectively. However, these rights are not always respected in practice. A number of labor strikes were harshly repressed throughout 2009, particularly in the north, which is still controlled by rebel military leaders. In

February 2009, while emergency services continued to be provided, medical workers went on strike for a few days to demand a pay increase. Voter registration workers have mounted repeated strikes over lack of pay and security, contributing to the delays in the process.

The judiciary is not independent. Judges are political appointees without tenure and are highly susceptible to external interference and bribes. Judges and clerks began to redeploy to the north in 2008, but they continue to encounter resistance from rebel soldiers who are unwilling to relinquish authority.

Cote d'Ivoire's cocoa and other industries have historically depended on workers from neighboring countries, but conflicts between immigrants and longer-term residents, coupled with the xenophobic concept of *Ivoirite*, have contributed to the current political crisis. The preliminary success of the voter-identification process in 2008 has begun to ease these tensions, but a strong and inclusive national identity has yet to emerge, and political parties typically form along ethnic lines.

More than 7,000 UN peacekeeping troops will remain in the country until elections are held. While reports of violence have decreased since the signing of the APO, the border areas with Liberia and Guinea are highly unstable and continue to be used for smuggling small arms.

Cote d'Ivoire has made symbolic efforts to combat child trafficking, but tens of thousands of children from all over the region are believed to be working on Ivorian plantations. A 2007 German study also found that 85 percent of women involved in prostitution in Cote d'Ivoire were juveniles.

Despite official support for their constitutional rights, women suffer widespread discrimination. Equal pay is offered in the small formal business sector, but women have few chances of obtaining formal employment. Rape was reportedly common during the civil war, and it has remained a serious problem in the country, with perpetrators generally enjoying impunity.

Croatia

Political Rights: 1 *
Civil Liberties: 2
Status: Free

Population: 4,433,000
Capital: Zagreb

Ratings Change: Croatia's political rights rating improved from 2 to 1 due to improvements in the treatment of minority Serb and Roma communities.

Ten-Year Ratings Timeline For Year Under Review (Political Rights, Civil Liberties, Status)

2000	2001	2002	2003	2004	2005	2006	2007	2008	2009
2,3F	2,2F	2,2F	2,2F	2,2F	2,2F	2,2F	2,2F	2,2F	1,2F

Overview: Halfway through his second term, Prime Minister Ivo Sanader unexpectedly resigned in June 2009, and Jadranka Kosor became Croatia's first female prime minister in the postcommunist period. The first round of presidential elections was held in December, with SDP candidate Ivo Josipovic and independent candidate Milan Bandic moving on to a second round scheduled for January 2010. Progress was made in public administration and judicial reform, and the treatment of ethnic minority communities also registered improvements.

As part of the Socialist Federal Republic of Yugoslavia, Croatia held its first multiparty elections in 1990, which resulted in a victory for former communist general turned nationalist dissident Franjo Tudjman and his Croatian Democratic Union (HDZ). Tudjman and the HDZ continued to rule Croatia throughout the decade. Even as the country declared independence from Yugoslavia in 1991, the predominantly Serb region known as Krajina declared its independence from Croatia, resulting in a de facto partition. In 1995, Croatian military offensives overran the Serb enclave, and a majority of Croatia's Serbs either fled or were forcibly expelled from the country.

Tudjman died in December 1999, and voters elected an estranged Tudjman ally, Stjepan Mesic, as president in January 2000. Parliamentary elections later that month resulted in a victory for a center-left coalition led by the Social Democratic Party (SDP), whose leader, Ivica Racan, assumed the position of prime minister.

The HDZ, under the leadership of Ivo Sanader, returned to power in 2003 and repositioned itself as a conventional European center-right party, although some of its more controversial nationalist figures remained in influential positions. Sanader's government worked to meet the conditions for European Union (EU) accession, including improving cooperation with the International Criminal Tribunal for the Former Yugoslavia (ICTY) in The Hague. The trial of top Croatian war crimes suspect, Ante Gotovina, was still in process at the end of 2009. Several other Croatian military and political figures are also on trial for alleged crimes committed during the 1991–95 conflict.

The HDZ led November 2007 parliamentary elections with nearly 37 percent of the vote, followed by the SDP with 31 percent. New laws on the State Electoral Commission (SEC), voter lists, and party financing had been enacted in 2006 and 2007 to remedy previous electoral problems. However, issues that remained outstanding included granting the SEC the power to independently verify campaign finance reports submitted by candidates, and streamlining the legal framework for dealing with election complaints and appeals.

Following weeks of negotiations, Sanader's new government took office in January 2008. The HDZ formed a governing coalition with the Croatian Peasant Party (HSS), the Croatian Social Liberal Party (HSLS), and seven out of eight ethnic minority representatives, including three members of the Independent Serbian Democratic Party (SDSS). One of the new cabinet's four deputy prime ministers was a Serb.

In July 2009, Sanader unexpectedly resigned from office, leading to allegations that he was irresponsibly leaving his post just as Croatia was facing serious economic difficulties and a deadlocked territorial dispute with Slovenia. He was replaced by HDZ deputy prime Minister Jadranka Kosor, who became the first female prime minister of Croatia. The first round of presidential elections to replace Croatia's other leading politician, President Stipe Mesic, were held in December, with Social Democratic Party candidate Ivo Josipovic and independent candidate Milan Bandic becoming the top two vote-getters from a field of twelve candidates. A runoff election was scheduled for January 10, 2010.

Croatia was invited to join NATO at the 2008 Bucharest Summit, and formally became a member state in April 2009. The country's other main foreign policy goal of joining the EU has been significantly delayed in recent years due to the country's territorial dispute with neighboring Slovenia over maritime and land borders. The EU cancelled accession talks with Croatia in June 2009, after Slovenia blocked the closing of several chapters of Croatia's accession negotiations. However, the two sides came to a mutual agreement in September to allow for international mediation in the dispute, unlocking Croatia's EU accession path. By year's end, negotiations had opened on 30 of 33 chapters for Croatia's EU accession, and 18 chapters had been successfully closed; the country is likely achieve full EU membership in late 2011 or early 2012.

Political Rights and Civil Liberties: Croatia is an electoral democracy. Both the 2009 presidential poll and the 2007 parliamentary elections were deemed generally free and fair. The 153-seat parliament (Sabor) is a unicameral body composed of 140 members from geographical districts, 8 representing ethnic minorities, and a variable number representing Croatians living abroad. All members are elected to four-year terms. The president of the republic, who serves as head of state, is elected by popular vote for up to two five-year terms. The prime minister is appointed by the president, but must then be approved by the parliament.

The largest parties are the center-right HDZ and center-left SDP, though several smaller parties, including the HSS–HSLS coalition and the Croatian People's Party (HNS), have won representation in the parliament. In recent years, there has been an overall modest improvement in the political climate for Serb and Roma communities, with high-ranking government officials making more public statements in support of ethnic minority rights. The current government coalition formed after the 2007 parliamentary elections included eight minority members of parliament. While Serbs control a number of Croatia's municipalities, ethnic minorities, particularly Serbs, remain underrepresented in government and the civil administration.

Corruption remains a problem in Croatia, often driven by a nexus of security institutions and businesspeople. Organized crime tied to political and business interests is thought to be behind several assassinations in Zagreb in 2008. In 2009, the Office for the Fight Against Corruption and Organized Crime issued indictments against two former vice presidents of Croatia's Privatization Fund and a former government minister. Croatia was ranked 66 out of 180 countries surveyed in Transparency International's 2009 Corruption Perceptions Index.

The constitution guarantees freedoms of expression and the press, and these rights are generally respected in practice. However, reporters remain vulnerable to political pressure, and prominent journalists have alleged that the media are becoming increasingly beholden to the interests of powerful advertisers. Moreover, intimidation of journalists working on corruption issues has taken on dangerous dimensions. During the 2009 local election campaign, journalists critical of particular candidates were sometimes barred from press conferences, and in June, journalist Hrvoje Appelt announced that he had been dismissed from his job at one of Croatia's largest media outlets, despite being under police protection related to his reporting on organized crime. Access to the internet is unrestricted.

Freedom of religion is guaranteed by the constitution. A group needs at least

500 members and five years of operation as a registered association to be recognized as a religious organization. Members of the Serbian Orthodox Church continue to report cases of intimidation and vandalism, although the number of such incidents appears to be declining. Little progress has been made in restoring property nationalized by the communists to non-Roman Catholic groups.

The constitution provides for freedoms of association and assembly. A variety of both international and domestic nongovernmental organizations operate in Croatia without governmental interference or harassment. Workers are free to form and join trade unions. Despite economic discontent and dissatisfaction with government performance, protests organized by the Croatian Association of Trade Unions in September 2009 attracted little support. Nevertheless, trade unions have been increasingly successful in influencing government policy and decision making.

The judicial system suffers from numerous problems, including questionable selection of judges, a large backlog of cases, excessively long trials, a lack of impartiality among the local courts, and poor implementation of court decisions, especially in cases related to the repossession of property owned by Serbs. Nevertheless, some progress has been registered on these fronts over the past year. The European Commission has cited progress in improving the efficiency of the judiciary as evidenced by a reduction in the overall case backlog in the judicial system; a new Law on Misdemeanors, an amended Law on the Courts, and a new Civil Procedure Code have reduced the number of cases brought before the courts. Croatia initiated approximately 30 war crimes trials in 2008 and 2009, and the European Commission's 2009 progress report for Croatia noted greater willingness on the part of Croatian authorities to prosecute individuals regardless of their ethnicity. Prison conditions do not fully meet international standards due to overcrowding and poor medical care.

Respect for minority rights has gradually improved since 1999. There has been a noticeable decrease in negative stereotyping of ethnic minorities in the country's media. Returning Serbs are still harassed by the local population, although the frequency of such incidents is on the decline. Approximately 80,000 Croatian Serbs remain registered as refugees in the region at the end of 2009; this difficult environment has deterred Serbs from returning to Croatia. The Roma population continues to face discrimination and significant social and economic obstacles.

The constitution prohibits discrimination on the basis of gender. However, women are paid significantly less than men with similar qualifications. There are currently 36 women in the 153-seat parliament. Women must comprise at least 40 percent of the candidate lists for each political party at the local, national, and EU levels, though it remains unclear whether the prescribed fines are large enough to deter violations. Domestic violence against women is believed to be widespread and underreported, though the government has helped to finance several shelters and counseling centers for victims. Trafficking in women for the purpose of prostitution continues to be a problem, and Croatia is a transit country for women trafficked to Western Europe.

Cuba

Political Rights: 7
Civil Liberties: 6
Status: Not Free

Population: 11,225,000
Capital: Havana

Ten-Year Ratings Timeline For Year Under Review (Political Rights, Civil Liberties, Status)

2000	2001	2002	2003	2004	2005	2006	2007	2008	2009
7,7NF	7,7NF	7,7NF	7,7NF	7,7NF	7,7NF	7,7NF	7,7NF	7,6NF	7,6NF

Overview: In March 2009, President Raul Castro fired several prominent cabinet ministers amid a worsening economic crisis. Also during the year, former leader Fidel Castro appeared to regain his health and wrote frequent essays in the state press, sparking speculation that his renewed influence could slow Cuba's reform process. In November, noted blogger Yoani Sanchez reported being beaten and intimidated by suspected government agents. Cuban authorities in December arrested a U.S. contractor for distributing communications equipment to religious groups, although he remained in detention without being formally charged.

Cuba achieved independence from Spain in 1898 as a result of the Spanish-American War. The Republic of Cuba was established in 1902 but remained under U.S. tutelage until 1934. In 1959, the U.S.-supported dictatorship of Fulgencio Batista, who had ruled Cuba for 18 of the previous 25 years, was overthrown by Fidel Castro's July 26th Movement. Castro declared his affiliation with communism shortly thereafter, and the island has been governed by a one-party state ever since.

Following the 1991 collapse of the Soviet Union and the end of some $5 billion in annual Soviet subsidies, Castro opened some sectors of the economy to direct foreign investment. The legalization of the U.S. dollar in 1993 created a new source of inequality, as access to dollars from remittances or through the tourist industry enriched some, while the majority continued to live on peso wages averaging less than $10 a month.

The authorities remained highly intolerant of political dissent. In 1999, the government introduced harsh sedition legislation, with a maximum prison sentence of 20 years. It stipulated penalties for unauthorized contacts with the United States and the import or distribution of "subversive" materials, including texts on democracy and material from news agencies and journalists. The government also undertook a series of campaigns to undermine the reputations of leading opposition figures by portraying them as agents of the United States.

In 2002, the Varela Project, a referendum initiative seeking broad changes in the decades-old socialist system, won significant international recognition. However, the referendum proposal was rejected by the constitutional committee of the National Assembly, and the government instead held a counterreferendum in which 8.2 million people supposedly declared the socialist system to be "untouchable." The government initiated a crackdown on the prodemocracy opposition in March 2003. Seventy-five people, including 27 independent journalists, 14 independent librarians, and dozens of signature collectors for the Varela Project, were sentenced to an average of 20 years in prison following one-day trials held in April.

On July 31, 2006, Fidel Castro passed power on a provisional basis to his younger brother, defense minister and first vice president Raul Castro, after serious internal bleeding forced him to undergo emergency surgery and begin a slow convalescence. The 81-year-old Fidel resigned as president in February 2008, and Raul, 76, formally replaced him. The new president appointed 77-year-old Jose Ramon Machado, a top Communist Party *apparatchik*, as the new first vice president and named 72-year-old Julio Casas as the new defense minister. Though officially retired, Fidel continued to write provocative columns in the newspaper *Granma*, and he remained in the public eye through the release of a small number of carefully selected photographs and video clips.

The government approved a series of economic reforms in March 2008. These included allowing ordinary Cubans to buy consumer electronic goods and stay in the country's top tourist hotels. After introducing a plan in April that permitted thousands of Cubans to receive titles to their homes, the government eliminated salary caps and raised pensions for the country's more than two million retirees. The state also began granting farmers a larger role in decisions about land use. In late August and early September, however, Cuba was struck in rapid succession by hurricanes Gustav and Ike; more than 100,000 homes were damaged, and 30 percent of the country's crops were destroyed. Combined with the global economic downturn that began shortly thereafter, the storms sent the Cuban economy into a dire crisis that halted the tentative reform process.

In 2009, the government began to distribute land leases to agricultural workers, but other key aspects of the reform agenda remained stalled. Cuba's heavy dependence on imports led to a shortage of foreign exchange, forcing layoffs and closures at many state enterprises, and the threat of blackouts led to electricity rationing during the summer.

In March, Raul Castro dismissed Vice President Carlos Lage and Foreign Minister Felipe Perez Roque as part of a major cabinet shakeup. Fidel Castro later accused the two figures of being seduced by "the honey of power." In all, 10 cabinet officials were replaced, and the president subsequently postponed the long-overdue Sixth Party Congress, a major leadership conference that had been scheduled for the second half of 2009. Fidel's health and influence seemed to improve during the year, casting further doubts on Raul's initial policies.

Cuba continued to deny political and civil liberties to regime opponents in 2009. According to the Cuban Commission on Human Rights, a nongovernmental group, the number of political prisoners grew slightly to 208 by mid-2009, but had declined to 201 by year's end. Harassment and short-term detentions replaced long prison terms as the preferred form of repression, although some dissidents won reprieves from the government. In June, prominent dissident and neurosurgeon Hilda Molina was granted a long-sought exit visa so that she could join family members in Argentina; the move, which came just before elections in Argentina, indicated a political compromise between Argentine and Cuban leaders. In October, political prisoners Nelson Alberto Aguiar Ramirez and Omelio Lazaro Angulo Borrero, who had been arrested in the 2003 crackdown, were released following an intercession on their behalf by the visiting Spanish foreign minister. Several dissident groups praised the government's decision to allow Colombian pop singer Juanes to organize a major Havana concert promoting "Peace Without Borders," which took place in September with more than one million Cubans in attendance.

In April, the administration of newly elected U.S. president Barack Obama repealed all restrictions on the ability of Cuban Americans to visit Cuba or send money to their Cuban relatives. In June, the United States joined in the repeal of a 1962 resolution that had suspended Cuba's membership in the Organization of American States, but the Castro government rejected any interest in rejoining the group. Nevertheless, diplomatic contacts between the United States and Cuba increased during the year, including the resumption of stalled bilateral migration talks and negotiations on the restoration of direct postal service. The tentative thaw in U.S.-Cuban relations was threatened in December, when Cuban authorities arrested U.S. contractor Alan Gross, reportedly for distributing communications equipment to religious nongovernmental organizations. While Cuban officials publicly claimed that Gross was a "spy," he remained in detention without being formally charged.

Political Rights and Civil Liberties:
Cuba is not an electoral democracy. Longtime president Fidel Castro and his brother, current president Raul Castro, dominate the one-party political system, in which the Communist Party of Cuba (PCC) controls all government entities. The 1976 constitution provides for a National Assembly, which designates the Council of State. That body in turn appoints the Council of Ministers in consultation with its president, who serves as chief of state and head of government. Raul Castro is now president of the Council of Ministers and the Council of State, and commander in chief of the armed forces, while Fidel remains first secretary of the PCC. The most recent PCC congress was held in 1997; the next one, which is more than six years overdue, has been indefinitely postponed.

In the January 2008 National Assembly elections, as in previous elections, voters were asked to either support or reject a single candidate for each of the 614 seats. All candidates received the requisite 50 percent approval, with Raul Castro winning support from over 99 percent of voters.

All political organizing outside the PCC is illegal. Political dissent, whether spoken or written, is a punishable offense, and dissidents frequently receive years of imprisonment for seemingly minor infractions. The regime has also called on its neighbor-watch groups, known as Committees for the Defense of the Revolution, to strengthen vigilance against "antisocial behavior," a euphemism for opposition activity. Several dissident leaders have reported intimidation and harassment by state-sponsored groups. The absolute number of political prisoners in Cuba decreased slightly from 205 to 201 during 2009. By year's end, 53 of the 75 people arrested in the March 2003 crackdown on independent journalists, librarians, and other activists remained behind bars. In November, former political prisoner Marta Beatriz Roque led a small group of dissidents on an eight-day hunger strike that ended amid serious health concerns.

Official corruption remains a serious problem, with a culture of illegality shrouding the mixture of private and state-controlled economic activities that are allowed on the island. Cuba was ranked 61 out of 180 countries surveyed in Transparency International's 2009 Corruption Perceptions Index.

The news media are controlled by the state and the PCC. The government considers the independent press to be illegal and uses Ministry of Interior agents to infiltrate and report on the outlets in question. Independent journalists, particularly those associated with the dozen small news agencies that have been established outside state control, are subjected to ongoing repression, including terms of hard labor and assaults by state security agents. Foreign news agencies may only hire local reporters through government offices, limiting employment opportunities for independent journalists. Nearly two dozen of the independent journalists arrested in March 2003 remain imprisoned in degrading conditions, including physical and psychological abuse; acts of harassment and intimidation have also been directed against their families. Nevertheless, some state media, such as the newspaper *Juventud Rebelde*, have begun to cover previously taboo topics such as corruption in the health and education sectors.

Access to the internet remains tightly controlled, and it is difficult for most Cubans to connect from their homes. Websites are closely monitored, and while there are state-owned internet cafes in major cities, the costs are prohibitive for most residents. Only select state employees have workplace access to e-mail and restricted access to websites deemed inappropriate by the Ministry of Communications. Cuban blogger Yoani Sanchez has emerged as a worldwide celebrity, though few on the island can access the ironic and critical musings about life in Cuba on her popular blog, Generation Y. In 2009, the Cuban government denied her a visa to receive Columbia University's prestigious Maria Moors Cabot Prize for Latin American journalism in New York, and in November, Sanchez reported that she and another opposition blogger, Orlando Luis Pardo Lazo, were forced into a car, beaten, and denounced as "counterrevolutionaries" by three men they assumed to be government agents.

In 1991, Roman Catholics and other believers were granted permission to join the PCC, and the constitutional reference to official atheism was dropped the following year. However, official obstacles to religious freedom remain substantial. Churches are not allowed to conduct educational activities, and church-based publications are subject to censorship by the Office of Religious Affairs. While Roman Catholicism is the traditionally dominant faith, an estimated 70 percent of the population practices some form of Afro-Cuban religion.

The government restricts academic freedom. Teaching materials for subjects including mathematics and literature must contain ideological content. Affiliation with PCC structures is generally needed to gain access to educational institutions, and students' report cards carry information regarding their parents' involvement with the party. In the March 2003 crackdown, security forces raided 22 independent libraries and sent 14 librarians to prison with terms of up to 26 years. Many were charged with working with the United States to subvert the Cuban government.

Limited rights of assembly and association are permitted under the constitution. However, as with other constitutional rights, they may not be "exercised against the existence and objectives of the Socialist State." The unauthorized assembly of more than three people, even for religious services in private homes, is punishable with up to three months in prison and a fine. This rule is selectively enforced and is often used to imprison human rights advocates. Workers do not have the right to strike or bargain collectively. Members of independent labor unions, which the government considers illegal, are often harassed, dismissed from their jobs, and barred from future employment.

The Council of State, led by Raul Castro, controls both the courts and the judicial process as a whole. Beginning in 1991, the United Nations voted annually to assign a special investigator on human rights to Cuba, which consistently denied the appointee a visa. In 2007, the UN Human Rights Council ended the investigator position for Cuba. However, Raul Castro authorized Cuban representatives to sign two UN human rights treaties in February 2008. Cuba does not grant the International Committee of the Red Cross or other humanitarian organizations access to its prisons.

Afro-Cubans have frequently complained about widespread discrimination against them by government and law enforcement officials. Many Afro-Cubans have only limited access to the dollar-earning sectors of the economy, such as tourism and joint ventures with foreign companies.

Freedom of movement and the right to choose one's residence and place of employment are severely restricted. Attempting to leave the island without permission is a punishable offense. Intercity migration or relocation requires permission from the local Committee for the Defense of the Revolution and other authorities.

In the post-Soviet era, only state enterprises can enter into economic agreements with foreigners as minority partners; ordinary citizens cannot participate. PCC membership is still required to obtain good jobs, suitable housing, and real access to social services, including medical care and educational opportunities. In April 2008, the government eliminated wage caps and said it would begin moving toward a system in which pay was more closely linked with productivity. Also that year, it lifted a nine-year ban on privately operated taxis, and opened up unused land to private farmers and cooperatives, giving producers greater freedom to manage their lands and set their own prices. Farmers are now able to buy their own basic supplies, rather than rely on state provisions, for the first time since the 1960s. In July 2009, the government began to implement a massive land distribution program that resulted in the approval of 78,113 leases.

Cuba positioned itself at the forefront of the gay rights movement in Latin America in 2008, due in part to the advocacy of Mariela Castro, Raul Castro's daughter. In May, the government helped to sponsor an International Day Against Homophobia that featured shows, lectures, panel discussions, and book presentations. The Ministry of Public Health in June authorized government-provided sex-change surgeries for transsexuals, a move that provoked a strong protest from the Catholic Church. By 2009, 19 individuals had been identified as meeting the requirements for the surgery, and officials were debating the possible approval of artificial insemination for lesbians who wished to bear children. Cuba had already ranked well on gender equality; about 40 percent of all women work, and they are well represented in most professions.

Cyprus

Political Rights: 1
Civil Liberties: 1
Status: Free

Population: 1,072,000
Capital: Nicosia

Note: The numerical ratings and status listed above do not reflect conditions in Northern Cyprus, which is examined in a separate report.

Ten-Year Ratings Timeline For Year Under Review (Political Rights, Civil Liberties, Status)

2000	2001	2002	2003	2004	2005	2006	2007	2008	2009
1,1F	1,1F	1,1F	1,1F	1,1F	1,1F	1,1F	1,1F	1,1F	1,1F

Overview:
Complaints against the police, especially for corrupt activities and abuse of detainees, made headlines in Cyprus in 2009. Meanwhile, in November, police rescued 110 Romanian workers from a camp where they were allegedly being held and forced to work without pay.

Cyprus gained independence from Britain in 1960 after a five-year guerrilla campaign by partisans demanding union with Greece. In July 1974, Greek Cypriot National Guard members, backed by Greece's military junta, staged an unsuccessful coup aimed at such unification. Five days later, Turkey invaded northern Cyprus, seized control of 37 percent of the island, and expelled 200,000 ethnic Greeks from the north. Today, the Greek and Turkish communities are almost completely separated in the south and north, respectively.

A buffer zone known as the Green Line has divided Cyprus, including the capital, since 1974. UN resolutions stipulate that Cyprus is a single country of which the northern third is illegally occupied. In 1983, Turkish-controlled Cyprus declared its independence, a move recognized only by Turkey.

Reunification talks accelerated after a more receptive Turkish government was elected in 2002; the European Union (EU), the United States, and the United Nations added pressure for an agreement, and a new pro-unification government was elected in Northern Cyprus in 2003. Then-UN secretary-general Kofi Annan led a round of negotiations that collapsed in 2004 after no consensus was reached. As previously agreed, Annan subsequently proposed a plan that was put to a vote in simultaneous, separate referendums on both sides of the island in April 2004. Ultimately, 76 percent of Greek Cypriots voted against the plan, while 65 percent of Turkish Cypriots voted in favor. With the island still divided, only Greek Cyprus joined the EU as scheduled in May 2004.

In parliamentary elections held in the south in 2006, the Democratic Party (DIKO) won 11 seats, while the Democratic Rally (DISY) and Progressive Party of the Working People (AKEL), a communist party, each took 18 seats; three other parties captured the remaining 9 seats. The 2004 referendum and the prospects for reunification were major campaign issues, and the results were considered a signal of support for President Tassos Papadopoulos of DIKO and his rejection of the UN plan. However, this sentiment was reversed in the 2008 presidential election, when AKEL leader

Demetris Christofias won 53 percent of the runoff vote, making him the only communist head of state in Europe. His cabinet includes ministers from DIKO as well as the Movement for Social Democrats (EDEK). Christofias's election paved the way for new reunification talks, and he has continued to meet with the Northern Cypriot leader regularly.

Political Rights and Civil Liberties: Cyprus is an electoral democracy. Suffrage is universal, and elections are free and fair. The 1960 constitution established an ethnically representative system designed to protect the interests of both Greek and Turkish Cypriots; the Greek Cypriots maintain that the constitution still applies to the entire island.

The president is elected by popular vote to serve a five-year term. The unicameral House of Representatives has 80 seats filled through proportional representation for five-year terms. Of these, 24 are reserved for the Turkish Cypriot community, but the Turkish Cypriot representatives withdrew in 1964 and have not been replaced to date. Instead, the Turkish Cypriots maintain their own parliament in the northern part of the island.

Following a ruling against Cyprus by the European Court of Human Rights (ECHR) in 2004, a law was passed allowing Turkish Cypriots living in the south to vote and run for office in Greek Cypriot elections. About 390 registered to vote before the 2008 presidential election, up from 270 in 2006, when one also ran for a seat in parliament. Turkish Cypriots cannot run for president, as the constitution states that a Greek Cypriot should hold that post and a Turkish Cypriot should be vice president. The Maronites (Catholics of Lebanese descent), Armenians, and Latins (Catholics of European descent) elect special nonvoting representatives. Women are very poorly represented politically, with only one woman in the cabinet and seven in parliament.

Corruption is not a major problem in Cyprus. New laws were passed in 2008 to prevent conflicts of interest by government officials and to make it a criminal offense to withhold information on bribery in defense procurement. Several corruption scandals involving the police were uncovered in 2009, including an officer who helped a murderer escape from prison and another who attempted to buy a rocket launcher while claiming to work on an arms-trafficking case. Cyprus was ranked 27 out of 180 countries surveyed in Transparency International's 2009 Corruption Perceptions Index.

Freedom of speech is constitutionally guaranteed and generally respected. A vibrant independent press frequently criticizes the authorities. Several private television and radio stations in the Greek Cypriot community compete effectively with public stations. Parliamentary hearings on freedom of information in May 2009 indicated that many legal requests for information are not fulfilled, mostly due to lack of resources. Although Turkish Cypriot journalists can enter the south, Turkish journalists based in the north have reported difficulties crossing the border. In April, a journalist was threatened by a mob during a march marking the fifth anniversary of the rejection of the Annan plan. Access to the internet is unrestricted.

Freedom of religion is guaranteed by the constitution and protected in practice. Nearly all inhabitants of the south are Orthodox Christians, and some discrimination against other religions has been alleged. In September 2009, more than 100 Muslims of two differing sects clashed at a mosque in the capital; nearly all involved were immigrants. The police controversially arrested 150 people in a subsequent sweep; 36 were found to be illegal and faced deportation, while the remainder were released. State schools use textbooks containing negative language about Turkish Cypriots and Turkey.

Freedoms of association and assembly are respected. Nongovernmental organizations (NGOs) generally operate without government interference. Workers have the right to strike and to form trade unions without employer authorization.

The independent judiciary operates according to the British tradition, upholding due-process rights. However, the ECHR ruled against Cyprus in 2009 for failure to provide a timely trial; the court case in question lasted nearly six years. In 2008, the Cyprus ombudswoman issued complaints on behalf of asylum seekers who were indefinitely detained in Nicosia's prison; while the situation has improved somewhat, long-term detention of migrants continues. The Council of Europe and other groups have noted cases of police brutality, including targeted beatings of minorities. There were 110 complaints reported against the police in 2008, sparking 42 investigations; 54 complaints concerned a violation of human rights. In March 2009, a black Cypriot sued the police after allegedly racially motivated physical abuse. Also in March, 10 plainclothes police officers who were videotaped beating two students in 2005 were cleared of all charges in a controversial criminal court decision; a Supreme Court appeals process began in November. Prison overcrowding has decreased but remains a problem.

A 1975 agreement between the two sides of the island governs treatment of minorities. Turkish Cypriots are now entitled to Republic of Cyprus passports, and thousands have obtained them. However, Turkish Cypriots in the south have reported difficulty obtaining identity cards and other documents, as well as harassment and discrimination. Asylum seekers face regular discrimination, especially in employment, and the ombudswoman continues to highlight discrimination against homosexuals.

Since accession to the EU in 2004, all citizens can move freely throughout the island, and a key border crossing in Nicosia was opened in 2008. While the Greek Cypriots have thwarted attempts to lift international trade and travel bans on the north, trade continues to increase between the two sides.

The status of property abandoned by those moving across the Green Line beginning in 1974 is a point of contention in reunification talks. Under changes in the law in the north, Greek Cypriots can appeal to a new property commission to resolve disputes, but the government in the south does not recognize this commission. A 1991 law states that property left by Turkish Cypriots belongs to the state. Several key cases in 2009 left the international status of the property commission unresolved, though it continues to issue decisions on property disputes.

Gender discrimination in the workplace, sexual harassment, and violence against women are problems. Local NGOs reported in 2009 that 80,000 Greek Cypriot women are subject to domestic violence, as well as an additional 30,000 foreign women. While the government has made genuine progress to prevent human trafficking, Cyprus remains a transit and destination country, and prosecution is weak. Slave labor has been occasionally uncovered in Cyprus. In November 2009, police saved 110 Romanian workers from a camp where they were allegedly being held and forced to work without pay.

Czech Republic

Political Rights: 1
Civil Liberties: 1
Status: Free

Population: 10,511,000
Capital: Prague

Ten-Year Ratings Timeline For Year Under Review (Political Rights, Civil Liberties, Status)

2000	2001	2002	2003	2004	2005	2006	2007	2008	2009
1,2F	1,2F	1,2F	1,2F	1,1F	1,1F	1,1F	1,1F	1,1F	1,1F

Overview:

Prime Minister Mirek Topolanek's center-right government was ousted by a vote of no confidence in March 2009, and President Vaclav Klaus appointed Jan Fischer as prime minister of a caretaker government in April. Because a majority of deputies opposed early parliamentary elections, Fischer's government was set to remain in place until regular elections in June 2010. Also during 2009, violence against Roma continued amid worsening economic conditions.

Czechoslovakia was created in 1918 amid the collapse of the Austro-Hungarian Empire. Soviet forces helped establish a communist government after World War II, and in 1968 they crushed the so-called Prague Spring, a period of halting political liberalization under reformist leader Alexander Dubcek.

In December 1989, a series of peaceful anticommunist demonstrations led by dissident Vaclav Havel and the Civic Forum opposition group resulted in the resignation of the government, in what became known as the Velvet Revolution. Open elections were held the following year. In 1992, a new constitution and the Charter of Fundamental Rights and Freedoms were adopted, and the country began an ambitious program of political and economic reform under Finance Minister Vaclav Klaus of the center-right Civic Democratic Party (ODS), who became prime minister that year. In 1993, the state dissolved peacefully into separate Czech and Slovak republics, and Havel became president of the former.

Close parliamentary elections in 1998 brought the center-left Czech Social Democratic Party (CSSD) to power, although an "opposition agreement" between the CSSD and the ODS limited meaningful political competition and brought about several years of political gridlock. Klaus was elected president by Parliament in 2003.

The Czech Republic joined the European Union (EU) in May 2004, but the CSSD's poor showing in June elections for the European Parliament led to Prime Minister Vladimir Spidla's resignation and a period of instability in the ruling coalition.

In the June 2006 lower house elections, the CSSD and the unreformed Communist Party of Bohemia and Moravia (KSCM) captured 100 seats (74 and 26, respectively), while three other parties—the ODS, the Christian and Democratic Union–Czechoslovak People's Party (KDU-CSL), and the Greens—also won 100 (81, 13, and 6, respectively). Months of negotiations failed to produce a viable government, as no party was willing to work with the KSCM, and the two largest parties were unable to agree on a grand coalition. A fragile government of the ODS, KDU-CSL, and Greens failed a confidence vote in October after serving only one month, but the ODS easily won regional and Senate elections in late October, strengthening its public position.

In January 2007, President Klaus reappointed Prime Minister Mirek Topolanek of the ODS, who had remained in office in a caretaker capacity since the last coalition collapsed. Klaus himself was narrowly reelected in February 2008, receiving 141 votes in Parliament. The CSSD led regional and Senate elections in October 2008, rising to a new total of 29 seats in the Senate and reducing the ODS to a total of 35, ending its majority in the chamber.

Topolanek's coalition government was ousted in a parliamentary vote of no confidence in March 2009, and Klaus appointed Jan Fischer to lead the caretaker government that took over in May. The president set early parliamentary elections for October, but the Constitutional Court blocked them in September, after an independent deputy argued that snap elections would violate his right to serve a full term. The CSSD, Greens, and KSCM defeated a subsequent constitutional amendment that would have allowed for early elections. As a result, the caretaker government was set to remain in place until regular parliamentary elections due in June 2010.

Klaus, a skeptic of EU integration, signed the long-delayed Lisbon Treaty in November 2009, after the Constitutional Court deemed it compatible with the Czech constitution and he received assurances that the country could opt out of the EU's Charter of Fundamental Rights. The Czech ratification cleared the way for implementation of the treaty, which was intended in part to make EU decision making more efficient.

Political Rights and Civil Liberties: The Czech Republic is an electoral democracy. Since the Velvet Revolution in 1989, the country has enjoyed free and fair elections. The Chamber of Deputies, the lower house of Parliament, has 200 members elected for four-year terms by proportional representation. The Senate has 81 members elected for six-year terms, with one-third up for election every two years. The president, elected by Parliament for five-year terms, appoints judges, the prime minister, and other cabinet members, but has few other formal powers. The prime minister, whose recommendations determine the cabinet appointments, relies on support from a majority in the Chamber of Deputies to govern.

The three largest political parties are the center-left CSSD; the center-right, market-oriented ODS; and the leftist KSCM. Parties must win at least 5 percent of the vote to enter the lower house.

Corruption affects many sectors of society, and the government has taken little action to improve transparency and prevent graft. National police began investigating former Defense Ministry officials in March 2009 for alleged involvement in fraudulent construction contracts. Separately, a lawmaker from the new centre-right party TOP 09 and two KSCM vice chairmen resigned in September after they were implicated in a newspaper's bribery investigation. The Czech Republic was ranked 52 out of 180 countries surveyed in Transparency International's 2009 Corruption Perceptions Index.

Freedom of expression is respected, although the Charter of Fundamental Rights and Freedoms, part of the Czech constitution, prohibits threats against individual rights, state and public security, public health, and morality. The country's print and electronic media are largely in private hands. In February 2009, an appeals court upheld a fine against journalist Sabina Slonkova for refusing to name the source of footage showing an illicit meeting between a lobbyist and a presidential adviser, despite a 2005 Constitutional Court ruling that journalists cannot be compelled to reveal their sources. A new law banning publication of police wiretap records and the names of victims and suspects in specific crimes took effect in April 2009. Critics argue that the law, which carries penalties of up to five years in prison and a fine of CZK 5 million (US$270,000), infringes on the public's right to know. Internet access is unrestricted.

The government generally upholds freedom of religion. In July 2009, the KDU-CSL voiced opposition to the construction of a second mosque in Brno, but there is no law that would prevent it. Academic freedom is widely respected.

Czechs may assemble peacefully, form associations, and petition the government. Trade unions and professional associations function freely. The 2007 labor code abolished several restrictions on freedom of association but requires unions within a single enterprise to act in concert when conducting collective bargaining.

The independent judiciary consists of the Constitutional Court, the Supreme Court, the Supreme Administrative Court, and high, regional, and district courts. A 2008 law streamlined the selection procedure for Constitutional Court and Supreme Court judges and established disciplinary measures for those caught accepting bribes. Prisons generally meet international standards, though abuse of vulnerable prisoners serving life-long sentences remains a problem. In December 2009, three policemen were charged with abuse of power for beating a suspected drug dealer to death.

The Charter of Fundamental Rights and Freedoms gives minorities the right to participate in the resolution of matters pertaining to their group. A 1999 law restored citizenship to many residents, including Roma, who continue to experience discrimination. Romany children are reportedly segregated in schools or even sent to schools for the mentally disabled. In April 2009, a two-year-old Romany girl was seriously injured during an arson attack on her family's home. In May, the anti-Roma National Party (Narodni Strana) aired a European Parliament campaign advertisement promising a, "final solution to the Gypsy question." Czech Television pulled the ad, but argued that it had no legal right to regulate the content of election material. In November, a representative of the National Party received a one-year suspended sentence and three year's probation for inciting hatred by airing the advertisement. The new Antidiscrimination Act, which took effect in September after the Chamber of Deputies overturned a presidential veto, provides for equal treatment regardless of sex, race, age, or sexual orientation. Promoting denial of the Holocaust and inciting religious hatred remain illegal.

Gender discrimination is legally prohibited. However, sexual harassment in the workplace appears to be fairly common, and women are underrepresented at the highest levels of government and business. They currently hold 14 seats in the 81-member Senate, and 35 of 200 in the Chamber of Deputies. Trafficking of women and girls for prostitution remains a problem. The government has taken steps in recent years to strengthen the reporting and punishment of domestic violence. The Council of Europe's Committee for the Prevention of Torture (CPT) raised concerns again in 2009 that convicted sex offenders were being surgically castrated without their consent or sufficient information on the surgery and its side effects. The CPT reported that most sex offenders had agreed to the castration to avoid long-term imprisonment and that more than 50 percent had committed nonviolent crimes.

Denmark

Political Rights: 1
Civil Liberties: 1
Status: Free

Population: 5,529,000
Capital: Copenhagen

Ten-Year Ratings Timeline For Year Under Review (Political Rights, Civil Liberties, Status)

2000	2001	2002	2003	2004	2005	2006	2007	2008	2009
1,1F	1,1F	1,1F	1,1F	1,1F	1,1F	1,1F	1,1F	1,1F	1,1F

Overview: Several riots and violent protests occurred in 2009, including in Copenhagen's Noerrebro neighborhood and during the December UN Climate Change Conference in the Danish capital. In October, two men were arrested in connection with a terrorist plot targeting the offices of the newspaper *Jyllands-Posten.* Meanwhile, a controversy erupted over the military's attempt to prevent the publication of a book on the grounds that it would reveal sensitive military information.

Denmark has been a monarchy since the Middle Ages, but after the promulgation of its first democratic constitution in 1849, the monarch's role became largely ceremonial. The country was occupied by Nazi Germany during World War II, despite its attempts to maintain neutrality, and in 1949, it joined NATO. In 1973, Denmark became a member of the European Economic Community (EEC), forerunner to the European Union (EU).

Postwar Danish politics have been dominated by the Social Democratic Party. However, in the 2001 elections, a right-wing coalition led by Anders Fogh Rasmussen's Liberal Party won control by pledging to reduce immigration and lower taxes. The coalition, which also included the Conservative People's Party, was supported by the anti-immigrant and Euroskeptic Danish People's Party. Denmark has had a conflicted relationship with the EU, rejecting the bloc's 1992 Maastricht Treaty on justice, foreign, and monetary policy and opting not to adopt the euro as its sole currency in 2000.

The Liberals won reelection in 2005, maintaining their coalition with the Conservatives and receiving external support from the Danish People's Party. Prime Minister Rasmussen was returned to office again in the 2007 elections, with the Liberals, Conservatives, and Danish People's Party receiving 45, 18, and 25 seats, respectively. The Social Democrats captured 45 seats, and the Socialist People's Party, one of the smaller opposition parties, more than doubled its share of seats, from 11 to 23. Rasmussen officially resigned his post on April 5, 2009, after being named NATO secretary general; he was replaced by finance minister Lokke Rasmussen (no relation).

In October 2009, two men, David Coleman Headley and Tahawwur Hussain Rana, were arrested in Chicago in connection with a terrorist bombing plot against the offices of the newspaper *Jyllands-Posten*; the paper had printed controversial cartoons of the prophet Mohammad in 2005. Authorities retrieved surveillance video of the buildings showing the men visiting two *Jyllands-Posten* offices over the course of the year. The men are alleged to have had ties to the terrorist attacks in Mumbai, India, in 2008.

A major controversy arose in 2009, when the country's military tried to prevent a former Danish soldier from publishing a memoir about his combat experiences in Iraq and Afghanistan on the grounds that it would reveal military secrets and endanger Danish soldiers. A leading Danish newspaper, *Politiken*, published the book in its entirety and included it as a "free supplement" on September 16. A Copenhagen court subsequently ruled that the military could not ban the book, since the information had already been released to the public.

Several violent clashes between law enforcement officials and protestors occurred during 2009. In August, police raided a church in the Noerrebro neighborhood of Copenhagen sheltering a group of Iraqis who had been denied asylum. Some 300 protestors attacked the police vehicle transporting the refugees, and police responded with pepper spray and batons. Also in August, a riot broke out in Copenhagen's Noerrebro district, the site of numerous violent clashes in recent year, prompted by a violent altercation between a police officer and a demonstrator, the exact nature of which remains contested.

During the UN Climate Change Conference held in December in the Danish capital, a series of small-scale protests culminated in a much larger demonstration on December 12, in which nearly 1,000 protestors were held under Denmark's controversial preventive detention law, which allows demonstrators to be administratively detained on the mere suspicion of disturbing the peace. Some demonstrators were kettled, a controversial police tactic in which a large group of protestors is contained in a limited area without access to food, water, or toilets. Law enforcement officials used pepper spray and tear gas against some of the activists. An investigation by the country's ombudsman into these incidents was ongoing at year's end.

Political Rights and Civil Liberties: Denmark is an electoral democracy. The current constitution, adopted in 1953, established a single-chamber parliament (the Folketing) and retained a monarch, currently Queen Margrethe II, with mostly ceremonial duties. The parliament's 179 representatives are elected at least once every four years through a system of modified proportional representation. The leader of the majority party or coalition is usually chosen to be prime minister by the monarch. Danish governments most often control a minority of seats in parliament, ruling with the aid of one or more supporting parties. Since 1909, no single party has held a majority of seats, helping to create a tradition of compromise.

The territories of Greenland and the Faeroe Islands each have two representatives in the Folketing. They also have their own elected institutions, which have power over almost all areas of governance.

Levels of corruption in Denmark are very low. The police began investigating a case in 2008 concerning the pharmaceutical company Missionpharma, which was suspected of bribing two consultants to secure a UN contract in the Democratic Republic of Congo; the charges were dropped in January 2009. Denmark was ranked 2 out of 180 countries surveyed in Transparency International's 2009 Corruption Perceptions Index.

The constitution guarantees freedom of expression. The media reflect a wide variety of political opinions and are frequently critical of the government. The state finances radio and television broadcasting, but state-owned television companies have independent editorial boards. Independent radio stations are permitted but tightly regulated. Internet use in Denmark is among the world's highest in terms of the percentage of the population with access.

Freedom of worship is legally protected. However, the Evangelical Lutheran Church is subsidized by the government as the official state religion. The faith is taught in public schools, although students may withdraw from religious classes with parental consent. At present, about half of all schoolchildren are exempted from the catechism taught in public schools. On May 29, the parliament amended the Administration of Justice Act to ban religious or political symbols from judicial attire.

The constitution provides for freedoms of assembly and association. Civil society is vibrant, and workers are free to organize. The labor market is mainly regulated by agreements between employers' and employees' organizations. Several protests in 2009 turned violent, including demonstrations against police harassment in the Copenhagen district of Norrebro and protests during an international climate conference in the Danish capital.

The judiciary is independent, and citizens enjoy full due-process rights. The court system consists of 100 local courts, 2 high courts, and the 15-member Supreme Court, with judges appointed by the monarch on the government's recommendation. A 2007 report by the International Commission of Jurists found ethnic bias in "a limited scope" of Danish court rulings and suggested mandatory training courses on discrimination for judges and lawyers. Prisons generally meet international standards.

Discrimination is prohibited under the law. However, Denmark introduced one of Europe's strictest immigration laws in 2002. The measure restricts citizens' ability to bring foreign spouses into the country, requiring both partners to be aged 24 or older. The law also requires the Dane to pass a solvency test, prove that he or she has not drawn social security for at least a year, and post a bond of almost $10,000. A reunified family's husband and wife must both prove "close ties to Denmark." The law came under scrutiny after the European Court of Justice ruled in July 2008 that a similar Irish law, which requires foreign spouses to prove residence in an EU country before taking up residence in Ireland, was incompatible with a 2004 EU directive allowing foreign spouses to live in EU member states regardless of prior residence. Denmark also denies religious worker visas, which restricts access to missionaries entering the country from abroad.

Denmark has closed many of its asylum centers since the introduction of the restrictive 2002 immigration law. In September 2009, Denmark was criticized by the United Nations High Commissioner for Human Rights for deporting 22 Iraqis even though Iraq had been deemed "dangerous."

Women enjoy equal rights in Demark and represent half of the workforce. However, disparities have been reported in the Faeroe Islands and Greenland. Denmark is a destination and transit point for women and children trafficked for the purpose of sexual exploitation. Following the 2003 adoption of legislation that defined and criminalized such trafficking, the government began working regularly with nongovernmental organizations in their trafficking-prevention campaigns. In March 2009, the Supreme Court handed down its first human trafficking convictions: a Croatian national and a Czech citizen received prison sentences of three and a half and two and a half years, respectively, for trafficking women from the Czech Republic to Denmark.

Djibouti

Political Rights: 5
Civil Liberties: 5
Status: Partly Free

Population: 864,000
Capital: Djibouti

Ten-Year Ratings Timeline For Year Under Review (Political Rights, Civil Liberties, Status)

2000	2001	2002	2003	2004	2005	2006	2007	2008	2009
4,5PF	4,5PF	4,5PF	5,5PF	5,5PF	5,5PF	5,5PF	5,5PF	5,5PF	5,5PF

Overview: Following clashes at the border in June 2008, Eritrean troops continued to occupy disputed territory in 2009, in defiance of a UN Security Council resolution. Also during the year, renewed violence by ethnic Afar rebels ended several years of relative calm, and drought and food insecurity remained significant hardships for much of the population.

Djibouti, formerly the French Territory of the Afars and Issas, gained independence in 1977. Its people are divided along ethnic and clan lines, with the Issa (Somali) and Afar peoples traditionally falling into opposing political camps. The Issa make up about 60 percent of the population, and the Afar about 35 percent. Ethnic conflict broke out in 1991, with Afar rebels of the Front for the Restoration of Unity and Democracy (FRUD) launching a guerrilla war against Issa domination. In 1994, the largest FRUD faction agreed to end its insurgency in exchange for inclusion in the government and electoral reforms.

President Hassan Gouled Aptidon controlled a one-party system until 1992, when a new constitution authorized four political parties. In 1993, Gouled won a fourth six-year term in Djibouti's first contested presidential election, which was considered fraudulent by international observers. In the 1997 legislative elections, which were also considered unfair, the ruling People's Progress Assembly (RPP) won all 65 legislative seats.

Gouled stepped down in 1999, but his nephew, Ismael Omar Guelleh, won that year's presidential poll with 74 percent of the vote. For the first time since elections began in 1992, no group boycotted the vote, and it was regarded as generally fair. In 2001, a comprehensive peace accord aimed at ending the decade-long Afar insurgency was signed. A bloc of four parties under the umbrella Union for the Presidential Majority (UMP) ran against the four-party opposition bloc, Union for a Democratic Alternative (UAD), in the 2003 parliamentary elections. The UMP captured all 65 seats.

Guelleh used Djibouti's strategic location to generate international support and development assistance. Beginning in 2004, approximately 2,000 U.S. military personnel were stationed in the country, alongside a similar number of French troops.

In 2005, Guelleh won a second six-year term. The only challenger withdrew from the election, citing government control of the media and repression of the opposition. The country's human rights league called the official turnout figure of 79 percent "highly unlikely."

Legislative elections took place in March 2008, but the main opposition parties did not participate, citing government abuses including the house arrest of opposition leaders and manipulation of the electoral process. In June of that year, an Eritrean military incursion along the disputed border resulted in the deaths of a number of Djiboutian soldiers. Eritrea ignored a UN Security Council resolution calling for a withdrawal, and the standoff continued through 2009.

Also in 2009, renewed clashes took place between government forces and elements of the FRUD, which accused the president of persecuting the Afar people and failing to hold transparent elections.

A severe drought affecting the entire Horn of Africa posed serious hardships for the majority of the population, more than 40 percent of which lives under the poverty line. Moreover, the country's dependence on imported food meant that persistently high global food prices in 2009 had a profound impact on the poor. UNICEF warned that malnutrition was becoming a serious problem in and around the capital, home to two-thirds of the population.

Political Rights and Civil Liberties: Djibouti is not an electoral democracy. The formal structures of representative government and electoral processes have little relevance to the real distribution and exercise of power. The ruling party has traditionally used state resources to maintain itself in government.

The elected president serves a maximum of two six-year terms, and the 65 members of the unicameral parliament, the National Assembly, are directly elected for five-year terms. Opposition parties are disadvantaged by electoral rules and the government's abuse of the administrative apparatus. In the 2003 legislative elections, the ruling UMP coalition won 62 percent of the vote. It captured all of the National Assembly seats, however, because the election law stipulates that the winner of the majority in each of the country's five electoral constituencies is awarded all seats in that district. Opposition parties boycotted the 2005 presidential election and the 2008 parliamentary polls.

Political parties are required to register with the government. In 2008, President Ismael Omar Guelleh issued a decree that dissolved the opposition Movement for Democratic Renewal party, whose leader had reportedly voiced support for that year's Eritrean military incursion.

Efforts to curb the country's rampant corruption have met with little success. According to the Heritage Foundation's 2009 Index of Economic Freedom, business activity is hampered by bureaucratic inefficiency, and the taking of bribes is commonplace. Djibouti was ranked 111 out of 180 countries surveyed in Transparency International's 2009 Corruption Perceptions Index.

Despite constitutionally mandated protections, freedom of speech is not upheld in practice. The domestic media sector is very limited. The government owns the principal newspaper, *La Nation*, as well as Radio-Television Djibouti (RTD), which operates the national radio and television stations. Strict laws governing libel and slander mean that journalists generally avoid covering sensitive issues, including human rights, the army, the FRUD, and relations with Ethiopia. The opposition-oriented *Le Renouveau* newspaper was permanently closed by the authorities in 2007 on grounds of libel, due to an article stating that a businessman had paid a bribe to the national bank governor, the president's brother-in-law. Djibouti is one of the few countries in Africa without any independent newspapers. The international press is sold freely in Djibouti, and foreign radio broadcasts are available from the British Broadcasting Corporation, Voice of America, and Radio France International, offering alternative sources of information to the public. The government places few restrictions on internet access, although the Association for Respect of Human Rights in Djibouti (ARDHD) claims that its site is regularly blocked.

Islam is the state religion, and 94 percent of the population is Muslim. Freedom of worship is respected. While academic freedom is generally upheld, higher educational opportunities are limited, with the government first authorizing the establishment of a university in 2006.

Freedoms of assembly and association are nominally protected under the constitution, but the government has demonstrated little tolerance for political protests and criticism by civil society groups. The Interior Ministry requires permits for peaceful assemblies and monitors opposition activities. Police have dispersed several demonstrations, including protests against high food prices. Local human rights groups do not operate freely. In 2007, the chairman of the Djibouti League of Human Rights was found guilty of "defamation and spread of false information" and sentenced to six months in prison. However, women's groups and some other nongovernmental organizations are able to work without much interference.

Workers may join unions and strike. In practice, however, the government discourages truly independent unions and has been accused of meddling in their internal elections and harassing union representatives.

The judicial system is based on the French civil code, although Sharia (Islamic law) prevails in family matters. The courts are not independent of the government. Corruption is a problem and led to the dismissal of two magistrates in 2007. A lack of resources often causes significant delays in legal proceedings. Security forces frequently make arrests without a proper decree from a judicial magistrate, in violation of constitutional requirements. Prison conditions remain harsh, with reports of detainees being physically abused, but there have been some improvements in recent years.

Minority groups including the Afar people, Yemeni Arabs, and non-Issa Somalis suffer social and economic discrimination.

Women continue to suffer serious discrimination under customary practices related to inheritance and other property matters, divorce, and the right to travel. Female genital mutilation is widespread, and legislation forbidding mutilation of young girls is not enforced. However, women's groups working under the patronage of the first lady are engaged in efforts to curb the practice, and they have reportedly achieved some progress in the capital. A law requiring at least 10 percent of elected offices to be held by women has had a positive effect. The 2008 parliamentary elections resulted in a record nine female lawmakers, representing 14 percent of the legislature.

Dominica

Political Rights: 1
Civil Liberties: 1
Status: Free

Population: 72,000
Capital: Roseau

Ten-Year Ratings Timeline For Year Under Review (Political Rights, Civil Liberties, Status)

2000	2001	2002	2003	2004	2005	2006	2007	2008	2009
1,1F	1,1F	1,1F	1,1F	1,1F	1,1F	1,1F	1,1F	1,1F	1,1F

Overview: Prime Minister Roosevelt Skerrit of the Dominica Labour Party was elected to a second five-year term in December 2009; his party received 60 percent of the vote and 18 of 21 seats in parliament. Still, strong outcry from the opposition over alleged government corruption and electoral fraud undermined the prime minister's chances of ending the political polarization that plagued his last term.

Dominica gained independence from Britain in 1978. The centrist Dominica Labour Party (DLP) swept to victory for the first time in 20 years in the January 2000 parliamentary elections, and formed a coalition with the right-wing Dominica Freedom Party (DFP). DLP leader Roosevelt "Rosie" Douglas was named prime minister, but died of a heart attack in October 2000. Douglas's replacement, Pierre Charles, died of heart failure in January 2004, and was succeeded by Roosevelt Skerrit, also of the DLP.

Skerrit's government inherited tremendous financial troubles and lost public support as it implemented austerity measures. Increased global competition hit the agriculturally based economy especially hard, and the imposition of an International Monetary Fund (IMF) stabilization and adjustment program proved highly unpopular. Despite those difficulties, the DLP confirmed its mandate by easily winning an April 2004 by-election.

Skerrit and the DLP secured 12 seats in the 2005 elections, ensuring a majority even without the support of the DFP. Former prime minister Edison James, leader of the opposition United Workers Party (UWP), initially accepted the results but later claimed that five of the DLP seats were obtained through fraud. Meanwhile, the DFP struggled to remain relevant and was not represented in the parliament.

In May 2009, Skerrit was forced to contend with the so-called "rubbish bin scandal," which exploded into a national controversy when opposition UWP spokesman Edison James accused the government of importing 2,700 garbage bins from Pennsylvania at an unusually high cost of $102.19 per bin, more than four times their average retail price. Skerrit attempted to deflect opposition claims that the high price reflected government corruption and lack of transparency, but then failed to deliver a promised refund. The incident dealt a significant blow to Skerrit's public image in the run-up to December elections.

In December, Skerrit and his DLP won both the popular vote (with 60 percent) and the majority of seats in the House of Assembly (18 of 21). Elections were deemed free and fair by observer teams from both the Organization of American States and a CARICOM mission, despite objections from opposition leaders. News agencies reported that the DLP had spent over $8 million on its campaign, and opposition candidates claimed that some of this money was spent on airline tickets for DLP supporters living abroad to return to the island to vote. Despite these allegations and others involving unfair access to television advertising, the reelection of Skerrit has been recognized worldwide.

Political Rights and Civil Liberties: Dominica is an electoral democracy. The government is headed by a prime minister, and the unicameral House of Assembly consists of 30 members serving five-year terms. Twenty-one members are elected, and nine senators are appointed—five by the prime minister and four by the opposition leader. The president is elected by the House of Assembly for a five-year term; the prime minister is appointed by the president.

The three main political parties are the ruling DLP, the opposition UWP, and the once-robust DFP, which ruled from 1980 to 1995 but no longer has a seat in the parliament.

Dominica was ranked 34 out of 180 countries surveyed in Transparency International's 2009 Corruption Perceptions Index.

The press is free, and there is no censorship or government intrusion. Four private newspapers and an equal number of political party journals publish without interference. Although the main radio station is state owned, there is also an independent station. Citizens have unimpeded access to cable television and regional radio broadcasts, as well as to the internet. In 2008, the government launched an official website designed to increase government transparency, although its impact to date has been limited.

Freedom of religion is recognized. While a majority of the population is Roman Catholic, some Protestant churches have been established. Certain religious and cultural minorities assert that the law infringes on their rights. The indigenous Kalinago population numbers less than 3,000 and has repeatedly complained of racial discrimination in Dominican law and practice. In 2009, Rastafarians claimed that members of their religion were discriminated against in hiring practices, and suggested that the nationwide ban on marijuana limited their religious expression. Academic freedom is respected.

The authorities uphold freedoms of assembly and association, and advocacy groups operate freely. Workers have the right to organize, strike, and bargain collectively. Although unions are independent of the government and laws prohibit anti-union discrimination by employers, only 13 percent of the workforce is unionized.

The judiciary is independent, and the rule of law is enhanced by the courts' subordination to the inter-island Eastern Caribbean Supreme Court. In 2009, Prime Minister Roosevelt Skerrit officially confirmed his government's intention to accept the Caribbean Court of Justice as its final court of appeal, instead of the Privy Council in London, but was unable to finalize the decision by year's end. The judicial system operated smoothly over the year, and its efficient handling of cases compared favorably with other islands in the region. However, staffing shortfalls in the judicial system remain a problem.

The island's only prison is overcrowded and has sanitation problems. In 2006, Dominica signed a prisoner transfer agreement with Britain that would allow convicted criminals to serve out their sentences in their countries of origin.

The Dominica police force became responsible for security after the military was disbanded in 1981, and operates professionally with few human rights complaints. Dominica in 2009 signed a deal with U.S. authorities to collaborate on eTrace, a paperless firearm tracking system designed to fight weapons trafficking and illegal gun possession in the Caribbean. While the homicide rate increased slightly in 2009, it remained one of the lowest in the region.

The Protection against Domestic Violence Act allows abused persons, usually women, to appear before a judge and request a protective order without seeking legal counsel. There are no laws mandating equal pay for equal work for men and women in private sector jobs, and inheritance laws do not fully recognize women's rights.

⬇ Dominican Republic

Political Rights: 2
Civil Liberties: 2
Status: Free

Population: 10,090,000
Capital: Santo Domingo

Trend Arrow: The Dominican Republic received a downward trend arrow due to the revelation through several major scandals of the level of drug traffickers' penetration of Dominican police and legal institutions, as well as new constitutional bans on abortion and gay marriage that are among the strictest in the world.

Ten-Year Ratings Timeline For Year Under Review (Political Rights, Civil Liberties, Status)

2000	2001	2002	2003	2004	2005	2006	2007	2008	2009
2,2F	2,2F	2,2F	3,2F	2,2F	2,2F	2,2F	2,2F	2,2F	2,2F

Overview: In 2009, support for President Leonel Fernandez of the Dominican Liberation Party began to wane amidst a worsening economic climate, as well as several major scandals involving collusion between drug traffickers and the police. The new constitution ratified in October included some of the toughest restrictions on abortion and gay marriage in the world.

After achieving independence from Spain in 1821 and from Haiti in 1844, the Dominican Republic endured recurrent domestic conflict, foreign occupation, and authoritarian rule. The assassination of General Rafael Trujillo in 1961 ended 30 years of dictatorship, but a 1963 military coup led to civil war and U.S. intervention. In 1966, under a new constitution, civilian rule was restored with the election of conservative president Joaquin Balaguer. His ouster in the 1978 election marked the first time an incumbent president peacefully handed power to an elected opponent.

Since the mid-1990s, Dominican politics have been defined by competition between the Dominican Liberation Party (PLD) and the Dominican Revolutionary Party (PRD), although Balaguer's Social Christian Reformist Party (PRSC) remained an important factor. Leonel Fernandez of the PLD was first elected president in 1996, but term limits prevented him from running in 2000. He was succeeded by the PRD's

Rafael Hipolito Mejia Dominguez, a former agriculture minister whose campaign appealed to those left behind by the country's overall economic prosperity. In 2001, Mejia successfully enacted a constitutional change to allow a second consecutive presidential term, but he decisively lost his 2004 reelection bid to Fernandez.

While his 1996–2000 presidential term had featured substantial economic growth, Fernandez returned to face a ballooning US$6 billion foreign debt, a 16 percent unemployment rate, annual inflation of some 32 percent, and a deep energy crisis. Within a short period, however, inflation had been brought into the single digits, and macroeconomic stability had improved dramatically, with the economy posting a 9 percent growth rate in 2005. In return for International Monetary Fund financing, the government agreed to cut subsidies on fuel and electricity and reduce the bloated government payroll.

The PLD, capitalizing on the president's successful economic management, won a majority in both houses of Congress in May 2006. In the Senate, the PLD took 22 seats, while the PRD won only 6 and the PRSC took 4. In the Chamber of Deputies, the PLD won 96 seats and the PRD took 60, leaving the PRSC with 22. Fernandez secured a third term in the May 2008 election with 54 percent of the vote. His opponent, the PRD's Miguel Vargas Maldonado, garnered just over 40 percent. Political violence associated with the balloting led to three deaths, but Fernandez called for a national celebration, dubbing the election a "democratic fiesta." Fernandez promoted a constitutional reform process that resulted in the ratification of the country's 38th constitution in October 2009. The new constitution has no restrictions on nonconsecutive presidential reelection, which would allow Fernandez to run for president again in 2016.

The Dominican Republic faced new troubles in 2009, stemming from a wave of scandals involving the Dominican National Police, as well as a worsening economic climate. In February, 27 police officers, including 2 colonels, were charged with allowing drug dealers to operate in their districts with impunity. In August, another police unit was dismantled, and authorities launched an investigation into the alleged ties between nearly 200 officers and drug trafficking. Separately, lawyers and staffers in the government's legal department were fired in relation to allegations of malfeasance in the Central Electoral Board. Controversy also erupted over bloated government payrolls after new reports revealed that some Dominican ministries had 10 times as many staff as equivalent ministries in neighboring countries. The Central Bank claimed 3.5 percent growth during 2009, but some analysts and rating agencies viewed that figure as optimistic, especially considering initial projections of a 1 percent contraction during the year.

Political Rights and Civil Liberties: The Dominican Republic is an electoral democracy. The 2008 presidential election and the 2006 legislative elections were determined to have been free and fair. The constitution provides for a president and a bicameral National Congress, both elected to four-year terms. The Congress consists of the 32-member Senate and the 178-member Chamber of Deputies. The three main political parties are the ruling PLD, the opposition PRD, and the smaller PRSC.

Official corruption remains a serious problem. President Leonel Fernandez, whose first term in the 1990s was marred by a scandal involving the disappearance of US$100 million in government funds, made fighting corruption a central theme of his 2004 election campaign. In his inaugural address, he pledged fiscal austerity and promised large cuts in the borrowing, hiring, and heavy spending that had characterized the outgoing administration. Still, the corruption problem has not improved much during his tenure, and the Dominican Republic was ranked 99 out of 180 countries surveyed in Transparency International's 2009 Corruption Perceptions Index. The uncovering in 2009 of bloated government payrolls in some ministries fueled charges of political patronage.

The law provides for freedom of speech and of the press, and the government generally respects those rights. There are five national daily newspapers and a large number of local publications. The state-owned Radio Television Dominicana operates radio and television services. Private owners operate more than 300 radio stations and over 40 television stations, most of them small, regional broadcasters. In March 2005, Fernandez signed implementation rules for a 2004 freedom of information law. Internet access is unrestricted but not widely available of large urban areas; the Fernandez government has worked to improve access to technology in rural areas.

Constitutional guarantees regarding religious and academic freedom are generally observed.

The government upholds the right to form civic groups, and civil society organizations in the Dominican Republic are some of the best organized and most effective in Latin America. Labor unions are similarly well organized. Although legally permitted to strike, they are often subjected to government crackdowns. In 2009, peasant unions were occasionally targeted by armed groups working for major landowners, and the rights of Haitian workers were routinely violated.

The judiciary, headed by the Supreme Court, is politicized and riddled with corruption, and the legal system offers little recourse to those without money or influence. However, reforms implemented in recent years, including measures aimed at promoting greater efficiency and due process, show some promise of increasing citizen access to justice. In 2004, a new criminal procedures code gave suspects additional protections, and a new code for minors improved safeguards against sexual and commercial exploitation.

Extrajudicial killings by police remain a problem, and low salaries encourage endemic corruption in law enforcement institutions. The Fernandez administration's police reform efforts faced serious setbacks in 2009, including drug corruption scandals involving hundreds of officers and reported increases in the use of extortion and intimidation by police. In July, the National Commission on Human Rights documented more than 70 instances of police forcing onions into suspects' mouths in order to extract confessions. Prisons suffer from severe overcrowding, poor health and sanitary conditions, and routine violence that has resulted in a significant number of deaths.

The Dominican Republic is a major transit hub for South American drugs, mostly cocaine, headed to the United States. Local, Puerto Rican, and Colombian drug smugglers use the country as both a command-and-control center and a transshipment point. The government estimates that some 20 percent of the drugs entering the country remain there as "payment in kind." The government has sought the right to shoot down planes that drop unauthorized packages onto its territory, but the United States opposes the measure.

The mistreatment of Haitian migrants continues to mar the Dominican Republic's international reputation, but no strategy has been adopted to handle this growing problem. More than 6,000 Haitians were forcibly deported from the Dominican Republic in 2009 in a practice that failed to meet minimal human rights standards. The situation is exacerbated by poor economic prospects in the Dominican Republic, which has intensified competition for work among local and migrant populations.

Violence and discrimination against women remain serious problems, as do trafficking in women and girls, child prostitution, and child abuse. The government has created the post of secretary for women's issues, and women regularly serve in Congress and at the cabinet level. In 2009, the new Dominican constitution included one of the most restrictive abortion laws in the world, making the practice illegal even in cases of rape, incest, or to protect the life of the mother. The measure was strongly opposed by Amnesty International and domestic women's rights groups, who feared the law would have severely negative consequences for women's health. The new constitution also defined marriage as solely between a man and a woman, making the country one of the few in the world to ban gay marriage at the constitutional level.

East Timor

Political Rights: 3
Civil Liberties: 4
Status: Partly Free

Population: 1,134,000
Capital: Dili

Ten-Year Ratings Timeline For Year Under Review (Political Rights, Civil Liberties, Status)

2000	2001	2002	2003	2004	2005	2006	2007	2008	2009
6,3PF	5,3PF	3,3PF	3,3PF	3,3PF	3,3PF	3,4PF	3,4PF	3,4PF	3,4PF

Overview: Internal security improved in 2009, but little was done to address the underlying causes of a period of political instability that began in 2006. Alleged perpetrators of a 2008 assassination attempt against Prime Minister Kay Rala Xanana Gusmao and President Jose Ramos Horta went on trial in July. In October, Gusmao's government narrowly survived a no-confidence motion after officials released a former militia leader accused of human rights abuses without a court order. Also that month, the country held generally free and fair village council elections.

Portugal abandoned its colony of East Timor in 1975, and Indonesia invaded when the leftist Revolutionary Front for an Independent East Timor (Fretilin) declared independence later that year. East Timor became Indonesia's 26th province in 1976. Over the next two decades, Fretilin's armed wing, Falintil, waged a low-grade insurgency against the Indonesian army, which committed widespread human rights abuses as it consolidated control. Civil conflict and famine may have killed up to 180,000 Timorese during Indonesian rule.

International pressure on Indonesia mounted following the 1991 Dili massacre, in which Indonesian soldiers were captured on film killing more than 200 people. In 1999, 78.5 percent of the East Timorese electorate voted for independence in a referendum approved by Indonesian president B. J. Habibie. The Indonesian army's scorched-earth response to the vote killed roughly 1,000 civilians, resulted in more than 250,000 refugees, and destroyed approximately 80 percent of East Timor's buildings and infrastructure before an Australian-led multinational force restored order.

In 2001 East Timor elected a Constituent Assembly to draft a constitution. Kay Rala Xanana Gusmao, a former head of Falintil and chairman of Fretilin until he broke from the party in 1988 to form a wider resistance coalition, won the presidency the following year. Independence was officially granted in May 2002. Fretilin, led by Prime Minister Mari Alkatiri, won the country's first local elections in 2004 and 2005.

In 2006, the firing of 600 soldiers, combined with frustration over corruption and high levels of unemployment, sparked widespread rioting and armed clashes with the police. The unrest led to numerous deaths and displaced 150,000 people. Australian troops were deployed to restore security, but instability continued, and Alkatiri was forced to resign in June amid allegations that he had formed a hit squad to kill off political opponents. While Alkatiri was not prosecuted, the interior minister at the time was convicted in 2007 of arming the hit squad and ultimately pardoned in 2008.

Jose Ramos Horta, who was appointed to replace Alkatiri, won a May 2007 presidential runoff election with 67 percent of the vote, defeating Fretilin's Francisco Guterres. Outgoing president Gusmao launched a new party, the National Congress for Timorese Construction (CNRT), to contest the June legislative elections. Frentilin led with 21 of the 65 seats, but the CNRT, which won 18, joined smaller parties to form the Alliance of the Parliamentary Majority (AMP). The new coalition held 37 seats, and Ramos Horta invited it to form a government, with Gusmao as prime minister.

In February 2008, former army major Alfredo Reinado—who had escaped from prison after being arrested for involvement in the 2006 uprising—led a group of former soldiers in an unsuccessful attempt to assassinate Gusmao and Ramos Horta. Reinado was killed during the attack, and his comrades later surrendered to security forces. They went on trial in July 2009, and the proceedings were ongoing at year's end.

Stability improved in 2009, but the conditions underlying the previous years' crises continued to simmer. These included politicization of the civil service and security forces, conflict over land and property, and the broader legacy of 35 years of internecine conflict. While the last of 65 camps for internally displaced persons closed in July, an estimated 72 families remained wary of returning to their communities and stayed in four transitional shelters near the capital as of December.

In August, the authorities captured Martenus Bere, an Indonesian citizen who had been indicted for his role as a militia leader in the 1999 violence, as he entered East Timor. However, the government later released him without a court order, and he returned to Indonesia in October. The release was ostensibly due to health concerns, but Gusmao and Ramos Horta acknowledged that it was a political concession to Indonesia Fretilin brought a no-confidence motion against the AMP government that month, but it failed, 25–39. Also in October, Fretilin claimed a major victory in village council elections, although council candidates are technically barred from representing political parties.

At the end of 2009, the total value of East Timor's fund for oil and gas royalties was estimated at more than US$4 billion, and the country has one of the highest aid-per-capita ratios in the world. Nevertheless, it remains the poorest country in Southeast Asia, with an unemployment rate of about 50 percent and more than 40 percent of the population living below the poverty line.

Political Rights and Civil Liberties: East Timor is an electoral democracy. Elections for the presidency and the unicameral Parliament held in 2007 were generally deemed free and fair, as were October 2009 local elections in 442 villages. The directly elected president is a largely symbolic figure, with formal powers limited to the right to veto legislation and make certain appointments. The leader of the majority party or coalition in the 65-seat, unicameral Parliament becomes the prime minister. Both the president and Parliament serve five-year terms, with the president eligible for up to two terms. Fretilin, now in opposition, remains the single largest political party, and personalities and old loyalties tied to the resistance movement of the 1970s influence political outcomes more than policy issues.

Voter frustration with corruption and nepotism was one reason for Fretilin's relatively poor showing in the 2007 elections. Accusations of graft have continued under the AMP government. Over 5,200 cases were awaiting investigation as of June 2009, indicating that high-level corruption is not effectively prosecuted. Parliament in June 2009 voted to create an anticorruption commission, but the composition and powers of the body were still under discussion at year's end. East Timor was ranked 146 out of 180 countries surveyed in Transparency International's 2009 Corruption Perceptions Index.

The free flow of information in East Timor is hampered primarily by poor infrastructure and scarce resources. An estimated 68 percent of Timorese are reached by the national broadcaster, Radio Timor-Leste, and a few community radio stations also operate. Since 2007, East Timor Television has been available via satellite beyond the Dili broadcast area. The country has two major daily newspapers and two major weekly papers. The daily *Suara Timor Lorosae* is generally considered to be pro-Fretilin, while the weekly *Jornal Nacional Diaro* is loosely affiliated with the CNRT. Less than 1 percent of the population has access to the internet. By March 2009, approximately 140,000 people had mobile-telephone subscriptions.

Journalists often feel intimidated and practice self-censorship. A new penal code promulgated in March 2009 excludes defamation as a criminal offense, and a widely criticized case against editor Jose Antonio Belo of the weekly *Tempo Semanal* was consequently dropped. Draft media laws publicized in March were criticized for several restrictive provisions, including a rule limiting the number of local radio stations to one per community and a requirement that journalists work for five years before becoming licensed professionals. The measures were under revision at year's end.

East Timor is a secular state, but the Roman Catholic Church plays a central role; 98 percent of the population is Roman Catholic. Church rules prohibit persons living under religious vows from holding political office. There are no significant threats to religious freedom or clashes involving the country's Muslim and evangelical Christian minorities. Academic freedom is generally respected, though religious education is compulsory in schools.

Freedoms of association and assembly are constitutionally guaranteed, but a 2004 law regulates political gatherings and prohibits demonstrations aimed at "questioning constitutional order" or disparaging the reputations of the head of state and other government officials. The law requires that demonstrations and public protests be authorized in advance.

East Timor's labor code, which is based on International Labor Organization standards, permits workers other than police and military personnel to form and join worker organizations. It also guarantees the rights to bargain collectively and to strike, although written notice must be given 10 days before a strike. Unionization rates are low due to high levels of unemployment and informal economic activity.

The country suffers broadly from weak rule of law, a prevailing culture of impunity, and flawed security forces. The fragile legal system has just 13 judges hearing cases in four district courts as well as a shortage of qualified public defenders. According to an October 2009 Independent Comprehensive Needs Assessment (ICNA) organized by the United Nations Integrated Mission In Timor-Leste (UNMIT), the courts are backlogged by approximately 300 civil cases and 1,500 criminal cases. Due process rights are often restricted or denied, largely because of a lack of resources and personnel. Alternative methods of dispute resolution and customary law are widely used, though they lack enforcement mechanisms and have other significant shortcomings, including unequal treatment of women.

The government's 2009 release without a court order of former pro-Indonesian militia leader Martenus Bere, who had been indicted by the UN Serious Crimes Unit in 2003 for alleged human rights violations in 1999, was widely decried as a violation of judicial independence and the rule of law. In August, Amnesty International called on the UN Security Council to establish an independent criminal tribunal for the country, but President Jose Ramos Horta stated on numerous occasions that East Timor would not pursue such a tribunal. He also said he would consider pardoning, in the interests of peace, some of the 28 defendants who went on trial in July 2009 for the 2008 attempt on his and the prime minister's lives. The remarks were seen as another political intrusion on the judicial process. In December, the Parliament adopted a resolution that empowers the parliamentary committee responsible for law and constitutional affairs to draft legislation that addresses the findings of reports by the Commission for Reception, Truth, and Reconciliation (CAVR) and the Commission on Truth and Friendship (CTF).

Internal security improved in 2009, though gang violence, sometimes directed by rival elites or fueled by land disputes, was still a problem. The UN mission began a phased transfer of policing responsibility to the national police in May. While approximately 1,579 UN police and military liaison officers remained in East Timor at year's end, four of the thirteen districts had been transferred to the national police, as well as responsibility for police training, maritime security, and the police intelligence department. Neither the Timorese police nor the military are well trusted by the population, and relations between the two forces remain tense due to political rifts dating to the independence struggle.

A draft land law that was undergoing public consultation at the end of 2009 is expected to settle many long-standing disputes, but it was criticized for not explicitly guaranteeing community lands. There was also uncertainty as to who would participate in bodies responsible for ruling on land conflicts.

Equal rights for women are constitutionally guaranteed, but domestic violence remains a persistent problem. It is estimated that half of all women were victims of gender-based crimes in 2008, while only a marginal fraction of cases of abuse were reported to the police, often due to fears that jailing the abuser would result in loss of financial support for the family. Trafficking of women and children is reportedly on the rise, as is the sex trade. The penal code promulgated in 2009 criminalizes abortion except in cases that endanger the health of the mother. While women's participation in government remains much lower than that of men, women hold three senior cabinet posts and 19 of 65 seats in Parliament.

Ecuador

Political Rights: 3
Civil Liberties: 3
Status: Partly Free

Population: 13,625,000
Capital: Quito

Ten-Year Ratings Timeline For Year Under Review (Political Rights, Civil Liberties, Status)

2000	2001	2002	2003	2004	2005	2006	2007	2008	2009
3,3PF	3,3PF	3,3PF	3,3PF	3,3PF	3,3PF	3,3PF	3,3PF	3,3PF	3,3PF

Overview: President Rafael Correa won a new term in April 2009 elections, the first to be held under a constitution adopted the previous year. Meanwhile, a new mining law and a proposed water law spurred fierce antigovernment protests by civil society groups, which argued that the measures failed to protect the environment and indigenous rights. Also during the year, the administration was implicated in a corruption scandal involving the award of lucrative government contracts to Correa's brother.

Established in 1830 after the region achieved independence from Spain in 1822, the Republic of Ecuador has endured many interrupted presidencies and military governments. The last military regime gave way to civilian rule after a new constitution was approved by referendum in 1978, although President Jamil Mahuad was forced to step down in 2000 after midlevel military officers led by Colonel Lucio Gutierrez joined large protests by indigenous groups. Mahuad was succeeded by Vice President Gustavo Noboa.

Gutierrez won a surprise victory in the 2002 presidential election, marking the first time that Ecuador's head of state shared the ethnicity and humble background of the country's large indigenous population. However, by the end of 2003, Gutierrez had been politically weakened by conflicts within his leftist coalition and the immediate effects of his fiscal austerity policies. The powerful Confederation of Indigenous Nationalities of Ecuador (CONAIE) movement soon withdrew support for the president, and dissent over fiscal and labor reforms spilled into the streets.

After a dismal showing by Gutierrez's Patriotic Society Party (PSP) in the October 2004 regional and municipal elections, the opposition began to press for his removal. The protest movement grew after Gutierrez dismissed the Supreme Court for political bias in December and replaced the panel with loyal judges, who granted immunity to several exiled politicians facing corruption accusations. The president sought to placate protesters by dismissing the new Supreme Court in April 2005, but he was ousted that month on the spurious charge of "abandonment of post," and Vice President Alfredo Palacio assumed the presidency.

Demonstrations against foreign oil companies and a proposed free-trade agreement (FTA) with the United States dominated the first half of 2006. In May, the government annulled the contract of U.S.-based Occidental Petroleum, accusing the company of violating its terms; the move prompted the United States to suspend FTA talks indefinitely.

Charismatic former finance minister Rafael Correa—who criticized free-market economic policies and pledged to renegotiate the country's foreign debt and end the FTA talks with the United States—won the 2006 presidential election, defeating banana magnate Alvaro Noboa with 57 percent of the vote in the November runoff. However, Noboa's Institutional Renewal Party of National Action (PRIAN) led concurrent congressional elections with 28 out of 100 seats. The PSP placed second with 24.

Correa soon began pressing Congress to authorize a referendum calling for a constituent assembly that would be empowered to write a new constitution. By the end of March 2007, the fight to determine the rules of the prospective assembly had led the congressional opposition to remove the head of the Supreme Electoral Tribunal (TSE). The tribunal subsequently dismissed 57 legislators, many of whom were replaced by alternates more sympathetic to the executive branch. When the Constitutional Court declared those dismissals illegal, the reshaped Congress removed all nine of its judges. According to Human Rights Watch, all of these decisions, "were without any credible basis in law."

In April 2007, some 82 percent of referendum voters approved the creation of a constituent assembly, and Correa's Proud and Sovereign Fatherland (PAIS) party captured 80 of the assembly's 130 seats in September delegate elections.

After nearly a year of fitful progress, the constituent assembly approved a draft constitution in late July 2008, and the charter was adopted in a September referendum, with 64 percent of the vote. A subset of 76 constituent assembly members were tasked with fulfilling legislative duties until fresh presidential and legislative elections could be held in 2009.

Supporters of the new constitution said it would guarantee an array of rights and services to all citizens, and praised the charter's separation of powers into five independent branches—executive, legislative, judicial, electoral, and transparency and social control. Critics of the document argued that it concentrated both political and economic power in the hands of the president, including through reduced central bank independence and increased budget control, and posited a long list of rights that the state would be hard pressed to uphold.

Correa won a new four-year term in the April 2009 general elections, taking 52 percent of the vote in the first round. Gutierrez placed second with 28 percent, followed by Alvaro Noboa with 11 percent. PAIS captured 59 of 124 seats in the new National Assembly, followed by the PSP with 19, the Social Christian Party (PSC) with 11, PRIAN with 7, and a range of smaller parties with the remainder. Parties allied with PAIS garnered over a dozen seats, giving it a working majority.

Political Rights and Civil Liberties: Ecuador is an electoral democracy. However, it suffers from an unstable political system that has brought it eight presidents since 1996. The 2009 elections, the first under the 2008 constitution, were deemed generally free and fair by international observers, although the European Union monitoring team noted some problems with vote-tabulation procedures and the abuse of state resources on behalf of government-aligned candidates.

The new constitution provides for a president elected to serve up to two four-year terms; in practice, this means that President Rafael Correa, who won his first term under the charter in 2009, could serve until 2017. To win without a runoff, presidential candidates must garner 40 percent of the first-round votes and beat their closest rival by at least 10 percentage points. The unicameral, 124-seat National Assembly is elected via open-list proportional representation for four-year terms. The president has the authority to dissolve the legislature once in his term, which triggers new elections for both the assembly and the presidency; the assembly can likewise dismiss the president, though under more stringent rules.

For decades, Ecuador's political parties have been largely personality based, clientelist, and fragile. Correa's PAIS party, though not fully ideologically coherent, is currently the largest in the legislature. Its competitors include the right-of-center PRIAN and PSC, the populist PSP, and the center-left Ethics and Democracy Network (RED).

Political representation of the indigenous population, which is centered in the country's interior, has increased greatly over the past 15 years; the CONAIE indigenous movement is one of the better-organized and more vocal social groups in the country.

Ecuador is racked by corruption, and numerous politicians and functionaries have been investigated for graft. In 2009, a corruption scandal erupted over the award of hundreds of millions of dollars in government contracts to Fabricio Correa, the president's brother and former fund-raiser, who responded with counteraccusations of bribery and conflict of interest in the president's inner circle. The case remained under investigation at year's end. Ecuador was ranked 146 out of 180 countries surveyed in Transparency International's 2009 Corruption Perceptions Index.

Freedom of expression is generally observed, and the media, most of which are privately owned, are outspoken. However, press freedom watchdog organizations warned that several vague articles in the new constitution could allow abusive forms of media regulation. Correa has accused the press of improper links with private interests and often lambastes journalists. This hostile rhetoric has been blamed for an increase in physical attacks on and harassment of reporters and news outlets. In 2009, there were 103 cases of harassment against journalists. The television station Teleamazonas has faced government interventions on several occasions, including three days of suspended transmission in December 2009 in response to coverage of potential damage to fisheries caused by oil production. Two television stations that were confiscated in July 2008 as part of the government's seizure of 250 businesses owned by the Grupo Isaias conglomerate remained under state control in 2009, despite a government pledge to sell the seized assets to compensate citizens whose savings were lost in the 1998 failure of an Isaias-owned bank. Internet access is unrestricted.

The constitution provides freedom of religion, and the authorities respect this right in practice, though tensions between the government and the Roman Catholic Church increased during the run-up to the constitutional referendum. Academic freedom is not restricted.

The right to organize political parties, civic groups, and unions is upheld by the authorities. Ecuador has numerous human rights organizations, and despite occasional acts of intimidation, they report openly on arbitrary arrests and instances of police brutality and military misconduct. While many protests occur peacefully, human rights groups strongly objected to repression by security forces—including a large number of arrests—during protests related to a draft mining law that was enacted in January 2009. Opposition to provisions of the mining law was among the issues that created friction between the government and Ecological Action, a nongovernmental organization (NGO) whose license was briefly suspended in March 2009. Critics decried the temporary shutdown as arbitrary and potentially chilling. More generally, however, thousands of NGOs operate throughout the country with relative freedom. The country's labor unions have the right to strike, though the labor code limits public sector strikes. As little as 1 percent of the workforce is unionized, partly because most people work in the informal sector.

The judiciary, broadly undermined by the corruption afflicting all government institutions, has in recent years also been subject to significant political pressures. The highest judicial bodies under the new constitution are the 9-member Constitutional Court and the 21-member National Court of Justice (CNJ). Following approval of the new charter, the majority of previous Supreme Court members selected to serve on the CNJ refused to take their seats. A standoff of several months ended with an agreement in which former alternate Supreme Court judges occupied a majority of the new court's positions.

Judicial processes remain slow, and many inmates reach the time limit for pretrial detention while their cases are still under investigation. The number of inmates in the prison system is more than double the intended capacity, and torture and ill-treatment of detainees and prisoners remain widespread. In March 2009, a new criminal procedure code and elements of a new penal code, which were designed to improve the system's efficiency and fairness, entered into force, though their effectiveness was difficult to ascertain by year's end.

In 2008, after the Colombian military launched a cross-border raid on leftist Colombian rebels encamped on Ecuadorean territory, it emerged that Ecuadorean military officials had provided information to their Colombian counterparts that had not been provided to Correa. The president consequently dismissed his defense minister and several senior commanders. Efforts to step up patrols along the border continued in 2009, as did attempts to regularize the status of the tens of thousands of Colombian refugees living in Ecuador.

Despite their significant political influence, indigenous people continue to suffer discrimination at many levels of society. In the Amazon region, indigenous groups have attempted to win a share of oil revenues and a voice in decisions on natural resources and development. Although the 2008 constitution recognizes indigenous justice and the right of indigenous groups to be consulted on matters affecting their communities, the government has maintained that it will not hand indigenous groups a veto on core matters of national interest. The new mining law, combined with the introduction of a draft water law in September 2009, has stirred conflict between the government and CONAIE-led indigenous groups. A September 2009 protest ended in the death of one indigenous man, dozens of injuries to demonstrators and police, and the suspension of an indigenous-language radio station's license for allegedly inciting violence.

Women took 40 of 124 seats in the 2009 legislative elections, and the new constitution calls for significant female presence throughout the public sphere. Violence against women is common, as is employment discrimination. Trafficking in persons, generally women and children, remains a problem.

Egypt

Political Rights: 6
Civil Liberties: 5
Status: Not Free

Population: 78,629,000
Capital: Cairo

Ten-Year Ratings Timeline For Year Under Review (Political Rights, Civil Liberties, Status)

2000	2001	2002	2003	2004	2005	2006	2007	2008	2009
6,5NF	6,6NF	6,6NF	6,6NF	6,5NF	6,5NF	6,5NF	6,5NF	6,5NF	6,5NF

Overview:
Ayman Nour, President Hosni Mubarak's main challenger in the 2005 presidential election, was released in February 2009 after serving three years in prison. In June, lawmakers approved legislation that would reserve 64 seats for women in the lower house of parliament. However, the regime avoided substantial political reform and continued to abuse civil liberties during the year, maintaining pressure on the opposition Muslim Brotherhood as well as independent journalists.

Egypt formally gained independence from Britain in 1922 and acquired full sovereignty following World War II. After leading a coup that overthrew the monarchy in 1952, Colonel Gamal Abdel Nasser ruled until his death in 1970. The constitution adopted in 1971 under his successor, Anwar al-Sadat, established a strong presidential system with nominal guarantees for political and civil rights that were not respected in practice. Sadat signed a peace treaty with Israel in 1979 and built an alliance with the United States, which provided the Egyptian government with roughly US$2 billion in aid annually.

Following Sadat's assassination in 1981, then vice president Hosni Mubarak became president and declared a state of emergency, which has been in force ever since. A deterioration in living conditions and the lack of a political outlet for many Egyptians fueled an Islamist insurgency in the early 1990s. The authorities responded by jailing thousands of suspected militants without charge and cracking down on political dissent. Although the armed infrastructure of Islamist groups had been largely eradicated by 1998, the government continued to restrict political and civil liberties as it struggled to address Egypt's dire socioeconomic problems.

Economic growth in the late 1990s temporarily alleviated these problems, but the country experienced a downturn after the 2001 terrorist attacks on the United States. Popular disaffection with the government spread palpably, and antigovernment demonstrations were harshly suppressed by security forces.

The government sought to cast itself as a champion of reform in 2004. Mubarak appointed a new cabinet of younger technocrats and introduced market-friendly economic reforms. However, associates of the president's son Gamal, a rising star in the ruling National Democratic Party (NDP), received key economic portfolios, stoking concerns that the changes were simply preparations for a hereditary transition.

Meanwhile, a consensus emerged among leftist, liberal, and Islamist political forces as to the components of desired political reform: direct, multicandidate presidential elections; the abrogation of the Emergency Law; full judicial supervision of elections; the lifting of restrictions on the formation of political parties; and an end to government interference in the operation of nongovernmental organizations (NGOs). The opposition nevertheless remained polarized between unlicensed and licensed political groups, with the latter mostly accepting the regime's decision to put off further reform until after the 2005 elections.

In December 2004, Kifaya (Enough), an informal movement encompassing a broad spectrum of secular and Islamist activists, held the first demonstration explicitly calling for Mubarak to step down. Despite a heavy-handed response by security forces, Kifaya persisted with demonstrations in 2005, leading other opposition groups to follow suit. The United States was also pressing Egypt to democratize at the time.

Mubarak proposed a constitutional amendment that would allow Egypt's first multicandidate presidential election, but it required candidates to be nominated by licensed parties or a substantial bloc of elected officials. Consequently, all major opposition groups denounced the measure and boycotted the May 2005 referendum that approved it.

The results of the September 2005 presidential election were predictably lopsided, with Mubarak winning 88 percent of the vote. His main opponent, Al-Ghad (Tomorrow) Party leader Ayman Nour, took just 8 percent. Having been charged earlier in the year with forging signatures in his party's petition for a license, Nour was convicted and sentenced to five years in prison a few months after the election.

Three rounds of parliamentary elections in November and December 2005 featured a strong showing by the formally banned Muslim Brotherhood, whose candidates ran as independents. The Brotherhood increased its representation in the lower house sixfold, to 88 of 454 seats, though the NDP remained dominant. Voter turnout was low, and attacks on opposition voters by security forces and progovernment thugs abounded. Judges criticized the government for failing to prevent voter intimidation and refused to certify the election results, prompting the authorities to suppress judicial independence in 2006.

The government postponed the 2006 municipal elections until 2008 and began a renewed crackdown on the Muslim Brotherhood. U.S. pressure for democratic reform had subsided after the Brotherhood's recent gains and the victory of Hamas in the January 2006 Palestinian elections. In March 2007, a set of 34 constitutional amendments were submitted to a national vote. Official reports stated that only 25 percent of eligible voters participated, with 76 percent of those approving the proposals, but independent monitors put the turnout closer to 5 percent. Opposition leaders boycotted the referendum on the grounds that the amendments would limit judicial monitoring of elections and prohibit the formation of political parties based on religious principles. The Judges' Club accused the government of ballot stuffing and vote buying. Upper house elections held that June were similarly marred by irregularities, and the Muslim Brotherhood was prevented from winning any seats after authorities detained potential candidates and found spurious reasons to prevent several candidates from registering. When the postponed municipal elections were finally held in 2008, the Brotherhood was again shut out in a similar manner, and the government's ongoing crackdown on the group led to lengthy prison terms for many senior members.

Ayman Nour was released in February 2009 after serving three years of his sentence, but he subsequently faced periodic harassment. His release was viewed as a sign of the regime's confidence rather than an opening of the space for political dissent.

Political Rights and Civil Liberties:

Egypt is not an electoral democracy. The political system is designed to ensure solid majorities for the ruling NDP at all levels of government. Constitutional amendments passed in 2007 banned religion-based political parties, ensuring the continued suppression of the Muslim Brotherhood, a nonviolent Islamist group that represents the most organized opposition to the government. President Hosni Mubarak, who has been in power since 1981, serves six-year terms and appoints the cabinet and all 26 provincial governors. The first multicandidate popular election for the presidency was held in 2005, and Mubarak's main challenger, Ayman Nour, was jailed on dubious charges soon after the vote.

The 454-seat People's Assembly (Majlis al-Sha'b), the parliament's lower house, exercises only limited influence on government policy, as the executive initiates almost all legislation. Ten of its members are appointed by the president, and the rest are popularly elected to five-year terms. The chamber is set to expand to 518 members in 2010 under reforms passed in June 2009, which set aside 64 new seats for women. There were just eight women in the People's Assembly as of 2009, half of whom were appointed. The 264-seat upper house, the Consultative Council (Majlis al-Shura), functions only in an advisory capacity. The president appoints 88 of its members, and the rest are elected to six-year terms, with half coming up for election every three years. Most of the 18 women in the chamber as of 2009 were appointed. As a result of restrictions on the licensing of political parties, state control over television and radio stations, and systemic irregularities in the electoral process, legislative elections do not meet international standards.

The 2007 constitutional amendments allow citizens to form political parties "in accordance with the law," but no party can be based on religion, gender, or ethnic origin. Previously, new parties had required approval from an NDP-controlled body linked to the Consultative Council. Religious parties have long been banned, but members of the Muslim Brotherhood compete as independents. Also under the new rules, a party must have been continuously operating for at least five years and occupy at least 5 percent of the seats in the parliament in order to nominate a presidential candidate. This means that it will be nearly impossible for any opposition candidate to participate in the presidential election scheduled for 2011.

The June 2007 Consultative Council elections put the new constitutional amendments into practice. Police detained a number of Muslim Brotherhood members on election day, including six candidates, for violating the ban on religious parties. Ahead of the 2008 municipal elections, the authorities arrested hundreds of would-be candidates and prevented thousands of others from registering.

The Muslim Brotherhood continues to suffer from a vigorous government crackdown that began in 2006. Members and supporters are regularly detained on dubious charges, and senior Brotherhood officials are sometimes charged in military courts. The arrests continued in 2009 as the government sought to prepare the field for the 2010 parliamentary elections.

Corruption remains pervasive at all levels of government. Egypt was ranked 111 out of 180 countries surveyed in Transparency International's 2009 Corruption Perceptions Index.

Freedom of the press is restricted in law and in practice. The state dominates the broadcast media and exercises influence over all privately owned publications through its monopoly on printing and distribution. The three leading daily newspapers are state controlled, and their editors are appointed by the president. Foreign publications and Egyptian publications registered abroad are subject to direct government censorship. Foreign journalists are sometimes harassed or expelled. In October 2009, authorities at Cairo airport prevented Swedish freelance reporter and blogger Per Bjorklund, who often reported on Egypt's labor movement, from entering the country. Several privately owned Egyptian satellite television stations have been established, but their programming is subject to state influence. Films, plays, and books are subject to censorship, especially for content deemed contrary to Islam or harmful to the country's reputation. A number of books and movies have been banned on the advice of the country's senior clerics.

Authorities continue to use an array of security-related and other laws to curb independent reporting. A 2006 press law abolished custodial sentences for libel, but it increased the possible fines, and journalists can still be jailed for other offenses. Nevertheless, Egyptian print journalists have resisted mounting government pressure in recent years, increasingly rejecting self-censorship despite the likelihood of harassment or prosecution. In February 2009, five journalists were fined for violating a court's ban on media coverage of the murder trial of Hisham Talaat Mostafa, a powerful businessman and member of parliament who was ultimately convicted of killing his onetime paramour, Lebanese singer Suzanne Tamim.

Internet journalists and bloggers have also defied more intense government harassment by reporting on sensitive issues that other media would not touch. The New York–based Committee to Protect Journalists (CPJ) has documented the detentions of several bloggers, including that of Dia Gad, who was detained for weeks without charge in February 2009 over his critical reporting on the situation at Egypt's border with the Gaza Strip. A number of previously arrested bloggers remained in detention at year's end. Abdel Karim Nabil Suleiman continued to serve a four-year prison sentence he had received in 2007 for criticizing Islam and the president. In addition to the detentions, bloggers like Wael Abbas, who documents cases of torture on his website, are routinely prevented from leaving the country, harassed, and monitored. CPJ has reported that the authorities examine internet traffic to gather information on potential targets for legal action.

Islam is the state religion. The government appoints the staff of registered mosques and attempts to closely monitor the content of sermons in thousands of small, unauthorized mosques. Most Egyptians are Sunni Muslims, but Coptic Christians form a substantial minority, and there are a very small number of Jews, Shiite Muslims, and Baha'is. A March 2009 ministerial decree recognized the right of adherents of "nonrecognized" religions to obtain identification papers, effectively ending the policy of forcing of Baha'is to identify as Muslims or Christians. Separately, a 2008 court ruling found that Christian converts to Islam were free to return to Christianity. Despite these positive developments, anti-Christian employment discrimination is evident in the public sector, especially the security services and military, and the government frequently denies or delays permission to build and repair churches. When clashes between Christians and Muslims occur, the authorities generally attempt to downplay the sectarian nature of the violence. However, sectarian clashes have been increasing in frequency, with Coptic Christians suffering the brunt of the violence. In addition, groups like the Cairo Institute for Human Rights Studies have reported that the state is becoming less tolerant of eating in public during Ramadan and has harassed and monitored Shiites in Egypt.

Academic freedom is limited. Senior university officials are appointed by the government, and the security services reportedly influence academic appointments and the curriculum's treatment of sensitive topics. University professors and students have been prosecuted for political and human rights advocacy outside of the classroom.

Freedoms of assembly and association are heavily restricted. Organizers of public demonstrations must receive advance approval from the Interior Ministry, which is rarely granted. The Emergency Law allows arrest for innocuous acts, such as insulting the president, blocking traffic, or distributing leaflets and posters. Authorities have cracked down more zealously on protesters and labor activists in recent years, partly because U.S. pressure for democratic reform has eased. In 2009, the government routinely arrested hundreds of demonstrators at the Gaza-Egypt border and held them without charge.

The Law of Associations prohibits the establishment of groups, "threatening national unity [or] violating public morals," bars NGOs from receiving foreign grants without the approval of the Social Affairs Ministry, requires members of NGO governing boards to be approved by the ministry, and allows the ministry to dissolve NGOs without a judicial order. Security services have rejected registrations, decided who could serve on boards of directors, harassed activists, and intercepted donations.

The 2003 Unified Labor Law limits the right to strike to "nonstrategic" industries and requires workers to obtain approval for a strike from the government-controlled Egyptian Trade Union Federation, the only legal labor federation. Nevertheless, Egypt has been swept by a wave of wildcat strikes since late 2006. The strikes continued throughout 2009, but the government has succeeded in infiltrating and weakening the labor movement to some degree.

The Supreme Judicial Council, a supervisory body of senior judges, nominates and assigns most members of the judiciary. However, the Justice Ministry controls promotions and compensation packages, giving it undue influence over the courts. The 2006 Judicial Authority Law offered some concessions to judicial independence, but fell short of reforms advocated by the Judges' Club.

Egypt remains subject to the Emergency Law, invoked in 1981 and repeatedly renewed since then, despite Mubarak's 2005 promise that it would be replaced with specific antiterrorism legislation. Under the Emergency Law, "security" cases are usually referred to exceptional courts that are controlled by the executive branch and deny defendants many constitutional protections. The special courts issue verdicts that cannot be appealed and are subject to ratification by the president. Although judges in these courts are usually selected from the civilian judiciary, they are appointed directly by the president. Arrested political activists are often tried under the Emergency Law. The 2007 constitutional amendments essentially enshrined many controversial aspects of the Emergency Law, such as the president's authority to transfer civilians suspected of terrorism to military courts.

Since military judges are appointed by the executive branch to renewable two-year terms, these tribunals lack independence. Verdicts are based on little more than the testimony of security officers and informers, and are reviewed only by a body of military judges and the president. Legislation passed in 2007 allows for limited appeal of military court decisions, but opposition figures denounced it as an inadequate attempt to bolster the rights guarantees of the new constitutional amendments.

The Emergency Law restricts many other basic rights, empowering the government to tap telephones, intercept mail, search persons and places without warrants, and indefinitely detain suspects without charge if they are deemed a threat to national security.

The Egyptian Organization for Human Rights has reported that as many as 16,000 people are detained without charge for security-related offenses, and thousands are serving sentences for such offenses. Prison conditions are very poor; inmates are subject to torture and other abuse, overcrowding, and a lack of sanitation and medical care.

Human rights groups have criticized Egypt's treatment of migrants and refugees from Sudan and other African states, and the Egyptian military has continued to shoot and kill migrants trying to enter Israel through Egypt and other border crossings. In 2009, at least 19 migrants were killed.

Although the constitution provides for equality of the sexes, some aspects of the law and many traditional practices discriminate against women. Job discrimination is evident even in the civil service. Muslim women are placed at a disadvantage by laws on divorce and other personal status issues, and a Muslim heiress typically receives half the amount of her male counterparts, though Christians are not subject to such provisions of Islamic law. Domestic violence is common, as is sexual harassment on the street. Spousal rape is not illegal, and the penal code allows for leniency in so-called honor killings. The government has been involved in a major public-information campaign against female genital mutilation, but it is still widely practiced.

El Salvador

Political Rights: 2
Civil Liberties: 3
Status: Free

Population: 7,339,000
Capital: San Savador

Ten-Year Ratings Timeline For Year Under Review (Political Rights, Civil Liberties, Status)

2000	2001	2002	2003	2004	2005	2006	2007	2008	2009
2,3F	2,3F	2,3F	2,3F	2,3F	2,3F	2,3F	2,3F	2,3F	2,3F

Overview:
Mauricio Funes led the leftist Farabundo Marti National Liberation Front (FMLN) to a historic victory in El Salvador's January legislative and March presidential elections, ending two decades of right-wing National Republican Alliance (ARENA) rule. The new administration faced serious challenges during the year, including an economic downturn and an unexpected increase in violent crime.

El Salvador gained independence from Spain in 1821 and broke away from a Central American federation in 1841. A republican political system dominated by the landowning elite, and subject to foreign interference, gave way to military rule in the mid-20th century. A 1979–92 civil war pitted the right-wing, military-dominated government against Marxist guerrillas led by the Farabundo Marti National Liberation Front (FMLN), leaving more than 75,000 people dead and 500,000 displaced.

The conservative National Republican Alliance (ARENA) party held the presidency for two decades beginning in 1989, but it faced growing competition from the FMLN, which evolved into a strong opposition party after the war.

In 2007, ARENA and the smaller National Conciliation Party (PCN) began to build an alliance aimed at preventing the FMLN from taking power in the 2009 elections. Responding in part to the rise of the left in neighboring Nicaragua and other Latin American countries, they mounted what many analysts deemed a fear-based campaign that sought to link the FMLN and its presidential candidate, former journalist and self-described moderate Mauricio Funes, to leftist Venezuelan president Hugo Chavez. The conservatives also suggested that an FMLN victory would jeopardize relations with the United States and the legal status of Salvadoran migrants, who currently benefitted from temporary protective status there. Political violence increased ahead of the elections, and the FMLN and ARENA accused each other of instigating the unrest. In October 2008, all major parties signed an agreement that obliged them to prevent violence among their supporters, avoid confrontational language while campaigning, and recognize the legitimacy of the election results.

A number of preelection decisions appeared to favor ARENA. For instance, the legislative and presidential polls were scheduled for different months, requiring parties to pay for consecutive rather than concurrent campaigns, and ARENA was known to have the largest budget. Moreover, Salvadorans living abroad were required to return and cast their ballots in person, limiting the vote to those who could afford the trip. In addition to these challenges, the Supreme Electoral Tribunal (TSE) failed to address well-documented irregularities in the voter registry, such as its inclusion of about 85,000 deceased voters. The TSE issued the final registry ahead of schedule in September 2008, days before data from the 2007 census was published. As a result, voter information and the distribution of legislative seats for 2009 were based on old census data that did not account for the past decade's growth in urban areas, which are home to 60 percent of the population.

Municipal and legislative elections were held in January 2009, with observers reporting irregularities such as voter cards being issued to residents of other districts. In San Isidro, Cabanas, opposition mayoral candidates filed a complaint stating that the ARENA candidate was distributing voter cards to Honduran citizens. The Municipal Electoral Committee responded by shutting down the city's vote at midday and holding a make-up election the following week. Community activist Gustavo Marcelo Rivera, who had been vocal in denouncing electoral fraud in San Isidro, was abducted and murdered in June. While police dismissed the crime as the work of gang members, Rivera's family maintained that it was politically motivated.

Although an ARENA candidate won the crucial mayoralty of San Salvador, the FMLN emerged as the winner nationally, taking 35 seats in the Legislative Assembly. ARENA placed second with 32 seats, followed by the PCN (11 seats), the Christian Democratic Party (5 seats), and Democratic Convergence (1 seat).

Observers reported that many of the irregularities noted during the January elections were rectified in the March presidential vote, although they continued to call on the TSE to update the voter registry. In an historic victory, Funes defeated ARENA's Rodrigo Avila, 51.3 percent to 48.7 percent. Funes assumed the presidency in June, inheriting a US$500 million budget deficit that has been attributed to a drop in exports as well as financial mismanagement by the outgoing administration.

The new administration faced major economic challenges in 2009. Remittances represent about 17 percent of gross domestic product, and, due in large part to the recession in the United States, they fell by 10.3 percent in the first half of the year. It is estimated that between 30 and 40 percent of all Salvadorans live in poverty, and 70 percent of the potential workforce is either underemployed or unemployed.

Political Rights and Civil Liberties: El Salvador is an electoral democracy. The 2009 legislative and presidential elections were deemed free and fair, although some irregularities were reported. The president is elected for a five-year term, and the 84-member, unicameral Legislative Assembly is elected for three years. The two largest political parties are the conservative ARENA and the FMLN, a former left-wing guerrilla organization that took power for the first time in 2009.

Corruption is regarded as a serious problem throughout government. A 2006 Ethics Law was designed to combat corruption in the public sector, but critics have stressed that it needs to be strengthened with an access-to-information component. El Salvador was ranked 84 out of 180 countries surveyed in Transparency International's 2009 Corruption Perceptions Index.

The constitution provides for freedom of the press, and this right is generally respected in practice. The media are privately owned, but ownership is confined to a small group of powerful businesspeople who often impose controls on reporters to protect their political or economic interests. The ARENA-aligned TeleCorporacion Salvadoreno (TCS) owns three of the five private television networks and dominates the market. Reporters are subject to criminal defamation laws, and judges can close legal proceedings to the media on national security grounds. Reporters do not have to reveal their sources if ordered to testify in a court case. Journalists with Radio Victoria in Cabanas reported receiving multiple threats in 2009 related to stories criticizing proposed mining projects. In September, French filmmaker Christian Poveda, director of the 2008 film *La Vida Loca*, about the 18th Street gang, was murdered in a suburb of San Salvador. Four alleged gang members and one police officer were arrested that month in connection with the crime. Some reporters have been accused of using their status for personal gain, raising ethical concerns. There is unrestricted access to the internet, and the government and private organizations have worked to extend internet access to the poor.

The government does not encroach on religious freedom, and academic freedom is respected.

Freedoms of assembly and association are generally upheld, but a vaguely worded 2006 antiterrorism law has raised concerns about the potential repression of left-leaning social movements. Police arrested 14 people on terrorism charges during a 2007 protest in Suchitoto against the privatization of water services; the charges were dropped in February 2008, but one of those arrested was assassinated by unknown assailants in May of that year. In 2009, multiple activists involved in protests against Canada's Pacific Rim Mining Corporation received threats or were attacked. El Salvador's wide array of nongovernmental organizations (NGOs) generally operate freely, but some have reported registration difficulties. Labor unions have long faced obstacles in a legal environment that has traditionally favored business interests.

The ineffectual and corrupt judicial system continues to promote impunity, especially for the well connected. In July 2009, the work of the Supreme Court was paralyzed for over two weeks as five judges whose terms had ended were not immediately replaced. Observers cited corruption and partisanship in the selection process as causes for the delay.

Violent crime continued unabated in 2009, registering the highest murder rate of the decade with 4,365 homicides during the year—a 37 percent increase from the 3,179 homicides reported in 2008. The forced repatriation of hundreds of Salvadoran criminals from the United States has contributed to the violence and reflects the international reach of major gangs like Mara Salvatrucha (also known as MS-13). There are an estimated 13,500 gang members in the country, 5,700 of whom are in prison.

The office of the human rights ombudsman, who is elected by the National Assembly for a three-year term, was created by the 1992 peace accords. While human rights abuses have declined steadily since the end of the war, civil liberties are still limited by sporadic political violence, repressive police measures, and vigilante groups. The ARENA government, like others in Central America, used "iron fist" (*mano duro*) tactics to combat gang violence, including house-to-house sweeps by the police and military. However, judges have often refused to approve warrants for such wide searches. Unofficial death squads and vigilantes, allegedly linked to the police and army, have also emerged to combat the gangs with extrajudicial killings.

Beyond the gang-related violence, law enforcement officials have been criticized for brutality, corruption, arbitrary arrest, and lengthy pretrial detention. In 2009, some 40 police officers, including three chiefs and the former head of the National Civil

Police's antinarcotics division, were investigated for alleged involvement in drug trafficking.

As of 2009, there were roughly 21,000 inmates in a prison system designed to house just 8,000, and about half of the inmates were believed to be awaiting trial. In February, more than 9,000 prisoners and their family members staged simultaneous peaceful protests to demand better conditions in the prison system. The event, organized with the help of NGOs, marked the first time that members of the country's two largest gangs, Mara Salvatrucha and 18th Street declared a temporary truce to protest together.

Salvadoran law, including a 1993 general amnesty, bars prosecution of crimes and human rights violations committed during the civil war, and the authorities have faced criticism from NGOs and the Inter-American Court of Human Rights for failing to adequately investigate such crimes. In a positive development, the new administration in August 2009 announced the creation of a commission to investigate the disappearances of children during the civil war.

There are no national laws regarding indigenous rights. According to the U.S. State Department's 2009 human rights report, access to land and credit remain problems for indigenous people.

Businesses are subject to regular extortion by organized criminal groups. Transport companies estimate that between 20 and 30 percent of their income is paid to criminal groups, and 36 transportation workers were killed in early 2009 for failure to pay bribes.

While women are granted equal rights under family and property law, they are occasionally discriminated against in practice; women also suffer discrimination in employment. A reform that would have enshrined bans on same-sex marriage and adoptions by same-sex couples in the constitution was defeated in the legislature in September 2009. Human trafficking for the purpose of prostitution is a serious problem. In 2009, El Salvador was ranked as a Tier 2 country in the U.S. State Department's Trafficking in Persons Report. Child labor also continues to be an area of concern, and one 2007 estimate held that up to a third of the workers on the country's sugarcane plantations were under the age of 18. Violence against women and children is widespread.

Equatorial Guinea

Political Rights: 7
Civil Liberties: 7
Status: Not Free

Population: 676,000
Capital: Malabo

Ten-Year Ratings Timeline For Year Under Review (Political Rights, Civil Liberties, Status)

2000	2001	2002	2003	2004	2005	2006	2007	2008	2009
7,7NF	6,6NF	7,6NF	7,6NF	7,6NF	7,6NF	7,6NF	7,6NF	7,7NF	7,7NF

Overview: Spanish authorities launched an investigation into alleged money laundering by Equatorial Guinea's government in

January 2009, and in February, unidentified gunmen attacked the presidential palace, prompting the authorities to deny speculation that the incident was a coup attempt. President Teodoro Obiang Nguema Mbasogo, the longest-serving ruler in sub-Saharan Africa, easily won a new term in the November presidential election, which was widely regarded as rigged.

Equatorial Guinea achieved independence from Spain in 1968. Current president Teodoro Obiang Nguema Mbasogo seized power in 1979 after deposing and executing his uncle, President Francisco Macias Nguema. International pressure forced Obiang to establish a multiparty system in 1992, though he and the ruling Democratic Party of Equatorial Guinea (PDGE) retained power over the next decade in a series of seriously flawed elections.

The president secured another seven-year term with nearly 100 percent of the vote in 2002, and then formed a national unity government with eight smaller parties, though key portfolios remained with presidential loyalists. The PDGE won 68 of 100 seats in the 2004 parliamentary elections, and allied parties took another 30. The opposition Convergence for Social Democracy (CPDS) won the remaining two seats.

Also in 2004, the government thwarted a coup attempt that reportedly aimed to install Severo Moto, an exiled opposition figure, as president. The accused coup plotters included former British commando Simon Mann, British financier Ely Calil, and Sir Mark Thatcher, son of former British prime minister Margaret Thatcher. Equatoguinean authorities sentenced Moto in absentia to 62 years in prison, and in 2008, they issued international arrest warrants for Calil and Thatcher. Mann was extradited to Equatorial Guinea to serve a 34-year prison sentence, but he was pardoned in November 2009.

Obiang dissolved the parliament in February 2008 and called legislative and municipal elections for May. A new coalition comprising the PDGE and nine smaller parties a reported 100 percent of the vote in many districts, taking 99 out of 100 seats in the parliament amid allegations of widespread irregularities. The CPDS, the sole opposition party, was reduced to a single seat.

Prime Minister Ricardo Mangue Obama Nfubea and his cabinet resigned in July 2008 over allegations of corruption and mishandling of the 2004 coup plot. However, Obiang reappointed most of the ministers to a new cabinet headed by Tang. Nfubea had taken office after a similar mass resignation in 2006.

In February 2009, a group of unidentified gunmen attacked the presidential palace in Malabo. The government blamed a Nigerian rebel group, the Movement for the Emancipation of the Niger Delta (MEND), for the attack, although the group rejected the accusation. Despite the authorities' denial that the incident was a coup attempt, they arrested several opposition figures in its aftermath.

Obiang swept the November 2009 presidential election with a reported 96 percent of the vote, though as with past balloting, the election was widely regarded as rigged. The president's main opponent, CPDS leader Placido Mico Abogo, was left with less than 4 percent.

Equatorial Guinea's abundant oil revenues do not reach the majority of its citizens; according to the watchdog group Global Witness, 60 percent of the population lives on less than $1 a day. Equatorial Guinea became an Extractive Industries Transparency Initiative (EITI) candidate country in 2008. It has until 2010 to be validated as a compliant country, but the International Monetary Fund has noted its lack of progress.

Political Rights and Civil Liberties: Equatorial Guinea is not an electoral democracy and has never held credible elections. The 2009 presidential election reportedly featured intimidation by security forces and restrictions on foreign observers, among other irregularities. President Teodoro Obiang Nguema Mbasogo, who won a new seven-year term, marked his 30th year in power in 2009, making him the longest-serving ruler in sub-Saharan Africa. The 100 members of the unicameral House of People's Representatives are elected to five-year terms but wield little power; all but one of the chamber's seats are held by the propresidential coalition. The few opposition parties, in particular the CPDS, are closely monitored by the government. A clan network linked to the president underlies the formal political structure.

Equatorial Guinea is considered one of the most corrupt countries in the world. Obiang and members of his inner circle have amassed huge personal fortunes stemming from the oil industry. The president has argued that information on oil revenues is a state secret, resisting calls for transparency and accountability. In January 2009, Spanish authorities began an investigation after a Spanish human rights organization filed a complaint accusing the Equatoguinean government of engaging in money laundering in Spain; the investigation was ongoing at year's end. Equatorial Guinea was ranked 168 out of 180 countries surveyed in Transparency International's 2009 Corruption Perceptions Index.

Although the constitution guarantees press freedom, the 1992 press law authorizes government censorship. A few private newspapers and underground pamphlets are published irregularly, but they face financial and political pressure. Libel remains a criminal offense, and all journalists are required to register with the government. The state holds a monopoly on broadcast media, with the exception of RTV-Asonga, a private radio and television outlet owned by the president's son. journalists were dismissed from the state broadcaster in January 2009 for "insubordination" and "lack of enthusiasm." In June, the only correspondent for foreign media in Equatorial Guinea, Rodrigo Angue Nguema, was imprisoned for four months after publishing an incorrect story about embezzlement by the head of the national airline. Satellite television is increasingly popular, and Radio Exterior, Spain's international shortwave service, has a large audience in the country The only internet service provider is state affiliated, and the government reportedly monitors internet communications.

The constitution protects religious freedom, although in practice it is sometimes affected by the country's broader political repression, and official preference is given to the Roman Catholic Church and the Reform Church of Equatorial Guinea. Academic freedom is also politically constrained, and self-censorship among faculty is common.

Freedoms of assembly and association are severely restricted, and political gatherings must have official authorization to proceed. There are no effective human rights organizations in the country, and the few international nongovernmental organizations are prohibited from promoting human rights. The constitution provides for the right to organize unions, but there are many legal barriers to collective bargaining. While it has ratified key International Labour Organization conventions, the government has refused to register the Equatorial Guinea Trade Union, whose members operate in secret. The country's only legal labor union, the Small Farmers' Syndicate, received legal recognition in 2000. In 2008, protests by Chinese construction workers over wages led to clashes with security forces. The were deported and replaced by new Chinese personnel.

The judiciary is not independent, and security forces generally act with impunity. Civil cases rarely go to trial, and military tribunals handle national security cases. In October 2008, opposition figure Cipriano Nguema Mba, who had political asylum in Cameroon, was abducted by two Cameroonian policemen and handed over to Equatorial Guinea, where he was incarcerated. In 2004, a military court had sentenced Nguema in absentia to 30 years in prison for allegedly plotting a coup and absconding with government funds. Prison conditions are deplorable. The UN Human Rights Council's Working Group on Arbitrary Detention cited the country in a 2007 report for holding detainees in secret, denying them access to lawyers, and jailing them for long periods without charge. In March 2009 Amnesty International report alleged that several opposition figures detained after the February attack on the presidential palace had been tortured. After visiting the country in 2008, the UN srapporteur on torture criticized the penal and judicial system, highlighting systematic torture and appalling detention conditions. These issues were underscored by the UN Universal Periodic Review of Equatorial Guinea in December 2009.

Obiang's Mongomo clan, part of the majority Fang ethnic group, monopolizes political and economic power. Differences between the Fang and the Bubi are a major source of political tension that has often erupted into violence. Fang vigilante groups have been allowed to abuse Bubi citizens with impunity.

All citizens are required to obtain exit visas to travel abroad, and some opposition figures have been denied such visas. Those who do travel are sometimes subjected to interrogation on their return.

Constitutional and legal guarantees of equality for women are largely ignored, and violence against women is reportedly widespread. Traditional practices including primogeniture and polygamy discriminate against women. Abortion is permitted to preserve the health of the mother, but only with spousal or parental authorization.

Eritrea

Political Rights: 7
Civil Liberties: 7*
Status: Not Free

Population: 5,073,000
Capital: Asmara

Ratings Change: Eritrea's civil liberties rating declined from 6 to 7 due to the government's persistent and intense repression of religious minorities, its dominance over the judiciary, and its harsh system of national service, which ties people to the state for much of their working lives.

Ten-Year Ratings Timeline For Year Under Review (Political Rights, Civil Liberties, Status)

2000	2001	2002	2003	2004	2005	2006	2007	2008	2009
7,5NF	7,6NF	7,6NF	7,6NF	7,6NF	7,6NF	7,6NF	7,6NF	7,6NF	7,7NF

Overview: The government of Eritrea intensified its suppression of human rights in 2009, using arbitrary arrests and an onerous conscription system to control the population. Religious minorities faced particular pressure from the authorities, who continued to use a pliant judicial system to detain political prisoners indefinitely. Meanwhile, Eritrea defied a UN Security Council resolution instructing it to withdraw its troops from the disputed border with Djibouti following clashes between the two countries' armies in 2008.

Britain ended Italian colonial rule in Eritrea during World War II, and the country was formally incorporated into Ethiopia in 1952. Its independence struggle began in 1962 as a nationalist and Marxist guerrilla war against the Ethiopian government of Emperor Haile Selassie. The seizure of power in Ethiopia by a Marxist junta in 1974 removed the ideological basis of the conflict, and by the time Eritrea finally defeated Ethiopia's northern armies in 1991, the Eritrean People's Liberation Front (EPLF) had discarded Marxism. Independence was achieved in May 1993 after a referendum supervised by the United Nations produced a landslide vote for statehood.

War with Ethiopia broke out again in 1998. In May 2000, an Ethiopian offensive made significant gains. The two sides signed a truce in June 2000, and a peace treaty was signed that December. The agreement called for a UN-led buffer force along the contested border and stipulated that further negotiations should determine the final boundary line. The war dominated the country's political agenda, reflecting the government's habitual use of real or perceived national security threats to generate popular support and justify the militarization of society.

In May 2001, a group of 15 senior ruling-party members publicly criticized President Isaias Afwerki and called for, "the rule of law and for justice, through peaceful and legal ways and means." Eleven members of the group were arrested for treason in September of that year. One is thought to have died in custody, and the others remain in secret detention. They have never been formally charged. The small independent media sector was also shut down, and a number of journalists were imprisoned.

The government clamped down on nongovernmental organizations (NGOs) in

2005, and ordered the U.S. Agency for International Development (USAID) to end its operations in the country. In 2006, reports emerged that hundreds of followers of various unregistered (mostly Protestant) churches were being detained, harassed, and abused.

The government continued this pattern of suppressing civil society and political dissent over the next three years, and arbitrary detention remained the authorities' most common method of stifling independent action by citizens. In 2009, Human Rights Watch released a report detailing Eritrea's practice of conscripting both men and women for mandatory and indefinite national service; a related article described the country as a "giant prison."

Eritrea maintained an aggressive stance toward its neighbors in 2009. Eritrean army units had attacked Djiboutian forces at the disputed border in June 2008, and there was no indication at year's end that Eritrea would comply with a UN Security Council resolution calling on it to withdraw its troops from the area. Eritrea was also accused of supporting rebel movements in Ethiopia, Sudan, and Somalia. According to the CIA World Fact Book, Eritrea spends 6.3 percent of its gross domestic product on the military, the ninth-highest percentage in the world. By contrast, the UN Development Programme's 2009 Human Development Index ranked Eritrea 165 out of 182 countries measured, and the World Bank put the country's gross national income per capita at just $630 for 2008, one of the worst figures in the world.

Political Rights and Civil Liberties: Eritrea is not an electoral democracy. Created in 1994 as a successor to the EPLF, the Popular Front for Democracy and Justice (PFDJ) is the only legal political party in the country. Instead of moving toward a democratic system, the PFDJ has taken significant steps backward since the end of the war with Ethiopia. The 2001 political crackdown and subsequent repressive measures clearly demonstrate the Eritrean government's authoritarian stance.

In 1994, a 50-member Constitutional Commission was established. A new constitution was adopted in 1997, authorizing "conditional" political pluralism with provisions for a multiparty system. The constitution calls for an elected 150-seat legislature, the National Assembly, to choose the president from among its members by a majority vote. However, national elections have been postponed indefinitely, and President Isaias Afwerki has remained in office since independence. In 2004, regional assembly elections were conducted, but they were carefully orchestrated by the PFDJ and offered no real choice to voters.

Eritrea long maintained a reputation for a relatively low level of corruption. In recent years, however, graft appears to have increased. The government's control over foreign exchange effectively gives it sole authority over imports. At the same time, those in favor with the regime are allowed to smuggle goods into the country at great profit. Eritrea was ranked 126 out of 180 countries surveyed in Transparency International's 2009 Corruption Perceptions Index.

There are no independent media in Eritrea. The government controls all broadcasting outlets and banned all privately owned newspapers in its 2001 crackdown, effectively blocking the dissemination of opposing or alternative views. A group of journalists arrested in 2001 remain imprisoned without charge; as many as 4 of the original 10 are believed to have died in custody. A fresh wave of arrests took place in February 2009, when 50 employees of Radio Bana, which produces educational programs for the government, were detained. A total of 19 journalists were behind bars in Eritrea as of December 2009, according to the U.S.-based Committee to Protect Journalists, which did not count nonjournalist staff members. The government controls the internet infrastructure and is believed to monitor online communications, though only a small fraction of the population has internet access.

The government places significant limitations on the exercise of religion. Since 2002, it has officially recognized only four faiths: Islam, Orthodox Christianity, Roman Catholicism, and Lutheranism as practiced by the Evangelical Church of Eritrea. Persecution of minority Christian sects has escalated, particularly for Jehovah's Witnesses, who were stripped of their basic civil rights in 1994, and evangelical and Pentecostal churches. Abune Antonios, patriarch of the Eritrean Orthodox Church, has been under house arrest since 2006. According to Amnesty International, members of other churches have been jailed and tortured or otherwise ill-treated to make them abandon their faith. Compass Direct, an NGO, estimates that up to 3,000 Christians are currently in prison because of their beliefs. At least two are believed to have died in custody in January 2009. In December, a group of 30 elderly women from a banned evangelical denomination were arrested while praying together in Asmara. Some Muslims have also been targeted for persecution.

Academic freedom is constrained. Secondary school students are subject to the highly unpopular policy of obligatory military service, and are often stationed at bases far from their homes. The official 18-month service period is frequently open ended in practice, and no conscientious-objector status is recognized. The government imposes collective punishment on the families of deserters, forcing them to pay heavy fines or putting them in prison.

Freedom of assembly is not recognized. The government maintains a hostile attitude toward civil society; independent NGOs are not allowed, and the legitimate role of human rights defenders is not recognized. In 2005, Eritrea enacted legislation to regulate the operations of all NGOs, requiring them to pay taxes on imported materials, submit project reports every three months, renew their licenses annually, and meet government-established target levels of financial resources. International human rights NGOs are barred from the country, and the government expelled three remaining development NGOs in 2006.

The civil service, the military, the police, and other essential services have some restrictions on their freedom to form unions. In addition, groups of 20 or more persons seeking to form a union require special approval from the Ministry of Labor.

The judiciary, which was formed by decree in 1993, has never issued rulings significantly at variance with government positions. Constitutional due process guarantees are often ignored in cases related to state security.

According to Amnesty International and Human Rights Watch, torture, arbitrary detentions, and political arrests are common. Prison conditions are poor, and outside monitors such as the International Committee of the Red Cross have been denied access to detainees. In some facilities, inmates are held in metal shipping containers or underground cells in extreme temperatures. Prisoners are often denied medical treatment. The government maintains a network of secret detention facilities and frequently refuses to disclose the location of prisoners to their families.

The Kunama people, one of Eritrea's nine ethnic groups, reportedly face severe discrimination. They reside primarily in the west and have resisted attempts to integrate them into the national society. They are also viewed with suspicion for having backed a rival group rather than the EPLF during the war of independence.

Freedom of movement is heavily restricted. Eritreans under the age of 50 are rarely given permission to leave the country, and those who try to travel without the correct documents face imprisonment. Eritrean refugees and asylum seekers who are repatriated from other countries are also detained. Written permission is often required even for internal travel.

Government policy is officially supportive of free enterprise, and citizens have the nominal freedom to choose their employment, establish private businesses, and operate them without government harassment. However, few private businesses remain in Eritrea. This is largely because of the conscription system, which ties most able-bodied men and women to an indefinite period of national service and can entail compulsory labor for enterprises controlled by the political elite. The 2009 Heritage Foundation Index of Economic Freedom cites other barriers to starting and operating a business in Eritrea, including burdensome regulations and the high cost of credit. It ranks Eritrea as the second-worst country in sub-Saharan Africa for economic freedom.

Women played important roles in the guerrilla movement prior to independence, and the government has worked to improve the status of women. Women hold some senior government positions. Equal educational opportunity, equal pay for equal work, and penalties for domestic violence have been codified. However, traditional societal discrimination against women persists in rural areas. Female genital mutilation was banned by the government in 2007, but there have been no arrests under the new law, and the practice remains widespread.

Estonia

Political Rights: 1
Civil Liberties: 1
Status: Free

Population: 1,340,000
Capital: Tallinn

Ten-Year Ratings Timeline For Year Under Review (Political Rights, Civil Liberties, Status)

2000	2001	2002	2003	2004	2005	2006	2007	2008	2009
1,2F	1,2F	1,2F	1,2F	1,1F	1,1F	1,1F	1,1F	1,1F	1,1F

Overview: Estonia's economy continued to worsen in 2009, with unemployment reaching a postindependence high of 14.5 percent. Disputes over how to cut government spending and lower the country's budget deficit while maintaining social guarantees led to the disintegration of the three-party ruling coalition.

Estonia gained independence from Russia in 1918, but it was captured—along with Latvia and Lithuania—by Soviet troops during World War II. Under Soviet rule, approximately one-tenth of Estonia's population was deported, executed, or forced to flee abroad. Subsequent Russian immigration reduced ethnic Estonians to just over 61 percent of the population by 1989. Estonia regained its independence with the disintegration of the Soviet Union in 1991. It adopted a new constitution in July 1992 and held its first legislative elections in September of that year. Russian troops withdrew from Estonia in 1994.

After the 2003 legislative elections, the newly formed right-leaning Res Publica party outmaneuvered the left-wing Center Party to form a centrist coalition government with the Reform Party and the People's Union. In March 2005, a parliamentary vote of no confidence against the justice minister prompted Res Publica leader Juhan Parts to step down as prime minister, leaving the position to the Reform Party's Andrus Ansip. Former foreign minister Toomas Hendrik Ilves defeated incumbent Arnold Ruutel in the country's 2006 presidential vote.

In the March 2007 parliamentary elections, the Reform Party captured 31 seats, followed closely by the Center Party with 29 seats. The Reform Party, the Union of Pro Patria and Res Publica (IRL), and the Social Democratic Party (SDP) formed a left-right coalition, and Ansip stayed on as prime minister.

The new government faced a major crisis in April 2007, when plans to relocate a Soviet World War II memorial and exhume the remains of Soviet soldiers buried at the site touched off protests, mostly by young ethnic Russians. The demonstrations erupted into two days of violence, as police responded with tear gas and water cannons to widespread looting and vandalism. The monument, the Bronze Soldier, was moved from its original place in the center of Tallinn to a nearby military cemetery. Meanwhile, protesters from the pro-Kremlin youth group Nashi surrounded the Estonian embassy in Moscow for days, harassing the country's diplomats, and large-scale cyberattacks took down Estonian commercial and governmental websites. The initial attacks were reportedly traced to internet addresses registered in Russia, including some in the presidential administration, although direct links to the Russian government could not be proven. In January 2009, four alleged organizers of the riots, members of pro-Kremlin groups, were acquitted for their role in the crisis due to lack of evidence. In June, the government revealed the Victory Monument of the War of Independence on Freedom Square in Tallinn, only a short walk from the Bronze Soldier's former location.

The economy took a turn for the worse in 2009—with unemployment reaching 14.5 percent in December—and disputes over budget cuts broke up the ruling coalition. At the center of the conflict was how to manage the budget deficit in light of the Employment Contracts Act (ECA) entering into law on July 1, which was meant to simultaneously increase social guarantees and labor market flexibility. The Reform Party and the IRL advocated further cuts to unemployment benefits, while the SDP proposed raising the unemployment insurance tax rate in lieu of benefit reductions. The SDP left the coalition on May 25, leaving the Reform Party and the IRL to rule as a 50-seat minority government through the end of the year. October's local election results, with the Center Party gaining twice as many votes as the Reform Party, raised further concerns about the future of the ruling coalition.

Political Rights and Civil Liberties:

Estonia is an electoral democracy. Elections have been free and fair, and the 2007 polls were the world's first parliamentary elections to employ internet voting; about 30,000 people voted online. The 1992 constitution established a 101-seat, unicameral Parliament, or Riigikogu, whose members are elected for four-year terms. A prime minister serves as head of government, and a president with a five-year term fills the largely ceremonial role of head of state. After the first president was chosen by popular vote in 1992, presidential elections reverted to parliamentary ballot. The prime minister is chosen by the president and confirmed by Parliament.

In advance of local elections in October 2009, the Tallinn City Council agreed on a plan to include the entire city of Tallinn into one electoral district. The plan would have provided the Center Party, which currently holds a majority on the Council, with an even greater advantage but was thwarted by Parliament in February. Estonia saw its largest voter turnout rate in October's local elections, with about 60 percent of the population showing up to the polls. Only citizens may participate in national elections, though resident noncitizens may vote (but not run as candidates) in local elections. About 10 percent of Parliament members are ethnic minorities.

Political parties organize freely, though only citizens may be members. The country's two main right-wing parties, Pro Patria and Res Publica, merged in 2006 to become the Union of Pro Patria and Res Publica. Major parties include the Center Party, the Reform Party, the Social Democratic Party, the Greens, and the People's Union. In the June 2009 European Parliamentary elections, journalist Indrek Tarand brought in the highest results in Estonia's electoral history for an independent candidate.

Corruption is regarded as a relatively minor problem in Estonia, which was ranked 27 out of 180 countries surveyed in Transparency International's 2009 Corruption Perceptions Index. In May 2009, three individuals, including a former government minister, were found guilty of attempted bribery regarding the sale of an environment ministry building; the former minister received a suspended jail sentence, and the other two defendants were given fines. A new anticorruption law is expected to come into force in 2010. Legal guarantees for public access to government information are respected in practice. Government decisions are almost instantly available on the internet, where Estonians may comment and exchange views.

The government respects freedom of the press. In addition to the public broadcaster, Estonian Television, there are a variety of commercial channels and independent newspapers and radio stations. In 2009, financial reasons were given for closing a Russian language television channel and a daily newspaper. There are no government restrictions on access to the internet, and Estonia is among the leading countries in the world with regard to internet penetration.

Religious freedom is respected in law and in practice. Estonia built its only synagogue in 2007 to serve the country's 2,500 person Jewish community. Estonia does not restrict academic freedom. In 2009, the government continued to implement a program calling for 60 percent Estonian-language instruction in the country's public Russian-language high schools by 2011.

The constitution guarantees freedoms of assembly association, and the government upholds those rights in practice. Public gatherings may be prohibited to ensure public safety. Civil society is vibrant, and the government involves nongovernmental organizations in the drafting of legislation. Although workers have the right to organize freely, strike, and bargain collectively, the Estonian Confederation of Trade Unions has reported antiunion discrimination in the private sector. Approximately 10 percent of the country's workers are union members. In June 2009, the Baltic Trade Union Youth Forum organized a protest of 500 people outside the Parliament building against the ECA.

The judiciary is independent and generally free from government interference. Laws prohibiting arbitrary arrest and detention and ensuring the right to a fair trial are largely observed, though lengthy pretrial detention remains a concern. There have been reports of police officers physically or verbally abusing suspects. The country's prison system continues to suffer from overcrowding and limited access to medical care, although the opening of a new prison in July 2008 reduced crowding. In March 2009, the Estonian court sentenced Herman Simm, a former civil servant who was allegedly passing state secrets to the Russian government, to 12 years and 6 months in prison on counts of treason and sharing classified information.

Many ethnic Russians arrived in Estonia during the Soviet era and are now regarded as immigrants who must apply for citizenship through a process that requires knowledge of the Estonian language. At the end of 2009, about 100,000 people, or just over 7 percent of the country's population, were of undetermined citizenship, according to the Estonian government. The authorities have adopted policies to assist those seeking Estonian citizenship, including funding Estonian language courses. The use of Estonian is mandatory in certain work environments, including among public sector employees, medical professionals, and service personnel. In 2009, an Estonian Integration Fund project offered classes for public safety, educational, management, and health-care employees with knowledge of basic Estonian to help improve their language skills. The same year, however, the government stopped translating law documents from Estonian to Russian, citing budget losses. The granting of asylum or refugee status in accordance with the 1951 UN Convention Relating to the Status of Refugees and its 1967 protocol is legally protected and provided in practice.

Though women enjoy the same legal rights as men, women earn on average about 30 percent less than men. About one-fifth of the members of Parliament are women. Violence against women, including domestic violence, remains a problem. Estonia is a source, transit point, and destination for women trafficked for the purpose of prostitution.

♦ Ethiopia

Political Rights: 5
Civil Liberties: 5
Status: Partly Free

Population: 82,825,000
Capital: Addis Ababa

Trend Arrow: Ethiopia received a downward trend arrow due to the narrowing of political space in advance of the 2010 elections, the government's crackdown on the operations of nongovernmental organizations, and its passing of a draconian antiterrorism law.

Ten-Year Ratings Timeline For Year Under Review (Political Rights, Civil Liberties, Status)

2000	2001	2002	2003	2004	2005	2006	2007	2008	2009
5,5PF	5,5PF	5,5PF	5,5PF	5,5PF	5,5PF	5,5PF	5,5PF	5,5PF	5,5PF

Overview:
Prime Minister Meles Zenawi's government bolstered restrictions on political activity in 2009 as it prepared for federal and regional elections scheduled for 2010. Opposition party activists were arrested, and a new antiterrorism law gave the government broad authority to crack down on perceived opponents. Other legislation enacted during the year imposed strict controls on civil society organizations.

One of the few African countries to avoid decades of European colonization, Ethiopia ended a long tradition of monarchy in 1974, when Emperor Haile Selassie was overthrown in a Marxist military coup. Colonel Mengistu Haile Mariam ruled the country until a coalition of guerrilla groups led by forces from the northern Tigray region overthrew his brutal dictatorship in 1991. The main rebel group, the Ethiopian People's Revolutionary Democratic Front (EPRDF), formed a new regime, and its leader, Meles Zenawi, became interim president.

Under the EPRDF, democratic institutions and a new constitution were introduced. Most of the opposition boycotted elections held in 1995, claiming harassment of its supporters precluded a fair vote, and Meles became prime minister. He began a second five-year term after the 2000 elections, which the EPRDF also won easily. Opposition parties and some observers criticized the government's conduct of the vote.

A border dispute with Eritrea, which had gained formal independence from Ethiopia in 1993 after a long guerrilla conflict, triggered a war that lasted from 1998 to 2000. The Eritrea-Ethiopia Boundary Commission was then established to draw a new border, but Ethiopia rejected its 2002 decision to assign the town of Badme to Eritrea.

In the 2005 elections for the powerful lower house of Parliament, the EPRDF and its allies won 327 seats, while the two main opposition parties took 161 seats, up from 12 in the previous Parliament. Notwithstanding their gains, opposition parties argued that fraud and interference in the electoral process had deprived them of outright victory. Street demonstrations led to violence and a harsh reaction by the authorities. At least 193 people were killed and more than 4,000 were arrested, including leading opposition figures, who were finally pardoned and released in 2007.

The opposition boycotted local elections in 2008, accusing the EPRDF of harassment. Opposition activities were further restricted in 2009, as the EPRDF prepared for the 2010 federal and regional elections. In June, 45 members of an unregistered political party were charged with trying to topple the government.

Ethiopia's relations with neighboring countries were tense but stable in 2009. The border dispute with Eritrea remained unresolved, but Ethiopian forces completed their withdrawal from Somalia, ending a disastrous three-year campaign aimed at destroying Islamist rebel groups and propping up the war-torn country's Transitional Federal Government.

Meanwhile, Ethiopia continued to face separatist movements in Oromiya and the Ogaden. Sporadic fighting persisted between government forces and Ogaden National Liberation Front (ONLF) guerrillas. The authorities have banned journalists from the region, preventing the outside world from accurately assessing the situation there.

Ongoing drought in parts of the country in 2009 led to a warning that five million people would be in need of food aid, in addition to the eight million who already received it. The drought also reduced Ethiopia's hydroelectric power output, causing frequent outages in Addis Ababa and contributing to a growth rate of less than 2 percent according to the United Nations, which was far less than the 10 percent claimed by the government.

Political Rights and Civil Liberties: Ethiopia is not an electoral democracy. However, the presence of a significant elected opposition at the federal level since 2005 does mark a possible step forward in the development of the country's democratic political culture.

The bicameral Parliament consists of a 108-seat upper house, the House of Federation, and a 547-seat lower house, the House of People's Representatives. The lower house is filled through popular elections, while the upper chamber is selected by the state legislatures, with both serving five-year terms. The House of People's Representatives selects the prime minister, who holds most executive power, and the president, who serves in a largely ceremonial capacity for six-year terms. The 1995 constitution has a number of unique features, including a federal structure that grants certain powers and the right of secession to ethnically based states. However, in 2003 the central government acquired additional powers to intervene in states' affairs when public security is deemed to be at risk.

More than 60 legally recognized political parties are active in Ethiopia, but the EPRDF dominates political life. Government harassment has seriously impeded the ability of opposition parties to function, although some have used rhetoric that could be interpreted as advocating violence, or have failed to conduct themselves in a manner consistent with a democratic political culture.

A recent series of arrests of opposition figures appeared to signal a crackdown on political freedoms in advance of the 2010 elections. Unity for Democracy and Justice party leader Birtukan Mideksa, who had received a sentence of life in prison after the 2005 postelection violence and was pardoned in 2007, was re-arrested in December 2008, after her pardon was revoked. In June 2009, 46 people were charged with plotting to overthrow the government on behalf of Ginbot 7, an unregistered party. In November, a court convicted 26 of the defendants after a trial that legal rights groups criticized as unfair. However, a high-profile opponent of the government, the singer Tewodros Kassahun, known as Teddy Afro, was released early from a two-year prison sentence in August 2009; he had been convicted for a hit-and-run automobile accident, but his supporters claimed that the case was politically motivated.

The government has taken a number of steps to limit corruption, including the imposition of asset-disclosure rules for state officials. However, graft remains a significant problem. Former prime minister Tamrat Layne and former defense minister Seye Abreha were convicted of corruption in 2007, but both had been released by the end of 2008, having already served several years in prison on other corruption charges. Ethiopia was ranked 120 out of 180 countries surveyed in Transparency International's 2009 Corruption Perceptions Index.

The news media are dominated by state-owned broadcasters and government-oriented newspapers. There are a number of independent newspapers, but they struggle financially and face intermittent government harassment. The only independent newspaper in the capital, *Addis Neger*, suspended operations in November, as staff said they feared prosecution by the authorities. A 2008 media law has had a chilling effect on freedom of speech. Although it barred government censorship of private media, the measure allowed prosecutors to seize material before publication in the name of national security and gave the government broader powers to pursue defamation cases. Journalists who fall foul of the government risk exile or imprisonment. In two separate cases in August 2009, journalists were given one-year prison sentences for spreading false information. Internet usage is confined mainly to major urban areas, and the government has blocked opposition-run websites.

Constitutionally mandated religious freedom is generally respected, although religious tensions have risen in recent years. The Ethiopian Orthodox Church is influential, particularly in the north. In the south there is a large Muslim community, made up mainly of the Somali, Oromo, and Afari ethnic groups.

Academic freedom is restricted. Prime Minister Meles Zenawi has accused universities of being friendly to the opposition, and their activities are closely monitored. In recent years, student protests against government policies have led to scores of deaths and injuries and hundreds of arrests. The government has tried to establish a more orderly and loyal academic community by creating 13 new state universities. Growing intolerance of dissent has dampened private discussion in the country, as even ordinary citizens face harassment or arrest for speaking out against the government.

Freedoms of assembly and association are limited. In January 2009, the House of People's Representatives passed the Charities and Societies Proclamation, which is designed to restrict the ability of foreign nongovernmental organizations (NGOs) to bypass government channels when they disburse funds. Foreign NGOs are defined as groups that receive more than 10 percent of their funding from abroad. The measure also gives the government broad authority to restrict NGO activities it deems unhelpful, such as campaigning for human and political rights. All civil society organizations are required to reregister with the government under the new rules.

Trade union rights are tightly restricted. Government workers in "essential industries," a term that is broadly defined, are not allowed to strike, and the Confederation of Ethiopian Unions is under government control. Some union leaders suspected of engaging in political activity have been removed from their elected offices or forced to leave the country. All unions must be registered, and the government retains the authority to cancel union registration.

The judiciary is officially independent, although there have been few significant examples of decisions at variance with government policy. Suspects are routinely held without warrants, and cases can take a long time to reach court. A draconian new counterterrorism law, passed by the government in July 2009, defines terrorist activity very broadly and gives great discretion to the security forces. According to Human Rights Watch, the law could be used to prosecute peaceful political protesters and impose the death penalty for offenses as minor as damaging public property. Conditions in Ethiopia's prisons are harsh, and the International Committee of the Red Cross is not permitted to inspect federal facilities and police stations. Detainees frequently report being abused or tortured.

The government has tended to favor Tigrayan ethnic interests in economic and political matters. Politics within the EPRDF have been dominated by the Tigrayan People's Liberation Front. Discrimination against other groups, especially the Oromo, has been widespread. According to the International Crisis Group, Ethiopia's federal system of government, which grants autonomy to the dominant ethnic group in each region, has increased tensions between communities. Repression of the Oromo and ethnic Somalis, and government attempts to co-opt their parties into subsidiaries of the EPRDF, have helped to fuel nationalism in both Oromiya and the Ogaden.

The government has established a Women's Affairs Ministry, and Parliament has passed legislation designed to protect women's rights. In practice, however, women's rights are routinely violated. Women have traditionally had few land or property rights, especially in rural areas, where there is little opportunity for female employment beyond agricultural labor. General deficiencies in education exacerbate the problems of rural poverty and gender inequality. According to the NGO Save the Children, Ethiopia has one of the lowest rates of school enrollment in sub-Saharan Africa.

Fiji

Political Rights: 6
Civil Liberties: 4
Status: Partly Free

Population: 844,000
Capital: Suva

Ten-Year Ratings Timeline For Year Under Review (Political Rights, Civil Liberties, Status)

2000	2001	2002	2003	2004	2005	2006	2007	2008	2009
6,3PF	4,3PF	4,3PF	4,3PF	4,3PF	4,3PF	6,4PF	6,4PF	6,4PF	6,4PF

Overview: In 2009, Fiji continued to be ruled by an interim government headed by the leaders of the 2006 military coup. A court ruled in April that the dismissal of Laisenia Qarase and the dissolution of Parliament in 2006, as well as Frank Bainimarama's 2007 appointment as interim prime minister, were illegal. President Josefa Iloilo subsequently suspended the constitution, reinstated Bainimarama as caretaker prime minister, and imposed Public Emergency Regulations. Throughout the year, the regime became increasingly intolerant of criticism, suppressing the media and voices of dissent through arrests and lawsuits.

Fiji, colonized by Britain in 1874, became an independent member of the Commonwealth in 1970. Intense rivalry between indigenous Fijians and Indo-Fijians is the main source of political and social tension. Indians were first brought to Fiji in the 19th century to work on sugar plantations, and Indo-Fijians have historically made up a majority of the population and controlled a large share of the economy. Armed coups by indigenous factions in 1987 and 2000 overthrew governments led by Indo-Fijian parties.

After the 2000 coup, the military installed Laisenia Qarase, an indigenous Fijian of the United Fiji Party (UFP), to lead an interim government. Qarase was elected prime minister in the 2001 elections, and he won a second term in 2006. That year, a destabilizing rift between Qarase and military chief Frank Bainimarama—an indigenous Fijian—emerged over the fate of the 2000 coup participants; Bainimarama wanted the suspects prosecuted and jailed, while Qarase proposed granting amnesty to those convicted and providing immunity to those not yet charged. When Qarase refused Bainimarama's demand for his resignation, he was ousted by Bainimarama in another military coup in December 2006. Parliament was dissolved, and Bainimarama assumed presidential powers, claiming that Qarase's removal was essential to tackling rampant official corruption and addressing discrimination against Indo-Fijians.

In January 2007, Bainimarama returned executive authority to former president Josefa Iloilo, a staunch Bainimarama supporter, who named Bainimarama the interim prime minister. Bainimarama also continued as the head of the military, and Iloilo granted him immunity. While the interim government undertook a number of reforms to address official corruption, public support for the coup quickly diminished when the government began intimidating its critics and suppressing the media through arrests and travel bans. Bainimarama also continued to ignore international appeals and pressure to return Fiji to civilian rule. The pledge for political reform lost credibility after the interim government cut wages in 2007 and 2008 for civil servants, but not cabinet members, and dismissals and appointments seemed largely a matter of opposition to or support for the interim government and Bainimarama.

In 2008, the interim government failed to set a date for elections and made electoral reforms and the approval of the new People's Charter for Change, Peace, and Progress preconditions for new elections. In 2007, the interim government had appointed a 45-member National Council for Building a Better Fiji—with representatives from government, provincial councils, and civil society—to draft the charter, which was intended to complement the constitution.

Bainimarama and Qarase continued to pursue rival lawsuits in 2008, with the former seeking to nullify the 2006 elections based on alleged vote rigging by the UFP, and the latter calling for the interim government to be declared illegal. The Suva High Court dismissed Qarase's suit against the interim regime in October, ruling that Iloilo's appointment of the interim government was valid. Qarase filed another suit to stop work on the charter, and the High Court granted an injunction in November to cease work on the document. However, the interim government subsequently obtained a stay on the injunction from the High Court to allow the drafting to continue.

In December, the final version of the charter was released with recommendations to address the many sources of ethnic tensions, including replacing the communal electoral rolls with a one-person-one-vote system; teaching Fijian and Hindi in all schools to promote multiculturalism; and designating all citizens as Fijians, a term previously reserved only for indigenous Fijians. The charter also officially confirmed the military's role in governing Fiji. Opposition members, the teacher's union, and the Methodist Church of Fiji and Rotuma all opposed the charter.

In February 2009, Bainimarama announced the appointments of additional military officers to the cabinet and other senior government posts. Commander Francis Kean—Bainimarama's brother-in-law, who was sentenced to 18 months in prison for manslaughter in 2007—was appointed as head of the navy.

In April, the October 2008 High Court decision was overturned, and the court of appeal ruled that the 2006 dismissal of Qarase and his cabinet, the dissolution of Parliament, and the 2007 appointment of Bainimarama as interim prime minister were illegal. The president was ordered to appoint a caretaker prime minister to dissolve Parliament and call elections, though Bainimarama and Qarase were barred from being selected. Iloilo suspended the 1997 constitution the following day, reconfirmed himself as president under a "new legal order," nullified all judicial appointments, and imposed Public Emergency Regulations (PER) to suppress public opposition; the PER remained in place through year's end. Bainimarama, who had resigned following Iloilo's abrogation of the constitution, was named as caretaker prime minister and reappointed his previous cabinet. In July, Iloilo retired from the presidency, and Epeli Nailatikau—a military officer and the vice president—became the interim president.

Bainimarama remained defiant of international criticism and pressure throughout the year, isolating Fiji in the process. In September, Bainimarama promised a new constitution based on the charter by 2013 and elections in September 2014, ignoring domestic and international requests to set earlier dates. In May, the European Union terminated millions in development aid, and Fiji was suspended from the Pacific Islands Forum (PIF), a regional political and economic bloc. In March and September, respectively, the United Nations and the British military said they would no longer recruit soldiers from Fiji. The country was officially suspended from the Commonwealth in September.

Bainimarama's relationship with traditional chiefs and the influential Methodist church also worsened throughout the year. He banned a Methodist Church conference scheduled for August and charged a traditional high chief with disobedience for his involvement in the event.

Political Rights and Civil Liberties: Fiji is not an electoral democracy. Under the 1997 constitution, which was suspended in April 2009, Parliament consists of the 32-seat Senate and the 71-seat House of Representatives. The president appoints 14 senators on the advice of the Great Council of Chiefs, 9 on the advice of the prime minister, 8 on the advice of the opposition leader, and 1 on the advice of the council representing outlying Rotuma Island. House members are elected for five-year terms, with 25 seats open to all ethnicities, 23 reserved for indigenous Fijians, 19 for Indo-Fijians, 3 for other ethnic groups (mainly citizens of European and East Asian extraction), and 1 for Rotuma voters. The president is appointed to a five-year term by the Great Council of Chiefs in consultation with the prime minister, who is in turn appointed by the president. The prime minister is generally the leader of the majority party or coalition in Parliament.

The two main political parties are the UFP, largely supported by indigenous Fijians, and the predominantly Indo-Fijian Labor Party.

Official corruption and abuse are widespread, and reform agendas by multiple governments have not produced significant results. Despite Frank Bainimarama's pledge to tackle official corruption, he received US$178,000 in March 2009 for leave accumulated since 1978. Fiji was not rated in Transparency International's 2009 Corruption Perceptions Index.

While the 1997 constitution provides for freedom of speech and the press, the interim government continued to harass and intimidate the media in 2009. A number of domestic and foreign journalists were detained, arrested, convicted, and deported throughout the year. The Australian-born editor of the *Fiji Times* was deported in January after the newspaper was convicted of contempt of court. The *Fiji Times* was fined US$54,500, and its editor-in-chief was given a three-month suspended sentence for publishing an article criticizing the judges who supported the 2006 military coup.

Media conditions deteriorated considerably following the April suspension of the constitution and enforcement of the PER. The state-owned Fiji Broadcasting Corporation provides radio and television broadcasts, and while there are several privately owned newspapers and radio and television stations, the PER allowed for daily government censorship of print publications and radio and television broadcasts. The military regime warned journalists against publishing or broadcasting content that was critical of Bainimarama or the interim government. In April, two Australian Broadcasting Corporation FM radio transmitters were shut down, and journalists with *Fijilive*, a web-based news service, were detained and questioned for a story on the devaluation of Fiji's currency. All broadcasting licenses were revoked in November. Internet access is expanding but remains limited by cost and connectivity constraints outside the capital.

Freedom of religion is generally respected, though the interim government detained several religious leaders opposed to the military regime in 2009. Most indigenous Fijians are Christians, and Indo-Fijians are Hindus. The number of attacks on places of worship, especially Hindu temples, has increased in recent years.

While academic freedom is generally respected, the education system suffers from a lack of resources, and indigenous Fijians are granted special privileges in education. Bainimarama's interim government has claimed that the promised new constitution seeks to eliminate such favoritism. Brij Lal, an Australian citizen of Fijian origin and an academic at the Australian National University, was deported to Australia in November 2009, after he commented to the media on the interim government's expulsion of diplomatic representatives from Australia and New Zealand.

Freedoms of assembly and association have also been restricted since the suspension of the 1997 constitution and the imposition of the PER in April. Bainimarama's government was permitted to stop public protests under the PER, and the few permits granted for pubic assemblies were often revoked. Since 2007, the interim government has banned several public demonstrations by the Methodist Church and teachers' union against the government's policies. Workers can form and join trade unions, though these rights have reportedly been constrained under the new interim government.

The 2009 abrogation of the constitution has raised concerns about the future independence of Fiji's judiciary. Josefa Iloilo dismissed the judiciary in April, though new judges aligned with the military regime were appointed, as well as the former chief justice and several judges loyal to Bainimarama. The already serious backlog of cases was exacerbated by a shortage of judges and lawyers due to the government's delayed replacement of dismissed personnel. Prisons are highly overcrowded with poor sanitary and living conditions.

Race-based discrimination is pervasive, and indigenous Fijians receive preferential treatment in education, housing, land acquisition, and other areas. Discrimination, economic hardship, and political turmoil have caused more than 140,000 Indo-Fijians to leave Fiji since the late 1980s. Part of the resulting void has been filled by migrants from China, who now control approximately 5 percent of the economy. Their growing economic strength has made them targets of indigenous Fijian resentment and attacks.

Discrimination and violence against women are widespread. Women's groups claim that rape, child abuse, incest, and infanticide cases are increasing, as well as the number of pregnancy-related deaths. Women are not well represented in government and leadership positions and do not receive equal pay. Legal protections against discrimination do not include homosexuality. Fiji is a source and destination country for the trafficking of women and children.

Finland

Political Rights: 1
Civil Liberties: 1
Status: Free

Population: 5,339,000
Capital: Helsinki

Ten-Year Ratings Timeline For Year Under Review (Political Rights, Civil Liberties, Status)

2000	2001	2002	2003	2004	2005	2006	2007	2008	2009
1,1F	1,1F	1,1F	1,1F	1,1F	1,1F	1,1F	1,1F	1,1F	1,1F

Overview:
Finland's murky campaign-funding law caused further political turmoil in 2009, as Prime Minister Matti Vanhanen resisted calls for resignation over a campaign finance scandal. Meanwhile, concerns over encroachments on freedom of expression continued throughout the year.

After centuries of Swedish and then Russian rule, Finland gained independence in 1917. The country is traditionally neutral, but its army has enjoyed broad popular support since it fended off a Soviet invasion during World War II. Finland joined the European Union (EU) in 1995 and is the only Nordic country to have adopted the euro currency. In the 2000 presidential election, Tarja Halonen of the Social Democratic Party (SDP) was elected as the country's first female president. She defeated six other candidates—including four women—from across the political spectrum.

Halonen won a second term as president in 2006, defeating the candidate of the opposition National Coalition Party. However, the 2007 parliamentary elections represented a victory for the center-right National Coalition. Although the ruling Center Party held on toits plurality by 1 seat, capturing 23.1 percent of the vote, the National Coalition Party gained 10 seats, winning 22.3 percent of the vote. Meanwhile, the left-leaning parties received record-low levels of support. Acknowledging the shift to the right, Prime Minister Matti Vanhanen formed a four-party coalition consisting of his Center Party, the National Coalition, the Greens, and the Swedish People's Party, leaving the SDP in opposition for the first time since 1995. In December 2009, Vanhanen announced that for personal reasons he would not seek reelection in 2011.

In April 2009, the Helsinki appeals court found Markus Pentikainen, a photographer for the current affairs magazine *Suomen Kuvalehti,* guilty of disobeying police orders during the 2006 "Smash Asem" demonstration in Helsinki against the Asia-Europe Summit. Pentikainen, while displaying full press credentials, had been arrested by law enforcement officials after he refused to leave the scene. The case was being pursued in the European Court of Human Rights at the year's end.

In September and October 2009, Prime Minister Vanhanen came under fire after public broadcaster YLE publicized allegations that he had received valuable supplies for the construction of his home in the 1990s in return for political favors. The scandal prompted calls from the opposition and the media for Vanhanen's resignation. The publicly funded company that allegedly supplied the construction materials, Nuorisosaatio, was also accused of financing the Centre Party's campaign in several previous elections. However, YLE failed to produce any evidence or disclose its sources in the matter, causing the National Bureau of Investigation to drop its investigation. Despite criticism for its failure to sufficiently investigate the claims, YLE was exonerated by the Council for Mass Media in Finland. The Council's chairman and one other member stepped down over the exoneration. These two resignations and the failure to reprimand YLE have exacerbated a debate over whether journalists should be required by law to reveal their source during the preliminary stages of an investigation. Potential legislation to address these issues was still pending at the year's end.

In December 2009, the government of Finland announced that Finland's six provinces will be abolished as of January 2010, along with its provincial governor posts. The provinces will become regions under the administration of the Regional State Administrative Agencies (AVI) and the Centers for Economic Development, Transport, and the Environment (ELY). The reform was initiated by Vanhanen in 2007.

Political Rights and Civil Liberties: Finland is an electoral democracy. The prime minister is responsible for running the government. The president, whose role is mainly ceremonial, is directly elected for a six-year term. The president appoints the prime minister and deputy prime minister from the majority party or coalition after elections. The selection must be approved by Parliament.

Representatives in the 200-seat unicameral Parliament, or Eduskunta, are elected to four-year terms. The Aland Islands—an autonomous region located off the southwestern coast whose inhabitants speak Swedish—have their own 29-seat parliament as well as a seat in the national legislature. The indigenous Saami of northern Finland also have their own parliament.

Finland failed to reform its campaign finance legislation in 2009 following corruption charges against several government officials in 2008. The current law contains loopholes allowing for undisclosed donations and lacks penalties for such violations. Prime Minister Matti Vanhanen was involved in campaign-funding scandals throughout September and October 2009. A separate investigation over campaign financing caused a member of Parliament to step down in September. Additional isolated corruption and bribery cases emerged throughout 2009, including a bribery scandal in which members of the Defense Forces were said to have bribed a company, Stena Metall, to scrap army tanks. A heated discussion on how to amend the campaign finance and bribery laws continued through the year's end. Finland was ranked 6 out of 180 countries surveyed in Transparency International's 2009 Corruption Perceptions Index.

Finnish law provides for freedom of speech, which is also respected in practice. Finland has a large variety of newspapers and magazines, grants every citizen the right to publish printed material, and protects the right to reply to public criticism. Newspapers are privately owned but publicly subsidized, and many are controlled by or support a particular political party. Authorities proposed legislation in 2008 that would hold bloggers responsible for comments posted to their sites containing hate speech; the law had not been adopted by the end of 2009. In August 2009, a Helsinki City Councilman and writer Jussi Halla-Aho was brought to trial on charges of inciting racial hatred on his blog. While cleared of these charges in September, Halla-Aho was subsequently found guilty of defamation of religion and fined EUR 330 (US$450) for calling the prophet Mohammad a pedophile. Public broadcaster YLE was cleared of libel charges in May after Halla-aho brought a case against them for calling him "Dr. Race" on a website in February. In August, media giant Alma Media made a "mandatory tender offer" for the stock of media group Talentum. In October, the Finnish government made broadband internet access a legal right for all Finns.

Finns enjoy freedom of religion. The Evangelical Lutheran Church and the Orthodox Church are both state churches and receive public money from income taxes, but citizens may exempt themselves from contributing to those funds. Under current legislation, religious communities other than the state churches may also receive state funds. According to the U.S. State Department, communities with 200 members or more can receive a statutory subsidy of over US$5 per member. The government officially recognizes some 55 religious groups. Religious education is part of the curriculum in all secondary public schools, but students may opt out of such classes in favor of more general instruction in ethics. The government respects academic freedom, and privacy rights are also protected.

Freedoms of association and assembly are upheld in law and in practice. Workers have the right to organize, bargain collectively, and strike. Approximately 70 percent of workers belong to trade unions.

The constitution provides for an independent judiciary, which consists of the Supreme Court, the supreme administrative court, and the lower courts. The president appoints Supreme Court judges, who in turn appoint the lower-court judges. The Ministry of the Interior controls police and Frontier Guard forces. Ethnic minorities and asylum seekers report occasional police discrimination.

The criminal code covers ethnic agitation and penalizes anyone who threatens a racial, national, ethnic, or religious group. Since 1991, the indigenous Saami, who make up less than 1 percent of the population, have been heard in the Eduskunta on relevant matters. The constitution guarantees the Saami cultural autonomy and the right to pursue their traditional livelihoods, which include fishing and reindeer herding. Their language and culture are also protected through public financial support. However, representatives of the community have complained that they cannot exercise their rights in practice and that they do not have the right to self-determination with respect to land use. While Roma also make up a very small percentage of the population, they are more significantly disadvantaged and marginalized.

The 2004 Aliens Act streamlined the procedures for asylum and immigration applications, as well as for work and residency permits. The law also allowed for the granting of residency permits for individual humane reasons. The state provides aid for skill recognition in the labor market and assists with language acquisition for immigrants. As immigration levels increased in 2009, Finland also received record numbers of asylum seekers.

Women enjoy equal rights in Finland. In 1906, the country became the first in Europe to grant women the vote and the first in the world to allow women to become electoral candidates. In the current cabinet, 12 out of 20 ministers are women. In addition, women hold about 42 percent of the seats in Parliament. However, women earn only about 80 percent as much as men of the same age, education, and profession, despite a law stipulating equal pay for equal work. Women are generally employed in lower-paid occupations due to a deeply entrenched idea of "men's jobs" and "women's jobs." Domestic violence is an ongoing concern in Finland.

Finland is both a destination and a transit country for trafficked people. Legislation enacted in 2004 made human trafficking a criminal offense. Amendments to the Alien Act in 2006 allow trafficked victims to stay in the country and qualify for employment rights.

France

Political Rights: 1
Civil Liberties: 1
Status: Free

Population: 62,621,000
Capital: Paris

Ten-Year Ratings Timeline For Year Under Review (Political Rights, Civil Liberties, Status)

2000	2001	2002	2003	2004	2005	2006	2007	2008	2009
1,2F	1,2F	1,2F	1,1F	1,1F	1,1F	1,1F	1,1F	1,1F	1,1F

Overview: Several commissions reviewed a range of issues in France in 2009, including those related to the judiciary, measuring the country's ethnic composition, the French administrative system, and the wearing of burqas. Meanwhile, a month-long general strike in Guadeloupe and Martinique led to a governmental increase in payments to low-wage workers.

After the French Revolution of 1789, republics alternated with monarchist regimes until the creation of the Third Republic in 1871. The Fourth Republic was established after World War II, but it eventually fell victim to domestic political turbulence and a series of colonial setbacks. In 1958, Charles de Gaulle, France's wartime leader, returned to create the strong presidential system of the Fifth Republic, which stands today.

Jacques Chirac, a right-leaning Gaullist, was first elected president in 1995. In the 2002 presidential election, Jean-Marie Le Pen, the head of the far-right, xenophobic National Front, stunned France and the world by receiving more votes than Lionel Jospin, the prime minister and head of the rival center-left Socialist Party (PS), in the first round. Chirac, with Socialist support, defeated Le Pen overwhelmingly in the second round. Support for the National Front has since declined but continues to impact politics in the form of certain law-and-order policies.

In early 2003, France joined Russia in blocking UN Security Council authorization for the U.S.-led invasion of Iraq. France's stance severely strained its relations with the United States, but bolstered Chirac's popularity at home. After the invasion, Chirac moved to strengthen the European Union (EU) as a counterweight to U.S. power.

A strong EU foreign policy was a key French goal in the drafting of a new EU constitutional accord. However, French voters rejected the proposed constitution in a 2005 referendum. Its successor, the Lisbon Treaty, which incorporated many of the key institutional changes of the failed constitution, was signed by the government in February 2008 without a referendum. In April 2009, France rejoined NATO's integrated military command, from which de Gaulle had withdrawn in 1966 because he believed it constrained French sovereignty.

In late 2005, the accidental deaths of two teenagers of North African descent who were fleeing police touched off weeks of violent riots. Most of the rioters were youths descended from immigrants from North and sub-Saharan Africa. Despite their French birth and citizenship, many reported discrimination and harassment by police in recent anticrime operations. The violence provoked a major discussion about the failure to fully integrate minorities into French society.

The ruling Union for a Popular Movement (UMP) nominated party leader Nicolas Sarkozy as its candidate for the 2007 presidential elections. Sarkozy had suffered a drop in popularity as interior minister following the 2005 riots, as he was associated with harsh policing tactics. Sarkozy's law-and-order message, pro-American foreign-policy views, opposition to Turkish EU membership, and other positions made him a controversial candidate. The PS nominated Segolene Royal, the first woman to be chosen by a major political party. Sarkozy won the May election in the second round, with 53 percent of the vote, and the UMP renewed its majority in subsequent parliamentary elections. Sarkozy appointed a popular Socialist, Bernard Kouchner, as foreign minister, and a North African–descended Muslim woman, Rachida Dati, as justice minister. Dati, who had always been a controversial figure, stepped down when she was elected to the European Parliament in June 2009.

The government's popularity declined in late 2007, when riots erupted after two teenagers of African descent were killed in a collision with a police car. Unlike in 2005, the riots were better organized, and scores of police were wounded. By May 2008, the president's popularity was the lowest of any first-year president in 50 years.

While Sarkozy's reputation recovered somewhat with a revived foreign and domestic agenda, including economic liberalization, his popularity again declined with the global financial crisis, when Sarkozy began vocally criticizing laissez-faire capitalism. The economic downturn has caused an increase in already high unemployment and incited many protests in 2009, including some militant demonstrations. The UMP won European Parliament elections in June despite Sarkozy's continuing unpopularity.

Sarkozy in 2009 proposed a plan to improve administrative efficiency by redrawing local and regional administrative boundaries. Socialists have criticized the plan, alleging that the reforms aim to reduce their influence in regions where they dominate. The proposals were still under review at year's end.

Political Rights and Civil Liberties:

France is an electoral democracy. The president and members of the key house of Parliament, the 577-seat National Assembly, are elected to five-year terms; the upper house, the 321-seat Senate, is an indirectly elected body. The prime minister must be able to command a majority in Parliament. Until 1986, the president and prime minister were always of the same party, and the president was the most powerful figure in the country. However, since 1986, there have been periods lasting several years (such as 1997–2002) in which the president and prime minister belonged to rival parties. In such circumstances, the prime minister has the dominant role in domestic affairs, while the president largely guides foreign policy.

Parties organize and compete on a free and fair basis. The center-left PS and the center-right UMP are the largest parties, but others with significant support range from the largely unreformed French Communist Party on the left to the anti-immigrant and anti-EU National Front on the right. France remains a relatively unitary state, with some political and administrative powers devolved to regions, departments, towns, and cities, but with key decisions made in Paris.

Members of the French elite, trained in a small number of prestigious schools, often move between politics and business, increasing opportunities for corruption. President Jacques Chirac used his immunity as head of state a number of times to avoid prosecution on corruption allegations stemming from his time as mayor of Paris from 1977 to 1995. However, formal corruption charges were brought against the former president in 2009, though no trial had begun by year's end. In October 2009, Chirac's interior minister, Charles Pasqua, was sentenced to a year in prison for involvement in arms trafficking to the Angolan government in the 1990s. France was ranked 24 out of 180 countries surveyed in Transparency International's 2009 Corruption Perceptions Index.

The media operate freely and represent a wide range of political opinion. Though an 1881 law forbids "offending" various personages, including the president and foreign heads of state, the press remains lively and critical. However, journalists covering events involving the National Front or the Corsican separatist movement have been harassed and have come under legal pressure to reveal sources. Journalists generally face difficulty covering unrest in the volatile suburbs, including several injuries during the 2005 and 2007 riots. An intern for *Le Monde* was arrested in July 2009 and held overnight for covering demonstrations against police violence in Montreuil, even after he had identified himself as a journalist to authorities. Journalists have been pressured by courts to reveal sources when they report on criminal cases and when they publish material from confidential court documents. In March 2009, the government raided the offices of a TV production company in search of the incriminating footage of an interview with a top Martinique businessman, although nothing was taken. While internet access is generally unrestricted, a controversial law passed by the National Assembly in September and approved by the Constitutional Court in October sanctions users who are found illegally downloading music and films. Under the new law, three warnings will be issued before internet access is disconnected, with suspensions lasting up to a year. Repeat offenders could face heavy fines of up to US$43,900 or two years in prison.

Freedom of religion is protected by the constitution, and strong antidefamation laws prohibit religiously motivated attacks. Denial of the Nazi Holocaust is illegal. France maintains the policy of *laicite,* whereby religion and government affairs are strictly separated. A 2004 law bans "ostentatious" religious symbols in schools. While widely believed to be aimed at the *hijab*—a headscarf worn by some Muslim women and girls—the controversial ban was supported by most voters, including many Muslims. In 2008, a woman was denied citizenship for wearing the burqa, which covers the entire body, and thus failing to assimilate. A commission to investigate the wearing of burqas in France is due to publish its report in early 2010, although reportedly less than 400 women—mostly French converts—wear them. Academic freedom is generally respected by French authorities.

Freedoms of assembly and association are respected. Civic organizations and nongovernmental organizations can operate freely. Trade union organizations are weak, and membership has declined over the past two decades. Nevertheless, civil service unions remain relatively strong, and strike movements generally gain wide public support.

France has an independent judiciary, and the rule of law is firmly established. Citizens are generally treated equally. However, the country's antiterrorism campaign has included surveillance of mosques, and unrelated government raids, such as those involving tax violations, have appeared to target businesses owned or frequented by Muslims, like butcher shops. Suspects can be detained for up to four days without being charged. Amnesty International accused French authorities in April 2009 of failing to investigate alleged police abuse, which the group claimed typically targets ethnic minorities. France has some of the most overcrowded prisons in Europe, and suicides are common, prompting a new penitentiary law in 2009 that includes alternatives to prison, such as parole and electronic bracelets. In August, a committee on penal reform controversially recommended the abolition of the investigative judge, a post that has been responsible for many corruption and other high-level investigations of French officials.

French law forbids the categorization of people according to ethnic origin, and no statistics are collected on ethnicity. However, the violence of 2005 and 2007 fueled concerns about Arab and African immigration and the failure of integration policies in France, where minorities are woefully underrepresented in leadership positions in both the private and public sectors. From 2007 to 2009, Rachida Dati served as the first Muslim justice minister and the first person of non-European descent to become a top minister in the French cabinet under the Fifth Republic. In 2007, legislation was passed that would have permitted the collection of certain kinds of ethnic data, though the Constitutional Council ruled that the law was unconstitutional. In anticipation of 2010 regional elections, the government initiated a "debate" on national identity in the fall of 2009, which quickly evolved into a political discussion of Islam and diversity by year's end. In September 2009, authorities evicted hundreds of migrants and asylum seekers living in makeshift encampments near Calais, detaining many and bulldozing the camps.

Corsica continues to host a sometimes violent separatist movement, and low-level attacks against property and government targets are frequent, though people are rarely harmed. In 2001, the government devolved some legislative powers to the island and allowed teaching in the Corsican language in public schools. In August 2009, the car of Enrico Porsia, an Italian investigative reporter for the Amnistia news website, was bombed in Corsica, but no injuries were reported.

In early 2009, major protests broke out in Guadeloupe and Martinique, two French overseas departments equal in status to those in mainland France. A month-long general strike began over the cost of living but also reflected tensions between the black majority and the ruling whites. French riot police were sent in and ultimately reached a deal whereby the government agreed to increase payments to low-wage workers.

Gender equality is protected in France. Constitutional reforms in 2008 institutionalized economic and social equality, though women still earn approximately 25 percent less than men with similar qualifications. Some electoral lists require the alternation of candidates by sex. In 2007, women won 18.5 percent of the seats in the legislature (up from 16.9 percent in 2002). Women have served as key ministers, as well as prime minister. The rights of homosexuals are protected in France, and a type of nonmarriage civil union, the PACS, or civil solidarity pact, is recognized.

Gabon

Political Rights: 6
Civil Liberties: 5*
Status: Not Free

Population: 1,475,000
Capital: Libreville

Status Change: Gabon's civil liberties rating declined from 4 to 5 and its status from Partly Free to Not Free due to increased restrictions on the media in the period surrounding the presidential election as well as a crackdown on postelection protesters.

Ten-Year Ratings Timeline For Year Under Review (Political Rights, Civil Liberties, Status)

2000	2001	2002	2003	2004	2005	2006	2007	2008	2009
5,4PF	5,4PF	5,4PF	5,4PF	5,4PF	6,4PF	6,4PF	6,4PF	6,4PF	6,5NF

Overview: President Omar Bongo, the world's longest-serving republican ruler, died in June 2009, and his son, Ali Bongo, was declared the winner of an August presidential election. Two other candidates contested the results, and postelection protests drew a violent police response, but the Constitution Court ultimately upheld Bongo's victory in October. During the year, the authorities suspended media outlets that reported on sensitive issues like Omar Bongo's health and the postelection unrest, and opposition figures were barred from leaving the country following the violence.

Gabon gained independence from France in 1960. Omar Bongo, then the vice president, took power after the incumbent president's death in 1967 and went on to establish a one-party regime. In 1990, protests prompted by economic hardship led to multiparty legislative elections, but Bongo and the ruling Gabonese Democratic Party (PDG) retained power over the subsequent years through a series of flawed votes.

In 2006 legislative elections, the PDG and allied parties won 97 of the 120 seats in the National Assembly, the bicameral parliament's lower house. Observers judged the elections to be credible and an improvement over the 2005 presidential contest, which had featured postelection violence and accusations of voter-registry manipulation, among other irregularities. Elections for the Senate, the upper house, were held in January 2009, with regional and municipal councilors voting to fill the chamber's 102 seats. PDG won 75 seats, reflecting its success in the 2008 local elections; it had taken 1,120 out of 1,990 council seats in those polls. No other party won more than six Senate seats.

Bongo died in June 2009, and in keeping with the constitution, Senate president Rose Francine Rogombe became interim head of state. Defense Minister Ali Bongo, son of the late president, was nominated as the PDG candidate for a snap presidential election, leading some senior PDG figures, including former interior minister Andre Mba Obame, to resign and run as independents. A total of 23 candidates contested the August 30 election, and Bongo was announced as the winner with almost 42 percent of the vote. Voter turnout was approximately 44 percent. Mba Obame and Pierre Mamboundou of the opposition Union of the Gabonese People party placed second and third, each with about 25 percent of the vote. The two men rejected the official results, and the opposition claimed that 15 people died in subsequent clashes between police and protesters. A recount took place in September, but the Constitutional Court ultimately upheld Bongo's victory. He was sworn in as president in October.

The country's dwindling oil production accounts for some 60 percent of state income. In 2008, the government signed a contract with a Chinese state-owned company to launch the Belinga iron-ore mining project, which was strongly opposed by environmentalist groups.

Political Rights and Civil Liberties: Gabon is not an electoral democracy. The 2009 presidential election was marred by irregularities, including allegations of vote rigging and intimidation of the press. Opposition candidates challenged the election results and petitioned the constitutional court, which called for a vote recount that supported Ali Bongo's victory. The president is elected for seven-year terms, and a 2003 constitutional change removed the two-term limit imposed in 1991. The president has extensive powers, including the authority to appoint judges and dissolve the parliament. The bicameral legislature consists of a 102-seat Senate, expanded from 91 seats in 2008, and a 120-seat National Assembly. Regional and municipal officials elect senators for six-year terms, while National Assembly members are elected by popular vote for five-year terms.

Freedom to form and join political parties is generally respected, but civil servants face harassment and discrimination if they affiliate with opposition groups. The PDG has held power continuously since 1968, and Ali Bongo's victory in the 2009 presidential election reinforced the party's dominance. Of some 50 other registered parties, 40 are part of the PDG's ruling coalition, the Union for the Gabonese Presidential Majority. In November, eight opposition parties formed a new political alliance, the Coalition of Groups and Political Parties for Change (CGPPA), with presidential runner-up Mba Obame as a leading member.

Corruption is widespread. Though a Commission Against Illicit Enrichment was established in 2003, it has yet to take major action. Rampant graft prevents the country's significant natural-resource revenue from reaching the majority of the population. In 2008, Transparency International brought a complaint against President Omar Bongo and two other African heads of state, alleging embezzlement of public funds to buy assets in France. In October 2009, however, a French appeals court dismissed the case, citing the organization's lack of legal standing. In November, Jean-Pierre Oyiba, the president's cabinet director, resigned amid accusations of graft. Gabon was ranked 106 out of 180 countries surveyed in Transparency International's 2009 Corruption Perceptions Index.

Press freedom is guaranteed in law but restricted in practice. The state has the power to criminalize civil libel suits, and because legal cases against journalists are relatively common, many reporters practice self-censorship. State-controlled outlets dominate the broadcast media, but there are some private broadcasters, and foreign news sources are available. In December 2008, two journalists and three civil society leaders were arrested for possession of a publicly available letter alleging financial mismanagement by Omar Bongo. The five were released, but the charges were not dropped. One of the civil society leaders, Marc Ona Essangui, won a court case against the government in November 2009, which found that the travel bans imposed on him infringed on his rights. In May 2009, two newspapers, *Ezombolo* and *Le Nganga*, were suspended and warnings were issued to Radio France Internationale over their coverage of the president's worsening health. In the run-up to the August presidential election, the government placed restrictions on the media, including curtailing the media's access to polling stations and denying accreditation to some foreign journalists. Additionally, a private television station owned by independent candidate Andre Mba Obame was taken off the air. The editor of the government-owned newspaper *L'Union* was arrested and interrogated in September after the outlet reported on postelection violence. Further media restrictions occurred in November, when the government suspended six independent newspapers and one private television channel. Access to the internet is not restricted by the government.

Religious freedom is enshrined in the constitution and generally upheld by authorities. The government does not restrict academic freedom.

The rights of assembly and association are guaranteed but not always respected. Following the 2009 presidential election, security forces violently dispersed hundreds of protesters staging a peaceful demonstration in front of the electoral commission.

Due to the lack of strong opposition parties, nongovernmental organizations (NGOs) serve as important vehicles for scrutiny of the government. However, it is difficult for these groups to operate freely. In 2008, the interior minister suspended

22 NGOs for a week after they issued a public statement criticizing the government. Civil society leader Marc Ona Essangui was prevented from leaving the country to attend international conferences on four occasions in 2008.

Virtually the entire private sector workforce is unionized. Collective bargaining is allowed by industry, not by firm. In June 2009, the government reached agreement with a number of public sector unions and ended most ongoing strikes, which had intermittently involved oil workers, health workers, and teachers over the past two years. However, the new government placed restrictions on trade unions in October 2009, including banning public sector employees from holding paid senior union positions and withholding wages from striking workers during strike action.

The judiciary is not independent. Judges may deliver summary verdicts in some cases, and torture is sometimes used to produce confessions. However, the rights to legal counsel and a public criminal trial are generally respected. Prison conditions are poor, and arbitrary arrest and long periods of pretrial detention are common.

Discrimination against immigrants is widespread. Though equal under the law, most of Gabon's several thousand indigenous Pygmies live in extreme poverty in isolated forest communities without access to government services, and they are often exploited as cheap labor.

While there are no legal restrictions on travel, interference by the authorities occurs regularly. In September 2009, the government banned opposition leaders from leaving the country pending an investigation into postelection violence. Business conditions remain difficult; Gabon ranked 158 out of 183 countries in the World Bank's 2010 Doing Business survey.

Gabon has been criticized for the exploitation of thousands of child laborers who arrive from other African countries to work as domestic servants. The government has cooperated with international organizations to fight child trafficking, but says it lacks sufficient resources to tackle the problem.

Legal protections for women include equal-access laws for education, business, and investment, but these laws favor educated women in urban areas. Several women hold high-level positions in the new government, including the minister of defense and the minister of justice. Women have no property rights in widely practiced common-law marriages, and they continue to face societal discrimination, particularly in rural areas. Domestic violence is reportedly widespread. Children and young adults are susceptible to ritual killings, and 12 such killings were reported ahead of the 2008 local elections. At least 11 ritual crimes were confirmed in 2009. Rape is illegal but seldom prosecuted, and abortion is prohibited.

The Gambia

Political Rights: 5
Civil Liberties: 5*
Status: Partly Free

Population: 1,609,000
Capital: Banjul

Ratings Change: The Gambia's civil liberties rating declined from 4 to 5 due to President Yahya Jammeh's enhanced personal control over the judiciary and threats of violence against civil society organizations.

Ten-Year Ratings Timeline For Year Under Review (Political Rights, Civil Liberties, Status)

2000	2001	2002	2003	2004	2005	2006	2007	2008	2009
7,5NF	5,5PF	4,4PF	4,4PF	4,4PF	5,4PF	5,4PF	5,4PF	5,4PF	5,5PF

Overview: **President Yahya Jammeh exerted growing personal control over state institutions in 2009, capriciously replacing the chief justice and other senior officials. Jammeh also publicly threatened journalists and warned that he would execute any human rights activists who destabilized the country.**

After gaining independence from Britain in 1965, The Gambia functioned for almost 30 years as an electoral democracy under President Dawda Jawara and his People's Progressive Party. A 1981 coup by leftist soldiers was reversed by intervention from Senegal, which borders The Gambia on three sides. The two countries formed the Confederation of Senegambia a year later, but it was dissolved in 1989.

Lieutenant Yahya Jammeh deposed Jawara in a 1994 military coup. The junior officers who led the coup quickly issued draconian decrees curtailing civil and political rights. A new constitution, adopted in a closely controlled 1996 referendum, allowed Jammeh to transform his military dictatorship into a nominally civilian administration.

Jammeh defeated human rights lawyer Ousainou Darboe in a 2001 presidential election, and the ruling Alliance for Patriotic Reorientation and Construction (APRC) won all but three seats in the 2002 National Assembly elections, thanks to a widespread boycott by opposition parties.

The government announced in March 2006 that it had foiled an attempted coup, leading to the arrest of dozens of people, including several prominent journalists and senior intelligence and defense personnel. Ten military officers were sentenced to lengthy prison terms in April 2007.

Jammeh won a new five-year term in the September 2006 presidential election, taking 67.3 percent of the vote. Darboe, running as the candidate of the United Democratic Party (UDP), received 26.6 percent, while another opposition leader, Halifa Sallah, captured the remaining share. The preelection period was marred by government repression of the media and the opposition, and Darboe rejected the results as a "sham." In January 2007 legislative elections, the APRC won 42 out of 48 contested seats and gained another 5 that are filled by presidential appointees. A Commonwealth election observation group called for, "a more level playing field and a more restrained utilization of the advantages of incumbency."

Jammeh has drawn criticism for erratic statements and behavior. He has claimed that he can personally cure HIV/AIDS using traditional herbs, and in 2008, the president threatened decapitation for any homosexuals who remained in the country. In September 2009, he publicly warned against causing instability through human rights activism, reportedly saying, "If you think that you can collaborate with so-called human rights defenders, and get away with it, you must be living in a dream world. I will kill you, and nothing will come out of it." Also in 2009, the president continued his practice of arbitrarily replacing top government officials, sacking the chief justice, the Speaker of parliament, and a number of cabinet ministers in June. Dozens of military officers were reportedly arrested in November on suspicion of planning a coup.

Although The Gambia is a poor, agrarian country, it has experienced modest economic growth thanks to its tourism industry and the government's increased emphasis on economic development, for which it received praise in 2009 from World Bank and African Development Bank officials.

Political Rights and Civil Liberties: The Gambia is not an electoral democracy. The 2006 presidential election was marred by serious government repression of the media and the opposition, and Commonwealth observers found similar flaws in the 2008 legislative elections. The president is elected by popular vote for unlimited five-year terms. Of the 53 members of the unicameral National Assembly, 48 are elected by popular vote and the remainder are appointed by the president; members serve five-year terms.

The opposition UDP, led by Ousainou Darboe, holds four National Assembly seats, and the National Alliance for Democracy and Development (NADD), led by Halifa Sallah, holds one. One other seat is held by an independent. However, the president and the ruling APRC are in clear control, and the system's pluralism is largely symbolic.

Official corruption remains a serious problem, although President Yahya Jammeh's recent focus on economic development policies has led to increased anticorruption efforts, including the establishment of an Anti-Corruption Commission. Separately, a special judiciary commission in late 2009 began investigating allegations that several High Court judges were involved in misappropriations of state funds as well as illicit real estate deals. The Gambia was ranked 106 out of 180 countries surveyed in Transparency International's 2009 Corruption Perceptions Index.

The government does not respect freedom of the press. Laws on sedition give the authorities great discretion in silencing dissent, and independent media outlets and journalists are subject to arrests, harassment, and violence. The 2004 assassination of journalist and press freedom activist Deyda Hydara is still unsolved, and the whereabouts of another journalist, "Chief" Ebrima Manneh, have remained unknown since he was arrested in 2006 for publishing a report that was critical of Jammeh in the privately owned *Daily Observer* newspaper. The managing directors of the *Daily Observer* and *Today* were each temporarily detained on sedition charges in 2008. In June 2009, nine journalists and managing directors of independent media outlets were held for several days and heavily fined for publicly denouncing the president over comments concerning Hydara. The president broadly threatened journalists in July by stating any, "who thinks that he or she can write whatever he or she wants and go free is making a big mistake." The government runs Radio Gambia as well as the sole television channel and the *Gambia Daily* newspaper. There are several private radio stations and newspapers, and foreign broadcasts are available. While the state generally does not restrict internet usage, some websites have been blocked.

Freedom of religion is legally guaranteed and generally upheld by the government. Academic freedom is respected on the surface, but the broader limitations on freedom of speech are thought to encourage self-censorship among scholars. Private discussion is limited by fears of surveillance, searches, and arrest by the National Intelligence Agency (NIA).

Freedoms of assembly and association are provided by law, though in practice they are constrained by state intimidation, including the president's public threats against human rights groups in 2009. Gambians, except for civil servants and members of the security forces, have the right to form unions, strike, and bargain for wages. However, the climate of fear generated by the state, and the NIA reportedly dissuades workers from taking action.

The constitution provides for an independent judiciary, but the courts are hampered by corruption and executive influence. The president has the authority to appoint and dismiss judges, and in June 2009, he replaced Chief Justice Abdou Karim Savage—appointed in 2006—with a Nigerian national, Emmanuel Agim. The judicial system recognizes customary law and Sharia (Islamic law), primarily with regard to personal status and family matters.

Impunity for the country's security forces, particularly the NIA, is a problem. A 1995 decree allows the NIA to search, arrest, or seize any person or property without a warrant in the name of state security. In such cases, the right to seek a writ of habeas corpus is suspended.

Torture of prisoners, including political prisoners, has been reported. Diplomatic relations with Ghana have been strained over The Gambia's failure to investigate the 2005 deaths of 50 African migrants, including 44 Ghanaians, reportedly while in Gambian custody. In 2009, Guinean "witch doctors" accompanied by Gambian security forces reportedly abducted and abused some 1,000 Gambians who were suspected of witchcraft.

The Gambia's various ethnic groups coexist in relative harmony, though critics have accused Jammeh of privileging members of the Jola ethnic group in the military and other positions of power. The constitution prohibits discrimination based on religion, language, ethnicity, gender, and other factors.

The government has encouraged female education by waiving primary school fees for girls, but women have fewer opportunities for higher education and wage employment than men, especially in rural areas. While the vice president and several cabinet ministers are women, there are just four women in the 53-seat National Assembly. Sharia provisions regarding family law and inheritance restrict women's rights, and female genital mutilation remains legal and widely practiced. The U.S. State Department placed The Gambia on Tier 2 in its 2009 Trafficking in Persons Report, removing it from the Tier 2 Watch List but noting ongoing problems with trafficking in women and children for forced labor and sexual exploitation.

Georgia

Political Rights: 4
Civil Liberties: 4
Status: Partly Free

Population: 4,611,000
Capital: Tbilisi

Note: The numerical ratings and status listed above do not reflect conditions in South Ossetia or Abkhazia, which are examined in separate reports.

Ten-Year Ratings Timeline For Year Under Review (Political Rights, Civil Liberties, Status)

2000	2001	2002	2003	2004	2005	2006	2007	2008	2009
4,4PF	4,4PF	4,4PF	4,4PF	3,4PF	3,3PF	3,3PF	4,4PF	4,4PF	4,4PF

Overview:
The fragmented opposition sought to rally public opinion against President Mikheil Saakashvili in 2009, as the country prepared for municipal elections in 2010. However, the political debate was often overshadowed by ongoing tension with Russia, with which Georgia fought a brief war in 2008. Russian troops continued to occupy a considerable portion of Georgia's internationally recognized territory, and in August Georgia, officially withdrew from the Russian-dominated Commonwealth of Independent States.

Georgia gained its independence from Russia in 1918, only to become part of the Soviet Union in 1922. In 1990, shortly before the Soviet Union's collapse, an attempt by the region of South Ossetia to declare independence from Georgia and join Russia's North Ossetia republic sparked a war between the separatists and Georgian forces. Although a ceasefire was signed in 1992, South Ossetia's final political status remained unresolved.

Following a national referendum in April 1991, Georgia declared its independence from the Soviet Union. Nationalist leader and former dissident Zviad Gamsakhurdia was elected president in May. The next year, he was overthrown by opposition militias and replaced with former Georgian Communist Party head and Soviet foreign minister Eduard Shevardnadze. Parliamentary elections held in 1992 resulted in more than 30 parties and blocs winning seats, although none secured a clear majority.

In 1993, Georgia was rocked by the violent secession of the Abkhazia region and an insurrection by Gamsakhurdia loyalists. Shevardnadze legalized the presence of some 19,000 Russian troops in Georgia in return for Russian support against Gamsakhurdia, who reportedly committed suicide after his defeat. In early 1994, Georgia and Abkhazia signed an agreement in Moscow that called for a ceasefire, the stationing of Commonwealth of Independent States (CIS) troops under Russian command along the Abkhazian border, and the return of refugees under UN supervision.

In 1995, Shevardnadze and his Citizens' Union of Georgia (CUG) party won presidential and parliamentary polls. The CUG won again in the 1999 parliamentary elections, and observers from the Organization for Security and Cooperation in Europe (OSCE) concluded that, despite some irregularities, the vote was generally fair. In the 2000 presidential poll, however, Shevardnadze's wide margin of victory led to fraud accusations that were supported by election monitors.

Shevardnadze faced growing opposition from prominent members of the CUG, including Justice Minister Mikheil Saakashvili, who criticized the president's failure to contain widespread corruption. While Shevardnadze resigned as CUG chairman in 2001, Saakashvili left to form his own party, the National Movement.

A flawed parliamentary vote in November 2003 sparked a campaign of street protests known as the Rose Revolution. While official results put a pro-Shevardnadze coalition in the lead with 21 percent, independent domestic monitors concluded that the National Movement had actually won with nearly 27 percent. OSCE monitors reported violations including ballot-box stuffing, inaccurate voter lists, biased media coverage, harassment of some domestic election monitors, and pressure on public employees to support progovernment candidates.

The postelection demonstrations ultimately forced Shevardnadze to resign, and Parliament speaker Nino Burjanadze, a Saakashvili ally, was named interim president. Meanwhile, the Supreme Court cancelled the results of the parliamentary elections. Saakashvili won a snap presidential election in January 2004, running virtually unopposed and capturing 96 percent of the vote. Fresh parliamentary elections in March gave two-thirds of the seats to the National Movement and allied parties.

Saakashvili's relations with Russia soured as he quickly reestablished Tbilisi's control over the semiautonomous southwestern region of Ajaria and pledged to reintegrate the separatist enclaves of Abkhazia and South Ossetia, which were tacitly supported by the Kremlin. Russia imposed a trade and transport embargo on Georgia in 2006—in response to Georgia's brief detention of several alleged Russian spies—and the two countries continued to exchange accusations of military provocation surrounding the two breakaway territories over the next two years.

Growing opposition to Saakashvili's dominance of the domestic political scene culminated in large street protests in late 2007. Demonstrations in November drew between 50,000 and 100,000 people, prompting a violent police crackdown and the imposition of a November 7–16 state of emergency that barred opposition media from the airwaves and restricted freedom of assembly. Responding to opposition demands for early elections, Saakashvili scheduled an early presidential vote for January 5, 2008, giving his opponents little time to prepare.

Saakashvili won reelection with roughly 53 percent of the vote, but his main challenger alleged fraud, and OSCE observers noted an array of irregularities. The ruling party and its allies captured 119 of the 150 seats in May parliamentary elections, with the opposition again declaring that the balloting was rigged. A dozen of the winning opposition candidates refused to take their seats, and international monitors found that the authorities had failed to correct the problems cited in the presidential vote.

Tensions with Russia over South Ossetia and Abkhazia mounted during the spring and summer of 2008. Open warfare erupted in South Ossetia in early August, and an ensuing Russian invasion pressed deep into Georgian territory. A French-brokered ceasefire took hold after more than a week of fighting, and by fall, Russian forces had largely withdrawn to the confines of the two separatist enclaves. Russia recognized the territories' independence in the wake of the conflict, but few other countries followed suit. Russia also established a substantial troop presence in both territories that remained in place at the end of 2009, despite the fact that the ceasefire deal called for a withdrawal of all forces to their positions before the fighting. A

European Union (EU) report released in September 2009 assigned blame to both Russia and Georgia for the 2008 hostilities.

Georgian opposition factions continued to press their case against Saakashvili in 2009, and the confrontations between the two sides—while still intense—took place in a somewhat more stable and permissive environment than in the previous two years. Opposition leaders demanded the president's resignation in April, and his refusal led to a series of street protests and arrests that lasted into the summer. At one point in April, opposition activist Kakha Khozelishvili was severely beaten by unknown assailants in Tbilisi, and dozens of protesters reported being assaulted by masked attackers as they left demonstrations.

The year's political standoff was often interwoven with looming national security concerns. Several members of the opposition Democratic Movement–United Georgia party, founded by Burjanadze after she broke with the president in 2008, were arrested in March for alleged involvement in arms purchases and plans to foment violence. Burjanadze claimed that the case was part of a government intimidation effort. Her husband, Badri Bitsadze, was swept into the intrigue later that month, when the media aired photographs of him meeting with Shalva Breus, a Georgian with Russian citizenship who had once served as a Russian deputy property minister. The episode stoked fears of collusion between the Kremlin and the Georgian opposition, though Bitsadze denied any impropriety. Adding to the tension, a tank battalion based east of Tbilisi allegedly launched an abortive mutiny in early May. One of the suspected ringleaders, Gia Krialashvili, was killed in a shootout with security forces later that month, and two other suspects were wounded. A trial of the accused officers had not yielded a verdict by year's end.

Cementing its rift with Moscow, Georgia formally withdrew from the Russian-dominated Commonwealth of Independent States in August. Saakashvili also drew criticism from Russia and many Georgians in December, when the government-ordered demolition of a Soviet-era World War II monument in the city of Kutaisi accidentally killed two local residents.

Political Rights and Civil Liberties:

Georgia is not an electoral democracy. The elections following the 2003 Rose Revolution were considered improvements over previous polls, but OSCE monitors have identified problems with more recent balloting, including the 2008 presidential and parliamentary elections. The flaws have included the abuse of state resources, reports of intimidation aimed at public employees and opposition activists, and apparent voter-list inaccuracies.

In September 2009, Parliament adopted a constitutional amendment that allowed 10 opposition politicians to assume their seats after refusing them in 2008 to protest the flawed elections. However, only one of the eligible candidates—Konstantine Gamsakhurdia, son of the late president—accepted this offer, and some observers said he had been persuaded by the government's pledge to reopen an investigation into his father's death.

According to the constitution, the president appoints the cabinet and serves up to two five-year terms, although current president Mikheil Saakashvili—first elected in 2004—was reelected in 2008 after calling an early vote. The cabinet's membership under Saakashvili has been fairly unstable; in February 2009, he named

Nika Gilauri to serve as his fifth prime minister, and in August, he appointed a 28-year-old defense minister. Parliament until the 2008 elections consisted of 235 members, with 100 elected by party list, 75 elected in single-member districts, and 10 others representing displaced citizens from Abkhazia. Under the new structure, Parliament has just 150 seats, with half chosen by party list and the other half in single-member districts. The amended electoral code did not require the constituencies to be of equal size, and the OSCE noted that the number of voters in each district ranged from 6,000 to 140,000.

Parliament in December 2009 passed a new elections law to govern municipal balloting scheduled for May 2010. It allows the direct election of Tbilisi's mayor for the first time, but opposition parties objected to a provision permitting the leading candidate to secure a first-round victory with as little as 30 percent of the vote, among other complaints.

Saakashvili's National Movement has been the dominant party since 2004. The fragmented opposition parties have formed a series of shifting alliances in recent years, and the defection of former Parliament Speaker Nino Burjanadze and other Saakashvili allies to the opposition in 2008 set off a new round of reorganization. Irakli Alasania, previously Georgia's ambassador to the United Nations, emerged as one of several potential leaders of a unified opposition in 2009, forming a new party called Our Georgia–Free Democrats.

Corruption remains a challenge in Georgia. While notable progress has been made in recent years with respect to lower- and mid-level corruption, efforts to combat high-level corruption that began in the mid-2000s have stalled. The government's achievements have included university-level education reforms that curbed bribery in admissions and grading. However, implementation of a 2005 plan aimed at improving the transparency and effectiveness of the civil service, in part by strengthening the role of inspectors general within public agencies, remains in its nascent stages. Moreover, apparently continues to suffer from corruption at elite levels, and the administration's growing insularity has fostered opportunities for cronyism and insider deals. Georgia was ranked 66 out of 180 countries surveyed in Transparency International's 2009 Corruption Perceptions Index.

The constitution provides guarantees for press freedom, and the print media, though limited in reach, feature a diversity of political opinions and perspectives. The state television and radio outlets were converted into public service broadcasters in 2005, but critics assert that the stations have become increasingly progovernment rather than striking an independent course. The private broadcast media, while retaining a considerable degree of pluralism, have not escaped the political turmoil of recent years. The opposition-oriented Imedi TV, whose broadcast facility was raided by security forces in November 2007, was taken over by a progovernment businessman in 2008, and relatives of the deceased previous owner, Badri Patarkatsishvili, have waged a campaign to reclaim control. Maestro TV, an opposition station that covers the Tbilisi area, was the target of a grenade attack in May 2009; no injuries were reported. In November, a wealthy businessman and former co-owner of the progovernment channel Rustavi-2, Erosi Kitsmarishvili, took over management of Maestro TV and announced his ambition to transform the station into a national enterprise with an emphasis on critical assessment of government policies.

The authorities do not restrict access to the internet, but high-speed connections are prohibitively expensive for many citizens. In October 2009, the authorities opened an investigation into the posting of web videos that mocked the head of the Georgian Orthodox Church, Catholicos-Patriarch Ilia II. Tea Tutberidze, the head of a progovernment civil society group, said she posted the material in response to the cleric's recent criticism of the president's handling of the 2008 war with Russia.

Freedom of religion is respected for the country's largely Georgian Orthodox Christian population and some traditional minority groups, including Muslims and Jews. However, members of newer groups, including Baptists, Pentecostals, and Jehovah's Witnesses, have faced harassment and intimidation by law enforcement officials and Georgian Orthodox extremists. The government does not restrict academic freedom.

Respect for the freedoms of association and assembly was tarnished by the November 2007 state of emergency and crackdown on opposition protests, in which several hundred people were injured. These rights were again constrained by the August 2008 conflict and Russia's weeks-long occupation of significant portions of Georgian territory beyond South Ossetia and Abkhazia. Opposition parties held a number of sizeable rallies during 2009, and there was no repeat of violence on the scale of 2007. Nevertheless, clashes with police were reported in several instances.

Nongovernmental organizations (NGOs) are able to register and operate without arbitrary restrictions. They play an active role in public debate, though their influence has decreased somewhat under the current administration.

The constitution and the Law on Trade Unions allow workers to organize and prohibit antiunion discrimination. The Amalgamated Trade Unions of Georgia, the successor to the Soviet-era union federation, is the principal trade union bloc. It is not affiliated with and receives no funding from the government. While Georgia replaced its Soviet-era labor code with a new framework in 2006, union influence remains marginal. In 2009, unions sought further reforms of the labor laws, complaining that the government ignored workers' rights in its pursuit of foreign investment and economic recovery from the war and the global financial crisis.

The judiciary has not undergone meaningful or durable reform in recent years, and continues to suffer from significant corruption and pressure from the executive branch. The payment of bribes to judges is reportedly common.

The police force has improved its performance since the government dismissed half of its personnel in 2004 as part of an anticorruption overhaul. Among other results, the changes virtually eliminated bribe-seeking vehicle stops by police, previously a part of daily life. However, human rights ombudsman Sozar Subari has repeatedly accused the police of abusing and torturing detainees; he joined the political opposition after his five-year term expired in September 2009. Prison conditions in Georgia remain grim.

The government generally respects the rights of ethnic minorities in areas of the country that are not contested by separatists. Freedom of residence and freedom to travel to and from the country are observed.

Although some women have achieved high positions in government, they remain seriously underrepresented, holding just nine seats in the current Parliament. Societal violence against women is a problem. The authorities have acknowledged the issue and in 2006 passed the first law on domestic violence, which allows victims to file immediate protective orders against their abusers and permits police to issue a temporary restrictive order against suspects. While there are no laws that specifically criminalize violence against women, the criminal code classifies rape and sexual coercion as crimes. Georgian law prohibits trafficking in persons, but the country remains a source, transit point, and destination for the trade.

Germany

Political Rights: 1
Civil Liberties: 1
Status: Free

Population: 81,980,000
Capital: Berlin

Ten-Year Ratings Timeline For Year Under Review (Political Rights, Civil Liberties, Status)

2000	2001	2002	2003	2004	2005	2006	2007	2008	2009
1,2F	1,2F	1,2F	1,1F	1,1F	1,1F	1,1F	1,1F	1,1F	1,1F

Overview: Parliamentary elections in September 2009 resulted in the formation of a majority coalition consisting of the two major center-right parties, the Christian Democratic Union and Christian Social Union (CDU/CSU) and the Free Democratic Party (FDP). The CDU's Angela Merkel was reelected as chancellor. The Social Democratic Party (SPD), part of the previous grand coalition with the CDU/CSU, experienced the greatest decline in voter support of any party in German federal elections in 60 years.

Modern Germany emerged in 1871, when the patchwork of German states united under Prussian leadership following the Franco-Prussian war. After Germany's defeat in World War I, the German Empire was replaced in 1919 by the Weimar Republic, which gave way in 1933 to Nazism and led to World War II. Following its defeat in World War II, Germany was divided into two states—the capitalist and democratic Federal Republic in the west and the communist German Democratic Republic in the east—during the ensuing Cold War. The Berlin Wall, which had kept East Berliners from fleeing west, was opened in 1989, and East Germany was absorbed into the Federal Republic the following year. Despite nearly two decades of massive subsidies, the federal states of former East Germany remain considerably poorer than the rest of the country. The economic situation has contributed to greater support for extremist political groups in the east.

After 16 years of rule by Chancellor Helmut Kohl and a coalition of his center-right Christian Democratic Union and Christian Social Union (CDU/CSU) and the socially liberal, market-oriented Free Democratic Party (FDP), Germans in 1998 elected the so-called "red-green coalition," consisting of the Social Democratic Party (SPD) and the Green Party, with the SPD's Gerhard Schroeder as chancellor. The red-green coalition won a narrow victory in the 2002 election, despite sluggish economic growth in its first term. In its second term, the Hartz I-IV labor market reforms were enacted, which aimed to create a more flexible market. However, the reforms eroded the support of labor unions, a key component of the SPD's electoral base, and failed to improve the economy quickly enough to please voters.

In 2005, Schroeder engineered a no-confidence vote against himself to trigger national elections. Neither the red-green coalition nor the CDU/CSU-FDP opposition was able to garner an outright majority, and both sides were unwilling to cooperate with the newly formed Left Party. After unusually protracted coalition negotiations, the CDU/CSU and the SPD were obliged to form a "grand coalition," and the CDU's Angela Merkel became Germany's first female chancellor.

Merkel enjoyed international prominence during 2007, hosting a Group of 8 summit and holding the rotating presidency of the European Union (EU) for the first half of the year. However, tensions between the two parties of the grand coalition began to build during the second half of its term, with each party trying to distinguish itself. Despite a lackluster political year, Merkel was overwhelmingly reelected as party leader at the end of 2008, and the SPD named Foreign Minister Frank-Walter Steinmeier as its chancellor candidate for the 2009 elections.

The political scene in 2009 was dominated by the federal election. The preelection period was characterized by low-key campaigning, as both the CDU/CSU and SPD focused on defending their records within the grand coalition. In the September poll, the CDU/CSU won 239 seats with approximately 34 percent of the vote, while the FDP took 93 seats, up from 61 in 2005. The SPD captured only 146 seats—an 11 percent decline over the 2005 results—representing its worst performance in a German federal election and the most significant decline in voter support of any party in federal elections in 60 years. Gains by the Greens were not significant enough to offset the SPD's losses, and once again, no party was willing to form a coalition with the Left Party. The CDU/CSU and FDP formed a majority coalition together without the SPD for the first time since 1998, and Merkel was reelected as chancellor. Although the election was free and fair, the Organization for Security and Cooperation in Europe sent election monitors after the parliamentary election commission barred several very small parties from participating, in some cases because of legal technicalities.

In November, the controversial trial of John Demjanjuk—a Ukrainian-born former U.S. citizen and alleged World War II Nazi concentration camp guard—began in Munich; Demjanjuk is suspected of facilitating the murder of thousands of Jews at the Sobibor concentration camp. The trial has been contentious because Mr. Demjanjuk is elderly and in poor health, and he is the only low-ranking official and the only foreign suspect to have been charged with Holocaust-related crimes. His trial is likely to be the last for Nazi-era war crimes.

Political Rights and Civil Liberties: Germany is an electoral democracy. The constitution provides for a lower house of parliament, the 622-seat Bundestag (Federal Assembly), elected at least every four years through a 50-50 mixture of proportional representation and single-member districts, as well as an upper house, the Bundesrat (Federal Council), which represents the states. The country's head of state is a largely ceremonial president, chosen jointly by the Bundestag and a group of state representatives to serve up to two five-year terms. In Germany's federal system, state governments have considerable authority over matters such as education, policing, taxation, and spending. The chancellor, the head of government, is elected by the Bundestag and usually serves for the duration of a four-year legislative session, which can be cut short only if the Bundestag chooses a replacement in a so-called constructive vote of no confidence.

Political pluralism has been constrained by laws restricting the far left and far right. The Communist Party of Germany was banned in the Federal Republic in 1956. However, the former ruling party of communist East Germany, renamed the Party of Democratic Socialism (PDS), was a legal and democratic far-left party that participated in state governments after reunification. It merged with former left-wing SPD members to form the new Left Party ahead of the 2005 elections.

The two main far-right parties, the National Democratic Party (NDP) and the German People's Union (DVU), are hostile to immigration and the EU, and have been accused of glorifying Adolf Hitler and the Third Reich. Efforts in 2003 to ban the NPD on the grounds that it is illegal to advocate Nazism failed in the Constitutional Court, when it was revealed that many of the witnesses testifying against the NPD were agents of the intelligence services. After the NDP gained a measure of success in 2008 local elections in Saxony, state intervention to curtail the NPD reemerged as a political issue. The CSU and SPD both stated in 2009 that a new attempt should be made to ban the NPD. However, the CDU disagreed, arguing that changes to the constitutional circumstances since 2003 were not significant enough to render success more likely. The CDU also contended that state intervention would only strengthen the NPD. In the run-up to the 2009 elections, the NPD—which captured less than 2 percent of the vote—made headlines by sending fake deportation notices to prominent Green and CDU politicians of immigrant or minority ethnic backgrounds.

The government is held accountable for its performance through open debates in the parliament, which are covered widely in the media. Germany is free of pervasive corruption and was ranked 14 out of 180 countries surveyed in Transparency International's 2009 Corruption Perceptions Index.

Freedom of expression is protected in the constitution, and the media are largely free and independent. The Constitutional Court ruled in 2003 that surveillance of journalists' telephone calls could be deemed legal by judges in "serious" cases, which threatens journalists' source confidentiality. Journalists have also been prosecuted for "divulging state secrets." Nevertheless, the press remains lively, investigative, and professional.

It remains illegal to advocate Nazism or deny the Holocaust. The Constitutional Court ruled in November 2009 that it is acceptable to ban speech glorifying the ideology of Hitler. The ruling was made in reference to 2005 legislation that outlawed a march in honor of one of Hitler's colleagues, Rudolf Hess, which had caused sporadic violence prior to its prohibition. The authorities have sought unsuccessfully to prosecute internet users abroad who post Nazi propaganda aimed at Germany.

Freedom of belief is protected under law. However, Germany has taken a strong stance against the Church of Scientology, which it deems an economic organization rather than a religion. The four biggest political parties deny membership to Scientologists, the group has been under surveillance by intelligence agencies, and local labor offices in some cases help employers screen prospective employees (and vice-versa) for membership of Scientology groups. Eight states have passed laws prohibiting female Muslim schoolteachers from wearing headscarves (*hijab*) on duty. The number of racially motivated crimes reached record highs in 2008 and 2009, confirming an environment of increasing hostility toward immigrants in general and

Muslims in particular. The far-right NPD, while not making any headway at the federal level, does have some regional strongholds in the former East Germany, where it has been represented in two state parliaments since 2004. Academic freedom is generally respected in Germany.

Civic groups and nongovernmental organizations operate without hindrance. The right of peaceful assembly is not infringed upon, except in the case of outlawed groups, such as those advocating Nazism or opposing the democratic order. Trade unions, farmers' groups, and business confederations are free to organize.

The judiciary is independent, and the rule of law prevails. The Federal Constitutional Court vets the compatibility of legislation with the basic law. In addition to having its own provisions, Germany is a party to the European Convention on Human Rights. Prison conditions are adequate, though the Council of Europe has criticized the practice of preliminary detention before formal arrest; people so detained may not contact a lawyer or family members.

Women's rights are well protected, with generous maternity policies and antidiscrimination laws. There are 6 women in the 16-member federal cabinet. Limited same-sex partnership rights are respected.

Ghana

Political Rights: 1
Civil Liberties: 2
Status: Free

Population: 23,837,000
Capital: Accra

Ten-Year Ratings Timeline For Year Under Review (Political Rights, Civil Liberties, Status)

2000	2001	2002	2003	2004	2005	2006	2007	2008	2009
2,3F	2,3F	2,3F	2,2F	2,2F	1,2F	1,2F	1,2F	1,2F	1,2F

Overview: President John Atta Mills, who took office in January 2009, spent his first year in power working to fulfill campaign promises by investigating corruption, increasing government transparency, and improving living standards for the poor. However, he also had to contend with the effects of the global economic crisis, and it remained unclear whether his administration would prove effective.

Ghana achieved independence from British rule in 1957. After the 1966 ouster of its charismatic independence leader, Kwame Nkrumah, the country was rocked for 15 years by a series of military coups. Successive military and civilian governments vied with one another in both incompetence and dishonesty.

In 1979, air force officer Jerry Rawlings led a coup against the ruling military junta, and although he returned power to a civilian government after a purge of corrupt senior army officers, he seized power again in December 1981. Rawlings's new administration proved to be brutally repressive, banning political parties and quelling all dissent. While he agreed under economic and political pressure to hold multiparty elections in the late 1980s, the elections were considered neither free nor fair, and Rawlings and his National Democratic Congress (NDC) party remained in power. The 1996 elections were generally respected at home and abroad, but Rawlings and the NDC again retained their positions.

In 2000, free and fair presidential and parliamentary polls led to a peaceful transfer of power from Rawlings—who was forced to step down due to term limits—and the NDC to opposition leader John Kufuor and his New Patriotic Party (NPP). Kufuor won soundly with 57 percent of the vote, while NDC candidate John Atta Mills captured 43 percent. Kufuor was reelected in 2004, defeating Atta Mills for a second time as the NDC alleged irregularities. The NPP won 128 seats in Parliament, and the NDC took 94. Sporadic violence was reported, as were a few incidents of intimidation and other irregularities, but domestic and international observers judged the elections to be generally free and fair.

In advance of the December 2008 presidential election, the NPP faced internal division as over 20 candidates vied for the party's nomination. Ultimately, Nana Akufo-Addo, most recently the foreign minister, was chosen over Kufuor's preferred candidate, Alan Kyerematen. The fact that Akufo-Addo and many of his supporters belonged to the Akyem tribe while Kufuor and Kyerematen were Ashanti meant that ethnic rifts often complicated the political ones. Meanwhile, the NDC easily chose John Atta Mills as its candidate for the third time, though it too experienced some internal conflict as Atta Mills and Rawlings continued to clash.

While problems with voter registration and fighting between NDC and NPP supporters were reported before and during the vote, the election was ultimately viewed as a success by both domestic and international observers. Akufo-Addo won the first round with 49 percent, while Atta Mills took 48 percent. However, Atta Mills won the runoff with just 50.23 percent. His inauguration in January 2009 marked the second-ever peaceful, democratic transfer of power in Ghana. The NDC also won concurrent parliamentary elections, taking 114 seats as the NPP secured 107.

In August 2009, the parliamentary vote at six polling stations in Akwatia was rerun, since the initial results from December 2008 had been disputed. While the seat was awarded to the NPP candidate as expected, the unhindered rerun served as another demonstration of the stability of Ghana's democratic system.

After assuming office, Atta Mills faced the difficult task of fulfilling at least some of his campaign pledges while also steering the country through the global economic crisis. Nonetheless, some NDC supporters, backed by Rawlings, soon began complaining about the new president's inability to fulfill his promises or "support those who supported him"—a reference to the patronage networks that continue to underlie Ghanaian politics. Perceived corruption within the NPP was an important election issue, so Atta Mills's decision to investigate a number of former cabinet ministers and NPP officials for corruption was well received, though NPP officials alleged that the cases were politicized.

While Ghana has been working to move away from donor dependency, the government was forced to make exceptions for the economic crisis in 2009. It was awarded US$1.2 billion in interest-free loans over three years from the World Bank and US$602.6 million from the International Monetary Fund to help tackle "macroeconomic instability." The government also expected to benefit from new oil production beginning in 2010.

Political Rights and Civil Liberties: Ghana is an electoral democracy. The December 2008 presidential and parliamentary elections were considered fair and competitive. The president and vice president are directly elected on the same ticket for up to two four-year terms. Members of the unicameral, 230-seat Parliament are also elected for four-year terms.

The political system is dominated by two rival parties, the NPP and the NDC, which won 114 and 107 Parliament seats, respectively, in the latest elections. Smaller parties and independents hold the remainder.

One of President John Atta Mills's campaign promises was to weed out corruption and improve governance. His predecessor, John Kufuor of the NPP, had a zero-tolerance policy on corruption, but his administration made less progress than anticipated. Critics often alleged that investigations were overly politicized, and corruption within the NPP government was believed to be extensive. The new NDC administration used the Bureau of National Investigation to examine corruption allegations against a number of former NPP officials, including Kufuor's chief of staff, the health and information ministers, and the foreign minister. While many Ghanaians supported these initial investigations, there were few real successes and no convictions by year's end. Nonetheless, in November the cabinet approved a Right to Information Bill that could pave the way to greater government transparency if passed by Parliament in 2010. Ghana ratified the UN Convention Against Corruption in 2007 and was ranked 69 out of 180 countries surveyed in Transparency International's 2009 Corruption Perceptions Index.

Freedom of expression is constitutionally guaranteed and generally respected. Numerous private radio stations operate, and many independent newspapers and magazines are published in Accra. However, in 2009, there were a large number of assaults on and acts of intimidation against journalists, often perpetrated by NPP or NDC supporters. Internet access is unrestricted.

Religious freedom is protected by law and generally respected. While relations between Ghana's Christian majority and Muslim minority are generally peaceful, Muslims often report feeling politically and socially excluded, and there are few Muslims in the top levels of government. Both domestic and international human rights observers have reported a high incidence of exorcism-related physical abuse at Pentecostal prayer camps.

Academic freedom is legally guaranteed and upheld in practice. In 2005, the government removed all fees for access to primary and secondary education, and in 2009, it was reported that primary school enrollment was as high as 85 percent for boys and 78 percent for girls. At the same time, many teachers have complained of neglect by Atta Mills, citing low salaries and recent reductions in some of their allowances.

The rights to peaceful assembly and association are constitutionally guaranteed, and permits are not required for meetings or demonstrations. With the election season over, there were fewer demonstrations in 2009 and no attempts by the government to prevent public gatherings. Nonetheless, disgruntled NDC supporters seeking greater rewards for their electoral work staged a number of protests, with some even attacking government buildings and demanding jobs.

Under the constitution and 2003 labor laws, which conform to International Labour Organization (ILO) conventions, workers have the right to form or join trade unions. However, the government forbids industrial action in a number of essential industries, including fuel distribution, public transportation, and the prison system.

Ghanaian courts have acted with increased autonomy under the 1992 constitution, but corruption remains a problem. Scarce resources compromise the judicial process, and poorly paid judges are tempted by bribes. The Accra Fast Track High Court is specifically tasked with hearing corruption cases involving former government officials, but many observers raised doubts about its impartiality and respect for due process under the Kufuor administration. It remains to be seen whether its performance will improve under the new government.

While Atta Mills pardoned 1,021 prisoners in 2009 to celebrate the birthday of Kwame Nkrumah, easing the strain on prison infrastructure, prisons remain seriously overcrowded and often feature life-threatening conditions.

While communal and ethnic violence occasionally flares in Ghana, often due to tribal rivalries in the north, no such violence was reported in 2009.

Ghanaians are generally free to travel throughout the country despite occasional police-imposed curfews and roadblocks erected by security forces or civilians seeking payments from motorists. Road conditions are dismal, and car accidents are one of the leading causes of death in the country. According to the United Nations' Integrated Regional Information Networks (IRIN), 602 people died in road accidents between January and March 2009, up from 399 in the same period in 2008.

Despite their equal rights under the law, women suffer societal discrimination, especially in rural areas where opportunities for education and wage employment are limited. And although a domestic violence law was passed in 2007, few victims report such crimes because of the persistent stigma attached to them. However, women's enrollment in universities is increasing, and there are a number of high-ranking women in the current government. For the first time, women hold the positions of Speaker of Parliament, police inspector general, and attorney general.

The country serves as a source and transit point for human trafficking, including for child labor and sexual exploitation. In 2009, following undercover work conducted by a journalist working for the *New Crusading Guide* newspaper, three Chinese nationals were sentenced to a combined 36 years of hard labor for trafficking fellow Chinese for prostitution in Ghana.

Greece

Political Rights: 1
Civil Liberties: 2
Status: Free

Population: 11,277,000
Capital: Athens

Ten-Year Ratings Timeline For Year Under Review (Political Rights, Civil Liberties, Status)

2000	2001	2002	2003	2004	2005	2006	2007	2008	2009
1,3F	1,3F	1,2F	1,2F	1,2F	1,2F	1,2F	1,2F	1,2F	1,2F

Overview:
In October 2009, the Panhellenic Socialist Movement returned to power, winning national elections and ending five years of rule by the center-right New Democracy party. The riots of late 2008 continued into early 2009 with the shooting of a police officer by the militant leftist group, Revolutionary Struggle, in January. In December, the country's debt reached critical levels, leading to social unrest.

The core of modern Greece gained independence from the Ottoman Empire in 1830. The ensuing century brought additional territorial gains at the Ottomans' expense, as well as domestic political struggles between royalists and republicans. Communist and royalist partisans mounted a strong resistance to Nazi German occupation during World War II, but national solidarity broke down in the early postwar period, when royalists won national elections and eventually defeated the Communists in a civil war. In 1967, a group of army officers staged a military coup, suspending elections and arresting hundreds of political activists. A 1974 referendum rejected the restoration of the monarchy, and a new constitution in 1975 declared Greece a parliamentary republic.

The Panhellenic Socialist Movement (PASOK) governed the country from 1981 to 2004, except for a brief period from 1990 to 1993, when the conservative New Democracy party held power. New Democracy returned to power in the 2004 elections and won another term in September 2007.

National elections were called in October 2009 by Prime Minister Costas halfway through his four-year mandate, partly due to a number of corruption scandals that had rocked his coalition. PASOK returned to power in the October elections, winning seats and ending five years of rule by Karamanlis's center-right New Democracy party, which captured only 91 seats. The Communist Party of Greece (KKE) took 21 seats, the Popular Orthodox Rally (LAOS)—a nationalist and xenophobic party—won 15, and the Coalition of the Radical Left (SYRIZA) took 13. George Papandrreou, the son and grandson of former prime ministers, was elected as the new prime minister.

The violent protests that erupted in December 2008 after the police shooting of a 15-year-old continued into early 2009. In January, a police officer was shot and seriously injured by the militant leftist group, Revolutionary Struggle, in an attack on riot police guarding the culture ministry in Athens; the group has also claimed responsibility for a 2007 attack on the U.S. embassy in Athens. The January attack was reminiscent of the domestic terrorism waged by the November 17 group for three decades, until 2002. In June, another police officer guarding a witness's home was shot dead by two gunmen; the witness was involved in a trial related to another left-wing terrorist group, the Revolutionary People's Struggle.

The Greek police faced criticism in 2009 over the mistreatment of civilians, including the abuse of protesters during the December 2008 riots. The police have also been accused of using excessive force against detainees and denying suspects prompt access to lawyers, as well as allegations of arbitrary detention and torture.

A report released in February by the Council of Europe Commissioner for Human Rights raised concerns about the treatment of minorities in Greece, citing issues surrounding associational rights, statelessness of certain minorities, and the implementation of Sharia (Islamic law) by government-appointed muftis in the region of Thrace.

In April, tens of thousands of people assembled to protest against the government's economic policies, which sought to address large deficits by freezing state wages and raising taxes. The protests were also focused on the government's bailout of large banks in the midst of the global recession.

In a September monitoring report, the European Commission against Racism and Intolerance (ECRI) cited some improvements in the country's efforts to reduce racism, but noted considerable room for improvement, particularly related to the discrimination of minority groups, the recognition of persons belonging to the Macedonian community, and strengthening the ombudsman in charge of overseeing the law.

In October, eight Afghan migrants drowned when their boat crashed off the coast of the island of Lesbos. It is believed that the migrants were being smuggled as part of a human-trafficking operation. In the first half of 2009, an estimated 14,000 migrants arrived in Greece by boat.

In December, Greece's debt reached over 400 billion dollars, its highest level in modern history, leading to considerable concern across Europe about its impact. Spending cuts announced that month aimed at restoring international confidence in the country's economy were met with public protests.

Political Rights and Civil Liberties: Greece is an electoral democracy. All 300 members of the unicameral Parliament are elected by proportional representation. The largely ceremonial president is elected by a supermajority of Parliament for a five-year term. The current president, Karolos Papoulias of PASOK, was elected unopposed in 2005. The prime minister is chosen by the president and is usually the leader of the majority party in Parliament.

The country has generally fair electoral laws, equal campaigning opportunities, and a system of compulsory voting that is weakly enforced. Some representatives of the Romany community complain that certain municipalities have failed to register Roma who did not fulfill basic residency requirements.

Corruption continues to be a problem, particularly within the police forces. During 2009, police officers were dismissed and suspended for taking bribes and other illegal activities, according to the U.S. State Department. The economic crisis further spotlighted the problem of corruption in the country; in December, the new prime minister, George Papandreou, held talks with opposition leaders and set out to create an anticorruption plan, including a reform of the tax system. In 2009, a former government minister was accused of taking bribes for shipping contracts, though

Parliament in May voted to not indict him; the incident contributed to the crisis of former prime minister Karamanlis, who eventually called for snap elections in October. Greece was ranked 71 out of 180 countries surveyed in Transparency International's 2009 Corruption Perceptions Index.

The constitution includes provisions for freedom of speech and the press, and citizens have access to a broad array of privately owned print and broadcast outlets. There are, however, some limits on speech that incites fear, violence, and public disharmony, as well as on publications that offend religious beliefs, are obscene, or advocate the violent overthrow of the political system. A 2007 media law mandates that the main transmission language of radio stations be Greek, and requires that radio stations keep a certain amount of money in reserve and hire a specific number of full-time staff, which places a disproportionate burden on smaller, minority-owned stations. While internet access is generally not restricted in Greece, officials blocked the Google search engine for privacy reasons in May and prohibited Google from taking pictures in Greece for the Google Maps's "street view" function. "Street view," which gives a 360-degree view of a street, has not been banned but suspended until the government receives further requests for information.

Freedom of religion is guaranteed by the constitution, though the Orthodox Church receives government subsidies and is considered the "prevailing" denomination of the country. Members of some minority religions face social discrimination and legal barriers, such as permit requirements to open houses of worship and restrictions on inheriting property. Proselytizing is prohibited, and consequently, Mormons and Jehovah's Witnesses are routinely arrested and have reported abuse by police officers. Anti-Semitism also remains a problem. Athens is still awaiting the construction of the city's first licensed mosque. Academic freedom is not restricted in Greece.

Freedoms of assembly and association are guaranteed by the constitution and generally protected by the government, though there are some limits on groups representing ethnic minorities. Nongovernmental organizations (NGOs) generally operate without interference from the authorities, and some domestic human rights groups receive government funding and assistance. Workers have the right to join and form unions. In December 2008, an outspoken trade union leader was attacked by an unknown assailant who threw acid on her face. The leader was known to advocate for basic worker rights, often for immigrants in the cleaning industry.

The judiciary is independent, and the constitution provides for public trials. Human rights groups have raised concerns about the ill-treatment of asylum seekers by law enforcement officials, and prison overcrowding remains a problem.

Despite government efforts to combat it, racial intolerance is still pervasive in society and is often expressed by public figures. Laws against racism and incitement to hatred are rarely enforced. In March 2009, an appeals court overturned an earlier conviction against Kostas Plevris, a nationalist writer accused of publishing anti-Semitic material and inciting hatred in his book, *Jews, the Whole Truth*. The 2009 ECRI report noted that the leader of the far-right LAOS party, which won nearly 6 percent in October elections, frequently made public anti-Semitic and racist statements, including blaming immigrants for criminal activities; however, in March, the court overturned an earlier ruling against him of inciting hatred. The government does not officially recognize the existence of any non-Muslim ethnic minority groups, particularly Slavophones. Macedonian is not recognized as a language, and using the terms Turkos or Tourkikos ("Turk" and "Turkish," respectively) in the title of an association is illegal and may lead to the dissolution of the group. The Romany community continues to face considerable discrimination and a general denial of justice.

Immigrants are disproportionately affected by institutional problems in the judicial system. Bureaucratic delays force many into a semilegal status when they are not able to renew their documents, putting them in jeopardy of deportation. In 2009, the conservative government began cracking down on "clandestine" immigrants and demolished a 13-year-old encampment housing approximately 1,800 immigrants in Patras. The new Socialist government has called for improvements in the country's treatment of immigrants, including stronger border control.

Women lack specific legislation to deal with domestic violence and face discrimination in the workplace. Women currently hold 17 percent of the seats in Parliament. Trafficking in women and children for prostitution remains a problem. While the government has attempted to address the issue in recent years, international NGOs continued to express concern over the country's punishment of trafficking offenders and the complicity of some officials in trafficking.

Grenada

Political Rights: 1
Civil Liberties: 2
Status: Free

Population: 106,000
Capital: St. George's

Ten-Year Ratings Timeline For Year Under Review (Political Rights, Civil Liberties, Status)

2000	2001	2002	2003	2004	2005	2006	2007	2008	2009
1,2F	1,2F	1,2F	1,2F	1,2F	1,2F	1,2F	1,2F	1,2F	1,2F

Overview: 2009, Prime Minister Tillman Thomas of the National Democratic Congress (NDC) marked his first year in office by reshuffling his cabinet and elevating several junior ministers. The attorney general resigned in July, after admitting he used his position to lobby for leniency on behalf of a relative who faced drug-dealing charges in Florida. Seven men, who represented the last of the "Grenada 17" convicted in the 1983 murder of Prime Minister Maurice Bishop, were set free after more than two decades in prison.

Grenada gained independence from Britain in 1974. Maurice Bishop's Marxist New Jewel Movement seized power in 1979, creating a People's Revolutionary Government (PRG). In 1983, Bishop was murdered by New Jewel hard-liners Bernard Coard and Hudson Austin, who took control of the country. However, a joint U.S.-Caribbean military intervention quickly removed the PRG and set the country on a path toward new elections. In 1986, Coard and 18 others were sentenced to death; subsequently, 2 of the 19 were pardoned, and the rest—who became known as the Grenada 17—had their sentences commuted to life imprisonment. In 2006, an additional 4 of the 17 were released. The London-based Privy Council ruled in February

2007 that the same findings that had invalidated the death sentences also rendered the life sentences unconstitutional. The 13 remaining inmates received reduced sentences in June 2007, and 3 were immediately released. The other 10, resentenced to 40 years in prison, would become eligible for release by 2010. The last seven were freed in September 2009.

Prime Minister Keith Mitchell of the New National Party (NNP) ruled Grenada from 1995 to 2008, when his party lost parliamentary elections to the opposition National Democratic Congress (NDC). Tillman Thomas, the NDC leader, was sworn in as prime minister in July 2008. The NDC captured 11 seats in the 15-member House of Representatives, leaving the NNP with just 4. Despite his defeat in the general elections, former prime minister Mitchell won the NNP leadership contest in July 2009.

Amidst the global economic downturn in 2009, Prime Minister Thomas reshuffled his cabinet and elevated several junior ministers. Significant changes included separating the portfolios for foreign affairs and tourism and naming a female senator as minister for health.

Political Rights and Civil Liberties: Grenada is an electoral democracy. The 2008 parliamentary elections were considered generally free and fair, although there were allegations of voter-list manipulation. The bicameral Parliament consists of the elected, 15-seat House of Representatives, whose members serve five-year terms, and the 13-seat Senate, to which the prime minister appoints 10 members and the opposition leader names 3. The prime minister is typically the leader of the majority party in the House of Representatives and is appointed by the governor-general, who represents the British monarch as head of state. Grenada's main political parties are the NDC, the NNP, the Grenada United Labor Party (GULP), and the People's Labor Movement (PLM).

Corruption remains a contentious political issue in Grenada, and the country compares unfavorably with several of its neighbors. In 2009, Grenada's attorney general admitted to writing a letter on official stationery to U.S. prosecutors pleading for clemency for his stepson, who faced sentencing in Florida on drug-dealing charges. At Prime Minister Thomas's request, the attorney general resigned in July. Grenada was not ranked by Transparency International in its 2009 Corruption Perceptions Index.

The right to free expression is generally respected. The media, including three weekly newspapers and several other publications, are independent and freely criticize the government. A private corporation, with a minority stake owned by the government, operates the principal radio and television stations. There are also nine privately owned radio stations, one privately owned television station, and a privately owned cable company. In 2009, the government drafted and circulated for comments a Freedom of Information Act to ensure greater government transparency. Access to the internet is unrestricted.

Citizens of Grenada generally enjoy the free exercise of religious beliefs, and there are no official restrictions on academic freedom.

Constitutional guarantees regarding freedoms of assembly and association are respected. Grenada has a robust civil society that participates actively in domestic and international discussions, although limited resources hamper its effectiveness.

Workers have the right to organize and bargain collectively. Labor unions represent an estimated 52 percent of the workforce, according to the Labor Ministry.

All unions belong to the government-subsidized Grenada Trades Union Council (GTUC). A 1993 law gave the government the right to establish tribunals empowered to make "binding and final" rulings when a labor dispute is considered to be of vital interest to the state; the GTUC has expressed concerns that the law is an infringement on the right to strike. Employers are not legally bound to recognize a union if less than half of the workers are unionized.

The independence and authority of Grenada's judiciary is generally respected by the Royal Grenada Police Force. Grenada is a member of the Organization of Eastern Caribbean States court system and a charter member of the Trinidad-based Caribbean Court of Justice, but the country still relies on the Privy Council in London as its final court of appeal. Detainees and defendants are guaranteed a range of legal rights, which the government respects in practice. However, a lack of judges and facilities has led to a backlog of six months to one year for cases involving serious offenses. In September 2009, the government released the final seven members of the Grenada 17, who had spent more than two decades in prison following convictions for their role in the 1983 murder of Prime Minister Maurice Bishop. This highly publicized case had been repeatedly criticized due to perceived political manipulation by the government, and Amnesty International had classified the group as political prisoners.

Grenada's prison conditions, though poor, meet minimum international standards, and the government allows visits by human rights monitors. Flogging is still legal but employed rarely, primarily as a punishment for sex crimes and theft.

Grenada has few significant minorities, although its gay population remains a target of discrimination. Women are represented in the government, including both houses of Parliament and the cabinet. Women generally earn less than men for equal work. Domestic violence against women is common, and most instances of abuse go unreported or are settled out of court. In 2009, NGOs such as the Grenada National Organization for Women and the Coalition on the Rights of the Child remained outspoken on incidents of rape and abuse.

Guatemala

Political Rights: 4*
Civil Liberties: 4
Status: Partly Free

Population: 14,027,000
Capital: Guatemala City

Ratings Change: Guatemala's political rights rating declined from 3 to 4 due to the government's inability to implement policies and legislation in the face of pervasive organized crime.

Ten-Year Ratings Timeline For Year Under Review (Political Rights, Civil Liberties, Status)

2000	2001	2002	2003	2004	2005	2006	2007	2008	2009
3,4PF	3,4PF	4,4PF	4,4PF	4,4PF	4,4PF	3,4PF	3,4PF	3,4PF	4,4PF

Overview: While President Alvaro Colom struggled in 2009 to curb the corruption and impunity that plague Guatemalan institutions, he himself was accused of involvement in a scandal surrounding the state-run Banrural bank and the murder of lawyer Rodrigo Rosenberg in May. Separately, the release of a new report on civil war–era human rights abuses in March led to the abduction and torture of the wife of human rights prosecutor Sergio Morales. Violent crime continued unabated during the year, and civil society activists suffered a number of threats and attacks.

The Republic of Guatemala, which was established in 1839, has endured a history of dictatorship, foreign intervention, military coups, and guerrilla insurgencies. Civilian rule followed the 1985 elections, and a 36-year civil war, which claimed the lives of more than 200,000 people, ended with a 1996 peace agreement. The Guatemalan National Revolutionary Unity (URNG) guerrilla movement became a legal political group, and a truth commission began receiving complaints of rights violations committed during the conflict. However, voters in 1999 rejected a package of constitutional amendments that had been prepared in accordance with the peace plan. The general consensus was that the government failed to implement substantive reforms, including ending military impunity, fully recognizing the rights of the Maya Indians, and reforming taxation to pay for health, education, and housing programs for the poor.

In 2003, the Constitutional Court ruled that retired general Efrain Rios Montt—who employed brutal tactics against the URNG during his 18 months as ruler of Guatemala in 1982 and 1983—could run for the presidency. Before the decision, the Guatemalan Republican Front (FRG) party mustered armed supporters to intimidate the Court's justices and critics, and Rios Montt was later chosen as the FRG's candidate. However, in the first round of the presidential election, he placed third behind Oscar Berger of the Grand National Alliance (GANA) and Alvaro Colom of the National Unity for Hope (UNE). Berger went on to defeat Colom in the runoff with 54 percent of the vote.

The 2007 general elections were the bloodiest in Guatemala's recent history, with more than 50 candidates, activists, and their relatives slain during the campaign period. This violence, some of which was not overtly political, was fueled by the drug trade, gang activity, and armed groups including rogue soldiers and paramilitary forces. The September vote was nevertheless regarded by international observers as largely free and fair. The UNE party captured 51 seats in Congress, followed by GANA with 37 seats, and former general Otto Perez Molina's Patriot Party with 29 seats. The FRG lost 65 percent of its congressional base, falling to just 14 seats, though the seat secured by Rios Montt gave him immunity from prosecution; a Spanish court in 2006 had issued arrest warrants for eight former military leaders, including Rios Montt, for crimes against humanity. In the presidential contest, Colom defeated Perez in a runoff vote, capturing 53 percent of the ballots amid a turnout of 45 percent.

Colom, who since taking office had dismissed several senior officials in response to scandals, corruption charges, or policy ineffectiveness, continued his attempts to curb official corruption and impunity in 2009. In March, he established a committee tasked with declassifying military archives from the civil war era. He also extended the mandate of the UN-backed International Commission against Impunity in Guatemala (CICIG), widely considered to be one of the only legitimate public institutions in the country, through September 2011. The biggest scandal of the year involved the May assassination of lawyer Rodrigo Rosenberg, who recorded a video prior to his death in which he accused Colom of ordering his murder. He also accused First Lady Sandra Torres and top government officials of covering up illegal business deals involving Banrural, a development bank. Colom denied the accusations and ordered an investigation into Rosenberg's murder, which was ongoing at year's end.

In other developments in the fight against impunity, in March 2009, the special prosecutor for human rights, Sergio Morales, released a landmark report on abuses committed during the civil war, based on military archives. The following day, Morales's wife, lawyer and professor Gladys Monterroso, was kidnapped and tortured by unknown assailants. A separate report released in September, based on archives from the presidency's social welfare department, indicated that at least 333 children and possibly thousands more were kidnapped by security forces during the war and sold abroad. In June, Guatemala's Forensic Anthropology Foundation opened the country's first DNA testing lab to identify victims from wartime mass graves. And in August, former paramilitary Felipe Cusanero became the first person in Guatemala to be convicted of forced disappearances. He was sentenced to 150 years in prison for ordering the disappearance of six civilians between 1982 and 1984.

Famine conditions in 2009 claimed the lives of at least 460 people, as a combination of rising food prices, prolonged drought, and a drop in migrant remittances linked to the global economic downturn exacerbated malnourishment, particularly in rural areas. Roughly 80 percent of the population lives below the poverty level and does not benefit from social security. The country also continues to rank high on inequality indicators, with some 63 percent of gross domestic product concentrated in the hands of 20 percent of the population. Guatemala is a party to the Dominican Republic–Central American Free Trade Agreement (DR-CAFTA) with the United States, and it joined Venezuela's Petrocaribe program in July 2008 to receive preferential rates on oil imports.

Political Rights and Civil Liberties: Guatemala is an electoral democracy. Despite intimidation and violence during the campaign period, the 2007 presidential and legislative elections were regarded by international observers as generally free and fair. The constitution stipulates a four-year presidential term and prohibits reelection. The unicameral Congress of the Republic, consisting of 158 members, is elected for four years. Elections take place within a highly fragmented and fluid multiparty system. Two notable traditional parties are the FRG and the National Advancement Party (PAN). Other parties include the URNG, formerly a guerrilla movement, and the UNE, led by current president Alvaro Colom. The GANA coalition, which had supported former president Oscar Berger, included the Patriot Party, the National Solidarity Party (PSN), and the Reformist Movement (MR) party. In 2008, divisions within GANA caused it to split into two factions.

Efforts to combat corruption, such as the introduction of an electronic procurement system for government entities, have made some progress. During 2009, former Congress president Eduardo Meyer, a close ally of Colom, was investigated in connection with a scandal involving the transfer of $10.9 million in congressional funds to a stockbroker. Opposition leader Otto Perez Molina was among a number of others implicated in the affair.

The Law for Free Access to Public Information took effect in April 2009, promoting transparency and granting citizens access to information on budgets and salaries, among other topics. The government has taken related steps to establish an institutional framework for transparency, including the creation of a Viceministry of Fiscal Transparency and Evaluation, and a Public Information Unit responsible for handling requests for public records. Guatemala was ranked 84 out of 180 countries surveyed in Transparency International's 2009 Corruption Perceptions Index.

While freedom of speech is protected by the constitution, those who vigorously condemn the government or past human rights abuses can face persecution. The press and most broadcast outlets are privately owned. A Mexican businessman, Angel Gonzalez, owns a monopoly of broadcast television networks and has significant holdings in radio. Newspaper ownership is concentrated in the hands of moderate business elites, and most papers have centrist or conservative editorial views. Twitter user Jean Anleu Fernandez was arrested in May 2009 for a posted comment in which he urged people to withdraw their money from the allegedly corrupt state-owned bank Banrural. He was charged with "inciting financial panic," and his arrest led tens of thousands of protesters to take to the streets in June. In August, publisher Raul Figueroa-Sarti was sentenced to one year in prison for publishing a photograph on the cover of a novel without the photographer's permission, but some argued that the case had been brought in retaliation for his publication of books on human rights abuses. Journalists often face threats and practice self-censorship when covering drug trafficking, corruption, and organized crime. Two television reporters were murdered separately in 2009, and other media workers suffered serious attacks.

The constitution guarantees religious freedom. However, members of indigenous communities have faced discrimination for the open practice of their Mayan religion. The government does not interfere with academic freedom, but scholars have received death threats for raising questions about past human rights abuses or continuing injustices.

Freedom of assembly is guaranteed and generally respected in practice. However, police often use force to end disruptive demonstrations, resulting in the injury and death of some protesters. In October 2009, police clashed with protesters in a long-running land dispute over a US$1 billion nickel-mining project, leaving one man dead and several others injured.

The constitution guarantees freedom of association, and a variety of nongovernmental organizations (NGOs) operate without major legal or government obstacles. However, labor, human rights, and environmental activists continued to face death threats or attacks in 2009, and even international agencies suffered intimidation and office burglaries. In one case, Juana Baca Velasco, coordinator of the Association of Ixhil Women, was assaulted in March and continued to receive death threats for several months thereafter.

Guatemala is home to a vigorous labor movement, but trade unions are subject to intimidation and violence, particularly in rural areas during land disputes. Workers are frequently denied the right to organize and face mass firings and blacklisting, especially in export-processing zones. Countless union members have been threatened or attacked, and some union activists' families have been targeted for rape and murder. In April 2008, the U.S.-based AFL-CIO labor federation, along with six Guatemalan unions, filed a complaint with the U.S. Labor Department for violations of the labor provisions of DR-CAFTA, citing Guatemala's failure to protect unionists. No action had been taken on this complaint at the end of 2009.

The judiciary is troubled by corruption, inefficiency, capacity shortages, and the intimidation of judges, prosecutors, and witnesses. Threats against judicial sector workers are common, and according to the NGO Lawyers' Rights Watch Canada, at least 40 judges and lawyers have been murdered since 2005, including 4 between January and July 2009. In September 2009, the CICIG reported irregularities in the selection of various judges, including cases of nepotism by members of the nominating committees. The CICIG has also reported that difficulties in working with the Office of the Public Prosecutor have impeded its investigations of corruption and organized crime within public institutions.

Pretrial detention is legally limited to three months, but inmates often spend years in jail before trial. Since 2007, the government has introduced 24-hour courts in some areas to increase efficiency. Prison conditions are harsh, and the facilities are rife with gang- and drug-related violence and corruption. Although the provision of indigenous language translators in courtrooms is legally mandated, a lack of funding has prevented proper implementation.

Police have been accused of torture, extortion, kidnapping for ransom, and extrajudicial killings of suspected gang members. Several police officers were charged with drug-related crimes in 2009, including the director general, assistant director, and director of operations of the National Civil Police, all of whom were fired in August over the disappearance of more than 100 kilograms of seized cocaine. The government's use of the military to maintain internal security remains controversial, since the 1996 peace accords placed limits on the practice.

Guatemala is one of the most violent countries in Latin America, and in 2009, it experienced its most violent year in recent history, with 6,451 homicide victims; the country registered an average of 18 murders a day in 2009, compared with 15 a day in 2008. It is estimated that only 2 percent of murder cases result in a conviction. Violence related to drug trafficking has spilled over border from Mexico, with rival gangs and cartels battling over territory. In March 2009, authorities discovered a training camp in Quiche run by the Zetas, a notorious Mexican drug gang; also that month, Colom received death threats from Mexico's Gulf cartel. Trafficking organizations operate with impunity in the jungles of northern Guatemala, which serve as a storage and transit hub for cocaine en route to the United States. These traffickers have also contributed to a growing local drug problem by paying Guatemalan associates in cocaine rather than cash. In the wake of the global economic downturn, Guatemala has been forced to cut funding for the military's efforts to fight drug smuggling and organized crime.

In other forms of violence, at least 200 transportation workers were murdered during 2009, with officials estimating that organized crime groups extorted nearly US$10,000 a day from bus drivers. Meanwhile, the continued practice of lynching, mutilation, torture, and political assassinations—carried out by plainclothes security forces, angered mobs, gangs, and other groups—has shocked the country.

Indigenous communities suffer from especially high rates of poverty and infant mortality. Indigenous women are particularly marginalized, and more than half of those over age 15 are illiterate. Discrimination against the Mayan community continues to be a major concern. The government in recent years has approved the eviction of indigenous groups to make way for mining, hydroelectric, and other development projects.

Sexual harassment in the workplace is not penalized. Young women who migrate to the capital for work are especially vulnerable to harassment and inhumane labor conditions, and women overall earn 60 percent of what men in the same jobs are paid. Violence against women and children is widespread. Guatemalan women and children are drawn into prostitution both locally and in neighboring countries. In 2008, Congress passed a law against femicide, the murder of a woman for gender-related reasons, which now carries a penalty of 25 to 50 years in prison; the law similarly recognized and increased penalties for a range of other crimes against women. Transgender women and gay men also continue to be targets of violent attacks.

Guatemala has the highest rate of child labor in the Americas, with one-third of school-aged children forced to work on farms or in factories. A new law against human trafficking came into force in April 2009, clarifying the legal definition of the crime and increasing penalties. However, Guatemala remained on the Tier 2 Watch List in the U.S. State Department's Trafficking in Persons Report in 2009, due to the government's failure to comply with minimum international standards to eliminate trafficking. Casa Alianza, the foremost nonprofit operator of shelters for trafficking victims, was forced to close its Guatemala facilities in 2009 due to lack of funding.

Guinea

Political Rights: 7
Civil Liberties: 6*
Status: Not Free

Population: 10,058,000
Capital: Conakry

Ratings Change: Guinea's civil liberties rating declined from 5 to 6 due to the military junta's repressive measures, including the massacre of more than 150 opposition protesters in September and the use of rape as a means of political intimidation.

Ten-Year Ratings Timeline For Year Under Review (Political Rights, Civil Liberties, Status)

2000	2001	2002	2003	2004	2005	2006	2007	2008	2009
6,5NF	6,5NF	6,5NF	6,5NF	6,5NF	6,5NF	6,5NF	6,5NF	7,5NF	7,6NF

Overview: Captain Moussa Dadis Camara, the leader of a military junta that took power in December 2008, refused in 2009 to adhere to an initial promise that he would not run in the presidential election set for early 2010. His erratic and repressive rule during the year culminated in the massacre of more than 150 opposition protesters in September. The incident, which also featured brutal rapes and beatings by security forces, triggered an investigation by the United Nations as well as a series of international sanctions. In Decem-

ber, Camara was shot and seriously injured by one of his officers, and the consequences remained uncertain at year's end.

Guinea gained independence from France in 1958 and grew increasingly impoverished under the repressive, one-party rule of President Ahmed Sekou Toure. After his death in 1984, a military junta led by Lieutenant Colonel Lansana Conte abolished all political parties and the constitution, and began a program of economic liberalization.

A new constitution was adopted in 1990. Conte won the country's first multiparty presidential elections in 1993, but international observers said the polls were deeply flawed. Presidential, legislative, and municipal elections over the next 12 years were similarly marred by state patronage, media bias, broad manipulation of the electoral process, and opposition boycotts; all resulted in lopsided victories for Conte and the ruling Party for Unity and Progress (PUP).

In early 2007, a general strike to protest corruption, the cost of basic goods, and inadequate government services grew into nationwide antigovernment demonstrations. Security forces opened fire on protesters, killing more than 130. The president agreed under pressure to vest some executive powers in a new prime minister, but named an ally to the post in February and declared martial law when the choice stirred protests into a near-revolt of unprecedented scale. With mediation by the Economic Community of West African States (ECOWAS), union leaders agreed to suspend the general strike, while Conte pledged to control inflation, organize legislative elections, and name a "consensus" prime minister backed by unions and civil society. He appointed veteran diplomat Lansana Kouyate, but initial optimism faded as the prime minister's reform plan was stymied by structural challenges, back-room opposition from the president and his associates, and perceptions that Kouyate was pursuing his own political agenda.

In May 2008, Conte unilaterally dismissed Kouyate. A faction of the army mutinied later that month, and security forces brutally suppressed a police mutiny in June as well as sporadic antigovernment demonstrations by civilians. The ailing president died in December, and junior officers quickly mounted a successful military coup, promising to hold elections in two years.

Captain Moussa Dadis Camara, the coup leader, initially enjoyed considerable popularity, especially as he sought to expose corruption among former officials. However, his arbitrary and personalized style of rule quickly engendered opposition. In August, under international and domestic pressure, the ruling junta—known as the National Council for Democracy and Development (CNDD)—set presidential and legislative elections for January and March 2010, respectively. Camara began to hint that he might renege on his earlier promise not to run for president, and opposition forces mounted a massive rally in late September. The gathering was viciously suppressed by security forces, who killed more than 150 people and raped and beat hundreds of others. The international community, including ECOWAS, the African Union, the European Union, and the United States, roundly condemned the crackdown and imposed sanctions on the Guinean regime. However, China broke ranks and signed a $9 billion mining agreement with the junta in October.

In December, as the International Criminal Court and a special UN panel investigated the September massacre, the commander of Guinea's presidential guard shot

Camara in the head, seriously injuring him. The country's leadership and the antici-pated elections remained in doubt at year's end.

Political Rights and Civil Liberties: Guinea is not an electoral democracy. Elections under presi-dents Ahmed Sekou Toure and Lansana Conte were heavily manipulated, and the December 2008 military coup sus-pended all political activity, civilian government institutions, and the constitution. The resulting junta, the CNDD, promised to hold open presidential and legislative elections in early 2010, but those plans were in doubt after the September 2009 mas-sacre of opposition supporters and the December assassination attempt on junta leader Moussa Dadis Camara.

There are several significant political parties, most of which have clear regional and ethnic bases. However, the country has no history of peaceful rotation of power, and prior to the 2008 coup, Conte's controlled much of the government as well as substantial patronage networks in the military and civil bureaucracy.

Corruption has been cited as a serious problem by international donors, and many government activities are shrouded in secrecy. Guinea was ranked 168 out of 180 countries surveyed in Transparency International's 2009 Corruption Perceptions Index. The CNDD promised to crack down on corruption, but, instead, it oversaw a continued disintegration of the rule of law and legal institutions. Camara instituted a practice of haranguing allegedly corrupt officials on television, although it was not clear whether this was aimed at rooting out corruption or taking control of it.

Under Conte, restrictive laws allowed media censorship and criminalized defa-mation, and private radio and print outlets were subject to suspensions and harass-ment. The state controls a radio station and the only television broadcaster. In 2009, the military junta sought to intimidate independent journalists through arbitrary ar-rest and other tactics, and several were beaten, threatened, and harassed in the wake of the September massacre. Some foreign journalists were forbidden from entering the country during the year. Internet access is limited to urban areas, but has gener-ally not been restricted by the government when available.

The constitution, which provides for the protection of religious rights, was sus-pended after the 2008 coup. Religious rights are generally respected in practice, though there have been instances of discrimination against non-Muslims in gov-ernment employment, as well as restrictions on Muslims' freedom to convert to other religions. Academic freedom has been hampered to some degree by government influence over hiring and curriculum content. Intimidation by the security forces eroded freedom of private discussion in 2009, particularly after the massacre.

The CNDD restricted freedoms of association and assembly, and the authori-ties clearly demonstrated their contempt for these rights during the brutal suppres-sion of the September 2009 opposition rally. Even before the coup, the law allowed authorities to ban any gathering that "threatens national unity," and troops had repeatedly fired into crowds of protesters. The junta banned all political and union activity, though union and political party leaders continued to make public state-ments and met with the CNDD on several occasions in 2009. Moreover, a number of nongovernmental organizations operated openly, and trade unions engaged in strike actions, most notably after the massacre. In October, for example, a coalition of trade unions declared a widely observed two-day mourning period.

Under Conte, the nominally independent courts were marred by corruption, a lack of resources, nepotism, ethnic bias, and political interference. Informal customary justice mechanisms operated in addition to official courts. The legal system was thrown into turmoil by the CNDD's initial suspension of judicial institutions, and in June 2009 court staff went on strike to protest political interference in judicial affairs. Security forces have long engaged in arbitrary arrests, torture of detainees, and extrajudicial execution with impunity. Prison conditions are harsh and sometimes life-threatening. In 2008, international analysts warned that Guinea was becoming a significant transit point for drug trafficking.

While the law prohibits ethnic discrimination, human rights reports have noted societal discrimination in employment, housing, and marriage patterns. People from the Guerze ethnic group, to which Camara belongs, received favored treatment in 2009. Also, despite Camara's alleged anticorruption campaign, in 2009 the government signed a number of highly questionable and nontransparent contracts with foreign companies for exploitation of Guinea's minerals sector.

Societal discrimination against women is common, and while women have legal access to land, credit, and business, the inheritance laws and the traditional justice system have favored men. Security personnel openly raped dozens of women in the 2007 and 2009 crackdowns. Human Rights Watch has reported that thousands of young girls serving as unpaid domestic workers in Guinea are subject to beatings or rape by their employers. Guinea was a source, transit point, and destination for human trafficking in 2009, according to the U.S. State Department. Advocacy groups are working to eradicate the illegal but nearly ubiquitous practice of female genital mutilation.

Guinea-Bissau

Political Rights: 4
Civil Liberties: 4
Status: Partly Free

Population: 1,611,000
Capital: Bissau

Ten-Year Ratings Timeline For Year Under Review (Political Rights, Civil Liberties, Status)

2000	2001	2002	2003	2004	2005	2006	2007	2008	2009
4,5PF	4,5PF	4,5PF	6,4PF	4,4PF	3,4PF	4,4PF	4,4PF	4,4PF	4,4PF

Overview: The assassinations of General Batista Tagme Na Wai and President Joao Bernardo Vieira in March 2009 plunged Guinea-Bissau into a period of acute disorder. However, despite an upsurge in political violence following the assassinations, Malam Bacai Sanha was elected president in a two-round vote in June and July that was deemed free and fair by international observers. The country's chronic instability continued to be fueled by military interference in politics and the influence of international drug cartels.

Guinea-Bissau declared independence from Portugal in 1973, following a 13-year guerrilla war by the leftist African Party for the Independence of Guinea-Bissau and Cape Verde (PAIGC). Luis Cabral became president in 1974, but disaffection with his repressive rule led to divisions within the PAIGC, and in 1980 he was toppled by the prime minister, former military commander Joao Bernardo "Nino" Vieira.

Vieira ruled from 1980 to 1984 as head of a Revolutionary Council composed primarily of military figures. A reconstituted single-party National People's Assembly approved a new constitution in 1984 and elected Vieira as head of state. His authoritarian grip on power was challenged by coup plots in 1983, 1985, and 1993, and international pressure from donors eventually led to economic liberalization and political reform. In 1994, the country held its first multiparty legislative and presidential elections, and Vieira was elected president.

An army mutiny broke out in June 1998, after Vieira fired General Ansumane Mane, accusing him of smuggling arms to separatist rebels in Senegal's Casamance region. Hostilities escalated when Vieira called on troops from neighboring Senegal and Guinea to put down the uprising. The war that ensued displaced hundreds of thousands of people and destroyed the country's infrastructure and economy. Vieira was ousted in May 1999 and went into exile in Portugal.

Presidential and legislative elections in November 1999 resulted in a sound defeat for the PAIGC. Kumba Yala, leader of the Social Renovation Party (PRS), became president in early 2000. Fighting broke out that year between military factions backing Yala and Mane after Mane declared himself head of the armed forces. Mane was subsequently killed. In 2002, Yala dissolved the parliament and called early elections, which were then postponed. The president ruled by decree until he was overthrown in a 2003 coup led by General Verisimo Correia Seabra.

Legislative elections held in March 2004 were declared free and fair by international observers, and the PAIGC returned with a plurality of seats. A new government was formed, and Carlos Gomes Junior became prime minister. Vieira returned from exile to stand for the June 2005 presidential election as an independent candidate, challenging Yala of the PRS and Malam Bacai Sanha of the PAIGC. Vieira was declared winner of the July presidential runoff, which international observers also judged to be free and fair, though many Bissau-Guineans insisted otherwise.

Vieira dismissed Gomes Junior and appointed former PAIGC ally Aristide Gomes to replace him as prime minister. This caused tensions between Vieira's supporters and the parliamentary opposition. After months of negotiations, the three dominant parties in the National People's Assembly—the PAIGC, the PRC, and the United Social Democrat Party (PUSD)—agreed on a national political stability pact in March 2007. Days later, the coalition passed a vote of no confidence against the prime minister. Gomes resigned, and despite considerable resistance from Vieira, Martinho Ndafa Cabi of the PAIGC took over the premiership.

Legislative elections scheduled for March 2008 were postponed to November due to insufficient funds and planning. Although the run-up to the voting was marred by uncertainty and an alleged coup plot by navy commander Bubo Na Tchuto, the PAIGC won a resounding victory, and the polls were hailed by the international community and Bissau-Guineans as free and transparent. The PAIGC won 67 seats in the 100-seat legislature, while the PRS won 28, and a newly created party backed by Vieira, the Republican Party for Independence and Development (PRID), won 3. Carlos Gomes Junior of the PAIGC once again became prime minister.

On March 1, 2009, General Batista Tagme Na Wai, the armed forces chief of staff, was killed in a bombing at military headquarters. The following morning, soldiers attacked the presidential palace and assassinated Vieira. National People's Assembly Speaker Raimundo Pereira was sworn in as interim president on March 3, in keeping with the constitution, and a new presidential election was eventually scheduled for June 28. Political violence escalated during the campaign. On June 5, presidential candidate Baciro Dabo and former defense minister Helder Proenca were both killed; the Interior Ministry claimed that they were shot while resisting arrest for involvement in an alleged coup plot. Several other prominent political figures were also arrested that day.

Despite a wave of violence and intimidation tactics, the first round of the presidential election was held as scheduled. Sanha of the PAIGC placed first with 39.6 percent of the vote, followed by Yala of the PRS with 29.4 percent and independent Henrique Rosa with 24.2 percent. In the July 26 runoff, Sanha defeated Yala, 63.5 percent to 36.5 percent. International observers reported that both rounds were peaceful, free, and transparent. Sanha was sworn in as president in September, pledging to work on security sector reform and combat drug trafficking.

Guinea-Bissau, one of the world's poorest countries, is currently carrying out reforms to improve fiscal stability as part of a $5.6 million Emergency Post-Conflict Assistance (EPCA) program initiated by the International Monetary Fund. Discussions are under way to begin work on a Poverty Reduction and Growth Facility (PRGF) program in 2010. Angolan investment in bauxite mining and a European Union–financed project to rehabilitate roadways have also been announced.

Political Rights and Civil Liberties: Guinea-Bissau is an electoral democracy. The 100 members of the unicameral National People's Assembly are elected by popular vote to serve four-year terms. The president is elected for five-year terms. Legislative and presidential elections held in 2008 and 2009 were declared free and fair by international observers. However, military intervention is a constant threat to democratically elected governments.

Political parties in Guinea-Bissau are competitive. While the PAIGC has been the dominant party for most of the country's history and currently holds power, it has also been in the opposition. Political parties and party leaders often suffer from military interference and shifting personal cliques.

Corruption is pervasive, driven in large part by the drug trade. Guinea-Bissau ranked 162 out of 180 countries surveyed in Transparency International's 2009 Corruption Perception Index (CPI).

Although the constitution provides for freedoms of speech and the press, the political disorder of 2009 led to grave violations. In March, former prime minister Jose Fadul and prominent lawyer Pedro Infanda were beaten and tortured, respectively, for criticizing the military. When Guinea-Bissau Human Rights League president Luis Vaz Martins condemned the violence, he was pursued by armed men who threatened to kill him. Journalists face harassment and practice self-censorship. There are a number of private and community radio stations in addition to the national broadcasters, and several private newspapers publish sporadically, largely due to financial constraints. Internet access is unrestricted.

Religious freedom is legally protected and usually respected in practice. Academic freedom is similarly guaranteed and upheld.

Freedoms of assembly and association are recognized and usually respected, but security forces have occasionally suppressed public demonstrations. Nongovernmental organizations generally operate freely. Workers are allowed to form and join independent trade unions, though few work in the wage-earning formal sector. The right to strike is protected, and government workers frequently exercise this right.

Scant resources and endemic corruption severely challenge judicial independence. The U.S. State Department has reported that there are essentially no resources to conduct criminal investigations and no formal detention facilities. Judges and magistrates sometimes go for months without pay and are highly susceptible to corruption. A culture of impunity is prevalent, particularly in the military. A law passed in 2008 provides amnesty to persons who have committed political crimes. High-level investigations of the assassinations of the president and army chief in 2009 were deemed inconclusive.

With its weak institutions and porous borders, Guinea-Bissau has become a major transit point for Latin American drug cartels moving cocaine to Europe. The UN Office on Drugs and Crime has estimated that as much as $2 billion in drugs are trafficked through the country each year. Powerful segments of the military, police, and government are reportedly complicit in the trade. Moreover, the absence of the rule of law has impeded legitimate private enterprise.

Ethnic identity is an important factor in politics, and the military is dominated by the Balanta ethnic group, the country's largest.

Women face significant traditional and societal discrimination, despite some legal protections. They generally do not receive equal pay for equal work and have fewer opportunities for education and jobs in the small formal sector. Women of certain ethnic groups cannot own or manage land or inherit property. Domestic violence, female genital mutilation, and early marriage are widespread.

⬇ Guyana

Political Rights: 2
Civil Liberties: 3
Status: Free

Population: 773,000
Capital: Georgetown

Trend Arrow: Guyana received a downward trend arrow due to the violation of detainees' rights by law enforcement officials.

Ten-Year Ratings Timeline For Year Under Review (Political Rights, Civil Liberties, Status)

2000	2001	2002	2003	2004	2005	2006	2007	2008	2009
2,2F	2,2F	2,2F	2,2F	2,2F	3,3PF	2,3F	2,3F	2,3F	2,3F

Overview: In 2009, President Bharrat Jagdeo retained a strong base of support despite a series of government scandals relating to sex, drugs, and credible allegations that police officers had tortured criminal suspects. Charges of corruption and police brutality spiked in 2009, with formal complaints increasing by 11 percent.

Guyana gained independence from Britain in 1966 and was ruled by the autocratic, predominantly Afro-Guyanese People's National Congress party (PNC) for the next 26 years. In 1992, Cheddi Jagan of the largely Indo-Guyanese People's Progressive Party (PPP) won the presidency in Guyana's first free and fair elections. He died in 1997, and the office passed to his wife, Janet, who resigned in 1999 for health reasons. She was succeeded by Finance Minister Bharrat Jagdeo of the PPP-C, an alliance of the PPP and the Civic Party. President Jagdeo was elected in his own right in 2001.

Guyanese politics are dominated by a tense split between descendants of indentured workers from India, known as Indo-Guyanese, who make up about half of the population and generally back the PPP-C, and Afro-Guyanese, who compose 36 percent of the population and largely support the PNC-R.

In 2004, the political climate showed brief signs of improving when the two main parties, the PPP-C and PNC-R, announced that they had reached agreement on a wide variety of issues. However, the emerging harmony was disrupted when a police informant revealed the existence of death squads that enjoyed official sanction and had killed some 64 people. An investigation exposed apparent links to the home affairs minister, Ronald Gajraj, but he was largely exonerated by an official inquiry in 2005.

Violence escalated in 2006 ahead of that year's elections. In the spring, Agriculture Minister Satyadeo Sawh was brutally slain by masked gunmen, and four newspaper employees were shot dead on the outskirts of the capital in early August. The National Assembly was dissolved amid acrimony and mudslinging, and the elections were delayed by several weeks, as deep conflicts within the seven-member Guyana Elections Commission undermined the credibility of the process. Despite those concerns, the elections unfolded without incident in August, due in part to the heavy presence of international observers.

President Jagdeo handily won another five-year term, as his PPP-C received 54 percent of the vote and 36 seats in the 65-member National Assembly. The main opposition PNC-Reform party (PNC-R) won 34 percent of the vote and 21 seats. A new party, the Alliance for Change (AFC), won 5 seats, and two minor parties, the United Force and the Justice for All Party, each won a single seat. The emergence of the multiracial AFC suggested that the fierce racial divide of Guyanese politics was on the wane. Nevertheless, relations between the government and opposition remained tense.

In 2009, President Jagdeo's strong support fueled speculation that he may seek to amend the constitution and seek a third term. While denying such claims, it remained unclear who his party would choose as a successor. Meanwhile, opposition leader Robert Corbin of the PNC-R led demonstrations and publicly charged that the Jagdeo government had links to convicted drug trafficker Robert Khan. The government also faced an array of lesser scandals. A former army chief forged paperwork in relation to an adoption application, and the U.S. visa of the president's press secretary was revoked for soliciting sex with a teenager. Additionally, Guyanese policemen were accused of torturing three suspects held in connection with a murder investigation, including a 15 year-old-boy whose genitals were doused with flammable liquid and set ablaze by local authorities.

Political Rights and Civil Liberties: Guyana is an electoral democracy. The 1980 constitution provides for a strong president and a 65-seat National Assembly, elected every five years. An Assembly Speaker is also elected, and two additional, nonvoting members are appointed by the president. The leader of the party with a plurality of parliamentary seats becomes president for a five-year term, and appoints the prime minister and cabinet.

The 2006 elections strengthened the hand of the ruling PPP-C but also demonstrated that some Guyanese are beginning to vote across racial lines, as symbolized by the establishment of the multiracial AFC. The main opposition party remains the PNC-R. Other significant political parties or groupings include the Alliance for Guyana, the Guyana Labor Party, the United Force, the Justice for All Party, the Working People's Alliance, and the Guyana Action Party, which enjoys strong support from indigenous communities in the south.

Guyana was ranked 126 out of 180 countries surveyed in Transparency International's 2009 Corruption Perceptions Index, the worst ranking in the English-speaking Caribbean. The country is a transshipment point for South American cocaine destined for North America and Europe, and counternarcotics efforts are undermined by corruption that reaches to high levels of the government. The informal economy is driven primarily by drug proceeds and may be equal to between 40 and 60 percent of formal economic activity.

Several independent newspapers operate freely, including the daily *Stabroek News* and *Kaieteur News*. The state owns and operates the country's sole radio station, which broadcasts on three frequencies. However, Guyana's courts ruled in 2009 that this represented an unfair media monopoly, and the government pledged to introduce new broadcast legislation to rectify it. In October 2009, police arrested opposition activist Mark Benschop during a search of his home, citing illegal radio transmission, but Benschop was exonerated of terrorism charges and released in November. Seventeen privately owned television stations freely criticize the government, although in March 2009, the government urged CNS TV not to air the opposition party program *AFC on the Move*, and the program was subsequently dropped. In 2009, the Guyana Press Association denounced a government initiative to license media professionals as an attempt to impose control over the profession. Opposition party leaders complain that they lack access to the state media. There are no government restrictions on the internet.

Guyanese generally enjoy freedom of religion, and the government does not restrict academic freedom.

The government largely respects freedoms of assembly and association in practice. The right to form labor unions is also generally upheld, and unions are well organized. However, employers are not required to recognize unions in former state enterprises that have been sold off by the government.

The judicial system is independent, but due process is undermined by shortages of staff and funds. In 2005, Guyana cut all ties to the Privy Council in London, the court of last resort for other former British colonies in the region, and adopted the Trinidad-based Caribbean Court of Justice as its highest appellate court. Prisons are overcrowded, and conditions are poor.

The Guyana Defence Force and the national Guyana Police Force are under civilian control. Racial polarization has seriously eroded law enforcement, with many Indo-Guyanese complaining that they are victimized by Afro-Guyanese criminals and ignored by the predominantly Afro-Guyanese police. Meanwhile, many Afro-

Guyanese claim that the police are manipulated by the government for its own purposes. Official inquiries have repeatedly pointed to the need for improved investigative techniques, more funding, community-oriented policing, better disciplinary procedures, greater accountability, and a better ethnic balance in the police force, but the government has taken few concrete steps to implement the proposed reforms. A series of violent crimes in 2008 left over 30 dead, raising public concerns about government ineffectiveness. Security forces responded forcefully to a July 2009 arson attack on the Ministry of Health, and an increase in reported police brutality followed. Formal complaints against corruption and police brutality increased by 11 percent in 2009, representing one complaint every two days. There were 78 unique allegations of unlawful arrest and 46 complaints of excessive use of police force throughout the year. In October, two police officers were charged following evidence that they had tortured three murder suspects, including lighting a teenager's genitals on fire. The officers were granted bail and the case remained unresolved at year's end.

Guyana is home to nine indigenous groups with a total population of about 80,000. Human rights violations against them, particularly with respect to land and resource use, are widespread and pervasive. Indigenous people's attempts to seek redress through the courts have been met with unwarranted delays by the judiciary. While racial clashes have diminished in the last decade, long-standing animosity between Afro- and Indo-Guyanese remains a serious concern. A Racial Hostility Bill passed in 2002 increased the penalties for race-based crimes. Guyana appointed its first female and first indigenous foreign minister in April 2008.

Domestic violence and violence against women in general are widespread. Rape, is illegal, but often goes unreported and is infrequently prosecuted. Furthermore, spousal rape is considered a lesser offense. In 2009, 60 persons were charged with rape, and a quarter were found guilty. Over 250 persons were charged with statutory rape, resulting in only 22 convictions. There is no pre-determined sentence for a rape conviction, and the average prison time ranges from 5 to 10 years in the event of a guilty verdict. The Guyana Human Rights Association has charged that the legal system's treatment of victims of sexual violence is intentionally humiliating. Sodomy is punishable with a maximum sentence of life in prison. Guyana has the second-highest HIV prevalence rate in Latin America and the Caribbean.

Haiti

Political Rights: 4
Civil Liberties: 5
Status: Partly Free

Population: 9,242,000
Capital: Port-au-Prince

Ten-Year Ratings Timeline For Year Under Review (Political Rights, Civil Liberties, Status)

2000	2001	2002	2003	2004	2005	2006	2007	2008	2009
6,5NF	6,6NF	6,6NF	6,6NF	7,6NF	7,6NF	4,5PF	4,5PF	4,5PF	4,5PF

Overview: Haitian politics remained turbulent in 2009. Following a vote of no confidence by the parliament, Prime Minister Michele Pierre-Louis was forced from her post in October after only a year in office. President Rene Preval named planning minister Jean-Max Bellerive as her replacement, and the appointment was quickly ratified by the parliament.

Since gaining independence from France in 1804 following a slave revolt, the Republic of Haiti has endured a history of poverty, violence, instability, and dictatorship. A 1986 military coup ended 29 years of rule by the Duvalier family, and the army held power for most of the next eight years. Under international pressure, the military in 1987 permitted the implementation of a French-style constitution, which remains in place today.

Jean-Bertrand Aristide, a popular former priest, was first elected president in 1990. He was deposed and exiled by a military triumvirate after only eight months in office. While paramilitary thugs terrorized the populace, the ruling junta engaged in blatant narcotics trafficking. The United States and the United Nations imposed a trade and oil embargo, and in 1994, the United Nations authorized a multinational force to restore the legitimate Haitian authorities. In September 1994, facing an imminent U.S. invasion, the military rulers stepped down. U.S. troops took control of the country, and Aristide was reinstated. He dismantled the military before the June 1995 parliamentary elections, but his support began to fracture when international observers questioned the legitimacy of the balloting. Aristide retained the backing of the more radical Lavalas Family (FL) party, which won an overwhelming parliamentary majority.

The FL nominated Rene Preval, who had been Aristide's prime minister in 1991, as its next presidential candidate, despite the fact that he was not a party member. Preval won the 1995 election and took office in February 1996. The United Nations had planned to withdraw its troops by the end of the month, but the new U.S.-trained Haitian National Police (HNP) lacked the competence to fill the void. The UN force extended its stay at Preval's urging, but cut its presence to 1,300 troops by June; the U.S. combat force had withdrawn two months earlier.

Aristide was voted back into the presidency in November 2000. The election was boycotted by all major opposition parties and held amid widespread civil unrest and voter intimidation. Aristide ran on a populist platform of economic revitalization; opponents claimed that he was bent on establishing a one-party state. His win with nearly 92 percent of the ballots followed similar results in that year's parliamentary elections, which gave his supporters 80 percent of the seats in the lower house and all but one seat in the upper house.

Despite the electoral victory, Aristide's second term as president was undermined by business elites and opposition groups who banded together to oppose him. Furthermore, foreign donors had cut their aid programs in 2000, when a standoff between Aristide and his opponents delayed the elections, and poverty had worsened. An armed revolt, led by a combination of political gangs and former army officers, threatened the president's hold on power in February 2004. The United States and France declined to send peacekeepers in the absence of a political settlement between Aristide and opposition groups. Faced with the possibility of a violent ouster, Aristide was spirited out of the country in a plane chartered by the United States and deposited in the Central African Republic. He denounced the circumstances of his departure, but eventually accepted exile in South Africa.

Aristide's sudden resignation was quickly papered over by a constitutional transition that elevated Boniface Alexandre, head of the Supreme Court, to the position of president. Prime Minister Yvon Neptune, an Aristide ally, agreed to remain in office to help the transition process, but was later jailed by the interim government. Political decay continued throughout the rest of the country. In March 2004, Gerard Latortue, a former foreign minister and longtime UN official, was named interim prime minister. Meanwhile, the UN peacekeeping force gradually expanded beyond the capital and was renewed with troop contributions from Brazil and other Latin American countries. The force eventually reached 9,000 troops and civilian police, and the United Nations extended its mandate several times.

Haitian electoral authorities held presidential and legislative elections in February 2006, with a second round of parliamentary elections in April. Despite initial turbulence when some polling stations opened late, the voting was deemed the cleanest and fairest in Haitian history, and turnout surpassed 50 percent. The elections yielded evidence of both political consensus and continued fragmentation. Former president Preval won a second term with 51 percent of the vote, triumphing over at least 33 other contenders, but his newly organized Lespwa party failed to win a majority in either house of parliament. Lespwa captured just over a third of the Senate seats and a quarter of the seats in the Chamber of Deputies. In December 2006, municipal elections were held successfully, along with a final round of voting to decide a handful of unresolved parliamentary races. Security improved the following year after UN forces cracked down on gangs in the capital.

Haiti entered a period of turmoil when the parliament forced out Prime Minister Jacques-Edouard Alexis amid rising food prices in April 2008 and then rejected the president's two initial nominees to replace him. Michele Pierre-Louis was finally approved as a compromise candidate in September, but she was dismissed by parliament in October 2009, following a contentious debate over allegations that hurricane recovery funds had been misspent, though the charge was never proven. Despite fears that Pierre-Louis's removal would spark new instability, the nomination and confirmation of her replacement, former planning minister Jean-Max Bellerive, occurred within two weeks, marking a succession that was surprisingly orderly. Elections to replace one third of the Haitian Senate were held in April, with a runoff in June, amid widespread disinterest and low voter turnout; Lespwa won 5 of the 11 seats contested in the runoff, thereby maintaining a legislative plurality in the parliament's upper chamber.

In order to ensure the country's stability in the short term, the UN Security Council extended the peacekeeping force's mandate until October 2010.

Political Rights and Civil Liberties: Haiti is an electoral democracy. In 2006, citizens changed their government in the most credible elections since 1990. The country's 1987 constitution provides for a president elected for a five-year term, a National Assembly composed of the 30-member Senate and the 99-member Chamber of Deputies, and a prime minister appointed by the president. Senators are elected for six-year terms, with one-third coming up for election every two years, deputies for four-year terms. There are no legislative term limits, but the president cannot serve consecutive terms. Many lawmakers remain sorely short of financial and administrative resources, and the parliament itself has played a largely reactive role in government, either opposing or accepting initiatives from the executive branch.

The legislature is currently divided among several small parties, with no single faction holding a majority. Most parties are driven by personality or support from a particular region. President Rene Preval's first-round election victory in 2006 helped to sweep many candidates from his untested Lespwa party into the parliament, although the party's grassroots support was not very substantial.

Endemic corruption continues to hobble Haiti's political and economic development. A number of lawmakers elected in 2006 have reportedly been involved in criminal activities, and they sought parliament seats primarily to obtain immunity from prosecution. Preval identified the fight against corruption as a major priority, demanding full disclosure of financial records for top government officials. Haiti was ranked 168 out of 180 countries surveyed in Transparency International's 2009 Corruption Perceptions Index.

Freedom of the press has been constrained by the absence of a viable judicial system and widespread insecurity, and violence against journalists remains a problem. Media outlets tend to practice self-censorship to avoid violent retribution for critical reporting. Haiti has two main newspapers, *Le Nouvelliste* and *Le Matin*, each with print runs of about 15,000. About five people are estimated to read each copy, which brings their total readership to about 75,000, including both Haitians and expatriates living in Haiti. The country also has three weekly news bulletins: the middle-of-the-road *Haiti en Marche*, the left-wing *Haiti Progres*, and the conservative *Haiti Observateur*. More than 90 percent of Haitians have access to radio, and more than 290 stations operate without a license on FM bandwidth. There are more than 70 community radio stations, often linked with political groups or parties. Television stations, by contrast, are far less common, with about 20 in Port-au-Prince and another 15 in the provinces. Several television stations have been established in recent years by radio station and newspaper owners seeking to increase their influence, but the total television audience in Haiti is below 10 percent due to lack of electricity and resources.

The government generally respects religious and academic freedoms. However, the absence of an effective police force means that there is little protection for those who are persecuted for their views.

Freedoms of assembly and association, including labor rights, are not respected in practice. Haiti has rich civil society traditions at the local level, but many of its formally organized civil society groupings have been co-opted by political and economic elites. Unions are too weak to engage in collective bargaining, and their organizing efforts are undermined by the country's high unemployment rate. In 2009, parliament ratified new labor regulations, including a stratified minimum wage system for the commercial and industrial sectors and minimum health and safety standards. Still, the minimum wage increases applied to only a small segment of the population, and enforcement of standards remained weak.

The judicial system continues to be corrupt, inefficient, and dysfunctional. It is burdened by a large backlog of cases, outdated legal codes, and poor facilities. Moreover, official business is conducted in French rather than Creole. Prison conditions are harsh, and the ponderous legal system guarantees lengthy pretrial detentions. In 2009, Amnesty International estimated that Haitian authorities are holding thousands of people without charge, mainly due to poor judicial functioning.

Haiti's police force virtually collapsed during the 2004 uprising and is only slowly evolving into a cohesive organization. Hundreds of police officers suspected of corruption have been purged from the HNP, and new recruitment and training expanded the total police force from 5,700 officers in 2006 to more than 11,000 in 2009, though the force was still far short of its target of 15,000 officers. Haiti's current police chief is well respected and has made important strides in purging corrupt officers and training new recruits. The UN peacekeeping force has helped to establish a minimum level of security in some parts of the country, but the HNP remains unprepared to take over in the peacekeepers' absence.

The trafficking of drugs and people remained a serious problem in 2009. There is widespread violence against women and children in Haiti. Up to 300,000 children serve in *restavec* ("live with," in Creole), a form of unpaid domestic labor with a long history in the country.

Honduras

Political Rights: 4*
Civil Liberties: 4*
Status: Partly Free

Population: 7,466,000
Capital: Tegucigalpa

Ratings Change: Honduras's political rights and civil liberties ratings declined from 3 to 4 due to the forced exile of President Manuel Zelaya and subsequent restrictions on citizens' civil liberties.

Ten-Year Ratings Timeline For Year Under Review (Political Rights, Civil Liberties, Status)

2000	2001	2002	2003	2004	2005	2006	2007	2008	2009
3,3PF	3,3PF	3,3PF	3,3PF	3,3PF	3,3PF	3,3PF	3,3PF	3,3PF	4,4PF

Overview: Democratically elected president Manuel Zelaya was deposed and forced into exile in a June 2009 coup that was widely condemned by the international community. The resulting de facto regime, led by Congress president Roberto Micheletti, oversaw the systematic violation of civil liberties by security forces, including the freedoms of assembly and the press. Zelaya managed to return to the country in September, but he was confined to the Brazilian embassy, and the de facto authorities refused to reinstate him as they pressed forward with the previously scheduled national elections in November. Porfirio Lobo Sosa of the National Party won the presidential vote and was due to take office in early 2010.

The Republic of Honduras was established in 1839, some 18 years after independence from Spain. The country endured decades of military rule and intermittent elected governments, with the last military regime giving way to civilian authorities in 1982. However, the military remained powerful in the subsequent decades; the first president to exercise his constitutional authority to veto the military and choose its leaders did so in 1999.

Under civilian rule, power has alternated between the Liberal Party (PL) and the National Party (PN). In the 2005 elections, Jose Manuel Zelaya Rosales of the PL defeated the PN's Porfirio Lobo Sosa to win the presidency. The PL also took control of Congress, winning 62 of the 128 seats. The PN was left with 55 seats, and three minor parties split the remainder. The run-up to the balloting had been marred by political violence that left several PL supporters injured and at least two dead.

Under Zelaya's administration, political polarization increased in an environment characterized by poor policy performance and faltering public institutions. The president deepened the country's political divisions, including within his own party, and pitted factions of the political and business elite against one another through increasingly populist posturing. In 2008, he brought Honduras into two Venezuelan-led regional trade initiatives, Petrocaribe and the Bolivarian Alternative for the Americas (ALBA), drawing objections from business organizations, the opposition, and elements of his own government.

Zelaya announced in March 2009 that he would push forward with a highly controversial overhaul of Honduras's constitution, including the elimination of presidential term limits. His opponents interpreted the proposal as a power grab, although the constitutional reform process would have begun only after the end of his nonrenewable four-year term in 2010. Zelaya's plan to hold a nonbinding referendum in June to gauge support for the overhaul sparked a political crisis, and in May, the president of Congress, Roberto Micheletti of the PL, declared that the proposed reforms were prohibited by the constitution and the June balloting would be illegal. The military, siding with Micheletti, announced that it would not participate in the mobilization of ballots, as is customary during Honduran elections. In response, Zelaya dismissed army commander Romeo Vasquez on June 24, in addition to accepting the resignation of Defense Minister Angel Edmundo Orellana. The following day, the Supreme Court ordered General Vasquez's reinstatement on the grounds that there was no reason for his removal. Zelaya refused, and led a group of supporters to collect ballots for the referendum, vowing to follow through with the vote as scheduled.

On June 28, the day of the intended poll, armed soldiers abducted Zelaya from the presidential palace and forcibly deported him to Costa Rica. Congress accepted a forged letter of resignation later that day and named Micheletti the acting president. While Micheletti argued that Zelaya's removal was allowed by the constitution, the international community condemned the coup and continued to recognize Zelaya as the legitimate president of Honduras. Both the UN General Assembly and the Organization of American States demanded Zelaya's reinstatement.

The de facto government curtailed civil and political liberties in the months after the coup. It imposed nationwide curfews that sometimes lasted up to 72 hours, often with little notice, and violently suppressed public demonstrations of support for Zelaya's reinstatement, reportedly resulting in the deaths of several protesters. Many media outlets and journalists reported harassment and threats, in addition to frequent power outages and blocked transmissions. The authorities temporarily shut down two radio stations and a television station in September, raiding their offices and confiscating equipment. Civil society organizations and human rights defenders also faced harassment, reporting increased surveillance, threats, and physical assaults. Many of these abuses were carried out under an executive decree issued by Micheletti in late September. It suspended civil liberties for 45 days, granting the police new powers of detention, banning all public meetings, and effectively licensing the security forces to act without regard for human rights or the rule of law. Micheletti reversed the decree under international pressure on October 5.

Zelaya succeeded in reentering the country on September 21, but took refuge in the Brazilian embassy, where he remained through the end of the year under threat of arrest by the de facto government. The international community fostered lengthy negotiations aimed at reinstating Zelaya and allowing him to serve out his legal term; many countries warned that they would not recognize the upcoming national elections, long scheduled for November, if the coup leaders refused to comply. Nevertheless, the talks repeatedly broke down, and the de facto authorities pressed ahead with the elections. Porfirio Lobo Sosa of the PN, Zelaya's opponent in 2005, won the presidency with 56 percent of the ballots, defeating Zelaya's vice president, Elvin Santos Lozano of the PL. The PN captured 71 seats in Congress, followed by the PL with 45 and three smaller parties with the remainder. While Zelaya had called for a boycott and turnout was reportedly below 50 percent, it was apparently not much lower than in previous elections. Lobo's inauguration was set for January 2010.

Honduras's 2009 political crisis severely inhibited economic activity, isolated the country from major trading partners, and combined with the global economic downturn to exacerbate existing poverty. In September 2009, the Central Bank announced that remittances from Hondurans working abroad dropped by 13.1 percent during the first eight months of the year, due to recession in the United States.

Political Rights and Civil Liberties: Honduras is not an electoral democracy. Elected president Manuel Zelaya was forcibly removed by the military in a June 2009 coup, and although his term ran through January 2010, he had not been reinstated by year's end. Roberto Micheletti, the president of Congress, was named the interim leader, and his de facto government oversaw previously scheduled general elections on November 29. Amid a climate of severely compromised civil liberties and press freedoms, November's elections were generally considered to have met international standards and resulted in a win for conservative candidate Porfirio Lobo.

The president and the 128-member, unicameral National Congress are elected for four-year terms; the president is limited to one term. The proportion of the votes received by a party's presidential candidate determines its representation in Congress. The PL was the ruling party at the time of the coup, with the PN in opposition and three smaller parties also holding seats. The PL then fractured between Zelaya supporters and opponents, and the PN won a majority in the November elections. The military has long exerted considerable influence on civilian governments.

Official corruption continues to cast a shadow over the political scene. Army officers have been found guilty of involvement in drug trafficking and related cartel conflicts. A 2006 transparency law was marred by claims that it contained amendments designed to protect corrupt politicians. In 2007, three commissioners were appointed to the regulatory Access to Public Information Institute in a reportedly politicized manner. Long-standing civil society complaints of corruption among the political and business elite led to the creation in May 2008 of the Comprehensive Movement for Dignity and Justice (MADJ), an umbrella group that included social and religious organizations, trade unions, and prosecutors. In April 2008, 25 prosecutors staged a 38-day hunger strike to protest the unwillingness of the attorney general's office to investigate alleged acts of corruption. The group also objected to a new law creating a criminal investigative unit within the office of the attorney general, arguing that it would concentrate power in the hands of corrupt officials. Honduras was ranked 130 out of 180 countries surveyed in Transparency International's 2009 Corruption Perceptions Index.

The authorities systematically violated the constitution's press freedom guarantees in 2009. The de facto government regularly restricted press coverage, shutting down the operations of Radio Globo, Radio Catracha, and television's Channel 36 for a period in September and October. Numerous radio and television stations reported harassment that included police surveillance, police assault, threats, blocked transmissions, and power outages. Three journalists were murdered during the year, in each case by unidentified gunmen. Two of the killings occurred well before the coup, and none appeared to be directly related to the political situation. Authorities linked at least one of the murders, that of Rafael Munguia Ortiz of Radio Cadena Voces in March 2009, to the victim's reporting on organized crime. Separately, in July police beat and temporarily detained a journalist with the state-owned Radio Nacional de Honduras.

Media ownership is concentrated in the hands of a few powerful business interests, and although the Supreme Court struck down restrictive defamation laws in 2005, many journalists practice self-censorship. Lack of access to public officials and information is a significant obstacle for reporters. Payments to journalists and manipulation of state advertising are reportedly used to secure favorable coverage or silence criticism. There is generally unrestricted access to the internet, but access was impaired following the coup by multiple politically motivated power outages and cuts in telephone service.

Freedom of religion is typically respected, though religious gatherings were included in the de facto government's announcement of restrictions on freedom of assembly in October 2009. Academic freedom is also usually honored, but scholars have faced pressure to support the privatization of the national university, and academic critics of the coup were subject to harassment in 2009.

Constitutional guarantees on the freedoms of assembly and association were not observed in 2009, and in late September, an executive decree suspended civil liberties for several days, including a ban on public meetings. The de facto government's October announcement on freedom of assembly required all public meetings and marches to be registered with the police 24 hours in advance. Security forces have violently suppressed peaceful demonstrations. More than a dozen civilians were killed during or after their participation in anticoup demonstrations in 2009, and more than 1,200 protesters were arrested.

The 2006 Citizen Participation Law protects the role of civil society groups and individuals in the democratic process. Labor unions are well organized and can strike, but labor actions often result in clashes with security forces. Labor, gay and transgender rights, land rights, environmental, and Afro-Honduran activists are regularly victims of threats and repression. In 2008, security officials at the National Autonomous University of Honduras seized a "blacklist" of 135 public figures from two plainclothes policemen who had been following the president of the student union. The list included indigenous and labor leaders, lawmakers, journalists, and clergy, many of whom were marked for surveillance. Human rights defenders and political activists faced significant threats following the coup in 2009, including harassment, surveillance, and detentions. A number of coup opponents and activists were murdered, including two members of the leftist Democratic Unification Party—a labor leader and a peasants' rights activist—who were killed on the same day in July, and an indigenous leader killed in October. Some individuals with links to the military or the coup leaders were also killed during the year. The motives and identities of the perpetrators of the various attacks were often unclear.

The judicial system is weak and inefficient, and there are reportedly high levels of politicization. The vast majority of inmates are awaiting trial, prison conditions are harsh, and the facilities are notoriously overcrowded. Two prison riots in 2008 left 27 inmates dead. There is an official human rights ombudsman, but critics claim that the office's work is politicized. In 2009, Human Rights Watch accused the attorney general's office of blocking investigations into human rights violations.

While the murder rate has dropped from the 1999 figure of 154 per 100,000 inhabitants, it remains among the highest in the region. Figures for 2009 are unknown, partly due to government censorship of politically motivated murders. Most homicides are attributed to youth gangs, including transnational groups like Mara Salvatrucha (MS-13) and 18th Street, or to Mexican drug-trafficking cartels that have become active in Honduras. However, the repression and violence associated with the coup resulted in an increase in deadly attacks on members of the Frente Nacional de Resistencia Popular (FNRP), a social movement against the coup. The violence is exacerbated by the presence of an estimated 600,000 firearms in private hands, only 40 percent of which are registered. The government has made membership in a gang punishable by up to 12 years in prison and uses the military to help maintain order. However, police officers and other vigilantes have committed extrajudicial killings, arbitrary arrests, and illegal searches. Hundreds of juveniles have reportedly been killed in "social cleansing" campaigns. The United States suspended nonhumanitarian aid to Honduras in the wake of the 2009 coup, potentially hampering government counternarcotics efforts.

Indigenous and Afro-Honduran residents have faced various abuses by property developers and their allies in recent years, including corrupt titling processes and acts of violence. In October 2009, the authorities raided a Garifuna-run community hospital in Ciriboya and eliminated physician stipends; the Fraternal Organization of Black Hondurans claimed that the hospital takeover was retaliation for Garifuna opposition to the coup.

Women remain vulnerable to exploitation by employers, particularly in the low-wage *maquiladora* (assembly plant) export sector. Child labor is a problem in rural areas and in the informal economy. The nongovernmental organization Casa Alianza has estimated that as many as 10,000 children are working as prostitutes. According to UNESCO, 29 percent of Honduran children drop out of school before the fifth grade, and youths head about 10 percent of households. The overall population is dominated by young people: 41 percent are under 15, and 20 percent are aged 15 to 24. The U.S. State Department's 2009 Trafficking in Persons Report ranked Honduras as a Tier 2 country, finding that while it does not fully comply with minimum international standards to combat trafficking, the government is making efforts to do so. The report also found that criminal gangs' use of forced child labor is a serious concern.

Hungary

Political Rights: 1
Civil Liberties: 1
Status: Free

Population: 10,024,000
Capital: Budapest

Ten-Year Ratings Timeline For Year Under Review (Political Rights, Civil Liberties, Status)

2000	2001	2002	2003	2004	2005	2006	2007	2008	2009
1,2F	1,2F	1,2F	1,2F	1,1F	1,1F	1,1F	1,1F	1,1F	1,1F

Overview:　　Prime Minister Ferenc Gyurcsany announced his resignation in March 2009 and was replaced by Economy Minister Gordon Bajnai in April. Right-wing parties dominated Hungary's European Parliament elections in June, as the ruling Hungarian Socialist Party was accused of failing to implement adequate reforms amid the global economic crisis. Also in 2009, the Romany community faced a wave of violent attacks.

Hungary achieved full independence from the Austro-Hungarian Empire following World War I, though it lost large portions of its previous territory. Soviet occupation after World War II led to communist rule, and Soviet troops crushed an uprising by Hungarians seeking to liberalize the political and economic system in 1956. However, in the late 1980s, the ruling Hungarian Socialist Workers' Party came under intense pressure to accept reforms. Free parliamentary elections were held in 1990, and over the next decade, power alternated between conservative and socialist blocs, both of which pursued European integration. Hungary formally entered the European Union (EU) in May 2004.

A ruling coalition of the Hungarian Socialist Party (MSzP) and the Alliance of Free Democrats (SzDSz) won reelection in April 2006, taking 210 seats in the National Assembly after a campaign in which Viktor Orban, leader of the conservative opposition Fidesz party, stressed populist themes. In September 2006, comments that Prime Minister Ferenc Gyurcsany had made at a closed party meeting in May, in which he admitted that his government had repeatedly lied to the electorate about its budgetary and economic performance, were leaked to the press. The revelation sparked major riots and severely damaged public confidence in the government as it struggled to rein in budget deficit equal to 9 percent of gross domestic product.

In late March 2008, the SzDSz withdrew from the coalition to protest the unilateral dismissal of the health minister, leaving the government with just 190 of the 386 parliament seats. However, the prime minister shuffled the cabinet and rejected calls for a confidence vote. In March 2009, Gyurcsany announced his resignation amid accusations that he had failed to address adequately the country's fiscal problems in the face of a global economic crisis that struck in late 2008. Following a constructive vote of no confidence in April, Economy Minister Gordon Bajnai, an independent, was approved as the new prime minister with support from the MSzP and SzDSz.

In the June 2009 European Parliament elections, Fidesz won 14 of Hungary's 22 seats, and the MSzP took 4. The Movement for a Better Hungary (Jobbik), a far-right party, won three seats, and the SzDSz carried only one.

Political Rights and Civil Liberties:

Hungary is an electoral democracy. Voters elect representatives every four years to the 386-seat, unicameral National Assembly under a mixed system of proportional and direct representation. The National Assembly elects both the president, whose duties are mainly ceremonial, and the prime minister. Elections in Hungary have been generally free and fair since the end of communist rule.

The main political parties are the MSzP and the conservative Fidesz, which has adopted an increasingly nationalist stance in recent years. The liberal SzDSz, which supports free-market policies, is the third-largest party but only narrowly cleared the 5 percent vote threshold to enter the parliament in 2002 and 2006.

Hungary's constitution guarantees the right of ethnic minorities to form self-governing bodies, and all 13 recognized minorities have done so. Despite the large population of Roma, only a small number have been elected to the National Assembly in recent elections. In March 2007, local minority representatives for the first time elected county-level governing bodies. However, the entities are limited to cultural affairs and lack jurisdiction over housing, education, and health matters.

Successive governments have introduced stronger penalties for bribery and implemented a long-term anticorruption strategy, though analysts raised questions about illegal campaign funding methods after the heated 2006 parliamentary elections. In December 2009, the parliament passed a new anticorruption bill that included the creation of a national anti-graft office, changes to public procurement legislation, and whistle-blower protections. However, President Laszlo Solyom returned parts of the legislation for parliament's review at year's end. Hungary was ranked 46 out of 180 countries surveyed in Transparency International's 2009 Corruption Perceptions Index.

Freedom of speech is respected, and independent media operate freely, albeit within a highly polarized atmosphere. Political controversy continues to trouble state television and radio, with opposition parties accusing the government of improperly attempting to influence content. Hungary's National Television and Radio Commission (ORTT) came under significant criticism in October 2009 for awarding the only two national commercial radio licenses to frequencies with suspected connections to the ruling and opposition Fidesz. The ORTT chairman subsequently resigned over the controversy, and an investigation into the tenders was pending at year's end. Foreign ownership of Hungarian media is extensive, but the successful introduction of private Hungarian television stations has challenged the argument that state-supported media are necessary for balanced coverage. Internet access is unrestricted.

The constitution guarantees religious freedom and provides for the separation of church and state. While adherents of all religions are generally free to worship in their own manner, the state provides financial support to four "historical" religious groups: the Roman Catholic Church, the Calvinist Church, the Lutheran Church, and the Alliance of Hungarian Jewish Communities. The state does not restrict academic freedom.

The constitution provides for freedoms of assembly and association, and the government generally respects these rights in practice. Nongovernmental organizations (NGOs) operate without restrictions, and a number of them mounted peaceful demonstrations in August 2009 to counter the rise in far-right rallies. Police used tear gas to prevent antigovernment protesters from reaching the parliament in March 2009, and made 35 arrests. In July, police again used tear gas to disperse crowds attending a demonstration by the far-right Hungarian Guard (Magyar Garda) and arrested 216 protesters. The Supreme Court upheld a ban on the Hungarian Guard in December on the grounds that its activities incited fear and hatred.

The government respects workers' rights to form associations, strike, and petition public authorities. Trade unions represent less than 30 percent of the workforce. Jobbik and the Ready to Act Hungarian Police (TMRSZ) trade union signed a cooperation agreement in May 2009, but an investigation by the public prosecutor's office found the deal unlawful in that it violated police political neutrality.

Hungary has an independent judiciary. Courts are generally fair, but the judiciary in recent years has faced criticism for lax regulations on asset statements and conflict of interest for judges. While Roma make up only about 10 percent of the population, they account for an estimated 50 percent of prison inmates, fueling accusations of police discrimination. NGOs raised concerns in 2009 over multiple complaints of harassment and excessive use of force against Romany detainees. Prisons are generally approaching Western European standards, though overcrowding, inadequate medical care, and poor sanitation remain problems.

Hungary has taken a number of steps to improve monitoring of Romany legal rights and treatment, but the community continues to face widespread discrimination, and Roma are five times more likely to live in poverty than the population as a whole. Increasing violence against Roma led to four deaths in 2009, and rising insecurity forced Romany men to patrol their own neighborhoods. Four men were arrested in August in connection with the recent string of arson attacks and deadly shootings.

In September 2009, the parliament passed a new civil code to fulfill obligations under the UN Convention on the Rights of Persons with Disabilities (CRPD). Under the previous code, the disabled were placed under guardianship and seriously restricted in their decision making with respect to place of residence, marriage, property, and employment. The new civil code bans plenary guardianship and grants the disabled more independence, though it had not taken effect by year's end. Separately, in a step forward for sexual minorities, the legal option of registered partnerships for same-sex couples became available in July 2009, having been approved by the parliament in 2007.

Women possess the same legal rights as men, but they face hiring and pay discrimination and tend to be underrepresented in high-level business and government positions. Women hold only 35 of 386 seats in the National Assembly. Rape, including rape within marriage, is recognized as a crime in the penal code, but a 2007 Amnesty International report found that women are overwhelmingly reluctant to report rapes and face widespread prejudice when it comes to prosecuting such cases. Hungary is a transit point, but also a source and destination country, for trafficked persons, including women trafficked for prostitution.

Iceland

Political Rights: 1
Civil Liberties: 1
Status: Free

Population: 321,000
Capital: Reykjavik

Ten-Year Ratings Timeline For Year Under Review (Political Rights, Civil Liberties, Status)

2000	2001	2002	2003	2004	2005	2006	2007	2008	2009
1,1F	1,1F	1,1F	1,1F	1,1F	1,1F	1,1F	1,1F	1,1F	1,1F

Overview: The credit crisis that began in late 2008 and led to an economic collapse in Iceland fueled widespread protests throughout the beginning of 2009. The increasing frequency of demonstrations and escalation of tensions between protesters and police led Prime Minister Geir Haarde to step down in January, creating an historic interim government which was eventually voted into power during early elections in May.

Iceland gained independence from Denmark in 1944. It became a founding member of NATO in 1949, despite having no standing army. The country declared itself a nuclear-free zone in 1985. David Oddsson of the center-right Independence Party (IP), first elected prime minister in 1991, finally stepped down in 2004. He was succeeded by Halldor Asgrimsson of the Progressive Party (PP), the coalition partner of the IP. After a poor government showing in local elections, Asgrimsson resigned the premiership in favor of the IP's Geir Haarde in June 2006.

The ruling coalition broke up following May 2007 parliamentary elections, in which the IP took 25 seats and the PP slipped to 7, leaving the pair with a razor-thin majority in the 63-seat legislature. The IP then formed a new coalition with the center-left Social Democratic Alliance, which held 18 seats, and Haarde returned as prime minister. A credit crisis forced the government to nationalize three large banks in 2008, resulting in widespread protests and Prime Minister Haarde's resignation on January 26, 2009.

In February, Johanna Sigurdardottir was named interim prime minister. Her center-left coalition, consisting of the Social Democratic Alliance and the Left-Green Movement, won early elections in May capturing 34 out of 63 seats, the first time that leftist parties have held a majority in Iceland. Elections also resulted in the highest number of first-time members and the highest percentage of women in parliament in Iceland's history.

While majority of Icelanders are still opposed to European Union (EU) membership, the grim economic situation appeared to alter public attitudes in favor of joining the EU, and the government formally applied for membership in July. Iceland is expected to join before 2011.

Political Rights and Civil Liberties: Iceland is an electoral democracy. The constitution, adopted in 1944, vests power in a president, a prime minister, the 63-seat unicameral legislature (the Althingi), and a judiciary. The president, whose duties are mostly ceremonial, is directly elected for a four-year term. The legislature is also elected for four years, but it can be dissolved for early elections in certain circumstances, as was the case in 2009. The prime minister is appointed by the president but responsible to the legislature. Olafur Ragnar Grimsson was reelected as president in the 2008 elections. The center-right IP dominated politics since the country's independence until May 2009, when Johanna Sigurdardottir's center-left coalition took power. Elections are free, fair, and competitive. Five political parties are represented in the Althingi.

Corruption is generally not a problem for Iceland, although it has experienced politically tinged business-fraud scandals in recent years. The government and leading businessmen were under investigation in 2009 for prior corruption that may have partially caused Iceland's financial collapse in 2008 and 2009, though no conclusions had been made public by the year's end. Iceland was ranked 8 out of 180 countries surveyed in Transparency International's 2009 Corruption Perceptions Index. In response to the Index, a national survey was held in November, indicating that 67 percent of Icelanders consider the level of corruption in government to be high or very high.

The constitution guarantees freedom of speech and of the press. Iceland's wide range of print publications includes both independent and party-affiliated newspapers. The autonomous Icelandic National Broadcasting Service competes with private radio and television stations. Private media ownership is concentrated, with the Nordurljos (Northern Lights) Corporation controlling most of the private television and radio outlets and two out of the three national newspapers. Some reporters practice self-censorship to avoid publishing libelous material. Internet access is unrestricted.

The constitution provides for freedom of religion, though nearly 90 percent of Icelanders belong to the Evangelical Lutheran Church. The state supports the church through a special tax, which citizens can choose to direct to the University of Iceland instead. A 2008 law requires the teaching of theology in grades 1–10. Academic freedom is respected, and the education system is free of excessive political involvement.

Freedoms of association and peaceful assembly are generally upheld. However, protests over Iceland's devastated economy in January 2009 ended when police fired tear gas on crowds, the first time tear gas had been used since NATO protests in 1949. Police also beat several protestors from the environmental organization "Saving Iceland" in August 2009, seriously injuring one woman; the protestors wanted to expose government tax breaks for the aluminum industry. Other large-scale peaceful protests occurred throughout the year against government economic policies. Many nongovernmental organizations operate freely and enjoy extensive government cooperation. The labor movement is robust, with over 80 percent of all eligible workers belonging to unions, though unemployment reached 10 percent in 2009 due to the economic crisis. All unions have the right to strike.

The judiciary is independent. The law does not provide for trial by jury, but many trials and appeals use panels of several judges. The constitution states that all people shall be treated equally before the law, regardless of sex, religion, opinion, ethnic origin, race, property, or other status. However, the charter does not specifically prohibit racial discrimination in other contexts. Prison conditions generally meet international standards.

The Act on Foreigners was amended in 2004 to allow home searches without warrants in cases of suspected immigration fraud, among other changes. Foreigners can vote in municipal elections if they have been residents for at least five years, or three years for citizens of Scandinavian countries. Protests broke out in March 2009, when the Directorate of Immigration decided to deport asylum seekers to Greece; the four men in question were deported in October. One of the men returned to Iceland in December and is appealing his asylum application.

Women enjoy equal rights, and more than 80 percent of women participate in the workforce. A pay gap exists between men and women in spite of laws designed to prevent disparities. While a five-year plan to reduce violence against women was launched in 2006, a 2009 report indicated that 42 percent of women over the age of 16 years have been subject to physical or sexual abuse or have been threatened with such violence. In 2008, the Althingi passed the Act on Equal Status and Equal Rights of Women and Men to advance gender equality. In the May 2009 elections, Johanna Sigurdardottir became the first woman leader of Iceland and the world's first openly lesbian head of state. Women captured nearly 43 percent of seats in the parliament, the highest number in the country's history. The government participates in the Nordic-Baltic Action Group against Human Trafficking. A committee was appointed in 2008 to develop new strategies to combat human trafficking in Iceland. In April 2009, parliament passed a law criminalizing human trafficking.

India

Political Rights: 2
Civil Liberties: 3
Status: Free

Population: 1,171,029,000
Capital: New Delhi

Note: The numerical ratings and status listed above do not reflect conditions in Indian-controlled Kashmir, which is examined in a separate report.

Ten-Year Ratings Timeline For Year Under Review (Political Rights, Civil Liberties, Status)

2000	2001	2002	2003	2004	2005	2006	2007	2008	2009
2,3F	2,3F	2,3F	2,3F	2,3F	2,3F	2,3F	2,3F	2,3F	2,3F

Overview:

The ruling United Progressive Alliance, a coalition led by the Congress Party, won a decisive victory in the April–May 2009 parliamentary elections, allowing Prime Minister Manmohan Singh to remain in office. The Congress-led alliance also maintained its majority in state elections in Maharashtra and Arunachal Pradesh in October, and won a plurality of seats in Haryana. While the year was relatively peaceful, ongoing Maoist and separatist insurgencies contributed to lawlessness and human rights violations in a number of states.

India achieved independence from Britain in 1947, as predominantly Muslim portions of British India were split off to form Pakistan. The centrist, secular Congress Party ruled at the federal level for nearly all of the first 50 years of independence. In the mid-1990s, however, the Hindu nationalist Bharatiya Janata Party (BJP) became a major factor in Parliament, leading a number of subsequent governments. In addition, the pattern shifted from single-party to coalition governments, typically involving large numbers of parties and an increasingly important role for parties based in a single state. The 1990s also featured major economic reform, with a Congress government initiating a shift toward market-oriented policies following a balance-of-payments crisis in 1991.

The BJP, which had held power since 1998, was unexpectedly defeated after calling early national elections in 2004. The Congress Party formed a ruling coalition with a number of regional parties, but Congress leader Sonia Gandhi decided to hand the premiership to former finance minister Manmohan Singh. The new Congress-led United Progressive Alliance (UPA) government agreed to reverse several of the previous government's policies, including controversial antiterrorism legislation and the injection of Hindu nationalist ideology into state-run schools. However, the UPA faced internal rifts and opposition from the Communist Party of India–Marxist, one of its leftist allies, on economic issues such as privatization and labor law reform. The government survived a contentious July 2008 confidence vote in Parliament triggered by the Communists' objections to a nuclear pact with the United States, though the vote was marred by bribery allegations.

The UPA gained strength in the April–May 2009 parliamentary elections, decisively defeating the BJP-led National Democratic Alliance, which remained its closest rival. Congress itself won 206 of 543 lower house seats, compared with 116 for the BJP, and the UPA won 260 seats overall. Moreover, the coalition made alliances with several independent parties, eventually giving it a majority of 322 seats. Mayawatti, the chief minister of Uttar Pradesh and a leader of low-caste Dalits, was thought to be a potential contender for the premiership before the elections, but her Bahujan Samaj Party (BSP) did not perform as well as expected, securing only 21 seats. Average voter turnout over all five phases of the election was approximately 60 percent.

Congress's electoral victory led to a more stable government, though the absence of communist parties from the ruling coalition did not lead to any major economic changes in its first budget, released in July. Liberal attempts to introduce reforms were weakened by India's comparative success during the global economic crisis.

A peace dialogue that began after India and Pakistan came close to war in 2002, but which faltered in 2008 due to a series of terrorist attacks attributed to Islamist militants, resumed in June 2009. The fresh talks came after Pakistan took steps to acknowledge the role of the Pakistani-based militant group Lashkar-e-Taiba in a November 2008 terrorist assault on hotels and other sites in Mumbai that killed 171 people. After a round of talks in July, India and Pakistan issued a joint statement declaring that acts of terrorism would not have any impact on the peace process, although the Indian government was forced to backtrack on the issue following vocal domestic criticism.

Political Rights and Civil Liberties: India is an electoral democracy. Members of the lower house of Parliament, the 545-seat Lok Sabha (House of the People), are directly elected for five-year terms (except for two appointed members representing Indians of European descent). The Lok Sabha determines the leadership and composition of the government. Most members of the less powerful 250-seat upper house, the Rajya Sabha (Council of States), are elected by the state legislatures using a proportional-representation system to serve staggered six-year terms; up to 12 members are appointed. Executive power is vested in a prime minister and cabinet. The president, who plays a largely symbolic role as head of state, is chosen for a five-year term by state and national lawmakers.

Under the supervision of the Election Commission of India (ECI), recent elections have generally been free and fair. The 2009 national polls were generally peaceful, although Maoist militant attacks throughout the country led to 17 deaths during the first phase of voting. Electronic voting machines, also used in 2004 elections, have helped reduce voting day irregularities such as booth capturing. Violence has also declined during state-level elections, which were held in 2009 in Andhra Pradesh, Orissa, Sikkim, Arunachal Pradesh, Maharashtra, and Haryana. Incumbents retained power in all elections. Badly maintained voter lists and the intimidation of voters in some areas continue to be matters of concern, although the ECI has made efforts to make voter lists available online.

A wide range of political parties operate freely. Due to the rising popularity of regional and caste-based parties, coalition governments have become the norm at the national level. The trend toward coalition governments is not as strong at the state level, although larger states are commonly led by coalitions.

Government effectiveness and accountability are undermined by criminality in politics, decrepit state institutions, and widespread corruption. India was ranked 84 out of 180 countries surveyed in Transparency International's 2009 Corruption Perceptions Index. The electoral system depends on "black money" obtained though tax evasion and other means. Politicians and civil servants are regularly caught accepting bribes or engaging in other corrupt behavior, although a great deal of corruption goes unnoticed and unpunished. During the 2009 election campaign, there were widespread allegations of vote buying: police in Andhra Pradesh seized US$600,000 in cash that was allegedly set to be used for bribes, while 500 cases of liquor destined for distribution to voters were seized in Karnataka. Despite laws requiring candidates to declare their financial assets, criminal records, and educational backgrounds, those with links to organized crime or whose election victories were at least in part dependent on unreported money continue to win election and serve as lawmakers, as do a number who face serious criminal charges. The 2005 Right to Information Act has reportedly been used heavily and successfully to improve transparency, although many information requests are still denied because of poor record keeping by government agencies. Those who try to expose bureaucratic corruption often receive threats or are otherwise penalized in terms of career prospects.

The predominantly private media are vigorous and diverse, and their investigations and scrutiny of politicians form an important component of India's democracy. Nevertheless, journalists continue to face a number of constraints. The constitution protects freedom of speech and expression but does not explicitly mention media freedom. The government occasionally uses its power under the Official Secrets Act to censor security-related articles. Authorities have also on occasion used other security laws, criminal defamation legislation, hate-speech laws, and contempt of court charges to curb critical voices, though a 2006 amendment to the Contempt of Courts Act introduced truth as a valid defense. In January 2009, B. V. Seetaram, chairman and chief editor of Chitra Publications, was arrested in Karnataka on defamation charges. He was released weeks later. In February, a Calcutta-based editor and a publisher with the *Statesman* newspaper were arrested under religious speech laws after reprinting a British news article that sparked protests by Muslim groups.

Journalists remain subject to intimidation. On a number of occasions during 2009, reporters were attacked, threatened, or detained by local authorities, right-wing groups, or insurgents. Members of the press are particularly vulnerable in rural areas and insurgency-racked states, such as Chhattisgarh, Kashmir, Assam, and Manipur. In March 2009, Anil Majumder, editor of the *Aji* newspaper in Assam, was shot and killed as he arrived home. While the motive behind the killing was unknown, the media speculated that Majumder was killed due to public support for peace talks between the government and the guerrilla group, the United Liberation Front of Asom. Police had not yet apprehended the perpetrator by year's end.

Internet access is largely unrestricted, although some states have passed legislation that requires internet cafes to register with the state government and maintain visitor registries. Under Indian internet crime law, the burden is on website operators to demonstrate their innocence. Potentially inflammatory books and films are occasionally banned or censored. In August 2009, the BJP government in Gujarat banned a book about Pakistan's founder, Mohammed Ali Jinnah, due to "defamatory references" to India's first home minister, Vallabhbhai Patel; in addition, the book's author was expelled from the BJP. However, the book ban was reversed by a court in September.

Freedom of religion is constitutionally guaranteed and generally respected. Hindus of various strains and ethnicities form a majority of the overall population, but the state is secular. Violence against religious minorities remains a problem in certain states, and prosecution of the culprits has been inadequate. Members of the so-called Sangh Parivar—a group of Hindu nationalist organizations that includes the BJP—and some local media outlets promote antiminority views. In 2007 and 2008, dozens of churches and Christian homes in Orissa were destroyed by Hindu militants. An estimated 30 Christians were killed, and 3,000 homes destroyed in Kandhamal, the state's most violent district. A UN religious freedom report released in January 2009 noted the "increased ghettoization and isolation" of Muslims in some parts of Gujarat, and commented that a "pervasive fear of mob violence" exists in many parts of the country. In August 2009, the U.S. Commission on International Religious Freedom placed India on its watch list, noting an increasing culture of impunity for those who perpetrate religious attacks. In 2009, Varun Gandhi, a Hindu nationalist youth leader, was jailed under the National Security Act for inciting religious hatred. During a speech, he had called a Muslim rival "Osama bin Laden" and proclaimed that he would cut off the hand of any Muslim who threatened a Hindu. Legislation in several states criminalizes religious conversions that take place as a result of "force" or "allurement." Academic freedom is generally quite robust, though intimidation of professors and institutions sometimes occurs.

There are some restrictions on freedoms of assembly and association. Section 144 of the criminal procedure code empowers the authorities to restrict free assembly and impose curfews; officials occasionally use it to prevent demonstrations. Police and hired thugs sometimes beat, arbitrarily detain, or otherwise harass villagers and members of nongovernmental organizations (NGOs) who protest forced relocation from the sites of development projects. In February 2009, the authorities cracked down on protests in Tamil Nadu against the treatment of the Tamil minority in Sri Lanka; several hundred protesters were arrested following clashes with the police. Prior to the demonstrations, the state government had shut down universities to discourage students from taking part.

Human rights organizations generally operate freely. However, they have expressed concern about threats, legal harassment, the use of excessive force by police, and occasionally lethal violence. In Gujarat, advocates for justice following anti-Muslim riots in 2002—in which an estimated 2,000 people were killed and 100,000 displaced with at least tacit support from the BJP-led state government—have faced harassment, including police or tax investigations and threatening telephone calls, according to Human Rights Watch. Due in part to public protest over his imprisonment, Binayak Sen, a doctor who was active in organizing local health care in Chhattisgarh and had been a vocal critic of the government's conduct in combating Maoist Naxalite rebels, was released on bail in May 2009 after 22 months of detention. Sen had been detained for allegedly passing letters to a Naxalite prisoner he was treating. The work of rights activists may be hindered by a 2001 Home Ministry order that requires organizations to obtain clearance before holding international conferences or workshops if the subject matter is, "political, semipolitical, communal, or religious in nature or is related to human rights," although this prohibition is often ignored. Foreign monitors are occasionally denied visas to conduct research trips to India on human rights issues.

Workers in the formal economy regularly exercise their rights to bargain collectively and strike. However, the Essential Services Maintenance Act enables the government to ban strikes in certain industries and limits the right of public servants to strike. Estimates of the number of child laborers vary widely, from 12 million to 55 million. Many work in the informal sector in hazardous conditions, and some are bonded laborers. Children younger than 14 are banned from working as domestic servants or at hotels, restaurants, or roadside food stalls, although in practice the law is routinely flouted.

The judiciary is independent of the executive branch. Judges have displayed considerable activism in response to public interest litigation on official corruption, environmental issues, and other matters. However, in recent years judges have initiated several contempt of court cases against activists and journalists who expose judicial corruption or question verdicts. Contempt of court laws were reformed in 2006 to make truth a defense with respect to allegations against judges, provided the information is in the public and national interest.

The lower levels of the judiciary in particular are reportedly rife with corruption, and most citizens have great difficulty securing justice through the courts. In August 2009, following a public debate over judicial accountability, India's 29 Supreme Court justices announced that they would disclose their assets publicly on the court's website. The court system is severely backlogged and understaffed, with about 38 million civil and criminal cases pending. This leads to lengthy pretrial detention for a large number of suspects, many of whom remain in jail beyond the duration of any sentence they might receive if convicted. A 2009 report by the Chief Justice of the Delhi High Court indicated that at the current pace it would take 466 years to clear the backlog.

Despite legal reforms in recent years, the criminal justice system still generally fails to provide equal protection to minorities, lower castes, and tribal members. Muslims, who make up some 13.4 percent of the population, are underrepresented in the security forces, with only 29,000 serving in an army of 1.1 million, according to the *Christian Science Monitor*. Muslims are also underrepresented in "influential" or "sensitive" areas of government, such as the foreign and intelligence services. A 2006 report released by the Sachar Committee—a high-level government committee convened to address the social and economic status of Muslims in India—suggested several measures to combat inequalities, but the report has had little impact.

Particularly in rural India, caste *panchayats* (informal councils) or Muslim religious leaders often issue edicts concerning marriage, divorce, and other social customs. While these bodies play a role in relieving the overburdened official courts, their edicts sometimes result in violence or persecution aimed at those perceived to have transgressed social norms, especially women and members of the lower castes.

Police often torture or abuse suspects to extract confessions or bribes. Custodial rape of female detainees continues to be a problem, as does routine abuse of ordinary prisoners, particularly minorities and members of the lower castes. The Asian Centre for Human Rights reported in 2009 that between 2001 and March 2009, 1,184 deaths in police custody were reported, nearly all as a result of torture. The group estimates that the actual number of deaths is far greater. The National Human Rights

Commission (NHRC) is headed by a retired Supreme Court judge and handles roughly 80,000 complaints each year. However, while it monitors abuses, initiates investigations, makes independent assessments, and conducts training sessions for the police and others, its recommendations are often not implemented, and it has few enforcement powers. The commission also lacks jurisdiction over the armed forces, which severely hampers its effectiveness.

Reports by the NHRC, Human Rights Watch, and other groups allege that the Gujarat state government instructed police not to intervene during the 2002 communal violence, and that police have since been reluctant to register complaints against or arrest those accused of murder, rape, or complicity in the rioting. The rehabilitation of displaced victims and the prosecution of the perpetrators have consequently made little progress, as witnesses and victims' advocates have faced intimidation by local authorities and Hindu nationalists. In 2006, a Mumbai special court sentenced 9 people to life imprisonment for their role in the Best Bakery massacre, and 13 people were convicted in 2008 for their roles in the riots, with 11 receiving life sentences. However, the majority of victims appear unlikely to see justice.

Security forces operating in the context of regional insurgencies continue to be implicated in disappearances, extrajudicial killings, rape, torture, arbitrary detention, and destruction of homes. Despite several calls for its repeal, the Armed Forces Special Powers Act (AFSPA) and the Disturbed Areas Act remain in effect in a number of states, granting security forces broad powers of arrest and detention. Security forces also continue to hold suspects under the National Security Act, which authorizes detention without charge for up to one year, as well as the Unlawful Activities Prevention Act. In response to spiraling Naxalite-related violence, the Chhattisgarh state government passed the Special Public Protection Act in 2006, with broad language allowing three-year detentions for "unlawful activities" and criminalizing the provision of support to the Naxalite rebels, even if under duress. The criminal procedure code requires the federal or relevant state government to approve prosecution of security force members, but such approval is rarely granted, leading to impunity for personnel implicated in human rights abuses.

The recent spread and growth in influence of the Naxalites are a serious concern. There are an estimated 14,000 armed fighters, supported by 40,000 cadre members, organized into a number of groups that since late 2004 have been loosely allied as the Communist Party of India–Maoist. The *Christian Science Monitor* reported in 2009 that Maoists operate in 20 of 28 states, and control some rural areas outright. Focusing on the tribal areas in states such as Andhra Pradesh, Orissa, Bihar, Chhattisgarh, and Jharkhand, they aim to establish a communist state on behalf of marginalized groups, including tribal peoples, lower castes, and the landless poor. According to a 2008 Human Rights Watch report, they have imposed illegal taxes; requisitioned food and shelter from villagers; engaged in abduction and forced recruitment, including recruitment of child soldiers; hampered aid deliveries; and planted land mines that have caused civilian casualties. In June 2009, the government banned the Communist Party of India–Maoist and labeled it a terrorist group. The move will give security forces greater leeway in arresting and detaining suspects.

Naxalite-related violence killed more than 998 security personnel and civilians during 2009, according to the South Asia Terrorism Portal (SATP). Particularly after the 2005 launch of the anti-Maoist Salwa Judum campaign in Chhattisgarh, local civilians who are perceived to be progovernment have been targeted by the Naxalites. The government, often working with the Salwa Judum militia, has routinely raided suspected Naxalite-controlled villages in recent years, with attacks continuing through 2009, often targeting civilians. A 2008 Human Rights Watch report documented a pattern of beatings and murders by security forces in the area. Around 50,000 civilians have been displaced by Naxalite-related violence and live in government-run camps.

In India's seven northeastern states, more than 40 insurgent factions—seeking either greater autonomy or complete independence for their ethnic or tribal groups—attack security forces and engage in intertribal violence. The rebels have been implicated in numerous bombings, killings, abductions, and rapes of civilians, and they also operate extensive extortion networks. Approximately 843 troops, militants, and civilians were killed in these northeastern states in 2009, according to the SATP. Tens of thousands of civilians have been displaced, and many live in squalid camps. In January 2009, the Assam Legislative Assembly passed the Assam Preventive Detention (Amendment) Act, lifting the maximum period for preventive detention of terrorist suspects from six months to two years.

The constitution bars discrimination based on caste, and laws set aside generous quotas in education and government jobs for the so-called scheduled tribes, scheduled castes (Dalits), and other backward classes (OBCs). In addition, women and religious and ethnic minorities are represented in national and local government; in 2004, Manmohan Singh became India's first Sikh prime minister, and in 2007, the BSP, formed chiefly to represent Dalits, won an absolute majority in Uttar Pradesh, India's most populous state. However, members of the lower castes and minorities continue to face routine unofficial discrimination and violence. The worst abuse is experienced by the country's 160 million Dalits, who are often denied access to land and other public amenities, abused by landlords and police, punished by village councils or members of the upper castes for alleged social transgressions, and forced to work in miserable conditions. A government proposal to reserve an extra 27 percent of places in universities and technical institutes for OBCs—taking the total portion of reserved slots to 49.5 percent—was approved in 2008. Indian Muslims are disproportionately more likely to be poor and illiterate, and less likely to have access to government employment, medical care, or loans.

Property rights are somewhat tenuous for tribal groups and other marginalized communities, and members of these groups are often denied adequate resettlement opportunities and compensation when their lands are seized for development projects. While many states have laws to prevent land transfers to nontribal groups, the practice is widespread, according to a 2008 Asian Indigenous and Tribal People's Network report. The 2006 Forest Rights Act gave tribal groups ownership rights over forestland they farmed, although recent reports suggest that the law has yet to be effectively implemented. A long-running protest by 1,738 landless Dalit families in Kerala, who demanded land held by a private rubber plantation, was resolved in 2009, when the government granted the families money to build housing elsewhere.

Each year, several thousand women are killed or driven to suicide, and countless others are abused or deserted by husbands, in the context of domestic disputes. Despite the criminalization of dowry demands and hundreds of convictions each year, the practice continues. Rape and other violence against women are serious problems, and lower-caste and tribal women are particularly vulnerable. A 2006 law banned dowry-related harassment, widened the definition of domestic violence to include emotional or verbal abuse, and criminalized spousal rape. However, reports released in 2009 by the Delhi-based Lawyers' Collective indicated that enforcement of the law was poor in many states. So-called honor killings, in which women are murdered by relatives for perceived sexual or moral transgressions, remain a problem, especially in the northwestern states of Punjab and Haryana.

Muslim personal-status laws and traditional Hindu practices discriminate against women in terms of inheritance, adoption, and property rights. The malign neglect of female children after birth remains a concern, as does the banned but growing use of prenatal sex-determination tests to selectively abort female fetuses. These trends have contributed to a significant imbalance in the male-female birth ratios in a number of states. In 2008, the government announced an award of nearly US$3,000 for families that raise female children. The trafficking of women and children to, from, and within India—primarily for prostitution and forced labor—remains a significant problem.

In a landmark decision in July 2009, a court scrapped colonial-era laws that banned homosexual behavior. The laws had contributed to the harassment of gay men and the NGOs that work with them, according to Human Rights Watch, and the court ruling came after a protracted campaign against the statutes by rights groups. Gay activist groups organize openly, despite harassment and occasional violence.

Indonesia

Political Rights: 2
Civil Liberties: 3
Status: Free

Population: 243,306,000
Capital: Jakarta

Ten-Year Ratings Timeline For Year Under Review (Political Rights, Civil Liberties, Status)

2000	2001	2002	2003	2004	2005	2006	2007	2008	2009
3,4PF	3,4PF	3,4PF	3,4PF	3,4PF	2,3PF	2,3F	2,3F	2,3F	2,3F

Overview: President Susilo Bambang Yudhoyono's (SBY) Democratic Party led legislative elections in April 2009, and Yudhoyono secured a second term in the July presidential election. Security forces in September killed terrorism suspect Noordin Mohammad Top, the alleged mastermind of twin suicide bombings that had struck hotels in the capital in July. Separately, the chief of Indonesia's anticorruption commission went on trial for murder during the year, and two of his deputies were accused of extortion, but their case led to the exposure of an apparent conspiracy by police and prosecutors to undermine the commission. The parliament passed legislation in September that would weaken the authority of the commission and a related anticorruption court. In addition, the parliament began investigating a controversial bailout of Bank Century in November, which pitted the House of Representatives against the SBY administration and shrunk his ruling coalition.

Indonesia won independence from its Dutch colonial rulers in 1949. After several parliamentary governments collapsed, the republic's first president, Sukarno, assumed authoritarian powers in 1957. The army, led by General Suharto, crushed a violence followed, ostensibly against suspected PKI members, resulting in an estimated 500,000 deaths. With military backing, Suharto formally became president in 1968.

Suharto's regime created Golkar, a progovernment party based on bureaucratic and military interests, and embarked on a development program that helped the economy grow by an annual average of 7 percent for three decades. In the 1990s, Suharto's children and cronies were the major beneficiaries of state privatization schemes and in many cases, ran business monopolies with little oversight. Soaring inflation and unemployment following the Asian financial crisis of 1997 prompted urban riots in 1998, and Suharto was forced to resign. He was succeeded by then vice president B. J. Habibie, who removed legal constraints on the press, labor unions, and political parties.

In 1999, Indonesia held its first free legislative elections since 1955. The Indonesian Democratic Party–Struggle (PDI-P), led by Sukarno's daughter, Megawati Sukarnoputri, won the largest number of seats, followed by Golkar. The People's Consultative Assembly, made up of elected lawmakers and appointed officials, chose Muslim leader Abdurrahman Wahid as president and Megawati as vice president, but Megawati rose to the presidency in 2001, after Wahid was impeached over corruption allegations. Megawati's administration was credited with stabilizing the economy but also with a rise in corruption, due in part to a hasty political decentralization process. Internal security threats increased, including a series of terrorist bombings.

Support for the PDI-P dropped in the 2004 elections, and Golkar once again became the largest party in the legislature. Later that year, Susilo Bambang Yudhoyono (SBY) of the new Democratic Party and his running mate, Jusuf Kalla of Golkar, won the presidency and vice presidency in the second round of the presidential election, taking 61 percent of the vote.

The Democratic Party won the April 2009 parliamentary elections, raising its share of seats to 148, from 55 in 2004. Golkar garnered 106 seats, and the PDI-P took 94. parties generally fared poorly, though the Prosperous Justice Party (PKS), with its strong anticorruption platform, captured 57 seats. The elections yielded a significant turnover in the parliament's membership, with approximately 75 percent of the chamber consisting of new lawmakers. SBY easily secured a second five-year term in the July presidential election, defeating Megawati and Kalla with 61 percent of the vote in the first round. SBY's new running mate, former central bank governor Boediono, became vice president.

Although SBY's solid electoral victory demonstrated public approval of his economic management and anticorruption efforts, the latter were undermined during the year as the leadership of the Corruption Eradication Commission (KPK) was implicated in criminal cases. KPK chairman Antasari Azhar was arrested in May and eventually put on trial for the murder of a businessman; a verdict had not been reached by year's end. In October, police arrested two deputy chairmen of the KPK on charges of extortion and abuse of power, but wiretap recordings that emerged the following month revealed an apparent conspiracy in which officials within the national police and the attorney general's office allegedly aimed to frame the two KPK members and discredit the commission itself. The scandal triggered persistent public protests in favor of the KPK, and in November, the president forced the resignations of a senior police official and the deputy attorney general. The case against the two deputy chairmen of the KPK was dropped in December, and both deputies returned to work.

The government's counterterrorism campaign suffered a setback in July, when bombings at two Jakarta hotels killed nine people and injured more than 50 others. However, the police killed the suspected mastermind of the bombings, the Malaysian-born Islamist militant Noordin Mohammad Top, in a September raid. Noordin had been implicated in a number of other bombings since 2003, and allegedly headed a splinter faction of Jemaah Islamiyah (JI), a transnational network of Southeast Asian militants that was loosely linked to al-Qaeda.

Also in 2009, Indonesia continued to grapple with separatist and sectarian tensions in a number of different regions. In Aceh, where a devastating 2004 earthquake and tsunami had paved the way for a peace agreement in 2005 with the separatist Free Aceh Movement (GAM) militant group, suspicions lingered between former GAM members and the Indonesian military amid a number of violent incidents. The unresolved murders in February and March of four members of the Aceh Party, the GAM's political successor organization, bolstered former GAM members' claims that the military had reneged on the peace agreement. Former GAM leaders also engaged in infighting over the inequitable division of reintegration funds. Sporadic violence against foreign nationals continued in 2009, including the nonfatal shooting of a Red Cross worker in November.

In Papua, where the central government's exploitation of natural resources has stirred resentment and demands for independence, rallies of between 5,000 and 10,000 people were mounted in three cities in October 2009 to express dissatisfaction with economic development and alleged human rights abuses by the military. The development of oil-palm plantations has also brought an influx of non-Papuan workers and firms, prompting land disputes, and tension has increased between local Christians and non-Papuan Muslim communities. The Free Papua Movement (OPM) has waged a low-grade insurgency since the early 1950s. Politically motivated violence increased in the latter half of 2009; the OPM claimed responsibility for some of the violence, including incidents in which it had no direct role. Unresolved violence surrounding the province's Grasberg gold mine increased in July and continued through the end of the year, with several attacks on mining personnel and Brimob, the Indonesian paramilitary police. Several shooting incidents were also reported, killing at least eight people, including three foreign nationals. In December, Kelly Kwalik, head of the West Papuan National Liberation Army (TPN) of the OPM, was killed by Indonesian police.

Political Rights and Civil Liberties: Indonesia is an electoral democracy. In 2004, for the first time, Indonesians directly elected their president and all members of the House of Representatives (DPR), as well as members of a new legislative body, the House of Regional Representatives (DPD). Previously, presidents had been elected by the People's Consultative Assembly (MPR), then made up of elected lawmakers and appointed officials. The MPR now performs tasks involving the swearing in and dismissal of presidents and the amendment of the constitution, and consists of elected DPR and DPD members. The DPR, which expanded from 550 seats in 2004 to 560 in 2009, is the main parliamentary chamber. The 132-member DPD is responsible for proposing and monitoring laws related to regional autonomy. Presidents and vice presidents can serve up to two five-year terms, and all legislators also serve five-year terms.

Parties or coalitions must attain 25 percent of the popular vote or 20 percent of the seats in the DPR to nominate candidates for president. Voters for the DPR can select either a party list or an individual candidate, but under a December 2008 Constitutional Court ruling on that year's Law on Legislative Elections, candidates are seated based on the number of votes they receive, regardless of their position on the party lists. The changes are expected to increase lawmakers' accountability to voters and reduce the power of party bosses, while making it more difficult for women to gain seats. The results of the 2009 legislative and presidential elections were accepted by all parties, but there were notable problems with the voter lists; the General Election Commission (KPU) was ordered by the Supreme Court to recount the legislative election votes before allocating seats, and after five months of confusion over conflicting seat allocation rules, the KPU followed the Constitutional Court ruling. A new national census scheduled for 2010 is expected to correct many of these irregularities for future elections.

Staggered, direct elections for regional leaders began in 2005 and have generally been considered free and fair. Independent candidates were allowed to contest local elections for the first time in 2008, although Aceh's 2006 governance law had already allowed independent candidates there as part of an effort to integrate former GAM separatists into the political process.

Corruption remains endemic. Indonesia was ranked 111 out of 180 countries surveyed in Transparency International's (TI) 2009 Corruption Perceptions Index, and TI's 2009 Global Corruption Barometer found the DPR to be the most corrupt institution in the country. The KPK's successes in a series of high-profile cases in 2008 and 2009 raised public expectations that acts of corruption, even by senior officials, would be punished. However, critics have accused entrenched elites of attempting to weaken anticorruption institutions, citing the alleged conspiracy against the KPK that was revealed in November 2009, as well as a new anticorruption bill passed by the parliament and signed into law in September. The legislation dilutes the authority and independence of the KPK and the Anticorruption Court (Tipikor), where cases brought by the KPK have been tried since 2004. It effectively decentralizes anticorruption efforts, placing them under the jurisdiction of district courts. However, original articles revoking the KPK's wiretapping and litigation powers—seen as key instruments of the KPK's success—were removed by SBY before signing the bill into law. A controversial 2008 bailout of Bank Century has led to accusations of large-scale graft at the cabinet level. The Committee for Financial Sector Stability, led by Finance Minister Sri Mulyani and then central bank governor Boediono, initially authorized a IDR 632 billion (US$70 million) financial rescue, but the final bailout figure, IDR 6.76 trillion (US$650 million), was almost nine times the original figure; there were also allegations that some depositors had preferential treatment and questions of whether bailout funds were embezzled. In November, the DPR voted to investigate the bailout; investigations were ongoing at the year's end. The Bank Century case is widely believed to be an attempt to undermine the SBY administration by targeting Mulyani and Boediono.

Indonesia is home to a vibrant and diverse media environment, though press freedom remains hampered by a number of legal and regulatory restrictions. There is a large independent media sector, but strict licensing rules mean that thousands of television and radio stations operate illegally. Foreign journalists are not authorized to travel to the restive provinces of Papua and West Papua without special permission. In addition to legal obstacles, reporters sometimes face violence and intimidation. Journalist A. A. Narendra Prabangsa of the daily *Radar Bali* was murdered in February 2009 after publishing a series of articles on local corruption. Police arrested several suspects in May, and the case against them was still pending at year's end. The Alliance of Independent Journalists reported a 30 percent decline in instances of violence against journalists in 2009.

Reporters often practice self-censorship to avoid running afoul of civil and criminal libel laws; Article 311 of the 2007 criminal code makes defamation punishable by four years in prison. In July 2009, a Jakarta court imposed a six-month suspended jail sentence on the writers of a complaint letter that was published in several newspapers and supposedly defamed a property developer. However, some court decisions have favored journalists in libel cases. In April, the Supreme Court overturned a previous ruling ordering the magazine *Time Asia* to pay 1 trillion rupiah (more than US$100 million) in damages for a 1999 story on the Suharto family's fortune and embezzlement. And in September, a district court in Makassar acquitted journalist and press freedom activist Upi Asmaradhana of defaming a police official.

The 2008 Law on Electronic Information and Transactions (ITE) extended libel and other restrictions to the internet and online media, criminalizing the distribution or accessibility of information or documents that are, "contrary to the moral norms of Indonesia" or related to gambling, blackmail, or defamation. Violators face a possible six-year prison sentence. Journalist and blogger Nurliswandi Piliang was charged under the ITE law in 2008 and appealed to the Constitutional Court, but the Court upheld the law in May 2009. Also that month, Prita Mulyasari was arrested under the ITE law for allegedly defaming a hospital where she had been a patient by distributing a complaint about it to friends via e-mail. Her case garnered significant public attention, and she was ultimately acquitted in December; the hospital dropped a parallel civil suit after she appealed a judgment instructing her to pay some US$20,000 in damages. Several other ITE cases emerged in 2009 for Facebook and Twitter usage.

Indonesia officially recognizes Islam, Protestantism, Roman Catholicism, Hinduism, Buddhism, and Confucianism. Members of unrecognized religions have difficulty obtaining national identity cards. Atheism is not accepted, and the criminal code contains provisions against blasphemy. The national government has often failed to respond to religious intolerance in recent years. Societal discrimination and violence against Ahmadiyya—a heterodox Islamic sect with 400,000 Indonesian followers—increased in 2008 after the Religious Affairs Department recommended that the group be banned. Seeking a compromise, the government banned Ahmadis from proselytizing, but the sect has been banned outright in several districts and in the province of South Sumatra. Some 130 Ahmadis remained in shelters in 2009, after sectarian violence in 2006 forced them from their homes in Mataram, Lombok. Separately, violence between Christians and Muslims in Poso continued to decrease in 2009, although underlying grievances and low public confidence in government remained unaddressed. The Wahid Institute reported 93 incidents of religious intolerance in 2009, a significant decline from the 232 cases recorded in 2008.

Academic freedom in Indonesia is generally respected. However, books deemed capable of inciting political instability are banned by the Attorney General's Office, which also monitors the circulation of books.

Freedom of assembly is usually upheld, and peaceful protests are commonplace in the capital. Authorities have restricted this right in conflict areas, however. Flag-raising ceremonies and independence rallies in Papua are routinely disbanded, and participants have been prosecuted.

Indonesia hosts a strong and active array of civil society organizations, though some human rights groups are subject to monitoring and interference by the government. Moreover, independence activists in Papua and the Moluccas, and labor and political activists in Java and Sulawesi, remain targets for human rights abuses. Progress in the case of Munir Said Thalib, a prominent rights activist who died of arsenic poisoning in 2004 while on a flight from Jakarta to Amsterdam, stalled in 2009, when the courts upheld the acquittal of the former head of the National Intelligence Agency (BIN), Muchdi Purwopranjono. No high-level official has been convicted in the Munir murder to date, or for any serious human rights violation since the fall of Suharto. The Human Rights Commission (Komnas HAM), which investigates abuses of human rights, is backlogged by thousands of public complaints. In December, Komnas HAM found that the Sidoarjo mudflow disaster had been caused by a human error, rather than by a natural disaster as the DPR and National Police had found in 2008. The mudflow has displaced over 45,000 people since 2006.

Workers can join independent unions, bargain collectively, and with the exception of civil servants, stage strikes. However, the labor movement is fragmented, and government enforcement of minimum-wage and other labor standards is weak. The 2003 Labor Law makes it difficult for employers to lay off workers, which has resulted in an increase in contract hires and a reduction in long-term employment and benefits. Domestic workers are currently excluded from labor law protections. A February 2009 report by Human Rights Watch found that many government officials continue to foster myths about the circumstances of domestic workers and deny widespread abuses.

The judiciary, particularly the Constitutional Court, has demonstrated its independence in some cases, but the court system remains plagued by corruption and other weaknesses. SBY made judicial reform a key objective after he took office in 2004, and he renewed his commitment following the revelation of the alleged conspiracy against the KPK in late 2009. Nevertheless, progress to date has been limited; while the president appointed well-known reformers to the positions of attorney general and chief justice of the Supreme Court during his first term, the Supreme Court remains the slowest of the country's judicial institutions to reform. Low salaries for judicial officials and impunity for illegal activity perpetuate the problems of bribery, forced confessions, and interference in court proceedings by military personnel and government officials at all levels.

A number of districts began issuing local ordinances based on Sharia (Islamic law) in 2006. Many are unconstitutional, contradict international treaties to which Indonesia is a signatory, or are unclear, leading to enforcement problems. The national government and various parties have failed to take decisive action on the issue, apparently for political reasons. Many of the ordinances seek to enforce an Islamic dress code, Koranic literacy requirements, and bans on prostitution. For example, a bylaw passed in October 2009 by the West Aceh legislature prohibits women from wearing pants. Other measures are more extreme: in September, the Aceh provincial parliament passed legislation that, among other provisions, allows stoning for adultery and public lashing for homosexual acts. The law has not been approved by the provincial governor, and the newly elected Aceh parliament, inaugurated in October, was set to review the measure along with three others passed by the outgoing legislature.

The DPR and the Ministry of Home Affairs have the power to overturn illegal ordinances passed at the subnational level, and concern over the constitutionality of local regulations has not been limited to those based on Sharia.

Members of the security forces regularly go unpunished for human rights violations. These include ongoing low-level abuses in conflict zones like Papua, but they are largely related to land disputes and military involvement in illegal activities such as logging and mining. In September 2009, members of the outgoing DPR dropped deliberations on a military justice bill that would have required soldiers to be tried in civilian courts for criminal offenses.

Effective police work has proven critical to Indonesia's recent successes in fighting terrorism, but the police force remains rife with corruption and other abuses, and officers have generally avoided criminal penalties. The head of the national police's legal division revealed in August that approximately 350 officers are dismissed annually for rights violations. A June Amnesty International report found that over a one-year period, police gunfire had killed 50 people and injured 60 others, with little evidence to suggest that the suspects had resisted arrest. The national police issued a new set of law enforcement standards that month.

Detention laws are generally respected, but there are many reports of abuse aimed at female and minority detainees. According to a report issued by the Indonesian Human Rights Monitor (IMPARSIAL) in August 2009, student activists are the most prone to arbitrary arrest, followed by farmers and journalists. Prisons have reportedly been significant recruiting sites for radical groups, primarily due to corruption and lax controls that allow the circulation of extremist media material.

Members of Indonesia's minority groups face considerable discrimination. The problems of mining and logging on communal land and state appropriation of land claimed by indigenous groups are most acute in Kalimantan. Ethnic Chinese, who make up less than 3 percent of the population but are resented for reputedly holding the lion's share of the country's wealth, continue to face harassment and occasional violence.

Discrimination against women persists, particularly in the workplace. Trafficking of women and children for prostitution, forced labor, and debt bondage also continues, despite the passage of new laws and stricter penalties. In 2009, special police units were established in each province to handle cases of trafficking, sexual abuse, and violence against women and children, and to protect witnesses and victims. Abortion is illegal, except to save a woman's life. Sharia-based ordinances in a number of districts infringe on women's constitutional rights; it is estimated that over 150 bylaws discriminate against women and minorities. Critics have also suggested that a new health law endorsed by the DPR in September 2009 discriminates against homosexuals through articles specifying health care for married couples. In 2008, the DPR passed an antipornography bill that critics said would victimize women, in part because it applies not just to published images but to speech and gestures that "incite sexual desire." Significantly, the measure invites the "public" to participate in the discouragement of pornographic acts, which could lead to extrajudicial enforcement. The Constitutional Court began hearing objections to the law in February 2009. Under a 2008 law, 30 percent of a political party's candidates and board members must be women. While only 101 women were elected to the 560-seat DPR in 2009, this was an increase over the 63 who served from 2004 to 2009.

⬇ Iran

Political Rights: 6
Civil Liberties: 6
Status: Not Free

Population: 73,244,000
Capital: Tehran

Trend Arrow: Iran received a downward trend arrow due to strong evidence of fraud in the June 2009 presidential election and the violent suppression of subsequent protests.

Ten-Year Ratings Timeline For Year Under Review (Political Rights, Civil Liberties, Status)

2000	2001	2002	2003	2004	2005	2006	2007	2008	2009
6,6NF	6,6NF	6,6NF	6,6NF	6,6NF	6,6NF	6,6NF	6,6NF	6,6NF	6,6NF

Overview: Mahmoud Ahmadinejad was awarded a second four-year term in the June 2009 presidential election, but public outrage at the allegedly fraudulent results sparked widespread demonstrations that persisted for the remainder of the year. The government responded by violently suppressing the protests and heavily restricting the flow of information. Security forces were accused of raping and torturing detained demonstrators and opposition supporters, many of whom were subjected to televised show trials. The regime continued its crackdown even as the troubled economy suffered from the effects of a global financial crisis and ongoing international sanctions.

In 1979, a revolution ousted Iran's monarchy, which had been marked by widespread corruption and misguided modernization efforts. The revolution mobilized much of the population and brought together diverse political interests, but democratic and secular elements were largely subsumed under the leadership of the previously exiled Ayatollah Ruhollah Khomeini. Although the constitution drafted by Khomeini's disciples provided for an elected president and parliament, an unelected body, the Council of Guardians, was empowered to approve candidates and certify that the decisions of elected officials were in accord with Sharia (Islamic law). Khomeini was named supreme leader and vested with control over the security and intelligence services, the armed forces, and the judiciary. Soon after the establishment of the Islamic Republic, Iraqi leader Saddam Hussein launched an invasion to settle a long-running border dispute. The ensuing war, which lasted from 1980 to 1988, cost over a million lives.

After Khomeini's death in 1989, the title of supreme leader passed to Ayatollah Ali Khamenei, a middle-ranking cleric who was a compromise candidate but lacked the religious credentials and popularity of his predecessor. The constitution was changed to consolidate his power and give him final authority on all matters of foreign and domestic policy.

Beneath its veneer of religious probity, the Islamic Republic had given rise to a new elite that accumulated wealth through opaque and unaccountable means. Basic freedoms had been revoked, and women in particular experienced a severe regression in their status and rights. By the mid-1990s, dismal economic conditions and a demographic trend toward a younger population had contributed to significant public dissatisfaction with the regime. A coalition of reformists began to emerge within the leadership, advocating a gradual process of political change, economic liberalization, and normalization of relations with the outside world that was designed to legitimize, but not radically alter, the existing political system.

Representing this coalition, former culture minister Mohammad Khatami was elected president in 1997 with nearly 70 percent of the vote. Under his administration, more than 200 independent newspapers and magazines with a diverse array of viewpoints were established, and the authorities relaxed the enforcement of restrictions on social interaction between the sexes. Reformists won 80 percent of the seats in the country's first nationwide municipal elections in 1999 and took the vast majority of seats in parliamentary elections the following year, with student activists playing a major role in their success.

The 2000 parliamentary elections prompted a backlash by hard-line clerics. Over the four years after the polls, the conservative judiciary closed more than 100 reformist newspapers and jailed hundreds of liberal journalists and activists, while security forces cracked down on the ensuing student protests. Khatami was reelected with 78 percent of the vote in 2001, but popular disaffection stemming from the reformists' limited accomplishments, coupled with the Council of Guardians's rejection of the candidacies of most reformist politicians, allowed hard-liners to triumph in the 2003 municipal and February 2004 parliamentary elections.

The Council of Guardians similarly rejected the candidacies of popular reformists ahead of the June 2005 presidential election, though the victory of Tehran mayor Mahmoud Ahmadinejad over other approved candidates reflected popular desires for change. As Iran's first nonclerical president in more than two decades, he had campaigned on promises to fight elite corruption and redistribute Iran's oil wealth to the poor and middle class. Nevertheless, his hard-line administration oversaw a crackdown on civil liberties and human rights, and a stricter enforcement of the regime's morality laws.

The new government also adopted a more confrontational tone on foreign policy matters, feeding suspicions that its expanding uranium-enrichment activity, ostensibly devoted to generating electricity, was in fact aimed at weapons production. In an effort to compel Iran to halt the uranium enrichment, the UN Security Council imposed sanctions on the country in December 2006, and subsequently expanded them as negotiations failed to make progress.

In the December 2006 municipal and Assembly of Experts elections, voters signaled their disapproval of the government's performance by supporting far more moderate officials. Carefully vetted conservative candidates won nearly 70 percent of the seats in the March 2008 parliamentary elections, but many were considered critics of Ahmadinejad, and particularly of his economic policies.

Despite crackdowns on human and women's rights activists and restrictions on internet freedom in the months prior to the June 2009 presidential election, supporters of all candidates seemed to enjoy a relatively relaxed and politically vibrant atmosphere. The Council of Guardians approved only 3 of 475 potential candidates to compete against Ahmadinejad, but all 3 were well-known and potentially formidable figures: Mir Hussein Mousavi, a reformist former prime minister; Mohsen Rezai, a conservative former head of the Iranian Revolutionary Guard Corps (IRGC); and Mehdi Karroubi, a reformist former Speaker of parliament and the only cleric approved. Mousavi emerged as the main challenger, confronting Ahmadinejad in unprecedented televised debates.

Despite polls that indicated a close race, Ahmadinejad was declared the winner soon after the election, credited with over 63 percent of the vote. Mousavi officially received only 33.75 percent, while Rezai and Karroubi reportedly garnered 1.73 percent and 0.85 percent, respectively. All three challengers lodged claims of fraud, and subsequent findings by independent analysts reinforced suspicions that irregularities had occurred. According to official data, the conservative vote increased by 113 percent compared with the 2005 election, and several provinces registered more votes than the number of eligible voters. In 10 provinces won by Ahmadinejad, his victory was only possible if he had secured the votes of all former nonvoters and all those who had voted for his main conservative opponent in 2005, as well as up to 44 percent of those who had previously voted for reformist candidates.

Protests broke out on a massive scale as voters rejected the official results. In a rare show of defiance, high-profile political figures publicly broke with Khamenei's validation of the election, with Khatami going so far as to publicly call for a referendum on the government's legitimacy. The security forces violently cracked down on all public expressions of dissent and tightened government control of both online and traditional media, but protesters continued to mount periodic demonstrations for the rest of the year, using mobile-telephone cameras and the internet to document abuses and communicate with the outside world.

Meanwhile, Iran's relations with the United States and Britain, which had seemed to improve earlier in 2009, worsened in the wake of the election as the regime accused those and other foreign governments of attempting to orchestrate a velvet revolution. Iranian authorities temporarily detained nine employees of the British embassy in late June, alleging that they played a "significant role" in the postelection unrest. At the end of July, three Americans were arrested when they strayed into Iranian territory while hiking in northern Iraq; they remained in custody at year's end. Separately, it was revealed in September 2009 that Iran had been secretly building a second uranium-enrichment plant near the city of Qom, stirring calls for additional international sanctions.

Political Rights and Civil Liberties: Iran is not an electoral democracy. The most powerful figure in the government is the supreme leader (*Vali-e-Faghih*), currently Ayatollah Ali Khamenei. He is chosen by the Assembly of Experts, a body of 86 clerics who are elected to eight-year terms by popular vote, from a vetted list of candidates. The supreme leader is head of the armed forces and appoints the leaders of the judiciary, the chiefs of state broadcast media, the commander of the IRGC, the Expediency Council, and half of the Council of Guardians. Although the president and the parliament, both with four-year terms, are responsible for designating cabinet ministers, the supreme leader exercises de facto control over appointments to the ministries of Defense, the Interior, and Intelligence.

All candidates for the presidency and the 290-seat, unicameral parliament are vetted by the Council of Guardians, which consists of six clergymen appointed by the supreme leader and six civil law experts selected by the head of the judiciary, all for six-year terms (the latter are nominally subject to parliamentary approval). The Council of Guardians also has the power to reject legislation approved by the parliament; disputes between the two are arbitrated by the Expediency Council, another unelected, conservative-dominated body. Both it and the Assembly of Experts are currently headed by former president Ali Akbar Hashemi Rafsanjani, who has, at times, sided with the reformist camp to curb the influence of his rival, current president Mahmoud Ahmadinejad.

The IRGC's influence within Iran continues to grow, as it now wields military, political, and economic power. Former members of the IRGC, including Ahmadinejad, hold key positions within the government, and its commercial arms have been awarded the right of first refusal for government contracts, some of which have been extremely lucrative.

Corruption is pervasive. The hard-line clerical establishment has grown immensely wealthy through its control of tax-exempt foundations that monopolize many sectors of the economy, such as cement and sugar production. Iran was ranked 168 out of 180 countries surveyed in Transparency International's 2009 Corruption Perceptions Index.

Freedom of expression is severely limited. The government directly controls all television and radio broadcasting. Satellite dishes are illegal, and while they are generally tolerated, there have been increasing reports of dish confiscation and steep fines. The authorities have had some success in jamming broadcasts by dissident satellite stations based overseas, and cooperation with Persian-language satellite channels is banned. Even the purchase of satellite images from abroad is illegal. The Ministry of Culture must approve publication of all books and inspects foreign books prior to domestic distribution.

The authorities frequently issue ad hoc orders banning media coverage of specific topics and events. Although some foreign media outlets had been specifically invited to cover the 2009 presidential election, the government officially banned the foreign media from reporting on the postelection demonstrations. Most foreign journalists were confined to their hotels and ultimately forced to leave as their visas expired. Reporters from a number of countries were arrested and temporarily detained during the year.

The Press Court has extensive power to prosecute journalists for such vaguely worded offenses as "insulting Islam" and "damaging the foundations of the Islamic Republic." The use of "suspicious sources" or sources that criticize the government is also forbidden. Fear of stepped-up penalties has reinforced a trend toward journalistic self-censorship. The Association of Iranian Journalists reported in 2007 that the profession had suffered in quality and investment due to the government's crackdown on independent newspapers. The organization was subsequently harassed by the government, and in August 2009, its offices were raided and closed.

Iran leads the world in the number of jailed journalists, with 39 behind bars at the close of 2009. Some received sentences of up to 15 years in prison, and at least one was sentenced to flogging. Several dozen other journalists were arrested and released on bail during the year, often after they issued coerced confessions on television.

Individuals used mobile-telephone cameras and social-networking websites to provide some of the only independent coverage of the aftermath of the 2009 presidential election, particularly given the crackdown on traditional media. The effectiveness of this type of reporting has improved as internet use in Iran has skyrocketed, reaching about 25 percent of the population by 2008. Recognizing the internet's growing influence, the government has forced service providers to block a growing list of "immoral" or politically sensitive sites. In 2006, the authorities announced the creation of a central filtering facility to block unauthorized websites, identify internet users, and keep a record of sites visited.

The number of blocked websites rose sharply ahead of the presidential election, affecting internationally known sites like Facebook, Twitter, and YouTube, as well as several political websites. In late 2009, a group calling itself the Iranian Cyber Army hacked Twitter, redirecting users to a message that appeared to support the current regime. Text-messaging services were completely shut down on the day of the election, and phone services were severely disrupted the next day. Sites associated with minority and human rights, and particularly women's rights, were also targeted during the year. Some women's rights activists who were detained by police later reported that their online activities had been monitored by officials, who produced copies of their instant-messaging discussions during interrogations.

Religious freedom is limited in Iran, whose population is largely Shiite Muslim but includes Sunni Muslim, Baha'i, Christian, Jewish, and Zoroastrian minorities. The Special Court for the Clergy investigates religious figures for alleged crimes and has generally been used to persecute clerics who stray from the official interpretation of Islam. Ayatollah Seyd Hussain Kazemeini Boroujerdi, a cleric who advocates the separation of religion and politics, is currently serving 11 years in prison for his beliefs.

Sunnis enjoy equal rights under the law but face discrimination in practice; there is no Sunni mosque in Tehran, and few Sunnis hold senior government posts. The Sunni militant group Jundallah, associated with the ethnic Baluchi minority, has waged a campaign of bombings and other attacks on the government in recent years, and the authorities have accused the United States and Britain of supporting the group. At least 13 Sunni men were executed in July 2009 for alleged involvement in a December 2008 bombing. In October 2009, a suicide bombing attributed to Jundallah struck a meeting between IRGC commanders and tribal leaders, killing more than 40 people.

Sufi Muslims have also faced persecution by the authorities. The constitution recognizes Zoroastrians, Jews, and Christians as religious minorities, and they are generally allowed to worship without interference, so long as they do not proselytize. Conversion by Muslims to a non-Muslim religion is punishable by death. The non-Muslim minorities are barred from election to representative bodies (though a set number of parliamentary seats are reserved for them), cannot hold senior government or military positions, and face restrictions in employment, education, and property ownership.

Some 300,000 Baha'is, Iran's largest non-Muslim minority, are not recognized in the constitution, enjoy virtually no rights under the law, and are banned from practicing their faith. Hundreds of Baha'is have been executed since the Islamic Revolution in 1979. Baha'i students are often barred from attending university and prevented from obtaining their educational records. Seven Baha'i leaders arrested in 2008 were officially accused of espionage in February 2009. After prominent human rights lawyer Shirin Ebadi became involved in their case in 2008, state-controlled media accused her daughter of converting to the Baha'i faith. Ebadi's colleague and fellow human rights lawyer, Abdolfattah Soltani, was arrested in June 2009 and released on bail in September; it was unclear whether the arrest was related to his involvement with the Baha'i case. In November and December, several more Baha'is were arrested, including at least four women.

Academic freedom is limited. Scholars are frequently detained, threatened, and forced to retire for expressing political views, and students involved in organizing protests face suspension or expulsion. Shortly after the 2009 presidential election, security forces broke into universities around the country. At least six students at Tehran University were killed, and the chancellor of Shiraz University reportedly resigned in protest over the violence, which reportedly left two of his students dead. At least five members of the Office for Strengthening Unity, a national student and alumni organization, were also killed in the attacks. Several other members were indicted in show trials in August, accused of fomenting a velvet revolution; four remained behind bars at year's end.

The constitution prohibits public demonstrations that, "violate the principles of Islam," a vague provision that was regularly invoked in 2009 to deny requests for demonstration permits. Vigilante and paramilitary organizations that are officially or tacitly sanctioned by the government—most notably the Basij militia and Ansar-i Hezbollah—regularly play a major role in breaking up demonstrations. They were instrumental in the violent dispersal of protesters in the second half of 2009.

Demonstrations were mounted nearly every day of the week after the June 12 election, drawing hundreds of thousands of peaceful protesters into the streets. However, a sermon by Khamenei on June 19 made clear that any further protests would be met with harsh violence. The next day, security forces reportedly killed 20 protesters. The death of one of the victims, 26-year-old Neda Agha-Soltan, was recorded on a mobile-phone camera and disseminated via the internet; her name quickly became a rallying cry for protesters. After the violence of June 20, protests were limited almost exclusively to national holidays or days of mourning. Dozens of people, including a nephew of presidential candidate Mir Hussein Mousavi, were killed during protests on December 27, which marked both the major Shiite holiday of Ashura and the seventh day of mourning following the death of Grand Ayatollah Hussein-Ali Montazeri, a harsh critic of the regime.

Under the pretense of "countering immoral behavior," the government also disrupts private gatherings. The Basij carried out thousands of home raids in 2007, arresting more than 150,000 people and forcing them to sign letters promising to observe official dress codes and adhere to moral standards. A group of women referred to as the Mourning Mothers were attacked and arrested by security forces in

December 2009 as they convened to remember their children, who had either gone missing or been killed since the elections.

The constitution permits the establishment of political parties, professional syndicates, and other civic organizations, provided that they do not violate the principles of "freedom, sovereignty, and national unity" or question the Islamic basis of the republic. Human rights discourse and grassroots activism are integral parts of Iranian society. However, the security services routinely arrest and harass secular activists as part of a wider effort to control the activities of nongovernmental organizations (NGOs). Although permits are not required by law, the Ministry of the Interior has been imposing them and shutting down organizations that do not seek or qualify for them. The offices of the Human Rights Defenders Center, run by Shirin Ebadi, were raided and closed by the authorities in December 2008 for allegedly operating without a license. Ebadi, an outspoken critic of the regime's human rights abuses and the 2003 Nobel Peace Prize laureate, argued that the organization had permission to operate but that the authorities refused to hand over the proper documentation. Jinous Sobhani, secretary at the center and a Baha'i, was arrested in January 2009 and released on bail in March.

Iranian law does not allow independent labor unions, though workers' councils are represented in the Workers' House, the only legal labor federation. In 2009, union members throughout the country were attacked and arrested by security forces for participating in May Day celebrations. At least five labor leaders were jailed in 2009 for their efforts on behalf of sugar refinery workers, with one remaining behind bars at year's end. Teachers unions have been banned since 2007, but have not yet been dissolved by courts. Three arrests were made at a Tehran rally to celebrate National Teachers' Day on May 4, and multiple union members were arrested in the wake of the June presidential elections. In October, security forces broke up a strike by workers at a pipe manufacturing company in Ahwaz, who were seeking 10 months of unpaid wages; the crackdown resulted in 50 arrests and a number of injuries.

The judicial system is not independent, as the supreme leader directly appoints the head of the judiciary, who in turn appoints senior judges. General Courts ostensibly safeguard the rights of defendants, but in practice suspects are frequently tried in closed sessions without access to legal counsel. Dissident clerics are tried before the Special Court for the Clergy. Political and other sensitive cases are tried before Revolutionary Courts, where due-process protections are routinely disregarded and trials are often summary. In August and September 2009, hundreds of journalists and dissidents were convicted of crimes related to national security in five mass trials, none of which met international standards. During each of these televised proceedings, the prosecutor read out a "general indictment" against the hundreds of detainees in attendance. Select individuals then issued confessions that are generally believed to have been coerced.

The country's penal code is based on Sharia and provides for flogging, amputation, and execution by stoning or hanging for a range of social and political offenses; these punishments are carried out in practice. A man convicted of adultery was stoned to death in Rasht in March 2009. Iran's overall execution rate has increased by nearly 300 percent under Ahmadinejad. In July 2009, 44 convicted drug traffickers were hanged, including 24 on the same day. By August, four detainees had been sentenced to death for their involvement in protests, and the December 27 demonstrations prompted the minister of the interior to declare that all protesters would be considered *muharib*—persons waging war against God—and thus subject to execution.

In 2009, at least three prisoners were executed for crimes they committed while juveniles, and 142 others remained on death row. The government had announced in 2008 that it would no longer execute juveniles, but it later clarified that the death penalty remained an option under the parallel "retribution" system, in which the sentence is imposed by the victim's family rather than the state. This would be allowed for male offenders over the age of 15 and female offenders as young as 9.

Although the constitution prohibits arbitrary arrest and detention, such abuses are increasingly routine, and family members of detainees are often not notified for days or weeks. Suspected dissidents are frequently held in unofficial, illegal detention centers, and allegations of torture are common there and in Tehran's infamous Evin prison. A 2004 law banned torture in interrogations, but reports of the practice persisted in 2009, particularly for political prisoners arrested after the June presidential election. Prison conditions in general are notoriously poor, and there are regular allegations of abuse and death in custody. Male and female detainees alleged rape by security forces in the second half of 2009; after reformist presidential candidate Mehdi Karroubi released a detainee's first-hand account of rape on his website, prosecutors initiated a case against him. The rape claims were reinforced, when a former member of the Basij confessed that security personnel were permitted to rape detainees as a "reward" for their work.

The constitution and laws call for equal rights for all ethnic groups, but in practice, these rights are restricted by the authorities. Ethnic Kurds, Arabs, Baluchis, and Azeris complain of political and economic discrimination. Kurdish opposition groups suspected of separatist aspirations, such as the Democratic Party of Iranian Kurdistan (KDPI), are brutally suppressed. The Free Life Party of Kurdistan (PJAK), a separatist militant group linked to the Kurdistan Workers' Party (PKK) of Turkey, has conducted a number of guerrilla attacks in recent years and was declared a terrorist organization by the United States in 2009. In May, after alleged PJAK attacks on police stations in border cities left multiple officers and rebels dead, Iranian aircraft attacked PJAK outposts in Iraq.

Freedom of movement is routinely restricted in Iran. Political activists are often banned from leaving the country after completing prison sentences or being released on suspended sentences. Security services have been known to confiscate passports or interrogate travelers on their return from conferences abroad. Shirin Ebadi, whose Nobel Peace Price was confiscated in November 2009, was in Spain at the time of the election and did not return to Iran for the rest of the year, although it is unclear whether this was by choice.

Women are widely educated; a majority of university students are female, and 94 percent of secondary-school-aged girls attend school, compared with only 80 percent of boys. Women currently hold seats in the parliament, though they are routinely excluded from running for higher offices. In a sign of female voters' growing political influence, the 2009 presidential candidates addressed issues that concerned women in the weeks preceding the election. Twice-elected parliament member Vahid-Dastjerdi became Iran's first female cabinet minister in September 2009, when she was appointed to head the Health Ministry. However, female judges may not issue final verdicts, and a woman cannot obtain a passport without the permission of her husband or a male relative. Women do not enjoy equal rights under Sharia-based statutes governing divorce, inheritance, and child custody, although some of these inequalities are accompanied by greater familial and financial obligations for men. A woman's testimony in court is given only half the weight of a man's, and the monetary damages awarded to a female victim's family on her death is half that owed to the family of a male victim. Women must conform to strict dress codes and are segregated from men in some public places, and there has been a crackdown in recent years on women deemed to be dressed immodestly. In February 2009, Alieh Eghdam Doust became the first women's rights defender in Iran to have her prison sentence implemented. She is now serving a three-year sentence for participating in a peaceful protest in 2006.

Iraq

Political Rights: 5*
Civil Liberties: 6
Status: Not Free

Population: 30,047,000
Capital: Baghdad

Ratings Change: Iraq's political rights rating improved from 6 to 5 due to free and competitive provincial elections in early 2009 and an increase in the Iraqi government's autonomy as U.S. troops began their phased withdrawal.

Ten-Year Ratings Timeline For Year Under Review (Political Rights, Civil Liberties, Status)

2000	2001	2002	2003	2004	2005	2006	2007	2008	2009
7,7NF	7,7NF	7,7NF	7,5NF	7,5NF	6,5NF	6,6NF	6,6NF	6,6NF	5,6NF

Overview: Iraq successfully held provincial elections in January 2009, with Prime Minister Nouri al-Maliki's Da'wa party emerging as the biggest winner. The parliament in November managed to pass legislation that would govern the scheduled 2010 national elections, but a veto by the presidency council threatened to hold up the polls, forcing lawmakers to pass a revised law in December. Also during the year, U.S. forces transferred security responsibilities to their Iraqi counterparts and began withdrawing from the country under a new bilateral security agreement. There were a series of sectarian killings and deadly attacks on government institutions in 2009, but widespread violence remained at an ebb.

The modern state of Iraq was established after World War I as a League of Nations mandate administered by Britain. The British installed a constitutional monarchy that privileged the Sunni Arab minority at the expense of Kurds and Shiite Arabs. Sunni Arab political dominance continued after independence in 1932 and a military coup that toppled the monarchy in 1958. The Arab nationalist Baath party seized power in 1968, and the new regime's de facto strongman, Saddam Hussein, assumed the presidency in 1979.

Hussein brutally suppressed all opposition and made foreign policy decisions that placed a heavy burden on the country. Iraq fought a destructive war with Iran from 1980 to 1988, and then invaded Kuwait in 1990, only to be ousted by a U.S.-led coalition the following year. After the war, the United Nations imposed economic sanctions on Iraq in a bid to limit its military capacity, force Hussein to allow international verification of the elimination of the country's weapons of mass destruction (WMD), and compel Iraq into resolving its border dispute with Kuwait. The sanctions remained in place for over a decade and caused widespread humanitarian suffering without achieving the intended goals.

Following the establishment of a U.S.-enforced no-fly zone north of the 36th parallel in 1991, most of the three northern provinces of Erbil, Duhok, and Sulimaniyah came under the control of the Kurdistan Democratic Party (KDP) and the Patriotic Union of Kurdistan (PUK). The two factions fought openly in the mid-1990s, but they eventually reconciled and established an autonomous Kurdistan Regional Government (KRG).

A U.S.-led coalition invaded Iraq in March 2003 and established a Coalition Provisional Authority (CPA) to administer the country. It disbanded the Iraqi military and prevented members of the Baath party from serving in government or the new security forces. The lack of a viable military and a dearth of foreign soldiers created a security vacuum, leading to widespread looting, damage to infrastructure, and acute electricity and water shortages. The alleged WMD that inspired the invasion were never found.

Sunni Arabs, who constitute roughly 20 percent of the population, were disproportionately affected by de-Baathification policies and wary of participating in a political transition that could hand power to the Shiite majority. Exploiting these sentiments, loose networks of former Baathist officials, Sunni Arab tribe members, and Islamist militants associated with al-Qaeda began organizing and funding an insurgency that rapidly gained strength in late 2003 and 2004.

Insurgents threatened Sunni Arabs and ensured that they boycotted the 2005 elections for a Transitional National Assembly (TNA) and provincial governments. As a result, Shiite and Kurdish parties won a landslide victory, and Sunni Arabs were not well represented in the new Iraqi Transitional Government (ITG) or the drafting process for a permanent constitution. The charter was approved by referendum in October 2005, though more than two-thirds of voters in two largely Sunni Arab provinces rejected it. Under a compromise brokered as a concession to Sunni demands, the first elected parliament would form a Constitutional Review Committee to determine whether the document should be amended.

Meanwhile, Shiite party militias were able to infiltrate the Interior Ministry's police and counterinsurgency forces, and extrajudicial detentions and killings by both the militias and militia-dominated police units became common during 2005 and 2006. Sunni militias responded in kind, and an intense cycle of sectarian conflict ensued. Ethnically cleansed or segregated neighborhoods soon became a fixture in Baghdad and other multiethnic provinces.

Sunni Arabs participated in the December 2005 elections for a full-term parliament, increasing their political representation. Nouri al-Maliki of the Shiite Da'wa party was chosen as prime minister. However, further political progress remained elusive; the main Sunni Arab bloc in parliament and a Shiite faction loyal to populist cleric and militia leader Moqtada al-Sadr both began a boycott of the legislature in 2007.

The parliament adopted several symbolic measures in 2008 to bring Sunni Arabs back into the political process. In January many former Baathists were permitted to return to jobs they lost under the CPA's de-Baathification process, and in February, the government granted amnesty to thousands of mainly Sunni Arab prisoners. The largest Sunni bloc returned to government in April, after a boycott of almost a year, and six Sunni ministers subsequently joined al-Maliki's cabinet.

In January 2009, Iraq held provincial elections that were originally scheduled for October 2008. Under electoral legislation passed in late 2008, voters could choose candidates rather than party lists, the use of religious symbols in campaigning was restricted, a 25 percent quota was set for female council members, and just 6 seats—down from 15 in an earlier draft—were set aside for Christians and other small minorities out of a total of 440 provincial council seats. The voting was largely peaceful, and turnout in most provinces ranged from 50 percent to 75 percent. On the whole, al-Maliki's Da'wa party emerged as the winner, though it needed to form coalitions to govern in most provinces. Sharp political and sectarian divisions remained, however; in five provinces the leading parties missed April deadlines, delaying the formation of governments.

The January elections did not include the autonomous Kurdish region or the contested province of Kirkuk. A referendum to determine whether Kirkuk would join the Kurdish region remained delayed, despite a constitutional provision that had required it before the end of 2007. In Ninewa—another province divided between Sunni Arabs and Kurds, as well as Turkmens and a number of smaller groups—the Kurds lost representation due to greater participation by Sunni Arab and Turkmen voters, who had largely abstained from earlier provincial balloting. Elections in July for the Kurdish regional parliament and presidency featured high turnout and a fairly strong showing by a new opposition bloc called Gorran (Change), which took about a quarter of the parliamentary vote. Nevertheless, the ruling PUK-KDP alliance maintained its dominance, and President Massoud Barzani of the KDP won reelection. Gorran alleged that many of its supporters were subsequently fired from government jobs.

In November, the parliament passed a new election law to govern the 2010 national elections. However, it was vetoed by the presidency council, as Vice President Tariq al-Hashimi, a Sunni, argued that it did not provide enough representation to Iraqis residing abroad. A slightly revised law was finally passed in December. It called for an open-list, proportional-representation voting system, with multimember districts corresponding to the 18 provinces. A total of eight seats were reserved for Christians and other small religious minorities. Under an internationally brokered compromise on Kirkuk, Sunni Arab, Turkmen, and Kurdish factions agreed to use a 2009 voter registry rather than an older version, despite their suspicions about the legitimacy of a large influx of Kurdish residents since 2003; however, the election results would be subject to a UN-led investigation if fraud was alleged.

Under a 2008 security agreement between Iraq and the United States, U.S. troops in 2009 completed a withdrawal from Iraqi cities and transferred authority over security and combat operations to Iraqi forces. Iraqi officials also obtained authority over prisoners and the power to prosecute U.S. personnel in some circumstances. About 140,000 U.S. troops were stationed in Iraq as of early 2009, and the U.S. government planned to withdraw most from the country by late 2010, though up to 50,000 could remain through the end of 2011, when all U.S. forces had to leave under the security pact. Despite the Iraqi government's increased autonomy, it was unable to provide basic services to its people; certain areas of Baghdad still received only six hours of electricity daily.

The U.S. withdrawal came in the context of apparently durable security improvements since 2007, when an additional 30,000 U.S. troops had been deployed to help suppress rampant sectarian and insurgent violence. Sunni militias had also increasingly turned against the insurgency and al-Qaeda in those years. Between 379 and 677 Iraqi civilians and security personnel were killed monthly between January and October 2009, a considerable decline from 2008 numbers. The violence that remained often had a sectarian character: 35 Shiite pilgrims were killed by a suicide bomber in February, as were another 140 in April, and Shiite mosques in Baghdad and Karbala were bombed in September. There were almost daily attacks in the ethnically, religiously, and politically contested city of Mosul. A coordinated series of bombings struck Christian sites in Baghdad and Mosul in July; other minorities, including Turkmens and Shabaks, were also targets of periodic violence.

Other attacks during the year focused on Iraqi government sites. The police academy was bombed in March, as were the offices of the Iraqi army. Insurgents attacked government food-distribution centers in April, and police officers at checkpoints across the country were targeted immediately after Ramadan. In October, the deadliest bombing in two years struck the Justice Ministry and the Baghdad provincial council complex, killing over 150 people and wounding more than 500.

Political Rights and Civil Liberties: Iraq is not an electoral democracy. Although it has conducted meaningful elections, the country remains under the influence of a foreign military presence and impairments caused by sectarian and insurgent violence. Under the constitution, the president and two vice presidents are elected by the parliament and appoint the prime minister, who is nominated by the largest parliamentary bloc. Elections are held every four years. The prime minister forms a cabinet and runs the executive functions of the state. The parliament consists of a 275-seat lower house, the Council of Representatives, and a still-unformed upper house, the Federal Council, which would represent provincial interests. The lower house is set to expand to 325 seats in 2010. Political parties representing a wide range of viewpoints operate without restrictions, but the Baath party is officially banned. The Independent Electoral Commission of Iraq (IECI), whose nine-member board was selected by a UN advisory committee, has sole responsibility for administering elections.

Home to one-fifth of the country's population, the autonomous Kurdish region constitutes a distinct polity within Iraq, with its own flag, military units, and language. The 111-seat regional legislature remains dominated by the allied PUK and KDP, despite the presence of the new Gorran opposition bloc following 2009 elections. The Kurdish region's political leaders profess their commitment to remaining part of a federal Iraqi state, but Kurdish security forces maintain a de facto border with the rest of Iraq, and Iraqi Arabs are often treated as foreigners.

Iraq is plagued by pervasive corruption at all levels of government, and most offenders reportedly enjoy impunity. A national Integrity Commission is tasked with fighting corruption, but it conducts its investigations in secret and does not publish its findings until the courts have issued final decisions. In April 2009, an attempt by anticorruption authorities to arrest several Trade Ministry officials resulted in gunfire from ministry guards. A number of the suspects were ultimately arrested and sentenced to prison, and the trade minister, a member of Prime Minister Nouri al-Maliki's Da'wa party, was forced to resign in May and face charges himself. Recruits allegedly pay bribes to enter the security forces. Iraq was ranked 176 out of 180 countries surveyed in Transparency International's 2009 Corruption Perceptions Index.

Freedom of expression is protected by the constitution and generally respected by the authorities. However, it has been seriously impeded by sectarian tensions and fear of violent reprisals. Over a dozen private television stations are in operation, and major Arab satellite stations are easily accessible. More than 150 print publications have been established since 2003 and are allowed to function without significant government interference. Internet access is not currently restricted.

Legislation passed in 2006 criminalized the ridicule of public officials, who often file suits when journalists report on corruption allegations. An Iraqi court in May 2009 ordered the German-based Iraqi news website Kitabat to pay a billion dinars (US$850,000) in damages for an article accusing al-Maliki's chief of staff of nepotism, though the prime minister then withdrew the lawsuit. In August, the Dubai-based satellite television station Al-Sharqiya was ordered to pay 100 million dinars for defamation against an Iraqi military spokesman, and Britain's *Guardian* newspaper was instructed to pay 100 million dinars in November for an article in which al-Maliki was accused of increasing authoritarianism.

Violent retribution against journalists has hindered their ability to report widely and objectively. The Committee to Protect Journalists (CPJ) and the Iraq-based Journalistic Freedoms Observatory in June 2009 reported more than 70 cases of harassment and assault against journalists by Iraqi security forces since January. However, in an indication of the overall improvement in the security situation, CPJ documented only 4 murders of journalists in 2009, down from at least 11 in 2008 and more than 30 in each of the previous two years. Impunity for such murders remained the norm.

Journalists operate more freely in the Kurdish region, although a 2008 press law imposes fines for creating instability, spreading fear or intimidation, causing harm to people, or violating religious beliefs. Journalists who offend local officials and top party leaders or expose high-level corruption remain subject to physical attacks, arbitrary detention, and harassment. Kurdish broadcast media are dominated by the two main political parties, but independent print outlets and internet sites have arisen in recent years.

Freedom of religion is guaranteed by the constitution, and religious institutions are allowed to operate with little formal oversight. However, all religious communities in Iraq have been threatened by sectarian violence. Estimates of the Christian population that has sought safety abroad since 2003 reach into the hundreds of thousands. Religious and ethnic minorities in northern Iraq—including Turkmens, Arabs, Christians, and Shabaks—have reported instances of discrimination and harassment by Kurdish authorities, though a number have fled to the Kurdish-controlled region due to its relative security. While sectarian violence declined in 2009, formerly mixed areas are now much more homogeneous, and terrorist attacks continue to be directed toward sectarian targets.

Academic institutions operate in a highly politicized and insecure environment. Hundreds of professors were killed during the peak of sectarian and insurgent violence, and many more stopped working or fled the country, though there have been some reports of scholars returning to their jobs following security improvements in the last two years.

Rights to freedom of assembly and association are recognized by the constitution and generally respected in practice. The constitution guarantees these rights, "in a way that does not violate public order and morality." Domestic and international nongovernmental organizations (NGOs) are able to operate without legal restrictions, and although safety concerns severely limit their activities in many areas, their situation improved along with general security conditions in 2009. The lack of a legal framework and registration system for NGOs also hinders their ability to function and attract donor funds.

The constitution provides for the right to form and join professional associations and unions. Union activity has flourished in nearly all industries since 2003, and strikes have not been uncommon. However, Iraq's 1987 labor law remains in effect, prohibiting unionization in the public sector, and a 2005 decree by the ITG gave authorities the power to seize all union funds and prevent their disbursal. A pro-union parliamentary committee was subsequently established to revise the decree and advance International Labour Organization–compliant labor laws that were drafted in 2004, but these have yet to be enacted.

Judicial independence is guaranteed in the constitution. The Higher Judicial Council—headed by the chief judge of the Federal Supreme Court and composed of Iraq's 17 chief appellate judges and several judges from the Federal Court of Cassation—has administrative authority over the court system. In practice, however, judges have come under immense political and sectarian pressure and have been largely unable to pursue cases involving organized crime, corruption, and militia activity, even when presented with overwhelming evidence. Iraqi citizens often turn to local militias and religious groups to dispense justice rather than seek redress with official law enforcement bodies that are seen as corrupt or ineffective.

Those accused of committing war crimes, genocide, and crimes against humanity fall under the jurisdiction of the Iraqi High Tribunal (IHT), previously known as the Iraq Special Tribunal. The IHT statute does not explicitly require that guilt be proven beyond a reasonable doubt and lacks adequate safeguards against self-incrimination. International observers noted numerous irregularities in the trial that culminated in the execution of former president Saddam Hussein in December 2006. Trials and sentencing procedures for a number of senior Hussein aides were ongoing in 2009.

The criminal procedure code and the constitution prohibit arbitrary arrest and detention, though both practices are common in security-related cases. The constitution prohibits all forms of torture and inhumane treatment and affords victims the right to compensation, but authorities have not established effective safeguards against the mistreatment of detainees. Allegations of torture by security services have been serious and widespread. While KRG laws similarly prohibit inhumane treatment, it is widely acknowledged that Kurdish security forces practice illegal detention and questionable interrogation tactics. Detainees in U.S. custody have also experienced torture and mistreatment, although U.S. forces in 2009 were transferring their remaining detainees to Iraqi control. In September, the U.S. military closed Camp Bucca, once its largest detention facility in the country.

The constitution promises women equal rights under the law, though in practice they face various forms of legal and societal discrimination. Women are guaranteed 25 percent of the seats in the legislature, and their participation in public life has increased as the security situation has improved; in 2009, women entered the officer corps of the Iraqi police for the first time. While they still faced serious social pressure and restrictions, women also returned in larger numbers to jobs and universities. Women enjoy somewhat greater legal protections and social freedoms in the Kurdish region, but their political power is limited. Moreover, domestic abuse and so-called honor killings remain serious problems both in the Kurdish region and across the country. The laws applicable outside the Kurdish region offer leniency to the perpetrators of honor killings, and though the laws in the Kurdish region are more favorable towards women, honor killings and suicides of women accused of honor crimes persist. The U.S. State Department placed Iraq on the Tier 2 Watch List in its 2009 Trafficking in Persons Report, noting problems including the trafficking and sexual exploitation of women from impoverished and displaced Iraqi families, and the abuse of foreign men and women who are recruited to work in Iraq.

Ireland

Political Rights: 1
Civil Liberties: 1
Status: Free

Population: 4,528,000
Capital: Dublin

Ten-Year Ratings Timeline For Year Under Review (Political Rights, Civil Liberties, Status)

2000	2001	2002	2003	2004	2005	2006	2007	2008	2009
1,1F	1,1F	1,1F	1,1F	1,1F	1,1F	1,1F	1,1F	1,1F	1,1F

Overview: The ruling Fianna Fail and Green parties saw a sharp drop in support in local elections in June 2009. While they continued to govern, a series of resignations and defections left them with equal support in Parliament to the opposition. Irish voters also reversed their 2008 decision and approved the European Union's Lisbon Treaty in October. Meanwhile, Ireland struggled with continued financial hardship throughout the year.

The Irish Free State emerged from the United Kingdom under the Anglo-Irish Treaty of 1921, though six counties in the province of Ulster remained within the United Kingdom. A brief civil war followed, ending in 1923. In 1937, the Irish Free State adopted a new constitution and a new name—Ireland, or Eire.

Ireland remained neutral in its foreign policy, staying out of World War II and NATO. It joined the European Community (now the European Union, or EU) along with Britain and Denmark in 1973. Thanks in part to large subsidies for poorer countries within the EU, Ireland enjoyed high rates of economic growth for many years, transforming from one of the poorest countries in Europe into one of the richest. It adopted the euro on its launch as an electronic currency in 1999 and introduced euro notes and coins in 2001.

Ireland has resisted any EU moves that would impinge on its neutrality, including plans to set up an EU military capability. Partly for this reason, Irish voters rejected the EU's Treaty of Nice in June 2001, temporarily blocking the enlargement of the bloc into Eastern Europe. In a second referendum, in October 2002, Irish voters approved the treaty.

The country achieved outstanding economic growth from 1998 through 2002, which slowed to a still-impressive 5.7 percent in 2006. With slower growth, budget tightening fueled voter disillusionment. However, a strong debate performance by Prime Minister Bertie Ahern, combined with voter comfort after 10 years of economic growth, helped Fianna Fail to win the May 2007 general elections. Ahern was given a third consecutive term as prime minister in June. Fianna Fail captured 78 of 166 seats in the lower house of Parliament, compared with opposition Fine Gael's 51. However, the poor performance by the Progressive Democrats, who lost six of their eight seats, forced Fianna Fail to take the Green Party, with its six seats, into the governing coalition for the first time in that party's history. The rest of the lower house's seats were held by the Labour Party (20), Sinn Fein (4), and independents (5).

In September 2007, Ahern narrowly won a vote of confidence over long-standing questions about his personal financial dealings as finance minister in the 1990s. He had denied granting favors in exchange for loans from businessmen friends, however evidence emerged in 2008 that money under his control as finance minister had been lent interest free to a former business partner. It was also revealed that he had received bank deposits in British pounds, something he had earlier denied. He finally agreed to step down, and Finance Minister Brian Cowen became prime minister in May.

Soon after Cowen's installation, Irish voters rejected the EU's Lisbon Treaty, designed to replace a draft EU constitution that had failed to pass in 2005. Despite their general enthusiasm for EU membership, Irish voters were swayed in part by a series of false allegations about the treaty, including that it would force Ireland to legalize abortion and would lead to the creation of an EU army. However, Irish voters reversed their decision in September 2009, strongly supporting the treaty in a second vote.

While the ruling Fianna Fail and Green parties saw a significant decline in support in local elections in June 2009, the coalition subsequently won a motion of confidence in Parliament. As a result of a series of resignations and defections—many in protest of government policies—the number of coalition backers had dropped to equal that of the opposition by early August 2009. However, Fianna Fail and the Green Party continued in power after agreeing on a governmental program in October, which provides for electoral reform, such as the establishment of an independent electoral commission and changes to rules for political donations.

Ireland has faced severe economic problems in conjunction with the global crisis, driven by a rapid decline in property prices. In 2009, the economy entered a technical depression, with public finances in deep crisis and the Irish banking system extremely fragile despite government intervention.

Political Rights and Civil Liberties: Ireland is an electoral democracy. The Parliament (Oireachtas) consists of a lower house (the Dail), whose 166 members are elected by proportional representation for five-year terms, and an upper house (the Seanad, or Senate) with 60 members, 11 appointed and 49 elected by representatives of various interest groups. The Senate is mainly a consultative body. The president, whose functions are largely ceremonial, is directly elected for a seven-year term. The prime minister, or taoiseach, is chosen by Parliament.

The political party system is open to the rise and fall of competing groupings. The two largest parties—Fianna Fail and Fine Gael—do not differ widely in ideological orientation but represent the opposing sides of the 1920s civil war. The smaller parties are the Labour Party, Sinn Fein, and the Greens. The Progressive Democrats disbanded in 2009.

Corruption has been a recurring problem, with many scandals involving members of Fianna Fail. In March 2009, a former department of justice official was jailed for his role in a scheme to extend visas for Chinese students in exchange for bribes. Separately, a former government press secretary was convicted in May of bribery related to land deals in Dublin in the 1990s. In October, the Speaker of the Parliament stepped down amid criticism that he had claimed personal expenses as a minister, though he denied the allegations against him. A 2009 report by Transparency International Ireland stated that the greatest concern was so-called legal corruption in the form of undue political influence through cronyism, political patronage and favors, donations, and other contacts that influence political decisions and behavior. Likely due to the low levels of petty corruption, Ireland was ranked 14 out of 180 countries surveyed in Transparency International's 2009 Corruption Perceptions Index.

The media are free and independent, and internet access is unrestricted. The print media present a variety of viewpoints. Television and radio are dominated by the state broadcaster, but the growth of cable and satellite television is weakening its influence. The state maintains the right to censor pornographic and violent material, which critics charge is an anachronistic practice and possibly a violation of the European Convention on Human Rights. A defamation bill passed in 2009 decriminalized defamation in Ireland; a controversial provision for the offense of blasphemy had not come into force by year's end.

Freedom of religion is provided in the constitution, and discrimination on the basis of religion is illegal. Although the country is overwhelmingly Roman Catholic, there is no state religion, and adherents of other faiths face few impediments to religious expression. Religious education is provided in most primary and secondary schools, whose boards include officials of the Catholic Church. However, parents may exempt their children from religious instruction, and the constitution requires equal funding for students wishing instruction in other faiths. Academic freedom is respected.

Freedom of association is upheld, and nongovernmental organizations can operate freely. The right of public assembly and demonstration is not legally infringed. Collective bargaining is legal and unrestricted, and labor unions operate without hindrance.

The legal system is based on common law, and the judiciary is independent. Council of Europe inspectors in 2006 found evidence of some beatings and other ill-treatment of detainees by police, mostly at the time of arrest. While prison conditions have improved in recent years, overcrowding remains a problem. Despite equal protection for all under the law, the Irish Travellers, a traditionally nomadic group of about 25,000 people, face social discrimination in housing, hiring, and other areas.

Ireland, which had been remarkably tolerant of a large influx of immigrants into its relatively homogenous population during the boom years, has seen public opinion move against immigration as the economy has worsened. A 2009 EU study found that there were 224 racially motivated crimes reported in Ireland in 2007, a 29.5 percent increase over 2006.

Inequality persists in pay rates for men and women, but discrimination in employment on the basis of sex or sexual orientation is forbidden under national and EU law. The past two presidents have been women: Mary McAleese (elected in 1997 and reelected in 2004) and Mary Robinson (1990–97). However, women are underrepresented politically, with just 20 elected to the Parliament in 2007. Abortion is legal only when the life of the mother is in danger, and women seeking abortions frequently travel to Britain to have them performed. An Irish nongovernmental organization that works with women in the sex trade has reported an increase in prostitution as well as human trafficking in Ireland.

A 2009 bill gives same-sex couples the right to civil partnership, but denies equal access to the protections received by families with married parents. The much-publicized Commission to Inquire into Child Abuse, investigating claims of abuse in state schools and orphanages since the 1940s, submitted two reports in 2009 that exposed widespread physical and emotional abuse against children in state institutions as well as by Catholic priests.

Israel

Political Rights: 1
Civil Liberties: 2
Status: Free

Population: 7,634,000 [Note: There are an estimated 187,000 Israeli settlers in the West Bank, about 20,000 in Golan Heights, and fewer than 177,000 in East Jerusalem.]
Capital: Jerusalem

Note: The numerical rating and status reflect the state of political rights and civil liberties within Israel itself. Separate reports examine the Israeli-occupied territories and the Palestinian-administered areas.

Ten-Year Ratings Timeline For Year Under Review (Political Rights, Civil Liberties, Status)

2000	2001	2002	2003	2004	2005	2006	2007	2008	2009
1,3F	1,3F	1,3F	1,3F	1,3F	1,2F	1,2F	1,2F	1,2F	1,2F

Overview: In January, Israeli forces concluded a major military campaign against the Islamist militant group Hamas in the Gaza Strip in an effort to halt rocket fire into Israel. The incursion, which had begun in December 2008, drew accusations of war crimes from international human rights groups and a UN Human Rights Council investigation. While the incumbent centrist Kadima party won the most seats in February's parliamentary elections, the rightist Likud party succeeded in forming a governing coalition, and Benjamin Netanyahu succeeded Kadima's Tzipi Livni as prime minister in April.

Israel was formed in 1948 from part of the British mandate of Palestine, which had been created by the League of Nations following World War I. A 1947 UN partition plan dividing Palestine into two states, Jewish and Arab, was rejected by the Arab Higher Committee and the Arab League, and Israel's 1948 declaration of independence led to war with a coalition of Arab countries. While Israel maintained its sovereignty and expanded its borders, Jordan (then known as Transjordan) seized East Jerusalem and the West Bank, and Egypt took control of the Gaza Strip.

As a result of its 1967 war with Egypt, Jordan, and Syria, Israel occupied the Sinai Peninsula, the West Bank, the Gaza Strip, East Jerusalem, and the Golan Heights. Israel annexed East Jerusalem in 1967 and extended Israeli law to the Golan Heights in 1981. It returned the Sinai to Egypt in 1982 as part of a peace agreement between the two countries.

In 1993, Israel secured an agreement with the Palestine Liberation Organization (PLO) that provided for a phased Israeli withdrawal from the West Bank and Gaza Strip and limited Palestinian autonomy in those areas, in exchange for Palestinian recognition of Israel and a renunciation of terrorism. In 1994, Israel and Jordan agreed to a U.S.-brokered peace agreement. However, Israeli-Palestinian negotiations on a future Palestinian state broke down in 2000, and Palestinian militant violence resumed.

In 2002, the Israel Defense Forces (IDF) reoccupied many of the West Bank areas that had been ceded to the Palestinian Authority (PA) in the 1990s. Israel also began construction of a security barrier in the West Bank that roughly followed the 1949 armistice line. Critics accused the Israelis of confiscating Palestinian property and impeding access to land, jobs, and services for those living in the barrier's vicinity. As a result, the barrier—which was about 70 percent complete by the end of 2009—has been rerouted six times by order of the Israeli Supreme Court; half of these orders have yet to be implemented.

After the death of Palestinian leader Yasser Arafat, Mahmoud Abbas was elected president of the PA in January 2005. A verbal ceasefire agreement between Israeli prime minister Ariel Sharon and Abbas led to a general decline, but not a halt, in violence. In September 2005, Sharon's government completed a unilateral withdrawal of Jewish settlers from the Gaza Strip, overcoming fierce right-wing opposition. Sharon subsequently left the right-wing Likud party and founded the centrist Kadima party. In January 2006, he suffered a stroke that left him in a coma, and then deputy prime minister Ehud Olmert succeeded him as prime minister and Kadima chairman. After the 2006 parliamentary elections, Olmert and Kadima headed a new coalition government that included the Labor Party, the religious Shas party, and other factions.

Israeli-Palestinian violence picked up after the Islamist group Hamas won elections to the Palestinian Legislative Council (PLC) in January 2006, displacing Abbas's Fatah party. Over the next two years, Israel experienced a decreasing number of terrorist attacks in Israel and regular rocket and mortar fire from the Gaza Strip, while the IDF continued to stage air strikes against militant leaders and destructive incursions into Palestinian territory, including an invasion of the Gaza Strip in the summer of 2006.

Also that summer, Israel went to war against the Lebanese Islamist militia Hezbollah after the group staged a cross-border attack. By the time a UN-brokered ceasefire took effect in mid-August, about 1,200 Lebanese, including many civilians, had been killed; 116 IDF soldiers and 43 Israeli civilians were also killed. A 2007 report by Israel's state comptroller described the government's efforts to protect civilian life during the conflict as "a grave failure."

Olmert resigned in September 2008 after being charged in a corruption case. Foreign Minister Tzipi Livni replaced him, but she was unable to form a new majority coalition in the Knesset (parliament), prompting early elections in February 2009. While Kadima led with 28 seats, Likud (27 seats) ultimately formed a mostly right-wing government with the secular nationalist Yisrael Beiteinu (15 seats), Shas (11 seats), and other parties. The center-left Labor Party (13 seats) also joined the coalition, leaving Kadima in opposition. The new government, headed by Likud leader Benjamin Netanyahu, took office in April.

Meanwhile, Israeli-Palestinian violence continued. Hamas had seized control of the Gaza Strip in June 2007, creating a rift with the Fatah-dominated West Bank. Israel thereafter regarded Gaza as a hostile entity and imposed an economic blockade, allowing only limited amounts of humanitarian aid through its border crossings. In June 2008, Israel and Hamas implemented a six-month truce agreement, leading to a significant decrease in clashes in and around Gaza. Separately, Israel had pursued accelerated peace talks with the Fatah-led PA in the West Bank. However, despite a series of confidence-building measures and increased involvement by the United States, any breakthrough remained far off by the end of 2009.

After the six-month truce expired and Hamas ramped up its rocket bombardment of Israeli towns near the Gaza border, the IDF in December 2008 launched a major offensive, including near-daily air strikes and a ground invasion. Israel declared a unilateral ceasefire in late January 2009, with Hamas following suit soon thereafter. Israeli forces had destroyed large swathes of Gaza's military, government, and civilian infrastructure; according to the British Broadcasting Corporation (BBC), more than 4,000 buildings were destroyed, with 20,000 severely damaged. Human casualty figures remained in dispute: while the Palestinian Centre for Human Rights reported 1,434 Palestinians killed, including 960 noncombatants, the IDF reported 1,166 Palestinians killed, including 295 to 460 noncombatants. Thirteen Israelis were killed, including three civilians.

International and domestic human rights organizations accused Israel of using excessive force and imposing collective punishment on Gaza residents, citing the casualty figures, destroyed civilian infrastructure and homes, the IDF's allegedly illegal use of white phosphorus, and austere humanitarian conditions stemming in part from the blockade. Amnesty International and Human Rights Watch accused Israeli forces of war crimes, as did a UN Human Rights Council investigation led by South African jurist Richard Goldstone. The Israeli government, which did not cooperate with the Goldstone probe, vociferously denied these charges, arguing that the campaign was necessary to protect Israeli civilians from Gaza-based rocket fire and that Palestinian civilian casualties were caused primarily by Hamas and other militant groups' use of civilian areas to stage and prepare attacks. Hamas and other Palestinian militant groups were also accused of war crimes for indiscriminately firing over 700 rockets into Israeli civilian areas during the war.

Political Rights and Civil Liberties:

Israel is an electoral democracy. A largely ceremonial president is elected by the 120-seat Knesset for seven-year terms. The prime minister is usually the leader of the largest party or coalition in the Knesset, members of which are elected by party-list proportional representation for four-year terms. At under 3 percent, Israel's threshold for parliamentary representation is the world's lowest, leading to the regular formation of niche parties and unstable coalitions.

Parties or candidates that deny the existence of Israel as a Jewish state, oppose the democratic system, or incite racism are prohibited. In January 2009, the Knesset's central election committee voted to ban two Arab parties—Balad and the United Arab List (UAL)–Ta'al —from the February elections on these grounds, citing their alleged support for Hamas in the Gaza conflict. The ban was rapidly overturned by the Supreme Court, and the parties were allowed to run (UAL-Ta'al won four seats and Balad won three). In 2007, Balad leader and Knesset member Azmi Bishara had resigned his seat and eventually left Israel for fear of prosecution on charges of espionage and aiding an enemy during war; Bishara had previously expressed support for Hezbollah during visits to Lebanon and Syria, both technically at war with Israel.

Thirteen members of the current Knesset are Arab Israelis. While the Arab population votes heavily for Arab-oriented parties, the left-leaning and centrist Zionist parties also draw strong support from the Arab community. No independent Arab party has been formally included in a governing coalition. After Israel annexed East Jerusalem in 1967, Arab residents were issued Israeli identity cards and given the option of obtaining Israeli citizenship, though most choose not to seek citizenship for political reasons. Noncitizens have the same rights as Israeli citizens, except the right to vote in national elections. They can vote in municipal as well as PA elections, and are eligible to apply for Israeli citizenship. However, Israeli law strips such Arabs of their Jerusalem residency if they remain outside the city for more than three months; in December 2009, the Interior Ministry revoked the residency rights of 4,570 Palestinians, whose cases represented more than a third of all such revocations since 1967. While the government claimed that most of the affected individuals lived abroad and had been receiving government stipends, Israeli and Palestinian rights groups accused Israel of manipulating the demographic balance in East Jerusalem. The city's Arab population does not receive a share of municipal services proportionate to its numbers.

Under the 1948 Law of Return, Jewish immigrants and their immediate families are granted Israeli citizenship and residence rights; other immigrants must apply for these rights. In 2003, the Knesset passed a measure that temporarily denied citizenship and residency status to West Bank or Gaza residents married to Israeli citizens. While the law was criticized as blatantly discriminatory, supporters cited evidence that 14 percent of suicide bombers acquired Israeli identity cards via family reunification laws, and the Supreme Court upheld the measure in 2006.

Israel was ranked 32 out of 180 countries surveyed in Transparency International's 2009 Corruption Perceptions Index. Corruption scandals in recent years have implicated senior officials, including a prime minister, a finance minister, and the heads of the tax authority and the police. Ehud Olmert resigned as prime minister in 2008 amid an investigation into some US$500,000 in donations and other gifts he had reportedly received from a U.S. businessman over many years, as well as several other alleged misdeeds dating to his previous posts in the cabinet and as mayor of Jerusalem. In August 2009, Olmert was indicted in three of these scandals. Separately, Yisrael

Beiteinu leader and current foreign minister Avigdor Lieberman is under investigation for money laundering, fraud, and breach of trust; in August, police recommended that the attorney general file charges against him.

Press freedom is respected in Israel, and the media are vibrant and independent. All Israeli newspapers are privately owned and freely criticize government policy. The Israel Broadcasting Authority operates public radio and television services, and commercial broadcasts are widely available. Most Israelis subscribe to cable or satellite television, and internet access is widespread and unrestricted. While print articles on security matters are subject to a military censor, the scope of permissible reporting is broad. The Government Press Office (GPO) has occasionally refused to provide press cards, especially to Palestinians, to restrict them from entering Israel, claiming security considerations. In February 2009, Israel threatened to not renew the work visas of some journalists with the Qatar-based satellite television station Al-Jazeera after Qatar cut trade ties with Israel. During the Gaza conflict, the IDF—which had declared Gaza off-limits to journalists—occasionally extended the exclusion zone two miles into Israeli territory, impeding both local and foreign journalists from reporting on developments at the border.

While Israel's founding documents define it as a, "Jewish and democratic state," freedom of religion is respected. Christian, Muslim, and Baha'i communities have jurisdiction over their own members in matters of marriage, divorce, and burial. Since the Orthodox establishment generally handles these matters among Jews, marriages between Jews and non-Jews are not recognized by the state unless conducted abroad. In 2009, there were a number of clashes between police and ultra-Orthodox residents opposed to the opening of a parking lot near Jerusalem's Old City on the Jewish Sabbath. In November, the arrest of a woman praying at the Western Wall with a *tallit* (or Jewish prayer shawl)—traditionally worn by men—sparked a significant controversy in the country.

Muslim and Christian communities occasionally claim discrimination in resource allocation and upkeep of religious sites, though the state budget officially assigns funds according to need. In November 2009, the newspaper *Haaretz* reported that ultra-Orthodox political pressure has impeded the planned construction of a mosque and a church at Ben Gurion International Airport in Tel Aviv. Citing security concerns, Israel occasionally restricts Muslim worshippers' access to the Temple Mount, or Haram al-Sharif, in Jerusalem. In October, Muslim youths at the site threw stones and firebombs at police and a tourist group, and police responded with rubber bullets and stun grenades.

Primary and secondary education are universal, with instruction for the Arab minority based on the common curriculum used by the Jewish majority, but conducted in Arabic. In 2007, the government approved an Arabic textbook that presents the founding of the state from the typical Palestinian perspective. However, in 2009, the Education Ministry ordered the word *Nakba* (catastrophe)—the term used by many Arabs to describe the establishment of Israel—removed from the text. School quality is generally worse in mostly Arab municipalities, and Arab children have reportedly had difficulty registering at mostly Jewish schools. Israel's universities are open to all students based on merit, and have long been centers for dissent. In October 2009, a court found that Tel Aviv University had closed an art exhibition by members of the Falun Gong spiritual movement in 2008 due to pressure from the Chinese embassy. The university was ordered to pay the organizers' court costs and to allow the exhibit during the next semester. Periodic road closures and other security measures in recent years have made it difficult for West Bank and Gaza residents to reach Israeli universities.

Freedoms of assembly and association are respected. Israel hosts an active civil society, and demonstrations are widely permitted. Groups committed to the destruction of Israel are not allowed to demonstrate. In July 2009, the cabinet approved a bill that prohibited state funding for activities by local authorities that mark the Nakba, considered a day of mourning by many Arab Israelis and commemorated on Israeli independence day. The measure—which must still pass three rounds of votes by the full Knesset—also bars state funding for any activities that reject Israel's existence as a Jewish and democratic state, or that fall within the official definition of armed struggle or terrorist activities against Israel. Also in 2009, the Foreign Ministry voiced concerns about the funding of antiwar groups by foreign governments. While the ministry reportedly asked the British, Spanish, and Dutch governments to stop funding one such group, Breaking the Silence, no additional steps were taken.

The largest of several demonstrations against the IDF's 2009 campaign in Gaza took place in Arab-majority towns in the north, including gatherings of 150,000 people in Sakhnin and 100,000 people in Baqa al-Gharbiyah. While most demonstrations were allowed to proceed, human rights organizations alleged that permits were more difficult to obtain in the north, that there were instances of "physical violence" by police, and that detained Arab Israeli protesters were more likely to be kept in custody during legal proceedings than their non-Arab counterparts.

Workers may join unions of their choice and have the right to strike and bargain collectively. Three-quarters of the workforce either belong to Histadrut, the national labor federation, or are covered by its social programs and bargaining agreements. General strikes are common but generally last under 24 hours. About 100,000 legal foreign workers enjoy wage protections, medical insurance, and guarantees against employer exploitation. However, those who leave their original employers are stripped of such rights and face deportation. Advocacy groups claim that there are at least 100,000 illegal workers in Israel, many of whom are exploited. In July 2009, a new immigration enforcement unit announced plans to deport nearly 300,000 illegal migrants and visa violators. Demonstrations were mounted across the country in October to protest the Interior Ministry's decision to deport 250 migrant families, including 1,200 children. The ministry was reevaluating the decision at year's end.

The judiciary is independent and regularly rules against the government. The Supreme Court hears direct petitions from citizens and Palestinian residents of the West Bank and Gaza Strip. The state generally adheres to court rulings, but the Association for Civil Rights in Israel reported in 2009 that the state was in contempt of eight rulings handed down by the Supreme Court since 2006, including a 2006 rerouting of the West Bank security barrier.

The Emergency Powers (Detention) Law of 1979 provides for indefinite administrative detention without trial. According to an October 2009 report by the human rights groups B'Tselem and HaMoked Center, there are about 7,150 Palestinians in Israeli custody: 5,000 serving sentences, 1,569 awaiting trial, and 335 in administrative detention. A 2006 temporary order (extended for three years in December 2007) permits the detention of suspects accused of security offenses for 96 hours without judicial oversight, compared with 24 hours for other detainees. In 2007, B'Tselem and HaMoked Center reported that Palestinian prisoners are held in terrible conditions and are subject to abusive interrogation techniques, including instances of torture. The government disputed the accuracy of the report.

While personal security in Israel deteriorated during the 2009 Gaza campaign, rocket attacks subsequently declined. The roughly 700 rockets and mortar shells fired into Israel during the conflict killed three people and injured scores, and the towns of Sderot and Gedera and the cities of Ashdod and Ashkelon were at least partially evacuated. From the ceasefire to the end of 2009, about 160 rockets hit Israel. In December, the country's Shin Bet intelligence agency reported that attacks on Israelis in 2009 fell to the lowest level since 2000, with 15 total fatalities. *Haaretz* has reported that over 12,000 rockets have been launched into Israel from Gaza since 2001. According to B'Tselem, about 500 Israeli civilians have been killed by Palestinian attacks since September 2000.

Although they have full political rights, the roughly one million Arab citizens of Israel (about 19 percent of the population) receive inferior education, housing, and social services relative to the Jewish population. Arab Israelis, except for the Druze minority, are not subject to the military draft, though they may volunteer. Those who do not serve are ineligible for the associated benefits, including scholarships and housing loans. In 2000, 13 Arabs were killed by police attempting to quell several days of often violent protests in support of the concurrent uprising in the Palestinian territories. A subsequent state-sponsored investigation (the Orr Commission) found that the government's "neglectful and discriminatory" management of the Arab population had led to, "poverty, unemployment, a shortage of land, serious problems in the education system and substantially defective infrastructure." In 2008, the attorney general announced that no police officers would be prosecuted for the 13 killings due to lack of evidence, drawing objections from human rights groups.

Separately, a July 2007 report by the state comptroller heavily criticized the government for failure to protect Arab Israeli villages—most of which did not have bomb shelters—during the 2006 conflict with Hezbollah. In 2008 and 2009, a number of Jewish towns in the north began insisting that prospective property buyers accept Israel's existence as a Jewish and democratic state as well as the towns' "Zionist ethos." These restrictions, widely perceived as attempts to exclude Arabs, are being challenged in court. In 2008, Jewish youths in the city of Akko attacked an Arab Israeli who drove through a mostly Jewish neighborhood during the Jewish holiday of Yom Kippur; this prompted retaliation by Arab youths and riots that spread to other cities.

Most Bedouin housing settlements are not recognized by the government or provided with essential services. International and domestic human rights groups have accused the government of pervasive land and housing discrimination against the Bedouin, and have urged authorities to stop demolishing unlicensed Bedouin homes. In December 2008, a Knesset-appointed committee called for the state to recognize villages and legalize buildings without permits as long as the settlements had a "minimal mass" of residents that would not affect existing regional plans. The state's Israeli Lands Administration owns 93 percent of the land in Israel; 13 percent of that is owned by the Jewish National Fund (JNF). In 2005, the Supreme Court and attorney general ruled that the JNF could no longer market property only to Jews.

The Knesset made a first attempt to override those rulings in 2007, but the process remained incomplete at the end of 2009.

Security measures can lead to delays at checkpoints and in public places. Security forces sometimes carry out random identity checks of civilians. By law, all citizens must carry national identification cards. The West Bank security barrier restricts the movements of some East Jerusalem residents. Formal and informal local rules that prevent driving on Jewish holidays can also hamper freedom of movement.

Women have achieved substantial parity at almost all levels of Israeli society. However, Arab women and religious Jewish women face some discrimination and societal pressures that negatively affect their professional, political, and social lives. In October 2009, the Transport Ministry outlawed so-called "modesty buses," on which women were forced to sit at the back, separate from men. The buses had recently been appearing in greater numbers in very religious Jewish neighborhoods of Jerusalem. The trafficking of women for prostitution has become a problem in recent years; both the United Nations and the U.S. State Department have identified Israel as a top destination for trafficked women. The government has opened shelters for victims, and in 2006, the Knesset passed a law mandating prison terms of up to 20 years for perpetrators. In March 2009, Israeli police uncovered a trafficking ring that allegedly smuggled 2,000 women from the former Soviet Union into Israel and Cyprus over a six-year period for sex work.

Sexual minorities have made significant strides in recent years. A 2005 Supreme Court decision granted guardianship rights to nonbiological parents in same-sex partnerships, and two lesbians were granted permission to legally adopt each other's biological children in 2006. Openly gay Israelis are permitted to serve in the armed forces. In August 2009, however, a gunman killed 2 people and wounded 15 at a gay, lesbian, and transgender support center in Tel Aviv.

Italy

Political Rights: 1
Civil Liberties: 2
Status: Free

Population: 60,274,000
Capital: Rome

Ten-Year Ratings Timeline For Year Under Review (Political Rights, Civil Liberties, Status)

2000	2001	2002	2003	2004	2005	2006	2007	2008	2009
1,2F	1,2F	1,1F	1,1F	1,1F	1,1F	1,1F	1,1F	1,2F	1,2F

Overview:

In October 2009, hundreds of thousands of people demonstrated in Rome against Prime Minister Silvio Berlusconi's attacks on the media, which had covered the premier's personal life, including allegations that he had sex with a teenage girl. Meanwhile, Parliament adopted a controversial new immigration law, and the country made gains against the influence of organized crime.

Italy was unified under the constitutional monarchy of Piedmont and Sardinia in the 19th century. Its liberal period ended in 1922, with the rise Benito Mussolini and his Fascist Party, which eventually led the country to defeat in World War II. A referendum in 1946 replaced the monarchy with a republican form of government.

The "clean hands" corruption trials of the early 1990s prompted the collapse of the major political factions that had dominated postwar Italian politics—the Christian Democrats, the Communists, and the Socialists. Since that time, many new parties and coalitions have emerged.

Parliamentary elections in 2006 ushered in a new center-left coalition government led by Romano Prodi, leaving Prime Minister Silvio Berlusconi's center-right bloc in opposition for the first time since 2001. Berlusconi's premiership had been marred by abortive attempts to prosecute him on money laundering, fraud, and tax evasion charges, and by his personal domination of the national media, including state outlets and his extensive private holdings. However, Prodi's new government proved unstable; in 2007, it lost key votes in Parliament over Italy's troop presence in Afghanistan, and it finally collapsed after a no-confidence vote in January 2008.

Berlusconi's rightist coalition, People of Freedom (PDL), handily won early parliamentary elections in April 2008, capturing a total of 344 seats in the lower house and 174 in the Senate in combination with two smaller allies. A center-left coalition led by Rome mayor Walter Veltroni's new Democratic Party placed second with 246 seats in the lower house and 132 seats in the Senate. Berlusconi ran on pledges to crack down on crime and illegal immigration, and the new Parliament passed a number of measures on those issues in 2008 and 2009.

A debate over the separation of church and state in Italy was sparked in 2009, after a teacher received a one-month suspension in February for removing a crucifix from his classroom. A November ruling by the European Court of Human Rights against the use of crucifixes in Italian classrooms was met with opposition. Also in February, the Supreme Court dismissed a seven-month jail sentence handed down to a judge for failing to perform his duties, after he refused to enter courts where crucifixes were hanging.

In June 2009, voters were presented with a national referendum on electoral laws during the European elections. The referendum, which sought to reduce further the number of parties in the system and move the country closer to a two-party model, was considered invalid when the number of respondents was less than the necessary quorum of 50 percent.

Berlusconi, the first head of Italian government to take legal action against Italian and European media, continued to interfere in journalists' efforts to cover conflicts between his private and political life. A national media group, *L'Espresso*, which owns *La Repubblica* newspaper, sued Berlusconi for defamation in July for calling the newspaper "subversive" and encouraging businesses to boycott advertising with the paper. Berlusconi's private life came under further scrutiny in May 2009, when his wife of 19 years accused him of "consorting with minors" and filed for divorce. *La Repubblica* subsequently began investigating the prime minister's personal life, alleging that he had also paid for sex. On October 3, 2009, between 150,000 and 300,000 people assembled in Rome for the "Right to Know, Duty to Inform" protest against Berlusconi's attacks on the media.

Twenty-two CIA agents, one U.S Air Force colonel, and two Italian secret agents were convicted in November in an Italian court for the 2003 kidnapping of a Muslim cleric in Milan. The cleric had been transferred to Egypt, where he was allegedly tortured as part of the U.S. policy of "extraordinary rendition." The Americans plan to appeal the conviction.

In December, Berlusconi was attacked while getting into a car in Milan by a man with a history of mental illness; Berlusconi suffered two broken teeth and a small nose fracture.

Political Rights and Civil Liberties:

Italy is an electoral democracy. The president, whose role is largely ceremonial but sometimes politically influential, is elected for a seven-year term by Parliament and representatives of the regions. Giorgio Napolitano, a former communist, was selected for the post in 2006. The president chooses the prime minister, who is often, but not always, the leader of the largest party in the 630-seat lower house, the Chamber of Deputies. The upper house is the Senate, with 315 seats. Members of both chambers serve five-year terms. The constitution also divides the country into 20 administrative regions.

A 1993 electoral law replaced the existing system of proportional representation with single-member districts for most of the seats in Parliament. The move was designed to reduce the number of political parties that could obtain seats and ensure a more stable majority for the parties in power; Italians had seen more than 50 governments since 1945. However, in 2005, proportional representation was restored, with a provision awarding at least 54 percent of the seats in the lower house to the winning party or coalition, no matter how small its margin of victory. For the Senate, victory in a given region assures the winning party or coalition a 55 percent majority of that region's allotment of seats. Just 6 parties won seats in the lower house in the 2008 elections, down from 26 the previous election.

In March 2009, Silvio consolidated the two main rightist parties—his Italia and former neo-fascist National Alliance—into a single party, of Freedom (*Il Popolo della Libertao* PDL). The regionalist and anti-immigration Lega Nord party, which is still part of the ruling coalition, decided to remain an independent party. The PDL first emerged as an electoral alliance with all three parties in 2008, while the Democratic Party, the main party of the left, allied itself with the Italy of Values party.

Corruption remains an issue in politics despite the changes in government over the past decade. Italy was ranked 63 out of 180 countries surveyed in Transparency International's 2009 Corruption Perceptions Index, the second lowest rating for Western Europe. Berlusconi has faced numerous corruption charges over the years, but has never been convicted. However, in October 2009, the Constitutional Court overturned a law granting Berlusconi immunity from prosecution while still in office. The ruling allows for a number of pending court cases against him to proceed; the first of which began in November, involving tax fraud related to the media group Mediaset, in which Berlusconi owns a significant stake. The trial was eventually adjourned as the prime minister could not attend due to state business.

Freedoms of speech and of the press are constitutionally guaranteed. However, the prime minister controls up to 90 percent of the country's broadcast media through state-owned outlets and his own private media holdings. There are many newspapers and news magazines, most of them with regional bases. Newspapers are primarily run by political parties or owned by large media groups. The Chamber of Deputies passed an amendment to a controversial bill in June 2009 that reintroduced jail sentences for journalists who use the transcripts from wiretaps without a judge's permission. The Senate had yet to approve the amendment at year's end. In August, Berlusconi sued several foreign newspapers covering his private life, including accusations that he had a sexual relationship with an 18-year-old girl. *Il Giornale*, a newspaper owned by the Berlusconi family, attacked the Catholic paper, *Avvenire*, after it ran stories criticizing Berlusconi's behavior. Also in August, the state broadcasting network, RAI, and the private media group, Mediaset, both refused to show a trailer for *Videocracy*, a film critical of Berlusconi's domination over the media. Although the internet is generally unrestricted, the government blocks foreign websites if they violate national laws.

Freedom of religion is respected and guaranteed by the constitution. Although Roman Catholicism is the dominant faith and the state grants some privileges to the Catholic Church, there is no official religion. The state provides support, if requested, to other sects represented in the country. The government has signed agreements with a number of religious groups but has yet to pass an omnibus religious freedom law. Academic freedom is respected and protected.

Italians are free to assemble and form social and political associations, and around 35 percent of the workforce is unionized. The constitution recognizes the right to strike, with the exception of those employed in essential services and a number of self-employed professions, such as lawyers, doctors, and truck drivers.

The judicial system is undermined by long trial delays and the influence of organized crime. A bill backed by Berlusconi's government that would place a six-year cap on the length of trials in Italy's three-tier justice system was pending before Parliament at year's end. The bill, which does not apply to Mafia crimes, has been criticized by the opposition, as it would apply retroactively and annul Berlusconi's current trials for tax fraud and corruption. Despite legal prohibitions against torture, there have been reports of excessive use of force by police, particularly against illegal immigrants. In August, the European Court of Human Rights ruled that an Italian police officer who shot dead a protester during the 2001 Group of 8 summit in Genoa was acting in self-defense. Some prisons suffer from overcrowding.

The country made some gains against organized crime in 2009. In March, 100,000 people marched in Naples against the Camorra—the Naples-based organized crime syndicate—one of the largest turnouts for this annual anti-Mafia event. In July, 49 members of a Sicilian Mafia crime family were jailed for extorting protection money from Sicilian stores. These were the first successful prosecutions for Sicilian businesses, who had cooperated and worked closely with police. Throughout the year, police arrested several top leaders in the Camorra and additional commanders in the Sicilian Mafia.

Italy is a major entry point for undocumented immigrants trying to reach Europe, and the government has been criticized for holding illegal immigrants in overcrowded and unhygienic conditions and denying them access to lawyers and other experts. The government began a crackdown on illegal immigration in 2008, including the arrests of hundreds of suspected illegal immigrants in May. In July 2009, a new immigration law was passed that fines illegal immigrants and gives authorities the power to detain them for up to six months without charge. A number of human rights groups raised concerns that the new law undermines the rights of asylum seekers. The law also allows for the formation of unarmed patrol groups to help police maintain order and imprison people who knowingly harbor undocumented immigrants. One such group, the Italian National Guard, was created in June and has been criticized for evoking the Blackshirt Legion of the fascist era. The group is currently under investigation by authorities in Milan for breaching laws prohibiting the display and use of Nazi and fascist insignia.

Women benefit from generous maternity-leave provisions, equality in the workforce, and considerable educational opportunities. However, violence against women continues to be a problem, and female political representation is low for the region. Women hold 21 percent of the seats in the Chamber of Deputies. In July 2009, Italy became the last European country to approve the abortion pill. However, unlike in the United States and other European countries, the pill can only be administered in hospitals, where the patient must remain until the pill has taken effect.

Italy is a destination country for the trafficking of women and children for sexual and labor exploitation. The Italian government has made efforts to tackle the problem by increasing its prosecution of traffickers and it also finances nongovernmental organizations that work to raise awareness of the problem and support trafficking victims.

Jamaica

Political Rights: 2
Civil Liberties: 3
Status: Free

Population: 2,702,000
Capital: Kingston

Ten-Year Ratings Timeline For Year Under Review (Political Rights, Civil Liberties, Status)

2000	2001	2002	2003	2004	2005	2006	2007	2008	2009
2,2F	2,3F	2,3F	2,3F	2,3F	2,3F	2,3F	2,3F	2,3F	2,3F

Overview:

In 2009, Jamaica experienced an increase in crime, with homicides reaching an all-time high of 1,680, surpassing the previous record from 2005. Gang violence persisted, especially in urban areas.

Jamaica achieved independence from Britain in 1962. Since then, power has alternated between the social democratic People's National Party (PNP) and the more conservative Jamaica Labour Party (JLP).

In 2002, Percival James Patterson of the PNP became the only prime minister in Jamaican history to be elected to three consecutive terms. His party won 34 of 60 seats in the House of Representatives, giving the PNP continued control of Parliament. The JLP remained in opposition with 26 seats.

In March 2006, Patterson announced that he would step down after 14 years in power, setting off a hard-fought PNP leadership battle between Minister for Local Government Portia Simpson Miller, National Security Minister Peter Phillips, and Finance Minister Omar Davies. Simpson Miller fended off her competition by securing 46 percent of the vote among 3,800 party delegates. Her victory was heralded as a major advance for the role of women in Jamaican politics, but her government foundered due to poor economic growth and the fallout from Hurricane Dean, which struck the island in August.

In parliamentary elections held in September 2007, the JLP won 33 seats in the House of Representatives, ending the 18-year rule of the PNP, which took 27 seats. Opposition leader Bruce Golding became the new prime minister, but Simpson Miller survived her party's defeat, easily winning reelection to her parliamentary seat. The popularity of the ruling JLP lagged behind that of the PNP in 2008, due to a sluggish economy and the new government's inability to stem the rising crime rate.

Under Golding's rule, Jamaica has continued to struggle with high levels of crime. In the first six months of 2009, 4,778 major crimes were reported, representing a 19 percent increase over the same period the previous year. The 1,680 homicides reported in 2009 represented an all-time high, marking a 4 percent increase over 2008 numbers. Over half of these murders were gang related and only 21 percent were solved in court.

In April 2009, Jamaica witnessed its first major airplane hijacking in years, when a gunman took six crew members hostage on a CanJet flight; however, the perpetrator was captured after an eight-hour standoff, and no injuries were reported.

Political Rights and Civil Liberties: Jamaica is an electoral democracy. Violence has often accompanied elections, but in the 2007 vote, there were only two shootings. The British monarch is represented as head of state by a governor-general, who is appointed by the monarch on the recommendation of the Jamaican prime minister. Following legislative elections, the governor-general appoints the leader of the majority party or coalition in the lower house, the House of Representatives, to be the prime minister. The bicameral Parliament consists of the 60-member House of Representatives, elected for five years, and the 21-member Senate, with 13 senators appointed on the advice of the prime minister and 8 on the advice of the opposition leader.

In recent years, the ideological gulf between the two main political parties—the center-left PNP and the more conservative JLP—has narrowed considerably due to the retirement of their respective veteran leaders.

Corruption remains a considerable problem. Government whistle-blowers who object to official acts of waste, fraud, or abuse of power are not well protected by Jamaican law, as is required under the Inter-American Convention against Corruption. In 2009, an overhaul of the customs service resulted in the firing of several employees allegedly linked to corruption, and customs revenue subsequently increased by 25 percent. The Corruption Prevention Act of 2002 requires that some government officials make their financial assets public, but implementation of this rule has been problematic; over 5,000 government employees have reportedly filed late or not at all. Jamaica was ranked 99 out of 180 countries surveyed in Transparency International's 2009 Corruption Perceptions Index.

The constitutional right to free expression is generally respected. While newspapers are independent and free of government control, circulation is generally low. Broadcast media are largely state owned but are open to pluralistic points of view. In 2008, one local television station began broadcasting the news in Jamaican Patois, breaking with the long-standing practice of using the dialect only in informal settings. Journalists occasionally face intimidation in the run-up to elections. The government does not restrict access to the internet; about 50 percent of Jamaicans have access, more than double the regional average of the Caribbean.

The constitution provides for freedom of religion, and the government generally respects this right in practice. The government does not hinder academic freedom. Freedoms of association and assembly are generally respected. Jamaica has a robust civil society, though the most influential nongovernmental actors tend to emanate from business interests. Approximately 20 percent of the workforce is unionized. Labor unions are politically influential and have the right to strike.

The judicial system is headed by the Supreme Court and includes several magistrates' courts and a court of appeals. The Privy Council in London was formerly the highest appellate court for Jamaica, but it was replaced with the Trinidad-based Caribbean Court of Justice, inaugurated in 2005. Privy Council rulings against the death penalty had angered many in Jamaica, and in 2009, the defendants in two separate murder cases were sentenced to death by hanging.

Despite government efforts to improve penal conditions, a mounting backlog of cases and a shortage of court staff at all levels continue to undermine the judicial system, which is slow and inefficient, particularly in addressing police abuses and violence in prisons. In July 2009, Amnesty International reported that 224 civilians had been killed by the police during the preceding year and criticized the lack of punishment for negligent officers. Police are officially allowed to use lethal force if an officer's life is threatened or a dangerous felon is escaping, but its use is widespread in practice. The system for investigating police abuse lacks personnel to pursue cases, protect crime scene evidence, take statements from officers in a timely manner, and conduct adequate autopsies of victims. Ill-treatment by police and prison guards has been reported, and conditions in detention centers and prisons are abysmal.

In 2009, violent crime continued to depress tourism and investment. High-crime areas often overlap with tourist destinations like Montego Bay, but Kingston's garrison communities were the epicenter of most violence in 2009. Jamaica is a transit point for cocaine shipped from Colombia to U.S. markets, and much of the island's violence is the result of warfare between drug gangs known as posses; contributing factors include the deportation of Jamaican-born criminals from the United States and an illegal weapons trade.

Amnesty International has identified homosexuals as a marginalized group that is targeted for extreme harassment and violence. Same-sex intercourse is punishable by 10 years' imprisonment at hard labor. In recent years, several Jamaicans have been granted asylum in Britain on the grounds that they were in danger because of their homosexuality. Activists for gay and lesbian rights remain targets of violence. Gareth Henry, a prominent member of the advocacy group Jamaica Forum for Lesbians, All-Sexuals, and Gays (J-FLAG), fled to Canada in 2008 and filed for refugee status following an escalating series of threats against his life. In 2009, Prime Minister Bruce Golding endorsed keeping homosexuality illegal and vowed never to allow gays in his cabinet. The antigay lyrics of Jamaican entertainers, particularly reggae singers, remain a source of contention.

Despite legal protections for women suffering from violence and discrimination, enforcement remains lacking, and violence against women continues to be widespread. In an April 2009 survey conducted by International Perspectives on Sexual and Reproductive Health, nearly 49 percent of female respondents between the ages of 15 and 17 had experienced sexual violence or coercion.

Japan

Political Rights: 1
Civil Liberties: 2
Status: Free

Population: 127,568,000
Capital: Tokyo

Ten-Year Ratings Timeline For Year Under Review (Political Rights, Civil Liberties, Status)

2000	2001	2002	2003	2004	2005	2006	2007	2008	2009
1,2F	1,2F	1,2F	1,2F	1,2F	1,2F	1,2F	1,2F	1,2F	1,2F

Overview: The 2009 election victory of the Democratic Party of Japan (DPJ) ended more than five decades of nearly continuous Liberal Democratic Party (LDP) rule. Although the new prime minister, Yukio Hatoyama, promised numerous domestic and foreign policy reforms, difficult economic conditions and tenuous party unity pose a serious challenge to the implementation of these policies.

Japan has operated as a parliamentary democracy with a largely symbolic monarchy since its defeat in World War II. The Liberal Democratic Party (LDP), which has ruled almost continuously since 1955, presided over Japan's economic ascent while maintaining close security ties with the United States during the Cold War. The so-called iron triangle—the close relationship between the LDP, the banks, and big-business representatives—was a key factor behind Japan's economic success. The LDP government mandated that corporations, specifically construction firms in charge of major public-works projects, rely on banks for capital, and the banks in turn took large equity stakes in the companies. Over time, companies engaged in politically expedient but financially unviable projects in order to reap government rewards. The iron triangle came to be cited as a major source of corruption in the government. The economy ran into trouble in the early 1990s, following a collapse in the stock and real-estate markets. While the fallout was extensive, the economy slowly returned to a healthy state in 2002.

In 2005, Prime Minister Junichiro Koizumi took a major political gamble. After the legislature's upper house failed to pass his bill to privatize the postal system, he called snap elections, hoping to remove LDP members who opposed his reform policies. Koizumi's gamble succeeded by giving him a landslide victory, widely seen as a popular mandate to implement privatization reforms, that left the LDP with 296 of the 480 seats in the lower house.

When Koizumi's term as party leader ended in 2006, Shinzo Abe—who had risen to prominence as a strong advocate of a popular movement to demand the return of Japanese citizens previously kidnapped by North Korea—succeeded him. Abe's tenure, however, was soon marred by repeated scandals and political gaffes. Five of his ministers had resigned in disgrace, and his agriculture minister committed suicide following revelations about questionable office expenses. Abe himself got into trouble after claiming there was no evidence that the government had any role in the creation of Japan's system of sexual slavery during World War II. Abe eventually resigned in September 2007, after losing control of the upper house to the opposition Democratic Party of Japan (DPJ) in the July 2007 elections. The DPJ won 60 of the 121 seats at stake, for a new total of 109, while the LDP fell to a total of 83 seats.

Yasuo Fukuda succeeded Abe as the head of the LDP and prime minister. Although the 71-year-old was considered a moderate and a consensus builder, like his predecessor, he lacked Koizumi's charisma and leadership. After Fukuda failed to rally support and govern effectively, he resigned in September 2008. Former foreign minister Taro Aso, the LDP secretary general, succeeded him later that month. The Aso government focused on rejuvenating the faltering economy, which remained burdened with a government debt equal to almost 200 percent of the country's gross domestic product.

After repeated failed leaderships and growing public disillusionment, the LDP's nearly 55-year dominance in the lower house ended when the DPJ captured 308 seats in the August 30, 2009, elections. The DPJ formed a coalition with two smaller parties, the Social Democratic Party and the People's New Party, and DPJ party leader Yukio Hatayama was selected to be the new prime minister. The DPJ's center-left platform, which challenged many of the LDP's long-standing policies, included greater independence from U.S. influence, improved relations with neighboring Asian countries, greater rights to traditionally marginalized groups (such women and ethnic minorities), and a more decentralized and accountable government concerned with social welfare and environmental issues. While many regard the DPJ's victory as an opportunity to enact various reforms and create a genuine two-party system in Japan, ongoing domestic economic problems and the DPJ's lack of party unity cast serious doubts on this prospect.

Political Rights and Civil Liberties: Japan is an electoral democracy. The prime minister—the leader of the majority party or coalition in the bicameral legislature's (Diet's) lower chamber, the House of Representatives—serves as head of government and appoints a cabinet of ministers. Members of the 480-seat House of Representatives serve four-year terms; 300 are elected in single-member constituencies, and 180 are elected by party list in 11 regional districts. An upper chamber, the House of Councilors, consists of 146 members elected in multiseat constituencies and 96 elected by national party list; members serve six-year terms, with half facing election every three years. Emperor Akihito serves as the ceremonial head of state.

Although several political parties compete for power, the center-right LDP dominated for almost 55 years. The DPJ's victory in the August 2009 elections to the House of Representatives opened the way for the development of a two-party system. Other minor opposition parties include the Japanese Communist Party and the Social Democratic Party.

Until leaving office in 2006, former prime minister Junichiro Koizumi focused his reform efforts on breaking down the corruption that resulted from the iron triangle system, mostly by loosening ties between the government and big business. Although Japan is a signatory of the U.N. Convention against Corruption, the Diet has not yet ratified it into law. Japan was ranked 18 out of 180 countries surveyed in Transparency International's 2009 Corruption Perceptions Index.

Japan's press is private and independent, but the presence of press clubs, or *kisha kurabu*, is an obstacle to press freedom. Press clubs ensure homogeneity of news coverage by fostering close relationships between the major media and bureaucrats and politicians. Government officials often give club members exclusive access to political information, leading journalists to avoid writing critical stories about the government and reducing the media's ability to pressure politicians for greater transparency and accountability. Reporters outside the press club system conduct most of Japan's investigative journalism. Internet access is not restricted.

Japanese of all faiths can worship freely. Religious groups are not required to be licensed, but registering with government authorities as a "religious corporation" brings tax benefits and other advantages. There are no restrictions on academic freedom.

The constitution guarantees freedoms of assembly and association. The political culture in Japan is strong, and there are active civic, human rights, social welfare, and environmental groups. Trade unions are independent, and with the exception of police and firefighters, all unionized workers have the right to strike.

Japan's judiciary is independent. There are several levels of courts, and suspects are generally given fair public trials by an impartial tribunal (there are no juries) within three months of being detained. The National Police Agency is under civilian control and is highly disciplined, though reports of human rights abuses committed by police persist. While arbitrary arrest and imprisonment are not practiced, there is potential for abuse due to a law that allows the police to detain suspects for up to 23 days without charge in order to extract confessions. Prison conditions comply with international standards, although prison officials have been known to use physical and psychological intimidation to enforce discipline or elicit confessions. The government sometimes restricts human rights groups' access to prisons. A 2006 Penal Facilities and Treatment of Prisoners Law provides for a monitoring body to inspect prisons, improved access to the outside world for prisoners, and human rights education for prison staff.

Although the constitution prohibits discrimination based on race, creed, sex, or social status, certain groups continue to face unofficial discrimination. Japan's three million *burakumin*, who are descendants of feudal-era outcasts, and the indigenous Ainu minority suffer from entrenched societal discrimination that prevents them from gaining equal access to housing and employment opportunities. Foreigners generally, and Koreans in particular, suffer similar disadvantages.

Although women in Japan enjoy legal equality, discrimination in employment and sexual harassment on the job are common. Violence against women often goes unreported because of concerns about family reputation and other social mores. While prostitution remains illegal, it is widespread. According to the U.S. State Department's 2009 Trafficking in Persons Report, Japan is primarily a destination country for people trafficked for forced labor and sexual exploitation. The issue of World War II–era sex slaves, known as comfort women, stirred controversy in 2007, when the U.S. House of Representatives passed a resolution calling on Japan to accept responsibility and provide compensation. The Japanese courts contend that compensation claims were settled by postwar treaties.

Jordan

Political Rights: 6*
Civil Liberties: 5
Status: Not Free

Population: 5,915,000
Capital: Amman

Status Change: Jordan's political rights rating declined from 5 to 6 and its status from Partly Free to Not Free due to King Abdullah's dismissal of the parliament and his announcement that elections would not be held until the end of 2010, as well as the security forces' increased influence over political life.

Ten-Year Ratings Timeline For Year Under Review (Political Rights, Civil Liberties, Status)

2000	2001	2002	2003	2004	2005	2006	2007	2008	2009
4,4PF	5,5PF	6,5PF	5,5PF	5,4PF	5,4PF	5,4PF	5,4PF	5,5PF	6,5NF

Overview: The king dissolved the parliament in November, about two years into its four-year term, and announced that new elections would not be held until late 2010; ordinarily, elections would be held within four months of the parliament's dissolution. The delay would allow the government to rule by decree for at least a year, and it was expected to enact a series of unpopular market liberalization measures as well as a new election law in the parliament's absence.

The Hashemite Kingdom of Jordan, known as Transjordan until 1950, was established as a League of Nations mandate under British control in 1921 and won full independence in 1946. The turbulent 46-year reign of King Hussein, which began in 1953, featured a massive influx of Palestinian refugees, the loss of the West Bank to Israel in 1967, and numerous assassinations and coup attempts. Nevertheless, with political and civil liberties tightly restricted, Hussein proved adept at co-opting his political opponents. After economic austerity measures in the late 1980s sparked rioting and pressure for greater freedom, the government progressively eased restrictions on civil liberties, though the reform process suffered some reversals in the mid-1990s.

By the time Crown Prince Abdullah succeeded his father as king in 1999, the kingdom faced severe economic problems. The expected "peace dividend" from Jordan's 1994 peace treaty with Israel had failed to improve conditions for most of the population, and Abdullah began major economic reforms. Meanwhile, additional restrictions on the media, public protests, and civil society activity were imposed after groups including Islamists, leftists, and Jordanians of Palestinian descent staged demonstrations to demand the annulment of the 1994 treaty and express support for the Palestinian uprising (*intifada*) against Israel that began in 2000.

In 2001, Abdullah dissolved the parliament, postponed elections scheduled for November, and replaced elected municipal councils with state-appointed local committees. He ruled by decree for over two years, issuing more than 200 "temporary laws" that weakened due process and restricted freedoms of expression and assembly.

The king allowed reasonably free and transparent—though not fair—parliamentary and municipal elections in 2003. In an informal understanding with the palace, dissident leftist and Islamist groups gained limited freedom of expression and political participation, and agreed to curtail their agitation against Jordan's pro-U.S. foreign policy.

The relationship between the government and political parties remained strained, however. In 2007, security forces arrested nine members of the Islamic Action Front (IAF), the main opposition party and the political arm of the Muslim Brotherhood in Jordan, for "threatening national security" ahead of that year's municipal and parliamentary elections. Only a handful of IAF candidates won seats in the polls, which were marred by irregularities. A new political party law in 2008 required parties to have broader membership bases, and the number of registered parties consequently fell to 14, from 37.

The king appointed a new government in February 2009, and then unexpectedly dismissed the parliament in November. While new elections would ordinarily be held within four months, the government announced that the polls would be postponed until late 2010, allowing it to rule by decree for at least a year. The parliament had failed to pass government-backed economic reforms in August, and the cabinet was expected to enact the legislation in the legislature's absence. There was also speculation that the government would issue a new election law in the coming year, potentially affecting the composition of any future parliament.

Political Rights and Civil Liberties:

Jordan is not an electoral democracy. King Abdullah II holds broad executive powers, appoints and dismisses the prime minister and cabinet, and may dissolve the National Assembly at his discretion. The 110-seat lower house of the National Assembly, the Chamber of Deputies, is elected through universal adult suffrage. It may approve, reject, or amend legislation proposed by the cabinet, but its ability to initiate legislation is limited. It cannot enact laws without the assent of the 55-seat upper house, the Senate, whose members are appointed by the king. Members of both houses serve four-year terms. Regional governors are appointed by the central government.

The electoral system is heavily skewed toward the monarchy's traditional base of support. Voters in the 45 multiseat parliamentary districts each choose a single candidate, which favors tribal and family ties over political and ideological affiliations. In addition, rural districts with populations of Transjordanian origin are overrepresented relative to urban districts, where most Jordanians of Palestinian descent reside. Activists have repeatedly called for a new electoral law based on proportional representation. A 2007 law cleared the way for that year's municipal elections, in which all mayors and council members were elected, though an exception for Amman meant that half of the city's council members would continue to be appointed.

The authorities have made some progress in combating persistent official corruption in recent years, and an independent Anticorruption Commission was established in 2007. Among other high-profile corruption cases in 2009, the minister of public works was accused of profiting from a housing project, and a lawmaker's brother allegedly used a parliamentary car to smuggle drugs. Jordan was ranked 49 out of 180 countries surveyed in Transparency International's 2009 Corruption Perceptions Index.

Freedom of expression is restricted, and those who violate redlines regarding the royal family and certain societal taboos face arrest, causing widespread self-censorship. As in previous years, private citizens were arrested in 2009 for criticizing the king. Laith Shbailat, a prominent Islamist opposition leader, was beaten by unidentified assailants after he gave a televised interview accusing the government of corruption and calling for abrogation of the peace treaty with Israel. Another member of the Muslim Brotherhood was arrested for allegedly plotting to set up a "militant faction." The security forces, whose leadership generally excludes Jordanians of Palestinian descent, continue to exercise significant influence over Jordanian political life by limiting citizens' freedoms of speech and assembly.

While prison was abolished as a penalty for press offenses in 2007, journalists can still be jailed under the penal code. A study released in 2009 by the Amman-based Center for Defending Freedom of Journalists found that 43 percent of journalists admitted receiving some form of "incentive" from the government, while 94 percent said they practiced self-censorship. In April, a newspaper columnist was acquitted of insulting the parliament in an article he had posted online. However, the parliament issued rules that month to limit journalists' physical access to the parliament building and offices, and to allow interviews of lawmakers only in the presence of a media officer. The authorities are also sensitive to criticism from foreign media. Security forces attacked a camera crew with the Qatar-based satellite television station Al-Jazeera during January demonstrations against the Israeli offensive in Gaza. And in July, the government closed the local offices of two Iranian state-funded television channels: the Arabic-language Al-Alam and the English-language Press TV.

Most broadcast news outlets remain under state control, but satellite dishes give residents access to foreign media. While there are dozens of private newspapers and magazines, the government has broad powers to close them. Authorities are routinely tipped off about potentially offensive articles by informers at printing presses, and editors frequently come under pressure to remove such material. Intelligence agents often call journalists with warnings about their writing. While the government denies restricting access to the internet, websites airing critical views have been blocked in the past, and authors of critical posts have faced intimidation or arrest.

Islam is the state religion. Christians and Jews are recognized as religious minorities and can worship freely, and while Baha'is and Druze are not officially recognized, they are allowed to practice their faiths. The government appoints Islamic clergy and monitors sermons at mosques, where political activity is banned. Preachers must obtain written government permission to lead services or teach the Koran. Only state-appointed councils may issue religious edicts, or fatwas, and it is illegal to criticize these rulings.

Academic freedom is generally respected, and Jordanians openly discuss political and societal developments. However, certain limits remain in place, and there have been reports of a heavy intelligence presence on some university campuses.

Freedom of assembly is heavily restricted. Provincial governors often deny permission to hold demonstrations, particularly when organizers seek to criticize Jordanian-Israeli relations. Police violently dispersed demonstrations protesting Israel's offensive in Gaza in January, as well as a protest against food imports from Israel in July. The Amman governorate also prevented an Islamist demonstration protesting clashes at Jerusalem's Al-Aqsa mosque in September.

Freedom of association is limited. While many nongovernmental organizations (NGOs) are able to operate without running afoul of the authorities, the government is considering new legislation that would severely limit their independence. Under the measure, the government would be able to supervise NGO budgets, reject foreign funding, and veto individual programs planned by the organizations. NGOs would be barred from engaging in "religious or sectarian" activities, and would have to open membership to anyone fulfilling the criteria in their bylaws. While the legislation had yet to be approved at the end of 2009, the government currently puts occasional pressure on NGOs' activities.

Workers have the right to bargain collectively but must receive government permission to strike. More than 30 percent of the workforce is organized into 17 unions. Foreign workers do not enjoy the same legal protections as Jordanians, and labor rights organizations have raised concerns about poor working conditions in so-called Qualifying Industrial Zones (QIZs), where mostly female and foreign factory workers process goods for export. In 2009, a foreign investor who owned a factory in a QIZ left the country without paying any of the employees, and the government was unable to offer any assistance to the affected workers.

The judiciary is subject to executive influence through the Justice Ministry and the Higher Judiciary Council, most of whose members are appointed by the king. While most trials in civilian courts are open and procedurally sound, the State Security Court (SSC) may close its proceedings to the public. A 2001 decree allows the prime minister to refer any case to the SSC and denies the right of appeal to people convicted of misdemeanors by the SSC.

Under the constitution, suspects may be detained for up to 48 hours without a warrant and up to 10 days without formal charges being filed; courts routinely grant prosecutors 15-day extensions of this deadline. Even these protections are denied to suspects referred to the SSC, who are often held in lengthy pretrial detention and refused access to legal counsel until just before trial. Provincial governors can also order indefinite administrative detention, and about a fifth of all Jordanian prisoners are held under this provision; there are approximately 10,000 new cases of administrative detention each year. The UN special rapporteur on torture found in 2006 that, "torture is systematically practiced" by the General Intelligence Department (GID), which interrogates suspects to obtain confessions in SSC cases. There is no independent complaint or monitoring mechanism for abuse in custody.

Prison conditions are poor, and inmates are reportedly subject to severe beatings and other abuse by guards. Prison staff allegedly force prisoners to take castor oil to prevent the bodily concealment of contraband. Islamist prisoners on a hunger strike in August 2009 were denied water; Islamists are typically isolated in small groups from the rest of the prison population. In one week in November, two Jordanians died after police beatings.

Freedom of movement and travel is generally respected. The size of the Iraqi refugee community in Jordan has decreased significantly in recent years, and Iraqis in Jordan receive better treatment than in other host countries. However, their entry into Jordan is strictly limited, and those who enter the country are subject to heavy restrictions, including the right to work or to use Jordanian public services.

Women enjoy equal political rights but face legal discrimination in matters involving inheritance, divorce, and child custody, which fall under the jurisdiction of

Sharia (Islamic law) courts. Government pensions and social security benefits also favor men. Although women constitute only about 14 percent of the workforce, the government has made efforts to increase the number of women in the civil service. Women are guaranteed a quota of six seats in the lower house of parliament and, under the 2007 municipalities law, 20 percent of the seats in municipal councils. Article 98 of the penal code allows for lenient treatment of those who commit a crime in a "state of fit or fury" resulting from an unlawful or dangerous act on the part of the victim. In practice, this provision is often applied to benefit men who commit "honor crimes" against women. At least 14 such crimes were reported in the first eight months of 2009.

⬇ Kazakhstan

Political Rights: 6
Civil Liberties: 5
Status: Not Free

Population: 15,880,000
Capital: Astana

Trend Arrow: Kazakhstan received a downward trend arrow due to a spate of politically motivated libel suits against critical media outlets, a restrictive new internet law, arbitrary arrests of officials and businesspeople, and the grossly deficient judicial proceedings against human rights activist Yevgeny Zhovtis.

Ten-Year Ratings Timeline For Year Under Review (Political Rights, Civil Liberties, Status)

2000	2001	2002	2003	2004	2005	2006	2007	2008	2009
6,5NF	6,5NF	6,5NF	6,5NF	6,5NF	6,5NF	6,5NF	6,5NF	6,5NF	6,5NF

Overview:
President Nursultan Nazarbayev and his Nur Otan party maintained almost complete control over the political sphere in 2009, using tactics including arbitrary arrests, restrictive new laws, and politically motivated prosecutions to muzzle critical media outlets and individuals. These long-standing authoritarian practices continued even as Kazakhstan prepared to assume the chairmanship of the Organization for Security and Cooperation in Europe in 2010.

Kazakh Communist Party leader Nursultan Nazarbayev won an uncontested presidential election in December 1991, two weeks before Kazakhstan gained its independence from the Soviet Union. In April 1995, Nazarbayev called a referendum on extending his five-year term, due to expire in 1996, until December 2000. A reported 95 percent of voters endorsed the move. An August 1995 referendum, which was boycotted by the opposition, approved a new constitution designed to strengthen the presidency. Nazarbayev's supporters captured most of the seats in December 1995 elections for a new bicameral Parliament.

In October 1998, Parliament amended the constitution to increase the presidential term from five to seven years and moved the presidential election forward from December 2000 to January 1999. The main challenger was disqualified on a technicality, and Nazarbayev was reelected with a reported 80 percent of the vote.

Progovernment parties captured all but one seat in 2004 elections for the lower house of Parliament. International monitors from the Organization for Security and Cooperation in Europe (OSCE) found some improvements over previous polls, but criticized the lack of political balance on election commissions, media bias in favor of propresidential candidates, and the politically motivated exclusion of candidates.

The president again secured reelection in 2005, with 91 percent of the vote amid opposition allegations of fraud. An international monitoring report found intimidation and media bias in favor of the incumbent.

Political violence flared in 2005-2006, with the suspicious suicide of opposition leader Zamanbek Nurkadilov in December 2005 and the murder of Altynbek Sarsenbayev, a leading member of the opposition coalition For a Just Kazakhstan, in February 2006. The investigation of Sarsenbayev's killing pointed to the involvement of state security officers but left many questions unanswered. The trial of Yerzhan Utembayev, former head of the Senate administration, and his sentencing to a 20-year prison term for organizing the murder were marred by reports of coerced confessions.

Constitutional changes in May 2007 removed term limits for Nazarbayev and eliminated individual district races for the lower house of Parliament, leaving only party-slate seats filled by nationwide proportional representation. Elections under the new rules in August produced a one-party legislature, with the propresidential Nur Otan party taking 88 percent of the vote and no opposition parties clearing the 7 percent threshold for representation. Opposition protests foundered, and the government ignored a critical OSCE report. No opposition candidates participated in the October 2008 indirect elections for the upper house of Parliament.

In 2009, some Nur Otan legislators proposed a lifetime presidency for Nazarbayev, which would eliminate the need for him to seek reelection. However, the president commented that his existing access to unlimited seven-year terms was sufficient.

Also during the year, Rakhat Aliyev, Nazarbayev's former son-in-law, published a muckraking book about the president that Kazakh prosecutors promptly banned, initially threatening to try anyone who even "touched" the volume. An exemplar of Kazakhstan's personalized and volatile politics, Aliyev had risen to positions as high as deputy foreign minister and built a media empire before falling out of favor in 2007. He then went into exile in Austria as Nazarbayev's daughter divorced him, his Kazakh business interests collapsed, and a Kazakh court sentenced him to two 20-year prison terms in absentia for illegal business practices and other crimes. In 2008, he issued a series of statements accusing the Kazakh leadership of corruption.

Kazakhstan maintained productive relations with all major powers in 2009. Its foreign policy included energy ties with China, which continued to expand its oil and gas pipeline network in Central Asia during the year, and cooperation with the United States, which began to ship nonmilitary supplies for operations in Afghanistan through Kazakhstan. Kazakhstan was also set to assume the chairmanship of the OSCE in 2010, despite its poor human rights record.

Political Rights and Civil Liberties: Kazakhstan is not an electoral democracy. The constitution grants the president considerable control over the legislature, the judiciary, and local governments. The removal of term limits for the country's "first president" in May 2007 cleared the way for President Nursultan Nazarbayev to seek reelection after the end of his current seven-year term in 2012.

The upper house of the bicameral Parliament is the 47-member Senate, with 32 members chosen by directly elected regional councils and 15 appointed by the president. The senators serve six-year terms, with half of the 32 elected members up for election every three years. The lower house (Mazhilis) has 107 deputies, with 98 elected by proportional representation on party slates and 9 appointed by the Assembly of Peoples of Kazakhstan, which represents the country's various ethnic groups. Members serve five-year terms. Parties must clear a 7 percent vote threshold to enter the Mazhilis, and once elected, deputies must vote with their party. A June 2007 law prohibited parties from forming electoral blocs. These rules effectively prevented opposition parties from winning seats in August 2007 parliamentary elections and 2008 Senate elections, producing a legislature that is devoid of opposition representation.

The country's broader law on political parties prohibits parties based on ethnic origin, religion, or gender. A 2002 law raised from 3,000 to 50,000 the number of members that a party must have to register.

Corruption is widespread at all levels. The U.S. Justice Department continues to investigate alleged bribes by U.S. oil companies to secure lucrative Kazakh contracts in the 1990s. Rakhat Aliyev's 2008 allegations of high-level corruption were accompanied by some documentary evidence and matched reports from numerous other sources. Kazakhstan was ranked 120 out of 180 countries surveyed in Transparency International's 2009 Corruption Perceptions Index.

While the constitution provides for freedom of the press, the government has repeatedly harassed or shut down independent media outlets. Libel is a criminal offense, and the criminal code prohibits insulting the president; self-censorship is widespread. Most media outlets, including publishing houses, are controlled or influenced by members of the president's family and other powerful groups. A new privacy law passed by Parliament in November and signed by President Nazarbayev in December contained a vague ban on, "interference into an individual's private life," sparking fears that it could be used to hamper investigative journalism.

Independent media in 2009 suffered attacks, arrests, and crippling libel judgments. The weeklies *Taszharghan* and *Respublika* faced closure after courts ordered them each to pay fines of US$300,000 to US$400,000 on dubious pretexts. Ramazan Yesergepov, editor of the weekly *Alma-Ata Info*, received a three-year sentence for revealing state secrets while reporting on a corruption investigation. In December, Gennady Pavlyuk, a journalist from Kyrgyzstan, was murdered in Almaty.

The government at times has blocked websites that are critical of the regime, and legislation signed in July 2009 classifies all websites in the ".kz" domain as media outlets and imposes stringent regulations. The independent online outlet *Zonakz* and the website of the weekly *Respublika* suffered multiple cyber attacks in 2009.

The constitution guarantees freedom of worship, and many religious communities practice without state interference. Laws passed in 2005 banned all activities by unregistered religious groups and gave the government great discretion in outlawing organizations it designated as "extremist." Local officials have harassed groups defined as "nontraditional," such as Hare Krishnas, Baptists, and Jehovah's Witnesses. In 2009, a Hare Krishna community in Almaty charged that the authorities had destroyed 26 homes belonging to its members.

The government reportedly permits academic freedom, except with respect to criticism of the president and his family. Corruption in the education system is widespread, and students frequently bribe professors for passing grades.

Despite constitutional guarantees, the government imposes restrictions on freedom of association Assembly. In February 2009, the opposition party Azat was refused a location to hold a protest, and courts fined protesters on several occasions during the year for unsanctioned demonstrations in support of jailed human rights activist Yevgeny Zhovtis. The government also banned demonstrations on World Journalism Day in June. Nongovernmental organizations continue to operate despite government harassment surrounding politically sensitive issues. Workers can form and join trade unions and participate in collective bargaining, although co-opted unions and close links between the authorities and big business make for an uneven playing field. Workers mounted several strikes in 2009 over unpaid wages, sometimes resorting to hunger strikes as well.

The constitution makes the judiciary subservient to the executive branch. Judges are subject to political bias, and corruption is evident throughout the judicial system. Conditions in pretrial facilities and prisons are harsh. Police at times abuse detainees and threaten their families, often to obtain confessions, and arbitrary arrest and detention remain problems. Investigations of several former associates of Rakhat Aliyev appeared to be politically motivated, as did several high-profile 2009 corruption cases against former officials. Also during the year, Zhovtis's flawed trial on charges of vehicular manslaughter ended quickly with a severe sentence, suggesting that the authorities were using the case to silence a well-known critic.

Members of the sizable Russian-speaking minority have complained of discrimination in employment and education. However, in 2007, the Constitutional Court affirmed the equality of the Russian and Kazakh languages. In January 2009, Kazakhstan decided to continue the practice of indicating ethnicity in citizens' passports.

While the rights of entrepreneurship and private property are formally protected, equality of opportunity is limited by bureaucratic hurdles and the control of large segments of the economy by clannish elites and government officials. A 2003 land code provides for private ownership, but critics have charged that the law primarily benefits wealthy individuals with close government ties. Astana residents whose homes have been demolished to make way for large construction projects have said they were denied legally guaranteed compensation. Banker Mukhtar Ablyazov, who fled the country after his bank was nationalized in early 2009, charged that a wave of arrests and prosecutions in the business sector during the year was politically motivated.

Traditional cultural practices and the country's economic imbalances limit professional opportunities for women. The current 107-member lower house of Parliament includes only 17 female deputies. Domestic violence often goes unpunished, as police are reluctant to intervene in what are regarded as internal family matters. Despite legal prohibitions, the trafficking of women for the purpose of prostitution remains a serious problem. The country's relative prosperity has drawn migrant workers from neighboring countries, who often face poor working conditions and a lack of legal protections, although a slower economy in 2009 reduced the number of migrant workers.

Kenya

Political Rights: 4
Civil Liberties: 4*
Status: Partly Free

Population: 39,070,000
Capital: Nairobi

Ratings Change: Kenya's civil liberties rating declined from 3 to 4 due to the government's failure to address abuses by the security forces, including their role in postelection violence in 2008.

Ten-Year Ratings Timeline For Year Under Review (Political Rights, Civil Liberties, Status)

2000	2001	2002	2003	2004	2005	2006	2007	2008	2009
6,5NF	6,5NF	4,4PF	3,3PF	3,3PF	3,3PF	3,3PF	4,3PF	4,3PF	4,4PF

Overview: Prominent international leaders criticized the Kenyan government in 2009 for its lack of progress on key reforms. These included the establishment of a tribunal to investigate postelection violence in 2008, much-needed land reform, a strengthened anticorruption campaign, and improved accountability for abuses by the security forces.

Kenya achieved independence from Britain in 1963. Nationalist leader Jomo Kenyatta served as president until his death in 1978, when Vice President Daniel arap Moi succeeded him. While the Kenyan African National Union (KANU) party remained in power, Moi diminished the influence of the previously dominant Kikuyu ethnic group, favoring his own Kalenjin group.

In 1992, after a lengthy period of single-party rule, domestic unrest and pressure from international donors forced Moi to hold multiparty elections. However, he and KANU continued to win elections during the 1990s by using political repression, state patronage, media control, and dubious electoral procedures. Government corruption remained common, as did police abuses, political influence in the judiciary, and state efforts to undermine independent civil society activity. Political polarization increased amid government-sponsored ethnic violence, perpetrated in most cases by Kalenjin or Maasai KANU supporters against members of the Kikuyu and Luhya ethnic groups, who were believed to support opposition parties. Despite these problems, political space for opposition views continued to open, and many of the core elements necessary for a democratic political system developed.

The opposition united to contest the 2002 elections as the National Rainbow Coalition (NARC). It won a majority in the National Assembly, and its presidential candidate, Mwai Kibaki, defeated KANU's Uhuru Kenyatta, the son of Kenya's first president. The new leadership's ambitious reform program achieved some successes, but the effort was blunted by a number of factors, including the fragility of the governing coalition, a complex and unsuccessful bid to overhaul the constitution, significant fiscal constraints, and the threat of terrorism. An independent anticorruption commission was established, but it produced few successful prosecutions. John Githongo, a respected anticorruption activist whom Kibaki had appointed to lead the Office of Governance and Ethics, resigned from that post in early 2005, citing his frustration with ongoing corruption and the Kibaki administration's failure to enact meaningful reforms.

The lively press and public investigative commissions became increasingly critical of the substance and slow pace of the government's reform agenda, and in November 2005, referendum voters soundly rejected a draft constitution that failed to shift power away from the presidency. In January 2006, Githongo issued an authoritative report indicating that corruption had reached the highest ranks of the government. The findings implicated the vice president and prompted the resignation of several cabinet ministers.

Kenya's democratic and economic development suffered a sharp reversal as a result of the apparent manipulation of the December 2007 presidential election. While the concurrent parliamentary polls showed major gains for the opposition Orange Democratic Movement (ODM), Kibaki was declared the winner of the presidential vote amid credible, multiple allegations of fraud. He had long been accused of favoring his Kikuyu ethnic group, and the presidential results sparked weeks of violence between the Kikuyu, the Luo, and other groups. More than 1,500 people were killed, and over 300,000 were displaced, although many eventually returned or were resettled by the government. In late February 2008, Kibaki and ODM presidential candidate Raila Odinga, a Luo, negotiated a compromise agreement in which Odinga gained the newly created post of prime minister and his party joined Kibaki's recently formed Party of National Unity (PNU) in a coalition cabinet.

A Commission of Inquiry into Post-Election Violence, also known as the Waki Commission, began work in June 2008. I ts report, issued in October, concluded that systemic failures in Kenya's security institutions, governmental impunity, and popular anger were the primary instigating factors in the crisis. The report called for the creation of a special tribunal to prosecute crimes committed during the postelection violence, and stated that in the absence of such a tribunal, the names of organizers of the violence should be sent to the International Criminal Court (ICC) for possible prosecution.

In 2009, the government and legislature made little progress in addressing the postelection violence. Their failure to act prompted former UN secretary general Kofi Annan, who had overseen negotiations for the 2008 power-sharing deal, to provide the ICC with a list of alleged perpetrators, although the names were not made public. Also during the year, the parliament rejected Kibaki's bid to reappoint the ineffective Aaron Ringera as head of the anticorruption commission, and General Mohammed Hussein Ali was fired as chief of the police force in the wake of a highly critical UN report on police brutality, though structural reforms to address the root of the problem were not implemented.

The Kenyan economy in 2009 continued to suffer from high inflation and a serious drought, which affected the important agricultural sector and caused food and energy shortages. An estimated 10 percent of the population required food aid.

Political Rights and Civil Liberties: Kenya is an electoral democracy. While there were few claims of irregularities in the December 2007 parliamentary polls, which the opposition won, reports on the flawed presidential vote highlighted apparent vote rigging and other administrative manipulations that had the effect of favoring the incumbent, Mwai Kibaki. The election commission nevertheless declared Kibaki the winner, and he was quickly sworn in. In September 2008, an international commission issued a final report, stating that the legitimacy of the election results was undermined by several factors, including a defective voter registry and widespread fraud. The report also recommended electoral reforms that have yet to be fully implemented.

The president is elected for a five-year term. Under the 2008 postelection compromise, he now shares power with a prime minister, who is the leader of the largest party or coalition in the National Assembly. The unicameral body consists of 210 members elected for five-year terms, with an additional 12 members appointed by the president and nominated by the parties on the basis of their shares of the popular vote. Political parties representing a range of ideological, regional, and ethnic interests are active and vocal, and there are no significant impediments to party formation.

Corruption remains a very serious problem. Political parties, nongovernmental organizations (NGOs), and the press, as well as some official bodies, have exposed many examples of government corruption and malfeasance. However, official probes and prosecutions have yielded meager results. Since 2003, the Kenya Anti-Corruption Commission's efforts have led to just 51 convictions: in 2009, the parliament rejected Kibaki's attempt to appoint its director for another five-year term. Transparency International's 2009 Corruption Perceptions Index ranked Kenya 146 out of 180 countries surveyed. The 2009 East African Bribery Index identified the Kenyan police as the most corrupt institution in East Africa, followed in Kenya by the Ministry of Defence and the judiciary.

The constitution provides for freedom of speech and a free press. These rights are generally respected in practice, and Kenya features one of the liveliest media environments on the continent. However, there have been intermittent restrictions on media freedom. In March 2006, security forces raided the independent KTN television station and stole documents and equipment. Amid the violence that followed the December 2007 elections, the authorities imposed a temporary ban on live broadcasts. Most Kenyans rely on the broadcast media, particularly radio, for news. A number of private television and radio stations operate, although their reach is limited. The government-owned Kenya Broadcasting Corporation continues to dominate the broadcast sector, particularly outside urban centers. The government does not restrict access to the internet.

The authorities generally uphold freedom of religion, though there have been some reports of government hostility toward Muslims. Religious groups are required to register with the government, which permits them to apply for tax-exempt status. Religious tension has risen since terrorist attacks in 1998 and 2002 that were associated with Islamic fundamentalism, but religion was not a major factor in the political and ethnic unrest of early 2008. A record 13 Muslims were appointed to the cabinet that year.

Academic freedom is the norm in Kenya, reflecting the country's broader respect for freedom of thought. In 2008, however, a leading education think tank, the Institute of Policy Analysis and Research, published a report stating that the education sector is "in crisis" due to structural deficiencies in the learning environment, poor education policy choices made by the government, and inadequate funding levels, among other problems. The 2008 postelection violence had at least a temporary chilling effect on freedom of private discussion, as many individuals became hesitant to discuss ethnic-related issues openly.

The constitution guarantees freedom of assembly. This right is generally respected, although there have been cases of unnecessary use of force at demonstrations, and public gatherings were curtailed during the 2008 postelection violence. One of the core strengths of Kenya's political culture, even in recent periods of political polarization, has been its robust civil society. However, two leading human rights activists who had been investigating police abuses in the deaths of individuals linked to the Mungiki criminal sect were murdered in 2009. A police whistle-blower who provided information to the national human rights body was also murdered during the year, and the police were unable to identify the perpetrators.

There are some 40 trade unions in the country, representing about 500,000 workers. Most of the unions are affiliated with the sole approved national federation, the Central Organization of Trade Unions. The Industrial Relations Charter gives workers the right to engage in legitimate trade union organizational activities, and all workers other than police officers are legally free to join unions. The 2007 Labour Relations Act explicitly establishes broad criteria for trade union registration, leaving authorities with limited grounds for suspending or refusing to register a union. Some unions have complained that employers resist unionization efforts, and that the relevant government bodies have been ineffective in enforcing the law. Historically, much of the trade union movement has been subservient to the authorities.

The judiciary's actions have reflected the primacy of the executive branch for much of the period since independence, and judicial corruption remains an impediment to the rule of law. The courts are understaffed and underfinanced, leading to long trial delays that violate defendants' right to due process. The 2008 inquiry on postelection violence noted the public's lack of confidence in the judiciary and called for the establishment of a truth, justice, and reconciliation commission, which began work in 2009. The country has officially recognized Kadhi courts, which administer Sharia (Islamic law) for issues including marriage and inheritance in areas with a predominantly Muslim population.

Legal checks on arbitrary arrest are not uniformly respected, and police still use force to extract information from suspects and deny them access to legal representation. Security forces engaged in extrajudicial killings during the 2008 postelection violence. Philip Alston, the UN special rapporteur on extrajudicial executions, visited Kenya in 2009 and found evidence of, "a systematic, widespread and clearly planned strategy to execute individuals carried out on a regular basis by the Kenya police." Such condemnations, however, have not resulted in any prosecutions. Also in 2009, the government admitted that the inmate population in Kenyan jails was almost 300 percent above their intended capacity.

Kenya's population comprises more than 40 ethnic groups, and friction between them has led to frequent allegations of discrimination and periodic episodes of violence. Land disputes frequently underlie ethnic clashes, as seen in the 2008 fighting, and long-awaited land reforms have languished. The Mungiki sect of mainly Kikuyu youth has been associated with postelection and other criminal violence. In addition, the continued presence of refugees from Somalia, and criminal activities by some of them, have exacerbated the problems faced by Kenya's own Somali minority. Other factors contributing to ethnic tension include widespread firearms possession, the commercialization of traditional cattle herding, poor economic conditions, drought, and ineffective security forces.

The Waki Commission's report cited specific cases of both state- and opposition-sponsored violence and massive internal population displacements during the 2008 postelection crisis. The population movements led in some cases to expropriation of property and belongings. Resettlement of internally displaced people has proceeded slowly, and in September 2009 Kibaki ordered that the remaining 7,000 individuals be resettled immediately.

Women in Kenya continue to face serious obstacles. They are denied equal property rights, putting them at greater risk of poverty, disease (including HIV/AIDS), violence, and homelessness. Kenyan women's rights groups have pointed out that 60 percent of the charges stemming from the 2008 postelection violence involved cases of rape, noting evidence that police committed the most abuses against women. Several bills aimed at strengthening women's rights with regard to marriage and property have been introduced by the government in recent years, but have yet to be enacted. Traditional attitudes limit the role of women in politics, although there are no legal restrictions and some progress has been made. In 2006, Kibaki declared that women would receive 30 percent of appointments in the public service, but this has yet to be realized. The 2007 elections increased the number of women in the National Assembly to 20, or about 8 percent of the total.

According to the Kenya AIDS Indicator Survey Report released in 2009, the national HIV prevalence rate among adults was 7.8 percent, with 1.4 million Kenyans living with HIV at the end of 2007. The national HIV prevalence rate had been 6.7 percent in 2003.

Kiribati

Political Rights: 1
Civil Liberties: 1
Status: Free

Population: 99,000
Capital: Tarawa

Ten-Year Ratings Timeline For Year Under Review (Political Rights, Civil Liberties, Status)

2000	2001	2002	2003	2004	2005	2006	2007	2008	2009
1,1F	1,1F	1,1F	1,1F	1,1F	1,1F	1,1F	1,1F	1,1F	1,1F

Overview:
Environment Minister Tetabo Nakara resigned in August 2009 in protest over the government's slow response to disputes between rival ruling groups on the Island of Maiana that turned violent in July.

Kiribati gained independence from Britain in 1979. The country consists of 33 atolls scattered across nearly 1.5 million square miles of the central Pacific Ocean, as well as Banaba Island in the western Pacific.

Chinese military ambitions in the Pacific and competing offers of development assistance from China and Taiwan have been major issues in Kiribati politics. Teburoro

Tito's refusal to release details about a land lease to China for a satellite-tracking facility led to his removal through a no-confidence vote in 2003. Tong, the opposition leader, was elected to replace him. Tong immediately terminated the 15-year lease and restored ties with Taiwan in 2004.

In the 2007 parliamentary elections, independent candidates took 19 seats, followed by Tong's Pillars of Truth (Boutokaan Te Koaua, or BTK) party with 18 seats, and former president Tito's Protect the Maneaba (Maneaban Te Mauri, or MTM) party with 7 seats. Tong secured a second four-year term in presidential elections the same year.

In July 2009, a dispute between the traditional elders' association (Te Bau Ni Maiana) and the island's elected council rapidly escalated into open violence. Te Bau Ni Maiana had ordered the abolition of Maiana's council and demanded new elections. The mayor and several council members rejected their demand and took the case to court, which ruled in the council's favor, indicating that a democratically elected body cannot be forced to disband. However, members of Te Bau Ni Maiana did not accept the court ruling and burned down the mayor's house. The mayor and his allies subsequently resigned in August amid increasing intimidation. Environment Minister Tetabo Nakara, who is from the island of Maiana, also resigned in protest over the government's failure to intervene in the disagreement.

The president has vigorously called for international attention to the growing threats of rising sea levels and dwindling fresh-water supplies facing the people of Kiribati. Tong has that relocation of the entire population may be necessary if ongoing climate change makes inundation inevitable.New Zealand has committed to accept some environmental refugees from Kiribati, and some have already relocated there.

The government is the main employer, and many residents practice subsistence agriculture. The economy depends considerably on foreign assistance and worker remittances, and the state generates a small sum from selling licenses to foreign fishing fleets. Interest from a well-managed trust fund built on royalties from phosphate mining has balanced the national budget and kept the country debt free.

Political Rights and Civil Liberties: Kiribati is an electoral democracy. The president is popularly elected in a two-step process, with Parliament nominating candidates from its own ranks and voters then choosing one to be president. Forty-four representatives are popularly elected to the unicameral House of Parliament (Maneaba Ni Maungatabu) for four-year terms. One additional member is nominated by the Rabi Island Council, and the attorney general holds a seat ex officio. (Although Rabi Island is a part of Fiji, many residents were originally from Kiribati's Banaba Island. British authorities forced them to move to Rabi when phosphate mining made Banaba uninhabitable.) The president, vested with executive authority by the constitution, is limited to serving three four-year terms.

The major parties are the BTK and MTM. Political parties are loosely organized and generally lack fixed ideologies or formal platforms. Geographical, tribal, and personal loyalties are more important determinants of political affiliation.

Official corruption and abuse are serious problems, and the government has not shown a commitment to address them. The number of businesses owned by mainland Chinese has increased rapidly in recent years, raising concerns over possible corruption in granting immigration status to Chinese investors and other legal wrongdoing in overseeing foreign investments. Kiribati was ranked 111 out of 180 countries surveyed in Transparency International's 2009 Corruption Perceptions Index.

Freedom of speech is generally respected. However, the government occasionally restricts opposition criticism. Newspapers can be prosecuted for criminal offenses but cannot be deregistered by the government. Kiribati has two weekly newspapers: the state-owned *Te Uekara* and the privately owned *Kiribati Newstar*. Churches publish several newsletters and other periodicals. There is also one television and two radio stations, all owned by the state. Internet access is limited outside the capital due to cost and lack of infrastructure.

There have been no reports of religious oppression or restrictions on academic freedom. The expansion of access to and quality of education at all levels, however, is seriously restricted by a lack of resources. Secondary education is not available on all islands, and there is a shortage of qualified teachers.

Freedoms of assembly and association and the right to organize unions and bargain collectively are generally respected. A number of nongovernmental groups are involved in development assistance, education, health, and advocacy for women and children. Only about 10 percent of the workforce belongs to unions, the largest of which is the Kiribati Trade Union Congress, with about 2,500 members. The law provides for the right to strike, though the most recent strike was in 1980.

The judicial system is modeled on English common law and provides adequate due-process rights. It consists of the high court, a court of appeal, and magistrates' courts; final appeals can go to the Privy Council in London. The president makes all judicial appointments. A 260-person police force performs law enforcement and paramilitary functions. Kiribati has no military; defense assistance is provided by Australia and New Zealand under bilateral agreements. Traditional customs permit corporal punishment, which can be used to discipline boys for criminal activity. Councils on some outer islands are used to adjudicate petty theft and other minor offenses.

Citizens enjoy freedom of movement, though village councils have used exile as a punishment.

Discrimination against women is common in the traditional, male-dominated culture. Sexual harassment is illegal and not reported to be widespread. Spousal abuse and other forms of violence against women and children are often associated with alcohol abuse.

Kosovo

Political Rights: 5*
Civil Liberties: 4*
Status: Partly Free

Population: 2,222,000
Capital: Pristina

Status Change: Kosovo's political rights rating improved from 6 to 5, its civil liberties rating from 5 to 4, and its status from Not Free to Partly Free due to municipal elections that were generally deemed to be in compliance with international standards, and greater recognition of minority rights.

Ten-Year Ratings Timeline For Year Under Review (Political Rights, Civil Liberties, Status)

2000	2001	2002	2003	2004	2005	2006	2007	2008	2009
6,6NF	6,6NF	5,5PF	5,5PF	6,5NF	6,5NF	6,5NF	6,5NF	6,5NF	5,4PF

Overview: Kosovo held municipal elections in November and December 2009, marking the first balloting since it declared independence in early 2008. The elections were praised by the European Union and featured notable participation by the Serb minority, though there were reports of fraud in some areas. The Serb enclave north of the Ibar River remained separated from the rest of Kosovo, and the country continued to suffer from harassment of independent media and high levels of corruption.

Ethnic Albanians and Serbs competed for control over Kosovo throughout the 20th century. In the late 1980s, the Serbian government began revoking much of Kosovo's provincial autonomy, but the Kosovo Albanians, under longtime leader Ibrahim Rugova, developed their own quasi-governmental institutions during the 1990s.

An ethnic Albanian guerrilla movement called the Kosovo Liberation Army (KLA) began attacking Serbs and suspected ethnic Albanian collaborators in late 1997, provoking harsh responses by government forces. In March 1999, after internationally sponsored negotiations failed to halt the violence, NATO launched a 78-day bombing campaign that compelled Serbia to relinquish control over the province. After the fighting ended, hundreds of thousands of ethnic Albanians who had been expelled by government forces returned. NATO and the United Nations took responsibility for Kosovo's security and civilian administration, though Serbian rule remained legally intact.

After the international takeover, tens of thousands of non-Albanians were forced to flee the province. Ethnic Albanians subsequently made up about 90 percent of the population, with Serbs accounting for most of the remainder. The largest Serb enclave was situated north of the Ibar River, while smaller communities were scattered throughout the province and protected by international forces. In March 2004, two days of rioting against non-Albanian groups left 20 people dead, 800 homes and 30 churches destroyed, and more than 4,000 Serbs and other non-Albanians homeless.

Parliamentary elections in October 2004 led to a governing coalition between

Rugova's Democratic League of Kosovo (LDK) and the Alliance for the Future of Kosovo (AAK), led by former KLA commander Ramush Haradinaj. However, Haradinaj resigned as prime minister to contest war crimes charges in 2005, and Rugova, who had served as Kosovo's president since 2002, died in January 2006. Subsequently, the Democratic Party of Kosovo (PDK), led by former KLA political leader Hashim Thaci, became the dominant party. It won the 2007 parliamentary elections with 36 of 120 seats, raising Thaci to the premiership in a governing coalition with the LDK, which took 25 seats. Of the other major parties, the New Kosovo Alliance (AKR) won 13 seats, a union of the Albanian Christian Democratic Party of Kosovo (PShDK) and the Democratic League of Dardania (LDD) won 11, and the AAK captured 10. Smaller factions took the remainder.

The 2004 riots had led to accelerated talks on Kosovo's final status, but Albanian negotiators demanded full independence, and Serbian officials offered only autonomy short of independence. In late 2007, Finnish mediator Martti Ahtisaari recommended that the UN Security Council grant Kosovo a form of internationally supervised independence. Russia continued to support Serbia's position, however, and the international community was unable to reach consensus.

Kosovo's parliament unilaterally declared independence on February 17, 2008. It was quickly recognized by the United States and most European Union (EU) countries, but over two-thirds of the world's states declined to follow suit. Moreover, resistance by Russia and China barred Kosovo from membership in the United Nations and other international organizations. In June 2008, Kosovo's Serb municipalities formed a separate assembly that affirmed its allegiance to Belgrade. The legal situation was further complicated by the ongoing supervision of international entities in Pristina, including the United Nations Interim Mission in Kosovo (UNMIK), an EU mission known as EULEX, and the NATO peacekeeping force.

Kosovo held municipal elections, its first balloting since the independence declaration, in two rounds in November and December 2009. Although they took place in a generally calm atmosphere and won praise from the EU, the elections were criticized for the widespread incidence of family voting (which effectively disenfranchises women) and the reliance of Kosovo officials on the international community to organize the polls. The PDK led the voting, followed by the LDK and AAK, but the contests in at least two of the three dozen municipalities were set for reruns in early 2010, after election officials found serious fraud in more than half of their polling centers. The elections were notable for the fact that Serbs took control of three municipalities, as well as the relatively high Serb turnout of 24 percent, a significant increase from the near total Serb boycotts of Kosovo elections in previous years. Overall voter turnout was about 45 percent in the first round and 38 percent in the second.

Also during 2009, reports about abuses stemming from the 1999 conflict heightened political and ethnic tensions. In November, a man identifying himself as a former assassin for the KLA's intelligence service claimed to have participated in 17 murders and other crimes, including attacks on potential witnesses in war crimes trials. He implicated senior PDK members in the killings, and said the victims were often LDK members. Other reports that emerged during the year involved torture camps that the KLA had allegedly operated, with captives including Serbs and anti-KLA ethnic Albanians (often LDK members). In August, a Human Rights Watch (HRW) official said up to 400 individuals may have been the victims of alleged KLA kidnapping and organ-harvesting schemes during the 1999 conflict.

By the end of 2009, a total of 64 countries had recognized Kosovo's independence. However, Serbia launched a suit before the International Court of Justice that year, claiming that the 2008 independence declaration violated international law. A decision was expected in 2010.

Since 1999, Kosovo has received 25 times more international aid per capita than Afghanistan, yet it remains the poorest country in Europe, with an unemployment rate of 40 percent and average per capita income of approximately $2,500.

Political Rights and Civil Liberties: Kosovo is not an electoral democracy. The International Civilian Representative (ICR) retains the power to override legislation and decisions deemed to be at odds with the Ahtisaari Plan, which calls for human rights and minority protections. The ICR doubles as the EU representative in Kosovo. Members of the unicameral, 120-seat Kosovo Assembly are elected to three-year terms, and 20 seats are reserved for ethnic minorities. The Assembly elects the president, who also serves a three-year term. The president nominates the prime minister, who must then be approved by the Assembly. In February 2009, ICR Pieter Feith criticized the Assembly for allowing the government to impose legislation without serious debate or scrutiny.

The 2009 municipal elections were generally considered free and fair, and Serbs reportedly participated in much larger numbers than in past elections. The electoral commission detected significant fraud in some areas, however, and most of the Serb population—particularly in the large enclave north of the Ibar River—remains loyal to the government in Belgrade. The main ethnic Albanian parties in Kosovo's multiparty system are organized to some extent around clan or regional ties. Other parties cater to various ethnic minorities, including Serbs.

Corruption in Kosovo is a serious problem, even by regional standards. It can be attributed in part to the country's history of underground institutions and wartime smuggling, and has been exacerbated by the multiplicity of legal regimes and authorities. Kosovo was not rated in Transparency International's 2009 Corruption Perceptions Index.

The 2008 constitution protects freedoms of expression and the press, with exceptions for speech that provokes ethnic hostility. Freedom of expression is limited in practice by lack of security, especially for ethnic minorities. Although there is a wide variety of print and electronic media, journalists report frequent harassment and intimidation. Defamation remains a criminal offense. In 2009, the newspaper *Infopress*, which receives large amounts of advertising revenue from the government, issued thinly veiled calls for the murder of prominent journalist Jeta Xharra, who has reported on government corruption. In October, the director of the European Broadcasting Union criticized the government for political interference at the public broadcaster, Radio-Television Kosovo (RTK). Access to the internet is not restricted.

The new constitution guarantees religious freedom, and ethnic Albanians, who are predominantly Muslim, generally enjoy this right in practice. However, since 1999, there have been systematic attacks on Orthodox Christian sites associated with the Serb population. There have also been attacks on Protestant places of worship in recent years, including several incidents during 2009. Overall, however, the number of attacks on religious sites not associated with the Albanian community has declined somewhat.

Academic freedom has not been formally restricted, but appointments at the University of Pristina are considered to be politicized, and Kosovo's educational system—including higher education—is for the most part ethnically segregated.

Freedom of assembly has occasionally been restricted for security reasons, and the 2008 constitution includes safeguards for public order and national security. Nongovernmental organizations generally function freely, although decreasing donor funding has led many to close. Groups that infringe on the constitutional order or encourage ethnic hatred can be banned by the courts. The constitution protects the right to form and join trade unions. UNMIK regulations on labor rights, which remain in force, do not recognize the right to strike, but workers have not been prevented from doing so. The largest labor group in Kosovo, the Association of Independent Trade Unions (BSPK), claims to represent some 100,000 workers.

The constitution calls for an independent judiciary, but courts at all levels are subject to political influence, intimidation, and corruption. A September 2009 report by the Kosovo Judicial Council (KJC) expressed alarm at the large backlog of cases and insufficient budgets and staffing. Implementation of court decisions is weak. In the municipality of Ferizaj/Urosevac, for instance, less than 10 percent of the 6,050 cases processed had their sentences imposed in 2008. Impunity for war crimes is also a problem. Former prime minister Ramush Haradinaj was acquitted by the International Criminal Tribunal for the former Yugoslavia (ICTY) in 2008 amid complaints of witness intimidation; several witnesses died under unclear circumstances. In October 2009, ICTY prosecutors asked for a partial retrial. Ethnic Albanian judges rarely prosecute cases involving Albanian attacks on non-Albanians. Prison conditions are generally in line with international standards, though overcrowding remains a problem and abuse of prisoners has been reported. The weak judicial system has led to the reemergence of familial blood feuds in some areas.

Organized crime remains a serious problem, with criminal networks extending into various economic sectors and politics. Kosovo is reportedly a key transit point for Central Asian heroin en route to Western Europe.

In 2009, HRW reported that the situation for ethnic minorities in Kosovo had not improved since the independence declaration, while Minority Rights Group International (MRGI) argued that the international community had ceded responsibility for ethnic minorities to the Pristina government, which had little interest in protecting their rights. Kosovo's smaller minorities—the Roma, Ashkali, Gorani, and others—face exceptionally difficult conditions. Numerous attacks on Roma were reported in two towns during 2009. Non-Albanians' freedom of movement is restricted by security concerns, and they have had difficulty in reclaiming properties they fled in 1999. Illegal property transfers remain common. In an indication of the often hostile atmosphere for returnees, houses built for Serb returnees near Prizren were vandalized in April 2009 before the new occupants could move in. Hopes for improving security for non-Albanian communities currently rest on Kosovo's decentralization plan, which will give them more control over local police forces and judicial institutions.

Gender inequality is a major concern, especially in rural areas; support for women's rights is strongest in the capital. Patriarchal attitudes often limit a woman's ability to gain an education, choose a marriage partner, or secure employment. Women are also underrepresented in politics, although election rules stipulate that women must occupy every third spot on each party's candidate list. In the 2007 parliamentary elections, women won 38 of 120 seats; none of the 11 female mayoral candidates were elected in 2009. In many rural areas, women are effectively disenfranchised by "family voting," in which the male head of a household casts ballots for the entire family. Domestic violence is a serious problem, as is discrimination against sexual minorities.

Kosovo serves as a source, transit point, and destination for women and children trafficked for prostitution. The international presence in Kosovo provides a relatively affluent clientele for the trade.

Kuwait

Political Rights: 4
Civil Liberties: 4
Status: Partly Free

Population: 2,985,000
Capital: Kuwait City

Ten-Year Ratings Timeline For Year Under Review (Political Rights, Civil Liberties, Status)

2000	2001	2002	2003	2004	2005	2006	2007	2008	2009
4,5PF	4,5PF	4,5PF	4,5PF	4,5PF	4,5PF	4,4PF	4,4PF	4,4PF	4,4PF

Overview: In May 2009, Kuwait held parliamentary elections for the third time in three years. For the first time Kuwait's history, four women won seats in the new parliament. In April, a former member of parliament was arrested and quickly released on bail for criticizing a member of the ruling family. Kuwait's Constitutional Court in October granted women the right to obtain a passport without the permission of their husbands. In December, the parliament questioned Prime Minister Nasser al-Sabah over concerns about corruption.

For more than 200 years, the al-Sabah dynasty has played a role in ruling Kuwait. A year after the country gained its independence from Britain in 1961, a new constitution gave broad powers to the emir and created the National Assembly. Iraqi forces invaded in August 1990, but a military coalition mandated by the United Nations and led by the United States liberated the country in February 1991.

Emirs have suspended the National Assembly two times, from 1976 to 1981 and from 1986 to 1992. After its restoration in 1992, the parliament played an active role in monitoring the emir and the government, often forcing cabinet ministers out of office and blocking legislation proposed by the ruling family. However, the legislature has also served as an impediment to progressive political change by rejecting measures on women's rights and economic reform.

After 28 years of rule, Sheikh Jaber al-Ahmad al-Sabah died in 2006. Despite fears of a contentious succession process, the cabinet and parliament removed his heir for health reasons and elevated Sheikh Sabah al-Ahmad al-Sabah, the half-brother of the previous emir, as the new emir.

Parliamentary elections held in 2006 were the first to include women, having won the right to vote and run for office the year before. However, none of the 27 female candidates secured seats. In 2007, continued pressure from the legislature to end government corruption forced two prominent cabinet ministers to resign.

The emir dissolved parliament in March 2008, leading to another round of elections in May. Members of parliament continued to press for the power to question cabinet members on corruption and the performance of public services. In November 2008, members of the Salafi bloc in parliament demanded the right to question Prime Minister Nasser al-Sabah, a nephew of the emir, on charges of corruption. As a result of parliamentary anger, the prime minister submitted his and the cabinet's resignation in November.

The emir accepted the cabinet's resignation in December 2008. In a display of his displeasure with the parliament, the emir immediately reappointed his nephew, Nasser al-Sabah, as prime minister, a move that ensured continued frustration. The prime minister finalized the new cabinet in January 2009, making no significant changes to the government. Opposition members of parliament quickly renewed calls to question members of the cabinet for the misuse of public funds. Tensions boiled over again just three months after the formation of the cabinet, leading the government to resign again on March 16. The emir dissolved the parliament two days later, setting up the country's third parliamentary elections in three years.

Elections for the new parliament were held in May 2009. Four women won seats, marking the first time women candidates have been elected in the country's history. Turnout was low, and the results were mixed, with Sunni Islamists, Shiites, liberals, and tribal representatives all winning seats.

After renewed calls to question the prime minister on corruption emerged in November, he appeared before the parliament in December, marking the first time a Kuwaiti prime minister had ever been questioned by the legislature. He survived the subsequent no-confidence vote, when 35 of the parliament's 50 members voted in support of him.

Kuwait, which holds about 10 percent of the world's proven oil reserves, suffered an economic slowdown in 2009 following the collapse of oil prices in late 2008. Oil dominates the economy, accounting for nearly 90 percent of public revenues.

Political Rights and Civil Liberties: Kuwait is not an electoral democracy. The ruling family largely sets the policy agenda and dominates political life. The emir has overriding power in the government system and appoints the prime minister and cabinet. Under the constitution, the emir shares legislative power with the 50-member National Assembly, which is elected to four-year terms by popular vote. The electorate consists of men and women over 21 years of age who have been citizens for at least 20 years; members of most security forces are barred from voting. A 2006 law reduced the number of multimember electoral districts from 25 to 5 in an effort to curb corruption and manipulation. The emir has the authority to dissolve the National Assembly at will but must call elections within 60 days. The parliament can overturn decrees issued by the emir while it was not in session. It can veto the appointment of the country's prime minister, but then it must choose from three alternates put forward by the emir. The parliament also has the power to remove government ministers with a majority vote.

Formal political parties are banned. While political groupings, such as parliamentary blocs, have been allowed to emerge, the government has impeded their activities through harassment and arrests.

Corruption has been a dominant political issue in recent years, with lawmakers placing considerable pressure on the government to tackle the problem. Kuwait was ranked 66 out of 180 countries surveyed in Transparency International's 2009 Corruption Perceptions Index.

While a 2006 press law requires officials to obtain a court order to close newspapers, the authorities continue to limit criticism and debate on politics in the press. Kuwait has more than 10 daily and weekly Arabic newspapers and 2 English-language dailies. The state owns four television stations and nine radio stations, but there are also a number of private outlets, including the satellite television station Al-Rai. Foreign media outlets work relatively freely in Kuwait. Kuwaitis have access to the internet, though the government has instructed internet service providers to block certain sites for political or moral reasons. Authorities curbed freedom of speech on several occasions in 2009. Daifallah Bouramia, a former member of parliament, was arrested in April for criticizing Kuwait's defense minister Jaber al-Mubarak al-Sabah at an election rally, stating that he was "not fit" to be prime minister. Bouramia was later released on bail. From April to June, an Australian woman visiting Kuwait on vacation with her family served four months in prison for insulting the emir during an argument with immigration officials at the airport.

Islam is the state religion, but religious minorities are generally permitted to practice their faiths in private, and Christian churches operate freely. Shiite Muslims, who make up around a third of the population, enjoy full political rights but are subject to some discrimination and harassment.

Academic freedom is generally respected. Kuwait has a tradition of allowing relatively open and free private discussion, often conducted in traditional gatherings (*diwaniyat*) that usually include only men. However, there are indications that these traditional sanctuaries of free speech are under pressure. In November 2009, police arrested the prominent journalist Abdulqader al-Jassem for criticizing the prime minister at a private diwaniya. He was released on bail and was awaiting trial at year's end.

The government imposes constraints on freedoms of assembly and association, although those rights are provided by law. Kuwaitis must notify authorities of a public meeting or protest, but do not need a permit. In October 2009, over 700 expatriate construction workers protested inhumane working and living conditions, as well as overdue salaries. Workers also claimed they had not been paid for overtime in a year. Kuwaiti authorities responded favorably, compelling employers to remedy the situation or face stiff fines.

The government routinely restricts the registration and licensing of associations and nongovernmental organizations (NGOs), forcing dozens of groups to operate without legal standing or state assistance. Representatives of licensed NGOs must obtain government permission to attend foreign conferences on behalf of their organizations. Workers have the right to join labor unions, but the country's labor law mandates that there be only one union per occupational trade.

Kuwait lacks an independent judiciary. The emir appoints all judges, and the executive branch approves judicial promotions. Authorities may detain suspects for four days without charge. The Ministry of the Interior supervises the main internal security forces, including the national police, the Criminal Investigation Division, and Kuwait State Security. The government permits visits to prisons by human rights activists, who report adherence to international standards, though with some concern about overcrowding.

Stateless residents, known as *bidoon*, are estimated to number 100,000. They are considered illegal residents, do not have full citizenship rights, and often live in wretched conditions. Kuwait is a destination country for human trafficking, with many people coming from Bangladesh, India, Pakistan, the Philippines, and Sri Lanka.

The 1962 constitution provides men and women with equal rights. Nevertheless, women face discrimination in several areas of law and society and remain underrepresented in the workforce. While women are offered some legal protections from abuse and discrimination, they are only permitted to seek a divorce in cases where they have been deserted or subject to domestic violence. Women are required to have a male guardian in order to marry and are eligible for only one-half of their brother's inheritance. Domestic abuse and sexual harassment are not specifically prohibited by law, and foreign domestic servants remain particularly vulnerable to abuse and sexual assault. Kuwait is a destination country for the trafficking of women. Despite efforts by some members of parliament to push forward desegregation, the country's public schools have been segregated since 2001. In December 2009, a parliamentary committee voted to segregate private schools as well, but the measure had not moved beyond the committee by year's end. Women comprise more than 60 percent of the student body at several leading universities in Kuwait. Kuwaiti women have the right to vote and run as candidates in parliamentary and local elections. In October 2009, Kuwait's Constitutional Court granted married women the right to obtain passports and to travel without their husband's permission, overturning a 1962 law.

Kyrgyzstan

Political Rights: 6*
Civil Liberties: 5*
Status: Not Free

Population: 5,304,000
Capital: Bishkek

Status Change: Kyrgyzstan's political rights rating declined from 5 to 6, its civil liberties rating from 4 to 5, and its status from Partly Free to Not Free due to a flawed presidential election, the concentration of power in the executive branch, and new legal restrictions on freedom of religion.

Ten-Year Ratings Timeline For Year Under Review (Political Rights, Civil Liberties, Status)

2000	2001	2002	2003	2004	2005	2006	2007	2008	2009
6,5NF	6,5NF	6,5NF	6,5NF	6,5NF	5,4PF	5,4PF	5,4PF	5,4PF	6,5NF

Overview: President Kurmanbek Bakiyev secured a new term in a
                       flawed presidential election in July, retaining power amid
a continuing deterioration of basic freedoms and a disturbing string of violent incidents targeting journalists and politicians. A new law restricted freedom of reli-

gion during the year, and former officials faced what appeared to be politically motivated criminal prosecutions.

Shortly after Kyrgyzstan gained independence from the Soviet Union in 1991, Askar Akayev, a respected physicist, was elected president. He easily won reelection in 1995, and constitutional amendments the following year substantially increased the powers of the presidency. International observers noted serious irregularities in the 2000 parliamentary and presidential elections, which yielded another term for Akayev.

Long-standing frustrations in the economically depressed and politically marginalized south culminated in public protests in 2002. Six protesters were killed when police fired into a crowd the village of Aksy. Four former regional prosecutors and police officials were sentenced to prison in December in connection with the shootings, and additional convictions came five years later, but opposition critics continued to argue that senior officials who authorized the use of force were never brought to justice.

After flawed February 2005 parliamentary elections, thousands of demonstrators took to the streets across the country to protest irregularities and ultimately call for Akayev's resignation. On March 24, protesters and opposition supporters stormed the presidential headquarters in Bishkek. Akayev fled abroad and later resigned.

In the July 2005 presidential poll, former prime minister and opposition leader Kurmanbek Bakiyev captured 89 percent of the vote. His victory was regarded as nearly inevitable after he and Feliks Kulov, his most serious rival, formed a political alliance in May: Kulov withdrew his presidential candidacy in exchange for the post of prime minister. Observers from the Organization for Security and Cooperation in Europe (OSCE) nevertheless concluded that the election, "marked tangible progress ... towards meeting OSCE commitments."

The Bakiyev-Kulov alliance held until early 2007, when Kulov joined the opposition. In April, opposition groups organized demonstrations in Bishkek calling for constitutional reform and Bakiyev's resignation. However, after demonstrators allegedly attacked police, the authorities violently dispersed the protests, dealing the opposition a significant blow.

In October 2007, referendum voters approved a new constitution that expanded the parliament from 75 to 90 seats and introduced party-slate balloting. The hastily called referendum drew criticism from civil society groups, which pointed to the government's use of administrative resources to ensure a favorable outcome.

Bakiyev dissolved the parliament the day after the referendum, and a progovernment party called Ak Zhol was quickly formed to contest elections in December. The disputed balloting, dubbed a "missed opportunity" by OSCE observers and held under new legislation, produced a parliament dominated by Ak Zhol and devoid of opposition representation. Amendments pushed through the new legislature later that month widened the executive's authority, and a government formed in the final days of 2007 was stacked with Bakiyev loyalists.

The president consolidated his power in 2008, sidelining the country's remaining well-known opposition figures. Kulov's departure from politics in May, when Bakiyev appointed him as head of an energy development project, reflected the broader disappearance of a viable political opposition.

In March 2009, Medet Sadyrkulov, Bakiyev's former chief of staff, was found dead in a burned-out car near Bishkek. Opposition representatives charged that Sadyrkulov, who had left the government earlier in the year, was assassinated because he planned to join the opposition. His relatives asked for an additional investigation in May, after initial inquiries failed to clarify the circumstances of his death.

Bakiyev won another five-year term in the July presidential election, taking 75 percent of the vote. OSCE observers concluded that the poll failed to meet international standards, citing evidence of fraud, intimidation of opposition supporters, and the misuse of administrative resources, among other problems.

Kyrgyzstan continued to balance strategic and economic relations with Russia and the United States in 2009. In February, after receiving US$2 billion in loan guarantees from Russia, the Kyrgyz government threatened to evict the U.S. military from a base at Manas airport. It then agreed in June to let U.S. forces remain in exchange for significantly higher rent payments.

Political Rights and Civil Liberties: Kyrgyzstan is not an electoral democracy. The 2005 presidential election drew praise for making substantial progress over previous elections, but observers found serious flaws in the 2007 parliamentary and 2009 presidential elections.

Constitutional changes adopted in the hastily organized 2007 referendum expanded the unicameral parliament from 75 to 90 deputies, with party-list voting replacing single-member districts. president and parliament serve five-year terms, and the majority party in the parliament nominates the prime minister.

The propresidential Ak Zhol party holds 71 of the 90 seats, and the only other parties represented—the Social Democratic Party, with 11 seats, and the Kyrgyzstan Communist Party, with 8—generally cooperate with the government. The fragmented opposition's periodic attempts to unite have only underscored the weakness of alternative forces.

Corruption is pervasive in Kyrgyz society, and bribes are frequently required to obtain lucrative government positions. The nepotistic practices of President Kurmanbek Bakiyev, whose sons and brothers are prominent in business and government, were evident in the October 2009 appointment of his son Maksim as head of the Central Agency for Development. Kyrgyzstan was ranked 162 out of 180 countries surveyed in Transparency International's 2009 Corruption Perceptions Index.

A variety of private print and broadcast outlets continue to operate alongside state-run television and radio stations, but the government has stepped up pressure on independent journalism in recent years, using licensing rules, criminal libel laws, and various forms of administrative harassment to suppress media scrutiny. Journalists have also faced increased extralegal harassment and violent attacks. Osh-based journalist Alisher Saipov, who ran an Uzbek-language newspaper that was critical of Uzbekistan's government, was killed in October 2007; the Kyrgyz government has failed to investigate the murder vigorously, although police said in October 2009 that they were seeking a suspect. Correspondent Syrgak Abdyldayev of the independent weekly *Reporter-Bishkek* was stabbed in March 2009 and left the country in August after receiving threats. Osh-based journalist Kubanychbek Joldoshev was beaten in November. U.S.-funded Radio Free Europe/Radio Liberty remained barred from the country's television and FM radio airwaves in 2009 after refusing in 2008 to submit programming for government screening before broadcast. In December, journalist Gennady Pavlyuk, who wrote for several newspapers in Kyrgyzstan, died in Almaty, Kazakhstan, after he was thrown from a window with his arms and legs bound with duct tape. After Pavlyuk's murder, the OSCE called on the Kyrgyz government to acknowledge a "safety crisis of Kyrgyzstan's press." The government has reportedly blocked some websites, but the primary obstacles to widespread internet access are economic and infrastructural.

The government has generally respected freedom of religion, but all religious organizations must register with the Ministry of Justice, a process that is often cumbersome. In January 2009, the president signed a new law that banned proselytizing, the distribution of religious literature in public places, and private religious education. The measure also requires at least 200 signatures to register a religious organization. The government monitors and restricts Islamist groups that it regards as a threat to national security, particularly Hizb ut-Tahrir, an ostensibly nonviolent international movement calling for the creation of a caliphate. In March 2009, the government banned the wearing of headscarves in schools.

Corruption is widespread in the educational system, and bribes are often required to obtain admission to schools or universities. Teachers have reportedly been forced to subscribe to government newspapers, and authorities in some municipalities require schoolchildren to perform during national holidays and visits by government officials.

The government has tightened restrictions on freedom of assembly in recent years. In August 2008, Bakiyev signed legislation requiring organizers to give the authorities 12 days' notice before all gatherings and allowing officials to ban protests on ill-defined grounds. Police blocked protests after the July 2009 presidential election.

Freedom of association is typically upheld, and nongovernmental organizations (NGOs) participate actively in social and political life. However, since 2007, they have made plausible claims that the authorities are attempting to exclude them as part of a broad push against alternative political and civic voices. Kyrgyz NGOs noted in a November 2008 statement that nine journalists and human rights activists had sought or received political asylum abroad in the previous two years.

The law provides for the formation of trade unions, and unions are generally able to operate without obstruction. However, strikes are prohibited in many sectors, and the Federation of Trade Unions has reportedly fallen under the political influence of the government. Legal enforcement of union rights is weak, and collective bargaining agreements are not always respected by employers.

Despite the enactment of various reform measures, the judiciary is not independent and remains dominated by the executive branch. Corruption among judges, who are underpaid, is widespread. Defendants' rights, including the presumption of innocence, are not always respected, and there are credible reports of violence against suspects during arrest and interrogation.

Two former officials faced charges in 2009 that appeared to be politically motivated. In June, former foreign minister and current opposition member Alikbek Jekshenkulov went on trial for a 2007 murder. Former defense minister Ismail Isakov went on trial on corruption charges in November.

Ethnic minority groups, including Uzbeks, Russians, and Uighurs, have complained of discrimination in employment and housing. Members of the country's sizable Uzbek minority, concentrated in the south, have long demanded more political and cultural rights, including greater representation in government, more Uzbek-language schools, and official status for the Uzbek language.

The government, which abolished the Soviet-era exit-visa system in 1999, generally respects the right of unrestricted travel to and from the country. There are barriers to internal migration, however, including a requirement that citizens obtain permits to work and settle in particular areas of the country.

Personal connections, corruption, organized crime, and widespread poverty limit business competition and equality of opportunity. Conscripted soldiers have reportedly been rented out to civilian employers under illegal arrangements, with some forced to work for no pay.

Cultural traditions and apathy among law enforcement officials discourage victims of domestic violence and rape from contacting the authorities. The trafficking of women and girls into forced prostitution abroad is a serious problem, and some victims report that the authorities are involved in trafficking. The practice of bride abduction persists despite being illegal, and few perpetrators are prosecuted. Women are well represented in the workforce, the parliament (where they hold nearly a third of all seats), and institutions of higher learning, but poor economic conditions have had a negative effect on women's professional and educational opportunities.

Laos

Political Rights: 7
Civil Liberties: 6
Status: Not Free

Population: 6,320,000
Capital: Vientiane

Ten-Year Ratings Timeline For Year Under Review (Political Rights, Civil Liberties, Status)

2000	2001	2002	2003	2004	2005	2006	2007	2008	2009
7,6NF	7,6NF	7,6NF	7,6NF	7,6NF	7,6NF	7,6NF	7,6NF	7,6NF	7,6NF

Overview: The Laotian government continued to encourage large-scale foreign investment and development projects in 2009, often at the expense of small farmers and tribal communities. The United States lifted trade restrictions on the country in June, despite objections from human rights activists. Also during the year, Laos reached a deal with Britain to repatriate two British citizens facing life in prison for drug smuggling. However, human rights advocates in December voiced concern over the fate of some 4,000 Hmong migrants to be deported by Thai authorities at the request of the Laotian government.

Laos won independence in 1953, after six decades of French rule and Japanese occupation during World War II. The new constitutional monarchy soon fell into a civil war with Pathet Lao guerrillas, who were backed by the Vietnamese Communist Party. As the conflict raged on, Laos was also drawn into the Vietnam War in 1964. The Pathet Lao seized power in 1975, and the Lao People's Revolutionary Party (LPRP) has ruled the country ever since. By the 1980s, the economy was in tatters after years of civil war and state mismanagement. Noting the success of China's economic opening, the LPRP began to relax controls on prices, encouraged foreign investment, and privatized farms and some state-owned enterprises.

The party's policy of maintaining tight political control while spurring economic development continued over subsequent decades, but the rapid expansion of extractive industries and an influx of thousands of Chinese businesses and workers increasingly drew public resentment. The seizure of land from subsistence farmers and tribal communities for leasing to foreign-owned agribusinesses proved especially problematic, sometimes triggering protests and violence. The government ordered a halt to land grants in 2007, but local and provincial authorities largely ignored the move. Given rampant corruption and the lack of a reliable land inventory or management system, critics have estimated that two to three million hectares have been transferred or fenced off for lease to foreign investors since the 2007 government order was issued.

In June 2009, the United States removed Laos from a trade blacklist that had prevented U.S. businesses operating in the country from receiving government-backed loans. The decision was based on Laos's shift toward open markets, but critics said it ignored human rights concerns.

Also in 2009, Laos and Britain reached an agreement that allowed two Britons serving life sentences for drug offenses in Laos to be transferred to Britain. The two cases drew international attention to Laos's harsh penalties for nonviolent drug crimes. Smuggling 500 or more grams of heroin carries the death penalty, and one of the Britons was arrested with 680 grams, but she was spared a death sentence after she became pregnant in custody under unclear circumstances.

In December, some 400 Hmong migrants were sent back to Laos by the Thai government, 158 of whom are officially recognized as UN refugees. The group was the first of 4,000 Hmong to be deported by Thai authorities at the request of the Laotian government. Human rights advocates have voiced concern over the welfare of the migrants, as it was not clear at year's end what the Laotian government planned to do with them.

Political Rights and Civil Liberties:

Laos is not an electoral democracy. The 1991 constitution makes the LPRP the sole legal political party and grants it a leading role at all levels of government. The LPRP vets all candidates for election to the rubber-stamp National Assembly, whose 115 members elect the president. Elections are held every five years, most recently in 2006, when former vice president and defense minister Choummaly Sayasone became head of the LPRP and state president.

Corruption and abuses by government officials are widespread. Official announcements and new laws aimed at curbing corruption are rarely enforced, and government regulation of virtually every facet of life provides many opportunities for bribery. Senior officials in government and the military are frequently involved in commercial logging, mining, and other enterprises aimed at exploiting Laotian natural resources. The country was ranked 158 out of 180 countries surveyed in Transparency International's 2009 Corruption Perceptions Index.

Freedom of the press is severely restricted. Any journalist who criticizes the government or discusses controversial political topics faces legal punishment. The state owns all media, including three newspapers with extremely low circulations. Residents within frequency range of Radio Free Asia and other foreign broadcasts from Thailand can access these alternative media sources. Internet access is heavily restricted, and content is censored.

Religious freedom is tightly constrained. Dozens of Christians have been detained on religious grounds, and several have been jailed for proselytizing or conducting other religious activities. The government forces Christians to renounce their faith, confiscates their property, and bars them from celebrating Christian holidays. The religious practice of the majority Buddhist population is restricted through the LPRP's control of clergy training and supervision of temples and other religious sites.

Academic freedom is not respected. University professors cannot teach or write about democracy, human rights, and other politically sensitive topics. Although some young people now go overseas for university- and graduate-level education, they are selected by the government and are generally children of senior officials and military leaders.

Government surveillance of the population has been scaled back in recent years, but searches without warrants still occur.

The government severely restricts freedom of assembly. Laws prohibit participation in organizations that engage in demonstrations or public protests, or that in any other way cause "turmoil or social instability." Those found guilty of violating these laws can receive sentences of up to five years in prison. Laos is home to some nongovernmental welfare and professional groups, but they are prohibited from pursuing political agendas and are subject to strict state control. All unions must belong to the official Federation of Lao Trade Unions. Strikes are not expressly prohibited, but workers rarely stage walkouts, and they do not have the right to bargain collectively.

The courts are corrupt and controlled by the LPRP. Long procedural delays are common, particularly for cases dealing with public grievances and complaints about government abuses. Security forces often illegally detain suspects, and some Laotians have allegedly spent more than a decade in jail without trial. Hundreds of political activists have also been held for months or years without trial. Prisoners are often tortured and must bribe prison officials to obtain better food, medicine, visits from family, and more humane treatment.

Discrimination against members of ethnic minority tribes is common. The Hmong, who fielded a guerrilla army allied with U.S. forces during the Vietnam War, are particularly distrusted by the government and face harsh treatment. Thousands have been forced off their land to make way for the exploitation of timber and other natural resources.

All land is owned by the state, though citizens have rights to use it. With no fair or robust system to protect land rights or ensure compensation for displacement, development projects often spur public resentment and sometimes violent protests.

Although laws guarantee women many of the same rights as men, gender-based discrimination and abuse are widespread. Tradition and religious practices have contributed to women's inferior access to education, equal employment opportunities, and worker benefits. Poverty exacerbates these hardships and puts many women at greater risk of exploitation and abuse by the state and society. An estimated 15,000 to 20,000 Laotian women and girls, including many tribal peoples, are trafficked each year for prostitution. In May 2009, amid growing concern about the spread of HIV/

AIDS, the government initiated a program targeting "katheoys," or transgender men, who typically turn to prostitution to make a living because of severe discrimination. The campaign included special clinics to provide testing and treatment.

Latvia

Political Rights: 2
Civil Liberties: 1
Status: Free

Population: 2,256,000
Capital: Riga

Ten-Year Ratings Timeline For Year Under Review (Political Rights, Civil Liberties, Status)

2000	2001	2002	2003	2004	2005	2006	2007	2008	2009
1,2F	1,2F	1,2F	1,2F	1,2F	1,1F	1,1F	2,1F	2,1F	2,1F

Overview: The public's deep distrust of Latvia's government in the face of a deepening economic crisis was underscored by a major protest in January 2009, which turned violent and resulted in more than two dozen injuries. In response, President Valdis Zatlers issued an ultimatum that the government pass certain reforms or he would call for a referendum to dissolve Parliament. After the government collapsed in February and a new coalition led by the New Era Party was formed the following month, several key reforms were adopted. The new government spent much of the rest of 2009 imposing budget cuts in the midst of an extremely severe contraction of Latvia's economy.

After centuries of foreign domination, Latvia gained its independence in 1918, only to be annexed by the Soviet Union during World War II. The long Soviet occupation featured a massive influx of Russians and the deportation, execution, and emigration of tens of thousands of ethnic Latvians. In 1991, Latvia regained its independence as the Soviet Union disintegrated, and a multiparty system took root during the 1990s.

Prime Minister Einars Repse's coalition government—including his center-right New Era Party, Latvia's First Party (LPP), the Union of Greens and Farmers (ZZS), and For Fatherland and Freedom/Latvian National Independence Movement (TB/LNNK)—collapsed in 2004. A subsequent ZZS-led government survived for just seven months and was replaced in December by a coalition of the New Era Party, the People's Party, LPP, and ZZS. Aigars Kalvitis of the People's Party was named prime minister. However, New Era withdrew in April 2006, after an economic crimes probe was launched against one of its leaders.

In the October 2006 parliamentary polls, the People's Party led with 23 seats, followed by the ZZS and New Era with 18 each, the Harmony Center with 17, LPP/Latvia's Way with 10, TB/LNNK with 8, and For Human Rights in a United Latvia with 6. The People's Party, LPP/Latvia's Way, ZZS, and TB/LNNK formed a new government, with Kalvitis remaining prime minister. Valdis Zatlers, an orthopedic surgeon, was elected president by Parliament in May 2007.

Kalvitis sparked a political crisis in September 2007 by suspending the director of the Bureau for the Prevention and Combating of Corruption (KNAB), Aleksejs Loskutovs, over alleged irregularities in the KNAB's accounting. Opponents of the decision characterized it as a politically motivated attack on an agency that had become increasingly active in pursuing corruption cases, including against senior government officials. Parliament's planned vote on the issue in October was postponed after several thousand people gathered outside the building to support Loskutovs and demand Kalvitis's resignation. In a second major rally in November, protesters denounced corruption and called for new elections.

In December, Kalvitis announced that his government would resign, Loskutovs was reinstated, and Parliament approved a new government, which—despite the public's call for political change—included the same four parties as its predecessor. Former prime minister Ivars Godmanis (1990-1993) of LPP/Latvia's Way was selected to replace Kalvitis. In June 2008, Loskutovs was finally dismissed by Parliament for inadequate oversight following revelations that two KNAB employees had stolen funds seized by the bureau over several years.

In the face of a deepening economic crisis, thousands of Latvians marched on the Parliament building in January 2009. The protest began as a peaceful demand for the government's resignation, but it escalated into the most violent protest the country had experienced since independence after several hundred people threw stones at the Parliament building and looted stores. More than two dozen people were injured, and more than 100 were detained by police. The following day, President Zatlers issued an ultimatum that the government adopt key reforms, including constitutional amendments that would provide for the appointment of a head of the KNAB, allow the public to dismiss Parliament by referendum, and increase oversight of economic development. If the reforms were not passed by the end of March, Zatlers said he would call for a referendum to dissolve Parliament.

On February 20, the four-party ruling coalition collapsed after two coalition partners withdrew their support. A new government was formed shortly thereafter, composed of the New Era Party, the People's Party, ZZS, TB/LNNK, and the Civic Union. New Era's Valdis Dombrovskis, a former finance minister and member of the European Parliament, was appointed prime minister. In March, Zatlers chose not to follow through with his threats to dissolve Parliament, citing progress on several of his reform demands, including strengthening oversight of international funding and the appointment of Normunds Vilitus as the new director of the KNAB. Subsequently, constitutional amendments were approved, allowing voters to initiate a national referendum to dissolve Parliament.

The new government spent the rest of 2009 enacting spending cuts, as Latvia suffered one of the deepest economic recessions in the world. Real GDP declined by about 18 percent at the end of the year, and unemployment had reached around 20 percent. Meanwhile, public dissatisfaction with the country's dominant parties continued to increase; the new Civic Union party and Harmony Center led in June European Parliament elections, and Harmony Center also won a majority in Riga's June municipal elections.

Political Rights and Civil Liberties: Latvia is an electoral democracy. The constitution provides for a unicameral, 100-seat Parliament (Saeima), whose members are elected for four-year terms. Parliament elects the president, who serves up to two four-year terms. The prime minister is nominated by the president and must be approved by Parliament. The October 2006 legislative elections were free and fair. Resident noncitizens may not vote in either national or local elections.

The country's major parties include the People's Party, ZZS, New Era, LPP/ Latvia's Way, TB/LNNK, and For Human Rights in a United Latvia. As a result of growing popular discontent with the parties associated with the previous ruling coalition, voters in 2009 began to favor lesser-known parties, including the center-left Harmony Center, which derives much of its support from the ethnic Russian population, and the Civic Union, a center-right group founded in 2008 on a platform of ending the country's often very close connections between business and politicians.

The government has adopted various anticorruption measures and made some progress against corruption in 2009. In March, the director of the KNAB—which had been without a leader since mid-2008—was finally appointed, and Parliament approved a law allowing plea bargaining by informants that is anticipated to help in the investigation of corruption cases. Meanwhile, the high-profile corruption case of the former mayor of Ventspils, Aivars Lembergs, continued at year's end. Latvia was ranked 56 out of 180 countries surveyed in Transparency International's 2009 Corruption Perceptions Index.

The government generally respects freedom of speech and of the press. Private television and radio stations broadcast programs in both Latvian and Russian, and newspapers publish a wide range of political viewpoints. Complete information on media ownership is not easily obtainable, although many newspapers are believed to be associated with business interests and political figures. In July, the highly respected newspaper *Diena* was suddenly sold to a foreign owner, although the true identity of the new owner remained a subject of dispute and controversy. Many of the paper's leading journalists and editors resigned in protest, and observers expressed concerns that the new owner would limit the newspaper's editorial independence. The government does not restrict access to the internet.

Freedom of religion is generally respected. However, so-called traditional religious groups enjoy certain rights, such as teaching religion to public school students, which are unavailable to newer groups. There are no government restrictions on academic freedom.

Freedoms of assembly and association are protected by law and in practice. There were numerous unrestricted gatherings in 2009, including by teachers and scientists against proposed pay cuts. A major antigovernment protest in January, organized by opposition parties and labor unions, began peacefully but turned violent, resulting in scores of arrests and a number of injuries. While the city council tried to ban a gay pride parade in Riga in May on the grounds that it posed a security risk, it was ultimately held after a court decision restored the parade's permit. The government does not restrict the activities of nongovernmental organizations (NGOs). Workers enjoy the right to establish trade unions, strike, and engage in collective bargaining. About 15 percent of the workforce is unionized.

While judicial independence is generally respected, inefficiency and corruption continue to be problems. In February 2009, two district court judges were sentenced to eight years in prison for bribery. Also in February, a new law entered into force requiring information on court decisions to be published on the internet. Legal prohibitions against arbitrary arrest and the right to a fair trial are largely observed in practice. However, lengthy pretrial detention remains a concern. Law enforcement officials have reportedly used excessive force against detainees, and prison inmates suffer from overcrowding and inadequate medical care.

Nearly one-fifth of Latvia's residents are noncitizens. Those who immigrated during the Soviet period, the majority of whom are ethnic Russians, must apply for citizenship and pass a Latvian language test. Only about 2,000 people were granted citizenship in 2009; some noncitizens have cited resentment at not having been granted citizenship automatically at independence in 1991 as a reason for not applying. An ombudsman responsible for protecting the rights of individuals in relation to the government was appointed by Parliament in 2007; however, the ombudsman's office has faced sharp budget cuts during the last two years, and some rights groups have criticized it for not responding adequately to human rights problems. Latvia is a party to the 1951 UN Convention Relating to the Status of Refugees and its 1967 protocol. A new law adopted in June 2009 on the treatment of asylum seekers includes provisions on detention procedures and appeals.

Women enjoy the same legal rights as men, but they often face employment and wage discrimination. There are 22 women in the 100-member Parliament. Domestic violence is reportedly a serious problem. Latvia is a source for women trafficked for the purpose of prostitution, mostly to Western Europe. In 2009, the government initiated a five-year antitrafficking program in conjunction with domestic NGOs and international organizations.

Lebanon

Political Rights: 5
Civil Liberties: 3*
Status: Partly Free

Population: 3,876,000
Capital: Beirut

Ratings Change: Lebanon's civil liberties rating improved from 4 to 3 due to a decline in political violence that had plagued the country since 2005, coupled with a series of positive reforms to combat sectarianism and limit arbitrary detention.

Ten-Year Ratings Timeline For Year Under Review (Political Rights, Civil Liberties, Status)

2000	2001	2002	2003	2004	2005	2006	2007	2008	2009
6,5NF	6,5NF	6,5NF	6,5NF	6,5NF	5,4PF	5,4PF	5,4PF	5,4PF	5,3PF

Overview: The March 14 Coalition retained its majority in the June 2009 parliamentary elections. However, the need to negotiate a national unity government with the rival March 8 Coalition, delayed the formation of a cabinet until five months after the election, as each political faction looked to its foreign patrons for guidance. Over the course of 2009, both the outgoing and incoming governments introduced modest but positive reforms aimed at limiting arbitrary detention and improving the rights of domestic workers and refugees. For the first time since 2005, Lebanon was largely free from political violence.

Lebanon was established as a League of Nations mandate under French control in 1920. After winning its independence in 1943, the new state maintained a precarious democratic system based on the division of power among the country's then 18 officially recognized sectarian communities. As demographic developments, including emigration, transformed the slight Christian majority into a minority, Muslim leaders demanded reform of the fixed 6 to 5 ratio of Christian-to-Muslim parliamentary seats and an end to exclusive Maronite Christian control of the presidency. In 1975, war erupted between a coalition of Lebanese Muslim and leftist militias aligned with Palestinian guerrilla groups on one side, and an array of Christian militias bent on preserving the political status quo on the other.

After the first few years of fighting, a loose consensus emerged among Lebanese politicians regarding a new power-sharing arrangement. However, following the entry of Syrian and Israeli troops into Lebanon in 1976 and 1978, the various militias and their foreign backers had little interest in disarming.

In 1989, the surviving members of Lebanon's 1972 parliament convened in Taif, Saudi Arabia, and agreed to a plan put forward by the Arab League that would weaken the presidency, establish equality in Christian and Muslim parliamentary representation, and mandate close security cooperation with occupying Syrian troops. A new Syrian-backed government then extended its writ to most of the country, with the exception of southern Lebanon, which remained under Israeli occupation until 2000.

Although Syria consolidated its control over Lebanese state institutions in the 1990s, Lebanon managed to preserve greater political and civil liberties than were allowed in most Arab countries. Lebanese who openly condemned the occupation risked arbitrary arrest, but criticism of the government was tolerated. By the end of the decade, Lebanon's economy was in deep recession, and growing public disaffection with the postwar establishment spurred demonstrations against Syrian domination.

In 2004, the United States joined with France and most other European governments in calling for an end to Syria's power over Lebanon. Damascus moved to defend its position by forcing the Lebanese parliament to approve a constitutional amendment extending the six-year tenure of President Emile Lahoud, a staunch Syrian ally and a rival of Prime Minister Rafiq Hariri. On the eve of the parliamentary vote, the UN Security Council issued a resolution calling for a presidential election, the withdrawal of all foreign forces, and the disarmament of militias. The amendment nevertheless passed, provoking an international outcry.

Encouraged by the international climate, Hariri and other politicians who had been loyal to Syria began defecting to the opposition. In February 2005, four months after resigning as prime minister, Hariri was killed along with 22 others in a car bombing. Widespread suspicions of Syrian involvement led to international pressure for an immediate Syrian withdrawal and to extensive anti-Syrian demonstrations in Beirut. An interim government was formed to oversee legislative elections. Syrian troops pulled out of the country in April, and in the May and June balloting, allies of the late Hariri—calling themselves the March 14 Coalition—expanded their parliamentary bloc to 72 out of 128 seats. The coalition, supported mainly by Sunni Muslims and certain Christian and Druze factions, went on to form a new government led by Prime Minister Fouad Siniora.

The March 14 Coalition lacked the two-thirds parliamentary majority needed to overturn Lahoud's term extension and elect a new president, leaving the pro-Syrian Lahoud in office; this division paralyzed the government. In October 2005, a UN panel charged with investigating Hariri's murder reported, "converging evidence pointing at both Lebanese and Syrian involvement" in the crime. Meanwhile, a series of assassinations and bombings that began in the months after the Syrian withdrawal targeted key anti-Syrian politicians.

In July 2006, the powerful militia of the Shiite Islamist movement Hezbollah attacked Israeli forces in a cross-border raid, sparking a six-week war that severely damaged Lebanon's infrastructure and killed some 1,500 people, most of them Lebanese civilians. After the war ended with a UN-brokered ceasefire, Lebanese politicians struggled to stabilize the government. The March 8 Coalition—a largely Shiite and Christian bloc that was backed by Hezbollah and aligned with Iran and Syria— left the national unity government in November, demanding a reorganized cabinet in which it would hold veto power. Hezbollah mounted a round-the-clock protest outside the cabinet offices, and street battles between supporters of the rival coalitions broke out with increasing frequency.

Political assassinations aimed at anti-Syrian lawmakers and public figures continued in 2007. Also during the year, the army waged a four-month campaign against a Sunni Islamist militant group based in Nahr el-Bared, a Palestinian refugee camp; the fighting killed some 400 people and displaced more than 30,000 others. The camp was completely destroyed, and reconstruction did not begin until late 2008.

Meanwhile, political deadlock continued as the pro- and anti-Syrian coalitions in the parliament repeatedly failed to elect a new president to replace Lahoud, whose term expired in November 2007. The two sides agreed on army commander Michel Suleiman as a compromise candidate, but they could not agree on the process for electing him. In May 2008, responding to a pair of government decisions they viewed as a threat, Hezbollah and its allies seized West Beirut by force. Battles between the opposition and government supporters raged across Lebanon for nearly a week, leaving nearly 100 people dead. A power-sharing agreement brokered by Qatar cleared the way for Suleiman's election later that month, the formation of a new national unity government, and the passage of a revised election law in September.

In parliamentary elections held in June 2009, the March 14 and March 8 coalitions won 71 and 57 seats, respectively, and Saad Hariri—the son of Rafiq Hariri— was named prime minister. Negotiations over the cabinet's composition, which continued to be heavily influenced by external actors, including Syria and Saudi Arabia, dragged on for several months, and the new government was not announced until November. The majority was granted 15 ministers and the minority 10, while the remaining 5 were named by the president and would be ostensibly neutral. This arrangement meant that the majority could not act unilaterally, but the minority would lack a clear veto.

Lebanon was largely free from political violence in 2009, although Lebanese authorities arrested dozens of people suspected of spying for Israel, including high-ranking security officials. Some fled to Israel to escape the crackdown. Also in 2009, Britain announced that it would meet with political representatives of Hezbollah, having shunned the organization since 2005 and designating its military wing as a terrorist organization in 2008.

Political Rights and Civil Liberties: Lebanon is not an electoral democracy. Although the 2009 parliamentary elections were conducted peacefully and judged to be free and fair in some respects, vote buying was reported to be rampant, and the electoral system retained a number of structural flaws linked to the country's sectarian political system.

The president is selected every six years by the 128-member National Assembly, which in turn is elected for four-year terms. The president and parliament nominate the prime minister, who, along with the president, chooses the cabinet, subject to parliamentary approval. The unwritten National Pact of 1943 stipulates that the president be a Maronite Christian, the prime minister a Sunni Muslim, and the speaker of the National Assembly a Shiite Muslim. Parliamentary seats are divided among major sects under a constitutional formula that does not reflect their current demographic weight. Shiites comprise at least a third of the population, but they are allotted only 21 percent of parliamentary seats. The sectarian political balance has been periodically reaffirmed and occasionally modified by foreign-brokered agreements like the 1989 Taif accords and the 2008 Doha Agreement.

The 2009 elections were conducted under the 2008 election law, which stemmed from the Doha agreement. It condensed nationwide voting into a single day, introduced some curbs on campaign finance and advertising, and created smaller, more religiously homogeneous districts. However, some important changes—including the reduction of the voting age to 18 from 21 and a system allowing expatriates to vote abroad—would not come into force until the 2010 municipal elections at the earliest, and the framers of the new law rejected the core recommendations of the Boutros Commission, which had been created in 2005 to advise the government on electoral reform. Among other changes, the panel had called for a bloc of the National Assembly seats to be filled through proportional representation, the establishment of an independent electoral commission, and a 20 percent quota for women on candidate lists. The 2008 law also retained restrictions on moving one's voter registration to a new district and failed to introduce preprinted ballots.

The sectarian political system and the powerful role of foreign patrons effectively limits the accountability of elected officials to the public at large, as seen during the protracted cabinet negotiations of 2009. Political and bureaucratic corruption is widespread. Businesses routinely pay bribes and cultivate ties with politicians to win contracts, and anticorruption laws are loosely enforced. In September 2009, a financier associated with Hezbollah was arrested for a large-scale Ponzi scheme that resulted in serious losses for political parties as well as many ordinary investors. Later in the year, the new justice minister suspended a judge without pay for alleged corruption, the first such disciplinary action in memory. Lebanon was ranked 130 out of 180 countries surveyed in Transparency International's 2009 Corruption Perceptions Index.

Lebanon has a long tradition of press freedom, though nearly all media outlets have ties to political groups. There are seven privately owned television stations and dozens of privately owned radio and print outlets that reflect a range of views. Internet access is not restricted. Vaguely worded laws that criminalize critical reporting on Syria, the military, the judiciary, and the presidency remain in force. The series of assassinations that targeted anti-Syrian journalists between 2005 and 2008 have all gone unpunished to date. Journalists cannot report from some Hezbollah-controlled areas without the group's explicit permission and oversight. The authorities banned two high-profile films in 2009, *Waltz with Bashir* and *Help*, the first because of the ban on Israeli products, and the second for discussing prostitution and drugs, though they were widely available informally as DVDs. Several major media outlets implemented layoffs during the year as a result of the global economic crisis, and in some cases the dismissals seemed to be politically motivated.

Freedom of religion is guaranteed in the constitution and protected in practice. However, informal religious discrimination is common. In 2009, the Interior Ministry allowed citizens not to list their religion on their national identity cards or national registration, the first time in Lebanese history that identification cards did not immediately identify individuals as a member of a religious group. Academic freedom is firmly established.

Rights to freedom of association and assembly are generally unrestricted. On several occasions in recent years, hundreds of thousands of Lebanese have rallied in favor of or in opposition to the government. Lebanon's civil society is vibrant, and nongovernmental organizations (NGOs), including human rights groups, operate openly. The government requires notification of an NGO's formation. The Interior Ministry has at times transformed the notification process into an approval process and has been known to conduct inquiries into an organization's founding members. NGOs must invite ministry representatives to general assemblies, where votes are held on bylaws or boards of directors. All workers except those in government may establish unions, which have the right to strike and bargain collectively. In recent years, union activity has been closely affiliated with political groupings, and labor concerns have thus taken a backseat to union-based political activity.

The judiciary is ostensibly independent, but it is subject to heavy political influence in practice. The Judicial Council nominates judges, who are then approved by the Justice Ministry. Both government and opposition parties vet judicial appointments. International standards of criminal procedure are generally observed in the regular judiciary, but not in the military court, which consists largely of military officers with no legal training.

The security forces' practice of arbitrary detention has declined since 2005. While the government has made some progress in fighting torture since 2007, new legislation and regulations on the issue are often not enforced, and the use of torture remains widespread in security-related cases. Prison conditions are poor. A reported 3,207 of Lebanon's 5,122 inmates had not faced trial as of May 2009, and many are held under "preventative arrest." This mechanism had allowed the government to hold individuals without trial indefinitely, but the Justice Ministry in 2009 announced new regulations that require such detainees to be tried within six months. This term is renewable once, and the rules will not apply to security cases. Four generals who had been held without charge since 2005 in connection with the assassination of former prime minister Rafiq Hariri were released in April 2009.

Nearly 350,000 Palestinian refugees living in Lebanon are denied citizenship rights and face restrictions on working, building homes, and purchasing property. Since 2008, the government has issued identification cards to nearly 750 of the 3,000 to 5,000 Palestinians believed to lack papers, though the process has slowed for administrative reasons. Residents of the Nahr el-Bared camp, which was devastated by fighting in 2007, live under extremely difficult conditions as they await reconstruction. The government formed in 2009 includes the country's first minister of state for Palestinian refugee affairs.

Women enjoy many of the same rights as men, but they experience some social and legal discrimination. Since family and personal-status matters are adjudicated by the religious authorities of each sectarian community, women are subject to discriminatory laws governing marriage, divorce, inheritance, and child custody. Women are underrepresented in politics, holding only four parliamentary seats, and do not receive equal social security provisions. Men convicted of so-called honor crimes against women usually receive lenient sentences. Female foreign domestic workers are routinely exploited and physically abused by employers, although the Labor Ministry introduced a uniform contract for domestic workers in 2009 that guaranteed weekly time off, paid sick days, and limits on working hours.

Lesotho

Political Rights: 3 *
Civil Liberties: 3
Status: Partly Free

Population: 2,135,000
Capital: Maseru

Status Change: Lesotho's political rights rating declined from 2 to 3 and its status from Free to Partly Free due to unresolved disputes over legislative seats from the 2007 and 2008 elections and a breakdown in internationally mediated negotiations between the government and opposition.

Ten-Year Ratings Timeline For Year Under Review (Political Rights, Civil Liberties, Status)

2000	2001	2002	2003	2004	2005	2006	2007	2008	2009
4,4PF	4,4PF	2,3F	2,3F	2,3F	2,3F	2,3F	2,3F	2,3F	3,3PF

Overview:

Unknown gunman opened fire on Prime Minister Pakalitha Mosisili's home in April 2009 in an apparent assassination attempt, which was widely linked to continuing disputes between the ruing Lesotho Congress for Democracy and opposition parties over results from the 2007 snap legislative elections and 2008 by-elections. Positions on both sides hardened in 2009, and in September, mediation efforts by the Southern African Development Community failed after Lesotho's government refused to negotiate any longer.

Lesotho gained independence from Britain in 1966, and the following 30 years featured a number of military coups, annulled elections, and suspensions of constitutional rule. Parliamentary elections in 1998, although judged free and fair by international observers, set off protests after the results gave the ruling Lesotho Congress for Democracy (LCD) party 79 out of 80 constituency seats with just 60.5 percent of the vote. Troops from South Africa and Botswana—under the mandate of the 14-country Southern African Development Community (SADC)—were summoned to restore order, and an agreement that year stipulated that future elections must be supervised by an independent commission and include 40 additional, proportionally determined seats in the National Assembly. In the 2002 elections, the LCD captured 57.7 percent of the vote and 77 of 80 constituency seats, while the opposition Basotho National Party (BNP) won 21 of the new proportional-representation seats.

Prime Minister Pakalitha Mosisili called snap elections in late 2006 after 18 members of the LCD—led by former cabinet minister Tom Thabane—defected to join a new opposition party, the All Basotho Congress (ABC). The February 2007 polls, originally set for May, left a shortened, 90-day timetable that resulted in hasty preparations by the Independent Electoral Commission (IEC). Nevertheless, the elections were declared free and fair by domestic and international observers. According to the IEC, the LCD won 61 of the 80 constituency seats, with the ABC capturing 17. The commission allocated 21 of the 40 proportional-representation seats to the LCD-allied National Independent Party (NIP) and 10 to the Lesotho Workers' Party (LWP), the ABC's ally. Six other parties were also awarded seats.

Opposition parties—including the ABC/LWP and the BNP, which lost 18 seats—disputed the allocations and called a general strike. The strike was halted after the SADC agreed to mediate, but the talks failed to formally resolve the dispute. In 2008, 43 by-elections were held, the results of which were also contested by the opposition. ABC supporters protested outside the office of the IEC and held some workers hostage until the protest was broken up by police. In July 2009, the head SADC mediator, former Botswana president Sir Ketumile Masire, ended his mission in Lesotho, accusing the government of avoiding direct talks with the opposition. The following month, a call by the opposition for a work boycott in Maseru failed to gain significant support. In late 2009, the Christian Council of Lesotho took over facilitating the dialogue from the SADC, but no progress had been made between the parties by year's end.

In April 2009, Prime Minister Mosisili was the target of an assassination attempt when several gunmen opened fire on his house; one of the assailants was killed in the ensuing gunfight. Government officials and some journalists linked the assassination attempt to the election dispute, depicting it as a failed coup. Seven people were subsequently arrested, and their trials were pending at year's end.

Drought has plagued the country since 2001, leading to critical food shortages and the dependence of some 450,000 people on food aid. Lesotho is also scarred by an adult HIV/AIDS prevalence rate of about 24 percent, one of the world's highest. The government announced in 2005 that it would offer free HIV testing to all citizens, the first such program in the world. By the end of 2006, approximately 28,000 of the country's 58,000 infected citizens were receiving anti-retroviral treatment.

Political Rights and Civil Liberties: Lesotho is an electoral democracy. King Letsie III serves as ceremonial head of state. Under a system introduced in 2002, 80 of the 120 seats in the lower house of Parliament, the National Assembly, are filled by first-past-the-post constituency votes, and 40 are filled by proportional representation. Members serve five-year terms, and the leader of the majority party becomes prime minister. The Senate, the upper house of Parliament, consists of Lesotho's 22 traditional principal chiefs, who wield considerable authority in rural areas, and 11 other members appointed on the advice of the prime minister.

Snap elections held in 2007 resulted in a landslide victory for the ruling LCD and its ally, the NIP. Opposition parties—including the ABC, LWP, and BNP—continue to contest the results of both the 2007 polls and 2008 by-elections, accusing the government of poll rigging, gerrymandering, and unfairly allocating seats. In 2008, the government announced a new digital voter-registration system designed to curtail fraud.

The government has aggressively prosecuted corruption cases. In recent years, over a dozen officials and international construction firms have been investigated— and a number of both convicted—for bribery and other crimes associated with the Lesotho Highlands Water Project (LHWP), a multibillion-dollar dam and watershed project. Lesotho was ranked 89 out of 180 countries surveyed in Transparency International's 2009 Corruption Perceptions Index.

The government generally respects freedom of speech and the press, though press freedom has declined in recent years. Independent newspapers and radio stations routinely criticize the government, while state-owned print and broadcast media tend to reflect the views of the ruling party. In 2008, the Lesotho Communications Authority (LCA) increased the cost of broadcasting licenses sevenfold, from US$400 to US$3,000, drawing objections from press freedom advocates. Among other problems, media criticism of the government can result in heavy libel penalties, the government has been accused of withdrawing advertisements from critical outlets, and reporters are occasionally harassed or attacked. In September 2009, Marafaele Mohloboli, a *Lesotho Times* journalist and local press freedom advocate, received a death threat at her home. The government does not restrict internet access.

Freedom of religion in this predominantly Christian country is widely observed. The government does not restrict academic freedom.

Freedoms of assembly and association are generally respected. Several nongovernmental organizations operate openly. In October 2009, the ruling LCD introduced the Public Meetings and Procession Bill to Parliament. If passed, the law would require prior approval from local chiefs, the police, or relevant government officials in order to hold a public meeting; the bill was still pending at year's end. While labor rights are constitutionally guaranteed, the union movement is weak and fragmented, and many employers in the textile sector do not allow union activity.

Courts are nominally independent, but higher courts are especially subject to outside influence. The large backlog of cases often leads to trial delays and lengthy pretrial detention. Mistreatment of civilians by security forces reportedly continues. Prisons are dilapidated and severely overcrowded and lack essential health services; instances of torture and excessive force have been reported. An independent ombudsman's office is tasked with protecting citizens' rights. A 2009 study by the Electoral Institute of Southern Africa found that while the office has largely fulfilled its tasks of combating maladministration, dealing with injustice in the public service, and protecting human rights, it has largely failed to effectively fight corruption.

Tensions between Basotho and the small Chinese business community have led to minor incidents of violence.

The constitution bars gender-based discrimination, but customary practice and law still restrict women's rights in areas including property and inheritance. While their husbands are alive, women married under customary law have the status of minors in civil courts and may not enter into binding contracts. Domestic violence is reportedly widespread, but is becoming less socially acceptable. In 2006, the government implemented a policy of improved medical care for victims of rape. A 2005 constitutional amendment reserves a third of the seats in municipal councils for women.

Liberia

Political Rights: 3
Civil Liberties: 4
Status: Partly Free

Population: 3,955,000
Capital: Monrovia

Ten-Year Ratings Timeline For Year Under Review (Political Rights, Civil Liberties, Status)

2000	2001	2002	2003	2004	2005	2006	2007	2008	2009
5,6NF	6,5NF	6,6NF	6,6NF	5,4PF	4,4PF	3,4PF	3,4PF	3,4PF	3,4PF

Overview: In 2009, the government failed to adopt critical legislation and constitutional amendments needed to facilitate legally sound presidential and legislative elections in 2011. As a result, it is likely that the 2011 polls will be delayed. Also during the year, the Truth and Reconciliation Commission completed its work and recommended public sanctions for numerous current officials and the establishment of an internationalized domestic court to try those recommended for prosecution.

Liberia was settled in 1821 by freed slaves from the United States and became an independent republic in 1847. Americo-Liberians, descendents of the freed slaves, long dominated the political landscape. During the 1970s, a number of groups agitated for multiparty democracy and an end to the marginalization of indigenous Liberians. In 1980, army master sergeant Samuel Doe murdered President William Tolbert in a coup. Doe's regime concentrated power among members of his Krahn ethnic group and suppressed others. In 1989, former government minister Charles Taylor recruited fighters from among the Gio and Mano ethnic groups and launched a guerrilla insurgency from Cote d'Ivoire. A year later, Nigeria, under the aegis of the Economic Community of West African States (ECOWAS), led an armed intervention, preventing Taylor from seizing the capital but failing to protect Doe, who was murdered by a splinter rebel group led by Prince Johnson.

After years of endemic violence, the proliferation of armed factions, and numerous failed transitional arrangements, a peace accord was signed in 1995, and Taylor won national elections in 1997. He made little effort to seek genuine reconciliation or undertake mandated security reforms. Violence erupted again in 1999, as the Liberians United for Reconciliation and Democracy (LURD) rebel group sought to overthrow Taylor and purportedly received backing from Sierra Leone and Guinea. Meanwhile, in 2001, the United Nations imposed an arms embargo and diamond sanctions for Liberia's alleged involvement in the conflict in Sierra Leone. By 2003, LURD controlled most of northern Liberia, and another rebel group, the Movement for Democracy in Liberia (MODEL), squeezed Taylor's government from the southeast. With the capital threatened and the United States calling for him to step down, Taylor resigned in August 2003 and accepted Nigeria's offer of asylum.

Taylor's departure ended 14 years of intermittent civil war that had spilled over into three neighboring countries and left 200,000 Liberians dead. ECOWAS helped negotiate an end to the fighting, and West African peacekeepers became part of a 15,000-strong UN peacekeeping force. In keeping with a 2003 Comprehensive Peace

Agreement (CPA), members of Taylor's government, LURD, MODEL, and civil society representatives formed the National Transitional Government of Liberia (NTGL) under the chairmanship of businessman Charles Gyude Bryant. The NTGL governed the country until the 2005 elections.

Unity Party (UP) candidate Ellen Johnson-Sirleaf won the presidential runoff in November 2005, defeating the first-round winner, Congress for Democratic Change (CDC) candidate George Weah. In the concurrent legislative polls, 12 parties and numerous independents secured seats. The CDC placed first with 18 seats, followed by the UP with 12. For the first time in Liberian history, the president's party did not hold the majority of seats in the legislature.

Strained relations between the executive and legislative branches characterized the first years of Johnson-Sirleaf's term. The controversial Speaker of the House of Representatives was removed in 2007, a deadlocked leadership crisis incapacitated the Senate in late 2008 and early 2009, and local elections slated for 2008 were cancelled, ostensibly for financial reasons. The Supreme Court subsequently granted the president the authority to appoint mayors instead.

In 2009, the president and legislature failed to finalize legislation needed to facilitate the conduct of elections scheduled for 2011, potentially forcing a delay and increasing the risk of political instability.

Also during the year, the Truth and Reconciliation Commission (TRC) completed its work. The panel's final report was submitted to the legislature in July, but lawmakers passed a resolution suspending any action on the report until the 2010 legislative session. The TRC recommended Johnson-Sirleaf and 49 others for public sanctions, including a prohibition from holding public office for 30 years. It also called for the establishment of an extraordinary criminal tribunal, in the form of an internationalized domestic court, to try those accused of gross human rights violations and economic crimes. A total of 106 individuals were recommended for prosecution, including Taylor and 7 other former faction leaders. The Independent National Human Rights Commission (INHCR) is mandated to implement TRC recommendations, but confirmation of its members was still pending at year's end. Separately, Taylor continued his trial, begun in 2007, before the UN-backed Special Court for Sierra Leone.

Political Rights and Civil Liberties: Liberia is an electoral democracy. International observers determined that the 2005 presidential and legislative elections were free and fair. The bicameral legislature consists of a 30-member Senate and a 64-member House of Representatives; senators are elected to nine-year terms, and representatives to six-year terms. The president serves up to two six-year terms.

The constitution requires the reapportionment of constituencies after the 2008 national census and prior to the next general elections. However, President Ellen Johnson-Sirleaf in September 2009 vetoed a reapportionment bill on the grounds that it would add too many new seats to the House and strain the national budget. The National Elections Commission (NEC) also submitted a bill of recommended constitutional amendments to shape the electoral framework and strengthen the political party system, and the House of Representatives adopted a number of elections-related amendments. Any constitutional amendments must be approved in a national referendum held no sooner than one year after passage by the legislature. At the close of the legislative session in late September, the Senate had yet to concur with the House on the reapportionment bill or the constitutional amendments. Delays in the passage of these measures could result in the postponement of the 2011 elections and undermine the country's political stability.

A number of political alliances and coalitions were formed in 2009. The UP, the Liberia Action Party, and the Liberty Party agreed to a merger, and a broad-based coalition between the CDC, the National Patriotic Party, and the Liberia National Union was set to contest the 2011 elections. Parties continue to be challenged by weak organizational capacity, poor relations between party leaders and legislators, and the dominant role of key personalities and ethnic affiliations.

The Liberian Anti-Corruption Commission (LACC) became fully operational in 2009. Former NTGL chairman Charles Gyude Bryant and four others were acquitted of corruption charges related to the state oil refinery during the year, but another corruption case against Bryant is still pending. The pending civil servants' code of conduct, corruption offenses, whistle-blower protections, and freedom of information bills have yet to be passed by the legislature, thus calling into question the government's commitment to accountability and transparency. The ad-hoc Dunn Commission, established to investigate claims of corruption by senior government officials, found that some had used their positions to promote private business interests and recommended further action by the LACC. In 2009, the legislature approved numerous concession agreements and large-scale contracts, including the Liberian International Ship and Corporate Registry (LISCR) contract, which was renewed despite the Dunn Commission's reservations regarding its renegotiation. Liberia was ranked 97 out of 180 countries surveyed in Transparency International's 2009 Corruption Perceptions Index.

Since the expulsion of former president Charles Taylor, the media environment has become decidedly more open. A variety of newspapers publish mainly in the capital, and dozens of radio stations operate across the country. The media have been vigilant in exposing corruption within government and actively participated in the TRC process. However, journalists sometimes face harassment by state officials. Two newspapers were suspended during the year for alleged improper registration. The government does not restrict internet access, but poor infrastructure, illiteracy, and cost limit usage to a small fraction of the population.

Religious freedom is respected in principle. While there is no official religion, Liberia remains a de facto Christian state, and the Muslim minority reports discrimination. The government does not restrict academic freedom, though the educational infrastructure remains insufficient to meet demand.

Freedoms of assembly and association are guaranteed and respected. Numerous civil society groups, including human rights organizations, operate in the country. In 2009, over 60 civil society organizations welcomed the TRC report and condemned threats made against the commissioners. The Liberian Council of Churches has engaged numerous stakeholders regarding the report's recommendations. The right of workers to strike, organize, and bargain collectively is recognized, but the labor minister has acknowledged the urgent need to modernize Liberia's labor laws. A number of protests sparked by ongoing economic hardship turned violent at rubber plantations in 2009, with a senator being taken hostage in one instance.

Shortcomings in the rule of law continue to threaten peace consolidation and economic development. The executive branch interfered less in the judicial system in 2009 than previously, but justice is undermined by a lack of public defenders, case backlogs, prolonged pretrial detention, and prison overcrowding. A spate of prison breaks in 2008 and 2009 highlighted the inadequacy of security at corrections facilities. Despite having signed an international agreement aimed at abolishing the death penalty, Liberia allows capital punishment for certain crimes.

While progress was made in the training and deployment of the Emergency Response Unit of the Liberian National Police (LNP) in 2008 and 2009, national security institutions cannot yet independently ensure public safety and security. There were three clashes between elements of the LNP and the military in 2009, raising serious disciplinary concerns.

Armed robbery, mob violence, and vigilantism remain public scourges. Harmful traditional practices are common; riots erupted in Harper during the year over allegations of ritualistic killings. Child trafficking within West Africa remains a concern to the international community. In 2009, the government placed a moratorium on adoptions based on allegations of mismanagement and corruption in the adoption process.

Ethnic violence over land issues remains a potential threat to peace. Such land disputes often escalate quickly and could be politicized as elections draw closer. In 2009, the Land Commission was established to propose and coordinate land policy reforms, particularly the harmonization of customary- and common-law property rights. The commission does not have adjudicatory or implementation powers and is not yet fully operational; only six of the seven commissioners have been confirmed.

While female representation in the legislature remains limited, numerous cabinet ministers and senior level officials are women, including the leader of the opposition CDC party. Women elsewhere in government and among civil society are very politically engaged. Violence against women, including rape, is pervasive. A court with exclusive jurisdiction over sexual and gender-based violence cases completed its first trial in 2009.

Libya

Political Rights: 7
Civil Liberties: 7
Status: Not Free

Population: 6,283,000
Capital: Tripoli

Ten-Year Ratings Timeline For Year Under Review (Political Rights, Civil Liberties, Status)

2000	2001	2002	2003	2004	2005	2006	2007	2008	2009
7,7NF	7,7NF	7,7NF	7,7NF	7,7NF	7,7NF	7,7NF	7,7NF	7,7NF	7,7NF

Overview: The Libyan government nationalized the country's only quasi-independent media group in 2009, although online censorship and the hacking of dissident websites appeared to decline somewhat. Also during 2009, a prominent dissident died after years of illness in custody, and the authorities sentenced two Swiss businessmen to jail terms on immigration charges, apparently as part of a diplomatic row with Switzerland.

Libya was part of the Ottoman Empire until the Italian conquest and occupation of the country in 1911. It achieved independence in 1951, after a brief period of UN trusteeship in the wake of World War II. Until 1969, Libya was ruled by King Idris, a relatively pro-Western monarch. A group of young army officers, led by 27-year-old captain Mu'ammar al-Qadhafi, overthrew the king's government while he was traveling abroad.

Al Qadhafi argued that foreign oil companies were profiting from the country's resources at the expense of the Libyan people, and he moved to nationalize oil assets, claiming that the revenues would be shared among the population. In the early years of his rule, al Qadhafi published a multivolume treatise, the *Green Book*, in which he expounded his political philosophy and ideology—a fusion of Arab nationalism, socialism, and Islam. Although he has been Libya's undisputed leader since 1969, making him one of the world's longest-serving rulers, he holds no official title and is referred to as Brother Leader or the Guide of the Revolution.

Al Qadhafi adopted decidedly anti-Western policies, and after his regime was implicated in several international terrorist attacks, the United States imposed sanctions on Libya in 1981. Relations between the two countries continued to worsen, and in 1986, the United States bombed targets in Libya, including al-Qadhafi's home. The attack led to more provocations. In 1988, a U.S. airliner exploded over Lockerbie, Scotland, killing all 259 people aboard as well as 11 residents of the town. After an exhaustive investigation, Scottish police issued arrest warrants for two Libyans, including an intelligence agent. The UN Security Council imposed trade sanctions on the country. Over the next several years, Libya became more economically and diplomatically isolated.

In 1999, al-Qadhafi moved to mend his international image and surrendered the two Lockerbie bombing suspects for trial. He accepted responsibility for past acts of terrorism and offered compensation packages to the families of victims. The United Nations suspended its sanctions, and the European Union (EU) reestablished diplomatic and trade relations with Tripoli. In 2001, a special Scottish court sitting in the Netherlands found one of the Lockerbie suspects guilty of masterminding the attack. Libya agreed to pay a US$10 million compensation package to the families of each of the 270 victims in 2003. The following year, al-Qadhafi made his first trip to Europe in more than 15 years, and European leaders in turn traveled to Libya. The EU subsequently lifted its arms embargo and normalized diplomatic relations; Libya purchased hundreds of millions of dollars in European weapons systems in 2007. The regime also improved its relations with the United States. In 2004, a year after al-Qadhafi's government announced that it had scrapped its nonconventional weapons program, the United States established a liaison office in Tripoli. The U.S. government eventually removed Libya from its list of state sponsors of terrorism, reestablishing a full embassy in Tripoli in 2006.

Many observers speculated that Saif al-Islam al-Qadhafi, the leader's son, was behind some of these policy moves. He facilitated visits by foreign human rights activists, and according to press reports, his charitable umbrella organization—the Qadhafi International Foundation for Charity Associations—made it possible for

Libyan citizens to report abuses by the authorities. Saif al-Islam also publicly criticized current conditions in Libya and advocated changes in the leadership.

Nevertheless, the diplomatic and economic shifts were not accompanied by noticeable improvements in political rights or civil liberties, and the regime has remained hostile to foreign criticism and other perceived affronts. Libyan authorities successfully sued three newspapers in Morocco for defamation in 2009, and imposed 16-month prison sentences on two Swiss businessmen for immigration offenses in December, apparently as part of a broader retaliation against Switzerland for the brief 2008 arrest of al-Qadhafi's son Hannibal and his wife, who had been accused of abusing servants in Geneva. Also in 2009, Libya offered a jubilant welcome for the convicted Lockerbie bomber, who was released by Scottish authorities due to a terminal illness.

Political Rights and Civil Liberties: Libya is not an electoral democracy. Power theoretically lies with a system of people's committees and the indirectly elected General People's Congress, but in practice, those structures are manipulated to ensure the continued dominance of Mu'ammar al-Qadhafi, who holds no official title. It is illegal for any political group to oppose the principles of the 1969 revolution, which are laid out in the *Green Book*, although market-based economic changes in recent years have diverged from the regime's socialist ideals.

Political parties have been illegal for over 35 years, and the government strictly monitors political activity. Organizing or joining anything akin to a political party is punishable by long prison terms and even the death penalty. Many Libyan opposition movements and figures operate outside the country.

Corruption is pervasive in both the private sector and the government in Libya, which was ranked 130 out of 180 countries surveyed in Transparency International's 2009 Corruption Perceptions Index.

There is no independent press. The regime hardened its monopoly on media outlets in mid-2009 with the nationalization of Al-Ghad media group, which was established in 2007 by al-Qadhafi's son, Saif al-Islam, and encompassed the country's only quasi-independent newspapers and radio stations. The satellite television station Al-Libiya, a subsidiary of Al-Ghad and the country's only private television outlet, had fallen under scrutiny after airing criticism of the Egyptian government. State-owned media largely operate as mouthpieces for the authorities, and journalists work in a climate of fear and self-censorship. Those who displease the regime face harassment or imprisonment on trumped-up charges. The government controls the country's only internet service provider. The OpenNet Initiative found that dissident websites were censored and hacked sporadically in 2009, although less often than in previous years. The government established the first wireless service provider for public use in January. This may increase internet usage, which stood at only 4.7 percent in 2008 due to poor telecommunications infrastructure.

Nearly all Libyans are Muslim. The government closely monitors mosques for Islamist activity, and there have been unconfirmed reports of Islamist militant groups allied to al-Qaeda operating against the government. In 2007, al-Qaeda declared that the so-called Libyan Islamic Fighting Group had joined its international network. The few non-Muslims in Libya are permitted to practice their faiths with relative freedom. Academic freedom is tightly restricted.

The government does not uphold freedom of assembly. Those demonstrations that are allowed to take place are typically meant to support the aims of the regime. In February 2007, the authorities arrested 13 men for planning a peaceful demonstration in Tripoli to commemorate clashes between security forces and demonstrators the previous year. Idris Boufayed, a prominent opposition figure who had led planning for the demonstration, received a 25-year sentence, but was released in October 2008 to undergo treatment for advanced lung cancer. Two of the others were held incommunicado and without charge, a common practice in Libya, and the remaining 10 received jail terms of between 6 and 15 years. All had reportedly been released by March 2009.

The law allows for the establishment of nongovernmental organizations, but those that have been granted authorization to operate are directly or indirectly linked to the government. There are no independent labor unions.

The People's Court, infamous for punishing political dissidents, was abolished in 2005, but the judicial authority has since created the State Security Court, which carries out a similar function. The judiciary as a whole remains subservient to the political leadership and regularly penalizes political dissent. Human Rights Watch, citing Libya's secretary of justice, reported in December 2009 that 500 political prisoners remained in custody despite having been acquitted of all charges or served their full prison sentences. The head of internal security, Colonel Al-Tohamy Khaled, defended the continued detention of such prisoners by arguing that they were undergoing mandatory rehabilitation programs designed to rid them of extremist beliefs. He reportedly criticized the judges who had ordered the prisoners' release, saying they did not understand the threat the inmates posed.

Prominent political opposition figure Fathi al-Jahmi died at a Jordanian hospital in May 2009, after some seven years in nearly continuous government custody, according to Human Rights Watch. Following a long decline in health, Al-Jahmi had been receiving treatment for cardiac disease and diabetes in a government hospital in Libya, where he was held in de facto detention despite government claims in March 2008 that he was a free man. He was not allowed to seek treatment elsewhere until he fell into a coma just over two weeks before his death.

A large number of migrants from sub-Saharan Africa work in Libya or pass through in attempts to reach Europe. Human rights organizations have documented and criticized the country's treatment of these migrants. The regime has been more aggressive in its crackdown on illegal laborers in recent years, increasingly the likelihood of abuses. The Nigerian government alleged that Libya executed dozens of Nigerians in 2009 and intended to execute more than 200 additional Nigerian nationals for simple immigration violations.

Women enjoy many of the same legal protections as men, but certain laws and social norms perpetuate discrimination, particularly in areas such as marriage, divorce, and inheritance. Women who have been cast out by their families are particularly vulnerable. The government considers such women wayward and can hold them indefinitely in "social rehabilitation" facilities, which are de facto prisons. Women are seriously underrepresented in Libya's political system, with only 36 gaining seats in March 2009 indirect elections for the 468-member General People's Congress.

Liechtenstein

Political Rights: 1
Civil Liberties: 1
Status: Free

Population: 36,000
Capital: Vaduz

Ten-Year Ratings Timeline For Year Under Review (Political Rights, Civil Liberties, Status)

2000	2001	2002	2003	2004	2005	2006	2007	2008	2009
1,1F	1,1F	1,1F	1,1F	1,1F	1,1F	1,1F	1,1F	1,1F	1,1F

Overview: In February 2009 parliamentary elections, the Patriotic Union's Klaus Tschuescher was elected prime minister and subsequently formed a coalition government with the Progressive Citizens' Party. As the economic crisis continued to worsen, Liechtenstein agreed to ease bank-secrecy laws, allowing for the country's removal from the Organization for Economic Cooperation and Development's list of uncooperative tax havens.

Liechtenstein was established as a principality in 1719 and gained its sovereignty in 1806. From 1938 to 1997, it was governed by a coalition of the Progressive Citizens' Party (FBP) and the Fatherland Union, now the Patriotic Union (VU). The latter party then ruled alone until the FBP won the 2001 elections.

In a 2003 referendum, voters approved a constitutional amendment that granted significantly more power to the monarch, Prince Hans-Adam II. The amendment gave the prince the authority to dismiss the government, veto legislation, and appoint judges, but removed his right to rule by emergency decree. In 2004, Hans-Adam handed his constitutional powers to his son, Hereditary Prince Alois, though the elder prince retained his title as head of state.

In two-stage elections in 2005, the VU and the FBP won 10 and 12 of Parliament's 25 seats, respectively. However, a small third party, the Free List, captured three seats, forcing the two larger parties to form a grand coalition. FBP leader Otmar Hasler—the prime minister since 2001—retained his post.

In the February 2009 parliamentary elections, the VU won 13 seats, while the FBP took 11; the Free List captured just one seat. Prime Minister Hasler was replaced in March by Vice Prime Minister Klaus Tschuetscher of the VU, who subsequently formed a coalition government with the FBP.

Liechtenstein declared in 2006 that it would make no further changes to its banking-secrecy laws. However, its European neighbors renewed their tax-related complaints in 2008, as the economic crisis prompted new concerns about tax havens. In December 2008, Liechtenstein and the United States came to an information-sharing agreement on tax evasion investigations. Liechtenstein agreed in March 2009 to adopt Organization for Economic Cooperation and Development (OECD) transparency and information-sharing standards, including a commitment to exchange data on clients in both tax fraud and tax evasion investigations by foreign governments.

Political Rights and Civil Liberties: Liechtenstein is an electoral democracy. However, the unelected monarchy won greater authority in 2003, making it the most politically powerful in Europe. The unicameral Parliament (Landtag) consists of 25 deputies chosen by proportional representation every four years. These freely elected representatives determine the policies of the government, but the monarch has the power to veto legislation, dismiss the government, and appoint judges. Voting is compulsory.

Political parties are able to freely organize. Two parties—the VU and the FBP—have dominated politics over the last half-century.

Liechtenstein's politics and society are largely free of corruption, and the country continues to work to build sufficient mechanisms to fight money laundering in its banking system. Due to recent commitments, the OECD removed Liechtenstein from its list of uncooperative tax havens in May 2009. Liechtenstein was not ranked by Transparency International in its 2009 Corruption Perceptions Index.

The constitution guarantees freedom of expression and of the press. There is one private television station, and the only radio station is privately held. The two daily newspapers are aligned roughly with the two major political parties. Broadcasts from Austria and Switzerland are available and popular in the country, as are foreign newspapers and magazines. Internet access is not restricted.

The constitution establishes Roman Catholicism as the state religion but protects freedom of belief. Catholic or Protestant religious education is mandatory, but exemptions are routinely granted. All religious groups are tax-exempt. The government respects academic freedom.

Freedoms of assembly and association are protected, and the principality has one small trade union. A 2008 law provides civil servants with the right to strike.

Judges are appointed by the prince. Despite controversy over the monarch's expanded powers, Liechtenstein has remained a law-based state with an independent judiciary. Due process is respected, and prison conditions meet international standards. Crime is rare in the country. Switzerland is responsible for its customs and defense.

A third of the population is foreign born. Some native citizens have expressed concern over the growing number of immigrants from non-German-speaking countries. The government has responded by seeking to teach newcomers the language and culture of Liechtenstein in formal integration programs. The country received 227 asylum applications in 2009, a significant increase over the 26 submitted in 2008.

Liechtenstein has been a member since 1995 of the European Economic Area, a free-trade area that links non–EU members Norway, Iceland, and Liechtenstein with the EU.

Under a 2005 reform, abortion is legal in the first 12 weeks of pregnancy. A 2003 court decision upheld the principle of equal pay for equal work for women, but Liechtenstein's society remains conservative. While women celebrated the 25th anniversary of full voting rights in 2009, they are underrepresented in upper levels of business and government, with only 6 women serving in the 25-seat Parliament. Women enjoy equal rights in family law.

Lithuania

Political Rights: 1
Civil Liberties: 1
Status: Free

Population: 3,399,000
Capital: Vilnius

Ten-Year Ratings Timeline For Year Under Review (Political Rights, Civil Liberties, Status)

2000	2001	2002	2003	2004	2005	2006	2007	2008	2009
1,2F	1,2F	1,2F	1,2F	2,2F	1,1F	1,1F	1,1F	1,1F	1,1F

Overview: As Lithuania's economy continued to worsen in 2009, concerns about the government's economic austerity measures led to antigovernment demonstrations in January in which nearly 40 people were injured and 150 arrested. In May, independent candidate Dalia Grybauskaite was elected the country's first female president.

Lithuania became independent at the end of World War I, but it was annexed by the Soviet Union in 1940 under a secret protocol of the 1939 Hitler-Stalin pact. The country regained its independence with the collapse of the Soviet Union in 1991, and it joined NATO and the European Union in April and May 2004, respectively.

Also in April 2004, President Rolandas Paksas was impeached on charges of corruption and of violating his oath of office and the constitution. Arturas Paulauskas, the speaker of Parliament, took over as acting president until elections were held in June. Valdas Adamkus defeated Kazimiera Prunskiene, the leader of the Union of Farmers and New Democracy (VNDS), in a tight runoff contest and was sworn in as president in July.

A right-wing coalition of the Homeland Union/Lithuanian Conservatives (HU) and the Liberal and Center Union (LCS) captured 43 seats in the October 2004 parliamentary elections. After negotiations between left- and right-wing parties broke down, a ruling center-left coalition emerged in November, consisting of the Labor Party, VNDS, the Lithuanian Social Democratic Party (LSDP), and New Union (Social Liberals).

Following the withdrawal of the Labor Party and New Union (Social Liberals) from the government in 2006, a new ruling coalition was organized in July, consisting of the LSDP, LCS, National Farmer's Union (formerly the VNDS), and the new Civic Democracy Party, which had formed following a split within the Labor Party. The four parties together held fewer than 60 seats in Parliament, marking the first time since independence that the country had a minority government. Defense Minister Gediminas Kirkilas of the LSDP was chosen as the new prime minister.

The New Union (Social Liberals) rejoined the ruling coalition in February 2008; the expanded coalition held a slim 72-seat majority in the 141-seat legislature. In the run-up to the October 12 parliamentary elections, the creation of new parties further fragmented the country's political scene. The Homeland Union-Lithuanian Christian Democrats (TS-LKD), an alliance of right-wing parties, was formed in May, as was the National Resurrection Party (TPP), which was created by a group of celebrities but did not espouse any particular ideology. Following a runoff vote on October 26, the TS-LKD emerged with 45 seats, followed by the LSDP, whose popularity had declined with the weakening economy, with 25 seats. The TPP captured 16 seats; Order and Justice (TT) party, 15 seats; Liberal Union (LRLS), 11 seats; the Labor Party, 10 seats; and the LCS, 8 seats. Smaller parties and independent candidates won the remaining 11 seats. A four-party, center-right majority coalition was formed in December consisting of the TS-LKD, TPP, LRLS, and LCS. Former prime minister Andrius Kubilius (1999-2000) was selected as the new premier.

As the country's economy continued to worsen—with rising unemployment and marked slowdowns in GDP growth—the ruling coalition came under growing public pressure over its economic austerity measures. On January 16, some 7,000 people gathered in Vilnius to protest tax increases and cuts in social spending. The peaceful demonstration turned violent when a small group began throwing bottles and stones and tried to storm the Parliament building; nearly 40 people were injured, and some 150 arrested in the riots that lasted a few hours.

Independent candidate Dalia Grybauskaite, who was supported by the TS-LKD, won the May presidential election with almost 70 percent of the vote, becoming the first woman ever to hold that office in Lithuania. She defeated her closest rival, Algirdas Butkevicius of the LSDP, who captured less than 12 percent of the vote. European Parliament elections the following month saw TS-LKD candidates secure the largest number of seats, in contrast to anti-incumbent results in other European countries. Meanwhile, a split in the TPP in mid-2009 resulted in some members of the party withdrawing from the ruling coalition, which was left with 71 members at year's end.

Political Rights and Civil Liberties: Lithuania is an electoral democracy. The 1992 constitution established a unicameral, 141-seat Parliament (Seimas), with 71 members elected in single-mandate constituencies and 70 chosen by proportional representation, all for four-year terms. The prime minister is selected by Parliament, and the president is directly elected for a five-year term. While the 2008 parliamentary elections were largely free and fair, there were reports of irregularities, including alleged bribery and forged ballots. Three members of ethnic minorities hold seats in Parliament. Lithuania's many political parties operate freely, but the Communist Party is banned.

Corruption remains a problem in Lithuania, with a number of government officials under investigation, facing trial, or convicted of corrupt practices in 2009. Former economy minister and Labor Party leader Viktor Uspaskich was arrested in September 2007 as he returned to Lithuania from his native Russia, where he had fled the previous year to escape charges of tax and electoral fraud. He was granted immunity from prosecution after being elected to Parliament in October 2008. Parliament waived his immunity in December, but it was restored in June 2009, after he was elected to the European Parliament. Vilnius city council member and former mayor Arturas Zuokas was convicted in March 2008 of a 2003 bribery attempt, but a court in Vilnius vacated his conviction in November 2009. According to a 2009 report by Transparency International (TI) Lithuania, more than half of the people surveyed believed that corruption in the country had increased during the last five years. Lithuania was ranked 52 out of 180 countries surveyed in TI's 2009 Corruption Perceptions Index.

The government generally respects freedom of speech and the press. Privately owned newspapers, as well as independent broadcast media outlets, express a wide variety of views. However, according to a 2009 TI Lithuania study, the Lithuanian press suffers from a lack of written codes of conduct or adequate standards for transparency of ownership. The government does not restrict access to the internet.

Freedom of religion is guaranteed by law and largely upheld in practice. However, so-called traditional religious communities enjoy certain government benefits, including annual government subsidies, not granted to other groups. The Seventh-Day Adventist Church, which received official government recognition in 2008, and the Evangelical Baptists are the only state-recognized nontraditional religious groups; they are entitled to some state privileges, including the right to perform marriages. Academic freedom is respected.

Freedoms of assembly and association are generally observed. There are no serious obstacles to the registration of nongovernmental organizations (NGOs), and human rights groups operate without restrictions. Workers have the right to form and join trade unions, to strike, and to engage in collective bargaining, though there have been reports of employees being punished for attempting to organize. About 10 percent of the country's workforce is unionized.

The constitution guarantees judicial independence, which is respected in practice. Defendants generally enjoy due-process rights, including the presumption of innocence and freedom from arbitrary arrest and detention, though lengthy pretrial detention remains a problem. A July 2009 report by the Council of Europe's s Committee for the Prevention of Torture reported allegations of police officers mistreating detainees, particularly juveniles, and judges and prosecutors failing to respond adequately to claims of such mistreatment. Prisons continue to suffer from overcrowding and inadequate access to health care.

The rights of ethnic minorities, who constitute approximately 15 percent of the population, are legally protected. However, according to a February 2009 report by Lithuania's Department of Ethnic Minorities and Lithuanians Living Abroad, 23 percent of Russians, 19 percent of Poles, and 29 percent of members of other ethnic groups reported job discrimination, with Roma facing the greatest ethnic intolerance. Amendments adopted in 2008 to the Law on Equal Rights added prohibitions against discrimination based on age, disability, sexual orientation, religion, and ethnicity; the amendments do not apply to religious schools. However, in July 2009, Parliament overrode a presidential veto and passed amendments to the Law on the Protection of Minors against the Detrimental Effect of Public Information, limiting or banning a wide range of public information considered harmful to young people, including materials promoting homosexual, bisexual, and polygamous relations among minors. Following criticisms by domestic and foreign human rights activists, Parliament in December replaced the prohibition with reportedly less controversial language. The granting of asylum or refugee status in accordance with the 1951 UN Convention Relating to the Status of Refugees and its 1967 protocol is legally protected.

Although men and women enjoy the same legal rights, women earn lower average wages than men for the same work and remain underrepresented in management positions. In 2009, Irena Degutiene became the first woman chosen to be Speaker of Parliament and Dalia Grybauskaite was elected the first female president of Lithuania. About 20 percent of the members of Parliament are women. Domestic violence remains a serious problem. Lithuania is a source, transit point, and destination for the trafficking of women and girls for the purpose of prostitution.

Luxembourg

Political Rights: 1
Civil Liberties: 1
Status: Free

Population: 498,000
Capital: Luxembourg

Ten-Year Ratings Timeline For Year Under Review (Political Rights, Civil Liberties, Status)

2000	2001	2002	2003	2004	2005	2006	2007	2008	2009
1,1F	1,1F	1,1F	1,1F	1,1F	1,1F	1,1F	1,1F	1,1F	1,1F

Overview:
In June 2009 parliamentary elections, the Christian Social Party's Jean-Claude Juncker secured a fourth term and formed a coalition government with the opposition Socialist Worker's Party of Luxembourg in July. Amid lingering economic problems, Luxembourg faced continued criticism over its bank-secrecy laws.

The Grand Duchy of Luxembourg was established in 1815 after the Napoleonic wars. Following a brief merger with Belgium, it acquired its current borders in 1839. The country was occupied by Germany during both world wars, and it abandoned neutrality to join NATO in 1949. After forming an economic union with Belgium and the Netherlands in 1948, Luxembourg became one of the six founding members of the European Community—now the European Union (EU)—in 1957; it adopted the euro currency in 1999.

In 2004 elections, the opposition Socialist Worker's Party of Luxembourg (POSL) replaced the center-right Democratic Party (PD) as the junior coalition partner of Prime Minister Jean-Claude Juncker's Christian Social Party (PCS).

Parliamentary elections were held in June 2009, alongside elections for the European Parliament. The PCS gained two seats for a total of 26, and the POSL lost 1 seat for a total of 13. The PD followed with 9 seats, the Green Party with 7, the Action Committee for Democracy and Pension Justice with 4, and the Left alliance with 1. Juncker remained as prime minister for the 15th consecutive year—the longest tenure of any EU head of state—and formed a coalition government with the POSL in July.

Luxembourg struggled with continued financial hardship in 2009, as the country experienced a 4 percent contraction in GDP during the year. Juncker resigned from his dual role as finance minister in July, but planned to continue as chairman of the Eurogroup of euro zone finance ministers until the end of his term in December 2010. Amid continued pressure to ease bank-secrecy rules, Juncker criticized the EU banking structure, especially its focus on Luxembourg and Switzerland during the financial crisis, and demanded that equal pressure be applied to the United Kingdom and elsewhere.

In July, the PCS announced the creation of an international section for its French-speaking members, the first time a political party has been restructured for members who do not speak Luxembourgish. Government documentation remains largely available only in Luxembourgish and German.

Political Rights and Civil Liberties: Luxembourg is an electoral democracy. The head of state is the unelected Grand Duke Henri, whose powers are largely ceremonial. The unicameral legislature, the Chamber of Deputies, consists of 60 members elected by proportional representation to five-year terms. Following a December 2008 constitutional amendment, the Chamber no longer requires the grand duke's approval to pass bills into law. The legislature chooses the prime minister. Voting is compulsory for Luxembourg's citizens. Citizens of EU countries may vote after six years' residency but are not required to do so; residents from non-EU countries may not vote. Foreigners constitute over a third of Luxembourg's population.

The political system is open to the rise of new parties. There are three traditionally strong parties: the PCS, historically aligned with the Catholic Church; the POSL, a formerly radical but now center-left party representing the working class; and the PD, which favors free-market economic policies.

The government is largely free from corruption. Luxembourg was ranked 12 out of 180 countries surveyed in Transparency International's 2009 Corruption Perceptions Index.

Freedom of expression is guaranteed by the constitution, and Luxembourg has a vibrant media environment. A single conglomerate, RTL, dominates broadcast radio and television, and its programming is popular in neighboring countries. Newspapers represent a broad range of opinion. Internet access is unrestricted.

Roman Catholicism is the dominant religion, but there is no state religion, and the state pays the salaries of clergy from a variety of sects. Students may choose to study either the Roman Catholic religion or ethics; most choose the former. Protestant education is available on demand. Academic freedom is respected.

Freedoms of assembly and association are protected. Civic groups and non-governmental organizations operate freely. In 2009, EU-wide protests over falling milk prices turned violent in Luxembourg, as clashes between farmers and police caused injuries on both sides. Luxembourgers may organize in trade unions, and a large proportion of the workforce does so. The right to strike is constitutionally guaranteed.

The judiciary is independent, but judges are appointed by the grand duke. Detainees are treated humanely in police stations and prisons, though overcrowding was reported at Schrassig Prison in 2009.

Luxembourg's Muslim minority, mainly of Bosnian origin, faces no official hostility but some mild social discrimination. In 2007, the government agreed to give Muslim leaders the same recognition and financial support enjoyed by religious leaders of other faiths.

In part because of Luxembourg's conservative social mores, women comprise just under 50 percent of the labor force, and a significant gap remains between men's and women's wages. Women are underrepresented in the highest levels of government: 15 women currently serve in the 60-member parliament, and only 4 hold seats in the 15-member cabinet. Though the law does not technically allow abortion on demand, a woman who has had an abortion while in "distress" is considered not to have violated the law, and "distress" is interpreted liberally.

♚Macedonia

Political Rights: 3
Civil Liberties: 3
Status: Partly Free

Population: 2,049,000
Capital: Skopje

Trend Arrow: Macedonia received an upward trend arrow due to presidential and local elections that were deemed fair and competitive by outside observers and the implementation of reforms recommended after the 2008 parliamentary elections.

Ten-Year Ratings Timeline For Year Under Review (Political Rights, Civil Liberties, Status)

2000	2001	2002	2003	2004	2005	2006	2007	2008	2009
4,3PF	4,4PF	3,3PF	3,3PF	3,3PF	3,3PF	3,3PF	3,3PF	3,3PF	3,3PF

Overview: The governing center-right party won the 2009 presidential and municipal elections, which observers deemed a significant improvement on the unruly parliamentary elections of 2006 and 2008. Macedonia made some progress on reforms related to its European Union candidacy during the year, but the remaining obstacles included a long-running dispute with Greece over the country's name, and unresolved questions about the level of autonomy granted to the ethnic Albanian minority.

Macedonia, a republic in the communist-era Yugoslav federation, gained independence in 1992 and was known internationally as the Former Yugoslav Republic of Macedonia. Since then, however, the country's existence and legitimacy has been threatened on several levels. Greece objects to the name "Macedonia," arguing that it implies a territorial and cultural claim to the Greek region of the same name. Bulgaria contends that the Macedonian language is a dialect of Bulgarian. And internally, poor relations between the Macedonian Slav majority and the ethnic Albanian minority have raised doubts about the country's long-term viability.

Since independence, power has alternated between center-left and center-right governments, although an important constant has been the inclusion of an ethnic Albanian party in each ruling coalition. In 2000–2001, Albanians mounted an armed insurgency, demanding greater use of the Albanian language in official institutions, an increase in the number of Albanians in the civil service, and a transfer of certain government powers to municipalities. Unofficially, however, the insurgency was motivated in part by a desire to control lucrative smuggling routes in northwestern Macedonia. An August 2001 agreement, known as the Ohrid Accords, temporarily satisfied most of the rebels' stated demands, though violent incidents continued to erupt periodically.

Parliamentary elections in 2002 returned the Social Democratic Party of Macedonia (SDSM) to power after a period of rule by the center-right Internal Macedonian Revolutionary Organization–Democratic Party for Macedonian National Unity (VMRO-DPMNE), and SDSM leader Branko Crvenkovski became prime minister. The Democratic Union for Integration (DUI), headed by the leader of the ethnic Albanian uprising, Ali Ahmeti, joined the SDSM government as a coalition partner.

Crvenkovski rose to the presidency in a special 2004 election after the incumbent died in a plane crash.

The VMRO-DPMNE won parliamentary elections in 2006, but the polls were marred by preelection violence and significant irregularities on election day. DUI supporters then mounted weeks of demonstrations to protest the VMRO-DPMNE's decision to form a coalition with a rival group, the Democratic Party of Albanians (DPA). DUI subsequently engaged in months of intermittent parliamentary boycotts, sometimes blocking key legislation related to the Ohrid Accords and Macedonia's European Union (EU) candidacy.

Early parliamentary elections held in 2008 were widely seen as the worst since independence. Irregularities—mainly in Albanian areas—included attacks on party offices, failure to guarantee equal access to the media, and ballot-box stuffing. The final results gave the ruling VMRO-DPMNE and its smaller allies 63 out of 120 seats. The opposition SDSM and its junior partners took only 27 seats. DUI, which won 18 seats, confirmed its position as the leading Albanian party and entered the new government, while the rival DPA garnered 11 and went into opposition.

University professor Georgi Ivanov, running for the VMRO-DPMNE, won the 2009 presidential election. He led by a wide margin in the March first round and then took 63 percent of the vote in the April runoff against the SDSM's Ljubomir Frckoski. After the Albanian candidates were eliminated in the first round, turnout for the run-off was negligible among Albanian voters, but the election was generally praised by international observers as an improvement on the 2008 polls. The VMRO-DPMNE also did well in the concurrent municipal elections, capturing 55 out of the country's 84 municipalities outright.

The parliament made progress on the remaining reforms called for in the Ohrid Accords, enacting the Law on Inter-Municipality Cooperation in June 2009. Other laws that enhanced the role of local governments in economic development issues had been enacted the previous year. However, ethnic Albanian and Macedonian Slav politicians continued to disagree over matters like the use of the Albanian language throughout Macedonia, display of the flag of neighboring Albania, and increasing the number of ethnic Albanians in government. Such rifts threatened the country's ongoing pursuit of EU membership. Macedonia was also seeking membership in NATO, but Greece had blocked an invitation for it to join in 2008.

Political Rights and Civil Liberties: Macedonia is an electoral democracy. Most elections held since independence have been deemed satisfactory according to international standards, though the 2008 parliamentary polls were marred by a number of irregularities. The political climate surrounding the 2009 presidential and parliamentary elections was much calmer than in 2008, and the electoral boards reverted to a mixed professional-political composition designed to limit the possibility for fraud.

Members of the unicameral, 120-seat Sobranie (Assembly) are elected to four-year terms by proportional representation. The president is elected to a five-year term through a direct popular vote, but the prime minister holds most executive power. According to reforms put in place by the Ohrid Accords, certain types of legislation need to be passed by a "double majority," meaning a majority of lawmakers from both of the main ethnic groups.

Corruption remains a serious problem, although Macedonia has made consistent progress in confronting it in recent years. In July 2009, the parliament adopted legislation designed to strengthen transparency in political party financing. The Law on Conflict of Interest was also amended the year, increasing the scope of the law—especially with regard to civil servants—and requiring government officials to submit a conflict of interest declaration. Macedonia was ranked 71 out of 180 countries surveyed in Transparency International's 2009 Corruption Perceptions Index.

The constitution provides for freedom of the press. Libel is punishable by fines, but not by imprisonment. Political appointees are frequently named to senior positions in state-owned media, a leading source of information for much of the population, and political parties either own or are closely linked to three of the five private television stations licensed to broadcast nationwide. The country's media outlets are strongly divided along ethnic lines. Ownership of print outlets is fairly concentrated, with a German media group controlling the three leading dailies. There were no reports of restrictions on access to the internet during 2009.

The constitution guarantees freedom of religion, but a law that took effect in 2008 favors established religious organizations over newer ones. Education officials in February 2009 upheld a school ban on the wearing of religious or ethnic markers after an Albanian student sought to wear a headscarf. In April, the Constitutional Court ruled that a 2008 law allowing religious classes in elementary schools was unconstitutional. A long-standing dispute between the breakaway Macedonian Orthodox Church and the canonically recognized Serbian Orthodox Church continues; the leader of a faction loyal to the Serbian Church has been repeatedly arrested and harassed for his religious activities. In October, he was again sentenced to two and a half years in prison for what most observers believe to be trumped-up charges. There have been reports of radical Islamists taking control of some local mosques with financial support from Middle Eastern countries.

Academic freedom is generally not restricted, but the country's ethnic divisions sometimes complicate education and research. In February 2009, school officials in the town of Struga decided to segregate classes after fights broke out between Albanian and Macedonian children. In November, the Macedonian Academy of Sciences and Arts was forced to withdraw a new encyclopedia and disband the editing team after Albanians argued that it presented a distorted and offensive version of the country's history.

Constitutional guarantees of freedoms of assembly and association are generally respected, although in 2009, the police intervened when a student group protested the planned construction of a new church in Skopje's main square. Nongovernmental organizations (NGOs) typically operate without government interference. The constitution recognizes the right of workers to organize and bargain collectively. More than 50 percent of the legal workforce (mostly in the public sector) is unionized, and strikes, though subject to a number of restrictions, are common. However, the EU's October 2009 progress report found few improvements in labor rights over the past year, and workers have little leverage due to the poor state of the economy. Some unions have reported obstacles in their efforts to register.

The EU's 2009 progress report noted a number of improvements in the functioning of the Macedonian judiciary over the past year. A new training academy for judges and prosecutors has begun graduating its first students, and a new system is in place for appraising the performance of judges and court presidents. During the year, however, the government publicly questioned the Constitutional Court's legitimacy after it ruled that the government-sponsored law allowing religious classes in state schools was unconstitutional. Prison conditions in the country have been improving, although they are still considered inadequate by international standards.

Women enjoy the same legal rights as men, but societal attitudes limit women's participation in nontraditional roles. Women currently hold 2 out of 22 cabinet positions and 39 out of 120 parliament seats, more than at any time since independence. Every third candidate on a party's electoral list must be female. In the 2009 municipal elections, however, none of the 84 available mayoral positions was filled by a woman. Domestic violence and trafficking of women remain serious problems. In Albanian Muslim areas, many women are subjected to proxy voting by male relatives and are frequently denied access to education.

Madagascar

Political Rights: 6*
Civil Liberties: 4*
Status: Partly Free

Population: 19,464,000
Capital: Antananarivo

Ratings Change: Madagascar's political rights rating declined from 4 to 6 and its civil liberties rating from 3 to 4 due to President Andry Rajoelina's unconstitutional rise to power, the suspension of the parliament, the repression of opposition protests, and limitations on press freedom, including the closure of opposition media outlets.

Ten-Year RatingsTimeline ForYear Under Review (Political Rights, Civil Liberties, Status)

2000	2001	2002	2003	2004	2005	2006	2007	2008	2009
2,4PF	2,4PF	3,4PF	3,3PF	3,3PF	3,3PF	4,3PF	4,3PF	4,3PF	6,4PF

Overview: The closure of an opposition media outlet at the end of 2008 touched off months of civil and political unrest in which dozens of demonstrators were killed. Facing intense pressure from the opposition and elements of the military, President Marc Ravalomanana resigned in March 2009 and was replaced by Andry Rajoelina, an opposition leader and mayor of Antananarivo. Rajoelina's unconstitutional accession to power, suspension of the parliament, and erratic leadership resulted in continued political uncertainty. In August, the various political factions reached a tentative power-sharing accord, but repeated attempts to form a transitional coalition government failed, and Rajoelina abandoned the talks in December.

After 70 years of French colonial rule and episodes of severe repression, Madagascar gained independence in 1960. A leftist military junta seized power in 1972. A member of the junta, Admiral Didier Ratsiraka, emerged as leader in 1975 and retained power until his increasingly authoritarian regime bowed to social unrest and nonviolent mass demonstrations in 1991.

Under a new constitution, opposition leader Albert Zafy won the 1992 presidential election. However, he failed to win reelection after being impeached by the Supreme Court in 1996. Ratsiraka won that year's presidential runoff election, which was deemed generally legitimate by international and domestic observers.

A decentralization plan was narrowly approved in a 1998 referendum amid a boycott by the country's increasingly fractious opposition. In the December 2001 presidential election, opposition candidate and Antananarivo mayor Marc Ravalomanana claimed that he had been denied an outright victory in the first round by polling irregularities. He declared himself president in February 2002, having refused to take part in a postponed runoff against the incumbent. After considerable violence between his and Ratsiraka's supporters, the High Constitutional Court announced that Ravalomanana had indeed won the election in the first round. Ratsiraka refused to acknowledge the result. Sporadic clashes continued until July 2002, when Ratsiraka left the country and the last of his forces surrendered. The extended crisis seriously damaged the Malagasy economy.

Ravalomanana's I Love Madagascar (TIM) party won a large majority in the December 2002 parliamentary elections. Observers from the European Union said the conduct of the polls was "generally positive." Political tensions increased in the run-up to the December 2006 presidential election, in which Ravalomanana secured a second term. While most observers agreed that the vote reflected the will of the people, the campaign was marred by opposition claims of a biased administration and electoral irregularities.

A constitutional referendum in April 2007 increased presidential powers, and Ravalomanana's authority was bolstered again in September parliamentary elections, as his TIM party won 106 of the 127 seats in the National Assembly. Local elections in December 2007 largely confirmed TIM's dominance, but Andry Rajoelina, a young and charismatic opposition candidate, won the mayoral race in the capital.

The closure of an opposition television station in December 2008 triggered months of violent protests in Antananarivo. Well over 100 people were killed, as protesters destroyed property and marched on government sites, and police responded with gunfire. Rajoelina called on Ravalomanana to resign, and declared himself president. As the political crisis deepened in March, with some army officers announcing their support for the opposition, Ravalomanana handed power to the military, which immediately transferred it to Rajoelina.

Now calling himself president of a "High Transitional Authority," Rajoelina suspended the parliament and established administrative bodies to govern the island. The new regime was largely shunned by the international community. In August, internationally mediated negotiations resulted in a tentative power-sharing agreement that would lead to elections in late 2010. Laborious talks on the composition of a coalition government ensued, and in October, the parties reached an initial accord under which Rajoelina would remain as the transitional president, and supporters of Ravalomanana and Ratsiraka would occupy other senior positions. Ravalomanana, however, objected to Rajoelina's continued status as president and withheld support. Another arrangement approved by the rivals in November also collapsed, and in December, Rajoelina declared that he was withdrawing from the power-sharing effort and named a new prime minister unilaterally.

Until 2009, Madagascar had experienced overall economic growth for seven years, due in part to large mining projects, but the World Bank estimates that annual per capita income remains around $300. Beginning in December 2008, the country's donor partners suspended aid disbursements, citing concerns about a lack of transparency in budget processes and possible conflicts of interest involving Ravalomanana's business assets. The 2009 political crisis resulted in continued suspension of foreign aid and significant economic dislocation.

Political Rights and Civil Liberties: Madagascar is not an electoral democracy. The undemocratic and unconstitutional manner in which Andry Rajoelina assumed the presidency in March 2009 demonstrated that the political culture has so far failed to incorporate a rules-based system and the practice of peaceful democratic succession.

According to the constitution, the president is directly elected for up to two five-year terms. The president is also legally required to be at least 40 years old; Rajoelina was 34 when he proclaimed himself president. The 2007 constitutional referendum continued a trend of steadily increasing presidential power. Among other provisions, it allowed the president to rule by decree during a state of emergency, and abolished autonomous provinces.

The parliament remained dormant at the end of 2009, after Rajoelina suspended it in March. The National Assembly, the bicameral legislature's lower chamber, has 127 members directly elected to four-year terms. The upper chamber, the Senate, has 33 members who serve four-year terms. Two-thirds of the senators are chosen by provincial lawmakers, and the rest are appointed by the president. The president has the power to appoint or dismiss the prime minister, who may come from a party that has a minority of seats in the National Assembly.

Approximately 150 parties are registered, although only a few have a national presence. Parties tend to suffer from internal divisions, shifting alliances, and a lack of resources and clear ideology. Prior to the suspension of the parliament, ousted president Marc Ravalomanana's TIM party had an overwhelming majority in both houses. Since Rajoelina's accession to power, opposition political activity in Madagascar has been circumscribed through bans on meetings and protests, killings of opposition supporters, and unsubstantiated government allegations of opposition party involvement in a series of explosions in Antananarivo in mid-2009. Following his ouster in March, Ravalomanana fled abroad and remained in South Africa at year's end.

Many observers have expressed concerns about the extent of and trends in corruption in Madagascar. According to the Heritage Foundation's 2010 Index of Economic Freedom, Madagascar ranks well below average on corruption, and "complicated administrative procedures introduce delays and uncertainties and multiply the opportunities for corruption." It was ranked 99 out of 180 countries surveyed in Transparency International's 2009 Corruption Perceptions Index.

The constitution provides for freedom of the press. A 1990 law on press freedom was followed by the introduction of privately owned FM radio stations and more critical political reporting by the print media. However, subsequent governments have at times curbed press freedom in practice. The media are highly polarized and partisan, and there are dozens of licensed television, radio, and print outlets. Because of the low literacy rate, the print media are mostly aimed at the French-speaking urban elite. Internet use, although not widespread, is becoming more popular. According to the International Telecommunications Union, there were approximately 315,000 internet users, or 1.5 percent of the population, as of June 2009.

The 2009 political crisis began when Ravalomanana ordered the closure of a private television station run by Rajoelina in December 2008 after it aired an interview with former president Didier Ratsiraka without official permission. One journalist was killed by gunfire from security forces during opposition protests in February, and several were beaten or harassed by the authorities or partisan thugs both before and after the change in power. Media outlets associated with each side were raided by security forces or ransacked by armed civilians during the turmoil, and a Ravalomanana-owned radio station was shut down by the authorities in April. The independent outlets that remain in operation increasingly practice self-censorship.

The Malagasy people have traditionally enjoyed religious freedom. The law strongly encourages, but does not require, religious organizations to register with the Ministry of Interior. There are no limitations on academic freedom.

Freedom of association is generally respected, and hundreds of nongovernmental organizations, including legal and human rights groups, are active. Freedom of assembly was severely affected by the unrest in early 2009, as protests degenerated into riots and looting, and security forces opened fire on demonstrators. After the change in power, Rajoelina's government sharply restricted opposition protests.

Workers' rights to join unions and strike are largely respected. The Ravalomanana administration endured a series of demonstrations and work stoppages, mainly over the high rate of inflation; strikes, often politically motivated, continued under the Rajoelina regime. Some of the country's labor organizations are affiliated with political groups. More than 80 percent of workers are engaged in agriculture, fishing, and forestry at a subsistence level.

The judiciary remains susceptible to corruption and executive influence. Its acquiescence in the face of Rajoelina's unconstitutional rise to power highlighted its weakness as an institution, and judicial decisions during the year were tainted by frequent intimidation. A lack of training, resources, and personnel hampers judicial effectiveness, and case backlogs are prodigious. Most of the approximately 20,000 people held in the country's prisons are pretrial detainees and suffer from extremely harsh and sometimes life-threatening conditions. In many rural areas, customary-law courts that lack due process often issue summary and severe punishments, and illegal activities, such as flogging, frequently occur. In the demonstrations and chaos surrounding the change in government, security forces often acted with impunity.

A political cleavage has traditionally existed between the coastal *cotier* and the highland *merina* peoples, of continental African and Southeast Asian origins, respectively. Due to past military conquest and long-standing political dominance, the status of the merina tends to be higher than that of the cotier. Ethnicity, caste, and regional solidarity often are factors that lead to discrimination.

Approximately 45 percent of the workforce is female. Malagasy women hold significantly more government and managerial positions than women in continental African countries. However, they still face societal discrimination and enjoy fewer opportunities than men for higher education and employment.

Malawi

Political Rights: 3*
Civil Liberties: 4
Status: Partly Free

Population: 14,214,000
Capital: Lilongwe

Ratings Change: Malawi's political rights rating improved from 4 to 3 due to a fairer and more competitive presidential election in 2009, greater electoral participation by women, and women's subsequent representation in governing institutions.

Ten-Year Ratings Timeline For Year Under Review (Political Rights, Civil Liberties, Status)

2000	2001	2002	2003	2004	2005	2006	2007	2008	2009
3,3PF	4,3PF	4,4PF	3,4PF	4,4PF	4,4PF	4,3PF	4,4PF	4,4PF	3,4PF

Overview: In the May 2009 presidential and parliamentary elections, President Bingu wa Mutharikaand his Democratic Progressive Party secured comfortable victories. Observers noted that the polls were more fair and competitive than in previous years, though incumbents enjoyed certain advantages, including positive coverage from government-run media outlets. While the climate for the judiciary improved during the year, the government failed to address ongoing corruption and bias in state-run media.

Malawi gained independence from Britain in 1963. President Hastings Kamuzu Banda ruled the country for nearly three decades, exercising dictatorial power through the Malawi Congress Party (MCP) and its paramilitary youth wing. Facing an economic crisis and strong domestic and international pressure, Banda accepted a referendum that approved multiparty rule in 1993. Bakili Muluzi of the United Democratic Front (UDF) won the presidency in a 1994 election that was generally perceived as free and fair. He was reelected in 1999.

Muluzi handpicked Bingu wa Mutharika, a relative political outsider, as his successor ahead of the May 2004 presidential election. Mutharika defeated his MCP opponent, while the MCP led the concurrent parliamentary elections. In early 2005, a rift between Mutharika and Muluzi, who remained the UDF chairman, worsened after several powerful UDF figures were arrested as part of Mutharika's new anticorruption campaign. Mutharika resigned from the UDF and formed the Democratic Progressive Party (DPP), which many lawmakers then joined. With the UDF and the MCP forming an opposition alliance against the president, the remainder of Mutharika's first term was characterized by acute tensions between the executive and legislative branches, sometimes leading to the paralysis of governing institutions, as well as ongoing conflict between Mutharika and Muluzi and his allies.

Despite predictions that Muluzi would emerge as Mutharika's primary challenger for the May 2009 presidential contest, the Malawi Electoral Commission (MEC) in March rejected Muluzi's candidacy on the grounds that the two-term limit outlined in the constitution proscribed him from standing again. After a court ruling upheld the MEC decision, Muluzi and the UDF formed an alliance with the head of the MCP,

John Tembo, and backed his candidacy for the presidency. Mutharika ran a highly effective cross-regional campaign focused on his provision of public goods, defeating Tembo with approximately 66 percent of the vote. In concurrent parliamentary elections, Mutharika's DPP won a total of 112 seats in the 193-seat legislature; the MCP took 26, and the UDF captured 17, leaving independent candidates and smaller parties with the remaining seats. Reflecting the dominance of the governing party, parliament has proved a more effective governing partner, as witnessed in the easy passage of legislation in the aftermath of the elections.

According to international and domestic election observers, the 2009 polls were more free and competitive than in previous years. Despite isolated instances of violence between party supporters, candidates enjoyed a more open campaign environment, polling day was peaceful, and there was little post election turmoil. However, incumbents had a clear advantage due to the use of state resources during the campaign period and a clear bias on government-controlled media outlets. In addition, irregularities in parliamentary races led to legal challenges after the announcement of results.

International donors, which account for 80 percent of Malawi's development budget, have widely applauded economic management under the Mutharika administration. In December 2007, the United States announced Malawi's eligibility for financial support under the Millennium Challenge Corporation (MCC) initiative. Separately, the IMF approved a $77.2 Million Exogenous Shocks Facility for Malawi in late 2008, making it the first country to receive funds under the facility. While relations with international financial institutions have been positive, President Mutharika criticized their policies in November 2009, claiming that they had contributed to foreign exchange shortages in the country. Dramatic improvements in agricultural output, partially credited to a popular fertilizer subsidy program, have helped the country to achieve solid economic growth rates over the last few years. The economy grew at a rate of 5.9 percent in 2009.

Political Rights and Civil Liberties: Malawi is an electoral democracy. The president is directly elected for five-year terms and exercises considerable executive authority. The unicameral National Assembly is composed of 193 members elected by popular vote to serve five-year terms. The 2009 presidential and parliamentary elections, though characterized by an uneven playing field in favor of the incumbents, were the most fair and competitive since the first multiparty elections in 1994. While in previous years opposition groups had questioned the impartiality and legitimacy of the MEC, key observers concluded that it operated during the 2009 elections with sufficient transparency.

The main political parties are the ruling DPP, the opposition MCP, and the UDF. In the past, the effectiveness of the opposition had been undermined by the president's refusal to call parliament into session, and the government had targeted members of the UDF with corruption charges. However, the opposition was able to organize and campaign freely during the 2009 elections.

While President Bingu wa Mutharika has pledged to fight corruption, opposition and civil society groups have charged that the effort has been directed primarily at Mutharika's political opponents. During his first term, a number of individuals associated with the previous government were investigated and charged with corruption, leading to several convictions. After years of investigation and two prior arrests, former president Bakili Muluzi was arrested again in 2009 and charged with 86 counts related to his alleged theft of public resources during his time in office. His trial remained ongoing at the year's end. Separately, a report by Malawi's auditor general issued in August 2009 indicated that government agencies had lost millions of dollars between 2005 and 2007, due to overcharging, theft, and dubious procurements. Anticorruption efforts have been undermined by the shifting leadership and personnel turnover at the Anti-Corruption Bureau. However, a new National Anti-Corruption Strategy was launched in 2009, which includes a plan to establish "integrity committees" in public institutions. Malawi ranked 89 out of 180 countries surveyed in Transparency International's 2009 Corruption Perceptions Index.

Freedom of the press is legally guaranteed. Despite occasional restrictions, Malawi's dozen or so newspapers present a diversity of opinion. There are some 20 radio stations and 2 television stations in the country. However, the government-controlled Malawi Broadcasting Corporation and TV Malawi—the historically dominant outlets in the country—display a significant bias in favor of the government. In the lead-up to the 2009 elections, broadcasts from these outlets took a strongly progovernment position, garnering criticism from local and international election observers. Independent media outlets are playing an increasingly important role and have been able to operate without substantial interference. However, those outlets associated with the political opposition have been the target of government harassment. During the May 2009 elections, Muluzi's Joy Radio was briefly closed for allegedly broadcasting a political message, which violated laws forbidding such broadcasts immediately before the polling period.

Religious freedom is generally respected, and the government does not restrict academic freedom.

The government generally upholds freedoms of association and assembly. In contrast to previous years, opposition groups, most notably the UDF, encountered few difficulties holding rallies in 2009. However, one student demonstration against the poor diet at a teacher-training college was disrupted by police in May.

Many nongovernmental organizations—including the constitutionally mandated Malawi Human Rights Commission—operate without interference. The right to organize labor unions and to strike is legally protected, with notice and mediation requirements for workers in essential services. Unions are active, and collective bargaining is practiced, but workers face harassment and occasional violence during strikes. Since only a small percentage of the workforce is formally employed, union membership is low.

During Mutharika's first term, the generally independent judiciary became involved in political disputes and faced government hostility. While there were no recorded instances of harassment of judges in 2009, Mutharika dismissed the inspector general of police in February 2009, allegedly for questioning the use of the police band for pro-government political rallies. Due process is not always respected by the overburdened court system, which lacks resources, personnel, and training. Police brutality is reportedly common, as are arbitrary arrests and detentions. Prison conditions are appalling, with many inmates dying from AIDS and other diseases.

The government maintains respect for private property and has generally embraced free-market principles. However, in May 2009 the president publically criticized tobacco purchasers from multi-national firms for the low prices offered to producers. Four representatives of such firms were served with deportation orders in September because their conduct was not "consistent with the development agenda of Malawi."

Despite constitutional guarantees of equal protection, customary practices perpetuate discrimination against women in education, employment, business, and inheritance and property rights. Violence against women and children remains a serious concern, though in recent years there has been greater media attention on and criminal penalties for abuse and rape. Abusive practices, including forced marriages and the secret initiation of girls into their future adult roles through forced sex with older men remain widespread. The practice of *kupimbira*, in which young girls of any age are sold by families to pay off debts, still exists in some areas. Trafficking in women and children, both locally and to locations abroad, is a problem. Penalties for the few successfully prosecuted traffickers have been criticized as too lenient.

Malawian women recorded significant gains in the 2009 elections. A large number of women ran as parliamentary candidates, and Joyce Banda became the first female vice president in the country's history. Women hold 22 percent of the seats in parliament and 26 percent in the cabinet.

Malaysia

Political Rights: 4
Civil Liberties: 4
Status: Partly Free

Population: 28,295,000
Capital: Kuala Lumpur

Ten-Year Ratings Timeline For Year Under Review (Political Rights, Civil Liberties, Status)

2000	2001	2002	2003	2004	2005	2006	2007	2008	2009
5,5PF	5,5PF	5,5PF	5,4PF	4,4PF	4,4PF	4,4PF	4,4PF	4,4PF	4,4PF

Overview:

Najib Razak, previously the deputy prime minister, rose to the premiership in April 2009 after Prime Minister Abdullah Ahmad Badawi stepped down. Abdullah had been discredited after presiding over the loss of the ruling coalition's long-standing two-thirds majority in the 2008 parliamentary elections. Also during 2009, a constitutional crisis erupted in the state of Perak, after the two main coalitions in the evenly divided legislature each claimed the right to govern, and a series of religious controversies threatened to undermine Najib's pledge to promote unity among Malaysia's racial and ethnic groups. Separately, the national anticorruption agency came under scrutiny in July when an opposition party official fell to his death after being questioned by agency investigators.

Malaya gained independence from Britain in 1957 and merged with the British colonies of Sarawak and Sabah to become the Federation of Malaysia in 1963. The ruling Barisan Nasional (National Front, or BN, known as the Alliance before 1969) won at least a two-thirds majority in 10 of the first 11 general elections after independence, the exception being the 1969 elections, which were nullified following race riots. The BN consists of mainly ethnic parties, dominated by the conservative, Malay-based United Malays National Organization (UMNO).

Racial tensions between the Malay majority and Chinese and Indian minorities have played a central role in Malaysian politics and economics since the country's founding. Independence was premised on a social contract, enshrined in the constitution, that granted citizenship to the non-Malay population in exchange for special rights and privileges, especially in education and economics, for all *bumiputera* (Malays and other indigenous peoples). After the outbreak of race riots in 1969, in which thousands of Chinese homes and businesses were destroyed and more than 180 people were killed, the government declared an 18-month state of emergency and tightened restrictions on free speech, assembly, and political organizations.

Modern Malaysia has been shaped by Mahathir Mohamed, one of the key architects of efforts to shift economic power from the Chinese to the Malays, first as education minister and then as prime minister from 1981 to 2003. His development policies transformed Malaysia into a hub for multinational corporations and high-technology exports. At the same time, he stunted democratic institutions, weakened the rule of law by curtailing the press and political opponents, and drew allegations of cronyism with his state-led industrial development. Mahathir criticized conservative Muslim leaders for failing to promote a more modern brand of Islam, and at the same time attempted to co-opt Islamist opposition forces by weaving their positions into UMNO's ideology.

In October 2003, Mahathir stepped down and left the premiership to his deputy, Abdullah Ahmad Badawi. The BN won 198 of the 219 seats in the lower house of Parliament in the 2004 elections, which were generally regarded as transparent. However, the three main opposition parties—the Democratic Action Party (DAP), the Islamic Party of Malaysia (PAS), and the People's Justice Party (PKR)—challenged the results on the grounds that the BN had engaged in vote rigging and other irregularities. Most specific challenges were rejected in court or withdrawn, although allegations of vote buying and problems with the electoral roll were substantiated.

Despite his strong popular mandate, Abdullah achieved little in the way of reform. In 2006, sharp divisions emerged within UNMO as Mahathir launched a series of harsh attacks on Abdullah. Meanwhile, Anwar Ibrahim, a former deputy prime minister who had been controversially removed by Mahathir in 1998, reemerged as a major opposition figure. A series of court rulings during the year that denied certain religious and legal rights for non-Muslims sparked a national debate on constitutional guarantees and the role of Islam in Malaysia. The government took action to suppress press coverage, public discussion, and related civil society activism on ethnic issues, citing the need to prevent national unrest.

Over the course of 2007, public frustration skyrocketed in response to government suppression of peaceful protests, the exposure of high-level political corruption cases, a related crackdown on online media, and a crisis involving alleged politicization of the judiciary. Demands for electoral reform in advance of the

2008 general elections—coupled with perceptions of rising crime, corruption, and inflation—triggered the largest antigovernment demonstrations in nearly a decade.

In the March 2008 elections, the BN lost its two-thirds majority in the lower house of Parliament for the first time since 1969, meaning it could no longer amend the constitution unilaterally. The BN managed to secure just 140 of the 222 lower-house seats, and Abdullah soon faced calls for his resignation. Anwar's PKR captured 31 seats, up from just 1 in the 2004 elections, followed by the DAP with 28 and PAS with 23. The opposition parties also won control of five of Malaysia's 13 states, and formed a coalition called the People's Alliance (PR) in the wake of the polls.

Anwar, emboldened by the opposition's historic electoral gains, claimed that he and the PR would capture a parliamentary majority through defections from the BN and form a new government by September 2008. However, he failed to meet his own deadline, costing him a measure of credibility.

The PR suffered another setback in February 2009, when one of its members in the Perak state assembly rejoined UMNO and three others declared themselves independent. This left both the BN and the PR with 28 representatives, setting off a constitutional crisis as each side put forward candidates for chief minister and laid claim to the state government. The dispute was taken up by the courts and remained unresolved at year's end.

Meanwhile, Abdullah, discredited by the BN's 2008 electoral setbacks, stepped down as UMNO leader and prime minister. He was succeeded in April 2009 by his deputy, Najib Razak, who pledged to promote unity among the country's racial and religious groups. However, over the course of the year, the government faced a number of contentious religious and ethnic disputes as well as serious corruption scandals. In one case in August, a group of 50 people claiming to be residents of a township outside Kuala Lumpur placed a severed cow's head in front of the Selangor state secretariat building to protest the proposed relocation of a Hindu temple to a Muslim-majority area. The act was considered highly offensive to the Hindu community, and Najib ordered a police investigation. Twelve men were eventually charged under the Sedition Act and for illegal gathering under the Police Act. The incident sparked a broader debate over inconsistencies in the application of the country's sweeping security laws, particularly the Sedition Act and the Internal Security Act (ISA). Critics accused the government of favoring Muslim Malays in general, noting that the home minister had initially failed to insist on a swift and thorough investigation of the cow-head protest. This contrasted with the quick arrests of minority protesters in the past. In September, police arrested 16 people who were participating in a march to condemn the cow-head incident.

Political Rights and Civil Liberties: Malaysia is not an electoral democracy. The leader of the party that wins a plurality of seats in legislative elections becomes prime minister. Executive power is vested in the prime minister and cabinet. The paramount ruler, the titular head of state, is elected for five-year terms by fellow hereditary rulers in 9 of Malaysia's 13 states. Mizan Zainal Abidin al-Marhum Sultan Mahmud al-Muktafi Billah Shah was elected to the post in 2006. The upper house of the bicameral Parliament consists of 44 appointed members and 26 members elected by the state legislatures, serving three-year terms. The lower house, with 222 seats, is popularly elected at least every five years.

The ruling BN is a coalition of 13 parties, most with an ethnic or regional base, including the dominant UMNO as well as the Malaysian Chinese Association (MCA) and the Malaysian Indian Congress (MIC). The three main opposition parties—the DAP, PAS, and PKR—formed their own coalition, the PR, after the March 2008 elections. dramatic electoral gains came despite serious obstacles, such as unequal access to the media and restrictions on campaigning and freedom of assembly, which left them unable to compete on equal terms with the BN. The country's first-past-the-post voting system also increases the power of the largest grouping, and national electoral outcomes have been affected by the malapportionment of constituencies in favor of East Malaysia. Despite winning more than 40 percent of the vote in the 2004 elections, opposition parties collectively captured only 18 out of 219 seats in the lower house. In 2008, the BN won just 51 percent of the vote but secured 140 of 222 lower-house seats.

The Election Commission (EC) is frequently accused of manipulating electoral rolls and gerrymandering districts to aid the ruling coalition, and the registrar of societies arbitrarily decides which parties can participate in politics. However, the EC was generally seen to have performed well in the 2008 elections.

The government and law enforcement bodies have suffered a series of corruption scandals in recent years, despite the BN's anticorruption campaign pledges. The Malaysian Anti-Corruption Commission (MACC), the agency tasked with restoring transparency to the government, came under scrutiny itself in July 2009, when an official with the opposition DAP was found to have fallen to his death from the window of an MACC building. The official, Teoh Beng Hock, was being questioned late at night about an investigation into the disbursement of state funds. An inquest into the death was ongoing at year's end. In another unresolved scandal, the MCA was implicated in the massive misuse of public funds for the Port Klang Free Zone project. Malaysia was ranked 56 out of 180 countries surveyed in Transparency International's 2009 Corruption Perceptions Index.

Freedom of expression is constitutionally guaranteed but restricted in practice, although the scope of political discussion in the media expanded noticeably after the 2008 elections. The 1984 Printing Presses and Publications Act (PPPA) gives the government the authority to revoke licenses without judicial review. It also requires that publications and printers obtain annual operating permits, encouraging self-censorship and limiting investigative journalism. Privately owned television stations have close ties to the BN and generally censor programming according to government guidelines. Books and films are directly censored for profanity, violence, and political and religious material.

With traditional media so heavily restricted, the internet has emerged as a primary outlet for free discussion and for exposing cases of political corruption. The government responded in 2007 with an escalating crackdown, including the first defamation charges against bloggers. Bloggers were also threatened with arrest under the ISA, the Official Secrets Act, and the Sedition Act, all of which can draw several years in prison. The BN significantly softened its efforts to curtail online expression immediately after the 2008 elections, but security laws were used to temporarily detain two bloggers later in the year. In 2009, the BN floated a government contract to carry out internet filtering, but the proposal had been withdrawn by year's end.

The Malaysian Communication and Multimedia Commission (MCMC), an agency responsible in part for regulating the internet, has become one of the greatest roadblocks for freedom of expression in the country. It has a record of being unnecessarily harsh toward the independent news website Malaysiakini.com, which is often critical of the government. The MCMC placed pressure on the outlet in 2009 for refusing to remove video clips related to the August cow-head protest from its website. The agency argued that the clips had the, "potential to annoy a particular racial group." Nevertheless, no further actions were taken regarding the issue.

While the BN government continues to promote a tolerant and inclusive form of Islam, religious freedom is restricted in Malaysia. Practicing a version of Islam other than Sunni Islam is prohibited. Muslim children and civil servants are required to receive religious education, using government-approved curriculums and instructors. Proselytizing among Muslims by other religious groups is prohibited, and a 2007 ruling by the country's highest court effectively made it impossible for Muslims to have their conversions to other faiths recognized by the state. In late December 2009, a judge overturned a government ban on Christians' use of the word "Allah" to refer to God. The ban had been imposed partly out of concern that the word could be used in attempts to convert Muslims to Christianity. Non-Muslims are not able to build houses of worship as easily as Muslims, and the state retains the right to demolish unregistered religious statues and houses of worship. In 2009, the cow-head protest drew attention to regulations that restrict the number of non-Muslim places of worship based in part on the relevant faith's share of the local population.

The government restricts academic freedom to the extent that teachers or students espousing antigovernment views may be subject to disciplinary action under the University and Colleges Act of 1971.

Freedoms of assembly and association are limited on the grounds of maintaining security and public order. A police permit is required for all public assemblies except picket lines, and the granting of permits is sometimes politically influenced. Demonstrators can be detained under laws including the Sedition Act, the Police Act, and the ISA. The Societies Act of 1996 defines a society as any association of seven or more people, excluding schools, businesses, and trade unions. Societies must be approved and registered by the government, which has periodically refused or revoked registrations for political reasons. Numerous nongovernmental organizations (NGOs) operate in Malaysia, but some international human rights organizations are not allowed to form Malaysian branches.

Most Malaysian workers—excluding migrant workers—can join trade unions, but the law contravenes international guidelines by restricting unions to representing workers in a single or similar trade. The Director General of Trade Unions can refuse or withdraw registration arbitrarily, and the union recognition process can take from 18 to 36 months. In practice, collective bargaining is limited. Unions in essential services must give advance notice of strikes, and various other legal conditions effectively render strikes impossible.

Judicial independence has been compromised by extensive executive influence. Arbitrary or politically motivated verdicts are not uncommon, with the most prominent case being the convictions of Anwar Ibrahim in 1999 and 2000 for corruption and sodomy. The sodomy conviction was overturned in 2004, and he was released from prison, but the corruption charge was upheld, delaying his return to elected office until 2008. Anwar was again accused of sodomy that year, and the new case was still pending at the end of 2009. Parliament enacted judicial reform legislation in late 2008, but it was criticized for allowing continued executive influence over judicial appointments.

Malaysia's secular legal system is based on English common law. However, Muslims are subject to Sharia (Islamic law), the interpretation of which varies regionally, and the constitution's Article 121 stipulates that all matters related to Islam should be dealt with in Sharia courts. In a high-profile case in 2009, a Sharia court sentenced a woman to caning for drinking beer, though the punishment had not been carried out by year's end.

There is no constitutional provision specifically banning torture, and police have been known to torture prisoners and use excessive force or inhumane tactics in conducting searches. Police reform has been inhibited by resistance at the highest levels of the police force and, according to many, by the attorney general. Individuals may be arrested without a warrant for some offenses and held for 24 hours without being charged. The ISA, in force since 1960, gives the police sweeping powers to hold any person acting, "in a manner prejudicial to the security of Malaysia," for up to 60 days, extendable to two years. The law has been used to jail mainstream politicians, alleged Islamist militants, trade unionists, suspected communist activists, ordinary criminal suspects, and members of "deviant" Muslim sects, among others. In 2009, despite the hard-line reputation of the new prime minister, the government released most detainees being held under the ISA, leaving just nine in custody at year's end.

Although the constitution provides for equal treatment of all citizens, the government maintains an affirmative-action program intended to boost the economic status of ethnic Malays and other indigenous people, known collectively as bumiputera. Bumiputera receive preferential treatment in areas including property ownership, higher education, civil service jobs, and business affairs, and bumiputera-owned companies receive the lion's share of large government contracts. Of the opposition-led states, only the DAP-controlled state of Penang has offered to eliminate the race-based preferential policy. However, no concrete measures had been put in place by year's end.

Foreign household workers are not covered by the Workmen's Compensation Act and are thus subject to exploitation by employers. Malaysians officially employ about 240,000 household workers, 90 percent of whom are Indonesian, representing roughly 20 percent of the national workforce. There are an estimated two million illegal workers in Malaysia. If arrested and found guilty, illegal workers can be caned and detained indefinitely pending deportation. An untrained volunteer reserve of hundreds of thousands of baton-wielding Malaysians, called Rela, has been pursuing illegal foreign workers and refugees since 2005, raising serious concerns among human rights groups.

Despite government initiatives and continued gains, women are still underrepresented in politics, the professions, and the civil service. Violence against women remains a serious problem. Muslim women are legally disadvantaged, because their family grievances are heard in Sharia courts, where men are favored in matters such as inheritance and divorce and women's testimony is not given equal weight. In its 2009 human trafficking report, the U.S. State Department placed Malaysia on its Tier 3 Watch List, noting that the country had made some progress in investigating and punishing sex trafficking offenses, but has not demonstrated efforts to investigate, prosecute, or convict offenders of labor trafficking.

Maldives

Political Rights: 3*
Civil Liberties: 4
Status: Partly Free

Population: 315,000
Capital: Male

Ratings Change: The Maldives' political rights rating improved from 4 to 3 due to largely fair and competitive legislative elections held in May 2009.

Ten-Year Ratings Timeline For Year Under Review (Political Rights, Civil Liberties, Status)

2000	2001	2002	2003	2004	2005	2006	2007	2008	2009
6,5NF	6,5NF	6,5NF	6,5NF	6,5NF	6,5NF	6,5NF	6,5NF	4,4PF	3,4PF

Overview:
Building on a historic transfer of power after the 2008 presidential election, the Maldives continued its democratic opening in 2009 with May legislative elections that were considered to be largely free and fair. A strong showing by former president Maumoon Abdul Gayoom's Maldivian People's Party ensured that the new parliament would remain balanced by competing political factions, but raised questions about Mohamed Nasheed's administration's ability to implement its ambitious reform agenda. The political transition was accompanied by a significantly improved environment for freedoms of expression and association, but corruption, religious restrictions, and abysmal prison conditions remained serious problems.

The Maldives achieved independence in 1965 after 78 years as a British protectorate, and a 1968 referendum replaced the centuries-old sultanate with a republican system. The first president, Amir Ibrahim Nasir, held office for 10 years. He was succeeded by Maumoon Abdul Gayoom, who went on to serve six five-year terms. He won and repeatedly renewed his mandate through a tightly controlled system of presidential referendums rather than competitive elections.

Gayoom initiated political reforms after the beating death of a prison inmate sparked riots in 2003. In May 2004, voters elected a People's Special Majlis (PSM)—composed of the ordinary 50-seat People's Majlis (parliament), another 50 members elected or appointed specifically to the PSM, and the cabinet—that was tasked with amending the constitution. The next several years brought incremental improvements to the legislative, judicial, and media frameworks, interspersed with bouts of unrest, crackdowns on the opposition Maldivian Democratic Party (MDP), and restrictions on freedom of expression.

As the reform process dragged on, political tensions remained high, and Gayoom was attacked in a failed assassination attempt in January 2008. The PSM approved the final set of constitutional amendments in June of that year. Under pressure from opposition demonstrators, the president in August ratified the new charter, which included protection for a range of civil liberties while maintaining restrictions on religious freedom. The country's first multiparty presidential election was held in two rounds in October. Gayoom outpolled five challengers in the first round, taking 41 percent of the vote, but MDP leader and former political prisoner Mohamed Nasheed went on to victory in the runoff with 54 percent. Nearly 87 percent of registered voters turned out for the second round.

The Nasheed administration's immediate priorities were anticorruption measures, democratization, government decentralization, and press freedom. In line with the third objective, the government in 2009 abolished the Atolls Ministry, appointed seven provincial state ministers, and published a draft decentralization bill for discussion. The president also abolished the Information Ministry, and introduced draft bills guaranteeing freedom of expression and press freedom that remained under consideration by the parliament at year's end.

In the May 2009 parliamentary elections, Gayoom's Maldivian People's Party (DRP) won 28 of 77 seats, while the MDP won 26, the DRP-allied People's Alliance (PA) took 7, and independents garnered 13. A Commonwealth observer team characterized the voting as largely transparent and competitive, with a turnout of 79 percent. The DRP's strong showing—and the election of DRP member Abdullah Shahid and PA member Ahmed Nazim as Speaker and Deputy Speaker, respectively, of the new Majlis—raised questions about the ability of the government to push through its ambitious reform agenda.

Political Rights and Civil Liberties: The Republic of Maldives is an electoral democracy. The first democratic presidential election in 2008 was deemed relatively free and fair, although observers reported flaws including some preelection violence, a compressed timeframe, and voter registration problems. The interim election commission established prior to the vote was considered generally professional, transparent, and impartial. Elections held in May 2009 were also judged to be largely credible despite minor problems related to the compilation of the voters' list as well as some intimidation and other irregularities.

Under the new constitution, the president is directly elected for up to two five-year terms. The Constituencies Act, passed in February 2009, increased the size of the unicameral People's Majlis to 77 seats, with all members elected from individual districts to serve five-year terms. The president, parliament members, and other key officials are required to be Sunni Muslims. Since political parties were legalized in 2005, a dozen have registered. The space for opposition parties to mobilize expanded significantly in the past few years, although interparty rivalries, which sometimes flare into violence, remain a concern.

Under former president Maumoon Abdul Gayoom, government accountability was limited by the executive branch's almost complete control over the legislature and judiciary. However, a new, independent auditor general and the revised constitution have provided greater transparency, shedding light on pervasive corruption. A new Anti-Corruption Commission (ACC), whose members are appointed by the president and approved by a parliamentary majority, was set up in October 2008. As of September 2009, it had opened 90 cases, many involving Gayoom and members of his administration. In addition, a presidential commission on corruption was formed in May to investigate allegations against the former government. The DRP denounced the move as politically motivated and of questionable legality. In September, President Mohamed Nasheed announced that he was seeking help from the World Bank to recover around US$2 billion in embezzled funds. The Maldives was ranked 130 out of 180 countries surveyed in Transparency International's 2009 Corruption Perceptions Index. Transparency International set up a branch in the Maldives in February.

The new constitution guarantees freedoms of expression and the press, but it places limits on speech deemed "contrary to the tenets of Islam." A defamation case brought against a former magazine editor in June 2009 prompted calls for the offense to be decriminalized, and the parliament passed legislation to that effect in November. Private print media have expanded, though some publications are still owned by Gayoom allies, and the sector's coverage presents a diversity of viewpoints. The number of private radio stations has also increased, and the country's first private television channels began operating in July and September 2008, while several others were preparing to open. However, these outlets were authorized through individual agreements with the government rather than new broadcasting legislation, limiting their legal protection. Reforms at state-run Television and Radio Maldives led to somewhat more balanced election coverage, but bias persisted, and planned legislation to transform the public broadcaster stalled during the year. Journalists remain subject to some harassment; a spate of cases in mid-2009 included separate attacks by political activists on a reporter for TV Maldives and an editor at the daily *Haveeru* in July. Oppositionist websites remained unblocked, but the Ministry of Islamic Affairs (MIA) announced in 2008 that Christian websites would be blocked, arguing that they could negatively affect belief in Islam, and a number of websites were blocked by the Telecommunication Authority at the MIA's request during 2009.

Freedom of religion remains severely restricted. Islam is the state religion, and all citizens are required to be Sunni Muslims. Imams must use government-approved sermons. Under Nasheed, the Supreme Council of Islamic Affairs has been transformed into a ministry with the sole authority to grant licenses to preachers; a number of members of the Islamist Adhaalath Party were appointed to senior positions in the ministry. In January 2009, Forum 18 reported that a man was prosecuted for denying both the existence of Allah and Muhammad's status as a prophet, but recanted before the judge. Non-Muslim foreigners, including approximately 70,000 guest workers on long-term visas, are only allowed to practice their religions in private, which is difficult in practice. There were no reported limitations on academic freedom, but many scholars self-censor. Maldivians are now palpably freer to discuss politically sensitive issues in public places.

The new constitution guarantees freedom of assembly, and a number of peaceful demonstrations were held during the year, but police sometimes disperse peaceful protesters with excessive force. In March 2009, additional members were appointed to the three-year-old Police Integrity Commission (PIC), which had largely been inactive under Gayoom. In October, the PIC launched an investigation into police conduct during a protest at which officers clashed with demonstrators and temporarily detained 20. There were no reports in 2009 of harassment of nongovernmental organizations (NGOs), whose numbers grew during the year.

The new constitution and the Employment Act, which took effect in 2008, provide for a minimum wage and grant workers the rights to form trade unions and strike, all of which had been excluded from the 1998 constitution. In response to a series of strikes, the country's first labor tribunal was established in December 2008 to enforce the Employment Act. In May 2009, Maldives joined the International Labour Organization. Foreign workers occasionally have trouble collecting wages from their employers.

The new constitution provides for an independent judiciary, and judges were sworn into the first Supreme Court and final court of appeals in September 2008. By the end of that year, courts were showing signs of increased independence from the executive. In July 2009, Nasheed established the Judicial Services Commission to further separate the two branches, although concerns remain about the composition of the commission. Civil law is used in most cases, but it is subordinate to Sharia (Islamic law), which is applied in matters not covered by civil law and in cases involving divorce or adultery. As a result, the testimony of two women is equal to that of one man, and punishments such as flogging and internal exile continue to be carried out. A revised penal code was under debate in the Majlis during 2009, but it had not been amended by year's end.

The new constitution bans arbitrary arrest, torture, and prolonged detention without adequate judicial review. It also requires compensation for those detained without legal justification. The Nasheed administration has initiated efforts to reform and retrain the police, and has established an eight-member parole board to recommend sentence reductions for unjustly detained inmates. However, progress on improving prison conditions has been slow, and abuses continue to take place. In October 2009, prisoners at Maafushi Jail rioted and set fires to protest deplorable conditions.

Women, who enjoy a 98 percent literacy rate, are increasingly entering the civil service and receiving pay equal to that of men, though traditional norms still limit opportunities for many women. Women hold few senior positions in the government, but there are five female members of parliament, and Nasheed appointed women to the posts of attorney general, minister of health and family, and deputy minister of education. Unlike the old charter, the new constitution allows a woman to become president. International human rights groups have urged reform of severe legal punishments that primarily affect women; in July 2009, Amnesty International noted that since 2006, nearly 200 people, the vast majority of them women, had been sentenced to flogging for extramarital sex.

Mali

Political Rights: 2
Civil Liberties: 3
Status: Free

Population: 13,010,000
Capital: Bamako

Ten-Year Ratings Timeline For Year Under Review (Political Rights, Civil Liberties, Status)

2000	2001	2002	2003	2004	2005	2006	2007	2008	2009
2,3F	2,3F	2,3F	2,2F	2,2F	2,2F	2,2F	2,3F	2,3F	2,3F

Overview:

Although a government military offensive in early 2009 appeared to have resolved some of the conflict with the Tuareg rebels in the north, increased threats from the regional terrorist organization, al-Qaeda in the Islamic Maghreb, within Mali kept the country's security situation tenuous. A new family law that had been under review for 10 years stalled again after religious groups protested the legislature's approval of the legislation in August.

Mali was ruled by military and one-party regimes for more than 30 years following independence from France in 1960. After soldiers killed more than 100 demonstrators demanding a multiparty system in 1991, President Moussa Traore was overthrown by the military.

Alpha Oumar Konare of the Alliance for Democracy in Mali (ADEMA) won the presidency in 1992 elections that were deemed credible by most observers. He secured a second and final term in 1997 amid a boycott by most of the opposition. Several opposition parties also boycotted that year's National Assembly elections, in which ADEMA captured 128 of 147 seats.

In the 2002 presidential election, independent candidate Amadou Toumani Toure, a popular former general who had led Mali during the post-Traore transition period, defeated his ADEMA opponent. During legislative elections that year, the Hope 2002 coalition emerged victorious over the ADEMA-led coalition.

Toure, running as the candidate of the Alliance for Democracy and Progress (ADP) coalition, was reelected with 71 percent of the second-round vote in the April 2007 presidential election. The ADP secured 113 seats, with 51 going to ADEMA, its largest constituent party, in elections for the National Assembly in July. The main opposition coalition, the Front for Democracy and the Republic (FDR), captured 15 seats, with a smaller party and independents securing the remaining 19 seats.

In the April 2009 municipal elections, ADEMA captured 30 percent of the available seats and five of the eight regional assemblies in the capital. While the government did not restrict opposition political parties from operating before or during the election, they did not perform well. The largest single opposition party, Rally for Mali (RPM), lost the only district it controlled in the capital, and a number of its young politicians broke off to form new political parties that performed well in the polls.

Tensions between the government and the marginalized ethnic Tuareg minority have erupted into violence over the years. Following a 1991 peace agreement and more than a decade of relative calm, a group of Tuareg army deserters attacked military barracks in 2006, demanding greater autonomy and development assistance. From 2006 to 2008, fighting continued amid a series of negotiations and ceasefires between the government and Tuareg rebels. Despite a 2008 peace agreement, the North Mali Tuareg Alliance for Change (ATNMC)—a rebel faction led by Ibrahim Bahanga—intensified its insurgency efforts. Violence throughout 2008 culminated in a December assault on an army base, followed by direct attacks on two pro-Toure Tuareg politicians that same month. The conflict had been transformed from a purely military operation isolated in the north to one that was both political and nationwide in scope, confirming President Toure's belief that negotiations with Bahanga were no longer possible. The army subsequently intensified its efforts, destroying the ATNMC's main base in January 2009. By April, hundreds of rebels had laid down their weapons and signed the 2008 agreement, while Bahanga fled to Libya.

While government relations with the Tuareg rebels appeared to have stabilized by the end of 2009, security in the north continued to be threatened by the growing activity of the terrorist organization al-Qaeda in the Islamic Maghreb (AQIM). As AQIM increases its operations, work or travel in the region has become nearly impossible, particularly for foreigners and known government supporters. At the end of 2008, AQIM kidnapped four European tourists, and one of them—a British national—was decapitated in May 2009, after the British government refused to release a radical cleric. While the other three hostages were released in July, the group assassinated a senior army intelligence officer in June, killed nearly 30 soldiers in an ambush on a military convoy in July, and took another European hostage in December. Originating during the Algerian civil war, AQIM is motivated by ideology rather than cultural grievances as the Tuareg rebels had been.

Although it is one of the world's least developed countries, Mali has undertaken significant political and economic reforms since the early 1990s, including a decentralization program that gave greater autonomy to local communities. Mali has benefited from international debt relief, and is currently working with the International Monetary Fund (IMF) to meet the targets under the Poverty Reduction and Growth Facility to improve Mali's budget.

Political Rights and Civil Liberties: Mali is an electoral democracy. During the 2007 presidential election, voting was peaceful, and international observers declared the results valid. The president, who appoints the prime minister, is elected by popular vote to serve up to two five-year terms. Members of the 147-seat unicameral National Assembly serve five-year terms, with 13 seats reserved to represent Malians living abroad.

Nearly 70 political parties operate in shifting electoral coalitions and are often organized around leading personalities, patronage, and ethnic or regional interests. The largest party is ADEMA, currently part of the ruling ADP coalition.

President Amadou Toumani Toure's government has launched anticorruption initiatives, including the creation of the Office of the General Auditor. However, corruption remains a problem, particularly in public procurement and contracting. Mali was ranked 111 out of 180 countries surveyed in Transparency International's 2009 Corruption Perceptions Index.

Mali's media have been considered among the freest in Africa. While dormant criminal libel laws were invoked by authorities in 2007, resulting in fines and suspended jail sentences, there have been no subsequent libel prosecutions, and there were no reports of harassment or intimidation of journalists in 2009. The government does not restrict internet access, although less than 1 percent of the population had access in 2009.

While Mali's population is predominantly Muslim and the High Islamic Council has a great deal of influence over politics, the state is secular, and minority religious rights are protected by law. Academic freedom is respected. In May 2009, the government launched a 10-year research and higher education reform plan in an effort improve both access to and quality of education at the nation's only institution of higher learning, the University of Bamako.

Freedoms of assembly and association are respected. In August 2009, some 50,000 people demonstrated peacefully in Bamako against the legislature's approval of a new family law. Many civic groups and nongovernmental organizations, including human rights groups, operate without interference, though the security situation in the north makes it very difficult to function there. The constitution guarantees workers the right to unionize, with the exception of those who provide "essential services," such as security force personnel or school principals.

The judiciary is not independent of the executive and is too weak to provide an adequate check on the other two branches of government. Local chiefs decide the majority of disputes in rural areas. Detainees are not always charged within the 48-hour period set by law, and there are lengthy delays in bringing defendants to trial. Police brutality has been reported, though courts have convicted some perpetrators. Prison conditions are harsh, and while human rights monitors are permitted to visit prisons, cumbersome administrative procedures reportedly make investigations difficult.

No ethnic group predominates in the government or security forces. Long-standing tensions between the marginalized Moor and Tuareg pastoralist groups on the one hand, and the more populous nonpastoralist ethnic groups on the other, have fueled intermittent instability.

Women are underrepresented in high political posts; 14 were elected to the National Assembly in 2007, and 5 of 27 cabinet ministers are women. Domestic violence against women is widespread, and cultural traditions have hindered reform. In August 2009, the National Assembly passed a new family law that had been under discussion for 10 years. The law would have raised the minimum age of marriage to 18 years and made both men and women the legal heads of the household. However, the law's approval was met with widespread opposition, including fervent protest from the High Islamic Council, and a 50,000-person demonstration. In response, the president asked the National Assembly to "reconsider" its decision and review the law before he approved it, leaving the law in limbo at year's end.

Although the constitution prohibits forced labor and child trafficking is punishable by 20 years in prison, adult trafficking is not criminalized. The U.S. State Department classifies Mali as a source, transit point, and destination country for women and children trafficked for the purposes of sexual exploitation and forced labor. While there were no child-trafficking prosecutions in 2009, a number of traffickers reportedly attempted to leave Mali with children; suspects were usually detained briefly and released without charge. Slavery remains a problem, particularly in the north, and according to some rights groups, there may be thousands living in conditions of servitude.

⬇ Malta

Political Rights: 1
Civil Liberties: 1
Status: Free

Population: 414,000
Capital: Valletta

Trend Arrow: Malta received a downward trend arrow due to its refusal to assist sea-going migrants in distress and the deplorable conditions of detention centers for migrants, which have yet to be brought up to European Union standards.

Ten-Year Ratings Timeline For Year Under Review (Political Rights, Civil Liberties, Status)

2000	2001	2002	2003	2004	2005	2006	2007	2008	2009
1,1F	1,1F	1,1F	1,1F	1,1F	1,1F	1,1F	1,1F	1,1F	1,1F

Overview:

Immigration issues emerged again for Malta in 2009 after the European Union Justice Commissioner publicly criticized the deplorable conditions for immigrants and asylum seekers in Malta's detention centers. In August, tensions arose with Italy, when Malta failed to rescue Eritrean migrants in distress off Malta's coast; Italian foreign minister Franco Frattini suggested Malta should hand over part of its search and rescue area to Italy.

After gaining independence from Britain in 1964, Malta joined the Commonwealth and became a republic in 1974. Power has alternated between the pro-Western, center-right Nationalist Party (PN) and the nonaligned, leftist Malta Labour Party (MLP). The PN pursued membership in the European Union (EU), which the country finally achieved in 2004.

In March 2004, the parliament elected Edward Fenech Adami, the outgoing prime minister and veteran PN leader, as president of the republic. Lawrence Gonzi, the deputy prime minister, took over the premiership.

Gonzi led the PN to a narrow victory over the MLP in the March 2008 elections; the PN won 49.3 percent of the overall vote, compared with 48.9 percent for the MLP. However, the results in the country's 13 five-seat electoral constituencies gave the MLP 34 seats and the PN just 31, triggering a constitutional provision that allowed extra seats to be added to ensure a legislative majority for the party winning the popular vote. The PN consequently received four additional seats. Voter turnout was 93 percent, the lowest the country had seen since 1971.

In January 2009, former Labour leader George Abela was nominated for president and was sworn in April. He was the first president to be nominated by a political party not in power and the first backed by both sides of the House since 1974. In June European Parliamentary elections, Simon Busuttil was reelected with a historical 69,000 votes.

In September 2008, the government welcomed the EU's adoption of the European Pact on Immigration and Asylum. Malta had long advocated a common EU immigration policy to help share the responsibility of integrating the influx of migrants it receives each year. Tensions over immigration flared up again in 2009, after

75 Eritrean migrants died at sea in August due to Malta's failure to send rescue vessels. Italian Foreign Minister Franco Frattini accused Malta of being ill-equipped to handle its vast search and rescue area (SAR), and urged Malta to either hand over part of its SAR to Italy or take in the asylum seekers that Italy saves within Malta's jurisdiction. However, Malta rejected Frattini's proposals. In March, EU Justice Commissioner Jacques Barrot criticized Malta for the deplorable conditions of its detention centers, including breakouts, riots, and overcrowding. The state of Maltese detention centers caused the nongovernmental organization (NGO) Medecins Sans Frontiers to leave Malta in protest that same month. The organization resumed its work in July, after improvements were made, allowing for medical practitioners to work under better conditions. Also in March, Malta struck an agreement with Libya, specifying that both countries would assist one another with search and rescue missions.

Political Rights and Civil Liberties: Malta is an electoral democracy. Members of the 65-seat unicameral legislature, the House of Representatives, are elected through proportional representation with a single-transferable-vote (STV) arrangement, allowing voters to rank competing candidates by preference. The parliament is elected for five-year terms, and lawmakers in turn elect the president, who also serves for five years. The president names the prime minister, usually the leader of the majority party or coalition. Elections are generally free and fair. After the 2008 elections, four extra seats were added to the parliament, for a total of 69 members, to ensure that the party winning the overall popular vote obtained a legislative majority.

The ruling PN and opposition MLP dominate national politics. The smaller Democratic Alternative party also competes, but is not currently represented in the parliament.

The EU has faulted Malta for its lack of a specific anticorruption program. In November 2009, the town mayor of Zebbug was accused of abuse of power for hiring council workers to work at his home. Also in November, Finance Minister Tonio Fenech was accused of corruption in property sales. Malta was ranked 45 out of 180 countries surveyed in Transparency International's 2009 Corruption Perceptions Index.

The constitution guarantees freedom of speech and of the press, though incitement to racial hatred is punishable by a jail term of six to eight months. Blasphemy is unlawful, and 162 criminal charges were initiated by authorities in 2009. There are several daily newspapers and weekly publications in Maltese and English, as well as radio and television stations, and residents have access to Italian television broadcasts. In February, *Malta Today* was fined EUR 7,000 (US$9,400) for an article printed four years earlier, which had mentioned the presence of slot machines at a local brasserie; the article was viewed as illegally promoting gambling. Mr. Fenech filed a libel suit against two *Malta Today* editors in October for casting doubts on his integrity as a minister. The lawsuit was pending at the year's end. After *Malta Today* broke the corruption story about Mr. Fenech in November, he filed judicial protest against *Malta Today* editor Matthew Vella, PL leader Joseph Muscat, who had confirmed the allegations, and the news head of One Production Ltd. Proceedings were still under way at the year's end. Also in November, University of Malta banned the student magazine *Ir-Realta'* for publishing a sexually charged story.

However, the editors sidestepped the ban by publishing the edition online. The government does not block internet access.

The constitution establishes Roman Catholicism as the state religion, and the state grants subsidies only to Catholic schools. While the population is overwhelmingly Roman Catholic, small communities of Muslims, Jews, and Protestants are tolerated and respected. There is one Muslim private school. Academic freedom is respected.

The constitution provides for freedoms of assembly and association, and the government generally respects these rights. NGOs investigating human rights issues are able to operate without state interference. The law recognizes the right to form and join trade unions, and limits on the right to strike were eased in 2002. However, a compulsory arbitration clause in the country's Employment and Industrial Relations Act allows the government to force a settlement on striking workers, contravening the International Labor Organization's Convention 87. The clause is reportedly used only when all other channels for arbitration have been exhausted. Approximately 55 percent of workers are unionized.

The judiciary is independent, and the rule of law prevails in civil and criminal matters. Prison conditions generally meet international standards, although the Council of Europe's Commission for Human Rights and the EU Justice Commissioner have criticized poor detention conditions for irregular migrants and asylum seekers, including overcrowding, rioting, and breakouts.

In a report released by the General Workers Union in September 2008, migrant workers are often exploited and subject to substandard working conditions. Malta faced criticism over immigration policies once again in 2009, though Malta and Libya reached an agreement in March to assist one another with rescue missions. In April 2009, Malta refused to assist a boat carrying 140 immigrants. Malta also ended a program called "Dar," which had paid for travel fare and had awarded a small stipend to migrants who voluntarily repatriated to their country of origin. In November, Malta won a bid to host the European Commission's European Asylum Support Office, which will facilitate communication and cooperation with EU member states on asylum applications. The office is projected to open in 2010.

Women occupy only 6 of the 69 seats in parliament, though they now hold two cabinet posts, the first to attain such senior government positions. Divorce is illegal, and violence against women continues to be a problem. Abortion is prohibited, even in cases of rape or incest. Malta is a destination for men and women trafficked for the purpose of sexual exploitation. Under European Commission directives, Malta changed the wording of its Equality for Men and Women Act in November 2009 to be more inclusive and in line with EU rules.

Marshall Islands

Political Rights: 1
Civil Liberties: 1
Status: Free

Population: 50,000
Capital: Majuro

Ten-Year Ratings Timeline For Year Under Review (Political Rights, Civil Liberties, Status)

2000	2001	2002	2003	2004	2005	2006	2007	2008	2009
1,1F	1,1F	1,1F	1,1F	1,1F	1,1F	1,1F	1,1F	1,1F	1,1F

Overview: Prime Minister Litokwa Tomeing survived his second vote of no confidence in March 2009 after he dismissed the foreign minister for publicly criticizing him. Another 1,500 residents left the Marshall Islands in 2009 for better work and education opportunities overseas; approximately one-third of the country's 54,000 citizens currently works or resides overseas.

The atolls and islands that make up the present-day Republic of the Marshall Islands (RMI) were claimed by Germany in 1885 and occupied by Japan during World War I. U.S. forces took control during World War II, and the RMI was placed under U.S. trusteeship in 1947. The country gained independence in 1986.

The RMI maintains close relations with the United States under a Compact of Free Association that first came into force in 1986. The pact allows the United States to maintain military facilities in the RMI in exchange for defense guarantees and development assistance. An amended compact that took effect in 2004 will run through 2023, promising annual U.S. transfers of US$57 million over the first 10 years and US$62 million per year for the following 10 years. The amended compact contains funding and accountability requirements that were absent in the original, but RMI citizens retain visa-free access to the United States to live, work, study, and seek medical services.

The 2004 compact extended use of the Kwajalein missile-testing range—the primary U.S. testing ground for long-range nuclear missiles and missile-defense systems since 1964—through 2066, and it has long been a source of controversy among the local people. Landowners have rejected the amended compact, demanding higher annual rent payments of US$19 million, instead of the U.S. offer of US$15 million. Their rejection has placed significant pressure on the national government, as the RMI relies on compact funds for nearly two-thirds of its annual budget.

Compensation for the victims of nuclear weapons testing conducted at the Bikini and Enewetak atolls more than 50 years ago has been another point of contention. Bikini remains uninhabitable and Enewetak is partly contaminated. While a US$150 million Nuclear Claims Fund is supposed to provide compensation for past, present, and future RMI claimants, victims argue that this sum is inadequate. The United States has refused to contribute more, maintaining that this sum is in addition to the US$1.5 billion already paid out for personal injury and property damages under the original compact.

Results of the January 2008 general elections gave no clear majority to any single party. However, the elections were considered free and fair by international observers. Former speaker and traditional chief Litokwa Tomeing of the Aelon Kein Ad (Our Islands) party was chosen as the new president by 18 of the 33 parliament members. Tomeing pledged transparency and good governance and assured Taiwan of continued diplomatic ties. He also promised renegotiation of the amended compact to obtain higher rents, more development assistance, and full compensation for those affected by weapons tests. In October 2008, Tomeing survived an opposition-led vote of no confidence. He defeated a second no-confidence vote in March 2009, which had been initiated by his supporters in protest of his dismissal of Foreign Minister Tony deBrum, a representative for Kwajalein. DeBrum had openly criticized the prime minister for failing to work with landowners to attain higher rent payments from the United States.

With limited education and employment opportunities, many residents take advantage of special privileges under the compact agreement and migrate to the United States. In 2009, a record 1,500 residents left the RMI. Approximately one-third of all RMI citizens currently reside overseas, primarily in the United States.

Political Rights and Civil Liberties: The RMI is an electoral democracy. The president is chosen for a four-year term by the unicameral House of Representatives (Nitijela), from among its members. The chamber's 33 members are directly elected to four-year terms. An advisory body, the Council of Chiefs (Iroij), consists of 12 traditional leaders, who are consulted on customary law. The two main political parties are Aelon Kein Ad and the United Democratic Party.

Corruption is a serious problem, and there has been little progress on reform efforts and improvements in transparency. A 2009 audit found that the Health Ministry could not account for US$273,000 spent in 2008. The country was not ranked in Transparency International's 2009 Corruption Perceptions Index.

The government generally respects freedom of speech and of the press. A privately owned newspaper, the *Marshall Islands Journal*, publishes articles in English and Marshallese. The government's *Marshall Islands Gazette* provides official news but avoids political coverage. Broadcast outlets include both government- and church-owned radio stations, and cable television offers a wide variety of international news and entertainment programs. Residents can also access U.S. armed forces radio and television in some parts of the country. The government does not restrict internet access, but penetration rates are low due to cost and technical difficulties.

Freedom of religion and academic freedom are respected in practice. The quality of secondary education remains low and four-year college education is rare. However, the College of the Marshall Islands offers two-year professional training courses and received full U.S. accreditation from the Western Association of Schools and Colleges in 2009 for the first time in seven years.

Citizen groups operate freely in the country. Many are sponsored by or affiliated with church organizations and provide social services. The government broadly interprets constitutional guarantees of freedom of assembly and association to cover trade unions. There is no formal right to strike or to engage in collective bargaining, but neither activity is prohibited.

The constitution provides for an independent judiciary. The government has raised judges' salaries in recent years to attract and retain more qualified jurists. Nearly all judges and attorneys are recruited from overseas. Police brutality is generally not a problem. Detention centers and prisons meet minimum international standards.

Despite the RMI's tradition of matrilineal inheritance in tribal rank and personal property, social and economic discrimination against women is widespread. Domestic violence against women is often alcohol related. Currently, only one woman sits in the parliament.

Mauritania

Political Rights: 6
Civil Liberties: 5
Status: Not Free

Population: 3,291,000
Capital: Nouakchott

Ten-Year Ratings Timeline For Year Under Review (Political Rights, Civil Liberties, Status)

2000	2001	2002	2003	2004	2005	2006	2007	2008	2009
6,5NF	5,5PF	5,5PF	6,5NF	6,5NF	6,4NF	5,4PF	4,4PF	6,5NF	6,5NF

Overview: General Mohamed Ould Abdel Aziz, who overthrew President Sidi Ould Cheikh Abdellahi in an August 2008 military coup, was declared the winner of a July 2009 presidential election. The results, while accepted by some foreign observers, were rejected by opposition parties.

Following independence from France in 1960, Mauritania was ruled by a series of civilian and military authoritarian regimes. In 1984, Colonel Maaouya Ould Sidi Ahmed Taya ousted President Mohamed Khouna Ould Haidallah. Although Taya introduced a multiparty system in 1991, he repeatedly secured poll victories for himself and his Democratic and Social Republican Party (PRDS) through the misuse of state resources, suppression of the opposition, and manipulation of the media and electoral institutions.

Soldiers led by Colonel Ely Ould Mohamed Vall finally overthrew Taya's government in August 2005, and the move was greeted with strong public support. Soon after taking power, the Military Council for Justice and Democracy (CMJD) pardoned and released hundreds of political prisoners, and dozens of political activists returned from exile. The CMJD set a timeline for holding elections and established an independent electoral commission to administer the process. Voters in June 2006 approved a constitutional amendment limiting presidents to two five-year terms. Legislative and municipal elections were held in November and December 2006, with independent candidates, mostly former PRDS members, securing a majority of the seats. Independents also won a majority of seats in January and February 2007 Senate elections. Sidi Ould Cheikh Abdellahi, running as an independent, won the presidency in March with 52 percent of the second-round vote. This series of elections were the first in Mauritania's history to be broadly viewed as generally free and fair.

Abdellahi drew criticism from military leaders and members of the National Party for Democracy and Development (PNDD), a propresidential party formed in early 2008, after he invited hard-line Islamists and former members of Taya's regime into the cabinet. The government resigned in June under the threat of a parliamentary no-confidence vote, and Abdellahi formed a new cabinet in July that included only PNDD members. This also failed to gain lawmakers' confidence, however, and 48 PNDD parliamentarians quit the party on August 4. On the morning of August 6, Abdellahi fired four leading generals. One of them, General Mohamed Ould Abdel Aziz, head of the Presidential Guard, then mounted a coup the same day. Security forces loyal to the coup leaders arrested the president, the prime minister, and several other officials.

Aziz and his allies announced that an 11-member junta, the High State Council (HSC), would run the country until new elections were held, but that other institutions, such as the parliament, could continue to function normally. While the international community strongly condemned the coup and key donors suspended nonhumanitarian aid, the domestic reaction was mixed. A majority of lawmakers and mayors expressed support, but a coalition of four pro-Abdellahi parties formed the National Front for the Defense of Democracy, and some parties refused to participate in the junta-led government, which was formed on September 1.

In April 2009, Aziz announced that he would resign from the military in order to run for president. The junta sought to hold a presidential election by June 2009 but faced resistance from opposition parties, civil society, and the international community. Opposition parties eventually agreed to participate in a vote after six days of negotiations in Senegal. Under international pressure, the HSC handed power in June to a transitional government made up of both opposition and coup supporters that would supervise an election set for July 18. As part of the deal, Abdellahi, who had been released from house arrest in late 2008, voluntarily resigned as president, and his former prime minister, who still faced corruption charges, was released on bail.

Aziz won the election in the first round with 52.6 percent of the vote. Four opposition parties challenged the results, claiming that they were prefabricated. The opposition also said electoral lists had been tampered with and voters had used fake ballot papers and identity cards. The parties lodged a formal appeal with the constitutional court, and the head of the electoral commission, Sid'Ahmed Ould Deye, resigned, saying he had doubts about the election's conduct. However, the constitutional court rejected the appeal. Observers from the International Organization of La Francophonie, the Arab League, and the African Union were satisfied with the fairness of the elections, though these groups are typically among the least critical of electoral conduct, and more credible observer groups were not present to assess the election.

Mauritania was one of only three Arab League members to have diplomatic relations with Israel, but in March 2009, the government closed the Israeli embassy in response to Israel's offensive in the Gaza Strip.

Despite the initiation of oil production in 2006, Mauritania remains one of the world's poorest countries, with some three-quarters of the population dependent on subsistence agriculture and livestock production. Mauritania imports about 70 percent of its food, and rising global food prices sparked social unrest in late 2007 and early 2008 that helped to weaken Abdellahi's presidency. In December 2009, the U.S. government reinstated Mauritania's preferential trading status under the African Growth and Opportunity Act (AGOA). The World Bank and the International Monetary Fund (IMF) also restarted their development programs, which had been suspended following the 2008 coup.

Political Rights and Civil Liberties: Mauritania is not an electoral democracy. The transitional elections of 2006 and 2007 were generally praised by independent observers, but constitutional government was suspended by the August 2008 military coup. Serious doubts have been raised about the legitimacy of the 2009 presidential election, which installed General Mohamed Ould Abdel Aziz as the civilian president almost exactly a year after he seized power.

Under the 1991 constitution, the president is responsible for appointing and dismissing the prime minister and cabinet, and a 2006 amendment imposed a limit of two five-year presidential terms. The bicameral legislature consists of the 95-seat National Assembly, elected to five-year terms by popular vote in single-member districts, and the 56-seat Senate, with 53 members elected by mayors and municipal councils and three members chosen by the rest of the chamber to represent Mauritanians living abroad. All senators serve six-year terms, with a third coming up for election every two years.

Elections for 17 Senate seats were held in November 2009. The Union for the Republic (UPR), formed in March by Aziz supporters, won 14 of the contests. The opposition accused the party of putting pressure on local authorities. Mauritania's party system is poorly developed, and clan and ethnic loyalties strongly influence the country's politics.

Corruption is believed to be a serious problem, and political instability has helped to prevent fiscal transparency from taking root in recent years. In September 2009, the World Bank suspended funding for the Global Fund to Fight AIDS, Tuberculosis, and Malaria after an audit uncovered embezzlement. The country coordinator and three other staff were arrested, but had not been tried by year's end. The Central Bank's former governor and his deputy were arrested in November for mismanaging and diverting nearly US$88 million in public funds. In December, two bank chairmen and a prominent businessman were arrested and charged with conspiracy for defrauding the Central Bank, though the opposition claimed they had been targeted for their support of an opposition candidate. Mauritania was ranked 130 out of 180 countries surveyed in Transparency International's 2009 Corruption Perceptions Index.

Press freedom improved during Abdellahi's presidency, but journalists continued to practice self-censorship, and private newspapers faced the threat of closure for material seen as offensive to Islam or threatening to the state. The military imposed new media restrictions after the 2008 coup, beginning with the takeover of state broadcast media. In March 2009, an online journalist for the website Taqadoumy was detained for three days after criticizing the government. Journalists attempted to stage a sit-in at the UN offices in Nouakchott in solidarity, but police raided the offices with tear gas. In May, the police assaulted a group of journalists and prevented them from covering a sit-in by the National Association of Lawyers. In August, the editor of *Taqadoumy*, Hanevy Ould Dehah, was fined and sentenced to six months in jail for "offending public decency." Press freedom groups denounced his punishment as excessive. Dehah completed his prison sentence on December 24, but was held through year's end without explanation.

Several private newspapers compete with state-run Arabic and French dailies, although their reach is limited by low circulation and literacy rates. There are no private radio or television stations licensed in the country, but Radio France Internationale broadcasts in the capital, and some residents have access to satellite television. The government sometimes attempts to restrict internet access, though little more than 1 percent of the population uses the medium.

Mauritania was declared an Islamic republic under the 1991 constitution, and proselytizing by non-Muslims is banned. In practice, however, non-Muslim communities have not been targeted for persecution. Academic freedom is respected.

The 1991 constitution guaranteed freedoms of association and assembly, and conditions grew more permissive when civilian rule was restored after the 2005 coup. In the wake of the 2008 coup, however, the junta banned protests and allowed only supporters to demonstrate. Amnesty International reports that the police violently broke up three peaceful protests against the proposed presidential election in April 2009.

Workers have the legal right to unionize and bargain for wages, but unions must be approved by the public prosecutor and often encounter hostility from employers. Although only about a quarter of Mauritanians are formally employed, the vast majority of workers in the industrial and commercial sectors are unionized. The right to strike is limited by notice requirements and bans on certain forms of strike action.

The judicial system is heavily influenced by the government. Many decisions are shaped by Sharia (Islamic law), especially in family and civil matters. Prison conditions are harsh, and security forces suspected of human rights abuses operate with impunity. There are reports that prisoners, particularly terrorism suspects, are subject to torture by authorities.

Mauritania has suffered a series of small-scale attacks by Islamist militants in recent years. In July 2009, a U.S. national was shot dead while trying to resist kidnapping; al-Qaeda in the Islamic Maghreb (AQIM) claimed responsibility, and three suspects have been arrested. AQIM also claimed responsibility for kidnapping three Spanish aid workers and two Italians in November and December. Also in December, the government introduced a new antiterrorism law, which expands the powers of security services.

The country's three main ethnic groups are the politically and economically dominant Moors of Arab and Berber descent; the black descendants of slaves, also known as Haratin or black Moors; and black Africans who are closer in ethnic heritage to the peoples of neighboring Senegal and Mali. Racial and ethnic discrimination persists in all spheres of political and economic life, almost universally to the disadvantage of darker-skinned communities. Despite a 1981 law banning slavery in Mauritania, an estimated half a million black Mauritanians are believed to live in conditions of servitude. A law that took effect in 2008 set penalties of 5 to 10 years in prison for slavery, but it drew criticism for not covering related practices such as forced marriage and indentured labor. In March 2009, the government announced a US$3.7 million program aimed at alleviating poverty among former slaves. Human trafficking is a serious problem, particularly the trafficking of children for various forms of forced labor and sexual exploitation. The U.S. State Department placed Mauritania in Tier 3, the worst possible ranking, in its 2009 Trafficking in Persons Report.

The Aziz government continued Abdellahi's initiative to facilitate the return of some 30,000 black Mauritanians who had been expelled to Senegal and Mali following communal violence in 1989. More than 17,000 reportedly returned during 2009. They have received housing assistance, but many faced difficulty recovering confiscated land.

Under rules established after the 2005 coup, party lists for the National Assembly elections had to include district-based quotas of female candidates. At the municipal level, women were guaranteed 20 percent of all seats. Women won 17 seats in the 2006 National Assembly elections and 30 percent of all municipal council seats. Nevertheless, discrimination against women persists. Under Sharia, a woman's testimony is given only half the weight of a man's. Legal protections regarding property and pay equity are usually respected only in urban areas among the educated elite. Female genital mutilation is illegal, but it is estimated that 65 percent of women have undergone some form of the practice. Abortion is prohibited except when the life of the mother is in danger.

Mauritius

Political Rights: 1
Civil Liberties: 2
Status: Free

Population: 1,276,000
Capital: Port Louis

Ten-Year Ratings Timeline For Year Under Review (Political Rights, Civil Liberties, Status)

2000	2001	2002	2003	2004	2005	2006	2007	2008	2009
1,2F	1,2F	1,2F	1,2F	1,1F	1,1F	1,2F	1,2F	1,2F	1,2F

Overview: The Mauritian economy was adversely affected in 2009 by the global recession and the expanding reach and incidence of piracy in the Indian Ocean. Meanwhile, Mauritius again was ranked highest among all African countries on the Ibrahim Index of African Governance.

Mauritius's ethnically mixed population is primarily descended from immigrants brought as laborers from the Indian subcontinent during the island's 360 years of Dutch, French, and British colonial rule. Since gaining independence from Britain in 1968, Mauritius has maintained one of the developing world's most successful democracies.

Navinchandra Ramgoolam served as prime minister from 1995 until 2000, when President Cassam Uteem called early elections. The opposition alliance, led by the Mauritian Socialist Movement (MSM), won the vote, and its leader, Sir Anerood Jugnauth, returned to the premiership, having previously held the post between 1982 and 1995. In a planned power shift, Paul Berenger, the leader of the Mauritian Militant Movement (MMM)—which was allied with the MSM—became prime minister in September 2003, the first person from outside the island's Indian-origin majority to hold the post.

In the 2005 parliamentary elections, frustration with rising unemployment and inflation contributed to victory for the opposition Social Alliance, led by Ramgoolam. However, in 2006, rising prices and concerns about increased criminal activity diminished the popularity of the new government, which had adopted a number of policies designed to further liberalize the economy, including the sale of government assets and reforms of the labor market, the pension system, social security, taxation, and facilities for foreign investors.

In 2008, the Mauritius National Assembly approved legislation establishing a Truth and Justice Commission to examine the country's history of slavery and indentured labor and to consider possible reparations. That same year, former inhabitants of the Chagos Islands, who had been evicted to Mauritius by Britain to make way for a military base in the 1960s, lost a long-running legal battle with the British government to secure their return.

The government has actively sought to promote itself as an economic gateway to Africa; Mauritius has reportedly attracted more than 9,000 offshore entities since independence in 1968, with the banking sector alone drawing more than US$1 billion in investments. The World Bank's 2010 report on the ease of doing business ranked Mauritius 17 out of 183 countries surveyed. However, real GDP growth declined from nearly 5 percent from 2005 to 2008 to approximately 2.5 percent in 2009. Although the Mauritian economy was adversely affected by the expanding reach and incidence of piracy in the Indian Ocean, the government declined to set up a facility to detain suspected pirates.

Political Rights and Civil Liberties: Mauritius is an electoral democracy. Since independence, Mauritius has regularly chosen its representatives in free, fair, and competitive elections. The head of state is a largely ceremonial president elected by the unicameral National Assembly for a five-year term. Executive power resides with the prime minister, who is appointed by the president from the party or coalition with the most seats in the legislature. Of the National Assembly's 70 members, 62 are directly elected and 8 are appointed from among unsuccessful candidates who gained the largest number of votes; all members serve five-year terms.

The main political groupings are the ruling Social Alliance coalition—which depends largely on the ethnic Indian majority—and the opposition alliance of the MMM and MSM; the two blocs have alternated in power for decades. Decentralized structures govern the country's small island dependencies. The largest of these is Rodrigues Island, which has its own government, local councils, and two seats in the National Assembly.

The country continues to enjoy a generally positive reputation for transparency and accountability. Mauritius was ranked 42 out of 180 countries surveyed in Transparency International's 2009 Corruption Perceptions Index. It also has ranked first in the Ibrahim Index of African Governance since its inception in 2007.

The constitution guarantees freedom of expression, and several private daily and weekly publications are often highly critical of both government and opposition politicians and their policies. The state-owned Mauritius Broadcasting Corporation (MBC) operates radio and television services and generally reflects government viewpoints. An MBC journalist was arrested in 2009 and suspended from his job for making derogatory remarks against the prime minister. A small number of private radio stations have been authorized, but the state-run media enjoy a monopoly in broadcasting local news. Internet use is widespread and unrestricted, with four different service providers.

Freedom of religion is respected, as is academic freedom.

The right to freedoms of assembly and association are honored, though police occasionally use excessive force in response to riots. The island's nine labor federations include 300 unions. A 2008 labor law gives employers greater flexibility in hiring and firing workers. In 2009, approximately 65,000 foreign workers were employed in 404 export processing zones, although their living and working conditions were generally very poor. Reports by the International Trade Union Confederation in both 2008 and 2009 criticized Mauritius for restricting internationally accepted labor rights practices. In March 2009, police dispersed a peaceful demonstration by Bangladeshis protesting against the Mauritian government's decision to terminate their work contracts. In July, the government announced plans to repatriate up to 6,000 Bangladeshi laborers.

The generally independent judiciary, headed by the Supreme Court, administers a legal system that is an amalgam of French and British traditions. Civil rights are for the most part well respected, although individual cases of police brutality have been reported.

Various ethnic cultures and traditions flourish in peace, and constitutional prohibitions against discrimination are generally respected. However, Mauritian Creoles, descendants of African slaves who comprise about a third of the population, live in poverty and complain of unfair treatment. Tensions between the Hindu majority and Muslim minority persist, constituting one of the country's few potential ethnic flashpoints. In addition, although they have not been the victims of formal discrimination, resettled Chagos Islanders have not been integrated into society and suffer from high levels of unemployment.

Women make up approximately 20 percent of the paid labor force and generally occupy a subordinate role in society. Women currently hold 17 percent of the seats in the National Assembly, though they occupy only 5 percent of the senior positions in the 100 top companies. Domestic violence against women continues to be a major problem.

Mexico

Political Rights: 2
Civil Liberties: 3
Status: Free

Population: 109,610,000
Capital: Mexico City

Ten-Year Ratings Timeline For Year Under Review (Political Rights, Civil Liberties, Status)

2000	2001	2002	2003	2004	2005	2006	2007	2008	2009
2,3F	2,3F	2,2F	2,2F	2,2F	2,2F	2,3F	2,3F	2,3F	2,3F

Overview: Violence associated with organized crime, particularly drug trafficking, again rose dramatically in 2009, resulting in the deaths of at least 7,700 people. The government continued to deploy troops to the areas most affected by violence even as allegations of rights abuses by the military increased. The opposition Institutional Revolutionary Party (PRI) and its allies captured a majority of seats in July elections for the lower house of Congress, and in December, President Felipe Calderon proposed a package of major political reforms.

Mexico achieved independence from Spain in 1810 and became a republic in 1822. Seven years after the Revolution of 1910, a new constitution established the United Mexican States as a federal republic. From its founding in 1929 until 2000, the Institutional Revolutionary Party (PRI) dominated the country through patronage, corruption, and repression. The formal business of government often took place in secret, and the rule of law was frequently compromised by arbitrary power.

In the landmark 2000 presidential election, Vicente Fox Quesada of the National Action Party (PAN) defeated the candidates of the PRI and the leftist Party of the Democratic Revolution (PRD), capturing 42.5 percent of the vote. The new president assembled a cabinet that included businessmen and intellectuals, announced plans to overhaul the notoriously corrupt and inefficient law enforcement agencies, and pledged to make Mexico an international leader in human rights.

By 2003, Fox's greatest achievements remained his defeat of the long-ruling PRI, providing for more open and accountable government, and arresting some leaders of the country's vicious drug cartels. However, solutions to the problems of poverty, corruption, crime, and unemployment proved elusive. Elections held in July 2003 confirmed the PRI as the most powerful party in Congress and in many state governments.

The 2006 presidential election was extremely close, with PAN candidate Felipe Calderon defeating Mexico City mayor Andres Manuel Lopez Obrador of the PRD by a mere 244,000 votes in the initial count. Lopez Obrador claimed that the result was fraudulent and declared himself the winner. For several months, he sought the annulment of the election and a full recount, but many Mexicans—and most international observers—were not convinced by the PRD's evidence of fraud. In September, after a partial recount, the Federal Electoral Tribunal formally declared Calderon the winner. Though the PAN won the most seats in the congressional elections, with 206 in the Chamber of Deputies and 52 in the Senate, the PRD's share of deputies exceeded the PRI's for the first time.

Several outbreaks of social unrest occurred in 2006. In April, a large demonstration in the town of San Salvador Atenco led to clashes between police and protesters that left two people dead, more than 200 arrested, and legal controversies over police conduct and protesters' harsh prison sentences. An even more serious crisis erupted in Oaxaca, where an attempt by Governor Ulises Ruiz of the PRI to forcefully disperse protesters led to months of violence that caused over a dozen deaths before Fox sent in federal police in late October.

In 2007, Calderon managed to forge legislative coalitions with opposition lawmakers to pass pension, tax, electoral, and judicial reforms, but political wrangling increased in 2008, due to an attempted reform of the petroleum sector and the approach of the 2009 congressional elections. The PRI emerged from the July 2009 balloting with control of the Chamber of Deputies, and for a third straight year, the party outperformed its rivals in state and local elections, which were held in six states in 2009.

Violence associated with organized crime, particularly drug trafficking, continued to worsen in 2009, despite Calderon's decision to deploy the military to the worst-affected areas after taking office in 2006. An expanded troop deployment in Juarez in early 2009 temporarily diminished the volume of killings there, but a subsequent upsurge dented local confidence in the authorities, as did mounting allegations of severe human rights violations by the military. December 2009 was the deadliest month of Calderon's term to date, causing increased criticism of the government's anticrime policies.

Mexico's economy also suffered during the year, with gross domestic product declining by an estimated 6.5 percent. The global economic downturn helped to reduce remittances from the United States and significantly slowed migration, even as U.S. authorities continued to step up deportations. The economy, particularly the tourism industry, was also buffeted by Mexico's status as the epicenter of an H1N1 influenza outbreak that began in March.

As the country prepared to enter its bicentennial year in 2010, a generalized sense of political dysfunction spurred Calderon to propose major political reforms in December. Among other changes, the package would allow limited reelection for many elected officials, permit candidates to run as independents, provide for a second round of voting in presidential elections, reduce the size of Congress, and grant the president a line-item veto on budget bills.

Political Rights and Civil Liberties: Mexico is an electoral democracy. The president is elected to a six-year term and cannot be reelected. The bicameral Congress consists of the 128-member Senate, elected for six years through a mix of direct voting and proportional representation, with at least two parties represented in each state's delegation, and the 500-member Chamber of Deputies, with 300 elected directly and 200 through proportional representation, all for three-year terms. Members of Congress are also currently barred from reelection. Each state has an elected governor and legislature.

Mexico's Federal Electoral Institute (IFE), which supervises elections and enforces political party laws, has come to be viewed as a model for other countries. The 2006 elections were considered generally free and fair, but there were many complaints, especially by the opposition PRD, concerning negative advertising and the use of administrative resources on behalf of the presidential victor, Felipe Calderon of the ruling PAN. In response, an electoral reform was passed in 2007 to regulate strictly campaign financing and the content of political advertising. Supporters argued that the reform would sever the links between politics and Mexico's often oligarchic business interests, while critics claimed that the new rules would weaken free speech and further increase the power of the main three parties—the PAN, the PRI, and the PRD. Opinion was mixed regarding the efficacy of the reform in its first major test, the 2009 Chamber of Deputies elections, but the contest overall was considered free and fair. The PRI garnered 237 seats, with its allied Green Party (PVEM) taking 21, thereby assuring PRI control of the chamber. The PAN's share fell to 143 seats, and the PRD declined to a distant third, with 71 seats.

Official corruption remains a serious problem. According to the 2009 Latinobarometro poll, 17 percent of Mexicans stated that they or a relative had been party to a corrupt act in the previous 12 months, though this represented a sharp decline from the 2002–2005 average of 54 percent. Billions of dollars in illegal drug money is believed to enter the country each year from the United States, and there is a perception that drug money affects politics, particularly on the state and local levels. In May 2009, federal officials arrested more than a dozen political functionaries in Michoacan for ties to the locally dominant La Familia criminal organization. Given the arrests' proximity to the July elections, the PRD state governor, Leonel Godoy, accused the government of politicizing justice. An arrest warrant was issued in July for Godoy's half-brother, a newly elected PRD congressman. Other scandals uncovered in 2009 involved the misappropriation of agricultural subsidies, the siphoning of oil from state-owned pipelines, and the opaque licensing of day-care facilities; the last came to light following a June fire that killed 48 children in Sonora. No senior politicians have been convicted of corruption in recent years, though many security officials have been dismissed or charged with links to drug traffickers. Mexico was ranked 89 out of 180 countries surveyed in Transparency International's 2009 Corruption Perceptions Index.

Legal and constitutional guarantees of free speech have been gradually improving, but the security environment for journalists has deteriorated markedly. No longer dependent on the government for advertising and subsidies, the competitive press has taken the lead in denouncing official corruption, though serious investigative reporting is scarce. Broadcast media are dominated by two corporations that control over 90 percent of the stations. Defamation was decriminalized at the federal level in 2007, and while it remains a crime in many states, a 2009 Supreme Court decision expanded the range of reporting protected from such state laws.

Since a sharp increase in violence in 2006, reporters probing police issues, drug trafficking, and official corruption have faced a high risk of physical harm. According to the National Human Rights Commission, 13 journalists were killed in 2009, making Mexico one of the world's most dangerous countries for journalists. Self-censorship has increased, and many newspapers in high-violence zones no longer publish bylines on stories involving organized crime. Press freedom groups have repeatedly noted that the special prosecutor's office devoted to investigating these acts has made only slow progress since opening in 2006. Mexico's 2002 freedom of information law, despite some limitations, has been considered successful at strengthening transparency at the federal level, though many states lag behind. The government does not restrict internet access.

Religious freedom is constitutionally protected and generally respected in practice. However, it is limited in some areas, and political battles over issues such as abortion and homosexual rights have led to an increase in religious discourse in the public sphere in recent years. The government does not restrict academic freedom.

Constitutional guarantees regarding free assembly and association are generally respected, but political and civic expression is restricted in some regions. In February 2009, the Supreme Court cleared top state officials of responsibility for the violence between police and protesters in Atenco in 2006. Nongovernmental organizations, though increasingly active, sometimes face violent resistance, including threats and occasional murders. The United Nations documented 128 acts of aggression against human rights defenders between 2006 and August 2009, with an impunity rate of over 98 percent.

Although Mexican trade unions' role as a pillar of the PRI has diminished significantly, independent unions have long faced government and management interference. Informal, nontransparent negotiations between employers and politically connected union leaders often result in "protection contracts" that govern employee rights but are never seen by workers. In addition, workers attempting to form independent unions are frequently fired by management. The government's closure of a state-run electric company in October 2009 angered the powerful electrical workers' union, which argued that the move was politically motivated. The government and many analysts maintained that the closure was necessary to improve the efficiency of state services.

The justice system remains plagued by delays and unpredictability. In June 2008, Congress passed a major constitutional reform that replaced the civil-inquisitorial trial system with an oral-adversarial one. An explicit presumption of innocence and stricter rules regarding evidence were also included, and the reform was widely expected to strengthen due process and increase efficiency and fairness. Nonetheless, human rights groups raised concerns about the vague definition of organized crime and the substantially weaker protections, including extended detention without charge, afforded to organized crime suspects. Implementation of the new system, expected to take eight years, proceeded slowly in 2009.

In rural areas, respect for laws by official agencies remains tenuous, and coordination between federal authorities and the state and local police is problematic, with purges of local police forces adding to the tension in 2008 and 2009. In many of the most crime-plagued zones, federal police and troops have, upon arrival, simply relieved local police of duty. Lower courts and law enforcement in general are undermined by widespread bribery, and a significant majority of crimes go unreported, because the underpaid police are viewed as either inept or in league with criminals. Torture, arbitrary arrest, and abuse of prisoners persist in many areas. Although the federal prosecutor's office announced in late 2009 that over 225,000 drug-related arrests had been made during Calderon's term, it acknowledged that nearly 75 percent of those arrested were subsequently freed. Prisons are violent and overcrowded, and pretrial detainees account for over 40 percent of inmates. Several prison riots in 2009 resulted in the deaths of scores of prisoners, while 53 prisoners fled a facility in Zacatecas in May without interference by guards. In the face of the government's seeming ineffectiveness, reports of vigilante activity increased in 2009.

Presidential authority over the armed forces is extensive, but the military has historically operated beyond public scrutiny, and human rights advocates have warned that its strengthened counternarcotics role has not been accompanied by increased clarity regarding limitations on its conduct. Complaints of abuse increased dramatically in 2009, including allegations of kidnapping, torture, rape, and murder. Although three soldiers were convicted of rape in a civil court in 2007, military personnel are generally tried in military courts, and most observers agree that the government's affirmations of these courts' effectiveness are not backed by credible evidence. In addition, an estimated 150,000 soldiers have deserted since 2000, providing a large pool of trained recruits for organized crime.

Although overall homicide rates have declined since the mid-1990s, the number of deaths attributed to drugs and organized crime has risen sharply in recent years, with over 7,700 in 2009 alone. The carnage was concentrated in northern Mexico, particularly in Ciudad Juarez, where over 2,600 killings occurred, making it one of the world's deadliest cities. The murders often featured extreme brutality and torture designed to maximize the psychological impact on civilians, authorities, and rival groups. On several occasions in 2009, apparent noncombatants were specifically targeted.

In addition to homicides, organized criminals have increased kidnappings, extortion, and other offenses. The government took a number of steps in 2008 and

2009 to curb the violence and ease popular frustration, including consultations with civic leaders, the signing of a US$1.4 billion counternarcotics aid agreement with the United States, the continued deployment of over 45,000 troops, the reformation of the federal police, the decriminalization of possession of small quantities of drugs, and numerous arrests.

Mexican law bans all forms of discrimination, including those based on ethnic origin, gender, age, and religion. Nevertheless, social and economic discrimination has marginalized indigenous peoples. Their ability to participate in decisions affecting their land and cultural traditions is usually negligible, and many are relegated to extreme poverty in rural villages that lack essential services. The government has attempted to improve indigenous-language services in the justice system, an area of major concern. In August and November 2009, the Supreme Court ordered the release of 29 indigenous prisoners who had been convicted in connection with a notorious 1997 massacre in Chiapas, citing severe procedural irregularities in their cases. Indigenous groups, particularly in Chihuahua and southern states, were harmed by the criminal violence in 2009. Rights groups also frequently detail the persecution and criminal predation faced by migrants from Central America, who are often bound for the United States.

Domestic violence and sexual abuse are common, and perpetrators are rarely punished. Implementation of a 2007 law designed to protect women from such crimes remains halting, particularly at the state level. Mexico is both a major source and a transit country for trafficked persons. Internal trafficking is also a problem. The murder of hundreds of women in the U.S. border zone over the last 15 years has remained a controversial subject; in Ciudad Juarez, the number of women killed, along with the overall murder rate, has risen substantially in recent years . Abortion became an increasingly contentious issue in 2009, as many states reacted to Mexico City's 2007 liberalization of abortion laws by strengthening their own criminal bans on the procedure in most circumstances.

Micronesia

Political Rights: 1
Civil Liberties: 1
Status: Free

Population: 111,000
Capital: Palikir

Ten-Year Ratings Timeline For Year Under Review (Political Rights, Civil Liberties, Status)

2000	2001	2002	2003	2004	2005	2006	2007	2008	2009
1,2F	1,2F	1,2F	1,1F	1,1F	1,1F	1,1F	1,1F	1,1F	1,1F

Overview: Following March 2009 congressional elections, the government of the Federated States of Micronesia (FSM) proposed an amendment to the constitution in May that would increase terms for representatives of single-member districts from two to four years. That same month, the FSM's former ambassador to the United States, Jesse Marehalau, was convicted of corruption.

The United States administered Micronesia, which included the Marshall Islands and other Pacific island groups, between 1947 and 1979 as a UN Trust Territory. In 1970, the Northern Marianas, Marshall Islands, and Palau demanded separate status from Kosrae, Pohnpei, Chuuk, and Yap; these latter four territories, representing 607 islands, became the Federated States of Micronesia (FSM). The FSM adopted a constitution and became self-governing in 1979 as the trusteeship expired and status negotiations with the United States continued.

In 1986, the FSM signed its first Compact of Free Association with the United States, which provides the FSM with U.S. economic and defense assistance in exchange for U.S. military bases in the islands. An amended compact, which extends this core commitment for another 20 years, came into effect in 2003. Compact funds, which represent about one-third of the FSM's national income, have contributed to education, health, the environment, capacity building, infrastructure, and private sector development. Money also goes to a trust fund overseen by a joint board of U.S. and FSM trustees. However, the allocation of funds has been a source of serious tension in federal-state relations, and several states threatened to leave the federation and seek separate bilateral treaties with the United States unless larger shares of the compact payments were distributed. The federal congress subsequently agreed to distribute larger shares to each of the four states. To improve transparency and accountability in its use of compact funds, a new record system was launched to track compact fund projects in November 2009.

Congressional elections held in March 2009 were deemed largely free and fair. Twenty-one independent candidates ran for the 10 two-year term seats up for election; no women competed. In May, the government passed an amendment to the constitution that would give all representatives of Congress four-year terms; the amendment must be approved by voters in the 2011 election. Five candidates competed in a special election for one of the Pohnpei seats in October after its incumbent, Resio Moses, died suddenly in June.

Political Rights and Civil Liberties: The FSM is an electoral democracy. The unicameral, 14-member Congress has one directly elected representative, serving four-year terms, from each of the four constituent states, and 10 representatives directly elected for two-year terms from single-member districts. Chuuk state, home to nearly half of the FSM's population, holds the largest number of congressional seats; this has been a source of resentment among the three smaller states. The president and vice president are chosen by Congress from among the four state representatives to serve four-year terms. By informal agreement, the two posts are rotated among the representatives of the four states. Emanuel Mori of Chuuk and Alik L. Alik of Kosrae were chosen as president and vice president, respectively, in 2007. Each state has its own constitution, elected legislature, and governor; the state governments have considerable power, particularly in budgetary matters. Traditional leaders and institutions exercise significant influence in society, especially at the village level.

There are no formal political parties, but there are no restrictions on their formation. Political loyalties are based mainly on geography, clan relations, and personality.

Official corruption and abuses are widespread and a major source of voter discontent. The United States suspended compact payments to the state of Chuuk in

August 2008 after it failed to implement plans for proper financial and management oversight; payments were resumed in 2009 after new oversight measures were put in place. In May, former FSM ambassador to the United States Jesse Marehalau was found guilty of corruption for his involvement in a fake passport scheme. He was sentenced to two concurrent prison terms, which were largely suspended except for 30 months, and a restitution fine of US$3,000. The FSM was not rated in Transparency International's 2009 Corruption Perceptions Index.

The news media operate freely. Print outlets include government-published newsletters and several small, privately owned weekly and monthly newspapers. Television stations operate in three of the four states. Each state government runs its own radio station, and the Baptist church runs a fifth station. Cable television is available in Pohnpei and Chuuk, and satellite television is increasingly common. Use of the internet is also growing, but low incomes and small populations make it difficult for service providers to expand coverage.

Religious freedom is respected in this mainly Christian country. There are no reports of restrictions on academic freedom, but lack of funds negatively affects the quality of and access to education.

Freedom of assembly is respected, and citizens are free to organize civic groups. A small number of student and women's organizations are active. No labor unions exist, though there are no laws against their formation. No specific laws regulate work hours, recognize the right to strike and bargain collectively, or set workplace health and safety standards. The economy is dependent on fishing, tourism, subsistence agriculture, and U.S. assistance.

The judiciary is independent, but it lacks funds to improve the functioning of the courts. There is also cultural resistance to using the court system, particularly for sex crimes.

Women enjoy equal rights under the law, including those regarding property ownership and employment. Women generally receive equal pay for equal work and are well represented in the lower and middle ranks of the state and federal governments. However, there are no women in parliament, and social and economic discrimination against women persists in the male-dominated culture. Domestic violence is common, and cases often go unreported because of family pressure, fear of reprisal, or an expectation of inaction by the authorities. Offenders rarely face trial, and those found guilty usually receive light sentences.

Moldova

Political Rights: 3*
Civil Liberties: 4
Status: Partly Free

Population: 4,133,000
Capital: Chisinau

Ratings Change: Moldova's political rights rating improved from 4 to 3 due to parliamentary elections that resulted in a rotation of power between the long-ruling Communist Party and a coalition of opposition parties.

Note: The numerical ratings and status listed above do not reflect conditions in Transnistria, which is examined in a separate report.

Ten-Year Ratings Timeline For Year Under Review (Political Rights, Civil Liberties, Status)

2000	2001	2002	2003	2004	2005	2006	2007	2008	2009
2,4PF	2,4PF	3,4PF	3,4PF	3,4PF	3,4PF	3,4PF	3,4PF	4,4PF	3,4PF

Overview:

The ruling Communist Party won April parliamentary elections amid claims of fraud, triggering antigovernment violence by young protesters in the capital. Police allegedly responded with severe beatings and other human rights abuses. The Communists, with their narrow legislative majority, were unable to elect a new president, leading to repeat parliamentary elections in July. An alliance of opposition parties won the vote and formed a new government, but they were also unable to muster the three-fifths majority required to elect a president, meaning a third round of parliamentary elections would have to be held in 2010.

Moldova gained independence from the Soviet Union in 1991, and free and fair elections were held in 1994. The Communist Party of Moldova (PCRM) took power at the head of a majority coalition in 1998 and won a landslide victory in 2001 on the promise of a return to Soviet-era living standards. Vladimir Voronin was elected president by Parliament.

The PCRM took 56 of 101 seats in the 2005 parliamentary elections and built a coalition to obtain the 61 votes needed to reelect Voronin. Election monitors highlighted a number of flaws during the campaign, including police harassment of the opposition, manipulation of the state media, and abuse of state funds by the PCRM.

After charting a foreign policy course away from Russia and toward the European Union (EU) in the period surrounding the elections, Voronin steered the country back toward Russia in 2007 and 2008. The Kremlin's cooperation was seen as essential in resolving the status of Transnistria, a separatist region that had maintained de facto independence from Moldova since 1992.

As Voronin repaired ties with Russia, his government's friction with Romania increased. After Romania joined the EU in January 2007, many Moldovans had applied for Romanian citizenship, taking advantage of the fact that much of Moldova had been part of Romania prior to World War II. This trend, coupled with the two countries' essentially identical dominant languages, stoked government concerns that Romania was seeking to undermine Moldovan nationhood.

The ruling PCRM won 60 seats in April 2009 parliamentary elections, though international monitors noted flaws in the voter lists, intimidation and harassment of opposition parties, and media bias, among other problems. Three opposition parties also won representation: the Liberal Party (PL) and the Liberal Democratic Party (PLD), each with 15 seats, and the Our Moldova Alliance (AMN), with 11. The results triggered youth-led protests in the capital on the day after the balloting, and the demonstrations turned violent on the second day, with some protesters ransacking government buildings. Police responded with beatings and hundreds of arrests, and three suspected deaths at the hands of police were reported.

The PCRM chose Voronin, who was constitutionally barred from seeking a third presidential term, as the new Parliament speaker. However, the party needed a three-fifths legislative majority, or 61 votes, to elect Prime Minister Zinaida Greceanii as the new president. It failed twice to elect its candidate, triggering fresh parliamentary elections in July. Although similar flaws were reported by observers, the balloting reduced the PCRM's share to 48 seats, with four opposition parties capturing the majority. The PLD took 18, followed by the PL with 15, the Democratic Party (PD) with 13, and the AMN with 7.

The new majority, calling itself the Alliance for European Integration (AIE), subsequently elected PLD leader Vlad Filat as prime minister and PL leader Mihai Ghimpu as Parliament Speaker. PD leader Marian Lupu was its presidential candidate; he had served as Parliament Speaker until May, and then defected from the PCRM to the opposition in June. However, the AIE failed twice—in November and December—to secure his election, meaning a third bout of parliamentary elections would have to be scheduled for 2010. In the interim, Filat's government would remain in place, with Ghimpu serving as acting president.

After convening in September, the new AIE-led Parliament began repairing relations with Bucharest. Voronin had blamed the April rioting on Romania, expelling the country's ambassador and imposing visa requirements on Romanian travelers; Romania had responded by making it easier for Moldovans to obtain Romanian citizenship. Among other steps, the AIE quickly reversed the visa rule and overturned a law barring public servants from holding dual citizenship.

Political Rights and Civil Liberties: Moldova is an electoral democracy. Voters elect the 101-seat unicameral Parliament proportional representation for four-year terms. Since 2000, Parliament has elected the president, who serves for up to two four-year terms. His choice for prime minister must then be approved by Parliament.

The April 2009 parliamentary elections, like previous elections, were marred by flawed voter lists, progovernment media bias, the abuse of administrative resources, and intimidation of opposition parties. Opposition critics focused on the voter lists, which had increased in size since 2005 despite a declining population. The voter rolls grew again ahead of the July repeat elections, which suffered from a similar set of flaws. In one apparent improvement between the April and July votes, the vote threshold for party representation in Parliament was lowered from 6 percent to 5 percent.

Corruption has been a major problem in Moldova, and high-profile antigraft prosecutions under the PCRM government often appeared politicized. Anticorruption officials reported in late 2008 that no public servant had ever been fired for missing or faulty income declarations. Access to information remains limited, and a bill on state secrets that was approved by Parliament in 2008 drew criticism for its broad scope and potential conflicts with the existing access to information law. Moldova was ranked 89 out of 180 countries surveyed in Transparency International's 2009 Corruption Perceptions Index.

Print media present a range of opinions, but they are not widely available in rural areas. The criminal code, along with June 2008 amendments to the Law on Editorial Activity, contains vague provisions banning defamation of the state and the people. Prison sentences for libel were abolished in 2004, but journalists practice self-censorship to avoid crippling fines. In the 2009 elections, public broadcasters and the PCRM-owned television station NIT favored the ruling party, while certain smaller stations like the Romanian-owned Pro TV and the radio station Vocea Basarabiei were more critical of the government. Outlets that air critical or opposition views were excluded from frequency distributions, threatened with license revocations, and harassed through criminal investigations in the months before the voting. During and after the April rioting, news websites and other internet-based media were temporarily disrupted, and many Romanian and foreign journalists were turned back at the border or expelled. Other journalists were briefly arrested and intimidated by police.

Although the constitution guarantees religious freedom, the government has shown its preferences through the selective enforcement of registration rules. A law passed in 2007 banned "abusive proselytism" and denied legal status to groups with fewer than 100 members. It also acknowledged the, "special significance and primary role," of the Orthodox Church; the PCRM government clearly favored the backed Moldovan Orthodox Church and showed hostility toward the Romanian-backed Bessarabian Orthodox Church. Authorities do not restrict academic freedom, but bribery and dismal salaries in the education system remain problems.

Citizens may participate freely in nongovernmental organizations (NGOs). However, private organizations must register with the state, and some NGOs have complained of bureaucratic obstruction and police harassment. Under legislation passed in February 2008, organizers of demonstrations must only give notice to authorities, but some local officials reportedly continued to require permits in 2009. Hundreds of people were arrested in connection with the April 2009 postelection protests, and many reported severe beatings and other abuse both before and after arrest. Organizers were charged with a range of offenses, though these charges were dropped under the new government in the fall. Civil society groups blamed for the unrest were scrutinized by tax officials in its wake. Nevertheless, human rights groups held a march in July to protest police abuses. Authorities have exerted pressure on unions and their members, and employers are rarely punished for violating union rights. During the 2009 campaign periods, public employees were reportedly pressured to attend political events.

Although the constitution provides for an independent judiciary, there is evidence of bribery and political influence among judicial and law enforcement officials. The authorities have pursued politicized criminal cases against government opponents, and long-standing concerns about abuse and ill-treatment in police custody were renewed in the aftermath of the April 2009 protests. At least three people reportedly died in the crackdown, and detainees were allegedly charged collectively with no access to counsel. In December, the new government filed charges against the former interior minister and the former Chisinau police chief in connection with the police response to the protests. Prison conditions in general are exceptionally poor. About a dozen inmates began a hunger strike in November to protest beatings and a lack of light and heat in their cells.

In an apparent act of political violence, an attacker threw a grenade into the crowd at an outdoor concert in October, injuring 40 people. Police linked the blast to telephone threats received by Prime Minister Vlad Filat's office the same day.

Members of the Romany community suffer the harshest treatment of the minority groups in Moldova. They face discrimination in housing and employment, are targets of police violence, and are considered vulnerable to voter intimidation and vote buying.

Women are underrepresented in public life. A total of 24 women were elected to Parliament in April 2009, and this increased to 25 in July. Moldova remains a significant source for women and girls trafficked abroad for forced prostitution, though the government's antitrafficking efforts led the U.S. State Department to raise the country out of the worst possible ranking in its 2009 Trafficking in Persons Report.

Monaco

Political Rights: 2
Civil Liberties: 1
Status: Free

Population: 35,000
Capital: Monaco

Ten-Year Ratings Timeline For Year Under Review (Political Rights, Civil Liberties, Status)

2000	2001	2002	2003	2004	2005	2006	2007	2008	2009
2,1F	2,1F	2,1F	2,1F	2,1F	2,1F	2,1F	2,1F	2,1F	2,1F

Overview: In a move toward greater financial transparency, Prince Albert II announced in March 2009 that foreign tax authorities will be given greater access to information on foreign account holders in Monaco. In April, Monaco's parliament voted to legalize abortion under certain conditions.

The Grimaldi family has ruled the Principality of Monaco for the past 700 years, except for a period of French occupation from 1793 to 1814. Under a treaty ratified in 1919, France pledged to protect the territorial integrity, sovereignty, and independence of the country in return for a guarantee that Monegasque policy would conform to French political, military, and economic interests.

Prince Rainier III, who ruled from 1949 until his death in 2005, is often credited with engineering Monaco's impressive economic growth. During his reign, the country ended its dependence on gambling and nurtured other sources of revenue—principally tourism and financial services. In February 2002, Monaco adopted the euro currency despite the fact that it is not a member of the European Union (EU).

Rainier's successor, Prince Albert II, has made global environmental awareness a priority of his reign, including the 2008 expansion of his organization, the Monaco Foundation, to include a chapter in the United States. In the 2008 legislative elections, the Union of Monaco (UPM) won 21 of the 24 seats in the Conseil National. The remaining three seats were won by the conservative opposition party Rally and Issues for Monaco (REM).

In an ongoing attempt to remove itself from the Organization for Economic Co-operation and Development's (OECD) list of uncooperative tax havens, Prince Albert announced plans to allow for greater financial transparency in March 2009. Monaco plans to begin granting foreign tax authorities access to information about foreign tax holder accounts in the principality. By September, Monaco had signed agreements with 12 countries to provide greater transparency and had made the OECD "white list" by October.

On April 1, the parliament voted to legalize abortion in cases where the mother's life is at risk due to pregnancy, the fetus has an incurable disease, or the pregnancy was the result of rape or domestic violence.

In December, Prince Albert revisited plans to expand the principality by building into the Mediterranean Sea. The plans were first announced in 2008 but were scrapped due to the financial crisis and environmental concerns.

Political Rights and Civil Liberties: Monaco is an electoral democracy. However, the prince, who serves as head of state, has the sole authority to initiate legislation and change the government. The 24 members of the unicameral Conseil National are elected for five-year terms; 16 are chosen through a majority electoral system and 8 by proportional representation.

The head of government, known as the minister of state, is traditionally appointed by the monarch from a list of three candidates, all French nationals, presented by the French government. The current minister of state, Jean-Paul Proust, has held the post since June 2005. The prince also appoints five other ministers (counselors), who make up the cabinet. All legislation and the budget require the assent of the Conseil National, which is currently dominated by the UPM party. The only other party represented is REM, which holds three seats.

Because of a lack of available financial information, the country's level of corruption is difficult to measure. Monaco was not ranked by Transparency International in its 2009 Corruption Perceptions Index. Monaco remains on the OECD list of uncooperative tax havens, but since July 2005, it has applied a withholding tax to accounts held by citizens of EU member states. Most of the resulting revenue goes back to the country where the account holder resides. In March 2009, Prince Albert II announced that the principality would start providing foreign tax authorities with information on foreign account holders.

The media in Monaco are free and independent. The constitution provides for freedom of speech and the press, although the penal code prohibits denunciations of the ruling family. Internet access is not restricted. In October 2009, Monaco began a massive effort to expand broadband capacities, which will link the country to 11 other nations.

The constitution guarantees freedom of religion. However, Roman Catholicism is the state religion. There are no laws against proselytizing by formally registered religious organizations, though proselytizing in public is strongly discouraged by authorities. Academic freedom is not restricted. The country's only institution of higher education, the private University of Monaco, offers degrees in business administration. Monegasque students are eligible to enter French and other postsecondary educational institutions on the basis of specific agreements.

The constitution provides for freedom of assembly, which is generally respected by the authorities. No restrictions are imposed on the formation of civic and human rights groups. Workers have the legal right to organize and bargain collectively, although they rarely do so. Less than 5 percent of the workforce is unionized. All workers except state employees have the right to strike.

The legal rights to a fair public trial and an independent judiciary are generally respected. The justice system is based on French legal code, and the constitution requires that the prince delegate his judicial powers to the courts. The prince names the five full members and two judicial assistants to the Supreme Court on the basis of nominations by the Conseil National and other government bodies. Jail facilities generally meet international standards. Once criminal defendants receive definitive sentences, they are transferred to a French prison.

The constitution differentiates between the rights of Monegasque nationals and those of noncitizens. Of the estimated 35,000 residents in the principality, only about 7,000 are actual Monegasques, who alone may participate in the election of the Conseil National. Monegasques also benefit from free education, unemployment assistance, and the ability to hold elective office. As long as they secure a residence permit, noncitizens are free to purchase real estate and open businesses.

Women generally receive equal pay for equal work. Although naturalized male citizens can transfer citizenship to their offspring, naturalized female citizens cannot. Women who become naturalized citizens by marriage cannot vote or run as candidates in elections until five years after the marriage. There are six women in the Conseil National. In what was seen as a historic win for women's rights, the Conseil National voted in April 2009 to legalize abortion in specific cases, after it had rejected a similar bill just two years earlier.

♠ Mongolia

Political Rights: 2
Civil Liberties: 2
Status: Free

Population: 2,708,000
Capital: Ulaanbaatar

Trend Arrow: Mongolia received an upward trend arrow due to a fair and competitive presidential election, as well as the peaceful transfer of authority from one prime minister to another.

Ten-Year Ratings Timeline For Year Under Review (Political Rights, Civil Liberties, Status)

2000	2001	2002	2003	2004	2005	2006	2007	2008	2009
2,3F	2,3F	2,2F	2,2F	2,2F	2,2F	2,2F	2,2F	2,2F	2,2F

Overview:
Tsakhiagiin Elbegdorj of the opposition Democratic Party won the May 2009 presidential election, which international observers deemed free and fair. The incumbent quickly conceded defeat, and the country avoided the sort of violent protests that had followed disputed parliamentary elections in 2008. Although many of those arrested in that year's unrest were freed under an amnesty law in 2009, observers raised concerns over beatings in detention and a lack of punishment for police who used deadly force to disperse the protesters. In October, the prime minister since 2007 resigned for health reasons, and power was transferred without incident to a new premier.

Once the center of Genghis Khan's sprawling empire, Mongolia was ruled by China for two centuries until Soviet-backed forces took control in the early 1920s. A people's republic was proclaimed in 1924, and the Mongolian People's Revolutionary Party (MPRP) established a one-party communist state. In response to persistent antigovernment protests, the MPRP legalized opposition parties in 1990. However, facing a poorly prepared and underfunded opposition, the MPRP easily won the first multiparty parliamentary elections that year, and won again in 1992.

The MPRP was voted out in the 1996 parliamentary elections after 72 years in office, power was transferred peacefully to the opposition Democratic Union Coalition. The new government sought to implement political and economic reforms, but with an economic downturn the following year, the MPRP regained power with victories in both the 1997 presidential election and the 2000 parliamentary vote.

The June 2004 parliamentary elections were marred by irregularities and gave neither side a majority. The MPRP consequently agreed to a power-sharing government with the Democracy Coalition (MDC), the latest incarnation of the opposition alliance. Former prime minister Elbegdorj of the MDC returned to the premiership, while Natsagiin Bagabandi of the MPRP carried on in the largely ceremonial presidency.

The MPRP's Nambaryn Enkhbayar, the parliament Speaker and a former prime minister, won the presidential election in May 2005, despite street demonstrations by protesters who accused him of corruption. In January 2006, the MDC-MPRP coalition government broke down, and the MPRP formed a new government with several small parties and defectors from the MDC. Miyeegombo Enkhbold of the MPRP became prime minister, but he was replaced in November 2007 by Sanjaa Bayar after being accused of excessive political favoritism and corruption.

The initial results of the June 28, 2008, parliamentary elections handed the MPRP a solid majority, and the opposition Democratic Party (DP) and others challenged the outcome. Small-scale political protests escalated into large demonstrations in the capital, and buildings, including the MPRP headquarters, were looted and burned. Five people were killed, scores were injured, and over 700 people were arrested. The government declared a four-day state of emergency on July 2. The final vote tally in August gave the MPRP 46 seats and the DP 27, and Bayar remained in office as prime minister.

Elbegdorj of the DP took 51.2 percent of the vote in the May 2009 presidential election, becoming the first DP president, though he had previously served twice as prime minister. Enkhbayar, the incumbent, quickly admitted defeat, averting a repeat of the previous year's unrest. International observers deemed the election generally free and fair. In October, Bayar resigned as prime minister for health reasons. He was replaced by Foreign Minister Sukhbaatar Batbold, reputedly one of the richest men in Mongolia.

The combined effects of the global economic downturn and extremely harsh winter exacerbated Mongolia's high poverty and unemployment rates in 2009. In October, a US$5 billion contract was signed with Ivanhoe/Rio Tinto, a Canadian and Australian company, to develop copper and gold mines. Though the deal was widely seen as a positive development, some observers expressed concerns over ongoing corruption and a lack of transparency surrounding the contract's negotiations. Also in 2009, the government set up a Human Development Fund to distribute mining royalties to citizens.

Political Rights and Civil Liberties: Mongolia is an electoral democracy. The 2009 presidential election was generally considered free and fair by international observers. Parliamentary balloting has varied over the years between multimember and single-member districts, and there is concern that these frequent changes make it difficult to stabilize the expectations of political elites or enhance popular confidence in democratic government. The prime minister, who holds most executive power, is nominated by the party or coalition with the most seats in the 76-member parliament (the State Great Hural) and approved by the parliament with the agreement of the president. There is no requirement that the prime minister be an elected member of parliament. The president is head of state and of the armed forces, and can veto legislation, subject to a two-thirds parliamentary override. Both the president and the parliament are directly elected for four-year terms.

The MPRP continues to be the most powerful party, but a number of smaller opposition groups are competitive, as evidenced by DP's victory in the 2009 presidential election.

Corruption remains a serious problem in Mongolia. A 2009 survey conducted by the Asia Foundation and Sant Maral Foundation found that one in five households had paid bribes, an increase from the findings of an earlier poll. Since its creation in 2007, the Independent Authority Against Corruption has been active in investigating allegations and verifying asset declarations. According to government figures, over 53,000 officials and civil servants complied with income-declaration rules in 2009; at least 54 people who gave false or late statements were punished with dismissal or other disciplinary measures. Transparency International ranked Mongolia 120 out of 180 countries surveyed in its 2009 Corruption Perceptions Index.

The government operates with limited transparency. In December 2009, however, an unprecedented public hearing was held on human rights abuses surrounding the 2008 postelection violence, with participation by civil society, the police, the parliament, and the National Commission on Human Rights (NCHR).

While the government generally respects press freedom, many journalists and independent publications practice a degree of self-censorship to avoid legal action under the State Secrets Law or libel laws that place the burden of proof on the defendant. The government at times filed libel suits or launched tax audits against publications or journalists in the wake of critical articles. The media faced tight restrictions during the state of emergency in 2008, but the situation returned to normal in 2009.

There are hundreds of privately owned print and broadcast outlets, but the main source of news in the vast countryside is the state-owned Mongolian National Broadcasting (MNB). MNB's coverage of the 2009 presidential election was reportedly balanced, while commercial stations largely favored the incumbent. Foreign content from satellite television and radio services like the British Broadcasting Corporation and Voice of America is also increasingly available. The government does not interfere with internet access.

Freedom of religion is guaranteed by the constitution. The fall of communism led to a growth in various Christian sects, as well as a revival of 's traditional Buddhism and Shamanism. Religious groups are required to register with the government and renew their status annually. While most registration requests are approved, according to the U.S. State Department, authorities in Tuv province have routinely denied registration to Christian churches. The Kazakh Muslim minority generally enjoys freedom of religion. Academic freedom is respected.

Freedoms of assembly and association are observed in law and in practice. However, in June 2009, the authorities denied registration to the Lesbian, Gay, Bisexual, and Transgender Center, claiming that the group's name conflicted with Mongolian traditions; following public and international pressure, the authorities recognized the center in December. A number of environmental, human rights, and social welfare groups, while largely reliant on foreign donors, operate without government restriction. Unions are independent and active, and the government has generally protected their rights in recent years, though the downsizing or sale of many state factories has contributed to a sharp drop in union membership. Collective bargaining is legal, but in Mongolia's poor economy, employers are often able to set wages unilaterally.

The judiciary is independent, but corruption among judges persists. The police force has been known to make arbitrary arrests, hold detainees for long periods, and beat prisoners. Deaths in prisons continue to be reported, due largely to disease—often tuberculosis—exacerbated by insufficient food, heat, and medical care. In an NCHR survey of 100 people detained following the 2008 postelection riots, 88 reported being abused in detention. In several cases, coerced confessions were allegedly used to convict detainees of offenses such as "creating mass disorder." Police reportedly used live ammunition during the riots, which killed at least five people. A total of 10 police officers and 4 senior police officials were under investigation regarding the deaths, and all have been removed from their posts. It remained unclear at year's end whether they would be formally charged or covered by a general amnesty law passed in July 2009. The measure applied to minor crimes committed before late June 2009, and covered most civilians still in detention for the 2008 unrest.

The NCHR consists of three senior civil servants nominated by the president, the Supreme Court, and the parliament for six-year terms. It has played an active role in investigating the alleged 2008 police abuses, but at least 11 cases it submitted for prosecution were dismissed with little explanation.

While Mongolia is not a party to the 1951 UN Convention Relating to the Status of Refugees and lacks legislation enabling the granting of asylum, the government frequently provides protection to refugees, including those fleeing persecution in China. However, in October 2009, a Chinese national, his wife, and his nine-year-old daughter were reportedly arrested by Chinese police officers with Mongolian police escorts outside the local office of the UN High Commissioner for Refugees in Ulaanbataar. The family was immediately taken back to China without a court hearing, and the arrested man, the operator of a Mongol-Tibetan medical, school in China, remained in detention there at year's end.

While women make up 60 percent of all university students as well as 60 percent of all judges, only five parliamentary seats are occupied by women. A 2005 law prohibited spousal abuse, and there have been dozens of convictions in recent years. However, social and cultural norms continue to discourage victims from reporting such crimes.

Montenegro

Political Rights: 3
Civil Liberties: 2*
Status: Free

Population: 628,000
Capital: Podgorica

Status Change: Montenegro's civil liberties rating improved from 3 to 2 and its status from Partly Free to Free due to the successful organization of parliamentary elections in March, progress in adopting anticorruption legislation, and an overall stabilization of country conditions.

Note: The ratings through 2002 are for the Federal Republic of Yugoslavia, of which Montenegro was a part, and those from 2003 through 2005 are for the State Union of Serbia and Montenegro.

Ten-Year Ratings Timeline For Year Under Review (Political Rights, Civil Liberties, Status)

2000	2001	2002	2003	2004	2005	2006	2007	2008	2009
4,4PF	3,3PF	3,2F	3,2F	3,2F	3,2F	3,3PF	3,3PF	3,3PF	3,2F

Overview: Parliamentary elections in March 2009 resulted in the best showing to date for longtime Montenegrin leader Milo Djukanovic's Democratic Party of Socialists. Also during the year, international monitoring organizations reported that Montenegro had made progress in combating corruption and reforming the judicial system. In December, the European Union (EU) granted visa-free travel privileges to Montenegrins, although the country had not yet achieved official EU candidate status.

Montenegro was first recognized as an independent state in 1878. In 1918, it joined the newly formed Kingdom of Serbs, Croats, and Slovenes, which after World War II became the Socialist Federal Republic of Yugoslavia. As that state collapsed in the early 1990s, Montenegro in 1992 voted to maintain its ties to Serbia as part of the truncated Federal Republic of Yugoslavia (FRY), dominated by Serbian leader Slobodan Milosevic. In 1997, however, a group of former Milosevic cohorts in Montenegro, led by then prime minister Milo Djukanovic, decided to break with Milosevic and set Montenegro on a slow course toward independence.

Milosevic's fall from power in 2000 did not improve relations between Montenegro and its larger federal partner, and the two republics signed an agreement in 2002 that loosened their bond, replacing the FRY with the State Union of Serbia and Montenegro. The deal allowed either republic to hold an independence referendum after three years, and Djukanovic chose to exercise this right in May 2006. Referendum voters approved the final break with Serbia by a relatively small margin, and in July, the Montenegrin parliament officially declared independence.

The September 2006 parliamentary elections confirmed voter support for the ruling proindependence coalition. Djukanovic retired from the premiership that October, but he returned to the office 18 months later. Aside from that hiatus, he has served as either president or prime minister of Montenegro since 1991.

Independence and national identity remained divisive issues, and a 2007 investigation stoked suspicions that Djukanovic's Democratic Party of Socialists (DPS) had manipulated the 2006 referendum and elections. Several police officers reported being pressured by the DPS to solicit votes in favor of independence and for the government. The government drew additional criticism from pro-Serbian factions in October 2008, when it officially recognized Kosovo's independence.

In January 2009, President Filip Vujanovic, a close Djukanovic ally, called snap parliamentary elections, allegedly because the government was concerned that the effects the global economic crisis could erode voter support by the time its full term ended. The early balloting, held in March, yielded the best outcome to date for the ruling party. With voter turnout at 66 percent, the DPS-led coalition won a comfortable majority of 48 seats in the 81-seat parliament. The opposition Socialist People's Party took 16 seats, followed by New Serb Democracy with 8, Movement for Change with 5, and four small ethnic Albanian parties with 1 seat each.

Montenegro has pursued European Union (EU) and NATO membership, joining NATO's Partnership for Peace program in 2006 and signing a Stabilization and Association Agreement with the EU in 2007. In December 2008, Montenegro submitted its application for EU membership and remained a potential candidate in 2009; the EU granted Montenegrins visa-free travel privileges in December 2009. Meanwhile, heavy Russian investment has generated significant controversy within the country. Some accounts suggest that as much as US$13 billion in Russian capital has entered Montenegro since the 1990s, making it the largest recipient of foreign investment per capita in Europe.

Political Rights and Civil Liberties: Montenegro is an electoral democracy. Recent elections have been considered free and fair, though with minor irregularities. Members of the unicameral, 81-seat Assembly (Skupstina) are elected for four-year terms. The president, directly elected for up to two five-year terms, nominates the prime minister, who must be approved by the legislature. Two presidential elections in 2002 failed to achieve the required voter turnout; the law was subsequently amended to eliminate the 50 percent turnout rule, and Filip Vujanovic of the DPS was finally elected in 2003 with a 48 percent turnout. He was reelected in April 2008 by a wide margin.

Numerous political parties compete for power, though the opposition remains relatively weak and divided. The current coalition government consists of the DPS, the Social Democratic Party (SDP), and two smaller parties representing Bosniaks and Croats. Other parties in the parliament represent ethnic Serbs and Albanians.

Corruption has traditionally been a very serious and widespread phenomenon in Montenegro, even by regional standards. Nevertheless, in its progress report on the country in 2009, the EU noted that Montenegro had made considerable advances in enacting anticorruption legislation. The current law on conflict of interest, adopted in December 2008, is seen as a marked improvement over previous such laws. Montenegro was ranked 69 out of 180 countries in Transparency International's 2009 Corruption Perceptions Index. The corruption problem is partly a legacy of the struggle against the Milosevic regime in the 1990s, when the small republic turned to various forms of smuggling to finance government operations. Prime Minister Milo Djukanovic has frequently been accused of involvement in cigarette smuggling, and a number of Montenegrin officials and businesspeople have been indicted in Italy for such activities.

Freedom of the press is generally respected, and there is a variety of private print and broadcast outlets, but journalists who criticize the government are frequently attacked. In August 2009, the mayor of Podgorica assaulted two journalists working on a story about official abuses of power. While criminal libel is not punishable by imprisonment, the threat of fines forces journalists to engage in self-censorship. Belgrade-based publications remain popular in the country, partly because a large segment of Montenegro's population identifies itself as Serb. Access to the internet has not been restricted.

The constitution guarantees freedom of religious belief. However, the canonically recognized Serbian Orthodox Church and a self-proclaimed Montenegrin Orthodox Church have repeatedly clashed over ownership of church properties and other issues.

Academic freedom is guaranteed by law, but politically charged debates about the nature of Montenegrin/Serb identity and Montenegrin history have sometimes spilled over into the educational realm. The Montenegrin government's decision to officially endorse use of the "Montenegrin language" has been challenged by citizens who consider themselves Serbs and who demand that their children be allowed to use the Serbian language in classrooms. In January 2009, the Serb National Council in Montenegro called for separate classrooms for students using Montenegrin and those using Serbian, although linguistically the two variants are completely mutually intelligible.

Citizens enjoy freedoms of association and assembly. Foreign and domestic nongovernmental organizations are able to pursue their activities without state interference. Some 95 percent of all employees in the formal economy belong to unions, and the right of workers to strike is generally protected. Collective bargaining, however, is still considered to be at a rudimentary level. The country has strict protections against employee dismissal and generous worker benefits, but these are thought to limit efficiency and encourage informality in the economy. Amendments to the Law on Strikes in 2009 expanded the right to strike to public administration employees.

The EU's 2009 progress report on Montenegro cites improvements in the area of judicial reform. The parliament has passed a new criminal procedure code and legislation governing the Constitutional Court. Gains have also been noted with respect to implementation of legislation intended to improve the professionalism of judges and prosecutors. Nevertheless, political interference with court cases remains a problem, and despite some progress, there is still a large backlog of cases. Most prison facilities are antiquated, overcrowded, and often unhygienic.

Ethnic minorities have access to media in their own languages. Ethnic Albanians, who make up roughly 7 percent of the population, claim that they are underrepresented in the civil service, particularly in the police and the judiciary. They have also sought proportional representation in government and greater autonomy at the municipal level.

Although women are legally entitled to equal pay for equal work, traditional patriarchal attitudes often limit their role in the economy. The gender gap in pay has widened in recent years to 19 percent. In general, women are underrepresented at higher levels of government. Only 11 percent of the current members of parliament are women, and there is 1 female minister in the 23-member government. Women make up 80 percent of the population considered to be illiterate in the country. Montenegro was ranked on the Tier 2 Watch List in the U.S. State Department's 2009 Trafficking in Persons Report, performing worse than all of its Balkan neighbors in efforts to combat human trafficking.

⬇ Morocco

Political Rights: 5
Civil Liberties: 4
Status: Partly Free

Population: 31,495,000
Capital: Rabat

Trend Arrow: Morocco received a downward trend arrow due to the increased concentration of power in the hands of political elites aligned with the monarchy.

Note: The numerical ratings and status listed above do not reflect conditions in Western Sahara, which is examined in a separate report.

Ten-Year Ratings Timeline For Year Under Review (Political Rights, Civil Liberties, Status)

2000	2001	2002	2003	2004	2005	2006	2007	2008	2009
5,4PF	5,5PF	5,5PF	5,5PF	5,4PF	5,4PF	5,4PF	5,4PF	5,4PF	5,4PF

Overview: The Modernity and Authenticity Party, recently founded by a friend of King Mohamed VI, placed first in the June 2009 local elections, signaling the growing concentration of political power in the hands of the king and his allies. The balloting was accompanied by reports of vote buying and other forms of electoral manipulation. Also during the year, the government and courts continued to batter the independent press with arrests, fines, and jail sentences.

Morocco gained independence in 1956 after more than four decades of French rule. The first ruler after independence, King Mohamed V, reigned until his death in 1961. His son, the autocratic Hassan II, then ruled the country until 1999. Thousands of his political opponents were killed, tortured, arrested, or disappeared. This repression was particularly acute in the years following two failed coup attempts in 1971 and 1972. In 1975, Morocco and Mauritania occupied Western Sahara; after three years of fighting the Algerian-backed Polisario Front, a Sahrawi nationalist guerrilla movement, Mauritania pulled out of the territory, which was then annexed in full by Morocco. A planned referendum on Western Sahara's future—attached to a UN-monitored ceasefire agreement in 1991—never took place. In the last few years of his life, Hassan initiated a political opening in Morocco. Several political prisoners were released, independent newspapers began publishing, and a new bicameral Parliament was established in 1997.

King Mohamed VI inherited the throne in 1999, at age 35. He declined to expand political freedom much further in the first years of his reign, apparently aiming to check the increased influence of Islamist political parties. However, he removed long-time interior minister Driss Basri, who had led much of the repression under King Hassan, and allowed exiled dissidents to return to the country.

Parliamentary elections held in 2002 were recognized as generally open. Over a dozen political parties participated, though independent journalists and other critics of the king were harassed and detained.

In May 2003, local Islamist militants with links to al-Qaeda mounted a series of suicide bombings targeting symbols of Morocco's Jewish community in Casablanca. The government responded by enacting a harsh antiterrorism law, but it was subsequently used to prosecute nonviolent opponents of the king.

In 2004, King Mohamed inaugurated the Equity and Reconciliation Commission (IER), tasked with addressing the human rights abuses perpetrated by the authorities from 1956 to 1999 and providing the victims with reparations. The commission, which was unprecedented in the Arab world, was headed by a former political prisoner and allowed victims to testify in public hearings. It submitted its final report to the king in 2006, including a series of recommendations for legal and institutional reforms designed to prevent future abuses. Critics of the IER have complained that it did not hold perpetrators to account for their actions, and that its recommendations have not led to major structural changes. Human rights abuses still occur on a regular basis, albeit on a smaller scale. Moreover, the authorities have been intolerant of further discussion of past abuses; in June 2008, a court in Rabat ordered the private daily *Al-Jarida al-Oula* to stop publishing IER testimony.

The 2007 elections for the Chamber of Representatives, the lower house of Parliament, drew the lowest turnout in Moroccan history, 37 percent. The Socialist Union of People's Forces (USFP), previously the lead party in the ruling coalition, fell to 38 seats. Its chief ally, the conservative Independence Party (Istiqlal), won a plurality of 52 seats. Opposition parties, which had criticized the elections' fairness, gained fewer seats than expected; the largest, the Islamist Justice and Development Party (PJD), placed second with 46 seats. Istiqlal leader Abbas el-Fassi was appointed prime minister.

El-Fassi appeared to have fallen out of favor by 2009, as former deputy interior minister Fouad Ali el-Himma, a close associate of the king, organized the Modernity and Authenticity Party (PAM) to contest local elections in June. The new party led the voting with more than 20 percent of local council seats, followed by Istiqlal with about 19 percent. Three other governing parties placed third, fourth, and fifth, leaving the PJD in sixth, with less than 6 percent, though it reportedly did well in urban areas. Widespread vote buying, bribery, intimidation, and other forms of manipulation were reported, and analysts regarded the official turnout figure of 52 percent with some skepticism.

Political Rights and Civil Liberties: Morocco is not an electoral democracy. Most power is held by the king and his close advisers. The monarch can dissolve Parliament, rule by decree, and dismiss or appoint cabinet members. He sets national and foreign policy, commands the armed forces, and presides over the judicial system. One of the king's constitutional titles is "commander of the faithful," giving his authority a religious dimension.

The lower house of Parliament, the Chamber of Representatives, has 325 directly elected members who serve for five-year terms. Members of the 270-seat upper house, the Chamber of Counselors, are chosen by an electoral college to serve nine-year terms. Thirty seats in the lower house are reserved for women, and under a rule that took effect in 2009, women are guaranteed 12 percent of the seats in local elections.

Given the concentration of power in the monarchy, the country's fragmented political parties and even the cabinet are generally unable to assert themselves. The most vocal opposition party that remains respectful of the monarchy is the PJD, which fared poorly in local elections in 2009. The popular Justice and Charity Movement, an Islamist group, is illegal but generally tolerated by the authorities. Other, more explicitly nonviolent Islamist groups that criticize the monarchical system are harassed by authorities and not permitted to participate in the political process.

Despite the government's rhetoric on combating widespread corruption, it remains a structural problem, both in public life and in the business world. Morocco was ranked 89 out of 180 countries surveyed in Transparency International's 2009 Corruption Perceptions Index.

The authorities have stepped up repression of the country's vigorous independent press in recent years, using the restrictive press law and an array of economic and other, more subtle mechanisms to punish critical journalists, particularly those who focus on the king, his family, or Islam. In an indication of their extreme sensitivity, government officials in August 2009 banned or destroyed copies of France's *Le Monde* daily, the French-language weekly *Tel-Quel*, and the Arabic weekly *Nichane* that reported the results of an opinion poll on the monarchy, despite the fact that 91 percent of respondents said they had a favorable view of the king. In September, police shuttered the daily *Akhbar al-Youm* for publishing a cartoon on the wedding of one of Morocco's princes; the courts later upheld the closure and imposed suspended jail sentences and fines on an editor and a cartoonist at the paper. In October, a court sentenced *Al-Michaal* editor Driss Chahtan to a year in jail after his paper allegedly published "false information" about the king's health. Two *Al-Michaal* reporters received shorter sentences, and an editor and reporter for *Al-Jarida al-Oula* received suspended sentences that month for a similar infraction.

Among several other court rulings against independent newspapers during the year, the Supreme Court in September upheld a 2006 defamation judgment against the trailblazing *Le Journal Hebdomadaire*, meaning the weekly's publishers owed over $350,000 in damages to the head of a Belgian think tank. *Le Journal* had alleged that a report by the research group on Western Sahara mirrored the Moroccan government's position. The case was seen as a politically motivated bid to destroy the paper without directly involving the government.

The state dominates the broadcast media, but residents have access to foreign satellite television channels. The authorities occasionally block websites and internet platforms, while bloggers and other internet users are sometimes arrested for posting content that offends the monarchy. In December 2009, a blogger and an internet cafe owner were sentenced to four months and one year in jail, respectively, for disseminating information about student protests.

Nearly all Moroccans are Muslims, but the small Jewish community is permitted to practice its faith without government interference. However, Moroccan authorities are growing increasingly intolerant of social and religious diversity as reflected in arrest campaigns against Shiites and Muslim converts to Christianity. Authorities have also detained several members of the Moroccan Alternative Movement for Individual Freedoms for planning a public "picnic" during the month of Ramadan to protest against the law that forbids eating during fasting hours. While university campuses generally provide a space for open discussion, professors practice self-censorship when dealing with sensitive topics like Western Sahara, the monarchy, and Islam.

Freedom of assembly is not well respected, and protests in Western Sahara especially have been controlled through violence and threats. According to Human Rights Watch (HRW), Moroccan authorities confiscated passports of Sahrawi activists in 2009 and prevented some from leaving the country. Civil society and independent nongovernmental organizations (NGOs) are quite active, though the authorities monitor Islamist groups and arrest suspected extremists. While NGOs in Morocco operate with more freedom than in many other Arab states, groups that offend the government face harassment.

Moroccan workers are permitted to form and join independent trade unions, and the 2004 labor law prevents employers from punishing workers who do so. However, the authorities have forcibly broken up labor actions that entail criticism of the government, and child laborers, especially girls working as domestic helpers, are denied basic rights.

The judiciary is not independent, and the courts are regularly used to punish opponents of the government. In the so-called Belliraj case, 35 people were arrested in February 2008 and convicted in July 2009 of forming a terrorist group, plotting attacks, and raising funds through criminal activities. However, according to HRW, the alleged acts were limited to one assassination attempt in 1996 and robberies committed a decade ago. The defendants claimed that confessions and statements in the case were made under torture and that they were simply members of political parties that the government wanted to eliminate.

Arbitrary arrest and torture still occur, though they are less common than under King Hassan. The security forces are given greater leeway for abuse with detainees advocating independence for Western Sahara.

Many Moroccans have a mixed Arab-Berber ancestry, and the government has officially recognized the language and culture of the Berbers.

Women continue to face a great deal of discrimination at the societal level. However, Moroccan authorities have a more progressive view on gender equality than leaders in many Arab countries. The 2004 family code has been lauded for granting women increased rights in the areas of marriage and child custody, and various other laws aim to protect women's interests.

Mozambique

Political Rights: 4*
Civil Liberties: 3
Status: Partly Free

Population: 21,971,000
Capital: Maputo

Ratings Change: Mozambique's political rights rating declined from 3 to 4 due to significant irregularities and a lack of transparency pertaining to the registration of candidates and the tabulation of votes in the October 2009 presidential, legislative, and provincial elections.

Ten-Year Ratings Timeline For Year Under Review (Political Rights, Civil Liberties, Status)

2000	2001	2002	2003	2004	2005	2006	2007	2008	2009
3,4PF	3,4PF	3,4PF	3,4PF	3,4PF	3,4PF	3,4PF	3,3PF	3,3PF	4,3PF

Overview: President Armando Guebuza and the ruling Front for the Liberation of Mozambique (FRELIMO) party won sweeping victories in the October 2009 national and provincial elections. International observers found that the overall outcome reflected the will of the people, but significant problems pertaining to the registration of candidates and the tabulation of results underscored the crucial need for greater transparency in the electoral process. Endemic corruption and weak judicial institutions also pointed to the broader challenge of securing transparency and accountability.

Mozambique achieved independence from Portugal in 1975. The Front for the Liberation of Mozambique (FRELIMO), a guerrilla group that had long fought to oust the Portuguese, subsequently installed itself as the sole legal political party of a Marxist-style state. Independence was followed by a 16-year civil war that pitted the Soviet-allied FRELIMO against the Mozambique National Resistance (RENAMO), a force sponsored by the white-minority governments of Rhodesia (Zimbabwe) and South Africa. The war resulted in nearly a million deaths and the displacement of several million people. President Samora Machel, the FRELIMO leader, was killed in a suspicious plane crash in 1986; he was succeeded by Joachim Chissano, a reform-minded FRELIMO moderate. A new constitution was enacted, calling for a multiparty political system, a market-based economy, and free elections. A peace accord signed in 1992 brought an end to the war, and a 7,500-strong UN peacekeeping force oversaw a disarmament and demobilization program and the transition to democratic government.

Mozambique held its first democratic elections in 1994. Chissano retained the presidency, and FRELIMO secured a majority of seats in the National Assembly. RENAMO accepted the outcome and transformed itself into a peaceful opposition political movement. Chissano was reelected in 1999, and FRELIMO once again won a majority of parliamentary seats. These results were deemed credible by the international community, despite technical difficulties and irregularities in the tabulation process. RENAMO nonetheless accused the government of fraud and at one point threatened to form its own government in the six northern and central provinces it controlled.

Chissano announced that he would step down as president on completion of his second elected term. In 2002, FRELIMO leaders chose Armando Guebuza, a hard-liner, to lead the party. Pledging to address corruption, crime, and poverty, Guebuza and FRELIMO won the 2004 presidential and legislative elections with a wide margin of victory, but RENAMO cited evidence of "massive fraud" and initially rejected the results announced by the National Electoral Commission (CNE). The commission subsequently admitted that 1,400 vote-summary sheets favoring RENAMO had been stolen, accounting for 5 percent of the total vote. It transferred one parliamentary seat from FRELIMO to RENAMO as compensation. International election observers expressed concerns about the CNE's conduct during the tabulation process, but ultimately determined that the abuses did not affect the overall outcome.

Guebuza's government has largely continued the liberal economic reforms and poverty-reduction policies of his predecessor. He has been criticized, however, for his heavy-handed management of FRELIMO and his uncompromising and confrontational stance toward the opposition.

Mozambique held presidential, legislative, and—for the first time—provincial elections in October 2009. Guebuza was reelected by a landslide, securing 75 percent of the vote. His opponents, Afonso Dhlakama of RENAMO and Daviz Simango of the newly formed Democratic Movement of Mozambique (MDM), received 16.4 percent and 8.6 percent, respectively. In the parliamentary contest, FRELIMO captured 191 of 250 seats, while RENAMO won 51 and the MDM won 8. FRELIMO also won absolute majorities in all 10 of the country's provincial assemblies.

RENAMO and MDM both alleged fraud. The European Union and other international observer groups reported that voting was conducted in a peaceful and orderly manner, though they were highly critical of many preelection and election-day processes. They noted that the CNE's rejection of party lists for ostensibly technical reasons—including the disqualification of MDM candidates' nomination papers in 9 of the country's 13 parliamentary constituencies—substantially restricted voter choice. The observers also documented irregularities that indicated ballot stuffing and tabulation fraud at some polling stations, though such distortions were considered insufficient to have impacted the overall result of the election.

Mozambique has achieved high levels of sustained economic growth since the end of the civil war, owing to relative political stability and the government's commitment to donor-backed market reforms. The economy has shown resilience in the face of the recent global downturn, with the International Monetary Fund estimating average real gross domestic product growth at 4.5 percent for 2009. Mozambique enjoys close relations with donors, who have helped to finance high spending levels on priority social sectors and poverty-reduction programs. The government is working to increase the share of domestic revenue in government spending by expanding the tax base and increasing foreign investment. Donors have also put pressure on the government to enact "second generation" liberalizing structural reforms to maintain the country's economic growth.

Political Rights and Civil Liberties: Mozambique is not an electoral democracy. While international observers have deemed the overall outcomes of Mozambique's national elections to have reflected the will of the people, electoral processes have repeatedly been riddled with problems. The 2009 elections were particularly criticized for widespread rejection of party lists and for "numerous irregularities" in the tabulation of results.

The president, who appoints the prime minister, is elected by popular vote for up to two five-year terms. Members of the 250-seat, unicameral Assembly of the Republic are also elected for five-year terms. The national government appoints the governors of the 10 provinces and the capital city. Despite the introduction of elected provincial assemblies and municipal governments, power remains highly centralized, particularly in the hands of the president.

Political parties are governed by a law that expressly prohibits them from identifying exclusively with any religious or ethnic group. Although RENAMO and the upstart MDM have won representation as opposition parties in the parliament, FRELIMO is the only party to have held power nationally, and its unbroken incumbency has allowed it to acquire significant control over state institutions. In the lead-up to the 2009 elections, the government was heavily criticized for disqualifying candidates from the MDM and a number of smaller parties in a majority of the country's constituencies on technical grounds that many saw as politically motivated. The campaign period was also marred by partisan violence. Three MDM campaign workers were injured when their offices were looted by a FRELIMO mob in Chokwe. Another was assaulted by RENAMO supporters in Nampula. RENAMO workers also suffered attacks by FRELIMO in Maputo, Sofala, and Nampula, as well as in Tete province, where RENAMO offices in Changara were burned and one RENAMO supporter was reportedly killed.

Corruption in government and business is pervasive. Mozambique was ranked 130 out of 180 countries in Transparency International's 2009 Corruption Perceptions Index. Local journalists and nongovernmental organizations (NGOs), such as the Center for Public Integrity, have played a crucial monitoring role by investigating and exposing high-profile corruption cases. Under considerable pressure from donors, President Armando Guebuza has stepped up efforts to fight corruption. As of the end of 2009, former transport minister Antonio Munguambe and four other defendants were on trial for allegedly stealing nearly US$2 million from Mozambique's national airline. Former interior minister Almerino Manhenje, who was arrested in

September 2008 for the alleged theft of about US$8.3 million from his ministry, was still awaiting trial.

While press freedoms are legally protected, journalists are sometimes harassed or threatened and often practice self-censorship. In March 2009, Bernardo Carlos received death threats after publishing a series of critical articles about the administration of Governor Ildefonso Muananthatha in Tete province. Mozambique has two government-run dailies—*Noticias* and *Diario de Mocambique*. There is also a state news agency and a state radio and television broadcaster. Since the introduction of multiparty democracy in 1994, new independent media sources have proliferated. These include several weeklies and the daily *O Pais*, a number of independent and community radio stations, and more recently, news websites. Although there are no official government restrictions on internet use, opposition leaders have claimed that government intelligence services monitor e-mail. International media operate freely in the country.

Religious freedoms are well respected, and academic freedoms are generally upheld, though there have been reports of teachers encountering pressure to support FRELIMO.

Associational and organizational rights are broadly guaranteed, but with substantial regulations. By law, the right to assembly is subject to notification and timing restrictions, and in practice, it is also subject to governmental discretion. Public demonstrations have occasionally turned violent. In some cases, security forces have broken up protests using disproportionate force. In 2008, riots broke out in Maputo following a 50 percent increase in public transport fees, leaving 4 people dead and more than 100 injured. Campaign rallies prior to the 2009 elections were at times disrupted by security forces or rival party activists. NGOs operate openly but face bureaucratic hurdles in registering with the government, as required by law. Workers have the right to form and join unions and to go on strike. The law was changed in 2008 to extend such provisions to government workers. The Organization of Mozambican Workers, the country's leading trade union confederation, is nominally independent and critical of the government's market-based reforms.

Judicial independence is undermined by endemic corruption, scarce resources, and poor training. The judicial system is further challenged by a dearth of qualified judges and a backlog of cases. Despite recent improvements, suspects are routinely detained well beyond the preventive detention deadline. Prison conditions are abysmal. According to Amnesty International, 13 detainees died from overcrowding in a police cell in Nampula province in March 2009, while 22 reportedly died, mainly from disease, in a prison in Manica province in early 2009. Abuses by security forces—including unlawful killings, excessive use of force, and arbitrary detention—remain serious problems despite human rights training. Public dissatisfaction with the police has also led to a rise in deadly vigilante violence.

Excessive bureaucracy, pervasive corruption, and insufficient legal redress unduly hinder private enterprise, especially at the local level.

Women are fairly well represented politically, holding the premiership and some 39 percent of the parliament, but they continue to face societal discrimination and violence despite recent advances in the law. Trafficking in persons, including the trafficking of children, is a serious problem along the highway from Maputo to Johannesburg in South Africa. Legal protections for women and children are rarely enforced.

Namibia

Political Rights: 2
Civil Liberties: 2
Status: Free

Population: 2,171,000
Capital: Windhoek

Ten-Year Ratings Timeline For Year Under Review (Political Rights, Civil Liberties, Status)

2000	2001	2002	2003	2004	2005	2006	2007	2008	2009
2,3F	2,3F	2,3F	2,3F	2,3F	2,2F	2,2F	2,2F	2,2F	2,2F

Overview:
Elections in November 2009 returned President Hifikepunye Pohamba and the South West Africa People's Organization to power. Although improvements were registered in the legal framework and conduct of the electoral contests, the incumbency enjoyed some advantages, and localized violence marred the campaigning process. While a number of opposition groups questioned the integrity of the elections process, observers declared the contests free and fair. A new communications law passed in July raised concerns about privacy rights, and media harassment continued throughout the year.

Namibia, formerly known as South West Africa, was claimed by German imperial forces in the late 19th century, and became a South African protectorate after World War I. In 1966, South Africa's mandate was revoked by the United Nations, and the South West Africa People's Organization (SWAPO) began a guerrilla campaign for independence. After years of war, a UN-supervised transition led to independence for Namibia in 1990, and SWAPO leader Sam Nujoma was chosen as president. The previous year, SWAPO had won 57 percent of the ballots in a free and fair vote for the Constituent Assembly, which became the National Assembly after independence.

Secessionist fighting in Namibia's Caprivi region between 1998 and 1999 led some 2,400 refugees to flee to neighboring Botswana. A mass trial of 120 defendants involved in the rebellion opened in 2003 and was ongoing at the end of 2009.

Nujoma and SWAPO retained control of the presidency and legislature in the 1994 and 1999 elections. In 2004, after a bitter succession contest within the party, Nujoma's longtime ally, Hifikepunye Pohamba, was chosen as the party's presidential candidate and went on to win elections. Divisions within SWAPO became a central concern for the new president. Rally for Democracy and Progress (RDP)—a breakaway party headed by several former prominent members of SWAPO—emerged in 2007. Pohamba also faced challenges from the hard-line SWAPO Party Youth League (SPYL) and, to a lesser degree, from Nujoma, who was especially critical of government policies and accused senior party leaders of corruption in 2008.

Despite these challenges, Pohamba won with 75 percent of the vote in the November 2009 presidential elections, while the first runner-up, RDP's Hidipo Hamutenya, obtained 11 percent. Twelve candidates contested in the elections, the greatest number to date. The party list for legislative seats reflected continuity in personnel rather than the infusion of "new blood" as had been called for by some.

In concurrent parliamentary elections, SWAPO won 54 seats in the 72-member legislature, while RDP took 8 seats.

The small white minority owns just under half of Namibia's arable land, and redistribution of property has been slow despite legislation passed in 2003 to speed up the process. Following the government's declaration in 2004 that all landholders were susceptible to expropriation, 30 farms have been targeted. However, as of 2009, the government had expropriated only five. Several farm owners have used the courts to contest the expropriation of their land or the prices offered by the government.

Namibia's economy has been among the strongest in the region, and the country has consistently been rated positively in terms of competitiveness and ease of doing business. While the economy grew at a rate of 3.3 percent in 2008, it contracted 0.7 percent in 2009. Namibia's Compact with the Millennium Challenge Corporation came into force in September 2009, having been one of three lower-middle-income countries to be granted eligibility by the U.S. government in 2005.

Political Rights and Civil Liberties: Namibia is an electoral democracy. The bicameral legislature consists of the 26-seat National Council, whose members are appointed by regional councils for six-year terms, and the 72-seat National Assembly, whose members are popularly elected for five-year terms using party-list proportional representation. The president, who is directly elected for five-year terms, appoints the prime minister and cabinet.

In advance of the 2009 elections, the government passed amendments to the existing electoral law to allow for the counting of ballots at polling places, among other changes. While these amendments were applauded by the opposition, other issues, such as the length of the polling period and the absence of an electoral tribunal, remained the subject of criticism. Another controversy concerned the electoral commission's decision to have ballots printed by a SWAPO-owned company. After complaints and pressure from opposition parties, this decision was rescinded, and a South African company was awarded the printing contract. Additionally, the government-run Namibian Broadcast Corporation (NBC) cancelled all free media time for parties in November, a move that hurt smaller opposition parties. Reports indicated that 82 percent of the news coverage was devoted to SWAPO rallies. The campaign period also witnessed some localized tension and violence between SWAPO supporters and the opposition RDP.

Following the contests, eight opposition parties announced that they would bring a list of irregularities—including reports of multiple registrations by individuals and suspiciously high turnout in some areas—to the courts to confirm the legitimacy of the results. Domestic and international observers declared the elections free and fair, although the latter raised some concerns about the pro-SWAPO bias on the government-owned radio station, delays in the counting process, and organizational mishaps during the polling process.

The ruling SWAPO party has dominated since independence. Significant opposition parties include the newly formed RDP, the Congress of Democrats, the Democratic Turnhalle Alliance, and the United Democratic Front. In 2008, individuals associated with the RDP were subjected to harassment and intimidation by SWAPO members, who disrupted RDP rallies and ignored police calls to disperse. The overall climate for the opposition improved in 2009, especially after the president called for more tolerance and respect for the law among SWAPO members, and a more aggressive police presence at opposition gatherings. However, the RDP did experience some difficulties in holding rallies immediately before the 2009 polls.

Although President Hifikepunye Pohamba has made anticorruption efforts a major theme of his presidency, official corruption remains a significant problem, and investigations of major cases proceed slowly. The Anti-Corruption Commission (ACC) is answerable only to the National Assembly and can recommend cases to the prosecutor-general, who has final say on whether to proceed. In 2008, the former head of the SPYL and six others were arrested and charged in a major fraud case. While the trial is scheduled for 2011, SWAPO lifted its suspension of the former SPYL head in July 2009, and placed him on the party list for legislative elections. Additional concerns have recently emerged that children of government officials are disproportionately favored with scholarships granted by the Chinese government. Namibia was ranked 56 out of 180 countries surveyed in Transparency International's 2009 Corruption Perceptions Index.

The constitution guarantees free speech, and Namibia's media have generally enjoyed a relatively open environment for their operations. Private broadcasters and independent newspapers usually operate without official interference. However, government and party leaders at times issue harsh criticism and even threats against the independent press, usually in the wake of unflattering stories. SWAPO and government figures have also repeatedly called for the establishment of a media council to regulate the activities and operations of the media.

While many insist that the NBC enjoys freedom to criticize the government, it has come under political pressure in recent years, as the loyalties of those running the corporation have been questioned. In February 2009, a high-ranking director was dismissed amidst allegations that he backed the opposition. In March, the NBC canceled a popular phone-in radio show, which had at times allowed for harsh criticism of the government and ruling party.

While there are no restrictions on internet sites, and many publications and organizations have websites that are critical of the government, the 2009 Communication Act has raised concerns about privacy rights. The new legislation—which was passed in the face of substantial opposition—includes an interceptions clause that allows the government to tap into private communications without a warrant.

Freedom of religion is guaranteed and respected in practice. The government does not restrict academic freedom.

Freedoms of assembly and association are guaranteed by law and permitted in practice, except in situations of national emergency. Although human rights groups generally have operated without interference, government ministers have in the past threatened and harassed nongovernmental organizations (NGOs) and their leadership. Constitutionally guaranteed union rights are respected. Although collective bargaining is not practiced widely outside the mining and construction industries, informal collective bargaining is increasingly common. Essential public sector workers do not have the right to strike.

The constitution provides for an independent judiciary, and the separation of powers is observed in practice. Access to justice, however, is obstructed by economic and geographic barriers, a shortage of public defenders, and delays caused by a lack of capacity in the court system, especially at lower levels. Traditional courts in rural areas have often ignored constitutional procedures. However, 2003 legislation to create greater uniformity in traditional court operations and better connect them to the formal judicial system was implemented in 2009. Allegations of police brutality persist, and conditions in prisons and military detention facilities are quite harsh.

Human rights are for the most part well respected in Namibia. However, minority ethnic groups have claimed that the government favors the majority Ovambo in allocating funding and services.

Despite constitutional guarantees, and one of highest percentages of women parliamentarians in Africa, women continue to face discrimination in customary law and other traditional societal practices. Widows and orphans have been stripped of their land, livestock, and other assets in rural areas. Lack of awareness of legal rights as well as informal practices have undermined the success of legal changes, such as the 2002 Communal Land Reform Act. Violence against women is reportedly widespread; rights groups have criticized the government for failing to enforce the country's progressive domestic violence laws. The government has been praised for providing antiretroviral drugs to Namibians infected with HIV/AIDS and for its 2007 policy outlawing societal and workplace discrimination against those living with the virus.

Nauru

Political Rights: 1
Civil Liberties: 1
Status: Free

Population: 10,000
Capital: Yaren

Ten-Year Ratings Timeline For Year Under Review (Political Rights, Civil Liberties, Status)

2000	2001	2002	2003	2004	2005	2006	2007	2008	2009
1,3PF	1,3F	1,2F	1,1F	1,1F	1,1F	1,1F	1,1F	1,1F	1,1F

Overview: Digicel, a private mobile telecommunications company, was given approval in June 2009 to provide wireless network services in Nauru. President Marcus Stephen declared September 1 a national holiday in celebration of the launch of nation-wide mobile service.

Nauru is the world's smallest republic. It was a German protectorate from 1888 until Australian troops seized it during World War I. The League of Nations granted a joint mandate to Australia, Britain, and New Zealand to govern the island in 1919. Japan occupied Nauru during World War II, and in 1947, the United Nations designated it as a trust territory under Australia. Nauru gained independence in 1968, became an associate Commonwealth member in 1969, and joined the United Nations in 1999.

The once-plentiful supplies of phosphate, mined by Australia for use as fertilizer, are now almost entirely exhausted in Nauru. Mining has made more than 80 percent of the eight-square-mile island uninhabitable, and the government has squandered much of its accumulated wealth through financial mismanagement. The country currently carries a large foreign debt, and rising sea levels threaten its survival.

Recent governments have tried different ways to generate income, mostly with limited success. With few viable economic alternatives, foreign development assistance had become a major source of government income. However, money laundering tied to Nauru's offshore banking operations had landed the country on international blacklists, restricting its access to international loans. Despite such restrictions, Nauru has received considerable aid from China and Taiwan by switching diplomatic recognition between the two rivals. Between 2001 and 2008, Nauru served as a refugee processing and detention center for Australia in exchange for rent and aid. International groups criticized the center for detaining refugees, including children, for years while awaiting processing, adjudication, and settlement. Its closure cost Nauru approximately one-fifth of the country's gross domestic product.

Intense political rivalry and the use of no-confidence votes have been a source of political instability. The election of Ludwig Scotty in 2004 and his re-election in August 2007 provided encouragement to some that a stable government and the implementation of much-needed economic reforms were possible. However, the president's apparent refusal to investigate allegations of corruption against Finance and Foreign Minister David Adeang led to Scotty's ouster in a no-confidence vote in December 2007. Marcus Stephen replaced Scotty as president, pledging good governance and transparency, though Stephen was soon challenged by a failed opposition-led vote of no confidence in March 2008. Political deadlock in Parliament followed, leading to Stephen's declaration of a state of emergency and calls for a snap election the following month. Stephen won a second term in office, and his supporters secured 12 of 18 seats in Parliament, ending the crisis.

To improve political stability and government accountability, the Scotty government launched a constitutional review in 2005. However, the 36-member Constitution Convention created to make recommendations to the government has yet to submit its suggestions, as delegates remained deeply divided over proposals including a directly elected president, making the state auditor an independent officer of Parliament, and requiring strict accounting for all public revenue and expenditures.

Nauru's distance from the rest of the world increases the importance of connectivity through telecommunications. The entry of the telecommunications company Digicel in June 2009 was greeted with considerable excitement, including the president's decision to make September 1—the day mobile telephone service and was officially launched in Nauru—a national holiday.

Political Rights and Civil Liberties:

Nauru is an electoral democracy. The 2007 elections were deemed free and fair by international observers. The 18-member unicameral legislature is popularly elected from 14 constituencies for three-year terms. Parliament chooses the president and vice president from among its members. Political parties include the Nauru First Party and the Democratic Party, but many politicians are independents.

Corruption is a serious problem in Nauru. Although there were allegations of government corruption in 2009, no cases were brought before the courts. In March, President Marcus Stephen signed a memorandum of understanding with Kiribati and Tuvalu to establish a subregional audit support program for more uniform and timely auditing of public accounts. Nauru was not rated in Transparency International's 2009 Corruption Perceptions Index.

The government does not restrict or censor the news media. Local journalists produce a number of weekly and monthly publications; foreign dailies, most in English, are freely admitted and widely available. The government publishes occasional bulletins, and the opposition publishes its own newsletters. Radio Nauru and Nauru TV, which the government owns and operates, broadcast content from Australia, New Zealand, and other international sources. There are no formal restrictions on internet usage, though cost and lack of infrastructure has limited access. The introduction of Digicel's wireless network services in 2009 made mobile phone service and internet access through mobile devices available to all areas of Nauru.

The constitution provides for freedom of religion, which the government generally respects in practice. There have been no reports of government suppression of academic freedom.

The government respects freedoms of assembly and association. There are several advocacy groups for women, development-focused groups, and religious organizations. The country lacks trade unions and labor protection laws, partly because there is little large-scale, private employment.

The judiciary is independent, and defendants generally receive fair trials and representation. The Supreme Court is the highest authority on constitutional issues, and Parliament cannot overturn court decisions. Appeals in civil and criminal cases can be lodged with the high court of Australia. Traditional reconciliation mechanisms, rather than the formal legal process, are frequently used, typically by choice but sometimes under communal pressure. A civilian official controls the 100-person police force. Police abuse is rare, although foreign workers have complained that the police are slow to act on cases filed against native employers. Nauru has no armed forces; Australia provides national defense under an informal agreement.

Societal pressures limit the ability of women to exercise their legal rights. Sexual harassment is a crime, but spousal rape is not. Domestic violence is frequently associated with alcohol abuse. There are currently no women serving in Parliament.

Nepal

Political Rights: 4
Civil Liberties: 4
Status: Partly Free

Population: 27,504,000
Capital: Kathmandu

Ten-Year Ratings Timeline For Year Under Review (Political Rights, Civil Liberties, Status)

2000	2001	2002	2003	2004	2005	2006	2007	2008	2009
3,4PF	3,4PF	4,4PF	5,4PF	5,5PF	6,5NF	5,4PF	5,4PF	4,4PF	4,4PF

Overview: In a blow to Nepal's recovery from a long-running civil conflict, the Maoist party withdrew from the government in May, after the president rejected the Maoist prime minister's attempt to fire the army chief. The Maoists physically blockaded the legislature for the remainder of the year and organized mass protests across the country. Despite the political unrest, Nepal maintained the significant improvements in law and order that followed the 2006 peace agreement. However, attacks on journalists remained commonplace, and ethnic violence continued in the south.

King Prithvi Narayan Shah unified the Himalayan state of Nepal in 1769. Following two centuries of palace rule, the left-leaning Nepali Congress (NC) party won Nepal's first elections in 1959. King Mahendra abruptly dissolved parliament and banned political parties in 1960, and in 1962, he began ruling through a repressive *panchayat* (village council) system. Many parties went underground until early 1990, when the NC and a coalition of Communist parties organized prodemocracy rallies that led King Birendra to lift the ban. An interim government introduced a constitution that vested executive power in a prime minister and cabinet responsible to parliament, but retained the monarch as head of state.

In Nepal's first multiparty elections in 32 years, Girija Prasad Koirala, a veteran dissident, led the NC to victory and formed a government in 1991. Torn by intraparty conflicts, the NC was forced in 1994 to call early elections, which it lost to the Communist Party of Nepal/United Marxist-Leninist, or CPN-UML. The Communists, however, failed to secure a majority in parliament. Separately, the more militant Communist Party of Nepal (Maoist) launched a guerrilla insurgency in 1996 that eventually engulfed much of the countryside. Hopes for a more stable government rose after the NC won a majority in 1999 elections.

In June 2001, King Birendra's brother Gyanendra took the throne after a bizarre palace incident in which the crown prince apparently shot and killed Birendra and nine other members of the royal family before killing himself. Gyanendra declared a state of emergency in November, and for the next several years, he ruled without parliament, appointing governments unilaterally. Moreover, he presided over a sharp escalation in the civil conflict, using the army to fight the Maoist rebels. The fighting, combined with periodic strikes and blockades, crippled the economy.

By 2005, Gyanendra's government was cracking down on political dissent and shutting down numerous media outlets and other means of communication, such as telephone and internet services. Realizing that their attempts to engage the king were unlikely to bear fruit, a seven-party alliance (SPA) of mainstream political factions entered into talks with the Maoists, yielding an agreement in November that called for the restoration of democracy.

In April 2006, thousands of people took part in daily demonstrations across the country, with the general public—led by professionals, civil society and human rights activists, and the civil service—forming the core of most marches. Gyanendra relented on April 24, agreeing to the provisions of the November 2005 SPA-Maoist pact. The restored parliament quickly removed most of the king's powers, and the SPA announced plans to elect a Constituent Assembly (CA) that would write a new constitution.

After months of tension over Maoist disarmament and the fate of the monarchy, SPA and Maoists concluded a Comprehensive Peace Agreement (CPA) in November 2006, stipulating that the Maoists would place their weapons under UN monitoring, confine their fighters to camps, disband their parallel government, and join a new interim government alongside members of the existing parliament. In January 2007, Maoists joined the parliament, weapons decommissioning was completed, and an interim constitution was promulgated. However, ethnic violence broke out in the Terrai plains region along the border with India. Combined with the lack of finalized election laws and ongoing disagreement over the monarchy, this led to a series of postponements of CA elections from their original date in June 2007.

The elections were finally held in April 2008, and international observers deemed them generally free and fair, with few incidents of violence on election day. However, the campaign period was marred by widespread violence, with regular attacks on candidates and campaign workers. Two candidates were killed, and Maoists were responsible for the bulk of the violence. The Maoist party won a conclusive victory, capturing 220 of the 601 seats. Its nearest rival was the NC (110 seats), followed by the CPN-UML (103 seats), the Madhesi People's Rights Forum (52 seats), and a range of smaller parties and independents. The CA quickly voted to replace the monarchy with a republican system, and in July, it chose the NC's Ram Baran Yadav as president. However, Maoist leader Prachanda was elected prime minister in August, and the Maoists formed a coalition government.

Faced with a hostile press, a vocal opposition, and deep suspicion from the upper echelons of the increasingly politicized military, the Maoists achieved little during their time in government. Antagonism between the Maoists and the army came to a head in May 2009, when Prachanda, frustrated by the military's resistance to integration with former Maoist fighters, ordered the firing of army chief Rookmangud Katawal. The order was legally dubious, since the president technically had control over such decisions, and it inspired widespread protest among coalition partners. The firing was ultimately rejected by Yadav. Prachanda resigned, and a new government led by the CPN-UML was formed. The Maoists maintained a physical blockade of the CA after leaving government, and Maoist protests were common throughout the country for the remainder of 2009. The siege was suspended for three days in late November to allow key budgetary legislation to pass.

Political Rights and Civil Liberties:

Nepal is not an electoral democracy. The CA elections held in April 2008 were found to be, "generally organized in a professional and transparent manner," by a European Union observation team. However, the observers noted that the elections did not fully meet international standards due to restrictions on freedoms of assembly, movement, and expression. Violence was fairly common during the campaign period, though election day was generally peaceful.

The government is operating under a 2007 interim constitution. In addition to its task of writing a permanent constitution, the 601-seat CA serves as the interim legislature. Members were selected through a mixed system of first-past-the-post constituency races (240 seats), proportional representation (335 seats), and appointments by the cabinet (26 seats). Both the president and the prime minister are elected by a majority of the CA, which abolished the monarchy shortly after convening in May 2008.

A wide range of political parties currently hold seats in the CA. Unlike the 1990 constitution, the interim constitution has no limitation on parties formed along ethnic lines. A third of the seats in the CA are reserved for women, and substantial allocations were also made for Madhesis, Dalits, and other minority groups. A 2007 civil service law reserves 45 percent of posts for women, minorities, and Dalits, but their representation in state institutions remains inadequate.

Corruption is perceived to be endemic in politics and government, and enforcement of anticorruption regulations remains weak. While the Commission for the Investigation of Abuse of Authority is active, high-level officials are rarely prosecuted. Many members of the CA have been accused or convicted of corruption in the past. Graft is particularly prevalent in the judiciary, with frequent payoffs to judges for favorable rulings. A 2009 government report suggested that corruption is also endemic in the police force, pointing to widespread acceptance of bribes and extensive police involvement in organized crime. Nepal was ranked 143 out of 180 surveyed in Transparency International's 2009 Corruption Perceptions Index.

The legal environment for the press has improved significantly since the April 2006 uprising, and several restrictive measures were repealed shortly after parliament was restored that year. The interim constitution provides for press freedom and specifically prohibits censorship, although these rules can be suspended during an emergency. Authorities are barred from closing or cancelling the registrations of media outlets due to content. The government maintains control of both the influential Radio Nepal, whose political coverage is supportive of official policies, and the country's main television station. However, there is a variety of independent radio and print outlets. Many mainstream media outlets showed a strong anti-Maoist bias during that party's short time in government.

Journalists are subject to serious violence and intimidation from sources including the military, police, Maoists, and a number of groups representing minorities. Harassment is particularly common for journalists reporting on sensitive ethnic issues in southern Nepal. In January 2009, radio journalist Uma Singh was murdered by a group of men in Janakpur. Five people were arrested in connection with the crime, which was thought to have been motivated by Singh's reporting on women's rights and caste issues.

The interim constitution identifies Nepal as a secular state, signaling a break with the Hindu monarchy. While religious tolerance is broadly practiced, proselytizing is prohibited, and members of some religious minorities occasionally complain of official harassment. There was a significant increase in harassment of the Tibetan community in 2009, according to the U.S. State Department's 2009 Report on International Religious Freedom. Tibetan groups have faced restrictions in organizing public events, and Christian groups have considerable difficulty registering as religious organizations, leaving them unable to own land. Two people were killed and at least 12 injured in a bomb blast at a Roman Catholic church in May 2009. While there was no claim of responsibility, police suspected an extremist Hindu group that had carried out similar bombings in the past.

The government does not restrict academic freedom. However, Maoist strikes in 2009 disrupted the school system; a UN report estimated there were 120 instances of school closures and approximately 80 cumulative school days lost during the year.

Freedom of assembly is guaranteed under the interim constitution. While peaceful protests are generally respected by the authorities, both Madhesi and Tibetan protests have been violently suppressed in recent years. Maoists began organizing large-scale, countrywide protests in May 2009, after the sacking of the army chief was blocked and they withdrew from government. The demonstrations, which lasted through year's end, included blockades of roads and government buildings and a call for a nationwide shutdown of schools. Several protests in the capital in May ended in violence by both protesters and police.

Nongovernmental organizations (NGOs) played an active role in the April 2006 protests, and after the king stepped down, the new government repealed a 2005 code of conduct that had barred NGOs from work that would disturb social harmony. Maoist cadres and the affiliated Young Communist League (YCL) at times threatened, attacked, or disrupted the activities of NGOs in 2009. Several attacks on NGOs aiding victims of sexual and domestic violence have been reported.

Labor laws provide for the freedom to bargain collectively, and unions generally operate without state interference. A draconian labor ordinance put in place by the king's government was repealed in 2006, and restrictions on civil service members forming unions were lifted. Workers in a broad range of "essential" industries cannot stage strikes, and 60 percent of a union's membership must vote in favor of a strike for it to be legal. Although bonded labor was outlawed in 2000, and the law sets the minimum age for employment at 14 years, both bonded and child labor persist in the informal sector. The United Nations reported in 2009 that the Maoist party continues to hold more than 3,000 children in cantonments. The Nepali Ministry for Labor and Transport Management estimates that there are approximately 2.4 million child laborers in Nepal.

The constitution provides for an independent judiciary, but most courts suffer from endemic corruption, and many Nepalese have only limited access to justice. In 2008, the chief justice of the Supreme Court acknowledged that it was often subject to political pressure. Because of heavy case backlogs and a slow appeals process, suspects are often kept in pretrial detention for periods longer than any sentences they would face if tried and convicted. Prison conditions are poor, with widespread overcrowding and detainees sometimes remaining handcuffed or otherwise fettered.

In ordinary criminal cases, police at times commit extrajudicial killings and cause the disappearance of suspects in custody. They also occasionally torture and beat suspects to punish them or extract confessions. The government generally has refused to conduct thorough investigations or take serious disciplinary measures against officers accused of brutality.

Both the state and the Maoists have been accused of committing an array of human rights abuses during the civil conflict, which claimed nearly 13,000 lives between 1996 and 2006. While a truth and reconciliation commission was called for in the 2006 peace agreement, a bill to create such a panel had yet to be enacted at the end of 2009. Under the terms of the peace deal, nearly 20,000 disarmed Maoist fighters are currently living in UN-monitored camps across the country. However, Maoists have been accused of continued human rights abuses. The YCL, established after the peace agreement, has kidnapped, harassed, and beaten political opponents and been accused of meting out vigilante justice in rural areas. Although the group's activities were scaled back somewhat in 2009, several YCL attacks on rival political parties were reported. Maoists repeatedly called for the integration of former Maoist fighters into the security forces during the year, but other parties and the military have blocked the process.

Members of the Hindu upper castes dominate government and business, and low-caste Hindus, ethnic minorities, and Christians face discrimination in the civil service and courts. Despite constitutional provisions that ban caste-based discrimination, Dalits continue to be subjected to exploitation, violence, and social exclusion. Separately, Nepal has provided asylum to more than 100,000 Bhutanese refugees since the early 1990s.

Madhesis, plains-dwelling people with close connections to groups across the border in India, are often described in contrast to Pahades, or hill-dwelling people. Madhesis are underrepresented in politics, have comparatively little economic support from the government, and—until an amendment to the citizenship law in 2006— had difficulty acquiring formal citizenship due to Nepali language requirements. Several armed separatist groups claiming to represent Madhesis operate in southern Nepal; security is poor and local governance nearly nonexistent in several southern states.

Women rarely receive the same educational and employment opportunities as men. The government has taken few steps to curb violence against women or to assist victims, and authorities generally do not prosecute domestic violence cases. Amnesty International and others have documented a number of cases of custodial rape of women and girls by security forces. Thousands of women and girls are trafficked annually, many to Indian brothels. Because most prostitutes who return to Nepal are HIV-positive, nearly all returnees are shunned. In December 2007, the Supreme Court ordered the government to abolish all laws that discriminate against homosexuals, and in November 2008, it gave its consent to same-sex marriage. The government has yet to implement these rulings, though citizens can now obtain third-gender identity documents.

Netherlands

Political Rights: 1
Civil Liberties: 1
Status: Free

Population: 16,527,000
Capital: Amsterdam

Ten-Year Ratings Timeline For Year Under Review (Political Rights, Civil Liberties, Status)

2000	2001	2002	2003	2004	2005	2006	2007	2008	2009
1,1F	1,1F	1,1F	1,1F	1,1F	1,1F	1,1F	1,1F	1,1F	1,1F

Overview:

Minority integration and freedom of speech remained top political concerns in the Netherlands throughout 2009. Geert Wilders, the leader of the anti-immigrant Party for Freedom (PVV), was charged with inciting hatred and discrimination in January for his comments about Muslims in recent years. The PVV won 17 percent of the Dutch vote in the June European Parliament elections, and polled well throughout the year. However, Rotterdam elected the Netherlands' first immigrant mayor that same month.

After the Dutch won their independence from Spain in the 16th century, the princely House of Orange assumed the leadership of the Dutch Republic, which later became the of the United Netherlands. Following a brief period of rule by Napoleonic France, the Kingdom of the Netherlands emerged in the 19th century as a constitutional monarchy with a representative government. The Netherlands remained neutral in both world wars, though the invasion of Nazi Germany in 1940 influenced the country to join NATO in 1949. In 1952, it became a founding member of the European Coal and Steel Community, a precursor to the European Union (EU).

The integration of immigrants has remained a prominent area of concern in Dutch politics since the murder of right-wing politician Pim Fortuyn in May 2002. His newly formed party, the Pim Fortuyn List (LPF), had placed second in that month's parliamentary elections, running on an anti-immigrant platform. However, party infighting led to the collapse of the new government in October. The center-right Christian Democratic Appeal (CDA) led the ensuing elections in 2003; it formed a coalition government with the People's Party for Freedom and Democracy (VVD) and the smaller Democrats-66 (D66) party.

In May 2006, immigration and integration minister Rita Verdonk moved to annul the citizenship of a fellow VVD member of parliament, the Somali-born Ayaan Hirsi Ali, after it was discovered that she had lied in her 1992 asylum application. Hirsi Ali had received death threats for being an outspoken critic of Islam and for the film *Submission*, which she had made in collaboration with controversial filmmaker Theo Van Gogh, who was killed by a radical Islamist in 2004. D66 quit the government over the handling of the incident, causing the coalition to collapse in June.

In November 2006 elections, the CDA again led the voting with 41 seats, followed by the Labor Party (PvdA) with 32, the Socialist Party with 26, and the VVD with 22. A new centrist coalition government took office in February 2007, consisting of the CDA, the PvdA, and the Christian Union party. The CDA's Jan-Peter Balkenende continued as prime minister. The coalition government included the country's first Muslim cabinet ministers—Ahmed Aboutaleb, deputy minister for social affairs, and Nebahat Albayrak, deputy minister of justice—and marked the morally conservative Christian Union's debut in government. The LPF gained no seats in the 2006 elections and has since disbanded.

The right-wing Party for Freedom (PVV), led by Geert Wilders, has continued to make immigration a dominant political issue. In the 2006 elections, the PVV gained nearly 15 percent of the vote, and 17 percent in the June 2009 European Parliament elections. The PVV states that its platform is not racist, but the party advocates ending immigration to the Netherlands from non-Western countries and takes an aggressive assimilationist attitude toward existing immigrants. Former integration minister Verdonk's party, Proud of the Netherlands (TON), also takes a hard line on immigration but has not garnered the same level of support as the PVV. Wilders was refused entry to the United Kingdom in February 2009, though the ban was subsequently overturned by the United Kingdom's Asylum and Immigration Tribunal in October.

In January 2009, Aboutaleb was inaugurated as mayor of Rotterdam, becoming the first mayor of a major Dutch city from a Muslim or immigrant background. However, controversy erupted in August over Aboutaleb's firing of Tariq Ramadan, his integration adviser, after it was discovered that Ramadan had been hosting a chat show on state-financed Iranian television. The Rotterdam government argued that Ramadan's action implied Dutch approval of Iran's regime. Meanwhile, Ramadan had been previously cleared in April of making homophobic remarks.

Political Rights and Civil Liberties: The Netherlands is an electoral democracy. The 150-member lower house of parliament, or Second Chamber, is elected every four years by proportional representation. The 75-member upper house, or First Chamber, is elected for four-year terms by the country's provincial councils. Foreigners resident in the country for five years or more are eligible to vote in local elections. The Netherlands extended voting rights to Aruba and the Netherlands Antilles for the first time in the June 2009 European Parliament elections.

The leader of the majority party or coalition is usually appointed prime minister by the monarch, currently Queen Beatrix. Mayors are appointed from a list of candidates submitted by the municipal councils. The monarch appoints the Council of Ministers (cabinet) and the governor of each province on the recommendation of the majority in parliament.

The country has few problems with political corruption. The Netherlands was ranked 6 out of 180 countries surveyed in Transparency International's 2009 Corruption Perceptions Index.

The news media are free and independent. In January 2009, Geert Wilders was charged with inciting hated and discrimination for editorials in which he called the Koran fascist and said it should be banned, as well as his controversial film *Fitna*. Wilders could face up to 16 months in prison and a fine of nearly US$13,000. His trial was scheduled for January 2010. In September 2009, the public prosecution office decided that the Arab European League (AEL) will be brought to trial for an anti-Semitic cartoon. The rarely enforced 1881 lese majesty law restricting defamation of the monarch was used in August, after the Associated Press published pictures of the royal family on vacation. The court ruled that the Associated Press should pay EUR 1,000 ($US1,400) every time the pictures are republished, up to a maximum fine of EUR 50,000 (US$70,000).

The constitution guarantees freedom of religion, and religious organizations that provide educational facilities can receive subsidies from the government. Members of the country's Muslim population have encountered an increase in hostility in recent years, including vandalism, arson, defacement of mosques or other Islamic institutions, harassment, and verbal abuse. The government requires all imams and other spiritual leaders recruited from Muslim countries to take a one-year integration course before practicing in the Netherlands. The government does not restrict academic freedom.

People have the right to assemble, demonstrate, and generally express their opinions. National and international human rights organizations operate freely without government intervention. Workers have the right to organize, bargain collectively, and strike. Two of the largest trade unions opened their ranks to self-employed workers in 2007.

The judiciary is independent, and the rule of law prevails in civil and criminal matters. The police are under civilian control, and prison conditions meet international standards.

The population is generally treated equally under the law, although human rights groups have criticized the country's recent asylum policies for being unduly harsh and violating international standards. Nongovernmental organizations had noted weak procedures for protecting asylum seekers who could face persecution at home. The government subsequently implemented a policy of automatically accepting asylum seekers based on country of origin. However, this policy was terminated in December 2009, and asylum applications will be assessed on an individual basis.

The country is a destination and transit point for trafficking in persons, particularly women and girls for sexual exploitation. A 2005 law expanded the legal definition of trafficking to include forced labor and increased the maximum penalty for traffickers to 12 years in cases of serious physical injury and 15 years in cases of death.

NewZealand

Political Rights: 1
Civil Liberties: 1
Status: Free

Population: 4,317,000
Capital: Wellington

Ten-Year Ratings Timeline For Year Under Review (Political Rights, Civil Liberties, Status)

2000	2001	2002	2003	2004	2005	2006	2007	2008	2009
1,1F	1,1F	1,1F	1,1F	1,1F	1,1F	1,1F	1,1F	1,1F	1,1F

Overview: In 2009, Prime Minister John Key tried to increase Maori and Pacific Islander support for the National Party-led coalition government by visiting important Maori sites and reaching out to these communities. Meanwhile, Taito Phillip Field, the first Pacific Islander elected to Parliament, was found guilty of bribery, corruption, and other criminal charges in August.

British sovereignty in New Zealand was established in 1840 under the Treaty of Waitangi, a pact between the British government and Maori chiefs that also guaranteed Maori land rights. New Zealand gained full independence from Britain in 1947, though the British monarch remained head of state.

General elections in 2005 gave the center-left Labour Party—which had been in office since 1999—a plurality of 50 parliamentary seats, compared with the center-right National Party's 48. Labour reached agreements with a number of smaller parties to secure a governing majority in the 121-seat Parliament.

Concerns about how immigration is changing the country's demographics have led the government to tighten immigration requirements in recent years. Residents must live in New Zealand for five years before they can apply for citizenship, and automatic citizenship is restricted to those born in Samoa between 1924 and 1948, when Samoa was under New Zealand's rule.

There is also increasing concern about immigrants as national security threats. The country's 2002 Terrorism Suppression Act (TSA) was used for the first time in 2008 to arrest 17 Maori activists suspected of plotting race-based terror attacks. After harsh criticism from Maori rights advocates and union leaders, the government dropped pending charges under the TSA and alternatively charged the defendants with the illegal possession and use of arms and ammunition under the Arms Act.

Prime Minister Helen Clark called for a snap general election in November 2008 in the midst of declining popularity, political scandals, and growing public anxiety about the domestic economic recession, exacerbated by the global financial crisis. The National Party, led by John Key, captured 58 seats, while Labour took 43 seats. With support from the Maori Party (5 seats), the United Future Party (1 seat), and the ACT New Zealand Party (5 seats), the coalition under Key's National Party took control of 69 of the 122 seats in Parliament, and Key was elected the new prime minister.

In 2009, Prime Minister Key tried to improve ties with the Maori population. In celebration of New Zealand's national day on February 4, he visited Waitangi—a practice terminated by his predecessor in 2004 after being jostled by protestors. Although two men did try to attack Key, they were arrested, and Key was unharmed. Also in February, the government officially acknowledged that the war dance (*haka*) performed by the national rugby team belongs to the Maori, in particular the Ngati Toa tribe. This was the first official designation of intellectual property protection for the Maori. While the Maori will not be awarded royalty claims, the tribe is permitted to address grievances over inappropriate use of the haka. In addition, the government agreed to pay $111 million in compensation—including both rent payments from government-owned forests and greenhouse gas emission credits—to eight tribes as a comprehensive settlement for grievances over land seizures and other breaches of the 1840 Treaty of Waitangi. In July, the government reversed the position of the previous administration and said it will endorse the United Nations Declaration on the Rights of Indigenous Peoples.

As of May 2009, nearly 5,000 foreign workers, mainly from neighboring Pacific islands, were working in the country under the 2006 Recognized Seasonal Employers Scheme (RSE). However, unemployment rates reached a record high of 7.3 percent in the December 2009 quarter. In response to popular pressure, the government implemented further restrictions on new migrant workers and their dependents. Beginning December 1, 2009, migrant workers must earn a minimum gross annual income of $33,675 in order for their children to receive visas to study in New Zealand. Many neighboring Pacific island countries welcomed the scheme as a way to increase remittance income, but critics in New Zealand argue that the plan takes jobs away from local people.

Political Rights and Civil Liberties: New Zealand is an electoral democracy. A mixed-member electoral system combines voting in geographic districts with proportional-representation balloting. New Zealand is a member of the Commonwealth, and Britain's Queen Elizabeth II is the head of state, represented by a governor-general. The prime minister, the head of government, is the leader of the majority party or coalition and is appointed by the governor-general. The unicameral Parliament, or House of Representatives, currently has 121 members, all elected for three-year terms.

The two main political parties are the center-left Labour Party and the center-right National Party. Five smaller parties (the Maori, United Future, ACT New Zealand, Green, and Progressive parties) also won representation in the 2008 parliamentary elections.

Seven of the Parliament's constituency seats are reserved for the native Maori population, which continues to increase. Approximately 15 percent of the country's 4.3 million people identify themselves as Maori, and nearly a quarter of all children are Maori. The Maori Party, the country's first ethnic party, was formed in 2004 to advance Maori rights and interests.

New Zealand is one of the least-corrupt countries in the world. It was ranked first out of 180 countries surveyed in Transparency International's 2009 Corruption Perceptions Index. However, public concern over high-level corruption has increased in recent years due to several cases of official abuse. In August 2009, Samoan-born, former member of Parliament Taito Phillip Field was convicted of corruption, bribery, and obstruction of justice for improperly influencing the immigration applications of eight Thai workers in return for free labor on five properties he owned; he was sentenced to six years in prison. This was the first time that a member of Parliament had been convicted of a serious breach of law.

The media are free and competitive. Newspapers are published nationally and locally in English, as well as in many other languages for the growing immigrant population. Television outlets include the state-run Television New Zealand, three private channels, and a Maori-language public network. A Maori-language radio station has been broadcasting since 1996. The government does not control or censor internet access, and competitive pricing promotes large-scale diffusion.

Freedom of religion is provided by law and respected in practice. Only religious organizations that intend to collect donations need to register with the government. Although New Zealand is a secular state, the government has fined businesses for operating on the official holidays of Christmas Day, Good Friday, and Easter Sunday. A 2001 law granted exemptions to several categories of stores in response to demands from non-Christian populations.

Academic freedom is enjoyed at all levels of instruction. The Education Act of 1964 bans religious education and observations during normal hours in primary schools. Some parents have complained about prayers and religious blessings at a number of primary and intermediate schools.

The government respects freedoms of assembly and association. Nongovernmental organizations are active throughout the country, and many receive considerable financial support from the government. The New Zealand Council of Trade Unions is the main labor federation. Fewer than 20 percent of the country's wage earners are union members. Under the 2001 Employment Relations Act (ERA), workers can organize, strike, and collectively bargain, with the exception of uniformed personnel.

The judiciary is independent, and defendants can appeal to the Privy Council in London. Prison conditions generally meet international standards, though there have been allegations of discrimination against the Moari, which make up more than half of the prison population. Over the past decade, the police force has been working to become more culturally sensitive in dealing with an increasingly racially and culturally diverse population.

Although no laws explicitly discriminate against the Maori, and their living standards have generally improved, most Maori and Pacific Islanders continue to lag behind the European-descended majority in social and economic status. The Maori population has become more assertive in its claims for land, resources, and compensation from the government. A special tribunal hears Maori tribal claims tied to the Treaty of Waitangi. In 2008, the government and Maori groups signed the Treelords agreement, which will transfer 435,000 acres of plantation forest and associated rents from the central government to eight North Island tribes of more than 100,000 people. In July 2009, the land transfer was completed, along with a payment of US$142 million, representing rent accumulated over the past 20 years. Additional rent and income from the sale and use of this land will be held in a trust-holding company to benefit tribe members.

Violence against women and children remains a significant problem, particularly among the Maori and Pacific Islander populations. Many governmental and nongovernmental programs work to prevent domestic violence and support victims, with special programs for the Maori community. A 2007 law banning the spanking of children remains controversial, as it grants police the authority to determine whether a parent should be charged with abuse. The law was rejected by the majority of voters in a non-binding referendum in August 2009, but the prime minister has said he will not overturn it. A 2005 Civil Union Bill grants same-sex partnerships recognition and legal rights similar to those of married couples.

Nicaragua

Political Rights: 4
Civil Liberties: 4*
Status: Partly Free

Population: 5,669,000
Capital: Managua

Ratings Change: Nicaragua's civil liberties rating declined from 3 to 4 due to President Daniel Ortega's continued use of violent intimidation and politicized courts to overcome obstacles to his plans for reelection.

Ten-Year Ratings Timeline For Year Under Review (Political Rights, Civil Liberties, Status)

2000	2001	2002	2003	2004	2005	2006	2007	2008	2009
3,3PF	3,3PF	3,3PF	3,3PF	3,3PF	3,3PF	3,3PF	3,3PF	4,3PF	4,4PF

Overview: President Daniel Ortega of the ruling Sandinista National Liberation Front (FSLN) pressed forward with his plans for reelection in 2009, securing a contentious Supreme Court ruling in October that struck down the constitutional ban on consecutive terms. Meanwhile, the international community condemned the results of the November 2008 municipal elections, which were marred by allegations of vote rigging in favor of the FSLN, and foreign donors announced the suspension of more than US$150 million in aid. Journalists, government critics, and civil society activists continued to face systematic harassment and intimidation during the year.

The independent Republic of Nicaragua was established in 1838, 17 years after the end of Spanish rule. Its subsequent history has been marked by internal strife and dictatorship. The Sandinista National Liberation Front (FSLN), a leftist rebel group, overthrew the authoritarian regime of the Somoza family in 1979. The FSLN then moved to establish a Marxist government, leading to a civil war. The United States intervened, in part by supporting irregular rebel forces known as the *contras*.

In 1990, National Opposition Union presidential candidate Violeta Chamorro defeated the FSLN's Daniel Ortega in free and open elections, leading to a peaceful transfer of power. Before leaving office, however, the Sandinistas revised laws and sold off state property to party leaders, ensuring that they would retain political and economic clout.

Former Managua mayor Arnoldo Aleman of the Liberal Constitutionalist Party (PLC) defeated Ortega in the 1996 presidential election, but he was accused of corruption throughout his presidency. In 1999, the PLC and FSLN agreed to a governing pact that guaranteed Aleman a seat in both the Nicaraguan and the Central

American parliaments, assuring him immunity from prosecution. It also included reforms that lowered the threshold for winning an election without a runoff from 45 to 40 percent (or 35 percent if the winner had a lead of 5 percentage points). Using their combined bloc in the legislature, the two parties solidified their political control over the Supreme Court, the electoral tribunal, the inspector general's office, and other institutions.

In the 2001 elections, PLC presidential candidate Enrique Bolanos, a respected conservative businessman, defeated Ortega. He vowed to prosecute Aleman and his aides for corruption, causing a break with the PLC; Bolanos later formed his own party, the Alliance for the Republic (APRE). The protracted effort to convict Aleman eventually yielded a 20-year prison sentence for money laundering in 2003. However, the former leader later used his alliance with Ortega to win concessions from the FSLN-controlled courts, and he was released from parole conditions in March 2007, so long as he did not leave the country.

Meanwhile, the PLC- and FSLN-dominated National Assembly blocked virtually all of Bolanos's proposed legislation. In 2005, the National Assembly voted to strip Bolanos of certain presidential powers and replace his appointees to autonomous state bodies. The Central American Court of Justice ordered the National Assembly to reverse the legislation, and after a long standoff, the two sides agreed to postpone implementation of the reforms until after Bolanos left office.

Ortega won the presidency in November 2006 elections, taking 38 percent in the first round. His closest challenger was a former finance minister under Bolanos, Eduardo Montealegre of the Nicaraguan Liberal Alliance (ALN), who took 29 percent. In the concurrent legislative elections, the FSLN obtained 38 out of 92 seats, while the PLC took 25, giving the allied parties a two-thirds majority. The ALN secured 22, and the Sandinista Renewal Movement (MRS) won 5. Bolanos also received a seat as outgoing president, and Montealegre took one as the presidential runner-up. The new National Assembly voted in January 2007 to postpone the 2005 constitutional reforms, which have not taken effect to date.

Later in 2007, Ortega consolidated presidential power through reforms that gave the executive branch more control over the central bank, the police, and the military. His administration also established a system of Citizens' Power Councils (CPCs), from the neighborhood to the federal level, to promote direct democracy and participate in the government's Zero Hunger food-production project. Critics argued that the bodies would blur the lines between state and party institutions. The president asserted his personal influence in June 2008 by appointing his wife to serve as head of the Social Cabinet, which put her in charge of programs like Zero Hunger as well as the National Social Welfare System.

The Supreme Electoral Council (CSE) took a number of steps in 2008 that appeared designed to ensure an FSLN victory in the November municipal elections. It postponed the elections in several municipalities in the Northern Atlantic Autonomous Region, where dissatisfaction with the government response to Hurricane Felix in 2007 had stoked anti-FSLN sentiment. The CSE annulled Montealegre's leadership of the ALN in April and granted it to an FSLN supporter, and in May, it revoked the legal status of two other opposition parties, the Conservative Party and the MRS, preventing them from contesting the elections. The CSE also refused accreditations to local and international electoral observers for the first time since 1990.

After the November balloting, the CSE announced that the FSLN had won 105 of 146 municipalities, including Managua. However, numerous independent observers documented fraud in at least 40 municipalities. In Managua, the CSE failed to report results from 660 polling places, and while observers asserted that Montealegre should have been declared mayor, the office went to Sandinista sympathizer Alexis Arguello. (In July 2009, Arguello was found dead in his home after an apparent suicide.)

Civil society groups led nationwide protests against electoral fraud in February 2009, but demonstrators were violently attacked by progovernment groups in Jinotega, Chinandega, and Leon, causing dozens of injuries. Opposition groups claimed that the police were complicit in the attacks, and in Chinandega two local officials and a progovernment union leader were charged with inciting violence. The international community condemned the municipal election results, leading to the suspension of more than $150 million in U.S. and European Union (EU) aid in 2009.

In July, Ortega publicly commented that Nicaragua should eliminate presidential term limits, stoking fears that he would resist giving up power at the end of his term in 2011. His proposal met with opposition in the National Assembly, where he lacked the support necessary to pass a constitutional amendment on the issue, but in October, he secured a ruling from the FSLN-controlled Supreme Court that struck down the ban on consecutive terms. In December, the National Assembly approved a resolution to oppose the Supreme Court's decision, leaving the electoral commission to decide which body of government to obey. The president of the electoral commission supported the Supreme Court's ruling, but is scheduled to leave his post in 2010. Thus, the future of the commission's decision remained in question at the year's end.

Political Rights and Civil Liberties: Nicaragua is an electoral democracy. The constitution provides for a directly elected president and a 92-member, unicameral National Assembly. Two seats in the legislature are reserved for the previous president and the runner-up in the last presidential election. Both presidential and legislative elections are held every five years. The governing FSLN party and its ally, the PLC, currently dominate state institutions and together hold a two-thirds majority in the legislature.

The 2006 presidential and legislative elections were regarded as free and fair by the CSE and the international community. However, independent observers reported fraud in at least 40 municipalities during the November 2008 local elections, which raised concerns about the impartiality of the CSE in the face of FSLN influence.

The political and civic climate is affected by corruption, political pacts, violence, and drug-related crime. Corruption cases against opposition figures often raise questions about political motivation. The 2007 Law on Access to Public Information requires public entities and private companies doing business with the state to disclose certain information. However, it preserved the government's right to protect information related to state security, and in 2009 government-run enterprises failed to publish financial information in accordance with the law.

The administration of President Daniel Ortega has created a network of private businesses under the auspices of the Bolivarian Alliance for the Americas (ALBA), a regional economic association through which the Venezuelan government provides Nicaragua with 10 million barrels of oil annually. Nicaragua pays half the cost up front and the rest over a 25-year period, with a 2 percent interest rate. The funds generated from the resale of Venezuelan oil are dedicated to social projects but administered directly by President Daniel Ortega's office, outside of the national budget. This has raised concerns that the money could be allocated in a corrupt or politicized manner. In June 2009, the Central Bank was required by the International Monetary Fund to reveal the amount of funding received from Venezuela on its website; Nicaragua reportedly received US$457 million in 2008, up from US$185 million in 2007. However, the Central Bank did not explain how the money was used. In February 2009, the director of the social program Zero Hunger, Gustavo Moreno, resigned amid charges of corrupt contracting and acquisition procedures. Nicaragua was ranked 130 out of 180 countries surveyed in Transparency International's 2009 Corruption Perceptions Index.

The constitution calls for a free press but allows some censorship. Radio remains the main source of information. Before leaving office in 1990, the Sandinistas privatized some radio stations and handed them to party loyalists. There are six television networks based in the capital, including a state-owned network, and many favor particular political factions. Three national newspapers cover the news from a variety of political viewpoints. Investigative journalism plays a major role in exposing corruption and official misconduct. The opposition has accused the office of the Communications and Citizenry Council, which oversees the government's press relations and is directed by First Lady Rosario Murillo, of limiting access to information and censoring the opposition. Access to the internet is unrestricted.

The press has faced increased political and judicial harassment since 2007, as the Ortega administration engages in systematic efforts to obstruct and discredit critics in the media. Journalists have received death threats, and some have been killed in recent years, with a number of attacks attributed to FSLN sympathizers. Amnesty International reported that at least 20 journalists and 5 independent radio stations were attacked following the 2008 municipal elections. Judges aligned with the FSLN have ordered restrictions on coverage of particular cases. In February 2009, citing a lack of evidence, the Interior Ministry dropped an embezzlement and money-laundering investigation it had launched in 2008 against 17 nongovernmental organizations (NGOs), with a focus on two groups headed by journalists. A poll released in April revealed that self-censorship had increased by 23 percentage points between February 2007 and February 2009; the share of respondents reporting that they did not feel safe discussing politics in public rose from 39 percent in 2007 to 68 percent in 2009.

Freedom of religion is respected, and academic freedom is generally honored.

Freedoms of assembly and association are recognized by law, but their observance in practice has come under mounting pressure. While public demonstrations are generally allowed, FSLN supporters used violence against antigovernment protesters in 2008. In February 2009, demonstrators calling for a recount of the November 2008 municipal elections were similarly attacked by FSLN supporters in the cities of Leon, Jinotega, and Chinandega. Opposition members accused the police of partisan behavior and failing to protect demonstrators.

Although NGOs are active and operate freely, they have faced harassment in recent years, and the emergence of the CPCs has weakened their influence. In 2009, the government introduced an "international cooperation manual" that would have regulated NGO activities and funding and placed restrictions on their cooperation with international organizations. Implementation of the manual was suspended in July, following widespread criticism by civil society organizations.

The FSLN controls many of the country's labor unions, and the legal rights of non-FSLN unions are not fully guaranteed. There are reports of employees being dismissed for union activities. Although the law recognizes the right to strike, unions must clear a number of hurdles first, and the requisite approval from the Ministry of Labor is almost never granted. Employers sometimes form their own unions to avoid recognizing legitimate organizations. Citizens have no effective recourse when labor laws are violated by those in power. Child labor and other labor abuses in export-processing zones continue to be problems, though child labor occurs most often in the agricultural sector.

The judiciary remains dominated by FSLN and PLC appointees, and the Supreme Court is a largely politicized body controlled by Sandinista judges. The court system also suffers from corruption, long delays, a large backlog of cases, and a severe shortage of public defenders. Access to justice is especially deficient in rural areas and on the Caribbean coast.

Despite long-term improvements in the conduct of security forces, abuses of human rights still occur, and law enforcement officials allowed progovernment groups to assault protesters with impunity following the 2008 municipal elections. Forced confessions remain a problem, as do arbitrary arrests, and insufficient funding has affected police performance and staffing levels. Conditions in the similarly underfunded prisons are poor. Nicaragua is an important transshipment point for South American drugs, but the police have been active in combating trafficking and organized crime.

The constitution and laws nominally recognize the rights of indigenous communities, but those rights have not been respected in practice. Approximately 5 percent of the population is indigenous and lives mostly in the Northern Atlantic Autonomous Region (RAAN) and Southern Atlantic Autonomous Region (RAAS). The government has taken no known steps to comply with a 2005 ruling by the Inter-American Court of Human Rights, which ordered it to pay damages to indigenous groups after the electoral commission prevented the majority-indigenous Yatama party from competing in 2000 municipal elections. Yatama won 16 percent of the vote in 2006 regional elections. In 2008, the CSE postponed municipal elections in seven municipalities of the RAAN; critics said the aim was to suppress anti-FSLN sentiment in the area following Hurricane Felix, which struck in September 2007. In April 2009, the Miskito Council of Elders announced the creation of a separatist movement demanding independence from Nicaragua; separatists have cited government neglect and grievances related to the exploitation of natural resources. Over a thousand separatist supporters held a demonstration in Bilwi, the RAAN capital, in May.

Violence against women and children, including sexual and domestic abuse, remains a widespread and underreported problem. In September 2009, the public defender's office increased free legal services for victims of domestic violence in 12 municipalities. Abortion is illegal and punishable by imprisonment, even when performed to save the mother's life or in cases of rape or incest. Scores of deaths stemming from the ban have been reported in recent years. The Autonomous Women's Movement, which has vocally opposed the abortion ban, was among the NGOs that faced criminal investigations in 2008 only to be cleared of wrongdoing in February 2009.

Nicaragua is a source for the trafficking of women and children for prostitution. A penal code reform prohibiting trafficking in persons took effect in July 2008, but the country was placed on the Tier 2 Watch List of the U.S. State Department's 2009 Trafficking in Persons Report due to its lack of progress in raising awareness of the problem, improving treatment of victims, and compiling reliable trafficking statistics.

Niger

Political Rights: 5*　　　　　　　　　　　　　　　　**Population:** 15,290,000
Civil Liberties: 4　　　　　　　　　　　　　　　　　　**Capital:** Niamey
Status: Partly Free

Ratings Change: Niger's political rights rating declined from 3 to 5 due to President Mamadou Tandja's antidemocratic moves to extend his power, including the dissolution of the Constitutional Court and National Assembly and the holding of a referendum to eliminate term limits and postpone the next presidential election—originally due in December 2009—until 2012.

Ten-Year Ratings Timeline For Year Under Review (Political Rights, Civil Liberties, Status)

2000	2001	2002	2003	2004	2005	2006	2007	2008	2009
4,4PF	4,4PF	4,4PF	4,4PF	3,3PF	3,3PF	3,3PF	3,4PF	3,4PF	5,4PF

Overview:　　　　　　　President Mamadou Tandja dissolved the National Assembly and Constitutional Court in May and June, respectively, after they stood in the way of his plan to eliminate term limits and postpone the next presidential election until 2012. The proposals were then adopted in a disputed August referendum. The government enacted a new constitution that same month, which called for the creation of a Senate and gave Tandja expanded power over the High Council for Communications, Constitutional Court, and National Assembly. Opposition parties boycotted legislative elections held in October, handing a lopsided victory to Tandja's party. The president's antidemocratic actions prompted the Economic Community of West African States (ECOWAS) to suspend Niger's membership following legislative elections.

After gaining independence from France in 1960, Niger was governed by a series of one-party and military regimes. General Ali Seibou took power in 1987, but his one-party regime yielded to international pressure and prodemocracy demonstrations, and a new constitution was adopted by popular referendum in 1992. Mahamane Ousmane of the Alliance of Forces for Change was elected president in 1993, then overthrown in January 1996 by Colonel Ibrahim Bare Mainassara, who became president in a sham election six months later.

After members of the presidential guard assassinated Mainassara in April 1999, the guard commander led a transitional government that organized a constitutional referendum in July and competitive elections in November. Retired lieutenant colonel Mamadou Tandja, supported by the National Movement for a Developing Society (MNSD) and the Democratic and Social Convention (CDS) parties, won the presidency in the generally free and fair balloting, and the MNSD and the CDS took a majority of seats in the National Assembly. Tandja was reelected in December 2004, and in concurrent legislative elections, four parties joined the MNSD and CDS to secure 88 of the National Assembly's 113 seats.

The next few years were marked by rising prices, food shortages, renewed fighting with ethnic Tuareg rebels in 2007, and allegations of government corruption that created tensions within the MNSD. Prime Minister Hama Amadou resigned over the charges in May 2007 and was arrested in 2008, though he claimed that the case was designed to prevent him from running for president in 2009.

In May 2009, Tandja asked the National Assembly to approve a referendum proposal to create a new constitution, which would postpone the next presidential election until 2012 and eliminate executive term limits, among other changes. After lawmakers voiced opposition to the plan, Tandja dissolved the National Assembly. In June, the Constitutional Court ruled against the proposed referendum, claiming that Tandja was in violation of the constitution. However, Tandja invoked article 53 of the Nigerien constitution and announced that he would rule by decree under emergency powers. He dissolved the Constitutional Court and nominated members for the creation of a new court. The referendum was held in August, and according to official results, the proposal passed with more than 92 percent of the vote amid a turnout of some 68 percent. However, the opposition, which had called for a boycott, rejected the results as fraudulent and estimated a turnout of less than 5 percent. Enacted on August 18, the new constitution eliminates the prime minister's role as head of government and gives Tandja expanded influence over the High Council for Communications, Constitutional Court, and National Assembly, as well as a new Senate, which had yet to be created at year's end.

Tandja lifted the emergency decree in August and announced legislative elections to replace the dissolved National Assembly. Key opposition parties boycotted legislative elections held in October, allowing Tandja's MNSD to capture 76 of the 113 seats, a gain of 30 seats. The elections were denounced by the international community, and the Economic Community of West African States (ECOWAS) suspended Niger's membership. Opposition parties announced that they would also boycott municipal elections scheduled for early 2010. By year's end, the United States and the European Union had withdrawn all non-humanitarian assistance.

In October, Libyan leader Mu'ammar al-Qadhafi declared an end to the Tuareg rebellion, and Tandja granted an amnesty to the rebels. Libya had led mediation efforts between the government and the rebels since August 2008, but at least one splinter group of the rebel Movement of Nigeriens for Justice (MNJ) rejected the peace deal, and the MNJ continued to demand greater Tuareg inclusion in the military and the mining sector.

Political Rights and Civil Liberties: Niger is not an electoral democracy. While observers considered the national polls held in 1999 and 2004 to be largely free and fair, President Mamadou Tandja's unconstitutional moves to extend his rule in 2009 dismantled much of the country's democratic progress.

The August 2009 constitutional referendum shifted power to the president, removing the previous limit of two five-year terms and giving him the exclusive power to appoint and dismiss the prime minister and cabinet. It also called for the creation of a Senate, with a third of the members appointed by the president and the remainder elected indirectly. The National Assembly, previously the unicameral legislature, has 113 directly elected members who serve five-year terms.

Ten political parties were represented in the National Assembly that was dissolved in May 2009, and leaders made efforts to include members of ethnic minorities and nomadic groups in positions of authority. However, major opposition parties boycotted the October elections, and a range of opposition politicians faced arrest during the year. In December, ECOWAS mediated peace talks between the government of Niger and the opposition, which continued through year's end.

Corruption is a serious problem in Niger, and observers have raised transparency concerns regarding uranium mining contracts as well as a US$5 billion oil-exploration deal signed in 2008 by the government and the China National Petroleum Corporation. Graft cases pursued by the authorities often appear politically motivated. In September 2009, more than thirty ex-lawmakers stood trial for "receiving illegal benefits." Twenty-eight were granted provisional release, and three deputies, two staff members, and two vendors were imprisoned. In October, international arrest warrants were issued for Mahamadou Issoufou, leader of the opposition Nigerien Party for Democracy and Socialism–Tarayya; former prime minister Hama Amadou; and former president of the CDS, Mahamane Ousmane, who had been Speaker of the National Assembly before its dissolution. All three men were accused of money laundering; Issoufou returned to Niger in November to face the charges. In November, the government placed a travel ban on 124 former assembly members. Niger was ranked 106 out of 180 countries surveyed in Transparency International's 2009 Corruption Perceptions Index.

The 2009 constitution gives the president the power to nominate the majority of the members of the High Council for Communications, the national media regulatory agency. The Council chairman is now also empowered to arrest any media outlet infringing upon "national security" without having to consult the rest of the council or issue a formal warning. The Niger Association of Independent Media Editors responded with a weeklong media blackout in July. Authorities regularly use libel laws to deter critical journalists. The privately owned media's outspoken support for the opposition in 2009 and its persistent critiques of the government's management of natural resource revenues meant that many journalists and outlets faced police pressure, arrests, and suspensions during the year. The charges included defamation, casting discredit on judicial rulings, and publishing false information. In June, the government ordered the private television and radio network Dounia to suspend broadcasting, but the order was reversed by the courts in July. Security forces held Alassane Karfi, a member of the Niger Party for Democracy and Socialism (PNDS), in prison from mid-July until October for his criticism of the referendum on Dounia television. The government does not restrict internet use, though less than 1 percent of the population has access to the medium.

Freedom of religion is generally respected. However, the Muslim majority is not uniformly tolerant of minority religions. Academic freedom is guaranteed in principle but not always observed in practice.

Constitutional guarantees of freedoms of assembly and association are largely upheld, but authorities restricted the operations of some nongovernmental organizations (NGOs) following the outbreak of Tuareg rebel activity in 2007. In 2009, a coalition of political parties, NGOs, and labor unions brought tens of thousands of demonstrators to the streets in the months surrounding the August referendum. In some instances, police clashed with demonstrators, using tear gas and batons and arresting participants. Separately, prominent human rights activist Marou Amadou was arrested and temporarily detained on multiple occasions beginning in May.

The constitution and other laws guarantee workers the right to join unions and bargain for wages, although over 95 percent of the workforce is employed in subsistence agriculture and small trading.

The constitution provides for an independent judiciary, and courts have shown some autonomy. However, Tandja demonstrated his willingness to disregard the separation of powers and rule of law in 2009, dissolving the Constitutional Court in June and replacing the members with his own nominees. While the new constitution increases the number of judges from seven to nine, it also increases the number nominated by the president from one to five.

The court system is overburdened and subject to executive and other interference. Public prosecutors are supervised by the Ministry of Justice, and the president has the power to appoint judges. Judicial corruption is fueled partly by low salaries and inadequate training. Prolonged pretrial detention is common, and police forces are also underfunded and poorly trained. Prisons are characterized by overcrowding and poor health conditions. Amnesty International has reported arbitrary detentions and extrajudicial killings of civilians by soldiers in retaliation for rebel attacks.

Insecurity plagues the northwest of the country along the Malian border. Disputes over land rights between herders and farmers have led to dozens of deaths in the Tillabery region. In January 2009, four Europeans were abducted by unknown assailants; three hostages were later released, but one was executed by his captors. In late December, four people from a convoy of Saudi citizens were killed near Tillabery. That same month, the Nigerien army clashed with reported drug traffickers, killing nine soldiers, seven traffickers, and a civilian at Telemses.

Discrimination against ethnic minorities persists, despite constitutional protections. Nomadic peoples continue to have poor access to government services.

A 2002 quota system requiring political parties to allocate 10 percent of their elected positions to women has increased their representation. Women continue to suffer discrimination, especially in rural areas. Family law gives women inferior status in property disputes, inheritance rights, and divorce. In the east, some women among the Hausa and Peul ethnic groups are rarely allowed to leave their homes without a male escort. Although sexual harassment was criminalized in 2001, domestic violence is reportedly widespread. Female genital mutilation was criminalized in 2003.

Although the government criminalized slavery in 2003, as many as 43,000 people still live in conditions of servitude. Niger was demoted to Tier 3, the worst-possible rating, in the U.S. State Department's 2009 Trafficking in Persons Report.

⬇ Nigeria

Political Rights: 5
Civil Liberties: 4
Status: Partly Free

Population: 152,616,000
Capital: Abuja

Trend Arrow: Nigeria received a downward trend arrow due to the ruling party's consolidation of power and clashes between the government and a religious sect that led to the deaths of several hundred people.

Ten-Year Ratings Timeline For Year Under Review (Political Rights, Civil Liberties, Status)

2000	2001	2002	2003	2004	2005	2006	2007	2008	2009
4,4PF	4,5PF	4,5PF	4,4PF	4,4PF	4,4PF	4,4PF	4,4PF	5,4PF	5,4PF

Overview:　　　　　　The ruling People's Democratic Party continued to consolidate power in 2009, with alleged partisan interference ensuring its victory in the April rerun of a 2007 gubernatorial election. In July, more than 700 people were killed in clashes between police and members of an Islamic fundamentalist sect. Separately, a government amnesty offer in August led to an apparent reduction in rebel violence in the Niger Delta region, though the situation remained volatile at year's end.

The military ruled Nigeria for much of its history after independence from Britain in 1960. Beginning with the first military coup in 1966, military officers claimed that their intervention was necessary to control simmering tensions among the country's 250 ethnic groups, as well as between religious communities. Muslims, who live mostly in the north, make up about 50 percent of the population, while Christians, who dominate in the south, account for most of the remaining 50 percent. Ethnic and regional tensions led to the attempted secession of Nigeria's oil-rich southeast as the Republic of Biafra in 1967, which touched off a three-year civil war and a devastating famine that together caused more than one million deaths.

A military-supervised political transition led to the inauguration of a civilian government in 1979, but the new democratic regime was burdened by factionalism, corruption, and communal polarization. Economic mismanagement and deeply flawed elections triggered another military intervention in 1983, followed by 16 more years of military rule.

After several years under the leadership of General Ibrahim Babangida, the country held a presidential election in June 1993. Moshood Abiola, a Muslim Yoruba from the south, was widely considered the winner, but Babangida annulled the election. A civilian caretaker administration governed briefly until General Sani Abacha, a principal architect of previous coups, took power in November 1993. Abacha's dictatorial regime dissolved all democratic structures and banned political parties, governing through a predominantly military Provisional Ruling Council (PRC). Abiola was jailed in 1994 and ultimately died in detention, just weeks after the unexpected demise of Abacha in 1998.

General Abdulsalami Abubakar emerged as the new military leader and presided over a transition to civilian rule. In 1999, Olusegun Obasanjo—a former general who had led a military regime from 1976 to 1979 and spent a number of years in prison under Abacha—won a presidential election on the ticket of the People's Democratic Party (PDP), which also captured the most seats in both the Senate and the House of Representatives.

Nigeria made its first transition from one elected government to another when Obasanjo won a second term in April 2003. The elections were preceded by violence, and observers documented widespread irregularities and fraud. Obasanjo, a southern Christian, took 62 percent of the vote. His main competitor was former general Muhammadu Buhari, a northern Muslim and member of the All Nigeria Peoples Party (ANPP), who won 32 percent. Buhari filed a petition to nullify the election results, but the Supreme Court in 2005 unanimously rejected the challenge, saying the documented fraud was not enough to have changed the vote's outcome.

Preparations in 2006 for the 2007 presidential, gubernatorial, and legislative elections were tumultuous and occasionally violent. Vice President Atiku Abubakar announced his intention to run for president, but his candidacy was threatened by corruption charges that he claimed were politically motivated. The opposition Action Congress (AC) party nominated him as its presidential candidate in December, and the Supreme Court cleared him to run just five days before the election. Umaru Yar'Adua, the Muslim governor of northern Katsina State who was widely perceived as Obasanjo's pick, won the PDP nomination, while the ANPP again chose Buhari as its candidate.

The April 2007 elections were marred by bloodshed and eyewitness reports of massive vote rigging and fraud. At least 200 people were killed in election-related violence, with victims including police and several candidates. International and local election monitors were highly critical of the vote, and opposition parties refused to accept the results, which gave Yar'Adua 70 percent of the presidential ballots, Buhari 19 percent, Abubakar 8 percent, and the Progressive People's Alliance candidate, Orji Uzor Kalu, 2 percent.

In the parliamentary vote, the PDP took 87 out of 109 Senate seats and 263 out of 360 House seats. The ANPP took 14 Senate seats and 63 House seats, while the AC took 6 Senate seats and 30 House seats; the remainder went to three smaller parties. The PDP also led the state elections, taking 29 out of 36 governorships.

The official results drew a raft of legal challenges that were adjudicated by election officials as well as the court system, with many appeals stretching well into 2008. In December 2008, the Supreme Court delivered its final ruling on the presidential contest, repudiating the opposition complaints and upholding Yar'Adua's victory. Separately, in a rare instance of an opposition candidate unseating a PDP rival through the appeals system, an appeals court in November overturned the election of the Edo State governor based on "voting irregularities," declaring the AC candidate the rightful governor. A February 2009 ruling annulled the gubernatorial victory of the PDP's Segun Oni in Ekiti State, calling for a rerun of the 2007 vote. However, political violence and misconduct attributed to PDP operatives accompanied the April 2009 runoff between Oni and the AC's Kayode Fayemi, and official results confirmed Oni as the winner.

In November, Yar'Adua left the country to seek medical treatment in Saudi Arabia, and he had not returned at year's end. Little information on his condition was released, and critics began calling for him to resign or temporarily hand power to the vice president.

Nigeria's economy is dominated by oil, which accounts for 95 percent of export revenues and almost all foreign investment. However, it is estimated that nearly US$400 billion in oil revenue has been stolen or squandered since Nigeria's independence in 1960. Wealth and political power are concentrated in the hands of a narrow elite, and much of the regular violence in the oil-rich yet impoverished Niger Delta region stems from unequal distribution of oil revenue.

Political Rights and Civil Liberties: Nigeria is not an electoral democracy. According to the constitution, the president is elected by popular vote for no more than two four-year terms. Members of the bicameral National Assembly, consisting of the 109-seat Senate and the 360-seat House of Representatives, are elected for four-year terms. The Brussels-based International Crisis Group found that the general elections of April 2007, "in the view of Nigerians and the many international observers alike, were the most poorly organized and massively rigged in the country's history." Civil society organizations reported numerous, widespread incidents of political harassment and violence surrounding the elections in six Niger Delta states, with the majority committed by PDP supporters or criminal gangs acting on behalf of PDP politicians.

Nearly 50 parties participated in the 2007 elections. The three major political parties are the ruling PDP; the ANPP, which is the largest opposition party and draws its strongest support from the Muslim north; and the AC, an opposition party formed from smaller groups ahead of the 2007 elections. Three other parties are represented in the federal legislature: the Progressive People's Alliance, the Labour Party, and the Accord Party. Although political parties represent a wide array of policy positions and openly engage in debate, they continue to be marginalized by the PDP. Many opposition parties have argued that the Independent National Electoral Commission is effectively an extension of the PDP.

Corruption remains pervasive despite government efforts to improve transparency and reduce graft. In a watershed case, former PDP deputy chairman Olabode George was sentenced in October 2009 to over two years in prison for graft dating to his tenure as head of the Port Authority. Also in 2009, U.S. oil-services firm Halliburton admitted distributing over US$180 million in kickbacks to Nigerian officials to secure more than US$6 billion in contracts. Seven former governors were charged with corruption in 2007 on orders from the Economic and Financial Crimes Commission (EFCC), the country's main anticorruption agency, but EFCC chairman Nuhu Ribadu was removed from his post in 2008 and fled the country following attempts on his life. The commission's current chairwoman, Farida Waziri, often faces politically motivated meddling in EFCC cases. Nigeria was ranked 130 out of 180 countries surveyed in Transparency International's 2009 Corruption Perceptions Index.

Freedom of speech and expression is constitutionally guaranteed, and Nigeria has a lively independent media sector. However, State Security Service (SSS) agents arrest journalists, confiscate newspapers, and harass vendors, notably when journalists are covering corruption or separatist and communal violence. Local authorities frequently condemn those who criticize them, and as cases of violence against journalists often go unsolved, suspicion surrounds the motives and perpetrators. A reporter and editorial board member with the newspaper *ThisDay*, Paul Abayomi Ogundeji, was killed in August 2008, making him the second *ThisDay* board member to be murdered in as many years. An assistant news editor for the *Guardian*, Bayo Ohu, was shot and killed in September 2009. Sharia (Islamic law) statutes in 12 northern states impose severe penalties for alleged press offenses. The government does not restrict internet access.

Religious freedom is guaranteed by the constitution, but many Nigerians, including government officials, discriminate against adherents of other religions. Religious violence frequently reflects regional and ethnic differences and accompanying competition for resources. At least 700 people were killed in July 2009 during clashes between police and an Islamic fundamentalist group in the city of Maiduguri; related violence was reported in neighboring states. The U.S. Commission on International Religious Freedom added Nigeria to its list of "countries of particular concern" in 2009, alleging government complicity and direct involvement in the deaths.

Academic freedom is generally honored, although government officials frequently pressure university administrators and faculty to ensure special treatment for their relatives and associates. Nigeria's public education system remains dismal; more than a third of the population is illiterate, and less than 60 percent of school-aged children are enrolled.

Freedoms of assembly and association are generally respected in practice. However, protests are often suppressed by state and private security forces, especially demonstrations organized by youth groups or in the Niger Delta. Human rights groups report that dozens of secessionist activists have been killed in recent years, and hundreds have been detained. Workers, except those in the military or "essential services," may join trade unions and have the right to bargain collectively. Public health workers strike frequently, and in 2009, Nigeria's largest labor union collective, the Nigeria Labour Congress, held several large demonstrations regarding workers' pay, deregulation in the petroleum sector, and election reforms. Also during the year, several months of strikes by faculty and staff unions crippled the university system.

The higher courts are relatively competent and independent, but they remain subject to political influence, corruption, and inefficiencies. Certain departments, particularly the Court of Appeals, have often overturned decisions on election challenges or allegations of corruption against powerful elites, raising doubts about their independence. Former PDP Delta State governor James Ibori, a leading financier of President Umaru Yar'Adua's 2007 campaign, was indicted that year on over 140 counts of corruption, but his case continues to be postponed in the courts. British police, in collaboration with the EFCC, have requested the extradition of both Ibori and former Akwa Ibom State governor Victor Attah for trial on money-laundering charges in Britain. However, in September 2009, Nigeria's attorney general Michael Aondoakaa blocked the request.

Ordinary defendants in Nigerian courts frequently lack legal representation and are often ill-informed about court procedures and their rights. Human rights groups have alleged that Islamic courts in the 12 northern states with Sharia statutes fail to respect due-process rights and discriminate against non-Muslims. Pretrial detainees, many of whom are held for several years, account for 65 percent of the country's inmates, and fewer than one in seven detainees has had access to a court-appointed lawyer. Amnesty International describes prison conditions in Nigeria as "appalling," and a 2008 report by the group found extensive human rights abuses in the prison system. Children are often held in prisons with adult populations.

Security forces commit abuses with impunity. In 2007, a UN special rapporteur found frequent extrajudicial killings by police and widespread torture and ill-treatment of suspects in police custody. Amnesty International reported 39 cases of extrajudicial killings by security forces between 2007 and 2009. Violent crime in certain cities and areas remains a serious problem, and the trafficking of drugs and small arms is reportedly on the rise.

The constitution prohibits ethnic discrimination and requires government offices to reflect the country's ethnic diversity, but societal discrimination is widely practiced, and ethnic clashes frequently erupt. Minorities in the Niger Delta feel particular discrimination, primarily with regard to distribution of the country's oil wealth, and their grievances have fueled rebel violence. The government launched an amnesty program in August 2009, and some militant factions reportedly accepted the offer. However, by year's end, the main rebel group, the Movement for the Emancipation of the Niger Delta (MEND), was threatening to cancel its tenuous ceasefire. Kidnappings, especially of oil workers, continued throughout the year.

The authorities often engage in forcible evictions to pave the way for development projects. Amnesty International estimated that between 2000 and 2009, more than two million Nigerians had been evicted.

Nigerian women face societal discrimination, although their educational opportunities have improved and several key governmental positions are held by women. Women in some ethnic groups are denied equal rights to inherit property, and spousal rape is not considered a crime. While the federal government publicly opposes female genital mutilation, it has taken no action to ban the practice. Women's rights have suffered serious setbacks in the northern states governed under Sharia statutes. Human trafficking to, from, and within the country for purposes of labor and prostitution is reported to be on the rise. The government in 2004 outlawed human trafficking and set up an agency to deal with offenders, but existing provisions are insufficient. According to UNICEF, there are 15 million child laborers in Nigeria, with 40 percent of them at risk of being trafficked. Several organizations have reported on an illegal trade in which pregnant teenagers are promised abortions, only to be held until their babies are delivered and sold for an average price of about US$2,400.

◢ North Korea

Political Rights: 7
Civil Liberties: 7
Status: Not Free

Population: 22,665,000
Capital: Pyongyang

Trend Arrow: North Korea received a downward trend arrow due to the government's tightening of control over a burgeoning private market and its repression of citizens' economic freedom.

Ten-Year Ratings Timeline For Year Under Review (Political Rights, Civil Liberties, Status)

2000	2001	2002	2003	2004	2005	2006	2007	2008	2009
7,7NF	7,7NF	7,7NF	7,7NF	7,7NF	7,7NF	7,7NF	7,7NF	7,7NF	7,7NF

Overview: The North Korean government carried out its second test of a nuclear weapon in May 2009, triggering new international sanctions. However, it indicated its openness to further disarmament negotiations later in the year, after former U.S. president Bill Clinton visited in August to secure the release of two American journalists. The Clinton trip and other official visits also dispelled speculation that North Korean leader Kim Jong-il was near death. In late November, the government announced a major revaluation of its currency and restricted the amount of old notes that individuals could exchange, effectively wiping out many citizens' cash savings. The move, part of a bid to crack down on private trading and bolster state controls on the economy, reportedly led to small protests and other disturbances by year's end.

The Democratic People's Republic of Korea (DPRK, or North Korea) was established in 1948 after three years of post–World War II Soviet occupation. The Soviet Union installed Kim Il-sung, an anti-Japanese resistance fighter, as the new country's leader. In 1950, North Korea invaded South Korea in an attempt to reunify the peninsula under communist rule. Drawing in the United States and then China, the ensuing three-year conflict killed at least 2.5 million people and ended with a ceasefire rather than a full peace treaty. Since then, the two Koreas have been on a continuous war footing, and the border remains one of the most heavily militarized places in the world.

Kim Il-sung solidified his control after the war, purging rivals, consigning thousands of political prisoners to labor camps, and fostering an extreme personality cult that promoted him as North Korea's messianic, superhuman "Great Leader." Marxism was eventually replaced by the DPRK's "Juche" (translated as "self-reliance") ideology, which combined extreme nationalism, xenophobia, and the use of state terror. After Kim Il-sung died in 1994, he was proclaimed "Eternal President," but power passed to his son, "Dear Leader" Kim Jong-il.

The end of the Cold War and its associated Soviet and Chinese subsidies led to the collapse of North Korea's command economy. Although severe floods in 1995 and 1996 compounded the problem, the famine of the 1990s, which killed at least a million people, was caused by decades of severe economic mismanagement. As many as 300,000 North Koreans fled to China in search of food, despite a legal ban on leaving the DPRK. In 1995, North Korea allowed the United Nations and private humanitarian aid organizations from Europe, North America, and South Korea to undertake one of the world's largest famine-relief operations. Despite continuing food shortages over the next decade, the DPRK in 2005 instructed the UN World Food Programme to either switch from humanitarian relief to development assistance or leave North Korea. The DPRK continues to force the international community to bear the burden of feeding its citizens while it devotes resources to its military.

The degraded state turned a blind eye as black markets emerged to deal with extreme shortages, and illicit traders smuggled in goods of all kinds from China. The regime instituted halting economic reforms in 2002, which included easing price controls, raising wages, devaluing the currency, and giving factory managers more autonomy. More extensive changes, which could ultimately undermine the dictatorship's grip on power, were rejected.

Kim Jong-il's regime was also kept afloat by Chinese and South Korean aid, as both neighbors feared that a state collapse could lead to massive refugee outflows, military disorder, the emergence of criminal gangs and regional warlords, and a loss of state control over nuclear weapons.

The DPRK had withdrawn from the Nuclear Non-Proliferation Treaty in 2003, and it raised alarm in the region by testing ballistic missiles and a nuclear device in 2006. In early 2007, the regime agreed to denuclearize in exchange for fuel aid and other concessions from its four neighbors and the United States, but further negotiations and implementation of the deal proceeded haltingly. In 2008, momentum picked up as Pyongyang handed over its declaration of nuclear assets and disabled its Yongbyon nuclear plant, and the United States removed North Korea from its list of state sponsors of terrorism. The so-called Six-Party Talks then broke down in December over the issue of verification of the nuclear assets declaration.

In April 2009, the DPRK tested a long-range missile and announced that it was withdrawing from the Six-Party Talks. The regime then conducted its second nuclear weapons test in May. In response, the UN Security Council unanimously passed Resolution 1874, which tightened weapons-related financial sanctions and called on all governments to search North Korean shipments for illicit weapons. Observers interpreted the new provocations by North Korea as an attempt to test newly elected U.S. president Barack Obama, force additional concessions from the international community, and rally hard-liners behind Kim Jong-il's third son and recently designated heir, Kim Jong-un. Kim Jong-il had reportedly suffered a stroke in August 2008, raising questions about the succession.

Former U.S. president Bill Clinton made a surprise visit to North Korea in early August to negotiate the release of two American journalists, who had been captured in May for trespassing along the Chinese border. Reports gleaned from the trip helped to dispel speculation that Kim Jong-il was too ill to rule. In addition, the visit and the reporters' release appeared to signal the DPRK's shift back toward diplomatic engagement, as confirmed by several meetings and positive gestures toward South Korea and China later in the year.

In late November, the government announced a currency revaluation and other measures designed to curb private trading and reassert state control over the economy. Citizens were allowed to exchange only a nominal amount of old currency for new notes, meaning their cash savings would be wiped out. In the face of public anger and confusion, reportedly including rare protests, the authorities later raised the limit somewhat on the amount of old notes that could be exchanged. Individuals could deposit larger amounts of old currency in state banks, but that carried the risk of being investigated for illegal trading. With the crippled black market unable to meet demand, prices rose sharply. The government caused further economic disruption at year's end by banning the use of foreign currency.

Political Rights and Civil Liberties: North Korea is not an electoral democracy. Kim Jong-il has led the DPRK since the 1994 death of his father, founding leader Kim Il-sung. He has many titles but rules as the chairman of the National Defense Commission, the "highest office of state" since the office of president was permanently dedicated to Kim Il-sung in a 1998 constitutional revision. North Korea's parliament, the Supreme People's Assembly (SPA), is a rubber-stamp institution elected to five-year terms. All candidates for office, who run unopposed, are preselected by the ruling Korean Workers' Party and two subordinate minor parties.

The latest SPA elections were held in March 2009, and in April, the new chamber reelected Kim Jong-il as defense commission chairman. Also that month, the SPA revised the constitution to reinforce Kim Jong-il's status as the undisputed "supreme leader," and to stipulate for the first time that the country respects and protects human rights. The move was interpreted as a response to international pressure, although protection of human rights remains virtually nonexistent in practice.

While North Korea was not ranked in Transparency International's 2009 Corruption Perceptions Index, corruption is believed to be endemic at every level of the state and economy.

All media outlets are run by the state. Televisions and radios are permanently fixed to state channels, and all publications are subject to strict supervision and censorship. Internet access is restricted to a few thousand people, and foreign websites are blocked. Still, the black market provides alternative information sources, including cellular telephones, pirated recordings of South Korean dramas, and radios capable of receiving foreign programs.

Although freedom of religion is guaranteed by the constitution, it does not exist in practice. State-sanctioned churches maintain a token presence in Pyongyang, and some North Koreans living near the Chinese border are known to practice their faiths furtively. However, intense state indoctrination and repression preclude free exercise of religion as well as academic freedom. Nearly all forms of private communication are monitored by a huge network of informers.

Freedom of assembly is not recognized, and there are no known associations or organizations other than those created by the state. Strikes, collective bargaining, and other organized-labor activities are illegal. Nevertheless, recent state efforts to crack down on the black market have reportedly sparked scattered protests.

North Korea does not have an independent judiciary. The UN General Assembly has recognized and condemned severe DPRK human rights violations, including torture, public executions, extrajudicial and arbitrary detention, and forced labor; the absence of due process and the rule of law; and death sentences for political offenses. Recent South Korean reports suggest that up to 154,000 political prisoners are held in six detention camps. Inmates face brutal conditions, and collective or familial punishment for suspected dissent by an individual is a common practice.

The government operates a semihereditary system of social discrimination, whereby all citizens are classified into 53 subgroups under overall security ratings— "core," "wavering," and "hostile"—based on their family's perceived loyalty to the regime. This rating determines virtually every facet of a person's life, including employment and educational opportunities, place of residence, access to medical facilities, and even access to stores.

There is no freedom of movement, and forced internal resettlement is routine. Access to Pyongyang, where the availability of food, housing, and health care is somewhat better than in the rest of the country, is tightly restricted. Emigration is illegal, but many North Koreans, especially women, have escaped to China or engaged in cross-border trade. Ignoring international objections, the Chinese government continues to return refugees and defectors to North Korea, where they are subject to torture, harsh imprisonment, or execution.

The economy remains both centrally planned and grossly mismanaged, with the military claiming over a third of the state budget. Development is also hobbled by a lack of infrastructure, a scarcity of energy and raw materials, and an inability to borrow on world markets or from multilateral banks because of sanctions, lingering foreign debt, and ideological isolationism. The growth of the black market in recent years gave many North Koreans a field of activity that was largely free from government control, but the currency reforms of late 2009 threatened to squelch such trading and the small measure of wealth it had produced.

There have been widespread reports of trafficked women and girls among the tens of thousands of North Koreans who have recently crossed into China. UN bodies have noted the use of forced abortions and infanticide against pregnant women who are forcibly repatriated from China.

Norway

Political Rights: 1
Civil Liberties: 1
Status: Free

Population: 4,827,000
Capital: Oslo

Ten-Year Ratings Timeline For Year Under Review (Political Rights, Civil Liberties, Status)

2000	2001	2002	2003	2004	2005	2006	2007	2008	2009
1,1F	1,1F	1,1F	1,1F	1,1F	1,1F	1,1F	1,1F	1,1F	1,1F

Overview: Violent clashes that broke out in Oslo at the end of 2008 between police and Palestinians demonstrating against Israel's military campaign in the Gaza Strip spilled over into January 2009. In September elections, the Red-Green coalition became the first ruling party to be reelected in 16 years, and Jens Stoltenberg was reappointed prime minister in October.

Norway's constitution, the Eidsvoll Convention, was first adopted in 1814, during a brief period of independence after nearly four centuries of Danish rule. Subsequently, Norway became part of a Swedish-headed monarchy. The country gained independence in 1905 and has since functioned as a constitutional monarchy with a multiparty parliamentary structure. Norway became a founding member of NATO in 1949.

Norwegian citizens narrowly rejected membership in the European Union (EU) in 1972 and 1994, despite government support for joining. Norwegians wanted to preserve their sovereignty and feared that membership would threaten the country's energy, agriculture, and fishing industries. As part of the European Economic Area, Norway has nearly full access to EU markets, and 71 percent of Norwegian exports go to EU countries. However, while Norway has adopted almost all EU directives, it has little power to influence EU decisions.

In December 2008, a group of Palestinians assembled outside the Israeli embassy in Oslo to protest against the Israeli Defense Forces' incursion into the Gaza Strip. The demonstration turned violent after protestors began throwing Molotov cocktails, resulting in the arrest of four protestors. The protests sparked widespread clashes between demonstrators and police during the first two weeks of 2009, leading to rioting in other parts of Oslo. Several instances of police force were reported, including the use of tear gas to disperse crowds. By mid-January, nearly 200 protestors had been arrested, most of whom were immigrants.

Norway was elected as a member of the UN Human Rights Council in May, and the President of the Norwegian Storting, Thorbjoern Jagland, was elected Secretary General of the Council of Europe in September. Also in 2009, the UN Development Programme's Human Development Report found Norway to have the best quality of life.

Prime Minister Jens Stoltenberg's center-left Red-Green coalition was reelected in the September 2009 parliamentary elections, making it the first government to win reelection in the last 16 years. The coalition—led by Stoltenberg's Labor Party, which won 64 seats—includes the Socialist Left Party and the Center Party (Agrarians), which captured 11 seats each. The Progress Party secured 41 seats; the Christian Democrats, 10 seats; and the Liberal Left, 2 seats. While the Norwegian Police Security Branch expressed fears of possible attacks against politicians leading up to the elections, no incidences of violence were reported; a revised national budget provided for an extra $4.5 million to strengthen protection for politicians.

In the Sami Assembly elections in September, the Labor Party captured 14 seats, the Progress Party took 3 seats, and various other Sami parties won a total of 22 seats.

Political Rights and Civil Liberties: Norway is an electoral democracy. The national Parliament, called the Storting, currently has 169 members. Lawmakers are directly elected for four-year terms through a system of proportional representation. The Parliament had been divided into two chambers, the Lagting and the Odelsting, until 2009, when it became unicameral. The leader of the majority party or coalition in the Storting is appointed prime minister by the constitutional monarch, currently King Harald V. Although officially the head of state and commander in chief of the armed forces, the monarch performs largely ceremonial duties.

The indigenous Sami population, in addition to participating in the national political process, has its own Consultative Constituent Assembly, or Sameting, which has worked to protect the group's language and cultural rights and to influence the national government's decisions about Sami land and its resources. The government supports Sami-language instruction, broadcast programs, and subsidized newspapers in Sami regions. A deputy minister in the national government deals specifically with Sami issues.

Norway remains one of the least corrupt countries in the world. However, isolated incidents of bribery and misconduct have occurred, and Norway's role in the international energy and mining industries has received particular scrutiny. In 2004, the Oslo Tax Office began investigating taxi drivers suspected of tax fraud. The investigation uncovered nearly 500 suspects who had failed to declare some US$84 million in taxes. In April 2009, approximately 300 taxi owners and drivers confessed to fraud totaling nearly US$100,000; several of the convicted individuals were sentenced to prison terms of up to two years. Norway was ranked 11 out of 180 countries surveyed in Transparency International's 2009 Corruption Perceptions Index.

Freedom of the press is constitutionally guaranteed. The state subsidizes many newspapers, the majority of which are privately owned and openly partisan, in order to promote political pluralism. The European Court of Human Rights ruled in December 2008 that the government ban on political advertisements had interfered with the Pensioner's Party's right to expression. As a consequence, the government changed the statutes of the Norwegian Broadcasting Corporation (NRK) to allow airtime for smaller political parties. Internet access is not impeded by the government.

The monarch is the constitutional head of the official Evangelical Lutheran Church of Norway, and at least half of the cabinet must belong to the church. Other denominations must register with the state to receive support, which is determined by size of membership. A course on religion and ethics focusing on Christianity is mandatory for students, but it is considered to be in violation of international human rights conventions, including the UN International Covenant on Civil and Political Rights (ICCPR) and the European Convention on Human Rights. While the Norwegian government has implemented some curriculum reforms, the UN Human Rights Committee in 2006 warned that the section of Norway's constitution requiring Evangelical Lutherans to raise their children in the faith could be a breach of the ICCPR. An April 2008 agreement gave the church the power to select bishops and deans, once the power of the government. Under political pressure, Justice Minister Knut Storberget in February 2009 was forced to withdraw a proposal that would have permitted Muslim police officers to wear a hijab. There was an increase in anti-Semitic incidents in 2009, particularly during the Israeli strike on the Gaza Strip. Clashes between Israeli and Palestinian protestors led to the detention of nearly 200 people in January. In May, a Jewish cemetery in Oslo was vandalized with Nazi symbols, and the government launched a celebration in August for Nobel Laureate Knut Hamsun, a Nazi sympathizer.

The constitution guarantees freedoms of assembly and association. However, in January 2009, police used tear gas to suppress protests in Oslo against the Israeli military campaign in the Gaza Strip. Tear gas was used again in April to disperse a group of Tamil demonstrators in the capital; the protesters demanded that Norway perform its role as mediator and order a ceasefire in Sri Lanka. Norwegians are very active in nongovernmental organizations (NGOs). Labor unions play an important role in consulting with the government on social and economic issues, and approximately 53 percent of the workforce is unionized. In January and March, several thousand police gathered to protest government-proposed changes to the Health and Safety at Work Act that would interfere with rest periods and curtail negotiation rights. An agreement was reached in July to add an hour to each work week for police officers, while protecting their rest time and negotiation rights.

The judiciary is independent, and the court system, headed by the Supreme Court, operates fairly at the local and national levels. The king appoints judges on the advice of the Ministry of Justice. The police are under civilian control, and there were no reports of human rights abuses committed by any domestic law enforcement authorities in 2009. Prison conditions generally meet international standards, though problems with overcrowding arose in 2009.

Overcrowding in Norwegian asylum centers has become a concern and may have contributed to the 2008 attacks on an asylum center near Oslo. As of September 2009, asylum seekers who voluntarily return to their homeland will receive approximately US$1,800 from the Norwegian government to assist in resettlement. The number of asylum seekers in Norway increased by 20 percent in 2009. As of October 2009, citizens within the EEA no longer need a residence permit to work in Norway, though the agreement excludes Romanians and Bulgarians. An ombudsman for equality and antidiscrimination was established in 2006 to counter ethnic and sexual bias. However, NGOs reported in 2009 that police used discriminatory racial profiling practices against ethnic minorities.

The Gender Equality Act provides equal rights for men and women. In 2009, nearly 40 percent of the seats in the Storting were won by women, a slight increase over the previous elections. Of the 19 government ministries, 10 are headed by women. A law that took effect in 2006 requires that at least 40 percent of board members at about 500 large companies traded on Norway's stock exchange be women. In December 2009, the same law was applied to municipal-owned company boards. Norway is a destination point for the trafficking of women for the purpose of sexual exploitation. The country, however, remains a leader in antitrafficking efforts, according to the U.S. State Department's 2009 Trafficking in Persons Report. A law went into effect in 2009 making the purchase of sex illegal; citizens caught paying for sex can receive up to six months in prison.

Oman

Political Rights: 6
Civil Liberties: 5
Status: Not Free

Population: 3,108,000
Capital: Muscat

Ten-Year RatingsTimeline ForYear Under Review (Political Rights, Civil Liberties, Status)

2000	2001	2002	2003	2004	2005	2006	2007	2008	2009
6,5NF	6,5NF	6,5NF	6,5NF	6,5NF	6,5NF	6,5NF	6,5NF	6,5NF	6,5NF

Overview: In April 2009, Oman sentenced civil aviation official Ali al-Zuwaidy to one month in prison for publishing comments on a popular website that were critical of the government. Separately, the country stripped Omani citizenship from a Yemeni political refugee in May for criticizing the deteriorating political situation in Yemen.

Except for a brief period of Persian rule, Oman has been an independent state since a native dynasty expelled the Portuguese from Muscat in 1650. After the expulsion, which ended more than a century of Portuguese involvement in the area, the sultan conquered neighboring territories and built a small empire that included parts of the eastern coast of Africa and the southern Arabian Peninsula. The overseas possessions were gradually lost beginning in the mid-19th century.

During the 1950s and 1960s, Oman experienced a period of civil unrest centered mostly in the interior regions of the country. In 1964, a group of separatists supported by Marxist governments, including that of the neighboring People's Democratic Republic of Yemen (South Yemen), started a revolt in Oman's Dhofar province. The insurgency was not completely quelled until the mid-1970s. Qaboos bin Said al-Said seized power in 1970 by overthrowing his father, Sultan Said bin Taimur, who had ruled for nearly four decades. The new sultan launched a program to modernize Oman's infrastructure, educational system, government, and economy.

In 1991, Qaboos replaced an appointed State Consultative Council, established in 1981, with a partially elected Consultative Council (Majlis al-Shura) designed to provide the sultan with a wider range of opinions on ruling the country. A limited number of women gained the right to vote and run as candidates in 1994. The 1996 basic law, promulgated by royal decree, created a bicameral parliament consisting of an appointed Council of State (Majlis al-Dawla) and a wholly elected Consultative Council. Only a limited number of citizens selected by tribal leaders were allowed to vote in the first elections. The basic law granted certain civil liberties; banned discrimination on the basis of sex, religion, ethnicity, and social class; and clarified the process for royal succession.

This limited political reform in the 1990s was overshadowed by a stronger effort, spearheaded by Qaboos in 1995, to liberalize and diversify Oman's oil-dependent economy. In preparation for Oman's accession to the World Trade Organization in 2000, the government lifted restrictions on foreign investment and ownership of enterprises in the country.

In 2003, the sultan decreed universal suffrage for all Omanis over the age of 21.

Parliamentary elections were held that year and again in October 2007. However, political reform has continued to lag behind economic reform, with Qaboos maintaining a strong grip on the state.

In May 2009, the government stripped Ali Salem al-Beidh, a Yemeni dissident living in exile in the country since 1994, of his Omani citizenship. A past supporter of the secessionist movement in southern Yemen, al-Beidh was punished for issuing a political statement critical of the Yemeni government's handling of the political crisis in the south.

Political Rights and Civil Liberties: Oman is not an electoral democracy. Citizens elect the 84-member Consultative Council for four-year terms, but the chamber has no legislative powers and can only recommend changes to new laws. The Consultative Council is part of a bicameral body known as the Council of Oman. The other chamber, the 59-member State Council, is appointed by the sultan, who has absolute power and issues laws by decree. The sultan serves as the country's prime minister; heads the ministries of Defense, Foreign Affairs, and Finance; and is the governor of Oman's central bank.

Under the country's constitution, citizens have the right to address public authorities on personal matters or on matters related to public affairs in a manner consistent with Omani law. Mechanisms exist for citizens to petition the government through local officials, and certain citizens are afforded limited opportunities to petition the sultan in direct meetings. Political parties are not permitted, and no meaningful organized political opposition exists.

Corruption is not perceived to be a serious problem in Oman. However, the legal code does not include freedom of information provisions. Oman was ranked 39 out of 180 countries surveyed in Transparency International's 2009 Corruption Perceptions Index.

Freedom of expression and democratic debate are limited, and criticism of the sultan is prohibited. The 2004 Private Radio and Television Companies Law established regulations for setting up private broadcast media outlets, a first for the country. The government permits private print publications, but many of these accept government subsidies and practice self-censorship. Omanis have access to the internet through the national telecommunications company, and the government censors politically sensitive and pornographic content. The sultan issued a decree in 2008 expanding government oversight and regulation of electronic communications, including communication on personal blogs. In April 2009, Ali al-Zuwaidy, a civil aviation official, was sentenced to one month in prison and fined US$520 for leaking a government document on a popular website. Al-Zuwaidy had posted a cabinet directive calling for a popular radio program to cease its antigovernment criticism. He served 11 days of the sentence, with the remainder suspended.

Islam is the state religion. Non-Muslims have the right to worship, although they are banned from proselytizing. Non-Muslim religious organizations must register with the government. The Ministry of Awqaf (Religious Charitable Bequests) and Religious Affairs distributes standardized texts for mosque sermons and expects imams to stay within the outlines of these texts. The government restricts academic freedom by preventing the publication of material on politically sensitive topics.

The right to peaceful assembly within limits is provided for by the basic law.

However, all public gatherings require official permission, and the government has the authority to prevent organized public meetings without any appeal process. The basic law allows the formation of nongovernmental organizations, but civic and associational life remains limited. The government has not permitted the establishment of independent human rights organizations and generally uses the registration and licensing process to block the formation of groups that are seen as a threat to stability.

Oman's 2003 labor law allows workers to select a committee to voice their demands and represent their interests but prevents them from organizing unions. Additional labor reforms enacted in 2006 brought a number of improvements, including protections for union activity, collective bargaining, and strikes. However, legal provisions covering migrant workers remain inadequate, and domestic servants are particularly vulnerable to abuse. Employers using child labor face increased penalties, including prison terms, under the law.

The judiciary is not independent and remains subordinate to the sultan and the Ministry of Justice. Sharia (Islamic law) is the source of all legislation, and Sharia Court Departments within the civil court system are responsible for family law matters, such as divorce and inheritance. In less populated areas, tribal laws and customs are frequently used to adjudicate disputes. Many of the civil liberties guarantees expressed in the basic law have not been implemented.

According to the law, arbitrary arrest and detention are prohibited. In practice, the police are not required to obtain an arrest warrant in advance. Government authorities must obtain court orders to hold suspects in pretrial detention, but the police and security services do not regularly follow these procedures. Prisons are not accessible to independent monitors, and former prisoners report overcrowding. The penal code contains broad and vague provisions for offenses against national security. These charges are prosecuted before the State Security Court, which usually holds proceedings that are closed to the public.

Omani law does not protect noncitizens from discrimination. Foreign workers risk deportation if they abandon their contracts without documentation releasing them from their previous employment, meaning employers could effectively keep workers from switching jobs and hold them in a relationship that is open to exploitation.

Although the basic law prohibits discrimination on the basis of sex, women suffer from legal and social discrimination. Oman's personal status law, based on Sharia, favors the rights of men over those of women in marriage, divorce, inheritance, and child custody. According to official statistics, women constitute only 10 percent of the total labor force in Oman. For the first time since women were granted the right to participate in 1994, no female candidates were elected in the October 2007 Consultative Council elections.

While Oman remains a destination and transit country for trafficking in women and men, a new antitrafficking law went into effect in December 2008. The government tried its first case under the new law in March 2009, convicting 11 men of bringing 13 women into the country for prostitution. The government also provided shelter for the women involved in the case. In April, the newly formed National Committee for Combating Trafficking in Persons convened its first meeting.

Pakistan

Political Rights: 4
Civil Liberties: 5
Status: Partly Free

Population: 180,808,000
Capital: Islamabad

Note: The numerical ratings and status listed above do not reflect conditions in Pakistani-controlled Kashmir, which is examined in a separate report.

Ten-Year Ratings Timeline For Year Under Review (Political Rights, Civil Liberties, Status)

2000	2001	2002	2003	2004	2005	2006	2007	2008	2009
6,5NF	6,5NF	6,5NF	6,5NF	6,5NF	6,5NF	6,5NF	6,5NF	4,5PF	4,5PF

Overview:
In March 2009, the civilian government of President Asif Ali Zardari yielded to political pressure and allowed Iftikhar Chaudhry, the chief justice of the Supreme Court who had been ousted by then military ruler Pervez Musharraf in 2007, to reclaim his post. The court subsequently struck down a Musharraf-era amnesty law in December, exposing a number of politicians to possible prosecution. Also during the year, Islamist militants attempted to extend their territorial control in North-West Frontier Province, provoking a sustained military response that began in the spring. This in turn led to the mass displacement of civilians and a wave of retaliatory terrorist attacks throughout the country.

Pakistan was created as a Muslim homeland during the partition of British India in 1947, and the military has directly or indirectly ruled the country for much of its independent history. As part of his effort to consolidate power, military dictator Mohammad Zia ul-Haq amended the constitution in 1985 to allow the president to dismiss elected governments. After Zia's death in 1988, successive civilian presidents cited corruption and abuse of power in sacking elected governments headed by prime ministers Benazir Bhutto of the Pakistan People's Party (PPP) in 1990 and 1996, and Nawaz Sharif of the Pakistan Muslim League (PML) in 1993.

Sharif, who returned to power in the 1997 elections, was deposed in a military coup after he attempted to fire the army chief, General Pervez Musharraf, in 1999. Musharraf appointed himself "chief executive" (and later president), declared a state of emergency, and suspended democratic institutions. The 2002 Legal Framework Order (LFO) gave Musharraf effective control over Parliament and changed the electoral rules to the detriment of opposition parties. The regime also openly promoted progovernment parties, such as the newly formed Pakistan Muslim League Quaid-i-Azam (PML-Q), which captured the largest share of seats in the 2002 parliamentary elections and led the new government.

While he managed to contain the secular opposition over the next several years, Musharraf was less willing to rein in radical Islamist groups, with which the military traditionally had a close relationship. These groups gradually extended their influence from outlying regions like the Federally Administered Tribal Areas (FATA) to major urban centers, carrying out attacks on both military and civilian targets.

Tensions between Musharraf and the increasingly activist judiciary came to a head in March 2007, when Musharraf suspended Iftikhar Chaudhry, the chief justice of the Supreme Court. The ensuing lawyers' protests sparked wider political unrest, and in July, the Supreme Court ruled against Musharraf and reinstated Chaudhry. When the Court attempted to rule on the validity of the October presidential election, which had confirmed Musharraf in office, he again took preemptive action and imposed martial law on November 3, suspending the constitution and replacing much of the higher judiciary. More than 6,000 civil society activists, political leaders, and lawyers and judges were arrested, although the vast majority were released after short detentions. The state of emergency was lifted in mid-December, and an amended version of the constitution was restored, but some restrictions on the press and freedom of assembly remained in place, as did the emasculated judiciary. Following the December 27 assassination of former prime minister Benazir Bhutto, parliamentary elections planned for early January 2008 were postponed until February, and Bhutto's widower, Asif Ali Zardari, assumed de facto leadership of the PPP.

The PPP led the February voting with 97 out of 272 directly elected seats in the National Assembly, followed by Nawaz Sharif's PML-N with 71. The ruling PML-Q was routed, taking only 42 seats, and the Muttahida Majlis-i-Amal (MMA), an alliance of Islamic parties, was also severely weakened. At the provincial level, the PML-N triumphed in its traditional stronghold of Punjab, while the PPP dominated in Sindh, and the Awami National Party, a secular and ethnic Pashtun group, won the most seats in the North-West Frontier Province (NWFP).

In March 2008, the PPP and PML-N reached a power-sharing deal and agreed to the key priorities of reinstating the judges ousted by Musharraf and stripping the president of his power to dissolve Parliament and dismiss the prime minister. A PPP-backed candidate, Yousuf Raza Gilani, was elected prime minister, and he immediately ordered an end to the house arrest of Chaudhry and other suspended Supreme Court justices. However, the coalition partners remained divided over the timing and method of reinstating the dismissed judges, and the PML-N withdrew from the cabinet in May. Musharraf, who had already stepped down as army chief in late 2007, resigned as president in the face of impeachment efforts in August. Less than a week later, the PML-N formally ended its coalition with the PPP, accusing it of breaking a promise to reinstate immediately all of the judges after Musharraf's exit; several of the judges were reappointed that month, but Chaudhry was not included. Zardari was thought to oppose the chief justice's return, because it could lead to the revival of long-dormant corruption cases against him. In September, Zardari won the indirect presidential election with 481 of the 702 votes cast; 368 national and provincial lawmakers abstained or boycotted the vote. The PML-N candidate received 153 votes, and the PML-Q took 44.

The PPP and its allies gained a simple majority in the March 2009 Senate elections, but this victory was overshadowed by Zardari's abortive attempt to sideline the opposition PML-N, which continued to push for Chaudhry's restoration. The crisis began with a February Supreme Court decision—widely presumed to have been influenced by the president—to ban Nawaz Sharif and his brother Shahbaz, the chief minister of Punjab, from office. The ruling led to the imposition of direct rule by Punjab's governor and rioting throughout the province. In response, the government filed cases against several hundred PML-N officials and activists, placed

Nawaz Sharif under house arrest, and ultimately banned political gatherings. Analysts argued that Zardari's concurrent purge of potential rivals within the PPP was also designed to consolidate his power. However, under pressure from the military and the United States, Zardari relented, ordering Chaudhry's reinstatement and asking the Supreme Court to review the case against the Sharif brothers. By the end of March, Chaudhry had resumed his position as chief justice, and the February ruling had been reversed.

The Supreme Court soon began dismantling the legal actions taken by Musharraf under the 2007 state of emergency, declaring them illegal and calling on Parliament to "regularize" them through ordinary legislation. In December, the Court specifically annulled the National Reconciliation Ordinance (NRO), a 2007 amnesty that had eliminated pending legal cases against Zardari and other exiled politicians so that they could return and participate in the 2008 elections. The ruling brought Zardari closer to possible prosecution on the old corruption charges, though he still enjoyed immunity as president. Many officials who lacked such protection, including cabinet ministers, faced immediate court proceedings at year's end.

Although the military had stepped up its operations against Islamist militants in the FATA and NWFP in 2008, terrorist attacks and other violence continued into 2009. In February, the government agreed to a peace deal in the NWFP's Swat district with an affiliate of the Tehrik-i-Taliban Pakistan (TTP, or Pakistani Taliban), a network of militant groups based in the FATA. Under the agreement, the first of its kind outside the FATA, the militants would observe a ceasefire in return for the establishment of Sharia (Islamic law) in the district. President Zardari approved legislation in April that formally imposed Sharia in seven districts of the NWFP, including Swat. Meanwhile, militants seized control of additional districts in the province and began implementing their harsh forms of justice. By May, the government had acknowledged the failure of the peace deal and resolved to retake the affected districts by force. In August, a missile reportedly fired by a U.S. drone aircraft killed TTP leader Baitullah Mehsud, and by year's end, the Pakistani military had expanded its campaign by reasserting control in Swat and occupying Mehsud's stronghold in South Waziristan, part of the FATA. Around two million civilians were displaced at various points by these military campaigns. Despite these territorial gains, Islamist militants continued to stage devastating suicide attacks throughout Pakistan.

Political Rights and Civil Liberties: Pakistan is not an electoral democracy. A civilian government and president were elected in 2008, ending years of military rule, but the military continues to exercise de facto control over many areas of government policy. The political environment is also troubled by corruption, partisan clashes, and Islamist militancy, among other problems.

The bicameral Parliament consists of a 342-seat National Assembly, which has 272 directly elected members and additional seats reserved for women (60 seats) and non-Muslim minorities (10 seats), all with five-year terms; and a 100-seat Senate, most of whose members are elected by the four provincial assemblies for six-year terms, with half up for election every three years. The president is elected for a five-year term by an electoral college consisting of the national and provincial legislatures. The 2002 LFO gave the president the right to dismiss unilaterally the prime minister and the national and provincial legislatures.

Although the 2008 parliamentary elections marked a distinct improvement over those held in 2002, they were not completely free and fair. The European Union observer mission noted the abuse of state resources and media, inaccuracies in the voter rolls, and rigging of the vote tallies in some areas. Opposition party workers faced police harassment, and more than 100 people were killed in political violence during the campaign period. Private media and civil society groups, such as the Free and Fair Election Network (FAFEN), played a significant watchdog role, publicizing incidents of violence, noting numerous irregularities, and otherwise monitoring the conduct of the balloting alongside foreign observers. Despite the irregularities, the balloting led to an orderly rotation of power, and the overall result reflected the will of the people.

Women's political participation is generally ensured by the reservation of legislative seats at the national, provincial, and local levels; women won an additional 16 National Assembly seats in the 2008 elections. In some parts of the country, women have difficulty voting and running for office due to objections from social and religious conservatives. Religious minorities also have reserved seats in both the national and provincial legislatures, allotted to different parties based on their share of the vote. However, members of the Ahmadiyya sect, who are required to register on a separate electoral list, largely boycotted the 2008 elections. Separately, a requirement that all candidates hold either a bachelor's degree or madrassa (Islamic school) qualification prevents roughly 95 percent of the population from running for office.

The FATA are subject to special rules that place local governance under the control of the president and unelected civil servants. Elected councils, set up in 2007 with the intention of increasing local representation, have not altered the established decision-making structures. President Asif Ali Zardari announced a reform package in August 2009 that would lift the long-standing ban on political parties in the tribal areas and rein in the arbitrary judicial and financial powers of the FATA's administration, but the necessary order had not been signed by year's end.

Pakistan's government operates with limited transparency and accountability, although this has improved somewhat with the resumption of civilian rule. The military has a stake in continuing to influence both commercial and political decision-making processes, in addition to its traditional dominance of foreign policy and security issues. Serving and retired officers have received top jobs in ministries, state-run corporations, and universities, and they enjoy a range of other privileges, but several thousand active-duty officers were withdrawn from civilian posts in 2008. In the fall of 2009, Zardari, over the objections of the army, accepted an aid package from the United States that included a range of conditionalities. The new Parliament has functioned more effectively than its predecessor, holding important policy debates and overturning key decisions of the former government. However, Zardari has been widely criticized for making appointments to top government and diplomatic positions based more on personal loyalty than professional competence.

Corruption is pervasive in politics and government. Under the NRO, issued by then president Pervez Musharraf in October 2007, Zardari and more than 8,000 other politicians, diplomats, and officials were granted immunity in ongoing cases. The Supreme Court's revocation of the NRO in December 2009 cleared the way for the revival of such cases, and though Zardari himself still enjoyed presidential immunity, several other high-ranking ministers were facing the threat of prosecution at year's end. The National Accountability Bureau (NAB), established in 1999 to try corruption cases, was slated to be abolished in January 2009 amid claims that it had grown overly politicized during the Musharraf era. At year's end, the National Assembly was considering legislation that would replace the NAB with a new and redefined anticorruption body. PILDAT criticized several provisions of the bill, particularly its adoption of a narrower definition of corruption and the restriction of the new entity's mandate to holders of political office. Pakistan was ranked 139 out of 180 countries surveyed in Transparency International's 2009 Corruption Perceptions Index.

Pakistan's outspoken newspapers and a recent growth in private television stations provide the public with a diverse range of views. However, media freedom in 2009 remained constrained by official attempts to silence critical reporting and by the high level of violence against journalists. In general, the constitution and other laws authorize the government to curb speech on subjects including the armed forces, the judiciary, and religion; blasphemy laws are occasionally used against the media. Particularly harsh ordinances imposed by Musharraf in late 2007 bar any content that defames the military or state institutions, or that is deemed "false or baseless." The penalties for violations include up to three years in prison, fines of up to 10 million rupees (US$165,000), and cancellation of media licenses. Although the rules have been routinely flouted, the new government has yet to act on promises to rescind them formally. Instead, it has engaged in its own sporadic efforts to suspend certain broadcasts or programs. For example, during the March 2009 demonstrations against Zardari, authorities temporarily shut down the cable service of the television stations GEO and Aaj, leading Information Minister Sherry Rehman to resign in protest. A number of stations were also blocked for several hours after a terrorist attack on army headquarters in October. Websites addressing sensitive subjects are periodically blocked. In July 2009, the government responded to a spate of jokes about Zardari that circulated via e-mail by warning that it would trace the messages and confront those responsible with prison sentences of up to 14 years.

The physical safety of journalists remains a concern, and at least four journalists were murdered in 2009, according to the Committee to Protect Journalists. Intimidation by the security forces—including physical attacks and arbitrary, incommunicado detention—appears to have declined, but Islamic fundamentalists, thugs hired by feudal landlords or local politicians, and police continued to harass journalists and attack media offices during the year. A number of reporters covering the conflict in the tribal areas and parts of NWFP were detained, threatened, expelled, or otherwise obstructed, either by government forces or militants.

Pakistan is an Islamic republic, and there are numerous legal restrictions on religious freedom. Blasphemy laws provide harsh sentences, including the death penalty, and injuring the "religious feelings" of individual citizens is prohibited. Incidents in which police officials take bribes to file false blasphemy charges against Ahmadis, Christians, Hindus, and occasionally Muslims continue to occur, with several dozen cases reported each year. No blasphemy convictions have withstood appeal to date, but the charges alone can lead to lengthy detentions, ill-treatment in custody, and persecution by religious extremists.

Ahmadis, who comprise approximately 2.5 percent of the population, consider themselves Muslims, but the constitution classifies them as a non-Muslim minority.

The penal code severely restricts their religious practice, and they must renounce their beliefs to vote or gain admission to educational institutions. Authorities occasionally confiscate or close Ahmadiyya publications and harass their staff. During 2009, dozens of Ahmadis faced criminal charges under blasphemy or other discriminatory laws.

Religious minorities also face unofficial economic and social discrimination, and they are occasionally subject to violence and harassment. In a growing trend, particularly in Sindh province, Hindu girls are kidnapped, forcibly converted, and compelled to marry their kidnappers. Terrorist and other attacks on places of worship and religious gatherings occur frequently, leading to the deaths of dozens of people every year; there was a notable upsurge in violence between members of the Sunni Muslim majority and the Shiite Muslim minority in 2009. A wave of attacks on Christians in August 2009, particularly in Punjab, was also attributed to the spread of Sunni extremist ideology. The government often fails to protect religious minorities from sectarian violence, and discriminatory legislation contributes to a climate of intolerance. On a positive note, the new government appointed a Roman Catholic as minister of minorities affairs in late 2008 and reserved 5 percent of federal jobs for religious minorities in May 2009.

The government generally does not restrict academic freedom. However, university student groups with ties to political parties or radical Islamist organizations intimidate students, teachers, and administrators and try to influence university policies. Girls' schools, particularly in the FATA and NWFP, face threats and attacks by Islamist militants; an April 2009 bombing at a girls' primary school in Malakand district killed and injured several dozen students. Girls living under Taliban rule in the Swat district were banned from attending school, and during the military's offensive there in the spring, at least 200 schools were damaged or destroyed. Nevertheless, many children returned to classes in August, often attending sessions in tents or outdoors.

Legal provisions for freedoms of assembly and association are selectively upheld. Authorities sometimes restrict public gatherings, disperse protests with excessive force, and use preventative arrest to forestall planned demonstrations. Some Islamist leaders have been held under house arrest or in preventive detention under the Maintenance of Public Order Act, which allows three months' detention without trial. In early 2009, the government banned public demonstrations in the capital for two months in an attempt to prevent marches in favor of the ousted chief justice. On March 10, police in Punjab arrested more than 300 members of the PML-N and other opposition parties to prevent them from joining such a demonstration; however, the protest ban was lifted in late March, when the judicial dispute was resolved.

Authorities generally tolerate the work of nongovernmental organizations (NGOs) and allow them to publish critical material. However, NGOs that focus on female education and empowerment, and female NGO staff in general, have faced threats, attacks, and a number of murders by radical Islamists, particularly in the north. Militant groups ordered NGOs to leave the Swat valley after they seized control there in February 2009. Citing security concerns, the government has, at times, prevented aid groups from operating in Baluchistan, exacerbating the province's humanitarian situation. Pakistan is also home to a large number of charitable or cultural organizations, such as the Jamaat-ud-Dawa (JD), that have links to Islamist militant groups.

The 2008 Industrial Relations Act allows workers to form and join trade unions, but it also places restrictions on union membership, the right to strike, and collective bargaining, particularly in industries deemed essential. According to an International Trade Union Confederation report, hundreds of workers have been fired for union activity since the act was passed. Despite legislation designed to combat it, illegal bonded labor is widespread, particularly in Sindh province. News reports have described a growing trend in which bonded laborers sell their organs to repay debts and escape servitude. The enforcement of child labor laws remains inadequate; recent surveys have indicated that there are at least 10 million child workers in Pakistan.

The judiciary consists of civil and criminal courts and a special Sharia court for certain offenses. Lower courts remain plagued by corruption, intimidation, and a backlog of some 1.5 million cases that leads to lengthy pretrial detentions. A new National Judicial Policy that took effect in June 2009 aims to tackle all three problems.

The Supreme Court was brought under the control of the executive during military rule. Increasing activism by the Court, particularly by Chief Justice Iftikhar Chaudhry, led Musharraf in late 2007 to dismiss a majority of superior court judges (13 from Supreme Court and 30 from provincial courts) and order the detention of Chaudhry as well as other judges, lawyers, and legal activists who opposed the executive's actions. The government elected in 2008 expanded the Supreme Court from 16 to 29 judges, but less than half of the dismissed judges were reinstated. Finally, after the political standoff in March 2009, Chaudhry was reinstated, as well as the remainder of the high court judges ousted by Musharraf. In July, the Supreme Court ruled that the decrees issued by Musharraf during the state of emergency in late 2007 were unconstitutional, and ordered that they be regularized by Parliament. For the judiciary, this meant that all of the appointments that had taken place under Chaudhury's replacement were deemed null and void and terminated immediately.

Other parts of the judicial system, such as the antiterrorism courts, operate with limited due-process rights. The Sharia court enforces the 1979 Hudood Ordinances, which criminalize extramarital sex and several alcohol, gambling, and property offenses. They provide for Koranic punishments, including death by stoning for adultery, as well as jail terms and fines. In part because of strict evidentiary standards, authorities have never carried out the Koranic punishments. Pressure to amend or do away with the ordinances, which are highly discriminatory toward women, has grown in recent years, and the Musharraf government made a degree of progress toward reversing some of the worst provisions.

The justice system in the FATA is governed by the Frontier Crimes Regulation, which allows collective punishment for individual crimes and preventative detention of up to three years. It also authorizes tribal leaders to administer justice according to Sharia and tribal custom. However, reforms announced in August 2009 would exclude women and minors from collective responsibility, establish an appellate tribunal and the right to bail, and curtail arbitrary powers of arrest and detention, according to the International Crisis Group, but these had not come into effect by year's end.

Feudal landlords and tribal elders throughout Pakistan adjudicate some disputes and impose punishments—including the death penalty and the forced exchange of brides between tribes—in unsanctioned parallel courts called jirgas. Militants in several tribal areas and districts of NWFP have reportedly set up their own parallel courts, dispensing harsh penalties with little regard for due process. After permission was granted to establish an exclusively Sharia-based swift justice system in Swat and several nearby districts in early 2009, many lawyers in the regular court system were left unemployed, and harsh punishments for behavioral transgressions, such as flogging and amputation, became the norm until the militants were ousted from Swat in April. Although the swift justice system remained in force, courts were staffed by judges appointed by the government, according to the U.S. State Department's 2009 human rights report.

Police routinely use excessive force, torture, and arbitrary detention; extort money from prisoners and their families; accept bribes to file or withdraw charges; rape female detainees; and commit extrajudicial killings. Conditions in the overcrowded prisons are extremely poor, and case backlogs mean that the majority of inmates are awaiting trial. Progress on creating an official human rights body empowered to investigate cases and redress grievances has been slow, and although a number of cases are investigated and some prosecutions do occur, impunity for human rights abuses remains the norm. Feudal landlords, tribal groups, and some militant groups operate private jails where detainees are regularly maltreated.

Although cases of politically motivated detention and disappearance have declined under civilian rule, the Human Rights Commission of Pakistan (HRCP)—an NGO—estimated that by November at least 1,100 people continued to be illegally detained by state agencies. Some are suspected of links to radical Islamist groups, but the detainees have also included Baluchi and Sindhi nationalists, journalists, researchers, and social workers. The military's Inter-Services Intelligence Directorate (ISI), which operates largely outside the control of civilian leaders and the courts, had faced growing pressure from Chaudhry's Supreme Court to end the practice of secret detentions, but his removal in 2007 stalled progress in this area. Government efforts to place the ISI under the control of the Interior Ministry in July 2008 were swiftly quashed by the military.

Tens of thousands of armed militants are believed to be active in Pakistan. These members of radical Sunni Islamist groups—including the TTP, Lashkar-i-Jhangvi, the JD, and the Sipah-i-Sahaba Pakistan (SSP)—have varying agendas and carry out terrorist attacks against foreign, Shiite, and Christian targets, killing hundreds of civilians each year. State institutions and security forces have also faced increased attacks in recent years. Sunni and Shiite groups engage in tit-for-tat sectarian violence, mostly bomb attacks against places of worship and religious gatherings. The murder of the SSP leader in August 2009 sparked countrywide riots in which a number of Shiites were killed. The New Delhi–based South Asia Terrorism Portal (SATP) reported that 190 people were killed and 398 were injured in sectarian violence in 2009, a decrease from the previous year. Islamist militants' expanding influence over territory in NWFP and the FATA has led to severe practical restrictions on local inhabitants' dress, social behavior, educational opportunities, and legal rights. In April, several dozen people were killed in clashes between local Urdu-speakers and refugees from the NWFP in Karachi.

The military's intermittent campaigns against Islamist guerrillas in the tribal areas since 2002 have been accompanied by human rights abuses, including arbitrary detention, property destruction, killing or displacement of civilians, and extrajudicial executions. Regular missile strikes attributed to U.S. drone aircraft have also reportedly killed or injured civilians. The authorities are sponsoring tribal militias, or lashkars, to help control the FATA, creating yet another unaccountable armed force. The army's spring 2009 offensive in the Swat district and surrounding parts of NWFP led to the temporary displacement of more than two million people. The SATP reported that 11,585 people were killed nationwide in terrorist- or insurgent-related violence in 2009, including 2,307 civilians, 1,011 security force personnel, and 8,267 militants, almost double the figures from 2008. Most were killed in suicide bomb blasts that targeted official installations, as well as religious buildings or events.

In addition to violence stemming from the Islamist movement, the separatist Baluchistan Liberation Army (BLA) has routinely attacked infrastructure and development projects since early 2005, and local tribal leaders have demanded greater political autonomy and control over Baluchistan's natural resources. The army, in turn, has stepped up counterinsurgency operations, leading to human rights violations and the displacement of thousands of civilians. Thousands of activists and other locals with suspected separatist sympathies have been detained, according to the International Crisis Group. In February 2009, a little known militant group, the Liberation United Front (BLUF), abducted U.S. citizen John Solecki, a UN refugee official based in Quetta. The kidnappers demanded the release of some 6,000 Baluchi activists they claimed had been "disappeared," but Solecki was released in April without the demands being met. In October, the BLUF claimed responsibility for the assassination of the province's education minister. Separately, three separatist politicians were killed after being abducted by armed men in April, triggering violence across the province. The unrest led to several deaths and calls for a strike from the Baluch National Front (BNF), a separatist political coalition.

A combination of traditional norms, discriminatory laws, and weak enforcement contributes to a high incidence of rape, domestic abuse, and other forms of violence against women; according to the HRCP, up to 80 percent of women are victims of such abuse during their lifetimes. Female victims of sexual crimes are often pressured by police not to file charges, and they are sometimes urged by their families to commit suicide. Gang rapes sanctioned by village councils to punish the targeted woman's relatives continue to be reported, despite the fact that harsh sentences have been handed down against the perpetrators in some cases. The discriminatory Hudood Ordinances, under which rape victims could be charged with adultery, were reformed with the passage of the 2006 Women's Protection Act. Under the new law, a woman is no longer required to produce four Muslim male witnesses to prove rape, and judges are required to try rape cases under criminal law rather than Sharia. However, extramarital sex is still criminalized, and spousal rape is not recognized as a crime.

According to the HRCP, at least 647 women were killed by family members in so-called honor killings in 2009, although many such crimes may go unreported. Activists have cast doubt on the authorities' willingness to enforce a 2005 law that introduced stiffer sentences and the possibility of the death penalty for honor killings. The incidence of acid attacks on women was also reportedly on the rise in 2009, with several hundred cases noted between April and June alone. The tribal practice of *vani*, in which women are offered in marriage to settle blood feuds, continues to occur in certain areas despite being outlawed in 2004. Other illegal forms of child and forced marriage also remain problems. Most interfaith marriages are considered illegal, and the children of such unions would be illegitimate. Severe restrictions on women's rights in areas controlled by the Taliban—including murders, public floggings, and limitations on dress and behavior—are a growing concern.

Pakistani inheritance law discriminates against women, who also face unofficial discrimination in educational and employment opportunities. The trafficking of women and children remains a serious concern, with female victims facing forced labor, sexual exploitation, or marriage to significantly older men.

Palau

Political Rights: 1
Civil Liberties: 1
Status: Free

Population: 21,000
Capital: Melekeok

Ten-Year Ratings Timeline For Year Under Review (Political Rights, Civil Liberties, Status)

2000	2001	2002	2003	2004	2005	2006	2007	2008	2009
1,2F	1,2F	1,2F	1,1F	1,1F	1,1F	1,1F	1,1F	1,1F	1,1F

Overview: Palau received a one-year extension of its Compact of Free Association with the United States in 2009, providing Palauans with continued access to education and employment in the United States and its territories. A number of senior political leaders, including former president Tommy Esang Remengesau, were convicted of official abuse and corruption during the year.

The United States administered Palau, consisting of 8 main islands and more than 250 smaller islands, as a UN Trust Territory from 1947 until 1981, when it became a self-governing territory. Palau gained full independence in 1994 under a Compact of Free Association with the United States, which stipulated that the United States would grant Palau a total of $442 million in economic aid between 1994 and 2009; allow Palauan citizens to reside, work, and study in the United States and its territories and have access to a variety of federal government programs; and defend Palau in exchange for U.S. military access to the archipelago until 2044.

Tommy Esang Remengesau was first elected president in 2000 and won a second term in the 2004 general election. Johnson Toribiong was elected president in the November 2008 elections, defeating Elias Camsek Chin, the former vice president. Parliamentary elections were held the same month, with all candidates running as independents. Seeking U.S. aid beyond 2009 was the central political issue, as the island's economy is highly dependent on compact funds. In July 2009, the United States agreed to extend the compact agreement for one year, beginning October 1, 2009, maintaining the same payment amounts. The extension provides Palau with much-needed financial relief, as the country carries a large national debt and has experienced a considerable decline in the tourism industry. Due to economic hardship, the parliament rejected Toribiong's request in August for significant salary increases for the president, vice president, and cabinet members.

Several high-ranking local and national public officials faced corruption charges in 2009, leading to a number of convictions. The Speaker of the Koror state government was convicted of perjury and misconduct in January, while the governor of Melekeok state was found guilty of using public funds for personal purposes in April. In November, former president Remengesau was found guilty of misconduct, including the stealing of public funds; he faces up to US$1.2 million in fines. In August, the former head of economic development was charged with unlawful fishing and employment of nonresident workers, and the ombudsman faced charges of forgery.

In June, the Palauan government accepted a U.S. request to resettle 17 Chinese Uighur Muslims who had been detained at the U.S. Naval Base at Guantanamo Bay in Cuba. By year's end, 6 of the 17 had moved to Palau. The Palauan government denied accusations by opponents that financial compensation was tied to the deal, stating that the decision was strictly humanitarian. In August, the parliament passed a bill to permit dual citizenship, an amendment supported by voters in a referendum that had been held alongside the November 2004 general elections.

Political Rights and Civil Liberties: Palau is an electoral democracy. The 2008 presidential and parliamentary elections were considered free and fair. The bicameral legislature, the Olbiil Era Kelulau, consists of the 9-member Senate and the 16-member House of Delegates. Legislators are elected to four-year terms by popular vote, as are the president and vice president. The president may serve only two consecutive terms. The country is organized into 16 states, each of which is headed by a governor, and each with a seat in the House of Delegates.

There are no political parties, though no laws prevent their formation. The current system of loose political alliances that quickly form and dismantle has had a destabilizing effect on governance.

Official corruption and abuse remain serious problems. Many public officials have been implicated and found guilty in recent years, including several convictions in 2009. To improve transparency and financial accountability, new anti-money-laundering measures were introduced in 2007, though evaluations have found significant deficiencies in due diligence, record keeping, and monitoring; the attorney general's office lacks the resources to oversee implementation of these measures. Palau was not rated in Transparency International's 2009 Corruption Perceptions Index.

Freedoms of speech and the press are respected. There are several print publications, five privately owned radio stations, and one privately owned television station. Cable television provides rebroadcasts of U.S. and other foreign programs. While internet access is not impeded by the government, diffusion is limited by cost and a lack of connectivity outside the main islands.

Citizens of Palau enjoy freedom of religion. Although religious organizations are required to register with the government, no application has ever been denied. There have been no reports of restrictions on academic freedom, and the government provides well-funded basic education for all.

Freedoms of assembly and association are respected. Many nongovernmental groups represent youth, health, and women's issues. Workers can freely organize unions and bargain collectively, though the economy is largely based on subsistence agriculture and is heavily dependent on U.S. aid and rent payments and remittances from Palauans working overseas.

The judiciary is independent, and trials are generally fair. A 300-member police and first-response force maintains internal order. Palau has no military. There have been no reports of prisoner abuse, though overcrowding is a problem in the country's only prison.

Foreign workers account for about one-third of the population and 75 percent of the workforce. There have been reports of discrimination against and abuse of foreign workers, who cannot legally change employers once they are in Palau and are paid far lower wages than Palauans. Foreigners are said to use fake marriages to exploit immigration privileges to the United States under the compact, making Palau a transit point for human trafficking from China, the Philippines, and Taiwan to the United States. In response to social tensions and a slower economy, the government in September 2009 decided to limit the number of foreign workers present in the country at any time to 6,000. In November, authorities began cracking down on illegal migrants and said that they would repatriate some 240 Bangladeshi workers with expired work permits.

Women are highly regarded in this matrilineal society, in which land rights and familial descent are traced through women. Many women are active in traditional and modern sectors of the economy and in politics, though there are no women in the parliament. The number of domestic violence and child abuse cases remains small. Sexual harassment and rape, including spousal rape, are illegal.

Panama

Political Rights: 1
Civil Liberties: 2
Status: Free

Population: 3,454,000
Capital: Panama City

Ten-Year Ratings Timeline For Year Under Review (Political Rights, Civil Liberties, Status)

2000	2001	2002	2003	2004	2005	2006	2007	2008	2009
1,2F	1,2F	1,2F	1,2F	1,2F	1,2F	1,2F	1,2F	1,2F	1,2F

Overview: Ricardo Martinelli of the Democratic Change party took office as president in July 2009 after defeating Balbina Herrera, the candidate of the incumbent Democratic Revolutionary Party, by the widest margin in a presidential election since Panama's transition to democracy. Martinelli faced challenges related to Panama's slowed economic growth, record crime rates, and increasing exposure to drug trafficking.

Panama was part of Colombia until 1903, when a U.S.-supported revolt resulted in the proclamation of an independent republic. A period of weak civilian rule ended with a 1968 military coup that brought General Omar Torrijos to power. After the signing of the 1977 Panama Canal Treaty with the United States, under which the canal was gradually transferred to Panamanian control by 1999, Torrijos promised democratization. However, a real transition to democracy would not come for another dozen years.

After Torrijos's death in 1981, General Manuel Noriega emerged as Panamanian

Defense Force (PDF) chief. He rigged the 1984 elections to bring the Democratic Revolutionary Party (PRD), then the PDF's political arm, to power. The Democratic Alliance of Civic Opposition (ADOC) won the 1989 elections, but Noriega annulled the vote and declared himself head of state. He was removed during a U.S. military invasion late that year, and ADOC's Guillermo Endara became president. Both the PRD and the Arnulfista Party (PA)—named after the late former president Arnulfo Arias—won elections in the 1990s. Presidential and legislative elections in 2004 returned the PRD to power, with Martin Torrijos, the son of the former strongman, winning the presidency.

By 2008, Torrijos faced mounting protests related to safety standards for construction workers and the rising cost of living. He also stoked opposition that year by issuing decrees during a legislative recess that created new security services and appeared to partly reverse the 1994 abolition of the military.

In Panama's May 2009 presidential and parliamentary elections, Ricardo Martinelli of the center-right, business-oriented Democratic Change (CD) party easily won the presidency with 60 percent of the vote, the largest margin of victory obtained by any president since the end of military rule. Balbina Herrera of the PRD, who had served as housing minister under the outgoing administration, placed second with 37.6 percent, and former president Endara garnered 2 percent. In the parliamentary contest, the PRD won 26 of the 71 seats, followed by the Panamenista Party with 21 seats, the CD with 15, and smaller parties and independents each taking less than 5 seats. Voter turnout was relatively high at 74 percent.

As of the end of 2009, the U.S. Congress had yet to ratify a bilateral free-trade pact signed with Panama in 2007. Meanwhile, Panama pushed ahead with its US$5.25 billion canal expansion project, set to be completed in 2014. Supporters of the project said it would boost Panama's economy, but opponents argued that the funds would be better spent on antipoverty programs, education, and health care. The canal is the country's largest source of income, but both it and the Colon Free Zone, a commerce and export-processing hub, felt the effects of the global economic slowdown in 2009. Workers in the free zone staged a strike in August to protest proposed increases in taxes and fees that they feared would do more damage to trade.

Political Rights and Civil Liberties: Panama is an electoral democracy. The 2009 national elections were considered free and fair by international observers. The president and deputies to the 71-seat unicameral National Assembly are elected by popular vote for five-year terms. Presidents may not seek consecutive terms. The constitution guarantees freedom for political parties and organizations.

In early 1999, Panama's largest political parties agreed to ban anonymous campaign contributions in an effort to stem the infiltration of drug money into the political process. Nevertheless, corruption remains widespread, and 2006 electoral reforms have been criticized as inadequate for improving transparency on campaign financing. President Martin Torrijos launched an anticorruption commission after taking power in 2004, and implemented a transparency law that had been suspended by his predecessor. However, he later worked to limit the law's scope, preventing the release of minutes from cabinet meetings and asset disclosures by public officials. In 2008, Torrijos came under scrutiny after it was revealed that his company had accepted US$1 million in dubious consulting fees from the government of the Dominican Republic between 2001 and 2004. Panama was ranked 84 out of 180 countries surveyed on Transparency International's 2009 Corruption Perceptions Index.

All of the country's media outlets are privately owned, with the exceptions of the state-owned television network and a network operated by the Roman Catholic Church. However, there is a considerable concentration of media ownership among relatives and associates of former president Ernesto Perez Balladares (1994–99) of the PRD. Internet access is unrestricted. Panama is notable for its harsh legal environment for journalists. In 2005, the country's restrictive gag rules were repealed and the censorship board was disbanded, but Torrijos in 2007 enacted criminal code reforms that lengthened sentences for offenses including libel.

Freedom of religion is respected, and academic freedom is generally honored.

Freedom of assembly is recognized, and nongovernmental organizations (NGOs) are free to operate. Although only about 10 percent of the labor force is organized, unions are cohesive and powerful. Construction workers mounted major strikes in February 2008 after one of their comrades was shot dead by police during protests over safety standards. In 2009, the construction workers' union SUNTRACS denounced the government to the International Labour Organization (ILO) for its failure to investigate the assassinations of three union leaders in 2007.

The judicial system remains overburdened, inefficient, politicized, and prone to corruption. Criminal code reforms that took effect in 2008 increased sentences for a number of offenses and raised questions about human rights. The prison system is already marked by violent disturbances in its decrepit, overcrowded facilities. The prisoner-to-public ratio is high, with approximately 300 inmates for every 100,000 residents.

The police and other security forces are poorly disciplined and corrupt. Security decrees issued by the Torrijos government in 2008 included the creation of a national aero-naval service, a border service, a council for public security and national defense, and a national intelligence service. Torrijos also named a former soldier to the post of police chief. He argued that the reforms were needed to combat drug trafficking and possible terrorist attacks on the Panama Canal, but opponents warned of a return to Panama's military past and said the changes lacked safeguards against abuse of power. President Ricardo nominated former Noriega military lieutenant Gustavo Perez as chief of police, who took office in July 2009 amid protests.

The government's counternarcotics campaign has been limited by a lack of resources, weak border enforcement, and corruption. Analysts believe that Panama is an emerging problem area for drug trafficking from Colombia to the United States, and the quantity of drug seizures, mostly cocaine, has grown from around 32,000 kilograms in 2005 to 54,000 kilograms in 2009. While crime rates have risen overall, the year 2009 saw a 23 percent increase in Panama's homicide rate from the previous year, with 806 homicides reported in 2009. It is believed that the majority of violent crimes are drug related.

Refugees from Colombia have faced difficulty obtaining work permits and other forms of legal recognition. There were approximately 1,900 recognized refugees living in Panama in 2009, mainly Colombians. The Martinelli administration had suggested measures to normalize the status of thousands of undocumented Colombians living in Panama without official refugee status, but no progress had been made on these measures at year's end. New immigration rules that took effect in 2008 tightened controls on foreigners, but other legislation gave recognized refugees who have lived in Panama for more than 10 years the right to apply for permanent residency. This law would apply mostly to long-standing refugees who fled Central American conflicts in the 1980s.

Discrimination against darker-skinned Panamanians is widespread. The country's Asian, Middle Eastern, and indigenous populations are similarly singled out. Indigenous communities enjoy a degree of autonomy and self-government, but some 90 percent of the indigenous population lives in extreme poverty. Since 1993, indigenous groups have protested the encroachment of illegal settlers on their lands and government delays in formally demarcating them. In March 2009, police leveled indigenous Naso communities in Bocas de Toro in response to a peaceful protest against a hydroelectric dam project. According to the NGO Cultural Survival, the action left over 200 people homeless. Separately, NGOs condemned the government before the Inter-American Commission on Human Rights for using force and intimidation to displace thousands of indigenous people in connection with a hydroelectric project on the Changuinola River, and in June 2009 the commission called on Panama to suspend all work on the dam.

Violence against women and children is widespread and common. Panama is a source, destination, and transit country for human trafficking. The government has worked with the ILO on information campaigns addressing the issue, and it has created a special unit to investigate cases of trafficking for the purpose of prostitution. However, the resources dedicated to such efforts remain insufficient. The U.S. State Department's 2009 Trafficking in Persons Report removed Panama from its Tier 2 Watch List, but the country remains classified as Tier 2 and does not fully comply with minimum international standards. In 2008, the government eliminated its *alternadora* visa category, which had been used to traffic foreign women for Panama's sex trade.

Papua New Guinea

Political Rights: 4
Civil Liberties: 3
Status: Partly Free

Population: 6,610,000
Capital: Port Moresby

Ten-Year Ratings Timeline For Year Under Review (Political Rights, Civil Liberties, Status)

2000	2001	2002	2003	2004	2005	2006	2007	2008	2009
2,3F	2,3F	2,3F	3,3PF	3,3PF	3,3PF	3,3PF	3,3PF	4,3PF	4,3PF

Overview: A March 2009 Ombudsman's report revealed serious misuse of government funds in Papua New Guinea. Despite growing domestic discontent and external criticism, lawmakers failed to address governance issues and rising violence, or improve economic and social welfare during the year. Meanwhile, lawmakers voted to significantly increase their own pay and other forms of compensation.

Papua New Guinea (PNG) gained independence from Australia in 1975. In 1988, miners and landowners on Bougainville Island began guerrilla attacks on a major Australian-owned copper mine, and by 1990, the islanders' demands for compensation and profit sharing became a low-grade secessionist war. Australia and New Zealand brokered a ceasefire in 1998 and a peace treaty in 2001, which called for elections for a semiautonomous Bougainville government and a referendum on independence in 10 to 15 years. Parliament approved a new constitution for Bougainville in 2004, and voters chose John Kabui, an independence advocate, as their first president in 2005. Australia remains deeply involved in recovery efforts, sending observers, peace-keepers, police officers and trainers, and material assistance.

In July 2007 general elections, Prime Minister Michael Somare's National Alliance captured 27 of the 109 seats in Parliament. In August, the new Parliament elected Somare to a second term. Somare's premiership has been plagued by controversy surrounding his alleged involvement in enabling Julian Moti—who was wanted in Australia for alleged sex crimes against a minor in Vanuatu in 2007—to escape to the Solomon Islands. Somare barred a 2006 special inquiry report into the incident from public release, though a leaked copy revealed recommendations for Somare's prosecution. A subsequent Ombudsman Commission's investigation into the Moti affair was not completed by the end of 2009.

Kabui died suddenly of a suspected heart attack in 2008, and James Tanis, vice president of Kabui's Bougainville People's Congress, was elected as the new president. Heavily armed roadblocks stopped residents of some regions from voting in by-elections, and many voters were unable to cast their ballots because their names were missing from the electoral rolls.

An ombudsman's report released in March 2009 noted that the education sector had misused US$13.3 million in allocated funds. The European Union subsequently requested that PNG return US$61 million provided for teacher training and the purchase of library books and textbooks. The report revealed that the government had also failed to account for tens of millions in the sales of mining and logging rights. Similarly, Australia reported in April that much of the US$9.6 billion in aid it has provided since 1976 has been misused.

Logging and other forms of natural resource exploitation have provided a significant increase in revenue for the government, spurring economic growth in recent years. However, poverty remains widespread, infrastructure is poor, and literacy, health, and other human development indicators all remain low. Parliament has failed to implement necessary reforms in the education and health-care sectors, and the courts and other public institutions are understaffed and poorly resourced. Meanwhile, lawmakers unanimously voted in January 2008 to increase funding for their own allowances and perks, amounting to an additional US$10 million annually for the national budget. Parliament approved the 2009 budget, which included US$11 million as part of a five-year loan repayment arrangement to purchase a US$46 million French-made jet airplane for the prime minister's use. Lawmakers voted unanimously again in 2009 to increase their accommodation and transportation allowances by 42 percent and 50 percent, respectively; the increase represents another US$35,000 per lawmaker each year, or US$3.8 million for all 109 members of Parliament.

Political Rights and Civil Liberties: PNG is an electoral democracy. However, the 2007 elections were marred by reports of fraud, lost ballots, attacks on journalists and candidates, and deaths. Voters elect a unicameral, 109-member Parliament to serve five-year terms. A limited preferential voting system allows voters to choose up to three preferred candidates on their ballots. The prime minister, the leader of the majority party or coalition, is formally appointed by the governor-general, who represents Britain's Queen Elizabeth II as head of state.

The major parties are the National Alliance, the United Resources Party, the Papua New Guinea Party, and the People's Progressive Party. Political loyalties are driven more by tribal, linguistic, geographic, and personal ties than party affiliation. Many candidates run as independents and align with parties after they are elected.

Official abuse and corruption are serious problems. Although a number of high-profile corruption cases are pursued each year and arrests are occasionally made, comprehensive reforms to increase transparency and the rule of law have not occurred. Senior officials generally avoid investigation by claiming executive privilege or parliamentary immunity and have occasionally silenced accusers through defamation and libel suits. In March 2009, the speaker of Parliament resigned amid allegations of misuse of parliamentary funds. In November, an investigation uncovered rampant corruption in the Foreign Affairs Ministry and the Immigration Department, though no one was charged or arrested by year's end. PNG was ranked 154 out of 180 countries surveyed in Transparency International's 2009 Corruption Perceptions Index.

Freedom of speech is generally respected, and the media provide independent coverage of controversial issues such as alleged police abuse, official corruption, and the views of the political opposition. However, the government and politicians have tried to limit critical reporting at times through the use of media laws and libel and defamation lawsuits. PNG has two state-owned and two privately-owned radio stations with national coverage, as well as a number of local radio stations. There are one commercial and three state-owned television stations. Internet access is limited by cost and lack of infrastructure, but the government does not restrict access.

The government upholds freedom of religion. Academic freedom is generally respected, but the government does not always tolerate criticism.

The constitution provides for freedoms of assembly and association, and the government generally observes these rights in practice. In October 2009, police rejected a request by the Salvation Army church group to hold a rally against poverty; no reason was given for the decision. Many civil society groups provide social services and advocate for women's rights, environmental conservation, and other causes. The government recognizes workers' rights to strike, organize, and engage in collective bargaining. Marches and demonstrations require 14 days' notice and police approval.

The judiciary is independent, and the legal system is based on English common law. The Supreme Court is the final court of appeal and has original jurisdiction on constitutional matters. The National Court hears most cases and appeals from the lower district courts. Laypeople sit on village courts to adjudicate minor offenses under both customary and statutory law. Suspects often suffer lengthy detentions and trial delays because of a shortage of trained judicial personnel.

Law enforcement officials have been accused of corruption, unlawful killings, extortion, rape, theft, the sale of firearms, and the use of excessive force in the arrest and interrogation of suspects. The correctional service is understaffed, and prison conditions are poor. Prison breaks are not uncommon: in 2009, 60 inmates escaped from a Port Moresby prison in September, 28 escaped from a jail in Garoka in October, and 70 escaped from a jail in Lae in December. Military control and effectiveness are hampered by a lack of training and equipment, poor morale, low pay, corruption, and disciplinary problems. In October 2009, police officers received a 5 percent pay raise, the first since 2006. The incidence of street and other serious crimes, including kidnapping and murder, continue to rise. Also, weak governance and law enforcement have allegedly made PNG a base for organized Asian criminal groups.

Native tribal feuds over land, titles, religious beliefs, and perceived insults frequently lead to violence and deaths. Inadequate law enforcement and the increased availability of guns have exacerbated this problem. Attacks on Chinese migrants and their businesses continue to increase, as the native population is generally frustrated by high unemployment and the increasing numbers of Chinese migrants opening businesses and working in mines. Their resentment is further fueled by government rhetoric and media reports that emphasize the influx of illegal Chinese migrants and their involvement in criminal activities.

Discrimination and violence against women and children are widespread. Females face high mortality rates from the lack of basic maternal health services, teenage pregnancy, and domestic violence. Despite pressure from women's rights groups, lawmakers generally oppose special seats for women in Parliament, and women are frequently barred from voting by their husbands. Although domestic violence is punishable by law, prosecutions are rare, as police commonly treat it as a private matter, and family pressure and fear of reprisal discourage victims from pressing charges. However, 25 women joined the military in July 2009 for the first time in PNG's history.

Paraguay

Political Rights: 3
Civil Liberties: 3
Status: Partly Free

Population: 6,349,000
Capital: Asuncion

Ten-Year Ratings Timeline For Year Under Review (Political Rights, Civil Liberties, Status)

2000	2001	2002	2003	2004	2005	2006	2007	2008	2009
4,3PF	4,3PF	4,3PF	3,3PF	3,3PF	3,3PF	3,3PF	3,3PF	3,3PF	3,3PF

Overview: President Fernando Lugo's election last year raised the expectation of social improvement for Paraguay's poor population. However, Lugo struggled to advance his reform agenda given his increasingly weak and unwieldy Patriotic Alliance for Change (APC) coalition and an obstructive Congress. After its principal conservative party left in July, the ruling coalition lost its majority in Congress. Meanwhile, corruption in the judiciary and conflict between landowners and peasants continued during the year.

Paraguay, which achieved independence from Spain in 1811, has been wracked by a series of crises since authoritarian president Alfredo Stroessner of the right-wing Colorado Party was ousted in 1989 after 35 years in power. The fragility of the country's emerging democratic institutions resulted in nearly 15 years of popular uprisings, military mutinies, antigovernment demonstrations, bitter political rivalries, and continued rule by the Colorados.

Senate leader Luis Gonzalez Macchi assumed the presidency in 1999, after the incumbent fled the country amid murder charges. In December 2002, Gonzalez Macchi offered to leave office early to avoid pending impeachment hearings against him for embezzlement. Gonzalez Macchi and many other members of the Colorado Party were also discredited by their failed efforts to reverse the country's downward economic spiral.

Former education minister Nicanor Duarte Frutos of the Colorado Party emerged victorious in the national elections of 2003. After taking office, Duarte moved to take control of the tax, port, and customs authorities to combat tax evasion and smuggling. Paraguay has a highly dollarized banking system, which facilitates the illegal transfer of funds to offshore accounts. This tax evasion as well as prevalent corruption deprived the state of about two-thirds of its legitimate revenues. Despite the difficult political environment, Duarte made some progress on his fiscal and tax reform agenda. In addition to a major tax reform bill passed in 2004, a personal income tax was enacted by Congress in January 2007. A 2006 standby agreement with the International Monetary Fund (IMF) boosted investor confidence in Paraguay.

Fernando Lugo, leader of the Patriotic Alliance for Change (APC) coalition—a heterogeneous coalition comprising 20 parties including Christian Democrats, socialists, communists, and peasant organizations—was elected president in April 2008. Lugo's election represented widespread disappointment in the Colorado Party, which had failed to address Paraguay's intractable problems of low public security, slow economic growth, endemic public corruption, and a poverty rate of more than 35 percent. His election also raised expectations that the standard of living for Paraguay's poor majority would improve. Land reform necessary to address Paraguay's highly skewed land distribution remains one of the administration's principal goals. However, in the 2009 UN Development Programme's Human Development Report, Paraguay was ranked 101 out of 182 countries in its Gini Index (measuring income inequality)—worse than nearby Ecuador, Peru, and Brazil.

Prospects for Lugo's reforms were dealt a blow when the coalition's largest member party—the conservative Authentic Liberal Radical Party (PLRA)—left the alliance in July 2009. With only of various small left-wing parties remaining, the APC no longer enjoys a majority in the Congress. The legislature is now controlled by the Colorados, who strongly oppose Lugo's reformist agenda. Amid calls by Lugo's critics for his resignation—including rumors of a pending military coup—Lugo replaced the heads of the army, navy, and air force in early November 2009.

The Lugo administration signed an historical agreement with Brazil in July 2009, which settled a decades-long dispute over payments for energy produced from the Itaipu hydroelectric dam. The agreement will triple Paraguay's income from the dam, but the agreement had yet to be approved by the Brazilian Congress by the year's end. Lugo has maintained a conventional economic program. However, the personal income tax, which came into effect in January 2009, was suspended a couple of months later following a Congressional defeat; it will not be changed until 2010 at the earliest.

Political Rights and Civil Liberties: Paraguay is an electoral democracy. The 2008 national elections were considered to be free and fair. The 1992 constitution provides for a president, a vice president, and a bicameral Congress, consisting of a 45-member Senate and an 80-member Chamber of Deputies, all elected for five-year terms. The president is elected by a simple majority vote, and reelection is prohibited. The constitution bans the active-duty military from engaging in politics.

Before Fernando Lugo and the APC came to power in 2008, the Colorado Party ruled Paraguay for over 60 years. The other major political groupings include the PLRA, the Beloved Fatherland Party, the National Union of Ethical Citizens, and the National Agreement Party.

Corruption cases languish for years in the courts without resolution, and corruption often goes unpunished, as judges favor the powerful and wealthy. The Lugo administration has pledged to increase overall transparency in government and reduce corruption, most notably in the judiciary. However, little progress was made in 2009. President Lugo was unable to depoliticize Paraguay's corrupt Supreme Court in August 2009, when he failed in his attempt to change the informal party quota system for judicial posts. Transparency International ranked Paraguay 154 out of 180 countries surveyed in its 2009 Corruption Perceptions Index, below all other countries in the Americas save Venezuela and Haiti.

The constitution provides for freedoms of expression and the press, and the government generally respects these rights in practice. There are a number of private television and radio stations and independent newspapers but only one state-owned media outlet, Radio Nacional, which has a limited audience. Journalists investigating corruption or drug trafficking are often the victims of threats and violent attacks. This climate of insecurity showed no improvement in 2009, as harassment of journalists continued. In January, the director of a community radio station was shot and killed; press groups speculated that he was murdered for his comments on connections between local police and drug traffickers. The government does not restrict use of the internet, nor does it censor internet content.

The government generally respects freedom of religion. All religious groups are required to register with the Ministry of Education and Culture, but no controls are imposed on these groups, and many informal churches exist. The government generally does not restrict academic freedom.

Freedoms of association and assembly were undermined by the government of former president Luis Gonzalez Macchi, which tolerated threats and the use of force against the opposition. However, the constitution does guarantee these freedoms, and President Lugo has respected these rights in practice. There are numerous trade unions, although they are weak and riddled with corruption. The labor code provides for the right to strike and prohibits retribution against strikers. However, employers often illegally dismiss and harass strikers and union leaders, and the government has failed in practice to address or prevent retaliation by employers against strikers.

The judiciary, under the influence of the ruling party and the military, is highly corrupt. Courts are inefficient, and political interference in the judiciary is a serious problem, with politicians routinely pressuring judges and blocking investigations. While the judiciary is nominally independent, 62 percent of judges are members of the Colorado Party. In August 2008, a court cleared former general Lino Oviedo of existing assassination charges, which permitted him to compete in the presidential elections and led to allegations of political involvement in judicial decision making. The constitution permits detention without trial until the accused has completed the minimum sentence for the alleged crime. Illegal detention by police and torture during incarceration still occur, particularly in rural areas. Poorly paid and corrupt police officials remain in key posts. Overcrowding, unsanitary conditions, and mistreatment of inmates are serious problems in the country's prisons; prisons and correctional centers held 60 percent more than capacity in 2009.

The lack of security in border areas, particularly in the tri-border region adjacent to Brazil and Argentina, has allowed organized crime groups to engage in money laundering and the smuggling of weapons and narcotics. The Shiite Islamist movement Hezbollah has long been involved in narcotics and human trafficking in the largely ungoverned tri-border area; in recent years, Hezbollah has developed ties with Mexican drug cartels.

The constitution provides Paraguay's estimated 108,000 indigenous people with the right to participate in the economic, social, and political life of the country. In practice, however, the indigenous population is unassimilated and neglected. A June 2008 census estimated that 48 percent of the indigenous were unemployed, and 88 percent lacked medical coverage. Peasant organizations sometimes occupy land illegally, and landowners often respond with death threats and forced evictions by hired vigilante groups. Violence between landless peasants and the predominantly Brazilian landowners practicing large-scale farming continued in 2009. However, the Itaipu agreement was expected to ease instability on the Paraguay-Brazil border.

An estimated 6 out of every 10 children born in Paraguay are not registered at birth and consequently lack access to public health and educational services. Sexual and domestic abuse of women continue to be serious problems. Although the government generally prosecutes rape allegations and often obtains convictions, many rapes go unreported, because victims fear their attackers or are concerned that the law will not respect their privacy. Employment discrimination against women is pervasive. Trafficking in persons is proscribed by the constitution and criminalized in the penal code, but there have been occasional reports of trafficking for sexual purposes and domestic servitude.

Peru

Political Rights: 2
Civil Liberties: 3
Status: Free

Population: 29,165,000
Capital: Lima

Ten-Year Ratings Timeline For Year Under Review (Political Rights, Civil Liberties, Status)

2000	2001	2002	2003	2004	2005	2006	2007	2008	2009
3,3PF	1,3F	2,3F	2,3F	2,3F	2,3F	2,3F	2,3F	2,3F	2,3F

Overview: In April 2009, former president Alberto Fujimori was sentenced to 25 years in prison for severe human rights violations committed during his authoritarian rule. A trend toward increasing social conflict continued during the year, as illustrated by a June incident in which at least 23 police officers and 10 protesters were killed following a months-long standoff over land rights.

Since achieving independence from Spain in 1821, Peru has experienced alternating periods of civilian and military rule. Civilians have held office since a 12-year dictatorship ended in 1980. However, that year, a Maoist guerrilla group known as the Shining Path launched a vicious two-decade insurgency.

Alberto Fujimori, a university rector and engineer, was elected president in 1990. In 1992, backed by the military, he suspended the constitution, took over the judiciary, and dissolved the Congress. A new constitution featuring a stronger presidency and a unicameral Congress was approved in a state-controlled 1993 referendum following the capture of Shining Path leader Abimael Guzman. Congress passed a law in 1996 that allowed Fujimori to run for a third term, despite a constitutional two-term limit.

According to official results, Fujimori outpolled Alejandro Toledo—a U.S.-educated economist who had been raised in one of Peru's urban squatter settlements—in the first round of the 2000 presidential election. Toledo boycotted the runoff, pointing to widespread doubts about the first-round vote count and a campaign of smears, threats, and assaults by Fujimori supporters linked to the government.

Beginning in September 2000, a series of videotapes emerged showing intelligence chief Vladimiro Montesinos bribing opposition congressmen and other figures. As a result, in late November, opposition forces assumed control of Congress, Fujimori fled to Japan and resigned, and respected opposition leader Valentin Paniagua was chosen as interim president.

Toledo's Peru Posible party led the April 2001 congressional elections with 25 percent of the vote, and he bested former president Alan Garcia (1985–90) in a runoff presidential election in June. A 2002 decentralization process gave new regional governments almost a quarter of the national budget and a range of powers that had long been concentrated in the capital.

In August 2003, Peru's Truth and Reconciliation Commission (CVR) reported that the Shining Path was the "principal perpetrator" of human rights abuses during the 1980–2000 civil conflict, but it also accused security forces of serious and repeated atrocities. The report more than doubled the estimated death toll; of the 69,000 killed, nearly three-fourths were residents of poor highland villages.

In June 2004, a special anticorruption court convicted Montesinos in the first of many cases against him, sentencing him to 15 years in prison. Fujimori, who remained in Japan, declared in September that he would run for president in 2006, despite being banned from holding office until 2011. In November 2005, he flew to Chile, where he was immediately detained, as Peru requested his extradition.

Ollanta Humala of the Peruvian Nationalist Party (PNP) won the first round of the presidential election in April 2006, with Garcia placing second. The PNP, allied with the Union for Peru (UPP) party, led the congressional elections with 45 seats, followed by Garcia's Peruvian Aprista Party (APRA) with 36 and the right-wing National Unity party with 17. The pro-Fujimori Alliance for the Future party won 13 seats. Although 15 of Peru's 24 regions voted for Humala in the June presidential runoff, Garcia garnered overwhelming support in Lima and won with 52.5 percent of the vote. In November regional elections, locally based independent candidates won in the vast majority of races.

Once in office, Garcia focused on macroeconomic growth and stability. In December 2006, he signed a controversial law requiring nongovernmental organizations (NGOs) to register with a state agency and detail their funding sources or face fines or suspension. The Constitutional Court in September 2007 struck down key provisions of the law, but NGOs continued to face harassment and hostility from the government.

Fujimori was extradited from Chile in September 2007, and in December he was sentenced to seven years in prison for ordering an illegal search of the home of Montesinos's wife in 2000. Also in December, Fujimori began a lengthy trial for murder and other more serious charges. The proceedings were initially disrupted by his supporters, but in April 2009, he was sentenced to 25 years in prison for overseeing death-squad killings and several kidnappings. International observers and local rights groups characterized the trial as fair and transparent, and hailed the verdict as an unprecedented example of a democratically elected leader convicted of human rights violations in his home country. Fujimori also pleaded guilty to corruption charges in September. However, as the year progressed, rights groups expressed disappointment that the Fujimori trial had failed to create momentum in other cases involving rights violations and that, in fact, the number of acquittals increased, including in cases where the prosecution's evidence appeared preponderant.

According to the national ombudsman's office, social conflict, often involving protests driven by local grievances, reached a peak of 288 active and latent disputes in September 2009 before declining to 260 at the end of the year. The largest share involved environmental issues. Analysts observed that the government's approach generally relied on reaction rather than mediation and early intervention.

The year's most serious case of social conflict stemmed from a packet of decree laws issued in June 2008. Indigenous groups in Bagua province said the measures would violate their land rights and lead to environmental degradation, and argued that the government had failed to consult with locals before issuing the decrees as required by law. Two of the decrees were quickly rescinded, but several more remained in force, and Congress failed to meet its own deadlines for reviewing them. Meanwhile, the government resorted to harsh rhetoric, including the accusation that foreign interests were behind the dispute, and vowed to use force against indigenous protesters if necessary.

In June 2009, the government mounted an operation to break up a highway road-block established by the protesters, resulting in violence at two sites that left 10 protesters and 23 police officers dead, with 1 other policeman missing. Over 200 people, mainly protesters, were injured, including more than 80 with gunshot wounds. Within two weeks, the disputed decrees were rescinded, and the government acknowledged its failure to consult with locals, but it maintained its claim—eventually discredited—that outside agitators were responsible for raising tensions. At year's end, multiple investigations into the deaths were ongoing. A commission appointed to produce an official report on the incident was unable to reach a consensus; a version backed by only four of the seven members blamed nonindigenous groups for radicalizing the protests and faulted the government merely for communication failures rather than what domestic and international rights groups described as a fundamentally misguided and inhumane strategy.

Political Rights and Civil Liberties: Peru is an electoral democracy. Elections in 2006 were generally free and fair, according to international observers. Complaints focused on poor logistics and information distribution in rural areas, as well as the disenfranchisement of the roughly one million Peruvians who lacked identification documents.

The president and the 120-member, unicameral Congress are elected for five-year terms. Congressional balloting employs an open-list, region-based system of proportional representation. A measure introduced in 2006 required parties to garner at least 4 percent of the total vote to win seats. Checks on campaign financing are weak, particularly at the local level.

A lack of programmatic coherence and occasional party switching by politicians have discredited political parties in the eyes of voters, reinforcing a broader trend toward political fragmentation.

Corruption is a serious problem. Public officials and judges are often dismissed or prosecuted for graft, but in 2009, 20 percent of Peruvians reported that they or a family member had paid a bribe in the previous year. In October 2008, evidence of favoritism in the awarding of oil exploration blocks triggered a major corruption scandal, dubbed Petrogate, that led to the resignation of Prime Minister Jorge del Castillo. The evidence, which consisted largely of illegally recorded telephone conversations, suggested a broader pattern of improper deals between officials and private interests. Investigations continued at a slow pace in 2009, with the focus shifting from the alleged corruption to the illegal recordings themselves. Meanwhile, a wave of graft scandals in Congress affected scores of legislators, further tarnishing the institution's credibility and prompting calls for structural reforms, including mid-term elections. Peru was ranked 75 out of 180 countries surveyed in Transparency International's 2009 Corruption Perceptions Index.

The lively press is for the most part privately owned. Journalists are at times intimidated and even attacked by officials and private actors angered by negative coverage. Low pay leaves reporters susceptible to bribery, and media outlets remain dependent on advertising by large retailers. Following the June 2009 clashes in Bagua, the government closed the radio station La Voz de Bagua, accusing it of inciting violence. Media watchdog groups condemned the move as censorship. In December 2009, President Alan Garcia stirred controversy by pardoning former television station owner Jose E. Crousillat, who had been serving a prison term for selling his station's editorial line to Vladimiro Montesinos. The government does not limit access to the internet.

The constitution provides for freedom of religion, and the government generally respects it in practice. However, the Roman Catholic Church receives preferential treatment from the state. The government does not restrict academic freedom.

The constitution provides for the right of peaceful assembly, and the authorities uphold this right for the most part. However, in 2007 the executive branch issued decrees that limited police responsibility in the event of injury or death during demonstrations. Freedom of association is also generally respected, but Garcia and other APRA leaders allege that NGOs hinder economic development and lack transparency. Antimining activists have faced questionable legal charges in recent years, and NGOs accuse the government's international cooperation agency of selective investigation. Several prominent activists faced harassment in 2009, including lawyer Carlos Rivera, who was temporarily arrested on a years-old charge, and former CVR head Salomon Lerner, who received death threats following his efforts to create a Museum of Memory to honor victims of the internal conflict.

Peruvian law recognizes the right of workers to organize and bargain collectively. Although workers exercise the right to strike, they must notify the Ministry of Labor in advance, with the result that nearly all strikes are categorized as illegal. Less than 10 percent of the formal-sector workforce is unionized, reflecting a legacy of free-market reforms and antiunion hostility by the Alberto Fujimori regime. Parallel unionism and criminal infiltration of the construction sector in Lima led to several murders in 2009.

The judiciary is widely distrusted and prone to corruption scandals. The Constitutional Court, once seen as independent, has been accused of favoring the government in recent years; civic groups criticized its December 2009 decision to close a corruption case against a former army general based on a procedural violation. A 2008 Judicial Career Law improved the entry, promotion, and evaluation system for judges, and the judiciary's internal disciplinary body has been highly active in recent years. Access to justice, particularly for poor Peruvians, remains problematic.

An estimated 70 percent of inmates are in pretrial detention, and as of November 2009, the inmate population had reached nearly 200 percent of the system's intended capacity. Since 2006, an adversarial justice system has been gradually introduced with the hope that it will speed up and ensure greater fairness in judicial proceedings.

In 2009, journalists and civic leaders denounced over 45 cases of extrajudicial killings of presumed criminals by police in Trujillo. The military has improved its human rights training, but it continues to stall on providing information to investigators regarding past violations. The Garcia government has not prioritized justice for cases of human rights abuses by state actors during the 1980s and 1990s. In 2006, it initiated a policy to provide legal defense to all state agents accused of human rights violations, even though many victims lack legal representation; rights advocates in 2009 complained of delays in the disbursement of funds to the Council of Reparations.

Remnants of the Shining Path, whose ideological motivations are increasingly fused with the economic incentives of the cocaine industry, continue to carry out attacks against security forces in the Apurimac-Ene River Valley (VRAE) zone. Citizens there have reported cases of abuse by the military. Meanwhile, the government's anticoca efforts and alternative-crop programs in other regions failed to halt overall increases in coca production in 2009.

Discrimination against the indigenous population remains pervasive, and the government's calls to step up exploitation of natural resources have raised indigenous groups' concerns about the environmental effects of mining, logging, and hydrocarbons exploration.

In recent years, women have advanced into leadership roles in various companies and government agencies. Although legal protections have improved, dviolence is epidemic, with over half of Peruvian women reporting instances of physical or emotional abuse. Forced labor, including child labor, persists in the gold-mining region of the Amazon.

◢ Philippines

Political Rights: 4
Civil Liberties: 3
Status: Partly Free

Population: 92,227,000
Capital: Manila

Trend Arrow: The Philippines received a downward trend ar,row due to a general decline in the rule of law in the greater Mindanao region and specifically, the massacre of 57 civilians on their way to register a candidate for upcoming elections.

Ten-Year Ratings Timeline For Year Under Review (Political Rights, Civil Liberties, Status)

2000	2001	2002	2003	2004	2005	2006	2007	2008	2009
2,3F	2,3F	2,3F	2,3F	2,3F	3,3PF	3,3PF	4,3PF	4,3PF	4,3PF

Overview: Political maneuvering escalated in 2009, as potential candidates prepared for the 2010 presidential election. Meanwhile, the administration remained unsuccessful in its long-standing efforts to amend the constitution and resolve the country's Muslim and leftist insurgencies. In November, President Gloria Macapagal-Arroyo declared martial law in the southern province of Maguindanao, after 57 people were massacred in an apparent bid by the area's dominant clan to prevent the electoral registration of a rival candidate.

After centuries of Spanish rule, the Philippines came under U.S. control in 1898 and won independence in 1946. The country has been plagued by insurgencies, economic mismanagement, and widespread corruption since the 1960s. In 1986, a popular protest movement ended the 14-year dictatorship of President Ferdinand Marcos and replaced him with Corazon Aquino, whom the regime had cheated out of an electoral victory weeks earlier.

Aquino's administration ultimately failed to implement substantial reforms and was unable to dislodge entrenched social and economic elites. Fidel Ramos, a key figure in the 1986 protests, won the 1992 presidential election. The country was relatively stable and experienced significant if uneven economic growth under his administration. Ramos's vice president, Joseph Estrada, won the 1998 presidential election by promising concrete socioeconomic reform, but his administration was dogged by allegations of corruption almost from the outset. Massive street protests forced him from office in 2001 after a formal impeachment process failed.

Gloria Macapagal-Arroyo, Estrada's vice president, assumed the presidency upon his departure, and her political coalition won the May 2001 legislative elections. She nevertheless faced questions about the legitimacy of her unelected administration. In the 2004 presidential election, Arroyo initially seemed to have defeated her challenger by some 1.1 million votes. However, claims of massive fraud triggered demonstrations and were verified by some members of the administration.

When an audiotape of a conversation between the president and election officials surfaced in June 2005, supporting the previous year's vote-rigging allegations, many cabinet officials resigned to join a new opposition movement. An ultimately unsuccessful impeachment bid was launched, and the first of years of frequent protests called for the president's resignation.

The administration mounted several efforts to undercut the opposition movement, including punitive prosecutions and executive orders in 2005 and a week-long state of emergency in 2006 in response to an alleged coup attempt. The congressional opposition responded with a second unsuccessful impeachment bid that June.

The Commission to Address Media and Activist Killings, also known as the Melo Commission, was established in August 2006 following a spate of assassinations that year and to address the larger issue of extrajudicial killings since Arroyo took office in 2001. A February 2007 report by the commission acknowledged military involvement, but the panel was not empowered to pursue the matter with criminal investigations or prosecutions. A November 2008 report by a UN special rapporteur also cited military involvement in a significant number of recent extrajudicial executions of leftist activists. The abuses were believed to be encouraged by a government mandate to crush the communist insurgency by 2010, blurred lines between legitimate leftist parties and illegal groups affiliated with the rebel New People's Army (NPA), the president's dependence on high-level military support to retain power, and a persistent culture of impunity.

Although the president's coalition increased its lower-house majority in May 2007 legislative elections, the opposition bolstered its control of the Senate. Later in the year, Arroyo was implicated in a major corruption scandal involving a national broadband contract with the Chinese company ZTE, which had been approved in April. Separately, Arroyo pardoned former president Estrada in October, a month after the country's antigraft court sentenced him to life imprisonment. His conviction had been the first of a former Philippine president, and Arroyo's pardon was widely perceived as a bid to set a favorable precedent for her own treatment on leaving office.

In November 2007, former navy lieutenant and current senator Antonio Trillanes and Brigadier General Danilo Lim led roughly 20 soldiers in a failed coup attempt. A former vice president and a Roman Catholic bishop joined the men in a live television broadcast to call for Arroyo's removal from office on the grounds of electoral fraud and corruption.

Yet another failed impeachment bid was launched against the president in October 2008, and likely 2010 presidential candidate Manny Villar was ousted as leader of the Senate in November and replaced with a staunch Arroyo supporter.

Amid the political turmoil of 2008, peace talks between the government and the rebel Moro Islamic Liberation Front (MILF) broke down. The negotiations, which aimed to end a Muslim insurgency that had plagued the southern provinces since the early 1970s, had made some progress in 2007, focusing on the creation of a Bangsamoro Juridical Entity (BJE)—a self-governing expansion of the existing Autonomous Region of Muslim Mindanao (ARMM). In July 2008, the MILF agreed to sign an initial agreement on August 5, defining the BJE as the ARMM plus 712 *barangays* (small administrative units), with a formal referendum on inclusion to be held in the affected districts one year later and a formal peace agreement to be signed in November. However, local officials joined opposition leaders in calling the agreement unconstitutional, and on August 4, the Supreme Court imposed a restraining order on the deal.

While the MILF leadership expressed interest in continuing talks, 800 MILF fighters responded to the ruling by occupying five towns and nine villages in provinces bordering the ARMM. Government troops were sent in, and clashes erupted. The government officially called off the peace agreement on August 21, and the negotiating panel was dissolved in September. The conflict reached the highest levels of violence since 2003, with more than 600,000 Filipinos displaced by the end of 2008.

With a presidential election set for 2010, political maneuvering escalated in 2009. The lower house mounted a renewed campaign to amend the constitution by replacing the bicameral legislature with a unicameral one and lifting the one-term limit on the presidency. In June, the House of Representatives approved a resolution calling for the House and Senate to form a joint constituent assembly, which would ease passage of constitutional amendments by allowing the progovernment, 269-seat House to overwhelm the opposition-dominated, 24-seat Senate. Business leaders, civic groups, and the Roman Catholic Church objected to the amendment proposals, and they failed to pass by year's end.

Meanwhile, the two leading progovernment parties merged to form a united front in the upcoming elections, nominating Defense Minister Gilberto Teodoro as their presidential candidate in November 2009. Arroyo herself said she would seek to represent her home district of Pampanga in the House and registered her candidacy the same month. Leading opposition contenders included Villar, the former senator and real-estate tycoon; former president Estrada, who faced new corruption and murder allegations; and Benigno "Noynoy" Aquino, son of former president Aquino, who was widely mourned after her death in early August.

Attempting to demonstrate progress before the end of Arroyo's term, the administration changed its approach to the country's long-standing insurgencies in 2009. It dropped preconditions for negotiations with the NPA, and the communist rebels did the same, but peace talks scheduled for September failed to get off the ground. The government also sought to resume negotiations with the MILF, ordering a suspension of military operations in July. Both sides then agreed to a truce based in part on recognition of the August 2008 agreement as unsigned but "initialed." In addition, they arranged to establish an international contact group that would include representatives of the European Union, Turkey, and the Organization of the Islamic Conference. Peace negotiations resumed in December, with talks held in Kuala Lumpur, and joint ceasefire mechanisms were reactivated.

In the worst case of political violence in the country's recent history, the wife of local vice mayor Ismail Mangudadatu was ambushed by 100 armed men in November 2009 while traveling with other family members and supporters to file her husband's candidacy for the Maguindanao provincial governorship. A total of 57 people were massacred in the incident, including 29 journalists and 3 media workers who were accompanying the unarmed group. The graves in which the bodies were found appeared to have been dug in advance, and the mutilation of female victims indicated sexual assault. Evidence soon emerged to implicate the Ampatuan clan, which dominated the province's politics and was closely allied with the Arroyo administration.

Arroyo responded in early December by declaring martial law for the first time in nearly 30 years. The declaration, which applied to Maguindanao province only, entailed the suspension of habeas corpus and other rights, invoking significant criticism; the administration justified the move by arguing that the Ampatuans were fomenting rebellion. A state of emergency was declared in three Mindanao provinces immediately following the massacre, which remained even after martial law was lifted in mid-December. At least 62 people were arrested, including Maguindanao governor Andal Ampatuan Sr., and the authorities dug up arms caches as part of a broad effort to weaken local clans. Nevertheless, the Arroyo administration was widely criticized for its longtime policy of tolerating local warlords and supporting clan patronage as part of its counterinsurgency strategy, and the massacre brought new international attention the country's deeply entrenched culture of impunity. Arroyo lifted martial law on December 12, just before a joint session of Congress was due to vote on the declaration, as the Senate had already registered opposition.

Political Rights and Civil Liberties: The Republic of the Philippines is not an electoral democracy. Elections in 2004 and 2007 were marred by fraud, intimidation, and political violence, and the country was shaken by alleged coup plots or attempts in 2005, 2006, and 2007.

The Philippines has a presidential system of government, with the directly elected president limited to a single six-year term. Gloria Macapagal-Arroyo, then the vice president, rose to the presidency in 2001, after military pressure and street protests drove President Joseph Estrada from power. She completed Estrada's first term and—despite some legal challenges—won her own full term in 2004. Her opponents have repeatedly called for her to step down, partly due to the constitutionally anomalous length of her tenure. She, in turn, has pushed for the creation of a parliamentary system of government with extended term limits, but these efforts proved ineffective in 2009.

The national legislature, the Congress, is bicameral. The 24 members of the Senate are elected on a nationwide ballot and serve six-year terms, with half of the seats up for election every three years. The 269 members of the House of Representatives serve three-year terms, with 218 elected by district and the remainder elected by party list to represent ethnic minorities. Legislative coalitions are exceptionally fluid, and members of Congress often change affiliation, effectively rendering political parties meaningless. In May 2009, the two leading progovernment parties merged to form Lakas-Kampi-CMD, which accounts for two-thirds of all House members, three-quarters of all governors, and 70 percent of all mayors. Opposition members hold a slimmer majority in the Senate. The main opposition party is the Struggle for a Democratic Philippines (Laban, or LDP).

Political violence is typically tied to local rivalries and clan competition, but it is especially common in the ARMM and has increasingly targeted leaders of legitimate left-wing parties that are perceived to be associated with leftist guerrillas. One far-left party, Bayan Muna, has endured the murders of more than 130 members since Arroyo took office.

The Philippines' Commission on Elections (Comelec) is entirely appointed by the president, and with the president's permission, it has the authority to unseat military, police, and government officials. Comelec was widely discredited by the 2005 audiotape scandal regarding cheating in the 2004 elections. No internal investigation was conducted, and the 2007 legislative elections were overseen by the same tainted officials. Comelec chairman Benjamin Abalos resigned in October 2007, after being accused of bribing a government official to approve the broadband deal with China's ZTE Corporation.

Corruption and cronyism are rife in business and government. Despite recent economic reforms, a few dozen leading families continue to hold an outsized share of land, corporate wealth, and political power. Local bosses often control their respective areas, limiting accountability and encouraging abuses of power. High-level corruption also abounds. For example, the ZTE contract scandal has entangled the president, her husband, Mike Arroyo, and a number of other top officials. In November 2009, a Senate committee recommended that the ombudsman reopen the ZTE contract investigation, and called for corruption charges to be brought against Mike Arroyo and eight others, including government ministers. Senate accusations early in the year also put the president's husband at the center of a scandal involving road-building contracts, in which he was accused of accepting bribes to influence the bidding process.

A culture of impunity, stemming in part from a case backlog in the judicial system, hampers the fight against corruption. More high-profile cases have been filed in recent years, and several civic organizations have emerged to combat corruption, but cases take an average of six to seven years to be resolved in the Sandiganbayan anticorruption court. The country's official anticorruption agencies, the Office of the Ombudsman and the Presidential Anti-Graft Commission (PAGC), have mixed records. Many maintain that the former has been compromised under the current administration, as convictions have declined, while the PAGC lacks enforcement capabilities. The president's 2008 withdrawal of Executive Order 464, which since 2005 had prevented government and security officials from attending congressional inquiries without presidential permission, was a positive development, but administration allies have continued to avoid testifying by invoking executive privilege. The Philippines was ranked 139 out of 180 countries surveyed in Transparency International's 2009 Corruption Perceptions Index.

The constitution provides for freedoms of expression and the press. The private media are vibrant and outspoken, although newspaper reports often consist more of innuendo and sensationalism than substantive investigative reporting. The country's many state-owned television and radio stations cover controversial topics and are willing to criticize the government, but they, too, lack strict journalistic ethics. While the censorship board has broad powers to edit or ban content, government censorship is generally not a serious problem. The internet is widely available and uncensored.

Potential legal obstacles to press freedom were raised in 2007, including Executive Order 608, which established a National Security Clearance System to protect classified information, and the new Human Security Act (HSA), which would allow journalists to be wiretapped based on mere suspicion of involvement in terrorism.

Libel is a criminal offense, and libel suits have been used frequently to quiet criticism of public officials. In September 2009, former president Estrada filed a libel complaint against the *Philippine Daily Inquirer* for a front-page story that included statements accusing his government of coercing a Chinese-Filipino tycoon into selling shares of the country's largest telecommunications firm.

The Philippines remains one of the most dangerous places in the world for journalists to work, and impunity for crimes against them remains the norm. Several journalists were killed in separate incidents in 2009, but a total of 29 (plus 3 additional media workers) were slain in the November massacre in Maguindanao province. The reporters had been invited to accompany the family members of local vice mayor Ismail Mangudadatu on their trip to file his candidacy for governor, reportedly in an effort to help ensure the family's safety. Press freedom groups and the head of the national police called for an independent commission to investigate the massacre. The Commission on Human Rights was conducting an investigation at year's end.

Freedom of religion is guaranteed under the constitution and generally respected in practice. While church and state are separate, the population is mostly Christian, with a Roman Catholic majority. The Muslim minority is concentrated on the southern island of Mindanao and, according to the most recent census, represents 5 to 9 percent of the total population. Perceptions of relative socioeconomic deprivation and political disenfranchisement, and resentment toward Christian settlement in traditionally Muslim areas, have played a central role in the Muslim separatist movement. The U.S. State Department's 2009 religious freedom report indicated no instances of religious persecution and praised the country for its efforts at interfaith dialogue.

Academic freedom is generally respected in the Philippines, and professors and other teachers can lecture and publish freely.

Citizen activism is robust, and demonstrations are common. However, permits are required for rallies, and antigovernment protests are often dispersed. Freedoms of assembly and association were suspended to varying degrees in the provinces of Maguindanao and Sultan Kudarat and in the city of Cotabato (all in Mindanao) in November 2009 following the declaration of a state of emergency in these areas and the imposition of martial law in Maguindanao. While martial law was lifted in Maguindanao in mid-December, the state of emergency in these areas was upheld.

The Philippines has many active human rights, social welfare, and other nongovernmental groups, as well as lawyers' and business associations. Various labor and farmers' organizations that are dedicated to ending extrajudicial killings and helping families of the disappeared face significant threats, and their offices are occasionally raided. Trade unions are independent and may align with international groups. However, in order to register, a union must represent at least 20 percent of a given bargaining unit. Moreover, large firms are stepping up the use of contract workers, who are prohibited from joining unions. Only about 5 percent of the labor force is unionized. Collective bargaining is common, and strikes may be called, though unions must provide notice and obtain majority approval from their members. Violence against labor leaders remains a problem and has been part of the greater trend of extrajudicial killings in recent years. Workers' groups claim nearly 90 cases of abduction or murder since Arroyo took office, while government records put the number at 35.

Judicial independence has traditionally been strong, particularly with respect to the Supreme Court. In 2007, it spearheaded efforts to resolve the issue of extrajudicial killings and similar abuses, promulgating the writ of *amparo* (protection) to prevent the military from delaying cases by denying that it has a given person in custody. Human rights lawyers generally describe the new writ as a success. In 2009, the Supreme Court issued a writ of amparo to protect a navy lieutenant from military authorities after she accused her commanding officers of embezzling U.S. military funds. In early December, an appeals court in Cagayan de Oro issued a writ of amparo on behalf of members of the Ampatuan family, who claimed they were unnecessarily detained when government troops sealed off their homes following the Maguindanao massacre.

Rule of law in the country is generally weak. A backlog of more than 800,000 cases in the court system contributes to impunity, and low pay encourages rampant corruption. The judiciary receives less than 1 percent of the national budget, and judges and lawyers often depend on local powers for basic resources and salaries, leading to compromised verdicts. At least 12 judges have been killed since 1999, but there have been no convictions for the attacks. In September 2009, a Sharia (Islamic law) court judge was killed by two gunmen on Jolo Island.

Reports of arbitrary detention, disappearances, kidnappings, and abuse of suspects continued in 2009. Mounting evidence has confirmed the military's responsibility for many of the numerous killings of leftist journalists, labor leaders, and senior members of legal left-wing political parties in recent years. Military officers maintain that the killings are the result of purges within the communist movement. The lack of effective witness protection has been a key obstacle to investigations. About 90 percent of extrajudicial killing and abduction cases have no cooperative witnesses. Especially problematic is the fact that the Department of Justice oversees both the witness-protection program and the entity that serves as counsel to the military. Similarly, the Philippine National Police, tasked with investigating journalist murders, falls under the jurisdiction of the military.

Convictions for extrajudicial killings are extremely rare, and not a single member of the military has been found guilty of such a murder since Arroyo took office. Overall numbers of extrajudicial killings have declined from an annual peak of 220 in 2006. However, there was a significant spike in death-squad killings at the local level in 2008 and 2009, especially in Davao. Local-level officials are believed to keep lists of suspected criminals who are abducted or killed if they fail to heed warnings to reform or leave the area. The death squads responsible reportedly collect about 5,000 pesos (US$100) for each job. In a positive development, the Commission on Human Rights launched independent investigations into the death squads in March 2009. There has also been a recent rise in kidnappings for ransom; authorities killed at least 47 suspected kidnappers during 2009, while 60 others were arrested in a government crackdown.

The Muslim separatist conflict has caused severe hardship for many of the 15 million inhabitants of Mindanao and nearby islands, and has resulted in more than 120,000 deaths since it erupted in 1972. Both government and rebel forces have committed summary killings and other human rights abuses. The escalation of violence in the south in late 2008 displaced more than 600,000 people; an estimated 300,000 remained displaced as of September 2009. Meanwhile, the communist NPA continues to engage in executions, torture, and kidnappings in the countryside, especially in central and southern Luzon.

Citizens may travel freely outside conflict zones, and there are no restrictions on employment or place of residence. The poor security situation inhibits individuals' ability to operate businesses.

Women have made many social and economic gains in recent years. The UN Development Programme notes that the Philippines is one of the few countries in Asia to significantly close the gender gap in the areas of health and education. Although more women than men now enter high school and university, women face some discrimination in private sector employment, and women in Mindanao enjoy considerably fewer rights.

The trafficking of women and girls abroad and internally for forced labor and prostitution remains a major problem, despite antitrafficking efforts by the government and civil society. The fact that many women trafficked for illicit labor are heavily indebted by the time they begin working exacerbates the problem. There are reports of bonded labor, especially of children, in black-market trades such as prostitution and drug trafficking. The country's various insurgent groups have been accused of using child soldiers.

Poland

Political Rights: 1
Civil Liberties: 1
Status: Free

Population: 38,146,000
Capital: Warsaw

Ten-Year Ratings Timeline For Year Under Review (Political Rights, Civil Liberties, Status)

2000	2001	2002	2003	2004	2005	2006	2007	2008	2009
1,2F	1,2F	1,2F	1,2F	1,1F	1,1F	1,1F	1,1F	1,1F	1,1F

Overview:
President Lech Kaczynski ratified the European Union's Lisbon Treaty in October 2009, after an opt-out clause concerning the Charter of Fundamental Rights was added. While Poland was the only country in the bloc to experience economic growth in 2009, its progress toward adoption of the euro currency stalled during the year.

After being destroyed by its powerful neighbors in a series of 18th-century partitions, Poland enjoyed a window of independence from 1918 to 1939, only to be invaded by Germany and the Soviet Union at the opening of World War II. The country then endured decades as a Soviet satellite state until 1989, when the Solidarity trade union movement forced the government to accept democratic elections.

Fundamental democratic and free-market reforms were introduced between 1989 and 1991, and additional changes came as Poland prepared its bid for membership in the European Union (EU). In the 1990s, power alternated between political parties with a background in Solidarity and those with communist origins. Former communist Alexander Kwasniewski of the Democratic Left Alliance (SLD) replaced Solidarity's Lech Walesa as president in 1995 and was subsequently reelected by a large margin in 2000. A government led by the SLD oversaw Poland's final reforms ahead of EU accession, which took place in May 2004.

Law and Justice (PiS), a conservative party headed by identical twin brothers Lech and Jaroslaw Kaczynski, won the September 2005 parliamentary elections. Kazimierz Marcinkiewicz, rather than Jaroslaw Kaczynski, was named prime minister–designate to avoid damaging Lech Kaczynski's presidential bid by raising the prospect of the two brothers controlling both presidency and premiership. Lech Kaczynski duly won the presidential contest in October, and PiS eventually formed a fragile majority coalition with the leftist-populist, agrarian Self-Defense Party (Samoobrona) and the socially conservative, Catholic-oriented League of Polish Families (LPR). In July 2006, Jaroslaw Kaczynski replaced Marcinkiewicz as prime minister. The ruling coalition broke apart in September, only to re-form in a weakened state the following month. When it collapsed again a year later, following the prime minister's firing of a number of senior officials, legislative elections were called for October 2007.

The center-right Civic Platform (PO) party won 209 seats in the Sejm, followed by PiS with 166, the Left and Democrats (LiD) coalition with 53, and the Polish People's Party (PSL) with 31. A representative of the German minority held the remaining seat. In the Senate, the PO took 60 seats, the PiS won 39, and the last seat went to an independent. The PO and PSL formed a coalition government in November, with PO leader Donald Tusk as prime minister.

The relationship between Tusk and Lech Kaczynski remained tense in 2008, as the president resisted the government's generally pro-EU policy initiatives. Kaczynski ratified the EU's Lisbon Treaty in October 2009, but only with an opt-out clause regarding the Charter of Fundamental Rights, which the PiS felt would infringe on Polish sovereignty and potentially allow more legal abortions, same-sex marriage, and euthanasia. While Tusk's government had laid out plans in 2008 for Poland to adopt the euro currency by 2012, it abandoned this target date in July 2009 due to the global financial crisis. In May, the country secured a US$20 billion credit line from the International Monetary Fund to help it endure the crisis, and it was the only country in the EU to achieve economic growth in 2009.

In the June 2009 elections for the European Parliament, the PO led with 25 seats, followed by the PiS with 15, an SLD-led coalition with 7, and the PSL with 3. Former center-right prime minister Jerzy Buzek was elected president of the European Parliament, making him the first Eastern European to hold such a high-ranking position in the EU.

In September, U.S. president Barack Obama canceled his predecessor's plans to build an antiballistic missile installation in Poland. However, the United States was expected to proceed with the related deployment of short- to medium-range air defense missiles, and an agreement was reached in December to station a U.S. Patriot antimissile battery in Poland.

Political Rights and Civil Liberties: Poland is an electoral democracy. Voters elect the president for up to two five-year terms and members of the bicameral National Assembly for four-year terms. The president's appointment of the prime minister is subject to confirmation by the 460-seat Sejm, the National Assembly's lower house. The prime minister is responsible for most government policy, but the president also has an important role, especially in foreign relations. The 100-member Senate, the upper house, can delay and amend legislation but has few other powers.

The conservative PiS and the center-right PO have become the two most important political parties. The SLD formed the LiD coalition with a number of smaller left-leaning parties in 2006, but the grouping ultimately dissolved in 2008. PiS's former governing coalition partners, Self-Defense and the LPR, failed to win representation in the 2007 legislative elections. There is one representative of the German minority in the Sejm.

Corruption remains a problem and often goes unpunished. Several high-ranking government officials, including the deputy prime minister, resigned in October 2009 for their alleged involvement in a gambling-industry lobbying scandal. Also that month, the head of the Central Anticorruption Bureau (CBA) was charged with abuse of power for encouraging his agents to engage in bribery and forgery. Such scandals adversely affect Poland's ability to attract foreign investment. Poland was ranked 49 out of 180 countries surveyed in Transparency International's 2009 Corruption Perceptions Index.

The 1997 constitution guarantees freedom of expression and forbids censorship. Libel is a criminal offense, though a November 2009 amendment to the criminal code eased criminal penalties for defamation. Infringements on media freedom include gag orders and arbitrary judicial decisions concerning media investigations of individuals affiliated with parties in power. Poland's print media are diverse and, for the most part, privately owned. The state-owned Polish Television (TVP) and Polish Radio are dominant in their media, but they face growing competition from private Polish and foreign outlets. Control over TVP has caused various political disputes in recent years, as several bills on the station's funding have been passed by parliament and then vetoed by the president. In November, the president signed hate-speech legislation that made the possession, production, sale, or distribution of communist or fascist symbols punishable by up to two years in prison. The government does not restrict internet access.

The state respects freedom of religion. Religious groups are not required to register with the authorities but receive tax benefits if they do. Academic freedom is generally respected.

Polish citizens can petition the government, assemble legally, organize professional and other associations, and engage in collective bargaining. However, complicated legal procedures and slow courts hinder workers' ability to strike. Public demonstrations require permits from local authorities. Poland has a robust labor movement, but groups including the self-employed and those working under individual contracts are barred from joining a union. Labor leaders have complained of harassment by employers.

Poland has an independent judiciary, but courts are notorious for delays in administering cases. State prosecutors have proceeded slowly on corruption investigations, contributing to concerns that they are subject to considerable political pressure. Prison conditions are fairly poor by European standards, and pretrial detention periods can be lengthy. A new human rights division was opened by the Justice Ministry in November 2009 to address properly human rights abuses and support victims.

Ethnic minorities generally enjoy generous protections and rights under Polish law, including funding for bilingual education and publications, and privileged representation in the parliament; their political parties are not subject to the minimum vote threshold of 5 percent to achieve representation. Some groups, particularly the

Roma, suffer discrimination in employment and housing, racially motivated insults, and, less frequently, physical attacks. Poland's homosexual community is active, but also faces discrimination.

Women have made inroads in the professional sphere and are employed in a wide variety of occupations; several hold high positions in government and the private sector. Female lawmakers hold 20 percent of the Sejm seats and 8 percent of the Senate. However, domestic violence against women is a serious concern. Trafficking in women and girls for the purpose of prostitution also remains a problem. Following an incest and pedophilia case in 2008, a bill stipulating that pedophiles convicted of certain crimes (such as incest) must be chemically castrated upon their release was signed by the president in November 2009, drawing significant criticism from human rights groups.

Portugal

Political Rights: 1
Civil Liberties: 1
Status: Free

Population: 10,639,000
Capital: Lisbon

Ten-Year Ratings Timeline For Year Under Review (Political Rights, Civil Liberties, Status)

2000	2001	2002	2003	2004	2005	2006	2007	2008	2009
1,1F	1,1F	1,1F	1,1F	1,1F	1,1F	1,1F	1,1F	1,1F	1,1F

Overview: In the run-up to the September 2009 parliamentary elections, in which Prime Minister Jose Socrates' Socialist Party narrowly won reelection, a scandal erupted over an allegation that the Socialist government was spying on President Anibal Cavaco Silva. Meanwhile, corruption continued to be an issue of concern throughout the year.

Portugal was proclaimed a republic in 1910, after King Manuel II abdicated during a bloodless revolution. Antonio de Oliveira Salazar became prime minister in 1932 and ruled the country as a fascist dictatorship until 1968, when his lieutenant, Marcello Caetano, replaced him. During the "Marcello Spring," repression and censorship were relaxed somewhat, and a liberal wing developed inside the one-party National Assembly. In 1974, a bloodless coup by the Armed Forces Movement, which opposed the ongoing colonial wars in Mozambique and Angola, overthrew Caetano.

A transition to democracy began with the election of a Constitutional Assembly that adopted a democratic constitution in 1976. A civilian government was formally established in 1982, after a revision of the constitution brought the military under civilian control, curbed the president's powers, and abolished the unelected Revolutionary Council. Portugal became a member of the European Economic Community (later the European Union, or EU) in 1986, and in early 2002, Portugal adopted the euro. In 1999, Portugal handed over its last colonial territory, Macao, to the People's Republic of China.

Anibal Cavaco Silva, a center-right candidate who had served as prime minister from 1985 to 1995, won the 2006 presidential election, marking the first time in Portugal's recent history that the president and prime minister hailed from opposite sides of the political spectrum.

Portugal held the rotating EU presidency for the second half of 2007, during which time Portugal oversaw the drafting the Treaty of Lisbon, which replaced the proposed EU constitution that had been rejected in 2005. Ratification of the treaty by the 27-country bloc was completed in November 2009.

In the September 2009 legislative elections, Jose Socrates' governing Socialist Party won a narrow victory with 37 percent of the vote. The centre-right Social Democratic Party captured 29 percent, followed by the Democratic and Social Centre/ People's Party with nearly 11 percent. After talks of forming a coalition fell apart, the Socialists formed a minority government in October.

Leading up to the September election, an espionage scandal overtook election coverage, when the newspaper *Publico* reported that President Silva feared that he was under surveillance by the Socialist government. The opposition newspaper, *Diario de Noticias,* alleged that the story was leaked by Silva's longtime adviser, Fernando Lima, who was subsequently fired by Silva at the end of September. The president addressed the scandal following the elections, denying reports that he thought the presidency was under surveillance and claiming that Lima had been let go due to the disruption caused by his supposed involvement.

Political Rights and Civil Liberties: Portugal is an electoral democracy. The 230 members of the unicameral legislature, the Assembly of the Republic, are elected every four years using a system of proportional representation. The president, elected for up to two five-year terms, holds no executive powers, though he can delay legislation with a veto and dissolve the Assembly to call early elections. The prime minister is nominated by the Assembly, and the choice is confirmed by the president. The constitution was amended in 1997 to allow resident noncitizens to vote in presidential elections.

The Portuguese have the right to organize and join political parties and other political groupings of their choice, except for fascist organizations. The main political parties are the Socialist Party, the Social Democratic Party, and the Social Centre/ People's Party. The autonomous regions of Azores and Madeira—two island groups in the Atlantic—have their own political structures with legislative and executive powers. In 2009, Jose Socrates sought to impose term limits on the autonomous regions in a broader attempt to further autonomy.

Corruption scandals continued to make headlines in 2009. In January, Prime Minister Jose Socrates was accused of having granted the British development company Freeport permission to build a shopping mall on protected land outside of Lisbon in exchange for bribes in 2002 during his tenure as environment minister. Jose da Mota, the head of Eurojust, an EU judicial body, allegedly tried to persuade investigators to curb their inquiries at the behest of the premier and the minister of justice. Da Mota stepped down as head of Eurojust in December after being suspended over the affair. Investigations continued at the year's end. Separately, Portuguese police in November carried out a wide-spread operation to expose suspects—including former cabinet minister Armando Vara—engaged in a scheme to illicitly obtain industrial waste contracts. Vara was on trial at year's end. Portugal was ranked 35 out of 180 countries surveyed in Transparency International's 2009 Corruption Perceptions Index.

Freedom of the press is guaranteed by the constitution, and laws against insulting the government or the armed forces are rarely enforced. The inadequately funded public broadcasting channels face serious competition from commercial television outlets. In the run-up to the 2009 elections, the television station TVI pulled a program about the Freeport scandal that implicated Socrates. The program's presenter and senior editors criticized the move as censorship and resigned in protest. Internet access in Portugal is generally not restricted.

Although the country is overwhelmingly Roman Catholic, the constitution guarantees freedom of religion and forbids religious discrimination. The Religious Freedom Act provides religions that have been established in the country for at least 30 years (or recognized internationally for at least 60 years) with a number of benefits formerly reserved for the Catholic Church, such as tax exemptions, legal recognition of marriage and other rites, and respect for traditional holidays. Academic freedom is respected.

Freedoms of assembly and association are honored, and national and international nongovernmental organizations, including human rights groups, operate in the country without government interference. Workers enjoy the right to organize, bargain collectively, and strike for any reason, including political ones. Despite months of protest by labor organizations, the government adopted a labor law in June 2008 making it easier for employers to hire and dismiss employees. In March 2009, Portugal saw its first general strike since 2002. Approximately 200,000 people marched in Lisbon to demand higher salaries and to protest rising unemployment and continued government proposals to adjust labor laws. Only 35 percent of the workforce is unionized.

The constitution provides for an independent court system. However, staff shortages and inefficiency have contributed to a considerable backlog of pending trials. Human rights groups have expressed concern about unlawful police shootings, deaths in police custody, and poor prison conditions, including overcrowding, poor sanitary conditions, and high rates of HIV/AIDS among inmates. The prison population—as a percentage of the total population—is larger than the EU average. A March 2009 report by the Council of Europe's Committee for the Prevention of Torture expressed continued concern over mistreatment of prisoners including the aforementioned infringements.

The constitution guarantees equal treatment under the law. The government has taken a number of steps to combat racism, including passing antidiscrimination laws and launching initiatives to promote the integration of immigrants and Roma. A 2007 immigration law facilitates family reunification and legalization for immigrants in specific circumstances, such as those who applied under "immigration amnesty." According to a 2008 study by the Observatory for Immigration, immigrants pay discriminatorily high taxes, little of which is channeled to projects directly benefiting foreign citizens.

Domestic violence against women remains a problem, and few cases are brought to trial; over 7,000 cases were reported in the first half of 2008. A 2008 report from the General Confederation of Portuguese Workers revealed that women earn four times less than men. In August 2009, a lesbian couple lost their court appeal to marry, as the Portuguese government declared gay marriage unconstitutional. After the September elections, a Secretary for Equality position was created to promote women as equal members of society, among other duties. The country is a destination and transit point for trafficked persons, particularly women from Eastern Europe and former Portuguese colonies in South America and Africa.

Qatar

Political Rights: 6
Civil Liberties: 5
Status: Not Free

Population: 1,409,000
Capital: Doha

Ten-Year Ratings Timeline For Year Under Review (Political Rights, Civil Liberties, Status)

2000	2001	2002	2003	2004	2005	2006	2007	2008	2009
6,6NF	6,6NF	6,6NF	6,6NF	6,5NF	6,5NF	6,5NF	6,5NF	6,5NF	6,5NF

Overview: Five years after agreeing to hold legislative elections for the Consultative Council, Qatar again failed to do so in 2009. As a result of government pressure, the director of the Doha Center for Media Freedom, an institution devoted to promoting free speech and protecting journalists, resigned in July.

Qatar gained independence from Britain in 1971. The following year, Khalifa bin Hamad al-Thani deposed his cousin, Emir Ahmad bin Ali al-Thani, and ruled until 1995 as an absolute monarch, with few government institutions checking his authority. In 1995, the emir was deposed by his son, Hamad bin Khalifa al-Thani, who began a program of gradual political, social, and economic reforms. Hamad dissolved the Ministry of Information shortly after taking power, an action designed to demonstrate his commitment to expanding press freedom.

In 1996, Hamad permitted the creation of Al-Jazeera, which has become one of the most popular Arabic-language satellite television channels in the Middle East. However, Al-Jazeera generally does not cover Qatari politics and focuses instead on regional issues.

Elections were held in 1999 for a 29-member Central Municipal Council, a body designed to advise the minister of municipal affairs and agriculture. The poll made Qatar the first state of the Gulf Cooperation Council to introduce universal suffrage for men and women over 18 years of age. Hamad also accelerated a program to build Qatar's educational institutions, inviting foreign universities to establish branches in the country.

Central Municipal Council elections were held again in 2003. Also that year, Qatari voters overwhelmingly approved a constitution that slightly broadened the scope of political participation without eliminating the monopoly on power enjoyed by the ruling family. Most rights in the new constitution do not apply to noncitizen residents, who form a majority of the population.

In 2007, citizens again voted for the Central Municipal Council, choosing 29 members from 125 candidates. One woman was elected. Turnout reached 51 percent, a considerable improvement over 2003, when just 30 percent of the eligible electorate voted. In July 2008, the emir appointed a new cabinet that included two women.

Qatar has hosted U.S. military forces for a number of years, and the U.S. presence grew significantly after 2001. The country has faced severe criticism in the region for its ties to the United States and its tentative links with Israel.

Political Rights Qatar is not an electoral democracy. The head of state is
and Civil Liberties: the emir, currently Hamad bin Khalifa al-Thani, whose family has a monopoly on political power. The emir appoints a
prime minister and cabinet. The constitution states that the emir appoints an heir
after consulting with the ruling family and other notables. Voters elect local government representatives with limited powers over municipal services; these representatives report to the appointed minister of municipal affairs and agriculture. Under the
constitution, which was ratified by public referendum in 2003 and promulgated by
the emir in 2004, elections are to be held for 30 of the 45 seats in a new Consultative
Council; the emir has the power to appoint the other 15 members. However, the elections had yet to be held at the end of 2009. The existing 35-member Consultative
Council is entirely appointed.

Only a small percentage of the country's population—about 200,000 people out
of 1,409,000 residents—is permitted to vote or hold office. The government does
not permit the existence of political parties.

Although critics have complained of a lack of transparency in government procurement, Qatar was ranked 22 out of 180 countries surveyed in Transparency
International's 2009 Corruption Perceptions Index, making it the best performer in
the Middle East.

The constitution guarantees freedom of expression. However, content in the
print and broadcast media is influenced by leading families, and journalists practice
a high degree of self-censorship. Reporters face possible jail sentences for slander.
The top five daily newspapers are privately owned, but their owners and boards
include members of the ruling family. In July 2009, Robert Menard, the director of the
Doha Center for Media Freedom—an institution launched in 2008 to promote freedom of speech and protect embattled journalists—resigned claiming government
pressure. Although the satellite television channel Al-Jazeera is privately owned,
the government has reportedly paid operating costs for the channel since its inception. As a result, Al-Jazeera rarely criticizes the ruling family. Qataris have access to
the internet, but the government censors content and blocks access to sites that are
deemed pornographic or politically sensitive.

Islam is Qatar's official religion. However, the 2004 constitution explicitly provides for freedom of worship. The Ministry of Islamic Affairs regulates clerical matters and the construction of mosques. The first of six churches to be built for Qatar's
Christian community was opened in Doha in March 2008, and the remaining five
were still under construction at the end of 2009. The constitution guarantees freedom of opinion and academic research, but scholars often practice self-censorship
on politically sensitive topics.

While the constitution grants freedom of assembly and the right to form nongovernmental organizations (NGOs), these rights are limited in practice. Protests are
rare, with the government restricting the public's ability to organize demonstrations.
All NGOs need state permission to operate, and the government closely monitors
the activities of these groups. After hosting the 2007 Conference on Democracy and
Reform in Doha, the Ministry of Foreign Affairs established the Arab Foundation
for Democracy to monitor progress on reform in the region. Sheikh Hamad has contributed US$10 million to the foundation. There are no independent human rights
organizations, but a National Human Rights Committee (NHRC), consisting of mem-

bers of civil society and government ministries, has done some work on investigating alleged abuses.

A 2005 labor law expanded some protections for citizens, but it prohibits noncitizen workers from forming labor unions. Foreign nationals make up most of the workforce, but fear of job loss and deportation often prevents them from exercising what rights they have. Many foreign workers face economic abuses, like the withholding of salaries or contract manipulation, while others endure poor living conditions and excessive work hours. Worker complaints have included charges as serious as torture, imprisonment, and forced labor. Foreign construction workers have repeatedly demonstrated against poor living and working conditions. Female domestic servants are particularly vulnerable to abuse and are often lured or forced into prostitution. In March 2008, the government announced plans to build a "worker's city" for 50,000 laborers near Doha in an effort to improve the living and health conditions of foreign workers. Although some infrastructure construction was completed by July 2009, the project was put on hold in December.

Despite constitutional guarantees, the judiciary is not independent in practice. The majority of Qatar's judges are foreign nationals who are appointed and removed by the emir. The judicial system consists of Sharia (Islamic law) courts, which have jurisdiction over a narrow range of issues including family law, and civil law courts, which have jurisdiction over criminal cases as well as commercial and civil suits. The Supreme Judiciary Council regulates the judiciary. The constitution protects individuals from arbitrary arrest and detention and bans torture. However, a 2002 law allows the suspension of these guarantees for the "protection of society." The law empowers the minister of the interior to detain a defendant for crimes related to national security on the recommendation of the director-general of public security.

The government discriminates against noncitizens in education, housing, health care, and other services that are offered free of charge to citizens. In March 2009, the government worked with local religious leaders in an outreach campaign aimed at raising awareness of the moral and legal implications of human trafficking. Qatar has also attempted to restrict visas for suspected prostitutes trying to enter the country, but enforcement remains inconsistent.

The constitution treats women as full and equal persons, and discrimination based on sex, of origin, language, or religion is banned. In 2006, Qatar implemented a codified family law, which regulates issues important for women, including inheritance, child custody, marriage, and divorce. While the law offers more protections for women than they enjoyed previously, they continue to face some disadvantages, including societal discrimination, and few effective legal mechanisms are available for them to contest incidents of bias.

Romania

Political Rights: 2
Civil Liberties: 2
Status: Free

Population: 21,474,000
Capital: Bucharest

Ten-Year Ratings Timeline For Year Under Review (Political Rights, Civil Liberties, Status)

2000	2001	2002	2003	2004	2005	2006	2007	2008	2009
2,2F	2,2F	2,2F	2,2F	3,2F	2,2F	2,2F	2,2F	2,2F	2,2F

Overview: President Traian Basescu narrowly won a second term in a December 2009 runoff election against Mircea Geoana of the Social Democratic Party (PSD), paving the way for a new coalition government led by the Basescu-allied Democratic Liberal Party (PDL). A fragile governing coalition between the PSD and PDL had collapsed in October, leading to months of political deadlock. Separately, a European Union progress report in July found that Romania's efforts to reform its judicial system and combat corruption were being hindered by political infighting and procedural delays.

In 1989, longtime dictator Nicolae Ceaucescu was overthrown and executed by disgruntled communists. A provisional government was formed under Ion Iliescu, a high-ranking communist, and regular multiparty elections soon followed. The former Communist Party, renamed the Social Democratic Party (PSD), took power in the 2000 parliamentary elections, with Adrian Nastase as prime minister.

In 2004, Traian Basescu of the Alliance for Truth and Justice (comprising the National Liberal Party, or PNL, and the Democratic Party, or PD) defeated Nastase in a presidential runoff. The PNL and PD then formed a coalition government with the Humanist Party (later renamed the Conservative Party, or PC), and the Democratic Union of Hungarians in Romania (UDMR). Calin Popescu Tariceanu of the PNL became prime minister.

The ruling coalition proved rather unstable, and after Romania's accession to the European Union (EU) in January 2007, the friction between the president and prime minister flared into direct confrontation. The PSD exploited the rift and gave tactical support to Tariceanu. Much of the disagreement appeared to stem from the president's aggressive pursuit of EU-backed judicial and anticorruption reforms, which his opponents accused him of politicizing.

Tariceanu ousted the Basescu-allied PD from the cabinet in April 2007. At the PSD's urging, Parliament voted to suspend Basescu and organize a referendum on his removal, but he easily won the vote in May. The new Democratic Liberal Party (PDL), a union of the PD and a PNL splinter faction, won parliamentary elections in November 2008, narrowly defeating a PSD-PC alliance in the lower house, 115 seats to 114, and in the Senate, 51 seats to 49. The rivals then formed a grand coalition in December, controlling a combined 329 out of 471 seats in both chambers. Meanwhile, the PNL was left with 65 seats in lower house and 28 seats in the Senate, followed by the UDMR with 22 and 9. The remaining 18 lower-house seats were set aside for ethnic minorities. Voter turnout was less than 40 percent; unlike in previous years, no major fraud allegations were reported. PDL leader and Cluj mayor Emil Boc was subsequently confirmed by Parliament as the new prime minister.

The grand coalition broke down in October 2009, after the PSD interior minister—Dan Nica, the country's third interior minister that year—was sacked for suggesting that the PDL was planning to engage in fraud in the upcoming presidential election. The PSD withdrew from the coalition, and Boc's resulting minority government was ousted in a no-confidence vote, leaving a caretaker government in place as the presidential campaign began. The opposition rejected Basescu's nominees to replace Boc in the weeks leading up to the vote.

Basescu and his PSD challenger, Mircea Geoana, led the first round in November, with 32 percent and 31 percent, respectively. PNL candidate Crin Antonescu, who placed third with 20 percent, then endorsed Geoana, as did the UDMR. Nevertheless, Basescu won the December runoff by some 70,000 votes amid 58 percent turnout, and the Constitutional Court confirmed the results after the PSD forced a partial recount. Parliament subsequently approved a new PDL-UDMR coalition government led by Boc.

The year's political clashes took place as the EU pressed Romania to follow through on judicial and anticorruption reforms, and as the global economic downturn placed serious strains on the national budget. The government agreed in March to a US$27 billion package of emergency loans from the International Monetary Fund and other lenders, pledging to undertake painful deficit reductions over the next several years. Separately, the EU released roughly US$200 million in agricultural aid that had been frozen in 2008, citing improvements in Romania's disbursement system.

Political Rights and Civil Liberties: Romania is an electoral democracy. Elections since 1991 have been considered generally free and fair. The president is directly elected for up to two five-year terms, and appoints the prime minister with the approval of Parliament. Members of the bicameral Parliament, consisting of the 137-seat Senate and 334-seat Chamber of Deputies, are elected for four-year terms. New rules governing the 2008 parliamentary elections replaced the old party-list voting system with single-member districts, although all districts with no majority winner were allotted based on collective proportional representation. In a referendum held concurrently with the 2009 presidential election, voters overwhelmingly endorsed a plan by President Traian Basescu to create a unicameral parliament with no more than 300 seats.

The constitution grants a lower-house seat to each national minority that passes a certain voting threshold, and 18 such seats were allotted in 2008. The UDMR has long represented the ethnic Hungarian minority. Political participation and representation of Roma is very weak. For the first time since its 1992 founding, the ultranationalist Greater Romania Party won no seats in Parliament in 2008, though it secured two seats in June 2009 elections for the European Parliament.

Romania has struggled to meet EU anticorruption requirements since joining the bloc in 2007. The latest EU progress report in July 2009 found that improved investigations by the National Anticorruption Directorate and the new National Integrity Agency, which vetted public officials' asset declarations, were offset by the inability of the courts and disciplinary bodies to adjudicate cases swiftly. The report also noted political resistance to anticorruption efforts, particularly in Parliament, which had moved slowly and inconsistently on requests to lift the immunity of accused members. The Chamber of Deputies voted in March 2009 to allow criminal proceedings against former prime minister Adrian Nastase, having rejected such a move the previous year. Two former cabinet ministers were indicted for corruption the same month, and three sitting ministers faced graft probes during the year. None of the roughly 20 current and former cabinet ministers accused of corruption since 2007 have been convicted to date. Romania was ranked 71 out of 180 countries surveyed in Transparency International's 2009 Corruption Perceptions Index, tying Greece and Bulgaria for the worst performance in the EU.

The constitution protects freedom of the press, and the media are characterized by considerable pluralism, though Romanian journalists often suffer verbal abuse and minor physical assaults. In January 2007, the Constitutional Court struck down reforms that had decriminalized libel and defamation, effectively reinstating them in the penal code. Long-standing concerns about political bias at state-owned media continue, and private outlets remain heavily influenced by the political and economic interests of their owners. During the 2009 presidential campaign, key media moguls turned their outlets against Basescu, though he ultimately won despite the hostile coverage. The government does not restrict access to the internet.

Religious freedom is generally respected, but "nontraditional" religious organizations encounter both difficulties in registering with the state and discrimination by some local officials and Orthodox priests. The government formally recognizes 18 religions, each of which is eligible for proportional state support. The Romanian Orthodox Church remains dominant and politically powerful. Religions are required to have a membership equal to at least 0.1 percent of the population to be officially acknowledged. Moreover, nontraditional religions must undergo a 12-year "waiting period" prior to recognition. The government does not restrict academic freedom, but the education system is weakened by unchecked corruption.

The constitution guarantees freedoms of assembly and association, and the government respects these rights in practice. The civil society sector is vibrant and able to influence public policy, increasingly by working through EU officials and mechanisms. Workers have the right to form unions and strike, but in practice, many employers work against unions, and illegal antiunion activity is rarely punished. Major labor protests took place throughout 2009, as public employees, including teachers, railway workers, judges, and police, fought budget cuts and demanded salary increases.

The judiciary is one of the most problematic institutions in Romania. The 2009 EU progress report praised the passage of new criminal and civil codes in June, but noted that they could not take effect until new procedural codes were also enacted, which was not expected until at least 2011. The courts continue to suffer from budgetary, staffing, and structural deficiencies, and existing laws allow criminal defendants to trigger lengthy delays in their cases. Conditions in Romanian prisons remain poor.

Romania's 18 recognized ethnic minorities have the right to use their native tongue with authorities in areas where they represent at least a fifth of the population, but the rule is not always enforced. Roma, homosexuals, people with disabilities, and HIV-positive children and adults face discrimination in education, employment, and other areas.

The constitution guarantees women equal rights, but gender discrimination is a problem. Only about 10 percent of the seats in Parliament are held by women. Trafficking of women and girls for forced prostitution has become a major concern. However, some law enforcement and victim-protection progress has been reported in recent years. The criminal code does not provide for restraining orders in domestic violence cases, and abortion is permitted after 14 weeks of pregnancy only to save the woman's life or in other extraordinary circumstances.

Russia

Political Rights: 6
Civil Liberties: 5
Status: Not Free

Population: 141,839,000
Capital: Moscow

Trend Arrow: Russia received a downward trend arrow due to electoral abuses, declining religious freedom, greater state controls over the presentation of history, growing police corruption, and the repeated use of political terror against victims, including human rights activists and journalists.

Note: The numerical ratings and status listed above reflect the addition of Chechnya to the Russia report; in previous years, Chechnya was the subject of a separate report.

Ten-Year Ratings Timeline For Year Under Review (Political Rights, Civil Liberties, Status)

2000	2001	2002	2003	2004	2005	2006	2007	2008	2009
5,5PF	5,5PF	5,5PF	5,5PF	6,5NF	6,5NF	6,5NF	6,5NF	6,5NF	6,5NF

Overview: The executive branch maintained its tight controls on the media, civil society, and the other branches of government in 2009, and took additional steps to rein in religious and academic freedom. The large-scale disqualification of opposition candidates helped secure a sweeping victory for the ruling United Russia party in local and regional elections in October. In November, a dissident police officer faced punishment after drawing attention to widespread police corruption. Insurgent and other violence in the North Caucasus continued during the year, as did assassinations of prominent human rights activists and journalists.

With the collapse of the Soviet Union in December 1991, the Russian Federation emerged as an independent state under the leadership of President Boris Yeltsin. In 1993, Yeltsin used force to thwart an attempted coup by parliamentary opponents of radical reform, after which voters approved a new constitution establishing a powerful presidency and a bicameral national legislature, the Federal Assembly. The 1995 parliamentary elections featured strong support for the Communist Party and ultranationalist forces. Nevertheless, in the 1996 presidential poll, Yeltsin defeated Communist leader Gennady Zyuganov with the financial backing of powerful business magnates, who used the media empires they controlled to ensure victory. The August 1998 collapse of the ruble and Russia's financial markets provided a traumatic but ultimately useful corrective to the Russian economy, ushering in years of rapid growth. In 1999, Yeltsin appointed Vladimir Putin, then the head of the Federal Security Service (FSB), as prime minister.

Conflict with the separatist republic of Chechnya, which had secured de facto independence from Moscow after a brutal 1994–96 war, resumed in 1999. Government forces reinvaded the breakaway region after Chechen rebels led an incursion into the neighboring Russian republic of Dagestan in August and a series of deadly apartment bombings—which the Kremlin blamed on Chechen militants—struck Russian cities in September. The second Chechen war dramatically increased Putin's popularity, and after the December 1999 elections to the State Duma, the lower house of the Federal Assembly, progovernment parties were able to form a majority coalition.

An ailing and unpopular Yeltsin—who was constitutionally barred from a third presidential term—resigned on December 31, 1999, transferring power to Putin. The new acting president subsequently secured a first-round victory over Zyuganov, 53 percent to 29 percent, in the March 2000 presidential election. After taking office, Putin moved quickly to consolidate his power, reducing the influence of the legislature, taming the business community and the news media, and strengthening the FSB. He considerably altered the composition of the ruling elite through an influx of personnel from the security and military services. Overall, Putin garnered enormous personal popularity by overseeing a gradual increase in the standard of living for most of the population; the improvements were driven largely by an oil and gas boom and economic reforms that had followed the 1998 ruble collapse.

In the December 2003 Duma elections, the Kremlin-controlled United Russia party captured 306 out of 450 seats. With the national broadcast media and most print outlets favoring the incumbent, no opponent was able to mount a significant challenge in the March 2004 presidential election. Putin, who refused to debate the other candidates, received 71.4 percent of the vote in a first-round victory, compared with 13.7 percent for his closest rival, the Communist-backed Nikolai Kharitonov.

Putin introduced legislative changes in 2004 that eliminated direct gubernatorial elections in favor of presidential appointments, citing a need to unify the country in the face of terrorist violence. The government also began a crackdown on democracy-promotion groups and other nongovernmental organizations (NGOs), especially those receiving foreign funding. The authorities removed another possible threat in 2005, when a court sentenced billionaire energy magnate Mikhail Khodorkovsky, founder of the oil firm Yukos, to eight years in prison for fraud and tax evasion. A parallel tax case against Yukos itself led to the transfer of most of its assets to the state-owned Rosneft. Khodorkovsky had antagonized the Kremlin by bankrolling opposition political activities.

A law enacted in 2006 handed bureaucrats wide discretion in shutting down NGOs that were critical of official policy. In another sign that safe avenues for dissent were disappearing, an assassin murdered investigative journalist Anna Politkovskaya in October of that year. She had frequently criticized the Kremlin's ongoing military campaign in Chechnya and the excesses of Russian troops in the region.

The heavily manipulated December 2007 parliamentary elections gave a solid majority to progovernment parties. The ruling United Russia party captured 315 of the 450 Duma seats, while two other parties that generally support the Kremlin,

Just Russia and the nationalist Liberal Democratic Party, took 38 and 40 seats, respectively. The opposition Communists won 57 seats in the effectively toothless legislature.

Putin's handpicked successor, First Deputy Prime Minister Dmitry Medvedev, won the March 2008 presidential election with 70.3 percent of the vote and nearly 70 percent voter turnout. As with the 2007 parliamentary elections, the Organization for Security and Cooperation in Europe (OSCE) refused to monitor the voting due to government constraints on the number of monitors and the amount of time they could spend in the country. Medvedev immediately appointed Putin as his prime minister, and the former president continued to play the dominant role in government, with some presidential powers shifting to the prime minister. In November and December, the leadership amended the constitution for the first time since it was adopted in 1993, extending the presidential term from four to six years.

In 2009, as a global recession took hold, the government drew on reserve funds it had amassed during the oil and gas boom to support the economy. Meanwhile, assassins continued to target the regime's most serious critics with impunity, murdering, among others, human rights activists Markelov in January and Natalia Estemirova in July. These deaths were often tied to the conflict in Chechnya, where Ramzan Kadyrov had used harsh tactics to suppress rebel activity with Putin's backing.

The tightly controlled October 2009 local and regional elections, which gave United Russia some 70 percent of the contested seats, provoked protests, including a short-lived walkout by other parties in the normally subservient Duma. Before the elections, the authorities had eliminated most of the opposition candidates by invalidating the signatures they had collected.

Political Rights and Civil Liberties:

Russia is not an electoral democracy. The 2007 State Duma elections were carefully engineered by the administration, handing pro-Kremlin parties a supermajority in the lower house, which is powerless in practice. In the 2008 presidential election, state dominance of the media was on full display, debate was absent, and incumbent Vladimir Putin was able to pass the office to his handpicked successor, Dmitry Medvedev.

The 1993 constitution established a strong presidency with the power to dismiss and appoint, pending parliamentary confirmation, the prime minister. However, the current political system no longer represents the constitutional arrangement, since Prime Minister Putin's personal authority and power base among the security services make him the dominant figure in the executive branch. The Federal Assembly consists of the 450-seat State Duma and an upper chamber, the 166-seat Federation Council. Beginning with the 2007 elections, all Duma seats were elected on the basis of party-list proportional representation. Parties must gain at least 7 percent of the vote to enter the Duma. Furthermore, parties cannot form electoral coalitions, and would-be parties must have at least 50,000 members and organizations in half of the federation's 83 administrative units to register. These changes, along with the tightly controlled media environment and the misuse of administrative resources, including the courts, make it extremely difficult for opposition parties to win representation. Half the members of the upper chamber are appointed by governors and half by regional legislatures, usually with strong federal input in all cases. Although the governors were previously elected, a 2004 reform gave the president the power to appoint them. Under constitutional amendments adopted in 2008, future presidential terms will be six years rather than the current four, though the limit of two consecutive terms will remain in place. The terms for the Duma will increase from four years to five.

Corruption in the government and business world is pervasive. A growing lack of accountability within the government enables bureaucrats to act with impunity. Although Medvedev enacted a package of anticorruption reforms at the end of 2008, Transparency International's Russia chapter reported an increase in bribes in 2009. The state closed the vast majority of Russia's casinos in July, but a presidential report found a growth in organized crime in the fall. A police major, Aleksei Dymovsky, posted videos on the internet in November to shed light on police corruption, including soliciting bribes and fabricating cases against innocent people to meet quotas for solving cases. He was subsequently fired and faced prosecution for abuse of office at year's end. Also during the year, businessmen complained about the extensive use of pliable courts and extralegal methods to seize commercial assets. At the same time, Medvedev criticized state corporations, whereas Putin's presidency had featured a rapid expansion of the state's role in the economy. Russia was ranked 146 out of 180 countries surveyed in Transparency International's 2009 Corruption Perceptions Index.

Although the constitution provides for freedom of speech, the authorities continue to put pressure on the dwindling number of critical media outlets. Since 2003, the government has controlled, directly or through state-owned companies, all of the national television networks. Only a handful of radio stations and publications with limited audiences offer a wide range of viewpoints. Discussion on the internet is free, but the government devotes extensive resources to manipulating the information and analysis available there. At least 19 journalists have been killed since Putin came to power, including 3 in 2009, and in no cases have the masterminds been prosecuted. The authorities have further limited free expression by passing vague laws on extremism that make it possible to crack down on any organization that lacks official support.

Freedom of religion is respected unevenly. A 1997 law on religion gives the state extensive control and makes it difficult for new or independent congregations to operate. Orthodox Christianity has a privileged position, and in 2009, the president authorized religious instruction in the public schools. Regional authorities continue to harass nontraditional groups, such as Jehovah's Witnesses and Mormons. In February 2009, the Justice Ministry empowered an Expert Religious Studies Council to investigate religious organizations for extremism and other possible offenses.

Academic freedom is generally respected, although the education system is marred by corruption and low salaries. The arrest and prosecution of scientists and researchers on charges of treason, usually for discussing sensitive technology with foreigners, has effectively restricted international contacts in recent years. In its treatment of history, the Kremlin has sought to emphasize the positive aspects of Soviet leader Joseph Stalin's dictatorship, while scholars who examine his crimes have faced accusations that they are unpatriotic, casting a chill over objective efforts to examine the past. In 2009, Medvedev established a Commission for Countering Attempts to Falsify History to the Detriment of Russia's Interests, tasked with exposing "falsifications" that could hurt the country. Also during the year, St. Petersburg State

University tried to monitor its professors' foreign publications and presentations, but quickly withdrew the new regulations after an international outcry.

The government has consistently reduced the space for freedoms of assembly and association. Overwhelming police responses and routine arrests have discouraged unsanctioned protests, though pro-Kremlin groups are able to demonstrate freely. A 2006 law imposed onerous new reporting requirements on NGOs, giving bureaucrats extensive discretion in deciding which organizations could register and hampering activities in subject areas that the state deemed objectionable. The law also places extensive controls on the use of foreign funds, and in July 2008, Putin lifted the tax-exempt status of most foreign foundations and NGOs. The state has sought to provide alternative sources of funding to local NGOs, including a handful of organizations that are critical of government policy, though such support generally limits the scope of the recipient groups' activities. In 2009, Medvedev amended the NGO law to make it less burdensome, but overall conditions for civil society groups remain difficult. In a positive development, a St. Petersburg court ruled that a 2008 police search of the human rights group Memorial's offices had been illegal, ordering the police to return confiscated computer hard drives.

While trade union rights are legally protected, they are limited in practice. Strikes and worker protests have occurred in prominent industries, such as automobile manufacturing, but antiunion discrimination and reprisals for strikes are not uncommon, and employers often ignore collective-bargaining rights. With the economy continuing to change rapidly after emerging from Soviet-era state controls, unions have been unable to establish a significant presence in much of the private sector. The largest labor federation works in close cooperation with the Kremlin.

The judiciary lacks independence from the executive branch, in part because judges are often dependent on court chairmen for promotions and bonuses and must follow Kremlin preferences in order to advance. Two members of the Constitutional Court were punished after decrying judges' lack of independence, with one forced to resign from the court in December 2009. The justice system has also been tarnished by the politically fraught cases of Mikhail Khodorkovsky, who faced trial on new charges in 2009 as he neared the end of his prison sentence, and Anna Politkovskaya, whose murderers have yet to be identified. In February 2009, a jury rejected prosecutors' arguments that four men charged with minor roles in the killing were guilty.

After judicial reforms in 2002, the government has made gains in implementing due process and holding timely trials, though Medvedev has complained that this progress is not adequate. Since 2003, the criminal procedure code has allowed jury trials in most of the country. While juries are more likely than judges to acquit defendants, these verdicts are frequently overturned by higher courts, which can order retrials until the desired outcome is achieved. Russia ended the use of jury trials in terrorism cases in 2008, and Medvedev in 2009 proposed doing the same for organized crime cases. Russian citizens often feel that domestic courts do not provide a fair hearing and have increasingly turned to the European Court of Human Rights.

Critics charge that Russia has failed to address ongoing criminal justice problems, such as poor prison conditions and law enforcement officials' widespread use of illegal detention and torture to extract confessions. The death of lawyer Sergei Magnitsky in pretrial detention provided evidence that the authorities were denying him necessary medical treatment after his client had charged government employees with embezzling millions of dollars. In some cases, there has also been a return to the Soviet-era practice of punitive psychiatry.

Parts of the country, especially the turbulent North Caucasus region, suffer from high levels of violence. Chechen president Ramzan Kadyrov's success in suppressing major rebel activity in his domain has been accompanied by numerous reports of extrajudicial killings and collective punishment. Moreover, related rebel movements have appeared in surrounding Russian republics, including Ingushetia, Dagestan, and Kabardino-Balkaria. Hundreds of officials, insurgents, and civilians die each year in bombings, gun battles, and assassinations. Among other attacks in 2009, an assassination attempt seriously injured Ingushetia's president in June, an Ingush opposition figure was murdered in October, and a train bombing between Moscow and St. Petersburg killed over 25 people in November.

Immigrants and ethnic minorities—particularly those who appear to be from the Caucasus or Central Asia—face governmental and societal discrimination and harassment. Foreign nationals, particularly Georgians, have been targeted for harassment during periods of friction between the Kremlin and their home governments. While racially motivated violence has increased in recent years, the number of murders and injuries fell in 2009, according to Sova, a group that tracks ultranationalist activity in the country. Homosexuals also encounter discrimination and abuse, and gay rights demonstrations are often attacked by counterdemonstrators or suppressed by the authorities.

The government places some restrictions on freedom of movement and residence. Adults must carry internal passports while traveling and to obtain many government services. Some regional authorities impose registration rules that limit the right of citizens to choose their place of residence. In the majority of cases, the targets are ethnic minorities and migrants from the Caucasus and Central Asia.

Property rights remain precarious. State takeovers of key industries, coupled with large tax liens on select companies, have reinforced perceptions that property rights are being eroded and that the rule of law is subordinated to political considerations. The government has forcibly changed the terms of contracts with foreign oil and gas companies working in Russia.

Women in Russia have particular difficulty achieving political power. They hold 14 percent of the Duma's seats and less than 5 percent of the Federation Council's. None of the key positions in the federal executive branch are held by women, and the female governor of St. Petersburg is the main exception at the regional level. Domestic violence continues to be a serious problem, and police are often reluctant to intervene in what they regard as internal family matters. Economic hardships contribute to widespread trafficking of women abroad for prostitution.

Rwanda

Political Rights: 6
Civil Liberties: 5
Status: Not Free

Population: 9,877,000
Capital: Kigali

Ten-Year Ratings Timeline For Year Under Review (Political Rights, Civil Liberties, Status)									
2000	2001	2002	2003	2004	2005	2006	2007	2008	2009
7,6NF	7,6NF	7,5NF	6,5NF	6,5NF	6,5NF	6,5NF	6,5NF	6,5NF	6,5NF

Overview: The process of judging perpetrators of the 1994 genocide neared completion in 2009 as the traditional *gacaca* courts officially concluded their work. The government arrested the leader of a rebel group from the neighboring Democratic Republic of Congo in January, despite claims that it continued to support the group. Meanwhile, as Rwanda moved toward a presidential election in 2010, the ruling Rwandan Patriotic Front seemed to step up its already tight control over civic and political life, particularly limiting press freedom.

Belgian colonial rule in Rwanda, which began after World War I, exacerbated and magnified tensions between the minority Tutsi ethnic group and the majority Hutu. A Hutu rebellion beginning in 1959 overthrew the Tutsi monarchy, and independence from Belgium followed in 1962. Hundreds of thousands of Tutsi were killed or fled the country in recurring violence over the subsequent decades. In 1990, the Tutsi-dominated Rwandan Patriotic Front (RPF) launched a guerrilla war from Uganda to force the Hutu regime, led by President Juvenal Habyarimana, to accept power sharing and the return of Tutsi refugees.

Habyarimana was killed when his plane was shot down near Kigali in April 1994. Hutu extremists immediately pursued the complete elimination of the Tutsi. During the genocide, which lasted some three and a half months, as many as a million Tutsi and moderate Hutu were killed. By July, however, the RPF had succeeded in taking control of Kigali and establishing an interim government of national unity.

The Hutu-dominated army and militia, along with as many as two million Hutu refugees, fled into neighboring countries, especially the Democratic Republic of Congo (DRC). These forces were able to retrain and rearm in the midst of international relief efforts to assist the refugees. The RPF responded by attacking refugee camps in the DRC in 1996.

Nearly three million refugees returned to Rwanda between 1996 and 1998 and were peacefully reintegrated into society. Security improved considerably after 1997, although isolated killings and disappearances continued. The RPF-led government closely directed the country's political life. In 2000, President Pasteur Bizimungu, a moderate Hutu installed by the RPF, resigned and was replaced by Vice President Paul Kagame, a Tutsi.

Rwanda's extended postgenocide political transition officially ended in 2003 with a new constitution and national elections. The RPF's preeminent position—combined with a short campaign period, the advantages of incumbency, and a pliant political culture traumatized by the effects of the genocide—ensured victory for

Kagame in the presidential vote and for the RPF and its allies in subsequent parliamentary elections. The largest opposition party, the Hutu-based Democratic Republican Movement (MDR), was declared illegal by the authorities before the elections for allegedly promoting ethnic hatred.

A 2004 parliamentary commission report criticized a number of nongovernmental organizations (NGOs) for propagating "genocide ideology," causing these organizations to significantly limit criticism of the government. Bizimungu was sentenced that year to 15 years in prison after being convicted of antistate activities, and Amnesty International and other independent observers questioned the trial's fairness. He was pardoned and released in April 2007, though one of his codefendants remained in prison.

A ban on political party offices at the local level was lifted in June 2007, and several parties began organizing efforts. However, party activity remained tightly constrained. The RPF-led coalition won handily in the September 2008 parliamentary elections, taking 42 out of 53 elected seats in the lower house. Monitoring by a European Union observer team indicated that the actual RPF share of the vote was higher than reported, suggesting an attempt to make the elections appear more democratic.

In 2009, the grassroots *gacaca* courts officially completed their work of adjudicating genocide cases, though plans for a continuation of the gacaca system were under way. Separately, by year's end, the Criminal Tribunal for Rwanda (ICTR) had arrested a total of 81 individuals and completed cases against 48 since its inception in 1994. Cases against 26 individuals were ongoing. Genocide trials for Rwandans also took place in Belgium, Canada, and Finland. Meanwhile, charges against RPF officials have been leveled in both Spain and France for war crimes allegedly committed during the genocide. Rose Kabuye, a key Kagame ally, who had been arrested in Germany in 2008 and extradited to France, remained there awaiting trial in 2009.

The Rwandan government improved its cooperation with the DRC during the year, conducting joint military operations in the eastern DRC against Rwandan Hutu rebels. In January, Rwanda arrested Laurent Nkunda, the leader of a Congolese Tutsi rebel group, the National Congress for the Defense of the People (CNDP). Nevertheless, the CNDP continued to carry out military operations and occupy territory in the eastern DRC, and observers accused the RPF of maintaining its alleged support for the group.

With considerable international aid, Rwanda has improved earnings from coffee exports and increased grain and potato production, helping to sustain an economic growth rate of nearly 8 percent. Economic development, however, has been unevenly distributed.

Political Rights and Civil Liberties: Rwanda is not an electoral democracy. International observers have noted that the 2003 presidential and 2003 and 2008 parliamentary elections, while administratively acceptable, presented Rwandans with only a limited degree of political choice. The 2003 constitution grants broad powers to the president, who can serve up to two seven-year terms and has the authority to appoint the prime minister and dissolve the bicameral Parliament. The 26-seat upper house, the Senate, consists of 12 members elected by regional councils, 8 appointed by the president, 4 chosen by a forum of political parties, and 2 representatives of universities, all serving eight-year terms. The Chamber of Deputies, or lower house, includes 53 directly elected members, 24 women chosen by local councils, and 3 members chosen by youth and disability groups. All serve five-year terms.

The constitution officially permits political parties to exist, but only under strict controls. The constitution's emphasis on "national unity" has the effect of limiting political pluralism. The RPF dominates the political arena, and parties closely identified with the 1994 genocide are banned, as are parties based on ethnicity or religion. These restrictions have been used to eliminate parties that have the potential to challenge the RPF's dominance. The constitutionally mandated Political Party Forum vets proposed policies and draft legislation before they are introduced in Parliament. All parties must belong to the forum, which operates on the principle of consensus, though in practice, the RPF guides its deliberations. Parliamentary committees have begun to question ministers and other executive branch officers more energetically, and some of these debates are reported in the local press. As the country moves toward the 2010 presidential election, the government appears to be tightening controls on independent political activity.

Government countermeasures have helped limit corruption, though graft remains a problem. A number of senior officials in recent years have been fired and faced prosecution for alleged corruption, embezzlement, and abuse of power. The Office of the Ombudsman, the auditor general, and the National Tender Board are all tasked with combating corruption. Rwanda was ranked 89 out of 180 countries surveyed in Transparency International's 2009 Corruption Perceptions Index.

The RPF has imposed numerous legal restrictions and informal controls on the media, and press freedom groups have accused the government of intimidating independent journalists. The British Broadcasting Corporation's Kinyarwanda service was banned for two months ending in June 2009 after it aired dissenting views on the genocide. In August, the Media High Council recommended the suspension for three months of the independent national weekly *Umuseso* for defaming the president, and in December, authorities arrested and released the editor, Didas Gasana, on another defamation charge. Also in August, the editor of *Rugari* was sentenced to two years in prison for attempted extortion, and a journalist from *Rushyashya* was sentenced to a three-month jail term for photographing a gacaca trial. The editor of *Umuvugizi*, Jean-Bosco Gasasira, was convicted of defamation and invasion of privacy in November for publishing an article about an affair between two government officials. He was fined about US$6,000. A new media law enacted in August contained a number of restrictive provisions, including educational requirements for journalists, a rule compelling journalists to reveal sources when it is deemed necessary for criminal cases, and increased capital requirements for starting new media outlets. Authorities do not restrict access to the internet, but its penetration in the country remains limited.

Religious freedom is generally respected, though the government has increasingly enforced regulations on religious organizations and has arrested clergy for comments construed as denying the genocide. The implication of some clergy in the genocide has complicated relations between the government and many churches. Academic freedom is constrained by fears among teachers and students of being labeled "divisionist" and potentially arrested.

Although the constitution codifies freedoms of association and assembly, in reality, these rights are limited. Some NGOs have complained that registration and reporting procedures are excessively onerous, and activities that the government defines as "divisive" are prohibited. Several organizations have been banned in recent years, leading others to refrain from criticizing the RPF. However, most civil society organizations that do not focus on sensitive subjects, such as democracy and human rights, function without direct government interference.

The constitution provides for the rights to form trade unions, engage in collective bargaining, and strike. According to the 2009 Annual Survey of Violations of Trade Union Rights compiled by the International Trade Union Confederation, relations between the government and trade unions have improved since the first union elections in 2007. Nevertheless, the government continues to pressure the unions, often in subtle and indirect ways. The list of "essential services" in which strikes are not allowed is excessively long. The largest union umbrella group, the Central Union of Rwandan Workers, was closely controlled by the previous regime but now has greater independence.

The judiciary has yet to secure full independence from the executive. Nevertheless, a 2008 report by Human Rights Watch noted some recent improvements in the judicial system, including an increased presence of defense lawyers at trials, improved training for court staff, and revisions to the legal code. The gacaca courts have faced criticism from legal experts because of government interference and their focus on genocide crimes to the exclusion of crimes allegedly committed by the RPF. Although the gacaca process was formally completed in June 2009, some trials and appeals continue, and the government announced plans to continue gacaca courts to try more serious genocide cases. An estimated 1.5 million cases were tried in the gacaca courts. While their behavior does not appear to reflect official policy, individual police officers sometimes use excessive force, and local officials periodically ignore due-process protections.

Equal treatment under the law is guaranteed, and legal protections against discrimination have increased in recent years. A national identity card is required when Rwandans wish to move within the country, but these are issued regularly. In previous years, there were cases of government officials forcing citizens to return to the districts listed on their identity cards, though this no longer appears to be a problem.

The 2003 constitution requires women to occupy at least 30 percent of the seats in each chamber of Parliament. After the 2008 elections, Rwanda became the first country in the world to have a female parliamentary majority, with 56 percent of seats in the lower house held by women. Both the Speaker of the lower house and the chief justice of the Supreme Court are women. Women's rights to inherit land have been strengthened through legislation. An international report found in 2006 that Rwanda had made significant strides toward achieving an equal balance of girls and boys in primary school education, and special incentives exist to promote the advancement of girls in science-related study topics. Despite these improvements, de facto discrimination against women continues. Economic and social dislocation has forced women to take on many new roles, especially in the countryside.

Saint Kitts and Nevis

Political Rights: 1
Civil Liberties: 1
Status: Free

Population: 50,000
Capital: Basseterre

Ten-Year Ratings Timeline For Year Under Review (Political Rights, Civil Liberties, Status)

2000	2001	2002	2003	2004	2005	2006	2007	2008	2009
1,2F	1,2F	1,2F	1,2F	1,2F	1,1F	1,1F	1,1F	1,1F	1,1F

Overview: In 2009, Prime Minister Denzil Douglas campaigned for reelection in advance of the January 2010 parliamentary elections. Meanwhile, the opposition denounced efforts to enforce a constitutional provision banning holders of dual citizenship from seeking elected office and criticized the sitting government's attempts to redraw district boundaries just months before the election.

Saint Kitts and Nevis gained independence from Britain in 1983 but remains a member of the Commonwealth. Denzil Douglas of the ruling Saint Kitts and Nevis Labour Party (SKNLP) has been prime minister since July 1995. In 2002 elections, the SKNLP won a stronger parliamentary majority, taking all eight Saint Kitts seats in the National Assembly and shutting out the opposition People's Action Movement (PAM).

Douglas called early elections for October 2004, and his SKNLP won seven Saint Kitts seats, while the opposition PAM took the eighth. The Concerned Citizens Movement (CCM), a pro-independence party that headed Nevis's local government, kept two seats, and the Nevis Reformation Party (NRP), which also historically has favored secession from Saint Kitts, retained one. In July 2006, the NRP defeated the CCM in elections for Nevis's local assembly, taking three of the five seats. The NRP's Joseph Parry was subsequently named the island's third premier.

In 2009, Prime Minister Douglas increasingly focused on his campaign to win a new term in the parliamentary elections scheduled for March 2010. In response to opposition claims that the government was engaged in voter padding, or registration of voters outside of their legal districts, the chairman of the Organization of Eastern Caribbean States announced that political developments in St. Kitts and Nevis would be closely monitored. A new initiative to enforce a constitutional provision barring dual citizens from holding elective office provoked controversy and forced several parliamentary candidates to publicly renounce their U.S. citizenship. A late push in November by the SKNLP to redraw district lines just before the election failed. Following economic contraction in 2008, the government had reportedly stabilized its finances in 2009, strengthening Douglas's political position ahead of the 2010 elections.

Political Rights   Saint Kitts and Nevis is an electoral democracy. The 2004
and Civil Liberties: elections were free and fair. The federal government consists of the prime minister, the cabinet, and the unicameral

National Assembly. A governor-general represents Britain's Queen Elizabeth II as ceremonial head of state. Elected National Assembly members—eight from Saint Kitts and three from Nevis—serve five-year terms. Senators are appointed to the body, and their number may not exceed two-thirds of the elected members, with one chosen by the leader of the parliamentary opposition for every two chosen by the prime minister.

Saint Kitts's main political parties are the SKNLP and the PAM. On Nevis, the two main parties are the CCM, which had long been the majority party there, and the NRP, which won a majority of seats in the Nevis Island Assembly in July 2006. Nevis's assembly is composed of five elected and three appointed members, and the local government pays for all of its own services except for those involving police and foreign relations. Saint Kitts has no similar body.

The constitution grants Nevis the option to secede if two-thirds of the elected legislators in Nevis's local assembly and two-thirds of Nevisian referendum voters approve. Though a 1998 referendum on independence failed, Nevisians continued to feel neglected by the central government.

Saint Kitts and Nevis has generally implemented its anticorruption laws effectively. Despite recently proposed legislation on financial integrity, government officials are not required to disclose financial assets. Saint Kitts and Nevis was not surveyed in Transparency International's 2009 Corruption Perceptions Index.

Constitutional guarantees of free expression are generally respected. The sole local television station is government owned, although it is managed by a Trinidadian company, and there are some restrictions on opposition access to the medium. The government radio station was privatized in 1997. There are four radio stations and two newspapers; one of them publishes daily and the other one weekly. Foreign media are available, and internet access is not restricted.

The free exercise of religion is constitutionally protected, and academic freedom is generally honored.

The right to organize civic organizations is generally respected, as is freedom of assembly. An estimated 10 percent of the workforce is unionized. The right to strike, while not specified by law, is recognized and generally respected in practice. The main labor union, the Saint Kitts Trades and Labour Union, is associated with the ruling SKNLP. In 2009, the government drafted a new labor code to bring the country's laws in line with the International Labor Organization.

The judiciary is for the most part independent, and legal provisions for a fair and speedy trial are generally observed. Capital punishment is legal, and in December 2008, the government hanged Charles Laplace for the murder of his wife. The highest court is the Eastern Caribbean Supreme Court on Saint Lucia, but under certain circumstances, there is a right of appeal to the Trinidad-based Caribbean Court of Justice. Additionally, an appeal may be made to the Privy Council in the United Kingdom.

The islands' traditionally strong rule of law continues to be tested by the prevalence of drug-related crime and corruption; the intimidation of witnesses and jurors is also a problem. The government reported 2,048 criminal cases in 2008, a 10 percent increase over the previous year. The national prison is overcrowded, with over 250 prisoners in a space intended for 150. The repatriation of felons from the United States has contributed to law enforcement agencies' sense that they are being overwhelmed.

The Domestic Violence Act criminalizes domestic violence and provides penalties for abusers, but violence against women remains a problem. The Ministry of Gender Affairs records an average of 25 to 30 reports of domestic violence per year and has offered counseling for abuse victims. There are no laws against sexual harassment. Legislation passed in November 2008 increased the age of consent for sexual activity from 16 to 18.

Saint Lucia

Political Rights: 1
Civil Liberties: 1
Status: Free

Population: 172,000
Capital: Castries

Ten-Year Ratings Timeline For Year Under Review (Political Rights, Civil Liberties, Status)

2000	2001	2002	2003	2004	2005	2006	2007	2008	2009
1,2F	1,2F	1,2F	1,2F	1,2F	1,1F	1,1F	1,1F	1,1F	1,1F

Overview: In 2009, St. Lucia was battered by economic uncertainty and rising crime as Prime Minister Stephenson King reshuffled his cabinet amidst strong criticism from the opposition.

Saint Lucia, a member of the Commonwealth, achieved independence from Britain in 1979. In May 1997, Kenny Anthony led the Saint Lucia Labour Party (SLP) to victory in legislative elections, defeating the United Workers' Party (UWP). As prime minister, Anthony began to address the concerns of an electorate that was weary of economic distress and reports of official corruption. In the December 2001 general elections, the SLP captured 14 of 17 seats in the House of Assembly.

John Compton, Saint Lucia's first prime minister after independence, came out of retirement to lead the UWP to an unexpected victory in the December 2006 elections; he was sworn in again as prime minister at the age of 81. Though his party won 11 seats in the House of Assembly, he pledged to, "govern in a spirit of cooperation," with the SLP. Compton was soon sidelined by illness and died in September 2007. He was replaced by Stephenson King, a cabinet member from the UWP, who had served as acting prime minister for several months before Compton's death.

The SLP in 2008 repeatedly threatened to mount public demonstrations and called for King's resignation. The opposition disagreed with the government over its signing of the International Criminal Court agreement, its initial reluctant stance on the Economic Partnership Agreement with Europe, and its failure to enter a drug interdiction agreement with Britain.

In 2009, Prime Minister King reshuffled his cabinet for the second time since taking office in an effort to regain political momentum in the face of a deteriorating economic situation. A 12 percent decline in the tourism sector precipitated an economic slowdown across most sectors and emboldened opposition leaders. King faced increasingly effective criticism from the opposition on topics including the planned privatization of the Water and Sewerage Authority and higher salary scales for public servants. In August, the opposition led protests in an effort to force out the minister of health and the attorney general. Meanwhile, problems with renovations at the country's High Court prompted a strike by court employees and members of the bar association.

Political Rights and Civil Liberties:

Saint Lucia is an electoral democracy. The December 2006 elections were deemed free and fair, marking the first time that observers from the Caribbean Community and the Organization of American States were invited to observe. A governor-general represents the British monarch as head of state. Under the 1979 constitution, the bicameral Parliament consists of the 17-member House of Assembly, elected for five years, and an 11-member Senate. The prime minister is chosen by the majority party in the House of Assembly. Six members of the Senate are chosen by the prime minister, three by the leader of the parliamentary opposition, and two in consultation with civic and religious organizations. The island is divided into 11 regions, each with its own elected council and administrative services.

Political parties are free to organize, but two parties—the UWP, in power since 2006, and the SLP, the official opposition—dominate politics.

The few incidents of official corruption recorded in 2009 were appropriately addressed through the judicial system, and the country generally scores well in international surveys. Government officials are required by law to present their financial assets annually. Saint Lucia was ranked 22 out of 180 countries surveyed in Transparency International's 2009 Corruption Perceptions Index, the best performer in Latin America and the Caribbean.

The constitution guarantees freedom of speech, which is respected in practice. Libel offenses were removed from the criminal code in 2006. The media carry a wide spectrum of views and are largely independent of the government. There are five privately owned newspapers, four privately held radio stations, one government-funded radio station, and four privately owned television stations. In June 2009, a political firestorm erupted when suspected criminals made public threats against law enforcement officials in television and radio interviews. Police commissioners denounced the reports as inflammatory and possibly illegal, and threatened to sue the television and radio stations involved. However, no legal actions were eventually taken. Internet access is not restricted.

The constitution guarantees free exercise of religion, and that right is respected. Academic freedom is generally honored.

Constitutional guarantees regarding freedoms of assembly and association are largely upheld. Civic groups are well organized and politically active, as are labor unions, which represent the majority of wage earners.

The judicial system is independent and includes a high court under the St. Lucia-based Eastern Caribbean Supreme Court. In recent years, the record of Saint Lucia's police and judicial system has been blemished by a series of high-profile incidents, including severe beatings of inmates by police and cases of police assault. In 2009, there were numerous complaints of physical abuse by police and prison officers, highlighted by the case of Keiran Herman, who reported physical abuse and torture at the La Toc station.

Although citizens traditionally have enjoyed a high degree of personal security, rising crime—including drug-related offenses—has created concern. As of October 2009, there had been 33 murders in St. Lucia, and the island seemed on pace to surpass the 39 murders recorded in 2008. Saint Lucia is third in the Caribbean, after Jamaica and Trinidad and Tobago, in terms of the interdiction of drug mules headed for Britain each year. Prison overcrowding remains a problem, with major backlogs in the judicial system leading to prolonged pretrial detentions.

Women are underrepresented in politics and other professions. Domestic violence is a serious concern, especially among women from low-income groups. Homosexuals are occasionally targeted in hate crimes.

Saint Vincent and the Grenadines

Political Rights: 2　　　　　　　　　　　　　　　**Population:** 110,000
Civil Liberties: 1　　　　　　　　　　　　　　　**Capital:** Kingstown
Status: Free

Ten-Year Ratings Timeline For Year Under Review (Political Rights, Civil Liberties, Status)

2000	2001	2002	2003	2004	2005	2006	2007	2008	2009
2,1F	2,1F	2,1F	2,1F	2,1F	2,1F	2,1F	2,1F	2,1F	2,1F

Overview:　　　　　　In November, the ruling Unity Labour Party and Prime Minister Ralph Gonsalves suffered a major blow when a national referendum on constitutional reform was soundly defeated, ending a hotly disputed debate that had dominated the political scene in 2009.

Saint Vincent and the Grenadines achieved independence from Britain in 1979, with jurisdiction over the northern Grenadine islets of Bequia, Canouan, Mayreau, Mustique, Prune Island, Petit Saint Vincent, and Union Island.

In the 2001 elections, the social-democratic Labour Party (ULP) captured 12 of the 15 contested legislative seats, and Ralph Gonsalves became prime minister. The incumbent, conservative New Democratic Party (NDP) was reduced to three seats. International observers monitored the elections, which had been preceded by large antigovernment protests and the first serious political unrest in the country's history.

In December 2005, Gonsalves led the ULP to reelection, again taking 12 of the 15 contested seats, while the opposition NDP won the remaining 3. The NDP later vowed to take legal action over alleged electoral irregularities, but the party's effort stalled after the Organization of American States gave the elections its stamp of approval.

Gonsalves was charged with sexual assaults on two women in 2008, though both cases were subsequently dropped. Opposition legislators boycotted a parliamentary session over the issue, but Gonsalves threatened to declare the seats vacant and open them for elections.

In 2009, the politics of St. Vincent and the Grenadines became increasingly polarized over a November referendum to replace the country's 1979 constitution with one produced by a government-appointed Constitution Review Commission. Following six years of deliberations, the proposed constitution featured several important changes, such as opening national elections to members of the clergy and dual citizens and the inclusion of strong provisions against forced labor. It also ruled that marriage could only exist between a biological man and a biological woman. The opposition strongly opposed the new constitution for falling short of fully reforming the government, and former prime minister James Mitchell said the document should be burned.

On November 25, the constitutional reform failed to pass a national referendum, receiving support from only 43 percent of voters with 56 percent opposed. The apparent unpopularity of the constitutional reform, which would have required approval from a two-thirds majority of voters, places the ruling ULP in an awkward position with one year of the prime minister's term remaining.

Political Rights and Civil Liberties: Saint Vincent and the Grenadines is an electoral democracy. The December 2005 legislative elections were considered free and fair by international observers. The constitution provides for the election of 15 representatives to the unicameral House of Assembly to serve five-year terms. The prime minister is the leader of the majority party. Six senators are appointed to the chamber—four chosen by the government and two by the opposition. A governor-general represents the British monarch as head of state.

The two main political parties are the ruling, left-leaning ULP and the conservative NDP.

In recent years, there have been allegations of drug-related corruption within the government and the police force and of money laundering through Saint Vincent banks. Nevertheless, Saint Vincent and the Grenadines was ranked 31 out of 180 countries surveyed in Transparency International's 2009 Corruption Perceptions Index, making it one of the best performers in the region.

The press is independent, with two privately owned, independent weeklies and several smaller, partisan papers. Some journalists allege that government advertising is used as a political tool. The only television station is privately owned and free from government interference. Satellite dishes and cable television are available to those who can afford them. The main news radio station is government owned, and call-in programs are prohibited. Equal access to radio is mandated during electoral campaigns, but the ruling party takes advantage of state control over programming. Internet access is not restricted.

Freedom of religion is constitutionally protected and respected in practice, and academic freedom is generally honored. Access to higher education is limited but improving, as the University of the West Indies initiates degree programs with community colleges in Saint Vincent and other members of the Organization of Eastern Caribbean States.

There are constitutional protections for freedoms of assembly and association. Nongovernmental organizations are free from government interference. Labor unions are active and permitted to strike. In 2009, unions represented a reported 16 percent of the workforce.

The judicial system is independent. The highest court is the Eastern Caribbean Supreme Court (based in Saint Lucia), which includes a court of appeals and a high court. Litigants have a right of ultimate appeal, under certain circumstances, to the Trinidad-based Caribbean Court of Justice. The independent Saint Vincent Human Rights Association has criticized long judicial delays and a large backlog of cases caused by personnel shortages in the local judiciary. It has also charged that the executive branch at times exerts inordinate influence over the courts.

Although the country remains one of the safest in the Caribbean, violent crime does occasionally occur. Prison conditions have improved but remain poor. The Belle Isle Correctional Facility opened in October 2009, easing the pressure on other long-overcrowded facilities. Murder convictions carry a mandatory death sentence, and while three people remain on death row, the last execution took place in 1995.

Violence against women, particularly domestic violence, is a major problem. The Domestic Violence Summary Proceedings Act, which provides for protective orders, offers some tools that benefit victims. Homosexuality remains a criminal offense.

Samoa

Political Rights: 2
Civil Liberties: 2
Status: Free

Population: 190,000
Capital: Apia

Ten-Year Ratings Timeline For Year Under Review (Political Rights, Civil Liberties, Status)

2000	2001	2002	2003	2004	2005	2006	2007	2008	2009
2,2F	2,2F	2,2F	2,2F	2,2F	2,2F	2,2F	2,2F	2,2F	2,2F

Overview: Village chiefs continued to deliver harsh sentences in 2009, ruling in March to banish a family from the village of Vaimoso. The September tsunami that struck Samoa and neighboring islands cost the country US$58 million in damages. In June, the parliamentary Speaker failed in his attempt to remove nine members of parliament for allegedly violating the Electoral Act.

Germany controlled what is now Samoa between 1899 and World War I. New Zealand then administered the islands under a League of Nations mandate; after World War II, a UN mandate. The country became independent in 1962 and changed its name from Western Samoa to Samoa in 1988.

The centrist Human Rights Protection Party (HRPP) has dominated politics since independence. Tuila'epa Aiono Sailele Malielegaoi secured a second term as prime minister in the 2006 general elections, with the HRPP winning 35 of the 49 legislative seats. The main opposition party, the Samoa Democratic United Party (SDUP), captured 10 seats, and independents took the remainder.

In May 2007, Samoa's head of state, Malietoa Tanumafili II, died at age 94, after serving for 45 years; he had been appointed for life at independence. The legislature in June elected former prime minister Tuiatua Tupua Tamasese Efi to serve a five-year term as the new head of state.

The role and powers of village chiefs continue to be source of controversy. *Matai*, or chiefs of extended families, control local government and churches through the village *fono*, or legislature, which is open only to them. Many provide leadership and help their communities to solve conflicts, but abuse of power and excessive punishment also occur. In February 2009, six matai were charged with arson for destroying a banished family's home in 2005. In a separate case that attracted national attention in March, the matai of the village of Vaimoso banished Vaiotu Mulitalo, a former cabinet minister, along with his wife and children, for bestowing three chiefly titles without approval from the matai and for other actions that allegedly insulted the dignity of the village; the matai rejected the family's plea for forgiveness and request to return. The family took the case to the land and titles court, which ruled in the matai's favor.

The parliamentary speaker disqualified and removed nine members of parliament in June, alleging they had violated the Electoral Act by joining the new Tautua Samoa Party midterm. The accused parliamentarians argued that they had created the party, but were not members, and the Supreme Court ruled in July that they should return to their seats.

In September, a massive tsunami hit Samoa and neighboring islands, killing more than 170 Samoans and causing US$58 million in damages. This disaster caused further economic hardships for Samoa despite a rapid inflow of aid from the United States and other countries.

The switch to driving on the right side of the road in September stirred a great deal of public debate in 2009, as citizens questioned the purpose of the change and the costs of buying new road signs and remodeling vehicles to comply with safety regulations.

Political Rights and Civil Liberties: Samoa is an electoral democracy. The 2006 legislative elections were deemed free and fair. Executive authority is vested in the head of state, who is elected for five-year terms by the Legislative Assembly. The head of state appoints the prime minister, who leads the government and names his own cabinet. All laws passed by the 49-member, unicameral Legislative Assembly must receive approval from the head of state to take effect. Although candidates are free to propose themselves for electoral office, the approval of the matai is essential. Two legislative seats are reserved for at-large voters, mostly citizens of mixed or non-Samoan heritage who have no ties to the 47 village-based constituencies. All lawmakers serve five-year terms. The main political parties are the HRPP and the SDUP.

Official corruption and abuses do not appear as widespread or serious as in some other states in the region. Samoa was ranked 56 out of 180 countries surveyed in Transparency International's 2009 Corruption Perceptions Index.

Freedoms of speech and the press are generally respected. Despite continued criticism of the Printers and Publishers Act of 1982 and the Law of Criminal Libel, there have been no reports of intimidation or law suits against journalists in recent years. Journalists are legally required to reveal their sources in defamation suits against them, but this law has not been tested in court. The government operates one of three television stations and there are several English-language and Samoan newspapers. A state monopoly provides telephone and internet services, though internet access is not restricted by the government. The government continues to ban movies deemed contradictory to Christian beliefs and values, including *Milk* and *Angels and Demons* in 2009.

The government respects freedom of religion in practice, and relations among religious groups are generally amicable. There were no reports of restrictions on academic freedom.

Freedoms of assembly and association are respected in practice, and human rights groups operate freely. Approximately 60 percent of adults work in subsistence agriculture, and about 20 percent of wage earners belong to trade unions. Workers, including civil servants, have the legal right to strike and bargain collectively. Samoa depends heavily on remittances from some 100,000 Samoans living abroad.

The judiciary is independent and upholds the right to a fair trial. The Supreme Court is the highest court, with full jurisdiction over civil, criminal, and constitutional matters. The head of state, on the recommendation of the prime minister, appoints the chief justice. Prisons generally meet international standards. A special program allows prisoners to return home on weekends to help them reintegrate with society. However, a January 2009 attack on a taxi driver by a parolee has strengthened critics' arguments for discontinuing the program.

Samoa has no military, and the small police force has little impact in the villages, where the fono settles most disputes. The councils vary considerably in their decision-making styles and in the number of matai involved. Light offenses are usually punished with fines in cash or kind; serious offenses result in banishment from the village. The Supreme Court ruled in 2000 that the 1990 Village Fono Act, which gives legal recognition to village fono decisions, could not be used to infringe on villagers' freedom of religion, speech, assembly, and association. Similar Supreme Court rulings followed in 2003 and 2004.

Domestic violence against women and children is common. Spousal rape is not illegal, and social pressure and fear of reprisal inhibit reporting of domestic abuse. Sexual abuse of young girls and illegal drug use are both increasing.

San Marino

Political Rights: 1
Civil Liberties: 1
Status: Free

Population: 31,000
Capital: San Marino

Ten-Year Ratings Timeline For Year Under Review (Political Rights, Civil Liberties, Status)

2000	2001	2002	2003	2004	2005	2006	2007	2008	2009
1,1F	1,1F	1,1F	1,1F	1,1F	1,1F	1,1F	1,1F	1,1F	1,1F

Overview:
In 2009, San Marino found itself embroiled in scandals, including a money laundering scheme that led to the arrests of five heads of the nation's top bank. However, in September, San Marino was removed from the Organization for Economic Cooperation and Development's "gray list" of tax havens.

Founded in the year 301, according to tradition, San Marino is considered the world's oldest existing republic and is one of the world's smallest states. The papacy recognized San Marino's independence in 1631, as did the Congress of Vienna in 1815. In 1862, Italy and San Marino signed a treaty of friendship and cooperation. Despite its dependence on Italy, from which it currently receives budget subsidies, San Marino maintains its own political institutions. It became a member of the Council of Europe in 1988 and a member of the United Nations in 1992. Tourism and banking dominate the country's economy.

The European Union (EU) Savings Taxation Directive, which provided a way to tax revenue from savings accounts held by EU citizens in a member state other than their country of residence or in certain non-EU countries, took effect in July 2005. San Marino was not an EU member, but it agreed to participate in the directive, which was intended to prevent harmful tax practices.

In June 2008, the left-wing leading government coalition—consisting of the Party of Socialists and Democrats (PSD), the Popular Alliance of Democrats (AP), the United Left (SU), and the new Democrats of the Center party (DdC)—collapsed when the AP withdrew its delegates. The move forced the Grand and General Council, San Marino's parliament, to call early elections for November, which put the center-right Pact for San Marino coalition—comprised of the San Marino Christian Democratic Party (PDCS), the AP, the Freedom List, and the Sammarinese Union of Moderates—in power with 54 percent of the vote and 35 parliamentary seats.

In 2009, San Marino faced a series of scandals amid a faltering economy. In May, five top executives from San Marino's largest bank, Cassa di Risparmio della Repubblica di San Marino, were arrested and held in preventative custody on charges of money laundering. All five were released six months later under the condition that they remain in Bologna, where they had been held, with the exception of Mario Fantini, who was permitted to return to San Marino and live under house arrest for age reasons. Investigations were still under way at the year's end. Following the arrests, Italy placed the bank's consumer finance group, Delta, under bankruptcy proceedings. Bids to save to the group were still pending and the future of the group remained uncertain at the year's end.

In July, the Italian economy minister announced a tax amnesty for Italians who repatriated offshore accounts. The amnesty ran from September through December and drained San Marino of many of its Italian accounts, causing increased financial hardship for the country. However, San Marino signed 14 tax-information accords with EU nations in September, which lifted secrecy between signatories and assisted San Marino's removal from the Organization for Economic Cooperation and Development's (OECD) "gray list" of tax havens.

Reports surfaced at the end of 2009 that companies were registering in San Marino under fictitious residences, facilitating fiscal advantages and black market trade. While false registration of residence was outlawed in 2003, the government currently lacks a body to investigate companies' claims of residency. An emergency census was arranged by the government in September to address the issue.

Political Rights and Civil Liberties: San Marino is an electoral democracy. The 60 members of the Great and General Council, the unicameral legislature, are elected every five years by proportional representation. Executive power rests with the 10-member Congress of State (cabinet), which is headed by two captains-regent selected every spring and fall by the Great and General Council from among its own members. The captains-regent serve as joint heads of state for a six-month period. Although there is no official prime minister, the secretary of state for foreign and political affairs is regarded as the head of government; Fiorenzo Stolfi was elected to the post in July 2006. As the result of a 2008 electoral law, the winning coalition must have captured a majority of 50 percent plus 1, as well as at least 30 of the 60 parliamentary seats. New rules were also implemented to make it easier for Sammarinese living abroad to vote in elections.

The PDCS, the PSD, and the AP are the three dominant political groups in the country. There are several smaller groups, however, and majority governments are usually formed by a coalition of parties.

There are few problems with government corruption in the country. San Marino was not ranked in Transparency International's 2009 Corruption Perceptions Index.

Freedoms of speech and the press are guaranteed. There are three daily private newspapers and one weekly paper, a state-run broadcast system for radio and television called RTV, and a private FM station, Radio Titiano. The Sammarinese have access to all Italian print media and certain Italian broadcast stations. Access to the internet is unrestricted.

Religious discrimination is prohibited by law. Roman Catholicism is the dominant, but not the state, religion. Citizens can voluntarily donate 0.3 percent of their income through their taxes to the Catholic Church or other groups, such as the Waldensian Church—the world's oldest Protestant church—or the Jehovah's Witnesses. Academic freedom is respected.

Residents are free to assemble, demonstrate, and conduct open public discussions. Civic organizations are active. Workers are free to strike, provided they do not work in military occupations, organize trade unions, and bargain collectively. Approximately half of the country's workforce is unionized.

The judiciary is independent. Lower-court judges are required to be noncitizens—generally Italians—to assure impartiality. The final court of review is the Council of Twelve, a group of judges chosen for six-year terms from among the members of the Grand and General Council. The country's prison system generally meets international standards, and civilian authorities maintain effective control over the police and security forces.

The population is generally treated equally under the law, although the European Commission against Racism and Intolerance has raised some concerns in the past about the status of foreigners in the country. San Marino has no formal asylum policy, and a foreigner must live in the country for 30 years to be eligible for citizenship. The European Convention on Nationality recommends that such residence requirements should not exceed 10 years.

Women are given legal protections from violence and spousal abuse, and gender equality exists in the workplace and elsewhere. There are, however, slight differences in the way men and women can transmit citizenship to their children. The country has restrictive laws regarding abortion, which is permitted only to save the life of the mother. Under the new 2008 electoral law, no more than two-thirds of candidates from each party can be of the same gender in an attempt to promote women's representation in government. Nine women were elected to the Great and General Council in 2008 and two to the Congress of State. In January 2009, an Authority of Equal Opportunities was established to curb gender-based violence.

SaoTome and Principe

Political Rights: 2
Civil Liberties: 2
Status: Free

Population: 163,000
Capital: Sao Tome

Ten-Year Ratings Timeline For Year Under Review (Political Rights, Civil Liberties, Status)

2000	2001	2002	2003	2004	2005	2006	2007	2008	2009
1,2F	1,2F	1,2F	2,2F	2,2F	2,2F	2,2F	2,2F	2,2F	2,2F

Overview: An alleged coup plot involving individuals who briefly ousted President Fradique de Menezes in a 2003 coup was uncovered in February 2009, and the trial of suspected conspirators began in October. Regional and municipal elections scheduled for August were postponed until 2010, when they may coincide with parliamentary elections. Meanwhile, a series of political scandals surrounding development aid emerged during the year.

Sao Tome and Principe gained independence from Portugal in 1975. President Manuel Pinto da Costa's Movement for the Liberation of Sao Tome and Principe (MLSTP)—later the for the Liberation of Sao Tome and Principe/Social Democratic Party (MLSTP-PSD)—was the only legal political party until a 1990 referendum established multiparty democracy. Miguel dos Anjos Trovoada, a former prime minister, returned from exile and won the first democratic presidential election in 1991. He was reelected for a final term in 1996.

Fradique de Menezes, backed by Trovoada's Independent Democratic Action (ADI) party, won the 2001 presidential election. In 2003, a group of military officers briefly ousted Menezes, but he was returned to power one week later.

The Force for Change Democratic Movement (MDFM), in coalition with the Democratic Convergence Party (PCD), took 23 of 55 seats in the 2006 parliamentary election. The MLSTP-PSD won 20 seats, while ADI took 11. Though peaceful, protesters prevented approximately 9,600 people from voting in 18 electoral districts. A rerun was held in April without incident. MDFM leader Tome Soares da Vera Cruz became prime minister, while Menezes won a second term in the 2006 presidential election.

Following growing criticism over price increases and its handling of a police mutiny in late 2007, the government collapsed twice in 2008. A new ruling coalition was formed in June with Joaquim Rafael Branco, leader of the MLSTP-PSD, at the head. The ADI refused to join, but the government gained a majority in the National Assembly with 43 seats. Municipal and regional elections scheduled for August 2009 were postponed until 2010, and legislative elections were tentatively scheduled for March 2010.

An alleged coup plot was uncovered in February 2009, when authorities arrested 38 suspects, including 6 members of a small political party, the Christian Democratic Front (FDC), as well as individuals involved in the 2003 coup. Several suspects were released, but the trial of the remaining suspects, which began in October, resulted in two convictions, including a five-year prison sentence for the FDC leader for illegal weapons possession.

Large oil and natural gas deposits are thought to lie off the coast, though production is not expected before 2010. A 2001 agreement with Nigeria created the Joint Development Zone (JDZ), with Sao Tome and Principe receiving 40 percent of oil and gas revenues. The government planned to establish a national oil company in 2010 with assistance from Angola. Corporate allegations have surrounded the process by which exploration blocks in the JDZ are awarded, and funds intended for Sao Tome's oil account were allegedly transferred to a Nigerian bank in 2008. That same year, the country became an Extractive Industries and Transparency Initiative (EITI) candidate country. Despite its potential wealth, the country faces serious poverty. Sao Tome ranked 131 out of 182 countries in the 2009 UN Development Programme's Human Development Report. In 2009, the local currency was pegged to the euro.

Political Rights and Civil Liberties: Sao Tome and Principe is an electoral democracy. Presidential and parliamentary elections in 2006 were free and fair. The president is elected for a five-year term and can serve up to two consecutive terms. Members of the unicameral, 55-seat National Assembly are elected by popular vote to four-year terms. Four party blocs currently hold seats in the legislature, but a number of other parties exist.

Development aid and potential oil wealth have fueled growing corruption among members of the ruling elite. In March 2009, an investigation into misappropriation by the agency formerly responsible for administering aid funds resulted in prison sentences for the former director and treasurer. Separately, the director of the new agency responsible for managing aid came under suspicion in May for misappropriating food aid from Italy. Another scandal emerged in July, after contaminated goods were imported under a Brazilian government credit line. Delfim Neves, the administrative director of the company involved in the scandal, is also the secretary-general of the PDC and was thus shielded by National Assembly immunity. In May, the national audit office accused the government of corruption following the National Assembly's decision to remove the office's oversight of the sale of public property and goods. In December, the national audit office also began the trial of five former government members charged with embezzling social welfare money. The country was ranked 111 out of 180 countries surveyed in Transparency International's 2009 Corruption Perceptions Index.

Freedom of expression is guaranteed and respected. While the state controls a local press agency and the only radio and television stations, no law forbids independent broadcasting. Opposition parties receive free airtime, and newsletters and pamphlets criticizing the government circulate freely. Residents have access to foreign broadcasters. Internet access is not restricted, though a lack of infrastructure limits penetration.

Freedom of religion is respected within this predominantly Roman Catholic country. The government does not restrict academic freedom.

Freedoms of assembly and association are respected. Citizens have the constitutional right to demonstrate with two days' advance notice to the government. Workers' rights to organize, strike, and bargain collectively are guaranteed and respected.

The judiciary is independent, though occasionally subject to manipulation. The Supreme Court has ruled in the past against both the government and the president. The court system is understaffed and inadequately funded. Prison conditions are harsh.

There is societal discrimination against homosexuals. While testing is free and antiretroviral drugs available, persons with HIV/AIDS have been shunned by their communities and families.

The constitution provides equal rights for men and women, but women encounter discrimination in all sectors. Women have been appointed to cabinet positions, including the premiership. Currently, two women serve in the 55-seat National Assembly. Domestic violence is common and rarely prosecuted.

Saudi Arabia

Political Rights: 7
Civil Liberties: 6
Status: Not Free

Population: 28,687,000
Capital: Riyadh

Ten-Year Ratings Timeline For Year Under Review (Political Rights, Civil Liberties, Status)

2000	2001	2002	2003	2004	2005	2006	2007	2008	2009
7,7NF	7,7NF	7,7NF	7,7NF	7,7NF	7,6NF	7,6NF	7,6NF	7,6NF	7,6NF

Overview: In January 2009, Saudi Arabia began implementing portions of an ongoing judicial reform agenda, including training programs for judges and the construction of new courts. In February, King Abdullah sacked two controversial religious leaders and appointed the first-ever female cabinet member, Deputy Minister for Girls' Education Noura al-Fayez. The government announced in May that the next municipal council elections would be postponed by two years. Sectarian tensions remained a serious concern during the year, particularly after religious police attacked Shiite pilgrims in Medina in February.

Since its unification in 1932 by King Abdul Aziz Ibn Saud, Saudi Arabia has been governed by the Saud family in accordance with a conservative school of Sunni Islam. In the early 1990s, Saudi Arabia embarked on a limited program of political reform, introducing an appointed Consultative Council, or Majlis al-Shura. However, this did not lead to any substantial shift in political power. In 1995, King Fahd bin Abdul Aziz al-Saud suffered a stroke, and Abdullah, then the crown prince, took control of most decision making in 1997.

After the country endured a series of terrorist attacks in 2003 and 2004, the authorities intensified their counterterrorism efforts, killing dozens of suspects and detaining thousands of others over the subsequent years. Officials also attempted to stem financial support for terrorist groups through new checks on money laundering and oversight of charitable organizations. Nevertheless, thousands of Saudis went to Iraq in the years following the U.S.-led invasion in 2003 to participate in what they saw as an anti-American and anti-Shiite jihad.

The formal transfer of power from King Fahd, who died in August 2005, to King Abdullah led to increased expectations of political reform. However, Abdullah enacted few significant changes. Municipal council elections were held in 2005, giving Saudi men a limited opportunity to select some of their leaders at the local level, but women were completely excluded. The eligible electorate consisted of less than 20 percent of the population: male citizens who were at least 21 years old, not serving in the military, and resident in their district for at least 12 months. Half of the council seats were open for election, and the other half were appointed by the monarchy. Candidates supported by conservative Muslim scholars triumphed in the large cities of Riyadh and Jeddah, and minority Shiite Muslim voters participated in large numbers. The government ultimately determined that the councils would serve only in an advisory capacity.

In 2007, Abdullah announced bylaws for the Allegiance Institution, a new body composed of the sons (or grandsons in the event of their deaths) of the founding king. The committee, chaired by the oldest surviving son, would make decisions on the succession by majority vote using secret ballots, and would require a quorum of two-thirds of the members. The arrangement would not apply until after the current crown prince, Sultan bin Abdul Aziz al-Saud, became king. The committee would also have the authority to deem a king or crown prince medically unfit to rule, based on the advice of an expert panel.

A cabinet shake-up in February 2009 resulted in the appointment of the first-ever female cabinet member, Noura al-Fayez, as the deputy minister for girls' education. The king also fired two controversial religious figures, the head of the judiciary and the leader of the Commission for the Promotion of Virtue and the Prevention of Vice, also known as the religious police. The move was interpreted as a sign that the monarchy felt less beholden to hard-line religious leaders and was seeking to promote more moderate clerics. This trend continued in October, when the king removed a senior religious scholar from the Higher Council of Ulama for his criticism of gender-desegregated classrooms in the new King Abdullah University of Science and Technology, which had opened the previous month.

In November and December, Saudi military forces carried out air and ground assaults on the Houthi rebel group, based in northern Yemen. The Shiite guerrillas had been engaged in a bloody conflict with the Yemeni government since 2004, raising Saudi concerns about instability along the border and broader Shiite militancy.

Saudi Arabia's growing youth population has added to pressure on the government to create new jobs. In response, it has deployed its immense oil wealth to strengthen the nonpetroleum sector and sought to encourage private investment. The global economic downturn that began in late 2008 placed new stresses on the kingdom, but careful budgeting allowed it to avoid any significant political fallout.

Political Rights and Civil Liberties: Saudi Arabia is not an electoral democracy. The 1992 Basic Law declares that the Koran and the Sunna (the guidance set by the deeds and sayings of the prophet Muhammad) are the country's constitution. The cabinet, which is appointed by the king, passes legislation that becomes law once ratified by royal decree. The king also appoints a 150-member Majlis al-Shura (Consultative Council) every four years, though it serves only in an advisory capacity. Limited elections for advisory councils at the municipal level were introduced in 2005, but women were excluded. The next round of municipal elections was postponed by two years in May 2009, having initially been scheduled for that year. The government cited the need to establish mechanisms to involve more voters, although it remained unclear whether women would be allowed to participate. In addition to these advisory councils, the monarchy has a tradition of consulting with select members of Saudi society, but the process is not equally open to all citizens.

Political parties are forbidden, and organized political opposition exists only outside the country, with many activists based in London. In early 2004, the authorities splintered a nascent domestic reform movement by arresting several key figures who had attempted to create an independent human rights organization. One such activist, Abdullah al-Hamed, has been jailed repeatedly since then, and in 2008, another political reform advocate, Matrouk al-Faleh, was arrested after criticizing the government's treatment of al-Hamed. Al-Faleh was released in January 2009, but remains unable to travel outside the country.

Corruption is a significant problem, with foreign companies reporting that they often pay bribes to middlemen and government officials to secure business deals. Saudi Arabia was ranked 63 out of 180 countries surveyed in Transparency International's 2009 Corruption Perceptions Index.

The government tightly controls domestic media content and dominates regional print and satellite-television coverage, with members of the royal family owning major stakes in news outlets in multiple countries. Government officials have banned journalists and editors who publish articles deemed offensive to the religious establishment or the ruling authorities. The regime has also taken steps to limit the influence of new media, blocking access to over 400,000 websites that are considered immoral or politically sensitive. In June 2009, Jamal Khashoggi was fired as editor of the daily *Al-Watan* for criticizing the country's religious police and engaging in a dispute with the interior minister. In October, television show guest Mazen Abd al-Jawad was sentenced to five years in prison and 1,000 lashes for discussing his sexual exploits during an interview on the Lebanese Broadcasting Corporation (LBC), a Saudi-owned satellite station. Saudi authorities subsequently closed LBC's offices in Jeddah and Riyadh, and other participants in the show received lesser sentences. Rozanna al-Yami, a female producer involved with the program, was sentenced to 60 lashes but received a royal pardon.

Islam is the official religion, and all Saudis are required by law to be Muslims. The government prohibits the public practice of any religion other than Islam and restricts the religious practices of the Shiite and Sufi Muslim minority sects. Although the government recognizes the right of non-Muslims to worship in private, it does not always respect this right in practice. In October 2009, authorities banned the building of Shiite mosques, marking a significant reversal of policies that had offered Shiites some religious freedom in recent years.

Academic freedom is restricted, and informers monitor classrooms for compliance with curriculum rules, such as a ban on teaching secular philosophy and religions other than Islam. Despite changes to textbooks in recent years, intolerance in the classroom remains an important problem, as some teachers continue to espouse discriminatory and hateful views of non-Muslims and Muslim minority sects. In September 2009, the kingdom celebrated the opening of the King Abdullah University for Science and Technology, which features gender-desegregated classrooms and a rule forbidding the religious police from entering the campus.

Freedoms of association and assembly are not upheld. The government frequently detains political activists who stage demonstrations or engage in other civic advocacy. In January 2009, police arrested two activists in Riyadh who attempted to protest Israeli military strikes in the Gaza Strip.

A labor law enacted in 2005, as the country prepared to join the World Trade Organization, extended protections to previously unregulated categories of workers, set end-of-service benefits, established clear terms for terminating employment, and required large companies to provide nurseries for working mothers. It also banned child labor, set provisions for resolving labor disputes, and stated that women are permitted to work in, "all sectors compatible with their nature." One provision of the legislation set a 75 percent quota for Saudi citizens in each company's workforce. The more than six million foreign workers in the country have virtually no legal protections. Many are lured to the kingdom under false pretenses and forced to endure dangerous working and living conditions. Female migrants employed in Saudi homes as domestic workers have reportedly suffered regular physical, sexual, and emotional abuse. In January 2009, over 200 Chinese workers went on strike to protest low pay. Twenty-three were arrested and subsequently deported. The government passed a law in July imposing fines of up to US$266,000 for those found guilty of human trafficking.

The government promised sweeping judicial reforms in 2005, and Abdullah in 2007 announced the establishment of a new Supreme Court and an Appeals Court, whose members would be appointed by the king. The new higher courts replaced the old judiciary council, which was widely considered reactionary and inconsistent. The cabinet announced in 2008 that it would form a Special Higher Commission of judicial experts tasked with writing laws to serve as the foundation for verdicts in the court system, which is grounded in Sharia (Islamic law). While Saudi courts have historically relied on the Hanbali school of Islamic jurisprudence, the commission would incorporate all four Sunni Muslim legal schools in drafting the new laws. In January 2009, the kingdom began a judicial training program and initiated the construction of new courts. Officials in November announced the creation of new commercial courts for each province as well as plans to publish verdicts online, which would open a new era of transparency in the judicial system.

The penal code bans torture, but allegations of torture by police and prison officials are common, and access to prisoners by independent human rights and legal organizations is strictly limited.

Substantial prejudice against ethnic, religious, and national minorities prevails. Shiites represent 10 to 15 percent of the population and are underrepresented in major government positions; no Shiite has ever served as a government minister. Shiites have also faced physical assaults. In February 2009, religious police attacked hundreds of Shiite pilgrims in Medina, triggering unrest in the Shiite-majority Eastern Province, where political activists threatened violence if the government did not better protect the Shiite community.

Freedom of movement is restricted in some cases. The government punishes activists and critics by limiting their ability to travel outside the country. Reform advocates are routinely stripped of their passports.

Saudis have the right to own property and establish private businesses. While a great deal of business activity is connected to members of the government, the ruling family, or other elite families, officials have given assurances that newly created industrial and commercial zones will be free from royal-family interference.

Women are not treated as equal members of society, and many laws discriminate against them. They were not permitted to vote in the 2005 municipal elections, they may not legally drive cars, and their use of public facilities is restricted when men are present. By law and custom, Saudi women cannot travel within or outside of the country without a male relative. Unlike Saudi men, Saudi women cannot pass their citizenship to their children or foreign-born husbands. Moreover, Saudi women seeking access to the courts must be represented by a male. According to interpretations of Sharia in Saudi Arabia, daughters generally receive half the inheritance awarded to their brothers, and the testimony of one man is equal to that of two women.

The religious police enforce a strict policy of gender segregation and often harass women, using physical punishment to ensure that they meet conservative standards of dress in public. In 2007, a court sentenced a Shiite woman from Qatif, who had been raped by seven men, to 200 lashes and six months in jail for being alone with a man who was not her relative at the time of the attack; the man was also raped by the attackers and punished by the court. The rapists were sentenced to flogging and jail terms ranging from two to nine years. After an international outcry, the king pardoned the two victims in December of that year.

Education and economic rights for Saudi women have improved somewhat in recent years. More than half of the country's university students are now female, though they do not have equal access to classes and facilities. In 2004, women won the right to hold commercial licenses, which opened the door for greater economic participation. In addition, women have generally become more visible in society. Saudi state television began using women as newscasters in 2005, and two women became the first females elected to Jeddah's chamber of commerce that year, a small step forward for women's leadership in business. In 2008, the Saudi Human Rights Commission established a women's branch to investigate cases of human rights violations against women and children.

Senegal

Political Rights: 3
Civil Liberties: 3
Status: Partly Free

Population: 12,534,000
Capital: Dakar

Ten-Year Ratings Timeline For Year Under Review (Political Rights, Civil Liberties, Status)

2000	2001	2002	2003	2004	2005	2006	2007	2008	2009
3,4PF	3,4PF	2,3F	2,3F	2,3F	2,3F	2,3F	2,3F	3,3PF	3,3PF

Overview: President Abdoulaye Wade continued to consolidate power in 2009, announcing his intention to stand for a third term as president in 2012 and creating the appointed position of vice president, apparently for his son. However, the political dominance of Wade's Senegalese Democratic Party and its broader Sopi (Change) coalition was threatened after the opposition scored victories in municipal elections that were finally held in March after years of delay.

Since independence from France in 1960, Senegal has avoided military or harsh authoritarian rule and has never suffered a successful coup d'etat. President Leopold Senghor exercised de facto one-party rule through the Socialist Party (PS) for nearly two decades after independence. Most political restrictions were lifted after 1981, when Abdou Diouf of the PS succeeded Senghor. He went on to win large victories in unfair elections in 1988 and 1993.

Abdoulaye Wade's victory in the 2000 presidential poll—his fifth attempt—ended four decades of rule by the PS. Wade, the leader of the Senegalese Democratic Party (PDS), defeated Diouf in a runoff that was deemed free and fair by international observers. A new constitution was approved in 2001, reducing presidential terms from seven to five years, setting the maximum number of terms at two, and abolishing the Senate created in 1999, among other changes. A coalition led by the PDS won 89 of 120 National Assembly seats in that year's legislative elections, with the PS taking only 10 seats. Wade secured a second term in the 2007 presidential election, which featured 70.5 percent turnout and fervent opposition accusations of vote rigging. The opposition coalition, including the PS and 11 other parties, boycotted legislative polls later that year, leading to an overwhelming victory for the PDS, whose Sopi (Change) coalition secured 131 of 150 seats, and a record low turnout of 35 percent.

Since taking office in 2000, Wade had disappointed observers by working to increase the power of the presidency and demonstrating a willingness to persecute those who threatened his authority. For example, in a move approved by the National Assembly in 2006, he amended the constitution to postpone legislative elections by a year and reestablish the Senate, where more than half of the members would be appointed by the president. The National Assembly also approved his 2008 measure to restore the seven-year presidential term beginning in 2012, and his 2009 decision to create the unelected position of vice president, believed to be intended for Wade's son, which will be filled for the first time in 2012.

Meanwhile, leading politicians had faced corruption allegations when they began to challenge Wade's dominance within the PDS. Idrissa Seck was dismissed as prime minister in 2004 based on accusations of embezzlement and threatening national security, and former National Assembly president Macky Sall was pushed out of office in 2008, when Wade shortened the term for his post from five years to one. Wade subsequently had Sall questioned by police about potential money laundering in January 2009. While all charges against Seck were finally dropped in May 2009 and he began working to reclaim his place in the ruling party, Sall formally resigned from the PDS in 2008, costing him both his seat in the parliament and his position as mayor of Fatick.

Wade also repeatedly postponed municipal elections. Originally scheduled for May 2007, they were first delayed until May 2008 and then pushed back to March 2009. When they were finally held that month, in conditions deemed free and fair, the PS and its opposition coalition, United to Boost Senegal (BSS), performed well. BSS members won in the majority of the main towns, including Saint Louis and Dakar, where Wade's son Karim was defeated. Despite the postponements and unfavorable results, the ruling coalition accepted its losses peacefully.

In September 2009, Wade announced that he intended to run for reelection in 2012. While the opposition argued that the bid for a third term was yet another example of Wade's authoritarian tendencies, other observers characterized the announcement as a ploy designed to stave off rivals within the ruling party until he could position Karim Wade as his successor.

The separatist conflict in the Casamance region remained unresolved in 2009. The peace process had wavered since the 2007 death of Augustine Diamacoune Senghor, head of the separatist Movement of the Democratic Forces of Casamance (MFDC), which left the group's leadership in disarray. While the region was quiet during the first half of 2009, sporadic violence started up again in May when separatists attacked a military convoy near the border with The Gambia. By September, regular clashes between the rebels and the army had resumed, including military air strikes against MFDC bases.

While Senegal's lucrative trade deal with France, under which it receives US$163 million in aid each year, is due to expire in 2010, France increased its aid to US$202 million in 2009, after the International Monetary Fund (IMF) offered its qualified approval of Senegal's financial performance. Also during the year, the U.S. Millennium Challenge Corporation announced that it had approved a five-year, US$540 million grant to Senegal to help reduce poverty.

Political Rights and Civil Liberties: Senegal is an electoral democracy. The National Observatory of Elections has performed credibly in overseeing legislative and presidential polls since its creation in 1997. The president is elected by popular vote for up to two terms, and the length of the term was extended from five to seven years by a constitutional amendment in 2008. According to President Abdoulaye Wade, who is currently serving his second term, that amendment also made it possible for him to seek a new term in 2012, although the opposition rejects this interpretation.

The president appoints the prime minister. In April 2009, Wade shuffled his cabinet and appointed a new prime minister, Souleymane Ndene Ndiaye, who had previously served as the president's spokesman. Wade has repeatedly replaced the prime minister in recent years, reducing the importance of the office.

Constitutional amendments that were put into effect in 2007 converted the National Assembly into a 150-seat lower house and created an upper house, the 100-member Senate. Members of the National Assembly are popularly elected every five years, though the most recent vote was postponed from 2006 to 2007 as part of the amendments. The Senate consists of 65 members appointed by the president and 35 members elected by public officials.

There are more than 75 legally registered political parties in Senegal. Major parties include the ruling PDS and the opposition PS. Many of the smaller parties revolve around individual personalities rather than firm party structures or policy platforms. The PDS currently controls most national political offices, but the opposition performed well in the 2009 municipal elections.

Corruption remains a serious problem. While the government pledged in 2009 to improve transparency and the management of public expenditures, it was revealed that officials had attempted to give US$200,000 in cash as a "gift" to a departing IMF representative. The representative had the money returned as soon as it was discovered, and the affair was seen as an attempt to smear him after he voiced criticism of government policies. Separately, an investigative journalist released a book accusing the agency responsible for organizing a 2008 summit of the Organization of the Islamic Conference of serious mismanagement; the agency was overseen by Karim Wade, the president's son. Senegal was ranked 99 out of 180 countries surveyed in Transparency International's 2009 Corruption Perceptions Index.

Freedom of expression is generally respected, and members of the independent media are often highly critical of the government, despite the risk of criminal defamation charges. In 2009, two journalists received three-month jail sentences for defaming a member of parliament, but two others were exonerated and pardoned after being convicted of defaming Wade. There are approximately 20 independent radio stations and many independent print outlets, but the government owns the only national television station, which provides favorable coverage. Access to the internet is not restricted.

Religious freedom is respected, and the government continues to provide free airline tickets to Senegalese Muslims and Christians undertaking pilgrimages overseas. Senegal is a predominantly Muslim country, with 94 percent of the population practicing Islam. The country's Sufi Muslim brotherhoods are very influential; Wade has close ties with the most powerful brotherhood, the Mouride.

Academic freedom is legally guaranteed and respected in practice. In one incident in 2009, police entered a university campus and damaged property while looking for students who had rioted earlier over unpaid grants.

Freedoms of association and assembly are guaranteed. While the number of street protests and demonstrations has been on the rise in recent years, the government has taken action to repress some of them. This occasionally degenerates into violent clashes between protesters and riot police, as with 2008 demonstrations over rising food prices. There were few such incidents in 2009, though police used tear gas to disperse a demonstration protesting the corruption allegations against former PDS politician Macky Sall.

Human rights groups and other nongovernmental organizations operate freely in Senegal. Although workers' rights to organize, bargain collectively, and strike are legally protected for all except security employees, the labor code requires the president's approval for the initial formation of a trade union. In February 2009, a teachers' union went on strike over late salary payments and severe overcrowding in student accommodations, and in May, unions threatened to strike following the government's announcement that it intended to sell a majority stake in the country's telecommunications company, Sonatel, to France Telecom. This threat, coupled with fervent objections from the opposition and local business owners, led the government to rescind its plans.

The judiciary is independent by law, but poor pay and lack of tenure expose judges to external influences and prevent the courts from providing a proper check on the other branches of government. Uncharged detainees are incarcerated without legal counsel far beyond the lengthy periods already permitted by law. Prisons are overcrowded, often leading to hygiene and health issues for the inmates.

Women's constitutional rights are often not honored, especially in rural areas, and women enjoy fewer opportunities than men for education and formal employment. A 2007 law required all political parties to introduce gender parity to their candidate lists, but the measure did not take effect in time for that year's legislative elections, and there are currently just 34 women in the 150-seat National Assembly.

Only two sexual harassment cases have been brought in the courts since 1995, and men remain the legal heads of households. Many elements of Sharia (Islamic law) and local customary law, particularly those regarding inheritance and marital relations, discriminate against women.

Child trafficking is a problem in Senegal. A 2007 study conducted by UNICEF, the International Labour Organization, and the World Bank found that boys had been taken in by religious teachers' promises to educate them, but had been physically abused and forced to beg instead; 6,480 such boys were found in Dakar alone.

Serbia

Political Rights: 2*
Civil Liberties: 2
Status: Free

Population: 7,322,000
Capital: Belgrade

Ratings Change: Serbia's political rights rating improved from 3 to 2 due to the consolidation of a stable multiparty system after several rounds of elections in the post-Milosevic period.

Note: The ratings through 2002 are for the Federal Republic of Yugoslavia, of which Serbia was a part, and those from 2003 through 2005 are for the State Union of Serbia and Montenegro. Kosovo is examined in a separate report.

Ten-Year Ratings Timeline For Year Under Review (Political Rights, Civil Liberties, Status)

2000	2001	2002	2003	2004	2005	2006	2007	2008	2009
4,4PF	3,3PF	3,2F	3,2F	3,2F	3,2F	3,2F	3,2F	3,2F	2,2F

Overview: The parliament in November approved a new statute regulating the autonomy of the northern province of Vojvodina, ending a long political debate over the issue and demonstrating the effectiveness of the Democratic Party–led government elected in 2008. The country also made progress in its relations with the European Union, securing visa-free travel rights and the implementation of a trade agreement in December. However, press freedom groups criticized a media law adopted in August, and tensions involving the ethnic Albanian population in the Presevo Valley remained a problem.

Serbia was recognized as an independent state in 1878 after several centuries under Ottoman rule. It formed the core of the Kingdom of Serbs, Croats, and Slovenes proclaimed in 1918. After World War II, Serbia became a constituent republic of the Socialist Federal Republic of Yugoslavia, under the communist rule of Josip Broz Tito. Within the boundaries of the Serbian republic as drawn at that time were two autonomous provinces: the largely Albanian-populated Kosovo in the south, and Vojvodina, with a significant Hungarian minority, in the north.

Following the disintegration of socialist Yugoslavia in 1991, the republics of Serbia and Montenegro in 1992 formed the Federal Republic of Yugoslavia (FRY).

Slobodan Milosevic and his Socialist Party of Serbia (SPS, the former League of Communists of Serbia) ruled Serbia throughout the 1990s by controlling the security forces, financial institutions, and state-owned media. An avowed Serb nationalist, Milosevic oversaw extensive Serbian involvement in the 1991–95 wars that accompanied the old federation's breakup, both in Bosnia and Herzegovina and in Croatia.

In 1998–99, an ethnic Albanian insurgency in Kosovo provoked increasingly violent reprisals by state forces against the guerrillas and the civilian population. In March 1999, NATO launched a 78-day bombing campaign to force the withdrawal of FRY and Serbian forces from the province. A NATO-led force then occupied Kosovo, and the United Nations oversaw institution-building efforts there.

Milosevic was driven from office in October 2000, after his attempt to steal the September Yugoslav presidential election from opposition candidate Vojislav Kostunica of the Democratic Party of Serbia (DSS) triggered massive protests. An anti-Milosevic coalition took power following Serbian parliamentary elections in December, and Zoran Djindjic of the Democratic Party (DS) became Serbia's prime minister. The FRY was replaced with a looser State Union of Serbia and Montenegro in 2003, and each republic was granted the option of holding an independence referendum after three years.

Djindjic was assassinated by organized crime groups allied with Milosevic-era security structures in March 2003, and after parliamentary elections in December, Kostunica became Serbia's prime minister at the head of a fragile coalition government. The new DS leader, Boris Tadic, won the Serbian presidency in a June 2004 election.

Montenegro held a successful referendum on independence in May 2006, and formally declared independence the following month. This necessitated new Serbian elections, and in January 2007, the main anti-Milosevic parties—including the DS, the DSS, and the liberal G17 Plus—collectively managed to outpoll the ultranationalist Serbian Radical Party (SRS) and the SPS. In May, Kostunica formed another coalition government. Tadic won a second term as president in early February 2008, taking 51 percent of the vote.

Later that month, Kosovo unilaterally declared its independence from Serbia. Debate over the proper response increased tensions within the Kostunica government, which ultimately resigned in March 2008, prompting new elections. The May balloting resulted in an undisputed victory for the DS and its smaller allies, which favored economic reform and European Union (EU) integration. The DS-led electoral bloc won 102 of 250 seats, and it formed a coalition government with an SPS-led bloc (20 seats), the Hungarian Coalition (4 seats), and the Bosniak List for European Sandzak (2 seats). The SRS took 78 seats, followed by the DSS with 30; the smaller Liberal Democratic Party took 13 seats, and the Coalition of Albanians of the Presevo Valley won the remaining seat.

The new government, led by Mirko Cvetkovic, was the first since 2000 to include the SPS, which was trying to reinvent itself as a mainstream center-left party. The election outcome also marked the first time since 2000 that a single party, in this case the DS, controlled the presidency, the premiership, and a working majority in parliament. In another sign of political normalization, hard-liners in the SRS were further isolated when the moderate wing of the party broke off to form the Serbian Progressive Party (SNS) in September.

The government successfully passed a number of important laws in 2009, including a long-awaited statute that defined and expanded Vojvodina's autonomy in November, and legislation to improve conditions for nongovernmental organizations (NGOs) in July. The country also made progress in improving relations with the United States and the EU. It received praise for its cooperation with the International Criminal Tribunal for the former Yugoslavia (ICTY), and in December, the EU eliminated visa requirements for Serbians and cleared the way for implementation of a 2008 trade agreement. Later that month, Serbia formally submitted its application for EU membership.

Meanwhile, Serbia continued to challenge Kosovo's secession through legal and diplomatic means, most importantly, by bringing a suit before the International Court of Justice in The Hague. The court began hearings on the case in December 2009.

Political Rights and Civil Liberties: Serbia is an electoral democracy. The president, elected to a five-year term, plays a largely ceremonial role. The National Assembly is a unicameral, 250-seat legislature, with deputies elected by party list to serve four-year terms. The prime minister is elected by the assembly. Both the presidential and parliamentary elections in 2008 were deemed free and fair by international monitoring groups.

In addition to the main political parties, numerous smaller parties compete for influence. These include factions representing Serbia's ethnic minorities, two of which belong to the current coalition government. A new Law on Political Parties, passed in May 2009, increased the number of signatures needed to form a party to 10,000, or 1,000 for ethnic minority parties.

Serbia has made some progress in reducing corruption since the ouster of former president Slobodan Milosevic, but it remains a serious concern. Problem areas include public procurement, privatization, taxation, customs, and licensing. An official Anti-Corruption Agency is due to become operational in 2010. Serbia was ranked 83 out of 180 countries surveyed in Transparency International's 2009 Corruption Perceptions Index.

The press is generally free and operates with little government interference, although most media outlets are thought to be aligned with specific political parties. In August 2009, the parliament passed a new media law despite opposition from press freedom groups, which objected to its high fines and other provisions. Investigative journalism in Serbia remains weak, and businesspeople and government agencies often try to influence outlets through advertising purchases. Libel remains a criminal offense punishable by fines, but not imprisonment. There were no reports of the government restricting access to the internet.

The constitution guarantees freedom of religion, which is generally respected in practice. However, increases in ethnic tension often take the form of religious intolerance. Critics have complained that the 2006 Law on Churches and Religious Communities privileges seven "traditional" religious communities by giving them tax-exempt status and forcing other groups to go through cumbersome registration procedures. Students are required to receive instruction in one of the seven traditional faiths or opt for a civic education class. There were no reports that the government attempted to restrict academic freedom during 2009.

Citizens enjoy freedoms of assembly and association. However, in May 2009, the parliament adopted legislation that bans meetings of neo-Nazi or fascist organizations and their use of neo-Nazi symbols. A September gay pride parade in Belgrade was cancelled, because the government claimed it could not guarantee the security of the participants. Foreign and domestic NGOs are generally free to operate without government interference, and a new Law on Associations clarifying the legal status of NGOs was adopted in July 2009. The laws and constitution allow workers to form or join unions, engage in collective bargaining, and strike. In November 2008, a new agreement between the government, trade unions, and employers' associations was signed, but the global economic crisis has prevented it from being implemented.

Judicial reform has proceeded slowly in recent years. The Council of Europe's Venice Commission has criticized the degree of control the Serbian parliament has over judges, and in April 2009, two new bodies—the High Judicial Council and the State Prosecutorial Council—were created to supervise the election and promotion of judges and prosecutors. While these bodies have reformed Serbia's judicial system somewhat, critics claim there is still too much room for political interference, especially concerning the reappointment procedure. The judicial system suffers from a large backlog of cases, long delays in filing formal charges against suspects, and the failure of legislative institutions to heed judicial rulings. The criminal procedure code adopted in 2006 is scheduled to enter into force at the end of 2010, after being delayed twice. Prisons are generally considered to meet international standards, although overcrowding, drug abuse, and violence among inmates remain serious problems.

Serbian cooperation with the ICTY has improved significantly in recent years. All but two of the tribunal's Serb indictees have been arrested, leaving only former Bosnian Serb military commander Ratko Mladic and a former Croatian Serb leader at large. Serbia has also begun to prosecute war crimes more vigorously in domestic courts, as demonstrated by a Belgrade court's March 2009 decision to impose prison sentences of up to 20 years on 13 Serbs convicted of a massacre of Croatian civilians in 1991.

Ethnic minorities have access to media in their own languages, their own political parties, and other types of associations. Nevertheless, they are underrepresented in government. The country's main minority groups are the Bosniaks (Muslim Slavs), concentrated in the Sandzak region adjacent to Montenegro; an ethnic Albanian population in the Presevo Valley, adjacent to Kosovo; and the Hungarian community in Vojvodina. Tensions in Kosovo have threatened to spill into Presevo. In June 2009, two Serbian police officers were attacked and wounded in the area. In August, ethnic Albanian officials initiated an effort to create a formal "Presevo Valley district" within Serbia. In addition, there are concerns about the spread of extreme forms of Islam and internal political rivalries in the Sandzak. Serbia is also home to a significant Romany community, which often faces police harassment and other forms of discrimination. In March 2009, the parliament adopted legislation that would establish an independent commissioner to protect ethnic, religious, and other vulnerable groups—including sexual minorities—from discrimination.

Women make up about 22 percent of the parliament, and five women currently serve as cabinet ministers. According to electoral regulations, women must account for at least 30 percent of a party's candidate list. Although women are legally entitled to equal pay for equal work, traditional attitudes often limit their roles in the economy. Domestic violence remains a serious problem. The 2005 Law on the Family criminalized physical and psychological abuse, but its implementation has been hampered by the reluctance of victims to report such abuse and by prevailing patriarchal social norms. Some towns in southern Serbia have become transit points for the trafficking of women from the former Soviet Union to Western Europe for the purpose of forced prostitution.

Seychelles

Political Rights: 3
Civil Liberties: 3
Status: Partly Free

Population: 87,000
Capital: Victoria

Ten-Year Ratings Timeline For Year Under Review (Political Rights, Civil Liberties, Status)

2000	2001	2002	2003	2004	2005	2006	2007	2008	2009
3,3PF	3,3PF	3,3PF	3,3PF	3,3PF	3,3PF	3,3PF	3,3PF	3,3PF	3,3PF

Overview: In 2009, the Seychelles' economy was buffeted by the global recession and by the expanding reach and incidence of piracy in the Indian Ocean.

The Seychelles gained independence from Britain in 1976 as a multiparty democracy and remained a member of the Commonwealth. In 1977, Prime Minister France-Albert Rene seized power from President James Mancham. Rene then made his Seychelles People's Progressive Front (SPPF) the sole legal party. In 1992, however, the SPPF passed a constitutional amendment legalizing opposition parties, and many exiled leaders returned. Rene won multiparty elections in 1993.

The Seychelles National Party (SNP), led by Wavel Ramkalawan, emerged as the strongest opposition group in 1998 elections. Rene won a narrow victory in the 2001 presidential election, engendering opposition complaints of fraud. In October 2002, Rene dissolved parliament and called for early legislative elections. Although the SPPF won, the SNP made significant gains.

Rene stepped down as president in 2004 and was replaced by Vice President James Michel. The Indian Ocean tsunami struck later that year, causing about US$30 million in damage to public infrastructure; the vital tourism and fishing industries also suffered. Michel defeated Ramkalawan in the July 2006 presidential election.

The SPPF's majority of 23 seats was left unchanged by the May 2007 legislative elections; the SNP took the remaining 11. Michel subsequently restructured his government, placing an emphasis on environmental issues that could affect the country's reputation as a tourist destination.

In recent years, the Seychelles' economy has been harmed by rising food and fuel costs. Recent International Monetary Fund missions have found that the country has one of the highest debt burdens in Africa and continues to suffer from rising inflation and depletion of the central bank's foreign reserves. By contrast, the political arena has remained relatively placid. The Seychelles' economy continued to worsen in 2009 due to the global recession and the expanding reach and incidence of piracy in the Indian Ocean.

Political Rights and Civil Liberties: The Seychelles is an electoral democracy. The July 2006 presidential election and the 2007 parliamentary polls were generally viewed as having met basic international norms. However, the ruling SPPF's control over state resources and most media gives its candidates a significant advantage at the polls. The president and the unicameral National Assembly are elected by universal adult suffrage for five-year terms. The head of government is the president, who appoints the cabinet. Of the National Assembly's 34 members, 25 are elected directly and 9 are allocated on a proportional basis to parties gaining at least 10 percent of the vote.

The SPPF remains the dominant party, and the opposition SNP has claimed that its sympathizers are harassed by police and victimized by job-related security investigations in the public sector.

Concerns over government corruption have focused on the lack of transparency in privatization and the allocation of government-owned land. Seychelles was ranked 54 out of 180 countries surveyed in Transparency International's 2009 Corruption Perceptions Index.

The government controls much of the islands' media, operating radio and television stations. The daily newspaper, the *Nation*, is government owned, and at least two other newspapers support, or are published by, the SPPF. The opposition weekly *Regar* has been sued for libel by government officials under broad constitutional restrictions on free expression, including the suspension of printing in 2006 after the paper received an exorbitant fine. The other major independent newspaper, *Le Nouveau Seychelles Weekly*, has also faced state interference in its functioning. The board of directors of the officially multipartisan Seychelles Broadcasting Corporation includes several non-SPPF members. A controversial 2006 law restricts private radio station ownership. High licensing fees have also discouraged the development of privately owned broadcast media. The government does not limit internet access.

The right of religious freedom is mandated by the constitution and exists in practice. Churches in this predominantly Roman Catholic country have been strong voices for human rights and democratization, and they generally function without government interference.

The constitution endorses freedoms of assembly and association. Private human rights groups and other nongovernmental organizations operate in the country. Public demonstrations are generally tolerated, although on occasion the government has impeded opposition gatherings. Workers have the right to strike. However, the Seychelles Federation of Workers' Unions, which is associated with the ruling party, has been the only active trade union since the Seychelles National Trade Union ceased operations in 2007.

Judges generally decide cases fairly but face interference in those involving major economic or political interests. The majority of the members of the Seychellois judiciary are foreign nationals, and the impartiality of the non-Seychellois magistrates can be compromised by the fact that they are subject to contract renewal. In September 2009, newly-appointed chief justice Frederick Egonda-Ntende from Uganda outlined a policy to reduce the number of pending court cases and accelerate judgment of new cases. Security forces have at times been accused of using excessive force, including torture and arbitrary detention.

Nearly all of the country's political and economic life is dominated by people of European and South Asian origin. Islanders of Creole extraction face de facto discrimination, and discrimination against foreign workers has been reported. The government does not restrict domestic travel but may deny passports for unspecified reasons of "national interest."

The Seychelles in recent years has boasted one of the highest percentages of women in parliament in Africa at 24 percent, despite the lack of a quota system. Inheritance laws do not discriminate against women. In general, however, women are less likely than men to be literate, as they enjoy fewer educational opportunities. While nearly all adult females are classified as "economically active," most are engaged in subsistence agriculture. Domestic violence remains a widespread problem. The government adopted a National Strategy on Domestic Violence in 2008 aimed at decreasing its incidence.

Sierra Leone

Political Rights: 3
Civil Liberties: 3
Status: Partly Free

Population: 5,696,000
Capital: Freetown

Ten-Year RatingsTimeline ForYear Under Review (Political Rights, Civil Liberties, Status)

2000	2001	2002	2003	2004	2005	2006	2007	2008	2009
4,5PF	4,5PF	4,4PF	4,3PF	4,3PF	4,3PF	4,3PF	3,3PF	3,3PF	3,3PF

Overview: Political violence erupted in March 2009 between supporters of the two main political parties, but party leaders were quick to condemn the violence and participate in conciliatory dialogues. Also during the year, the Special Court for Sierra Leone sentenced three former leaders of the Revolutionary United Front rebel group for crimes committed during the civil war, and the Truth and Reconciliation Commission launched its reparations program.

Founded by Britain in 1787 as a haven for liberated slaves, Sierra Leone achieved independence in 1961. Siaka Stevens, who became prime minister in 1967 and then president in 1971, transformed Sierra Leone into a one-party state under his All People's Congress (APC) party. In 1985, Stevens retired and handed power to his designated successor, General Joseph Momoh. The Revolutionary United Front (RUF) launched a guerrilla insurgency from Liberia in 1991. Military officer Valentine Strasser ousted Momoh the following year, but failed to deliver on the promise of elections. General Julius Maada-Bio deposed Strasser in 1996, and elections were held despite military and rebel intimidation. Voters chose former UN diplomat Ahmad Tejan Kabbah of the Sierra Leone People's Party (SLPP) as president.

In 1997, Major Johnny Paul Koroma toppled the Kabbah government and invited the RUF to join his ruling junta. Nigerian-led troops under the aegis of the Economic Community of West African States Monitoring Group (ECOMOG) restored Kabbah to power in 1998, and a 1999 peace agreement led to the beginning of disarmament and the deployment of UN peacekeepers. British paratroopers were called in to restore order after 500 peacekeepers were taken hostage amid renewed violence in 2000. By 2002, the 17,000-strong UN peacekeeping force had started disarmament in rebel-held areas, and the war was declared over.

Kabbah won a new term in the May 2002 presidential election, defeating the APC's Ernest Koroma (no relation to Johnny Paul Koroma). The SLPP took 83 of 112 available seats in parliamentary elections that month. However, the SLPP government failed to address adequately the country's entrenched poverty, dilapidated infrastructure, and endemic corruption, and in 2007, Ernest Koroma won a presidential runoff election with 55 percent of the vote, leaving SLPP candidate Solomon Berewa with 45 percent. In the legislative polls, the APC led with 59 seats, followed by the SLPP with 43 and the People's Movement for Democratic Change (PMDC) with 10.

Local council elections were held without incident in 2008, but violence between APC and SLPP supporters broke out ahead of a local by-election in Pujehun district in March 2009. The fighting, which spread to Freetown, caused serious injuries and damage to SLPP offices and city council buildings. It also included vehicle arson and alleged acts of sexual violence.

The Political Parties Registration Commission and the UN Integrated Peacebuilding Office were quick to facilitate interparty dialogue, and in April, the APC and SLPP issued a joint communiqué calling for an end to all acts of political intolerance, the tempering of hostility between the party youth wings, and the establishment of independent mechanisms to investigate the events of March. The communiqué also provided a framework for bipartisan consensus-building.

In July, Koroma swore in the Commission of Inquiry to investigate allegations of rape and sexual violence during the March 16 attack on SLPP headquarters. The Commission found no evidence to sustain the allegations of rape but noted that outrages upon personal dignity and inhumane conduct had occurred. In October, the Independent Review Panel, to investigate the causes of political violence, was sworn in. APC and SLPP leaders adopted conciliatory postures in the wake of the March violence, and indicated their commitment to peaceful politics. Numerous interparty dialogues were held for the remainder of the year. Despite such measures, the relationship between the two parties continues to be plagued by mutual mistrust and suspicion. In September 2009, the president signed into law the Chieftaincy Act. Chieftaincy elections commenced in December, and some instances of violence were again reported.

Sierra Leone has vast natural resources, including diamonds, minerals, and unexploited off-shore oil wells. However, due to the legacies of war, the country remains one of the least developed in the world. Its large jobless population includes many former combatants, and some 42 percent of the country's inhabitants are under age 15, raising concerns about the potential for a return to violence. In December, Parliament adopted a law that will facilitate the establishment of a National Youth Commission to address issues of youth unemployment and the associated threats to peace.

Political Rights and Civil Liberties:

Sierra Leone is an electoral democracy. International observers determined that the 2007 presidential and parliamentary elections were free and fair, and power was transferred peacefully to the opposition. Of the unicameral Parliament's 124 members, 112 are chosen by popular vote, and 12 are indirectly elected paramount chiefs. Parliamentary and presidential elections are held every five years, and presidents may seek a second term. The APC, SLPP, and PMDC are the main political parties.

Corruption is a major problem in Sierra Leone. However, after winning office on an antigraft platform in 2007, President Ernest Koroma required ministers to sign performance contracts and all public officials, including himself, to declare their assets within three months of taking office. Almost 17,000 civil servants have declared their assets to the Anti-Corruption Commission (ACC). The government pledged in April 2009 that ministerial performance contracts would be publicly disclosed. Also during 2009, an ACC prosecution unit was established, and by October, it had already secured 15 convictions. The Minister of Health was dismissed and charged with corruption in November, and the Head of the National Revenue Authority was suspended in December pending the outcome of investigations by the ACC. The ACC has called for the creation of a fast-track anticorruption court, and it engaged with Parliament in drafting a code of conduct for lawmakers that was ongoing at year's end. Sierra Leone was ranked 146 out of 180 countries surveyed in Transparency International's 2009 Corruption Perceptions Index.

Freedoms of speech and the press are constitutionally guaranteed, but at times these rights are restricted. Libel is a criminal offense punishable by imprisonment, and in November 2009, the Supreme Court upheld the libel portions of the 1965 Public Order Act, rejecting a bid by the Sierra Leone Association of Journalists to have them repealed. In July, Parliament passed legislation to transform the state-owned Sierra Leone Broadcasting Service into an independent national broadcaster. Numerous independent newspapers circulate freely, and there are dozens of public and private radio and television outlets. The government shut down radio stations operated by the APC and SLPP following the March 2009 riots on the grounds that they contributed to the unrest. In July, the Independent Media Commission withdrew their licenses, and they remained closed at year's end. The government does not restrict internet access, though the medium is not widely used.

Freedom of religion is protected by the constitution and respected in practice. Academic freedom is similarly upheld. A code of conduct for teachers was finalized in 2009, and numerous absentee or nonexistent "ghost" teachers were deleted from the state payroll.

Freedoms of assembly and association are constitutionally guaranteed and generally observed in practice. Workers have the right to join independent trade unions, but serious violations of core labor standards occur regularly. Nongovernmental organizations (NGOs) and civic groups operate freely, though a 2008 law requires NGOs to submit annual activity reports and renew their registration every two years.

The judiciary has demonstrated a degree of independence, and a number of trials have been free and fair. However, corruption, poor salaries, police unprofessionalism and a lack of resources threaten to impede judicial effectiveness. Arbitrary arrests are common, as are lengthy pretrial detentions under harsh conditions. Many backlogged cases were resolved in 2009, easing overcrowding in prisons. Renovations at the Mafanta prison also relieved some crowding. The Sierra Leone Bar Association launched a pilot legal aid program in Freetown during the year.

Drug trafficking and other crimes, including armed robbery, pose a threat to the rule of law. Following the seizure of over 700 kilograms of cocaine in July 2008, government and international partners established the Joint Drug Interdiction Task Force. In April 2009, the High Court ruled on the case and convicted 18 people, including 8 foreigners. In September, civilians took to the streets to protest increases in common crime. Police opened fire killing three demonstrators and injuring numerous others. In October, the president invoked the Military Assistance to Civil Power Act that provides for joint military-police operations to combat crime.

The Special Court for Sierra Leone, a hybrid international and domestic war crimes tribunal, has been working since 2004 to convict those responsible for large-scale human rights abuses during the civil war. In April 2009, the court sentenced three senior RUF leaders to lengthy prison terms. In October, the Appeals Chamber upheld the previous judgments of the Trial Chamber, and to date, a total of eight persons from the three main factions that participated in the conflict have been convicted. Following the findings of the Appeals Chamber, all convicts were transferred to Rwanda, where they will be serving their prison terms. Former Liberian president Charles Taylor has been on trial at the court since 2007, accused of fostering the RUF insurgency. Separately, in the latter half of 2009, the Truth and Reconciliation Commission launched its reparations program for war victims including micro-grants for identified beneficiaries and fistula surgeries for victims of sexual violence. In December, President Koroma launched the Special Trust Fund for War Victims to mobilize much-needed resources for the program.

In 2007, Parliament passed laws to prohibit domestic violence, grant women the right to inherit property, and outlaw forced marriage. Despite these laws and constitutionally guaranteed equality, gender discrimination remains widespread. The country's maternal and child mortality rates are among the highest in the world, and female genital mutilation is a common practice, though traditional chiefs have pledged not to subject girls under the age of 18 to this practice. Women hold 13 percent of the seats in Parliament. Umu Jalloh was sworn in as chief justice in December 2008, becoming the first female to head one of Sierra Leone's branches of government. Conflicting interpretations of the constitution and cultural mores prevented women from standing as candidates in some parts of the country in the chieftaincy elections held in December 2009; cases filed by human rights lawyers challenging such exclusions were still before the courts at year's end.

Singapore

Political Rights: 5
Civil Liberties: 4
Status: Partly Free

Population: 5,113,000
Capital: Singapore

Ten-Year Ratings Timeline For Year Under Review (Political Rights, Civil Liberties, Status)

2000	2001	2002	2003	2004	2005	2006	2007	2008	2009
5,5PF	5,5PF	5,4PF	5,4PF	5,4PF	5,4PF	5,4PF	5,4PF	5,4PF	5,4PF

Overview: The authorities continued to restrict freedoms of speech and assembly in 2009. In April, Singapore's legislature passed a measure that would require police permission for public assemblies of all sizes, removing a previous threshold of five or more people. In October, the *Far Eastern Economic Review* lost an appeal in a defamation case brought by the prime minister and his father; the magazine agreed to settle the case in November and was shuttered by its owners in December.

The British colony of Singapore obtained home rule in 1959, entered the Malaysian Federation in 1963, and gained full independence in 1965. During his three decades as prime minister, Lee Kuan Yew and his People's Action Party (PAP) transformed the port city into a regional financial center and exporter of high-technology goods but restricted individual freedoms and stunted political development in the process.

Lee transferred the premiership to Goh Chok Tong in 1990 but stayed on as "senior minister," and the PAP retained its dominance. Lee's son, Lee Hsien Loong, became prime minister in 2004, and the elder Lee assumed the title of "minister mentor." In 2005, President Sellapan Ramanathan began a second term as the largely ceremonial head of state.

Despite his expressed desire for a "more open society," Lee Hsien Loong did little to change the authoritarian political climate. He called elections in May 2006, a year early, to secure a mandate for his economic reform agenda. With a nine-day campaign period and defamation lawsuits hampering opposition candidates, the polls resembled past elections in serving more as a referendum on the prime minister's popularity than as an actual contest for power. The PAP retained 82 of the 84 elected seats, with 66 percent of the vote, although the opposition offered candidates for a greater number of seats and secured a larger percentage of the vote than in previous years. The opposition Workers' Party and Singapore Democratic Alliance (SDA) each won a single seat despite receiving 16.3 percent and 13 percent of the vote, respectively.

Over the next three years, Lee continued to pursue his economic agenda while using the legal system and other tools to keep the opposition in check. The government also maintained that racial sensitivities and the threat of Islamist terrorism justified draconian restrictions on freedoms of speech and assembly. Such rules were repeatedly used to silence criticism of the authorities. Singapore Democratic Party (SDP) leader Chee Soon Juan faced multiple convictions and heavy fines for defamation and other crimes in 2007 and 2008, while the *Far Eastern Economic Review*, a 63-year-old magazine owned by the U.S.-based News Corporation, was forced to pay some US$300,000 in November 2009 to settle a defamation case brought by the Lees.

Political Rights and Civil Liberties: Singapore is not an electoral democracy. The country is governed through a parliamentary system, and elections are free from irregularities and vote rigging, but the ruling PAP dominates the political process. The prime minister retains control over the Elections Department, and the country lacks a structurally independent election authority. Opposition campaigns are hamstrung by a ban on political films and television programs, the threat of libel suits, strict regulations on political associations, and the PAP's influence on the media and the courts.

The largely ceremonial president is elected by popular vote for six-year terms, and a special committee is empowered to vet candidates. The prime minister and cabinet are appointed by the president. Singapore has had only three prime ministers since independence. Of the unicameral legislature's 84 elected members, who serve five-year terms, 9 are elected from single-member constituencies, while 75 are elected in Group Representation Constituencies (GRCs), a mechanism intended to foster minority representation. The winner-take-all nature of the system, however, limits the extent to which GRCs actually facilitate minority representation and, in effect, helps perpetuate the return of incumbents. Up to nine additional, nonpartisan members can be appointed by the president, and up to three members can be appointed to ensure a minimum of opposition representation.

Singapore has traditionally been lauded for its relative lack of corruption. There is no special legislation facilitating access to information, however, and management of state funds came under question for the first time in 2007. Critics lamented the state's secret investment of national reserves, and investigations into the state investment arm, Temasek Holdings, were launched by Indonesian and Thai watchdog agencies. Singapore was ranked 3 out of 180 countries surveyed in Transparency International's 2009 Corruption Perceptions Index.

Singapore's media market remains tightly constrained. All domestic newspapers, radio stations, and television channels are owned by government-linked companies. Although editorials and news coverage generally support state policies, newspapers occasionally publish critical pieces. Self-censorship is common among journalists. The Sedition Act, in effect since the colonial period, outlaws seditious speech, the distribution of seditious materials, and acts with "seditious tendency." Media including videos, music, and books are sometimes censored, typically for sex, violence, or drug references.

Foreign broadcasters and periodicals can be restricted for engaging in domestic politics, and regulations in place since 2006 require all foreign publications to appoint legal representatives and provide significant financial deposits. The leadership's practice of using defamation suits and license revocations to silence critical media is often applied to foreign-owned outlets. In October 2009, the *Far Eastern Economic Review* lost its appeal of an earlier judgment finding that it had defamed Prime Minister Lee Hsien Loong and his father, Lee Kuan Yew, by publishing a 2006 interview with an opposition figure. The magazine agreed to settle the case for about US$300,000 in November, and it was discontinued as of December 2009 by its owner, the U.S.-based News Corporation, which cited falling revenues and readership. The Lees have never lost a defamation case in Singapore.

The internet is widely accessible, but the authorities monitor online material and block some content through directives to licensed service providers. In 2008, lawyer and blogger Gopalan Nair was sentenced to three months in jail for insulting judges on his blog and in an e-mail message.

The constitution guarantees freedom of religion as long as its practice does not violate any other regulations, and most groups worship freely. However, religious actions perceived as threats to racial or religious harmony are not tolerated, and unconventional groups like the Jehovah's Witnesses and the Unification Church are banned. All religious groups are required to register with the government under the 1966 Societies Act. In October 2009, five adherents of the Falun Gong spiritual movement, including Singapore nationals and mainland Chinese, were arrested and briefly detained after putting up posters in a public park that described the persecution of Falun Gong practitioners in China; the case was pending at year's end.

All public universities and political research institutions have direct government links that bear at least some influence. Academics engage in political debate, but their publications rarely deviate from the government line on matters related to Singapore.

The Societies Act restricts freedom of association by requiring most organizations of more than 10 people to register with the government, and only registered parties and associations may engage in organized political activity. Political speeches are tightly regulated, and public assemblies must be approved by police. Legislation passed in April 2009 eliminated a previous threshold requiring permits for public assemblies of five or more people, meaning political events involving just one person could require official approval. Permits are not needed for private, indoor gatherings as long as the topic of discussion is not race or religion.

Unions are granted fairly broad rights under the Trade Unions Act, though restrictions include a ban on government employees joining unions. A 2004 amendment to the law union members from voting on collective agreements negotiated by union representatives and employers. Strikes are legal for all except utility workers, but they must be approved by a majority of a union's members, as opposed to the internationally accepted standard of at least 50 percent of the members who vote. In practice, many restrictions are not applied. All but 5 of the country's 64 unions are affiliated with the National Trade Union Congress, which is openly allied with the PAP. Singapore's 180,000 domestic workers are excluded from the Employment Act and regularly exploited. A 2006 standard contract for migrant domestic workers addresses food deprivation and entitles replaced workers to seek other employment in Singapore, but it fails to provide other basic protections, such as rest days.

The government's overwhelming success in court cases raises questions about judicial independence, particularly because lawsuits against opposition politicians and parties often drive them into bankruptcy. Many judges have ties to PAP leaders, but it is unclear whether the government pressures judges or simply appoints those who share its conservative philosophy. The judiciary is efficient, and defendants in criminal cases enjoy most due-process rights.

The government generally respects citizens' right to privacy, but the Internal

Security Act (ISA) and the Criminal Law Act (CLA) permit the authorities to conduct warrantless searches and arrests to preserve national security, order, and the public interest. The ISA, previously aimed at communist threats, is now used against suspected Islamist terrorists. Suspects can be detained without charge or trial for an unlimited number of two-year periods. A 1989 constitutional amendment prohibits judicial review of the substantive grounds for detention under the ISA and of the constitutionality of the law itself. The CLA is mainly used to detain organized crime suspects; it allows preventive detention for an extendable one-year period. The Misuse of Drugs Act empowers authorities to commit suspected drug users, without trial, to rehabilitation centers for up to three years.

Security forces are not known to commit serious abuses. The government has in recent years jailed police officers convicted of mistreating detainees. The penal code mandates caning, in addition to imprisonment, for about 30 offenses; it is discretionary for certain other crimes involving the use of force. Caning is reportedly common in practice.

There is no legal discrimination, and the government actively promotes racial harmony and equity. Despite government efforts, ethnic Malays have not on average reached the schooling and income levels of ethnic Chinese or ethnic Indians, and they reportedly face discrimination in private sector employment.

Citizens enjoy freedom of movement, although the government occasionally enforces its policy of ethnic balance in public housing, in which most Singaporeans live, and opposition politicians have been denied the right to travel.

Women enjoy the same legal rights as men in most areas, and many are well-educated professionals, though relatively few women hold top positions in government and the private sector. Of the current Parliament's 84 elected seats, 17 are held by women, all of whom belong to the PAP. In 2007, Parliament voted to maintain provisions of the penal code that make acts of "gross indecency" between men punishable by up to two years in prison.

⬇Slovakia

Political Rights: 1
Civil Liberties: 1
Status: Free

Population: 5,417,000
Capital: Bratislava

Trend Arrow: Slovakia received a downward trend arrow due to an increase in civil defamation cases against journalists, with plaintiffs including the prime minister and the head of the Supreme Court.

Ten-Year Ratings Timeline For Year Under Review (Political Rights, Civil Liberties, Status)

2000	2001	2002	2003	2004	2005	2006	2007	2008	2009
1,2F	1,2F	1,2F	1,2F	1,1F	1,1F	1,1F	1,1F	1,1F	1,1F

Overview: Ivan Gasparovic won a second term as president in an April 2009 runoff vote against Iveta Radicova of the Slovak Democratic and Christian Union–Democratic Party. New signs of discrimination against the Romany community emerged during the year, including police abuse of Romany children and the construction of an ethnic separation wall in an eastern Slovakian town. Separately, rising numbers of libel cases, including suits brought by the prime minister and Supreme Court president, contributed to self-censorship among journalists.

Anticommunist opposition forces brought about the collapse of the Czechoslovak government in 1989, and the country held its first free elections the following year. After another round of elections in June 1992, negotiations began on increased Slovak autonomy within the Czech and Slovak Federative Republic. This process led to a peaceful dissolution of the federation and the establishment of an independent Slovak Republic in January 1993.

From 1993 to 1998, Vladimir Meciar—who served twice as prime minister during this period—and his Movement for a Democratic Slovakia (HZDS) dominated politics, opposed direct presidential elections, flouted the rule of law, and intimidated independent media. In the 1998 parliamentary elections, voters rejected Meciar's rule and empowered a broad right-left coalition. The new parliament selected Mikulas Dzurinda as prime minister and worked to enhance judicial independence, combat corruption, undertake economic reforms, and actively seek membership in the EU and NATO.

The HZDS led the 2002 parliamentary elections with 19.5 percent of the vote, but Dzurinda's Slovak Democratic and Christian Union (SDKU) formed a center-right government with the Party of the Hungarian Coalition (SMK), the Christian Democratic Movement (KDH), and the Alliance of the New Citizen (ANO).

In April 2003, the legislature ratified Slovakia's accession to NATO. In a binding national referendum held the following month, Slovaks voted overwhelmingly in favor of EU membership. Slovakia duly joined the two organizations in April and May 2004, respectively.

Meciar lost the 2004 presidential runoff election to a former HZDS ally, Ivan Gasparovic. After the government lost support due to unpopular economic reforms, the KDH left the coalition in February 2006, prompting early elections in June. The leftist, populist Smer (Direction–Social Democracy) party won 50 of 150 seats, followed by the SDKU, now allied with the Democratic Party (DS), with 31; the far-right Slovak National Party (SNS) with 20; the SMK with 20; the HZDS, now allied with the People's Party (LS), with 15; and the KDH with 14. Smer's leader, Robert Fico, formed an unusual coalition with the SNS and LS-HZDS, raising concerns abroad that the allied left and right wings of Slovak politics could adopt destabilizing policies.

Following a corruption scandal in November 2007, Fico dismissed the deputy director of the Slovak Land Fund and the agriculture minister selected by the LS-HZDS. The ensuing conflict between Fico and Meciar almost broke up the coalition. In January 2008, the three opposition parties brought an unsuccessful no-confidence motion against Fico, accusing him of complicity in the Slovak Land Fund corruption case.

A two-round presidential election held in March and April 2009 was considered free and fair. Gasparovic, supported by Smer and the SNS, outpolled five challengers in the first round, winning nearly 47 percent of the vote. His leading opponent, sociologist Iveta Radicova of the SDKU-DS, took 38 percent. Gasparovic then defeated Radicova in the second round, securing 55 percent of the vote. Slovakia, which had formally adopted the euro currency in January, posted the EU's lowest voter turnout for European Parliament elections in June, with less than 20 percent participation. The three opposition parties each won two seats, while Smer garnered five and its coalition partners each took one.

Political Rights and Civil Liberties: Slovakia is an electoral democracy. Parliamentary elections in 2006 and the presidential election in 2009 were considered free and fair. Voters elect the president for up to two five-year terms and members of the 150-seat, unicameral National Council (parliament) for four-year terms. The prime minister is appointed by the president but must have majority support in the parliament to govern.

Slovakia's political party system is fragmented. The current governing parties are Smer, the LS-HZDS, and the SNS. The SDKU-DS, the KDH, and the SMK, which represents ethnic Hungarians, form the opposition. All other parties failed to reach the 5 percent electoral threshold required for representation in the parliament.

Corruption remains a problem, especially in law enforcement, the health-care and business sectors, and the judiciary. A special court tasked with adjudicating high-profile corruption cases was abolished in May 2009, after the Constitutional Court ruled it unconstitutional. Separately, presidential candidate Iveta Radicova resigned from her parliament seat in April, after violating the chamber's rules by casting a vote on behalf of an SDKU-DS colleague. In October, the European Commission ruled that the controversial "bulletin board" tender—a 2007 deal worth approximately US$170 million between the Construction Ministry and two companies with alleged connections to SNS leader Jan Slota—had violated EU regulations. Slovakia was ranked 56 out of 180 countries surveyed in Transparency International's 2009 Corruption Perceptions Index.

Slovakia's media are largely free but remain vulnerable to political interference. Journalists have faced increasing verbal attacks by politicians. The 2008 Press Act obliges print media to publish an offended reader's replies. Prime Minister Robert Fico filed multiple libel cases against the press in 2009, receiving up to US$135,000 in damages. In one case, Fico in September demanded roughly US$47,000 from the parent company of the daily *SME* after it published a caricature that mocked the secrecy surrounding his supposed health problems. The threat of lawsuits has reportedly led to growing self-censorship among journalists. The government does not limit access to the internet.

The government respects religious freedom. Registered religious organizations are eligible for tax exemptions and government subsidies. The Roman Catholic Church is the largest denomination and consequently receives the largest share of subsidies. A 2007 legal change requires a religious group to have at least 20,000 members to register, effectively excluding the small Muslim community and others. Academic freedom is respected in Slovakia. The parliament passed an amendment to the Education Act in February 2009 allowing for "deeply rooted" Hungarian place names to be stated in Hungarian first, followed by the Slovak translation, in Hungarian minority textbooks.

The authorities uphold the rights to assemble peacefully, petition state bodies, and associate in clubs, political parties, and trade unions. However, civil society is not as active as in other countries in Central Europe. Nongovernmental organizations criticized the police in June 2009 for failing to respond to violence that erupted between Slovak protestors and supporters of Chinese president Hu Jintao's visit in June; police arrested nine demonstrators.

The constitution provides for an independent judiciary and a Constitutional Court. An independent Judicial Council oversees the assignment and transfer of judges. Corruption, intimidation of judges, and a significant backlog of cases have raised questions about the judicial system's capacity to meet EU standards. The Supreme Court chairman, Stefan Harabin, has been criticized for intimidating the media and demanding out-of-court libel settlements amounting to some € 600,000 (US$820,000). Harabin has also been accused of intimidating judges and having connections to organized crime. In October 2009, 105 judges signed a document entitled "Five Sentences," drawing attention to unjust disciplinary measures within the judiciary, including Harabin's suspension of critical judges.

While ethnic minorities have a constitutional right to contribute to the resolution of issues that concern them, Roma continue to experience widespread discrimination and inequality in education, housing, employment, public services, and the criminal justice system. National policies to remedy these problems have been unsuccessful at the local level, where Roma are segregated in settlements and their children are frequently placed in special education programs or never enrolled in school. Roma face the persistent threat of racially motivated violence. In April 2009, *SME* released footage of Slovak policemen abusing and humiliating six Romany boys. Also that month, eight Slovak Romany women were awarded approximately US$5,000 each by the European Court of Human Rights as compensation for forced sterilization by Slovak hospitals. A wall separating the Romany and non-Romany populations of a small town in eastern Slovakia was erected in October, drawing accusations of collective punishment.

An amendment to the State Language Act that took effect in September 2009 requires the use of the Slovak language in public offices and official documents, as well as in public officials' dealings with citizens. Failure to comply will result in fines of up to US$7,000 for state bodies, except in areas where an ethnic minority makes up more than 20 percent of the local population. While disputes over the law strained relations between Slovakia and Hungary in 2009, the high commissioner of the Organization for Security and Cooperation in Europe (OSCE) stated that the law meets European and international requirements.

Although women enjoy the same legal rights as men, they continue to be underrepresented in senior-level business positions and in the government. Only 29 women hold seats in the 150-seat National Council. Radicova was Slovakia's first female presidential candidate. Domestic violence is punishable by imprisonment but remains widespread. Human trafficking from and through Slovakia, mainly for the purpose of sexual exploitation, also remains a problem.

Slovenia

Political Rights: 1
Civil Liberties: 1
Status: Free

Population: 2,043,000
Capital: Ljubljana

Ten-Year Ratings Timeline For Year Under Review (Political Rights, Civil Liberties, Status)

2000	2001	2002	2003	2004	2005	2006	2007	2008	2009
1,2F	1,2F	1,1F	1,1F	1,1F	1,1F	1,1F	1,1F	1,1F	1,1F

Overview:
Prime Minister Borut Pahor's government came under attack in the fall of 2009 from a number of trade unions demanding better pay or an increase in the minimum wage rate, both of which are opposed by business groups. The long-awaited construction of a mosque in Ljubljana was delayed again in 2009, as the Islamic Community in Slovenia continued to face challenges. Meanwhile, a number of lingering issues kept Slovenia and Croatia from resolving a long-running border dispute, despite a tentative agreement made between Pahor and his Croatian counterpart in September.

The territory of modern Slovenia, long ruled by the Austro-Hungarian Empire, became part of the Kingdom of Serbs, Croats, and Slovenes (renamed the Kingdom of Yugoslavia in 1929) after World War I, and a constituent republic of the Socialist Federal Republic of Yugoslavia following World War II. After decades of relative prosperity in Josip Broz Tito's Yugoslavia, various elements in Slovene civil society began to part ways with the Communist system in the 1980s. In 1990, the Democratic United Opposition (DEMOS) defeated the ruling League of Communists in democratic elections, although former Communist leader Milan Kucan was elected president. The country declared independence in June 1991 and secured its status after a short 10-day conflict, escaping the war and destruction suffered by much of the rest of Yugoslavia as it disintegrated.

After 1990, Slovenia was generally ruled by center-left governments, the most important component of which was Janez Drnovsek's Liberal Democratic Party (LDS). Drnovsek served as prime minister almost continuously from 1992 to 2002, when he was elected president. In the 2004 parliamentary elections, Janez Jansa's center-right Slovenian Democratic Party (SDS) finally unseated the LDS-led government, and Jansa became prime minister.

In Slovenia's 2007 presidential elections, Danilo Turk, a law professor and former diplomat, ran as an independent with the backing of the Social Democrats (SD) and several other parties. He won the November runoff with 68 percent of the vote, defeating the government's candidate, Alojz Peterle.

In the September 2008 parliamentary elections, the SD captured 29 seats and some 30 percent of the vote, followed by the SDS with 28 seats. SD leader Borut Pahor, who became prime minister, formed a coalition government with three small parties: the center-left Zares (9 seats), the Democratic Party of Pensioners of Slovenia (7 seats), and the once-powerful LDS (5 seats). The remaining seats in the 90-member lower house went to the far-right Slovene National Party (5 seats), an alliance of the Slovene People's Party and the Slovene Youth Party (5 seats), and the Hungarian and Italian ethnic minorities (1 seat each).

Slovenia has widely been considered one of the Eastern European success stories of the postcommunist period. In 2004, the country joined both the European Union (EU) and NATO, and from January–June 2008, Slovenia was the first former communist bloc state to hold the EU's rotating presidency. In 2006, Slovenia became the first former communist state to adopt the euro as its official currency.

Slovenia's most important foreign policy problem is resolving its 18-year-old border dispute with neighboring Croatia. The dispute concerns the delineation of the two countries' maritime border in the Bay of Piran, and parts of their common territorial border. In September 2009, Pahor and his Croatian counterpart, Jadranka Kosor, agreed to submit the dispute to international arbitration, pending ratification of their agreement by both states' parliaments. However, the two parliaments had not endorsed the agreement by year's end.

Political Rights and Civil Liberties: Slovenia is an electoral democracy. The country has a bicameral Parliament: members of the 90-seat National Assembly, which chooses the prime minister, are elected to four-year terms; and the 40-seat National Council, a largely advisory body, represents professional groups and local interests. The president is directly elected for up to two five-year terms. Elections since independence have been considered free and fair. Slovenia's main political parties are the center-left SD, led by current prime minister Borut Pahor, and the center-right SDS of former prime minister Janez Jansa. Such large parties generally govern in coalition with smaller parties.

One seat each in the National Assembly is reserved for Slovenia's Hungarian and Italian minorities, and Roma are automatically given seats on 20 municipal councils. Citizens with origins in other former Yugoslav republics have reported discrimination in Slovenia.

Corruption, while less extensive than in some other Central and Eastern European countries, remains a problem in Slovenia, usually taking the form of conflicts of interest and contracting links between government officials and private businesses. Just over 6 percent of the country's 80,000 public servants are legally required to disclose personal financial information. In September 2009, Finnish television broadcaster YLE reported that the Finnish company Patria had paid €21 million (US$26 million) to help finance the electoral campaign of then prime minister Janez Jansa's SDS. The allegations were connected to a larger scandal in which Patria allegedly bribed Slovene officials to obtain a weapons contract in 2006. Slovenia was ranked 27 out of 180 countries surveyed in Transparency International's 2009 Corruption Perceptions Index.

Freedoms of speech and of the press are guaranteed by the constitution. However, insulting public officials is prohibited by law. There have been reports of self-censorship and increasing government pressure on both media outlets and advertisers. Newspapers that are critical of the government, such as *Dnevnik* and *Mladina*, have faced difficulty securing advertisers. In October 2009, a Ljubljana appeals court lifted a widely criticized judicial order that had barred the Ljubljana daily *Dnevnik* from publishing articles about an Italian business since August. Internet access is unrestricted.

The constitution guarantees freedom of religion. Most Slovenians (approximately 58 percent) are Roman Catholics, although the number of practicing Catholics has dropped in recent years. The 2007 Religious Freedoms Law remained under review in 2009 by the Constitutional Court; the National Council objects to some aspects of Article 20 of the law regulating the legal status of religious communities. However, the law remained in effect at year's end.

Societal discrimination against the small Muslim community remains a problem. A forty-year effort to build a mosque in Ljubljana continues to face a variety of legal challenges. Although a contract was signed in December 2008 for the acquisition of land on which the mosque would be built, a Ljubljana city council member announced plans in January 2009 to launch a referendum to prevent the construction of a minaret. Following court appeals, Ljubljana's administrative court ultimately rejected the petition for a referendum on the issue. While architectural plans for the mosque were drawn up throughout 2009, construction had yet to begin at year's end. The government does not restrict academic freedom.

Freedoms of assembly and association are respected. Numerous nongovernmental organizations operate freely, and the government generally supports the role they play in the policy-making process. Workers enjoy the right to establish and join trade unions, strike, and bargain collectively, though there are some exceptions for public sector employees, primarily police and the military. The Association of Free Trade Unions of Slovenia (ZSSS) has some 300,000 members and controls the four trade union seats in the National Council. Organized labor's main concerns are pension reform, increasing the minimum wage, and halting privatizations in health care. In September 2009, workers at Slovenia's two largest industrial enterprises went on strike to demand increases in the minimum wage. Separately, police officers launched a one-day protest action in October, forcing the government to abandon plans to freeze pensions.

The Slovenian judiciary enjoys a high degree of independence, and the constitution guarantees citizens due process, equality before the law, and a presumption of innocence. However, the judiciary is plagued by a large backlog of cases. Some 416,000 cases were pending as of September 2009. Political infighting over the appointment of judges remains a problem. Prison conditions meet international standards, although overcrowding has been reported.

Incitement to racial hatred is a criminal offense. However, Slovenia has had persistent problems in dealing with various minorities—Italians, Muslim residents and guest workers, and citizens of the former Yugoslavia. Police harassment of Roma and residents from other former Yugoslav republics, the so-called new minorities, remains a problem. Some 20,000 non-Slovene citizens of the former federation who remained in Slovenia after independence had been removed from official records in 1992, after they failed to apply for citizenship or permanent resident status during a brief window of opportunity. In 2009, the Slovenian government began enforcing a 2003 Constitutional Court ruling intended to provide retroactive permanent residency status to the estimated 4,000 to 6,000 people that remain in the category of "the erased." The group of effectively stateless individuals has been systematically denied driver's licenses, pensions, and access to state health care.

Women hold the same legal rights as men but remain underrepresented in political life. Currently, there are 12 women serving in the 90-seat National Assembly and only one in the 40-seat National Council. After his election as prime minister in 2008, Pahor named five women to his 18-member cabinet—the highest number in any postindependence Slovenian government. By law, 40 percent of the electoral lists for Slovenia's European parliamentary elections must be reserved for women. Over 50 percent of the candidates in the June 2009 elections for the European Parliament were women. On average, Slovenian women receive 93 percent of the pay of their male counterparts, which compares favorably with rates in Western European countries.

Domestic violence remains a concern. Amendments to the penal code in November 2008 prohibit sexual harassment in the workplace. Slovenia is a transit and destination country for women and girls trafficked from Eastern Europe for the purpose of prostitution.

Solomon Islands

Political Rights: 4
Civil Liberties: 3
Status: Partly Free

Population: 519,000
Capital: Hoiara

Ten-Year Ratings Timeline For Year Under Review (Political Rights, Civil Liberties, Status)

2000	2001	2002	2003	2004	2005	2006	2007	2008	2009
4,4PF	4,4PF	3,3PF	3,3PF	3,3PF	3,3PF	4,3PF	4,3PF	4,3PF	4,3PF

Overview: A Truth and Reconciliation Commission was launched in April 2009 to investigate and address human rights violations committed during ethnic violence that lasted from 1998 to 2003. Throughout the year, Prime Minister Derek Sikua continued efforts to improve governance and political stability, including the creation of an Anti-Corruption Taskforce in November.

The Solomon Islands gained independence from Britain in 1978. Tensions between the two largest ethnic groups—the Guadalcanalese and the Malaitans—over jobs and land rights erupted into open warfare in 1998. Scores were injured or killed before peace was restored with the 2000 Townsville Peace Agreement, brokered by Australia and New Zealand. Order was maintained initially by a UN mission and after 2003 by the Australian-led Regional Assistance Mission to the Solomon Islands (RAMSI).

No single party secured a majority in the April 2006 parliamentary elections, with independents winning 30 of the 50 seats. The new chamber chose Snyder Rini as prime minister, though bribery allegations against him sparked two days of riots in the capital, leading to Rini's resignation. In May, Parliament elected former prime minister Manasseh Sogavare to replace Rini. Sogavare was ousted in a no-confidence vote in December 2007 following a series of controversial decisions, including the appointment to attorney general of his close friend Julian Moti—who was wanted in Australia for alleged sex crimes against a minor. Lawmakers then chose Derek Sikua as prime minister, who immediately tried to rectify some of his predecessor's most egregious and controversial actions, including making a formal apology to the Malaitans and a pledge to address official corruption.

National efforts to promote political stability and national reconciliation continued in 2009. The government launched a Truth and Reconciliation Commission in April to investigate crimes and address impunity connected to the 1998–2003 ethnic war. The Commission, which is modeled after South Africa's Truth and Reconciliation Commission and has received international financial backing, will begin hearings in 2010.

There was considerable public dissatisfaction throughout the year surrounding allegations that legislators and their wives had received thousands of dollars per year in special entitlements. In October, the High Court ruled against the Parliament Entitlement Commission's decision to award US$6,700 in annual allowances to the spouses of legislators.

In May, the government announced an indefinite freeze on hiring and the creation of new positions in public services due to a significant shortfall in the budget. The country's economic crisis, fueled by the global recession, has increased unemployment, and Sikua openly stated in October that idle youths are a threat to public safety.

Political Rights and Civil Liberties: The Solomon Islands are not an electoral democracy. Recent elections, including the 2006 parliamentary elections, have been marred by allegations of fraud. A governor-general, appointed on the advice of Parliament for a five-year term, represents the British monarch as head of state. Members of the 50-seat, unicameral National Parliament are elected for four-year terms. A parliamentary majority elects the prime minister, and the cabinet is appointed by the governor-general on the advice of the prime minister.

There are several political parties, but most politicians run as independents and then align themselves with parties and interests. Political activity is driven more by personalities and clan identities than party affiliation.

Rampant corruption at all levels of government is a major source of public discontent and hinders economic development. In November 2009, several officials, including four former lawmakers, faced corruption charges for allegedly selling passports. Prime Minister Derek Sikua vowed to improve governance, appointing a new ombudsman in 2008 to investigate alleged government abuses. In February 2009, the government launched a new Anti-Corruption Taskforce to develop a national anticorruption policy and make recommendations on reforms. The country was ranked 111 out of 180 countries in Transparency International's 2009 Corruption Perceptions Index.

Freedoms of expression and the press are generally respected, but legal and extralegal means are sometimes used by politicians and elites to intimidate journalists. The print media include a daily, a weekly, and two monthly publications. The government operates the only radio station. There is no local television station, but foreign broadcasts can be received via satellite. Although government harassment of the media has eased since Manasseh Sogavare's administration, Sikua sued a newspaper, *Island Sun*, for defamation in May for an article alleging that he and a cabinet minister had been drunk and acted inappropriately at their New York hotel while attending the 2008 UN General Assembly. Separately, the Leadership Code Commission, the government's top accountability watchdog agency, was criticized for intimidation and violating media freedom by requesting that two journalists reveal their sources in relation to articles alleging wrongdoing by members of Parliament. Internet penetration is low, mainly due to technical and cost barriers.

Freedom of religion is generally respected. Academic freedom is observed, but the lack of public funds severely undermines the quality of education.

The constitution guarantees freedom of assembly, and the government generally recognizes this right. Organizers of demonstrations must obtain permits, which are typically granted. Civil society groups operate without interference. Workers are free to organize, and strikes are permitted.

Threats against judges and prosecutors have weakened the independence and rigor of the judicial system. Judges and prosecutors have also been implicated in corruption and abuse scandals. A lack of resources limits the government's ability to provide legal counsel and timely trials. Traditional chiefs have sought more funds for traditional courts in rural areas to ease the strain on the formal court system. The ombudsman's office has potentially far-reaching powers to investigate complaints of official abuse and unfair treatment, but generally lacks the funds to do so.

There is no military. Domestic security and law enforcement are provided by a civilian-controlled police force of about 1,000 people, but poor training, the widespread abuse of power, and factional and ethnic rivalries have undermined public trust in the service. Six police officers were suspended in May 2009 for helping several Chinese nationals in custody for visa violations to escape from prison. Prison conditions meet minimum international standards.

Growing anti-Chinese sentiment in reaction to their perceived economic dominance and influence over politicians was a central factor in the 2006 riot, which destroyed nearly 80 percent of Chinese-owned businesses in the capital. In April 2009, the government released a report that found no evidence of a conspiracy to instigate the riots.

Discrimination limits the economic and political roles of women. Rape and other forms of abuse against women and girls are widespread. While rape is illegal, no law prohibits domestic violence.

Somalia

Political Rights: 7
Civil Liberties: 7
Status: Not Free

Population: 9,133,000
Capital: Mogadishu

Note: The numerical ratings and status listed above do not reflect conditions in Somaliland, which is examined in a separate report.

Ten-Year Ratings Timeline For Year Under Review (Political Rights, Civil Liberties, Status)

2000	2001	2002	2003	2004	2005	2006	2007	2008	2009
6,7NF	6,7NF	6,7NF	6,7NF	6,7NF	6,7NF	7,7NF	7,7NF	7,7NF	7,7NF

Overview:

As Ethiopian forces completed their withdrawal from the country in January 2009, Somalia's transitional parliament was expanded to include opposition factions, and the new body elected moderate Islamist leader Sheikh Sharif Sheikh Ahmed as president. He formed a broader government that enjoyed international support and a moderate amount of domestic goodwill, but it struggled to impose its authority over more than a small portion of the country during the year. Meanwhile, its radical Islamist opponents, the Shabaab and Hizbul Islam, fought among themselves and alienated most Somalis with their brutal interpretation of Islamic law. A suicide bombing at a university graduation ceremony in December killed four cabinet ministers and several other officials, raising new doubts about the government's ability to defend itself.

Somalia gained independence in 1960 as an amalgam of former British and Italian colonies populated largely by ethnic Somalis. A 1969 coup by army general Siad Barre led to two decades of instability, civil strife, and the manipulation of clan loyalties for political purposes. After Barre's regime was finally toppled in 1991, the country descended into warfare between clan-based militias, and an effective national government was never restored.

Extensive television coverage of famine and civil conflict that killed approximately 300,000 people in 1991 and 1992 prompted a UN humanitarian mission led by U.S. forces. The intervention soon deteriorated into urban guerrilla warfare with Somali militias, and over 100 UN peacekeepers, including 18 U.S. soldiers, were killed. The operation was eventually terminated, and international forces had left by March 1995. Civil strife continued over the subsequent decade with varying degrees of intensity.

At a 2000 peace conference in Djibouti, many of Somalia's factional leaders agreed to participate in a three-year transitional government with a 245-seat Transitional National Assembly. The government and more than 20 rival factions signed a ceasefire in 2002, but serious fissures developed as some groups launched separate power-sharing negotiations in Mogadishu.

The political process was revitalized in 2004 and resulted in the establishment of a 275-seat Transitional Federal Assembly (TFA) and a new Transitional Federal Government (TFG), in which the leading clans took an equal number of seats. In October

2004, TFA members elected the controversial Ethiopian-backed warlord Abdullahi Yusuf Ahmed to serve a five-year term as president. Yusuf had previously been the leader of the breakaway region of Puntland.

By early 2005, strong divisions had emerged within the TFG between Yusuf's supporters and an alliance of clan leaders and Islamists; the president was perceived as hostile to the influence of Islamists in politics and social services in Mogadishu. The Islamist Courts Union (ICU), a broad coalition of Islamists, eventually emerged as the dominant force within the capital, and over the course of 2006, the group gained control of most of southern Somalia. Unable to assert power in Mogadishu, the TFG established itself in the town of Baidoa. Meanwhile, hard-liners within the ICU, backed by Eritrea, grew increasingly hostile toward Ethiopia. With tacit U.S. support, Ethiopia invaded Somalia to oust the ICU in December 2006, forcing the Islamists to retreat to the extreme south of the country.

The departure of the ICU triggered renewed instability and an insurgency against the Ethiopian-backed TFG by groups including the Shabaab (Arabic for "youth"), a radical ICU faction. All sides in the conflict committed severe human rights abuses, and as many as 400,000 people were displaced from Mogadishu during 2007. By the end of the year, a group of moderate exiled ICU leaders had joined forces with non-Islamist opposition members to form the Alliance for the Reliberation of Somalia (ARS), though hard-line Shabaab supporters did not participate.

Insurgent groups continued to battle Ethiopian and TFG forces in 2008, and increased attacks on aid workers led to a reduction in humanitarian assistance. UN-sponsored negotiations between the TFG and a more moderate faction of the ARS began in Djibouti in June, and by November, the two sides had agreed to a power-sharing arrangement that would double the size of the 275-member parliament. The Shabaab did not join the talks and vowed to fight on.

In January 2009, Ethiopian forces completed their withdrawal from the country, and the newly expanded TFA was sworn in. It elected the chairman of the ARS, Sheikh Sharif Sheikh Ahmed, as Somalia's new president, and he appointed Omar Abdirashid Ali Sharmarke as prime minister in February, along with a 36-member cabinet.

Radical Islamist forces responded by launching a major offensive. Their ranks were bolstered by significant numbers of foreign extremists, and they managed to seize control of much of southern and central Somalia. While the militants proved unable to oust the TFG from Mogadishu during the year, they landed a number of serious blows. The interior minister was wounded in a March attack, and the security minister was assassinated in a car bombing in June. A suicide bombing at a university graduation ceremony in December killed the ministers of health, education, higher education, and youth and sports, along with other officials and a number of students. Moreover, fierce fighting erupted in Mogadishu in May, killing hundreds of civilians and forcing more than 200,000 residents to flee their homes. Chaos in the country intensified when the Shabaab and a rival faction, Hizbul Islam, fought pitched battles for control of the southern port of Kismayo in October.

The United States tried to fortify the beleaguered government during the year, sending 40 tons of arms and ammunition to the TFG in the summer. It also targeted suspected terrorists on Somali soil, killing an alleged member of al-Qaeda, Saleh Ali Saleh Nabhan, in September. The Shabaab responded with a bomb attack on the

Mogadishu base of an undermanned African Union peacekeeping force, killing its deputy commander and some 20 others.

Meanwhile, the situation in the semiautonomous region of Puntland in northeastern Somalia also deteriorated. A resurgence of clan rivalries triggered renewed insecurity and a breakdown in governance, and pirates based along the Puntland coast continued to launch audacious raids on foreign ships, holding crew members and cargo for ransom. The problem spiked in early 2009, prompting the international community to mount joint naval patrols in the Gulf of Aden and parts of the Indian Ocean.

Somalia's ongoing conflict and a chronic drought combined during the year to create what Refugees International described as the world's worst humanitarian crisis. More than 3 million people were in need of assistance, yet the UN World Food Programme had to scale back its operations due to the murder of two staff members in January and the reluctance of foreign donors to contribute money for food supplies that could be seized and exploited by Islamist militant groups.

Political Rights and Civil Liberties: Somalia is not an electoral democracy. The state has in many respects ceased to exist, and there is no governing authority with the ability to protect political rights and civil liberties. The TFG is recognized internationally, but its actual territorial control is minimal. The TFA, or parliament, was expanded in early 2009, following a 2008 agreement between the TFG and a wing of the opposition ARS. It now has 550 members, with 200 of the new seats allocated to the ARS and the remaining 75 to civil society groups. The TFA elects the president, choosing the moderate Islamist Sheikh Sharif Sheikh Ahmed in January after his predecessor resigned in late 2008. Sharif named Omar Abdirashid Ali Sharmarke as prime minister in February. The TFG was given a five-year mandate when it was established in 2004, and a new constitution and national elections were supposed to follow. However, the TFA voted in January 2009 to extend the TFG's mandate until 2011. The country has no effective political parties, and the political process is driven largely by clan loyalty.

Since May 1991, the northwestern region of Somaliland, roughly comprising the territory of the former British colony, has functioned with relative stability as a self-declared independent state, though it has not received international recognition. The region of Puntland has not sought full independence, declaring only a temporary secession until Somalia is stabilized. However, sentiment there has recently been hardening in favor of independence. In December 2008, elections for Puntland's 66-member legislature were held. The new parliament elected former finance minister Abdirahman Muhammad Mahmud "Farole" for a four-year term as president in January 2009. The result was seen as a fair reflection of the will of the legislature, and power was transferred peacefully from the defeated incumbent.

Because of the breakdown of the state, corruption in Somalia is rampant and grew worse following the overthrow of the ICU in 2006. Somalia was ranked as the worst performer among 180 countries surveyed in Transparency International's 2009 Corruption Perceptions Index. Corruption is also pervasive in Puntland.

Although Somalia's Transitional Federal Charter (TFC) calls for freedoms of speech and the press, these rights are minimal in practice. A TFG press law passed in 2008 allowed for significant government control over the media, and journalists have struggled to operate in areas controlled by the Shabaab. In 2009, the militants closed down a number of media organizations and stopped reporters from going about their duties. At least nine journalists were killed during the year, according to the Committee to Protect Journalists, including four from Radio Shabelle who were slain in separate attacks. In the most deadly incident, two cameramen and a reporter were killed in the December bombing of a graduation ceremony in Mogadishu. Two foreign journalists kidnapped near Mogadishu in 2008 were released in November 2009, reportedly after ransom was paid.

Journalists also faced a difficult and dangerous media environment in Puntland, where they were restricted from reporting on the January 2009 presidential election. Several reporters were arrested during the year, and three correspondents for Voice of America were temporarily barred from operating. Two foreign journalists who had been kidnapped in Bossasso in 2008 were freed in January.

Despite the fragmented state of the Somali media environment, photocopied dailies and low-grade radio stations have proliferated since 1991. Radio is the primary news medium, although there is no national broadcaster. Somalis living abroad maintain a rich internet presence, and internet and mobile-telephone services are widely available in large cities. Nevertheless, poverty, illiteracy, and the displacement of Somalis from urban areas limit access to these resources.

Nearly all Somalis are Sunni Muslims, but there is a very small Christian community. Both the TFC and Puntland's charter recognize Islam as the official religion. The TFC provides for religious freedom, though these rights are not respected in practice. The Shabaab and other radical Islamist groups imposed crude versions of Islamic law in areas under their control in 2009, banning music, films, certain clothing, and any other items they deemed immoral or un-Islamic. Anyone accused of apostasy risked execution. A clan leader was executed in Kismayo in January for alleged apostasy, and two sons of a Christian leader were beheaded near the city in February. A man was stoned to death for adultery in the town of Merka, near Mogadishu, in November; the death sentence on his pregnant partner was deferred until she had given birth. Members of other Muslim groups were also targeted by the Shabaab. Two clerics belonging to the government-allied Islamist group Ahlu Sunna wal Jammaa were beheaded in the Middle Shabelle region in March. The Shabaab caused deep offense among many Somalis by destroying the graves of Sufi Muslim saints.

The education system is severely degraded due to the breakdown of the state, and there is no system of higher education outside of Mogadishu. Academics reportedly practice self-censorship. The Shabaab has begun interfering in the education system in areas under its control, ordering the removal from schools of UN-distributed textbooks it considered to be "un-Islamic." The bombing of a graduation ceremony in December, which killed young medical students and two education ministers, among others, was widely seen as a direct attack on the education system itself.

Freedom of assembly is not respected amid the ongoing violence, and the largely informal economy is inhospitable to organized labor. The conflict has forced nongovernmental organizations and UN agencies operating in Somalia to reduce or suspend their activities. Staff from one of the few that remains, the UN World Food Programme, have faced attack, and piracy off the Somali coast has increased the cost of shipping humanitarian supplies.

There is no judicial system functioning effectively at the national level. The TFA passed a law to implement Sharia (Islamic law) in May 2009, but the government was unable to carry out the legislation in practice. Local authorities administer a mix of Sharia and traditional Somali forms of justice and reconciliation. The harshest codes are enforced in areas under the control of the Shabaab. People convicted of theft or other minor crimes are flogged or have their limbs amputated, usually in public.

The human rights situation in Somalia remained grim in 2009, with civilians caught up in fighting between the Islamist militias, the TFG, and African Union peacekeepers. There was no effective process in place to investigate allegations of human rights abuses by any of the warring parties. The office of the UN High Commissioner for Refugees estimated that there were 1.5 million internally displaced people by the year's end, most of them living in appalling conditions. An estimated 500,000 were taking refuge in neighboring countries.

Most Somalis share the same ethnicity and religion, but clan divisions have long fueled violence in the country. The larger, more powerful clans continue to dominate political life and are able to use their strength to harass the weaker clans.

Women in Somalia face a great deal of discrimination. Female genital mutilation is still practiced in some form on nearly all Somali girls. Sexual violence is rampant due to lawlessness and impunity for perpetrators, and rape victims are often stigmatized.

South Africa

Political Rights: 2
Civil Liberties: 2
Status: Free

Population: 50,674,000
Capital: Tshwane/Pretoria

Ten-Year Ratings Timeline For Year Under Review (Political Rights, Civil Liberties, Status)

2000	2001	2002	2003	2004	2005	2006	2007	2008	2009
1,2F	1,2F	1,2F	1,2F	1,2F	1,2F	2,2F	2,2F	2,2F	2,2F

Overview:

Jacob Zuma, head of the ruling African National Congress (ANC) party, faced renewed corruption charges in January 2009, but prosecutors dropped the case just before national elections in April. The ANC easily won the vote despite competition from a splinter party that had formed in 2008, and Zuma was elected president by the new National Assembly. Also during the year, residents intensified demonstrations to protest the government's slow delivery of public services including electricity, water, and housing.

In 1910, the Union of South Africa was created as a self-governing dominion of the British Empire. The Afrikaner-dominated National Party (NP) came to power in 1948 on a platform of institutionalized racial separation, or "apartheid," that was designed to maintain white minority rule. Partly as a result, South Africa declared formal independence in 1961 and withdrew from the Commonwealth. The NP went on to govern South Africa under the apartheid system for decades. Mounting domestic and international pressure prompted President F. W. de Klerk to legalize the antiapartheid African National Congress (ANC) and release ANC leader Nelson Mandela from prison in 1990. Between then and 1994, when the first multiracial elections were held, almost all apartheid-related legislation was abolished, and an interim constitution was negotiated and enacted.

The ANC won the April 1994 elections in a landslide, and Mandela was elected president. As required by the interim constitution, a national unity government was formed, including the ANC, the NP, and the Zulu-nationalist Inkatha Freedom Party (IFP). A Constitutional Assembly produced a permanent constitution, which was signed into law in December 1996. The ANC claimed almost two-thirds of the vote in 1999 elections, and Thabo Mbeki, Mandela's successor as head of the ANC, won the presidency. In 2004, the ANC won an even greater victory, taking nearly 70 percent of the national vote and majorities in seven of nine provincial legislatures. Mbeki easily secured a second five-year term.

Rifts within the ruling party and its "governing alliance" with the South African Communist Party (SACP) and the Congress of South African Trade Unions (COSATU) dominated South African politics over the subsequent years, as did ongoing controversies surrounding former deputy president Jacob Zuma. Mbeki sacked Zuma in 2005, after he was implicated in the corruption trial of his financial adviser, Schabir. Zuma's supporters—including COSATU, the SACP, the ANC Youth League, and many ethnic Zulus—claimed that the scandal was engineered by Mbeki's allies in the ANC and the media; these accusations were redoubled after Zuma was accused of raping a family friend. In 2006, he was acquitted of the rape charge, and his corruption trial was dismissed on procedural grounds. Zuma was again charged with corruption in 2007.

At the ANC's national conference in December 2007, Zuma defeated Mbeki in a heated battle for the party presidency, and Zuma's allies were elected to a majority of other ANC executive positions. By late 2008, relations between the ANC and Mbeki's government were seriously strained. In September, after a High Court judge set aside the remaining corruption charges against Zuma due to prosecutorial misconduct, the ANC's national executive committee forced Mbeki to resign as state president. The party nominated its deputy president, Kgalema Motlanthe, to serve as interim state president, and he was quickly confirmed by the National Assembly. After Mbeki's ouster, recently resigned defense minister Mosiuoa "Terror" Lekota quit the ANC and formed a new opposition party. A series of ANC leaders—nearly all of them Mbeki allies—moved to the new party, which was formally registered as Congress of the People (COPE) in December 2008.

While Zuma was once again charged with corruption in January 2009, head national prosecutor Mokotedi Mpshe dropped the case for good in April, just two weeks before national elections. He argued that the timing of the 2007 charges was politically motivated, citing wiretap evidence of conversations to that effect between top law enforcement officials, who denied Mpshe's claims.

Despite the new competition from COPE, the ANC won another sweeping victory in the April 2009 elections, taking 65.9 percent of the national vote (for 264 seats in the 400-seat National Assembly) and clear majorities in eight of nine provinces. The Democratic Alliance (DA) retained its status as the largest opposition party, winning 16.7 percent of the national vote (67 seats) and outright control of Western Cape Province. COPE won 7.4 percent (30 seats), the IFP won 4.6 percent (18 seats), and a collection of smaller parties took the remainder. Zuma was easily elected state president by the National Assembly the following month, winning 277 of 400 votes.

Some 5.5 million South Africans, about 11 percent of the population, are infected with HIV/AIDS. A 2008 Harvard University study claimed that 330,000 people had died between 2000 and 2005 as a result of the Mbeki government's skepticism about the link between HIV and AIDS, and the disease caused average life expectancy to drop from 62 in 1990 to 50 in 2007. While state-funded access to antiretroviral drugs expanded rapidly in 2008, it slowed in 2009. In September, the AIDS Law Project reported that 40 percent of HIV-positive South Africans were not receiving treatment.

Political Rights and Civil Liberties: South Africa is an electoral democracy. Elections for the 400-seat National Assembly are determined by party-list proportional representation, and the 90 members of the National Council of Provinces are selected by the provincial legislatures. The National Assembly elects the president to serve concurrently with its five-year term.

The ANC, which has won supermajorities in every democratic election, dominates the political landscape. The DA is the leading opposition party, followed by COPE and the IFP. The electoral process is generally free and fair, although the state-owned South African Broadcasting Corporation (SABC) has been accused of pro-ANC bias. Political violence, while never severe, increased in the run-up to the 2009 elections. According to the *Mail & Guardian*, there were 40 incidents of electoral violence in 2009, most, "at the level of intimidation or clashes," in KwaZulu-Natal and the Eastern Cape. Between January and April, five politicians were killed in election-related violence, including four in KwaZulu-Natal. In addition, party officials engaged in inflammatory rhetoric during the campaign.

Several agencies are tasked with combating corruption, but enforcement is inadequate. servants regularly fail to declare their business interests as required by law, and the ANC has been criticized for charging fees to business leaders for access to top government officials. In 2007, police commissioner Jackie Selebi was arrested on charges of corruption related to his association with an organized crime boss; his trial began in October 2009. In 2008, Parliament abolished the Directorate of Special Operations, known as the Scorpions, an independent unit that had pursued several high-profile corruption investigations, including the case against current president Jacob Zuma. The Scorpions were replaced by the Directorate for Priority Crime Investigation (or the "Hawks"). In November 2009, the Human Settlement Department, which deals with housing, announced that over 920 government officials were being charged with corruption linked to housing fraud. South Africa was ranked 55 out of 180 countries surveyed in Transparency International's 2009 Corruption Perceptions Index.

Freedoms of expression and the press are protected in the constitution and generally respected in practice. A number of private newspapers and magazines are sharply critical of powerful figures and institutions. Most South Africans receive the news via radio outlets, a majority of which are controlled by the SABC. The SABC also dominates the television market, but two commercial stations are expanding their reach. Internet access is unrestricted and growing rapidly, although many South Africans cannot afford the service fee.

The government is increasingly sensitive to media criticism and has encroached on the editorial independence of the SABC. Government critics have been barred or restricted from SABC airwaves. In March 2009, the SABC canceled a television puppet show based on the work of cartoonist Jonathan Shapiro; in December 2008, Zuma had sued Shapiro and the *Sunday Times* for defamation over a cartoon in the paper, seeking over US$700,000 in damages. Rifts within the ANC have recently found their way into SABC leadership battles. In February 2009, President Motlanthe refused to sign legislation that would have allowed Parliament to fire SABC board members; the measure was seen as a means of ousting the board recently appointed by former president Thabo Mbeki. An amended bill requires a, "proper inquiry by Parliament," before such dismissals, but the bill had not been passed by year's end. In addition, both the ANC and COPE accused the SABC of biased coverage of the events surrounding the ANC split. SABC journalists in turn accused members of both parties of intimidation in the run-up to the 2009 elections.

Freedom of religion and academic freedom are constitutionally guaranteed and actively protected by the government.

Freedoms of association and peaceful assembly are also secured by the constitution, and South Africa hosts a vibrant civil society and an embedded protest culture. Nongovernmental organizations (NGOs) can register and operate freely. Lawmakers regularly accept input from NGOs on pending legislation. A recent trend of protests over the pace and extent of public service delivery—including housing, electricity, and water—escalated significantly in both scope and violence in 2009, particularly during the winter months. Police used rubber bullets and water cannons to disperse protests throughout the year.

South Africans are free to form, join, and participate in independent trade unions. COSATU, which claims over two million members, is part of a tripartite governing alliance with the ANC and the SACP. Strike activity is common. In July 2009, 70,000 construction workers building soccer stadiums for the upcoming World Cup went on strike; that same month, municipal workers also struck across the country. In August, a demonstration by over 1,500 soldiers demanding higher pay turned violent, as the soldiers rioted in Pretoria. Subsequently, the government considered banning the unionization of the defense forces.

Judicial independence is guaranteed by the constitution, and the courts—particularly the Constitutional Court and the Supreme Court—operate with substantial autonomy. In 2008, however, judicial and prosecutorial independence came under fire. In June of that year, the Constitutional Court (CC) filed a complaint with the Judicial Service Commission against senior Cape High Court judge John Hlophe, alleging that he had attempted to influence the Zuma corruption case. ANC secretary general Gwede Mantashe labeled the CC's actions "counterrevolutionary," and the Johannesburg High Court later ruled that the CC had violated Hlophe's rights by filing its complaint in a public manner. Meanwhile, in dismissing corruption charges against Zuma that year, High Court judge Christopher Nicholson stated that he believed Zuma's prosecution to have been at least partially motivated by political interference from the executive branch.

In October 2009, Zuma appointed four new judges and a new chief justice to the CC; the appointments were welcomed by opposition parties and legal organizations. However, his November appointment of former justice ministry general Menzi Simelane as the new head of the National Prosecuting Authority (NPA) was condemned by many opposition parties and civil society organizations, who pointed to Simelane's lack of qualifications and allegedly unlawful role in the politically tainted dismissal of former NPA head Vusi Pikoli in 2008.

Staff and resource shortages undermine defendants' procedural rights, including the rights to a timely trial and state-funded legal counsel. While pretrial detainees wait an average of three months before trial, some wait up to two years. The lower courts have proven more susceptible to corruption than the higher panels, and there have been reports of violent intimidation of judges and magistrates.

Despite constitutional prohibitions and government countermeasures, there have been reports of police torture and excessive force during arrest, interrogation, and detention. According to Amnesty International, deaths in custody increased in 2009. The Judicial Inspectorate of Prisons investigates prisoners' assault allegations but has limited resources and capacity. Prisons often fail to meet international standards and feature overcrowding, inadequate health care, and abuse of inmates by staff or other prisoners; both HIV/AIDS and tuberculosis are problems. Recent inquiries have found that corruption, maladministration, and sexual violence are rife in the penal system.

South Africa has one of the highest violent-crime rates in the world. The Zuma administration has given the police more latitude to use force against criminals, and in 2009 a number of police officials made statements alluding to a "shoot to kill" policy. However, after a string of civilian deaths in police actions, Zuma announced that no such policy existed.

The constitution prohibits discrimination based on a range of categories, including race, sexual orientation, and culture. State bodies such as the South African Human Rights Commission (SAHRC) and the Office of the Public Prosecutor (OPP) are empowered to investigate and prosecute cases of discrimination. Affirmative action legislation has benefited previously disadvantaged groups (defined as "Africans," "Coloureds," and "Asians") in public and private employment as well as in education. Racial imbalances in the workforce persist, and a majority of the country's business assets remain white owned. The government's Black Economic Empowerment (BEE) program aims to increase the black stake in the economy, mostly by establishing race-based ownership thresholds for government tenders and licenses. In 2008, the Pretoria High Court ruled that Chinese South Africans should also enjoy access to such benefits and thus included them in the official definition of "black." In November 2009, the Solidarity trade union sued the government for racial discrimination in police hiring on behalf of a group of white applicants; the union had already filed nine similar cases against the police and one against the prison service. Also that month, the cabinet approved a new policy prohibiting discrimination against HIV-positive soldiers.

Increased illegal immigration, particularly from Zimbabwe and Mozambique, has led to a rise in xenophobic violence by police and vigilantes, including a wave of attacks in May 2008 killed 62 suspected foreigners (21 were in fact South African) and temporarily displaced some 80,000 others. Sporadic attacks picked up in 2009, particularly during the service-delivery protests in July. In November, about 2,500 Zimbabweans were forced to flee the de Doorns informal settlement in the Western Cape after being attacked by other residents. Immigration and police forces have been accused of abusing illegal immigrants and detaining them longer than allowed under the Immigration Act.

The number of foreign nationals in South Africa is contested, with estimates ranging from two to seven million, including between one and three million Zimbabweans. In April 2009, the government announced a moratorium on the deportation of Zimbabweans, and granted most 90-day visa waivers. The government also announced plans to create six-month "special dispensation permits" for many Zimbabweans, legalizing their presence and giving them access to workers' rights and basic health care and education. However, the program had not been implemented by year's end. Separately, the nomadic Khoikhoi and Khomani San peoples, indigenous to South Africa, suffer from social and legal discrimination.

South Africa has one of the world's most liberal legal environments for homosexuals. The 2006 Civil Unions Act legalized same-sex marriage, and a 2002 Constitutional Court ruling held that homosexual couples should be allowed to adopt children. Nevertheless, homosexuals are subject to attacks.

The state generally protects citizens from arbitrary deprivation of their property. However, some 80 percent of farmland is owned by white South Africans, who make up 14 percent of the population. As a result, thousands of black and colored farmworkers suffer from insecure tenure rights; illegal squatting on white-owned farms is a serious problem, as are attacks on white owners. The government has vowed to transfer 30 percent of land to black owners by 2014; however, only 6.7 percent of land had been transferred by the end of 2009, and over half of the affected farms had failed or were failing, according to the Ministry for Land Reform and Rural Development. In July, the state-owned Land Bank told Parliament that 350 redistributed farms would have to be repossessed if the new owners continued to fail to repay their loans.

Separately, a state-sponsored effort to revamp downtown Johannesburg has evicted hundreds—and potentially thousands—of squatters from inner-city buildings. In May 2009, the rights group Abahlali baseMjondolo sued the government over plans to demolish shantytowns in Durban; the case was set to appear before the CC.

Equal rights for women are guaranteed by the constitution and promoted by Commission on Gender Equality. While the constitution allows the option and practice of customary law, it does not allow such law to supersede the rights assured to women as South African citizens. Nevertheless, women suffer de facto discrimination with regard to marriage (including forced marriage), divorce, inheritance, and property rights. Despite a robust legal framework, domestic violence and rape, both criminal offenses, are serious problems. South Africa has one of the world's highest rates of sexual abuse. In June 2009, a survey by the South African Medical Research Council found that two-fifths of male respondents admitted to being physically violent with a sexual partner, and one-quarter admitted to committing rape. Women are also subject to sexual harassment and wage discrimination in the workplace, and are not well represented in top management positions. However, women hold 45 percent of seats in the National Assembly and lead five of nine provincial governments; the main opposition DA party is led by Helen Zille, who became premier of Western Cape Province after the 2009 elections.

South Korea

Political Rights: 1
Civil Liberties: 2
Status: Free

Population: 48,747,000
Capital: Seoul

Ten-Year Ratings Timeline For Year Under Review (Political Rights, Civil Liberties, Status)

2000	2001	2002	2003	2004	2005	2006	2007	2008	2009
2,2F	2,2F	2,2F	2,2F	1,2F	1,2F	1,2F	1,2F	1,2F	1,2F

Overview:
Although South Korea faced economic uncertainty and renewed provocations from North Korea during 2009, the domestic political situation was calm compared with the large street protests of 2008. There were some expressions of public frustration, such as after the May suicide of former president Roh Moo-hyun and in response to layoffs by the automaker Ssangyong Motor, but they did not escalate into broader unrest.

The Republic of Korea (ROK) was established on the southern portion of the Korean Peninsula in 1948, three years after the Allied victory in World War II ended Japan's 35-year occupation. U.S. and Soviet forces had divided the peninsula between them, initially to accept the surrender of the Japanese army. The subsequent Korean War (1950–53) pitted the U.S.- and UN-backed ROK, or South Korea, against the Soviet- and Chinese-backed Democratic People's Republic of Korea (DPRK), or North Korea, and left some three million Koreans dead or wounded. In the decades that followed the 1953 armistice, South Korea's mainly military rulers crushed dissent and maintained a tightly controlled society in response to the continuing threat from the North. During this period, South Korea implemented an export-led industrialization drive that transformed the poor, agrarian land into one of the world's leading economies.

South Korea began its democratic transition in 1987, when military strongman Chun Doo-hwan acceded to widespread protests by students and the middle class, allowing his successor to be chosen in a direct presidential election. In the December balloting, Roh Tae-woo, Chun's ally and fellow general, defeated the country's two best-known dissidents, Kim Young-sam and Kim Dae-jung, as the opposition failed to unite behind a single candidate.

After joining the ruling party in 1990, Kim Young-sam defeated Kim Dae-jung in the 1992 presidential election to become South Korea's first civilian president since 1961. As president, he tried to reduce corruption, sacked hard-line military officers, curbed the domestic security services, and successfully prosecuted former presidents Chun and Roh for corruption and treason. However, anger over the government's failure to better supervise the country's banks and business conglomerates in the midst of a regional financial crisis led South Koreans in 1997 to elect Kim Dae-jung as president, making him the first opposition candidate to win a presidential election.

Kim Dae-jung's efforts to reach out to North Korea culminated in a historic 2000 summit with North Korean leader Kim Jong-il. With Kim Dae-jung constitutionally barred from seeking a second term, Roh hyun, a human rights lawyer and former cabinet minister, won the 2002 presidential election on the ruling liberal party's ticket; he narrowly defeated Lee Hoi-chang of the opposition conservative Grand National Party (GNP).

Roh took office in February 2003 facing an economic slowdown, an opposition-led parliament, and public moves by North Korea to revive its nuclear weapons program. In addition, just one year into his term, the opposition brought a parliamentary motion to impeach Roh over a minor technical breach of election rules, and he stepped down temporarily. The Constitutional Court then overturned the impeachment vote, and Roh was reinstated. Nevertheless, his popularity entered a period of sustained decline.

Former Seoul mayor, Lee Myung-bak of the GNP, won the December 2007 presidential election with 48.7 percent of the vote, defeating former unification minister Chung Dong-young of the liberal Uri Party, who took 26.1 percent. The GNP scored another victory in the April 2008 parliamentary elections, winning 131 seats outright and an additional 22 seats through proportional representation; the opposition Democratic Party (formerly the Uri Party) captured 66 seats outright and received 15 proportional seats. Four smaller parties and independents accounted for the remainder.

After taking office, President Lee focused his foreign policy on strengthening relations with the United States rather than improving ties with North Korea. South Korea's decision to resume U.S. beef imports in April drew weeks of protests in the form of mass candlelight vigils. The demonstrations were driven in part by broader disappointment with the new administration's alleged "authoritarian style" of governance, business-friendly reform agenda, and other changes from the policies of the two previous presidents. The crippling protests ultimately forced a cabinet reshuffle and backtracking on much of Lee's agenda.

Government and public attention shifted to the economy in late 2008 as a global financial crisis emerged. With aggressive fiscal intervention and heavy spending, the Lee administration was able to stabilize the financial sector, save the job market from massive layoffs, and steer the economy toward recovery after an initial plummet.

The domestic political situation remained fairly calm in 2009 compared with the previous year. There were many occasions that could have led to large and sustained protests. For example, former president Roh Moo-hyun committed suicide in May amid corruption allegations, and former president Kim Dae-jung's death from natural causes in August provided Lee's opponents with another opportunity to muster. In addition, workers facing layoffs by the automaker Ssangyong Motor occupied a factory from May through August, at times clashing with police. However, the president avoided major instability in part through increased sensitivity to public opinion and a greater emphasis on helping the poor and needy in society rather than simply promoting probusiness policies.

Relations with North Korea grew more tense in the first half of 2009, as Pyongyang announced in April that it was withdrawing from the multilateral Six-Party Talks on its nuclear weapons program. It also tested a long-range missile that month, and conducted its second nuclear weapons test in May. The UN Security Council tightened sanctions on the North in response. A number of events later in the year served to ease tensions somewhat, including Pyongyang's decision to send a delegation to Dae-jung's funeral.

Political Rights and Civil Liberties: South Korea is an electoral democracy. Elections are free and fair, and electoral processes have improved since 2002. The 1988 constitution vests executive power in a directly elected president, who is limited to a single five-year term. Of the unicameral National Assembly's 299 members, 245 are elected in single-member districts, and 54 are chosen through nationwide proportional representation, all for four-year terms.

Political pluralism is robust in South Korean politics, with multiple political parties competing for power. The two largest parties are the GNP and the Democratic Party, formerly the Uri Party.

Despite the overall health of the South Korean political system, bribery, influence peddling, and extortion by officials have not been eradicated from politics, business, and everyday life. In 2009, President Lee Myung-bak made anticorruption efforts a top administrative priority, particularly in the defense sector. Former president Roh Moo-hyun came under investigation in April for soliciting approximately US$6 million from a shoe manufacturer while in office, driving the humiliated former leader to take his own life in May. South Korea was ranked 39 out of 180 countries surveyed in Transparency International's 2009 Corruption Perceptions Index.

South Korea's news media are free and competitive. Newspapers are privately owned and report fairly aggressively on government policies and alleged official and corporate wrongdoing. The government directly censors films for sex and violence, though it has been increasingly liberal in recent years. Violent and sexually explicit websites are also censored. The National Security Law stipulates that South Koreans may not listen to North Korean radio. However, no effective measures are in place to block access to broadcasts by North Korean stations.

In 2009, a number of events suggested that the government was attempting to curb critical media. Legislation to deregulate media ownership was passed in July, potentially allowing large conservative newspaper companies to take over progressive broadcast outlets that tend to be critical of the Lee administration. Although proper voting procedures for the bill were violated, the Constitutional Court ruled that it was still valid. Separately, a blogger known as Minerva was arrested in January and charged with spreading false economic information that caused instability in the markets. He was acquitted in April, however. In June, four producers and a writer for the television program *PD Notebook* were indicted on defamation charges for a 2008 report on U.S. beef imports that had sparked weeks of protests; the accused face five-year prison sentences. A series of six hearings began in September and would continue into 2010.

The constitution provides for freedom of religion. Academic freedom is also unrestricted, with the exception of limits on statements of support for the North Korean regime or communism, in accordance with the National Security Law. This law is applied selectively and only rarely.

South Korea respects freedom of assembly, and the Law on Assembly and Demonstrations requires only that the police be informed in advance of all demonstrations, including political rallies. However, local nongovernmental organizations (NGOs) have alleged that while protestors are convicted under this law, police have not been equally penalized for mistreating demonstrators. In September 2009, the Constitutional Court struck down a rule banning demonstration activities at night and called for revised legislation by the end of June 2010. Human rights groups, social welfare organizations, and other NGOs are active and for the most part operate freely.

The country's independent labor unions advocate workers' interests, organizing high-profile strikes and demonstrations that sometimes lead to arrests. However, labor unions in general have been diminishing in strength and popularity. The violent that began in May 2009 at a Ssangyong Motor factory in Pyeongtaek weakened public support for the unions, especially as many companies struggled amid the economic downturn. Significant labor reforms that would allow multiple unions to compete within companies and no longer require employers to pay for union leaders who are not direct employees were pending at year's end.

South Korea's judiciary is generally considered to be independent. There is no trial by jury; judges render verdicts in all cases. Police occasionally engage in verbal and physical abuse of detainees. While South Korea's prisons lack certain amenities, such as hot water in the winter, there have been few reports of beatings or intimidation by guards.

Because South Korean citizenship is based on parentage rather than place of birth, residents who are not ethnic Koreans face extreme difficulty obtaining citizenship. Lack of citizenship bars them from the civil service and also limits job opportunities at some major corporations. The country's few ethnic minorities face legal and societal discrimination.

The government generally respects citizens' right to privacy. An Anti-Wiretap Law sets out the conditions under which the government can monitor telephone calls, mail, and e-mail. However, the number of reported wiretaps increased significantly between 2008 and 2009., Political and business elites often carry two mobile phones and change their numbers frequently to evade what they perceive as intrusive government eavesdropping. Travel both within South Korea and abroad is unrestricted; the only exception is travel to North Korea, for which government approval is required.

Although women in South Korea enjoy legal equality, they face discrimination in practice, with men enjoying more social privileges and better employment opportunities. However, a 2005 Supreme Court ruling granted married women equal rights with respect to inheritance. Previously, married women were considered to be part of their husband's family and were not eligible to inherit family property. Korea is one of the few countries outside the Muslim world where adultery is a criminal offense.

Spain

Political Rights: 1
Civil Liberties: 1
Status: Free

Population: 46,916,000
Capital: Madrid

Ten-Year Ratings Timeline For Year Under Review (Political Rights, Civil Liberties, Status)

2000	2001	2002	2003	2004	2005	2006	2007	2008	2009
1,2F	1,2F	1,1F	1,1F	1,1F	1,1F	1,1F	1,1F	1,1F	1,1F

Overview:
In 2009, government plans to liberalize abortion laws were met with criticism from groups including opposition conservatives and the Catholic Church. The Basque parliament voted in a non-nationalist government in May for the first time in 30 years, sparking a bombing spree by the Basque separatist group Euskadi Ta Askatasuna (ETA).

Peninsular Spain's current borders were largely established by the 16th century, and after a period of great colonial expansion and wealth, the country declined in relation to its European rivals. Most of its overseas possessions were lost in wars or revolts by the end of the 19th century. The Spanish Civil War of 1936–39 ended in victory for General Francisco Franco's right-wing Nationalists, who executed, jailed, and exiled the leftist Republicans. During Franco's long rule, many countries cut off diplomatic ties, and his regime was ostracized by the United Nations from 1946 to 1955. The militant Basque separatist group Euskadi Ta Askatasuna (ETA), or Basque Fatherland and Freedom, was formed in 1959 with the aim of creating an independent Basque homeland and went on to carry out a campaign of terrorist bombings and other illegal activities. After a transitional period following Franco's death in 1975, Spain emerged as a parliamentary democracy, joining the European Economic Community, the precursor to the European Union (EU), in 1986.

During the 2004 parliamentary elections, the Spanish Socialist Workers' Party (PSOE) defeated the conservative Party (PP), which had been in power for 11 years. However, lacking an outright majority, the PSOE relied on regionalist parties to support its legislation. The elections came only days after multiple terrorist bombings of commuter trains in Madrid that killed almost 200 people. The conservative government blamed ETA, which angered voters when it was discovered that the attacks were carried out by Islamic fundamentalists in response to the conservative government's support of the U.S.-led war in Iraq. After becoming prime minister, the PSOE's Jose Luis Rodriguez Zapatero pulled Spain's troops out of Iraq. In 2007, a Spanish court handed down long prison sentences for 21 of the 28 defendants charged in connection with the 2004 bombings; 7 of the accused were acquitted. In 2008, a key suspect in the bombings was sentenced to 20 years in prison.

ETA announced its first ceasefire in March 2006, but peace talks with the Spanish government broke down in January 2007, after the separatist group claimed responsibility for a December 2006 bombing in a parking garage at the Barajas Airport. The Supreme Court banned hundreds of candidates from participating in 2007 local elections in the Basque region, accusing them of links to ETA.

Parliamentary elections held in March 2008 returned the PSOE to power. The PSOE, which had focused on liberal reforms, such as gender equality and same-sex marriage, won 43.5 percent of the vote in the lower house, followed by the PP, which captured 40.1 percent.

For the first time in 30 years, the Basque Nationalist Party lost its absolute majority in the Basque parliament election in March 2009. The new coalition of the PSOE and the center-right PP pledged to focus on security and economy and not press for regional autonomy.

ETA carried out at least 17 violent attacks throughout 2009, marking the 50th anniversary of the group's founding. In June, a senior police officer was killed in a bomb attack in Bilbao, the capital of the Basque region. The resort island of Majorca was hit with a series of bombings in July, including an explosion that killed two police officers, the deadliest attack by ETA since 2007. In October, French authorities arrested two leaders of ETA, including Aitor Elizaran Aguilar, who had allegedly replaced Javier Lopez Pena, a senior ETA commander captured by French police in 2008.

In September, the government released plans to liberalize abortion laws in Spain, making the procedure "on demand" for the first time in this primarily Catholic country. The move was met with criticism from the opposition conservatives and the Catholic Church. A massive anti-abortion protest in mid-October, sponsored by 40 religious and civic groups, called on the government to repeal the bill. In December, the bill was passed by the Congress of Deputies, and final approval from the Senate was expected in early 2010.

In October, parliament passed a controversial law that increases the time illegal immigrants can be held before deportation from 40 to 60 days and imposes restrictions on parents joining their immigrant children.

Political Rights and Civil Liberties: Spain is an electoral democracy. The Congress of Deputies, the lower house of the National Assembly, has 350 members elected from party lists in provincial constituencies. The Senate has 259 members, with 208 elected directly and 51 chosen by regional legislatures. Members of both the Senate and Congress serve four-year terms. Following legislative elections, the prime minister, known as the president of the government, is selected by the monarch and is usually the leader of the majority party or coalition. The candidate must also be elected by the National Assembly. The country's 50 provinces are divided into 17 autonomous regions with varying degrees of power, in addition to the two North African enclaves of Ceuta and Melilla.

People generally have the right to organize in political parties and other competitive groups of their choice. The Basque separatist Batasuna party, which had previously garnered between 5 and 10 percent of the regional vote, was permanently banned in 2003 for its alleged ties to the armed group ETA.

Spain was ranked 32 out of 180 countries surveyed in Transparency International's 2009 Corruption Perceptions Index. In July, the country's espionage chief stepped down after being accused of using taxpayer money to fund his exotic vacations.

The country has a free and lively press, with more than 100 newspapers covering a wide range of perspectives and actively investigating high-level corruption. Daily newspaper ownership, however, is concentrated within large media groups like Prisa and Zeta. Journalists who oppose the political views of ETA are often targeted by the group. ETA carried out a bomb attack in January 2009 near a TV repeater station in Guipuzcoa Province and another in November in front of a local newspaper office in Pamplona. In December, two Spanish journalists were given suspended sentences of one year and nine months for revealing state secrets by publishing the names of people implicated in a registration scandal involving the Popular Party; they were also barred from practicing journalism during the period of their suspended sentences. Internet access is not restricted.

Freedom of religion is guaranteed through constitutional and legal protections. Roman Catholicism is the dominant religion and enjoys privileges that other religions do not, such as financing through the tax system. Jews, Muslims, and Protestants have official status through bilateral agreements with the state, while other groups (including Jehovah's Witnesses and the Mormons) have no such agreements. The government does not restrict academic freedom.

The constitution provides for freedom of assembly, and the government respects this right in practice. Domestic and international nongovernmental organizations operate without government restrictions. With the exception of members of the military, workers are free to organize and join unions of their choice and to strike. About 15 percent of the workforce is unionized. In February 2009, almost half of all magistrates went on strike for 24 hours to protest their working conditions, stressing the need for 1,000 additional judges to bring the country up to European standards.

The constitution provides for an independent judiciary. However, there have been concerns about the functioning of the judicial system, including the impact of media pressure on sensitive issues such as immigration and Basque terrorism. Baltasar Garzon, the most controversial judge in Spain, faced the Supreme Court in September 2009 on charges by a right-wing group that he had overstepped his judicial powers with his 2008 inquiry into the atrocities committed by General Francisco Franco. The case had not gone to trial by year's end. There have been reports of police abuse of prisoners, especially immigrants. Police can also hold suspects of certain terrorism-related crimes for up to five days with access only to a public lawyer. Prison conditions generally meet international standards.

Spain's universal justice law allows judges to try suspects for crimes committed abroad if they are not facing prosecution in their home country. However, in June 2009, Spain's lower house voted in favor of limiting the universal justice law to cases involving either victims with Spanish citizenship or some other link to Spain, as well as cases where the alleged perpetrators are in Spain. Prior to this change, the country's attorney general in April rejected an attempt to bring top U.S. officials to trial for torture allegations at Guantanamo Bay, saying the case had no merit, as the defendants were not present at the time of the crimes.

Women enjoy legal protections against rape, domestic abuse, and sexual harassment in the workplace. However, violence against women, particularly within the home, remains a serious problem. Women hold 36 percent of the seats in the lower house. Legislation enacted in 2005 legalized same-sex marriages and allowed gay couples to adopt children. Trafficking in men, women, and children for the purpose of sexual exploitation and forced labor remains a problem in Spain. However, the government prosecuted 135 trafficking cases in 2008, 33 more than in 2007.

Sri Lanka

Political Rights: 4
Civil Liberties: 4
Status: Partly Free

Population: 20,502,000
Capital: Colombo

Ten-Year Ratings Timeline For Year Under Review (Political Rights, Civil Liberties, Status)

2000	2001	2002	2003	2004	2005	2006	2007	2008	2009
3,4PF	3,4PF	3,4PF	3,3PF	3,3PF	3,3PF	4,4PF	4,4PF	4,4PF	4,4PF

Overview: The government ended its long-running civil war with the rebel Liberation Tigers of Tamil Eelam in May, destroying the Tigers' leadership in a final battle on the coast. Several hundred thousand civilians displaced by the last months of fighting remained forcibly interned in camps for much of the year, before the majority were allowed to leave or exercise somewhat greater freedom of movement in late November. Despite the war's completion and an improvement in security throughout the country, the situation for human rights defenders and journalists remained grim, with numerous attacks and cases of intimidation occurring amid a climate of nationalist rhetoric and impunity.

After Sri Lanka gained independence from Britain in 1948, political power alternated between the conservative United National Party (UNP) and the leftist Sri Lanka Freedom Party (SLFP). While the country made impressive gains in literacy, basic health care, and other social needs, its economic development was stunted and its social fabric tested by a long-running civil war between the government and ethnic Tamil rebels. The conflict was triggered by anti-Tamil riots in 1983 that claimed hundreds of lives, but it came in the context of broader Tamil claims of discrimination in education and employment by the Sinhalese majority. By 1986, the Liberation Tigers of Tamil Eelam (LTTE, or Tamil Tigers), which called for an independent Tamil homeland in the northeast, had eliminated most rival Tamil guerrilla groups and was in control of much of the northern Jaffna Peninsula. At the same time, the government was also fighting an insurgency in the south by the leftist People's Liberation Front (JVP). The JVP insurgency, and the brutal methods used by the army to quell it in 1989, killed an estimated 60,000 people.

In 1994, Chandrika Kumaratunga ended nearly two decades of UNP rule by leading the SLFP-dominated People's Alliance (PA) coalition to victory in parliamentary elections and then winning the presidential election. After her initial attempt to negotiate with the LTTE failed, she reverted to focusing on a military solution. Kumaratunga won an early presidential election in 1999, but the UNP and its allies gained a majority in 2001 parliamentary elections, and UNP leader Ranil Wickremasinghe became prime minister.

Following a 2002 permanent ceasefire accord (CFA), the government and LTTE agreed to explore a political settlement based on a federal system, and while the Tigers suspended their participation in peace talks in 2003, they stated that they remained committed to a political solution. The peace process was also constrained by infighting between the main political parties about how to approach the LTTE.

Kumaratunga called parliamentary elections in early 2004, and bolstered by the support of the JVP, her new PA-led United People's Freedom Alliance (UPFA) coalition won 105 out of 225 seats and formed a minority government. Apart from the JVP, other extremist and ethnic-based parties also made inroads, including a new party formed by Buddhist clergy, the National Heritage Party (JHU). The peace process was subsequently hampered by the addition of the JVP to the ruling coalition and the presence of pro-Sinhalese forces like the JHU in Parliament.

The gradually eroding ceasefire was shaken in 2004 when Colonel Karuna Amman (the nom de guerre of Vinayagamoorthi Muralitharan), an LTTE commander in the east, formed a breakaway faction called the Tamil People's Liberation Tigers (TMVP) and alleged discrimination in the treatment of eastern Tamils by the LTTE leadership. By 2006, the Karuna faction had become loosely allied with the government.

Prime Minister Mahinda Rajapaksa, the PA nominee, narrowly won the 2005 presidential election with 50.3 percent of the vote, as opposed to 48.4 percent for Wickremasinghe, largely due to a boycott and voter intimidation by the LTTE. Rajapaksa cultivated a more authoritarian style of rule, relegating Parliament to a secondary role, and appointed his brothers to lead key ministries. Furthermore, the process by which a constitutional council nominated members of independent commissions, as required by the 17th amendment, was sidestepped; the council was not reconstituted after the terms of its members expired in 2006, and in its absence, the president unilaterally appointed loyalists to the commission posts.

Prospects for the peace process dimmed further in 2006 and 2007, as consensus-building among the southern parties stalled, fighting with the LTTE escalated, and both sides engaged in targeted killings of key leaders. A pattern of daily attacks in the north and east resumed, punctuated by LTTE land mine and suicide attacks in other parts of the country. Ground operations and largely indiscriminate aerial shelling by the military killed hundreds of people and displaced tens of thousands. Civilians' mobility and commercial and social activities were increasingly curtailed by curfews, road closures, and security checkpoints. All parties to the conflict engaged in human rights abuses. Even outside the conflict areas, emergency and antiterrorism legislation facilitated the detention of perceived security threats and critics of government policy.

The government formally annulled the CFA in January 2008, and the military stepped up its offensive, deepening the humanitarian crisis. In March 2008, the government began detaining civilians who fled rebel-held areas at special "welfare centers," which ostensibly protected them from LTTE reprisals but also allowed the army to screen them for LTTE infiltrators.

In May 2008 elections for a new provincial council in Eastern Province, the ruling UPFA, boosted by its alliance with the TMVP, secured 20 of the 37 seats. TMVP deputy leader Pillayan, who had assumed control of the group, was sworn in as the province's chief minister, prompting criticism in light of the TMVP's rebel past and its continued use of violence to intimidate political rivals.

The military continued its advance in early 2009, and had gained control of Mullaitivu, the last big town held by the LTTE, by late January. With thousands of civilians trapped in the remaining patch of rebel territory, fighting proceeded slowly, but in a decisive final battle over a small strip of coastal land in May, government forces killed the Tigers's leadership, including founder Prabhakaran. An official end to the war was declared on May 9. At least 100,000 people had been killed in the 26-year conflict. According to the South Asia Terrorism Portal, a total of 15,565 people (including 11,111 civilians, 1,315 security force personnel, and 3,139 LTTE militants) were killed in 2009 alone.

Approximately 300,000 civilians were displaced during the final phases of the war, and many of those were interned in government-run camps. They faced severe food shortages and outbreaks of disease. While the government promised that internally displaced persons (IDPs) would be released and resettled by the end of the year, it initially limited aid groups' access to the camps, with the primary aim of screening all residents for any rebels hiding among them. The safe return of IDPs to their homes was also hampered by the large number of mines laid across the conflict zone by both sides. In late November, under considerable pressure, officials announced that the IDPs remaining in the camps would be allowed to come and go somewhat more freely. Nevertheless, more than 100,000 IDPs remained in the camps at year's end. Thousands more had left the camps, but were unable to return to their homes due to damage caused by the fighting as well as danger from mines.

In August, local elections were held in the northern cities of Jaffna and Vavuniya for the first time in more than a decade, though the Jaffna campaign was marred by accusations of intimidation. The UPFA won a majority of the 23 seats in the Jaffna municipal council, while the Tamil National Alliance (TNA) secured the largest share of seats in the Vavuniya council. Further normalization occurred with the reopening of the A9 Jaffna–Kandy highway, the only land route connecting the capital with the northernmost part of the country.

The All-Party Representatives Committee (APRC), which had been convened years earlier to build political consensus on measures aimed at resolving ethnic grievances, remained deadlocked throughout 2009 on the issue of devolving powers to the provinces as envisaged in the 13th amendment to the constitution. Rajapaksa's SLFP and its allies opposed giving increased authority to the provinces. Separately, Karu Jayasuriya, the public administration and home affairs minister, resigned and rejoined the opposition UNP in December, citing the government's continued failure to reestablish the independent appointments process laid out in the 17th amendment.

The SLFP strengthened its political position ahead of the 2010 parliamentary elections by drawing a number of senior TMVP defectors, including Karuna himself, into its ranks, despite the fact that the TMVP was a fellow member of the ruling UPFA coalition. Karuna received a noncabinet post in the government as national integration and reconciliation minister, and tensions continued to grow between him and Pillayan, leading to the risk of violence between their respective factions. Meanwhile, in addition to its municipal election win in Jaffna, the UPFA recorded landslide victories in local elections held in Central and North-Western Provinces in February, as well as provincial elections held in April and August, respectively, in the traditional UNP strongholds of Western Province and Uva Province. The victories were seen as a public endorsement of the government's military successes.

Buoyed by this voter support, the government continued to crack down on dissent after the end of the war, harassing prominent journalists and human rights advocates as well as international critics. Rajapaksa also called for the presidential election to be held nearly two years early, in January 2010. However, in a surprise move, General Sarath Fonseka resigned as head of the armed forces and declared his candidacy on behalf of an opposition coalition in December. At year's end, both main candidates were engaged in a heated campaign, trading charges of fraud, nepotism, and misconduct.

Political Rights and Civil Liberties: Sri Lanka is an electoral democracy. The 1978 constitution vested strong executive powers in the president, who is directly elected for a six-year term and can dissolve Parliament. The prime minister heads the leading party in Parliament but otherwise has limited powers. The 225-member unicameral legislature is elected for a six-year term through a mixed proportional-representation system.

While elections are generally free and fair, they continue to be marred by some irregularities, violence, and intimidation, and the LTTE long refused to allow free elections in areas under its control. The independent Center for Monitoring Election Violence (CMEV) reported that the 2004 parliamentary elections were considerably less beleaguered by violence and malpractice than previous polls. The European Union's Election Observation Mission noted that the 2005 presidential vote proceeded fairly smoothly in the south, despite some inappropriate use of state resources and biased reporting by both state-run and private media outlets. However, voting in the north was suppressed by the LTTE, which enforced a boycott through acts of violence. After the election, intimidation by armed groups dramatically reduced the space for nonviolent Tamil politics in the north and east, while the escalating war led to more muted opposition from southern political parties. Provincial council elections held in Eastern Province in May 2008 were accompanied by widespread reports of irregularities and intimidation by the TMVP, while those held in other provinces in 2009 were acknowledged to be generally free and fair despite isolated instances of violence and the abuse of state resources by the ruling alliance, according to the CMEV.

Some observers charge that President Mahinda Rajapaksa's centralized, authoritarian style of rule has led to a lack of transparent, inclusive policy formulation. The Centre for Policy Alternatives (CPA) and others have noted the concentration of power in the hands of the Rajapaksa family. Several of the president's brothers hold important posts—Gotabaya serves as defense secretary—and therefore control a significant proportion of the national budget and take a lead role in policy formulation. Other trusted party stalwarts serve as implementers and advisers.

The 17th amendment to the constitution was designed to depoliticize key institutions by creating a constitutional council responsible for appointing independent commissions to oversee the police, the judiciary, human rights, and civil servants. Owing to a parliamentary impasse, Rajapaksa failed to reconstitute the council in 2006, after the terms of its previous members expired, and instead made unilateral appointments to several commissions in 2007. Some local groups allege that these actions have threatened the independence of the institutions and created a class of appointees who owe their positions to the president. Rajapaksa has expressed his opposition to the 17th amendment, and the constitutional council remained dormant in 2009.

Official corruption is a continuing concern. The current legal and administrative framework is inadequate for promoting integrity and punishing corrupt behavior, and weak enforcement of existing safeguards has been a problem. For example, legislators routinely ignore wealth-declaration requirements stipulated in the 1994 Bribery Amendment Act. Although hundreds of cases are being investigated or prosecuted by the Commission to Investigate Allegations of Bribery or Corruption (CIABOC), no current or former politician has been sentenced. Corruption watchdogs have found that government interference and the Treasury's ability to withhold funding compromise the CIABOC's independence and render it ineffective. Corruption cases can only be initiated by members of the public, who have been reluctant to do so because of a lack of whistleblower protections. Sri Lanka was ranked 97 out of 180 countries surveyed in Transparency International's 2009 Corruption Perceptions Index.

Media freedom declined further in 2009 amid escalating intimidation of journalists, particularly those covering the war or other political issues. Although freedom of expression is guaranteed in the constitution, a growing number of laws and regulations restrict this right, including the Official Secrets Act, emergency regulations reintroduced in 2005, the Prevention of Terrorism Act (PTA), additional antiterrorism regulations issued in December 2006, and defamation and contempt-of-court laws. Senior journalist J. S. Tissainayagam was detained without charge in March 2008 and indicted five months later under the PTA, marking the first time the law was used against a journalist. He was sentenced to a 20-year prison term in September 2009. While state-run media outlets have increasingly fallen under the influence of the government, private media have become more polarized. Official rhetoric toward critical journalists and outlets has grown more hostile, often equating any form of criticism with treason.

War coverage during the first half of 2009 was restricted by bans on journalists' physical access to conflict zones. Some of these bans continued after the war's end, and reporters were denied entry to cover local elections in Vavuniya and Jaffna in August. Over the past several years, Tamil-language newspapers have faced bans, seizures, harassment, intimidation of distributors, and threat-induced closures at the hands of various factions. Journalists throughout Sri Lanka, particularly those who cover human rights or military issues, encountered considerable levels of intimidation in 2009, leading to increased self-censorship. State-controlled media, as well as the Defense Ministry website, are regularly used to smear individual journalists and other activists. A number of journalists received death threats in 2009, while others were subject to attempted or actual kidnapping and assaults. In the most serious incident, prominent editor Lasantha Wickrematunga of the *Sunday Leader* was shot dead in January by unknown assailants in Colombo; he had previously received threats and predicted his own murder in an article that was published posthumously. Previous cases of attacks on journalists have not been adequately investigated or prosecuted, leading to a climate of complete impunity. Internet access is generally not restricted, although the government occasionally blocked access to pro-LTTE websites.

Religious freedom is respected, and members of all faiths are generally allowed to worship freely, but the constitution gives special status to Buddhism, and there is some discrimination and occasional violence against religious minorities. Tensions between the Buddhist majority and the Christian minority—particularly evangelical Christian groups, who are accused of forced conversions—sporadically flare into attacks on churches and individuals by Buddhist extremists. The U.S. State Department's 2009 International Religious Freedom Report describes several cases of harassment and violence aimed at Christian churches. Work permits for foreign clergy, formerly valid for five years, are now being issued for only one year with the possibility of extension. Conditions for Muslims in the north and east improved with the demise of the LTTE, which had discriminated against them in the past, but relations between Muslims and the predominantly Hindu Tamils remained somewhat tense. In recent years, the minority Ahmadiyya Muslim sect has faced increased threats and attacks from members of the Sunni Muslim community, who accuse Ahmadis of being apostates.

The government generally respects academic freedom, and no official restrictions were reported in 2009. However, the LTTE had a record of silencing intellectuals who criticized its actions, and progovernment Tamil groups have also allegedly made threats.

Freedom of assembly is typically upheld. Although the 2005 emergency regulations give the president the power to restrict rallies and gatherings, permission for demonstrations is usually granted. Police occasionally use excessive force to disperse protesters. The LTTE did not allow freedom of association in the areas under its control. International staff of humanitarian groups were subject to new government visa and work-permit regulations starting in 2006, and were occasionally barred from rebel-held areas. Following the end of the war in May 2009, many humanitarian workers' access to the conflict zone and the IDP camps remained restricted. Over the past few years, human rights and pro-peace nongovernmental organizations (NGOs), particularly those considered "unpatriotic" or unwilling to support the official line, have faced greater threats and harassment from authorities across the country, including assaults on their gatherings and proposed parliamentary investigations into their activities. In August 2009, Paikiasothy Saravanamuttu, head of the CPA, received death threats and was then detained for questioning upon his return from a trip to the United States. Several dozen NGO and humanitarian workers have been killed in recent years, while others have been subject to forced disappearance, as was the case with Stephen Sunthararaj in May 2009. Several foreign staffers of UN agencies and NGOs were deported during the year after making critical remarks about official policies.

Most of Sri Lanka's 1,500 trade unions are independent and legally allowed to engage in collective bargaining. Except for civil servants, most workers can hold strikes, but the 1989 Essential Services Act allows the president to declare a strike in any industry illegal. Even though more than 70 percent of the mainly Tamil workers on tea plantations are unionized, employers routinely violate their rights. The government has increased penalties for employing minors, and complaints involving child labor have risen significantly. Nevertheless, thousands of children continue to be employed as domestic servants, and many face abuse.

Successive governments have respected judicial independence, and judges can generally make decisions without overt political intimidation. However, concerns about politicization of the judiciary have grown in recent years, particularly with respect to Sarath Nanda Silva, who served as chief justice of the Supreme Court from 1999 until his retirement in June 2009. An International Crisis Group report released in June 2009 on the judiciary highlighted a number of problems, including the president's refusal to implement the 17th amendment; the executive's power to make high-level judicial appointments; the chief justice's control over the Judicial Service

Commission, which makes lower-level appointments; and the lack of a mechanism to sanction biased or corrupt judges. On a positive note, newly appointed chief justice Ashoka de Silva has expressed a commitment to reform, and in September, it was announced that some 50 new courts would be established to expand services and reduce processing times for cases. Corruption remains fairly common in the lower courts, and those willing to pay bribes have better access to the legal system.

Heightened political and military conflict beginning in 2006 led to a sharp rise in human rights abuses by security forces, including arbitrary arrest, extrajudicial execution, forced disappearance, torture, custodial rape, and prolonged detention without trial, all of which predominantly affect Tamils. Torture occurred in the context of the insurgency but also takes place during routine interrogations. Such practices are facilitated by the 2005 emergency regulations, which allow detention for up to a year without trial. In December 2006, the government reinstated certain provisions of the PTA, permitting arrests and indefinite detention of suspects without court approval. The Prevention and Prohibition of Terrorism and Specified Terrorist Activities Regulations, also introduced in 2006, were criticized for providing an overly broad definition of terrorism and granting immunity to those security personnel accused of rights abuses. These laws have been used to detain a variety of perceived enemies of the government, including political opponents, critical journalists, and members of civil society, as well as Tamil civilians suspected of supporting the LTTE.

Most past human rights abuses are not aggressively prosecuted, while victims and witnesses are inadequately protected, contributing to a climate of almost complete impunity. The National Human Rights Commission (NHRC) is empowered to investigate abuses, but it has traditionally suffered from insufficient authority and resources. Moreover, a result of the impasse over the 17th amendment, appointments to the NHRC and the National Police Commission, among other bodies, have been made unilaterally by the executive branch, raising questions about the suitability and independence of the appointees and further weakening these institutions.

A Presidential Commission of Inquiry, established to examine egregious human rights violations committed since 2006, was disbanded in June 2009 after its mandate was not extended. It had investigated only 7 of the 16 cases referred to it and produced initial reports on 5; its reports were not made public. The commission's chairman, Mahanama Tillekeratne, stated in November 2008 that at least 1,100 missing or abducted persons remained unaccounted for. Human rights groups have claimed that insufficient registration policies in the IDP camps contributed to widespread disappearances and removals from the camps without accountability. Following the August 2009 release of a video that appeared to show extrajudicial killings of captured rebels by government forces, the United Nations called for a full investigation and rights groups urged the government to lift its censorship policy for war coverage. The government rejected calls by the United Nations and international NGOs for an inquiry into abuses committed by both sides during the war.

For many years, the LTTE effectively controlled 10 to 15 percent of Sri Lankan territory and operated a parallel administration that included schools, hospitals, courts, and law enforcement. It raised money through extortion, kidnapping, theft, and the seizure of property. The LTTE also imposed mandatory military and civil-defense training on civilians, and regularly engaged in summary executions, assassinations, disappearances, arbitrary detentions, torture, and the forcible conscription of children. The Tigers's leadership and territorial control were essentially eliminated by the end of the war in May 2009, though the possibility of terrorist attacks by any surviving fighters remained a concern.

Tamils maintain that they face systematic discrimination in areas including government employment, university education, and access to justice. Legislation that replaced English with Sinhala as the official language in 1956 continues to disadvantage Tamils and other non-Sinhala speakers. Thousands of Tamils whose ancestors were brought from India to work as indentured laborers during the 19th century did not qualify for Sri Lankan citizenship and faced discrimination and exploitation. However, in 2003, Parliament granted citizenship to about 170,000 of these stateless "Indian" Tamils, and the majority of these have received papers since then, leaving approximately 30,000 in limbo at the end of 2009. Tensions between the three major ethnic groups (Sinhalese, Tamils, and Muslims) occasionally lead to violence, as occurred in Eastern Province in 2008, and the government generally does not take adequate measures to prevent or contain it.

The war left Sri Lanka with hundreds of thousands of IDPs, while a smaller number live as refugees in the southern Indian state of Tamil Nadu. While many of those displaced in the east returned to their homes following the end of fighting there, new rounds of displacement occurred as the battlefront shifted across Northern Province in early 2009. Several hundred thousand civilians were caught in the final phases of the war in May; after being used as human shields by the LTTE and subjected to shelling by government forces, many were kept in the internment camps under extremely poor conditions for much of the year, with small numbers being gradually released starting in August. At the end of November, bowing to international pressure, the government granted freedom of movement to the roughly 130,000 who remained in the camps as of December 1, and pledged to resettle them and close the camps as soon as possible. In the wake of the war, earlier groups of IDPs who have been displaced for many years, including a large group of 70,000 Muslims forcibly ejected from the north by the LTTE in the early 1990s, also contemplated returning to their original homes, but many faced difficulty doing so.

The general militarization of the conflict area led to serious restrictions on freedom of movement—citizens from the north and east are required to obtain a pass to travel and live in other parts of the country—as well as military control over many aspects of civilian administration. In August 2009, the governor of Northern Province confirmed the continuation, pending Supreme Court review, of a requirement that residents of the Jaffna Peninsula obtain army passes to travel beyond it. However, in November, the government eased restrictions on the ability of Tamils based in the south to travel to and from Jaffna using public transportation.

Women are underrepresented in politics and the civil service. Female employees in the private sector face some sexual harassment as well as discrimination in salary and promotion opportunities. Rape and domestic violence remain serious problems, with hundreds of complaints reported annually; existing laws are weakly enforced. Violence against women, including rapes, increased along with the general fighting in conflict areas and has also affected female prisoners and IDP internees. Although women have equal rights under civil and criminal law, matters related to the family—including marriage, divorce, child custody, and inheritance—are adjudicated under the customary law of each ethnic or religious group, and the application of these laws sometimes results in discrimination against women. The government remains committed to ensuring that children have good access to free education and health care, and it has also taken steps to prosecute those suspected of sex crimes against children. At least 500 former child soldiers conscripted by the LTTE were being rehabilitated in government-run centers at year's end.

Sudan

Political Rights: 7
Civil Liberties: 7
Status: Not Free

Population: 42,272,000
Capital: Khartoum

Ten-Year RatingsTimeline ForYear Under Review (Political Rights, Civil Liberties, Status)

2000	2001	2002	2003	2004	2005	2006	2007	2008	2009
7,7NF	7,7NF	7,7NF	7,7NF	7,7NF	7,7NF	7,7NF	7,7NF	7,7NF	7,7NF

Overview: The International Criminal Court issued an arrest warrant for President Omar al-Bashir in March 2009, citing evidence of crimes against humanity and war crimes in Darfur, but the government rejected the move. Fighting in Darfur continued at a lower level, but violence surged in Southern Sudan, where at least 2,500 people were killed in ethnic clashes. North-South tensions continued to undermine the 2005 Comprehensive Peace Agreement between al-Bashir's National Congress Party and the main Southern political force, the Sudan People's Liberation Movement. National elections scheduled for mid-2009 were consequently postponed until April 2010. The two sides also haggled over how the 2011 referendum on Southern secession would be organized and who would get to vote. Meanwhile, an international arbitration panel determined the boundaries of the oil-rich territory of Abyei, placing its main oil field in the North.

Sudan has been embroiled in nearly continuous civil wars since it gained independence from Britain and Egypt in 1956. Between 1956 and 1972, the Anyanya movement, representing mainly Christian and animist black Africans in southern Sudan, battled Arab Muslim–dominated government forces. In 1969, General Jafar Numeiri toppled an elected government and established a military dictatorship. The South gained extensive autonomy under a 1972 accord, and an uneasy peace prevailed for the next decade. In 1983, Numeiri restricted the South's autonomy and imposed Sharia (Islamic law), igniting a civil war that lasted until 2004 and caused the deaths of an estimated two million people and the displacement of millions more. Numeiri was ousted in 1985, and a civilian government elected in 1986 was overthrown three years later by General Omar al-Bashir. Over the next decade, al-Bashir governed with the support of senior Muslim clerics including Hassan al-Turabi, who served as leader of the ruling National Congress Party (NCP) and speaker of the National Assembly.

Mounting tensions between al-Bashir and al-Turabi prompted the former to dissolve the legislature and declare a state of emergency in 1999. Al-Bashir fired al-Turabi and oversaw deeply flawed presidential and parliamentary elections in 2000, which the

NCP won overwhelmingly. Al-Turabi was arrested in 2001 after he signed a memorandum of understanding with the Sudan People's Liberation Army (SPLA), the main Southern rebel group, whose political arm was known as the Sudan People's Liberation Movement (SPLM).

After sidelining al-Turabi, the chief proponent of Sudan's efforts to export Islamic extremism, al-Bashir began to lift Sudan out of international isolation. The government also ended the long-running civil war with the South by signing the Comprehensive Peace Agreement (CPA) with the SPLA in January 2005. The pact included provisions for power sharing in a Government of National Unity (GoNU), with the NCP retaining a slight majority in the parliament, as well as plans to share state oil revenues. The CPA granted autonomy to a Government of Southern Sudan (GoSS) led by the SPLM, and allowed for a referendum on Southern independence to be held after a six-year transitional period, during which the Khartoum government was obliged to withdraw 80 percent of its troops stationed in the South. However, the agreement failed to address human rights abuses committed by both sides, excluded non-SPLM opponents of the NCP, and left the status and boundaries of the oil-rich Abyei region undecided. Moreover, in a serious setback to the pact's implementation, longtime SPLM leader John Garang died in a July 2005 helicopter crash, just 20 days after he was sworn in as first vice president. Garang's death deprived the South of its leading advocate of continued unity with the North and tilted the political balance in favor of the secessionists. His deputy, Salva Kiir, replaced him as SPLM leader and first vice president.

The North-South peace process coincided with a separate conflict in Darfur. It had begun in 2003, when rebels—drawn from Muslim but non-Arab ethnic groups—attacked military positions, citing discrimination by the Arab-dominated government. In 2004, government-supported Arab militias known as *janjaweed* began torching villages, massacring the inhabitants, slaughtering and stealing livestock, and raping women and girls. The military also bombed settlements from the air. More than two million civilians were displaced. The scale of the violence led to accusations of genocide by international human rights groups and the United States, among others. While a special commission's report to the UN Security Council in 2005 stated that the mass killings and rape fell short of genocide, it requested that the case be referred to the International Criminal Court (ICC).

In 2006, the government reached a peace agreement with a faction of the Sudan Liberation Army, one of Darfur's rebel groups. All the other major groups refused to sign the pact. Khartoum finally agreed to allow UN peacekeepers to replace a beleaguered African Union force in February 2007, but deployments stalled due to Sudanese obstruction and contributing countries' reluctance to commit troops and equipment.

In May 2008, members of one of the main Darfur rebel groups launched an attack on Khartoum that was intended to oust al-Bashir, but it was repulsed on the city's outskirts. In July, ICC prosecutors requested an arrest warrant for al-Bashir on charges of war crimes, crimes against humanity, and genocide. The request was partially granted in March 2009, when the ICC decided that there was enough evidence to prosecute Sudan's president for war crimes and crimes against humanity, but not enough to charge him with genocide. The Arab League and the African Union refused to recognize the arrest warrant, and al-Bashir continued to travel freely in the region.

Violence continued in Darfur during 2009, albeit at a lower level. The first three months of the year saw the worst violence, with more than 400 people killed. The international community worked to revive the peace process and persuade the fragmented rebel groups to adopt a common position, but peace talks scheduled to resume in Qatar in October were delayed.

To some extent, events in Darfur in 2009 were overshadowed by those in Southern Sudan, where more than 2,500 people died in inter- and intraethnic violence, and a quarter of a million others were displaced. In the worst incident, 185 people died when armed youth from the Murle ethnic group attacked Lou Nuer civilians in Jonglei State in August. The GoSS noted the use of heavy weapons in the attacks and accused the NCP of arming proxy forces to destabilize the South and create an excuse to postpone the 2011 referendum, though the NCP denied involvement.

In July, an international tribunal in The Hague ruled that the main oil field in the disputed Abyei region lay in Northern territory. Al-Bashir in 2007 had refused to recognize a special panel's initial decision to place the Abyei region within Southern Sudan; fighting between the SPLM and Arab Misseriya militias, which the government was suspected of backing, had erupted in Abyei late that year, leaving scores of people dead.

Another area of contention centered on the CPA provision that national elections should take place before the independence referendum. Scheduled for 2009, they were postponed until April 2010, partly because of disputes over the census upon which the electoral roll was to be based. The GoSS rejected the census, claiming it undercounted the population of Southern Sudan. Voter registration proceeded at the end of the year in spite of the row, but participation was low in Darfur, North and South Kordofan, and much of Southern Sudan. Meanwhile, after difficult negotiations on the terms of the referendum, both sides eventually decided that a vote in favor of secession would be invalid unless it was approved by a simple majority of the Southern electorate, with 60 percent voter turnout. The referendum bill also resolved the issue of who could vote in 2011 and laid out the registration requirements necessary to do so. Less progress was made on other issues. The SPLM boycotted the GoNU in October to protest delays in security-sector reform. A new national security law passed in December contained no mechanism for holding the security services accountable.

Sudan's economy continues to rely on oil exports and is, therefore, vulnerable to price fluctuations on the international market. Oil revenue makes up 98 percent of Southern Sudan's budget and approximately 60 percent of the North's. While most of Sudan's oil is located in the South, the oil infrastructure and banking facilities are in the North. For this reason, the CPA provision for sharing Sudan's oil wealth is a source of rancor between the two sides. The SPLM expressed frustration after a report in September 2009 suggested that Khartoum was underreporting oil production to deprive the South of its share of the revenue. This friction was compounded by a budget crisis in Southern Sudan that raised serious questions about the GoSS's ability to provide its people with essential goods and services and develop the institutions necessary for an independent state.

Sudan's relations with Chad remained tense in 2009. The two neighbors signed a reconciliation pact in May, but just two days later, Chad accused Sudan of violating the deal by backing a Chadian rebel attack. Khartoum denied the allegations.

Political Rights and Civil Liberties: Sudan is not an electoral democracy. The last national elections, held in 2000, were boycotted by major opposition parties. President Omar al-Bashir and his NCP won easily and remained dominant until the peace agreement with the SPLM was implemented in 2005. The SPLM and the existing Sudanese government formed a joint transitional administration, with the SPLM leader as first vice president. Eight of Sudan's 30 cabinet ministries are now headed by members of the SPLM. The joint presidency appointed members of the 450-seat lower house of parliament, the National Assembly, with the NCP holding 52 percent, the SPLM controlling 28 percent, and the remaining seats divided among other Northern and Southern parties. The 50 members of the upper house, the Council of States, are indirectly elected by state legislatures. Although the current members of parliament were appointed, members of both chambers will serve five-year terms after the next elections, currently scheduled for April 2010.

In keeping with the CPA, a census will be used to determine electoral districts and verify revenue- and power-sharing arrangements between North and South. The census results were released in May 2009 after a long delay, and they were immediately rejected by the SPLM. The dispute remained unresolved at year's end. Under the 2008 election law, 60 percent of the lower-house's seats will be allocated by a majoritarian system, and 40 percent will be elected by proportional representation; 25 percent of the proportionally elected seats will be reserved for women.

Sudan is considered one of the world's most corrupt states. It was ranked 176 out of 180 countries surveyed in Transparency International's 2009 Corruption Perceptions Index. Corruption is also a serious problem in the GoSS.

The 2005 interim constitution recognizes freedom of the press, but the news media continue to face significant obstacles. A new Press and Publication Act, passed in 2009, drew angry protests from journalists. The measure formalizes the powers of the government-appointed Press Council, which can prevent publication or broadcast of material it deems unsuitable, temporarily shut down newspapers, and impose heavy fines on those who flout the rules.

Throughout 2009, journalists faced arrest for writing articles that offended the NCP. The newspaper *Al-Midan* was temporarily closed in February and unable to publish at least three separate editions because its articles failed to satisfy the censors. Other newspapers, including *Ajras al-Hurria* and even the traditionally progovernment *Al-Wifaq*, had to pull stories and were denied permission to publish individual editions. A contributing writer to the newspaper *Ray al-Shaab* was sentenced in February to six months in prison for defamation. Others were arrested and fined during the year, and at least two foreign journalists were expelled from Sudan for their work.

Although al-Bashir in September announced the end of prepublication censorship, which had forced journalists to submit their articles for approval by the National Intelligence and Security Services (NISS), reporters were asked to abide by a code of honor that narrowly defines the issues they are allowed to discuss. Stories about the ICC, Darfur, and the 2010 elections are closely scrutinized. In spite of the restrictions, numerous privately owned dailies and weeklies provide a range of views, including those of the opposition and the GoSS. While some private radio stations operate in Khartoum and the South, they are closely monitored. The state controls the only television broadcaster. Internet penetration is among the highest in sub-Saharan Africa, but the government monitors e-mail messages.

Press freedoms in Southern Sudan are generally greater than in areas controlled directly by Khartoum, and journalists have more leeway to criticize government policies. Nevertheless, journalists who criticize the SPLM face harassment and in some cases arrest.

Religious freedom, though guaranteed by the 2005 interim constitution, is not upheld in many parts of the country. Islam was previously the state religion, and Sharia was regarded as the source of legislation. Northern states, which are predominantly Sunni Muslim, are still subject to Sharia, unlike those in the South, which are predominantly Christian and animist. The North-South conflict was characterized as jihad by the government, and in some cases non-Muslims were forced to convert to Islam. The Christian minority in the North continues to face discrimination and harassment. Under the 1994 Societies Registration Act, religious groups must register in order to legally assemble, and registration is reportedly difficult to obtain. There were reports of attacks on churches in 2009, particularly in flashpoint regions such as South Kordofan. The GoSS generally respects religious freedom.

Respect for academic freedom is limited. The government administers public universities and is responsible for determining the curriculum. Authorities do not directly control private universities, but self-censorship among instructors is common.

Freedom of assembly is restricted. The authorities have clamped down on public activities, lectures, and rallies related to the 2010 elections. The NISS has broken up opposition party gatherings, denied permission for political meetings, and raided party offices. In December, demonstrators calling for democratic reform were tear gassed and rounded up in the city of Omburman.

The operating environment for nongovernmental organizations (NGOs) deteriorated in 2009. The government responded to the ICC's decision to approve an arrest warrant for al-Bashir by expelling international humanitarian aid organizations from the country. It revoked the permits of 13 foreign NGOs and closed down 3 domestic organizations. This had an immediate impact in Darfur, where 1.1 million people depended on food supplies distributed by the expelled organizations. While some foreign NGOs were allowed to return in May, they were unable to operate freely.

Trade union rights are minimal, and there are no independent unions operating in the country. The Sudan Workers Trade Unions Federation has been co-opted by the government and is not a credible advocate of workers' interests. Strikes are essentially illegal, as the required government approval has never been granted.

The judiciary is not independent. Lower courts provide some due-process safeguards, but the higher courts are subject to political control, and special security and military courts do not apply accepted legal standards. Sudanese criminal law is based on Sharia and allows punishments such as flogging and amputation, although such laws apply only to Northern, Muslim states. Under the CPA, the government created the National Judicial Service Commission (NJSC) to manage the judicial system; coordinate the relationships between judiciaries at the national, Southern Sudan, and state levels; and oversee the appointment, approval, and dismissal of judges. Nevertheless, the NJSC is subject to government pressure.

The police and security forces practice arbitrary arrest, holding people at secret locations without access to lawyers or their relatives. According to Human Rights Watch, the fate of 200 people arrested following the attack on Khartoum by Darfur rebels in 2008 remains unknown. Torture is prevalent, and prison conditions do not meet international standards.

The National Assembly passed a new national security bill in December despite complaints by the SPLM and other opposition parties. The act retains the repressive elements of its predecessor, giving the NISS sweeping powers to seize property, conduct surveillance, search premises, and detain suspects. The new legislation contains no public accountability mechanism.

It is widely accepted that the government has directed and assisted the systematic killing of tens or even hundreds of thousands of people in Darfur since 2003, including through its support for militia groups that have terrorized civilians. Human rights groups have documented the widespread use of rape, the organized burning of villages, and the forced displacement of entire communities. In the South, the GoSS has proved unable to provide a modicum of law and order, leaving communities exposed to violence from rival ethnic groups or clans, often sparked by competition for scarce resources. In a departure from previous tactics, the attackers have recently targeted women and children. The GoSS has done little to address the proliferation of small arms in the South.

Female politicians and activists play a role in public life but face extensive discrimination. Islamic law denies Northern women equitable rights in marriage, inheritance, and divorce. Female genital mutilation is practiced throughout the country. Sudan has not ratified the international Convention on the Elimination of All Forms of Discrimination Against Women, arguing that it contradicts traditional values. The restrictions faced by women in Sudan were brought to international attention in 2009 by the case of journalist Lubna Hussein, who was arrested along with several other women for wearing trousers in public. They faced up to 40 lashes under the penal code for dressing indecently, and 10 of the women reportedly received 10 lashes each after pleading guilty. Hussein, who challenged the charges, was sentenced to one month in jail after she refused to pay a fine of about $200. However, she was freed after one day in jail, when the Sudanese Union of Journalists paid the fine on her behalf.

The U.S. State Department considers Sudan to be a source, transit, and destination country for persons trafficked for forced labor and sexual exploitation. Legislation does not criminalize all forms of human trafficking, and enforcement of existing laws is weak. The Sudanese military, Darfur rebel groups, Southern Sudanese forces, and various militia groups continue to use child soldiers.

Suriname

Political Rights: 2
Civil Liberties: 2
Status: Free

Population: 502,000
Capital: Paramaribo

Ten-Year RatingsTimeline ForYear Under Review (Political Rights, Civil Liberties, Status)

2000	2001	2002	2003	2004	2005	2006	2007	2008	2009
1,2F	1,2F	1,2F	1,2F	1,2F	2,2F	2,2F	2,2F	2,2F	2,2F

Overview:
Following controversies and delays, the trial of opposition politician and former coup leader Desi Bouterse for the

"December murders" of 15 political opponents in 1982 remained the top political issue in Suriname in 2009. Meanwhile, the forced deportations of Guyanese migrants from Suriname heightened tensions between the two countries.

The Republic of Suriname achieved independence from the Netherlands in 1975, after more than three centuries of colonial rule. In 1980, a military coup led by Desi Bouterse established a regime that brutally suppressed civic and political opposition and initiated a decade of military intervention in politics. In 1987, Bouterse permitted elections that were won handily by the center-right New Front for Democracy and Development (NF), a coalition of mainly East Indian, Creole, and Javanese parties. The National Democratic Party (NDP), organized by the military, won just 3 out of 51 seats in the National Assembly.

The army ousted the elected government in 1990, and Bouterse again took power in a bloodless coup. International pressure led to new elections in 1991. The NF won a majority in parliament, and the NF's candidate, Ronald Venetiaan, was selected as president. Bouterse quit the army in 1992 in order to lead the NDP. In the May 2000 legislative elections, the NF again secured a strong majority of National Assembly seats.

In May 2001, Fred Derby—the star witness in the trial of Bouterse and others for 15 political killings committed in December 1982—suffered a fatal heart attack that initially appeared to rob the prosecution of key testimony. However, the government vowed that testimony given by Derby during a preliminary hearing would be submitted at trial.

In 2004, the NF government's fiscal austerity program helped to stabilize prices and the economy generally, but there were signs that the policy's negative side effects had increased voter discontent. In the 2005 elections, the NF managed to remain the single largest political force, winning 41 percent of the vote, although its failure to win a two-thirds majority in the National Assembly prevented it from electing a president. In August, a United People's Assembly consisting of 891 members—including national, regional, and local lawmakers—gave Venetiaan his third term as president, with 560 votes for the incumbent and 315 for the NDP candidate, Rabindre Parmessar.

In 2007, Suriname's courts ordered officials to proceed with the long-delayed prosecution of Bouterse and nine other suspects for the 1982 "December murders." Bouterse has denied any involvement in the killings, although in March 2007, he accepted political responsibility for the slayings while offering a public apology. The trial, which is regarded as a landmark test of Suriname's judicial system, began in November 2008 and has dominated the political debate over the past two years. In 2009, following frequent delays, the Bouterse trial advanced, including the testimony of six bystanders who had fled the country and settled in the Netherlands after witnessing the executions. The former dictator, who consistently failed to appear in court, faces a sentence of up to 20 years in prison if convicted.

President Venetiaan announced that legislative elections would be held on May 25, 2010, and called for a peaceful electoral campaign, although the political climate with the opposition remained tense.

Political Rights and Civil Liberties: Suriname is an electoral democracy. The 1987 constitution provides for a unicameral, 51-seat National Assembly, elected by proportional representation to five-year terms.

The body elects the president to five-year terms with a two-thirds majority. If it is unable to do so, a United People's Assembly—consisting of lawmakers from the national, regional, and local levels—convenes to choose the president by a simple majority. A Council of State (Raad van State) made up of the president and representatives of major societal groupings—including labor unions, business, the military, and the legislature—has veto power over legislation deemed to violate the constitution.

Political parties largely reflect the cleavages in Suriname's ethnically diverse society, although political-racial discord is much less acute than in neighboring Guyana. Suriname's major parties include the NDP, the National Party Suriname (NPS), and the People's Alliance for Progress (VVV). The current administration has support from the NF, a political alliance of which the NPS is a leading member.

Suriname has been plagued by corruption cases in recent years, and organized crime and drug networks continue to hamper governance. Former minister of public works Dewanand Balesar was put on trial for corruption in June 2006, having been stripped of his immunity by the National Assembly in 2005. In late 2008, Balesar was sentenced to jail for two years under charges of forgery, fraud, and conspiracy to commit theft, and was banned from holding a public office for a period of five years. In May 2009, Siegfried Gilds, a former trade minister in President Ronald Venetiaan's administration, was sentenced to 12 months in prison for money laundering and bribing a witness. Suriname was ranked 75 out of 180 countries surveyed in Transparency International's 2009 Corruption Perceptions Index.

The constitution provides for freedoms of expression and of the press, and the government generally respects these rights in practice. However, some media outlets engage in occasional self-censorship due to fear of reprisal from members of the former military leadership or pressure from senior government officials and others who object to critical stories about the administration. There are two privately owned daily newspapers, *De Ware Tijd* and *De West*. A number of small commercial radio stations compete with the government-owned radio and television broadcasting systems, resulting in a generally pluralistic range of viewpoints. Public access to government information is recognized in law, although it is very limited in practice. In 2009, the trial of Desi Bouterse for the "December murders" was freely covered by the local press. The government does not restrict access to the internet.

The authorities generally respect freedom of religion and do not infringe on academic freedom.

Freedoms of assembly and association are provided for in the constitution, and the government respects these rights in practice. Although civic institutions remain weak, human rights organizations function freely. Workers can join independent trade unions, though civil servants have no legal right to strike. Collective bargaining is legal and conducted fairly widely. The labor movement is active in politics.

The judiciary is susceptible to political influence and suffers from a significant shortage of judges and a large backlog of cases. In 2009, the Ministry of Justice and Police added six new judges in order to address the shortage. The courts and prisons are seriously overburdened by the volume of people detained for narcotics trafficking. Police abuse detainees, particularly during arrests, and prison guards mistreat inmates. Suriname is a signatory to the 2001 agreement establishing the Trinidad-based Caribbean Court of Justice (CCJ) as the final venue of appeal for member states of the Caribbean Community, but has yet to ratify the CCJ as its final court of appeal.

Suriname is a major transit point for cocaine en route to Europe, and poor law enforcement capabilities have resulted in a rising tide of drug money entering the country.

Discrimination against indigenous and tribal groups is widespread, and Surinamese law offers such groups no special protection or recognition. As a result, Amerindians, who live mostly outside urban areas, have only a marginal ability to participate in decisions affecting their lands, cultures, traditions, and natural resources. Tribal people known as Maroons are the descendants of escaped African slaves who formed autonomous communities in the interior during the 17th and 18th centuries. Their rights to lands and resources, cultural integrity, and the autonomous administration of their affairs are not recognized in Surinamese law. In September 2009, around 65 Guyanese migrants were forcefully deported from the western districts of Suriname during "Operation Koetai." The deportations, while aimed at cracking down on smuggling and other illegal border activity, fueled tensions between the two countries.

Constitutional guarantees of gender equality are not adequately enforced. Despite their central role in agriculture and food production, 60 percent of rural women, particularly those in tribal communities, live below the poverty level. Trafficking in persons remains a problem, and the country lacks a comprehensive law specifically banning the practice. However, several organizations specifically address violence against women and related issues.

Swaziland

Political Rights: 7
Civil Liberties: 5
Status: Not Free

Population: 1,185,000
Capital: Mbabane

Ten-Year Ratings Timeline For Year Under Review (Political Rights, Civil Liberties, Status)

2000	2001	2002	2003	2004	2005	2006	2007	2008	2009
6,5NF	6,5NF	6,5NF	7,5NF	7,5NF	7,5NF	7,5NF	7,5NF	7,5NF	7,5NF

Overview: The authorities in Swaziland continued to crack down on democracy advocates and curb critical media outlets in 2009, often by invoking the 2008 Suppression of Terrorism Act. However, in September, a court acquitted and released Mario Masuku, leader of the People's United Democratic Movement, who had been arrested on terrorism and sedition charges in 2008.

Swaziland regained its independence from Britain in 1968, and an elected Parliament was added to the traditional monarchy. In 1973, King Sobhuza II repealed the 1968 constitution, ended the multiparty system in favor of a *tinkhundla* (local council) system, and declared himself an absolute monarch. After Sobhuza's death in 1982, a protracted power struggle ended with the coronation of King Mswati III in 1986.

A new constitution implemented in 2006 removed the king's ability to rule by decree, but it reaffirmed his absolute authority over the cabinet, Parliament, and the judiciary. It also maintained the tinkhundla system—in which local chiefs control elections for 55 of the 65 seats in the House of Assembly, the lower house of Parliament—and did not overturn the ban on political parties. The charter provided for limited freedoms of speech, assembly, and association, as well as limited rights for women, but the king could suspend those rights at his discretion.

Also in 2006, security forces arrested members of the prodemocracy People's United Democratic Movement (PUDEMO) following bomb attacks the previous year. Sixteen PUDEMO members, including Secretary General Bonginkosi Dlamini, were charged with treason, attempted murder, and malicious damage to government property. The suspects were later freed on bail.

During 2008, there were over 10 bomb attacks on government targets, although none killed any officials or civilians. In September, a bomb blast at a bridge near the king's palace in Lozitha killed one of the bombers, a member of PUDEMO. The government later banned PUDEMO, along with four other groups, under the newly enacted Suppression of Terrorism Act (STA). PUDEMO leader Mario Masuku was arrested on charges of terrorism and sedition, but a court acquitted him in September 2009, citing lack of evidence. Security forces later violently dispersed about 50 activists and journalists gathered outside the Matsapha correctional facility to await Masuku's release.

Swaziland has the world's highest rate of HIV infection; estimates range from 26 to 33.4 percent of the sexually active population. In 2009, only about 32,000 Swazis were receiving antiretroviral drug treatment, out of an estimated 62,000 who require it. Swaziland also has the highest rate of tuberculosis infection. That disease, aggravated by HIV/AIDS, remains the country's leading cause of death.

Political Rights and Civil Liberties: Swaziland is not an electoral democracy. King Mswati III is an absolute monarch with ultimate authority over the cabinet, legislature, and judiciary. Of the House of Assembly's 65 members, 55 are elected by popular vote within the tinkhundla system, in which local chiefs vet all candidates. The king appoints the other 10 members. The king also appoints 20 members of the 30-seat Senate, with the remainder selected by the House of Assembly. Parliament members, all of whom serve five-year terms, are not allowed to initiate legislation. Traditional chiefs govern designated localities and typically report directly to the king.

Political parties are banned, but there are political associations, the two largest being PUDEMO and the Ngwane National Liberatory Congress (NNLC), although PUDEMO was declared a terrorist organization in 2008. It and other prodemocracy groups boycotted the November 2008 House of Assembly elections.

Corruption is a major problem. The monarchy spends lavishly despite the largely impoverished population, and members of Parliament engage in fraud and graft. The government's Anti-Corruption Unit was not authorized to seize assets or enforce penalties on both bribe payers and bribe takers until 2006, nearly a decade after it was created. Swaziland was ranked 79 out of 180 countries surveyed in Transparency International's 2009 Corruption Perceptions Index.

The king can suspend constitutional rights to free expression at his discretion, and these rights are severely restricted in practice, especially with respect to speech on political issues or the royal family. Publishing criticism of the monarchy is banned, and self-censorship is widespread, as journalists are routinely subject to threats and attacks by the authorities. The attorney general and other officials have threatened journalists with arrest under the STA since its passage in 2008. Several defamation lawsuits were filed in 2009, though some were dismissed by the courts. South African media are available, and both the *Swazi Observer* and independent *Times of Swaziland* occasionally criticize the government. The country's only independent radio station broadcasts religious programming; four radio stations that received operating licenses in 2008 had them revoked in 2009. The government does not restrict access to the internet, but few Swazis can afford access.

Freedom of religion is respected in practice but not explicitly protected in the constitution. Academic freedom is limited by self-censorship. While Swazis criticize the government in private discussions, they are less free to criticize the monarchy itself.

The government has restricted freedoms of assembly and association, and permission to hold political gatherings has often been denied. Prodemocracy protesters are routinely dispersed and arrested by police. The STA grants the government sweeping powers to declare an organization a "terrorist group," and it has already been widely abused by authorities, according to Amnesty International. Police harassment and surveillance of civil society organizations has increased. In April 2009, a demonstration by church and labor groups calling for free education resulted in clashes between police and demonstrators.

Swaziland has active labor unions, and the Swaziland Federation of Trade Unions (SFTU), the largest labor organization, has led demands for democratization. However, government pressure—including the repeated arrest of SFTU leader Jan Sithole—has greatly limited union operations. Workers in all areas of the economy, including the public sector, can join unions, and 80 percent of the private workforce is unionized. Security forces violently dispersed large March 2008 strikes by public transport and textile workers in the country's worst labor unrest for decades. Some of the strikers vandalized Asian-owned shops; Swaziland's textile factories are owned by Taiwanese firms.

The dual judicial system includes courts based on Roman-Dutch law and traditional courts using customary law. The judiciary is independent in most civil cases, although the king has ultimate judicial powers, and the royal family and government often refuse to respect rulings with which they disagree. The Swazi High Court has made a number of notable antigovernment rulings in recent years, and this trend continued in 2009 with the acquittal of Mario Masuku.

According to the U.S. State Department, there were numerous incidents of police torture, beatings, and suspicious deaths in custody in 2009. Security forces generally operate with impunity. In the last four months of 2008, the army was deployed to man checkpoints throughout the country due to unrest, and new army camps were set up in parts of northern Swaziland that were believed to be sympathetic to PUDEMO. This military presence continued at a reduced level in 2009. Prisons are overcrowded, and inmates are subject to torture, beatings, rape, and a lack of sanitation. While the constitution prohibits torture, the ban is not enforceable in court. The spread of HIV/AIDS is a major problem in Swazi prisons.

The constitution grants women equal rights and legal status as adults. However, women's rights are still very restricted in practice. While both the legal code and customary law provide some protection against gender-based violence, it is common and often tolerated with impunity. In 2007, a survey found that one-third of Swazi women had been subjected to sexual violence, and two-thirds had been beaten or abused.

Sweden

Political Rights: 1
Civil Liberties: 1
Status: Free

Population: 9,288,000
Capital: Stockholm

Ten-Year Ratings Timeline For Year Under Review (Political Rights, Civil Liberties, Status)

2000	2001	2002	2003	2004	2005	2006	2007	2008	2009
1,1F	1,1F	1,1F	1,1F	1,1F	1,1F	1,1F	1,1F	1,1F	1,1F

Overview:
The controversial 2008 wiretapping law continued to cause political turmoil in 2009, leading to the adoption of a revised version in October. Demonstrations during the year over a range of issues resulted in several arrests, as well as an attack on the Iranian Embassy in Stockholm.

After centuries of wars and monarchical unions with its neighbors, Sweden emerged as a liberal constitutional monarchy in the 19th century. Norway ended its union with the country in 1905, leaving Sweden with its current borders. Its tradition of neutrality, beginning with World War I, was altered somewhat by its admission to the European Union (EU) in 1995 and was further eroded by a more pragmatic approach to security presented in 2002. However, Sweden has continued to avoid military alliances, including NATO.

Voters rejected the adoption of the EU's euro currency in a September 2003 referendum, despite strong support from government and business leaders. The "no" vote was attributed to skepticism about the EU and fears regarding the possible deterioration of welfare benefits and damage to the economy. Just days before the referendum, Foreign Minister Anna Lindh was killed in a knife attack in Stockholm. Her killer, Mijailo Mijailovic, was sentenced to life in prison.

In the September 2006 parliamentary elections, a four-party, center-right alliance headed by Fredrik Reinfeldt of the Moderate Party defeated the Social Democratic Party, which had been in power for 12 years and all but 10 of the previous 89 years. High unemployment was a major issue in the elections.

Parliament passed the Signals Intelligence Act in June 2008, giving Sweden's National Defense Radio Establishment the authority to tap international phone calls, e-mails, and faxes without a court order. Following widespread public protest, the law was changed in September to allow wire-tapping only in cases where external military threats were suspected and called for the creation of a special court to monitor the eavesdropping. The law went into effect January 1, 2009, amid continued protest, including the resignation of the head of the Swedish Intelligence Commission in February. The Riksdag narrowly passed an amended version of the bill in October, specifying that only the government and military can request surveillance, communication sent and received inside Sweden are exempt from surveillance, raw materials must be destroyed after one year, and those who have been monitored must be notified.

In March 2009, four men who ran the file-sharing website Pirate Bay were sentenced to one year in prison for violating copyright law, and faced a fine of $3.5

million for damages caused by their site. An appeal was rejected in June. Following their convictions, 25,000 people joined the Pirate Party, a political party that supports open online exchange. The Pirate Party won two seats in the European Parliamentary elections in June. Sweden held the EU Presidency from July to December 2009.

In April, information emerged that the government knew Swedish airports were used in 2005 as a stopping point for clandestine CIA planes flying terror suspects out of the United States. The government had previously denied such knowledge in 2006.

A series of protests in 2009 led to several arrests. The most severe occurred in June, when nearly 100 demonstrators protesting the reelection of Iranian president Mahmoud Ahmadinejad stormed the Iranian Embassy in Stockholm and attacked an embassy worker.

Political Rights and Civil Liberties: Sweden is an electoral democracy. The unicameral Parliament, the Riksdag, has 349 members elected every four years by proportional representation. A party must receive at least 4 percent of the vote nationwide or 12 percent in 1 of the 29 electoral districts to win representation. The prime minister is appointed by the speaker of the Riksdag and confirmed by the body as a whole. King Carl XVI Gustaf, crowned in 1973, is the largely ceremonial head of state.

Seven political parties are currently represented in the Riksdag. The largest is the Social Democratic Party, also known as the Workers' Party, which ruled for most of the last century with the aid of the Left Party and the Green Party. Other parties include the Moderates, the center-right Liberals, the Christian Democrats, and the Center Party, which focuses on rural issues.

The principal religious, ethnic, and immigrant groups are represented in Parliament. Since 1993, the indigenous Sami community has elected its own parliament, which has significant powers over community education and culture and serves as an advisory body to the government.

Corruption rates are very low in Sweden, which was ranked 3 out of 180 countries surveyed in Transparency International's 2009 Corruption Perceptions Index. According to the U.S. State Department's human rights report, there were 23 prosecutions in corruption cases during the year. In August 2009, it came to light that sensitive police information on violent criminals was being sold and circulated among Sweden's criminal underground. After an investigation, the Stockholm police department claimed that the documents had not been leaked by their unit, but argued instead that the data had been accessed by computer. Also in August, Minister Gunilla Carlsson called for investigations into international aid management after a corruption scandal broke involving aid money to Zambia. Approximately US$7 million in Swedish aid to the Health Ministry had disappeared.

Freedom of speech is guaranteed by law, and the country has one of the most robust freedom of information statutes in the world. However, hate-speech laws prohibit threats or expressions of contempt based on race, color, national or ethnic origin, religious belief, or sexual orientation. Sweden's media are independent. Most newspapers and periodicals are privately owned, and the government subsidizes daily newspapers regardless of their political affiliation. Public broadcasters air weekly radio and television programs in several immigrant languages. The ethnic press is entitled to the same subsidies as the Swedish-language press. In April 2009, the Intellectual Property Rights Enforcement Directive (IPRED) law went into effect, which will force internet service providers (ISPs) to reveal information about users and facilitate the conviction of those engaged in illegal file sharing. The Left and Green parties opposed the law, as well as groups that support file-sharing websites like Pirate Bay.

Religious freedom is constitutionally guaranteed. Although the population is 87 percent Lutheran, all churches, as well as synagogues and mosques, receive some state financial support. In 2009, over 200 hate crimes were reported against Muslims. Several lawsuits ruled in favor of Muslims who had faced discrimination throughout the year. Anti-Israel protests in January led to an increase in anti-Semitic incidents as well. The Jewish community reported an increase in Nazi symbols, personal threats, and isolated attacks on the Jewish cemetery. Academic freedom is ensured for all.

Freedoms of assembly and association are respected in law and in practice. Protests in 2009 on a range of issues, including demonstrations in January against the Israeli invasion of the Gaza Strip and protests against Iranian President Mahmoud Ahmadinejad's reelection in June, led to several arrests. The rights to strike and organize in labor unions are guaranteed. Trade union federations, which represent about 80 percent of the workforce, are strong and well organized.

The judiciary is independent. Swedish courts are allowed to try suspects for genocide committed abroad. The government maintains effective control of the police and armed forces. However, an investigation revealed in October 2009 that Johan Liljeqvist had been suffocated to death by police officers after kicking a car at a rally in Gothenburg in April 2008. The Council of Europe's antitorture body criticized Sweden in August 2009 for its treatment of prisoners, who are often kept in solitary confinement for inhumane lengths of time, among other violations.

Sweden was ranked at the top of the 2007 Migrant Integration Policy Index. However, the country changed its immigration policy that year, disallowing family reunification for "quota refugees." Family members must now apply separately for visas. A new Equality Ombudsman position was created in July 2008 to oversee efforts to prevent discrimination on the basis of gender, ethnicity, disability, and sexual orientation, and in April 2009, a permanent national hate-crime police unit was established. In November, a stream of demonstrations and counterdemonstrations were sparked after a youth hostel in Vellinge was turned into temporary housing for children seeking asylum. In protest, a fire was deliberately set outside the hostel on November 22. The government subsequently began talks about legislation that would force municipalities to house young asylum seekers. The law was still under discussion at the end of 2009.

The state gave formal recognition to adoption by gay couples for the first time in 2003. In 2005, the country granted lesbian couples the same rights regarding artificial insemination and in vitro fertilization as heterosexual couples.

Sweden is a global leader in gender equality. Some 47 percent of Riksdag members are female, and half of government ministers are women. Although 80 percent of women work outside of the home, they still earn only 70 percent of men's wages in the public sector and 76 percent in the private sector. The country is a destination and transit point for trafficking in women and children for sexual exploitation. The 2004 Aliens Act helped to provide more assistance to trafficking victims, and a "special ambassador" has been appointed to aid in combating human trafficking.

◆ Switzerland

Political Rights: 1
Civil Liberties: 1
Status: Free

Population: 7,754,000
Capital: Bern

Trend Arrow: Switzerland received a downward trend arrow due to referendum voters' approval of a constitutional ban on the construction of minarets.

Ten-Year Ratings Timeline For Year Under Review (Political Rights, Civil Liberties, Status)

2000	2001	2002	2003	2004	2005	2006	2007	2008	2009
1,1F	1,1F	1,1F	1,1F	1,1F	1,1F	1,1F	1,1F	1,1F	1,1F

Overview: In a highly controversial national referendum in November 2009, Swiss citizens approved a ban on the future construction of minarets on mosques, sparking domestic and international condemnation. Following a series of deals with European countries that allowed for the sharing of bank information, Switzerland was removed from the Organization for Economic Co-operation and Development's "gray list" of tax havens in September.

Switzerland, which has existed as a confederation of cantons since 1291, emerged with its current borders and a tradition of neutrality at the end of the Napoleonic wars in 1815. The country's four official ethnic communities are based on language: German, French, Italian, and Romansh (the smallest community).

Switzerland remained neutral during the wars of the 20th century, and it joined the United Nations only after a referendum in 2002. Membership in international institutions has long been a controversial issue in Switzerland. The Swiss have resisted joining the European Union (EU), and even rejected membership in the European Economic Area, a free-trade area that links non–EU members with the EU. However, Switzerland has joined international financial institutions and signed a range of free-trade agreements.

Hostility to both EU membership and immigration has been a hallmark of the right-wing Swiss People's Party (SVP). During the 2003 legislative elections, the SVP made blatantly xenophobic appeals, while insisting that it was not opposed to legal immigrants. The SVP led the vote, followed closely by the center-left Social Democratic Party (SP). The center-right Christian Democratic People's Party (CVP) received barely half the total of the SVP. Christoph Blocher, leader of the SVP, successfully called for a second SVP seat on the seven-member Federal Council, at the expense of the CVP.

A package of bilateral accords with the EU was passed in a June 2005 referendum. Switzerland agreed to join the Schengen area, a passport-free travel zone consisting of 2 other non-EU countries (Norway and Iceland) and 13 of the 25 EU member states. The accord also deepened Switzerland's cooperation with the EU on asylum policy, justice, and home affairs. A second referendum in September extended the free movement of labor to the 10 countries that had joined the EU in 2004.

The SVP opposed both referendums, and their passage led to speculation that the party had passed its political peak. However, the SVP successfully championed a 2006 referendum on tightening asylum and immigration laws. The new laws required asylum seekers to produce an identity document within 48 hours of arrival or risk repatriation. The tightening of immigration policy effectively limited immigration mainly to those coming from EU countries; prospective immigrants from outside the EU would have to possess skills lacking in the Swiss economy.

In the October 2007 elections, the SVP triumphed with 29 percent of the vote—more than any party since 1919. The SP captured 19.5 percent, and the Free Democratic Party (FDP) took only 15.6 percent, its worst-ever showing. The SVP campaign received international attention for its anti-immigrant appeals. An SVP rally and counterdemonstration in Bern resulted in violence rarely seen in Switzerland.

The new parliament surprised the SVP by refusing to reappoint Blocher to the cabinet, choosing instead Eveline Widmer-Schlumpf from the party's moderate wing. The SVP responded by entering into opposition, the first time that a major party had done so in decades. The party expelled Widmer-Schlumpf and Samuel Schmid, the other SVP minister, and the two became part of a new moderate-right party, the Burgeois-Democratic Party, which constituted itself formally at the national level in November 2008. However, the SVP returned to the cabinet by year's end.

Switzerland, a major banking center, was severely hit by the global financial crisis in 2008, which renewed international criticism of the country's strict bank secrecy laws. In March 2009, Switzerland agreed to adopt international transparency standards established by the Organization for Economic Cooperation and Development (OECD) by providing foreign governments with financial information for tax evasion cases, in addition to tax fraud investigations. However, financial data sharing will be assessed on a case by case basis, and significant evidence will be required before information on individuals can be released.

The SVP continued its efforts to ban the construction of minarets on mosques in 2009 and successfully petitioned for a November referendum on the issue. Despite government opposition, nearly 58 percent of the population and 22 out of 26 cantons voted in favor of the referendum, effectively prohibiting the future construction of minarets at the constitutional level. However, the four mosques with existing minarets would not be affected. The ban was met with considerable domestic and international criticism, and human rights organizations considered it a violation of the European Human Rights Convention.

Political Rights and Civil Liberties: Switzerland is an electoral democracy. The constitution of 1848, significantly revised in 1874 and 2000, provides for a Federal Assembly with two directly elected chambers: the Council of States (in which each canton has two members and each half-canton has one) and the 200-member National Council. All lawmakers serve four-year terms. The Federal Council (cabinet) is a seven-person executive council, with each member elected by the Federal Assembly. The presidency is largely ceremonial and rotates annually among the Federal Council's members.

The Swiss political system is characterized by decentralization and direct democracy. The cantons and half-cantons have significant control over economic and social policy, with the federal government's powers largely limited to foreign affairs and some economic matters. Referendums are common; any measure that modifies the constitution must be put to a referendum. A new or revised law must also be put to a referendum and requires 50,000 signatures in favor of doing so. Voters may even initiate legislation themselves with 100,000 signatures. The main political parties have long been the SVP, the SP, the right-wing and free-market FDP, and the CVP.

The government is free from pervasive corruption. As the world's largest offshore financial center, the country had long been criticized for failing to comply with recommended international norms on money laundering and terrorist financing. However, Switzerland reached bilateral deals with several countries on financial information sharing in 2009 and was removed from the OECD's "gray list" of tax havens in September. Switzerland was ranked 5 out of 180 countries surveyed in Transparency International's 2009 Corruption Perceptions Index.

Freedom of expression is guaranteed by the constitution. Switzerland has a free media environment, although the state-owned Swiss Broadcasting Corporation dominates the broadcast market. Consolidation of newspaper ownership in large media conglomerates has forced the closure of some small and local newspapers. The penal code prohibits public incitement to racial hatred or discrimination. A controversial SVP poster in support of the minaret ban in 2009 was prohibited in several cantons but allowed in others out of respect for free speech. Internet access is unrestricted.

Freedom of religion is guaranteed by the constitution, and most cantons support one or several churches. The country is split roughly between Roman Catholicism and Protestantism, though some 400,000 Muslims form the largest non-Christian minority. A 2008 law requires that immigrant clerics receive integration training, including language instruction, before practicing. Most public schools provide religious education, depending on the predominant creed in each canton. Religion classes are mandatory in some schools, although waivers are regularly granted upon request. The government respects academic freedom.

Freedoms of assembly and association are upheld in practice, and civil society is especially active in Switzerland. The right to collective bargaining is respected, and roughly one-third of the workforce is unionized.

The judiciary is independent, and the rule of law prevails in civil and criminal matters. Most judicial decisions are made at the cantonal level, except for the federal Supreme Court, which reviews cantonal court decisions when they pertain to federal law. Refusal to perform military service is a criminal offense for males. Prison conditions are generally acceptable, though a September 2009 report by the European Commission against Racism and Intolerance (ECRI) noted incidents of police discrimination and excessive use of force against detainees in asylum detention centers. An independent 12-member National Commission for the Prevention of Torture was appointed in October by the Federal Council to conduct prison inspections.

The rights of cultural, religious, and linguistic minorities are legally protected, though increasing anxiety about the large foreign-born population has led to a tightening of asylum laws and societal discrimination, especially against non-European immigrants and their descendants. The mosque in Geneva was vandalized three times in the lead-up to the November 2009 referendum on the construction of minarets.

Women were only granted universal suffrage at the federal level in 1971, and the half-canton of Appenzell-Innerrhoden denied women the vote until 1990. The constitution guarantees men and women equal pay for work of equal value, but pay differentials remain. There are 3 women in the 7-member Federal Council, and 59 in the 200-member National Council, which is above the European average. Abortion in the first 12 weeks of pregnancy was decriminalized following a 2002 referendum.

Syria

Political Rights: 7
Civil Liberties: 6
Status: Not Free

Population: 21,906,000
Capital: Damascus

Ten-Year Ratings Timeline For Year Under Review (Political Rights, Civil Liberties, Status)

2000	2001	2002	2003	2004	2005	2006	2007	2008	2009
7,7NF	7,7NF	7,7NF	7,7NF	7,7NF	7,7NF	7,6NF	7,6NF	7,6NF	7,6NF

Overview:
Freedoms of expression, association, and assembly remained tightly restricted throughout 2009, especially with regard to certain groups, such as the Kurdish minority. Syria's opposition in exile split during the year, ending an uneasy alliance between secularists and Islamists. On the international front, Syria and Lebanon exchanged ambassadors, and although the United States announced that it would send an ambassador to Damascus, none had been named by year's end.

The modern state of Syria was established by the French after World War I and gained formal independence in 1946. Democratic institutions functioned intermittently until the Arab Socialist Baath Party seized power in a 1963 coup and transformed Syria into a one-party state governed under emergency law. During the 1960s, power shifted from civilian ideologues to army officers, most of whom belonged to Syria's Alawite minority (adherents of an Islamic sect who make up 12 percent of the population). This trend culminated in General Hafez al-Assad's rise to power in 1970.

The regime cultivated a base of support that spanned sectarian and ethnic divisions, but relied on Alawite domination of the security establishment and the suppression of dissent. In 1982, government forces stormed the northern city of Hama to crush a rebellion by the opposition Muslim Brotherhood, killing as many as 20,000 insurgents and civilians.

Bashar al-Assad took power after his father's death in 2000, pledging to liberalize Syria's politics and economy. The first six months of his presidency featured the release of political prisoners, the return of exiled dissidents, and open discussion of the country's problems. In February 2001, however, the regime abruptly halted this so-called Damascus Spring. Leading reformists were arrested and sentenced to lengthy prison terms, while others faced constant surveillance and intimidation by the secret police. Economic reform fell by the wayside, and Syria under Bashar al-Assad proved resistant to political change.

Reinvigorated by the toppling of Iraq's Baathist regime in 2003, Syria's secular and Islamist dissidents began cooperating and pushing for the release of political prisoners, the cancellation of the state of emergency, and the legalization of opposition parties. Syria's Kurdish minority erupted into eight days of rioting in March 2004. At least 30 people were killed as security forces suppressed the riots and made some 2,000 arrests.

Despite hints that sweeping political reforms would be drafted at a major Baath Party conference in 2005, no substantial measures were taken. In October 2005, representatives of all three segments of the opposition—the Islamists, the Kurds, and secular liberals—signed the Damascus Declaration for Democratic National Change (DDDNC), which called for the country's leaders to step down and endorsed a broad set of liberal democratic principles.

In May 2006, exiled opposition leaders announced the creation of the National Salvation Front (NSF) to bring about regime change. Also that month, a number of Syrian political and human rights activists signed the Beirut-Damascus Declaration, which called for a change in Syrian-Lebanese relations and the recognition of Lebanese sovereignty. Many of the signatories were subsequently detained or sentenced to prison as part of a renewed crackdown that reversed the previous partial leniency on personal freedom.

In 2007, al-Assad won another term as president with 97.6 percent of the vote. In results that were similarly preordained by the electoral framework, the ruling Baath-dominated coalition won the majority of seats in that year's parliamentary and municipal polls. Meanwhile, supporters of the DDDNC formed governing bodies for their alliance and renewed their activities, prompting a government crackdown that extended into 2008.

In 2009, the NSF fell apart, largely because the Muslim Brotherhood, in deference to the Syrian government's support for the Palestinian militant group Hamas, suspended its opposition activities in the aftermath of Israel's offensive in the Gaza Strip in January. One prominent secular NSF member, Bashar al-Sha'i, quit the opposition in April and returned to Syria after publicly apologizing to the government in July, and another DDDNC member, Michel Kilo, was released from prison at the end of his three-year sentence in May. Other leading human rights figures within Syria were jailed or faced new charges of "weakening national morale" or "spreading false information" during the year. Separately, al-Assad reshuffled his government in April, replacing five ministers and creating an environment ministry.

Syria's diplomatic isolation eased somewhat in 2009. High-ranking officials from the United States met with Syrian leaders for the first time since 2005, Washington pledged to return an ambassador to Damascus, and Saudi Arabian diplomats held talks with Syrian officials. However, the U.S. ambassador had not been named by year's end, the United States renewed existing sanctions on Syria, and progress on an Association Agreement with the European Union stalled.

Political Rights and Civil Liberties: Syria is not an electoral democracy. Under the 1973 constitution, the president is nominated by the ruling Baath Party and approved by popular referendum for seven-year terms. In practice, these referendums are orchestrated by the regime, as are elections for the 250-seat, unicameral People's Council, whose members serve four-year terms and hold little independent legislative power. Almost all power rests in the executive branch.

The only legal political parties are the Baath Party and its several small coalition partners in the ruling National Progressive Front (NPF). Independent candidates, who are heavily vetted and closely allied with the regime, are permitted to contest about a third of the People's Council seats, meaning two-thirds are reserved for the NPF.

Regime officials and their families benefit from a range of illicit economic activities. Syria is slowly opening itself economically by removing heavy tariffs and eliminating subsidies, but these limited reforms benefit a small minority at the expense of average citizens. Corruption is widespread, and bribery is often necessary to navigate the bureaucracy. Syria was ranked 126 out of 180 countries surveyed in Transparency International's 2009 Corruption Perceptions Index.

Freedom of expression is heavily restricted. Vaguely worded articles of the penal code, the Emergency Law, and a 2001 Publications Law criminalize the publication of material that harms national unity, tarnishes the image of the state, or threatens the "goals of the revolution." Many journalists, writers, and intellectuals have been arrested under these laws. Apart from a handful of radio stations with nonnews formats, all broadcast media are state owned. However, satellite dishes are common, giving most Syrians access to foreign broadcasts. More than a dozen privately owned newspapers and magazines have sprouted up in recent years, and criticism of government policy is tolerated, provided it is nuanced and does not criticize the president. The 2001 press law permits the authorities to arbitrarily deny or revoke publishing licenses and compels private print outlets to submit all material to government censors. It also imposes punishment on reporters who do not reveal their sources in response to government requests. Since the Kurdish protests in 2004, the government has cracked down on journalists calling for the expansion of Kurdish or regional rights; the information minister fired a newspaper editor in Homs in August 2009 for publishing a column about regional identity.

Though a ban on the Saudi-owned, pan-Arab daily *Al-Hayat* was lifted in 2009, journalists in Syria continued to face harassment and intimidation in the form of short jail terms, travel bans, and confiscations of their notes. The Damascus office of the Dubai-based television station Al-Mashreq was closed in July for security reasons; 15 employees were held for questioning. Ibrahim al-Jaban, a prominent television journalist known for touching on taboo subjects, was banned from Syrian television in August.

Syrians access the internet only through state-run servers, which block more than 160 sites associated with the opposition, Kurdish politics, Islamic organizations, human rights, and certain foreign news services, particularly those in Lebanon. Social-networking and video-sharing websites, such as Facebook and YouTube, are also blocked. E-mail is reportedly monitored by intelligence agencies, which often require internet cafe owners to monitor customers. In practice, internet users often find ways around these restrictions, and poor connections and high costs tend to hinder access more effectively than government regulations. The government has been more successful in fostering self-censorship through intimidation; a dozen cyberdissidents are currently imprisoned. In September 2009, blogger Karim Antoine Arabji, who had written about corruption, was sentenced to three years in prison after already serving nearly two years in pretrial detention.

Although the constitution requires that the president be a Muslim, there is no state religion in Syria, and freedom of worship is generally respected. However, the government tightly monitors mosques and controls the appointment of Muslim clergy. All nonworship meetings of religious groups require permits, and religious fund-raising is closely scrutinized. The Alawite minority dominates the officer corps of the security forces.

Academic freedom is heavily restricted. Several private universities have recently been founded, and the extent of academic freedom within them varies. University professors have been dismissed or imprisoned for expressing dissent.

Freedom of assembly is closely circumscribed. Public demonstrations are illegal without official permission, which is typically granted only to progovernment groups. The security services intensified their ban on public and private gatherings in 2006, forbidding any group of five or more people from discussing political and economic topics. This rule has been enforced through surveillance and informant reports. Such activity by the intelligence services has ensured that a culture of self-censorship and fear prevails, and ordinary Syrians are unwilling to discuss politics under most circumstances.

Freedom of association is severely restricted. All nongovernmental organizations must register with the government, which generally denies registration to reformist or human rights groups. Leaders of unlicensed human rights groups have frequently been jailed for publicizing state abuses. Professional syndicates are controlled by the Baath Party, and all labor unions must belong to the General Federation of Trade Unions, a nominally independent grouping that the government uses to control union activity. Strikes in nonagricultural sectors are legal, but they rarely occur.

While the lower courts operate with some independence and generally safeguard defendants' rights, politically sensitive cases are usually tried by the Supreme State Security Court (SSSC), an exceptional tribunal established under emergency law that denies the right to appeal, limits access to legal counsel, tries many cases behind closed doors, and routinely accepts confessions obtained through torture. SSSC judges are appointed by the executive branch, and only the president and interior minister may alter verdicts. The SSSC suspended its operations in late 2008, following riots in Syria's largest prison for political detainees, but reopened its docket in 2009.

The security agencies, which operate independently of the judiciary, routinely extract confessions by torturing suspects and detaining their family members. In 2009, police killed several civilians who were protesting the demolition of illegally constructed homes outside Damascus. The state of emergency in force since 1963 gives security agencies virtually unlimited authority to arrest suspects and hold them incommunicado for prolonged periods without charge. Many of the estimated 2,500 to 3,000 political prisoners in Syria have never been tried. The majority are probably Islamists; those suspected of involvement with the Muslim Brotherhood or radical Islamist groups are regularly detained by the authorities. Possession of recordings or books by clerics whom the regime deems dangerous is often enough for arrest. After release from prison, political activists are often monitored and harassed by security services. The Syrian Human Rights Committee has reported that hundreds of government informants are rewarded for or coerced into writing reports on relatives, friends, and associates who are suspected of involvement in "antiregime" activities.

The Kurdish minority faces severe restrictions on cultural and linguistic expression. The 2001 press law requires that owners and top editors of print publications be Arabs. Some 200,000 Syrian Kurds are deprived of citizenship and are unable to obtain passports, identity cards, or birth certificates, which in turn prevents them from owning land, obtaining government employment, and voting. Suspected Kurdish activists are routinely dismissed from schools and public sector jobs. In 2009, the government made it more difficult to hire noncitizens, resulting in the dismissal of many Kurds. While one demonstration to demand more rights for the Kurdish community was allowed to take place in northern Syria, security forces stopped four demonstrations in February and March, detaining dozens of people and referring some to the judiciary for prosecution. Intelligence services generally monitor Kurdish leaders closely, sometimes excluding them and their families from public sector employment. At least 15 such leaders are barred from leaving Syria.

Opposition figures, human rights activists, and relatives of exiled dissidents are similarly prevented from traveling abroad, and many ordinary Kurds lack the requisite documents to leave the country. Other Syrians are generally allowed greater freedom of movement, residence, and employment.

The government has appointed some women to senior positions, including one of the two vice presidential posts. However, women remain underrepresented, holding 12.4 percent of the seats in the legislature. The government provides women with equal access to education, but many discriminatory laws remain in force. A husband may request that the Interior Ministry block his wife from traveling abroad, and women are generally barred from leaving the country with their children without proof of the father's permission. Violence against women is common, particularly in rural areas. The government imposed two-year minimum prison sentences for killings classified as "honor crimes" in 2009; previously, there had been a maximum one-year sentence. State-run media estimate that there are 40 such killings each year, whereas women's rights groups put the figure at 200. Personal status law for Muslim women is governed by Sharia (Islamic law) and is discriminatory in marriage, divorce, and inheritance matters; church law governs personal status issues for Christians, in some cases barring divorce. A draft personal status law introduced in 2009 was subsequently withdrawn after women's rights activists criticized its content and Christians denounced it as an attempt to take authority away from their respective churches.

Taiwan

Political Rights: 1*
Civil Liberties: 2*
Status: Free

Population: 23,079,000
Capital: Taipei

Ratings Change: Taiwan's political rights rating improved from 2 to 1 due to enforcement of anticorruption laws, including the prosecution of former high-ranking officials. However, the country's civil liberties rating declined from 1 to 2 due to flaws in the protection of criminal defendants' rights and limitations on academic freedom, including passage of a law restraining scholars at public educational facilities from participating in certain political activities.

Ten-Year Ratings Timeline For Year Under Review (Political Rights, Civil Liberties, Status)

2000	2001	2002	2003	2004	2005	2006	2007	2008	2009
1,2F	1,2F	2,2F	2,2F	2,1F	1,1F	2,1F	2,1F	2,1F	1,2F

Overview: Former president Chen Shui-bian of the Democratic Progressive Party was sentenced to life in prison on corruption charges in September 2009, though some observers raised concerns over flaws in the handling of his and other corruption cases. Following criticism of the government's response to Typhoon Morakot, Prime Minister Liu Chao-shiuan resigned in September. The Kuomintang government continued to improve relations with China during the year, leading to Taiwanese participation in UN-affiliated institutions for the first time since 1971. However, there were also growing concerns over restrictions on free expression, including limitations on academic freedom and pressure to limit criticism of Taiwanese and Chinese government policy.

Taiwan, also referred to sometimes as the Republic of China (ROC), became home to the Chinese nationalist Kuomintang (KMT) government-in-exile in 1949. Although the island is independent in all but name, the People's Republic of China (PRC) considers it a renegade province and has threatened to take military action if de jure independence is declared.

Taiwan's transition to democracy began in 1987, when the KMT ended 38 years of martial law. In 1988, Lee Teng-hui became the first native Taiwanese president, breaking the mainland emigres' stranglehold on politics. The media were liberalized and opposition political parties legalized in 1989. Lee oversaw Taiwan's first full multiparty legislative elections in 1991–92 and the first direct presidential election in 1996.

Chen Shui-bian's victory in the 2000 presidential race, as a candidate of the proindependence Democratic Progressive Party (DPP), ended 55 years of KMT rule. Chen narrowly won reelection in March 2004, but the KMT-led opposition retained its majority in the Legislative Yuan (LY) in parliamentary elections later that year, and political gridlock between the executive and legislative branches continued.

The KMT secured an overwhelming majority in the January 2008 legislative elections, taking 81 of 113 seats. The DPP took 27, and the remainder went to independents and smaller parties. The polls were the first to be held under a new electoral system. The fact that the KMT and DPP respectively secured 72 percent and 24 percent of the seats after winning 51 percent and 37 percent of the votes prompted some calls for a reexamination of the reforms. Taipei mayor Ma Ying-jeou of the KMT won the March presidential election, defeating the DPP's Frank Hsieh by a 16-point margin. Both elections were deemed generally free and fair, and an improvement over the 2004 polls, by international observers. They also marked the island's second peaceful, democratic transfer of power. The DPP's poor showing was attributed to voters' economic concerns, frustration at political gridlock, wariness of the DPP's proindependence policies, and recent corruption scandals involving Chen and other top officials.

Chen was indicted in December 2008, after his immunity had expired, and in September 2009, he was sentenced to life in prison for embezzlement, money laundering, and bribery. Some observers viewed the case as a milestone for the rule of law. However, there were also concerns raised over irregularities and possible political bias, including Chen's detention before and during trial, prosecutorial leaks to the media, and disciplinary charges against his defense counsel.

The KMT government's popularity was hurt during 2009 by the effects of the global economic downturn, although the economy had begun to recover by year's end. Separately, Prime Minister Liu Chao-shiuan was replaced by former KMT secretary general Wu Den-yih in September, amid a broader cabinet reshuffle after the government drew criticism for its slow response to Typhoon Morakot. The natural disaster caused over 500 deaths and hundreds of millions of dollars in damage in August.

The DPP won an important parliamentary by-election in September, giving it a quarter of the LY and increased oversight powers, including the ability to petition the Constitutional Court for interpretations of the validity of official policies and actions. The KMT retained a majority of the contested posts in December local elections, but the DPP made notable gains.

The Ma administration continued its policy of establishing closer relations with the PRC government in 2009. Bilateral talks led to agreements on mutual judicial and law enforcement assistance, loosened Taiwanese restrictions on mainland investment, and the removal of PRC objections to Taiwan's participation—with observer status under the name "Chinese Taipei"—in the World Health Assembly. This enabled Taiwanese representatives to partake in a UN specialized agency event for the first time since 1971.

Though many Taiwanese supported improved economic ties with China, critics argued that the administration was conceding elements of Taiwan's sovereignty, moving too quickly, and acting with minimal transparency. Several incidents during 2009 stoked fears that growing economic and diplomatic reliance on the PRC would increase pressure to self-censor on issues Beijing deemed sensitive or important. For example, the government in September refused to issue a visa to Rebiya Kadeer, a prominent advocate for the rights of China's Uighur minority. Meanwhile, Beijing maintained an aggressive legal and military stance on the prospect of eventual Taiwanese independence; an estimated 1,300 missiles remained aimed at the island at year's end.

Political Rights
and Civil Liberties:
Taiwan is an electoral democracy. The 1946 constitution, adopted while the KMT was in power on the mainland, created a unique structure with five branches of government (*yuan*). The president, who is directly elected for up to two four-year terms, wields executive power, appoints the prime minister, and can dissolve the legislature. The Executive Yuan, or cabinet, consists of ministers appointed by the president on the recommendation of the prime minister. The prime minister is responsible to the national legislature (Legislative Yuan), which, under constitutional amendments that took effect in 2008, consists of 113 members serving four-year terms; 73 are elected in single-member districts, and 34 are chosen through nationwide proportional representation. The six remaining members are chosen by indigenous people. The three other branches of government are the judiciary (Judicial Yuan), a watchdog body (Control Yuan), and a branch responsible for civil service examinations (Examination Yuan).

The two main political parties are the proindependence DPP and the Chinese nationalist KMT, which hold a combined 108 of 113 legislative seats and dominate the political landscape. Opposition parties are generally able to function freely, as indicated by the DPP's relatively strong performance in the December 2009 local elections. Nevertheless, there were credible reports during the year of increased political pressure on government critics and individuals whose activities could displease the Chinese authorities.

Though significantly less pervasive than in the past, corruption remains a feature of political life and an ongoing problem in the security forces. In 2009, the authorities took additional measures to enforce anticorruption laws, resulting in the prosecution of former top officials and the removal of four legislators from office due to vote buying. Former president Chen Shui-bian and his wife were sentenced in September to life in prison on charges of embezzlement and money laundering; an appeal was pending at year's end. The authorities also launched investigations of over 200 candidates for alleged vote buying in the December local elections. Though several KMT members were investigated or punished during the year, some observers raised concerns about selective prosecution of DPP politicians. Among other high-profile cases, a retired high-ranking military officer was indicted in April on bribery and blackmail charges, and five police officers were convicted in December of accepting bribes from casino operators, receiving terms ranging from 12 to 20 years in prison. Taiwan was ranked 37 out of 180 countries surveyed in Transparency International's 2009 Corruption Perceptions Index.

In March 2009, Taiwan ratified two UN human rights treaties—the International Covenant on Civil and Political Rights and the International Covenant on Economic, Social, and Cultural Rights—and passed an implementing law allowing two years to bring relevant regulations and practice into line with the treaties. The United Nations in June refused to accept formally the ratifications, citing the PRC as the only recognized representative of China.

The Taiwanese media reflect a diversity of views and report aggressively on government policies and corruption allegations. Given that most Taiwanese can access about 100 cable television stations, the state's influence on the media is, on balance, minimal. However, reforms and personnel changes at publicly owned media since 2008 have raised concerns about politicization. A former spokesperson for

President Ma Ying-jeou's electoral campaign was appointed as deputy president of the Central News Agency (CNA) in late 2008, and CNA staff reported receiving directives to alter certain content. Local and international observers noted that criticism of the government in subsequent CNA coverage was markedly toned down. In 2009, legislation requiring government approval of Public Television Service programming was dropped after public protests. However, local press freedom advocates and the Control Yuan criticized subsequent government measures to expand the service's board and replace its management.

Actions by private media owners, economic pressures resulting from the global financial crisis, and potential PRC influence on free expression were also of concern in 2009. Most private news outlets are seen as sympathetic to one of the two main political parties. Observers reported an increase in paid news placements in print and electronic media during the year. After a businessman with mainland commercial interests purchased the China Times Group in late 2008, incidents raised concerns of increased editorial pressure to soften criticism of the Ma administration and Beijing; in June 2009, the company threatened to sue several journalists and press freedom advocates for defamation over criticism of its actions in a dispute with the National Communications Commission. In September, the Kaohsiung Film Festival came under pressure—albeit unsuccessful—to not screen a documentary about exiled Uighur rights activist Rebiya Kadeer for fear that it could indirectly harm growing tourism from the mainland. There are generally no restrictions on the internet, which was accessed by over 65 percent of the population in 2009.

Taiwanese of all faiths can worship freely. Religious organizations that choose to register with the government receive tax-exempt status. Despite pressure from Beijing, the government in September 2009 allowed the Tibetan spiritual leader, the Dalai Lama, to visit the island and participate in memorial services for victims of Typhoon Morakot.

Although Taiwanese educators can generally write and lecture freely, the ability of scholars to engage in political activism outside the classroom came under pressure in 2009. The LY in July 2009 passed the Act Governing the Administrative Impartiality of Public Officials, which contained provisions restraining scholars at public academic facilities from participating in certain political activities. In addition, two professors known for their involvement in human rights groups faced prosecution for organizing peaceful protests surrounding the 2008 visit of a Chinese envoy; the cases were still pending at year's end.

Freedom of assembly is generally respected, and several large-scale demonstrations took place during 2009. Nevertheless, adherents of the Falun Gong spiritual movement, which is persecuted in China, occasionally faced pressure from local authorities to limit their protests at sites frequented by Chinese tourists. Unlike during his 2008 visit, demonstrations during Chinese envoy Chen Yunlin's December 2009 trip to Taiwan passed without significant violence between police and protesters. In May, the Control Yuan urged disciplinary measures against Taipei's police chief and precinct captain for police misconduct during the 2008 clashes, but some observers criticized the body's decision not to impeach any officials. The Parade and Assembly Law includes restrictions on demonstration locations and permit requirements for outdoor meetings. Although permits are generally granted, at least 26 people were under investigation in 2009 for allegedly failing to obtain a permit or obey police orders to disperse. All civic organizations must register with the government, though registration is freely granted. Nongovernmental organizations (NGOs) focusing on human rights, social welfare, and the environment are active and operate without harassment.

Trade unions are independent, and most workers enjoy freedom of association. However, government employees and defense-industry workers are barred from joining unions or bargaining collectively. According to the U.S. State Department's 2009 human rights report, unions may be dissolved if their activities "disturb public order," while other restrictions undermine collective bargaining and make it difficult to strike legally. The number of labor disputes increased in 2009 amid the economic downturn. Taiwan's 350,000 foreign workers are not covered by the Labor Standards Law or represented by unions, and many decline to report abuses for fear of deportation.

The judiciary is independent, and trials are generally fair. However, prominent cases in 2009 exposed flaws in the protection of criminal defendants' rights. Several suspects were detained for extended periods prior to conviction, including former president Chen, who was held in custody throughout the year as his trial proceeded. Legal experts also noted other irregularities in Chen's case, including government efforts to pursue disciplinary measures against his counsel for comments to the media. Prosecutorial leaks to the media continued during the year, sullying defendants' reputations before trial and conviction. The legal system partially responded to shortcomings in Chen's case, as the Grand Council of Justices ruled in January that prosecutors' recording of meetings between the defendant and his counsel was unconstitutional.

Police largely respect the ban on arbitrary detention, and suspects are allowed attorneys during interrogations to prevent abuse. However, three defendants in the high-profile Lu Cheng murder case, who were allegedly tortured in the 1980s to extract a confession, continued to be detained after 22 years as appeals proceeded. They remained in custody at year's end following a May 2009 High Court ruling. An estimated 187 criminal cases in Taiwan have lasted over 10 years. Although no executions have been carried out since 2005, 44 people remained on death row at year's end. Searches without warrants are allowed only in particular circumstances, and a 1999 law imposes strict punishments for illicit wiretapping.

The constitution provides for the equality of all citizens. Apart from the unresolved issue of ownership of ancestral lands, the rights of indigenous people are protected by law. Six LY seats are reserved for indigenous people, giving them representation that exceeds their share of the population. Thousands of indigenous people were left homeless by Typhoon Morakot, leading to their resettlement in nearby areas.

Taiwanese law does not allow for the granting of asylum or refugee status. However, amendments to the Immigration Act in 2009 facilitated the granting of residency certificates to over 100 Tibetans and 400 descendants of soldiers left behind in Thailand and Burma in 1949. In December, the Executive Yuan passed a refugee draft bill; it had yet to be debated by the legislature at year's end.

With the exception of civil servants and military personnel traveling to China, freedom of movement is generally unrestricted. Direct cross-strait air travel has expanded significantly since 2008, though PRC tourists are required to travel in chaperoned groups within Taiwan.

Taiwanese women face private sector job discrimination and lower pay than men on average. After the 2008 elections, women held 30 percent of the LY seats. Rape and domestic violence remain problems despite government programs to protect women and the work of numerous NGOs to improve women's rights. Although authorities can pursue such cases without the victims formally pressing charges, cultural norms inhibit many women from reporting the crimes. Taiwan is both a source and destination for trafficked women. In January 2009, the legislature passed a law that specifically criminalized sex and labor trafficking while increasing penalties for such offenses.

Tajikistan

Political Rights: 6
Civil Liberties: 5
Status: Not Free

Population: 7,450,000
Capital: Dushanbe

Ten-Year Ratings Timeline For Year Under Review (Political Rights, Civil Liberties, Status)

2000	2001	2002	2003	2004	2005	2006	2007	2008	2009
6,6NF	6,6NF	6,5NF	6,5NF	6,5NF	6,5NF	6,5NF	6,5NF	6,5NF	6,5NF

Overview: President Emomali Rahmon continued to tighten controls over religious practice in 2009. The promotion of two of Rahmon's children to government posts exposed increasing nepotism within his regime. The economy remained stalled, as remittances from Tajiks working abroad fell, and an audit revealed $1 billion in irregularities at the National Bank.

Former Communist Party leader Rakhmon Nabiyev was elected president of Tajikistan after the country declared independence from the Soviet Union in 1991. Long-simmering, clan-based tensions, combined with various anti-Communist and Islamist movements, soon plunged the country into a five-year civil war. In September 1992, Communist hard-liners forced Nabiyev's resignation; he was replaced later that year by Emomali Rakhmonov, a leading Communist Party member.

Rakhmonov was elected president in November 1994, after most opposition candidates either boycotted or were prevented from competing in the poll. Similarly, progovernment candidates won the 1995 parliamentary elections amid a boycott by the United Tajik Opposition (UTO), a coalition of secular and Islamic groups that had emerged as the main force fighting against Rakhmonov's government.

Following a December 1996 ceasefire, Rakhmonov and UTO leader Said Abdullo Nuri signed a formal peace agreement in 1997. The accord called for the merging of opposition forces into the regular army, granted an amnesty for UTO members, provided for the UTO to be allotted 30 percent of senior government posts, and established a 26-member National Reconciliation Commission, with seats evenly divided between the government and the UTO.

A September 1999 referendum that permitted the formation of religion-based political parties paved the way for the legal operation of the Islamic opposition, including the Islamic Renaissance Party (IRP). The referendum also extended the president's term from five to seven years. In November, Rakhmonov was reelected with a reported 97 percent of the vote in a poll that was criticized by international observers for widespread irregularities.

In February 2000 parliamentary elections, Rakhmonov's People's Democratic Party (PDP) received nearly 65 percent of the vote. Although the participation of six parties provided some political pluralism, a joint monitoring mission by the Organization for Security and Cooperation in Europe (OSCE) and the United Nations cited serious problems.

After the elections, the National Reconciliation Commission was formally disbanded, and a UN observer mission withdrew in May 2000. However, important provisions of the peace accord remained unimplemented, with demobilization of opposition factions incomplete and the government failing to meet the 30 percent quota for UTO members in senior government posts.

A 2003 constitutional referendum cleared a path for Rakhmonov to remain in office until 2020. The PDP easily won 2005 parliamentary elections, taking 52 of 63 seats in the lower house. OSCE monitors concluded that, "despite some improvement over previous elections, large-scale irregularities were evident." In the run-up to the polls, a number of Rakhmonov's prominent former allies were jailed, often on dubious charges.

Also in 2005, Russian border guards who had long patrolled the frontier with Afghanistan completed their withdrawal. However, a Russian army division that had been in place since the Soviet period maintained its permanent presence in the country.

Rakhmonov won the November 2006 presidential election with more than 70 percent of the vote, although the OSCE pointed in its report to lackluster campaigning and a general absence of real competition. The president broadened his influence to the cultural sphere in 2007, de-Russifying his surname to "Rahmon" in March and signing legislation in May to establish spending limits on birthday and wedding celebrations.

The severe winter between 2007 and 2008 power outages and demonstrations; in February 2008, the United Nations appealed for US$25 million in emergency assistance for the country to stave off famine. Economic hardships continued in 2009 amid falling remittances from workers in Russia and Kazakhstan.

Tajikistan's generally good relations with Russia suffered somewhat after an October 2009 Tajik law stripped the Russian language of its status as the language of interethnic communication. Ties with the United States warmed, as Tajikistan agreed to allow the overland transport of nonmilitary supplies to support U.S. and NATO operations in Afghanistan. Uzbekistan's late 2009 decision to withdraw from the unified Central Asian power grid amid tension with Tajikistan over water usage raised the prospect of severe electricity shortages in Tajikistan.

Political Rights and Civil Liberties: Tajikistan is not an electoral democracy. The 1994 constitution provides for a strong, directly elected president, who enjoys broad authority to appoint and dismiss officials. A full-time, bicameral parliament was created in 1999, while amendments in 2003 allowed current president Emomali Rahmon to serve two additional seven-year terms beyond the 2006 election. In the Assembly of Representatives (lower chamber), 63 members are elected by popular vote to serve five-year terms. In the 33-seat National Assembly (upper chamber), 25 members are chosen by local assemblies, and 8 are appointed by the president, all for five-year terms. Elections are neither free nor fair.

Patronage networks and regional affiliations are central to political life, with officials from the president's native Kulyob region dominant in government. In 2009, Rahmon's daughter Ozoda was appointed deputy foreign minister, while his son became deputy head of the Youth Union.

Rahmon's PDP is the ruling political party. Secular opposition parties are weak. The August 2006 death of the IRP's widely respected leader, Said Abdullo Nuri, further reduced the limited influence of the only legal religion-based party in Central Asia.

Corruption is reportedly pervasive. Members of the president's family allegedly maintain extensive business interests. In 2008, the National Bank revealed that it falsified its reserves to secure a US$48 million loan from the International Monetary Fund. An April 2009 audit by Ernst & Young revealed US$1 billion in irregularities in the National Bank's accounting, though it remains unclear whether these revelations sparked any meaningful reform. Tajikistan was ranked 158 out of 180 countries surveyed in Transparency International's 2009 Corruption Perceptions Index.

Despite constitutional guarantees of freedom of speech and the press, independent journalists face harassment and intimidation, and the penal code criminalizes defamation. The government controls most printing presses, newsprint supplies, and broadcasting facilities, leaving little room for independent news and analysis. Most television stations are state owned or only nominally independent, and the process of obtaining broadcast licenses is cumbersome. In August 2007, the president signed legislation that criminalized libel on the internet and allowed courts to sentence journalists to up to two years in prison for libel in print publications. In April 2009, Rahmon warned that "enemies" were using the internet to undermine his rule and urged mobilization against them.

The government has imposed increasing restrictions on religion in recent years in this predominantly Muslim country. In 2005, the minister of education banned the wearing of the *hijab* (headscarf) in schools and higher educational institutions. In 2007, the authorities shut down large numbers of unauthorized mosques and instituted more restrictive rules for licensing religious leaders. In January 2009, the Supreme Court banned Salafi Islam, a conservative movement. In March, a new law limited religious rituals to state-approved venues and banned the promotion of any religion except traditional Hanafi Islam. Reports indicate that conservative religiosity is on the rise despite official restrictions.

The government, at times, limits freedoms of assembly and association. Local government approval is required to hold public demonstrations, and officials reportedly refuse to grant permission in virtually all cases, rendering gatherings illegal. All nongovernmental organizations (NGOs) must register with the Ministry of Justice. Citizens have the legal right to form and join trade unions and to bargain collectively, but trade unions are largely subservient to the authorities and indifferent to workers' interests.

The judiciary lacks independence. Many judges are poorly trained and inexperienced, and bribery is reportedly widespread. Police often conduct arbitrary arrests and beat detainees to extract confessions. Conditions in prisons—which are overcrowded and disease-ridden—are often life-threatening. In June 2009, Deputy Justice Minister Rustam Mengliyev called the penitentiary system "closed," and in August, the authorities restricted visits by international representatives.

Tajikistan is a major conduit for the smuggling of narcotics from Afghanistan to Russia and Europe. A side effect has been an increase in drug addiction within Tajikistan, as well as a rise in the number of cases of HIV/AIDS.

In April 2008, Dushanbe Mayor Mahmadsaid Ubaydulloyev asked city residents to "donate" money from their salaries to fund the Roghun hydropower plant, a move critics described as state-sponsored extortion (although it was unclear how many people were affected). President Rahmon made a similar call in December 2009.

Sexual harassment, traditional discrimination, and violence against women, including spousal abuse, are reportedly common, but cases are rarely investigated. Reports indicate that women sometimes face societal pressure to wear headscarves, even though official policy discourages the practice. A November 2009 report by Amnesty International called domestic violence in Tajikistan "widespread." Despite some government efforts to address human trafficking, Tajikistan remains a source and transit country for persons trafficked for prostitution. Child labor, particularly on cotton farms, also remains a problem.

Tanzania

Political Rights: 4
Civil Liberties: 3
Status: Partly Free

Population: 43,739,000
Capital: Dar-es-Salaam

Ten-Year Ratings Timeline For Year Under Review (Political Rights, Civil Liberties, Status)

2000	2001	2002	2003	2004	2005	2006	2007	2008	2009
4,4PF	4,4PF	4,3PF	4,3PF	4,3PF	4,3PF	4,3PF	4,3PF	4,3PF	4,3PF

Overview:
In 2009, the ruling Chama Cha Mapinduzi (CCM) party secured overwhelming victories in local elections. Relations between the Zanzibar opposition and the CCM remained tense throughout the year. Meanwhile, Tanzania's economy suffered from the impact of the global recession.

Three years after mainland Tanganyika gained independence from Britain in 1961, the Zanzibar archipelago—consisting of Zanzibar, Pemba, and a number of smaller islands—merged with Tanganyika to become the United Republic of Tanzania. The ruling Chama Cha Mapinduzi (CCM) party, under longtime president Julius Nyerere, dominated the country's political life. Nyerere's collectivist economic philosophy—known in Swahili as *ujaama*—promoted a sense of community and nationality, but also resulted in significant economic dislocation and decline. During Nyerere's tenure, Tanzania played an important role as a "frontline state" in the international response to white-controlled regimes in southern Africa. Nyerere's successor, Ali Hassan Mwinyi, was president from 1985 to 1995 and oversaw a carefully controlled political liberalization process.

A CCM landslide victory in the 1995 parliamentary elections was seriously tainted by poor organization of the electoral process, fraud, and administrative irregularities; voting in Zanzibar was plainly fraudulent. The 2000 legislative and presidential polls showed modest improvements over the 1995 vote. However, the opposition Civic United Front (CUF) and independent observers charged that the CCM had engaged in fraud to retain power. Benjamin Mkapa, who first took office in 1995, was reelected as president.

Rioting in Zanzibar in 2001 resulted in the deaths of more than 40 people. The CCM and the CUF reached a reconciliation agreement designed to resolve the political crisis, but implementation of the agreement was delayed, and continues to strain relations with the mainland. The ongoing failure of the authorities and parties to resolve the Zanzibar crisis in recent years has negatively affected perceptions of Tanzania's political and governance system as a whole.

In presidential and parliamentary elections in December 2005, Foreign Minister Jakaya Kikwete, a CCM stalwart, was elected president with approximately 80 percent of the vote. The CCM captured 206 of 232 directly elected parliament seats. There were incidents of violence in the run-up to the polls in Zanzibar, and the postelection atmosphere was tense, as the CUF once again accused the victorious CCM of electoral fraud. Intermittent negotiations failed to resolve complaints about the 2005 elections in Zanzibar. Four opposition parties sought to form a united front for the next general elections, scheduled for late 2010, despite a constitutional prohibition on party coalitions.

In October 2009, the CCM won overwhelming victories in local elections. However, relations between the Zanzibar opposition and the CCM remained tense. Meanwhile, negotiations to legitimate the 2005 elections or prepare for the 2010 elections remained deadlocked.

Tanzania is one of the poorest countries in the world, with an annual per capita income of approximately US$1,200. According to the International Monetary Fund, the global recession has played a significant role in reducing GDP growth from over 7 percent in 2008 to about 5 percent in 2009.

Political Rights and Civil Liberties: Tanzania is not an electoral democracy. Elections have consistently been marred by widespread allegations of improprieties that largely benefit the CCM. Executive power rests with the president, who is elected by direct popular vote for a maximum of two five-year terms. Legislative power is held by a unicameral National Assembly, the Bunge, which currently has 323 members serving five-year terms. Of these, 232 are directly elected in single-seat constituencies; 75 are women chosen by the political parties according to their representation in the Bunge; 10 are appointed by the president; and 5 are members of the Zanzibar legislature, whose 50 deputies are elected to five-year terms. The attorney general is also an ex-officio member of the Bunge.

Although opposition parties were legalized in 1992, the ruling CCM continues to control the country's political life. The constitution prohibits political coalitions, which has impeded efforts by other parties to contest seriously the CCM's dominance. Opposition politics are highly fractious; the opposition fielded nine separate presidential candidates in the 2005 polls. The opposition CUF, based in Zanzibar, has sought to establish significant support on the Tanzanian mainland. To register in Tanzania, political parties must not be formed on religious, ethnic, or regional bases and cannot oppose the union of Zanzibar and the mainland. Parties with parliamentary representation receive government subsidies, but they criticize the low level of funding and the formula by which it is allocated.

Corruption remains a serious problem. A 2007 anticorruption bill gave the government greater power to target abuses in procurement and money laundering, but critics claim it is insufficient. In 2008, several scandals led to the resignation of the prime minister and three cabinet ministers. Tanzania was ranked 126 out of 180 countries surveyed in Transparency International's 2009 Corruption Perceptions Index.

Although the constitution provides for freedom of speech, it does not specifically guarantee freedom of the press. Print and electronic media are active, but their reach is largely limited to major urban areas. While the country has more than 50 regular newspapers, including 17 dailies, the government is allowed to ban newspapers without judicial recourse. The growth of the broadcast media has been hindered by a lack of capital investment, both public and private. However, a number of independent television and private FM radio stations have gone on the air in recent years. The number of journalists has increased from just 230 in 1991 to more than 4,000, according to the 2008 Media Sustainability Index, but journalists work under very difficult conditions with little compensation. Internet access, while limited to urban areas, is growing.

Press freedom rights in Zanzibar are constrained by its semiautonomous government, which has not permitted private broadcasters or newspapers. However, many islanders receive mainland broadcasts and read the mainland press. The Zanzibari government often reacts to media criticism by accusing the press of being a "threat to national unity."

Freedom of religion is generally respected in Tanzania, and relations between the various faiths are mainly peaceful. In recent years, however, religious tensions have increased. The Zanzibari government appoints a mufti, a professional jurist who interprets Islamic law, to oversee Muslim organizations. Some Muslims have been critical of this law, arguing that it represents excessive government interference in the exercise of religion. Academic freedom is respected in the country.

The constitution guarantees freedoms of assembly and association. However, these rights are not always respected, particularly in Zanzibar, where on several occasions in 2009, authorities either banned demonstrations or arrested peaceful protestors. Organizers of political events are required to obtain permission from the police. Many nongovernmental organizations (NGOs) are active, and some have influenced the public-policy process. However, some observers have critiqued flaws in a 2002 NGO act, including compulsory registration backed by criminal sanctions, lack of appeal to the courts, alignment of NGO activities with government plans, and the prohibition of national networks and coalitions of NGOs.

Less than 5 percent of the labor force is unionized, and workers' rights are limited. Essential workers are barred from striking, and other workers are restricted by complex notification and mediation requirements. In recent years, there have been sporadic strikes and protests by public sector employees over lack of pay. According to the International Trade Union Confederation, workers are commonly dismissed for involvement in trade union activity. Strikes are often declared illegal, and according to the International Confederation of Free Trade Unions, Zanzibar has outlawed strikes completely.

Tanzania's judiciary has displayed some signs of autonomy after decades of subservience to the one-party CCM regime, but it remains subject to considerable political influence. Arrest and pretrial detention rules are often ignored. Prisons suffer from harsh conditions, including overcrowding and safety and health concerns, and police abuse is common. Crime remains a significant concern despite low levels of violence. Narcotics trafficking is a growing problem, especially given the challenge of controlling Tanzania's borders.

The 2002 Prevention of Terrorism Act has been criticized by NGOs for its inconsistencies and anomalies. Acts of terrorism include attacks on a person's life, kidnapping, and serious damage to property. The law gives the police and immigration officials sweeping powers to arrest suspected illegal immigrants or anyone thought to have links with terrorists.

Compared with many of its neighbors, Tanzania has enjoyed tranquil relations among its many ethnic groups. The presence of refugees from conflicts in Burundi, Rwanda, and the Democratic Republic of Congo, however, has in the past raised tensions; according to the 2009 World Refugee Survey, approximately 320,000 refugees remain in the country. The final group of Burundian refugees in Tanzania who fled in 1972 returned home in October 2009.

Women's rights are guaranteed by the constitution, but are not uniformly protected. Traditional or Islamic customs that discriminate against women prevail in family law, especially in rural areas and in Zanzibar, and women enjoy fewer educational and economic opportunities than men. Domestic violence against women is reportedly common and rarely prosecuted. Nevertheless, women are relatively well represented in parliament, with over 30 percent of seats. Human rights groups have sought laws to bar forced marriages, which are most common among Tanzania's coastal peoples. Albinos are subject to violence and discrimination, with more than 50 suspected murders since 2006. In September 2009, four men were sentenced to death for murdering an albino boy, the first albino murder convictions in Tanzania's history.

Thailand

Political Rights: 5
Civil Liberties: 4
Status: Partly Free

Population: 67,764,000
Capital: Bangkok

Ten-Year Ratings Timeline For Year Under Review (Political Rights, Civil Liberties, Status)

2000	2001	2002	2003	2004	2005	2006	2007	2008	2009
2,3F	2,3F	2,3F	2,3F	2,3F	3,3PF	7,4NF	6,4PF	5,4PF	5,4PF

Overview: The government of Prime Minister Abhisit Vejjajiva continued to rule without a voter mandate in 2009, having taken power in late 2008 following a court decision to dissolve the ruling People's Power Party (PPP). Abhisit struggled during the year to maintain control over his coalition and deflect corruption charges against his allies. Meanwhile, deposed prime minister Thaksin Shinawatra continued to advocate the overthrow of the government from abroad, and a PPP-aligned protest movement mounted antigovernment demonstrations throughout the year. The protests turned violent in April, prompting Abhisit to declare emergency rule in Bangkok for nearly two weeks. Also in 2009, the government dramatically increased its coercive use of lese majeste laws to curb freedom of expression and political speech.

Known as Siam until 1939, Thailand was the only Southeast Asian country to avoid European colonial rule. A 1932 coup transformed the kingdom into a constitutional monarchy, but Thailand endured multiple military coups, constitutional overhauls, and popular uprisings over the next six decades. The army dominated the political scene during this period, with intermittent bouts of unstable civilian government. Under the leadership of General Prem Tinsulanonda in the 1980s, the country underwent a rapid economic expansion and a gradual transition toward democratic rule. The military seized power again in 1991, but Thailand's revered monarch, King Bhumipol Adulyadej, intervened to appoint a civilian prime minister in 1992. Fresh elections held in September of that year ushered in a 14-year period of elected civilian leadership.

The Asian financial crisis of 1997 sparked street protests by middle-class Thais in Bangkok against corruption and economic mismanagement. The parliament voted out the existing government and returned Democrat Party (DP) leader Chuan Leekpai, a former prime minister with a clean reputation, to the premiership. Lawmakers also approved a reformist constitution, which created a fully bicameral legislature with a directly elected Senate, strengthened executive authority, and promoted transparency by establishing independent election and anticorruption agencies.

Thaksin Shinawatra, a former deputy prime minister who built his fortune in telecommunications, unseated Chuan in the 2001 elections. Thaksin and his Thai Rak Thai (TRT, or Thais Love Thais) party mobilized voters in the north, northeast, and rural areas in part by criticizing the government for favoring urban, middle-class Thais.

As prime minister, Thaksin won praise for pursuing populist economic policies designed to stimulate aggregate demand. However, critics accused him and his government of undercutting the constitution, and he faced several serious corruption charges and investigations. Human rights groups also condemned Thaksin for media suppression and a violent counternarcotics campaign that resulted in at least 2,500 killings in a three-month period in 2003.

In 2004, separatist violence increased in Thailand's four southernmost provinces, home to most of the country's four million Muslims. Thaksin mounted a hardline response, and the provinces of Narathiwat, Yala, and Pattani were placed under martial law that year. The government was accused of human rights abuses in its effort to put down the insurgency, with two cases in particular, known as the Krue Se and Tak Bai incidents, resulting in the deaths of 191 people and drawing international condemnation.

The TRT swept the February 2005 parliamentary elections, making Thaksin the first prime minster to serve out a full four-year term, be elected to two consecutive terms, and lead a party to win outright without the need for a coalition partner. However, anti-Thaksin sentiment rose markedly during the year, particularly in Bangkok and the south. In January 2006, the prime minister's family was criticized for the tax-free, US$1.9 billion sale of its Shin Corporation to the investment arm of the

Singaporean government. Facing a wave of protests led by the People's Alliance for Democracy (PAD)—a right-wing grouping of royalists, business elites, and military leaders with support in the urban middle class—the prime minister called snap elections in early April. All three opposition parties boycotted the vote, and a fresh round of elections was ultimately scheduled for October.

However, a military coup in September preempted the new vote and ousted Thaksin, who was abroad at the time. The coup leaders' Council for National Security (CNS) abrogated the constitution, dissolved the parliament, and replaced the Constitutional Court with its own tribunal. In May 2007, the tribunal found the TRT guilty of paying off smaller parties in the April 2006 elections and dissolved it, specifically prohibiting Thaksin and 111 other party leaders from participating in politics for the next five years.

Referendum voters in August 2007 approved a new constitution, which contained a number of antidemocratic provisions. The poll results, with 57 percent in favor and 41 percent opposed, showed a significant protest vote in the northeast, Thaksin's regional stronghold.

Former TRT members regrouped under the banner of the People's Power Party (PPP) and won the December 2007 parliamentary elections with 233 of 480 lower-house seats. The DP placed second with 165 seats. The PPP quickly assembled a coalition government. Throughout 2008, yellow-shirted PAD supporters led protests accusing the government of serving as a corrupt proxy for Thaksin and demanding its dissolution. At the height of the protests in November, the PAD seized Bangkok's main airports, seriously disrupting travel and economic activity in the country and region. Meanwhile, in October, Thaksin was sentenced in absentia to two years in prison for abuse of office.

The PPP-led government—under intense pressure from the PAD, military commanders, and the judiciary—finally fell in December 2008, when the Constitutional Court disbanded the ruling party on the grounds that it had engaged in fraud during the December 2007 elections. DP leader Abhisit Vejjajiva, the head of the opposition, subsequently formed a new coalition and won a lower-house vote to become prime minister. He secured the support of 235 out of the 437 lower-house members who were present with the help of opportunistic members of Thaksin's alliance, including the Buam Jai Thai (BJT) party, which he rewarded with key ministerial posts. The government consolidated its power in January 2009 by-elections, capturing 20 of the 29 seats contested. Nevertheless, Abhisit struggled throughout 2009 to maintain control of his coalition partners, cope with opposition protests, and counter corruption charges filed against his allies. He survived a no-confidence motion in March, garnering 246 out of 449 votes.

The red-shirted United Front for Democracy Against Dictatorship (UDD), which had mounted large protests during the period of military rule following Thaksin's ouster, resumed its activities to oppose the PPP's dissolution and carried out antigovernment protests throughout 2009. The demonstrations intensified ahead of the Songkran holiday, which marked the Thai new year, in April. The UDD gathered over 100,000 protesters in Bangkok and stormed the venue of the East Asia Summit in Pattaya, forcing international delegations to be evacuated by air. At the height of the protests, Thaksin, speaking from Dubai, called for a people's revolution. Prominent UDD leader Jakrapob Penkair, who was in hiding to escape arrest, advocated a campaign of violence to depose the government. On the eve of Songkran, April 12, Abhisit imposed emergency rule in Bangkok and ordered the army to disperse the crowds. At least two people were killed and over 100 injured in the ensuing street battles. UDD leaders called on their supporters to disperse peacefully, averting further violence.

Abhisit's government moved swiftly to crack down on the opposition by revoking Thaksin's remaining passport, issuing arrest warrants for protest leaders, and shutting down radio stations involved in mobilizing support for the UDD. The government also invoked the Internal Security Act to curtail UDD protests and arrested red-shirt leaders on lese majeste grounds. Separately, on April 17, one of the PAD's leaders, Sondhi Limthongkul, was seriously injured when gunmen opened fire on his motorcade with automatic weapons.

Emergency rule in Bangkok was lifted on April 24, and Abhisit led a genuine reconciliation effort beginning in May. However, a multiparty reconciliation panel was unable to agree on draft changes to the 2007 constitution and the question of amnesty for the 111 party officials banned from politics as part of the dissolution of the TRT. Abhisit also faced potential opposition from the New Politics Party, formed by the PAD in late June and led by labor activist Somsak Kosaisuk. Separately, the red shirts infuriated their opponents over the summer by garnering over 3.5 million signatures to petition the king for a pardon for Thaksin. In October, General Chavalit Yongchaiyudh, who had served as prime minister from 1996 to 1997, became chairman of the PPP's successor party, the Phuea Thai Party (PTP, or For Thais Party).

Political Rights and Civil Liberties: Thailand is not an electoral democracy. The most recent parliamentary elections in December 2007 proceeded without major disruptions and returned Thailand to civilian rule, but they were not free and fair. The military retained significant influence, and martial law remained in effect in 25 provinces at the time of the elections. The CNS maintained tight control over the electoral process and deliberately maneuvered to influence the outcome against the PPP. Moreover, the PPP-led government that emerged from the voting was toppled in December 2008 in what many observers regarded as a judicial coup. Prime Minister Abhisit Vejjajiva, who took power after the PPP's ouster, did not seek a popular mandate in 2009, although by-elections were held without incident in January and June. The ruling coalition performed well in the January voting, but in the two by-elections held in June in the northeast, the opposition PTP defeated the BJT, which had defected from the PPP-led alliance to join Abhisit's government.

The current constitution was drafted under the supervision of the military-backed government and approved in an August 2007 referendum. It called for an amnesty for the 2006 coup leaders, and in a clear response to the premiership of Thaksin Shinawatra, whose government the coup overthrew, the charter contains a number of measures designed to restrict the power of the executive. It limited prime ministers to two four-year terms and set a lower threshold for launching no-confidence motions. The constitution also reduced the role of elected lawmakers. Whereas the old Senate was fully elected, the Senate created by the new charter consists of 76 elected members and 74 appointed by a committee of judges and members of independent government bodies. Senators, who serve six-year terms, cannot belong to political parties. For the 480-seat lower chamber, the House of Representatives, the new constitution altered the system of proportional representation to curtail the voting power of the northern and northeastern provinces, where support for Thaksin remains strong. Members serve four-year terms, and the prime minister is elected from among them. King Bhumibol Adulyadej is the head of state, and while he has little responsibility in day-to-day politics, he retains tremendous moral and symbolic influence, particularly in times of national or constitutional crisis.

The CNS-appointed interim legislature passed the Internal Security Act (ISA) shortly before elections in 2007. The law created an Internal Security Operations Command (ISOC)—headed by the prime minister and the army chief—that retains the authority to override civilian administration and restrict basic civil liberties to suppress disorder, even without a formal state of emergency. The ISA also provides legal immunity to those who commit human rights abuses under its auspices.

Corruption is widespread at all levels of Thai society. It ranked among Thais' top frustrations with the Thaksin government and was cited as part of the military's justification for the 2006 coup. Despite Abhisit's clean image, his party and coalition cohorts faced numerous corruption charges in 2009. Related controversies included irregularities in the government's Community Self-Sufficiency Project, a costly bus-leasing scheme managed by the BJT-controlled Transport Ministry, and BJT leader Newin Chidchob's acquittal in a contentious rubber-sapling procurement project. In July, 13 DP members of parliament were disqualified for breaching shareholder rules. In late December, the minister of public health resigned after he was implicated in a graft scandal. Thailand was ranked 84 out of 180 countries surveyed in Transparency International's 2009 Corruption Perceptions Index.

The 2007 constitution restored freedom of expression guarantees that were eliminated by the 2006 coup. The 2007 Publishing Registration Act, while less draconian than its predecessor, increased journalists' vulnerability by eliminating provisions that automatically included newspaper editors and publishers in defamation suits brought against their writers. Harsh defamation provisions remain in the penal code, and suits are often used to silence government critics. A Computer Crimes Act that took effect in 2007 assigns significant prison terms for the publication of false information deemed to endanger the public or national security. Under this law, the individual records of internet users must be kept by internet service providers for 90 days and may be inspected by the authorities without a warrant.

There was a surge in 2009 in the use of the country's lese majeste laws to stifle freedom of expression. The laws prohibit the defamation of the monarchy, but the authorities increasingly used them to target activists, scholars, students, journalists, foreign authors, and politicians who were critical of the government. Some of the accused faced decades in prison for multiple counts, while others fled the country. Defense Ministry and the Ministry of Information and Communication Technology (MICT) were the prime enforcers of lese majeste laws. In August 2009, the MICT created a police task-force to monitor online content and identify users who post objectionable material.

Thailand's broadcast media are also subject to restrictions; the six main television stations and all 525 radio frequencies are controlled by the government and military. In April and May 2009, radio stations supporting the UDD were pressured to shut down. Authorities forced a journalist to resign in September after he aired an interview of Thaksin on a radio show. Print publications are for the most part privately owned and have been subject to fewer restrictions than the broadcast media. The country's endless street protests inhibited the ability of journalists to carry out their work during 2009.

The constitution prohibits discrimination based on religious belief. There is no official state religion, but the constitution requires the monarch to be a Buddhist, and speech considered insulting to Buddhism is prohibited by law. The conflict in the south—which pits ethnic Malay Muslims against ethnic Thai Buddhists—continues to undermine citizens' ability to practice their religion. Buddhist monks reported that they were unable to travel freely through southern communities to receive alms, while Muslim academics and imams faced government scrutiny.

The 2007 constitution restored freedom of assembly guarantees, and major political protests were ongoing for much of 2009. UDD protests forced the postponement of the East Asia Summit in April, and the government invoked the ISA to discourage a repeat scenario for the rescheduled summit in October. In March and April, the protests devolved into violent street battles, with several people killed and hundreds injured. Human Rights Watch praised Thai law enforcement personnel and military forces for often showing great restraint in the face of provocation, but noted that they used live ammunition to disperse protesters in some cases.

Thailand has a vibrant nongovernmental organization (NGO) community, with groups representing farmers, laborers, women, students, and human rights interests. However, according to the U.S. State Department's 2009 human rights report, NGOs that dealt with sensitive political issues or obstructed government-backed development projects faced harassment. Human rights groups focused on the volatile southern provinces reportedly met with intimidation by both sides in the conflict.

Thai trade unions are independent, and more than 50 percent of state-enterprise workers belong to unions, but less than 2 percent of the total workforce is unionized. Antiunion discrimination in the private sector is common, and legal protections for union members are weak and poorly enforced. There are some restrictions on private sector strikes, and strikes by state-enterprise workers are prohibited, though such workers sometimes engage in walkouts in practice. Exploitation and trafficking of migrant workers from Burma, Cambodia, and Laos are serious and ongoing problems, as are child and sweatshop labor.

The 2007 constitution restored judicial independence and reestablished an independent Constitutional Court. A separate military court adjudicates criminal and civil cases involving members of the military, as well as cases brought under martial law. Sharia (Islamic law) courts hear certain types of cases pertaining to Muslims. In 2008, the Thai courts played an important role in resolving political disputes, generating complaints of judicial activism and political bias. Key rulings that year resulted in the removal of two prime ministers, the Speaker of the lower house, and the foreign minister, as well as the dissolution of the ruling party and a transfer of power to the opposition.

Pretrial detention—often lasting up to 84 days in criminal cases—is a serious problem, and trials frequently take years to complete. Prison conditions are grim, with inmates and detainees facing shackling and abuse by police and military personnel. State officials are rarely prosecuted for such acts.

A combination of martial law, emergency decree, and the ISA is in effect in the four southernmost provinces. Military sweeps since June 2007 have involved the indiscriminate detention of thousands of suspected insurgents and sympathizers, and there are credible reports of torture and other human rights violations, including extrajudicial killings, by security forces. To date there have been no successful criminal prosecutions of security personnel for these transgressions. Separatist fighters and other armed groups regularly attack government workers, religious figures, and civilians. In June 2009, 10 people were killed while praying at a mosque in Narathiwat province, spurring several reprisal killings aimed at Buddhist Thais. As of the end of 2009, more than 3,500 people had been killed in the conflict since 2004, making the insurgency one of the world's deadliest.

Thailand's hill tribes are not fully integrated into society and face restrictions on their freedom of movement. Many reportedly lack citizenship, which renders them ineligible to vote, own land, attend state schools, or receive protection under labor laws. Thailand has not ratified UN conventions on refugees, and the authorities continue to repatriate Burmese and Laotian refugees forcibly. In January 2009 the government drew international condemnation for towing boatloads of incoming Burmese Rohingya refugees back out to sea, which reportedly led to a number of deaths. Also during the year, several thousand Hmong refugees were forcibly repatriated to Laos.

While women have the same legal rights as men, they remain subject to economic discrimination in practice; underrepresented in local and national government bodies, with about 13 percent of the seats in the lower house of parliament; and vulnerable to domestic abuse, rape, and sex trafficking. Some 200,000 to 300,000 Thai women and children work as prostitutes, according to NGO estimates, and sex tourism remains a problem.

Togo

Political Rights: 5
Civil Liberties: 4*
Status: Partly Free

Population: 6,619,000
Capital: Lome

Ratings Change: Togo's civil liberties rating improved from 5 to 4 due to the launch of a Truth and Reconciliation Commission to investigate past human rights abuses, as well as a decrease in violence throughout the country.

Ten-Year Ratings Timeline For Year Under Review (Political Rights, Civil Liberties, Status)

2000	2001	2002	2003	2004	2005	2006	2007	2008	2009
5,5PF	5,5PF	6,5NF	6,5NF	6,5NF	6,5NF	6,5NF	5,5PF	5,5PF	5,4PF

Overview: The government oversaw notable reforms to the electoral code and election commission in 2009 as the country prepared for a presidential election in early 2010. The political environment was generally more peaceful than in previous years, and a Truth and Reconciliation Commission was launched in May to address past human rights abuses. However, President Faure Gnassingbe's tolerance for dissent remained limited, and in April, the army violently repressed an alleged coup plot led by his brother.

Originally part of a German colony that fell under the control of France after World War I, Togo gained its independence in 1960. Gnassingbe Eyadema, a demobilized sergeant, overthrew the civilian government in a bloodless coup in 1967. Using mock elections and a loyal military, he then presided over close to 40 years of repressive rule.

In 1991, under pressure from European governments, Eyadema agreed to set up a transitional government and prepare for free elections. However, his soldiers and secret police attacked opposition supporters, ultimately forcing thousands to flee abroad, and the transitional government was later dissolved. A series of elections were held during the 1990s under a new constitution approved in 1992, but military harassment and legal manipulation ensured that Eyadema and his Rally of the Togolese People (RPT) party remained in power. The president secured a new five-year term with 57 percent of the vote in 2003, defeating Emmanuel Bob-Akitani, who ran for the opposition Union of Forces for Change (UFC) after candidate Gilchrist Olympio was eliminated through a manufactured technicality.

Eyadema died in February 2005, and the military quickly installed his son, Faure Gnassingbe, in his stead. Protests and opposition activity were formally banned, but demonstrations were nonetheless frequent, and the police response was brutal.

Under international pressure, Gnassingbe held an April 2005 election that confirmed him as president. The Economic Community of West African States (ECOWAS) was the only international organization to endorse the poll, which featured over a million phantom voters on the electoral rolls, widespread intimidation, and a complete communications blackout on election day. Subsequent clashes between opposition supporters and security forces killed almost 500 people, injured thousands, and forced 40,000 to flee the country. According to the United Nations, most of the victims were killed by security forces in their homes.

In August 2006, the promise of renewed economic aid from the European Union (EU)—which had cut off support in 1993—spurred the RPT and opposition parties to form a unity government and schedule legislative elections. The RPT won 50 of the 81 National Assembly seats in the October 2007 polls, with 85 percent voter turnout. The UFC secured 27 seats, while the Action Committee for Renewal (CAR), another opposition party, captured the remainder. Many observers noted that the lopsided electoral system enabled the RPT to win 62 percent of the seats with just 39 percent of the vote. Nonetheless, most international election monitors deemed the polls to have been transparent.

By the end of 2008, the EU had restored full economic aid, and the World Bank and International Monetary Fund also resumed cooperation that year. Relations with international donors were bolstered in part by Gnassingbe's appointment of Gilbert Fossoun Houngbo, a former UN Development Programme official, as prime minister in September.

In June 2009, the government, opposition parties, and civil society members reached agreement on the reformation of the electoral code and the composition of the main electoral commission in preparation for the 2010 presidential election. By October, the government had agreed to drop residency requirements that previously barred Gilchrist Olympio of the UFC from running, and the electoral code reform was adopted by year's end. However, in November, both major opposition parties threatened to boycott the poll unless the government agreed to hold a runoff if no candidate won a majority in the first round.

While there were a number of minor confrontations between security forces and opposition demonstrators during 2009, Gnassingbe showed the least tolerance for opposition within the RPT and his own family. In April, the army raided the home of his elder brother, Kpatcha, on suspicion that he was planning a coup. The raid led to a gun battle that left three people dead. Kpatcha Gnassingbe, 18 soldiers, and 10 civilians were eventually arrested and charged with rebellion.

Political Rights and Civil Liberties: Togo is not an electoral democracy. Despite international consensus that the 2007 legislative elections were relatively free and fair, the 2005 presidential vote was blatantly fraudulent and marked by serious violence. The president is elected to five-year terms and appoints the prime minister. Members of the 81-seat, unicameral National Assembly are also elected to five-year terms, using a party-list system in multimember districts. The RPT remains the dominant party, but the opposition UFC and CAR parties won a significant share of seats in 2007.

Corruption continues to be a serious impediment to development, and the government took no significant steps to tackle the problem in 2009. Togo was ranked 111 of 180 countries surveyed in Transparency International's 2009 Corruption Perceptions Index.

Freedom of the press is guaranteed by law, though it is often disregarded. Blatant impunity for past crimes against journalists encourages self-censorship. Following the crackdown on Kpatcha Gnassingbe's alleged coup plot in April 2009, the government announced a temporary ban on all call-in radio and television programs, ostensibly to, "prevent public opinion from prejudicing the case against Kpatcha." In October, a new law gave the state broadcasting council the power to impose severe penalties, including suspending publications for up to six months, withdrawing press cards, and seizing equipment, on journalists responsible for "serious errors." The government runs Togo's only daily newspaper, *Togo Press*, as well as the only national television station. Private print and broadcast outlets exist, but they are limited in capacity and often heavily politicized. Access to the internet is generally unrestricted, but few people use the medium due to high costs.

Constitutionally protected religious freedom is generally respected, though tensions sometimes arise between Togo's southern Christian majority and northern Muslim minority. Islam and Christianity are recognized as official religions, but other religious groups must register as associations. Political discussion is prohibited on religious radio and television outlets.

While government informers and security forces are believed to maintain a presence on university campuses and in other public places, ordinary citizens are now able to speak more openly than in previous years.

Respect for freedoms of assembly and association has improved since 2006. In 2009, a number of opposition and civil society demonstrations were held in Lome, and only a few drew a police response. Togo's constitution guarantees the right to form and join labor unions, and most workers have the right to strike, but collective bargaining is limited to a single nationwide wage agreement. Workers' right to organize is restricted in export-processing zones.

The judicial system is understaffed, inadequately funded, and heavily influenced by the presidency. While the death penalty was abolished in 2008, extrajudicial killings remain a serious concern. Human rights groups and victims have repeatedly called for the prosecution of those responsible for the campaign of killings, abductions, and intimidation linked to the 2005 presidential election. In May 2009, a Truth and Reconciliation Commission was formally launched, with representatives from academia, civic and religious groups, and business, but not from political parties. The commission does not have the power to prosecute perpetrators, and can only recommend such action.

Discrimination is common among the country's 40 ethnic groups, and tensions have historically divided the country between north and south. While President Faure Gnassingbe's father came from the northern Kabiye group and his mother is an Ewe from the south, Kpatcha Gnassingbe is fully Kabiye. The army is traditionally composed primarily of Kabiye soldiers.

Despite constitutional guarantees of equality, women's opportunities for education and employment are limited. Nonetheless, in 2009, Victoire Dogbe Tomegah became the first woman to serve as presidential chief of staff. Customary law discriminates against women in divorce and inheritance, giving them the legal rights of minors, and a husband may legally bar his wife from working or choose to receive her earnings. As in much of West Africa, child trafficking for the purpose of slavery is a serious problem in Togo. Prosecutions under a 2005 child-trafficking law are rare.

Tonga

Political Rights: 5
Civil Liberties: 3
Status: Partly Free

Population: 103,000
Capital: Nuku'alofa

Ten-Year Ratings Timeline For Year Under Review (Political Rights, Civil Liberties, Status)

2000	2001	2002	2003	2004	2005	2006	2007	2008	2009
5,3PF	5,3PF	5,3PF	5,3PF	5,3PF	5,3PF	5,3PF	5,3PF	5,3PF	5,3PF

Overview: An electoral reform commission, which issued its final report in November 2009, made a number of recommendations, including that the king appoint the prime minister only on the advice of the parliament. Five elected lawmakers were acquitted in September of sedition charges associated with the 2006 riots. An inter-island ferry sank in September, killing 74 passengers, and the ensuing investigation deepened public discontent over the government's mismanagement in its handling of the disaster.

Tonga consists of 169 islands that King George Tupou I united under his rule in 1845. It became a constitutional monarchy in 1875 and a British protectorate in 1900, gaining independence in 1970 as a member of the Commonwealth. King Taufa'ahau Tupou IV ruled from 1945 to 2006. His son, Crown Prince Tupouto'a, assumed the title King Siaosi Tupou V in 2006 and was officially crowned in 2008.

Politics and the economy are dominated by the monarchy, hereditary nobles, and a few prominent commoners. The economy is heavily dependent on foreign aid and remittances from Tongans living abroad. Prodemocracy candidates were first elected to the parliament in 2002, winning seven of nine directly elected seats for commoners. Prodemocracy candidates again won the majority of commoners' seats in the 2005 elections, and for the first time, two popularly elected representatives joined the cabinet.

Growing public demand for political reform pushed the former king in 2005 to approve the formation of a constitutional review committee. In October 2006, the committee submitted its recommendations to the government, which responded with a counterproposal. Prodemocracy advocates, who rejected the counterproposals as too conservative and slow, launched a street protest in November that quickly escalated into violent rioting, leaving several people dead, hundreds injured, and 80 percent of the capital's business district in ruins. The king declared a state of emergency, and nearly 700 people were arrested, including 5 popularly elected members of parliament who were charged with sedition; the latter were acquitted of sedition charges in September 2009, though the state of emergency remained in place at year's end. Meanwhile, talks between the king and prodemocracy advocates resulted in an agreement—to be enacted with the 2010 parliamentary elections—whereby the parliament will consist of 17 popularly elected representatives, 9 nobles elected by their peers, and 2 governors and 2 ministers appointed by the king.

In the April 2008 legislative elections, the Human Rights and Democracy Movement won four seats, the People's Democratic Party captured two seats, and independents took the remaining three popularly elected seats. The new parliament passed legislation in July 2008 to establish a five-member Constitution and Electoral Commission to determine necessary reforms for the November 2010 legislative elections, including the role of the monarch and the composition and selection of the legislature. In November 2009, the commission issued its final report, which included over 80 recommendations. Among the suggested changes were that all members of parliament would be popularly elected and that the king could appoint the prime minister only on the advice of the legislature. The king's support for the various recommendations eased concerns of possible renewed violence.

In September 2009, a domestic inter-island ferry sank about 50 miles from the country's capital, killing 74 people. The tragedy had a profound impact on Tonga, which has a population of only about 100,000 and whose 170 islands rely heavily on the use of ferries. In November, the transport minister resigned, and over 5,000 people petitioned the king to remove Prime Minister Feleti Sevele for his poor handling of the disaster, including rescue efforts, investigation of the disaster, and aid for families affected by the tragedy. During hearings in November, the vessel's captain acknowledged that he had known the ferry was unsafe, and in December, a former senior transportation ministry official stated that the government did not survey the vessel before its purchase. The investigation into the disaster continued at year's end.

In September, the parliament rejected ratification of the UN Convention on the Elimination of All Forms of Discrimination Against Women on the grounds that it conflicts with Tongan culture, citing that it would provide women with land ownership rights and allow abortion and same-sex marriage.

Political Rights and Civil Liberties: Tonga is not an electoral democracy. The parliament has 9 popularly elected members, 9 nobles elected by their peers, 10 members of the privy council, and 2 governors selected by the king. The king appoints the prime minister (a lifelong position) and the cabinet.

There are several nascent political parties, and prodemocracy candidates typically align with the Human Rights and Democracy Movement, which is not a formal party. In November 2009, a new political party, Paati Langafonua Tu'uloa, was formed to compete in the November 2010 elections.

Widespread official corruption is a major source of public discontent. The royals, nobles, and their top associates have allegedly used state assets for personal benefit, and transparency and accountability are also lacking. Tonga was ranked 99 out of 180 countries surveyed in Transparency International's 2009 Corruption Perceptions Index.

Despite constitutional guarantees of freedom of the press, the government has a history of suppressing media criticism. A Department of Information oversees all media reporting. Nevertheless, letters to the editor and commentaries critical of the government appear regularly in all newspapers, including those owned by the state or in which the state owns shares. In April 2009, the Supreme Court ruled that the prodemocracy newspaper *Kale'a* was liable for damages related to a letter to the editor published in 2007 that allegedly defamed the prime minister and his economic adviser; a court of appeal upheld this ruling in July. The government does not restrict access to the internet. The number of users has rapidly increased despite high costs and lack of infrastructure.

Freedom of religion is generally respected, but the government requires all religious references on broadcast media to conform to mainstream Christian beliefs. Academics reportedly practice self-censorship to avoid conflicts with the government.

Freedoms of assembly and association are upheld for apolitical or uncritical groups, though those engaging in protests and marches have faced government harassment. The state of emergency in force since the 2006 riots restricts public assembly in the capital. The 1963 Trade Union Act gives workers the right to form unions and to strike, but regulations for union formation were never promulgated.

The judiciary is generally independent and efficient, and traditional village elders frequently adjudicate local disputes. Criminal suspects may exercise the right to an attorney and a court hearing. While prisons are basic, there have been no reports of prisoner abuse.

Tensions between Tongans and ethnic Chinese have worsened in recent years, largely due to resentment stemming from the perceived Chinese domination of the economy.

Women enjoy equal access to education and health care and receive fairly equal treatment in employment. Women hold several senior government jobs, including cabinet positions and the majority of commissioned officer posts in the police force. Nevertheless, women cannot own land, and domestic violence against women is not uncommon.

Trinidad and Tobago

Political Rights: 2
Civil Liberties: 2
Status: Free

Population: 1,333,000
Capital: Port-of-Spain

Ten-Year Ratings Timeline For Year Under Review (Political Rights, Civil Liberties, Status)

2000	2001	2002	2003	2004	2005	2006	2007	2008	2009
2,2F	3,3PF	3,3PF	3,3PF	3,3PF	3,2F	2,2F	2,2F	2,2F	2,2F

Overview: In 2009, Trinidad and Tobago enjoyed the international spotlight by hosting the Fifth Summit of the Americas in Port-of-Spain. However, political and security difficulties continued to fester, including cases of political corruption and violent crime.

Trinidad and Tobago, a member of the Commonwealth, achieved independence from Britain in 1962 and became a republic in 1976.

Prime Minister Patrick Manning of the People's National Movement (PNM) returned to the premiership in December 2001 after a previous term in office from 1991 to 1995. Disputed elections in 2001, resulted in an evenly divided lower house, and Manning sought to break the deadlock by calling fresh elections in October 2002. The PNM won 20 of the chamber's 36 seats, but the opposition United National Congress (UNC) also had a strong showing, reinforcing the dominance of the two parties.

Former prime minister Basdeo Panday was sentenced to two years of hard labor in April 2006 for having failed to declare London bank accounts that he held while serving as prime minister in the late 1990s. He retained the UNC chairmanship while appealing his conviction, which was overturned in April 2007. Nevertheless, the UNC was embroiled in infighting, and several high-level defections fueled speculation that a three-party system could emerge. In September 2006, former UNC leader Winston Dookeran created a new party, Congress of the People.

Manning handily won another term in office in the November 2007 elections, with the PNM capturing 26 of the 41 seats in the lower house. The UNC won the remaining 15, leaving Congress of the People shut out of Parliament. About half of the country's one million registered voters cast their ballots, a lower turnout than in previous elections.

Violent crime rates remained among the highest in the region, but dropped slightly to 509 homicides in 2009, down from a high of 550 the previous year. In addition, Amnesty International reported that police had killed more than 40 people in 2008, and singled out the country for condemnation of extra-judicial police killings. Most investigations of extrajudicial crimes go unpunished, with only 6 percent resulting in charges filed against the police since 1999.

In 2009, Trinidad and Tobago gained international attention by hosting the Fifth Summit of the Americas, a major quadrennial gathering of the 34 elected heads of government from the Western Hemisphere. While the government tried to frame the summit as a major diplomatic achievement, popular discontent with the costs of the event and the related disruptions for security purposes cut into Manning's support.

Political Rights and Civil Liberties: Trinidad and Tobago is an electoral democracy. The November 2007 elections were generally considered to be free and fair by observers. A Caribbean Community (CARICOM) electoral observation mission reported that voting was orderly and peaceful, which represented a marked reduction in tension compared to previous elections. The president is elected to a five-year term by a majority of the combined houses of Parliament, though executive authority rests with the prime minister. Parliament consists of the 41-member House of Representatives, elected for five years, and the 31-member Senate, also serving for five years. The president appoints 16 senators on the advice of the prime minister, 6 on the advice of the opposition, and 9 at his own discretion.

Political parties are free to organize, but in practice, the dominance of the PNM and UNC has led to a two-party system. The parties are technically multiethnic, though the PNM is favored by Afro-Trinidadians, while the UNC is affiliated with Indo-Trinidadians.

The country is believed to suffer from high levels of official corruption. Trinidad's Integrity Commission, established under the 2000 Integrity in Public Life Act to uphold standards of transparency and accountability, has the power to investigate the financial and ethical performance of public functionaries. Former prime minister Basdeo Panday of the UNC was the first person to be investigated by the commission. In 2009, the Integrity Commission endured a series of controversies, as three of its five members resigned in rapid succession after their legal eligibility to serve in this capacity came under scrutiny. The UNC opposition attempted to use the scandal to force President George Richards from office, but the motion failed. Trinidad and Tobago was ranked 79 out of 180 countries surveyed in Transparency International's 2009 Corruption Perceptions Index.

Freedom of speech is legally guaranteed by the constitution. Press outlets are privately owned and vigorous in their pluralistic views. There are four daily newspapers and several weeklies, as well as both private and public broadcast media outlets. In 2009, inaccurate news reports about endangered children prompted the Telecommunications Authority of Trinidad and Tobago to investigate implementing a new broadcast code to curb false reporting; legal groups have protested that such a move could lead to curbs on press freedom. Access to the internet is not restricted.

Freedom of religion is guaranteed under the constitution, and the government honors this provision. Foreign missionaries are free to operate, but the government allows only 35 representatives of each denomination. Academic freedom is generally observed.

Freedoms of association and assembly are respected. Civil society is relatively robust, with a range of interest groups engaged in the political process. Labor unions are well organized, powerful, and politically active, although union membership has declined in recent years. Strikes are legal and occur frequently.

The judicial branch is independent, though subject to some political pressure and corruption. As a result of rising crime rates, the court system is severely backlogged, in some cases for up to five years, with thousands of criminal cases awaiting trial. The government permits human rights monitors to visit prisons, which are severely overcrowded.

The government has struggled in recent years to address the problem of violent crime. Many Trinidadians of East Indian descent, who are disproportionately targets of abduction, blame the increase in violence and kidnapping on government corruption and police collusion. Drug-related corruption extends to the business community, and a significant amount of money is believed to be laundered through front companies. The Proceeds of Crime Act provides severe penalties for money laundering and requires that major financial transactions be strictly monitored. The government works closely with U.S. law enforcement agencies to track drug shipments in and out of the country. Corruption in the police force, which is often drug related, is endemic, and law enforcement inefficiency results in the dismissal of some criminal cases. The police have won praise, however, for establishing a branch of Crime Stoppers, an international organization that promotes community involvement in preventing and informing on crime through a telephone hotline.

Trinidad and Tobago is one of the few countries in Latin America and the Caribbean that is grappling with the problem of Islamic extremism. In 2007, a four-person terrorist plot to blow up a fuel line at JFK airport in New York involved a Trinidadian suspect, but no formal links were found to Jamaat al-Muslimeen, a small radical Muslim group that had staged a coup attempt in Port-of-Spain in 1991, causing 23 deaths. In 2009, alleged police mistreatment of a Saudi diplomat drew protest from local Muslim leaders.

The population is multiethnic, consisting of Afro-Trinidadians, Indo-Trinidadians, and those of mixed race. The Indo-Trinidadian community continues to edge toward numerical, and thus political, advantage. Accusations of racial discrimination are often leveled in Parliament, and racial disparities persist, with Indo-Trinidadians composing a disproportionate percentage of the country's upper class. However, the country's leadership does alternate among the two dominant parties, and voting does not occur along strict ethnic lines.

Women participate in high-level politics, including 26 percent of the seats in the House of Representatives and 42 percent in the Senate. However, men still dominate most leadership positions, and salary gaps continue to favor men. Domestic violence remains a significant concern. While serious crimes such as murder and rape are reported, other instances of domestic abuse go unreported. In September 2009, the Network of NGOs for the Advancement of Women complained that the government was withholding a draft version of a new gender policy, a violation of the country's Freedom of Information Act.

Tunisia

Political Rights: 7
Civil Liberties: 5
Status: Not Free

Population: 10,429,000
Capital: Tunis

Ten-Year Ratings Timeline For Year Under Review (Political Rights, Civil Liberties, Status)

2000	2001	2002	2003	2004	2005	2006	2007	2008	2009
6,5NF	6,5NF	6,5NF	6,5NF	6,5NF	6,5NF	6,5NF	7,5NF	7,5NF	7,5NF

Overview: President Zine el-Abidine Ben Ali easily won a fifth term in the tightly controlled October 2009 general elections, while the ruling party captured three-quarters of the seats in the lower house of parliament. Throughout the year, the authorities continued to harass, arrest, and imprison journalists and bloggers, human rights activists, and political opponents of the government.

Tunisia, which had been a French protectorate since 1881, gained its independence in 1956. The country was then ruled for more than 30 years by President Habib Bourguiba, a secular nationalist who favored economic and social modernization along Western lines but severely limited political liberties. Bourguiba succeeded in advancing women's rights and economic development, and his government maintained strong relations with the West and fellow Arab states.

In 1987, Prime Minister Zine el-Abidine Ben Ali ousted Bourguiba and seized the presidency in a bloodless coup. Ben Ali's rise to power had little effect on state policy. He continued to push market-based economic development and women's rights, but he also repressed political opponents. Independent journalists, secular activists, and Islamists faced imprisonment, torture, and harassment. The Islamists, particularly those in the banned movement Ennahda, were jailed following sham trials in the early 1990s.

Ben Ali's hold on government institutions remained strong, and he won a fifth five-year term in the October 2009 presidential election, taking nearly 90 percent of the vote amid tight media and candidacy restrictions. In the concurrent elections for the Chamber of Deputies, the lower house of the legislature, the ruling Democratic Constitutional Rally (RCD) captured 161 of 214 seats. Of the six other parties that won representation, none took more than 16 seats. The Progressive Democratic Party (PDP), one of the few critical independent parties, boycotted the 2009 election after it was barred from campaigning, meaning only three candidates qualified to challenge the incumbent.

The government's efforts to control the 2009 election process were evident in restrictions imposed on the media, retaliation against journalists and bloggers, and a concerted bid by official media to discredit critical coverage. Although this was the first Tunisian election in which all presidential candidates were given airtime to discuss their platforms, the authorities manipulated the scheduling and edited the speeches. The RCD monopolized prime-time advertising and campaigning, while independent journalists and commentators were arrested or assaulted, and their publications, broadcast outlets, and even blogs and web pages were blocked.

Some political prisoners have been freed in recent years, and Ben Ali has stated that the press and opposition should feel free to promote their ideas. However, the president's critics still face beatings and incarceration, and even political activists who are released from jail often have their movements monitored and restricted.

Political Rights and Civil Liberties: Tunisia is not an electoral democracy. President Zine el-Abedine Ben Ali has exercised authoritarian rule since seizing power in a coup in 1987. Beginning in 1989, he won five consecutive five-year terms in tightly controlled elections, either running unopposed or easily defeating token challengers. A 2002 referendum removed the constitution's three-term limit for the presidency and raised the maximum age for presidential candidates from 70 to 75. A package of amendments in 2008 lowered the voting age from 20 to 18 and effectively barred presidential candidates other than the elected leaders of political parties who had served at least two years or those who obtained nominations from at least 30 lawmakers or local councilors. Both before and after the 2009 elections, the authorities cracked down on media outlets and human rights activists to minimize public expressions of dissent.

The president appoints the cabinet, the prime minister, regional governors, and the head of the official election-monitoring organization. Members of the 214-seat Chamber of Deputies are directly elected to serve five-year terms. Of the 126 members of Chamber of Advisors, the upper house of the legislature, 85 are indirectly elected by local officials and 41 are appointed by the president, all for six-year terms.

Opposition parties that are genuinely independent of state influence are weak and have almost no role in the formation of public policy. The state strictly monitors and severely curbs their activities. For example, according to Human Rights Watch, an edition of the Ettajdid party's weekly, *Ettarik al-Jadid*, was seized by officials on October 10, 2009, on the grounds that it published presidential candidate Ahmed Brahim's campaign platform before the official start of campaigning on October 11. However, the newly printed edition had not been scheduled to be distributed until that date.

Although Tunisia is considered less corrupt than several other Arab and African states, Ben Ali and his close relatives and associates have used their positions to create private monopolies in several sectors of the economy. Tunisia was ranked 65 out of 180 countries surveyed in Transparency International's 2009 Corruption Perceptions Index.

Tunisia has one of the worst media environments in the Arab world. Despite constitutional guarantees and a press law that promise freedom of expression, the government uses an array of legal, penal, and economic measures to silence dissenting voices. Libel and defamation are criminal offenses, and journalists also risk punishment under laws against disturbing public order. Only a handful of private television and radio stations have received licenses, including one owned by the president's son-in-law that was launched in 2009. Government-approved media regularly feature praise of Ben Ali and his associates, and criticism of the president is not tolerated.

Tunisian journalists in 2009 were detained, physically assaulted, fired from their jobs, prevented from leaving the country, and subjected to seemingly arbitrary police surveillance. More than 100 Tunisian journalists live in exile, according to Canadian Journalists for Free Expression. The authorities monitor foreign media, denying accreditation to critical journalists, and foreign publications or reporters can be seized or expelled if they offend the government. Ahead of the 2009 elections, the Qatar-based satellite television station Al-Jazeera was the target of a smear campaign, and its Tunisia-based correspondent was denied accreditation.

Stations that operate without approval via satellite or internet broadcasts face severe repression. For example, in January 2009, the authorities shut down the independent radio station Kalima soon after it began broadcasting via satellite, arresting or detaining several of its employees and confiscating materials from its offices. In February, three journalists for the London-based satellite television station Al-Hiwar al-Tounissi were arrested and charged with working for an "illegal station," according to the Observatoire pour la Liberte de Presse, d'Edition et de Creation.

The government bans access to an array of internet sites dealing with topics like democracy and human rights, and opposition media websites are often defaced. Social-networking and video-sharing sites like Facebook and YouTube were intermittently blocked during 2009. Online journalists and bloggers are routinely monitored, harassed, and arrested. The Committee to Protect Journalists has ranked Tunisia among the 10 worst places to be a blogger.

Tunisia's state religion is Islam, but the small population of local Jews and Christians are generally free to practice their religions. The government closely monitors mosques for extremist activity. They receive state funding and may remain open only during prayer time; imams are appointed and paid by the state. "Sectarian" dress like the *hijab* (headscarf) is prohibited, and both men and women with conservative religious appearances face police harassment.

Authorities limit academic freedom. While academics may discuss sensitive topics with relative openness in private settings, the government does not allow such discussion in public forums. In July 2009, professor Khedija Arfaoui was sentenced to eight months in prison for spreading rumors on Facebook, though she remained free at year's end pending an appeal.

Freedoms of association and assembly are guaranteed in the constitution and in several international treaties to which Tunisia is a party, but the government restricts these rights in practice. Nongovernmental organizations are legally prohibited from pursuing political objectives and activities, and independent human rights groups are routinely denied registration, forcing them to operate precariously as illegal bodies. Public-funding requirements and foreign-funding reporting rules make it extremely difficult for registered associations to maintain independence from the government and benefit from foreign sponsorship. Rights activists are routinely harassed, slandered, and abused. In September 2009, for example, human rights lawyer Radhia Nasraoui and her husband were assaulted by plainclothes police following a critical interview with Al-Jazeera.

Recognized trade unions, including the only labor federation, the General Union of Tunisian Workers, are progovernment in orientation. Authorities limit independent labor activity, especially when it resembles or threatens to become organized political opposition. Progovernment forces orchestrated a virtual coup within the year-old National Syndicate of Tunisian Journalists in mid-2009, taking over key leadership positions and endorsing Ben Ali's candidacy in the presidential election.

Despite constitutional guarantees, the judiciary lacks independence, and the executive branch controls the appointment and assignments of judges. Courts do not ensure due process in politically motivated cases and regularly issue convictions, including post-prison terms of "administrative control," or internal exile. Trials of suspected Islamists, human rights activists, and journalists are typically condemned as grossly unfair and politically biased by credible domestic and international observers. Prominent government critic and journalist Taoufik Ben Brik was sentenced in November 2009 to six months in prison following a trial in which his lawyers were prevented from fully presenting his case or cross-examining witnesses, according to Amnesty International. Human Rights Watch reports that other activists have been punished arbitrarily, including human rights defender Abdallah Zouari, who was released from internal exile in August 2009, some two years after his original sentence ended. Even after his release, Zouari continued to be monitored and harassed, and was briefly arrested in September. Suspected Islamists have been subjected to harsh prison sentences and reported ill-treatment in prison. Detention facilities in general are plagued by overcrowding and lack of medical care, and credible local and international sources report that detainees are routinely tortured in prison and in police custody.

Tunisian authorities have been fairly progressive on social policy, especially in the area of women's rights. The country ratified the Optional Protocol to the UN Convention on the Elimination of All Forms of Discrimination against Women in late 2008, and women in Tunisia enjoy more social freedoms and legal rights than their counterparts in other Arab countries. The personal status code grants women equal rights in divorce, and children born to Tunisian mothers and foreign fathers are automatically granted citizenship, which is not the case in many neighboring countries.

⬇ Turkey

Political Rights: 3
Civil Liberties: 3
Status: Partly Free

Population: 74,816,000
Capital: Ankara

Trend Arrow: Turkey received a downward trend arrow due to the Constitutional Court's decision to ban the pro-Kurdish Democratic Society Party.

Ten-Year Ratings Timeline For Year Under Review (Political Rights, Civil Liberties, Status)

2000	2001	2002	2003	2004	2005	2006	2007	2008	2009
4,5PF	4,5PF	3,4PF	3,4PF	3,3PF	3,3PF	3,3PF	3,3PF	3,3PF	3,3PF

Overview: The government in 2009 made promising overtures to Kurdish separatists in the southeast, raising hopes for an end to fighting and an expansion of Kurdish rights. However, violent protests erupted late in the year after the Constitutional Court banned the major pro-Kurdish party in December. Also in 2009, the government continued its expansive investigation into an alleged right-wing conspiracy to trigger a military coup.

Turkey emerged as a republic following the breakup of the Ottoman Empire at the end of World War I. Its founder and the author of its guiding principles was Mustafa Kemal, dubbed Ataturk (Father of the Turks), who declared that Turkey would be a secular state. He sought to modernize the country through measures such as the pursuit of Western learning, the use of the Roman alphabet instead of Arabic script for writing Turkish, and the abolition of the Muslim caliphate.

Following Ataturk's death in 1938, Turkey remained neutral for most of World War II, joining the Allies only in February 1945. In 1952, the republic joined NATO to secure protection from the Soviet Union. However, Turkey's domestic politics have been unstable, and the military—which sees itself as a bulwark against both Islamism and Kurdish separatism—has forced out civilian governments on four occasions since 1960.

The role of Islam in public life has been one of the key questions of Turkish politics since the 1990s. In 1995, the Islamist party Welfare won parliamentary elections and joined the ruling coalition the following year. However, the military forced the coalition government to resign in 1997, and Welfare withdrew from power.

The governments that followed failed to stabilize the economy, leading to growing discontent among voters. As a result, the Justice and Development (AK) Party won a sweeping majority in the 2002 elections. The previously unknown party had roots in Welfare, but it sought to distance itself from Islamism. Abdullah Gul initially served as prime minister, because AK's leader, Recep Tayyip Erdogan, had been banned from politics due to a conviction for crimes against secularism after he read a poem that seemed to incite religious intolerance. Once in power, the AK majority changed the constitution, allowing Erdogan to replace Gul in March 2003.

Erdogan oversaw a series of reforms linked to Turkey's bid to join the European Union (EU). Accession talks officially began in October 2005, but difficulties soon arose. Cyprus, an EU member since 2004, objected to Turkey's support for the Turkish Republic of Northern Cyprus, which is not recognized internationally. EU public opinion and some EU leaders expressed opposition to Turkish membership for a variety of other reasons. This caused the reform process to stall, and Turkish popular support for membership declined even as Turkish nationalist sentiment increased.

Ahmet Necdet Sezer's nonrenewable term as president ended in May 2007. Sezer had been considered a check on any extreme measures the AK-dominated parliament might introduce, and the prime minister's nomination of a new president was closely watched. Despite objections from the military and the secularist Republican People's Party (CHP), Erdogan chose Gul. In a posting on its website, the military tacitly threatened to intervene if Gul's nomination was approved, and secularists mounted huge street demonstrations to protest the Islamist threat they perceived in his candidacy. An opposition boycott of the April presidential vote in the parliament prevented a quorum, leading the traditionally secularist Constitutional Court to annul the poll. With his nominee thwarted, Erdogan called early parliamentary elections for July.

AK won a clear victory in the elections, increasing its share of the vote to nearly 50 percent. However, because more parties passed the 10 percent threshold for entering the legislature than in 2002, AK's share of seats decreased slightly to 340. The CHP, together with its junior partner, the Democratic Left Party, won 112 seats. The Nationalist Movement Party (MHP) entered the assembly for the first time, with

70 seats. A group of 20 candidates from the pro-Kurdish Democratic Society Party (DTP) also gained seats for the first time by running as independents, since they did not have the national support required to enter as a party. Other independents won the remaining eight seats. The MHP decided not to boycott the subsequent presidential vote, and Gul was elected president in August.

In an October 2007 referendum, voters approved constitutional amendments that, among other changes, reduced the presidential term to five years with a possibility for reelection, provided for future presidents to be elected by popular vote, and cut the parliamentary term to four years. The new parliament began drafting a new constitution, but progress later stalled.

In 2008, long-standing tensions between the AK government and entrenched, secularist officials erupted into an ongoing investigation focused on an alleged secretive ultranationalist group called Ergenekon. A total of 194 people were charged in three indictments in 2008 and 2009, including military officers, academics, journalists, and union leaders. A trial against 86 people began in October 2008, and a second trial against 56 people began in July 2009. Ergenekon was blamed for the 2006 bombing of a secularist newspaper and a court shooting that killed a judge the same year; its alleged goal was to raise the specter of Islamist violence so as to provoke a political intervention by the military. Critics argued that the government was using the far-reaching case to punish its opponents.

The government in 2009 made positive overtures to the Kurdish Workers' Party (PKK), a separatist group that has fought a decades-long guerrilla war against government forces in the southeast. The moves raised hopes of a permanent ceasefire; an earlier halt in fighting had lasted from 1999 to 2004. However, the state's relations with the Kurdish minority suffered a serious blow in December, when the Constitutional Court banned the DTP on the grounds that it had become, "a focal point for terrorism."

Political Rights and Civil Liberties: Turkey is an electoral democracy. The 1982 constitution provides for a 550-seat unicameral parliament, the Grand National Assembly. Reforms approved in a 2007 referendum reduced members' terms from five to four years. The changes also envision direct presidential elections for a once-renewable, five-year term, replacing the existing system of presidential election by the parliament for a single seven-year term. The president appoints the prime minister from among the members of parliament. The prime minister is head of government, while the president has powers including a legislative veto and the authority to appoint judges and prosecutors. The July 2007 elections were widely judged to have been free and fair, with reports of more open debate on traditionally sensitive issues.

A party must win at least 10 percent of the nationwide vote to secure representation in the parliament. The opposition landscape changed in 2007, with the entrance of the MHP and representatives of the DTP into the legislature. By contrast, only the two largest parties—the ruling AK and the opposition CHP—won seats in the 2002 elections.

A party can be shut down if its program is not in agreement with the constitution, and this criterion is interpreted broadly. In December 2009, the Constitutional Court closed the DTP and banned many of its members from politics, including the removal of two parliamentarians from office. Those remaining in parliament regrouped under the new Peace and Democracy Party. Major protests followed that were often violent and even deadly.

Reforms have increased civilian oversight of the military, but restrictions persist in areas such as civilian supervision of defense expenditures. The military continues to intrude on issues beyond its purview, commenting on key domestic and foreign policy matters. The fact that the military ultimately did not act on its tacit threats to disrupt the 2007 election of Abdullah Gul as president was considered a sign of progress. A 2009 law restricting the use of military courts brought Turkey closer to EU norms, but the measure is being contested by the opposition.

Turkey struggles with corruption in government and in daily life. The AK government has adopted some anticorruption measures, but reports by international organizations continue to raise concerns, and allegations have been lodged against AK and CHP politicians. Prime Minister Recep Tayyip Erdogan has been accused of involvement in a scandal over the misuse of funds at a charity called Lighthouse. A German court handling charges related to the scandal has implicated the head of Turkey's broadcasting authority. Government transparency has improved under a 2004 law on access to information. Turkey was ranked 61 out of 180 countries surveyed in Transparency International's 2009 Corruption Perceptions Index.

The right to free expression is guaranteed in the constitution, but legal impediments to press freedom remain. A 2006 antiterrorism law reintroduced jail sentences for journalists, and Article 301 of the 2004 revised penal code allows journalists and others to be prosecuted for discussing subjects such as the division of Cyprus and the 1915 mass killings of Armenians by Turks, which many consider to have been genocide. People have been charged under the same article for crimes such as insulting the armed services and denigrating "Turkishness"; very few have been convicted, but the trials are time-consuming and expensive. An April 2008 amendment changed Article 301's language to prohibit insulting "the Turkish nation," with a maximum sentence of two instead of three years, but cases continue to be brought under that and other clauses. For example, in 2009, a journalist who wrote an article denouncing what he said was the unlawful imprisonment of his father, also a journalist, was himself sentenced to 14 months in prison. A journalist was also shot near his office in December 2009. In a positive development the previous year, a court overturned a government ban on reporting about Ergenekon. Journalists have been among those implicated in the Ergenekon case.

Nearly all media organizations are owned by giant holding companies with interests in other sectors, contributing to self-censorship. In 2009, the Dogan holding company, which owns many media outlets, was ordered to pay crippling fines for tax evasion in what was widely described as a politicized case stemming from Dogan's criticism of AK and its members. The internet is subject to the same censorship policies that apply to other media, and a 2007 law allows the state to block access to websites deemed to insult Ataturk or whose content includes criminal activities. This law has been used to block access to the video-sharing website YouTube since 2008, as well as several other websites in 2009.

Kurdish-language publications are now permitted. The last restrictions on television broadcasts in Kurdish, which began in 2006, were lifted in 2009, some months after a 24-hour Kurdish-language channel began broadcasting. However, Kurdish newspapers in particular are often closed down and their websites blocked, and some municipal officials in the southeast have faced criminal proceedings for communicating in Kurdish.

The constitution protects freedom of religion, but the state's official secularism has led to considerable restrictions on the Muslim majority and others. Observant men are dismissed from the military, and women are barred from wearing headscarves in public universities and government offices. An AK-sponsored constitutional amendment passed in February 2008 would have allowed simple headscarves tied loosely under the chin in universities, but the Constitutional Court struck it down in June of that year. In the interim, many universities had defied the changes and continued to enforce the total ban. Separately in 2008, the parliament passed a new law that eases restrictions on religious foundations.

Three non-Muslim groups—Jews, Orthodox Christians, and Armenian Christians—are officially recognized, and attitudes toward them are generally tolerant, although they are not integrated into the Turkish establishment. Other groups, including non-Sunni Muslims like the Alevis, lack legal status, and Christian minorities have faced hostility; three Protestants were killed in April 2007 at a publishing house that distributed Bibles.

The government does not regularly restrict academic freedom, but self-censorship on sensitive topics is common. An academic who suggested that the early Turkish republic was not as progressive as officially portrayed was sentenced to a 15-month suspended jail term in 2008.

Freedoms of association and assembly are protected in the constitution. Prior restrictions on public demonstrations have been relaxed, but violent clashes with police still occur. The annual clashes between police and May Day protesters were less severe in 2009. A 2004 law on associations has improved the freedom of civil society groups, although 2005 implementing legislation allows the state to restrict groups that might oppose its interests. Members of local human rights groups have received death threats and sometimes face trial. Nevertheless, civil society is active on the Turkish political scene.

Laws to protect labor unions are in place, but union activity remains limited in practice. While some obstacles have been removed in recent years, Turkey still does not comply with international standards on issues such as collective bargaining.

The constitution envisions an independent judiciary. The government in practice can influence judges through appointments, promotions, and financing, though much of the court system is still controlled by strict secularists who oppose the current government. A 2009 scandal revealed official wiretapping of judges, leading to accusations of political interference. The judiciary has been improved in recent years by structural reforms and a 2004 overhaul of the penal code, and a promising reform strategy was approved in 2009. The death penalty was fully abolished in 2004, and State Security Courts, where many human rights abuses occurred, were replaced by so-called Heavy Penal Courts. However, Amnesty International has accused the Heavy Penal Courts of accepting evidence extracted under torture. The court system is also undermined by procedural delays, with some trials lasting so long as to become a financial burden for the defense.

The current government has enacted new laws and training to prevent torture, including a policy involving surprise inspections of police stations announced in

2008. The 2009 government human rights report found that torture and ill-treatment are declining, although the Human Rights Foundation of Turkey in 2008 reported much higher numbers and a slight increase in violence and ill-treatment since 2005. A man arrested for participating in a demonstration died in custody in October 2008, after he was allegedly beaten; 60 police and prison officials were indicted. Prison conditions can be harsh, with overcrowding and practices such as extended isolation in some facilities. In 2009, jailed PKK leader Abdullah Ocalan was moved to a new facility, ending his controversial solitary confinement.

Also in 2009, the government began serious peace negotiations with the PKK to end the Kurdish conflict in the southeast, including the announcement of a major government initiative to improve democracy and minority rights. However, the fate of this initiative is in doubt, since the banning of the DTP sparked protests at year's end. Bombings in other parts of the country by various radical groups are not infrequent, although there were no serious incidents in 2009.

The state claims that all Turkish citizens are treated equally, but because recognized minorities are limited to the three defined by religion, other minorities and Kurds in particular have faced restrictions on language, culture, and freedom of expression. The situation has improved with EU-related reforms, including the introduction of Kurdish-language postgraduate courses in 2009. However, alleged collaboration with the PKK is still used as an excuse to arrest Kurds who challenge the government.

A 2008 Human Rights Watch report found that gay and transgender people in Turkey face "endemic abuses," including violence, and a local report found widespread discrimination, especially in the workplace. Istanbul's largest gay and transgender organization, Lambda, won an appeal against its closure in 2009, but a prominent transgender human rights activist was stabbed to death soon thereafter. Advocates for the disabled have criticized lack of implementation of a law designed to reduce discrimination. Also in 2009, an Amnesty International report criticized Turkey's asylum policy, which does not recognize non-Europeans as refugees, and the European Court of Human Rights ruled that two Iranian refugees had been unlawfully detained while seeking asylum in Turkey.

Property rights are generally respected in Turkey, with the exception of the southeast, where tens of thousands of Kurds were driven from their homes during the 1990s. Increasing numbers have returned under a 2004 program, and some families have received financial compensation, but progress has been slow. Local paramilitary "village guards" have been criticized for obstructing the return of displaced families through intimidation and violence.

The amended constitution grants women full equality before the law, but the World Economic Forum ranked Turkey 129 out of 134 countries surveyed in its 2009 Global Gender Gap Index. Women held just 49 seats in the 550-seat parliament after the 2007 elections, though that was nearly double the previous figure. Domestic abuse and so-called honor crimes continue to occur; a 2007 study from the Turkish Sabanci University found that one in three women in the country was a victim of violence. Suicide among women has been linked to familial pressure, as stricter laws have made honor killings less permissible; the 2004 penal code revisions included increased penalties for crimes against women and the elimination of sentence reductions in cases of honor killing and rape. In 2009, the European Court of Human

Rights ruled that a 2002 honor killing constituted gender discrimination. In response, the government introduced a new policy, whereby police officers responding to calls for help regarding domestic abuse would be held legally responsible should any subsequent abuse occur.

Turkmenistan

Political Rights: 7
Civil Liberties: 7
Status: Not Free

Population: 5,110,000
Capital: Ashgabat

Ten-Year Ratings Timeline For Year Under Review (Political Rights, Civil Liberties, Status)

2000	2001	2002	2003	2004	2005	2006	2007	2008	2009
7,7NF	7,7NF	7,7NF	7,7NF	7,7NF	7,7NF	7,7NF	7,7NF	7,7NF	7,7NF

Overview: President Gurbanguly Berdymukhammedov appeared more interested in diversifying his country's natural gas exports in 2009 than in political and economic reforms at home. Progress away from the repressive legacy of former president Saparmurat Niyazov, who died in 2006, remained slow, producing token improvements rather than systemic change.

Turkmenistan gained formal independence from the Soviet Union in 1991. Saparmurat Niyazov, the former head of the Turkmenistan Communist Party, had been the sole candidate in elections to the newly created post of president in October 1990. He won reelection in 1992, with a reported 99.5 percent of the vote. A 1994 referendum extended his term until 2002. In the December 1994 elections to the Mejlis (National Assembly), only Niyazov's Democratic Party of Turkmenistan (DPT), the former Communist Party, was permitted to field candidates.

In the 1999 Mejlis elections, every candidate was selected by the government, and virtually all were members of the DPT. The Organization for Security and Cooperation in Europe (OSCE), citing numerous procedural inadequacies, refused to send even a limited assessment mission. The Mejlis unanimously voted in late December to make Niyazov president for life.

In November 2002, Niyazov survived an alleged assassination attempt in Ashgabat. The incident sparked a widespread crackdown on the opposition and perceived critics of the regime, drawing condemnation from foreign governments and international organizations. Mejlis elections in 2004 followed the established pattern of executive control.

Niyazov's rule was marked by frequent government reshuffles, the gutting of formal institutions, the muzzling of media, and an elaborate personality cult. The *Ruhnama*, a rambling collection of quasi-historical and philosophical writings attributed to Niyazov, became the core of educational curriculums. Limited information about the true state of affairs in Turkmenistan pointed to crises in health care, education, and agriculture.

Niyazov's death in December 2006 from an apparent heart attack was followed by the rapid and seemingly well-orchestrated ascent of Deputy Prime Minister Gurbanguly Berdymukhammedov to the position of acting president. The succession appeared to circumvent constitutional norms, as criminal charges were brought against Mejlis Ovezgeldy Atayev, who would have become acting president according to the constitution. Berdymukhammedov subsequently cemented his formal status, easily besting five obscure ruling-party candidates in a February 2007 presidential election that was not monitored by any international observers.

Berdymukhammedov gradually removed high-ranking Niyazov loyalists, with the resignation of Defense Minister Agageldy Mamedgeldiyev in January 2009 apparently ending the process. He also took steps to phase out Niyazov's cult of personality, ordering the removal of public portraits and a reduced emphasis on the *Ruhnama.* In August 2008, the Halk Maslahaty (People's Council), formally the country's supreme representative body, voted without public debate to approve a new constitution, effectively dissolving itself and dispersing its powers to the Mejlis and the president. Elections for an expanded Mejlis were held in December 2008, but as with previous votes, all of the nearly 300 candidates were preapproved by the presidential administration.

Berdymukhammedov changed Niyazov's isolationist foreign policy, parlaying Turkmenistan's natural gas reserves into broader foreign ties. In 2009, gas exports to Russia halted—and relations cooled—after an April pipeline explosion that Turkmenistan blamed on Russia. Meanwhile, a $7 billion pipeline to China opened in December, ending Russia's near-monopoly on gas exports from Turkmenistan. Turkmenistan also held talks with the United States on possible logistical support for NATO operations in Afghanistan, and relations with the European Union warmed amid ongoing discussions of potential energy exports.

Political Rights and Civil Liberties: Turkmenistan is not an electoral democracy. The late president Saparmurat Niyazov wielded near-absolute power until his death. None of the country's elections—including the February 2007 vote that gave Niyazov's successor, Gurbanguly Berdymukhammedov, a five-year term in office—have been free or fair.

The Halk Maslahaty, a legislative body of 2,500 elected and appointed members, approved a new constitution in August 2008, dissolving itself and shifting its legislative powers to the Mejlis (National Assembly). That body expanded from 50 to 125 seats in the December 2008 elections, with members serving five-year terms. The new constitution also gives citizens the right to form political parties, although only one party, the ruling DPT, is officially registered at present. Local council elections held in July 2009 mimicked previous elections amid reports of low turnout.

Corruption is widespread, with public officials often forced to bribe their way into their positions. State profits from gas exports remain opaque. Turkmenistan was ranked 168 out of 180 countries surveyed in Transparency International's 2009 Corruption Perceptions Index.

Freedom of speech and the press is severely restricted by the government, which controls all broadcast and print media. Internet access has expanded somewhat since Niyazov's death, although the sole service provider, run by the government, reportedly blocks undesirable websites. Radio Free Europe/Radio Liberty (RFE/RL) correspondents Osman Hallyev and Dovletmurat Yazguliev were threatened in January

2009. Unanswered questions still surround the death in custody of RFE/RL correspondent Ogulsapar Muradova in 2006.

The government restricts freedom of religion, and independent groups face persecution. Practicing an unregistered religion remains illegal, with violators subject to fines. In a small opening, a European representative of the Seventh Day Adventist Church was allowed into the country in October 2009, and a church spokesperson pointed to limited improvements in religious freedom.

The government places significant restrictions on academic freedom, and the *Ruhnama* is still used in the school system, although its prominence appears to be declining gradually. A concerted reform effort is needed to undo the damage of the Niyazov years. The restoration of the Academy of Sciences in 2009 was a small but welcome step.

The constitution guarantees freedoms of peaceful assembly and association, but these rights are severely restricted in practice. Sporadic protests, usually focused on social issues, have taken place; in July 2009, demonstrators in the port of Turkmenbashi protested water shortages. While not technically illegal, nongovernmental organizations (NGOs) are tightly controlled, and Turkmenistan has no civil society sector to speak of. Environmentalist Andrei Zatoka received a five-year prison term for "hooliganism" in October 2009, although the sentence was replaced with a fine in November. Doctors Without Borders, the last international humanitarian NGO active in Turkmenistan, withdrew from the country in December 2009 due to a lack of cooperation from the Turkmen government. The organization warned of a, "health crisis looming in Turkmenistan."

The government-controlled Colleagues Union is the only central trade union permitted. There are no legal guarantees for workers to form unions or strike, though the constitution does not specifically prohibit these rights. Strikes in Turkmenistan are extremely rare.

The judicial system is subservient to the president, who appoints and removes judges without legislative review. The authorities frequently deny rights of due process, including public trials and access to defense attorneys. The new constitution bars judges and prosecutors from membership in political parties.

Prisons suffer from overcrowding and inadequate nutrition and medical care, and international organizations are not permitted to visit. The government has released some two dozen political prisoners since Niyazov's death, but without a coordinated review. The release of accused dissident Muhammetguly Aymuradov after 14 years in prison in May 2009 was typical in this regard. Nothing is known about the condition of jailed former foreign ministers Boris Shikhmuradov and Batyr Berdyev. Rights activists Annakurban Amanklychev and Sapardurdy Khajiev, convicted on dubious espionage charges in 2006, remained behind bars in 2009.

Turkmenistan is a smuggling corridor for drugs from neighboring Afghanistan, with Niyazov-era reports suggesting the involvement of high-level officials in the narcotics trade as well as a growing problem of drug addiction within Turkmenistan.

Employment and educational opportunities for ethnic minorities are limited by the government's promotion of Turkmen national identity, although some of the more onerous restrictions on the educational and cultural institutions of ethnic minorities have been eased since Niyazov's death.

Freedom of movement is restricted, with a reported blacklist preventing some individuals from leaving the country. Approximately 50 students were unable to secure permits to study abroad at U.S.-funded institutions in 2009.

A Soviet-style command economy and widespread corruption diminish equality of opportunity, although some changes are taking place. The new constitution establishes the right to private property, but it remains unclear how this will be implemented. The government unified the commercial and official exchange rates in May 2008. A World Bank official noted in March 2009 that the country was moving cautiously toward market reforms, with plans to privatize 70 percent of the economy.

Traditional social and religious norms and a lack of employment prospects limit professional opportunities for women, and anecdotal reports suggest that domestic violence is common.

Tuvalu

Political Rights: 1
Civil Liberties: 1
Status: Free

Population: 11,000
Capital: Funafuti

Ten-Year Ratings Timeline For Year Under Review (Political Rights, Civil Liberties, Status)

2000	2001	2002	2003	2004	2005	2006	2007	2008	2009
1,1F	1,1F	1,1F	1,1F	1,1F	1,1F	1,1F	1,1F	1,1F	1,1F

Overview: Global climate change remained a key issue for Tuvalu's government in 2009, as rising sea levels continue to threaten the island's existence. In January, Tuvalu received a US$2 million grant from the Asian Development Bank to advance public financial management and governance systems.

The Gilbert and Ellice Islands, situated in the central South Pacific Ocean, became a British protectorate in 1892 and a British colony in 1916. Polynesian Ellice Islanders voted to separate themselves from the Micronesian Gilbertese in 1974. In 1978, the Ellice Islands became independent under the name of Tuvalu, while the Gilbert Islands become part of Kiribati.

The country has had several changes of government since 2001 due to intense personal and political rivalries and the frequent use of no-confidence votes. Individual and tribal loyalties rather than formal party affiliations drive political alliances, and elected representatives frequently change sides while in office. This situation has sustained a decade-long debate over proposals to introduce direct popular elections for prime minister.

Disappointment with incumbent lawmakers prompted a large voter turnout—some 6,000 out of a population of 10,000—in the 2006 general elections, and newcomers took 7 of the 15 seats in Parliament. Apisai Ielemia, a former civil servant, was chosen as prime minister.

Global climate change and rising sea levels pose significant challenges to Tuvalu and other low-lying island states. The premier of Niue, a small island off the coast of

New Zealand, offered refuge to Tuvaluans in August 2008, and many have accepted the invitation and migrated to the island.

In January 2009, the Asian Development Bank awarded Tuvalu a US$2 million grant to support its public financial management and governance systems. Tuvalu's other aid providers, including the United Nations and New Zealand, have stressed the necessity of improving governance, fiscal management, and transparency.

Political Rights and Civil Liberties: Tuvalu is an electoral democracy. The 2006 elections were free and fair. The head of state, Britain's Queen Elizabeth II, is represented by a governor-general who must be a citizen of Tuvalu. The prime minister, chosen by Parliament, leads the government. The unicameral, 15-member Parliament is elected to four-year terms. A six-person council administers each of the country's nine atolls. Council members are chosen by universal suffrage for four-year terms.

There are no formal political parties, although there are no laws against their formation. Political allegiances revolve around geography and personalities.

Tuvalu is one of the few places in the Pacific Islands where corruption is not a serious problem. The country was not ranked in Transparency International's 2009 Corruption Perceptions Index.

The constitution provides for freedoms of speech and the press, and the government generally respects these rights in practice. The semipublic Tuvalu Media Corporation (TMC) operates the country's sole radio station, television station, the biweekly newspaper *Tuvalu Echoes*, and the government newsletter *Sikuelo o Tuvalu*. Human rights groups have criticized the TMC for limited coverage of politics and human rights issues, but there have been no allegations of censorship or imbalances in reporting. Many residents use satellite dishes to access foreign programming. Internet access is largely limited to the capital because of cost and connectivity challenges, but authorities do not restrict access.

Religious freedom is generally respected. Religion is a major part of life in this overwhelmingly Christian country, and Sunday service is typically considered the most important weekly event. Academic freedom is also generally respected.

The constitution provides for freedoms of association and assembly, and the government upholds these rights. Public demonstrations are permitted, and nongovernmental organizations (NGOs) provide a variety of health, education, and other services for women, youth, and the population at large. In 2007, Parliament approved a bill allowing the incorporation of NGOs, strengthening legal protection for civil society groups. Workers have the right to strike and can freely organize unions and choose their own representatives for collective bargaining. Public sector employees, numbering fewer than 1,000, are members of professional associations that do not have union status. With two-thirds of the population engaged in subsistence farming and fishing, Tuvalu has only one registered trade union—the Tuvalu Seaman's Union—with about 600 members who work on foreign merchant vessels.

The judiciary is independent and provides fair trials. Tuvalu has a two-tier judicial system. The higher courts include the Council in London, the court of appeal, and the high court. The lower courts consist of senior and resident magistrates, the island courts, and the land courts. The chief justice, who is also the chief justice of Tonga, sits on the high court about once a year. A civilian-controlled constabulary force maintains internal order. Prisons are basic, but there have been no reports of abuse.

Major sources of revenue for the state include the sale of coins and stamps, sale of tuna-fishing licenses to foreign fleets, and leasing of the country's internet domain name, ".tv," to foreign firms. Copra and handicrafts are Tuvalu's main exports. About 10 percent of the annual budget is derived from the Tuvalu Trust Fund, a well-run overseas investment fund set up by Britain, Australia, and South Korea in 1987 to provide development assistance.

Traditional customs and social norms condone discrimination against women and limit their role in society. Women enjoy equal access to education, but they remain underrepresented in positions of leadership in business and government. There are currently no women in Parliament. Violence against women is rare. Rape is a crime punishable by law, but spousal rape is not included in the definition. No law specifically targets sexual harassment.

Uganda

Political Rights: 5
Civil Liberties: 4
Status: Partly Free

Population: 30,700,000
Capital: Kampala

Ten-Year Ratings Timeline For Year Under Review (Political Rights, Civil Liberties, Status)

2000	2001	2002	2003	2004	2005	2006	2007	2008	2009
6,5PF	6,5PF	6,4PF	5,4PF	5,4PF	5,4PF	5,4PF	5,4PF	5,4PF	5,4PF

Overview: The ruling National Resistance Movement party dominated the May 2009 local elections amid low voter turnout. In August, President Yoweri Museveni reappointed the electoral commission despite opposition claims that it was biased. Simmering tensions between the government and the traditional Kingdom of Buganda erupted into violence in September. Also during the year, press freedoms were increasingly restricted, and the Ugandan military undertook joint operations against the rebel Lord's Resistance Army in northern Democratic Republic of Congo with Congolese and Southern Sudanese forces, though the long-running conflict remained unresolved at year's end.

Following independence from Britain in 1962, Uganda experienced considerable political instability. President Milton Obote, an increasingly authoritarian leader, was overthrown by Major General Idi Amin in 1971. Amin's brutality made world headlines as hundreds of thousands of people were killed. However, his 1978 invasion of Tanzania led to his ouster by Tanzanian forces and Ugandan exiles. After Obote returned to power in 1980 through fraudulent elections, opponents, primarily from southern Ugandan ethnic groups, were savagely repressed.

Obote was overthrown a second time in a 1985 military coup, and in 1986, the rebel National Resistance Army, led by Yoweri Museveni, took power. Museveni introduced a "no party" system, with only one supposedly nonpartisan political organization—the National Resistance Movement (NRM)—allowed to operate unfettered. This system lasted for two decades.

Museveni and the NRM won presidential and legislative elections in 2001. While a ban on most formal party activities restricted the opposition, observers generally deemed the voting transparent and held that Museveni would have won in an open contest. The opposition boycotted the parliamentary elections, and the NRM's comfortable legislative majority was buttressed by dozens of special-interest representatives.

The National Assembly passed the Political Parties and Organizations Act in 2002, setting conditions under which political parties could be registered and function. The Constitutional Court ruled in 2003 that parts of the law were unconstitutional, and in 2004, it voided restrictions on the freedom of political parties to function. Ugandan voters in 2005 approved constitutional amendments that lifted the ban on political parties and repealed the prohibition on sitting presidents running for a third term, allowing Museveni to seek reelection in 2006.

A leading Museveni opponent, Kizza Besigye of the Forum for Democratic Change (FDC), returned from exile to contest the 2006 presidential election. He was arrested on charges including treason and rape, and was defeated at the polls by Museveni, who took 59 percent of the vote. The NRM also won a large majority in concurrent parliamentary elections. Besigye was later cleared of the rape charges, but the treason case remained outstanding.

In February 2009, Besigye was reelected as FDC party chairman, and was the party's favored candidate for the 2011 presidential election, in which Museveni was also expected to run. Adding to the field, former foreign minister and UN undersecretary general Olara Otunnu returned to Uganda in August after 23 years abroad.

Local council elections were held in May amid low voter turnout. The NRM dominated the balloting, doing well in areas outside its traditional power base. The only opposition party to make an impact was the FDC.

In September, growing tensions between the government and the Buganda region concerning land-reform legislation erupted into violence after police stopped Ronald Muwenda Mutebi II, monarch of the Baganda ethnic group, from attending a rally. At least 20 people were killed in two days of rioting in Kampala, and hundreds were arrested.

The government continued to struggle during the year with the Lord's Resistance Army (LRA), a cult-like rebel movement that had waged a vicious guerrilla war since the 1980s. From December 2008 to March 2009, the Ugandan military conducted a joint operation the armies of Southern Sudan and the Democratic Republic of Congo (DRC) in an effort to finally eliminate the border-crossing LRA. In another sign of improved ties between Uganda and the DRC, the two countries restored full diplomatic relations in August after a 12-year rift.

Uganda is home to more than 500,000 people infected with HIV. Due to concerted efforts, the overall prevalence rate is approximately 5.4 percent, although the United Nations reports that the infection rate may be increasing.

Political Rights and Civil Liberties: Uganda is not an electoral democracy. The single-chamber National Assembly and the powerful president, who faces no term limits, are elected for five-year terms. Of the current legislature's 332 members, 215 are directly elected, and 104 are indirectly elected from special interest groups including women, the military, youth, the disabled, and trade unions. Thirteen ex-officio seats are held by cabinet ministers, who are not elected members and do not have voting rights.

The National Assembly has asserted some independence, censuring high-level executive officials and exercising oversight to influence a number of government actions and policies. However, there are significant concerns regarding the ability of opposition parties to compete with the ruling NRM. A long-standing ban on political party activity was formally lifted in 2005, but the opposition is still hindered by restrictive party registration requirements, voter and candidate eligibility rules, the use of government resources to support NRM candidates, and paramilitary groups—such as the Kiboko Squad and the Black Mambas—that intimidate voters and government opponents. Army representatives in the National Assembly have openly campaigned for Museveni. The independence of the electoral commission has also been called into question, but nevertheless renewed the panel and reappointed its incumbent chairman in August 2009.

Although Uganda has certain measures in place to combat corruption, including the 2009 Anti-Corruption Bill and the Anti-Corruption Court, the resources to enforce them are generally lacking. A 2008 National Integrity Survey by the Inspector General of Government (IGG) reported widespread corruption in the public sector. Auditing and procurement agencies, in addition to the prosecution service, are understaffed and underfinanced. In 2008, evidence emerged that leading government officials had pressured the National Social Security Fund (NSSF) to pay inflated prices for land purchases; the fund's managing director and his deputy were suspended, and in a February 2009 cabinet reshuffle, the finance minister was demoted due to his connection to the scandal. Uganda was ranked 130 out of 180 countries surveyed in Transparency International's 2009 Corruption Perceptions Index.

The constitution provides for freedom of speech. Independent print outlets, including more than two dozen daily and weekly newspapers, are often critical of the government, and several private radio and television stations report on local politics. However, the government is increasingly demonstrating intolerance of press freedom. A sedition law is applied selectively to punish those who cross the NRM. In 2009, four journalists with the largest independent newspaper, the *Monitor*, faced criminal prosecutions. Three others with the *Independent*, including editor Andrew Mwenda, faced charges of sedition after publishing a caricature of Museveni. Mwenda faces another 21 criminal charges, including a 2005 sedition charge. A challenge to the sedition law is currently pending at the Supreme Court, and prosecutions under the legislation have been suspended. In September 2009, the government closed four radio stations and banned live debate programs after violent clashes in Kampala between security forces and supporters of the Baganda king. The ban on live debate programs lasted through the end of 2009. The authorities do not restrict internet usage, although access is limited to major urban centers.

There is no state religion, and freedom of worship is constitutionally protected and respected in practice. Various Christian sects and the country's Muslim minority practice their creeds freely. Academic freedom is also generally respected.

Freedoms of association and assembly are officially recognized. However, in August 2009, police halted a demonstration and arrested eight FDC members who protested Museveni's decision to renew the electoral commission. Nongovernmental organizations (NGOs) encourage the expression of different views and are willing to address politically sensitive issues. However, their existence and activities are vulnerable to the abuse of legal restrictions, including the manipulation of registration requirements. The 2006 NGO Registration Amendment Act requires NGOs and religious organizations to reregister with the Internal Affairs Ministry each year, though enforcement is currently suspended pending a review of the law.

Workers' rights to organize, bargain collectively, and strike are recognized by law, except for those providing essential government services, but legal protections often go unenforced. Many private firms refuse to recognize unions, and strikers are sometimes arrested. According to a 2008 report prepared by the Uganda African Peer Review Mechanism Commission, only one out of three companies comply with labor and employment laws.

The executive does not guarantee the independence of the judiciary. Prolonged pretrial detention, inadequate resources, and poor judicial administration combine to impede the fair exercise of justice. In 2007, the East African Court of Justice found Uganda guilty of violating the rights of its citizens due to repeated military interference with court processes.

The prison system is reportedly operating at three times its intended capacity, and dozens of inmates died during 2009 as a result of poor conditions. Pretrial detainees constitute more than half of the prison population. In April 2009, Human Rights Watch released a report alleging that the country's Joint Anti-Terrorism Task Force has unlawfully detained more than 100 people and tortured at least 25 over the past two years.

Human rights issues, such as police brutality, rape, and vigilante justice, remain serious concerns. The Uganda Human Rights Commission is established in the constitution as an independent government agency, but the National Assembly held its first discussion of the commission's recommendations over the last decade only in May 2009. In addition, members of an agency tasked with addressing discrimination, the Equal Opportunities Commission, have yet to be appointed.

The numbers of internally displaced persons (IDPs) have diminished in recent years due to reduced tensions in the northern part of the country and a government policy to phase out IDP camps. Concerns remain, however, about serious human rights violations related to the unresolved conflict between LRA rebels and the military. In addition to widespread LRA abuses, torture by security forces has occurred.

Although the constitution enshrines the principle of equality between women and men, discrimination against women remains pronounced, particularly in rural areas. Uganda has legislated quotas for women in all elected bodies. Almost 20 percent of National Assembly members are female, and one-third of local council seats are reserved for women. The law gives women the right to inherit land, but customary practices often trump legal provisions in practice. There are no laws protecting women from domestic violence, and incidents often go unreported and are rarely investigated. Cultural practices such as female genital mutilation persist. Sexual abuse of minors appears to be increasing, and according to the International Labour Organization, more than 2.7 million children are employed as workers. The government maintains a hostile attitude toward homosexual rights, and in October 2009, an NRM lawmaker introduced a bill that would create new offenses, including "aggravated homosexuality," and impose harsher penalties, including capital punishment. The bill was still under review by year's end.

Ukraine

Political Rights: 3
Civil Liberties: 2
Status: Free

Population: 46,030,000
Capital: Kyiv

Ten-Year Ratings Timeline For Year Under Review (Political Rights, Civil Liberties, Status)

2000	2001	2002	2003	2004	2005	2006	2007	2008	2009
4,4PF	4,4PF	4,4PF	4,4PF	4,3PF	3,2F	3,2F	3,2F	3,2F	3,2F

Overview:
Infighting among Ukraine's top politicians ahead of the 2010 presidential election left key offices vacant for many months in 2009, and populist fiscal policies further jeopardized the country's economy amid a serious global recession. Perceptions of widespread corruption grew, although the exclusion of a suspicious intermediary company from gas deals between Russia and Ukraine indicated some progress. Also during the year, the authorities arrested a key suspect in the 2000 murder of journalist Heorhiy Gongadze, but investigators had yet to identify the officials who ordered the killing. Despite its numerous problems, Ukraine continued to boast a vibrant civil society and a pluralistic political environment.

In December 1991, Ukraine's voters approved independence from the Soviet Union in a referendum and elected Leonid Kravchuk as president. Communists won a plurality in parliamentary elections in 1994, and Leonid Kuchma defeated Kravchuk in that year's presidential poll. Over time, Kuchma's government faced growing criticism for extensive, high-level corruption and the erosion of political rights and civil liberties.

The 1999 presidential election—in which Kuchma defeated Communist Party challenger Petro Symonenko—was marred by media manipulation, intimidation, and the abuse of state resources. The 2000 murder of independent journalist Heorhiy Gongadze and credible evidence that appeared to implicate Kuchma contributed to mass demonstrations and calls for the president's dismissal.

Reformist former prime minister Viktor Yushchenko's Our Ukraine bloc led the party-list portion of the 2002 parliamentary elections, marking the first electoral success for the democratic opposition since independence. However, propresidential factions were able to create a parliamentary majority, partly through successes in the half of the chamber that was filled through single-member district races at the time.

In the significantly tainted first round of the October 2004 presidential election, Yushchenko came in first among 24 candidates with 39.7 percent of the vote; Prime Minister Viktor Yanukovych, a representative of the eastern, Russian-speaking Donbas region who enjoyed backing from Russian president Vladimir Putin, won 39.3 percent. In the November runoff, the results from the Central Election Commission showed Yanukovych to be the winner by less than three percentage points. However, voting irregularities in Yanukovych's home region led the domestic opposition and international monitors to declare his apparent victory "not legitimate."

In what became known as the Orange Revolution because of Yushchenko's ubiquitous campaign color, millions of people massed peacefully in Kyiv and other cities to protest fraud in the second-round vote. The Supreme Court on December 4 struck down the results and ordered a rerun on December 26. In the middle of the crisis, the parliament ratified constitutional reforms that shifted certain powers from the president to the parliament, effective January 1, 2006. The compromise changes effectively lowered the stakes of the upcoming rerun, making it more palatable to Yushchenko's opponents. However, it created a semiparliamentary system with an unclear division of power, which later led to constant conflict between the president and prime minister.

The repeat of the second round was held in a new political and social atmosphere. The growing independence of the media, the parliament, the judiciary, and local governments allowed for a fair and properly monitored ballot. As a result, Yushchenko won easily with 52 percent of the vote, while Yanukovych took 44 percent. Some 75 percent of eligible voters participated. Former deputy prime minister Yulia Tymoshenko, Yushchenko's chief ally, was approved as prime minister in February 2005.

Despite the high expectations that accompanied the Orange Revolution, Yushchenko and Tymoshenko failed to establish themselves as effective leaders, and members of the government succumbed to infighting over privatization issues, with many implicated in a variety of scandals. In September 2005, Yushchenko dismissed his key allies, Tymoshenko and Petro Poroshenko, the head of the National Security and Defense Council. The March 2006 parliamentary elections prolonged the political stalemate, in which neither the fractured Orange coalition (the Yulia Tymoshenko Bloc and Yushchenko's Our Ukraine) nor Yanukovych's Party of the Regions could form a majority. In July, Socialist Party leader Oleksandr Moroz abandoned the Orange alliance to join the Party of the Regions and the Communist Party in a coalition that made him speaker of parliament and Yanukovych prime minister.

Yanukovych quickly sought to limit Yushchenko's power as president, targeting his ability to control foreign and national security policies. After a period of considerable infighting, Yushchenko dissolved the parliament in April 2007 and was ultimately able to schedule new elections on September 30. The Party of the Regions won 175 seats, followed by the Tymoshenko Bloc with 156 seats and the Our Ukraine–People's Self-Defense bloc with 72. The Communist Party won 27 seats, and the Lytvyn Bloc secured 20. Voter participation was 62 percent. Tymoshenko returned to the premiership in December, thanks to a restoration of the Orange alliance.

Despite the new alignment of forces, the power struggle between president and prime minister continued unabated in 2008 and 2009, as both leaders—along with Yanukovych—eyed the presidential election set for January 2010. Battles among these rivals left many key ministerial posts vacant for long periods in 2009, and at the instigation of the prime minister, the courts invalidated presidential decrees appointing governors and local leaders. The political strife also affected the media, as a Kyiv court banned any "unfair advertisements" against Tymoshenko in September.

Meanwhile, the global recession continued to weigh on Ukraine's export-dependent economy, which contracted by roughly 15 percent in 2009. With the election approaching, the government failed to launch unpopular but necessary reforms, such as raising domestic natural gas prices by cutting existing subsidies, and instead worsened its fiscal position by increasing wages and pensions. The International Monetary Fund had called for greater fiscal discipline when it provided a crucial $16.5 billion loan to prop up the economy in late 2008.

Political Rights and Civil Liberties: Ukraine is an electoral democracy. Massive citizen protests and a court-ordered rerun thwarted an attempt to rig the 2004 presidential election, and parliamentary elections in 2006 and 2007 were deemed free and fair, with only minor polling-place violations.

Citizens elect delegates to the Verkhovna Rada (Supreme Council), the 450-seat unicameral parliament, for four-year terms. Under an electoral law first used in the 2006 elections, all seats are chosen on the basis of party-list proportional representation. Parties must garner at least 3 percent of the vote to win representation. A related package of constitutional reforms shifted power from the president to the parliament, which now approves the prime minister proposed by the president on the recommendation of the majority coalition. The president, who is elected to a maximum of two five-year terms, no longer has the right to dismiss the cabinet. However, the president still issues decrees, is responsible for defending the constitution, and exercises power over the courts, the military, and law enforcement agencies. Political parties are typically little more than vehicles for their leaders and financial backers, and they generally lack coherent ideologies or policy platforms.

Corruption remains one of the country's most serious problems. Business magnates are presumed to benefit financially from their close association with top politicians, while the party-list electoral system reinforces legislators' loyalty to party bosses and leaves them less accountable to voters. In a positive development, the January 2009 resolution of a prolonged gas-price dispute between Ukraine and Russia finally ended the intermediary role of RosUkrEnergo, a secretive gas-trading company that was suspected of serving as a vehicle for corruption. Ukraine was ranked 146 out of 180 countries surveyed in Transparency International's 2009 Corruption Perceptions Index.

The constitution guarantees freedoms of speech and expression, and libel is not a criminal offense. Since the 2004 Orange Revolution, the government has abstained from direct political interference in the media, which have consequently grown more pluralistic, offering a broad range of opinions to the public. In November 2008, the National Council for Television and Radio Broadcasting instituted a local broadcast ban on Russia's most influential television networks, though it has proven ineffective. In 2009, the authorities barred Russian television cameraman Ihor Belokopytov from entering the country. His films have accused Ukraine of hosting secret CIA prisons and claimed that Ukrainian soldiers fought with Georgia against Russia in the 2008 conflict over South Ossetia.

Many media outlets are owned and influenced by business magnates with political interests, while local governments often control the local media. Journalists who investigate wrongdoing at the local level still face physical intimidation, and local police and prosecutors do not energetically pursue such cases. Three former police officers were convicted of taking part in the 2000 murder of independent journalist Heorhiy Gongadze in 2008, and in July 2009, the authorities arrested Oleksiy Pukach, a former senior Interior Ministry officer, who was accused of personally committing the murder. However, investigators had yet to identify those who ordered the killing. Internet access is not restricted and is generally affordable; lack of foreign language skills is the main barrier.

The constitution and the 1991 Law on Freedom of Conscience and Religion define religious rights in Ukraine, and these are generally well respected. Some religious leaders have complained that President Viktor Yushchenko actively supports the merger of the country's two major Orthodox Christian churches into one that would be independent of Moscow, but his activities on behalf of unity haven't amounted to much. Incidents of vandalism at religious sites continue to be reported, and Uzhhorod mayor Serhiy Ratushnyak was charged in August 2009 with making anti-Semitic remarks about presidential candidate Arseniy Yatsenyuk and attacking one of his campaign workers. Muslims are occasionally subjected to document checks by local police, particularly in the eastern parts of Ukraine. Local officials sometimes block the attempts of nontraditional religious groups to register and buy property and typically side with the dominant local religious group. Religious leaders complain about the slow restoration of religious buildings confiscated by the Soviet authorities.

Academic freedom is generally respected. Private universities now augment state-supported higher education, but bribes for entrance exams and grades remain a problem.

The constitution guarantees the right to peaceful assembly but requires organizers to give the authorities advance notice of any demonstrations. Ukraine has one of the most vibrant civil societies in the region. Citizens are increasingly taking issues into their own hands, protesting against unwanted construction, and exposing corruption. There are no limits on the activities of nongovernmental organizations. Trade unions function, but strikes and worker protests are infrequent. Factory owners are still able to pressure their workers to vote according to the owners' preferences.

Before the Orange Revolution, the judiciary was inefficient and subject to corruption. These problems remain, but to a marginally lesser degree than in the past. Although the president, members of parliament, and judges enjoy extensive immunity, the courts are considering new guidelines and will issue a decision on the matter in 2010. The judiciary has become an important arbiter in the political battles between the president and prime minister, but there is little respect for the separation of powers, and all political factions have attempted to manipulate courts, judges, and legal procedures. The Constitutional Court has largely remained silent in the face of politicians' attempts to grab power, lowering its legitimacy in the eyes of the public. In a sign of politicians' low regard for the courts, Prime Minister Yulia Tymoshenko proceeded with a tender to privatize a chemical plant in Odessa on September 29 despite a September 23 court order blocking the sale. The tender was ultimately aborted because the bids were too low.

Torture by police and poor conditions in overcrowded prisons have been persistent problems. However, a reform measure enacted in 2008 aimed to bring Ukraine's criminal justice system up to international standards, with a focus on improving pretrial detention procedures and strengthening victim's rights.

While the country's Romany population suffers from discrimination, the government has actively interceded to protect the rights of most ethnic and religious minorities, including the Crimean Tatar community. Tatars continue to suffer discrimination at the hands of local authorities and communities in Crimea in terms of land ownership, access to employment, and educational opportunities. Even though Ukraine decriminalized homosexuality, members of the gay and lesbian community report discrimination against them. In one violent example, antigay thugs disrupted a book event in Lviv in the summer of 2009.

The government generally respects personal autonomy and privacy, and the constitution guarantees individuals the right to own property, work, and engage in entrepreneurial activity. However, when the interests of powerful businesspeople are involved, cronyism and the protection of insider interests prevail.

Gender discrimination is prohibited under the constitution, but women's rights have not been a priority for government officials. While there are a relatively large number of women in prominent executive and legislative posts, including the premiership, women still do not have the same opportunities as men. Human rights groups have complained that employers advertising for jobs often specify the gender of the desired candidate and discriminate on the basis of physical appearance and age. The trafficking of women abroad for the purpose of prostitution remains a major problem and a threat to women's rights and security.

United Arab Emirates

Political Rights: 6
Civil Liberties: 5
Status: Not Free

Population: 5,066,000
Capital: Abu Dhabi

Ten-Year Ratings Timeline For Year Under Review (Political Rights, Civil Liberties, Status)

2000	2001	2002	2003	2004	2005	2006	2007	2008	2009
6,5NF	6,5NF	6,5NF	6,6NF	6,6NF	6,6NF	6,5NF	6,5NF	6,5NF	6,5NF

Overview: In May 2009, authorities of the United Arab Emirates detained a member of the ruling family who was caught on videotape allegedly torturing an Afghani man. In July, the Abu Dhabi Federal Court of Appeal ruled to suspend the newspaper *Emarat al-Yawm* for an article critical of the ruling family. Meanwhile, the country's economy struggled as a result of the global economic crisis. In December, Abu Dhabi provided Dubai a US$10 billion bailout to help ease the latter's debt crisis and stave off financial collapse.

Attacks on shipping off the coast of what is now the United Arab Emirates (UAE) led the British to mount military expeditions against the local tribal rulers in the early 19th century. A series of treaties followed, including a long-term maritime truce in

1853 and an 1892 pact giving Britain control over foreign policy. The seven sheikh-doms of the area subsequently became known as the Trucial States. In 1971, Britain announced that it was ending its treaty relationships in the region, and six of the seven Trucial States formed the UAE federation. Ras al-Khaimah, the seventh state, joined in 1972. The provisional constitution left significant power in the hands of each emirate.

The government in 2001 cracked down on corruption, arresting some senior officials. In the wake of that year's terrorist attacks on the United States, the government introduced reforms in its financial services and banking sectors to block the financing of terrorism. In 2004, new legislation established stricter punishments for crimes involving terrorism.

In January 2006, Sheikh Mohammed bin Rashid al-Maktoum succeeded his brother as ruler of the emirate of Dubai and prime minister of the UAE. His ascension did not result in any substantive changes in the UAE's political balance, with the ruling families maintaining a firm grip on power.

The first-ever elections for half of the 40-seat, largely advisory Federal National Council were held in December 2006. However, participation was limited to a small electoral college appointed by the emirates' seven rulers in September. The UAE government appointed the remaining 20 members in February 2007.

In May 2009, UAE police detained Sheikh Issa bin Zayed al-Nahyan, brother of the crown prince of Abu Dhabi, after he was caught on videotape torturing an Afghani merchant in 2008. He has been implicated in 25 additional incidents. Al-Nahyan's case went to trial in late 2009 and remained before the courts at year's end.

In contrast to many of its neighbors, the UAE has achieved some success in diversifying its economy to reduce dependency on the petroleum sector. The country has built a leading free-trade zone in Dubai and a major manufacturing center in Sharjah, and it has invested resources to expand its tourism industry. In spite of these efforts, however, the UAE has suffered from the recent global economic downturn. Property values have plummeted, and thousands of foreigners who had been working in the real estate and financial sectors have fled the country or been laid off. In December, Dubai received a US$10 billion bailout package from Abu Dhabi to help the state-owned Dubai World repay a US$4.1 billion bond.

Political Rights and Civil Liberties: The UAE is not an electoral democracy. All decisions about political leadership rest with the dynastic rulers of the seven emirates, who form the Federal Supreme Council, the highest executive and legislative body in the country. The seven leaders select a president and vice president, and the president appoints a prime minister and cabinet. The UAE has a 40-member Federal National Council (FNC), half of which was elected for the first time in 2006 by a 6,689-member electoral college chosen by the seven rulers. The other half of the council is directly appointed by the government for two-year terms. UAE officials have said they intend to grant universal suffrage for the 2010 FNC elections. The council serves only as an advisory body, reviewing proposed laws and questioning federal government ministers.

There are no political parties in the country. Instead, the allocation of positions in the government is largely determined by tribal loyalties and economic power. The emirate of Abu Dhabi, the major oil producer in the UAE, has controlled the federation's presidency since its inception. Citizens have a limited opportunity to express their interests through traditional consultative sessions.

The UAE is considered one of the least corrupt countries in the Middle East. It was ranked 30 out of 180 countries surveyed in Transparency International's 2009 Corruption Perceptions Index.

Although the UAE's constitution provides for some freedom of expression, the government has historically restricted this right in practice. The 1980 Printing and Publishing Law applies to all media and prohibits, "defamatory material and negative material about presidents, friendly countries, [and] religious issues, and [prohibits] pornography." Consequently, journalists commonly practice self-censorship, and the leading media outlets frequently publish government statements without criticism or comment. However, Dubai has a "Media Free Zone," where few restrictions have been reported on print and broadcast media produced for audiences outside of the UAE. Government officials continue to ban a variety of publications and internet websites. In 2009, the government continued its consideration of a restrictive press law that will reintroduce prison terms for journalists who "disparage" government officials or write stories that "harm the country's economy." The draft law also threatens fines of up to US$136,000 for commentary on the poor economy and up to US$1.35 million for articles "insulting" to the ruling family or government. In July, the Abu Dhabi Federal Court of Appeal suspended the newspaper *Emarat al-Yawm* for three weeks and fined its editor US$5,445 for an October 2006 article that claimed some of the ruling family's thoroughbred racehorses were given steroids.

The constitution provides for freedom of religion. Islam is the official religion, and the majority of citizens are Sunni Muslims. However, the minority Shiite Muslim sect and non-Muslims are free to worship without interference. The government controls content in nearly all Sunni mosques. In March 2009, the minister of State and Foreign Affairs, who also heads the National Human Rights Commission, rejected several recommendations by the United Nations for improving religious freedom in the UAE, including protections for citizens to convert or change religious beliefs. Academic freedom is limited, with the Ministry of Education censoring textbooks and curriculums in both public and private schools.

The government places limits on freedoms of assembly and association. In March 2009, Dubai outlawed public dancing, kissing, and the playing of loud music. Small discussions on politics in private homes are generally tolerated, but there are limits on citizens' ability to organize broader gatherings. Public meetings require government permits. All nongovernmental organizations (NGOs) must register with the Ministry of Labor and Social Affairs, and registered NGOs reportedly receive subsidies from the government.

The UAE's mostly foreign workers do not have the right to organize, bargain collectively, or strike. Workers continue to protest poor working and living conditions, with the government reportedly using military force to crack down on demonstrations. However, after hosting a joint UAE-United Nations conference on labor and human rights in May, the country's minister of labor committed to expand efforts to ensure that workers be paid fairly and in a timely manner as well as to improve housing standards. Amid the global recession, a growing number of expatriate workers were dismissed from their jobs and sent home.

The judiciary is not independent, with court rulings subject to review by the political leadership. The legal system is divided into Sharia (Islamic law) courts, which handle family and criminal matters, and secular courts, which cover civil law. Although the constitution bans torture, members of the royal family and the country's police have allegedly used torture against political rivals and business associates. Sharia courts sometimes impose flogging sentences for drug use, prostitution, and adultery. Recent violence among the nonindigenous community has led to arbitrary arrests and detention, and prisons of the larger emirates are overcrowded. While the federal Ministry of the Interior oversees police forces in the country, each emirate's force enjoys a great deal of autonomy.

Discrimination against noncitizens and foreign workers occurs in many aspects of life. Fewer than 20 percent of the country's residents are UAE citizens. There are also more than 100,000 stateless residents, often known as *bidoon*, who are unable to secure regular employment and face systemic discrimination. In 2008, the Ministry of Interior set up registration centers, where the bidoon could apply for citizenship. However, the government retains the final authority to approve or reject requests for citizenship, and selection criteria remain unclear. Hundreds of Lebanese Shiites and Palestinians were expelled by the government between August and October 2009 for reportedly refusing to spy on their fellow countrymen in the UAE.

The constitution does not specifically mention gender equality, and women's social, economic, and legal rights are not always protected. Muslim women are forbidden to marry non-Muslims and are eligible for only one half of their brother's inheritance. Women are underrepresented in government, though women have received appointments at various levels in recent years. The prime minister, Sheikh Mohammed bin Rashid al-Maktoum, added two new women to the country's cabinet in 2008, and Sheikh Sultan al-Qasimi, ruler of the emirate of Sharjah, has appointed five women to his consultative council. Abu Dhabi swore in the country's first woman judge in October 2008, after the judicial law was amended to allow women to serve as prosecutors and judges.

Foreigners lured into the country by employment opportunities are often subjected to harsh working conditions, physical abuse, and the withholding of passports. Despite government efforts to combat human trafficking—including a 2006 antitrafficking law and the opening of two shelters for women victims—the government has failed to address the problem adequately.

United Kingdom

Political Rights: 1
Civil Liberties: 1
Status: Free

Population: 61,823,000
Capital: London

Ten-Year Ratings Timeline For Year Under Review (Political Rights, Civil Liberties, Status)

2000	2001	2002	2003	2004	2005	2006	2007	2008	2009
1,2F	1,2F	1,1F	1,1F	1,1F	1,1F	1,1F	1,1F	1,1F	1,1F

Overview: A scandal over lawmakers' personal expenses erupted in May 2009, resulting in a loss of public faith in Parliament. Scotland's justice secretary stirred controversy in August by releasing a Libyan man who had been convicted for the 1988 bombing of an airliner over the town of Lockerbie. Separately, the new Supreme Court began functioning in October, replacing a panel of the House of Lords as the country's highest court and increasing the structural separation of powers.

The English state emerged before the turn of the first millennium and was conquered by Norman French invaders in 1066. Wales, Scotland, and lastly Ireland were subdued or incorporated into the kingdom over the course of centuries, culminating in the creation of the United Kingdom of Great Britain and Ireland in 1801. The Glorious Revolution of 1688–89 began a gradual—but eventually total—assertion of the powers of Parliament, as Britain became one of the modern world's first democracies. A significant extension of voting rights was passed in 1832, and subsequent reforms led to universal adult suffrage.

Most of Ireland won independence after World War I, with Protestant-majority counties in the north remaining a restive part of what became, as of 1927, the United Kingdom of Great Britain and Northern Ireland. Significant powers were devolved to a Scottish Parliament, and fewer to a Welsh Assembly, in 1997. Peace negotiations tentatively restored home rule to Northern Ireland in 1998.

The Labour Party won the 1997 general elections after adopting more centrist positions, ending nearly two decades of Conservative Party rule. Prime Minister Tony Blair led Labour to another major victory in 2001, though he faced opposition within the party for his support of the U.S.-led war in Iraq beginning in 2003.

A combination of slow progress in improving public services and the continuation of the Iraq war led to a far less decisive Labour victory in May 2005 elections, and the margin of the party's parliamentary majority fell from 165 seats to 66. Blair remained prime minister, but he was considerably weakened by speculation about when he would hand the premiership to Gordon Brown, the chancellor of the exchequer.

On July 7, 2005, three suicide bombings in London's Underground railway system and one on a London bus killed more than 50 people and wounded hundreds. The culprits were British Muslims—three of Pakistani descent and one a convert to Islam. The attacks set off a public debate about the integration of immigrants and racial and religious minorities into British society. They also led to wide-ranging government proposals to toughen antiterrorism laws, which in turn sparked concerns about civil liberties.

In previous decades, Britain's main source of internal violence had been the struggle between unionists and Irish nationalists in Northern Ireland. This largely ended with the Good Friday peace agreement, signed in 1998. However, the locally elected Assembly called for in the agreement was suspended in 2002 after Sinn Fein— the political party linked to the Irish Republican Army (IRA), an outlawed Irish nationalist paramilitary group—was caught spying on rival politicians and security officials. Further peace talks and the formal disarmament of the IRA paved the way for fresh elections for the Assembly in March 2007 and the formation of a power-sharing local government by Sinn Fein and the Democratic Unionist Party (DUP). The DUP's longtime leader, Ian Paisley, became first minister.

In June 2007, Blair resigned and Brown took office as prime minister. Although he won some praise for his response to failed terrorist attacks that month, Brown subsequently suffered from flagging public support and a Labour Party fund-raising scandal later that year. Meanwhile, David Cameron, a younger politician who had led the Conservative Party since late 2005, gained in the polls as he modernized and softened his party's right-wing image.

Brown acted decisively to counter the international financial crisis in late 2008 and early 2009 by shoring up ailing banks with public money, and his approach was hailed abroad as a model response. Nevertheless, Labour was left far behind by the Conservatives in the June 2009 European Parliament elections, which also handed the nationalist—and many say racist—British National Party its first two seats.

The European voting took place amid a major scandal concerning the widespread exploitation of parliamentary expense accounts by lawmakers. In May, the media had revealed that many Parliament members routinely used public funds for luxury items, home renovations, and other dubious purposes. Both major parties were implicated, and the image of the entire institution was tarnished. The Speaker of the House of Commons resigned as a result.

In August, Scotland's justice secretary made the controversial decision to release Abdelbaset al-Megrahi, the only person convicted in the 1988 bombing of a U.S. airliner over the Scottish town of Lockerbie. Al-Megrahi was allowed to return home to Libya on compassionate grounds, as he was terminally ill. The move drew criticism in Britain and the United States, and led to accusations that the British government had pushed for the release to bolster economic relations with Libya, though officials in London rejected the claims.

Political Rights and Civil Liberties: The United Kingdom is an electoral democracy. Each of the 646 members of the House of Commons, the dominant lower chamber of the bicameral Parliament, is elected in a single-member district. This procedure multiplies the power of the two largest parties—the Labour Party and the Conservative Party—at the expense of smaller parties. The Liberal Democrats, the third-largest party, are the most disadvantaged; although they won 22.1 percent of the vote in the 2005 elections, they received only 9.4 percent of the seats in the House of Commons. The parliamentary opposition holds ministers accountable in debates that are widely covered in the press. Parliamentary elections must be held at least every five years.

The House of Lords, Parliament's upper chamber, can delay legislation initiated in the Commons. If it defeats a measure passed by the Commons, the Commons must reconsider, but it can ultimately overrule the Lords. The Lords membership, currently more than 700, was reformed under Prime Minister Tony Blair, and all but 92 hereditary peers (nobles) were removed. The rest are "life peers," chosen by governments to serve for life; Law Lords, who until late 2009 served as the country's highest court; and a small number of bishops and archbishops of the Church of England. The monarch, currently Queen Elizabeth II, plays a largely ceremonial role as head of state.

In addition to the Labour and Conservative parties and the left-leaning Liberal Democrats, other parties include the Welsh nationalist Plaid Cymru and the Scottish National Party. In Northern Ireland, the main Catholic and republican parties are Sinn Fein and the Social Democratic and Labour Party, while the leading Protestant and unionist parties are the Ulster Unionist Party and the DUP.

After a period of centralization under Conservative governments from 1979 to 1997, the Labour Party delivered a far-reaching devolution of power to Northern Ireland, Scotland, and Wales. The first elections to the Scottish Parliament and the Welsh Assembly were held in 1999. The Scottish body has more power, including some tax-raising authority, than its Welsh counterpart. Welsh nationalism is primarily cultural. The Northern Ireland Assembly was temporarily suspended in 2002 after complications in the peace process, but restored in 2007.

Corruption is not pervasive in Britain, but high-level scandals have damaged the reputation of the political class under both Labour and Conservative governments. Instances of political donations made in exchange for "honors" (peerages and titles) have been reported under the Labour government, and a party-funding scandal tarnished the government in 2007. In 2009, a parliamentary expenses scandal drew a great deal of attention, although there was only limited corruption involved. At the same time, two members of the House of Lords were suspended for accepting bribes to amend legislation. Britain was ranked 17 out of 180 countries surveyed in Transparency International's 2009 Corruption Perceptions Index.

The law provides for press freedom, and the media in Britain are lively and competitive. Daily newspapers span the political spectrum, though the combined effects of the economic crisis and rising internet use have driven some smaller papers out of business. The state-owned British Broadcasting Corporation (BBC) is editorially independent and faces significant private competition. England's libel laws are among the most claimant-friendly in the world, leading wealthy foreign litigants—known as libel tourists—to use Britain's libel laws to silence their critics. Anyone can sue for libel in a British court as long as the material was accessed in Britain, and the burden of proof is on the defendant. In some cases, this practice has led to self-censorship. The government is also increasingly using so-called super-injunctions to forbid the media from reporting certain information and even from reporting on the injunction, as occurred in one high-profile case with the *Guardian* newspaper in 2009. The government has faced criticism for rampant delays in fulfilling freedom of information requests. In 2009, the government refused to fulfill a request on security grounds for the first time; the query sought the minutes of cabinet meetings leading up to the 2003 Iraq invasion. Internet access has not been restricted by the government. However, in 2009 the government announced that internet firms will be required to store increased information on user activities, including visits to foreign websites, and additional proposals designed to combat internet piracy have raised protests for their severity.

Although the Church of England and the Church of Scotland have official status, the government both prescribes freedom of religion in law and protects it in practice. Nevertheless, Muslims especially report discrimination, harassment, and occasional assaults. A 2006 law banned incitement to religious hatred, with a maximum penalty of seven years in prison. Academic freedom is respected by British authorities.

Freedoms of assembly and association are respected. However, police were criticized in April 2009 for corralling and striking protesters during an international summit, and for abusing a passerby who later died. Civic and nongovernmental organizations are allowed to operate freely. Workers' right to organize in unions is protected. Trade unions have traditionally played a leading role in the Labour Party, though this connection weakened as the party moved toward the center beginning in the 1990s.

A new Supreme Court began functioning in October 2009, improving the separation of powers by moving the highest court out of the House of Lords. An earlier round of reform in 2005 had removed the judicial and legislative functions of the Lord Chancellor, who remains a senior figure in the cabinet. The police maintain high professional standards, and prisons generally adhere to international guidelines.

Britain's antiterrorism laws are some of the strongest in the democratic world, and are frequently criticized by rights groups. Terrorism suspects can be detained without charge for 28 days, and in 2009, the European Court of Human Rights awarded compensation to 11 people who had been detained without trial after 2001 terrorist attacks in the United States. Also in 2009, a government report found that many people arrested under the antiterrorism laws had been subsequently charged with different crimes, indicating that the laws may have been misused. It also showed that people of Asian descent have been arrested on flimsier grounds than others. In June, the Law Lords ruled that the evidence used against a defendant may not be kept secret under so-called control orders—restrictive conditions placed on terrorism suspects—as was previously the case.

In several cases, the government has been accused of "outsourcing" torture by extraditing terrorism suspects to their home countries, where they could be abused in custody. According to a 2009 UN report, at least 15 people claimed to have been tortured in other countries with the knowledge of British authorities.

Violence in Northern Ireland has been rare in recent years. However, the murders of two soldiers and a policeman in March 2009 were claimed by IRA splinter groups that oppose the peace agreement. Four splinter groups remain active, but they may not total more than a few hundred people. Also in March, Parliament passed a law allowing devolution of responsibility for policing and criminal justice to the Northern Ireland government, though the transfer was not finalized by year's end.

In September 2009, the director of public prosecutions published guidelines describing circumstances in which a person was unlikely to be prosecuted for assisting another person's suicide, a topic that has been hotly debated in the country. While such assistance remained illegal, the factors that could dissuade a prosecution included the age, intent, and illness of the deceased, and the motives of those assisting them.

Britain has large numbers of immigrants and locally born descendants of immigrants, who receive equal treatment under the law. In practice, their living standards are lower than the national average, and they complain of having come under increased suspicion amid the terrorist attacks and plots of recent years. Racist incidents are more common in Northern Ireland than in other parts of the country. In a particularly severe incident in June 2009, thugs drove more than 100 Romanians, mostly Roma, from their homes; many ended up temporarily leaving the country.

Women receive equal treatment under the law but are underrepresented in politics and the top levels of business. Women on average earn 23 percent less than men. Abortion is legal in Great Britain but heavily restricted in Northern Ireland, where it is allowed only to protect the life or the long-term health of the mother. Northern Irish women seeking abortion typically travel to Great Britain.

United States of America

Political Rights: 1
Civil Liberties: 1
Status: Free

Population: 306,805,000
Capital: Washington, D.C.

Note: The numerical ratings and status listed above to not reflect conditions in Puerto Rico, which is examined in a separate report.

Ten-Year Ratings Timeline For Year Under Review (Political Rights, Civil Liberties, Status)

2000	2001	2002	2003	2004	2005	2006	2007	2008	2009
1,1F	1,1F	1,1F	1,1F	1,1F	1,1F	1,1F	1,1F	1,1F	1,1F

Overview: President Barack Obama's first year in office was dominated by efforts to revive the economy and enact a series of sweeping domestic reforms. While the administration succeeded in passing a major spending package to stimulate the economy, other proposals—such as an overhaul of the country's health insurance system—encountered significant obstacles in Congress. Also during the year, Obama made important changes to the counterterrorism programs inherited from his predecessor, George W. Bush, but he left many elements of previous policy in place.

The United States declared independence in 1776, during a rebellion against British colonial rule. The current system of government began functioning in 1789, following ratification of the country's constitution. Because the founders of the United States distrusted concentrated government authority, they set up a system in which the federal government has three coequal branches—executive, legislative, and judicial—and left many powers with state governments and the citizenry.

For most of the country's history, power has alternated between the Democratic and Republican parties. President George W. Bush of the Republicans was reelected for a second four-year term in 2004, but he subsequently suffered from major policy setbacks and declining public-approval ratings. In the 2006 midterm elections, the Democrats won control of both houses of Congress for the first time since 1994, and in 2008, Democratic Senator Barack Obama won the presidency, defeating the Republican nominee, Senator John McCain.

Obama, the first black candidate to become president, triumphed in the November general election amid fears of economic collapse triggered by a steep decline in the stock market, a housing crisis that entailed hundreds of thousands of home-mortgage foreclosures, and a major increase in the unemployment rate. He ultimately secured 53 percent of the popular vote, with McCain receiving 46 percent. In the Electoral College balloting, which determines the presidential election outcome, Obama and his vice presidential nominee, Senator Joseph Biden, received 365 votes, compared with 173 for McCain and his running mate, Governor Sarah Palin of Alaska. Although McCain did well among white men, Obama scored substantial majorities among several groups, including black, Hispanic, and younger voters. The turnout rate, at over 61 percent of eligible voters, was one of the highest recorded in recent years. In concurrent legislative elections, the Democrats increased their majorities in both the House of Representatives and the Senate.

Once in office, Obama moved to fulfill campaign pledges to reverse a number of Bush administration counterterrorism policies. He issued a policy document that forbade the use of torture by U.S. personnel, and announced plans to quickly shut down the detention facility at Guantanamo Bay, Cuba. However, many civil libertarians criticized the new administration for its unwillingness to roll back other Bush-era practices. For example, it declined to end the collection of Americans' voice and internet communications by the National Security Agency, and it invoked the doctrine of state secrets to block information requests in several court cases.

Likewise, the Obama administration showed little interest in investigating the actions of former Bush officials, as many civil libertarians and Democratic Party leaders had asked. Even the plan to shut down the Guantanamo detention facility remained incomplete at year's end, as the administration encountered resistance from ordinary citizens and political representatives in mainland U.S. areas to which the detainees might be transferred. A further complication emerged when defense officials reported that a number of former Guantanamo detainees had joined militant groups and taken up arms against the United States after being released. While the administration announced its intention to try some high-profile terrorism defendants in civilian courts, it indicated that others would be tried before military tribunals, asserting that the Bush-era tribunal system would first be reformed.

On domestic policy, Obama had entered office with an ambitious legislative agenda, including sweeping health insurance reform, measures to combat climate change and shift the country's energy policy, and new regulations for the financial industry. By year's end, with the exception of a spending package designed to stimulate the economy, little of the administration's domestic agenda had been passed by Congress despite the robust Democratic majorities in both houses. The president's difficulties were due in part to divisions within the Democratic Party, but more significant was the vocal and unified opposition of the Republican Party. The Republicans particularly relied on the filibuster in the Senate, a mechanism that requires a supermajority of 60 senators to bring legislation to a vote.

In his two most important foreign policy actions, Obama announced a plan for a phased withdrawal from Iraq that would have most U.S. combat forces out of the country in 2011, but also initiated a major increase in U.S. troop levels in Afghanistan, where the United States and other NATO countries were fighting a difficult conflict with the Taliban.

Political Rights and Civil Liberties: The United States is an electoral democracy with a bicameral federal legislature. The upper chamber, the Senate, consists of 100 members—two from each of the 50 states— serving six-year terms, with one-third coming up for election every two years. The lower chamber, the House of Representatives, consists of 435 members serving two-year terms. At the end of 2009, the Democrats controlled the House, 257–178. In the Senate, the Democrats held a substantial lead, with 58 seats as opposed to 40 for the Republicans; there were also two independents who voted with the Democratic caucus. All national legislators are elected directly by voters in the districts or states they represent. The president and vice president are elected to four-year terms. Under a 1951 constitutional amendment, the president is limited to two terms in office.

Presidential elections are decided by an Electoral College, meaning it is possible for a candidate to win the presidency while losing the national popular vote. Electoral College votes are apportioned to each state based on the size of its congressional representation. In most cases, all of the electors in a particular state cast their ballots for the candidate who won the statewide popular vote, regardless of the margin. Two states, Maine and Nebraska, have chosen to divide their electoral votes between the candidates based on their popular-vote performance in each congressional district, and other states are now considering similar systems.

In the U.S. political system, a great deal of government responsibility rests with the 50 states. Most law enforcement matters are dealt with at the state level, as are education, family matters, and many land-use decisions. States also have the power to raise revenues through various forms of taxation. In some states, citizens have a wide-ranging ability to influence legislation through institutions of direct democracy, such as referendums, which have been conducted on issues including tax rates, affirmative action, and immigrant rights. Direct-democracy mechanisms have been hailed by some as a reflection of the openness of the U.S. system. However, they have also been criticized on the grounds that recalling elected officials in the middle of their terms or making policy through referendums can lead to incoherent governance, undermine the institutions of representative democracy, and weaken the party system.

The intensely competitive U.S. political environment is dominated by the two major parties, the right-leaning Republicans and the left-leaning Democrats. The country's "first past the post" or majoritarian electoral system tends to discourage the emergence of additional parties, as do a number of specific legal and other hurdles. However, on occasion, independent or third-party candidates have significantly influenced politics at the presidential and state levels, and a number of newer parties, such as the Green Party, have modestly affected politics in certain municipalities in recent years. While the majoritarian system has discouraged the establishment of parties based on race, ethnicity, or religion, religious groups and minorities have been able to gain political influence through participation in the two established parties. Conservative Christian groups, for example, play a substantial role in Republican Party affairs, while black, Hispanic, and homosexual rights advocates play important roles in the Democratic Party. A number of laws have been enacted to ensure the political rights of minorities, especially blacks. In June 2009, the Supreme Court upheld a provision of the 1965 Voting Rights Act that allows the federal government to vet changes to election laws in certain states and municipalities with histories of discriminatory balloting rules.

Election campaigns in the United States are long and expensive. Serious candidates frequently find themselves in a "permanent campaign," with a never-ending process of fundraising. The two parties and the constituency and interest groups that support them have used various methods to circumvent legal restrictions on campaign spending, and the Supreme Court on several occasions has struck down such restrictions, finding that they violated free speech rights. Election spending for the 2008 contests easily surpassed that of previous years, reaching over $5 billion; the presidential race alone cost $2.4 billion.

American society has a tradition of intolerance toward corrupt acts by government officials, corporate executives, or labor leaders. In 2009, charges of corruption were brought against government officials in a number of states, including New York, New Jersey, and Illinois. In one notable case, the former governor of Illinois, Rod Blagojevich, was indicted in April for what prosecutors said was a broad graft scheme that included efforts to sell the Senate seat vacated by newly elected president Barack Obama, which the governor had the authority to fill by appointment. Blagojevich had been impeached and removed from office in January following his arrest in late 2008. The U.S. media are aggressive in reporting on cases of corporate and official corruption; newspapers often publish investigative articles that delve into questions of private or public malfeasance. At the same time, the expanding influence of interest groups and lobbyists on the legislative and policymaking processes, combined with their crucial role in campaign fundraising, has given rise to public perceptions of enhanced corruption in Washington. The United States was ranked 19 out of 180 countries surveyed in Transparency International's 2009 Corruption Perceptions Index.

The federal government has a high degree of transparency. A substantial number of auditing and investigative agencies function independently of political influence. Such bodies are often spurred to action by the investigative work of journalists. Federal agencies regularly place information relevant to their mandates on websites to broaden public access. In an action widely praised by scholars and civil libertarians, Obama in 2009 ordered that millions of government documents from the Cold War era be declassified and made available to the public.

The United States has a free, diverse, and constitutionally protected press. A long-standing debate over the impact of ownership consolidation—either by sprawling media companies with outlets in many states and formats, or by corporate conglomerates with little or no previous interest in journalism—has evolved into doubts about the financial viability of newspapers. Various papers in 2009 either shut down, made sharp cuts in staffing and print production, or opted to abandon print and produce web-only versions. Some analysts have argued that the end of the newspaper era is at hand, and that Americans will get nearly all of their news from online sources in the future. Already, internet journalists and bloggers play an important and growing role in the coverage of political news, and internet access is widespread in the country. Meanwhile, the traditional news divisions of major broadcast television networks have increasingly given way to 24-hour cable news stations and their internet sites.

Controversy has emerged in recent years over attempts by federal prosecutors and private attorneys to compel journalists to divulge the names of confidential sources or turn over notes and background material in legal cases. A bill that would provide journalists with limited protection from demands for information about confidential sources in federal cases was pending in Congress in 2009. Such press shield laws already exist in 37 states.

The United States has a long tradition of religious freedom. Adherents of practically every major religious denomination, as well as many smaller groupings, can be found throughout the country, and rates of both religious belief and religious-service attendance are high. The constitution protects religious freedom while barring any official endorsement of a religious faith, and there are no direct government subsidies to houses of worship. The debate over the role of religion in public life is ongoing, however, and religious groups often mobilize to influence political discussions on the diverse issues in which they take an interest, including gay marriage, abortion, civil rights, and immigration.

The academic sphere enjoys a healthy level of intellectual freedom. There are regular discussions on university campuses over such issues as the global economy, Israel and the Palestinians, and the alleged of curriculums on Middle Eastern affairs.

In general, officials respect the right to public assembly. Protest demonstrations directed at government policies are frequently held in Washington, New York, and other major cities. The United States gives wide freedom to trade associations, non-governmental organizations, and issue-oriented pressure groups to organize and argue their cases through the political process. In recent years, local authorities have sometimes employed strict crowd-control tactics at the presidential nomination conventions of the two major parties, large antiwar demonstrations, and protests at gatherings of the World Bank or other transnational institutions.

Federal law guarantees trade unions the right to organize workers and engage in collective bargaining with employers. The right to strike is also guaranteed. Over the years, however, the strength of organized labor has declined, so that less than 8 percent of the private sector workforce is currently represented by unions. An important factor in this trend is the country's labor code, which is regarded as an impediment to organizing efforts. The National Labor Relations Board, which adjudicates labor-management disputes, has been accused of circumscribing unions' ability to organize and represent workers effectively. This could change with Obama's appointment of board members who are more sympathetic to unions. Organizing efforts are also impeded by strong resistance from private employers. Several attempts to modify core labor laws have been defeated in Congress over the years, and in 2009, even with the enlarged Democratic majority, the legislature failed to adopt a union-supported reform measure that would have made it easier to organize workers. Despite its institutional decline, organized labor continues to play a vigorous role in electoral politics.

Judicial independence is respected. Although the courts have occasionally been accused of intervening in areas that are best left to the political branches, most observers regard the judiciary as a linchpin of the American democratic system. In recent years, much attention has been paid to the ideological composition of the Supreme Court, which has issued a number of significant decisions by a one-vote margin. In 2009, Obama named Sonia Sotomayor, a federal appeals court judge and former advocate for the rights of Puerto Ricans, to fill a vacancy on the Supreme Court, making her the first Hispanic and third woman to serve on the nine-member panel.

While the United States has a strong rule-of-law tradition, the criminal justice system's treatment of minority groups has long been a concern. A disproportionately large percentage of defendants in criminal cases involving murder, rape, assault, and robbery are black or Hispanic. Minority groups also account for an outsized share of the prison population.

Indeed, civil liberties organizations and other groups have advanced a broad critique of the criminal justice system, arguing that there are too many Americans in prison, that prison sentences are often excessive, and that too many people are prosecuted for minor drug offenses. Over two million Americans are behind bars in federal and state prisons and local jails at any given time, producing the highest national incarceration rate in the world. The number of incarcerated Americans has continued to increase even as the national rate of violent crime has declined in recent years. There is also a disturbing number of juveniles serving lengthy prison terms in adult penitentiaries. Concerns have been raised about prison conditions, especially the unsettling incidence of violence and rape.

The United States has the highest rate of legal executions in the democratic world. Reflecting growing doubts about the death penalty, several states have announced a moratorium on capital punishment pending studies on the practice's fairness, and the number of executions has declined steadily in recent years. Of particular importance in the campaign against the death penalty has been the exoneration of some death-row inmates based on new DNA testing. The Supreme Court has in recent years struck down the death penalty in cases where the perpetrator is a juvenile or mentally handicapped.

The United States is one of the world's most racially and ethnically diverse societies. In recent years, residents and citizens of Latin American ancestry have replaced blacks as the largest minority group, and the percentage of whites in the population has declined somewhat. An array of policies and programs designed to protect the rights of minorities, including laws to prevent workplace discrimination, affirmative action plans for university admissions, quotas to guarantee representation in the internal affairs of some political parties, and policies to ensure that minorities are not treated unfairly in the distribution of government assistance. Blacks, however, continue to lag in economic standing, educational attainment, and other social indicators. Affirmative action in employment and university admissions remains a contentious issue. The Supreme Court has given approval to the use of race or ethnicity as a factor in university admissions under certain narrow conditions. However, affirmative action has been banned, in whole or in part, through referendums in five states, and the Supreme Court further circumscribed the use of race in job promotions in a case involving firefighters from New Haven, Connecticut, in 2009.

Since its immigration laws underwent major changes during the 1960s, the United States has generally maintained liberal immigration policies. In recent years, there has been a prominent debate over the degree to which new immigrants are assimilating into American society. Most observers, however, believe that the country has struck a balance that both encourages assimilation and permits new legal immigrants to maintain their religious and cultural customs. Americans remain troubled by the large number of illegal immigrants in the country, and the federal government has responded by strengthening security at the border with Mexico. In a departure from previous policy, the Obama administration announced in 2009 that it would focus its enforcement efforts on employers rather than raiding job sites in search of undocumented workers who were subject to deportation.

Citizens of the United States enjoy a high level of personal autonomy. The right to own property is protected by law and is jealously guarded as part of the American of life. Business entrepreneurship is encouraged as a matter of government policy.

The United States prides itself as a society that offers wide access to economic and social advancement and favors government policies that enhance equality of opportunity. Historically, the opportunities for economic advancement have played a key role in the successful assimilation of new immigrants. Recently, however, studies have shown a widening inequality in wealth and a narrowing of access to upward mobility. Among the world's prosperous, stable democracies, the United States is unique in having a large underclass of poor people who have, at best, a marginal role in economic life.

Women have made important strides toward equality over the past several decades. They now constitute a majority of the American workforce; are heavily represented in the legal profession, medicine, and journalism; and predominate in university programs that train students for these careers. Although the average compensation for female workers is roughly 80 percent of that for male workers, women with recent university degrees have effectively attained parity with men. Nonetheless, many female-headed families continue to live in conditions of chronic poverty.

Federal law does not include homosexuals as a protected class under antidiscrimination legislation, though many states have enacted such protections. Since Massachusetts's highest court ruled in 2003 that the state constitution gave homosexual couples the same right to marry as heterosexual couples, many states have passed laws or constitutional amendments explicitly banning same-sex marriage. At the same time, an increasing number of states have granted gay couples varying degrees of family rights, and a handful have endorsed full marriage rights.

Uruguay

Political Rights: 1
Civil Liberties: 1
Status: Free

Population: 3,364,000
Capital: Montevideo

Ten-Year Ratings Timeline For Year Under Review (Political Rights, Civil Liberties, Status)

2000	2001	2002	2003	2004	2005	2006	2007	2008	2009
1,1F	1,1F	1,1F	1,1F	1,1F	1,1F	1,1F	1,1F	1,1F	1,1F

Overview: Jose Mujica of the ruling center-left Broad Front (FA) coalition emerged as the victor in Uruguay's November 2009 presidential runoff elections, defeating former president Luis Lacalle. Mr. Mujica's victory was helped by the continued popularity of the FA government, brought about by Uruguay's economic growth. The ruling FA government maintained its parliamentary majority. Separately, Tabare Vazquez's government continued investigations into atrocities committed during the military dictatorship of 1973 to 1985.

After gaining independence from Spain, the Republic of Uruguay was established in 1830. The ensuing decades brought a series of revolts, civil conflicts, and incursions by neighboring states, followed by a period of relative stability in the first half of the 20th century. The rival Colorado and Blanco parties vied for political power in the 1950s and 1960s, but economic troubles and an insurgency by the leftist Tupamaro National Liberation Front led to a military takeover by 1973. From that year until 1985, the country was under the control of a military regime whose reputation for incarcerating the largest proportion of political prisoners per capita in the world earned Uruguay the nickname "The Torture Chamber of Latin America."

The military era came to an end after elections held in 1984, in which Julio Maria Sanguinetti of the Colorado Party won the presidency. A 1986 amnesty law promoted by the new civilian president, who had been the military's favored candidate, granted members of the armed forces immunity for human rights violations committed during the years of dictatorship. The military extracted the concession as its price for allowing the democratic transition the year before.

In the next general election, held in November 1989, Luis Lacalle of the Blanco Party was elected president. The 1990s were marked by relative economic stability and prosperity. Jorge Batlle of the Colorado party was elected president in 1999. He immediately sought an honest accounting of the human rights situation under the former military regime, while showing equally firm determination to reduce spending and privatize state monopolies. In 2001, crises in the rural economy and an increase in violent crime, as well as growing labor unrest, set off alarms in what was still one of Latin America's safest countries.

A currency devaluation and default in Argentina at the end of 2001 caused a dramatic drop in foreign exchange reserves and unprecedented economic insecurity. By mid-2002, the government was forced to impose a weeklong bank holiday, Uruguay's first in 70 years, to stanch a run on the country's banks.

In October 2004, Uruguayans elected Tabare Vazquez of the Broad Front (FA) coalition as president in the first round of voting, dealing a crushing blow to the Colorado Party. Vazquez's coalition also captured a majority of seats in both houses of parliament, marking the first time in nearly 40 years that the president's party enjoyed a parliamentary majority. Faced with the challenge of creating a stable macroeconomic framework and attracting foreign capital, Vazquez began his term by implementing a floating exchange rate, fiscal discipline, and an inflation-targeted monetary policy in a once-again growing economy.

Uruguay fully repaid its International Monetary Fund (IMF) obligations in November 2006. Nevertheless, the Vazquez administration has continued its commitment to economic orthodoxy. In 2007, a revenue-neutral tax reform that introduced a personal income tax and simplified the tax system came into effect. Aided by increased commodity prices, in his five years as president, Vazquez has tripled foreign investment, maintained steady inflation, reduced poverty from 37 to 26 percent of the population, and cut unemployment in half.

Vazquez has proved willing to reopen the issue of some 200 Uruguayans who disappeared during the military's political dominance in the 1970s, or Uruguay's dirty war. Under its reinterpretation of the 1986 amnesty law, which allowed for higher-level officers to be tried, the administration arrested several police chiefs and army leaders in 2006 and 2007 for human rights violations committed during the military dictatorship. The government's investigation into those who disappeared in the dirty war included excavating military barracks where victims were suspected to be buried. In November 2006, former president Juan Maria Bordaberry was charged for the 1976 kidnapping and murder of two parliamentary leaders. A federal appeals court in 2008 confirmed the multiple murder charges against Bordaberry, but he was still awaiting trial at the end of 2009.

Former military dictator Gregorio Alvarez was arrested in December 2007 for abducting political opponents during the military rule. In October 2009, Alvarez was sentenced to 25 years in prison for murder and human rights violations. Still, most human rights violations cases are left in impunity. While the Supreme Court declared the amnesty law unconstitutional in mid-October, voters rejected a referendum several days later that would have overturned amnesty for those accused of human rights abuses during the military regime.

Helped by the ongoing popularity of President Vazquez, Jose Mujica of the ruling FA coalition won the runoff presidential election held in November 2009 with more than 53 percent of the vote. Mr. Mujica, a socialist senator who spent 14 years in prison for waging a guerrilla movement against the military regime, beat his top challenger, Luis Lacalle, former president and candidate of the conservative National (or Blanco) Party. The FA coalition maintained its majority in parliament.

Political Rights and Civil Liberties: Uruguay is an electoral democracy. The 2009 elections were free and fair. The 1967 constitution established a bicameral General Assembly consisting of the 99-member House of Representatives and the 30-member Senate, with all members serving five-year terms. The president is directly elected for a single five-year term.

The major political parties and groupings are the Colorado Party, the Independent Party, the Blanco Party, and the ruling FA coalition. The latter includes the Movement of Popular Participation (MPP), the New Space Party, the Socialist Party, and the Uruguayan Assembly, among other factions.

The Transparency Law (Ley Cristal) criminalizes a broad range of potential abuses of power by officeholders, including the laundering of funds related to public corruption cases. In 2005, the government announced that it had reached an important antinarcotics agreement with the United States, including tight controls on money laundering in a country previously known as a bank-secrecy haven. Uruguay was ranked 25 out of 180 countries surveyed in Transparency International's 2009 Corruption Perceptions Index.

Constitutional guarantees regarding free expression are generally respected, and violations of press freedom are rare. The press is privately owned, and broadcasting includes both commercial and public outlets. Numerous daily newspapers publish, many of them associated with political parties; there are also a number of weeklies. In June 2009, Congress approved a bill eliminating criminal penalties for defamation of public officials. The government does not place restrictions on internet usage.

Freedom of religion is a cherished political tenet of democratic Uruguay and is broadly respected. The government does not restrict academic freedom.

Rights to freedom of assembly and association are provided for by law, and the government generally observes these in practice. Civic organizations have proliferated since the return of civilian rule. Numerous women's rights groups focus on problems such as violence against women and societal discrimination. Workers exercise their right to join unions, bargain collectively, and hold strikes. Unions are well organized and politically powerful. Wage negotiations are completed by Uruguay's wage councils—the collective bargaining entities comprising representatives from the business sector, the government, and the unions.

Uruguay's judiciary is relatively independent. However, the court system is severely backlogged, and pretrial detainees often spend more time in jail than they would if convicted of the offense in question and sentenced to the maximum prison term. Overcrowded prisons reached almost 130 percent capacity in 2009, and violence among inmates remained a problem. Medical care for prisoners is substandard, and many rely on visitors for food.

The small black minority, comprising an estimated 9 percent of the population, continues to face economic difficulties. Official estimates state that 50 percent of Afro-Uruguayans are poor and suffer from discrimination.

Women enjoy equal rights under the law but face traditional discriminatory attitudes and practices, including salaries averaging about two-thirds those of men. As of the end of 2009, no gender discrimination cases had ever reached a courtroom. Violence against women remains a problem and was on the rise in 2009. On a positive note, women hold 15 parliamentary seats, and 4 of the 13 cabinet members are women. Congress approved gay civil unions in 2007, making Uruguay the first South American country to approve these rights nationwide.

Uzbekistan

Political Rights: 7
Civil Liberties: 7
Status: Not Free

Population: 27,562,000
Capital: Tashkent

Ten-Year Ratings Timeline For Year Under Review (Political Rights, Civil Liberties, Status)

2000	2001	2002	2003	2004	2005	2006	2007	2008	2009
7,6NF	7,6NF	7,6NF	7,6NF	7,6NF	7,7NF	7,7NF	7,7NF	7,7NF	7,7NF

Overview: Uzbekistan continued to rebuild relations with the United States and the European Union in 2009 amid growing cooperation on logistical support for NATO operations in Afghanistan. At the same time, the government of President Islam Karimov maintained repressive state controls at home, denying citizens their basic human rights.

Uzbekistan gained independence from the Soviet Union through a December 1991 referendum. In a parallel vote, Islam Karimov, the former Communist Party leader and chairman of the People's Democratic Party (PDP), the successor to the Communist Party, was elected president amid fraud claims by rival candidate Mohammed Solih, leader of the Erk (Freedom) Party. Solih fled the country two years later, and his party was forced underground. Only progovernment parties were allowed to compete in elections to the first post-Soviet legislature in December 1994 and January 1995. A February 1995 referendum to extend Karimov's first five-year term in office until 2000 was allegedly approved with 99 percent support.

All of the five parties that competed in the December 1999 parliamentary elections, which were strongly criticized by international monitors, supported the president. In the January 2000 presidential poll, Karimov defeated his only opponent, allegedly winning 92 percent of the vote. The government refused to allow the participation of genuine opposition parties. A 2002 referendum extended presidential terms from five to seven years.

A series of suicide bomb attacks and related violent clashes in late March and early April 2004 killed some 50 people. Police appeared to be the main targets. The authorities blamed radical international Islamist groups—particularly the al-Qaeda-linked Islamic Movement of Uzbekistan (IMU) and the banned Hizb ut-Tahrir (Party of Liberation). Suicide bombers killed several people outside the U.S. and Israeli embassies in July 2004 amid conflicting claims of responsibility. In December, elections for the lower house of a new bicameral parliament were held, with only the five legal, propresidential parties allowed to participate.

The city of Andijon in the Ferghana Valley witnessed a popular uprising and violent security crackdown in May 2005. On May 10 and 11, family members and supporters of 23 local businessmen charged with involvement in a banned Islamic group staged a peaceful demonstration in anticipation of the trial verdict. The situation turned violent on the night of May 12, when armed men stormed a prison, freed the 23 businessmen and other inmates, and captured the local government administration building. Thousands of local residents subsequently gathered in the city center, where people began to speak out on political and economic issues, often making antigovernment statements.

Security forces responded by opening fire on the crowd, which included many women and children. Although the authorities maintained that the protesters were the first to open fire, eyewitnesses reported that the security forces began shooting indiscriminately. Official figures put the death toll at 187, but unofficial sources estimated the dead at nearly 800, most of them unarmed civilians. The government accused Islamic extremists of orchestrating the demonstrations, though most of the demonstrators appeared to have been motivated by economic and social grievances, and many of those present had come to witness the events rather than participate in protests.

Karimov repeatedly rejected calls from the European Union (EU), the Organization for Security and Cooperation in Europe (OSCE), and the United States for an independent international inquiry into the violence. In July 2005, Uzbekistan gave the United States six months to leave its military base at Karshi-Khanabad, which it had been allowed to use to support operations in Afghanistan since late 2001. Russia and China endorsed the official account of the violence.

The Uzbek authorities instituted a wide-ranging crackdown after the Andijon incident, targeting nongovernmental organizations (NGOs) with foreign funding, potential political opposition figures, human rights defenders, and even former officials.

Karimov's seven-year term ended in January 2007, and the constitution barred him from running for reelection. Nevertheless, he won a new term in December 2007, with an official 88 percent of the vote.

Uzbekistan began repairing relations with the EU and United States in 2007, eventually agreeing to the overland transportation of nonmilitary supplies to support NATO operations in Afghanistan. In 2009, the EU lifted the last of the sanctions it had imposed after Andijon. Ties with Russia were mixed during the year, with significant Russian involvement in Uzbekistan's energy sector and strenuous Uzbek objections to Russian plans for a new military base in neighboring Kyrgyzstan.

Political Rights Uzbekistan is not an electoral democracy. President Islam
and Civil Liberties: Karimov uses the dominant executive branch to repress all
political opposition. His December 2007 reelection appeared to flout constitutional rules on term limits. A dubious referendum in 2002 replaced the country's single-chamber legislature with a bicameral parliament, consisting of a 120-seat lower house (with members elected by popular vote for five-year terms) and a 100-member upper house, or Senate (with 84 members elected by regional councils and 16 appointed by the president).

Only four political parties, all progovernment, are currently registered, and no genuine opposition parties function legally. A 2007 law intended to expand the role of registered parties had no real effect on the moribund political arena. Unregistered opposition groups, like Birlik and Erk, function primarily in exile. Exiled opposition activist Bahodir Choriyev returned to Uzbekistan in 2009, but the authorities limited his movements and harassed activists who tried to meet with him. December 2009 parliamentary elections offered voters no meaningful choice, although the four progovernment parties indulged in mild criticism of one another.

Corruption is pervasive. Uzbekistan was ranked 174 out of 180 countries surveyed in Transparency International's 2009 Corruption Perceptions Index.

Despite constitutional guarantees, freedoms of speech and the press are severely restricted. The state controls major media outlets and related facilities. Although official censorship was abolished in 2002, it has continued through semiofficial mechanisms that strongly encourage self-censorship. U.S.-funded Radio Free Europe/Radio Liberty was forced out of Uzbekistan in December 2005. State-controlled television has aired "documentaries" smearing perceived opponents, including a program in 2007 on journalist Alisher Saipov, who was subsequently murdered in Kyrgyzstan. The Committee to Protect Journalists charged in 2009 that at least seven journalists are behind bars in Uzbekistan, including activist Dilmurod Saidov, who received a 12.5-year sentence in February on dubious fraud charges. The OpenNet Initiative has found that the government systematically blocks websites with content that is critical of the regime.

The government permits the existence of mainstream religions, including approved Muslim, Jewish, and Christian denominations (primarily Protestant), but treats unregistered activities as a criminal offense. The state exercises strict control over Islamic worship, including the content of sermons. Suspected members of banned Muslim organizations and their relatives have been subjected to arrest, interrogation, and torture.

The government limits academic freedom, according to the U.S. State Department's

2009 human rights report. Bribes are commonly required to gain entrance to exclusive universities and obtain good grades.

Open and free private discussion is limited by the *mahalla* committees, traditional neighborhood organizations that the government has turned into an official system for public surveillance and control.

Despite constitutional provisions for freedom of assembly, the authorities severely restrict this right in practice. Law enforcement officials broke up a small rally of human rights activists in Tashkent in February 2009.

Freedom of association is tightly constrained, and unregistered NGOs face extreme difficulties and harassment. After the unrest in Andijon, the government shut down virtually all foreign-funded organizations in Uzbekistan. A local advocate in 2008 described membership in the government-controlled association for NGOs as "voluntary but compulsory." In 2009, members of the Human Rights Alliance faced harassment and imprisonment.

The Council of the Federation of Trade Unions is dependent on the state, and no genuinely independent union structures exist. Organized strikes are extremely rare.

The judiciary is subservient to the president, who appoints all judges and can remove them at any time. The creation in 2008 of a Lawyers' Chamber with compulsory membership increased state control over the legal profession. A 2007 report by Human Rights Watch described torture as "endemic" in the criminal justice system. Law enforcement authorities routinely justify the arrest of suspected Islamic extremists or political opponents by planting contraband or filing dubious charges of financial wrongdoing. In October 2009, rights activist Farhod Mukhtarov received a five-year prison sentence for fraud. The next month, the authorities released Sanjar Umarov, the leader of the opposition Sunshine Coalition, who had been held since 2005.

Prisons suffer from severe overcrowding and shortages of food and medicine. As with detained suspects, prison inmates—particularly those sentenced for their religious beliefs—are often subjected to abuse or torture. Human Rights Watch has documented a number of torture-related deaths in custody during the last few years. Reports in 2009 indicated that the poet Yusuf Juma, who received a five-year sentence after calling for Karimov's resignation in 2007, was targeted for abuse in prison. Rights organizations also highlighted several credible allegations in 2009 that police raped detained prisoners during investigations.

Although racial and ethnic discrimination is prohibited by law, the belief that senior positions in government and business are reserved for ethnic Uzbeks is widespread. Moreover, the government appears to be systematically closing schools for the Tajik-speaking minority.

Permission is required to move to a new city, and bribes are commonly paid to obtain the necessary registration documents. Restrictions on foreign travel include the use of exit visas, which are often issued selectively. Nevertheless, millions of Uzbeks, primarily men of working age, seek employment abroad, particularly in Russia and Kazakhstan.

Widespread corruption and the government's tight control over the economy limit equality of opportunity. The country's agricultural sector has seen few reforms since the Soviet period. As part of the government's economic stimulus plan, small farmers in 2009 were required to hire new employees, whether or not they had the resources to do so. A series of regulations and decrees over the last few years have placed numerous restrictions on market traders. Small businesses are freer to develop than large enterprises, which are often enmeshed in high-level corruption schemes. New regulations in 2009 ended tax privileges for foreign investors.

Women's educational and professional prospects are limited by cultural and religious norms and by ongoing economic difficulties. Victims of domestic violence are discouraged from pressing charges against perpetrators, who rarely face prosecution. The trafficking of women abroad for prostitution remains a serious problem. The parliament passed legislation in November 2009 that imposed tougher penalties for child labor, but the practice reportedly remained widespread during the year's cotton harvest.

Vanuatu

Political Rights: 2
Civil Liberties: 2
Status: Free

Population: 239,,000
Capital: Port Vila

Ten-Year Ratings Timeline For Year Under Review (Political Rights, Civil Liberties, Status)

2000	2001	2002	2003	2004	2005	2006	2007	2008	2009
1,3F	1,3F	1,2F	2,2F	2,2F	2,2F	2,2F	2,2F	2,2F	2,2F

Overview: In 2009, bitter political rivalries resulted in failed opposition-led votes of no confidence against Prime Minister Edward Natapei, who was also briefly stripped of his seat in Parliament and position as prime minister in November. In September, Iolu Abil was chosen as Vanuatu's new president. Meanwhile, Viran Molisa Trief was appointed the country's first female solicitor general in March.

Vanuatu was governed as an Anglo-French "condominium" from 1906 until independence in 1980. The Anglo-French legacy continues to split society along linguistic lines in all spheres of life, including politics, religion, and economics.

Widespread corruption and persistent political fragmentation have caused many governments to collapse or become dysfunctional. No-confidence votes have forced several changes of government in recent years, and parliamentary coalitions have been frequently formed and dissolved.

In March 2007, the government declared a two-week state of emergency in the capital following deadly clashes between people from Tanna and Ambrym islands. The violence, sparked by allegations of black magic, killed 3 people, injured 20, and led to 200 arrests.

In the 2008 parliamentary elections, the Vanua'aku Party (VP) won 11 seats, the National United Party (NUP) took 8, and the Union of Moderate Parties (UMP) and the Vanuatu Republican Party (VRP) each captured 7. In September, Parliament elected the VP's Edward Natapei—former prime minister from 2001 to 2004—to succeed Ham Lini as the new prime minister. International observers deemed the elections largely credible despite reports of bribery and fraud. Fractious politics in 2008 led to three failed no-confidence motions against Natapei before the year's end.

Natapei survived a no-confidence vote in June 2009 and forestalled another in mid-November, when he replaced half of his cabinet with members of the opposition alliance. However, his failure to submit a written explanation for missing three consecutive sittings of the Parliament resulted in Natapei being stripped of his seat in Parliament and his position as prime minister at the end of November. The chief justice reinstated Natapei in December, after ruling that the decision to remove him had been unconstitutional, and Natapei survived yet another no-confidence vote on December 10. In September, the electoral college chose Iolu Abil to replace Kalkot Mataskelekele as the country's president.

Vanuatu secured US$66 million in development assistance over five years from the U.S. Millennium Challenge Account in 2006, and the U.S. Government Accountability Office reported in 2008 that Vanuatu was making progress in creating jobs and increasing per capita income. However, unemployment rates are high, and crime has worsened, particularly in the capital. Real progress on economic reform and strengthening the rule of law remains difficult, as politics is dominated by ethnic, tribal, and personal rivalries.

Political Rights and Civil Liberties: Vanuatu is an electoral democracy. The constitution provides for parliamentary elections every four years. The prime minister, who appoints his own cabinet, is chosen by the 52-seat unicameral Parliament from among its members. Members of the parliament and the heads of the six provincial governments form an electoral college to select the largely ceremonial president for a five-year term. The National Council of Chiefs works in parallel with the Parliament, exercising authority mainly over language and cultural matters.

Many political parties are active, but individual rivalries are intense and politicians frequently switch affiliations. Politics is also driven by linguistic and tribal identity. The leading parties are the VP, NUP, and the francophone UMP.

Corruption remains a serious problem. National leaders have been forced from office in recent years amid corruption scandals. Elected officials have also been accused of threatening journalists for critical reporting. In March 2009, a member of Parliament was charged with unlawful sexual intercourse with a minor and indecent assault, though the charges were dropped when the victim refused to testify. Another lawmaker was charged in March with harboring a prisoner and obstructing officers on duty. Vanuatu was ranked 95 out of 180 countries surveyed in Transparency International's 2009 Corruption Perceptions Index.

The government generally respects freedoms of speech and the press. The state-owned Television Blong Vanuatu broadcasts in English and French. Radio Vanuatu is the only radio station. The state-owned *Vanuatu Weekly* and several privately owned daily and weekly papers supply international, national, and local news. In 2008, the government ended its monopoly over telecommunications services. The number of internet users is increasing, though access is largely limited to the capital due to cost and lack of infrastructure.

The government generally respects freedom of religion in this predominantly Christian country. Members of the clergy have held senior government positions, including the posts of president and prime minister. There were no reports of restrictions on academic freedom.

The law provides for freedoms of association and assembly, and the government typically upholds these rights. Public demonstrations are permitted by law and generally allowed in practice. Civil society groups are active on a variety of issues. Five independent trade unions are organized under the umbrella Vanuatu Council of Trade Unions. Workers can bargain collectively and strike.

The judiciary is largely independent, but it is weak and inefficient. Lack of resources hinders the hiring and retention of qualified judges and prosecutors. Long pretrial detentions are common. Tribal chiefs often adjudicate local disputes, but their punishments are sometimes deemed excessive. Despite reported improvements in 2009, prisons fail to meet minimum international standards. Ill-treatment of prisoners and police brutality allegedly provoke outbreaks. In March 2009, a detainee was allegedly beaten to death while in police custody. Approximately 70 inmates escaped from the main prison in Port Vila in December 2008, and another 5 escaped from the same facility in January 2009.

Local traditions are frequently sources of discrimination against women. There are only two women in Parliament. In March 2009, the government appointed Viran Molisa Trief as the first female solicitor general. Spousal rape is not a crime, and no law prohibits domestic abuse or sexual harassment, which women's groups claim are common and increasing. Most cases go unreported due to victims' fear of reprisal or family pressure, and the police and courts rarely intervene or impose strong punishments on offenders. The traditional practice of "bride payment," or dowry, remains common. Vanuatu is a transit point for victims trafficked for prostitution and labor.

Venezuela

Political Rights: 5*
Civil Liberties: 4
Status: Partly Free

Population: 28,368,000
Capital: Caracas

Ratings Change: Venezuela's political rights rating declined from 4 to 5 due to the adoption of laws designed to further marginalize the political opposition, including provisions that were rejected by referendum voters in December 2007.

Ten-Year Ratings Timeline For Year Under Review (Political Rights, Civil Liberties, Status)

2000	2001	2002	2003	2004	2005	2006	2007	2008	2009
3,5PF	3,5PF	3,4PF	3,4PF	3,4PF	4,4PF	4,4PF	4,4PF	4,4PF	5,4PF

Overview: In February 2009, referendum voters approved reforms backed by President Hugo Chavez Frias that abolished term limits for the presidency and other elected offices. Nevertheless, a weak economy, continued political polarization, and problems with the provision of key public services led to increased street protests during the year. Meanwhile, new laws threat-

ened to further marginalize the political opposition, and tensions with Colombia
increased the risk of armed conflict.

The Republic of Venezuela was founded in 1830, nine years after independence
from Spain. Long periods of instability and military dictatorship ended with the establishment of civilian rule in 1958 and the approval of a constitution in 1961. Until
1993, the center-left Democratic Action (AD) party and the Social Christian Party
(COPEI) dominated politics under an arrangement known as the Punto Fijo pact.
President Carlos Andres Perez (1989–93) of the AD, already weakened by the violent political fallout from his free-market reforms, was nearly overthrown by Lieutenant Colonel Hugo Chavez Frias and other nationalist military officers in two 1992
coup attempts, in which dozens of people were killed. Perez was subsequently impeached as a result of corruption and his inability to stem the social consequences
of economic decline, which had coincided with lower oil prices beginning in the 1980s.
Rafael Caldera, a former president (1969–74) and founder of COPEI, was elected president in late 1993 as head of the 16-party Convergence coalition, which included both
left- and right-wing groups.

Chavez won the 1998 presidential contest on a populist, anticorruption platform,
and in 1999, voters approved a new constitution that strengthened the presidency
and introduced a unicameral National Assembly. Although Chavez retained his post
in elections held under the new charter in 2000, opposition parties won most governorships, about half of the mayoralties, and a significant share of the National Assembly seats.

In April 2002, following the deaths of 19 people in a massive antigovernment
protest, dissident military officers attempted to oust Chavez, the vice president, and
the National Assembly with backing from some of the country's leading business
groups. However, the coup was resisted by loyalist troops and protesters, and Chavez
moved swiftly to regain control of the military, replacing dozens of senior officers.

The country was wracked by continued protests, and in December 2002, opposition leaders called a general strike that lasted 62 days but ultimately weakened
their political position as well as the economy. While fending off his opponents with
legal maneuvers and intimidation tactics, Chavez launched bold social-service initiatives, including urban health-care and literacy projects, many of which were staffed
by thousands of experts from Cuba. Chavez survived a 2004 presidential recall referendum triggered by an opposition signature campaign, taking 58 percent of the vote
amid high turnout.

Even as Venezuela faced multiple social and economic problems, Chavez continued to focus on increasing his influence over the judiciary, the media, and other
institutions of civil society. The National Assembly, controlled by his supporters,
approved a measure allowing it to remove and appoint judges to the Supreme Tribunal of Justice, which controlled the rest of the judiciary. The legislation also expanded
the tribunal's membership from 20 to 32 justices.

National Assembly elections in 2005 were boycotted by the opposition, which
accused the National Electoral Council (CNE) of allowing violations of ballot secrecy. A mere 25 percent of eligible voters turned out, and all 167 deputies in the
resulting National Assembly were government supporters, although a small number defected to the opposition in subsequent years.

In the 2006 presidential election, Chavez defeated Zulia state governor Manuel Rosales of the opposition New Time party, 61 percent to 38 percent. The incumbent exploited state resources during the campaign and drew on enduring support among poorer Venezuelans, who had benefited from his social programs. The balloting generally proceeded without incident and was pronounced fair by international observers.

Soon after the vote, Chavez pressed forward with his program of institutional changes. Nearly all progovernment parties merged into the Unified Socialist Party of Venezuela (PSUV), and the "Bolivarian revolution" deepened economically with a series of nationalizations. At the end of January 2007, the National Assembly voted to allow the president to issue decrees on a broad array of topics for 18 months.

In May 2007, the state seized the broadcast frequency and equipment of the country's oldest television station, RCTV, drawing strong objections from human rights and press freedom organizations. The renewal of its license was denied based on what Chavez claimed were the station's ongoing efforts to destabilize the government. University students mounted large street protests in support of RCTV that gained wide sympathy but were at times forcibly repressed. Meanwhile, the station soon returned to operation as a cable channel.

Referendum voters in December 2007 narrowly defeated a package of constitutional amendments that had been drafted by the government and National Assembly with little outside consultation. The most prominent amendment—which the opposition considered the key motivation behind the larger package—would have removed presidential term limits. The vote reflected robust opposition participation, public disappointment with rising inflation and crime rates, and a degree of disaffection among current and former Chavez supporters.

Chavez pledged to continue his efforts to enact the proposed amendments. In late July 2008, as his decree-making authority was about to expire, he unveiled a set of 26 new laws. Some appeared designed to institute measures that were rejected in the referendum, including presidential authority to name new regional officials and the reorganization of the military hierarchy.

Also that month, the nominally independent but government-friendly comptroller general disqualified over 300 candidates for the November state and local elections, including a number of opposition leaders, primarily on charges of corruption. PSUV and other Chavez-aligned candidates enjoyed massive publicity in state-controlled media and other resource advantages, while opposition candidates focused on perceived failures in public services and benefited from coverage in the opposition press. In balloting deemed fair by the Organization of American States (OAS), the opposition captured the mayoralty of greater Caracas as well as Venezuela's second-largest city and 5 of 22 states, including the three richest and most populous. Meanwhile, government candidates won 17 states and some 80 percent of the mayoralties.

Following the elections, Chavez moved forward with plans for a new referendum on abolishing term limits. Unlike the 2007 ballot, which focused on the presidential term, this referendum proposal would also lift term limits for mayors, governors, and state and national legislators. The government's efforts included mobilization of state resources and pressure on public employees, as well as arguments that only a continuation of the Bolivarian revolution would assure social services and political power for poorer Venezuelans. The February 2009 poll was characterized by observers as generally free, and Chavez prevailed with over 54 percent of the vote.

In March and April, the legislature passed laws allowing the national government to strip states of key governing functions and cut budget allocations; in practice, opposition-governed states and particularly the Caracas mayor's office were most affected. In August, the National Assembly passed a new electoral law that analysts suspected would lead to gerrymandering in favor of the ruling party. Battles between the government and the media also continued, with the primary opposition-aligned television broadcaster, Globovision, facing multiple investigations and several attacks on its headquarters by Chavez supporters. In July, the National Telecommunications Commission (CONATEL) stripped 32 radio stations of their licenses for what it described as procedural and administrative problems. Many of the stations insisted that any licensing flaws were the result of CONATEL's own errors.

Street protests increased during the year, as the global economic crisis contributed to rising unemployment and shrinking state revenue. According to local rights group PROVEA, workers were responsible for the largest number of protests, followed by community groups demonstrating against high crime and poor service provision, including ongoing water and electricity shortages caused by drought and poor planning. Political and student-led protests were also abundant. The state responded with harsh rhetoric that sought to delegitimize protesters, in part by linking them to antigovernment conspiracies. Although most protests occurred without incident, the state increased the degree of repression and brought criminal charges against numerous demonstrators.

Venezuelan relations with neighboring Colombia deteriorated further in 2009, having soured in early 2008 after Colombian forces raided a rebel camp in Ecuador and found alleged evidence of ties between the Colombian rebels and Venezuelan officials. News of a military accord in which Colombia would allow a U.S. presence on several of its bases prompted Chavez to freeze trade ties in July, and the agreement's official signing led him to warn of war and order troops to the border in November. Relations with the United States improved somewhat but remained tense, despite the return of the two countries' ambassadors to their respective posts in June; in September 2008, Chavez had expelled the U.S. ambassador following a series of real and perceived bilateral irritants, prompting the United States to respond in kind. Chavez continued to accuse the United States of seeking his ouster, pointing to Washington's allegedly weak response to a coup in Honduras as evidence of its militarist intentions in the region. Over the past several years, Chavez has increased friction with the United States and its allies by creating ostensible leftist alternatives to U.S.-backed trade pacts, garnering regional support with generous oil subsidies, seeking weapons purchases and other cooperation from Iran and Russia, and either explicitly or tacitly supporting favored electoral candidates in neighboring countries.

Political Rights and Civil Liberties: Venezuela is not an electoral democracy. While the act of voting is relatively free and the count is fair, the political opposition is forced to operate under extremely difficult conditions, and the separation of powers is nearly nonexistent.

The opposition boycotted the 2005 National Assembly elections due to concerns that ballot secrecy would be compromised by mechanized voting machines and fingerprint-based antifraud equipment. After the failed 2004 presidential recall referendum, tens of thousands of people who had signed petitions in favor of the effort found that they could not get government jobs or contracts, or qualify for public assistance programs; they had apparently been placed on an alleged blacklist of President Hugo Chavez Frias's political opponents. The opposition decided to actively contest the 2006 presidential election, and the voting was generally considered free and fair, but the CNE was ineffectual at limiting Chavez's use of state resources. He enjoyed a massive advantage in television exposure, and the promotion of social and infrastructure projects often blurred the line between his official role and his electoral campaign. Public employees were also subjected to heavy pressure to support the government.

Public resources were similarly exploited ahead of the December 2007 and February 2009 constitutional referendums and the November 2008 state and local elections. As in 2007, the referendum balloting in 2009 was conducted largely without incident, but full, final results, which could have allayed any lingering suspicions, were not released. A new Electoral Processes Law was promulgated in 2009 in preparation for the 2010 National Assembly elections. The opposition charged that the redistricting provisions in the law gave the Chavista-dominated CNE broad authority to gerrymander districts in a manner that would benefit the ruling PSUV and violate the constitutional principle of proportional representation.

The unicameral, 167-seat National Assembly is popularly elected for five-year terms. Chavez's control of the Assembly allows him to curb the independence of institutions including the judiciary, the intelligence services, and the Citizen Power branch of government, which was created by the 1999 constitution to fight corruption and protect citizens' rights. On several occasions during his tenure, Chavez has also been granted authority to legislate by decree on a wide range of topics. The president serves six-year terms, but due to the results of the 2009 referendum, he and other elected officials are no longer subject to term limits.

The merger of government-aligned parties into the PSUV is largely complete, though several groups retain nominal independence. In 2009, opposition parties established the Unity Roundtable and began preparations to select unity candidates for the 2010 elections. While the opposition considered the 2008 state and local elections a comeback, its victories were blunted by new laws allowing the national government to strip important functions from subnational administrations.

The government plays a major role in the economy and has done little to remove vague or excessive regulatory restrictions that increase opportunities for corruption. Several large development funds are controlled by the executive branch without independent oversight. The government's sporadic anticorruption efforts focus on its political opponents; in 2009 this included former Zulia state governor and presidential candidate Manuel Rosales, who sought political asylum in Peru, and former defense minister Raul Isaias Baduel, who was arrested in April and held in a military prison. In late 2009, however, several businessmen allied to high-ranking Chavistas were also arrested on charges of fraud and embezzlement. Transparency International ranked Venezuela 162 out of 180 countries surveyed in its 2009 Corruption Perceptions Index.

Although the constitution provides for freedom of the press, the media climate is permeated by intimidation, sometimes including physical attacks, and strong antimedia rhetoric by the government is common. The 2004 Law on Social Responsibility of Radio and Television gives the government the authority to control radio and television content. The local nongovernmental organization (NGO) Public Sphere reported 165 violations of free expression between January and September 2009. These included several incidents in which armed progovernment groups assaulted the offices of opposition outlets; the actions were disavowed by the government, and prominent progovernment agitator Lina Ron was arrested after leading a group that attacked the television station Globovision. A large portion of the print media, and a number of opposition broadcast outlets remain hostile toward the government, but their share of the broadcast media has declined in recent years. During all electoral processes in recent years, coverage by state media has been overwhelmingly biased in favor of the government; private outlets also exhibited bias, though to a somewhat lesser degree. In 2009, the government issued new regulations that effectively provided additional opportunities for the cancellation or takeover of private outlets' licenses. The government does not restrict internet access.

Constitutional guarantees of religious freedom are generally respected by the government, though tensions with the Roman Catholic Church remain high. Government relations with the small Jewish community have also been strained, particularly due to Chavez's cooperation with Iran and anti-Israel rhetoric. Academic freedom has come under mounting pressure in recent years with the formulation of a new curriculum that emphasizes socialist concepts. A new Organic Education Law was enacted in August 2009. Rights groups lauded provisions explicitly detailing the state's obligations, while opponents noted ambiguities that they said could lead to restrictions on private education and increased control by the government and communal councils. In universities, elections for student associations and administration positions have become more politicized, and rival groups of students have clashed repeatedly over both academic and political matters.

Freedom of peaceful assembly is guaranteed in the constitution, but the right to protest has become a sensitive topic in recent years. The rise of the student movement in 2007 caused a spike in confrontations with the government, but in 2009, it was workers, particularly employees of state-owned enterprises, who demonstrated most frequently, followed by citizens protesting poor services. The state's harsh rhetorical and legal response has fallen most heavily on the labor sector.

In 2000, the Supreme Tribunal of Justice ruled that NGOs with non-Venezuelan leaders or foreign government funding are not part of "civil society." As a result, they may not represent citizens in court or bring their own legal actions. The government has also made an effort to undermine the legitimacy of human rights and other civil society organizations by questioning their ties to international groups. Dozens of human rights defenders have been subject to threats and even violent attacks in recent years.

Workers are legally entitled to form unions, bargain collectively, and strike, with some restrictions on public sector workers' ability to strike. Control of unions has increasingly shifted from traditional opposition-allied labor leaders to new workers' organizations. Antigovernment groups allege that Chavez intends to create government-controlled unions, while the president's supporters maintain that the old labor regime was effectively controlled by the AD, COPEI, and employers. The growing competition has contributed to a substantial increase in labor violence as well as confusion during industry-wide collective bargaining. Labor strife rose significantly in 2008 and 2009, due in part to the addition of thousands of employees of nationalized companies to the state payroll and the government's failure to implement new collective-bargaining agreements in a context of reduced state resources. The government also encourages the formation of workers' militias and socialist patrols to deepen the "revolution" within industrial enterprises.

Politicization of the judicial branch has increased under Chavez, and the courts are undermined by the chronic corruption—including the growing influence of drug traffickers—that permeates the entire government system. Conviction rates remain low, the public-defender system is underfunded, and judges often lack tenure. High courts generally do not rule against the government. In December 2009, a judge ordered the release of a prominent banker who had been held without conviction on corruption charges for more than the maximum of two years. The judge was herself arrested hours later on corruption charges, and Chavez called for her to receive the maximum sentence.

At approximately 50 homicides per 100,000 inhabitants, Venezuela's murder rate is now one of the world's highest. The police and military have been prone to corruption, widespread arbitrary detention and torture of suspects, and extrajudicial killings. In 2009, the justice minister admitted that police were involved in up to 20 percent of crimes. Although hundreds of police are investigated each year, few are convicted. A plan to modify and purge the police was completed in early 2008, and in late 2009, a new national police force began operations. Although the prison budget has moderately increased and pretrial detention has been limited to two years, prison conditions in Venezuela remain among the worst in the Americas. The NGO Venezuelan Prison Observatory reported at least 366 violent deaths within prison walls in 2009, a modest decline from the death tolls of the previous two years.

The increasingly politicized military has stepped up its participation in social development and the delivery of public services. While Chavez's institutional control is solid, a faction of the military is perceived as wary of the Bolivarian project. Foreign officials assert that the military has adopted a more permissive attitude toward drug trafficking and Colombian rebel activity inside Venezuela. In recent years, the division of responsibility between the military and civilian militias has become less clear. There is also concern that the government has lost control over some of its supporters; in 2009, arrest warrants were issued, though never executed, against the head of the "La Piedrita collective," which controls a Caracas neighborhood, after its leader threatened government opponents.

Property rights are affected by the government's penchant for nationalization. The expropriation of large, idle landholdings has slowed in the last several years, but the nationalization of industrial enterprises continues apace. In 2009, several food producers were nationalized, along with small banks owned by the Chavista-linked businessmen who were accused of corruption during the year.

The formal rights of indigenous people have improved under Chavez, although those rights are seldom enforced by local political authorities. The constitution reserves three seats in the National Assembly for indigenous people and provides for, "the protection of indigenous communities and their progressive incorporation into the life of the nation." Indigenous communities trying to defend their land rights are subject to abuses, particularly along the Colombian border. In October 2009, the government granted more than 40,000 hectares of land to members of the Yukpa indigenous group in the border state of Tachira. A day later, two members of the group were killed as part of a broader land dispute involving indigenous groups, ranchers, and miners in the area.

Women enjoy progressive rights enshrined in the 1999 constitution, as well as benefits offered under a major 2007 law. However, Amnesty International reported in 2008 that while some programs, such as a hotline for victims of domestic abuse, have been established to assist women, much greater efforts at implementation are necessary for the law to have a tangible impact. Meanwhile, domestic violence and rape remain common, and the courts have provided limited means of redress for victims. The problem of trafficking in women remains inadequately addressed by the authorities. Women are poorly represented in government, with just 31 seats in the National Assembly.

⬇Vietnam

Political Rights: 7
Civil Liberties: 5
Status: Not Free

Population: 87,263,000
Capital: Hanoi

Trend Arrow: Vietnam received a downward trend arrow due to a serious tightening of space for civil society to comment on and criticize the government, including arrests of reform advocates and an effective ban on private think tanks.

Ten-Year Ratings Timeline For Year Under Review (Political Rights, Civil Liberties, Status)

2000	2001	2002	2003	2004	2005	2006	2007	2008	2009
7,6NF	7,6NF	7,6NF	7,6NF	7,6NF	7,5NF	7,5NF	7,5NF	7,5NF	7,5NF

Overview:
The state continued to seize land for development in 2009, despite the global economic downturn, and those who protested such moves were harshly punished. The authorities also displayed a growing intolerance for political dissent, cracking down on democracy activists and critical bloggers. In September, a government ban on public criticism of the Communist Party of Vietnam took effect, leading to the closure of the country's only independent think tank.

Vietnam won full independence from France in 1954, but it was divided into a Western-backed state in the south and a Communist-ruled state in the north. Open warfare between the two sides erupted in the mid-1960s. A 1973 peace treaty officially ended the war, but fighting did not cease until 1975, when the north completed its conquest of the south. Vietnam was formally united in 1976.

War and poor economic policies mired Vietnam in deep poverty, but economic reforms that began in 1986 drastically transformed the country over the next two decades. Tourism became a major source of revenue, as did the export of foodstuffs and manufactured products. However, political reform and a loosening of the one-party system were rejected by the ruling Communist Party of Vietnam (CPV). Criticism of the government continued to be harshly suppressed, and official corruption remained widespread. To protect the regime's legitimacy, the government began to call openly for an end to corruption, and acknowledged that some reforms were needed. The leadership also focused on closing the widening income gap between rural and urban populations.

At the 10th party congress in April 2006, Nong Duc Manh was reelected as CPV general secretary, and the delegates approved a proposal to allow CPV members to engage in business, partly to attract young entrepreneurs into the party. Nguyen Minh Triet was elected state president by the National Assembly in June, and Nguyen Tan Dung was chosen as prime minister.

After Vietnam secured entry into the World Trade Organization in January 2007, the government embarked on one of the strongest crackdowns against peaceful dissent in recent years, arresting nearly 40 dissidents and sentencing more than 20 to long prison terms. National Assembly elections were held in May of that year, and only 50 of the 500 deputies chosen did not belong to the CPV.

The government's reduced tolerance for open criticism and prodemocracy activism continued through 2008 and 2009. Among other prominent dissidents arrested or sentenced during 2009, Le Cong Dinh, a U.S.-trained lawyer who had defended many democracy supporters, was arrested in June for allegedly distributing antigovernment materials, libeling top political leaders, and colluding with domestic and foreign reactionaries to sabotage the state. In October, nine prodemocracy activists received prison sentences of up to six years for "spreading propaganda" against the government by hanging banners advocating multiparty democracy and through blogging that criticized the CPV. In other actions during the year, the government forced the closure of Vietnam's only independent think tank, and the security forces and courts continued to punish residents who objected to state confiscations of land for development.

Political Rights and Civil Liberties: Vietnam is not an electoral democracy. The CPV, the sole legal political party, controls politics and the government, and its Central Committee is the top decision-making body. The National Assembly, whose 500 members are elected to five-year terms, generally follows CPV dictates. The Vietnam Fatherland Front, an arm of the CPV, vets all candidates. The president, elected by the National Assembly for a five-year term, appoints the prime minister, who is confirmed by the legislature.

Corruption and abuse of office are serious problems. Although senior CPV and government officials have acknowledged growing public discontent, they have mainly responded with a few high-profile prosecutions of corrupt officials and private individuals rather than comprehensive reforms. Vietnam was ranked 120 out of 180 countries surveyed in Transparency International's 2009 Corruption Perceptions Index.

The government tightly controls the media, silencing critics through the courts and other means of harassment. A 1999 law requires journalists to pay damages to groups or individuals found to have been harmed by press articles, even if the reports are accurate. A 2006 decree imposes fines on journalists for denying revolutionary achievements, spreading "harmful" information, or exhibiting "reactionary ideology." Foreign media representatives cannot travel outside Hanoi without government approval. The CPV or state entities control all broadcast media. Although satellite television is officially restricted to senior officials, international hotels, and foreign businesses, many homes and businesses have satellite dishes. All print media outlets are owned by or are under the effective control of the CPV, government organs, or the army. A number of newspaper editors and reporters were dismissed in 2009 for reporting on corruption or criticizing official policy. In April 2009, the government temporarily suspended *Du Lich*, a biweekly newspaper, for running articles about the country's territorial dispute with China on the 30th anniversary of the Vietnamese-Chinese war.

The government restricts internet use through legal and technical means. A 2003 law bans the receipt and distribution of antigovernment e-mail messages, websites considered "reactionary" are blocked, and owners of domestic websites must submit their content for official approval. Internet cafes must register the personal information of and record the sites visited by users. Internet service providers face fines and closure for violating censorship rules. A 2008 decree specifies the types of information that private bloggers may legally post on their blogs. Several political bloggers were harassed, temporarily detained, or jailed during 2009; one, Me Nam, was released 12 days after her August arrest on the condition that she stop blogging, while another, a former army officer and leading prodemocracy activist, was given a five-year prison sentence for publishing subversive articles on the internet. Three more were charged in December and will face trials in January 2010; two of the accused were charged with attempting to overthrow the government, which could result in long prison terms or even death sentences.

Religious freedom remains restricted. All religious groups and most individual clergy members must join a party-controlled supervisory body and obtain permission for most activities. The Roman Catholic Church can now select its own bishops and priests, but they must be approved by the government. Many restrictions on charitable activities have been lifted, and clergy enjoy greater freedom to travel domestically and internationally. However, several religious leaders and adherents remain in prison or face other forms of government harassment. In March 2009, the courts upheld the convictions of eight people for disturbing public order and damaging property while protesting the state's confiscation of Catholic Church land, and in September, a police-backed mob forced Buddhist monks and nuns to leave their monastery in the central highlands.

Academic freedom is limited. University professors must refrain from criticizing government policies and adhere to party views when teaching or writing on political topics. Although citizens enjoy more freedom in private discussions than in the past, the authorities continue to suppress open criticism of the state.

Freedoms of association and assembly are restricted. Organizations must apply for official permission to obtain legal status and are closely regulated and monitored by the government. A small but active community of nongovernmental groups promotes environmental conservation, women's development, and public health. Human rights organizations and other private groups with rights-oriented agendas are banned. In September 2009, Vietnam's only independent think tank, the Institute of Development Studies, closed after a government decree restricted political research to the ruling party only and banned such organizations from publicly criticizing official policy. The institute's researchers had included prominent former state and party officials.

The Vietnam General Conference of Labor (VGCL), closely tied to the CPV, is the only legal labor federation. All trade unions are required to join the VGCL. In recent years, the government has permitted hundreds of independent "labor associations" to represent workers at individual firms and in some service industries. Farmer and worker protests against local government abuses, including land confiscations and unfair or harsh working conditions, have become more common. The central leadership uses such demonstrations to pressure local governments and businesses to comply with tax laws, environmental regulations, and wage agreements. Enforcement of labor laws covering child labor, workplace safety, and other issues remains poor. Critics also allege that the government has intentionally kept minimum wages low to attract foreign investment.

Vietnam's judiciary is subservient to the CPV, which controls courts at all levels. Defendants have a constitutional right to counsel, but lawyers are scarce, and many are reluctant to take on human rights and other sensitive cases for fear of harassment and retribution by the state. Defense attorneys cannot call or question witnesses and are rarely permitted to request leniency for their clients. Police can hold individuals in administrative detention for up to two years on suspicion of threatening national security. The police are known to abuse suspects and prisoners, and prison conditions are poor. Many political prisoners remain behind bars. Nguyen Van Ly, a Catholic priest and prominent prodemocracy activist currently serving an eight-year sentence, is said to be in solitary confinement and suffering from poor health, and is reportedly denied legal counsel.

Ethnic and religious minorities face discrimination in mainstream society, and some local officials restrict their access to schooling and jobs. Minorities generally have little input on development projects that affect their livelihoods and communities.

Land disputes have become more frequent, as the government seizes property to lease to domestic and foreign investors. Affected residents and farmers rarely find the courts helpful, and their street protests have resulted in harassment and arrests by the state. The harsh treatment of displaced citizens has stirred criticism from a few former senior party and state officials.

Although economic opportunities have grown for women, they continue to face discrimination in wages and promotion. Many are victims of domestic violence, and thousands of women each year are trafficked internally and externally and forced into prostitution. A number of cases of international adoption fraud have been exposed in recent years. In September 2009, 16 people—including 2 heads of provincial welfare centers, doctors, nurses, and government legal officials—were convicted of fraud in obtaining more than 250 babies between 2005 and 2008 and putting them up for international adoption, which typically involves considerable fees and donations by prospective parents.

Yemen

Political Rights: 6*
Civil Liberties: 5
Status: Not Free

Population: 22,880,000
Capital: Sanaa

Status Change: Yemen's political rights rating declined from 5 to 6 and its status from Partly Free to Not Free due to the two-year postponement of parliamentary elections, the renewal of fighting between central authorities and al-Houthi rebels in the north, and an escalation in violence between the government and opposition groups in the south.

Ten-Year Ratings Timeline For Year Under Review (Political Rights, Civil Liberties, Status)

2000	2001	2002	2003	2004	2005	2006	2007	2008	2009
5,6NF	6,6NF	6,5NF	5,5PF	5,5PF	5,5PF	5,5PF	5,5PF	5,5PF	6,5NF

Overview:

Parliamentary elections scheduled for April 2009 were postponed by two years in February, after opposition parties threatened a boycott to protest anticipated electoral manipulation by the government. In August, government forces and Houthi rebels in the northern province of Saada renewed fighting in a five-year-old civil conflict. The violence escalated in November, when Saudi Arabia began bombing Houthi positions inside Yemen in response to rebel attacks on Saudi military personnel near the border. Also during the year, oppositionists and secessionists in southern Yemen continued public protests against their political marginalization, and dozens of people were killed in clashes between the demonstrators and security forces. Militants associated with al-Qaeda carried out several attacks in 2009, including assaults on South Korean tourists and officials.

For centuries after the advent of Islam, a series of dynastic imams controlled most of northern Yemen and parts of the south. The Ottoman Empire ruled many of the cities from the 16th to the early 20th centuries, and the British controlled areas in the southern part of the country, including the port of Aden, beginning in the 19th century.

After the reigning imam was ousted in a 1960s civil war and the British left the south in 1967, Yemen remained divided into two countries: the Yemen Arab Republic (North Yemen) and the People's Democratic Republic of Yemen (South Yemen). The two states ultimately unified in 1990, and northern forces put down a southern attempt to secede in 1994. In the face of widespread poverty and illiteracy, tribal influences that limited the central government's authority in certain parts of the country, a heavily armed citizenry, and the threat of Islamist terrorism, Yemen took limited steps to improve the status of political rights and civil liberties in the years after unification.

In 2006, Yemen held its second presidential election since unification. President Ali Abdullah Saleh was reelected with 77 percent of the vote, and the ruling General People's Congress (GPC) party won by a similar margin in concurrent provincial and local council elections. The 2006 presidential race was the first in which a serious opposition candidate challenged the incumbent. Saleh's main opponent, Faisal Ben Shamlan, was supported by a coalition of Islamist and other opposition parties and received 22 percent of the vote.

In May 2008, Yemen held its first-ever elections for 20 provincial governors, who had previously been appointed. Opposition groups refused to participate, claiming electoral manipulation by the government. Progovernment candidates were elected in 17 of the 20 provinces that participated, and independents won in the remaining 3. One province did not hold elections due to protests by unemployed Yemenis.

Tensions between the government and the opposition escalated in late 2008, and the opposition Joint Meeting Parties—a coalition that includes the Yemeni Socialist Party and Islah, an Islamist party—threatened to boycott parliamentary elections scheduled for April 2009. The two sides agreed in February 2009 to postpone the vote by two years pending electoral reforms.

Fighting in the northern province of Saada, part of a five-year-old uprising by some members of Yemen's large community of Zaidi Shiite Muslims, resumed in August 2009 after a ceasefire that was declared a year earlier. In November, the rebels killed Saudi military personnel near the Yemeni-Saudi border, prompting Saudi forces to carry out bombing raids on rebel positions inside Yemen. The Saudi intervention came amid claims that the rebels—who were led by the family of slain Zaidi cleric Hussein Badreddin al-Houthi—were receiving financial and material support from Iran, though those claims remained unproven. Thousands of people have been killed in the conflict since 2004, and tens of thousands have been displaced.

Yemen also continued to suffer in 2009 from terrorist violence associated with al-Qaeda. In March, a suicide bombing killed four South Korean tourists in the southeastern town of Shibam. A second attack struck a convoy of South Korean officials sent to investigate the deaths. Also in March, four policemen were killed in a gun battle with Islamist militants in Jaar.

Political Rights and Civil Liberties: Yemen is not an electoral democracy. The political system is dominated by the ruling GPC party, and there are few limits on the authority of the executive branch. President Ali Abdullah Saleh has been serving continuously since 1978, when he became president of North Yemen in a military coup.

The president is elected for seven-year terms, and appoints the 111 members of the largely advisory upper house of parliament, the Majlis al-Shura (Consultative Council). The 301 members of the lower house, the House of Representatives, are elected to serve six-year terms. Provincial councils and governors are also elected. There is limited competition between the GPC, which took 238 lower house seats in the last parliamentary elections in 2003, and the two main opposition parties—the Islamist party Islah (46 seats) and the Yemeni Socialist Party (8 seats). There is also a handful of smaller factions and independent lawmakers. In February 2009, the GPC and the opposition agreed to postpone parliamentary elections, which had been scheduled for April, by two years; the opposition, demanding electoral reforms, had threatened to boycott the vote. Past elections have been marred by the abuse of state resources, voter registration irregularities, and other flaws.

Corruption is an endemic problem. Despite some recent efforts by the government to fight graft, Yemen lacks most legal safeguards against conflicts of interest. Auditing and investigative bodies are not sufficiently independent of the executive authorities. was ranked 154 out of 180 countries surveyed in Transparency International's 2009 Corruption Perceptions Index.

The state maintains a monopoly over the media that reach the most people—television and radio. Article 103 of the Press and Publications Law outlaws direct personal criticism of the head of state and publication of material that, "might spread a spirit of dissent and division among the people," or, "leads to the spread of ideas contrary to the principles of the Yemeni Revolution, [is] prejudicial to national unity or [distorts] the image of the Yemeni, Arab, or Islamic heritage." Access to the internet is not widespread, and the authorities block websites they deem offensive. In May 2009, the government officially suspended or effectively halted the publication of *Al-Ayyam*, the country's most popular daily, and seven other periodicals for their reporting on the southern opposition movement. Officials also blocked a number of websites and arrested at least one website owner and blogger. The authorities accused *Al-Ayyam* of "harming national unity" and stormed its headquarters in Aden later that month in an attempt to break up a protest against its closure; several security guards were killed in the assault.

The constitution states that Islam is the official religion and declares Sharia (Islamic law) to be the source of all legislation. Yemen has few non-Muslim minorities, and their rights are generally respected in practice. The government has imposed some restrictions on religious activity in the context of the rebellion in the northern province of Saada. Mosques' hours of operation have been limited in the area, and imams suspected of extremism have been removed. Strong politicization of campus life, including tensions between supporters of the ruling GPC and the opposition Islah party, places limits on academic freedom.

Yemenis enjoy some freedom of assembly, with periodic restrictions and sometimes deadly interventions by the government. Opposition political rallies were permitted across the country during the 2006 election season. However, over the past three years, southern Yemenis have mounted growing protests to challenge the GPC's alleged corruption and abuse of power, the marginalization of southerners in the political system, and the government's inability to address pressing social and economic concerns. The protest movement has increasingly called for secession by the south. The authorities have responded with mass arrests of organizers and attempts to break up demonstrations by force. Dozens of protesters and security officials were killed in such clashes between April and July 2009.

Yemenis have the right to form associations according to Article 58 of the constitution, and several thousand nongovernmental organizations operate in the country. The law acknowledges workers' right to form and join trade unions, but some critics claim that the government and ruling party elements have stepped up efforts to control the affairs of these organizations. Virtually all unions belong to a single labor federation, and the government is empowered to veto collective-bargaining agreements.

The judiciary is nominally independent, but in practice it is susceptible to interference from the executive branch. Authorities have a poor record on enforcing judicial rulings, particularly those issued against prominent tribal or political leaders.

Lacking an effective court system, citizens often resort to tribal forms of justice or direct appeals to executive authorities.

Arbitrary detention occurs, partly because law enforcement officers lack proper training and senior government officials lack the political will to eliminate the problem. Security forces affiliated with the Political Security Office (PSO) and the Ministry of the Interior torture and abuse detainees, and PSO prisons are not closely monitored.

Yemen is relatively homogeneous ethnically and racially. The Akhdam, a small minority group, live in poverty and face social discrimination.

Thousands of refugees seeking relief from war and poverty in the Horn of Africa are smuggled annually into Yemen, where they are routinely subjected to theft, abuse, and even murder.

Women continue to face pervasive discrimination in several aspects of life. A woman must obtain permission from her husband or father to receive a passport and travel abroad. Unlike men, women do not have the right to confer citizenship on a foreign-born spouse, and they can transfer Yemeni citizenship to their children only in special circumstances. Yemen's penal code allows lenient sentences for those convicted of "honor crimes"—assaults or killings of women by family members for alleged immoral behavior. In April 2008, the parliament voted down legislation that would have banned female genital mutilation. Women are vastly underrepresented in elected office; there is just one woman in the lower house of parliament. School enrollment and educational attainment rates for girls fall far behind those for boys.

Zambia

Political Rights: 3
Civil Liberties: 4*
Status: Partly Free

Population: 12,555,000
Capital: Lusaka

Ratings Change: Zambia's civil liberties rating declined from 3 to 4 due to new legal restrictions on the activities of nongovernmental organizations.

Ten-Year Ratings Timeline For Year Under Review (Political Rights, Civil Liberties, Status)

2000	2001	2002	2003	2004	2005	2006	2007	2008	2009
5,4PF	5,4PF	4,4PF	4,4PF	4,4PF	4,4PF	3,4PF	3,4PF	3,3PF	3,4PF

Overview:
The government and ruling party stepped up pressure on civil society and the media in 2009, including passing a law that increases restrictions on the activities of nongovernmental organizations. Former president Frederick Chiluba, found guilty of corruption in a British high court in 2007, was acquitted of the charges and has enjoyed a political rehabilitation at the hands of President Rupiah Banda. Meanwhile, two foreign governments suspended funding to Zambia's health sector in the wake of corruption scandals in the Ministry of Health.

Zambia gained independence from Britain in 1964. President Kenneth Kaunda and his United National Independence Party (UNIP) subsequently ruled Zambia as a de facto—and, from 1973, a de jure—one-party state. In the face of domestic and international pressure, Kaunda agreed to a new constitution and multiparty democracy in 1991. In free elections that October, former labor leader Frederick Chiluba and his Movement for Multiparty Democracy (MMD) captured both the presidency and the National Assembly by wide margins. However, in the 1996 elections, the MMD-led government manipulated candidacy laws, voter registration, and media coverage in favor of the incumbents. Most opposition parties boycotted the polls, and the MMD renewed its parliamentary dominance.

Dissent within the MMD, as well as protests by opposition parties and civil society, forced Chiluba to abandon an effort to change the constitution and seek a third term in 2001. Instead, the MMD nominated Levy Mwanawasa, who went on to win the 2001 elections. The MMD also captured a plurality of elected parliament seats. Domestic and international election monitors cited vote rigging and other serious irregularities. In the September 2006 presidential poll, Mwanawasa won a second term with 43 percent of the vote. In concurrent legislative elections, the MMD won 72 seats in the 150-seat parliament, while the Patriotic Front (PF) took 44 and the United Democratic Alliance captured 27. The remaining seats were split between smaller parties and independents. The polls were deemed the freest and fairest in 15 years.

Mwanawasa suffered a stroke in July 2008 and died in August. Prior to his death, Mwanawasa and his one-time fierce political rival, Michael Sata of the opposition Patriotic Front (PF), publicly declared an end to their feuding, which had been a source of tension. After years of public rancor over the constitutional reform process, a National Constitutional Conference (NCC) was under way in 2008, although it was boycotted by elements of civil society and the opposition.

The presidential by-elections in October 2008 that followed Mwanawasa's death pitted his vice president, Rupiah Banda, against Sata and Hakainde Hichilema of the United Party for National Development (UPND). Banda was elected president with 40 percent of the vote, against Sata's 38 percent, and Hichilema's 20 percent. Sata claimed that the elections were fraudulent and filed a legal challenge calling for a recount, but his request was rejected by the Supreme Court in March 2009.

During Banda's time in office, the overall political situation in the country has been characterized by contentious politics and governance challenges. Banda has been in conflict with members of his party who have sought to challenge his leadership and presumed candidacy for polls scheduled for 2011. Meanwhile, government and ruling party actors have taken aggressive and sometimes violent actions against the political opposition and elements of civil society thought to be against the president.

Despite substantial progress from 2004–2007, economic growth slowed in 2008 and 2009 owing to the global economic recession. Increases in the global price of copper in 2009 may generate improvements in 2010, however. Zambia experienced considerable debt relief in 2005 and 2007, and has obtained substantial investment in recent years from China. The International Monetary Fund (IMF) in 2008 pledged US$79 million to support poverty alleviation and economic growth, and in 2009, it agreed to provide over US$250 million to strengthen and stabilize the kwacha.

Political Rights and Civil Liberties: Zambia is an electoral democracy. While local and international observers declared the 2008 presidential elections to be free and fair, opposition parties and civil society groups raised concerns about fraud, including the printing of additional ballot papers and the incumbent's use of state resources for campaigning. The president and the unicameral National Assembly are elected to serve concurrent five-year terms. The National Assembly includes 150 elected members, as well as 8 members appointed by the president.

The opposition has been able to operate, although under some duress. PF leader Sata has been arrested and charged with various offenses, including sedition, since 2001. While violent clashes took place between supporters of the PF and the MMD in both 2008 and 2009, there is no evidence of systematic harassment of the PF by the government. In March 2009, the PF joined hands with the UPND to challenge the MMD in the 2011 elections.

While President Rupiah Banda's government launched an official anticorruption policy in July 2009, concerns have emerged over his administration's commitment to anticorruption efforts. One of Banda's ministers was forced to resign in April 2009 after being found guilty by a judicial tribunal of inappropriate behavior. However, a high court ruling overturned the verdict, and the minister was subsequently reappointed to a cabinet position. Banda has also abetted the political rehabilitation of former president Frederick Chiluba. A 2007 British high court judgment against Chiluba on corruption charges has not yet been registered or enforced in Zambia. Another corruption trial in a Zambian high court in August 2009 found the former president not guilty of embezzlement charges. When the head of a special task force on corruption attempted to appeal this ruling, he was dismissed from his position. Separately, an auditor general report issued in early 2009 stated that huge sums of money had been lost in 2007 through misuse, theft, and misappropriation of public resources. Also in 2009, the Swedish and Dutch governments both suspended funding to the health sector after it was revealed that millions of dollars had been embezzled from the ministry of health. Zambia was ranked 99 out of 180 countries surveyed in Transparency International's 2009 Corruption Perceptions Index.

Freedom of speech is constitutionally guaranteed, but the government often restricts this right in practice. The government controls two widely circulated newspapers, and owing to prepublication review, journalists commonly practice self-censorship. The state-owned, progovernment Zambia National Broadcasting Corporation (ZNBC) dominates the broadcast media, although several independent stations have the capacity to reach large portions of the population. The government has the authority to appoint the management boards of ZNBC and the Independent Broadcasting Authority, which regulates the industry and grants licenses to prospective broadcasters. The government has also delayed passage of a bill designed to give the public and journalists free access to official information. The independent media continue to play a significant role, although journalists have been arrested, detained, and harassed by government and MMD supporters in previous years. Criminal libel and defamation suits have been brought against journalists by MMD leaders in response to stories on corruption.

Conditions for the independent press and media deteriorated considerably in 2009. The government and ruling party aggressively harassed and interfered with press outlets deemed opponents of the administration, specifically the leading independent newspaper, the *Post*. As of July 2009, the *Post*'s staff had been physically or verbally attacked by MMD members on at least six occasions. In July, the government brought charges against the *Post*'s editor for distributing obscene material after a photo of a woman giving birth on the street was circulated. In August, the government threatened to introduce a bill to regulate the media if it failed to come up with its own regulatory body.

Constitutionally protected religious freedom is respected in practice. The government does not restrict academic freedom.

Under the Public Order Act, police must receive a week's notice before all demonstrations. While the law does not require permits, the police have frequently broken up "illegal" protests because the organizers lacked permits. In 2009, police detained nine individuals who participated in a public campaign of blowing car horns to protest the acquittal of Chiluba and threatened to disperse meetings of nongovernmental organizations (NGOs) seeking to organize the protests. Although NGOs have operated freely in the past, the government passed legislation in 2009 placing new constraints on their activities. The law requires the registration of NGOs and reregistration every five years and establishes a board to provide guidelines and regulate NGO activity in the country.

Zambia's trade unions are among Africa's strongest, and union rights are constitutionally guaranteed. The Zambia Congress of Trade Unions operates democratically without state interference. About two-thirds of the country's 300,000 formal-sector employees are union members. While collective bargaining rights are protected by statute, labor laws also require labor organizations to have at least 100 members to be registered, a potentially burdensome rule. While unions remain engaged in public affairs, they have become weaker both financially and organizationally in recent years.

Judicial independence is guaranteed by law. However, several decisions in 2009, including Chiluba's acquittal, tainted the public image of the judiciary and raised concerns that the executive branch was exercising undue influence over the institution. Legislation was also passed in 2009 that allows the executive to increase the number of judges serving on the High and Supreme Courts. The lack of qualified personnel, in part because of poor working conditions, contributes to significant trial delays. Pretrial detainees are sometimes held for years under harsh conditions, and many accused lack access to legal aid owing to limited resources. In rural areas, customary courts of variable quality and consistency—whose decisions often conflict with the constitution and national law—decide many civil matters.

Allegations of police corruption, brutality, and even torture are widespread, and security forces have generally operated with impunity. Prison conditions are very harsh; poor nutrition and limited access to health care have led to many inmate deaths. Despite government efforts in 2007 to reduce crowding, in part by pardoning convicts, overcrowding remains a serious problem.

Societal discrimination remains a serious obstacle to women's rights. Domestic violence and rape are major problems, and traditional norms inhibit many women from reporting assaults. Women are denied full economic participation and usually require male consent to obtain credit. Discrimination against women is especially prevalent in customary courts, where they are considered subordinate with respect to property, inheritance, and marriage. In 2005, an amended penal code banned the traditional practice of "sexual cleansing," in which a widow is obliged to have sex with relatives of her deceased husband. In an alleged effort to intimidate members of civil society, Vice President George Kunda stated in 2009 that the government could prosecute the known homosexuals in the country using legislation passed in 2005 against homosexuality.

Zimbabwe

Political Rights: 6*
Civil Liberties: 6
Status: Not Free

Population: 12,523,000
Capital: Harare

Ratings Change: Zimbabwe's political rights rating improved from 7 to 6 due to the formation of a national unity government and the swearing in of opposition leader Morgan Tsvangirai as prime minister.

Ten-Year Ratings Timeline For Year Under Review (Political Rights, Civil Liberties, Status)

2000	2001	2002	2003	2004	2005	2006	2007	2008	2009
6,5PF	6,6NF	6,6NF	6,6NF	7,6NF	7,6NF	7,6NF	7,6NF	7,6NF	7,6NF

Overview: In keeping with a power-sharing agreement that followed flawed elections and political violence in 2008, opposition leader Morgan Tsvangirai was sworn in as prime minister of a national unity government in February 2009. The new government took steps to ease Zimbabwe's dire economic situation, and foreign donors provided an influx of aid. However, allies of President Robert Mugabe continued to persecute supporters of Tsvangirai's Movement for Democratic Change party during the year, and little progress was made on fundamental reforms envisioned in the power-sharing deal.

In 1965, a white-minority regime in what was then colonial Southern Rhodesia unilaterally declared independence from Britain. A guerrilla war led by black nationalist groups, as well as sanctions and diplomatic pressure from Britain and the United States, contributed to the end of white-minority rule in 1979 and the recognition of an independent Zimbabwe in 1980. Robert Mugabe and the Zimbabwe African National Union–Patriotic Front (ZANU-PF), first brought to power in relatively democratic elections, have since ruled the country.

Zimbabwe was relatively stable in its first years of independence, but from 1983 to 1987, the Shona-dominated government violently suppressed opposition among the Ndebele ethnic minority, and between 10,000 and 20,000 civilians were killed by government forces. Widespread political unrest in the 1990s, spurred by increasing authoritarianism and economic decline, led to the creation in 1999 of the opposition Movement for Democratic Change (MDC), an alliance of trade unions and other civil society groups. However, Mugabe and ZANU-PF claimed victory over the MDC in parliamentary elections in 2002 and 2005, as well as in a 2002 presidential poll. All three elections were seriously marred by political violence aimed at MDC supporters, fraudulent electoral processes, and the abuse of state resources, including state-run media. Security forces crushed mass protests and strikes called by MDC leader Morgan Tsvangirai in 2003.

The 2005 parliamentary elections gave the ruling party a two-thirds majority and the ability to amend the constitution. It subsequently enacted amendments that nationalized all land, brought all schools under state control, and reintroduced an upper legislative house, the Senate. In November 2005 elections for the chamber, ZANU-PF secured 59 out of 66 seats; the MDC, deeply split over whether to participate, fielded just 26 candidates and won 7 seats. Voter turnout was less than 20 percent.

Also in 2005, the government implemented a slum-clearance effort known as Operation Murambatsvina, which means "drive out the trash" in the Shona. It resulted in the destruction of thousands of informal businesses and dwellings as well as thousands of arrests. According to the United Nations, approximately 700,000 people were made homeless, and another 2.4 million were directly or indirectly affected. Initially moved into transit camps near cities, many displaced residents were forced to return to the rural areas designated on their national identity cards. Analysts maintain that the operation, billed as part of a law-and-order campaign, actually targeted urban areas that were considered MDC strongholds and sources of antigovernment agitation. According to a June 2009 report by Amnesty International (AI), most victims still lacked adequate housing and had no means of redressing the destruction of their property.

In January 2008, police violently dispersed an MDC protest in Harare and detained Tsvangirai, despite a court ruling declaring the protest legal. The MDC was protesting unfair conditions ahead of the March general elections. Together with the independent Zimbabwe Election Support Network, the party accused the government of politicizing food aid and making preparations for large-scale vote fraud.

Violence before the March elections, though serious, was less severe than expected. In the parliamentary poll, the Tsvangirai-led MDC won 99 seats, followed by ZANU-PF with 97 seats and a breakaway faction of the MDC, led by Arthur Mutambara, with 10. The results denied ZANU-PF a legislative majority for the first time in the country's 28-year history. However, when the Zimbabwe Election Commission (ZEC) finally released the presidential results in May, it found that Tsvangirai had outpolled Mugabe, 47.9 percent to 43.2 percent, requiring a runoff between the two. The MDC accused the ZEC of fraud and claimed that Tsvangirai had won the election outright with over 50.3 percent of the vote. The regime was apparently prevented from engaging in more substantial fraud thanks to an extensive parallel vote count mounted by civic groups that quickly reported tallies from polling stations across the country.

Following the March balloting, ZANU-PF militias and state security forces began a brutal campaign of violence aimed at punishing and intimidating MDC members and their suspected supporters. The effort expanded in May and June to target civil society groups, church-affiliated organizations, human rights lawyers, trade unionists, and journalists. Tsvangirai ultimately withdrew from the June 27 runoff and took refuge in the Dutch embassy, allowing the unopposed Mugabe to win 85 percent of the vote amid low turnout and many spoiled ballots.

Political violence continued even after the election. According to international and domestic human rights organizations, some 200 MDC activists and supporters were killed over the course of 2008, about 5,000 were tortured by security forces or militias, and more than 10,000 required medical treatment for injuries.

In September 2008, ZANU-PF and the MDC reached a power-sharing agreement brokered by the Southern African Development Community (SADC) that allowed Mugabe to remain president, created the post of prime minister for Tsvangirai, and distributed ministries to ZANU-PF (14, including defense, state security, and justice), Tsvangirai's MDC faction (13, including finance, health, and constitutional and parliamentary affairs), and Mutambara's faction (3). The fate of the Home Affairs Ministry, which controls the police, was left to subsequent negotiations, and the issue—along with the abduction and detention of at least 20 MDC activists and officials by state security forces—nearly derailed the agreement on a number of occasions. A constitutional amendment creating the post of prime minister was enacted in February 2009, and the new government was sworn in that month. The cabinet included two home affairs ministers, one from ZANU-PF and one from the MDC.

The survival of the unity government remained in doubt throughout 2009. In April, Mugabe ordered the ZANU-PF-controlled Transport Ministry to take over the MDC-controlled Information Ministry, leaving an MDC member as deputy minister. Mugabe also refused to swear in MDC provincial governors and failed to consult the MDC in appointing loyalists as central bank governor and attorney general. MDC activists and supporters continued to suffer from violent attacks by security forces and militias, and invasions of white-owned farms picked up in the middle of the year. A group of 18 prominent human rights and political activists who had recently been released from jail were indicted on terrorism charges in May, and in June, an MDC cabinet minister reported that party officials were receiving death threats on a near-daily basis. In October, an audit revealed that over 10,000 ZANU-PF youth militia members were on the payroll of the Youth Development Ministry. Citing the ongoing crackdown, as well as the re-arrest of MDC stalwart Roy Bennett on terrorism and other charges, Tsvangirai announced that the MDC would not cooperate with the national unity government, but SADC-brokered talks led the party to reverse its move in November.

Also in 2009, the new government began to repair Zimbabwe's devastated economy. In January, it formally abandoned the Zimbabwean dollar—whose inflation rate had reached an astounding 13 billion percent in 2008—in favor of South African and U.S. currencies, leading to the first positive economic growth rates in nine years. The country also received an influx of international aid during the year. In December, the finance ministry cited improved revenues and forecast a seven percent growth rate in 2010. Nevertheless, unemployment in 2009 was estimated at over 90 percent.

The economic collapse of recent years, which had been accelerated by the government's seizure of most white-owned farmland beginning in 2000, fueled the emigration of as many as three residents and led to a serious breakdown in public services, including heath care and sanitation. An outbreak of cholera that ran from 2008 to mid-2009 infected over 100,000 people and killed more than 4,200, according to Doctors Without Borders.

Political Rights and Civil Liberties: Zimbabwe is not an electoral democracy. President Robert Mugabe and the ZANU-PF party have dominated the political landscape since independence in 1980, overseeing 18 amendments to the constitution that have expanded presidential power and decreased executive accountability. Presidential and legislative elections in March 2008 were marred by a wide-ranging campaign of violence and intimidation, flawed voter registration and balloting, biased media coverage, and the use of state resources—including food aid—to bribe and threaten voters. The government failed to implement changes to electoral, security, and press laws that were agreed to in a 2007 constitutional amendment. The period leading up to the presidential runoff in June 2008 featured accelerated violence against oppositionists, prompting a UN Security Council resolution declaring the impossibility of a fair poll. The election, in which Mugabe ultimately ran unopposed, was declared illegitimate by observers from the African Union and the SADC. Although the September 2008 power-sharing agreement between ZANU-PF and the opposition MDC—known as the Global Political Agreement (GPA)—called for a new, independent election commission, the body had not been formally constituted by the end of 2009.

Since the restoration of the Senate in 2005, Zimbabwe has had a bicameral legislature. A 2007 constitutional amendment removed appointed seats from the House of Assembly, increased the number of seats of both chambers (to 210 seats in the House of Assembly and 93 seats in the Senate), and redrew constituency boundaries. In 2008, despite political violence and vote rigging, the two factions of the MDC won 109 seats in the House of Assembly, leaving ZANU-PF with 97. In the Senate, where 33 seats are held by traditional chiefs, presidential appointees, and other unelected officials, ZANU-PF retained its majority; the 60 elected seats were divided evenly between ZANU-PF and the MDC factions. All elected officials serve five-year terms. A 2009 constitutional amendment stemming from the GPA created the post of prime minister (and two deputy prime ministers) while retaining the presidency, leaving the country with a split executive branch.

The GPA called for a new constitution following consultations with the public and the presentation of a draft in a referendum, but efforts to draft the charter formally made little progress in Parliament in 2009. In July, police had to forcefully disperse a constitutional conference intended as the official start of national consultations after ZANU-PF militants disrupted the conference, and a series of fights broke out among ZANU-PF and MDC delegates. Major civil society organizations like the National Constituent Assembly (NCA) and the Zimbabwe Congress of Trade Unions (ZCTU) opposed Parliament's role in drafting the new constitution, calling for greater participation by civic groups and the general public.

Corruption is rampant throughout the country, including at the highest levels of government. The collapse in public-service delivery and the politicization of food and agricultural aid has made the problem ubiquitous at the local level. A 2009 independent audit of the Agriculture Ministry revealed that the illegal reselling of agricultural inputs was widespread, as was corruption in the state-run Grain Marketing Board. Anticorruption prosecutions are almost exclusively motivated by political vendettas. An anticorruption commission envisioned in the GPA has yet to be formed. Zimbabwe was ranked 146 out of 180 countries surveyed in Transparency International's 2009 Corruption Perceptions Index.

Freedoms of expression and the press are severely restricted. The country's draconian legal framework includes the Access to Information and Protection of Privacy Act (AIPPA), the Official Secrets Act, the Public Order and Security Act (POSA), and the Criminal Law (Codification and Reform) Act. In general, these laws restrict who may work as a journalist, require journalists to register with the state, severely limit what they may publish, and mandate harsh penalties—including long prison sentences—for violators. Under the GPA, a new and independent Zimbabwe Media Commission (ZMC) is supposed to replace the state-controlled and highly discriminatory Media and Information Commission (MIC). By the end of 2009, however, the ZMC had not been formed, and the MIC had significantly raised the accreditation fees for foreign journalists, local journalists working for foreign media outlets, and foreign media outlets themselves. Journalists are routinely subjected to verbal intimidation, physical attacks, arrest and detention, and financial pressure by the police and ZANU-PF supporters. In 2008, scores of local and foreign journalists were beaten or detained both before and after the elections. While these attacks decreased in 2009, a number of journalists—including some working for state-owned outlets—were detained on defamation charges.

The government dominates the print and broadcast media. In 2009, retired military and intelligence officers loyal to Mugabe were appointed to the boards of state-owned newspapers, the state-controlled Zimbabwe Broadcasting Corporation (ZBC), and the NewZiana news agency. The *Daily News*, long the country's only independent daily, was shuttered in 2003 for not adhering to the AIPPA. While it has since been licensed to operate again, the seizure of its computers and archives in the run-up to the 2008 elections prevented it from publishing in 2009. A new independent daily, *NewsDay*, had not received a license by year's end due to the delay in the creation of the ZMC. Access to international news via satellite television is prohibitively expensive for most Zimbabweans, and in 2005, the government began jamming the shortwave radio signals of foreign-based stations that are perceived as hostile. Mugabe enacted the Interception of Communications Bill in 2007, empowering the state to monitor telephonic and electronic communication with sophisticated technology acquired from China. In July 2009, the government lifted a ban on international news organizations such as the British Broadcasting Corporation (BBC) and the U.S.-based Cable News Network (CNN).

While freedom of religion has generally been respected in Zimbabwe, church attendance has become increasingly politicized, with church groups such as the Solidarity Peace Trust and the Zimbabwe Christian Alliance at the forefront of opposition to the Mugabe government. Other groups, such as the Zimbabwe Council of Churches, are widely perceived as pro-Mugabe. In late 2007, the Anglican Church in Zimbabwe split along political lines, leading to restrictions on freedom of worship at a number of churches.

Academic freedom is limited. All schools are under state control, and educational aid has often been based on parents' political loyalties. Security forces and ZANU-PF thugs harass dissident university students, who have been arrested or expelled for protesting against government policy. In August 2009, four Zimbabwe National Students Union leaders were arrested while addressing students at the University of Zimbabwe in Harare; they were released the following day. In the political violence of 2008, thousands of teachers—many of whom served as polling officials—were beaten by ZANU-PF militias, and many rural schools were closed. According to the Progressive Teachers' Union of Zimbabwe, 7 teachers were killed, 60 were tortured, about 600 were hospitalized, and over 230 teachers' houses were burned down. In May 2009, AI reported that teachers continued to be attacked and threatened by ZANU-PF supporters, especially in rural areas. Despite reduced school fees, teachers' strikes and a lack of resources prevented 94 percent of rural schools from opening on schedule in February, according to the UN Children's Fund.

The small nongovernmental sector is active, but NGOs have faced increasing legal restrictions and extralegal harassment. The 2004 Non-Governmental Organizations Act increased scrutiny of human rights groups and explicitly prohibited them from receiving foreign funds. The 2002 POSA requires police permission for public meetings and demonstrations; such meetings are often broken up, and participants are subject to arbitrary arrest as well as attacks by ZANU-PF militias. The POSA also allows police to impose arbitrary curfews and forbids criticism of the president. A number of large demonstrations were prevented or violently dispersed in 2008, and an April ban on political rallies ahead of the presidential runoff severely restricted the opposition campaign; a court overturned a similar ban in June of that year. Between June and August 2008, most NGOs—except those explicitly concerned with HIV/AIDS, children, the elderly, or the disabled—were barred from operating.

The Labor Relations Act allows the government to veto collective-bargaining agreements that it deems harmful to the economy. Strikes are allowed except in "essential" industries. Because the ZCTU has led resistance to Mugabe's rule, it has become a particular target for repression, and trade unionists were attacked and detained throughout 2008. In February 2009, a strike by teachers, health workers, and other public sector employees ended after the government agreed to pay salaries in foreign currency. Some teachers and health workers struck again in May, impeding the already limited operations of hospitals, clinics, and schools. In November, the home of the secretary general of the General Agriculture and Plantation Workers' Union, Gertrude Hambira, was invaded by alleged members of a ZANU-PF militia in an apparent abduction attempt; Hambira was not at home at the time.

Pressure from the executive branch has substantially eroded judicial independence in recent years, although the situation improved somewhat in 2009. The accused are often denied access to counsel and a fair, timely trial, and the government has repeatedly refused to enforce court orders. It has also replaced senior judges or pressured them to resign by stating that it could not guarantee their security; judges have been subject to extensive physical harassment. The vacancy of nearly 60 magistrate posts has caused a backlog of some 60,000 cases. Among other signs of decreased politicization in 2009, a judge in February dropped treason charges against MDC official Tendai Biti, and in July, a magistrate ordered the government to investigate the alleged assault of four women arrested at a peaceful demonstration on World Refugee Day. In October, the Supreme Court ordered a permanent stay of prosecution against Jestina Mukoko and eight other human rights activists, citing torture by police. However, in March police arrested a magistrate who had ordered the release of the MDC's Roy Bennett on bail.

Security forces abuse citizens with impunity, often ignoring basic rights regarding detention, searches, and seizures. The government has taken no clear action to halt the rising incidence of torture and mistreatment of suspects in custody. ZANU-

PF militias operate as de facto enforcers of government policies and have committed assault, torture, rape, extralegal evictions, and extralegal executions without fear of punishment; the incidence of these abuses increased significantly in 2008 and continued, though at a decreased rate, in 2009. Security forces have taken on major roles in crop collection, food distribution, and enforcement of monetary policy, and both the police and the military are heavily politicized. In October 2009, UN torture investigator Manfred Nowak, whom Prime Minister Morgan Tsvangirai had invited to inspect the police and some jails, was denied entry into Zimbabwe.

Pretrial detention is a major problem, with some inmates held for over 10 years without trial. Scores of MDC officials and activists were abducted, charged with treason, and detained without due process throughout 2008. Prison conditions are harsh and life-threatening. Severe overcrowding and a major shortage of funds have contributed to a rise in HIV and tuberculosis infections among inmates and the deterioration of already poor sanitation facilities. The Zimbabwe Association for Crime Prevention and Rehabilitation reported in April 2009 that Zimbabwe's prisons hold more than double their intended capacity of 17,000 inmates. Deaths in prisons are often caused by disease or beatings by guards, and many prisoners rely on family members for food. In June, the International Committee of the Red Cross began feeding some 6,500 inmates after a South African documentary exposed severe malnourishment and extremely high fatality rates in the country's jails. According to the weekly *Standard*, 700 of the 1,300 inmates held at the high-security Chikurubi prison near Harare died in 2008.

People living in the two Matabeleland provinces continue to suffer political and economic discrimination, and these areas are often targeted by security forces as opposition strongholds. Restrictive citizenship laws discriminate against Zimbabweans with origins in neighboring African countries.

The state has extensive control over travel and residence. The government has seized the passports of its domestic opponents, and foreign critics are routinely expelled or denied entry. In 2008, the authorities confiscated the passports of several MDC officials, including Tsvangirai. High passport fees inhibit legal travel.

Property rights are not respected. Operation Murambatsvina in 2005 entailed the eviction of hundreds of thousands of city dwellers and the destruction of thousands of residential and commercial structures, many of which had been approved by the government. Fewer than 400 white-owned farms remain out of the 4,500 that existed when land invasions started in 2000, and any avenues of legal recourse for expelled farmers have been closed. A 2007 law stipulates that 51 percent of shares in all—including foreign—companies operating in Zimbabwe must be owned by black Zimbabweans. In 2008, the government dismissed an SADC court ruling that found land seizures affecting a group of 70 white farmers to be discriminatory and in violation of SADC rules. In July 2009, the deputy mayor of Harare announced plans to evict people from illegal settlements and marketplaces, raising fears of another Operation Murambatsvina and sparking a successful campaign by civil society organizations to halt the evictions.

Women enjoy extensive legal protections, but societal discrimination and domestic violence persist. Women serve as ministers in national and local governments and hold 32 and 24 seats in the House of Assembly and Senate, respectively. The World Health Organization has reported that Zimbabwean women's "healthy life expectancy" of 34 years is the world's shortest. Sexual abuse is widespread, including the use of rape as a political weapon. A recent upsurge in gender-based violence spurred renewed calls for the enactment of the Prevention of Domestic Violence Bill, which has lingered in Parliament for nine years. Female members of the opposition often face particular brutality at the hands of security forces. The prevalence of customary laws in rural areas undermines women's civil rights and access to education. Homosexuality is illegal.

Abkhazia

Political Rights: 5
Civil Liberties: 5
Status: Partly Free

Population: 216,000

Ten-Year Ratings Timeline For Year Under Review (Political Rights, Civil Liberties, Status)

2000	2001	2002	2003	2004	2005	2006	2007	2008	2009
6,5NF	6,5NF	6,5NF	6,5NF	6,5NF	5,5PF	5,5PF	5,5PF	5,5PF	5,5PF

Overview:
Following its recognition of Abkhazia's independence in 2008, Russia significantly tightened its grip on the territory in 2009. In June, the United Nations Observer Mission in Georgia (UNOMIG) ended its 16-year mission in Abkhazia after an extension was vetoed by Moscow. During an August visit, Russian prime minister Vladimir Putin pledged funding to reinforce the Abkhaz border and establish a military base in the territory. Abkhazia later announced that it would transfer control of strategic assets to Russia, prompting protests by the Abkhaz opposition. In September, Venezuela became the third country, after Russia and Nicaragua, to recognize the territory's independence; Nauru followed suit in December. Also that month, Abkhaz president Sergei Bagapsh easily won reelection.

Annexed by Russia in 1864, Abkhazia became an autonomous republic within Soviet Georgia in 1930. After the 1991 collapse of the Soviet Union, Abkhazia declared its independence from Georgia in 1992, leading to a year-long war that left thousands dead and displaced more than 200,000 residents, mainly ethnic Georgians. Abkhaz forces won de facto independence for the republic in September 1993, and in May 1994, an internationally brokered ceasefire was signed in Moscow.

Incumbent Abkhaz president Vladislav Ardzinba ran unopposed for reelection in 1999, and a reported 98 percent of voters supported independence in a concurrent referendum. Deputies loyal to Ardzinba won all 35 seats in the 2002 parliamentary elections, after the opposition withdrew to protest bias by the election commission and state-backed media.

Under pressure from a powerful opposition movement, Prime Minister Gennady Gagulia resigned in April 2003 and was succeeded by Defense Minister Raul Khadjimba, though Ardzinba refused to step down as president.

An opposition candidate, former prime minister Sergei Bagapsh, defeated Khadjimba in the December 2004 presidential election, but he was pressured into a January 2005 rerun with Khadjimba—who was backed by Ardzinba and the Kremlin—as his vice-presidential running mate. The new ticket won the rerun with 91 percent of the vote.

In July 2006, Georgian troops occupied the strategic Kodori Gorge, the only portion of Abkhazia under Georgian control, after a Kodori-based Georgian paramilitary group refused orders from Tbilisi to disarm its fighters. The pro-Tbilisi government-in-exile for Abkhazia, composed of ethnic Georgians, was transferred to the gorge later that year.

Candidates from more than a dozen parties competed in the March 2007 Abkhaz parliamentary elections. Members of the three pro-Bagapsh parties captured more than 20 seats, and a number of opposition candidates were elected as well despite claims that Bagapsh had interfered with the electoral process.

In April 2008, Moscow increased its deployment of peacekeepers in Abkhazia to more than 2,500, drawing sharp international criticism. After several years of rising tension, war broke out in August between Georgian forces on the one hand and Russian, South Ossetian, and Abkhaz forces on the other. Although the brief conflict centered on South Ossetia, another Russian-backed Georgian territory that had won de facto independence in the early 1990s, Abkhaz troops succeeded in capturing the Kodori Gorge and additional territory on the Georgian-Abkhaz border.

In late August, following a French-brokered ceasefire, Russia formally recognized both Abkhazia and South Ossetia as independent states. It was joined by Nicaragua in September, Venezuela a year later, and Nauru in December 2009. Most of the international community continued to view the two territories as de jure parts of Georgia.

Throughout 2009, Russia steadily increased its influence in Abkhazia, leading the Abkhaz opposition to accuse the government of ceding undue control to Moscow and call for a diversification of the territory's political and economic ties abroad.

The United Nations Observer Mission in Georgia (UNOMIG), which had monitored the conflict for 16 years, ended its mission in June after Russia refused to extend its mandate unless the organization recognized Abkhazia's independence. UNOMIG was subsequently replaced by European Union (EU) monitors, who could only operate on the Georgian side of the de facto border.

In August, Russian prime minister Vladimir Putin made his first postwar visit to Abkhazia, pledging hundreds of millions of dollars in social spending and additional funding to establish a military base and reinforce the Abkhaz-Georgian border. Abkhazia later announced that it would transfer control of its railway and airport to Moscow, and the government licensed Russia's state-owned oil company Rosneft to explore for oil in the territory.

Bagapsh won reelection as president of Abkhazia in December, capturing more than 59 percent of the vote in the first round amid 73 percent turnout. Khadjimba placed a distant second with just 15 percent. All five candidates reportedly endorsed Russia's preeminent role in the territory.

Political Rights and Civil Liberties: Residents of Abkhazia can elect government officials, but the more than 200,000 Georgians who fled the region during the war in the early 1990s cannot vote in the elections held by the separatist government. Most of the ethnic Georgians who remain in Abkhazia are also unable to vote in local polls, as they lack Abkhaz passports. None of the elections have been recognized internationally.

The 1994 constitution established a presidential-parliamentary system, but the president exercises substantial control. The president and vice president are elected for five-year terms. The parliament, or People's Assembly, consists of 35 members elected for five-year terms from single-seat constituencies.

Corruption in Abkhazia is believed to be extensive, and government officials are not required to provide declarations of income. The republic was not listed separately on Transparency International's 2009 Corruption Perceptions Index.

Electronic media, the main source of information in Abkhazia, are partly controlled by the state. There are some privately owned and independent news outlets, including several newspapers, but they have reported pressure from the authorities. The government increased its scrutiny of private outlets ahead of the December 2009 presidential election. One private television channel was denied a broadcast license, and a journalist was sentenced to three years in prison for libeling the president in an online article.

Religious freedom in Abkhazia is affected by the political situation. In April 2009, three Georgian Orthodox priests were expelled for alleged spying, and several Georgian Orthodox monks and nuns were expelled from the Kodori Gorge after refusing to recognize Abkhaz authority in the area. The Abkhaz Orthodox Church declared its separation from the Georgian Orthodox Church in September. Though a 1995 decree bans Jehovah's Witnesses, they continue to practice openly in Abkhazia, as do other denominations.

The Abkhaz constitution offers some protection to ethnic minorities seeking education in their native languages. Armenian-language schools generally operate without government interference, but unofficial Georgian-language schools have reported significantly increased pressure since the 2008 war. Ethnic Georgian residents who hold Georgian passports are restricted from studying at Sokhumi State University.

Freedom of assembly is somewhat limited, but the opposition and civil society groups mounted a number of protests in 2009 to challenge the government's allegedly excessive concessions to Russia as well as a proposal to offer citizenship to some ethnic Georgian returnees. Although most nongovernmental organizations (NGOs) in Abkhazia rely on funding from outside the territory, the NGO sector is relatively vibrant and exerts a significant degree of influence on government policies. Abkhaz NGOs accepted EU grants for the first time in September 2009, following the rewording of the grant terms to make them acceptable to Abkhazia. Abkhaz NGOs are not permitted by the government to monitor local elections.

Defendants' limited access to qualified legal counsel, violations of due process, and lengthy pretrial detentions are among the chronic problems in Abkhazia's criminal justice system, though several Abkhaz NGOs are working on programs to make the judiciary more independent and transparent.

The human rights situation for the ethnic Georgian population in Gali worsened in 2009. Residents reported increased pressure from the Abkhaz authorities, and they also continued to suffer from widespread poverty, particularly after the closure of UNOMIG, which supplied many jobs in the region. A July amendment to a law on citizenship that would have made many of Gali's approximately 45,000 ethnic Georgians eligible for Abkhaz passports—entitling them to vote, own property, run a business, and obtain Russian citizenship and pensions—if they gave up their Georgian passports was scrapped in August following protests by the opposition, which claimed the move would undermine Abkhaz security.

Travel and choice of residence are limited by the ongoing separatist dispute. Most of the ethnic Georgians who fled Abkhazia during the early 1990s are living in Tbilisi and western Georgia. Russian border guards took over the de facto border in May 2009 and hampered freedom of movement for Gali Georgians, many of whom rely on unofficial cross-border trade and receive pensions from Tbilisi. Since the war, ethnic Abkhaz have had greater difficulty receiving visas to travel abroad, including to the United States and EU countries.

As many as 85 percent of Abkhazia's residents hold Russian passports and receive social benefits as Russian citizens, which they claim is a matter of necessity in light of the fact that Abkhaz travel documents are not internationally recognized.

Equality of opportunity and normal business activities are limited by corruption, criminal organizations, and the Abkhaz economy's almost complete reliance on Russia. Russia's successful bid to hold the 2014 Olympics in nearby Sochi will likely have an additional economic impact on the region.

Hong Kong

Political Rights: 5
Civil Liberties: 2
Status: Partly Free

Population: 7,037,000

Ten-Year Ratings Timeline For Year Under Review (Political Rights, Civil Liberties, Status)

2000	2001	2002	2003	2004	2005	2006	2007	2008	2009
5,3PF	5,3PF	5,3PF	5,3PF	5,2PF	5,2PF	5,2PF	5,2PF	5,2PF	5,2PF

Overview: A record 150,000 people attended a candlelight vigil in June 2009 to commemorate the 20th anniversary of the massacre in which Chinese security forces crushed prodemocracy protests in Beijing and other cities. In November, the Hong Kong government proposed reforms to the electoral system. The plan included expansions of the legislature and the election committee that chooses the chief executive, but would largely preserve the existing semidemocratic system. Separately, Beijing's growing influence over Hong Kong's media landscape and immigration policies was evident during the year.

Hong Kong Island was ceded in perpetuity to Britain in 1842; adjacent territories were subsequently added, and the last section was leased to Britain in 1898 for a period of 99 years. In the 1984 Sino-British Joint Declaration, London agreed to restore the entire colony to China in 1997. In return, Beijing—under its "one country, two systems" formula—pledged to maintain the enclave's legal, political, and economic autonomy for 50 years.

Under the 1984 agreement, a constitution for the Hong Kong Special Administrative Region (SAR), known as the Basic Law, took effect in 1997. Stating that universal suffrage was the "ultimate aim" for Hong Kong, the Basic Law allowed direct elections for only 18 seats in the 60-member legislature, known as the Legislative Council (Legco), with the gradual expansion of elected seats to 30 by 2003. After China took control, it temporarily suspended the Legco and installed a provisional legislature that repealed or tightened several civil liberties laws during its 10-month tenure.

Tung Chee-hwa was chosen as Hong Kong's chief executive by a Beijing-organized election committee in 1997, and his popularity waned as Beijing became increasingly involved in Hong Kong's affairs, raising fears that civic freedoms would be compromised. Officials were forced to withdraw a restrictive antisubversion bill—Basic Law Article 23—after it sparked massive protests in July 2003.

Pro-Beijing parties retained control of the Legco in 2004 elections, which were marred by intimidation that was thought to have been organized by Beijing. In 2005, with two years left to serve, the deeply unpopular Tung resigned. He was replaced by career civil servant Donald Tsang, who China's National People's Congress (NPC) decided would serve out the remainder of Tung's term before facing election. In 2007, Hong Kong held competitive elections for chief executive after democracy supporters on the 800-member election committee nominated a second candidate, Alan Leong. However, Tsang won a new term by a wide margin, garnering 82 percent of the votes in the mostly pro-Beijing committee.

Pro-Beijing parties again won Legco elections in September 2008, taking 30 seats, although few of those members were elected by popular vote. The prodemocracy camp won 23 seats, including 19 by popular vote, enabling them to retain a veto over proposed constitutional reforms.

In November 2009, the government published a consultation document on proposed electoral reforms for the 2012 polls that would ostensibly serve as a transitional arrangement until the anticipated adoption of universal suffrage in 2017 for the chief executive and 2020 for the Legco. The system outlined in the plan did not represent substantive progress toward full democracy. Observers noted that the Hong Kong government's reluctance to make more drastic changes was partly due to restrictions imposed by several decisions of China's National People's Congress (NPC) Standing Committee, the most recent in 2007, and the requirement that any reforms obtain its approval. At year's end, the proposal remained open for public consultation, and Tsang was expected to submit a draft to the Legco in February 2010.

Beijing's growing influence over Hong Kong's media landscape and immigration policies remained evident during 2009. However, partly in response to comments by Tsang in which he downplayed the 1989 Tiananmen Square massacre, a record turnout of 150,000 people joined an annual candlelight vigil in June to commemorate the incident, in which Chinese security forces had crushed prodemocracy protests in Beijing and other cities. Public events marking the anniversary were not permitted in the rest of China.

Political Rights and Civil Liberties: Hong Kong's Basic Law calls for the election of a chief executive and a unicameral Legislative Council (Legco). The chief executive is elected by an 800-member committee: some 200,000 "functional constituency" voters—representatives of various elite business and social sectors, many with close ties to Beijing—elect 600 members, and the remaining 200 consist of Legco members, Hong Kong delegates to the NPC, religious representatives, and 41 members of the Chinese People's Political Consultative Conference (CPPCC), a mainland advisory body. The chief executive serves a five-year term.

The Legco consists of 30 directly elected members and 30 members chosen by the functional constituency voters. Legco members serve four-year terms. The Basic Law restricts the Legco's lawmaking powers, prohibiting legislators from introducing bills that would affect Hong Kong's public spending, governmental operations, or political structure. In the territory's multiparty system, the five main parties are the prodemocracy Democratic Party, Civic Party, and League of Social Democrats; the pro-Beijing Democratic Alliance for the Betterment and Progress of Hong Kong; and the business-oriented Liberal Party.

The 2008 Legco elections were procedurally free and fair, but the semidemocratic structure of the legislature meant that the prodemocracy camp remained a minority despite winning nearly 60 percent of the popular vote. Unlike in 2004, the elections were not accompanied by overt intimidation or threats, though indirect pressure and influence from Beijing was nonetheless evident.

The consultation document on electoral reform, introduced in November 2009, proposed several modest changes to the current system. The election committee for the chief executive would expand from 800 to 1,200 members, but would otherwise retain its existing composition. The Legco would expand from 60 to 70 seats, with direct elections for 5 of the new seats and the remaining 5 chosen indirectly by elected members of Hong Kong's 18 district councils. The consultation document did not include a blueprint for adopting universal suffrage in 2017 and 2020, contravening the government's earlier promises and heightening fears that the transition would be pushed further into the future.

Politically motivated violence is rare in Hong Kong. However, a total of 11 suspects—1 in Hong Kong and 10 in China—involved in a 2008 plot to shoot prominent prodemocracy politician Martin Lee and media tycoon Jimmy Lai, known for his vocal criticism of the Chinese Communist Party, received sentences of up to 18 years in prison in 2009. The plot's alleged mastermind was said to reside in Taiwan and remained at large at year's end.

Hong Kong is generally regarded as having low rates of corruption, although business interests have considerable influence on the Legco. In May 2009, the territory's internationally respected Independent Commission Against Corruption reported a 23 percent increase in graft complaints during the first three months of the year, compared with the same period in 2008. This was widely viewed as a result of the economic downturn, as officials were more inclined to engage in graft to compensate for personal financial losses. The right to access government information is protected by law and observed in practice. Hong Kong was ranked 12 out of 180 countries surveyed in Transparency International's 2009 Corruption Perceptions Index.

Under Article 27 of the Basic Law, Hong Kong residents enjoy freedoms of speech, press, and publication. These rights are generally respected in practice, and political debate is vigorous. There are dozens of daily newspapers, and residents have access to international radio broadcasts and satellite television. International media organizations operate without interference. Nonetheless, Beijing's growing influence over the media, book publishing, and film industries in recent years has led to self-censorship, particularly on issues deemed sensitive by the central government. This influence stems in part from the close relationship between Hong Kong media owners and the central authorities; at least 10 such owners sit on the CPPCC. In one incident during 2009, managers of the Hong Kong edition of *Esquire* magazine barred the publication of a 16-page feature about the Tiananmen Square massacre, and the feature's author was subsequently fired. More broadly, the Hong Kong Journalists' Association reported that, "only two or three newspapers devoted significant coverage to the anniversary, while leading TV stations aired just a few special programs, with some appearing to follow [the Communist Party's] line."

Hong Kong journalists face a number of restrictions when covering events on the mainland. In February 2009, Chinese authorities issued regulations requiring Hong Kong journalists to obtain temporary press cards from Beijing's liaison office prior to each reporting trip to the mainland, and to secure the prior consent of interviewees. While violence against journalists is rare in Hong Kong, reporters from the territory have repeatedly faced surveillance, intimidation, beatings, and occasional imprisonment when reporting on the mainland. In September, three journalists—a television reporter and two cameramen—were reportedly detained and beaten by police while covering unrest in Xinjiang. An official Chinese investigation concluded that the journalists had been at fault for "instigating protests," prompting a demonstration and a petition by hundreds of Hong Kong journalists.

The Hong Kong government, rather than an independent regulator, controls media licensing in the territory. Authorities continued to obstruct broadcasts by the prodemocracy station Citizens' Radio in 2009, after its license application was rejected in 2006. In November and December, more than a dozen prodemocracy activists and lawmakers were fined between US$125 and US$1,500 each for participating in unlicensed radio broadcasts, though one of the judges ruling on the case acknowledged the act of civil disobedience as "noble." Separately, in September, the government rejected proposals to convert the state-owned but editorially independent Radio Television Hong Kong (RTHK) into a fully independent public broadcaster, or to create such an outlet. Officials instead announced the creation of a government-appointed board to advise RTHK's director of broadcasting, potentially curbing the station's editorial autonomy. A period for public consultation on the issue began in October and had not concluded by year's end.

The Basic Law provides for freedom of religion, which is generally respected in practice. Religious groups are excluded from the Societies Ordinance, which requires nongovernmental organizations (NGOs) to register with the government. Adherents of the Falun Gong spiritual movement remain free to practice in the territory and hold occasional demonstrations, despite facing repression on the mainland. University professors can write and lecture freely, and political debate on campuses is lively.

The Basic Law guarantees freedoms of assembly and association. Police permits for demonstrations are required but rarely denied, and protests on politically sensitive issues are held regularly. In June 2009, a record 150,000 people participated in a candlelight vigil to mark the 20th anniversary of the Tiananmen Square massacre. Nevertheless, outside activists who planned to participate in events highlighting rights abuses in China continued to be denied entry or prevented from leaving the mainland in 2009.

Hong Kong hosts a vibrant and largely unfettered NGO sector, and trade unions are independent. However, there is limited legal protection for basic labor rights. Collective-bargaining rights are not recognized, protections against antiunion discrimination are weak, and there are few regulations on working hours and wages. While strikes are legal and several occurred in 2009, many workers sign contracts stating that walkouts could be grounds for summary dismissal.

The judiciary is independent, and the trial process is fair. The NPC reserves the right to make final interpretations of the Basic Law, effectively limiting the power of Hong Kong's Court of Final Appeals. While the NPC has not directly intervened in court cases for a number of years, several recent incidents raised concerns about growing influence from Beijing over law enforcement matters. In 2008, U.S.-based Tiananmen Square activist Zhou Yongjun was detained while visiting Hong Kong on a fake Malaysian passport, and in an unusual move, he was handed over to authorities on the mainland. He was tried there on bank fraud charges in 2009, although it remained unclear whether he or the person named on the fake passport was wanted by the authorities; a verdict was pending at year's end. Also in 2009, Hong Kong officials decided not to prosecute family members and acquaintances of Zimbabwean president Robert Mugabe, a close Beijing ally, after they physically assaulted several foreign journalists. Chief justice Andrew Li Kwok-nang, who has headed the judiciary since the handover, announced his retirement in September 2009; at year's end, observers were watching to see who would be his successor and whether that individual would uphold the same standards of independence.

Police are forbidden by law to employ torture and other forms of abuse. However, official figures indicated that police conducted over 1,600 strip searches in 2008, leading to the adoption in February 2009 of additional measures to monitor and limit the use of such searches. Arbitrary arrest and detention are illegal; suspects must be charged within 48 hours of their arrest. Prison conditions generally meet international standards.

Citizens are treated equally under the law, though Hong Kong's population of 200,000 foreign domestic workers remains vulnerable to abuse, and South Asians routinely complain of discrimination in employment. Since foreign workers face deportation if dismissed, many are reluctant to bring complaints against employers. A Race Discrimination Ordinance that took effect in July 2009 created an independent Equal Opportunities Commission to enforce its protections. However, in September, the UN Committee on the Elimination of Racial Discrimination criticized the ordinance for failing to cover certain government actions, neglecting the issue of indirect discrimination, and effectively excluding immigrants.

The government does not control travel, choice of residence, or employment within Hong Kong, although documents are required to travel to the mainland, and employers must apply to bring in workers from China; direct applications from workers are not accepted. Hong Kong maintains its own immigration system. In September 2009, an appeals court criticized the government for lack of candor and destruction of relevant documents in a lawsuit challenging the denial of entry to four Taiwanese Falun Gong practitioners in 2003; however, the court was reluctant to conclude that the immigration department had acted in an unlawful fashion in denying the plaintiffs' entry. Five Legco members and several human rights activists from Hong Kong were barred entry to Macau in March 2009, shortly after that territory passed new national security legislation; many of those affected are regularly barred from the mainland as well.

Women are protected by law from discrimination and abuse and are entitled to equal access to schooling, as well as to property in divorce settlements. However, women continue to face discrimination in employment opportunities, salary, inheritance, and welfare. Despite robust efforts by the government, Hong Kong remains a point of transit and destination for persons trafficked for sexual exploitation or forced labor.

Indian Kashmir

Political Rights: 4*
Civil Liberties: 4
Status: Partly Free

Population: 12,219,000

Ratings Change: Indian Kashmir's political rights rating improved from 5 to 4 due to reports that the December 2008 elections were generally fair and competitive, drawing a comparatively high voter turnout despite militant groups' calls for a boycott.

Ten-Year Ratings Timeline For Year Under Review (Political Rights, Civil Liberties, Status)

2000	2001	2002	2003	2004	2005	2006	2007	2008	2009
6,6NF	6,6NF	5,5PF	5,5PF	5,5PF	5,5PF	5,5PF	5,4PF	5,4PF	4,4PF

Overview:
Talks between India and Pakistan on the resolution of Kashmir's status continued in 2009, and in November, Kashmiri separatist leaders agreed to meet with the Indian government for the first time in four years. In the wake of successful elections in late 2008, the overall level of violence declined, continuing a seven-year trend; in October, India announced plans to withdraw 15,000 troops from the Jammu region. Nevertheless, separatist violence continued during the year, and a number of noncombat killings by security forces were reported. Impunity for human rights abuses remained the norm.

When British India was partitioned into India and Pakistan in 1947, the Hindu maharajah of Jammu and Kashmir tried to maintain his principality's independence, but he eventually ceded it to India in return for autonomy and future self-determination. Within months, India and Pakistan went to war over the territory. As part of a UN-brokered ceasefire in 1949 that established the present-day boundaries, Pakistan gained control of roughly one-third of Jammu and Kashmir. India retained most of the Kashmir Valley, along with Jammu and Ladakh. Under Article 370 of India's constitution and a 1952 accord, the territory received substantial autonomy, but India annulled such guarantees in 1957 and formally annexed the portion of Jammu and Kashmir under its control. Since then, it has largely been governed like other Indian states, with an elected legislature and chief minister. Under the 1972 Simla accord, New Delhi and Islamabad agreed to respect the Line of Control (LOC) dividing the region and to resolve Kashmir's status through negotiation.

The pro-India National Conference (NC) party won state elections in 1987 that were marred by widespread fraud, violence, and arrests of members of a new, Muslim-based opposition coalition, leading to widespread unrest. An armed insurgency against Indian rule gathered momentum after 1989, waged by the Jammu and Kashmir Liberation Front (JKLF) and other proindependence groups, consisting largely of Kashmiris, as well as Pakistani-backed Islamist groups seeking to bring Kashmir under Islamabad's control.

New Delhi placed Jammu and Kashmir under federal rule in 1990 and attempted to quell the uprising by force. The JKLF abandoned its armed struggle in 1994, and the insurgency was thereafter dominated by Pakistani-backed extremist groups, which included fighters from elsewhere in the Muslim world.

Although opposition parties joined together to form the All Parties Hurriyat Conference (APHC) in 1993, they boycotted the 1996 state elections, and the NC was able to form a government. The APHC also declined to participate in the 2002 elections, but the NC nevertheless lost more than half of its assembly seats, allowing the Congress Party and the People's Democratic Party (PDP) to form a coalition government.

Despite several setbacks, relations between the Indian government and moderate Kashmiri separatist groups generally improved after the 2002 elections. In 2004, talks were held for the first time between Kashmiri separatists and the highest levels of the Indian government. Moderate APHC leaders reiterated their renunciation of violence in 2005 and called for Kashmiris to become more deeply involved in the negotiating process. However, the latter was hampered by an emerging split within the APHC between those who favored a continuation of the insurgency and those who favored a political solution.

The PDP-Congress alliance collapsed in June 2008, when the PDP withdrew its support amid a high-profile dispute over land set aside for a Hindu pilgrimage site. State elections were held from November 17 to December 28. Turnout was higher than expected, exceeding 60 percent on most polling dates, as voters largely ignored calls for a boycott from separatist groups. While early voting dates were generally peaceful, some violence marred later polling—particularly in early December—when antielection protesters clashed with security forces. The elections were considered mostly free and fair, however, with significantly reduced levels of voter intimidation, harassment, and violence compared with previous elections. The NC won a plurality of 28 seats, followed by the PDP with 21 seats and Congress with 17. The NC then allied itself with Congress to form a coalition government.

Umar Farooq, chairman of one APHC faction, offered in November 2009 to begin direct talks with the Indian government within the next few months. The talks would be the first of their kind in four years.The security situation also improved during 2009, with the number of fatalities decreasing for the seventh consecutive year. According to the South Asia Terrorism Portal (SATP), about 377 people were killed during the year, compared with 541 in 2008. In October, New Delhi announced plans to withdraw 15,000 troops from the Jammu region, granting local police more responsibility over the area. Nevertheless, there were several incidents of violence, including bombings in public places and other attacks directed at security forces, politicians, and minority groups.

Relations between India and Pakistan improved somewhat in mid-2009, following a rift over a November 2008 terrorist attack in Mumbai that was linked to a Pakistani-based militant group. In July, the two sides agreed to separate their Kashmir talks from discussions related to terrorist attacks, but India was forced to backtrack from that position due to vocal domestic criticism.

Political Rights and Civil Liberties: Jammu and Kashmir, like India's other states, is governed by an elected bicameral legislature and a chief minister entrusted with executive power. An appointed governor serves as titular head of state. Members of the 87-seat lower house, or state assembly, are directly elected, while the 46-seat upper house has a combination of members elected by the state assembly and nominated by the governor.

India has never held a referendum allowing Kashmiri self-determination as called for in a 1948 UN resolution. The state's residents can change the local administration through elections, which are supposed to be held at least once every five years. The polls are monitored by the Election Commission of India, but historically, they have been marred by violence, coercion by security forces, and balloting irregularities. Militants have enforced boycotts called for by separatist political parties, threatened election officials and candidates, and killed political activists and civilians during balloting. More than 800 people were killed during the 2002 campaign period, including over 75 political activists and candidates.

However, the November and December 2008 legislative elections, which were considered generally free and fair, were largely peaceful despite some cases of violence. Turnout was significantly higher than in previous years, according to a *Times of India* report. A January 2009 ReliefWeb report noted that the election was the most peaceful in two decades.

Political violence has included high-profile assassinations of party and government officials, although the number of political killings has fallen somewhat in recent years. A prominent NC activist was killed by separatists in Srinigar in September 2009.

Corruption remains widespread despite apparent government efforts to combat it. The State Vigilance Organization has been active in recent years, charging several local officials with fraud and misappropriation of funds. Nevertheless, higher officials are seldom targeted, and convictions are rare. In January 2008, Education Minister Peerzada Mohammad Sayeed resigned after being charged with receiving a bribe, but he rejoined the cabinet in January 2009. Several whistle-blowers have reported harassment after filing complaints. Indian-controlled Kashmir was not ranked separately on Transparency International's 2009 Corruption Perceptions Index.

Though it is generally not used, India's 1971 Newspapers (Incitement to Offences) Act, which is in effect only in Jammu and Kashmir, gives district magistrates the authority to censor publications in certain circumstances. Pressure to self-censor has been reported at smaller media outlets that rely on state government advertising for the majority of their revenue. Despite these restrictions, newspapers report on controversial issues such as alleged human rights abuses by security forces. The authorities generally allow foreign journalists to travel freely, meet regularly with separatist leaders, and file reports on a range of issues, including government abuses. As with the rest of India, print media are thriving in Kashmir, with 145 dailies available across the state.

Journalists remain subject to pressure from militants, and many practice some degree of self-censorship for this reason. Militant groups threaten and sometimes kidnap, torture, or kill journalists. Reporters are also occasionally harassed or detained by the authorities. Incidents of violence against the press declined in 2009, with no reported cases of assault or murder, although journalists reporting on the alleged rape and murder of two women by Indian police in Shopian faced harassment and death threats. In July, police threatened two Srinagar-based journalists for reporting on the suspected disappearance of a youth while in police custody.

Freedom of worship and academic freedom are generally respected by Indian and local authorities. Since 2003, the state government has permitted separatist groups to organize a procession marking the prophet Muhammad's birthday. However, Islamist militants at times attack Hindu and Sikh temples or villages. The offer and subsequent retraction of land for a Hindu pilgrimage site in June 2008 inspired large and sometimes violent protests throughout the summer. However, pilgrimages to the site began again in mid-2009 and continued peacefully for the rest of the year.

Freedoms of assembly and association are often restricted. Although local and national civil rights groups are permitted to operate, they sometimes encounter harassment by security forces. The separatist APHC is allowed to function, but its leaders are frequently subjected to short-term preventative detention, and its requests for permits for public gatherings are often denied. Politically motivated general strikes, protest marches, and antigovernment demonstrations take place on a regular basis, though some are forcibly broken up by the authorities. During the summer protests of 2008, there were several reports of police shooting indiscriminately into stone-throwing crowds. The February 2009 killing of two unarmed youths by police in Bumai led to mass protests in the area in March; four people were injured when a mob attacked a police station, and local authorities imposed a day-long curfew to prevent further violence. In a separate incident, two people died during protests in June following the alleged rape and murder of two women by the police in Shopian.

Courts were regularly in session in Jammu and Kashmir in 2009, according to the U.S. State Department's human rights report. Nevertheless, judges, witnesses, and the families of defendants remain subject to intimidation by militants. In addition, the government and security forces frequently disregard court orders, including those quashing detentions. Two broadly written laws—the Armed Forces Special Powers Act (AFSPA) and the Disturbed Areas Act—allow Indian forces to search homes and arrest suspects without a warrant, shoot suspects on sight, and destroy buildings believed to house militants or arms. In a widely criticized decision in May 2007, India's Supreme Court effectively reversed previous rulings requiring the armed forces to involve civilian police in their operations and thus removed an important safeguard for detainees. Following the two killings in Bumai in February 2009, Chief Minister Omar Abdullah pledged to have the AFSPA repealed during his new government's six-year term; it was still in effect at year's end.

In a continuing cycle of violence, hundreds of militants, security personnel, and civilians are killed each year, although the number continued to decline in 2009. The SATP reported that 55 civilians, 78 security personnel, and 244 militants were killed during the year. The total of 377 was a significant decrease from the previous year's death toll of 541.

Indian security personnel based in Kashmir, numbering about 500,000, carry out arbitrary arrests and detentions, torture, "disappearances," and custodial killings of suspected militants and alleged civilian sympathizers. As part of the counterinsurgency effort, the government has organized former militants into progovernment militias. Members of these groups act with impunity and have reportedly carried out a range of human rights abuses against pro-Pakistani militants and civilians. Official figures released in August 2009 estimated that 3,429 people had disappeared between 1990 and July 2009. Human rights groups have suggested a number closer to 8,000. Security personnel are often rewarded—with either cash or a promotion—for producing a dead militant, and holding militants in custody is considered a security risk. This has led to the practice of fake "encounter" killings, in which militants as well as civilians are killed in custody and then passed off as combatants killed in battle.

While the state human rights commission examines several dozen complaints a year, it is hampered by inadequate resources and infrastructure. In addition, it cannot directly investigate abuses by the army or other federal security forces, nor can it take action against those found to have committed violations. Impunity for rights abuses by Indian armed forces has been the norm, in part because under the AFSPA, New Delhi is required to approve any prosecutions. However, the discovery of apparent victims of fake encounter killings in 2007 prompted an unusually thorough investigation, and at least 18 policemen were charged, including a number of senior officers and a former superintendent. While the government initially denied any wrongdoing in the two killings in Bumai in 2009, a subsequent investigation acknowledged that three police officers were guilty of "lapses," and disciplinary action was ordered against them. The Central Bureau of Investigation's probe of the alleged rape and murder of two woman in Shopian was ongoing.

Armed with increasingly sophisticated and powerful weapons, and relying to a greater degree on suicide squads, militant groups based in Pakistan continue to kill pro-India politicians, public employees, suspected informers, members of rival factions, soldiers, and civilians. The roughly 800 active militants also engage in kidnapping, rape, extortion, and other forms of intimidation. Violence targeting Pandits, or Kashmiri Hindus, is part of a pattern dating to 1990 that has forced several hundred thousand Hindus to flee the region; many continue to reside in refugee camps near Jammu. Other religious and ethnic minorities, such as Sikhs and Gujjars, have also been targeted.

Kashmiris are generally free to move around the state. A bus service across the LOC was launched in 2005, and trade across the line reopened in early 2008 for the first time in 60 years.

As in other parts of India, women face some societal discrimination as well as domestic violence and other forms of abuse. Female civilians continue to be subjected to harassment, intimidation, and violent attacks, including rape and murder, at the hands of both the security forces and militant groups.

Israel-Occupied Territories

Political Rights: 6
Civil Liberties: 6
Status: Not Free

Population: 3,933,000

Note: The areas and total number of persons under Israeli jurisdiction changed periodically during the year as a result of the fluid nature of Israel's military presence in the West Bank and Gaza Strip.

Ten-Year Ratings Timeline For Year Under Review (Political Rights, Civil Liberties, Status)

2000	2001	2002	2003	2004	2005	2006	2007	2008	2009
6,6NF	6,6NF	6,6NF	6,6NF	6,6NF	6,5NF	6,5NF	6,6NF	6,6NF	6,6NF

Overview:
Intense fighting between Israeli forces and Hamas in the Gaza Strip ended with a ceasefire in January 2009, but the

territory continued to suffer during the year from infrastructural damage, unexploded ordnance, and ongoing Israeli border restrictions. Meanwhile, Israeli authorities continued to break up protests against the growing security barrier in the West Bank, and approved additional construction at existing Jewish settlements near Jerusalem.

Israel declared its statehood in 1948 on land allotted for Jewish settlement under a UN partition plan. It gained additional territory in the ensuing conflict with neighboring Arab states. Meanwhile, Jordan captured East Jerusalem and the West Bank, and Egypt took the Gaza Strip. In the 1967 Six-Day War, Israel seized the West Bank, East Jerusalem, and the Gaza Strip, as well as the Sinai Peninsula (from Egypt) and the Golan Heights (from Syria). The Sinai was later returned to Egypt.

After 1967, Israel began establishing Jewish settlements in the West Bank and Gaza Strip, an action regarded as illegal by most of the international community. Israel maintained that the settlements were legal, since under international law, the West Bank and Gaza were disputed territories. In what became known as the first *intifada* (uprising), Palestinians living in the West Bank and Gaza began attacking mainly Israeli settlers and Israel Defense Forces (IDF) troops in 1987. Israel and Yasser Arafat's Palestine Liberation Organization (PLO) reached an agreement in 1993 that provided for a PLO renunciation of terrorism and recognition of Israel, Israeli troop withdrawals, and gradual Palestinian autonomy in the West Bank and Gaza.

In subsequent years, the IDF granted the new Palestinian Authority (PA) control over most of Gaza and up to 40 percent of West Bank territory, including 98 percent of the Palestinian population outside of East Jerusalem. However, the IDF reentered most PA areas after the September 2000 eruption of the second intifada. While the Israeli incursions targeted Islamist and secular militant groups, they also caused the deaths of many civilians.

After Arafat's death in 2004 and the election of Mahmoud Abbas as the new PA president in 2005, violence declined markedly. In February 2005, Abbas and Israeli prime minister Ariel Sharon agreed on a formal truce that lasted through June 2006. Israel unilaterally withdrew all settlers from the Gaza Strip in August 2005. However, it retained control of Gaza's airspace, its coastline, and most of its land border.

The Islamist faction Hamas won the 2006 Palestinian legislative elections, allowing it to form a PA government without Abbas's Fatah party. Israel, the United States, and the European Union (EU) refused to recognize the Hamas-led government, citing the group's involvement in terrorism and refusal to recognize Israel or past Israel-PA agreements.

In June 2006, in response to the killing of eight Palestinian civilians by an artillery shell, Hamas declared an end to the 2005 truce and accelerated the firing of Qassam rockets at Israel from Gaza. The source of the artillery fire remained in dispute. Hamas and other militant groups subsequently carried out a raid near Gaza, killing two IDF soldiers and capturing a third, Corporal Gilad Shalit. Israel responded by invading Gaza, where the IDF destroyed Qassam launchers and ammunition sites but failed to locate Shalit. The fighting killed dozens of civilians. PA-controlled areas of the West Bank also faced Israeli incursions in 2006.

IDF operations in the West Bank dropped significantly following the fracturing of the PA in June 2007 between the Hamas-controlled Gaza Strip and the Fatah-controlled West Bank. By contrast, Israel declared the Gaza Strip a "hostile entity" in response to the continued barrage of Qassam rockets and closed its borders with the territory, granting passage only to food deliveries and a restricted list of other humanitarian supplies. However, arms and goods were regularly smuggled through a tunnel network dug between Egypt and Gaza. Israeli forces continued to attack targets in the Gaza Strip and clash with Palestinian militants near the border for the remainder of the year.

After several more months of fighting, Israel and Hamas agreed to a six-month ceasefire in June 2008, leading to an easing of the blockade. Meanwhile, Israeli troops staged a number of raids in the West Bank during 2008, in addition to regular patrols. The IDF reportedly controlled about 60 percent of the West Bank, and construction continued on a security barrier that ran roughly along the West Bank side of the 1949 armistice line (Green Line) and sometimes jutted farther into the West Bank. Palestinians complained that the barrier, which by the end of 2009 was about 70 percent complete, expropriated West Bank land and collectively punished ordinary Palestinians for acts committed by terrorists.

Before his resignation in late 2008, Israeli prime minister Ehud Olmert sought to finalize peace talks with Abbas's Fatah-led government that had accelerated after the latter's 2007 split with the Hamas-controlled Gaza Strip. Olmert proposed a plan that involved the return of 93 percent of the West Bank to the Palestinians, international control of Jerusalem's "Holy Basin," and the ceding of the city's Arab neighborhoods to the Palestinians. The plan also called for a land swap, whereby Israel would retain three West Bank settlement blocs in exchange for land adjacent to Gaza (in the Negev desert) equal to 5.5 percent of the West Bank. The Palestinians would also receive free crossing between the West Bank and Gaza. Abbas rejected the plan, citing core Palestinian demands for a contiguous state within the 1967 borders with Jerusalem as its capital, and a "right of return" for Palestinian refugees.

War erupted between Hamas and Israeli forces in December 2008, after the six-month truce expired, and Hamas ramped up its rocket bombardment of Israeli towns near the border with Gaza. The IDF launched a campaign of near-daily air strikes and an almost three-week ground invasion of the coastal territory. Israel declared a unilateral ceasefire in late January 2009, and Hamas soon did the same. During the conflict, Israeli forces destroyed large portions of Gaza's military, government, and civilian infrastructure; according to the British Broadcasting Corporation, more than 4,000 buildings were destroyed, with 20,000 severely damaged. Tens of thousands of Gazans were left homeless by the fighting. While the Palestinian Centre for Human Rights reported that 1,434 Palestinians were killed, including 960 noncombatants, the IDF reported that 1,166 Palestinians were killed, including 295 to 460 noncombatants. Thirteen Israelis were killed, including three noncombatants. In January, the International Committee of the Red Cross (ICRC) reported that electricity and water were "severely limited" for two-thirds of Gaza's population, and vaccinations were in short supply. According to the UN Relief and Works Agency (UNRWA), some 150,000 Gazans continued to lack access to tap water as of April.

International and domestic human rights organizations accused Israel of using excessive military force in Gaza and imposing collective punishment on its residents. Amnesty International and Human Rights Watch argued that Israeli forces had committed war crimes, a charge echoed by an investigation commissioned by the

UN Human Rights Council and led by South African jurist Richard Goldstone. The Israeli government, which did not cooperate with the Goldstone commission, denied the allegations, arguing that the military campaign was necessary to protect Israeli civilians from Hamas rocket attacks; according to the IDF, over 7,500 rockets and mortar shells had been launched at Israel since 2005. Israel also asserted that Palestinian civilian casualties were caused primarily by Hamas and other militant groups' use of civilian areas to stage and prepare attacks, that Israeli actions—including the use of white phosphorus munitions—fell within the bounds of international law, and that the blockade of Gaza was limited to materials with potential military uses. Hamas and other Palestinian militant groups were also accused of war crimes for indiscriminately firing over 700 rockets into Israeli civilian areas during the war.

After the outbreak of hostilities, Israel had tightened its blockade of Gaza to allow only humanitarian goods and reduced the number of crossing openings. Aid agencies called for a full opening of crossing points; according to the UNRWA, the Israeli authorities in January were permitting only a fraction of the necessary number of trucks to enter Gaza each day. Following the ceasefire, crossings were opened on a limited basis to transfer grains, certain types of fuels, and other authorized goods, as well as international aid workers and individuals with specified medical and humanitarian needs. The Rafah border crossing with Egypt opened on an ad hoc basis. In August, Israel allowed cement and heavy building materials into Gaza for the first time in seven months.

Political Rights and Civil Liberties:

Since they are not citizens of Israel, Palestinians under Israeli control in the West Bank and Gaza cannot vote in Israeli elections. They are permitted to vote in PA elections. Israel was generally credited with allowing relatively free movement during the 2005 presidential and 2006 legislative elections for the PA, although some during the campaign, with electoral preparations, and with Israeli roadblocks were reported.

After Israel annexed East Jerusalem in 1967, Arab residents were issued Israeli identity cards and given the option of obtaining Israeli citizenship. However, by law, Israel strips Arabs of their Jerusalem residency if they remain outside the city for more than three months. Those who do not choose Israeli citizenship have the same rights as Israeli citizens, except the right to vote in national elections; they can vote in municipal elections. Many choose not to seek citizenship out of solidarity with Palestinians in the West Bank and Gaza Strip, believing East Jerusalem should be the capital of an independent Palestinian state. East Jerusalem's Arab population does not receive a share of municipal services proportionate to its size.

Arabs in East Jerusalem have the right to vote in PA elections, but are subject to restrictions imposed by the Israeli municipality of Jerusalem. In the 2006 PLC elections, Israel barred Hamas from campaigning in the city.

Druze and Arabs in the Golan Heights cannot vote in Israeli national elections, but they are represented at the municipal level.

International press freedom groups regularly criticize Israel for blocking journalists' access to conflict zones, harming and sometimes killing reporters during battles, and harassing Palestinian journalists. Israel insists that reporters risk getting caught in crossfire but are not targeted deliberately. Israeli journalists have been prohibited from entering the Gaza Strip since 2006 under a military decree that cites their personal safety. A broader ban that also applied to foreign journalists was in place from November 2008 to January 2009, though it was lifted briefly by court order in December. During the war, Israeli forces bombed Hamas-affiliated media stations and destroyed satellite equipment on the roof of a building that housed the local offices of Iran's English- and Arabic-language television networks. The IDF also interfered with a Gazan radio and television station, broadcasting calls to abandon Hamas. According to the International Freedom of Expression Exchange (IFEX), five Gazan journalists were killed by Israeli forces during the war.

Israel generally recognizes the right to freedom of worship and religion. On several occasions since 2000, Israeli authorities have restricted Muslim men under age 45 from praying at the Temple Mount/Haram al-Sharif compound in Jerusalem, citing the possibility of violent confrontations. In October 2009, hundreds of Muslim youths and Israeli police clashed at the site after the youths threw stones and firebombs at police and a tourist group; police responded with rubber bullets and stun grenades. The next day, prayers at the Haram al-Sharif were limited to women and men over age 50.

While academic freedom is generally respected, IDF-imposed closures and curfews in the West Bank, and the growing security barrier, have crippled the operations of many Palestinian academic institutions. Schools have sometimes been damaged during military actions, and student travel between the Gaza Strip and the West Bank has been limited. Schoolchildren have been injured or killed during fighting. In September 2009, the UN Office for the Coordination of Humanitarian Affairs reported that at least 280 of Gaza's 641 schools were damaged and 18 were destroyed during the fighting that ended in January, and that many schools lacked essential materials in the aftermath. Despite a nonbinding 2008 ruling by the Israeli Supreme Court calling on the government to allow Gazan students to study abroad, Israel's border restrictions have prevented them from doing so. According to the Association for Civil Rights in Israel (ACRI), East Jerusalem's schools are badly underfunded compared with schools in West Jerusalem.

While freedom of assembly is sometimes respected, demonstrations often turn violent and are forcibly dispersed, resulting in deaths on some occasions. Israel has imposed strict curfews in the West Bank at various times since 2000. In 2009, Israeli police continued to break up frequent demonstrations in opposition to the security barrier in the West Bank. An American protestor, Tristan Anderson, was critically injured in March after being hit by an IDF tear-gas canister. In a similar incident in April, a protestor, Bassem Ibrahim Abu-Rahma, was killed at a protest near Bil'in. The Israeli Supreme Court in July ordered the military to impose stronger charges on the officer and soldier filmed shooting a rubber bullet at the feet of a bound Palestinian arrested at a barrier protest in 2008.

There are many Palestinian nongovernmental organizations (NGOs) and civic groups, and their activities are generally not restricted by Israel. Associations that espouse violence enjoy significantly less freedom. Workers may establish and join unions without government authorization. Palestinian workers in Jerusalem are subject to Israeli labor law.

Israel's Supreme Court hears petitions from non-Israeli residents of the occupied territories regarding home demolitions, land confiscations, road closures, and

IDF tactics. Decisions in favor of Palestinian petitioners, while rare, have increased in recent years. Rights groups often charge that such petitions are not adjudicated in a timely fashion and are sometimes dismissed without sufficient cause. The Supreme Court has repeatedly ordered changes to the route of the West Bank security barrier after hearing NGO and Palestinian petitions. By the end of 2009, the Ministry of Defense had altered or pledged to alter the route in response to three of six such rulings.

Palestinians accused of broadly defined security offenses are tried in Israeli military courts, which grant some due-process protections but limit rights to counsel, bail, and appeal. Administrative detention without charge or trial is widely used. According to an October 2009 report by the human rights groups B'Tselem and HaMoked Center, there are about 7,150 Palestinians in Israeli custody: 5,000 serving sentences, 1,569 awaiting trial, and 335 in administrative detention. Most convictions in Israeli military courts are based on confessions, sometimes obtained through coercion. Israel outlawed the use of torture to extract security information in 2000, but milder forms of coercion are permissible when the prisoner is believed to have vital information about impending terrorist attacks. Human rights groups criticize Israel for continuing to engage in what they consider torture.

Israel frequently releases prisoners in the context of peace negotiations or mutual exchanges. In March 2009, Israel detained 10 senior Hamas leaders in the West Bank after talks over the release of Gilad Shalit collapsed; in September, authorities released 20 Palestinian women in exchange for a video of Shalit. While 7 Hamas lawmakers were released in 2009, including parliament Speaker Aziz Dweik, 15 remain in prison.

According to B'Tselem, Israeli security forces killed more than 4,790 Palestinians in the West Bank and Gaza between the beginning of the second intifada and the war in Gaza, about 47 percent of whom were noncombatants and about 20 percent of whom were minors. About 500 Israelis were killed in the territories during the same period, about 50 percent of whom were noncombatants. Following the war in Gaza, approximately 70 Palestinians had been killed by Israeli security forces as of the end of 2009, about 34 percent of whom were noncombatants. Violence between Palestinians and Israeli settlers is not uncommon. Settler assaults on Palestinians and their property continued to increase in 2009, particularly after Israeli forces dismantled illegal settler outposts in the West Bank. Rights groups accused the authorities of failing to adequately prosecute settlers for such offenses.

The easing of checkpoints and roadblocks in the West Bank and the wider deployment of PA security forces there led to increased economic activity in 2009, particularly in Nablus, Ramallah, and Jenin. However, despite the removal of 6 central checkpoints during the year, Israel maintains about 35 external and 50 internal checkpoints in the West Bank, as well as over 450 roadblocks. These measures impose extensive delays on local travel, stunt trade within the territory and with the outside world, and restrict Palestinian access to jobs, hospitals, and schools. Israel's security barrier has also cut off many Palestinians from their farms and other parts of the West Bank. All West Bank and Gaza residents must have identification cards to obtain entry permits to Israel, including East Jerusalem. Israel often denies permits without explanation. While most West Bank roads are open to both Israelis and Palestinians, about 10 roads are restricted to drivers with Israeli documents, ostensibly for security reasons. In October 2009, the Israeli Supreme Court ordered the military to open one of these roads to Palestinian traffic. In 2008, B'Tselem and HaMoked accused the government of stepping up enforcement of residency-permit requirements to deport hundreds of Gazans from the West Bank.

The extensive damage in Gaza following Israel's war with Hamas was a major impediment to freedom of movement in the territory in 2009. In August, the UN Development Programme reported that unexploded ordnance was still a serious hazard in Gaza and had been responsible for at least 17 deaths and 15 injuries, many of them suffered by minors. According to the United Nations, Israel's campaign destroyed some 1,700 hectares of agricultural land in Gaza, some of which could not be planted in time for the fall harvest.

Israel has not honored past agreements calling for a freeze in West Bank settlement construction. In 2008, the Israeli antisettlement group Peace Now claimed that Israel had built 60 percent more structures in existing West Bank settlements than in 2007; the report also documented the construction of 261 unofficial settler outposts. Peace Now accused the government of approving fewer than 6 percent of Palestinian building requests and demolishing 33 percent of illegal Palestinian-built structures in 2008, compared with 7 percent of illegal Jewish-built structures. In January 2009, the Israeli daily *Ha'aretz* reported on a censored database of West Bank settlements, suggesting that nearly 75 percent of construction since 1967 had occurred without the correct permits, and that over 30 settlements had constructed at least one building on private Palestinian land. In 2009, Israel approved construction of about 900 new homes in existing settlements near Jerusalem.

While Palestinian women are underrepresented in most professions and encounter discrimination in employment, they have full access to universities and to many professions. Palestinian laws and societal norms, derived in part from Sharia (Islamic law), put women at a disadvantage in matters of marriage, divorce, and inheritance. Rape, domestic abuse, and "honor killings," in which women are murdered by relatives for perceived sexual or moral transgressions, are not uncommon; these murders often go unpunished.

Nagomo-Karabakh

Political Rights: 5
Civil Liberties: 5
Status: Partly Free

Population: 145,000

Ten-Year Ratings Timeline For Year Under Review (Political Rights, Civil Liberties, Status)

2000	2001	2002	2003	2004	2005	2006	2007	2008	2009
5,6NF	5,6NF	5,5PF	5,5PF	5,5PF	5,5PF	5,5PF	5,5PF	5,5PF	5,5PF

Overview:
In October 2009, Turkey and Armenia signed a historic agreement to establish diplomatic relations and reopen their mutual border, raising concerns in Azerbaijan and potentially affecting negotiations between Baku and Yerevan over a settlement of Nagorno-Karabakh's status. The presidents of Armenia and Azerbaijan met several times in 2009, and

although the talks were hailed as a breakthrough by international negotiators, no concrete progress was reported by year's end.

Nagorno-Karabakh, populated largely by ethnic Armenians, was established as an autonomous region inside Soviet Azerbaijan in 1923. In February 1988, the regional legislature adopted a resolution calling for union with Armenia. The announcement led to warfare over the next several years between Armenian, Azerbaijani, and local Nagorno-Karabakh forces.

In 1992, Nagorno-Karabakh's new legislature adopted a declaration of independence, which was not recognized by the international community. By the time a Russian-brokered ceasefire was signed in May 1994, Karabakh Armenians, assisted by Armenia, had captured essentially the entire territory, as well as seven adjacent Azerbaijani districts. Virtually all ethnic Azeris had fled or been forced out of the enclave and its surrounding areas, and the fighting had resulted in thousands of deaths and created an estimated one million refugees and internally displaced persons (IDPs).

In December 1994, the head of Nagorno-Karabakh's state defense committee, Robert Kocharian, was selected by the territory's National Assembly for the newly established post of president. Parliamentary elections were held in 1995, and Kocharian defeated two other candidates in a popular vote for president the following year.

In September 1997, Foreign Minister Arkady Ghukassian was elected to replace Kocharian, who had been named prime minister of Armenia in March of that year. Kocharian was elected Armenia's president in 1998. In the territory's June 2000 parliamentary vote, the ruling Democratic Artsakh Union (ZhAM), which supported Ghukassian, won a slim victory, taking 13 seats.

Ghukassian won a second term as president in August 2002, with 89 percent of the vote. While a number of domestic and international nongovernmental organizations (NGOs) concluded that the elections marked a further step in Nagorno-Karabakh's democratization, they did note some flaws. An upsurge in shooting along the ceasefire line during the summer of 2003 fueled concerns of a more widespread escalation of violence.

Nagorno-Karabakh held parliamentary elections in June 2005, with the opposition accusing the authorities of misusing state resources to influence the outcome. According to official results, Ghukassian's renamed Democratic Party of Artsakh (AZhK) received 12 of the 33 seats, while opposition parties won only 3.

In a December 2006, a reported 98 percent of voters supported a referendum calling for Nagorno-Karabakh's independence. The referendum was not recognized by the international community.

Nagorno-Karabakh security chief Bako Saakian reportedly took more than 85 percent of the vote in a July 2007 presidential election. His main opponent, Deputy Foreign Minister Masis Mailian, received 12 percent. The government subsequently absorbed or co-opted most political opposition. In September 2007, Saakian appointed as prime minister Arayik Harutyunian, one of Nagorno-Karabakh's wealthiest businessmen.

The OSCE's Minsk Group—established in the 1990s to facilitate negotiations on Nagorno-Karabakh's status—has organized a number of meetings between Armenian and Azerbaijani leaders in recent years, but hope for progress was shaken in 2008 by a series of external political developments. Kosovo's declaration of independence from Serbia, and Russia's subsequent recognition of the independence of the breakaway Georgian regions of Abkhazia and South Ossetia, raised delicate questions about Nagorno-Karabakh's status. Moreover, postelection violence in Armenia was followed by skirmishes along the ceasefire line that killed 16 soldiers on both sides, marking one of the worst violations of the ceasefire in years. On March 14, 2008, the UN General Assembly passed a resolution identifying Nagorno-Karabakh as part of Azerbaijan and calling on Armenia to withdraw its troops. The measure was supported by 39 member states and rejected by 7, including Russia, France, and the United States, the three co-chairs of the Minsk Group.

The presidents of Armenia and Azerbaijan met again on several occasions in 2009, and while the talks were hailed as a breakthrough by members of the Minsk Group, no immediate progress was reported by year's end. In September, Matthew Bryza, a U.S. deputy assistant secretary of state who had co-chaired the Minsk Group since 2006 and was frequently accused of taking a pro-Azerbaijan stance, was replaced as the U.S. representative by ambassador Robert Bradtke.

Separately, following a year of delicate negotiations, the governments of Turkey and Armenia in October signed a historic agreement to establish diplomatic relations and reopen their shared border, which Turkey had sealed in 1993 to show solidarity with Azerbaijan. To Baku's consternation, Turkey did not make resolution of Karabakh's status a precondition for the agreement, but international negotiators were closely watching for any effects the renewed Turkish-Armenian relations could have on talks between Baku and Yerevan.

Political Rights and Civil Liberties: Nagorno-Karabakh has enjoyed de facto independence from Azerbaijan since 1994 and retains close political, economic, and military ties with Armenia. While most previous elections were regarded as relatively free and fair, parliamentary and presidential votes held in 2005 and 2007 were criticized by the opposition for alleged fraud and other irregularities. All of these elections were considered invalid by the international community, which does not recognize Nagorno-Karabakh's independence.

The president, who is directly elected for up to two five-year terms, appoints the prime minister. Of the unicameral National Assembly's 33 members, 22 are elected from single-mandate districts and 11 by party list, all for five-year terms. The main political parties in Nagorno-Karabakh are the AZhK, Free Motherland, Movement 88, and the Armenian Revolutionary Federation–Dashnaktsutiun. The latter two ran as an opposition alliance in the 2005 elections, but most of the opposition groups have since been brought into the government. The authorities have actively discouraged political dissent in recent years, warning that disunity could be dangerous in light of the territory's unresolved status. This rhetorical pressure has led to the gradual silencing of opposition voices.

Nagorno-Karabakh continues to suffer from significant corruption, particularly in the construction industry, as well as favoritism in filling civil service positions. The territory was not listed separately in Transparency International's 2009 Corruption Perceptions Index.

The region officially remains under martial law, which imposes restrictions on civil liberties, including media censorship and the banning of public demonstrations. However, the authorities maintain that these provisions have not been enforced since 1995, a year after the ceasefire was signed.

The government controls many of the territory's media outlets, and most journalists practice self-censorship, particularly on subjects related to Azerbaijan and the peace process. The underfunded public television station Karabakh Television, which has a monopoly on electronic media, broadcasts only three hours a day. Internet access is limited. The popular independent newspaper *Demo* and Karabakh-Open.com, the territory's only independent news website, were both closed by their publishers in 2008.

Most residents of Nagorno-Karabakh belong to the Armenian Apostolic Church, and the religious freedom of other groups is limited. A new law that took effect in January 2009 reportedly made it more difficult for minority religious groups to register, and apparently banned religious activity by unregistered groups. The law also banned proselytism by minority faiths. Although at least three minority groups were registered during the year, a Protestant group and the Jehovah's Witnesses were reportedly denied registration. Jehovah's Witnesses have been jailed for refusing to serve in the Karabakh army.

Freedoms of assembly and association are limited, but trade unions are allowed to organize. The handful of NGOs that are active in the territory, virtually all of them progovernment, suffer from lack of funding and competition from government-organized NGOs, or GONGOs.

The judiciary, which is not independent in practice, is influenced by the executive branch as well as powerful political, economic, and criminal groups.

The majority of Azeris who fled the territory during the separatist conflict continue to live in poor conditions in IDP camps in Azerbaijan. Land mine explosions cause deaths and injuries each year. According to the International Committee of the Red Cross, at least 50,000 antipersonnel mines were laid during the war, but in many cases, records of minefield locations were never created or were lost.

The continued control of major economic activity by powerful elites limits opportunities for most residents, though the government has instituted a number of economic rehabilitation projects in the past year.

Northern Cyprus

Political Rights: 2
Civil Liberties: 2
Status: Free

Population: 295,000

Note: See also the country report for Cyprus.

Ten-Year Ratings Timeline For Year Under Review (Political Rights, Civil Liberties, Status)

2000	2001	2002	2003	2004	2005	2006	2007	2008	2009
2,2F	2,2F	2,2F	2,2F	2,2F	2,2F	2,2F	2,2F	2,2F	2,2F

Overview: Parliamentary elections in April 2009 brought the opposition antiunification National Unity Party to power. Meanwhile, talks between the leaders of the north and south again failed to produce results.

Cyprus gained independence from Britain in 1960 after a 10-year guerrilla campaign by partisans demanding union with Greece. In July 1974, Greek Cypriot National Guard members, backed by the military junta that ruled Greece, staged an unsuccessful coup aimed at union. Five days later, Turkey invaded northern Cyprus, seized control of 37 percent of the island, and expelled 200,000 Greek Cypriots from the north. Today, the Greek and Turkish communities are almost completely separated in the south and north, respectively.

A buffer zone called the Green Line has divided Cyprus, including the capital city of Nicosia, since 1974. UN resolutions stipulate that Cyprus is a single country of which the northern third is illegally occupied. In 1983, Turkish-controlled Cyprus declared its independence as the Turkish Republic of Northern Cyprus (TRNC), an entity recognized only by Turkey.

Reunification talks accelerated after a more receptive Turkish government was elected in 2002, as well as added pressure for an agreement from the European Union (EU), the United States, and the United Nations. A pro-unification TRNC government led by Prime Minister Mehmet Ali Talat was elected in 2003.

In April 2004, a reunification plan proposed by then UN secretary general Kofi Annan was put to a vote in simultaneous, separate referendums on both sides of the island. Amid accusations that the proposed plan favored the Turkish side, 76 percent of Greek Cypriots voted against the plan, while 65 percent of Turkish Cypriots, led by the Talat government, voted in favor. With the island still divided, only Greek Cyprus joined the EU as planned in May 2004. The EU had used the prospect of membership as a bargaining tool to push for reunification, and since EU membership was granted, a new plan became more difficult to achieve.

Talat's Republican Turkish Party (CTP) won the 2005 legislative elections, governing in coalition with the Democratic Party (DP) of Serdar Denktash, son of former president Rauf Denktash. When three deputies resigned to form the new, progovernment Free Party in September, the coalition collapsed, and Serdar Denktash quit the government. The DP and the National Unity Party (UBP) blamed the collapse in part on Turkey, which had cooled to the elder Denktash's anti-EU and antiunification positions and allegedly extended its disfavor to the son, despite his more positive stance on those issues. Prime Minister Ferdi Sabit Soyer kept his post when his CTP formed a new coalition government with the Free Party. Meanwhile, Talat defeated UBP leader Dervish Eroglu, 56 percent to 23 percent, in presidential elections held the same year.

The UBP, which favors stronger ties to Turkey and draws many of its supporters from among the Turkish immigrant population, won legislative elections held in April 2009, capturing 26 of 50 seats. Polls indicated that voters turned against the CTP, which secured just 15 seats, for failing to achieve reunification and because of the economic downturn. The DP won five seats, and the Free Party and the Communal Democracy Party each captured two. UBP leader and former prime minister Eroglu was again selected as prime minister. The UBP victory was considered potentially damaging to reunification talks, which are led by the president but require the prime minister's support.

No major progress was made in talks between Talat and Greek Cypriot president Tassos Papadopoulos during 2009. In September, Eroglu claimed that more than 50 percent of Turkish Cypriots supported maintaining two separate states.

Turkey's investigations into the alleged secretive ultranationalist group, Ergenekon, spread to Cyprus in 2009, amid allegations that the group had used money and threats to increase electoral support for Eroglu in the late 1990s. A separate inquiry requested in April into whether Eroglu or Rauf Denktash had ties to the group was still pending at year's end.

Economic opportunities in the north are more limited than in the south. The economy depends heavily on the government of Turkey, and the public sector provides most jobs. State salaries have been frozen for three years due to austerity measures imposed by Turkey, while the cost of living has increased. Unemployment stands at 13 percent and 24 percent for 18- to 24-year-olds. However, Talat and Christofias jointly supported a business initiative in 2009 to build stronger economic links between the two communities. Also in 2009, southern Cyprus approved a EUR 259 million (US$345 million) aid package for the Turkish Cypriot community after years of delay.

Political Rights and Civil Liberties: Elections in the TRNC are free and fair. The president and 50-seat Assembly are elected to five-year terms. The powers of the president are largely ceremonial; the prime minister is head of government. The main parties are the ruling UBP, which has opposed unification, and the pro-unification CTP.

The roughly 1,000 Greek and Maronite Christian residents of the north are disenfranchised in the TRNC, but many vote in elections in the southern Republic of Cyprus. Minorities are not represented, and women are underrepresented, in the Assembly.

The government has made efforts to combat corruption in recent years, but graft and lack of transparency remain problems. After the 2009 elections, Serdar Denktash announced that all TRNC political parties had bought votes and admitted to distributing EUR 10,000 (US$13,300) himself. The TRNC is not listed separately on Transparency International's Corruption Perceptions Index.

Freedom of the press is generally respected, though some problems persist. The criminal code allows authorities to jail journalists for what they write, and the government has been hostile to the independent press. The government does not restrict access to the internet.

A 1975 agreement with Greek Cypriot authorities provides for freedom of worship, which is generally respected. The government does not restrict academic freedom. In 2004, Turkish Cypriot schools began teaching a less partisan account of Cypriot history, in accordance with Council of Europe recommendations.

The rights of freedom of assembly and association are respected. Civic groups and nongovernmental organizations generally operate without restrictions. Workers may form independent unions, bargain collectively, and strike, although union members have been subject to harassment. Protesters were arrested and some injured during November demonstrations against economic austerity measures.

The judiciary is independent, and trials generally meet international standards of fairness. Turkish Cypriot police, under the control of the Turkish military, sometimes fail to respect due-process rights, and there have been allegations of abuse of detainees. The police have also been accused of corruption related to narcotics trafficking.

Census results released in 2007 showed that about half of the north's population consisted of indigenous Turkish Cypriots. The rest include people of mainland

Turkish origin and many foreign workers, as well as Greek Cypriots and Maronites. The latter three groups face difficulties at Green Line checkpoints and discrimination, and they are allegedly subject to official surveillance. Male homosexuality is punishable with jail time, and while this is rarely enforced, homosexuals do face discrimination.

There are no direct flights between northern Cyprus and the rest of the world due to Greek Cypriot resistance and international regulations, which restrict the operation of the north's ports and airports. However, north-south trade on the island has continued to increase since restrictions were loosened after the 2004 referendum on reunification. In addition, all EU citizens, including Greek Cypriots, can now travel to the north by presenting identity cards, and passports or visas are no longer required. Most governments do not recognize Turkish Cypriots' travel documents, so thousands have obtained Republic of Cyprus passports since the option became available in 2004. However, in 2008, Turkey began forbidding Turkish Cypriots from leaving the country through Turkey without passports from the north.

In 2005, the European Court of Human Rights (ECHR) ruled that the TRNC must take more effective steps to address the restitution of Greek Cypriots who had owned property in the north before the island's division. In 2006, the northern authorities announced the formation of a property commission to adjudicate complaints. The commission, which the south does not recognize, had resolved 81 cases out of 432 applications by November 2009, although critics claim that compensation amounts are far below the value of the property. In January 2009, the property commission's effectiveness came into question after the ECHR ruled that all domestic remedies had been exhausted in the case of eight Greek Cypriots who had owned land in the north and had not appealed to the commission. However, the ECHR endorsed a separate commission decision in July, in which Turkey agreed to return part of a Greek Cypriot's former property along with some financial compensation. Also in July, the property commission announced settlements in two other cases that would return large pieces of land to Greek Cypriots and provide cash compensation, representing the largest compensation settlements decided by the commission to date.

Legal provisions for equal pay for women are not always enforced, especially in blue-collar jobs. A 2007 survey found that three-quarters of women were victims of violence at least once in their lives, with most attacks occurring at home. Police have proven unwilling to intervene, and many women choose not to report the crimes. The TRNC is a destination for trafficking in women, and little effort has been made to address this problem.

♥ Pakistani Kashmir

Political Rights: 6
Civil Liberties: 5
Status: Not Free

Population: 5,113,000

Trend Arrow: Pakistani Kashmir received an upward trend arrow due to largely peaceful elections for the reformed Gilgit-Baltistan Legislative Assembly in November.

Ten-Year Ratings Timeline For Year Under Review (Political Rights, Civil Liberties, Status)

2000	2001	2002	2003	2004	2005	2006	2007	2008	2009
--	--	7,5NF	7,5NF	7,5NF	7,5NF	7,5NF	7,5NF	6,5NF	6,5NF

Overview:
Conditions in Pakistani-administered Kashmir improved in 2009 due to reforms affecting the Northern Areas, which were renamed Gilgit-Baltistan, and elections for that region's new legislative assembly in November. Nevertheless, nationalist groups' demands for representation in Pakistan's parliament remained unfulfilled. Substantive progress on the dispute over Kashmir between India and Pakistan largely stalled in 2009, following November 2008 terrorist attacks in Mumbai, India, by a Pakistan-based militant group, although bilateral talks between the two countries did resume in June.

When British India was partitioned into India and Pakistan in 1947, the Hindu maharajah of Jammu and Kashmir tried to maintain his principality's independence, but he eventually ceded it to India in return for autonomy and future self-determination. Within months, India and Pakistan went to war over the territory. As part of a UN-brokered ceasefire in 1949 that established the present-day boundaries, Pakistan gained control of roughly one-third of Jammu and Kashmir, but unlike India, it never formally annexed its portion. The Karachi Agreement of April 1949 divided Pakistani-administered Kashmir into two distinct entities—Azad (Free) Kashmir and the Northern Areas. Pakistan retained direct administrative control over the Northern Areas, while Azad Kashmir was given a degree of nominal self-government.

A legislative assembly for Azad Kashmir was set up in 1970, and the 1974 interim constitution established a parliamentary system headed by a president and a prime minister. However, the political process was disrupted for long periods by military rule in Pakistan as a whole. Even when elections were held, Islamabad's influence over the voting and governance in general remained strong, and few observers considered the region's elections to be free and fair. In the 1996 polls, the Azad Kashmir People's Party (AKPP) won a majority in the legislative assembly after the rival Muslim Conference (MC) party mounted a boycott due to fraud allegations. The MC won the 2001 elections, but within weeks, Pakistani leader General Pervez Musharraf installed his own choice of president. In 2006, the MC again won a majority of the 41 directly elected seats, and MC candidate Raja Zulqarnain Khan emerged as president. MC leader Sardar Attique Ahmed Khan became prime minister after receiving Musharraf's nomination.

Meanwhile, the lack of political representation in the Northern Areas fueled demands for both formal inclusion within Pakistan and self-determination. In 1999, the Pakistani Supreme Court directed the administration to act within six months to give the Northern Areas an elected government with an independent judiciary, and to extend fundamental rights to the region's residents. The Pakistani government then announced a package that provided for an appellate court as well as an expanded and renamed Northern Areas Legislative Council (NALC). Elections to the NALC were held in October 2004, but the body had few real fiscal or legislative powers. The court of appeals was established in 2005.

Nationalist and proindependence groups in the Northern Areas continued to agitate for increased political representation, and in 2008, the Pakistani government began implementing structural reforms that yielded modest improvements while leaving most authority in federal hands. Islamabad approved the Gilgit-Baltistan Empowerment and Self Governance Order (GBESGO) in August 2009, officially renaming the Northern Areas as Gilgit-Baltistan and introducing a number of administrative, political, and judicial changes. The new order, which replaced the Northern Areas Legal Framework Order (LFO) of 1994, provided for a more powerful legislative body, the Gilgit-Baltistan Legislative Assembly (GBLA), with the authority to choose a chief minister and pass legislation on 61 subjects. While the government argued that the GBESGO established full internal autonomy, nationalist groups noted that a governor appointed by the Pakistani president would still be the ultimate authority and could not be overruled by the new assembly.

In November elections for the GBLA, the Pakistan People's Party (PPP), which governed at the federal level, won 12 of 24 directly elected seats; 10 of the remainder were divided among four other parties and four independents, and voting for two seats was postponed. Syed Mehdi Shah, head of the Gilgit-Baltistan chapter of the PPP, was nominated by his party to become the region's chief minister.

Despite periodic talks and high-level meetings between India and Pakistan, little progress has been made toward a comprehensive resolution of the Kashmir dispute. The process stalled after Pakistani militants were deemed responsible for a November 2008 terrorist attack on the Indian city of Mumbai, and India called on Pakistan to arrest the attack's organizers. A number of suspects were arrested in February 2009, and in November, the Pakistani government charged seven, including alleged mastermind Zaki-ur-Rehman Lakhvi, a leader of the militant group Lashkar-e-Taiba (LeT). The main objectives of the group, founded in the early 1990s, was to end Indian rule in Kashmir and reestablish Muslim rule throughout the Indian subcontinent.

Political Rights and Civil Liberties: The political rights of the residents of Pakistani-administered Kashmir remain severely limited, despite a number of improvements tied to the end of military rule and the election of a civilian government at the federal level in 2008, and elections for the new GBLA in November 2009. Neither Gilgit-Baltistan nor Azad Kashmir has representation in Pakistan's parliament.

Gilgit-Baltistan, previously known as the Northern Areas, continues to be directly administered by the Pakistani government, meaning its status still falls short of compliance with a 1999 Supreme Court ruling on the issue. The region is not included in the Pakistani constitution and has no constitution of its own, meaning there is no fundamental guarantee of civil rights, democratic representation, or separation of powers.

Under the August 2009 GBESGO, the political structure now includes the 33-member GBLA and a chief minister, as well as a 12-member Gilgit Baltistan Council (GBC) headed by the Pakistani prime minister and vice-chaired by a federally appointed governor. The GBC consists of 6 members of the GBLA and 6 Pakistani parlimentarians appointed by the governor, while the GBLA is composed of 24 directly elected members, 6 seats reserved for women, and 3 seats reserved for technocrats; the reserved seats are filled through a vote by the elected members. Ultimate authority rests in the hands of the governor, who has significant powers over judicial appointments and whose decisions cannot be overruled by the GBLA. In addition, many financial powers remain with the GBC rather than the elected assembly.

A local nationalist coalition, the Gilgit-Baltistan Democratic Alliance (GBDA), fielded 10 candidates in the November GBLA elections, while the Balawaristan National Front (BNF) ran 2, but none of these proindependence candidates won seats. GBDA leaders accused federal authorities of preventing nationalist parties from holding rallies and public gatherings, and of favoring Pakistani parties with funding and other forms of support. The leadership of the GBDA and three of its candidates were arrested prior to a nationalist rally shortly before the elections, and several proindependence leaders boycotted the vote. Although 2 people were killed and some 40 injured in violence between supporters of rival candidates, the elections were largely peaceful, and female voters were able to participate in most areas. Observer missions from the independent Human Rights Commission of Pakistan and the Free and Fair Election Network characterized the elections as competitive, despite procedural flaws including an inaccurate voter list, allegations of rigging and interference, and misuse of state resources to benefit the ruling PPP.

Azad Kashmir has an interim constitution, an elected unicameral assembly, a prime minister, and a president who is elected by the assembly. Both the president and the legislature serve five-year terms. Of the 49 assembly seats, 41 are filled through direct elections and 8 are reserved seats (5 for women and 1 each for representatives of overseas Kashmiris, technocrats, and religious leaders). However, Pakistan exercises considerable control over the structures of government and electoral politics. Islamabad's approval is required to pass legislation, and the federal minister for Kashmir affairs handles daily administration and controls the budget. The Kashmir Council—composed of federal officials and Kashmiri assembly members, and chaired by the prime minister of Pakistan—also holds some executive, legislative, and judicial powers. The Pakistani military retains a guiding role on issues of politics and governance.

Those who do not support Azad Kashmir's accession to Pakistan are barred from the political process, government employment, and educational institutions. They are also subject to surveillance, harassment, and sometimes imprisonment by Pakistani security services. The 2006 legislative elections in Azad Kashmir were marred by rigging allegations, but unlike the 2001 voting, they featured few instances of physical violence and harassment, possibly because of the greater international presence in the wake of a devastating 2005 earthquake in the region.

Azad Kashmir receives a large amount of financial aid from the Pakistani government, especially following the earthquake, but successive administrations have been tainted by corruption and incompetence. Aid agencies have also been accused of misusing funds meant for rebuilding schools and hospitals. A lack of official accountability has been identified as a key factor in the poor socioeconomic condition of both Azad Kashmir and Gilgit-Baltistan. However, the region has recently benefited from improvements in accountability at the federal level and the transfer of some budgetary powers to the GBLA in 2009. Pakistani-controlled Kashmir was not rated separately in Transparency International's 2009 Corruption Perceptions Index.

The Pakistani government uses the constitution and other laws to curb freedom of speech on a variety of subjects, including the status of Kashmir and sectarian violence. Media owners cannot publish in Azad Kashmir without permission from the Kashmir Council and the Ministry of Kashmir Affairs, and publications with a proindependence slant are unlikely to receive such permission, according to the U.S. State Department. Several dailies and weeklies operate in Gilgit-Baltistan, mostly under the auspices of the K-2 publishing house, and provide some scrutiny of official affairs. In recent years, authorities have banned several local newspapers and detained or otherwise harassed Kashmiri journalists. After three local journalists were charged with contempt of court against the chief justice of the Azad Kashmir Supreme Court in July 2009, police prevented the media from covering the case by barring all observers from the court premises. In addition to official pressure, local journalists have sometimes faced harassment and attacks from nonstate actors. Internet access is not usually restricted but remains confined to urban centers. Deliberately limited telephone and mobile-telephone access has been expanded since the 2005 earthquake. The presence of foreign media and aid organizations has also helped to open partially the tightly controlled information environment.

Pakistan is an Islamic republic, and there are numerous restrictions on religious freedom. Religious minorities also face unofficial economic and societal discrimination, and are occasionally subject to violent attack. Sectarian strife continues between Shiite Muslims, who form a majority in Gilgit-Baltistan, and the increasing number of Sunni Muslims, who are tacitly encouraged by the federal authorities to migrate to the Kashmir region from elsewhere in Pakistan. In 2009, groups such as the New Delhi–based Institute for Defence Studies and Analyses noted an upsurge in sectarian violence, with the number of killings exceeding the combined total from the previous two years. In April, Shiite leader Asad Zaidi, deputy speaker of the NALC, was assassinated. In September, a bomb blast in Gilgit precipitated sectarian violence in which about 12 people died.

Freedoms of association and assembly are limited. The constitution of Azad Kashmir forbids individuals and political parties from taking part in activities that are prejudicial to the region's accession to Pakistan. Police in recent years have regularly suppressed antigovernment demonstrations, sometimes violently, but there were no reports of deaths or lengthy detentions in 2009. During a February political standoff between the ruling PPP and its main rival in Pakistan, hundreds of people demonstrated in Muzzafarabad, the capital of Azad Kashmir.

Nongovernmental organizations (NGOs) are generally able to operate freely. Programs run by the Aga Khan Foundation, an international development organization that focuses on members of the Ismaili sect of Shia Islam, have faced harassment and violence by Sunni extremist groups, but no such attacks were reported in 2009. The situation for labor rights in Pakistani-controlled Kashmir is similar to that in Pakistan.

Pakistani laws apply in Gilgit-Baltistan at the executive's approval, according to the U.S. State Department's human rights report. The judiciary is not empowered to hear cases concerning fundamental rights or cases against the executive. All judicial appointments in Gilgit-Baltistan are based on three-year contracts subject to discretionary renewal by the bureaucracy, leaving the judiciary largely subservient to the executive. Meanwhile, cases concerning Gilgit-Baltistan are considered outside the jurisdiction of the Supreme Court of Pakistan. Judicial reforms in the GBESGO provide for the appointment of the chief judge and of other judges by the chairman of the new Gilgit Baltistan Council, "on the advice of the governor." Other judges would also be appointed by the chairman.

Azad Kashmir has its own system of local magistrates and high courts, whose heads are appointed by the president of Azad Kashmir. Appeals are adjudicated by the Supreme Court of Pakistan. There are also Islamic judges who handle criminal cases concerning Islamic law. In April 2007, local lawyers protested the appointment of Justice Mohammad Reaz Akhtar Chaudhry as chief justice to the Azad Kashmir Supreme Court over the court's most senior judge, arguing that it violated constitutional conventions and rules of seniority. The newspaper *Dawn* later reported that the court rejected the lawyers' petition on the issue.

Pakistan's Inter-Services Intelligence Directorate reportedly operates throughout Azad Kashmir and Gilgit-Baltistan and engages in extensive surveillance—particularly of proindependence groups and the press—as well as arbitrary arrests and detentions. In some instances, those detained by the security forces are tortured, and several cases of death in custody have been reported. Impunity for mistreatment of civilians by the military and intelligence services remains the norm. The territory also continues to be governed by the colonial-era Frontier Crimes Regulations, under which residents are required to report to local police stations once a month.

A number of Islamist militant groups, including those that receive patronage from the Pakistani military, operate from bases in Pakistani-administered Kashmir. Militant groups that have traditionally focused on attacks in Indian-administered Kashmir are reportedly expanding their influence and activities in Pakistani Kashmir, including the establishment of new *madrassas* (religious schools) in the area. They have also increased cooperation with other militants based in Pakistan's tribal areas, such as the Tehrik-i-Taliban Pakistan (TTP). In Pakistani Kashmir's first suicide attack, a bomber from the tribal areas targeted an army barracks in June 2009, killing two soldiers and injuring three; the TTP claimed responsibility. In August, the Pakistani government banned 25 militant groups operating within the country, including those focused on Kashmir. Although the government claimed to have raided and sealed off the Muzaffarabad headquarters of the LeT, also known as the Jamaat-ud-Dawa, other reports indicated that the group continued to operate training camps in the region. Tension between Islamist pro-Pakistan groups and proindependence Kashmiri groups—as well as some local residents—has reportedly increased in recent years.

Several hundred families displaced from the Line of Control (LOC) area by shelling between Indian and Pakistani forces prior to a 2003 ceasefire remain unable to return to their homes and have largely been excluded from earthquake-related assistance schemes. An estimated 90 percent of the housing destroyed by the 2005 quake, which killed at least 88,000 people and left several million homeless, had been rebuilt by mid-2009, but reconstruction of education and health facilities continued to proceed at a much slower pace, according to local authorities. The Azad Kashmir government also manages relief camps for refugees from Indian-administered Kashmir, the bulk of whom arrived after the situation on the Indian side worsened in 1989. Many more of the refugees (roughly 1.5 million) live elsewhere in Azad Kashmir and throughout Pakistan. A bus service across the LOC was launched in 2005, linking the capitals of Indian and Pakistani Kashmir and allowing some Kashmiri civilians to reunite with family members.

The status of women in Pakistani-administered Kashmir is similar to that of women in Pakistan. While honor killings and rape reportedly occur less frequently than in Pakistan, domestic violence, forced marriage, and other forms of abuse continue to be issues of concern. Women are not granted equal rights under the law, and their educational opportunities and choice of marriage partners remain circumscribed. in some parts of Pakistan, suspected Islamists occasionally mount attacks against NGOs that employ women and on their female employees.

PalestinianAuthority-AdministeredTerritories

Political Rights: 6*
Civil Liberties: 6
Status: Not Free

Population: 3,933,000

Ratings Change: The Palestinian Authority–administered territories' political rights rating declined from 5 to 6 due to the expiration of President Mahmoud Abbas's four-year term in January 2009, the ongoing lack of a functioning elected legislature, and an edict allowing the removal of elected municipal governments in the West Bank.

Note: The areas and total number of persons under Palestinian jurisdiction changed periodically during the year due to the fluid nature of Israel's military presence and activities in the West Bank and Gaza Strip.

Ten-Year Ratings Timeline ForYear Under Review (Political Rights, Civil Liberties, Status)

2000	2001	2002	2003	2004	2005	2006	2007	2008	2009
5,6NF	5,6NF	5,6NF	5,6NF	5,6NF	5,5PF	4,6PF	5,6NF	5,6NF	6,6NF

Overview:
Intense fighting between Israel and Hamas in the Gaza Strip ended with a ceasefire in January 2009, but Gaza residents continued to suffer from infrastructure damage, unexploded ordnance, and ongoing border restrictions. Economic and security conditions improved somewhat in the West Bank, but Palestinians' political rights deteriorated as Palestinian Authority president Mahmoud Abbas continued to govern after the expiration of his mandate in January. Abbas loyalists subsequently removed elected municipal officials from office when their terms expired later in the year.

In the 1967 Six-Day War, Israel occupied the Sinai Peninsula, the West Bank, the Gaza Strip, East Jerusalem, and the Golan Heights. It annexed East Jerusalem that year and the Golan Heights in 1981, though the Sinai was returned to Egypt. In what became known as the *intifada* (uprising), Palestinians living in the West Bank and Gaza began attacking mainly Israeli settlers and military targets in 1987 to protest Israeli rule.

Israel and Yasser Arafat's Palestine Liberation Organization (PLO) reached an agreement in 1993 that provided for Israeli troop withdrawals and gradual Palestinian autonomy in the West Bank and Gaza in exchange for PLO recognition of Israel and an end to Palestinian terrorism. The resulting Palestinian Authority (PA) subsequently obtained full or partial control of up to 40 percent of the West Bank, more than 50 percent of the Gaza Strip, and 98 percent of the Palestinian population, excluding East Jerusalem.

As negotiations on a final settlement and the creation of a Palestinian state headed toward collapse, a second intifada began in September 2000, and violence flared throughout the occupied territories. The Israeli government responded by staging raids into PA territory, targeting Islamist and secular militant groups but also causing the deaths of many civilians.

After Arafat died in November 2004, the PA in January 2005 held its second-ever presidential election, which had been repeatedly postponed; the first voting for president and the Palestinian Legislative Council (PLC) had taken place in 1996. Mahmoud Abbas of Arafat's Fatah faction won the 2005 contest, with 62 percent of the vote. In subsequent municipal voting in Gaza, the Islamist group Hamas won 77 out of 118 seats in 10 districts, to Fatah's 26 seats. In a second round of West Bank and Gaza municipal voting, Fatah won most municipalities, but Hamas posted impressive gains. Each group accused the other of fraud, and there was some election-related violence. Later that year, Israel unilaterally removed all Jewish settlers from the Gaza Strip, giving the PA full control within the territory.

Hamas won the January 2006 elections for the PLC, which Abbas had postponed in 2005. It secured 74 of 132 seats, while Fatah took just 45. Israel, the United States, and the European Union (EU) refused to recognize the resulting Hamas-led government, citing the group's involvement in terrorism and its refusal to recognize Israel or past Israel-PA agreements. The United States and the EU, then the largest donors to the PA, cut off assistance to the government.

Armed clashes between Hamas and Fatah supporters escalated in 2007, and in June, Hamas militants successfully took over Fatah-controlled facilities in Gaza. Thousands of Gazans, particularly those loyal to Fatah, fled along with most Fatah militants to the West Bank. Abbas subsequently dismissed the Hamas-led government, declared a state of emergency, and accused Hamas of staging a coup in Gaza. He appointed an emergency cabinet led by former finance minister Salam Fayad. This resulted in a bifurcated PA, with Hamas governing Gaza and Abbas and Fayad governing the roughly 40 percent of the West Bank not directly administered by Israel. The two sides later engaged in reciprocal crackdowns in their respective territories, arresting hundreds of partisan supporters, shutting down suspect civic organizations and media, and allegedly torturing some detainees.

After the split, the Fatah-controlled PA in the West Bank benefited from renewed U.S. and EU aid as well as tax revenues released by Israeli authorities. Peace negotiations between Israel and Abbas accelerated over the next two years, and while they did not yield progress on a final settlement, related confidence-building measures included the release of hundreds of Palestinian prisoners held in Israel, the wider deployment of Palestinian security forces, and the lifting of a number of checkpoints in the West Bank.

Meanwhile, Israel declared the Hamas-led Gaza Strip a "hostile entity" in response to ongoing rocket attacks, and imposed an economic blockade on the territory, granting passage only to food shipments and a restricted list of other humanitarian supplies. However, arms and goods were regularly smuggled through a developing tunnel network between Egypt and Gaza. The blockade was eased after Hamas and Israel declared a six-month truce in June 2008.

War erupted between Hamas and Israeli forces in December 2008, after the six-month truce expired, and Hamas ramped up its rocket bombardment of Israeli towns near the border with Gaza. The Israel Defense Forces (IDF) launched near-daily air strikes and an almost three-week ground invasion of the coastal territory. Israel declared a unilateral ceasefire in late January 2009, and Hamas soon did the same. During the conflict, Israeli forces destroyed large portions of Gaza's military, government, and civilian infrastructure; according to the British Broadcasting Corporation, more than 4,000 buildings were destroyed, with 20,000 severely damaged. Tens of thousands of Gazans were left homeless by the fighting. While the Palestinian Centre for Human Rights reported that 1,434 Palestinians were killed, including 960 noncombatants, the IDF reported that 1,166 Palestinians were killed, including 295 to 460 noncombatants. Thirteen Israelis were killed, including three noncombatants. In January, the International Committee of the Red Cross reported that electricity and water were "severely limited" for two-thirds of Gaza's population, and vaccinations were in short supply. According to the UN Relief and Works Agency (UNRWA), some 150,000 Gazans continued to lack access to tap water as of April.

During the fighting, Israel had again tightened its blockade of Gaza to allow only humanitarian goods, and reduced the number of crossing openings. Aid agencies called for a full opening of crossing points; according to the UNRWA, the Israeli authorities in January were permitting only a fraction of the necessary number of trucks to enter Gaza each day. Following the ceasefire, crossings were opened on a limited basis to transfer grains, certain types of fuels, and other authorized goods, as well as international aid workers and individuals with specified medical and humanitarian needs. The Rafah border crossing with Egypt opened on an ad hoc basis. In August, Israel allowed cement and heavy building materials into Gaza for the first time in seven months.

Also in 2009, sporadic violence between Hamas and Fatah continued. In May, five people—two PA policemen, two Hamas members, and a bystander—were killed when PA security officials arrested Hamas members based in the northern West Bank town of Qalqilya. The following month, another two Hamas members and one PA policeman were killed in a similar raid, also in Qalqilya.

Egyptian-brokered negotiations to form a new Palestinian unity government floundered throughout the year. In October, Abbas announced that presidential and parliamentary elections would be held in January 2010, whether or not an agreement with Hamas was in place by that time. Hamas rejected the announcement, claiming that Abbas—whose term as president had officially expired in January 2009—was an illegitimate ruler and had no right to call elections. By year's end, the January election date had been canceled, and it remained unclear when the polls would be held.

Political Rights and Civil Liberties: The Palestinian Authority (PA) is a quasi-governmental entity that has no real authority over its borders or defense policy. Moreover, its integrity and legitimacy have been undermined in recent years by the 2007 split between the Hamas-controlled Gaza Strip and the Fatah-controlled West Bank, repeated Israeli military incursions, and the breakdown or replacement of its elected political institutions. Laws governing Palestinians in the West Bank and Gaza Strip derive from Ottoman, British Mandate, Jordanian, Egyptian, and PA law, as well as Israeli military orders.

The PA president is elected to four-year terms, and international observers judged the 2005 presidential election to be generally free and fair. The prime minister is nominated by the president. The unicameral, 132-seat Palestinian Legislative Council (PLC) also serves four-year terms. While the January 2006 PLC elections were deemed largely fair by international observers, there were credible reports of PA resources being used for the benefit of Fatah candidates, as well as campaigning by Hamas candidates in mosques, in violation of electoral rules. Some voters reported having difficulty reaching polling stations because of Israeli roadblocks, though Israel was generally credited with allowing relatively free access during the elections.

After the fracturing of the PA in 2007, elected officials on both sides of the split were prevented from holding office and performing their duties. Hamas forcibly expelled Fatah officials from the Gaza Strip, while President Mahmoud Abbas appointed a new cabinet in the West Bank, creating an unelected authority in that territory. In 2008, Hamas forces in Gaza arrested hundreds of Fatah members and supporters and shut down the Fatah office in northern Gaza, while in the West Bank, forces aligned with Abbas arrested hundreds of Hamas members and supporters. The rift, combined with Israel's detention of many Palestinian lawmakers, has prevented the PLC from functioning in recent years, leaving the PA without an elected legislature.

In January 2009, Abbas's term as president officially expired. However, because presidential and legislative elections were tentatively scheduled for 2010, PA officials in the West Bank contended that he was entitled to serve another year under the PA's Basic Law. Hamas rejected this claim, arguing that if the president's term expires before elections can be held, the Basic Law empowers the head of the PLC—Aziz Dweik of Hamas, who was released from an Israeli prison in 2009—or his deputy to serve as acting president. In December, the indefinite extension of Abbas's term was approved by the Fatah-dominated PLO, and it remained uncertain at year's end whether elections would indeed be held in 2010. In another blow to democratic governance, Abbas issued a law in 2009 permitting the Fatah-affiliated local government minister to dissolve municipal councils after their four-year mandates expired. In October, PA security forces deposed the municipal government of Qalqilya, the largest Hamas-controlled municipality in the West Bank.

Palestinian residents of the West Bank, Gaza, and East Jerusalem do not have the right to vote in Israeli national elections. Arabs in East Jerusalem who hold Israeli identity cards can vote in the city's municipal elections and in PA elections. However, ahead of the 2006 PLC polls, Israeli authorities restricted campaigning in East Jerusalem to parties that registered with the Israeli police, effectively excluding Hamas.

Corruption was rampant during the PA presidency of Yasser Arafat, and after Abbas took over in 2005, he instituted budget controls, ended the old system of cash handouts to political loyalists and security personnel, and launched a widespread corruption probe. While the Hamas-led government that took control following the 2006 PLC elections expressed a willingness to subject itself to budgetary oversight, many foreign governments were reluctant to provide aid out of concern that it would be used for terrorist operations. Prime Minister Salam Fayad, who was appointed by Abbas after the PA schism in 2007, is highly regarded for his commitment to transparent government. Transparency International did not rank Palestine in its 2009 Corruption Perceptions Index.

The media are not free in the West Bank and Gaza. Under a 1995 press law, journalists may be fined and jailed, and newspapers closed, for publishing "secret information" on PA security forces or news that might harm national unity or incite violence. Several small media outlets are routinely pressured to provide favorable coverage of the PA, Fatah, or Hamas. Journalists who criticize the PA or the dominant factions face arbitrary arrests, threats, and physical abuse. Hamas has banned all journalists not accredited by its Information Ministry and closed down Gaza outlets that were not affiliated with it, while both the Fatah-led PA and Israeli forces have shut down Hamas-affiliated radio stations in the West Bank. During the Gaza conflict that ended in January 2009, Israel banned foreign journalists from traveling to Gaza through Israeli checkpoints. It also bombed Hamas-affiliated media stations and destroyed satellite equipment on the roof of a building that housed the local offices of Iran's English- and Arabic-language television networks. In July 2009, the PA banned the Qatar-based satellite television station Al-Jazeera from operating in the West Bank for a week after it aired remarks by an Abbas rival in which he accused Abbas of having collaborated with Israel to kill Arafat.

The PA generally respects freedom of religion, though no law specifically protects religious expression. The Basic Law declares Islam to be the official religion of Palestine and also states that, "respect and sanctity of all other heavenly religions (Judaism and Christianity) shall be maintained." Personal status law, which governs marriage and divorce, is based on religious law: for Muslims, it is derived from Sharia (Islamic law), and for Christians, from ecclesiastical courts. Some Palestinian Christians have experienced intimidation and harassment by radical Islamist groups and PA officials. Since the 2007 fracturing of the PA, Hamas-controlled security forces and militants have increasingly harassed Muslim worshippers at non-Hamas-affiliated mosques in Gaza, while Fatah-controlled authorities have directed similar pressure at Hamas-affiliated religious bodies.

The PA has authority over all levels of education. Some Palestinian schools teach hatred of Israel. Israeli military closures, curfews, and the West Bank security barrier restrict access to Palestinian academic institutions. Israeli authorities have at times shut universities, schools have been damaged during military operations, and schoolchildren have periodically been injured or killed during fighting. In September 2009, the UN Office for the Coordination of Humanitarian Affairs reported that at least 280 of Gaza's 641 schools were damaged and 18 were destroyed during the conflict that ended in January, and that many schools lacked essential materials in the aftermath.

The PA requires permits for rallies and demonstrations and prohibits violence and racist sloganeering. Nevertheless, large rallies, often marked by violent rhetoric, are regular occurrences in Palestinian areas. Hamas has significantly restricted freedoms of assembly and association in Gaza, with security forces dispersing public gatherings of Fatah and other groups and killing a number of people. There is a broad range of Palestinian nongovernmental organizations and civic groups, and Hamas itself operates a large network that provides social services to certain Palestinians. Following the January 2009 ceasefire between Hamas and Israel, Hamas restricted the activities of aid organizations that would not submit to its regulations or coordinate with its relief efforts. Many civic associations have been shut down for political reasons in both the West Bank and Gaza since the 2007 split in the PA.

Workers may establish and join unions without government authorization. Palestinian workers seeking to strike must submit to arbitration by the PA Labor Ministry. There are no laws in the PA-ruled areas to protect the rights of striking workers. Palestinian workers in Jerusalem are subject to Israeli labor law. The Fatah-aligned Palestinian General Federation of Trade Unions (PGFTU) is the largest union body in the territories. In 2007, the PGFTU building in Gaza City was taken over by Hamas militants, and operations generally ceased in the territory. In December 2008, the building was severely damaged in an Israeli air raid.

The judicial system is not independent, and Palestinian judges lack proper training and experience. In 2007, Abbas ordered judges to boycott judicial bodies in Gaza, and Hamas began appointing new prosecutors and judges in 2008. Israeli demands for a crackdown on terrorism have given rise to state security courts, which lack almost all due-process rights. There are reportedly hundreds of administrative detainees currently in Palestinian jails. The same courts are also used to try those suspected of collaborating with Israel or accused of drug trafficking. Defendants are not granted the right to appeal sentences and are often summarily tried and sentenced to death. According to the Palestinian Human Rights Monitoring Group, alleged collaborators are routinely tortured in Palestinian jails. These practices are not prohibited under Palestinian law.

While armed factions continued to exercise de facto rule over significant portions of PA-administered areas, PA security forces asserted increased control in Nablus, Ramallah, Jericho, and Jenin in 2009. Frequent and violent clashes occurred between Hamas and Fatah gunmen. Violence between Palestinians and Israeli settlers in the West Bank is also common.

The intifada and Israeli restrictions have exacted a serious toll on the Palestinian economy in recent years. The easing of checkpoints and roadblocks in the West Bank and the wider deployment of PA security forces there led to increased economic activity in 2009, particularly in Nablus, Ramallah, and Jenin. However, despite the removal of 6 central checkpoints in 2009, Israel maintains about 35 external and 50 internal checkpoints in the West Bank, and has constructed over 450 roadblocks. These measures impose extensive delays on local travel, stunt trade, and restrict Palestinian access to jobs, hospitals, and schools. Israel's security barrier has also cut off many Palestinians from their farms and other parts of the West Bank.

In Gaza, the Israeli blockade in place since 2007 grew even more stringent after a period of eased restrictions during the truce in the second half of 2008. The extensive damage inflicted during the conflict that ended in January 2009 became a major impediment to freedom of movement in the territory. The UN Development Programme reported in August that unexploded ordnance was still a serious hazard and was responsible for at least 17 deaths and 15 injuries, many of them suffered by minors. According to the United Nations, Israel's campaign destroyed some 1,700 hecatres of agricultural land in Gaza, some of which could not be planted in time for the fall harvest. In August, the Rafah crossing on Gaza's border with Egypt was opened for five days, the longest period since June 2007.

While Palestinian women are underrepresented in most professions and encounter discrimination in employment, they have fuller access to higher education. A political quota system was instituted in 2005, guaranteeing women a certain degree of representation on each party's candidate list for PLC elections. Personal status law, derived in part from Sharia, puts women at a disadvantage in matters of marriage, divorce, and inheritance. Rape, domestic abuse, and "honor killings," in which women are murdered by relatives for perceived sexual or moral transgressions, are not uncommon. These murders often go unpunished. Women's treatment in instances of rape or abuse is often determined by tribal leaders or PA-appointed governors, and not by the courts. Legal options for victims of domestic abuse are extremely limited. The UN Development Fund for Women (UNIFEM) and other groups reported an increase in domestic violence and sexual assault in Gaza during and after the war between Hamas and Israel.

Puerto Rico

Political Rights: 1   **Population:** 3,971,000
Civil Liberties: 1
Status: Free

Ten-Year Ratings Timeline For Year Under Review (Political Rights, Civil Liberties, Status)

2000	2001	2002	2003	2004	2005	2006	2007	2008	2009
1,2F	1,2F	1,2F	1,2F	1,2F	1,1F	1,1F	1,1F	1,1F	1,1F

Overview: Former governor Anibal Acevedo-Vila was found not guilty of corruption charges by a U.S. federal court in March 2009. Meanwhile, Puerto Rico's economy continued to worsen amid the global financial crisis.

Having been captured by U.S. forces during the Spanish-American War in 1898, Puerto Rico acquired the status of a commonwealth of the United States following approval by plebiscite in 1952. As a commonwealth, Puerto Rico exercises approximately the same control over its internal affairs as do the 50 states. Although they are U.S. citizens, residents of Puerto Rico cannot vote in presidential elections and are represented in the U.S. Congress by a delegate to the House of Representatives with limited voting rights.

Power has alternated between the pro-commonwealth Popular Democratic Party (PPD) and the pro-statehood New Progressive Party (PNP) for several decades. Anibal Acevedo-Vila of the PPD won the 2004 gubernatorial election by a razor-thin margin over his PNP opponent. Acevedo-Vila was indicted on corruption charges by a U.S. grand jury in March 2008, but he refused to withdraw his candidacy ahead of the 2008 gubernatorial election. The result was a major shift in Puerto Rican politics. PNP candidate Luis Fortuno, who had served as the island's representative in the U.S. Congress, firmly defeated the incumbent, while the PNP secured overwhelming majorities in both the House and Senate elections. Acevedo-Vila was acquitted in March 2009 of nine counts of violating the island's campaign finance laws. Nine of his associates reached plea agreements with the government, and several testified against the former governor.

Fortuno's agenda has been dominated by a fiscal crisis that was exacerbated by the global economic turndown. His proposals to raise taxes and cut 30,000 workers from the state payroll triggered a series of trade union protests at various times in 2009. Although Puerto Rico had for years been showcased as one of the Caribbean's major economic success stories, its performance has moved from stagnation to outright decline over the past several years. Per capita income stands at just over one-half the level of the poorest state in the United States, labor-force participation is low, and poverty rates are high.

For years, Puerto Ricans have been nearly equally divided between those who support the continuation of commonwealth status and those who favor full U.S. statehood. Commonwealth supporters argue that the special status allows the island to maintain its separate culture and an exemption from federal income taxes, while advocates of statehood seek presidential voting rights and full representation in Congress. A third option, independence, has little popular support; the Independence Party (PIP) candidate for governor received just 2 percent of the popular vote in 2008. While many Puerto Ricans have looked to the new American president, Barack Obama, to resolve the island's status, no initiatives emerged from the administration during its first year.

Political Rights and Civil Liberties:

The commonwealth constitution, modeled after that of the United States, provides for a governor elected for four-year terms and a bicameral legislature, currently consisting of a 27-member Senate and a 51-member House of Representatives, elected for four-year terms. As U.S. citizens, Puerto Ricans are guaranteed all civil liberties granted in the United States.

The commonwealth is represented in the U.S. Congress by a single delegate. In January 2007, the U.S. House of Representatives restored limited voting rights to the delegates from Puerto Rico, the District of Columbia, and several other U.S. territories. The change allows Puerto Rico's delegate to vote on floor amendments to legislation but not on final passage of bills.

The major political parties are the pro-commonwealth PPD, the pro-statehood PNP, and the pro-independence PIP.

Corruption is an endemic problem in commonwealth politics. Puerto Rico was ranked 35 out of 180 countries surveyed in Transparency International's 2009 Corruption Perceptions Index.

Puerto Rico's tradition of varied and vigorous news media has been under strain by a decline in newspapers due to the economic crisis and other factors. The *San Juan Star,* the commonwealth's principal English-language print outlet, was forced to close for financial reasons in 2008. While plans for a cooperatively owned English-language replacement were discussed, a new paper had not been established by the end of 2009.

Freedom of religion is guaranteed in this predominantly Roman Catholic territory. A substantial number of evangelical churches have been established on the island in recent years. Academic freedom is guaranteed.

Freedom of assembly is protected by law, and Puerto Ricans frequently mount protest rallies against local or federal government policies. There is a robust civil society, with numerous nongovernmental organizations representing the interests of different constituencies. The government respects trade union rights, and unions are generally free to organize and strike.

The legal system is based on U.S. law, and a Supreme Court heads an independent judiciary. Crime is a serious problem for the island. The murder rate is three times that of the United States, with a large proportion of drug-related homicides. The center of the narcotics trade has shifted from San Juan to smaller communities, leaving housing projects in some towns under virtual siege by drug gangs. The enforcement of drug laws has been accompanied by an increase in police corruption. In 2009, police officers were charged with involvement in a high-profile case in which a fake traffic stop was set up to steal drugs from a dealer.

In recent years, there has been an upsurge in attempts by illegal migrants from various Caribbean countries to reach Puerto Rico, often in flimsy boats. Many are brought to the island by smugglers.

Women enjoy equal rights under the law in education, at the workplace, and in other aspects of society. However, women's rights organizations maintain that women are still subject to widespread discrimination.

Somaliland

Political Rights: 5
Civil Liberties: 5*
Status: Partly Free

Population: 3,500,000

Ratings Change: Somaliland's civil liberties rating declined from 4 to 5 due to further restrictions on press freedom and the suppression of demonstrations following the postponement of the presidential election.

Ten-Year Ratings Timeline For Year Under Review (Political Rights, Civil Liberties, Status)

2000	2001	2002	2003	2004	2005	2006	2007	2008	2009
--	--	--	--	--	--	4,4PF	4,4PF	5,4PF	5,5PF

Overview: Somaliland plunged deep into crisis in 2009, as presidential elections were delayed yet again, and a constitutional deadlock forced the suspension of parliament. The government responded by clamping down on press freedoms and curtailing public demonstrations.

The modern state of Somalia was formed in 1960, when the newly independent protectorates of British Somaliland and Italian Somaliland agreed to unite. In 1969, General Siad Barre took power in Somalia, ushering in a violent era of clan rivalries and political repression. A prolonged struggle to topple Barre lasted until January 1991, when he was finally deposed. Heavily armed militias, divided along traditional clan lines, fought for control in the ensuing power vacuum. The current Somaliland, largely conforming with the borders of the former British Somaliland in the north-western corner of the country, took advantage of Somalia's political chaos and declared independence in May 1991.

In a series of clan conferences, Somaliland's leaders formed a government system combining democratic elements, including a parliament, with traditional political structures, such as an upper house consisting of clan elders. Somaliland's first two presidents were appointed by clan elders. In 2003, Dahir Riyale Kahin became Somaliland's first elected president; although he won by fewer than 100 votes, the runner-up accepted the outcome. Clan elders also appointed members of Somaliland's lower house of parliament until direct elections were held for the first time in 2005. In that poll, the president's United People's Democratic Party (UDUB) won 33 seats, with the Peace, Unity, and Development Party (Kulmiye) and the Justice and Development Party (UCID) following close behind. While the 2003 presidential and 2005 legislative elections did not meet international standards, there were no reports of widespread intimidation or fraud.

In May 2006, President Riyale violated the constitution by postponing elections for the upper house and extending its term by four years; under the constitution, only the lower house was empowered to extend the term. In October 2007, the government and opposition members agreed to postpone local and presidential elections, originally scheduled for December 2007 and April 2008, respectively, until later in 2008.

In April 2008, the upper house voted to extend President Riyale's term for an extra year. Negotiations between the government and opposition yielded a new electoral timetable; the presidential election would be held in March 2009, and the municipal elections were postponed indefinitely. Voter registration failed to produce an electoral roll that was acceptable to all sides. The process was mishandled by the National Electoral Commission (NEC) and plagued by fraud. Half of those who registered did not provide a verifiable fingerprint to prove their identity. Registration was almost derailed by several coordinated suicide bombings in Somaliland's main city, Hargeisa, which killed at least 23 people. Somaliland officials accused the Shabaab, the Somali jihadist group, of carrying out the attacks.

Somaliland's political crisis intensified in 2009. Presidential elections were postponed twice more, in March and September, because of the ongoing dispute over voter registration. President Riyale's plan to hold the election without a list was opposed by the UCID and Kulmiye, which contended that a flawed list was better than none at all and pledged to boycott the polls. Tensions increased in late August, when an opposition motion to impeach the president led to a brawl in parliament. President Riyale responded to the impeachment debate by ordering troops to occupy parliament. Although he soon reversed that decision, street protests erupted; during a parliamentary debate a few days later, another fight broke out, and a gun was reportedly drawn. When opposition supporters staged a demonstration on September 12, the police responded with live ammunition, killing four people.

A transitional agreement was eventually reached between the parties that prohibited the government from extending its term without consultation, called for the replacement of the NEC, and asked the international community for help in introducing a computerized voting system. However, the agreement did not allow enough time to hold elections before Riyale's extended term expired on October 29. A revised date of January 2010 was set.

Somaliland's relations with neighboring Puntland, which claims autonomy but not independence from Somalia, have been strained due to border disputes over the Sool and Sanaag regions. Periodic clashes continued in 2009. Tensions intensified in November, when a senior military official from Somaliland was killed by a roadside bomb in Sool.

Poverty is rife in Somaliland, and the government struggles to provide basic goods and services to much of the population. Because Somaliland is not internationally recognized, it receives little assistance from foreign governments and international lending institutions. International donors suspended funding for the elections during the constitutional deadlock, but restored it following the signing of the transitional agreement by Somaliland's three parties.

Political Rights and Civil Liberties: According to Somaliland's constitution, the president is directly elected for a maximum of two five-year terms and appoints the cabinet. Members of the 82-seat lower house of the bicameral parliament are directly elected for five-year terms, while members of the 82-seat upper house (Guurti) are indirectly elected by local communities for six-year terms. The legislature is weak and provides very little oversight of the executive.

Somaliland's constitution allows for a maximum of three political parties, and parties defined by region or clan are technically prohibited. Nevertheless, party and clan affiliations tend to coincide: the UDUB is identified with a subclan of the Dir clan; the UCID is largely supported by members of other Dir subclans; and the Darood clan tends to support Kulmiye.

Transparency International did not rank Somaliland separately in its 2009 Corruption Perceptions Index. However, corruption is a serious problem, fueled by the low salaries paid to public officials and the common practice whereby politicians offer tax relief in return for support.

While freedoms of expression and the press are guaranteed by Somaliland's constitution, journalists face interference and harassment. The protracted political crisis in 2009 led to increased government sensitivity over media reports. At least 10 journalists were arrested during the year, generally on charges of spreading false information or inciting violence. Two reporters with Horyaal Radio, an independent station, were sentenced to six months in prison in August, although they were released 15 days later. That same month, one of their colleagues was detained for 22 days without charge. Also in August, a freelance journalist, Adan Dahir, was badly beaten. Four men arrested a day later in connection with the attack were released without charge. Reporters with the online news services *Baadiyenews* and *Berberanews* were also detained. Two independent television stations began broadcasting in recent years. However, the stations face harassment from the government, which claims that liberalizing the airwaves would result in incendiary content and lead to clan violence. One of the channels, Horn Cable TV, was shut down in July on the orders of a judge for "threatening the peace." The main radio station is the government-run Radio Hargeisa, although the British Broadcasting Corporation (BBC) is available in the capital. There are seven private daily newspapers in Somaliland in addition to the state-owned *Mandeeq*, although they have limited circulations and are subsidized by journalists' relatives and Somalilanders living abroad.

Nearly all Somaliland residents are Sunni Muslims, and Islam is the state religion. Proselytizing by members of other faiths is prohibited.

Freedom of association is constitutionally guaranteed, and international and local nongovernmental organizations operate in Somaliland without serious government interference. However, the government is increasingly intolerant of opposition, and used the country's fragile political balance and precarious security situation as a justification to ban public demonstrations in March 2009. Opposition supporters were prevented by security forces from staging a march to celebrate Somalia National Movement Day in April, and police used excessive force to disperse a demonstration outside parliament in September, killing four protestors. The ban on public demonstrations remained in place at year's end.

According to the constitution, the judiciary is independent, and the laws cannot violate the principles of Sharia (Islamic law). In practice, the government bypasses the courts and use secret security committees to try many defendants without due process. Suspects are routinely held for long periods without charge. The judiciary is seriously underfunded, and the Supreme Court is ineffective. Somaliland has approximately 100 judges, most of whom do not have formal legal training. Somaliland police and security forces, while well organized, have at times used excessive force.

Societal fault lines are largely clan based; most Somalilanders belong to the Dir or Darood clans, which are made up of multiple subclans. Larger, wealthier clans have more political clout than the less prominent groups, and clan elders often intervene to settle conflicts.

Society in Somaliland is patriarchal. While women are present in the workplace and hold some public positions, men make the political decisions. As in the rest of Somalia, female genital mutilation is practiced on the vast majority of women.

⬇ South Ossetia

Political Rights: 7
Civil Liberties: 6
Status: Not Free

Population: 70,000

Ratings Change: South Ossetia received a downward trend arrow due to Russia's increased control over the economy and political system, and Russian aid that has fueled rampant corruption among local elites.

Ten-Year Ratings Timeline For Year Under Review (Political Rights, Civil Liberties, Status)

2000	2001	2002	2003	2004	2005	2006	2007	2008	2009
--	--	--	--	--	--	--	--	7,6NF	7,6NF

Overview:　　　　　Russia tightened its grip on South Ossetia in 2009, formalizing the presence of Russian border guards in the territory and constructing a new military base in Tskhinvali. Russian president Dmitri Medvedev pledged additional funds for South Ossetia in July, but reconstruction efforts have been painfully slow and mired in corruption. Meanwhile, a series of incidents in the summer increased the threat of new fighting with Georgia, and the more than 18,500 ethnic Georgians who fled South Ossetia during the 2008 war remained unable to return during the year.

South Ossetia first declared its independence from Georgia in 1920, igniting a war that left thousands dead. Both Georgia and South Ossetia were incorporated into the Soviet Union in 1922, with South Ossetia designated an autonomous *oblast* (region) within Georgia. The Ossetians exercised modest control over the territory during the Soviet period, and Georgian-South Ossetian relations were marked by relative peace and stability.

In 1989, a South Ossetian independence movement, responding in part to growing nationalism within Georgia, demanded that the oblast be upgraded to a republic, a move that was rejected by the Georgian government. South Ossetia declared full independence from Georgia in 1990, prompting Tbilisi to abolish its autonomous status. Fierce fighting broke out in January 1991, resulting in a thousand deaths and civilian displacement on both sides; some 40,000 to 100,000 Ossetians fled to North Ossetia, then part of the Russian Soviet Federated Socialist Republic. In March 1991, a reported 99 percent of South Ossetian referendum voters endorsed independence, and 90 percent voted in favor of seeking to join Russia in a January 1992 referendum, after the final dissolution of the Soviet Union. Both plebiscites were rejected by Tbilisi.

In June 1992, the Sochi Agreement—a ceasefire pact signed by Tbilisi, Moscow, and Tskhinvali—established a Russian-led peacekeeping force with Georgian and Ossetian components and created the Joint Control Commission (JCC), a negotiating framework co-chaired by Georgia, Russia, and both North and South Ossetia. The Organization for Security and Cooperation in Europe (OSCE) was put in charge of monitoring the ceasefire and facilitating negotiations.

Torez Kulumbegov led separatist South Ossetia from 1992 to 1993. He was succeeded by Lyudvig Chibirov, who went on to win the newly created post of president in 1996. Though relations with Tbilisi were calm and often cordial for the rest of the 1990s, the 2001 election of hard-liner Eduard Kokoity as president of South Ossetia renewed tensions. His Unity Party took the majority of seats in 2004 parliamentary elections; though four seats were reserved for the territory's ethnic Georgian population, only five Georgian villages were able to vote. All of the separatist regime's elections went unrecognized by Georgia and the international community.

In May 2004, recently elected Georgian president Mikheil Saakashvili ordered a campaign to dismantle the multimillion-dollar smuggling operation controlled by Kokoity's regime. Georgian Interior Ministry troops moved in and forcibly shut down the Ergneti Market, a major trading post and smuggling center. Skirmishes soon escalated, with dozens of people killed in August amid fears of all-out war. Ossetians, many of whom depended on the market for their livelihood, rallied around Kokoity. By August 19, the sides had agreed to a ceasefire, and in September, Saakashvili offered a proposal for expanded autonomy, which was rejected by Tskhinvali.

South Ossetia held a joint referendum and presidential election in November 2006, with 99.8 percent of voters on Ossetian-controlled territory reaffirming the bid for independence, according to Tskhinvali. Kokoity, who faced no genuine opposition, was reelected with a reported 98.1 percent of the vote.

On the same day, Tbilisi organized a parallel election and referendum for South Ossetia's Georgian-controlled areas. Dmitry Sanakoyev, an ethnic Ossetian and South Ossetia's former defense minister, won the presidency with the support of about 96 percent of the 57,000 participating voters, according to the electoral commission established for the poll. A reported 94 percent voted in favor of a proposal calling for South Ossetia to form a federation with Georgia. Neither the separatist nor the Tbilisi-backed election was monitored by international organizations. Sanakoyev's parallel government was established in 2007, but it was never able to draw significant support away from Kokoity.

Following weeks of skirmishes along the border in 2008, Tbilisi launched an attack on Tskhinvali on August 7. Russia immediately retaliated by sending tanks and ground troops into South Ossetia, pushing back Georgian forces. Russia then expanded the zone of conflict by invading Georgia via Abkhazia—another breakaway Georgian territory in the northwest—and by blocking Georgian ports and bombing Georgian towns.

Both sides had signed a French-brokered ceasefire deal by August 16, and Russia eventually withdrew its troops to the confines of South Ossetia and Abkhazia. However, they did not immediately return to prewar positions as called for by the ceasefire, and for several months continued to hold portions of the territories that were previously controlled by Tbilisi. Moscow, defying international criticism, formally recognized South Ossetia and Abkhazia as independent states on August 26 and, subsequently, concluded bilateral security agreements with the separatist governments.

In May 2009, South Ossetia held parliamentary elections that resulted in a legislature dominated by Kokoity loyalists. The victory came amid accusations that Kokoity had shut out and threatened opposition parties.

The OSCE, which had monitored the conflict for 17 years, ended its mission in June, after Russia refused to extend its mandate unless the organization recognized the independence of South Ossetia and Abkhazia. The OSCE was replaced by European Union (EU) monitors, though they could only operate on the Georgian side of the de facto border.

An exhaustive EU report released in September faulted both Tbilisi and Moscow for instigating the war, and accused both sides of violating international law. The report found that Tbilisi had initiated the assault on South Ossetia, which Georgian officials denied.

In the summer of 2009, Georgia accused Russian troops of attempting to take additional Georgian territory, and each side accused the other of kidnapping and cross-border shelling, stirring fears of a new outbreak of war.

By year's end, Russia had significantly tightened its grip on South Ossetia. An agreement signed between Moscow and Tskhinvali in April established a formal and permanent role for the Russian border guards, who had patrolled the de factor border since 2008. Moscow also constructed a new military base in Tskhinvali, and discussed the establishment of an additional base in the town of Akhalgori which had been controlled by Tbilisi until the 2008 war.

Russian president Dmitri Medvedev made a surprise visit to South Ossetia in July, promising additional reconstruction aid. Yet, despite the influx of funds from

Moscow, the rebuilding remained painfully slow, with many Ossetians accusing Kokoity of embezzlement. In December, Russian officials released a report finding that only a fraction of the aid to Tskhinvali had been used for its intended purposes.

As of the end of 2009, only Nicaragua, Venezuela, and Nauru had joined Russia in recognizing the independence of South Ossetia and Abkhazia.

Political Rights and Civil Liberties: Though South Ossetia conducts elections, they are not monitored or recognized by independent observers. Most ethnic Georgians have either declined to or been unable to participate in such elections.

During the May 2009 parliamentary elections, opposition parties reported significant government violations, including sealed ballot boxes, observers being given limited access to polling stations, and residents allegedly being forced to vote for Eduard Kokoity. Election laws enacted in 2008 set a 7 percent vote threshold for parties to enter the parliament and required all lawmakers to be elected by proportional representation; the rules helped to substantially decrease opposition representation in 2009.

Under the separatist constitution, the president and the 33-seat parliament are elected for five-year terms. In October 2008, President Kokoity dismissed his cabinet and replaced most ministers with officials from Russia, allegedly under pressure from Moscow. In August 2009 Kokoity appointed a Russian businessman, Vadim Brovtsev, as prime minister.

Corruption is believed to be extensive, particularly in the reconstruction effort, though South Ossetia was not listed separately on Transparency International's 2009 Corruption Perceptions Index. The territory has been linked to extensive smuggling and black-market activities, including the counterfeiting of U.S. currency.

South Ossetia's electronic and print media are entirely controlled by separatist authorities, and private broadcasts are prohibited. Russia's top-selling newspaper, *Komsomolskaya Pravda*, claimed to have launched a weekly publication for South Ossetia in 2009. Tskhinvali also operates an English- and Russian-language website.

The South Ossetian Orthodox Church, which the Georgian and Russian Orthodox Churches do not recognize, continues to operate freely, according to the religious monitoring group Forum 18.

The educational system reflects government views, and many South Ossetians receive higher education in Russia.

There were two protests in Tskhinvali in 2009: one in June by the opposition following the May parliamentary elections, and an unsanctioned demonstration in September by Tskhinvali residents complaining of the slow construction of new homes. Though several nongovernmental organizations operate in South Ossetia, at least one that claims to be independent has been linked to the government, and all organizations operate under close scrutiny from Tskhinvali.

South Ossetia's criminal code adheres to the Soviet Georgian and 1996 Russian models. Though the death penalty exists in law, South Ossetia has maintained an unofficial moratorium on executions since 1996.

Indiscriminate attacks by both sides in the 2008 war killed and displaced civilians, and Ossetian forces seized or razed property in Georgian-controlled villages. According to UN data cited by Amnesty International, about 30,000 people, most of them ethnic Georgians, remained displaced from their homes in and around South Ossetia as of May 2009, and 18,500 from South Ossetia faced long-term displacement. The majority of the displaced in Georgian-controlled territory have been housed in rapidly constructed developments provided by the Georgian government. Nearly all of the estimated 38,500 people who fled to Russia during the war are said to have returned to South Ossetia.

A UN envoy reported in August 2009 that South Ossetia's tiny remaining ethnic Georgian population had complained of being pressured to accept Russian passports and vote in the May parliamentary elections under threat of expulsion.

Russian authorities have barred ethnic Ossetians from entering Georgia, but they can travel freely into Russia.

As Russia increased its economic control over the territory in 2009, local elites also siphoned funds earmarked for rehabilitation projects, including construction.

Tibet

Political Rights: 7
Civil Liberties: 7
Status: Not Free

Population: 5,300,000 [This figure from China's 2000 census includes 2.4 million Tibetans living in the Tibet Autonomous Region (TAR) and 2.9 million Tibetans living in areas of eastern Tibet that were incorporated into various Chinese provinces.]

Ten-Year Ratings Timeline For Year Under Review (Political Rights, Civil Liberties, Status)

2000	2001	2002	2003	2004	2005	2006	2007	2008	2009
7,7NF	7,7NF	7,7NF	7,7NF	7,7NF	7,7NF	7,7NF	7,7NF	7,7NF	7,7NF

Overview: Although Tibet was more accessible to tourists and journalists for parts of the year, the high level of repression established in 2008 was generally maintained in 2009, particularly ahead of politically sensitive anniversaries. There were few large-scale demonstrations, though many Tibetans resorted to passive protest tactics, such as a farming boycott and abstention from Tibetan New Year celebrations. At least 715 political and religious prisoners reportedly remained in custody as of September. In October, three Tibetans were executed, marking the first use of the death penalty in the territory since 2003. Talks between the government and representatives of the Dalai Lama did not resume in 2009. Instead, the authorities continued ideological indoctrination campaigns and the vilification of the Dalai Lama through official rhetoric.

The eastern portions of Tibetan-populated areas were gradually incorporated into various Chinese provinces over several centuries. The Tibetan plateau was ruled by a Dalai Lama in the early 20th century, until the People's Liberation Army invaded Tibet in 1950, defeating the local army. In 1951, the Chinese Communist Party formally extended control over the Tibetan plateau. This territory was designated as the Tibet Autonomous Region (TAR) in 1965.

In 1959, Chinese troops suppressed a major uprising in Lhasa, in which tens of thousands of people were reportedly killed. Tibet's spiritual and political leader—the 14th Dalai Lama, Tenzin Gyatso—was forced to flee to India with some 80,000 supporters. During the next six years, China closed 97 percent of the region's Buddhist monasteries and defrocked more than 100,000 monks and nuns. During the Chinese Cultural Revolution (1966–76), nearly all of Tibet's estimated 6,200 monasteries were destroyed.

Under reforms introduced in 1980, religious practice was allowed again—with restrictions—and tourism was permitted in certain areas. Beginning in 1987, some 200 mostly peaceful demonstrations were mounted in Lhasa and surrounding areas. After antigovernment protests escalated in March 1989, martial law was imposed; it was not lifted until May 1990.

In the 1990s, Beijing reinvigorated efforts to control religious affairs and undermine the exiled Dalai Lama's authority. Six-year-old Gendun Choekyi Nyima was detained by the authorities in 1995, and his selection by the Dalai Lama as the 11th Panchen Lama was rejected; he has not been seen since. Beijing then orchestrated the selection of another six-year-old boy as the Panchen Lama. Since one of the roles of the Panchen Lama is to identify the reincarnated Dalai Lama, the move was seen as a bid by Beijing to control the eventual selection of the 15th Dalai Lama. China hosted envoys of the Dalai Lama in 2002, the first formal contacts since 1993. The Tibetan government-in-exile sought to negotiate genuine autonomy for Tibet, particularly to ensure the survival of its Buddhist culture, but no progress was made during subsequent rounds of dialogue. Meanwhile, other Tibetan exile groups have increasingly demanded independence.

Under Zhang Qingli, who was appointed as secretary of the Chinese Communist Party (CCP) in the TAR in 2005, the authorities amplified their repressive policies. To protest religious restrictions and the previous arrest of several monks, 300 monks conducted a peaceful march in Lhasa on March 10, 2008, the 49th anniversary of the 1959 uprising; security agents suppressed the march. A riot erupted four days later, with Tibetans attacking Chinese—civilians as well as those suspected of being plainclothes police—and burning Han- or Hui-owned businesses and government offices. The authorities reported that 19 people, mostly Chinese civilians, were killed, primarily in fires. Most observers believed the protests and riots to have been spontaneous outbursts of ethnic tension. Some, including prominent Chinese human rights activists, raised concerns of official malfeasance in terms of police not taking necessary steps to prevent violence or deliberately allowing it to escalate. Over 150 other protests, most of them reportedly peaceful, soon broke out in all Tibetan-populated areas of the plateau, as well as in other provinces. The government responded with a massive deployment of armed forces and barred entry to foreign media and tourists. According to overseas Tibetan groups, between 100 and 218 Tibetans were killed as security forces suppressed the demonstrations.

Although the region was accessible to tourists and journalists under special conditions for part of 2009, the high level of repression established in 2008 was generally maintained. Security measures were especially tight surrounding a series of politically sensitive dates. These included the Tibetan New Year (Losar) in February and both the 50th anniversary of the 1959 uprising and the one-year mark of the 2008 protests in March. During this period, security forces increased their presence in Lhasa, raided homes and businesses, detained hundreds of Tibetans accused of not having permits to be in Lhasa, established roadblocks throughout the region, and restricted access for foreign tourists and journalists. Tight restrictions were imposed again ahead of the 60th anniversary of CCP rule in October.

These security efforts largely prevented major demonstrations during the year, though several Tibetans carried out one-person protests; most were immediately detained. Many Tibetans instead resorted to passive methods of protest, such as participating in a farming boycott or refusing to partake in Losar celebrations.

Talks between the government and representatives of the Dalai Lama, which had last taken place in November 2008, did not resume in 2009. Meanwhile, official statements, state-run media, and "patriotic education" campaigns continued to vilify the exiled leader. Beijing also pursued an increasingly aggressive, and often effective, policy of pressuring foreign governments to refrain from meeting with the Dalai Lama and to publicly express support for the official Chinese position on Tibet.

The government's economic development programs have disproportionately benefited ethnic Han and a select category of Tibetans, such as businesspeople or government employees. Most other Tibetans cannot take advantage of economic development and related unities for higher education and employment. The development activity has also increased Han migration and stoked Tibetan fears of cultural assimilation.

Political Rights and Civil Liberties:

The Chinese government rules Tibet through administration of the TAR and 10 Tibetan autonomous prefectures in nearby Sichuan, Qinghai, Gansu, and Yunnan provinces. Under the Chinese constitution, autonomous areas have the right to formulate their own regulations and implement national legislation in accordance with local conditions. In practice, decision-making power is concentrated in the hands of senior CCP officials; in the case of the TAR, Zhang Qingli, an ethnic Han, has served as the region's CCP secretary since 2005. The few ethnic Tibetans who occupy senior positions serve mostly as figureheads, often echoing official statements that condemn the Dalai Lama and emphasize Beijing's role in developing Tibet's economy. Jampa Phuntsog, an ethnic Tibetan, served as chairman of the TAR government from 2003 through the end of 2009.

Since 1960, the Dalai Lama has overseen the introduction of a partly democratic system to the government-in-exile in Dharamsala, India. Current institutions include a popularly elected 46-member Assembly of Tibetan People's Deputies, a Supreme Judicial Commission overseeing civil disputes, and more recently, the direct election of a prime minister. In 2001, Buddhist scholar and lama Samdhong Rinpoche was chosen as prime minister and reelected in 2006. Participating in the polls were Tibetans in exile in India, Nepal, the United States, and Europe; an estimated 120,000 are eligible to vote, though in practice, voter turnout was reportedly 30 percent. Observers have noted that such arrangements fall short of a fully democratic system due to an absence of political parties and the ongoing role of the unelected Dalai Lama in decision making; a significant number in the exile community have resisted proposals by the Dalai Lama to completely step down from his political responsibilities, however.

Corruption is believed to be extensive in Tibet, as in the rest of China. Nevertheless, little information was available during the year on the scale of the problem or official measures to combat it. Tibet is not ranked separately on Transparency International's 2009 Corruption Perceptions Index.

Chinese authorities control the flow of information in Tibet, tightly restricting all media. International broadcasts are jammed. Increased internet penetration in urban areas has provided more access to information, but online restrictions and internet cafe surveillance in place across China are enforced even more stringently in the TAR. Officials repeatedly shut down mobile-telephone networks surrounding politically sensitive dates in March 2009. Security forces have also been known to periodically confiscate mobile phones, computers, and other communication devices from monasteries and private homes, and to routinely monitor calls in and out of the region. Tibetans who transmitted information abroad often suffered repercussions, while some internet users were arrested solely for accessing banned information. In August, 19-year-old Pasang Norbu was reportedly detained after viewing online images of the Dalai Lama and the Tibetan flag at a Lhasa internet cafe. In November, Kunchok Tsephel was sentenced to 15 years in prison, on charges of, "leaking state secrets," for writings posted on a literary website he had founded. In December, a Qinghai court sentenced Tibetan filmmaker Dhondup Wangchen to six years in prison; he had been detained in March after filming interviews with Tibetans for a documentary he was making titled *Leaving Fear Behind*.

Authorities continued to restrict access to Tibet for foreign journalists in 2009, though not as consistently as in 2008. Journalists were denied entry throughout the year, especially around politically sensitive dates. During other periods, journalists were required to travel in groups, and access was contingent on prior official permission, with Tibet being the only area of China to require such special authorization. Residents who assisted foreign journalists were reportedly harassed.

The authorities regularly suppress religious activities, particularly those seen as forms of political dissent or advocacy of Tibetan independence. Possession of Dalai Lama–related materials can lead to official harassment and punishment. CCP members and government employees must adhere to atheism and cannot practice a religion. The Religious Affairs Bureaus (RABs) control who can and cannot study religion in the monasteries and nunneries in the TAR; officials allow only men or women over the age of 18 to become monks or nuns, and they are required to sign a declaration rejecting Tibetan independence, expressing loyalty to the Chinese government, and denouncing the Dalai Lama. Regulations announced in 2007 require government approval for the recognition and education of reincarnated teachers. The government manages the daily operations of monasteries through Democratic Management Committees (DMCs) and the RABs. Only monks and nuns deemed loyal to the CCP may lead DMCs, and laypeople have also been appointed to these committees. Since 2008, monasteries in Kardze (Ganzi in Chinese) have been required to have a police station within their confines.

Since March 2008, the authorities have intensified ideological education campaigns that had been conducted sporadically since 1996 and began to escalate after Zhang Qingli's appointment in 2005. According to official statements, over 2,300 officials had been sent out to 505 monasteries across the TAR by March 2009 to carry out "patriotic education" programs among monks and nuns. The campaign had been extended beyond monasteries to reach Tibet's general population in 2008, forcing students, civil servants, farmers, and merchants to recognize the CCP claim that China "liberated" Tibet and to denounce the Dalai Lama. Monks and nuns who refuse face expulsion from monasteries or nunneries, while others risk loss of employment, or arrest. In a move that further reinforced the CCP's version of Tibetan history, the government designated March 28 as a new holiday called Serf Emancipation Day.

University professors cannot lecture on certain topics, and many must attend political indoctrination sessions. The government restricts course materials to prevent the circulation of unofficial versions of Tibetan history.

Freedoms of assembly and association are severely restricted in practice. Trade unions, civic groups, and human rights groups are illegal, and even nonviolent protests are harshly punished. Nongovernmental organizations (NGOs) focusing on development and health care operate under highly restrictive agreements. Domestic groups that challenge government policy on Tibet risk punishment. In July 2009, the authorities shut down the Beijing-based Open Constitution Initiative, a prominent legal-aid NGO, shortly after it published a report attributing the March 2008 protests to legitimate Tibetan grievances, thereby challenging the official line that the unrest was masterminded by external actors.

Despite the risks, Tibetans continued to seek avenues for peacefully expressing dissent in 2009. In the first large gathering since the 2008 protests, at least 100 people marched peacefully in Lhasa to assert religious freedom; 6 Tibetans were reportedly detained for several days for participating. Smaller or even one-person demonstrations were more common, though in most cases, participants were immediately arrested. Tibetans also staged passive protests, such as a widespread boycott of Losar celebrations in February. In Kardze (Ganzi in Chinese) Tibetan Autonomous Prefecture, farmers expressed disapproval of the post–March 2008 crackdown by refusing to till their land. Authorities responded with eviction threats, and at least one individual reportedly died after being beaten by police for putting up posters supporting the farming boycott.

The judicial system in Tibet remains abysmal. Defendants lack access to meaningful legal representation, and trials are closed if state security is invoked. Chinese lawyers who offer to defend Tibetan suspects have been harassed or disbarred. Security forces routinely engage in detention without due process and torture. Tibetan human rights groups and Amnesty International documented at least five Tibetans who reportedly died in custody, or immediately after release, as a result of torture in 2009. In the first executions in Tibet since 2003, three people were put to death in October for their role in the 2008 protests. Widespread and arbitrary arrests continued in 2009, though not on the same scale as in 2008. Due to government restrictions on prison access for independent monitors, precise figures of Tibetan detainees were unavailable. However, a partial list of political prisoners published by the U.S. Congressional-Executive Commission on China included 715 Tibetans as of September 2009, the vast majority of whom were arrested on or after March 10, 2008.

The deployment of an estimated 70,000 soldiers and the erection of roadblocks following the March 2008 protests exacerbated already severe restrictions on freedom of movement. Similar measures were employed sporadically during 2009, particularly surrounding the politically sensitive anniversaries. Increased security efforts kept the number of Tibetans who successfully crossed the border into Nepal at around 500 in 2009, compared with over 2,000 in 2007.

As members of an officially recognized "minority" group, Tibetans receive preferential treatment in university admissions. However, the dominant role of the Chinese language in education and employment limits opportunities for many Tibetans. The illiteracy rate among Tibetans, at over 47 percent, remains five times greater than that among ethnic Han. Private sector employers favor ethnic Han for many jobs, especially in urban areas. Tibetans find it more difficult than Han residents to obtain permits and loans to open businesses. General discrimination increased after the 2008 riots, as television broadcasts showed footage of Tibetans attacking Han residents and burning down Han and Hui businesses.

The authorities have intensified efforts to forcibly resettle traditionally nomadic Tibetan herders in permanent-housing areas with no provisions for income generation. According to official reports, in 2008, the government relocated some 312,000 Tibetan farmers and herders to housing projects. A program to resettle a further 57,000 herders would reportedly be completed in 2010.

China's restrictive family-planning policies are more leniently enforced for Tibetans and other ethnic minorities than for ethnic Han. Officials limit urban Tibetans to having two children and encourage—but do not usually require—rural Tibetans to stop at three children.

Transnistria

Political Rights: 6
Civil Liberties: 6
Status: Not Free

Population: 525,000

Ten-Year Ratings Timeline For Year Under Review (Political Rights, Civil Liberties, Status)

2000	2001	2002	2003	2004	2005	2006	2007	2008	2009
6,6NF	6,6NF	6,6NF	6,6NF	6,6NF	6,6NF	6,6NF	6,6NF	6,6NF	6,6NF

Overview: Russian president Dmitri Medvedev hosted a meeting between Moldovan president Vladimir Voronin and Transnistrian president Igor Smirnov in March 2009, and the three leaders signed a declaration that effectively endorsed a continued Russian troop presence in Transnistria until a political settlement on the breakaway region's status could be reached. Follow-up talks between Voronin and Smirnov were scuttled later that month, however, and an opposition victory in Moldovan elections in July added a new element of uncertainty to the negotiation process.

The Pridnestrovskaia Moldavskaia Respublica (PMR), bounded by the Dniester River to the west and the Ukrainian border to the east, is a breakaway region in eastern Moldova with a large population of ethnic Russians and ethnic Ukrainians. In the rest of Moldova, where the dominant language is nearly identical to Romanian, the separatist region is commonly known as Transnistria. It was attached to the territory that became Moldova when the borders were redrawn under Soviet leader Joseph Stalin in 1940. As the Soviet Union began to collapse in 1990, pro-Russian separatists in Transnistria, fearing that Moldova would unite with neighboring Romania, declared independence from Moldova and established the PMR under an authoritarian presidential system.

With weapons and other assistance from the Russian army, the PMR fought a military conflict with Moldova that ended with a 1992 ceasefire. A new Moldovan constitution in 1994 gave the territory substantial autonomy, but the conflict remained unresolved, and the separatist regime maintained a de facto independence that was not recognized internationally. The Organization for Security and Cooperation in Europe (OSCE), Russia, and Ukraine have attempted to mediate a final settlement between Moldova and the PMR. In 2005, the United States and the European Union (EU) were invited to join the negotiations as observers, creating the so-called 5+2 format.

The latest round of formal multilateral talks collapsed in early 2006, and Transnistrian referendum voters in September 2006 overwhelmingly backed a course of independence with the goal of eventually joining Russia, although the legitimacy of the vote was not recognized by Moldova or the international community.

In the absence of active 5+2 negotiations, Moldovan president Vladimir Voronin pursued bilateral talks with Russia and took a number of steps to bring Moldova's foreign policy into line with the Kremlin's. For much of 2008, he unsuccessfully urged Russia to accept a proposal whereby Transnistria would receive substantial autonomy within Moldova, a strong and unitary presence in the Moldovan Parliament, and the right to secede if Moldova were to unite with Romania in the future. The failed proposal also sought to replace the hundreds of Russian troops who remained stationed in Transnistria with civilian observers.

PMR president Igor Smirnov met with Voronin for the first time since 2001 in April 2008, then again in December. In March 2009, Russian president Dmitri Medvedev hosted the two leaders in Russia, and together they signed the so-called Moscow Declaration, which called for Russian troops in Transnistria to be replaced by an OSCE peacekeeping mission, but only after a political settlement was reached. Critics of the document said it amounted to a Moldovan acceptance of the Russian troop presence, and argued that Russia could use its leverage with the PMR to delay a political settlement indefinitely.

A planned bilateral meeting between Voronin and Smirnov was scuttled later in March, after Smirnov responded to an extension of EU travel bans on PMR officials by imposing his own travel bans on European envoys to Moldova. An opposition victory in Moldovan national elections in July drove Voronin and his party out of power, and it remained unclear how Moldova's negotiating strategy would change as a result.

Most of Moldova's industrial infrastructure is within Transnistria's borders, although economic isolation limits its potential. Ukraine, in early 2006,   agreed to require that all goods imported from Transnistria be cleared by Moldovan customs officers, and the EU has established a program to help Ukraine control smuggling along the Transnistrian border.

Political Rights and Civil Liberties: Residents of Transnistria cannot elect their leaders democratically, and they are unable to participate freely in Moldovan elections. While the PMR maintains its own legislative, executive, and judicial branches of government, no country recognizes its independence. Both the president and the 43-seat, unicameral Supreme Council are elected to five-year terms. Having won reelection in December 2006 with 82 percent of the vote, Igor Smirnov is now serving his fourth term as president, and he has said that he will not step down until Transnistria is independent. The international community has generally considered the presidential and parliamentary elections held since 1992 to be neither free nor fair, although they have not been monitored.

Opposition presidential candidates have often been barred from participating on technical grounds. In December 2005 parliamentary elections, the opposition group Obnovlenye (Renewal)—backed by Transnistria's dominant business conglomerate, Sheriff Enterprises—won 23 of the 43 seats. Obnovlenye leader Yevgeny Shevchuk seeks business-oriented reforms and has been accused of taking a softer line on Moldova, though his party supports PMR independence. He became Speaker of parliament after the elections, but the parliament has traditionally held very little power, and he stepped down as speaker in July 2009 after a disagreement with Smirnov over constitutional reform. The changes backed by Obnovlenye would have shifted significant power from the presidency to the parliament, but Smirnov submitted a counterproposal that would increase presidential power even further. No changes had been enacted by year's end.

Native Moldovan speakers are not represented in government and are under constant political pressure. PMR authorities prevented voters in the village of Corjova, which recognizes the Moldovan government, from participating in Moldova's 2009 national elections, though a few thousand Transnistrians were able to cast ballots at special voting sites on the west bank of the Dniester.

Corruption and organized crime are serious problems in Transnistria. The authorities are entrenched in the territory's economic activities, which rely in large part on smuggling schemes designed to evade Moldovan and Ukrainian import taxes. Russia has a major stake in the Transnistrian economy and supports the PMR through loans, direct subsidies, and low-cost natural gas. Upon resigning as parliament Speaker in 2009, Shevchuk reportedly accused the government of corruption, nepotism, and economic mismanagement. Transnistria is not listed separately on Transparency International's Corruption Perceptions Index.

The media environment is restrictive. Nearly all media are state owned or controlled and do not criticize the authorities. The few independent print outlets have small circulations. Critical reporting draws harassment by the authorities, who also use tactics such as bureaucratic obstruction and the withholding of information to inhibit independent media. The *Individual and His Rights*, an independent newspaper, has experienced intimidation and violent attacks. Journalists exercise a certain amount of self-censorship. Sheriff Enterprises dominates the limited private broadcasting, cable television, and internet access. There were no reports of censorship of internet content.

Religious freedom is limited. Orthodox Christianity is the dominant faith, and authorities have denied registration to several smaller religious groups, at times in defiance of court decisions. Other court rulings in favor of minority faiths have been routinely overturned. Unregistered groups, including Jehovah's Witnesses and Pentecostals, have difficulty renting space for prayer meetings and face harassment by police and Orthodox opponents.

Although several thousand students study Moldovan using the Latin script, this practice is restricted. The Moldovan language and Latin alphabet are associated with support for unity with Moldova, while Russian and the Cyrillic alphabet are associated with separatist goals. Parents who send their children to schools using Latin script, and the schools themselves, have faced routine harassment from the security services.

The authorities severely restrict freedom of assembly and rarely issue required permits for public protests. Freedom of association is similarly circumscribed. Non-governmental activities must be coordinated with local authorities, and groups that do not comply face harassment, including visits from security officials. The region's trade unions are holdovers from the Soviet era, and the United Council of Labor Collectives works closely with the government.

The judiciary is subservient to the executive and generally implements the will of the authorities. Defendants do not receive fair trials, and the legal framework falls short of international standards. Politically motivated arrests and detentions are common. Human rights groups have received accounts of torture in custody. Prison conditions are considered harsh, and the facilities are severely overcrowded. A Moldovan civil society group reported in October 2009 that 90 inmates were on a hunger strike to protest long pretrial detentions, beatings, and poor living conditions; family members of the strikers were allegedly threatened by police. Military conscripts have reportedly been mistreated, and at least two died in 2009.

Authorities discriminate against ethnic Moldovans, who make up about 40 percent of the population. It is believed that ethnic Russians and ethnic Ukrainians together comprise a slim majority, and as many as a third of the region's residents reportedly hold Russian passports.

Women are underrepresented in most positions of authority, and domestic violence against women is a problem. Transnistria is a significant source and transit point for trafficking in women for the purpose of prostitution. Homosexuality is illegal in Transnistria.

Western Sahara

Political Rights: 7   **Population:** 511,000
Civil Liberties: 6
Status: Not Free

Ten-Year Ratings Timeline For Year Under Review (Political Rights, Civil Liberties, Status)

2000	2001	2002	2003	2004	2005	2006	2007	2008	2009
7,6NF	7,6NF	7,6NF	7,6NF	7,6NF	7,6NF	7,6NF	7,6NF	7,6NF	7,6NF

Overview: Talks between the Moroccan government and the proindependence Polisario Front continued in 2009, but the two sides remained at odds over whether to allow a referendum on independence. Pro-independence activists continued to be detained and harassed, and the conditions on the ground for most Sahrawis remained poor.

Western Sahara was ruled by Spain for nearly a century, until Spanish troops withdrew in 1976, following a bloody guerrilla conflict with the proindependence

Popular Front for the Liberation of Saguia el-Hamra and Rio de Oro (Polisario Front). Mauritania and Morocco both ignored Sahrawi aspirations and claimed the resource-rich region for themselves, agreeing to a partition in which Morocco received the northern two-thirds. However, the Polisario Front proclaimed an independent Sahrawi Arab Democratic Republic and continued its guerrilla campaign. Mauritania renounced its claim to the region in 1979, and Morocco filled the vacuum by annexing the entire territory.

Moroccan and Polisario forces engaged in a low-intensity armed conflict until the United Nations brokered a ceasefire in 1991. The agreement called for residents of Western Sahara to vote in a referendum on independence the following year, to be supervised by the newly established UN Mission for a Referendum in Western Sahara (MINURSO). However, the vote never took place, with the two sides failing to agree on voter eligibility.

Morocco tried to bolster its annexation by offering financial incentives for Moroccans to move to Western Sahara and for Sahrawis to move to Morocco. Morocco also used more coercive measures to assert its control, engaging in forced resettlements of Sahrawis and long-term detention and "disappearances" of pro-independence activists.

In 2004, the Polisario Front accepted the UN Security Council's Baker II plan (named after former UN special envoy and U.S. secretary of state James Baker), which called for up to five years of autonomy followed by a referendum on the territory's status. However, Morocco rejected the plan, as it could lead to independence, and in 2007, offered its own autonomy plan.

Because the Polisario Front remained committed to an eventual referendum on independence, the two sides failed to make meaningful progress in several rounds of talks that started in 2007 and continued through 2009. Also in 2009, some UN Security Council members expressed concern about the human rights situation and proposed that the council consider expanding MINURSO's mandate.

Political Rights and Civil Liberties: As the occupying force in Western Sahara, Morocco controls local elections and works to ensure that independence-minded leaders are excluded from both the local political process and the Moroccan Parliament.

Western Sahara is not listed separately on Transparency International's Corruption Perceptions Index, but corruption is believed to be at least as much of a problem as it is in Morocco.

According to the Moroccan constitution, the press is free, but this is not the case in practice. There is little in the way of independent Sahrawi media. Moroccan authorities are sensitive to any reporting that is not in line with the state's official position on Western Sahara, and they continue to expel or detain Sahrawi, Moroccan, and foreign reporters who write critically on the issue. Human Rights Watch (HRW) reported that in October 2009, plainclothes police told two Morocco-based Spanish journalists to leave the El-Aaiun home of Sidi Mohamed Dadach, who heads the Committee to Support Self-Determination in Western Sahara (CODAPSO). Online media and independent satellite broadcasts are largely unavailable to the impoverished population.

Nearly all Sahrawis are Sunni Muslims, as are most Moroccans, and Moroccan authorities generally do not interfere with their freedom of worship. There are no major universities or institutions of higher learning in Western Sahara.

Sahrawis are not permitted to form independent political or nongovernmental organizations, and their freedom of assembly is severely restricted. As in previous years, activists supporting independence and their suspected foreign sympathizers were subject to harassment in 2009. HRW, which has documented several violations, reported that Moroccan authorities referred seven Sahrawi activists to a military court in October after charging them with harming state security; there were no verdicts at year's end. Moroccan officials appear to be particularly wary of Sahrawis who travel abroad to highlight the plight of their people and argue for independence. According to HRW, police in October 2009 began breaking up visits by foreign reporters and human rights activists to the homes of Sahrawi activists, rather than simply monitoring them; the police said the visits required clearance from Moroccan authorities.

Among Sahrawi activists themselves, HRW documented the case of Naama Asfari of the Paris-based Committee for the Respect of Freedoms and Human Rights in Western Sahara (CORELSO), who has been detained and harassed on numerous occasions over the years. In August 2009, he was sentenced to four months in jail after an argument with a police officer over the Sahrawi flag that Asfari had on his keychain. Asfari's cousin, who was with him during the encounter, was also sentenced to jail time. In another high-profile case, activist Aminatou Haidar, head of the Collective of Sahrawi Human Rights Defenders (CODESA), returned in November to Western Sahara from the United States, where she had received a human rights award. She indicated on her reentry paperwork that she lived in Western Sahara, and when she refused to change the document to indicate Morocco, she was detained and eventually deported without a passport to Spain's Canary Islands. Haidar was able to return home in December 2009 after a month-long hunger strike and considerable diplomatic pressure, but the authorities continued to monitor her and restrict her movements.

Sahrawis are technically subject to Moroccan labor laws, but there is little organized labor activity in the resource-rich but poverty-stricken territory.

International human rights groups have criticized Morocco's record in Western Sahara for decades. A highly critical September 2006 report by the UN High Commissioner for Human Rights—intended to be distributed only to Algeria, Morocco, and the Polisario Front—was leaked to the press that October. The human rights situation in the territory tends to worsen during periods of increased demonstrations against Moroccan rule. The Polisario Front has also been accused of disregarding human rights.

Morocco and the Polisario Front both restrict free movement in potential conflict areas. Morocco has been accused of using force and financial incentives to alter the composition of Western Sahara's population.

Sahrawi women face much of the same cultural and legal discrimination as Moroccan women. Conditions are generally worse for women living in rural areas, where poverty and illiteracy rates are higher.

Freedom in the World 2010 Methodology

INTRODUCTION

The *Freedom in the World* survey provides an annual evaluation of the state of global freedom as experienced by individuals. The survey measures freedom—the opportunity to act spontaneously in a variety of fields outside the control of the government and other centers of potential domination—according to two broad categories: political rights and civil liberties. Political rights enable people to participate freely in the political process, including the right to vote freely for distinct alternatives in legitimate elections, compete for public office, join political parties and organizations, and elect representatives who have a decisive impact on public policies and are accountable to the electorate. Civil liberties allow for the freedoms of expression and belief, associational and organizational rights, rule of law, and personal autonomy without interference from the state.

The survey does not rate governments or government performance per se, but rather the real-world rights and freedoms enjoyed by individuals. Thus, while Freedom House considers the presence of legal rights, it places a greater emphasis on whether these rights are implemented in practice. Furthermore, freedoms can be affected by government officials, as well as by nonstate actors, including insurgents and other armed groups.

Freedom House does not maintain a culture-bound view of freedom. The methodology of the survey is grounded in basic standards of political rights and civil liberties, derived in large measure from relevant portions of the Universal Declaration of Human Rights. These standards apply to all countries and territories, irrespective of geographical location, ethnic or religious composition, or level of economic development. The survey operates from the assumption that freedom for all peoples is best achieved in liberal democratic societies.

The survey includes both analytical reports and numerical ratings for 194 countries and 14 select territories.[1] Each country and territory report includes an overview section, which provides historical background and a brief description of the year's major developments, as well as a section summarizing the current state of

---

[1] These territories are selected based on their political significance and size. Freedom House divides territories into two categories: related territories and disputed territories. Related territories consist mostly of colonies, protectorates, and island dependencies of sovereign states that are in some relation of dependency to that state, and whose relationship is not currently in serious legal or political dispute. Disputed territories are areas within internationally recognized sovereign states whose status is in serious political or violent dispute, and whose conditions differ substantially from those of the relevant sovereign states. They are often outside of central government control and characterized by intense, longtime, and widespread insurgency or independence movements that enjoy popular support. Generally, the dispute faced by a territory is between independence for the territory or domination by an established state.

political rights and civil liberties. In addition, each country and territory is assigned a numerical rating—on a scale of 1 to 7—for political rights and an analogous rating for civil liberties; a rating of 1 indicates the highest degree of freedom and 7 the lowest level of freedom. These ratings, which are calculated based on the methodological process described below, determine whether a country is classified as Free, Partly Free, or Not Free by the survey.

The survey findings are reached after a multilayered process of analysis and evaluation by a team of regional experts and scholars. Although there is an element of subjectivity inherent in the survey findings, the ratings process emphasizes intellectual rigor and balanced and unbiased judgments.

HISTORY OF THE SURVEY

Freedom House's first year-end reviews of freedom began in the 1950s as the *Balance Sheet of Freedom*. This modest report provided assessments of political trends and their implications for individual freedom. In 1972, Freedom House launched a new, more comprehensive annual study called *The Comparative Study of Freedom*. Raymond Gastil, a Harvard-trained specialist in regional studies from the University of Washington in Seattle, developed the survey's methodology, which assigned political rights and civil liberties ratings to 151 countries and 45 territories and, based on these ratings, categorized them as Free, Partly Free, or Not Free. The findings appeared each year in Freedom House's *Freedom at Issue* bimonthly journal (later titled *Freedom Review*). The survey first appeared in book form in 1978 under the title *Freedom in the World* and included short, explanatory narratives for each country and territory rated in the study, as well as a series of essays by leading scholars on related issues. *Freedom in the World* continued to be produced by Gastil until 1989, when a larger team of in-house survey analysts was established. In the mid-1990s, the expansion of *Freedom in the World*'s country and territory narratives demanded the hiring of outside analysts—a group of regional experts from the academic, media, and human rights communities. The survey has continued to grow in size and scope; the 2010 edition is the most exhaustive in history.

RESEARCH AND RATINGS REVIEW PROCESS

This year's survey covers developments from January 1, 2009, through December 31, 2009, in 194 countries and 14 territories. The research and ratings process involved 50 analysts and 18 senior-level academic advisers—the largest number to date. The analysts used a broad range of sources of information—including foreign and domestic news reports, academic analyses, nongovernmental organizations, think tanks, individual professional contacts, and visits to the region—in preparing the country and territory reports and ratings.

The country and territory ratings were proposed by the analyst responsible for each related report. The ratings were reviewed individually and on a comparative basis in a series of six regional meetings—Asia-Pacific, Central and Eastern Europe and the Former Soviet Union, Latin America and the Caribbean, Middle East and North Africa, sub-Saharan Africa, and Western Europe—involving the analysts, academic advisers with expertise in each region, and Freedom House staff. The ratings were compared to the previous year's findings, and any major proposed numerical shifts or category changes were subjected to more intensive scrutiny. These reviews were followed by cross-regional assessments, in which efforts were made to ensure comparability and consistency in the findings. Many of the key country reports were also reviewed by the academic advisers.

CHANGES TO THE 2010 EDITION OF *FREEDOM IN THE WORLD*

The survey's methodology is reviewed periodically by an advisory committee of political scientists with expertise in methodological issues. Over the years, the committee has made a number of modest methodological changes to adapt to evolving ideas about political rights and civil liberties. At the same time, the time series data are not revised retroactively, and any changes to the methodology are introduced incrementally in order to ensure the comparability of the ratings from year to year.

The following changes were made to the 2010 edition of the survey:

Territories – Entities designated as related and disputed territories are no longer being identified with any particular country in order to avoid potential misunderstandings about the sometimes unclear relationship between the territory and the principal country or countries relating to them.

Kosovo – Kosovo was removed from the list of territories and added as an independent country due to the handover of governance functions from the international community to domestic authorities, and as a result of its recognition by a significant number of states, most of which are classified by Freedom House as Free or Partly Free.

Chechnya – Chechnya was dropped as a separate territory, and developments in this jurisdiction are now being addressed in the Russia report, due to the consolidation of power by pro-Kremlin forces, which have effectively eliminated any viable, active independence movement.

RATINGS PROCESS

(NOTE: see the complete checklist questions and keys to political rights and civil liberties ratings and status at the end of the methodology essay.)

Scores – The ratings process is based on a checklist of 10 political rights questions and 15 civil liberties questions. The political rights questions are grouped into three subcategories: Electoral Process (3 questions), Political Pluralism and Participation (4), and Functioning of Government (3). The civil liberties questions are grouped into four subcategories: Freedom of Expression and Belief (4 questions), Associational and Organizational Rights (3), Rule of Law (4), and Personal Autonomy and Individual Rights (4). Scores are awarded to each of these questions on a scale of 0 to 4, where a score of 0 represents the smallest degree and 4 the greatest degree of rights or liberties present. The political rights section also contains two additional discretionary questions: question A (For traditional monarchies that have no parties or electoral process, does the system provide for genuine, meaningful consultation with the people, encourage public discussion of policy choices, and allow the right to petition the ruler?) and question B (Is the government or occupying power deliberately changing the ethnic composition of a country or territory so as to destroy a culture or tip the political balance in favor of another group?). For additional discretionary question A, a score of 1 to 4 may be added, as applicable, while for discretionary question B, a score of 1 to 4 may be subtracted (the worse the situation, the more that may be subtracted). The highest score that can be awarded to the political rights checklist is 40 (or a total score of 4 for each of the 10 questions). The highest score that can be awarded to the civil liberties checklist is 60 (or a total score of 4 for each of the 15 questions).

The scores from the previous survey edition are used as a benchmark for the current year under review. In general, a score is changed only if there has been a real-world development during the year that warrants a change (e.g., a crackdown on the media, the country's first free and fair elections) and is reflected accordingly in the narrative.

In answering both the political rights and civil liberties questions, Freedom House does not equate constitutional or other legal guarantees of rights with the on-the-ground fulfillment of these rights. While both laws and actual practices are factored into the ratings decisions, greater emphasis is placed on the latter.

For states and territories with small populations, the absence of pluralism in the political system or civil society is not necessarily viewed as a negative situation unless the government or other centers of domination are deliberately blocking its operation. For example, a small country without diverse political parties or media outlets or significant trade unions is not penalized if these limitations are determined to be a function of size and not overt restrictions.

Political Rights and Civil Liberties Ratings – The total score awarded to the political rights and civil liberties checklist determines the political rights and civil liberties rating. Each rating of 1 through 7, with 1 representing the highest and 7 the lowest level of freedom, corresponds to a range of total scores (see tables 1 and 2).

Status of Free, Partly Free, Not Free – Each pair of political rights and civil liberties ratings is averaged to determine an overall status of "Free," "Partly Free," or "Not Free." Those whose ratings average 1.0 to 2.5 are considered Free, 3.0 to 5.0 Partly Free, and 5.5 to 7.0 Not Free (see table 3). The designations of Free, Partly Free, and Not Free each cover a broad third of the available scores. Therefore, countries and territories within any one category, especially those at either end of the category, can have quite different human rights situations. In order to see the distinctions within each category, a country or territory's political rights and civil liberties ratings should be examined. For example, countries at the lowest end of the Free category (2 in political rights and 3 in civil liberties, or 3 in political rights and 2 in civil liberties) differ from those at the upper end of the Free group (1 for both political rights and civil liberties). Also, a designation of Free does not mean that a country enjoys perfect freedom or lacks serious problems, only that it enjoys comparably more freedom than Partly Free or Not Free (or some other Free) countries.

Indications of Ratings and/or Status Changes – Each country's or territory's political rights rating, civil liberties rating, and status is included in a statistics section that precedes each country or territory report. A change in a political rights or civil liberties rating since the previous survey edition is indicated with a symbol next to the rating that has changed. A brief ratings change explanation is included in the statistics section.

Trend Arrows – Positive or negative developments in a country or territory may also be reflected in the use of upward or downward trend arrows. A trend arrow is based on a particular development (such as an improvement in a country's state of religious freedom), which must be linked to a score change in the corresponding checklist question (in this case, an increase in the score for checklist question D2, which covers religious freedom). However, not all score increases or decreases warrant trend arrows. Whether a positive or negative development is significant enough to warrant a trend arrow is determined through consultations among the report writer, the regional academic advisers, and Freedom House staff. Also, trend arrows are assigned only in cases where score increases or decreases are not sufficient to warrant a ratings change; thus, a country cannot receive both a ratings change and a trend arrow during the same year. A trend arrow is indicated with an arrow next to the name of the country or territory that appears before the statistics section at the top of each country or territory report. A brief trend arrow explanation is included in the statistics section.

GENERAL CHARACTERISTICS OF EACH POLITICAL RIGHTS AND CIVIL LIBERTIES RATING

POLITICAL RIGHTS

Rating of 1 – Countries and territories with a rating of 1 enjoy a wide range of political rights, including free and fair elections. Candidates who are elected actually rule, political parties are competitive, the opposition plays an important role and enjoys real power, and minority groups have reasonable self-government or can participate in the government through informal consensus.

Rating of 2 – Countries and territories with a rating of 2 have slightly weaker political rights than those with a rating of 1 because of such factors as some political corruption, limits on the functioning of political parties and opposition groups, and foreign or military influence on politics.

Ratings of 3, 4, 5 – Countries and territories with a rating of 3, 4, or 5 include those that moderately protect almost all political rights to those that more strongly protect some political rights while less strongly protecting others. The same factors that undermine freedom in countries with a rating of 2 may also weaken political rights in those with a rating of 3, 4, or 5, but to an increasingly greater extent at each successive rating.

Rating of 6 – Countries and territories with a rating of 6 have very restricted political rights. They are ruled by one party or military dictatorships, religious hierarchies, or autocrats. They may allow a few political rights, such as some representation or autonomy for minority groups, and a few are traditional monarchies that tolerate political discussion and accept public petitions.

Rating of 7 – Countries and territories with a rating of 7 have few or no political rights because of severe government oppression, sometimes in combination with civil war. They may also lack an authoritative and functioning central government and suffer from extreme violence or warlord rule that dominates political power.

CIVIL LIBERTIES

Rating of 1 – Countries and territories with a rating of 1 enjoy a wide range of civil liberties, including freedom of expression, assembly, association, education, and religion. They have an established and generally fair system of the rule of law (including an independent judiciary), allow free economic activity, and tend to strive for equality of opportunity for everyone, including women and minority groups.

Rating of 2 – Countries and territories with a rating of 2 have slightly weaker civil liberties than those with a rating of 1 because of such factors as some limits on media independence, restrictions on trade union activities, and discrimination against minority groups and women.

Ratings of 3, 4, 5 – Countries and territories with a rating of 3, 4, or 5 include those that moderately protect almost all civil liberties to those that more strongly protect some civil liberties while less strongly protecting others. The same factors that undermine freedom in countries with a rating of 2 may also weaken civil liberties in those with a rating of 3, 4, or 5, but to an increasingly greater extent at each successive rating.

Rating of 6 – Countries and territories with a rating of 6 have very restricted civil liberties. They strongly limit the rights of expression and association and frequently hold political prisoners. They may allow a few civil liberties, such as some religious and social freedoms, some highly restricted private business activity, and some open and free private discussion.

Rating of 7 – Countries and territories with a rating of 7 have few or no civil liberties. They allow virtually no freedom of expression or association, do not protect the rights of detainees and prisoners, and often control or dominate most economic activity.

Countries and territories generally have ratings in political rights and civil liberties that are within two ratings numbers of each other. For example, without a well-developed civil society, it is difficult, if not impossible, to have an atmosphere supportive of political rights. Consequently, there is no country in the survey with a rating of 6 or 7 for civil liberties and, at the same time, a rating of 1 or 2 for political rights.

ELECTORAL DEMOCRACY DESIGNATION

In addition to providing numerical ratings, the survey assigns the designation "electoral democracy" to countries that have met certain minimum standards. In determining whether a country is an electoral democracy, Freedom House examines several key factors concerning the last major national election or elections.

To qualify as an electoral democracy, a state must have satisfied the following criteria:

1) A competitive, multiparty political system;

2) Universal adult suffrage for all citizens (with exceptions for restrictions that states may legitimately place on citizens as sanctions for criminal offenses);

3) Regularly contested elections conducted in conditions of ballot secrecy, reasonable ballot security, and in the absence of massive voter fraud, and that yield results that are representative of the public will;

4) Significant public access of major political parties to the electorate through the media and through generally open political campaigning.

The numerical benchmark for a country to be listed as an electoral democracy is a subtotal score of 7 or better (out of a possible total score of 12) for the political rights checklist subcategory A (the three questions on Electoral Process) *and* an overall political rights score of 20 or better (out of a possible total score of 40). In the case of presidential/parliamentary systems, both elections must have been free and fair on the basis of the above criteria; in parliamentary systems, the last nationwide elections for the national legislature must have been free and fair. The presence of certain irregularities during the electoral process does not automatically disqualify a country from being designated an electoral democracy. A country cannot be an electoral democracy if significant authority for national decisions resides in the hands of an unelected power, whether a monarch or a foreign international authority. A country is removed from the ranks of electoral democracies if its last national election failed to meet the criteria listed above, or if changes in law significantly eroded the public's possibility for electoral choice.

Freedom House's term "electoral democracy" differs from "liberal democracy" in that the latter also implies the presence of a substantial array of civil liberties. In the survey, all Free countries qualify as both electoral and liberal democracies. By contrast, some Partly Free countries qualify as electoral, but not liberal, democracies.

FREEDOM IN THE WORLD 2010
CHECKLIST QUESTIONS AND GUIDELINES

Each numbered checklist question is assigned a score of 0-4 (except for discretionary question A, for which a score of 1-4 may be added, and discretionary question B, for which a score of 1-4 may be subtracted), according to the survey methodology. The bulleted sub-questions are intended to provide guidance to the writers regarding what issues are meant to be considered in scoring each checklist question; the authors do not necessarily have to consider every sub-question when scoring their countries.

POLITICAL RIGHTS CHECKLIST
A. ELECTORAL PROCESS

1. Is the head of government or other chief national authority elected through free and fair elections?

• Did established and reputable national and/or international election monitoring organizations judge the most recent elections for head of government to be free and fair? (*Note*: Heads of government chosen through various electoral frameworks, including direct elections for president, indirect elections for prime minister by parliament, and the electoral college system for electing presidents, are covered under this and the following sub-questions. In cases of indirect elections for the head of government, the elections for the legislature that chose the head of government, as well as the selection process of the head of government himself, should be taken into consideration.)

• Have there been undue, politically motivated delays in holding the most recent election for head of government?

• Is the registration of voters and candidates conducted in an accurate, timely, transparent, and nondiscriminatory manner?

• Can candidates make speeches, hold public meetings, and enjoy media access throughout the campaign free of intimidation?

• Does voting take place by secret ballot or by equivalent free voting procedure?

• Are voters able to vote for the candidate or party of their choice without undue pressure or intimidation?

• Is the vote count transparent, and is it reported honestly with the official results made public? Can election monitors from independent groups and representing parties/candidates watch the counting of votes to ensure their honesty?

• Is each person's vote given equivalent weight to those of other voters in order to ensure equal representation?

• Has a democratically elected head of government who was chosen in the most recent election subsequently been overthrown in a violent coup? (*Note*: Although a peaceful, "velvet coup" may ultimately lead to a positive outcome—particularly if it replaces a head of government who was not freely and fairly elected—the new leader has not been freely and fairly elected and cannot be treated as such.)

• In cases where elections for regional, provincial, or state governors and/or other subnational officials differ significantly in conduct from national elections, does the conduct of the subnational elections reflect an opening toward improved political rights in the country, or, alternatively, a worsening of political rights?

  2. Are the national legislative representatives elected through free and fair elections?

• Did established and reputable domestic and/or international election monitoring organizations judge the most recent national legislative elections to be free and fair?

• Have there been undue, politically motivated delays in holding the most recent national legislative election?

• Is the registration of voters and candidates conducted in an accurate, timely, transparent, and nondiscriminatory manner?

• Can candidates make speeches, hold public meetings, and enjoy media access throughout the campaign free of intimidation?

• Does voting take place by secret ballot or by equivalent free voting procedure?

• Are voters able to vote for the candidate or party of their choice without undue pressure or intimidation?

• Is the vote count transparent, and is it reported honestly with the official results made public? Can election monitors from independent groups and representing parties/candidates watch the counting of votes to ensure their honesty?

• Is each person's vote given equivalent weight to those of other voters in order to ensure equal representation?

• Have the representatives of a democratically elected national legislature who were chosen in the most recent election subsequently been overthrown in a violent coup? (*Note*: Although a peaceful, "velvet coup" may ultimately lead to a positive outcome—particularly if it replaces a national legislature whose representatives were not freely and fairly elected—members of the new legislature have not been freely and fairly elected and cannot be treated as such.)

• In cases where elections for subnational councils/parliaments differ significantly in conduct from national elections, does the conduct of the subnational elections reflect an opening toward improved political rights in the country, or, alternatively, a worsening of political rights?

3. Are the electoral laws and framework fair?

• Is there a clear, detailed, and fair legislative framework for conducting elections? (*Note*: Changes to electoral laws should not be made immediately preceding an election if the ability of voters, candidates, or parties to fulfill their roles in the election is infringed.)

• Are election commissions or other election authorities independent and free from government or other pressure and interference?

• Is the composition of election commissions fair and balanced?

• Do election commissions or other election authorities conduct their work in an effective and competent manner?

• Do adult citizens enjoy universal and equal suffrage? (*Note*: Suffrage can be suspended or withdrawn for reasons of legal incapacity, such as mental incapacity or conviction of a serious criminal offense.)

• Is the drawing of election districts conducted in a fair and nonpartisan manner, as opposed to gerrymandering for personal or partisan advantage?

• Has the selection of a system for choosing legislative representatives (such as proportional versus majoritarian) been manipulated to advance certain political interests or to influence the electoral results?

B. POLITICAL PLURALISM AND PARTICIPATION

1. Do the people have the right to organize in different political parties or other competitive political groupings of their choice, and is the system open to the rise and fall of these competing parties or groupings?

• Do political parties encounter undue legal or practical obstacles in their efforts to be formed and to operate, including onerous registration requirements, excessively large membership requirements, etc.?

• Do parties face discriminatory or onerous restrictions in holding meetings, rallies, or other peaceful activities?

• Are party members or leaders intimidated, harassed, arrested, imprisoned, or subjected to violent attacks as a result of their peaceful political activities?

2. Is there a significant opposition vote and a realistic possibility for the opposition to increase its support or gain power through elections?

• Are various legal/administrative restrictions selectively applied to opposition parties to prevent them from increasing their support base or successfully competing in elections?

• Are there legitimate opposition forces in positions of authority, such as in the national legislature or in subnational governments?

• Are opposition party members or leaders intimidated, harassed, arrested, imprisoned, or subjected to violent attacks as a result of their peaceful political activities?

3. Are the people's political choices free from domination by the military, foreign powers, totalitarian parties, religious hierarchies, economic oligarchies, or any other powerful group?

• Do such groups offer bribes to voters and/or political figures in order to influence their political choices?

• Do such groups intimidate, harass, or attack voters and/or political figures in order to influence their political choices?

• Does the military control or enjoy a preponderant influence over government policy and activities, including in countries that nominally are under civilian control?

• Do foreign governments control or enjoy a preponderant influence over government policy and activities by means including the presence of foreign military troops, the use of significant economic threats or sanctions, etc.?

4. Do cultural, ethnic, religious, or other minority groups have full political rights and electoral opportunities?

• Do political parties of various ideological persuasions address issues of specific concern to minority groups?

• Does the government inhibit the participation of minority groups in national or subnational political life through laws and/or practical obstacles?

• Are political parties based on ethnicity, culture, or religion that espouse peaceful, democratic values legally permitted and de facto allowed to operate?

C. FUNCTIONING OF GOVERNMENT

1. Do the freely elected head of government and national legislative representatives determine the policies of the government?

• Are the candidates who were elected freely and fairly duly installed in office?

• Do other appointed or non-freely elected state actors interfere with or prevent freely elected representatives from adopting and implementing legislation and making meaningful policy decisions?

• Do nonstate actors, including criminal gangs, the military, and foreign governments, interfere with or prevent elected representatives from adopting and implementing legislation and making meaningful policy decisions?

2. Is the government free from pervasive corruption?

• Has the government implemented effective anticorruption laws or programs to prevent, detect, and punish corruption among public officials, including conflict of interest?

• Is the government free from excessive bureaucratic regulations, registration requirements, or other controls that increase opportunities for corruption?

• Are there independent and effective auditing and investigative bodies that function without impediment or political pressure or influence?

• Are allegations of corruption by government officials thoroughly investigated and prosecuted without prejudice, particularly against political opponents?

• Are allegations of corruption given wide and extensive airing in the media?

• Do whistle-blowers, anticorruption activists, investigators, and journalists enjoy legal protections that make them feel secure about reporting cases of bribery and corruption?

• What was the latest Transparency International Corruption Perceptions Index score for this country?

3. Is the government accountable to the electorate between elections, and does it operate with openness and transparency?

• Are civil society groups, interest groups, journalists, and other citizens able to comment on and influence pending policies of legislation?

• Do citizens have the legal right and practical ability to obtain information about government operations and the means to petition government agencies for it?

• Is the budget-making process subject to meaningful legislative review and public scrutiny?

• Does the government publish detailed accounting expenditures in a timely fashion?

• Does the state ensure transparency and effective competition in the awarding of government contracts?

• Are the asset declarations of government officials open to public and media scrutiny and verification?

ADDITIONAL DISCRETIONARY POLITICAL RIGHTS QUESTIONS:

A. For traditional monarchies that have no parties or electoral process, does the system provide for genuine, meaningful consultation with the people, encourage public discussion of policy choices, and allow the right to petition the ruler?

• Is there a non-elected legislature that advises the monarch on policy issues?

• Are there formal mechanisms for individuals or civic groups to speak with or petition the monarch?

• Does the monarch take petitions from the public under serious consideration?

B. Is the government or occupying power deliberately changing the ethnic composition of a country or territory so as to destroy a culture or tip the political balance in favor of another group?

• Is the government providing economic or other incentives to certain people in order to change the ethnic composition of a region or regions?

• Is the government forcibly moving people in or out of certain areas in order to change the ethnic composition of those regions?

• Is the government arresting, imprisoning, or killing members of certain ethnic groups in order change the ethnic composition of a region or regions?

CIVIL LIBERTIES CHECKLIST
D. FREEDOM OF EXPRESSION AND BELIEF

1. Are there free and independent media and other forms of cultural expression? (*Note*: In cases where the media are state controlled but offer pluralistic points of view, the survey gives the system credit.)

• Does the government directly or indirectly censor print, broadcast, and/or internet-based media?

• Is self-censorship among journalists common, especially when reporting on politically sensitive issues, including corruption or the activities of senior officials?

• Does the government use libel and security laws to punish those who scrutinize government officials and policies through either onerous fines or imprisonment?

• Is it a crime to insult the honor and dignity of the president and/or other government officials? How broad is the range of such prohibitions, and how vigorously are they enforced?

• If media outlets are dependent on the government for their financial survival, does the government withhold funding in order to propagandize, primarily provide official points of view, and/or limit access by opposition parties and civic critics?

• Does the government attempt to influence media content and access through means including politically motivated awarding of broadcast frequencies and newspaper registrations, unfair control and influence over printing facilities and distribution networks, selective distribution of advertising, onerous registration requirements, prohibitive tariffs, and bribery?

• Are journalists threatened, arrested, imprisoned, beaten, or killed by government or nongovernmental actors for their legitimate journalistic activities, and if such cases occur, are they investigated and prosecuted fairly and expeditiously?

• Are works of literature, art, music, or other forms of cultural expression censored or banned for political purposes?

2. Are religious institutions and communities free to practice their faith and express themselves in public and private?

• Are registration requirements employed to impede the free functioning of religious institutions?

• Are members of religious groups, including minority faiths and movements, harassed, fined, arrested, or beaten by the authorities for engaging in their religious practices?

• Does the government appoint or otherwise influence the appointment of religious leaders?

• Does the government control the production and distribution of religious books and other materials and the content of sermons?

• Is the construction of religious buildings banned or restricted?

• Does the government place undue restrictions on religious education? Does the government require religious education?

3. Is there academic freedom, and is the educational system free of extensive political indoctrination?

• Are teachers and professors free to pursue academic activities of a political and quasi-political nature without fear of physical violence or intimidation by state or nonstate actors?

• Does the government pressure, strongly influence, or control the content of school curriculums for political purposes?

• Are student associations that address issues of a political nature allowed to function freely?

• Does the government, including through school administration or other officials, pressure students and/or teachers to support certain political figures or agendas, including pressuring them to attend political rallies or vote for certain candidates? Conversely, does the government, including through school administration or other officials, discourage or forbid students and/or teachers from supporting certain candidates and parties?

4. Is there open and free private discussion?

• Are people able to engage in private discussions, particularly of a political nature (in places including restaurants, public transportation, and their homes) without fear of harassment or arrest by the authorities?

• Does the government employ people or groups to engage in public surveillance and to report alleged antigovernment conversations to the authorities?

E. ASSOCIATIONAL AND ORGANIZATIONAL RIGHTS

1. Is there freedom of assembly, demonstration, and open public discussion?

• Are peaceful protests, particularly those of a political nature, banned or severely restricted?

• Are the legal requirements to obtain permission to hold peaceful demonstrations particularly cumbersome and time consuming?

• Are participants of peaceful demonstrations intimidated, arrested, or assaulted?

• Are peaceful protestors detained by police in order to prevent them from engaging in such actions?

2. Is there freedom for nongovernmental organizations? (*Note*: This includes civic organizations, interest groups, foundations, etc.)

• Are registration and other legal requirements for nongovernmental organizations particularly onerous and intended to prevent them from functioning freely?

• Are laws related to the financing of nongovernmental organizations unduly complicated and cumbersome?

• Are donors and funders of nongovernmental organizations free of government pressure?

• Are members of nongovernmental organizations intimidated, arrested, imprisoned, or assaulted because of their work?

3. Are there free trade unions and peasant organizations or equivalents, and is there effective collective bargaining? Are there free professional and other private organizations?

• Are trade unions allowed to be established and to operate free from government interference?

• Are workers pressured by the government or employers to join or not to join certain trade unions, and do they face harassment, violence, or dismissal from their jobs if they do?

• Are workers permitted to engage in strikes, and do members of unions face reprisals for engaging in peaceful strikes? (*Note*: This question may not apply to workers in essential government services or public safety jobs.)

• Are unions able to bargain collectively with employers and able to negotiate collective bargaining agreements that are honored in practice?

• For states with very small populations or primarily agriculturally based economies that do not necessarily support the formation of trade unions, does the government allow for the establishment of peasant organizations or their equivalents? Is there legislation expressively forbidding the formation of trade unions?

• Are professional organizations, including business associations, allowed to operate freely and without government interference?

F. RULE OF LAW

1. Is there an independent judiciary?

• Is the judiciary subject to interference from the executive branch of government or from other political, economic, or religious influences?

• Are judges appointed and dismissed in a fair and unbiased manner?

• Do judges rule fairly and impartially, or do they commonly render verdicts that favor the government or particular interests, whether in return for bribes or other reasons?

• Do executive, legislative, and other governmental authorities comply with judicial decisions, and are these decisions effectively enforced?

• Do powerful private concerns comply with judicial decisions, and are decisions that run counter to the interests of powerful actors effectively enforced?

2. Does the rule of law prevail in civil and criminal matters? Are police under direct civilian control?

• Are defendants' rights, including the presumption of innocence until proven guilty, protected?

• Are detainees provided access to independent, competent legal counsel?

• Are defendants given a fair, public, and timely hearing by a competent, independent, and impartial tribunal?

• Are prosecutors independent of political control and influence?

• Are prosecutors independent of powerful private interests, whether legal or illegal?

• Is there effective and democratic civilian state control of law enforcement officials through the judicial, legislative, and executive branches?

• Are law enforcement officials free from the influence of nonstate actors, including organized crime, powerful commercial interests, or other groups?

3. Is there protection from political terror, unjustified imprisonment, exile, or torture, whether by groups that support or oppose the system? Is there freedom from war and insurgencies?

• Do law enforcement officials make arbitrary arrests and detentions without warrants or fabricate or plant evidence on suspects?

• Do law enforcement officials beat detainees during arrest and interrogation or use excessive force or torture to extract confessions?

• Are conditions in pretrial facilities and prisons humane and respectful of the human dignity of inmates?

• Do citizens have the means of effective petition and redress when their rights are violated by state authorities?

• Is violent crime either against specific groups or within the general population widespread?

• Is the population subjected to physical harm, forced removal, or other acts of violence or terror due to civil conflict or war?

4. Do laws, policies, and practices guarantee equal treatment of various segments of the population?

• Are members of various distinct groups—including ethnic and religious minorities, homosexuals, and the disabled—able to exercise effectively their human rights with full equality before the law?

• Is violence against such groups widespread, and if so, are perpetrators brought to justice?

• Do members of such groups face legal and/or de facto discrimination in areas including employment, education, and housing because of their identification with a particular group?

• Do women enjoy full equality in law and in practice as compared to men?

• Do noncitizens—including migrant workers and noncitizen immigrants—enjoy basic internationally recognized human rights, including the right not to be subjected to torture or other forms of ill-treatment, the right to due process of law, and the rights of freedom of association, expression, and religion?

• Do the country's laws provide for the granting of asylum or refugee status in accordance with the 1951 UN Convention Relating to the Status of Refugees, its 1967 Protocol, and other regional treaties regarding refugees? Has the government established a system for providing protection to refugees, including against *refoulement* (the return of persons to a country where there is reason to believe they fear persecution)?

G. PERSONAL AUTONOMY AND INDIVIDUAL RIGHTS

1. Do citizens enjoy freedom of travel or choice of residence, employment, or institution of higher education?

• Are there restrictions on foreign travel, including the use of an exit visa system, which may be issued selectively?

• Is permission required from the authorities or nonstate actors to move within the country?

• Do state or nonstate actors determine or otherwise influence a person's type and place of employment?

• Are bribes or other inducements needed to obtain the necessary documents to travel, change one's place of residence or employment, enter institutions of higher education, or advance in school?

2. Do citizens have the right to own property and establish private businesses? Is private business activity unduly influenced by government officials, the security forces, political parties/organizations, or organized crime?

• Are people legally allowed to purchase and sell land and other property, and can they do so in practice without undue interference from the government or nonstate actors?

• Does the government provide adequate and timely compensation to people whose property is expropriated under eminent domain laws?

• Are people legally allowed to establish and operate private businesses with a reasonable minimum of registration, licensing, and other requirements?

• Are bribes or other inducements needed to obtain the necessary legal documents to operate private businesses?

• Do private/nonstate actors, including criminal groups, seriously impede private business activities through such measures as extortion?

3. Are there personal social freedoms, including gender equality, choice of marriage partners, and size of family?

• Is violence against women, including wife-beating and rape, widespread, and are perpetrators brought to justice?

• Is the trafficking of women and/or children abroad for prostitution widespread, and is the government taking adequate efforts to address the problem?

• Do women face de jure and de facto discrimination in economic and social matters, including property and inheritance rights, divorce proceedings, and child custody matters?

• Does the government directly or indirectly control choice of marriage partners through means such as requiring large payments to marry certain individuals (e.g., foreign citizens) or by not enforcing laws against child marriage or dowry payments?

• Does the government determine the number of children that a couple may have?

• Does the government engage in state-sponsored religious/cultural/ethnic indoctrination and related restrictions on personal freedoms?

• Do private institutions, including religious groups, unduly infringe on the rights of individuals, including choice of marriage partner, dress, etc.?

4. Is there equality of opportunity and the absence of economic exploitation?

• Does the government exert tight control over the economy, including through state ownership and the setting of prices and production quotas?

• Do the economic benefits from large state industries, including the energy sector, benefit the general population or only a privileged few?

• Do private interests exert undue influence on the economy through monopolistic practices, cartels, or illegal blacklists, boycotts, or discrimination?

• Is entrance to institutions of higher education or the ability to obtain employment limited by widespread nepotism and the payment of bribes?

• Are certain groups, including ethnic or religious minorities, less able to enjoy certain economic benefits than others? For example, are certain groups restricted from holding particular jobs, whether in the public or the private sector, because of de jure or de facto discrimination?

• Do state or private employers exploit their workers through activities including unfairly withholding wages and permitting or forcing employees to work under unacceptably dangerous conditions, as well as through adult slave labor and child labor?

KEY TO SCORES, PR AND CL RATINGS, AND STATUS

Table 1		Table 2	
Political Rights (PR)		**Civil Liberties (CL)**	
Total Scores	**PR Rating**	**Total Scores**	**CL Rating**
36-40	1	53-60	1
30-35	2	44-52	2
24-29	3	35-43	3
18-23	4	26-34	4
12-17	5	17-25	5
6-11	6	8-16	6
0-5*	7	0-7	7

Table 3

Combined Average of the PR and CL Ratings	Country Status
1.0 - 2.5	Free
3.0 - 5.0	Partly Free
5.5 - 7.0	Not Free

* It is possible for a country's total political rights score to be less than zero (between -1 and -4) if it receives mostly or all zeros for each of the 10 political rights questions *and* it receives a sufficiently negative score for political rights discretionary question B. In such a case, a country would still receive a final political rights rating of 7.

Tables and Ratings

Table of Independent Countries

Country	PR	CL	Freedom Rating	Country	PR	CL	Freedom Rating
Afghanistan	6 ▾	6	Not Free	Djibouti	5	5	Partly Free
Albania*	3	3	Partly Free	Dominica*	1	1	Free
Algeria	6	5	Not Free	Dominican Republic*	2	2	Free
Andorra*	1	1	Free				
Angola	6	5	Not Free	East Timor*	3	4	Partly Free
Antigua and Barbuda*	3*	2	Free	Ecuador*	3	3	Partly Free
				Egypt	6	5	Not Free
Argentina*	2	2	Free	El Salvador*	2	3	Free
Armenia	6	4	Partly Free	Equatorial Guinea	7	7	Not Free
Australia*	1	1	Free	Eritrea	7	7 ▾	Not Free
Austria*	1	1	Free	Estonia*	1	1	Free
Azerbaijan	6	5	Not Free	Ethiopia	5	5	Partly Free
Bahamas*	1	1	Free	Fiji	6	4	Partly Free
Bahrain	6 ▾	5	Not Free ▾	Finland*	1	1	Free
Bangladesh*	3 ▴	4	Partly Free	France*	1	1	Free
Barbados*	1	1	Free	Gabon	6	5 ▾	Not Free ▾
Belarus	7	6	Not Free	The Gambia	5	5 ▾	Partly Free
Belgium*	1	1	Free	Georgia	4	4	Partly Free
Belize*	1	2	Free	Germany*	1	1	Free
Benin*	2	2	Free	Ghana*	1	2	Free
Bhutan	4	5	Partly Free	Greece*	1	2	Free
Bolivia*	3	3	Partly Free	Grenada*	1	2	Free
Bosnia-Herzegovina*	4	3	Partly Free	Guatemala*	4 ▾	4	Partly Free
				Guinea	7	6 ▾	Not Free
Botswana*	3 ▾	2	Free	Guinea-Bissau*	4	4	Partly Free
Brazil*	2	2	Free	Guyana*	2	3	Free
Brunei	6	5	Not Free	Haiti*	4	5	Partly Free
Bulgaria*	2	2	Free	Honduras	4 ▾	4 ▾	Partly Free
Burkina Faso	5	3	Partly Free	Hungary*	1	1	Free
Burma	7	7	Not Free	Iceland*	1	1	Free
Burundi*	4	5	Partly Free	India*	2	3	Free
Cambodia	6	5	Not Free	Indonesia*	2	3	Free
Cameroon	6	6	Not Free	Iran	6	6	Not Free
Canada*	1	1	Free	Iraq	5 ▴	6	Not Free
Cape Verde*	1	1	Free	Ireland*	1	1	Free
Central African Republic	5	5	Partly Free	Israel*	1	2	Free
				Italy*	1	2	Free
Chad	7	6	Not Free	Jamaica*	2	3	Free
Chile*	1	1	Free	Japan*	1	2	Free
China	7	6	Not Free	Jordan	6 ▾	5	Not Free ▾
Colombia*	3	4	Partly Free	Kazakhstan	6	5	Not Free
Comoros*	3	4	Partly Free	Kenya	4	4 ▾	Partly Free
Congo (Brazzaville)	6	5	Not Free	Kiribati*	1	1	Free
Congo (Kinshasa)	6	6	Not Free	Kosovo	5 ▴	4 ▴	Partly Free ▴
Costa Rica*	1	1	Free	Kuwait	4	4	Partly Free
Cote d'Ivoire	6	5	Not Free	Kyrgyzstan	6 ▾	5 ▾	Not Free ▾
Croatia*	1 ▴	2	Free	Laos	7	6	Not Free
Cuba	7	6	Not Free	Latvia*	2	1	Free
Cyprus*	1	1	Free	Lebanon	5	3 ▴	Partly Free
Czech Republic*	1	1	Free	Lesotho*	3 ▾	3	Partly Free ▾
Denmark*	1	1	Free	Liberia*	3	4	Partly Free

Country	PR	CL	Freedom Rating	Country	PR	CL	Freedom Rating
Libya	7	7	Not Free	Senegal*	3	3	Free
Liechtenstein*	1	1	Free	Serbia*	2 ▲	2	Free
Lithuania*	1	1	Free	Seychelles*	3	3	Partly Free
Luxembourg*	1	1	Free	Sierra Leone*	3	3	Partly Free
♯ Macedonia*	3	3	Partly Free	Singapore	5	4	Partly Free
Madagascar	6 ▼	4 ▼	Partly Free	♨ Slovakia*	1	1	Free
Malawi*	3 ▲	4	Partly Free	Slovenia*	1	1	Free
Malaysia	4	4	Partly Free	Solomon Islands	4	3	Partly Free
Maldives	3 ▲	4	Partly Free⠎	Somalia	7	7	Not Free
Mali*	2	3	Free	South Africa*	2	2	Free
♨ Malta*	1	1	Free	South Korea*	1	2	Free
Marshall Islands*	1	1	Free	Spain*	1	1	Free
Mauritania	6	5	Not Free†	Sri Lanka*	4	4	Partly Free
Mauritius*	1	2	Free	Sudan	7	7	Not Free
Mexico*	2	3	Free	Suriname*	2	2	Free
Micronesia*	1	1	Free	Swaziland	7	5	Not Free
Moldova*	3 ▲	4	Partly Free	Sweden*	1	1	Free
Monaco*	2	1	Free	♨ Switzerland*	1	1	Free
♯ Mongolia*	2	2	Free	Syria	7	6	Not Free
Montenegro*	3	2 ▲	Free ▲	Taiwan*	1 ▲	2 ▼	Free
♨ Morocco	5	4	Partly Free	Tajikistan	6	5	Not Free
Mozambique	4 ▼	3	Partly Free	Tanzania	4	3	Partly Free
Namibia*	2	2	Free	Thailand	5	4	Partly Free
Nauru*	1	1	Free	Togo	5	4 ▲	Partly Free
Nepal	4	4	Partly Free	Tonga	5	3	Partly Free
Netherlands*	1	1	Free	Trinidad and Tobago*	2	2	Free
New Zealand*	1	1	Free				
Nicaragua*	4	4 ▼	Partly Free	Tunisia	7	5	Not Free
Niger	5 ▼	4	Partly Free	♨ Turkey*	3	3	Partly Free
♨ Nigeria	5	4	Partly Free	Turkmenistan	7	7	Not Free
♨ North Korea	7	7	Not Free	Tuvalu*	1	1	Free
Norway*	1	1	Free	Uganda	5	4	Partly Free
Oman	6	5	Not Free	Ukraine*	3	2	Free
Pakistan	4	5	Partly Free⠎	United Arab Emirates	6	5	Not Free
Palau*	1	1	Free				
Panama*	1	2	Free	United Kingdom*1	1	Free	
Papua New Guinea*	4	3	Partly Free	United States*	1	1	Free
				Uruguay*	1	1	Free
Paraguay*	3	3	Partly Free	Uzbekistan	7	7	Not Free
Peru*	2	3	Free	Vanuatu*	2	2	Free
♨ Philippines	4	3	Partly Free	Venezuela	5 ▼	4	Partly Free
Poland*	1	1	Free	♨ Vietnam	7	5	Not Free
Portugal*	1	1	Free	Yemen	6 ▼	5	Not Free ▼
Qatar	6	5	Not Free	Zambia*	3	4 ▼	Partly Free
Romania*	2	2	Free	Zimbabwe	6 ▲	6	Not Free
♨ Russia	6	5	Not Free				
Rwanda	6	5	Not Free				
St. Kitts and Nevis*	1	1	Free				
St. Lucia*	1	1	Free				
St. Vincent and the Grenadines*	2	1	Free				
Samoa*	2	2	Free				
San Marino*	1	1	Free				
Sao Tome and Principe*	2	2	Free				
Saudi Arabia	7	6	Not Free				

PR and CL stand for Political Rights and Civil Liberties, respectively; 1 represents the most free and 7 the least free rating. The ratings reflect an overall judgment based on survey results.

▲ ▼ up or down indicates a change in Political Rights, Civil Liberties, or Status since the last survey.

♯ ♨ up or down indicates a trend of positive or negative changes that took place but were not sufficient to result in a change in Political Rights or Civil Liberties of 1-7.

* indicates a country's status as an electoral democracy.

Note: The ratings reflect global events from January 1, 2009, through December 31, 2009.

Table of Related Territories

Country	PR	CL	Freedom Rating
Hong Kong	5	2	Partly Free
Puerto Rico	1	1	Free

Table of Disputed Territories

Country	PR	CL	Freedom Rating
Abkhazia	5	5	Partly Free
Indian Kashmir	4 ▲	4	Partly Free
Israeli-Occupied Territories	6	6	Not Free
Nagorno-Karabakh	5	5	Partly Free
Northern Cyrus	2	2	Free
✦ Pakistani Kashmir	6	5	Not Free
Palestinian Authority-Administered Territories	6 ▼	6	Not Free
Somaliland	5	5 ▼	Partly Free
♦ South Ossetia	7	6	Not Free
Tibet	7	7	Not Free
Transnistra	6	6	Not Free
Western Sahara	7	6	Not Free

Combined Average Ratings: Independent Countries

FREE	Israel	3.5	NOT FREE
1.0	Italy	Bangladesh	**5.5**
Andorra	Japan	Bosnia-Herzegovina	Algeria
Australia	Latvia	Colombia	Angola
Austria	Mauritius	Comoros	Azerbaijan
Bahamas	Monaco	East Timor	Bahrain
Barbados	Panama	Liberia	Brunei
Belgium	St. Vincent and the	Malawi	Cambodia
Canada	Grenadines	Maldives	Congo (Brazzaville)
Cape Verde	South Korea	Moldova	Cote d'Ivoire
Chile	Taiwan	Mozambique	Egypt
Costa Rica		Papua New Guinea	Gabon
Cyprus	**2.0**	Philippines	Iraq
Czech Republic	Argentina	Solomon Islands	Jordan
Denmark	Benin	Tanzania	Kazakhstan
Dominica	Brazil	Zambia	Kyrgyzstan
Estonia	Bulgaria		Mauritania
Finland	Dominican Republic	**4.0**	Oman
France	Mongolia	Burkina Faso	Qatar
Germany	Namibia	Georgia	Russia
Hungary	Romania	Guatemala	Rwanda
Iceland	Samoa	Guinea-Bissau	Tajikistan
Ireland	Sao Tome and	Honduras	United Arab
Kiribati	Principe	Kenya	Emirates
Liechtenstein	Serbia	Kuwait	Yemen
Lithuania	South Africa	Lebanon	
Luxembourg	Suriname	Malaysia	**6.0**
Malta	Trinidad and Tobago	Nepal	Afghanistan
Marshall Islands	Vanuatu	Nicaragua	Cameroon
Micronesia		Sri Lanka	Congo (Kinshasa)
Nauru	**2.5**	Tonga	Iran
Netherlands	Antigua and Barbuda		Swaziland
New Zealand	Botswana	**4.5**	Tunisia
Norway	El Salvador	Bhutan	Vietnam
Palau	Guyana	Burundi	Zimbabwe
Poland	India	Haiti	
Portugal	Indonesia	Kosovo	**6.5**
Saint Kitts and	Jamaica	Morocco	Belarus
Nevis	Mali	Niger	Chad
Saint Lucia	Mexico	Nigeria	China
San Marino	Montenegro	Pakistan	Cuba
Slovakia	Peru	Singapore	Guinea
Slovenia	Ukraine	Thailand	Laos
Spain		Togo	Saudi Arabia
Sweden	**PARTLY FREE**	Uganda	Syria
Switzerland	**3.0**	Venezuela	
Tuvalu	Albania		**7.0**
United Kingdom	Bolivia	**5.0**	Burma
United States	Ecuador	Armenia	Equatorial Guinea
Uruguay	Lesotho	Central African	Eritrea
	Macedonia	Republic	Libya
1.5	Paraguay	Djibouti	North Korea
Belize	Senegal	Ethiopia	Somalia
Croatia	Seychelles	Fiji	Sudan
Ghana	Sierra Leone	The Gambia	Turkmenistan
Greece	Turkey	Madagascar	Uzbekistan
Grenada			

Combined Average Ratings: Related Territories

FREE
1.0
Puerto Rico

PARTLY FREE
3.5
Hong Kong

Combined Average Ratings: Disputed Territories

FREE	PARTLY FREE	NOT FREE
2.0	**4.0**	**5.5**
Northern Cyprus	Indian Kashmir	Pakistani Kashmir
	5.0	**6.0**
	Abkhazia	Israeli-Occupied
	Nagorno-Karabakh	Territories
	Somaliland	Palestinian Authority-Administered Territories
		Transnistria
		6.5
		South Ossetia
		Western Sahara
		7.0
		Tibet

Electoral Democracies (116)

Albania
Andorra
Antigua and Barbuda
Argentina
Australia
Austria
Bahamas
Bangladesh
Barbados
Belgium
Belize
Benin
Bolivia
Bosnia-Herzegovina
Botswana
Brazil
Bulgaria
Burundi
Canada
Cape Verde
Chile
Colombia
Comoros
Costa Rica
Croatia
Cyprus
Czech Republic
Denmark
Dominica
Dominican Republic
East Timor
Ecuador
El Salvador
Estonia
Finland
France
Germany
Ghana
Greece
Grenada
Guatemala
Guinea-Bissau
Guyana
Haiti
Hungary

Iceland
India
Indonesia
Ireland
Israel
Italy
Jamaica
Japan
Kiribati
Latvia
Lesotho
Liberia
Liechtenstein
Lithuania
Luxembourg
Macedonia
Malawi
Maldives
Mali
Malta
Marshall Islands
Mauritius
Mexico
Micronesia
Moldova
Monaco
Mongolia
Montenegro
Namibia
Nauru
Netherlands
New Zealand
Nicaragua
Norway
Palau
Panama
Papua New Guinea
Paraguay
Peru
Poland
Portugal
Romania
St. Kitts and Nevis
St. Lucia
St. Vincent and the Grenadines

Samoa	Suriname
San Marino	Sweden
Sao Tome and Principe	Switzerland
Senegal	Taiwan
Serbia	Trinidad and Tobago
Seychelles	Turkey
Sierra Leone	Tuvalu
Slovakia	Ukraine
Slovenia	United Kingdom
South Africa	United States
South Korea	Uruguay
Spain	Vanuatu
Sri Lanka	Zambia

The Survey Team

CONTRIBUTING AUTHORS

Amanda Abrams is a Washington, DC–based freelance writer. Previously, she was a communications officer for Freedom House. She holds an MA in international development from Georgetown University's Master of Science in Foreign Service program. She served as a Central and Eastern Europe analyst for *Freedom in the World*.

Fatima Ayub is a senior advocate for the Open Society Institute based in London. She was previously a consultant on Afghanistan projects for the International Center for Transitional Justice and has worked with Amnesty International in London and at Human Rights Watch. She holds an MA in international studies, with a specialization in international law and organizations from the Johns Hopkins School of Advanced International Studies. She served as a South Asia analyst for *Freedom in the World*.

Scott H. Baker is the director of the International Business Program at Champlain College, where he teaches international business strategies within the context of socioeconomic and political development frameworks. He has worked on issues of political enfranchisement in conflict societies for the United Nations, and serves as an adviser and board member for several nonprofits in Nigeria and Southern Sudan dedicated to political rights and civil liberties. He is a doctoral candidate at the University of Vermont, focusing on the relationship between political disenfranchisement and conflict in Nigeria. He served as a West Africa analyst for *Freedom in the World*.

Michael Balz is an MA candidate at Princeton University's Woodrow Wilson School. He previously worked in Lebanon, Syria, and Egypt, as well as in the Middle East Program at the Center for Strategic and International Studies. He served as a Middle East analyst for *Freedom in the World*.

Gordon N. Bardos is assistant director of the Harriman Institute at Columbia University's School of International and Public Affairs. He also serves as executive director of the Association for the Study of Nationalities (ASN), the world's largest scholarly organization dedicated to the problems of nationalism, ethnicity, and ethnic conflict management. He served as a Balkans analyst for *Freedom in the World*.

Jaimie Bleck is a PhD candidate in the Government Department at Cornell University, where her research focuses on social service provision, citizenship, and democratization in West Africa. Previously, she worked for Winrock International as a program assistant on USAID's Africa Education Initiative Ambassadors Girls' Scholarship Program. She served as a Sahel analyst for *Freedom in the World*.

Julia Breslin is a freelance researcher, writer, and editor. Previously, she was the research and editorial associate for Freedom House's 2010 publication, *Women's Rights in the Middle East and North Africa*. She has written for various other publications, including the Max Planck Institute's Encyclopedia of Public International Law. Her research focus is the Middle East, and she has carried out research assignments in Kuwait, Bahrain, and the United Arab Emirates. She holds a law degree from Florida State University and an LLM in international human rights law from Lund University in Sweden, earned through a program taught in conjunction with the Raoul Wallenberg Institute of Human Rights and Humanitarian Law. She served as a Middle East analyst for *Freedom in the World*.

Jaclyn Burger has worked as a political affairs officer for the United Nations Mission in Liberia and as a background investigator and civics instructor for the bilateral U.S.-Liberia Security Sector Reform program. Her research interests include transitional justice, national reconciliation, security sector reform, and governance issues in sub-Saharan Africa. She holds an MA in international peace and conflict resolution with a specialization in postconflict peace-building from American University. She served as a West Africa analyst for *Freedom in the World*.

Sarah Cook is an Asia research analyst at Freedom House and assistant editor for *Freedom on the Net*, Freedom House's index of internet and digital media freedom. She recently served as assistant editor for the 2010 edition of *Countries at the Crossroads*, Freedom House's annual survey of democratic governance. Prior to joining Freedom House, she coedited the English version of Chinese attorney Gao Zhisheng's memoir, *A China More Just*. She holds an MSc in politics and an LLM in public international law from the School of Oriental and African Studies in London, where she was a Marshall Scholar. She served as an East Asia analyst for *Freedom in the World*.

Britta H. Crandall recently completed her PhD at the Johns Hopkins School of Advanced International Studies and is now finishing a book on U.S. policy toward Brazil. Prior to her doctoral studies, she was associate director for Latin American sovereign risk analysis at Bank One and worked as a Latin American program examiner for the Office of Management and Budget. She served as a South America analyst for *Freedom in the World*.

Jake Dizard is the managing editor of *Countries at the Crossroads*, Freedom House's annual survey of democratic governance. His area of focus is Latin America, with a specific emphasis on the Andean region and Mexico. He is a 2005 graduate of the Johns Hopkins School of Advanced International Studies. He served as a South America analyst for *Freedom in the World*.

Richard Downie is a fellow on the Africa Program at the Center for Strategic and International Studies. Previously, he was a journalist for the British Broadcasting Corporation (BBC). He received an MA in international public policy at the Johns Hopkins School of Advanced International Studies. He served as a Horn of Africa analyst for *Freedom in the World*.

Camille Eiss is policy director of the Truman National Security Project. She previously worked as a senior associate for the international development organization Endeavor, a research analyst and assistant editor of *Freedom in the World* at Freedom House, and an editor of the *Washington Quarterly* at the Center for Strategic and International Studies. She holds an MA in the history of international relations from the London School of Economics, with a focus on political Islam. She served as a Southeast Asia analyst for *Freedom in the World*.

Daniel P. Erikson was senior associate for U.S. policy and director of Caribbean programs at the Inter-American Dialogue until June 2010, when he was appointed senior adviser for Western Hemisphere affairs at the U.S. Department of State. He has published more than 50 academic and opinion articles on Latin America and the Caribbean, and he is the author of *The Cuba Wars: Fidel Castro, the United States, and the Next Revolution*. His previous positions include research associate at the Harvard Business School and Fulbright scholar in U.S.-Mexican business relations. He served as a Caribbean analyst for *Freedom in the World*.

Elizabeth Floyd is currently working on developing public relations strategies for the German-American Heritage Museum in Washington, DC. Previously, she was the Democracy Web project director and editor of special reports for Freedom House. She has served as an analyst for Belgium, the Netherlands, and the German-speaking countries for *Freedom of the Press*. She holds an MA in modern European history from Hunter College, with a focus on German history. She served as a Western Europe analyst for *Freedom in the World*.

Thomas W. Gold is a former assistant professor of comparative politics at Sacred Heart University and the author of *The Lega Nord and Contemporary Politics in Italy*. He earned his PhD in political science from the New School for Social Research and received a Fulbright Fellowship to conduct research in Italy. He served as a Western Europe analyst for *Freedom in the World*.

Cambria Hamburg completed her MA in international affairs at the Johns Hopkins School of Advanced International Studies in 2009, where she focused on Southeast Asian studies and international economics. She previously worked for the International Rescue Committee and the Council on Foreign Relations, and in 2004, she studied in Thailand on a Fulbright scholarship. She served as a Southeast Asia analyst for *Freedom in the World*.

Sinéad Hunt has worked previously for the Center for Strategic and International Studies and the Carter Center researching human rights and postconflict reconstruction in Central and North Africa. She holds an MA in international relations from Yale University, with a focus on politics and conflict in sub-Saharan Africa. She served as a Central Africa analyst for *Freedom in the World*.

Toby Jones is an assistant professor of Middle East history at Rutgers University. Previously, he was a visiting assistant professor and Mellon Postdoctoral Fellow at Swarthmore College and the Persian Gulf analyst for the International Crisis Group.

He has published in the *International Journal of Middle East Studies, Middle East Report, Foreign Affairs,* and *Arab Reform Bulletin.* He is the author of *Desert Kingdom: How Oil and Water Forged Modern Saudi Arabia* (forthcoming in fall 2010 from Harvard University Press). He served as a Middle East analyst for *Freedom in the World.*

Karin Deutsch Karlekar is a senior researcher at Freedom House and the managing editor of Freedom House's annual *Freedom of the Press* index. A specialist on media freedom trends and measurement indicators, she also developed the methodology for and edited the pilot *Freedom on the Net* index of internet and digital media freedom. She has written South Asia reports for several Freedom House publications, and has been on research missions to Afghanistan, Nigeria, Pakistan, Sri Lanka, Zambia, and Zimbabwe. She previously worked as a consultant for Human Rights Watch and as an editor at the Economist Intelligence Unit. She holds a PhD in Indian history from Cambridge University. She served as a South Asia analyst for *Freedom in the World.*

Sanja Kelly is a senior researcher at Freedom House and the managing editor of *Freedom on the Net,* Freedom House's index of internet and digital media freedom. She was also the managing editor of Freedom House's 2010 publication, *Women's Rights in the Middle East and North Africa.* She previously served as the managing editor of *Countries at the Crossroads,* Freedom House's annual survey of democratic governance. She has written reports for various publications and has been on research assignments in the former Yugoslavia, the Caucasus, Southeast Asia, Africa, and the Middle East. She served as a Balkans analyst for *Freedom in the World.*

Abraham Kim is vice president at the Korean Economic Institute. Previously, he was the research manager of government services and the principal Korea analyst at Eurasia Group. He has published a number of articles in major newspapers, including the *Asian Wall Street Journal,* the *Washington Times, Joongang Ilbo,* and the *Korea Times,* and has appeared on CNBC, Fox Business, and BNN-TV. He was a project manager for Science Application International Corporation (SAIC) and a policy analyst at the Center for Strategic and International Studies. He received his PhD in political science from Columbia University. He served as an East Asia analyst for *Freedom in the World.*

Daniel Kimmage is an independent consultant and senior fellow at the Homeland Security Policy Institute in Washington, DC. Previously, he was a regional analyst at Radio Free Europe/Radio Liberty, where he focused on politics, business, and media issues in Central Asia and Russia. He coauthored *Iraqi Insurgent Media: The War of Images and Ideas* (2007) and authored *The Al-Qaeda Media Nexus* (2008). His work has appeared in the *New York Times,* the *New Republic, Foreign Policy,* and *Slate.* He holds an MA in Russian and Islamic history from Cornell University. He served as a Central Asia analyst for *Freedom in the World.*

Astrid Larson is the Language Center Coordinator for the French Institute Alliance Francaise. She has served as an analyst for Western Europe, sub-Saharan Africa, and the South Pacific for Freedom House's *Freedom of the Press* survey. She received her MA in international media and culture from the New School University. She served as a Western Europe analyst for *Freedom in the World.*

Ming Kuok Lim focuses his research on the relationship between the use of new media, such as social-networking sites, and the development of democracy. He has conducted a series of interviews with prominent bloggers in Malaysia. He holds a PhD in communications from Pennsylvania State University. He served as a Southeast Asia analyst for *Freedom in the World.*

Timothy Longman is an associate professor of political science and director of the African Studies Center at Boston University. He has researched and published extensively on state-society relations, human rights, religion, and politics in Burundi, Rwanda, and the Democratic Republic of Congo, and authored the book *Christianity and Genocide in Rwanda.* Prior to coming to Boston University, he taught for 13 years at Vassar College. He has served as a consultant for Human Rights Watch, the International Center for Transitional Justice, and USAID in Burundi, Rwanda, and Congo. He served as an East Africa analyst for *Freedom in the World.*

Mary McGuire is the press officer at Freedom House. Previously, she was director of integrated communications at the University of California at Los Angeles. She has lived and worked in Latin America and has 10 years of experience in media and communications. She received an MA in international organizations at Dublin City University in Ireland, with a specialization in Latin American governments. She served as a South America analyst for *Freedom in the World.*

Eleanor Marchant is the program officer at Media Development Loan Fund, a New York–based nonprofit that supports independent journalism in developing countries. A former research analyst and assistant editor of the *Freedom of the Press* survey at Freedom House, she has also served as a visiting fellow at the Media Institute, an East Africa press freedom organization based in Kenya. She received her MA in international relations from New York University, where she wrote her thesis on democratization in West Africa. She served as a West Africa analyst for *Freedom in the World.*

Edward R. McMahon holds a joint appointment as research associate professor in the Political Science Department and the Department of Community Development and Applied Economics at the University of Vermont. Previously, he was the Dean's Professor of Applied Politics and the director of the Center on Democratic Performance at Binghamton University. He has also served as regional director for West, East, and Central Africa at the National Democratic Institute for International Affairs and as a diplomat with the U.S. Department of State. He served as an East Africa analyst for *Freedom in the World.*

Alysson A. Oakley is program director for the United States–Indonesia Society. (Any views expressed herein are hers alone, and do not represent those of USINDO.) She has lived in Indonesia and East Timor working on political development, with a focus on political parties and local legislatures. She holds an MA in international relations from the Johns Hopkins School of Advanced International Studies, with a concentration in Southeast Asia studies and international economics. She served as a Southeast Asia analyst for *Freedom in the World*.

Manuel Orozco is a senior associate and director of remittances and development at the InterAmerican Dialogue. He is also chair of Central America and the Caribbean at the U.S. Foreign Service Institute, as well as an adjunct professor and senior researcher at the Institute for the Study of International Migration at Georgetown University. He holds a PhD in political science from the University of Texas at Austin. served as a Central America analyst for *Freedom in the World*.

Robert Orttung is president of the Resource Security Institute and a visiting scholar at the Center for Security Studies at the Swiss Federal Institute of Technology (ETH) in Zurich. He is a coeditor of the *Russian Analytical Digest* and the *Caucasus Analytical Digest*. His recent books include *Energy and the Transformation of International Relations: Toward a New Producer-Consumer Framework* and *Russian Energy Power and Foreign Relations: Implications for Conflict and Cooperation* (both coedited with Andreas Wenger and Jeronim Perovic). He received his PhD in political science from the University of California–Los Angeles. He served as a Central and Eastern Europe analyst for *Freedom in the World*.

Sam Patten is the senior program manager for Eurasia at Freedom House. He brings a decade of experience in the former Soviet Union together with a background of foreign policy, democratization, and communications work at the U.S. Department of State and the U.S. Senate. Previously, he served as senior adviser for democracy promotion to the former undersecretary of state for democracy and global affairs, Paula Dobriansky. As a private consultant, he has helped manage the campaigns of democratically focused political leaders in Ukraine, Georgia, Romania, Albania, and northern Iraq. He holds a BA in American government from Georgetown University. He served as a Caucasus analyst for *Freedom in the World*.

Aili Piano is a senior researcher at Freedom House and the managing editor of *Freedom in the World*. She has been a country analyst for several Freedom House publications: *Nations in Transit*, a survey of democratization in Central and Eastern Europe and Eurasia; *Countries at the Crossroads 2004*, a survey of democratic governance; and *Freedom of the Press*. Previously, she worked as a diplomatic attaché at the Estonian Mission to the United Nations. She holds an MA from Columbia University's School of International and Public Affairs. She served as a Central and Eastern Europe analyst for *Freedom in the World*.

Arch Puddington is director of research at Freedom House and coeditor of *Freedom in the World*. He has written widely on American foreign policy, race relations, organized labor, and the history of the Cold War. He is the author of *Broadcasting Freedom: The Cold War Triumph of Radio Free Europe and Radio Liberty* and *Lane Kirkland: Champion of American Labor*. He served as a United States and Canada analyst for *Freedom in the World*.

Courtney C. Radsch is the senior program officer for Freedom House's Global Freedom of Expression Campaign and for the Southeast Asia Human Rights Program. She has worked as a journalist in the United States, Lebanon, Egypt, and Dubai. She is a PhD candidate in international relations at American University, where her research focuses on new media, activism, and politics in the Middle East. She served as a Middle East analyst for *Freedom in the World.*

Sarah Repucci is an independent consultant based in New York. She has previously worked as a senior research coordinator at Transparency International and a senior researcher at Freedom House. She holds an MA in European studies from New York University. She served as a Western Europe analyst for *Freedom in the World.*

Sara Rhodin is an assistant editor of *Nations in Transit* at Freedom House. She has written for the *New York Times* and the *Harvard Crimson* and was a Fulbright scholar in Estonia from 2006 to 2007. She holds an MA in regional studies (Russia, Eastern Europe, and Central Asia) from Harvard University. She served as a Central and Eastern Europe analyst for *Freedom in the World.*

Mark Y. Rosenberg is a PhD candidate in political science at the University of California–Berkeley. His research focuses on single-party dominance and the political economy of heterogeneous societies, mostly in sub-Saharan Africa. He is a former researcher at Freedom House and assistant editor of *Freedom in the World.* He served as a Southern Africa and Israel/Palestinian Territories analyst for *Freedom in the World.*

Tyler Roylance is a staff editor at Freedom House and the line editor for *Freedom in the World.* Previously, he worked as a senior editor for Facts on File's *World News Digest.* He holds an MA in history from New York University. He served as a Central and Eastern Europe analyst for *Freedom in the World.*

Hani Sabra has been a consultant for Freedom House for several years. Previously, he worked for the Committee to Protect Journalists and the International Center for Transitional Justice, both in New York. He served as a North Africa analyst for *Freedom in the World.*

Martin Smith is an MA candidate at Johns Hopkins University and a freelance consultant for small North American businesses expanding into Europe. He holds a degree in European studies from the University of London and has worked in European Union–related policy fields in Brussels. He has experience researching human rights issues in Central and Eastern Europe and Central Asia for members of the British Parliament, and has lived in the United Kingdom, Germany, Belgium, and the United States. He served as a Western Europe analyst for *Freedom in the World.*

Maxwell Sobolik is a Freedom House staff member. He holds an MA in humanities from Towson University. He served as a Western Europe analyst for *Freedom in the World.*

Daria Vaisman is a journalist working on her first book, a narrative nonfiction account of U.S. foreign policy in the former Soviet Union, to be published in 2011. She previously worked at Transparency International and the Eurasia Foundation, and holds an MA in international affairs from Columbia University. She served as a Caucasus analyst for *Freedom in the World*.

Peter VonDoepp is an associate professor of political science at the University of Vermont. A specialist in African politics, he has published numerous articles on democratization processes in Africa. He is also coeditor (with Leonardo Villalon) of and contributor to *The Fate of Africa's Democratic Experiments: Elites and Institutions*. He has obtained research grants from the National Science Foundation and Fulbright Hays Program. He served as a Southern Africa analyst for *Freedom in the World*.

Christopher Walker is director of studies at Freedom House and coeditor of *Countries at the Crossroads*, Freedom House's annual survey of democratic governance. He has written extensively on European and Eurasian political and security affairs. He holds an MA from Columbia University's School of International and Public Affairs. He served as a Caucasus analyst for *Freedom in the World*.

Thomas Webb is a law student at Fordham Law School. He is a former research assistant at Freedom House. He served as a South Asia analyst for *Freedom in the World*.

Sonya Weston is a research assistant at the Woodrow Wilson International Center for Scholars in Washington, DC. Previously, she worked for the International Foundation for Education and Self-Help in Guinea. She holds a BA in government and a specialization in international studies from Lawrence University. She served as a West Africa analyst for *Freedom in the World*.

Anny Wong is a political scientist with the RAND Corporation. Her research covers science and technology policy, international development, army manpower, and U.S. relations with states in the Asia-Pacific region. She holds a PhD in political science from the University of Hawaii at Manoa. She served as a Pacific Islands and Southeast Asia analyst for *Freedom in the World*.

Eliza Young is a research analyst and the assistant editor for *Freedom in the World*. She holds an MA in international relations from King's College London. She served as a Central and Eastern Europe analyst for *Freedom in the World*.

ACADEMIC ADVISERS

Jon B. Alterman directs the Middle East Program at the Center for Strategic and International Studies.

David Becker is an emeritus professor of government at Dartmouth College.

John P. Entelis is a professor of political science and director of the Middle East Studies Program at Fordham University.

Robert Lane Greene writes for the *Economist* and is an adjunct assistant professor of global affairs at New York University.

John W. Harbeson is an emeritus professor of political science at the City University of New York and professorial lecturer at the Johns Hopkins School of Advanced International Studies.

Steven Heydemann is vice president of the Grant and Fellowship Program at the U.S. Institute of Peace.

Thomas R. Lansner is an adjunct associate professor of international affairs in the School of International and Public Affairs at Columbia University.

Peter Lewis is an associate professor and director of the African Studies Program at the Johns Hopkins School of Advanced International Studies.

Rajan Menon is the Monroe J. Rathbone Professor of International Relations at Lehigh University.

John S. Micgiel is an adjunct professor of international affairs and director of the East Central European Center at Columbia University.

Alexander J. Motyl is a professor of political science at Rutgers University–Newark.

Andrew J. Nathan is the Class of 1919 Professor of Political Science at Columbia University.

Philip Oldenburg is an adjunct associate professor in the Department of Political Science and a research scholar at the South Asia Institute at Columbia University.

Eric L. Olson is a senior adviser to the Security Initiative at the Mexico Institute at the Woodrow Wilson International Center for Scholars.

Martin Schain is a professor of politics at New York University.

Peter Sinnott is an independent scholar who has been working on Central Asia issues for more than 25 years.

Bridget Welsh is an associate professor of political science at Singapore Management University.

Coletta Youngers is a senior fellow at the Washington Office on Latin America (WOLA) and an independent consultant specializing in human rights and democracy issues in Latin America.

PRODUCTION TEAM
Tyler Roylance, Line Editor

Ida Walker, Proofreader

Mark Wolkenfeld, Production Coordinator

Selected Sources

PUBLICATIONS/BROADCASTS

ABC Color [Paraguay], www.abc.com.py
Africa Confidential, www.africa-confidential.com
Africa Daily, www.africadaily.com
Africa Energy Intelligence, www.africaintelligence.com
AFRICAHOME dotcom, www.africahome.com
Africa News, http://www.africanews.com
AfricaOnline.com, www.africaonline.com
African Elections Database, http://africanelections.tripod.com
Afrol News, www.afrol.com
Aftenposten [Norway], www.aftenposten.no
Agence France Presse (AFP), www.afp.com
Al Arab al Yawm [Jordan]: alarabalyawm.net
Al Arabiya, www.alarabiya.net
Al Ahram, http://www.ahram.org.eg/
Al-Ahram Weekly [Egypt], www.weekly.ahram.org.eg
Al Akhbar [Beirut], www.al-akhbar.com
Al-Dustour [Egypt], http://www.addustour.com/
Al-Hayat, http://www.alhayat.com/
Al Jazeera, http://english.aljazeera.net
allAfrica.com, www.allafrica.com
Al-Masry Al-Youm [Egypt], http://www.almasryalyoum.com/
Al-Ray Al-'am [Kuwait], www.alraialaam.com
Al-Raya [Qatar], www.raya.com
Al-Sharq Al-Awsat, http://www.asharqalawsat.com/english/
Al-Quds Al-Arabi, www.alquds.co.uk
Al-Thawra [Yemen], www.althawra.gov.ye
Al-Watan [Qatar], www.al-watan.com
American Broadcasting Corporation News (ABC), www.abcnews.go.com
American RadioWorks, www.americanpublicmedia.publicradio.org
The Analyst [Liberia], www.analystliberia.com
Andorra Times, www.andorratimes.com
An-Nahar [Lebanon], http://www.annahar.com/http://web.naharnet.com/default.asp
Annual Review of Population Law (Harvard Law School), annualreview.law.harvard.edu
Arab Advisors Group, http://www.arabadvisors.com/
Arabianbusiness.com, www.arabianbusiness.com
Arabic Network for Human Rights Information (ANHRI), www.anhri.net
Arab Media, http://arab-media.blogspot.com/
Arab News [Saudi Arabia], www.arabnews.com

Arab Reform Bulletin, http://www.carnegieendowment.org/
Asharq Alawsat, www.asharqalawsat.com
Asia Sentinel, http://www.asiasentinel.com/
Asia Times, www.atimes.com
As-Safir [Lebanon], www.assafir.com
Associated Press (AP), www.ap.org
The Atlantic Monthly, www.theatlantic.com
Austrian Times, www.austriantimes.at
Australia Broadcasting Corporation News Online, www.abc.net.au/news
The Australian, www.theaustralian.news.com.au
Awareness Times [Sierra Leone], www.news.sl
Bahrain Post, www.bahrainpost.com
Bahrain Tribune, www.bahraintribune.com
Balkan Insight, www.balkaninsight.com
The Baltic Times, www.baltictimes.com
Bangkok Post, www.bangkokpost.co.th
The Boston Globe, www.boston.com
British Broadcasting Corporation (BBC), www.bbc.co.uk
BruDirect.com [Brunei], www.brudirect.com/
The Budapest Sun, www.budapestsun.com
Budapest Times, http://www.budapesttimes.hu/
Business Day [South Africa], www.bday.co.za
Cabinda.net, www.cabinda.net
Cable News Network (CNN), www.cnn.com
Cameroon Tribune, www.cameroon-tribune.cm
The Caribbean & Central America Report (Intelligence Research Ltd.)
CBS News, www.cbsnews.com
The Central Asia-Caucasus Analyst (Johns Hopkins University), www.cacianalyst.org
The China Post, www.chinapost.com.tw
Chosun Ilbo [South Korea], http://english.chosun.com/
The Christian Science Monitor, www.csmonitor.com
CIA World Factbook, www.cia.gov/cia/publications/factbook
Civil Georgia, www.civil.ge
The Copenhagen Post [Denmark], www.cphpost.dk
The Contemporary Pacific, http://pidp.eastwestcenter.org/pireport/tcp.htm
Corriere della Sera [Italy], www.corriere.it
Czech News Agency, http://www.ceskenoviny.cz/news/
Daily Excelsior [India-Kashmir], www.dailyexcelsior.com

Daily Star [Bangladesh], www.dailystar.net
Daily Star [Lebanon], www.dailystar.com.lb
The Daily Times, www.dailytimes.bppmw.com/
Danas [Serbia],
  http://www.danas.rs/danasrs/
  naslovna.1.html
Dani [Bosnia-Herzegovina], www.bhdani.com
Dawn [Pakistan], www.dawn.com
Der Spiegel [Germany], www.spiegel.de
Der Standard [Austria], www.derstandard.at
Die Zeit [Germany], www.zeit.de
Deutsche Presse-Agentur [Germany],
  www.dpa.de
Deutsche Welle [Germany], www.dwelle.de
The East Africa Standard [Kenya],
  www.eastandard.net
East European Constitutional Review (New
  York University), www.law.nyu.edu/eedr
East Timor Law Journal [East Timor],
  http://www.eastimorlawjournal.org/
The Economist, www.economist.com
The Economist Intelligence Unit reports,
  http://www.eiu.com/
EFE News Service [Spain], www.efenews.com
Election Watch, www.electionwatch.org
Election World, www.electionworld.org
El Mercurio [Chile], www.elmercurio.cl
El Nuevo Herald [United States],
  www.miami.com/mld/elnuevo
El Pais [Uruguay], www.elpais.com.uy
El Tiempo [Colombia], www.eltiempo.com
El Universal [Venezuela],
  www.eluniversal.com.ve
Expreso [Peru], www.expreso.co.pe
Far Eastern Economic Review, www.feer.com
Federal Bureau of Investigation Hate Crime
  Statistics, www.fbi.gov/ucr/2003/
  03semimaps.pdf
Fijilive, www.fijilive.com
FijiSUN, www.sun.com.fj
Fiji Times Online, www.fijitimes.com
Fiji Village, www.FijiVillage.com
The Financial Times, www.ft.com
Finnish News Agency, http://virtual.finland.fi/stt
Folha de Sao Paulo, www.folha.com.br
Foreign Affairs, www.foreignaffairs.org
Foreign Policy, www.foreignpolicy.com
France 24, www.france24.com
Frankfurter Allgemeine Zeitung [Germany],
  www.faz.net
The Friday Times [Pakistan],
  www.thefridaytimes.com
The Frontier Post [Pakistan],
  www.frontierpost.com
FrontPageAfrica [Liberia],
  www.frontpageafrica.com
Gazeta.ru [Russia], gazeta.ru
Global Insight, http://www.globalinsight.com/

Global News Wire, *www.lexis-nexis.com*
Globus [Croatia], www.globus.com.hr
The Guardian [Nigeria],
  www.ngrguardiannews.com
The Guardian [United Kingdom],
  www.guardian.co.uk
Gulf Daily News [Bahrain],
  www.gulf-daily-news.com
Gulf News Online [United Arab Emirates],
  www.gulf-news.com
Gulf Times [Qatar], www.gulf-times.com
Haaretz [Israel], www.haaretz.com
Hankyoreh Shinmun [South Korea],
  http://english.hani.co.kr/kisa/
Harper's Magazine, www.harpers.org
Haveeru Daily [Maldives],
  www.haveeru.com.mv
The Hindustan Times [India],
  www.hindustantimes.com
The Honolulu Advertiser,
  http://www.honoluluadvertiser.com/
Iceland Review, www.icelandreview.com
The Independent [United Kingdom],
  www.independent.co.uk
Index on Censorship,
  www.indexoncensorship.org
India Today, www.india-today.com
The Indian Express, www.indian-express.com
Info Matin [Mali], www.info-matin.com
Insight Magazine, www.insightmag.com
Insight Namibia Magazine,
  www.insight.com.na
Integrated Regional Information Networks
  (IRIN), www.irinnews.org
Inter Press Service, www.ips.org
Interfax News Agency,
  www.interfax-news.com
International Herald Tribune, www.iht.com
IRIN news, http://www.irinnews.org/
Irish Independent,
  www.unison.ie/irish_independent
Irish Times, www.ireland.com
Islands Business Magazine,
  www.islandsbusiness.com
Izvestia, www.izvestia.ru
The Jakarta Globe, http://
  www.thejakartaglobe.com/home/
The Jakarta Post, http://
  www.thejakartapost.com/
Jamaica Gleaner,
  http://www.jamaica-gleaner.com/
Jawa Pos [Indonesia],
  http://www.jawapos.co.id/utama/
Jeune Afrique [France],
  http://www.jeuneafrique.com/
Johnson's Russia List,
  www.cdi.org/russia/johnson/
Joongang Ilbo [South Korea],

http://joongangdaily.joins.com/
?cloc=homeltoplidaily
The Jordan Times, www.jordantimes.com
Journal of Democracy,
www.journalofdemocracy.org
Jyllands-Posten [Denmark], www.jp.dk
The Kaselehlie Press [Micronesia],
http://www.bild-art.de/kpress/
Kashmir Times [India-Kashmir],
www.kashmirtimes.com
Kathmandu Post [Nepal],
www.nepalnews.com.np/ktmpost.htm
Kedaulatan Rakyat [Indonesia],
http://www.kedaulatan-rakyat.com/
Khaleej Times [United Arab Emirates],
www.khaleejtimes.com
Kommersant [Russia], www.kommersant.ru
Kompas [Indonesia], http://www.kompas.com/
Korea Herald [South Korea],
http://www.koreaherald.com/index.jsp
The Korea Times [South Korea],
http://times.hankooki.com
Kuensel [Bhutan], www.kuenselonline.com
Kurier [Austria], www.kurier.at
Kuwait Post, www.kuwaitpost.com
L'Informazione di San Marino,
http://www.libertas.sm/News_informazione/
news_frameset.htm
La Jornada [Mexico], www.jornada.uam.nx
La Nacion [Argentina], www.lanacion.com.ar
La Repubblica [Italy], www.repubblica.it
La Semaine Africaine [Congo (Brazzaville)],
http://www.lasemaineafricaine.com/
La Tercera [Chile], www.tercera.cl
Lanka Monthly Digest [Sri Lanka],
www.lanka.net/LMD
Latin American Regional Reports,
www.latinnews.com
Latin American Weekly Reports,
www.latinnews.com
Le Faso [Burkina Faso], www.lefaso.net
Le Figaro [France], www.lefigaro.fr
Le Messager [Cameroon],
www.lemessager.net
Le Monde [France], www.lemonde.fr
Le Quotidien [Senegal] -
http://www.lequotidien.sn/
Le Temps [Switzerland], www.letemps.ch
Le Togolais [Togo],
http://www.letogolais.com/
Lexis-Nexis, www.lexis-nexis.com
The Local [Sweden], www.thelocal.se
L'Orient-Le Jour [Lebanon],
www.lorientlejour.com
The Los Angeles Times, www.latimes.com
Mail & Guardian [South Africa],
www.mg.co.za
The Manila Times, www.manilatimes.net/

Marianas Variety [Micronesia],
www.mvariety.com
Matangi Tonga Magazine,
www.matangitonga.to
The Messenger [Georgia],
www.messenger.com.ge
The Miami Herald,
www.miami.com/mld/miamiherald
Middle East Desk, www.middleeastdesk.org
Middle East Online,
www.middle-east-online.com
Middle East Report, www.merip.org
Minivan News [Maldives],
www.minivannews.com
Mirianas Variety [Micronesia],
www.mvariety.com
Misr Digital, http://misrdigital.blogspirit.com/
Moldova Azi, www.azi.md
Mopheme News [Lesotho],
www.lesoff.co.za/news
Mother Jones, www.motherjones.com
The Moscow Times,
www.themoscowtimes.com
Nacional [Croatia], www.nacional.hr
The Namibian, www.namibian.com.na/
The Nation, www.thenation.org
The Nation [Thailand],
www.nationmultimedia.com
The Nation Online [Malawi],
www.nationmalawi.com
The National [Papua New Guinea],
www.thenational.com.pg
The National [UAE], www.thenational.ae
National Business Review [New Zealand],
http://www.nbr.co.nz
National Public Radio (NPR), www.npr.org
National Review, www.nationalreview.com
Neue Zurcher Zeitung [Switzerland],
www.nzz.ch
The New Democrat Online [Liberia],
www.newdemocratnews.com
New Mandala, http://asiapacific.anu.edu.au/
newmandala/
News Agency of the Slovak Republic,
http://www.tasr.sk/30.axd?lang=1033
The New York Times, www.nytimes.com
The New Yorker, www.newyorker.com
The New Zealand Herald, www.nzherald.co.nz
Nezavisimaya Gazeta [Russia], www.ng.ru
NIN [Serbia], http://www.nin.co.rs/
Nine O'Clock [Romania], www.nineoclock.ro
NiuFM News [New Zealand],
http://www.niufm.com/
Noticias [Argentina],
www.noticias.uolsinectis.com.ar
Notimex [Mexico], www.notimex.com
Novi Reporter [Bosnia-Herzegovina],
http://www.novireporter.com

Nyasa Times [Malawi], www.nyasatimes.com
The Observer [Liberia],
    www.liberianobserver.com
O Estado de Sao Paulo, www.estado.com.br
O Globo [Brazil], www.oglobo.globo.com
OFFnews [Argentina], www.offnews.info
Oman Arabic Daily, www.omandaily.com
Oman Daily Observer,
    www.omanobserver.com
Oslobodjenje [Bosnia-Herzegovina],
    www.oslobodjenje.com.ba
Outlook [India], www.outlookindia.com
Pacific Business News,
    http://pacific.bizjournals.com/pacific/
Pacific Daily News, www.guampdn.com/
Pacific Islands Report,
    http://pidp.eastwestcenter.org/pireport
Pacific Magazine,
    http://www.pacificmagazine.net
Pagina/12 [Argentina], www.pagina12.com.ar
PANAPRESS, www.panapress.com
Papua New Guinea Post-Courier,
    www.postcourier.com.pg
The Perspective Newspaper [Liberia],
    www.perspective.org
The Philippine Daily Inquirer,
    http://www.inquirer.net/
Phnom Penh Post,
    www.phnompenhpost.com
The Pioneer [India], www.dailypioneer.com
Planet Tonga, http://www.planet-tonga.com
Political Handbook of the World,
    http://phw.binghamton.edu
Politics.hu [Hungary], http://www.politics.hu/
Politika [Serbia], http://www.politika.rs/
Port Vila Presse [Vanuatu], www.news.vu/en/
The Post [Zambia],
    www.zamnet.zm/zamnet/post/post.html
The Prague Post, www.praguepost.com
Radio and Television Hong Kong,
    www.rthk.org.hk
Radio Australia, www.abc.net.au/ra
Radio France Internationale, www.rfi.fr
Radio Free Europe-Radio Liberty reports,
    www.rferl.org
Radio Lesotho,
    www.lesotho.gov.ls/radio/radiolesotho
Radio Okapi [Congo-Kinshasa],
    www.radioOkapi.net
Radio New Zealand, www.rnzi.com
Republika [Indonesia],
    http://www.republika.co.id/
Reuters, www.reuters.com
Ritzau [Denmark], www.ritzau.dk
The Samoa News, www.samoanews.com
Samoa Observer, http://www.samoaobserver.ws/
San Marino Notizie,
    http://www.sanmarinonotizie.com/

Semana [Colombia], www.semana.com
The Sierra Leone News,
    www.thesierraleonenews.com
Slobodna Bosna [Bosnia-Herzegovina],
    www.slobodna-bosna.ba
The Slovak Spectator,
    www.slovakspectator.sk
Slovak News Agency,
    http://www.sita.sk/eng/services/online/en/
    content.php
SME [Slovakia], http://www.sme.sk/
Sofia Echo, www.sofiaecho.com
Solomon Islands Broadcasting Corporation,
    www.sibconline.com.sb
Solomon Star, www.solomonstarnews.com
The Somaliland Times,
    www.somalilandtimes.net
South Asia Tribune [Pakistan],
    www.satribune.com
South China Morning Post [Hong Kong],
    www.scmp.com
Star Radio News [Liberia],www.starradio.org.lr
The Statesman [India], www.thestatesman.net
Straits Times [Singapore],
    www.straitstimes.asia1.com.sg
Sub-Saharan Informer,
    http://www.ssinformer.com/
Suddeutsche Zeitung [Germany],
    www.sueddeutsche.de
Tageblatt [Luxembourg], www.tageblatt.lu
Tahiti Presse, www.tahitipresse.pf
Taipei Times, www.taipeitimes.com
Tamilnet.com, www.tamilnet.com
Tax-News.com, www.tax-news.com
Téla Nón Diário de São Tomé e Príncipe,
    http://www.telanon.info/
Tempo [Indonesia],
    http://www.tempointeraktif.com/
This Day [Nigeria], www.thisdayonline.com
The Tico Times [Costa Rica],
    www.ticotimes.net
Time, www.time.com
The Times of Central Asia, www.times.kg
The Times of India, www.timesofindia.net
Times of Zambia, www.times.co.zm/
TomPaine.com, www.TomPaine.com
Tonga Now, www.tonga-now.to
Tonga USA Today, www.tongausatoday.com
Tongan Broadcasting Commission,
    http://tonga-broadcasting.com/
Transcaucasus: A Chronology,
    http://www.anca.org/resource_center/
    transcaucasus.php
Trinidad Express,
    http://www.trinidadexpress.com/
Tuvalu News, http://www.tuvalu-news.tv/
U.S. News and World Report,
    www.usnews.com

U.S. State Department Country Reports on Human Rights Practices, www.state.gov/g/drl/rls/hrrpt

U.S. State Department Country Reports on Human Trafficking Reports, www.state.gov/g/tip

U.S. State Department International Religious Freedom Reports, www.state.gov/g/drl/irf

The Vanguard [Nigeria], www.vanguardngr.com

Vanuatu Daily Post, www.vanuatudaily.com

Venpres [Venezuela], www.venpres.gov.ve

Voice of America, www.voa.gov

The Wall Street Journal, www.wsj.com

The Washington Post, www.washingtonpost.com

The Washington Times, www.washingtontimes.com

The Weekly Standard, www.weeklystandard.com

World of Information Country Reports, www.worldinformation.com

World News, www.wn.com

Xinhua News, www.xinhuanet.com

Yedioth Ahronoth [Israel], *www.ynetnews.com*

Yemen Observer, *www.yobserver.com*

Yemen Times, www.yementimes.com

Yokwe Online [Marshall Islands], www.yokwe.net

Zawya, www.Zawya.com

ORGANIZATIONS

ActionAid Australia, http:/www.actionaid.org.au/

Afghan Independent Human Rights Commission, www.aihrc.org.af

Afghanistan Research and Evaluation Unit, www.areu.org.pk

Afrobarometer, www.afrobarometer.org

The Alliance of Independent Journalists [Indonesia], www.ajiindonesia.org/index.php

Alternative ASEAN Network on Burma, http://www.altsean.org/

American Bar Association Rule of Law Initiative, www.abanet.org/rol/

American Committee for Peace in the Caucasus, www.peaceinthecaucasus.org

American Civil Liberties Union, www.aclu.org

Amnesty International, www.amnesty.org

Annan Plan for Cyprus, www.cyprus-un-plan.org

Assistance Association for Political Prisoners [Burma], http://www.aappb.org/

Anti-Slavery International, www.antislavery.org

The Asia Foundation, http://asiafoundation.org/

Asian Center for Human Rights [India], www.achrweb.org

Asian Human Rights Commission [Hong Kong], www.ahrchk.net

Asian Philanthropy Forum, www.asianphilanthropyforum.org

Balkan Human Rights Web, www.greekhelsinki.gr

Bangladesh Center for Development, Journalism, and Communication, www.bcjdc.org

Belarusian Institute for Strategic Studies, www.belinstitute.eu

British Helsinki Human Rights Group, www.oscewatch.org/default.asp

Brookings Institution, www.brookings.edu

Cabindese Government in Exile, www.cabinda.org

Cairo Institute for Human Rights,` www.cihrs.org

Cambridge International Reference on Current Affairs, www.circaworld.com

Canadian Department of Foreign Affairs and International Trade, www.dfait-maeci.gc.ca

Carnegie Endowment for International Peace, www.carnegieendowment.org

The Carter Center, www.cartercenter.org

The Centre for International Governance, http://www.cigionline.org/

Centre for Monitoring Electoral Violence [Sri Lanka], www.cpalanka.org/cmev.html

Centre for Policy Alternatives [Sri Lanka], www.cpalanka.org

Centre for the Study of Violence and Reconciliation, www.csvr.org.za

Chad/Cameroon Development Project, www.essochad.com

Charter '97 [Belarus], charter97.org

Chatham House [United Kingdom], www.chathamhouse.org.uk

Child Rights Information Network, www.crin.org/resources/ infodetail.asp?ID=22188

Committee for the Prevention of Torture, www.cpt.coe.int

Committee to Protect Journalists, www.cpj.org

Coordinating Ministry of Economic Affairs [Indonesia], http://www.ekon.go.id/

Council of Europe, www.coe.int

Council on Foreign Relations, www.cfr.org/ index.html

The Danish Institute for Human Rights, www.humanrights.dk

Danish Ministry of Foreign Affairs, the Global Advice Network, www.business-anti-corruption.com

Ditshwanelo—The Botswana Centre for Human Rights, www.ditshwanelo.org.bw

Earth Institute Advisory Group for Sao Tome and Principe, www.earthinstitute.columbia.edu

Election Commission of India, www.eci.gov.in

Electoral Institute of Southern Africa, www.eisa.org.za

Electronic Iraq, www.electroniciraq.net

Eurasia Group, www.eurasiagroup.net

European Bank for Reconstruction and Development, www.ebrd.org

European Commission Against Racism and Intolerance, www.ecri.coe.int

European Institute for the Media, www.eim.org

European Roma Rights Center, http://www.errc.org/

European Union, www.europa.eu.int

European Union Agency for Fundamental Rights, http://fra.europa.eu

Executive Mansion of Liberia, www.emansion.gov.lr

Extractive Industries Transparency Initiative, www.eitransparency.org

Federal Chancellery of Austria, www.bka.gv.at

Forum 18, www.forum18.org

Forum for Human Dignity [Sri Lanka], www.fhd.8m.net

Forum of Federations/Forum des Federations, www.forumfed.org

Friends of Niger, www.friendsofniger.org

Global Integrity, www.globalintegrity.org

Global Policy Forum, www.globalpolicy.org

Global Rights, www.globalrights.org

Global Witness, www.globalwitness.org

The Government of Botswana Website, www.gov.bw

The Government of Mauritania Website, www.mauritania.mr

Government of Sierra Leone State House, www.statehouse.gov.sl

Habitat International Coalition, http://home.mweb.co.za/hi/hic/

Heritage Foundation, www.heritage.org

Hong Kong Human Rights Monitor, www.hkhrm.org.hk

Human Rights Center of Azerbaijan, http://mitglied.lycos.de/hrca

Human Rights Commission of Pakistan, www.hrcp-web.org

Human Rights Commission of Sierra Leone, www.humanrightssl.org

Human Rights First, www.humanrightsfirst.org

Human Rights Watch, www.hrw.org

Indolaw [Indonesia], www.indolaw.com.au/

Indonesian Institute of Sciences, www.lipi.go.id/

Indonesian Survey Institute, www.lsi.or.id/

INFORM (Sri Lanka Information Monitor)

Institute for Democracy in Eastern Europe, www.idee.org

Institute for Democracy in South Africa, www.idasa.org.za

Institute for Security Studies, www.iss.co.za

Institute for War and Peace Reporting, www.iwpr.net

Inter-American Dialogue, www.thedialogue.org

Inter American Press Association, www.sipiapa.com

Internal Displacement Monitoring Center, www.internal-displacement.org/

International Alert, www.international-alert.org

International Bar Association, www.ibanet.org

International Campaign for Tibet, www.savetibet.org

International Centre for Ethnic Studies, www.icescolombo.org

International Commission of Jurists, www.icj.org

International Confederation of Free Trade Unions, www.icftu.org

International Crisis Group, www.crisisweb.org

International Federation of Journalists, www.ifj.org

International Foundation for Electoral Systems, www.ifes.org

International Freedom of Expression Exchange, www.ifex.org

International Helsinki Federation for Human Rights, www.ihf-hr.org

International Institute for Democracy and Electoral Assistance, www.idea.int

International Labour Organization, www.ilo.org

International Legal Assistance Consortium, www.ilacinternational.org

International Lesbian and Gay Association, www.ilga.org

International Monetary Fund, www.imf.org

International Network for Higher Education in Africa, www.bc.edu/bc org/avp/soe/cihe/inhea/

International Organization for Migration, www.iom.int

International Press Institute, www.freemedia.at

International Republican Institute, www.iri.org

International Society For Fair Elections And Democracy [Georgia], www.isfed.ge

Jamestown Foundation, www.jamestown.org

Kashmir Study Group, www.kashmirstudygroup.net

Kyrgyz Committee for Human Rights, www.kchr.elcat.kg

Liberia Institute of Statistics and Geo-Information Services, www.lisgis.org/nada

Macedonian Information Agency, www.mia.mk

The Malawi Human Rights Commission, http://www.malawihumanrightscommission.org/

Malta Data, www.maltadata.com

Media Institute of Southern Africa, www.misa.org
Media Rights Agenda [Nigeria], www.mediarightsagenda.org
Migrant Assistance Programme Thailand, http://www.mapfoundationcm.org/eng/top/index.html
Millennium Challenge Corporation, www.mcc.gov
MONUC, http://monuc.unmissions.org/
National Anti-Corruption Network [Burkina Faso], www.renlac.org
National Democratic Institute for International Affairs, www.ndi.org
National Elections Commission of Liberia, www.necliberia.org
National Elections Commission of Sierra Leone, www.nec-sierraleone.org
The National Endowment for Democracy, www.ned.org
National Human Rights Commission [India], www.nhrc.nic.in
National Organization for Human Rights in Syria, www.nohr-s.org
National Peace Council of Sri Lanka, www.peace-srilanka.org
National Society for Human Rights [Namibia], www.nshr.org.na
Nicaragua Network, www.nicanet.org
Observatory for the Protection of Human Rights Defenders, www.omct.org
Odhikar [Bangladesh], www.odhikar.org
Office of the High Representative in Bosnia and Herzegovina, www.ohr.int
Open Society Institute, www.soros.org
Organization for Economic Cooperation and Development, www.oecd.org
Organization for Security and Cooperation in Europe, www.osce.org
Oxford Analytica, www.oxan.com/
Pacific Media Watch, www.pmw.c20.org
Parliament of Kiribati, http://www.tskl.net.ki/parliament/index.html
People's Forum for Human Rights [Bhutan]
Population Reference Bureau, www.prb.org
Publish What You Pay Campaign, www.publishwhatyoupay.org
Refugees International, www.refugeesinternational.org
Reporters Sans Frontieres, www.rsf.org
Republic of Angola, www.angola.org
Royal Institute of International Affairs, www.riia.org

Save the Children, www.savethechildren.org
Shan Women's Action Network, www.shanwomen.org
South African Human Rights Commission, www.sahrc.org.za
South African Press Association, www.sapa.org.za
South Asia Analysis Group [India], www.saag.org
South Asia Terrorism Portal [India], www.satp.org
South East Europe Media Organisation, http://seemo.org/
The Special Court for Sierra Leone, www.sc-sl.org
Sweden.se, www.sweden.se
Syria Comment, www.joshualandis.com
Tibet Information Network, www.tibetinfo.net
Transitions Online, www.tol.cz
Transparency International, www.transparency.org
Truth and Reconciliation Commission of Liberia, www.trcofliberia.org
Turkish Ministry of Foreign Affairs, www.mfa.gov.tr
United Nations Development Program, www.undp.org
United Nations High Commissioner for Refugees, www.unhcr.org
United Nations High Commissioner on Human Rights, www.unhchr.ch
United Nations Integrated Peacebuilding Office in Sierra Leone (UNIPSIL), http://unipsil.unmissions.org/
United Nations Interim Mission in Kosovo, www.unmikonline.org
United Nations Mission in Liberia (UNMIL), www.unmil.org
United Nations Population Division, www.un.org/esa/population
United Nations Security Council, www.un.org
U.S. Agency for International Development, www.usaid.org
U.S. Department of State, www.state.gov
University Teachers for Human Rights-Jaffna, www.uthr.org
Washington Office on Latin America, www.wola.org
The World Bank, www.worldbank.org
World Markets Research Centre, www.wmrc.com
World Press Freedom Committee, www.wpfc.org

1301 Connecticut Avenue, NW
Washington, DC 20036
(202) 296-5101

120 Wall Street, New York, NY 10005
(212) 514-8040

www.freedomhouse.org

Freedom House is an independent watchdog organization that supports the expansion of freedom around the world. Freedom House supports democratic change, monitors freedom, and advocates for democracy and human rights.

Founded in 1941, Freedom House has long been a vigorous proponent of the right of all individuals to be free. Eleanor Roosevelt and Wendell Willkie served as Freedom House's first honorary co-chairpersons.

William H. Taft IV
Chair
Freedom House Board of Trustees

Jennifer L. Windsor
Executive Director

Arch Puddington
Director of Research

www.freedomhouse.org

Support the right of every individual to be free.
Donate now.

Breinigsville, PA USA
03 October 2010
246541BV00002B/2/P